KV-409-344

Alex R. Piquero · David Weisburd
Editors

Handbook of Quantitative Criminology

YORK ST. JOHN
LIBRARY & INFORMATION
SERVICES

 Springer

Editors
Alex R. Piquero
Florida State University
College of Criminology and Criminal Justice
  Hecht House
634 W. Call Street
Tallahassee, Florida
apiquero@fsu.edu

David Weisburd
Hebrew University of Jerusalem
Inst. Criminology
91905 Jerusalem
Mount Scopus
Israel
msefrat@mscc.huji.ac.il
dweisbur@gmu.edu

ISBN 978-0-387-77649-1   (hardcover)   e-ISBN 978-0-387-77650-7
ISBN 978-1-4614-1388-2   (softcover)
DOI 10.1007/978-0-387-77650-7
Springer New York Dordrecht Heidelberg London

Library of Congress Control Number: 2009942233

© Springer Science+Business Media, LLC 2010, First softcover printing 2011
All rights reserved. This work may not be translated or copied in whole or in part without the written permission
of the publisher (Springer Science+Business Media, LLC, 233 Spring Street, New York, NY 10013, USA), except
for brief excerpts in connection with reviews or scholarly analysis. Use in connection with any form of information
storage and retrieval, electronic adaptation, computer software, or by similar or dissimilar methodology now known
or hereafter developed is forbidden.
The use in this publication of trade names, trademarks, service marks, and similar terms, even if they are not identified
as such, is not to be taken as an expression of opinion as to whether or not they are subject to proprietary rights.

Printed on acid-free paper

Springer is part of Springer Science+Business Media (www.springer.com)

Foreword

Quantitative criminology has certainly come a long way since I was first introduced to a largely qualitative criminology some 40 years ago, when I was recruited to lead a task force on science and technology for the President's Commission on Law Enforcement and Administration of Justice. At that time, criminology was a very limited activity, depending almost exclusively on the Uniform Crime Reports (UCR) initiated by the FBI in 1929 for measurement of crime based on victim reports to the police and on police arrests. A typical mode of analysis was simple bivariate correlation. Marvin Wolfgang and colleagues were making an important advance by tracking longitudinal data on arrests in Philadelphia, an innovation that was widely appreciated. And the field was very small: I remember attending my first meeting of the American Society of Criminology in about 1968 in an anteroom at New York University; there were about 25–30 people in attendance, mostly sociologists with a few lawyers thrown in. That Society today has over 3,000 members, mostly now drawn from criminology which has established its own clear identity, but augmented by a wide variety of disciplines that include statisticians, economists, demographers, and even a few engineers.

This Handbook provides a remarkable testimony to the growth of that field. Following the maxim that "if you can't measure it, you can't understand it," we have seen the early dissatisfaction with the UCR replaced by a wide variety of new approaches to measuring crime victimization and offending. There have been a large number of longitudinal self-report studies that provided information on offending and on offenders and their characteristics to augment the limited information previously available from only arrest data. The National Crime Victimization Survey (NCVS, formerly the NCS) was initiated in 1973 as an outgrowth of the Commission's recommendation to provide a measure of the "dark figure of crime" that did not get reported to the police. These initiatives had to be augmented by analytic innovations that strengthen the quality of their data. Inevitably, some data would be missing and imputation methods had to be developed to fill the gaps. Self-reports were hindered by recall limitations, and life calendars were introduced to facilitate memory recall.

Economists became interested in crime shortly after Garry Becker, building on the notion that the "demand" for crime would be reduced by increasing the punishment, or "price." He proposed an initial model of deterrence and his successors brought multivariate regression as a standard tool in criminology. That opened the door to variations such as logistic or probit models, for analysis of natural experiments when randomized design was not feasible, and for the use of propensity scores to better match treated and control populations. That brought time series models and hierarchical models into criminology also.

Experimentation was used to a limited degree early in criminology, but those experiments were largely limited to the kinds of psychological treatments that could be tested on a randomly separated treatment and control groups of offenders. Largely under the initiative of Lawrence Sherman, who led with the Kansas City Preventive Patrol experiment, we have seen a striking variety of randomized social experiments testing various means of operating elements of the criminal justice system, including police or courts as well as corrections, and new methods had to be developed to enhance the validity of those experiments and to compensate for the difficulty of incorporating a placebo into a social experiment.

Since there were limits to the degree to which one could experimentally manipulate the criminal justice system, a wide variety of modeling approaches developed. These include simulation models to analyze the flow of offenders through the system, models of criminal careers, and their dynamics from initiation to termination. Daniel Nagin introduced trajectory models as an important means of aggregating the dynamics of hundreds of individual longitudinal trajectories into a small number of distinct patterns that could capture the essential characteristics of longitudinal phenomena. Other models included spatial models of the diffusion of criminal activity within a community or across communities, network models characterizing the linkages among groups of offenders, and many more.

These are just a sampling of the many analytic innovations that Alex Piquero and David Weisburd have admirably assembled in this Handbook. This allows someone seeking an appropriate and innovative method for collecting some new data or for analyzing a particular set of data to explore a wide variety of approaches that have already been used, and hopefully to build on them in new ways that will provide an additional chapter for a future edition of the Handbook.

Alfred Blumstein
Heinz College, Carnegie Mellon University

Contents

Contributors

Lynn A. Addington, Department of Justice, Law, and Society, Washington, DC, American University, USA

Robert J. Apel, School of Criminal Justice, University at Albany, State University of New York, Albany, NY, USA

Barak Ariel, Institute of Criminology, University of Cambridge, Cambridge, UK

Richard Berk, Department of Statistics, The Wharton School, University of Pennsylvania, Philadelphia, PA, USA

Wim Bernasco, Netherlands Institute for the Study of Crime and Law Enforcement (NSCR), Amsterdam, Netherlands

Alfred Blumstein, Heinz College, Carnegie Mellon University, Pittsburgh, PA, USA

Robert Boruch, Center for Research and Evaluation in Social Policy, University of Pennsylvania, Philadelphia, PA, USA

Jeffrey A. Bouffard, College of Criminal Justice, Sam Houston State University, Huntsville, TX, USA

Roger Bowles, Centre for Criminal Justice Economics and Psychology, The University of York, York, UK

Robert Brame, Department of Criminal Justice, University of North Carolina at Charlotte, Charlotte, NC, USA

Chester L. Britt, College of Criminal Justice, Northeastern University, Boston, MA, USA

Shawn D. Bushway, School of Criminal Justice, University of Albany, State University of New York, Albany, NY, USA

Mark A. Cohen, Resources for the Future, Inc., Washington, DC, USA *and* Owen Graduate School of Management, Vanderbilt University, Nashville, TN, USA

Laura Dugan, Department of Criminology and Criminal Justice, University of Maryland, College Park, MD, USA

Henk Elffers, Netherlands Institute for the Study of Crime and Law Enforcement (NSCR), Amsterdam, Netherlands

M. Lyn Exum, Department of Criminal Justice & Criminology, University of North Carolina Charlotte, Charlotte, NC, USA

David P. Farrington, Institute of Criminology, University of Cambridge, Cambridge, UK

John S. Goldkamp, Department of Criminal Justice, Temple University, Philadelphia, PA, USA

Julie Horney, Department of Sociology & Crime, Law and Justice, Pennsylvania State University, University Park, PA, USA

Brian D. Johnson, Criminology and Criminal Justice, University of Maryland, College Park, MD, USA

David S. Kirk, University of Texas, Department of Sociology, Austin, TX, USA

Pamela K. Lattimore, RTI International, Research Triangle Park, NC, USA

Rolf Loeber, Western Psychiatric Institute and Clinic, University of Pittsburgh, Pittsburgh, PA, USA

Thomas A. Loughran, Department of Criminology, University of South Florida, Tampa, FL, USA

James P. Lynch, John Jay College of Criminal Justice, City University of New York, New York, NY, USA

John M. MacDonald, Department of Criminology, University of Pennsylvania, Philadelphia, PA, USA

Michael D. Maltz, Criminal Justice Research Center, Ohio State University, Columbus, OH, USA

Shadd Maruna, School of Law, Queen's University Belfast, Belfast, Northern Ireland

John D. McCluskey, Department of Criminal Justice, University of Texas at San Antonio, San Antonio, TX, USA

Jean Marie McGloin, Department of Criminology and Criminal Justice, University of Maryland, College Park, MD, USA

Stephen D. Mastrofski, Administration of Justice Department, George Mason University, Mannases, VA, USA

Katherine Masyn, Department of Human and Community Development, University of California Davis, Davis, CA, USA

Edward P. Mulvey, Western Psychiatric Institute and Clinic, University of Pittsburgh School of Medicine, Pittsburgh, PA, USA

Daniel S. Nagin, Heinz College, Carnegie Mellon University, Pittsburgh, PA, USA

D. Wayne Osgood, Department of Sociology, Pennsylvania State University, State College, PA, USA

Roger B. Parks, School of Public and Environmental Affairs, Indiana University, Bloomington, IN, USA

Ray Paternoster, Department of Criminology, University of Maryland, College Park, MD, USA

John Pepper, Department of Economics, University of Virginia, Charlottesville, VA, USA

Amanda E. Perry, Centre for Criminal Justice Economics and Psychology, University of York, Heslington, York, UK

Hanno Petras, Department of Criminology and Criminal Justice, University of Maryland, College Park, MD, USA

Carol Petrie, Committee on Law and Justice, National Research Council, Washington, DC, USA

Alex R. Piquero, Florida State University, College of Criminology and Criminal Justice Hecht House, 634 W. Call Street, Tallahassee, Florida

Jerry Ratcliffe, Department of Criminal Justice, Temple University, Philadelphia, PA, USA

Anne Giuranna Rhodes, Administration of Justice, George Mason University, Manassas, VA, USA

Steven M. Radil, Department of Geography, University of Illinois at Urbana-Champaign, Champaign, IL, USA

Anne Giuranna Rhodes, Administration of Justice, George Mason University, Manassas, VA, USA

Jennifer Roberts, Department of Criminology, Indiana University of Pennsylvania, Indiana, PA, USA

Lawrence W. Sherman, Institute of Criminology, University of Cambridge, Cambridge, UK

Sean Sullivan, Department of Economics, University of Virginia, Charlottesville, VA, USA

Gary Sweeten, School of Criminology and Criminal Justice, Arizona State University, Scottsdale, AZ, USA

Faye S. Taxman, Administration of Justice Department, George Mason University, Manassas, VA, USA

George E. Tita, Department of Criminology, Law and Society, University of California, Irvine, Irvine, CA, USA

Michael G. Turner, Department of Criminal Justice, University of North Carolina at Charlotte, Charlotte, NC, USA

David Weisburd, Administration of Justice, George Mason University, Manassas, VA, USA *and* Institute of Criminology, Hebrew University of Jerusalem, Jerusalem, Israel

Brandon C. Welsh, College of Criminal Justice, Northeastern University, Boston, MA, USA

David B. Wilson, Administration of Justice Department, George Mason University, Manassas, VA, USA

CHAPTER 1

Introduction

ALEX R. PIQUERO AND DAVID WEISBURD

Quantitative methods are at the heart of social science research generally, and in criminology/ criminal justice in particular. Since the discipline's birth, researchers have employed a variety of quantitative methods to describe the origins, patterning, and response to crime and criminal activity, and this line of research has generated important descriptive information that has formed the basis for many criminological/criminal justice theories and public policies. And in the past quarter-century, the advent and expansion of computers and advanced software applications has led to a burgeoning of methodological and statistical tools that have been put to use to address many criminological/criminal justice research issues. In short, the field of quantitative criminology now routinely employs quantitative techniques of all levels of complexity, not only to deal with the advances in longitudinal, experimental, and multilevel data structures but also to study substantive methodological or evaluative concerns of interest in the criminological/criminal justice community.

Unfortunately, many of the quantitative methods used in criminology/criminal justice have tended to appear in journal articles and book chapters such that a handbook-oriented reference guide has not existed that contains, in one volume, many of the important contemporary quantitative methods employed in criminology/criminal justice, especially those that have been developed to study difficult criminological questions, which have been previously examined using limited and/or inappropriate methodologies applied to particular types of data structures.

As a result, we reached out to leading quantitative researchers to develop chapters on many of the important methodological and statistical techniques used by criminologists to study crime and the criminal justice system. As such, *The Handbook of Quantitative Criminology* is designed to be the authoritative volume on methodological and statistical issues in the field of criminology and criminal justice.

Like handbooks available in other disciplines (economics, psychology, sociology), this book is designed to be a reference for new and advanced methods in criminology/criminal justice that provide overviews of the issues, with examples and figures as warranted, for students, faculty, and researchers alike. Authored by leading scholars in criminology/criminal justice, the handbook contains 35 chapters on topics in the following areas that have served witness to a proliferation of data collection and subsequent empirical research: (1) Innovative Descriptive Methods for Crime and Justice Problems; (2) New Estimation Techniques for Assessing Crime and Justice Policy; (3) New Directions in Assessing Design, Measurement

A.R. Piquero and D. Weisburd (eds.), *Handbook of Quantitative Criminology*, 1
DOI 10.1007/978-0-387-77650-7_1, © Springer Science + Business Media, LLC 2010,
First softcover printing 2011

and Data Quality; (4) Topics in Experimental Methods; (5) Innovation in Quasi-Experimental Design; and (6) Nonexperimental Approaches to Explaining Crime and Justice Outcomes. And although there exists many other methodological and quantitative techniques and issues in the study of criminology/criminal justice, the coverage of which would have been too difficult to include in a single handbook, *the Handbook of Quantitative Criminology* is intended to provide readers with a useful resource containing a comprehensive and contemporary treatment of research methodologies used in criminology/criminal justice.

We are honored to have this impressive list of contributors who have taken time out of their busy schedules and have worked carefully to construct entries in such a manner that they are as widely accessible as possible to readers of all levels, especially those who are seeking to learn the basic issues surrounding key methodological and quantitative methods. In this regard, we asked the chapter authors to follow as common a format as possible to be illustrative and to help guide readers of all levels of experience. We hope that readers learn as much about these methods and issues as we have.

Part I-A
Descriptive Approaches for Research and Policy: *Innovative Descriptive Methods for Crime and Justice Problems*

CHAPTER 2

Crime Mapping: Spatial and Temporal Challenges

JERRY RATCLIFFE

INTRODUCTION

Crime opportunities are neither uniformly nor randomly organized in space and time. As a result, crime mappers can unlock these spatial patterns and strive for a better theoretical understanding of the role of geography and opportunity, as well as enabling practical crime prevention solutions that are tailored to specific places. The evolution of crime mapping has heralded a new era in spatial criminology, and a re-emergence of the importance of *place* as one of the cornerstones essential to an understanding of crime and criminality. While early criminological inquiry in France and Britain had a spatial component, much of mainstream criminology for the last century has labored to explain criminality from a dispositional perspective, trying to explain why a particular offender or group has a propensity to commit crime. This traditional perspective resulted in criminologists focusing on individuals or on communities where the community extended from the neighborhood to larger aggregations (Weisburd et al. 2004). Even when the results lacked ambiguity, the findings often lacked policy relevance. However, crime mapping has revived interest and reshaped many criminologists appreciation for the importance of local geography as a determinant of crime that may be as important as criminal motivation. Between the individual and large urban areas (such as cities and regions) lies a spatial scale where crime varies considerably and does so at a frame of reference that is often amenable to localized crime prevention techniques. For example, without the opportunity afforded by enabling environmental weaknesses, such as poorly lit streets, lack of protective surveillance, or obvious victims (such as overtly wealthy tourists or unsecured vehicles), many offenders would not be as encouraged to commit crime.

This chapter seeks to make the case for crime mapping as an essential tool in the examination of criminal activity; it also charges mainstream criminology to re-engage with the practitioner interest in spatially targeted crime prevention. In the next section, I briefly outline the theoretical support for a spatial approach to the crime problem and warn of the negative outcomes that can potentially arise by ignoring the spatial dimensional of crime. After a basic primer in mapping crime locations, the chapter looks at different ways that crime hotspots can be identified. It also discusses the benefits of spatio-temporal crime mapping.

A.R. Piquero and D. Weisburd (eds.), *Handbook of Quantitative Criminology*, DOI 10.1007/978-0-387-77650-7_2, © Springer Science + Business Media, LLC 2010, First softcover printing 2011

The final section considers the future of crime mapping, both within the practitioner arena and the academic sphere, concluding that a closer relationship between academics versed in environmental criminology and the crime control field provides the best mechanism for mainstream criminology to regain relevance to practitioners and policy makers. Readers looking for extensive statistical routines, a "crime mapping for dummies" or a checklist of mapping requirements will be disappointed as there are few equations and no elaborate discussions of parameter choices; however, there is a section at the end of the chapter that will serve to point the reader to these resources. Furthermore, this chapter should be read in conjunction with the excellent chapter by Bernasco and Elffers in this book.

DEVELOPING A SPATIAL UNDERSTANDING

The earliest studies that explicitly explored the role of geography in the distribution of crime immediately noted various spatial relationships (see the discussions in Chainey and Ratcliffe 2005, and Weisburd et al. 2009). Both Guerry (1833) and Quetelet (1842) examined nationwide statistics for France, the latter identifying that higher property crime rates were reported in more affluent locations, and that seasonality had a role to play in crime occurrence. British government studies followed, but data were only collected for large administrative units, and local crime data at the neighborhood (or smaller) level were not available. Shaw and McKay (1942) resolved this issue by mapping juvenile delinquents by hand for Chicago, Philadelphia, and other cities. It is hard to imagine the effort that went into both data collection and address verification for their map showing individual dots for the distribution of 5,859 juvenile delinquents in Philadelphia (1942); however, as a result of their painstaking work Shaw, McKay, and their graduate students were able to confirm patterns they had previously observed in Chicago. These patterns suggested delinquency rates varied by zones of community characteristics that, they hypothesized, were the result of city expansion and migration patterns within cities over time. They found these patterns to be "regular and consistent" and that "in the absence of significant disturbing influences the configuration of delinquency in a city changes very slowly, if at all" (1942: 222).

Guerry, Quetelet, and the research team at the Chicago School (at the University of Chicago's sociology department) where Shaw and McKay did their pioneering work were all hampered by the requirement to conduct their research by hand. The early foundations of digital mapping technology that emerged in census bureaux in the 1970s – foundations that were built from the development of computer technology – gave little indication of the potential to follow. Early attempts to map crime using digital processes were hampered by technological and data limitations (Maltz et al. 1991; Weisburd and McEwen 1997), organizational issues (Openshaw et al. 1990), an inability to convert digital addresses into points on a map (Bichler and Balchak 2007; Harries 1999; Ratcliffe 2001, 2004b) and the functional obstacle that many police and criminal justice databases were simply not organized to record the address or other spatial information in a usable format (Ratcliffe and McCullagh 1998b). In recent years, technological limitations have largely melted away and organizational hurdles are being increasingly addressed (for example, the role of crime analysts in police departments: Taylor et al. 2007), such that crime mapping has seen a surge in adoption, especially among larger US police agencies (Weisburd and Lum 2005).

Prevention requires criminal justice agencies to be proactive rather than reactive, and proactivity requires the ability to predict crime hotspots and concentrations. Prediction is rarely possible from individual events, thus there is a direct link between prevention and patterns of criminality, in the form "prevention *requires* proactivity *requires* predictability *requires* patterns" (Ratcliffe 2009). The importance of identifying patterns as a precursor to effective crime prevention has been identified by practitioners who recognize the inherent ability of crime mapping to identify patterns and hotspots, taking advantage of Tobler's first rule of geography, that "Everything is related to everything else, but near things are more related than distant things" (Tobler 1970: 236).

The growth of interest in crime mapping from police departments has thus spurred practitioners to seek out both theoretical explanations for the patterns they see and remedies to the crime problems that plague the communities they police. Many crime prevention practitioners have thus been drawn to environmental criminology researchers, an eclectic group of crime scientists that are bringing a fresh and practical perspective to the problem of crime (for a list of the most prominent environmental criminologists/crime scientists, see the preface to Wortley and Mazerolle 2008). This expanding group actively engages with police and crime prevention agencies and does so armed with theories that lend themselves to crime prevention solutions, including; routine activity theory (Cohen and Felson 1979; Felson 1998), the rational choice perspective (Clarke and Felson 1993; Cornish and Clarke 1986; 1987), and crime pattern theory (Brantingham and Brantingham 1993). An understanding of these theoretical positions enables practitioners and action-oriented researchers to promote a range of practical and direct interventions that may reduce crime.

Each of these theoretical statements articulates a model for the interaction of offenders with crime opportunities, opportunities that are of varying attractiveness and distributed in a nonrandom manner across both place *and* time. Monthly and seasonal trends have long been documented (Harries 1980); for example, there is an increase in domestic violence (Farrell and Pease 1994) and violent crime (Field 1992) during summer months, while commercial robberies can increase during the winter (van Koppen and De Keijser 1999). Changes are even detectable hour-by-hour; vehicle crimes concentrate at night in residential neighborhoods but during the middle of the day in nonresidential areas (Ratcliffe 2002), and Felson and Poulsen (2003) found robbery tends to be an evening activity (though there was variation among the 13 US cities they studied). These findings all have potential policy implications; for example, with the timing of police directed patrol strategies, improvements to street lighting, and whether cities invest in surveillance cameras with night vision capability.

The introduction of spatially oriented research agendas has helped to address a growing problem of aspatiality in criminological research. Issues of spatial concentration are fundamental to crime mapping, yet many researchers are happy to labor along with tools that do not include a measure of, or control for, the spatial autocorrelation of values measured within areas (Arbia 2001; Cliff and Ord 1969). Spatial autocorrelation relates to the degree of dependency between the spatial location and the variable measured at that location (Chainey and Ratcliffe 2005). This spatial dependency could mean that the crime rate in one census area is partly influenced by the crime rate in a neighboring tract; for example, a drug set may sell drugs in one area and their presence may influence the growth of a drug market in the neighboring location. An OLS regression model could incorporate the existence of both drug sets in the model, but could not account for the interaction affect. Research that ignores the reality that crime problems and socio-demographic characteristics from one area can influence the volume of crime in another area can run afoul of the problem of independence. Traditional aspatial analytical techniques, such as OLS regression, can often be statistically unreliable unless this issue is explicitly addressed because, as Ward and Gleditsch (2008) point out, failing to account for first order correlation in the dependent variable will tend to underestimate the real variance in the data, increasing the likelihood of a Type I statistical error.

Numerous solutions to this problem exist and are increasingly becoming mainstream research tools for spatially aware researchers. Examples include the use of geographically weighted regression (Cahill and Mulligan 2007; Fotheringham et al. 2002), by incorporating a localized spatial lag measure to control for crime spillover effects (see Anselin 1988, 1996; Anselin and Bera 1998; with crime examples in the work of Andresen 2006; Martin 2002; Mencken and Barnett 1999), or through the adoption from regional science of two-stage least squares processes to estimate spatial effects (for example, Land and Deane 1992).

A secondary concern for researchers who fail to demonstrate spatial awareness is the modifiable areal unit problem (MAUP) (Bailey and Gatrell 1995; Openshaw 1984). The MAUP exists "where the results of any geographic aggregation process, such as the count of crimes within a set of geographic boundaries, may be as much a function of the size, shape and orientation of the geographic areas as it is of the spatial distribution of the crime data. In essence, when thematically mapped, different boundaries may generate different visual representations of where the hotspots may exist" (Chainey and Ratcliffe 2005: 151–152). Unfortunately, some researchers in the past have appeared either unaware of the MAUP or chose to ignore its potentially serious implications. Recognition of the MAUP has prompted the crime mapping community to employ hotspot mapping techniques that are not influenced by police beats, census tracts, or any other arbitrary administrative boundaries within the study region. These techniques enable crime mappers to see the underlying distribution of crime unhindered by the necessity to aggregate to areas that are unrelated to the crime problem (Chainey et al. 2003; Chainey et al. 2008; Ratcliffe and McCullagh 1999).

When cognizant of some of the forementioned issues, crime mapping provides the opportunity for greater insight into the spatial and temporal distributions of crime than just about any other technique available, at least for high volume crime, and it is of benefit to the research community as well as the practitioner and professional world. The next section of the chapter provides a brief overview of the basics of plotting crime events.

GETTING CRIME ONTO A MAP

It is still possible to conduct rudimentary crime mapping by sticking pins into maps; but crime data (both collectively and individually) contain a wealth of spatio-temporal information. Unless the data are computerized and analyzed using appropriate software, statistical tests and descriptive processes, that information will remain largely unavailable to both researchers and practitioners. The appropriate software solutions are commonly referred to as geographic information systems, or GIS.

GIS retain spatial information in three main ways: data are stored as *points*, *lines* or *polygons*.[1] A map of points could show school locations, bars or crime events. Lines can be used to map streets, railway lines, or routes that an offender might have taken between home and a crime location. Polygons are used to store all areal information. For example, census data, while collected from individuals and households, are distributed as polygons to

---

[1] An additional data structure is common outside of the crime field; the raster. A raster-based data model 'represents spatial features using cells or pixels that have attribute information attached to them' (Chainey and Ratcliffe 2005: 43). Rasters are common in many areas of geography; however, crime researchers tend to overwhelmingly favor the vector approach of points, lines and polygons. Both approaches have their advantages and disadvantages and are not mutually exclusive.

protect the privacy of individuals and so that individual houses within a census unit cannot be identified. While spatial data are retained as points, lines and polygons, attribute data are vital if the spatial information is to have more than superficial value. Within a GIS, attribute information is stored in table form while an index maintains a link to the appropriate spatial data. For example, a point on a map might indicate a burglary location while the associated attribute data will list the type of crime, the time of the offense, the value of property stolen, and the details of the police unit that responded. The ability to search and filter attribute information provides considerable value to a crime analyst wishing, for example, to map only late night assaults or thefts of a particular model of car.

Crime event locations are stored as points the vast majority of the time, and this requires a process to convert the address location of a crime into a point on a map. Crime data are mapped by a process called *geocoding*. Geocoding involves interpreting an address location and either scouring a database of possible matching addresses (known as a *gazetteer*), or using a computer algorithm to identify a suitable street line segment with an appropriate number range and street name and from this interpolate a likely location of the street address in question. For the latter to take place, the street lines of the city or area under examination must have been previously mapped, and the necessary attribute information (street name, house numbers and so on) added to the attribute file. Fortunately, for most advanced economies[2] countries, these files are available either freely or from commercial companies.

If the geocoding process is successful, the result is usually a location in Cartesian coordinates $(x - y)$,[3] and the GIS uses these coordinates to locate the crime in relation to other spatial data sets being mapped (Ratcliffe 2001). This means that a crime event can be viewed on a map relative to its proximity to bars or restaurants, sports stadiums or police stations (if these locations have also been geocoded). The *geocoding hit rate* (the percentage of address locations that has been successfully geocoded) is used to indicate the success rate of the geocoding process. Estimates vary, but one quantitative estimate suggests that at least 85% of crime events must be geocoded for subsequent maps to retain overall accuracy (Ratcliffe 2004b). This being said, experienced police departments and researchers can regularly achieve geocoding hit rates of 95% or better. Geocoded crime locations can be viewed individually, as a group of dots with other crime events, or can be aggregated to polygons. Using a point-in-polygon counting process, the number of crimes occurring in police beats or census tracts can be calculated – simply the number of points that fall within each boundary area.

GIS differ from mapping tools such as Google Maps or Microsoft MapPoint in that a GIS is able to answer complex spatial questions over different spatial data sets. Spatial questions typically come in the form of spatial relationship queries, with terms such as "near," "close," and "within"; for example, "Do robberies cluster near bars?" "Are sexual assaults concentrated close to red-light districts?" and "What percentage of car thefts are within the Central Business District?" It is this ability to pose queries of a spatial nature that differentiates a GIS from mapping programs, most online applications, and cartographic software packages.

---

[2] 'Advanced economies' is a term used by the International Monetary Fund. The current 32 countries on the list (at the time of writing) would be the most likely countries to have street indices for most of the country.

[3] Projected coordinate systems, where locations are identified with x-y coordinate pairs, are preferable because they enable simple distance calculations between points; however, geographic coordinate systems that locate places with latitude and longitude coordinates are still used in some crime mapping applications. A useful reference and free download online is Harries (1999); see http://www.ncjrs.gov/html/nij/mapping/pdf.html.

There are various commercial software solutions available, but the two main GIS programs come from the Pitney Bowes MapInfo (MapInfo) and the suite of ArcGIS programs available from Environmental Systems Research Institute Inc. (ESRI). These GIS are large, powerful and complex with steep learning curves. They are also rather unforgiving of mistakes and often lack defensive features that allow a user to roll-back errors. Training is therefore always recommended, unless the user is particularly resolute, foolhardy, or can tolerate a fair degree of frustration!

Much of the value in using a GIS for crime mapping emanates from the ability to integrate different spatial data sets into a single analysis. Crime events displayed on their own rarely tell the whole story. Additional data sets that can enhance understanding of the crime layer might include the locations of taverns or bars if the user believes they may be driving late night violence, the locations of parks and abandoned places if the user thinks they encourage illicit drug use, or the inclusion of particular census data if it is believed that increased crime is related to higher numbers of juveniles living in the vicinity. Theory therefore drives the selection of supplemental data sets that help us to understand crime distributions found in our primary data sets (Eck 1997), and this places an additional requirement on crime mappers. It is not sufficient to understand crime mapping to be a good analyst; understanding the theories of environmental criminology is also vital if the underlying patterns of behavior that drive the crime picture are to be accurately interpreted. With access to spatial crime data, a grasp of environmental criminology theory, and a suitable research tool (GIS), it is possible to engage in exploratory spatial data analysis (ESDA) of crime patterns (a useful reference for ESDA is found in Bailey and Gatrell 1995).

CRIME HOTSPOTS

One of the most common and innovative uses of crime mapping is to aggregate numerous crime events into hotspot maps. As explained earlier, aggregation to administrative units can run afoul of the MAUP: using different boundaries can result in significantly different maps. For much police operational work, this is not a problem for the user; police departments are often interested in the volume of crime in beats or districts, and city managers take interest in the crime level in city neighborhoods. Point-in-polygon aggregation, as can be conducted by any GIS, will easily complete this task. However the MAUP does pose a significant barrier to accurate data interpretation for people wishing to study a problem in greater depth.

Of considerable interest to researchers, and increasingly to more sophisticated crime prevention practitioners with a nuanced understanding of crime problems, is the use of techniques that do not force crime events to be the members of a group of fixed boundaries. Such techniques include spatial ellipses (Craglia et al. 2000), grid thematic mapping, and continuous surface maps using techniques such as kernel density estimation (Chainey et al. 2008: this citation also serves as a useful quantitative evaluation of these techniques). These new approaches free the geographer from artificially constraining hotspot areas to comply with local areal boundaries, boundaries that often mean little to police, offenders or the community. The resulting maps do ask more from the mapper as regards the selection of parameters (Eck et al. 2005), especially "when little regard is given to the legend thresholds that are set that help the analyst decide when a cluster of crimes can be defined as a hotspot. This visual definition of a hotspot being very much left to the 'whims and fancies' of the map designer" (Chainey et al. 2003: 22). As a result, some understanding of the underlying process to aid parameter selection is required.

FIGURE 2.1. Philadelphia robbery hotspots, from quartic kernel density estimation.

These hotspot surface maps are reminiscent of weather maps found in newspapers and on television. Areas that are shaded with the same color (or in the example of Fig. 2.1, same shade of grayscale) are deemed to contain approximately the same density or frequency of crime. An example is found in Fig. 2.1. This map shows 2005 robbery hotspots for the City of Philadelphia, PA, and is constructed using the kernel density estimate interpolation routine available from the software program, CrimeStat,[4] to produce intensity calculations $g(x)$ such that;

$$g(x_j) = \sum \left\{ [W_i I_i] \left[\frac{3}{\pi h^2} \right] \left[1 - \frac{d_{ij}^2}{h^2} \right]^2 \right\}$$

where d_{ij} represents the distance between a crime location and a reference point (usually the centroid of a grid cell), h is the bandwidth (radius) of a search area beyond which crime events are not included in the calculation, W_i is a weighting and I_i an intensity value at the crime event location (see Levine 2007).

Hotspot surface maps such as shown in Fig. 2.1 are often at the nexus where crime prevention practitioner and academic researchers differ on the next stage of an analysis. The divergence is grounded in the need for different outcomes. Practitioners often recognize that a substantial density of crime in a location is sufficient information to initiate a more detailed analysis of the problem regardless of statistical significance or any consideration of

---

[4] For the technically-minded, the city was divided into grid cells such that there were at least 250 columns, and then a quartic kernel estimation process was applied with a bandwidth of 2,000 feet.

the population at risk. Academic thinking is often engrossed in considering if this clustering of crime is meaningfully non-random, and if the patterns observed are still present once the analysis has controlled for the population at risk or other key demographic features of the broader community or regional structure.

For academic researchers, it has long been known that the issue of determining a population at risk is particularly problematic for crime (Boggs 1965). Too often, a simple measure of total number of people living in an area is used even when, as Keith Harries points out, the "uncritical application of population as a denominator for all crime categories may yield patterns that are at best misleading and at worst bizarre" (1981: 148). The problem can be demonstrated with a couple of examples. When examining crime in general, one might detect differences in crime *incidence* rates (the number of crimes per person in the population of the area) which may be related to the area *prevalence* rate (proportion of victims amongst the population) and/or the area crime *concentration* rate, an indication of the number of victimizations per victim (Hope 1995; Trickett et al. 1995). However, the denominator for residential burglary might be better represented as the number of occupied households, given populations shift throughout the work day and over weekends (Harries 1981).

Vehicle crime presents particular challenges, as the appropriate denominator for vehicle thefts would usually be the number of vehicles available to steal; however, this is confounded by dynamically changing patterns of vehicle location during the day compared to at night, the number of vehicles in private and public garages that could be considered unavailable for theft, the availability of street parking places and so on. Similarly, studies of aggravated assaults in entertainment areas are best when the appropriate control is a measure of the number of people in the area at the time; the residential population (as is usually available from the census) tells the researcher little about the real number of people outside nightclubs at 2 a.m. This *denominator dilemma* is the problem associated with identifying an appropriate target availability control that can overcome issues of spatial inequality in the areal units used to study crime.

Andresen (2006) addressed this denominator dilemma in Vancouver, BC with an imaginative approach to vehicle theft, burglary and violent crime using both residential and ambient populations as denominators, the latter providing daily estimates of a population in a spatial unit and calculated from the LandScan Global Population Database, at a resolution of one square kilometer. This approach is, however, not easily available for everyone, is computationally demanding, and is limited in terms of spatial resolution currently available. For many of the theoretical explanations of criminal activity mentioned earlier in the chapter, the size of a LandScan grid square may be at present too coarse for a detailed picture of criminal behavior.

Denominator issues aside, statistically significant crime hotspots can be determined with various spatial tools that are able to explain more about an individual datum point or area in relation to the spatial dependency of the location with neighboring places (Chainey and Ratcliffe 2005). Improved data quality now allows for analysis at a finer spatial resolution across numerous regimes of spatial association (Anselin 1996). For example, the geographically weighted regression technique is able to model and quantify significant non-static variation across independent variables (Fotheringham et al. 2002).

The most common spatial significance tool is the local variant of the Moran's I statistic (Anselin 1995, 1996; Moran 1950) with more recent variants that consider population density (Assuncao and Reis 1999; Oden 1995). For example, the local Moran's I has been used to explain spatial characteristics of homicide (Mencken and Barnett 1999; Messner and Anselin

2004; Messner et al. 1999). The global Moran's I statistic is a linear association between a value and the weighted average of neighboring values, and its takes the form:

$$I = \frac{1}{2} \sum_{ij} W_{ij} Z_i Z_j \ \forall i \neq j$$

where W_{ij} is a vector from a connectivity weight matrix W that is zero for all non-neighbors and a row-normalized value for all neighbors such that the sum of all vectors for a single spatial unit W_i is one, and z is a standardized variable under examination (from Ward and Gleditsch 2008). Closely related to this, the local Moran's I statistic for an observation i is defined as:

$$I_i = \sum_j w_{ij} z_j \ \forall j \in J_i$$

where only neighbors of i are included in the summation, and where $w_{ii} = 0$ (see Anselin 1995). Local Moran's I (and similar statistics such as the Getis and Ord Gi^*, see Getis and Ord 1992) provides a mechanism to make inferences about a population from a sample. It can be argued that if a crime analyst has access to all recorded crime, then the analyst does not have access to a sample but the actual population of all events. In this case, statistical inference is not required; however, as Fotheringham and Brunsdon (2004) argue, *sampling inference* is not the only value of a statistical test. Crime analysts may also be interested in the value of *process inference*, where "the null hypothesis is a statement about the data-generating process rather than about the population" (p. 448). For example, the positive relationship between alcohol establishments and crime has been known for some time (Murray and Roncek 2008; Roncek and Maier 1991), and even with all recorded crime and a map of all bar locations, there is value in knowing if the relationship is beyond a spurious or coincidental one.

Taking the Philadelphia example from Fig. 2.1, even though we have all of the recorded robbery data for the city, there is still value in identifying significant clusters as a starting point to exploring the underlying conditions that might be fuelling hotspots. While a global Moran's I test can show that crime events cluster in a non-random manner, this simply explains what most criminal justice students learn in their earliest classes. For example, a global Moran's I value (range −1 to 1) of 0.56 suggests that police sectors with high robbery counts adjoin sectors that also have high robbery counts, and low crime sectors are often neighbors of other low crime sectors. This is hardly a surprise given what can be seen in Fig. 2.1.

Figure 2.2 uses the same robbery data, this time aggregated to the 419 sectors of the Philadelphia Police Department. This time, a local indicator of spatial association (LISA) is applied (Anselin 1995, 1996; Getis and Ord 1996; Ord and Getis 1995). The most common LISA is the local Moran's I (mentioned earlier), an approach that enables us to identify clusters of high crime areas based on their locational similarity and crime rate similarity. This is done with the construction of a spatial weights matrix that identifies a spatial relationship, often contiguity, between areal units (Anselin et al. 2008). In other words, areas that are neighbors are deemed to be spatially close. Monte Carlo simulation techniques can be used to determine if crime rates cluster in a variety of ways (Besag and Diggle 1977; Hope 1968; Mooney 1997; Ratcliffe 2005). If a group of neighboring areas are found to have concentrated levels of high crime such that the chances of discovering these patterns by random is highly unlikely, then these areas are not only statistically significant, but also are worthy of further research and inquiry.

FIGURE 2.2. Philadelphia robbery clusters, statistical significance estimated with local Moran's I.

In Fig. 2.2, there are small clusters of high robbery areas in south and southwest Philadelphia, and a larger robbery problem in the inner north and northeast of the city. The northwest, in the area of Fairmount Park (a large public park) and smaller areas of the periphery of the city limits are shown to have clusters of low robbery police sectors.[5] The global Moran's I value of 0.56 indicates a general clustering as expected; however, the local Moran's I LISA approach indicates areas of statistically significant clusters where robberies are higher or lower than would be expected if robberies were randomly distributed around the city sectors. These could form the basis for a more detailed and spatially focused study. The chapter in this book by Bernasco and Elffers discusses in greater depth other approaches to, and measures of, spatial autocorrelation.

SPATIO-TEMPORAL CRIME MAPPING

At present, the most under-researched area of spatial criminology is that of spatio-temporal crime patterns. It would appear that significant research activity is still focused on fine-tuning methods of crime hotspot detection (Chainey et al. 2003) and geographic determination of crime clusters (Murray and Roncek 2008) while the temporal component of the underlying

---

[5] Again for the technically-minded, the output was created using a first order, Queen's contiguity spatial weights matrix, with pseudo significance limit set at 0.01 with 999 permutations. The software used to perform the analysis was the freely-available GeoDa. For map clarity and simplification, areas of low robbery surrounded by high robbery count, and high surrounded by low are not indicated.

crime distributions has languished as a largely ignored area of study. This is a shame, given the wealth of information that can be gleaned from an understanding of spatio-temporal crime mapping. Originating with the work of Hagerstrand (1970), time geography provides a conceptual framework for understanding constraints on human activity and how participation in activities (such as crime) is influenced by the constraints imposed by space and time (Miller 2005). As the relevant actors – victims, offenders, guardians, and place managers – adjust their relative densities over time and around specific places, the opportunities for crime shift and coagulate. These coagulations of crime opportunity, where victims and offenders come together in greater concentrations, help explain crime hotspots around bars late at night, in downtown areas of cities during weekend evenings, and in city centers during the workday. Temporal constraint theory provides a model to understand these shifting patterns and consider crime prevention solutions (Ratcliffe 2006).

The repeat victimization literature provides a direct indication of the temporal element of crime as a research frontier with significant policy significance. With regard to burglary, repeat victimization occurs when the location of a previous burglary is later targeted again. Early research into repeat victimization identified that "the chance of a repeat burglary over the period of one year was around four times the rate to be expected if the events were independent" (Polvi et al. 1991: 412). The same study found that the rate within a month of an initial event was over twelve times the expected rate, declining over the next few months. While a body of research that has been largely ignored in the US, further research has highlighted the crime prevention benefits of addressing repeat victimization (Farrell et al. 1998; Farrell and Pease 1993; Laycock 2001; Pease 1998), with one project in the UK being spectacularly successful at reducing crime (Forrester et al. 1988). From a crime mapping perspective, the existence of discernable repeat victimization timelines emphasizes the multidimensionality of crime: patterns are identifiable not only in terms of x and y coordinates, but also on a temporal plane.

While largely ignored by the crime mapping fraternity for many years (Lersch 2004), there is a growing number of techniques that incorporate a spatio-temporal analytical capacity. Even when the exact time of a crime is not known (such as with many burglaries or vehicle thefts), *aoristic analysis* (Ratcliffe and McCullagh 1998a) can be employed to calculate the probability that an event occurred within given temporal parameters, and sums the probabilities for all events that might have occurred to produce a temporal weight in a given area (Ratcliffe 2000). This technique has identified that many crime hotspots display temporal or aoristic signatures (Ratcliffe 2002), signatures that can be combined with the spatial pattern of the crime hotspot to identify effective crime reduction strategies (Ratcliffe 2004c). The aoristic value (t) can be calculated as:

$$t_{is} = \frac{\Delta}{\beta i - \alpha i}$$

where i(α, β) is a crime incident with start time (α) and end time (β), s is a temporal search parameter with start time (α) and end time (β), Δ represents a temporal unit (e.g., 1 min, hour, or day), start times (α) are rounded down to unit Δ end times (β) are rounded up to unit Δ, and where $i(\alpha, \beta) \cup s$. Individual aoristic values, for example, hour by hour, can be mapped for a single crime event of undetermined time, or the aoristic value can be used as a weighting parameter in a kernel density estimation surface (see Ratcliffe 2002, for more details and an example).

Figure 2.3 shows statistically similar clusters for vehicle thefts across Philadelphia in 2005. Comparing this image with Fig. 2.2, it can be seen that the large cluster is in the same

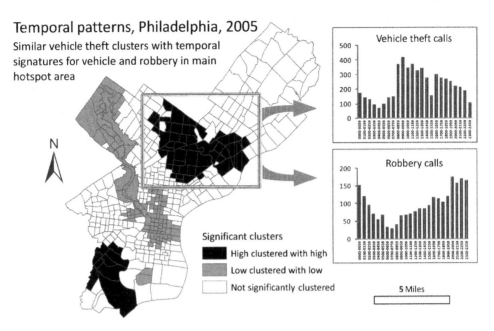

FIGURE 2.3. Significant vehicle theft clusters, with temporal signature charts for vehicle theft and robbery calls for the main high crime cluster. Charts show hourly call volume from 0000–0059 to 2300–2359.

area for both robbery and vehicle theft. The two side graphics in Fig. 2.3 isolate the crime events that occurred in this cluster area (loosely identified with a rectangle) and chart the event time on a bar chart. The charts show 24 vertical lines, each reporting the volume of crime calls for service in each hour of the day. The leftmost bar shows the volume from midnight to 1 a.m, 1 a.m to 2 a.m., and so on across to 11 p.m. to midnight on the far right. It can be seen that the temporal pattern of robbery calls is significantly different to vehicle theft calls.[6]

Issues of spatio-temporality and repeat victimization feature in the latest insight from the crime mapping research front: the near repeat phenomenon. Near repeat victimization stems from the realization that when a home is burgled, the risk of further victimization is not only higher for the targeted home, but also for homes nearby. As with repeat victimization, near repeat victimization also has a time period that appears to decay after some weeks or months. This communication of risk to nearby locations was first examined by Shane Johnson, Kate Bowers, and Michael Townsley and colleagues (Bowers and Johnson 2004; Johnson and Bowers 2004a, b; Townsley et al. 2003). While the exact spatio-temporal parameters of the infectiousness of burglary differ from place to place, the British and Australian studies were similar enough (usually a month or two and for a few hundred meters) to merit a multi-national comparison. This collaborative venture confirmed the consistency of the near repeat phenomenon across different countries (Johnson et al. 2007). Early studies concentrated on burglary; however, recent work has identified a near repeat pattern with shootings in Philadelphia (Ratcliffe and Rengert 2008) and even in the spatio-temporal distribution of improvised explosive device attacks on coalition forces in Baghdad (Townsley et al. 2008).

---

[6] Cluster map created using the same parameter choices as for Fig. 2.2. In Fig. 2.3's temporal charts, please note the change in vertical scale.

The preventative value of the near repeat phenomenon is still being uncovered. Informed by near repeat patterns, researchers have developed predictive mapping approaches that give greater weight to more recent and local crime, thus creating predictive hotspot maps that are more accurate predictors of short-term crime problems (Bowers et al. 2004; Johnson et al. 2009). Software to allow analysts to examine the near repeat phenomenon in their own data is now freely available with the Near Repeat Calculator (details available at the end of this chapter).

All of this evidence suggests fascinating new frontiers for crime analysts wishing to use mapping to explore beyond the flat two-dimensional patterns of crime events. The introduction of the temporal characteristics of crime opens up a range of avenues that are not only interesting from a theoretical sense, but also have real possibilities in better understanding and preventing crime and criminality.

CHALLENGES FOR THE FUTURE

The most prominent requisite to a lecturer, though perhaps not really the most important, is a good delivery; for though to all true philosophers science and nature will have charms innumerable in every dress, yet I am sorry to say that the generality of mankind cannot accompany us one short hour unless the path is strewed with flowers.[7]

When conducted correctly and with attention to detail and clarity, mapping can "strew flowers" across a wide variety of fields, and succinctly convey information in a format that is ideally suited to operational decision-making. The power of maps to convey both spatial (Tufte 2001) and spatio-temporal (Dorling and Openshaw 1992; MacEachren 1994; Peuquet 1994) information is well-known; what is also known by some cartographers is the capacity of poorly designed maps to be erroneous and misleading (Monmonier and Blij 1996). Spatio-temporal information can be effectively understood in map animation form (Dorling and Openshaw 1992), yet both training and tools are still too underdeveloped for mainstream use of animation within the policing domain. Even with basic maps that are now easy to create, few academics or police analysts receive any training in map design, computer graphics, or even basic cartography. The result is often an underwhelming map that fails to convey the key information and leaves the map reader confused rather than enlightened. Too often, the analytical community fixates on analytical techniques to the detriment of the vital role of the analyst: the conveyance of analysis and intelligence to influence decision-making (Ratcliffe 2008).

While crime mapping has become a clear subfield of both geography and criminal justice, many questions and problems remain. One particular problem among crime analysts is the incorrect tendency to map real values with choropleth (thematic) maps, resulting in the misleading impression that is often given by larger or unequal areas (Harries 1999). One easy solution is to map the location quotient:

$$LQ = \frac{\dfrac{c_i}{a_i}}{\dfrac{c_R}{a_R}}$$

---

[7] Michael Faraday, chemist, physicist, 1791–1867. From personal letters quoted in Thompson (1898).

where c is the frequency of crime and a is the area of a subset location (i) of a larger region (R). When mapped with a diverging visual scale, the map can show crime areas at the expected region-wide rate, areas that have lower levels of crime, and areas that are "hotter" than expected. First introduced to the criminological field by Brantingham and Brantingham (1993), location quotients have been recently used as a preliminary stage of more complex analyses of drug market distribution (Rengert et al. 2005; McCord and Ratcliffe 2007).

Other problems surround the appropriateness of the many different techniques available to analyze crime patterns. As police executives and decision-makers in the criminal justice system become more interested in predictive mapping and using intelligence-led policing to anticipate crime problems, the relative accuracy of different hotspot techniques has become a significant policy issue. Tools such as the prediction accuracy index (Chainey et al. 2008) are first steps in a direction that should provide greater clarity to analysts seeking predictive crime mapping that is statistically and empirically robust. Continued development into spatio-temporal patterns would appear to be a fertile research avenue with real policy implications, and with enough enthusiasm from the practitioner community we may find that GIS vendors start to develop software that will enable easy creation of animated maps of crime.[8] Without easy animation processes, it is unlikely that decision-makers and policy makers will be as engaged as they should with the temporal and spatio-temporal aspects of crime. Understanding the spatial dimensions of crime flux over time is a key component of cost-effective crime reduction in many situations.

Further theoretical enhancements that will in future provide a better idea of the spatial extent of noxious locations are in need of development. For example, it is well known that some bars and other licensed premises are not only the crime attractors and generators at their specific location, but they also influence the formation of crime hotspots in their immediate vicinity, with an influence that decays as distance from the specific site increases. The spatial extent of the decay is still indistinct; moreover, the mechanism to accurately assess the noxious influence of crime generating places is not yet clear.

As Ron Clarke noted, "Quite soon, crime mapping will become as much an essential tool of criminological research as statistical analysis is at present" (Clarke 2004: 60). This may be the case; however, it is apparent that much crime mapping potential is not currently realized. In a survey of the American crime analysis field, researchers found that few analysts engaged in true analysis but rather conducted basic management statistics and descriptive work (O'Shea and Nicholls 2002). Wilson charted by social science discipline the percentage of articles published from 1996 to 2005 that used some form of mapping or spatial analysis. While showing a "healthy growth" (Wilson 2007: 140), the percentage never crept above 0.1% for any field, including criminology and sociology.

The power of GIS lies in the ability of the researcher to discover the underlying patterns and characteristics of crime clusters and for practitioners to target high crime areas with effective crime prevention measures (Anselin et al. 2008). Crime mapping itself should rarely be the end of the analytical process. Researchers should be familiar with spatial statistics in order to differentiate between random patterns and characteristics of the data that are truly worth exploring (the Bernasco and Elffers chapter on spatial statistics in this book will serve as a good start). Equally, crime analysts should understand that crime mapping is but one stage in an intelligence-led crime reduction process; there is still a requirement to influence the

---

[8] As an example, an animated map showing hour-by-hour changes in violent crime hotspots in Camden, NJ, is available to download from the chapter author's web site at www.jratcliffe.net/var/violence.wmv.

thinking of decision-makers and steer them in the direction of effective crime reduction tactics. This will not only impact on the training requirements of crime analysts, but also on police managers (Ratcliffe 2004a).

The development of crime mapping in police departments, and the enthusiasm for environmental criminology as a mechanism to effect change resulting from a better understanding of the spatio-temporal characteristics of crime, has placed traditional criminology in somewhat of a quandary. As Clarke (2008: 192) points out, traditional academics have little enthusiasm for an approach to the crime problem that does not advance "the welfarist, social reform agendas of most criminologists" and cares less for an understanding of the long-term motivations of offenders but rather examines the dynamics of the crime event, seeking an understanding of the immediate location and circumstances surrounding each and every burglary, robbery and car theft. This has resulted in some claims that the practical outcomes of environmental criminology theory, such as situational crime prevention (Brantingham and Brantingham 1990; Clarke 1992; Ekblom and Tilley 2000) and crime prevention through environmental design (Cozens 2008; Feins et al. 1997) engage in social exclusion (for examples, see Tilley 2004; White and Sutton 1995). These arguments have not only been dismissed (Clarke 2008), but also perhaps suggest a disconnect of some parts of the broader criminology field to recognize the applicability of situational and geographic responses to crime control. A closer relationship between academics versed in environmental criminology and the crime control policy arena will provide the best mechanism for mainstream criminology to regain some relevance to practitioners, policy makers, and the community, all of whom recognize that while improvements in employment, poverty and education might reduce criminality over the course of decades, there is still a need for a crime control solution to the problems of today. Crime mapping provides a cartography of the problem, an analytical chart to uncover the answers, and influences the development of theories that can provide a route map to the solution.

GETTING STARTED

The standard text on crime mapping theory and practice is provided by Chainey and Ratcliffe (2005), while the book edited by Wortley and Mazerolle (2008) supports an understanding of the theoretical component and resultant crime prevention and policing responses. Anselin and colleagues (2008) provide a chapter that documents the most common methods of determining crime hotspots (see also Eck et al. 2005 which can be downloaded from the National Institute of Justice MAPS program below), while the website of the Center for Problem Oriented Policing is the single most comprehensive website dedicated to crime reduction analysis and solutions (www.popcenter.org). Connection to the crime mapping community is available through a list server, administered by the Mapping and Analysis for Public Safety (MAPS) program of the National Institute of Justice; details at www.ojp.usdoj.gov/nij/maps/. Their website is also a source for information regarding GIS, training and conferences – all with a crime focus. The International Association of Crime Analysts maintains a web site (www.iaca.net) that details training and resources regarding crime analysis, sometimes with a crime mapping component. Readers are welcome to visit this chapter author's website for additional links and resources (www.jratcliffe.net).

The two central GIS software solutions mentioned earlier, Pitney Bowes MapInfo (MapInfo) and the suite of ArcGIS programs available from ESRI are the main entry points for researchers and analysts, and they retain enough analytical power for most users. They are not, however, the only possibilities. An online search for the term "free GIS" will elicit over half-a-million hits, though the difficulty with free GIS programs is the lack of availability of base datasets such as road networks and census data in an appropriate spatial format. ArcGIS and MapInfo are continually developing and new analytical tools are regularly introduced. Furthermore, there is a growing library of downloadable routines for both ArcGIS and MapInfo that can extend the capacity of the programs. Numerous small programs written and donated by the analytical community in MapBasic (for MapInfo) and ArcObjects (for ArcGIS) formats are available and accessible on the Internet.

For more advanced crime analysis needs, there are additional software options. The mainstream statistical software solutions such as SPSS, SAS and Stata, are increasingly equipped with routines that provide some spatial analysis routines for point pattern data sets. Their processes are well documented and the interfaces are improving; however, they do not integrate directly with MapInfo or ArcGIS and some conversion of files back and forward is often necessary. Fortunately, there are a number of free software options for more advanced analysis.

CrimeStat (Levine 2006) is a free software program that comes with a substantial manual and workbook to assist with advanced spatial analysis questions (Levine 2006). It was developed through funding from the National Institute of Justice specifically for spatial crime analysis tasks and is able to read and write both MapInfo's tables and ArcGIS's shapefiles, aiding interface of the software with the data. In addition, GeoDa is also free, and is available online. While GeoDa has a relatively modest interface, and final map production is best done with a GIS, it does provide a range of tools to analyze and model spatial autocorrelation.

Finally, for advanced users seeking to take their spatial crime analysis to the frontier of the field, the latest development from the academic field is often first available in routines written for the programmable analytical software package called R. R is a free download, but is a command-line driven program where a little programming experience is helpful. The program and supporting library of routines is supported by a community of academics and researchers around the world, and doctoral students interested in spatial crime analysis are encouraged to explore the variety of spatial routines available. The statistical analysis and graphics environment and language called R is available from http://cran.r-project.org.

The GIS used to create the maps in this chapter was ESRI's ArcGIS (www.esri.com), while much of the analysis was conducted with CrimeStat (http://www.icpsr.umich.edu/CRIMESTAT/) and GeoDa (www.geoda.uiuc.edu). The latter two programs are free downloads, as is the Near Repeat Calculator mentioned in this chapter (www.temple.edu/cj/misc/nr).

Acknowledgement The author would like to thank the Philadelphia Police Department for continued support and provision of data over many years, and Ralph B. Taylor, Martin Andresen, Shane Johnson, George Rengert, Liz Groff and Travis Taniguchi for comments on an earlier draft of this chapter; however, opinions, omissions and errors remain firmly the fault of the author.

REFERENCES

Andresen MA (2006) Crime measures and the spatial analysis of criminal activity. Br J Criminol 46(2):258–285
Anselin L (1988) Spatial econometrics: methods and models. Kluwer, Dordrecht
Anselin L (1995) Local indicators of spatial association – LISA. Geogr Anal 27(2):93–115

Anselin L (1996) The Moran scatterplot as an ESDA tool to assess local instability in spatial association. In: Fischer M, Scholten HJ, Unwin D (eds) Spatial Analytical Perspectives on GIS. Taylor and Francis, London, pp 111–125

Anselin L, Bera A (1998) Spatial dependence in linear regression models with an introduction to spatial econometrics. In: Ullah A, Giles D (eds) Handbook of applied economic statistics. Marcel Dekker, New York, pp 237–289

Anselin L, Griffiths E, Tita G (2008) Crime mapping and hot spot analysis. In: Wortley R, Mazerolle L (eds) Environmental criminology and crime analysis. Willan Publishing, Cullompton, Devon, pp 97–116

Arbia G (2001) The role of spatial effects in the empirical analysis of regional concentration. Geogr Syst 3(3): 271–281

Assuncao RM, Reis EA (1999) A new proposal to adjust Moran's I for population density. Stat Med 18:2147–2162

Bailey TC, Gatrell AC (1995) Interactive spatial data analysis, 2nd edn. Longman, London

Besag J, Diggle PJ (1977) Simple Monte Carlo tests for spatial pattern. Appl Stat 26(3):327–333

Bichler G, Balchak S (2007) Address matching bias: ignorance is not bliss. Policing: An Int J Police Strateg Manage 30(1):32–60

Boggs SL (1965) Urban crime patterns. Am Sociol Rev 30(6):899–908

Bowers KJ, Johnson SD (2004) Who commits near repeats? A test of the boost explanation. West Criminol Rev 5(3):12–24

Bowers KJ, Johnson SD, Pease K (2004) Prospective hot-spotting: the future of crime mapping? Br J Criminol 44(5):641–658

Brantingham PL, Brantingham PJ (1990) Situational crime prevention in practice. Can J Criminol 32(1):17–40

Brantingham PL, Brantingham PJ (1993) Environment, routine, and situation: toward a pattern theory of crime. In: Clarke RV, Felson M (eds) Routine activity and rational choice, Vol 5. Transaction, New Brunswick, pp 259–294

Cahill M, Mulligan G (2007) Using geographically weighted regression to explore local crime patterns. Soc Sci Comput Rev 25(2):174–193

Chainey S, Ratcliffe JH (2005) GIS and crime mapping. Wiley, London

Chainey S, Reid S, Stuart N (2003) When is a hotspot a hotspot? A procedure for creating statistically robust hotspot maps of crime. In: Kidner DB, Higgs G, White SD (eds) Socio-economic applications of geographic information science. Taylor and Francis, London, pp 21–36

Chainey S, Tompson L, Uhlig S (2008) The utility of hotspot mapping for predicting spatial patterns of crime. Secur J 21(1–2):4–28

Clarke, RV (ed) (1992) Situational crime prevention: successful case studies. Harrow and Heston, Albany, NY

Clarke RV (2004) Technology, criminology and crime science. Eur J Crim Policy Res 10(1):55–63

Clarke RV (2008) Situational crime prevention. In: Wortley R Mazerolle L (eds) Environmental criminology and crime analysis. Willan Publishing, Cullompton, Devon, pp 178–194

Clarke RV, Felson M (1993) Introduction: criminology, routine activity, and rational choice. In: Clarke RV, Felson M (eds) Routine activity and rational choice. Vol 5. Transaction, New Brunswick, pp 259–294

Cliff AD, Ord JK (1969) The problem of spatial autocorrelation. In: Scott AJ (ed) London papers in regional science. Pion, London, pp 25–55

Cohen LE, Felson M (1979) Social change and crime rate trends: a routine activity approach. Am Sociol Rev 44: 588–608

Cornish DB, Clarke RV (1987) Understanding crime displacement: an application of rational choice theory. Criminology 25(4):933–947

Cornish D, Clarke R (1986) The reasoning criminal: rational choice perspectives on offending. Springer, New York

Cozens P (2008) Crime prevention through environmental design. In: Wortley R, Mazerolle L (eds) Environmental criminology and crime analysis. Willan Publishing, Cullompton, Devon, pp 153–177

Craglia M, Haining R, Wiles P (2000) A comparative evaluation of approaches to urban crime pattern analysis. Urban Stud 37(4):711–729

Dorling D, Openshaw S (1992) Using computer animation to visualize space-time patterns. Environ Plann B Plann Des 19(6):639–650

Eck JE (1997) What do those dots mean? Mapping theories with data. In D. Weisburd T. McEwen (eds) Crime mapping and crime prevention, Vol 8. Criminal Justice Press, Monsey, NY, pp 379–406

Eck JE, Chainey S, Cameron JG, Leitner M, Wilson RE (2005) Mapping crime: understanding hot spots (Special Report). National Institute of Justice, Washington DC

Ekblom P, Tilley N (2000) Going equipped: criminology, situational crime prevention and the resourceful offender. Br J Criminol 40(3):376–398

Farrell G, Chenery S, Pease K (1998) Consolidating police crackdowns: findings from an anti-burglary project (Police Research Series paper 113). Policing and Reducing Crime Unit, Research, Development and Statistics Directorate, Home Office, London

Farrell G, Pease K (1993) Once bitten, twice bitten: repeat victimisation and its implications for crime prevention. Police Res Group: Crime Prev Unit Ser Pap 46:32

Farrell G, Pease K (1994) Crime seasonality – domestic disputes and residential burglary in Merseyside 1988–90. Br J Criminol 34(4):487–498

Feins JD, Epstein JC, Widom R (1997) Solving crime problems in residential neighborhoods: comprehensive changes in design, management, and use. NIJ Issues Pract 157

Felson M (1998) Crime and everyday life: impact and implications for society 2nd edn. Pine Forge Press, Thousand Oaks, CA

Felson M, Poulsen E (2003) Simple indicators of crime by time of day. Int J Forecast 19(4):595–601

Field S (1992) The effect of temperature on crime. Br J Criminol 32(3):340–351

Forrester D, Chatterton M, Pease K (1988) The Kirkholt burglary prevention project, Rochdale (No. 13). Crime Prevention Unit (Home Office), London

Fotheringham AS, Brunsdon C, Charlton M (2002) Geographically weighted regression. Wiley, Chichester, UK

Fotheringham SA, Brunsdon C (2004) Some thoughts on inference in the analysis of spatial data. Int J Geogr Inf Sci 18(5):447–457

Getis A, Ord JK (1992) The analysis of spatial association by use of distance statistics. Geogr Anal 24(3):189–206

Getis A, Ord JK (1996) Local spatial statistics: an overview. In: Longley P, Batty M (eds) Spatial analysis: modelling in a gis environment, 1st edn. GeoInformation International, London p 374

Guerry A-M (1833) Essai sur la statistique morale de la France: precede d'un rapport a l'Academie de sciences. Chez Crochard, Paris

Hagerstrand T (1970) What about people in regional science? Pap Reg Sci 24:7–21

Harries KD (1980) Crime and the environment. Charles C. Thomas, Springfield, IL

Harries KD (1981) Alternative denominators in conventional crime rates. In: Brantingham PJ, Brantingham PL (eds) Environmental criminology. Sage, London, pp 147–165

Harries KD (1999) Mapping crime: principles and practice. US Department of Justice, Washington DC

Hope ACA (1968) A simplified Monte Carlo significance test procedure. J R Stat Soc Ser B 30:583–598

Hope T (1995) The flux of victimization. Br J Criminol 35(3):327–342

Johnson SD, Bowers KJ (2004a) The burglary as clue to the future: the beginnings of prospective hot-spotting. Eur J Criminol 1(2):237–255

Johnson SD, Bowers KJ (2004b) The stability of space-time clusters of burglary. Br J Criminol 44(1):55–65

Johnson SD, Bernasco W, Bowers KJ, Elffers H, Ratcliffe JH, Rengert GF, Townsley M (2007) Space-time patterns of risk: a cross national assessment of residential burglary victimization. J Quant Criminol 23(3):201–219

Johnson SD, Bowers KJ, Birks D, Pease K (2009) Predictive mapping of crime by ProMap: accuracy, units of analysis and the environmental backcloth. In: Weisburd D, Bernasco W, Bruinsma G (eds) Putting crime in its place: units of analysis in spatial crime research Springer, New York, pp 165–192

Land K, Deane G (1992) On the large-sample estimation of regression models with spatial effect terms: a two-stage least squares approach. Sociol Methodol 22:221–248

Laycock G (2001) Hypothesis-based research: the repeat victimization story. Crim Justice 1(1):59–82

Lersch KM (2004) Space, time, and crime. North Caroline Press, Durham, NC

Levine N (2006) Crime Mapping and the Crimestat Program. Geogr Anal 38(1):41–56

Levine N (2007) CrimeStat: a spatial statistics program for the analysis of crime incident locations (v 3.1). Ned Levine & Associates, Houston, TX, and the National Institute of Justice, Washington, DC. Mar [http://www.icpsr.umich.edu/CRIMESTAT/]. Chapter 8

MacEachren A (1994) Time as a cartographic variable. In: Hearnshaw H, Unwin D (eds) Visualisation in geographical information systems. Wiley, London, pp 115–130

Maltz MD, Gordon AC, Friedman W (1991) Mapping crime in its community setting: event geography analysis. Springer, New York

Martin D (2002) Spatial patterns in residential burglary: assessing the effect of neighborhood social capital. J Contemp Crim Justice 18(2):132–146

McCord E, Ratcliffe JH (2007) A micro-spatial analysis of the demographic and criminogenic environment of drug markets in Philadelphia. Aust N Z J Criminol 40(1):43–63

Mencken FC, Barnett C (1999) Murder, nonnegligent manslaughter and spatial autocorrelation in mid-South counties. J Quant Criminol 15(4):407–422

Messner SF, Anselin L (2004) Spatial analyses of homicide with areal data. In: Goodchild MF, Janelle DG (eds) Spatially integrated social science. Oxford University Press, New York, NY, pp 127–144

Messner SF, Anselin L, Baller RD, Hawkins DF, Deane G, Tolnay SE (1999) The spatial patterning of county homicide rates: an application of exploratory spatial data analysis. J Quant Criminol 15(4):423–450

Miller HJ (2005) A measurement theory for time geography. Geogr Anal 37(1):17–45

Monmonier M, Blij HJd (1996) How to lie with maps, 2nd edn. University of Chicago Press, Chicago

Mooney CZ (1997) Monte carlo simulation. Sage, Thousand Oaks, CA

Moran PAP (1950) Notes on continuous stochastic phenomena. Biometrika 37:17–23

Murray RK, Roncek DW (2008) Measuring diffusion of assaults around bars through radius and adjacency techniques. Crim Justice Rev 33(2):199–220

O'Shea TC, Nicholls K (2002) Crime analysis in America (Full final report), Office of Community Oriented Policing Services, Washington DC

Oden N (1995) Adjusting Moran's I for population density. Stat Med 14(1):17–26

Openshaw S (1984) The modifiable areal unit problem. Concepts Tech Mod Geogr 38:41

Openshaw S, Cross A, Charlton M, Brunsdon C, Lillie J (1990) Lessons learnt from a Post Mortem of a failed GIS. Paper presented at the 2nd National Conference and Exhibition of the AGI, Brighton, Oct 1990

Ord JK, Getis A (1995) Local spatial autocorrelation statistics: distributional issues and an application. Geogr Anal 27(4):286–306

Pease K (1998) Repeat victimisation: taking stock. Police Res Group: Crime Detect Prev Ser Pap 90 1–48

Peuquet DJ (1994) It's about time – a conceptual-framework for the representation of temporal dynamics in Geographical Information Systems. Ann Assoc Am Geogr 84(3):441–461

Polvi N, Looman T, Humphries C, Pease K (1991) The time course of repeat burglary victimization. Br J Criminol 31(4):411–414

Quetelet A (1842) A treatise in man. Chambers, Edinburgh

Ratcliffe JH (2000) Aoristic analysis: the spatial interpretation of unspecific temporal events. Int J Geogr Inf Sci 14(7):669–679

Ratcliffe JH (2001) On the accuracy of TIGER-type geocoded address data in relation to cadastral and census areal units. Int J Geogr Inf Sci 15(5):473–485

Ratcliffe JH (2002) Aoristic signatures and the temporal analysis of high volume crime patterns. J Quant Criminol 18(1):23–43

Ratcliffe JH (2004a) Crime mapping and the training needs of law enforcement. Eur J Crim Policy Res 10(1):65–83

Ratcliffe JH (2004b) Geocoding crime and a first estimate of an acceptable minimum hit rate. Int J Geogr Inf Sci 18(1):61–73

Ratcliffe JH (2004c) The Hotspot Matrix: a framework for the spatio-temporal targeting of crime reduction. Police Pract Res 5(1):5–23

Ratcliffe JH (2005) Detecting spatial movement of intra-region crime patterns over time. J. Quant Criminol 21(1):103–123

Ratcliffe JH (2006) A temporal constraint theory to explain opportunity-based spatial offending patterns. J Res Crime Delinq 43(3):261–291

Ratcliffe JH (2008) Intelligence-led policing. Willan Publishing, Cullompton, Devon

Ratcliffe JH (2009) The structure of strategic thinking. In: Ratcliffe JH (ed) Strategic thinking in criminal intelligence, 2nd edn. Federation Press, Sydney

Ratcliffe JH, McCullagh MJ (1998a) Aoristic crime analysis. Int J Geogr Inf Sci 12(7):751–764

Ratcliffe JH, McCullagh MJ (1998b) Identifying repeat victimisation with GIS. Br J Criminol 38(4):651–662

Ratcliffe JH, McCullagh MJ (1999) Hotbeds of crime and the search for spatial accuracy. Geogr Syst 1(4):385–398

Ratcliffe JH, Rengert GF (2008) Near repeat patterns in Philadelphia shootings. Secur J 21(1–2):58–76

Rengert GF, Ratcliffe JH, Chakravorty S (2005) Policing illegal drug markets: geographic approaches to crime reduction. Criminal Justice Press, Monsey, NY

Roncek DW, Maier PA (1991) Bars, blocks and crimes revisited: linking the theory of routine activities to the empiricisms of 'Hot Spots'. Criminology 29(4):725–753

Shaw CR, McKay HD (1942) Juvenile delinquency and urban areas. Chicago University Press, Chicago

Taylor B, Kowalyk A, Boba R (2007) The integration of crime analysis Into law enforcement agencies. Police Q 10(2):154–169

Thompson SP (1898) Michael Faraday: his life and work. MacMillan, New York

Tilley N (2004) Karl Popper: a philosopher for Ronald Clarke's situational crime prevention. In: Shoham S, Knepper P (eds) Israeli studies in criminology, Vol 8. de Sitter, Willowdale, Ontario, pp 39–56

Tobler W (1970) A computer movie simulating urban growth in the Detroit region. In: Economic geography, 46(Supplement: Proceedings. International Geographical Union. commission on quantitative methods. (June, 1970)) pp 234–240

Townsley M, Homel R, Chaseling J (2003) Infectious burglaries: a test of the near repeat hypothesis. Br J Criminol 43(3):61–633

Townsley M, Johnson SD, Ratcliffe JH (2008) Space time dynamics of insurgent activity in Iraq. Secur J 21(3): 139–146

Trickett A, Ellingworth D, Hope T, Pease K (1995) Crime victimization in the eighties – changes in area and regional inequality. Br J Criminol 35(3):343–359

Tufte ER (2001) The visual display of quantitative information, 2nd edn. Graphics Press, London

van Koppen PJ, De Keijser JW (1999) The time to rob: variations in time of number of commercial robberies. J Res Crime Delinq 36(1):7–29

Ward MD, Gleditsch KS (2008) Spatial regression models. (Quantitative Applications in the Social Sciences Series). Sage, Thousand Oaks, CA

Weisburd D, Bernasco W, Bruinsma GJN (2009) Units of analysis in geographic criminology: historical development, critical issues, and open questions. In: Weisburd D, Bernasco W, Bruinsma GJN (eds) Putting crime in its place: units of analysis in geographic criminology Springer, New York, pp 3–31

Weisburd D, Bushway S, Lum C, Yang S-M (2004) Trajectories of crime at places: a longitudinal study of street segments in the City of Seattle. Criminology 42(2):283–321

Weisburd D, Lum C (2005) The diffusion of computerized crime mapping in policing: linking research and practice. Police Pract Res 6(5):419–434

Weisburd D, McEwen T (1997) Crime mapping and crime prevention, Vol 8. Criminal Justice Press, New York

White R, Sutton A (1995) Crime prevention, urban space and social exclusion. Aust N Z J Sociol 31(1):82–99

Wilson RE (2007) The impact of software on crime mapping. Soc Sci Comput Rev 25(2):135–142

Wortley R, Mazerolle L (eds) (2008) Environmental criminology and crime analysis. Willan Publishing, Cullompton, Devon

## CHAPTER 3

Look Before You Analyze: Visualizing Data in Criminal Justice

MICHAEL D. MALTZ

INTRODUCTION AND RATIONALE

First, a confession. I taught statistics for 30 years, and for most of that time, I stuck pretty close to the topics covered in standard social science and statistics textbooks, explaining correlation, regression, statistical significance, t-tests, ANOVA, etc. In other words, I ended up teaching the same-old, same-old statistical methods (sorry, students), primarily inferential statistics, without stopping to consider how well they filled the students' needs. Of course, students need to know these methods, since they have to be able to interpret the findings of papers written by researchers who learned, and were applying the same-old, same-old methods. But they also need to know what assumptions are implicit in these methods; many are based on random sampling, which is often not the case, and on linearity, normality, independence, and other idealizations that are rarely found in real data – which does not stop researchers from applying them (Maltz 1994, 2006).

For the most part, these methods were developed early in the last century, when collecting data was an expensive proposition. For this reason, to reduce the cost of data collection, many of the methods were predicated on taking random samples. Moreover, analyzing data could take hours or days, even with small datasets.

Neither of these conditions still holds. Rather than a trickle of data, we are now confronted with a fire hose of data. Of course, this does not mean that there are no longer problems of data quality; much of the data is entered by humans, not automatically recorded, and dates, names, and other entries are not always entered correctly.[1]

And the computer horsepower we now command on our desktops (and in our pockets!) was undreamt of when the methods were developed (or when I started teaching). Using statistical packages like SPSS or SAS or Systat or Stata, one can pour the data into one of

---

[1] Regarding data entry, one of my favorite quotes is from an economist in the 1920s (Stamp 1929: 258): "The Government are very keen on amassing statistics. They collect them, add them, raise them to the nth power, take the cube root and prepare wonderful diagrams. But what you must never forget is that every one of these figures comes in the first place from the *chowty dar* [village watchman]. who just puts down what he damn pleases."

A.R. Piquero and D. Weisburd (eds.), *Handbook of Quantitative Criminology*,
DOI 10.1007/978-0-387-77650-7_3, © Springer Science + Business Media, LLC 2010,
First softcover printing 2011

these powerful analytic engines, select different "models" of the process under investigation,[2] and test theories (i.e., relationships among variables) to one's heart's content, scrutinizing the results for statistically significant findings.

Statistical significance has been the mainstay of social science statistical analysis ever since the pioneering work of R. A. Fisher. In more recent years, however, many questions about its value have arisen (Lieberson 1985; Cohen 1994; Maltz 1994, 2006; Wilkinson et al. 1999; Harmon et al. 2001). Regardless of its value in some situations, it is clear that it has been overused in the social sciences.

Moreover, using canned statistical routines can be likened to using the computer as an autopilot rather than as power steering (Maltz et al. 1991: 46). This is fine if you know where the data are going to take you (i.e., if you have specific hypotheses that you want to test), but these routines only go along well-trodden paths. Most assume that relationships among the variables are linear and additive, like the recipe for a cake – take two parts poor education, one part impulsivity, and three parts poverty and you cook up a delinquent. They are of limited benefit if you want to use the data to generate hypotheses, to explore the properties of the data and the relationships they may contain.

Of course, we all have preconceived notions about relationships among variables, i.e., conceptual models of the process under study. That is, we do not include shoe size as one of the variables we collect in delinquency studies. But using canned routines restricts our thinking about how the variables might relate. Looking at the data – and "playing" with the data (for example, transforming it, as will be seen in some of the examples) provides some insight into the nature of the relationships among the variables and into the appropriate way to model the processes generating the data.

Another problem with these canned routines is that they make assumptions about the relationship between variables that are implicit – and are rarely tested to see the extent to which they have any validity. Rall (2008) comes uncomfortably close to the truth in his depiction of how these programs assume that "rational" offenders make decisions about their targets (Fig. 3.1).[3]

That is not to say that all statistical analyses are suspect – they do have their place. However, there is another thread of data analysis that has been with us even longer than canned routines and tests based on statistical significance: drawing pictures of the data to discern patterns. Yet this practice is controversial in some quarters. Many social scientists still feel that it is improper to actually look at the data before analyzing them, referring to the practice as "data snooping" or "data dredging," going through the data to spot patterns or relationships. While in some cases researchers may use it improperly, to find relationships that they then incorporate in a hypothesis test that is not the only reason for looking at the data. When one is dealing with very large data sets, it is often the only way to determine what kinds of patterns exist within the data, and the field of data mining (see Chap. 34) has been

---

[2] Freedman (1985: 308) notes that "investigators often talk about 'modeling the data.' This is almost perverse: surely the object is to model the phenomenon, and the data are interesting only because they contain information about that phenomenon. Whatever it is that most social scientists are doing when they construct regression models, discovering natural laws does not seem to be uppermost in their minds."

[3] As the president of the American Statistical Association recently (Morton, 2009) said: "[D]on't trust complicated models as far as you can throw them – protect yourself and examine those data every which way. Are your assumptions correct? What are those pesky outliers up to? Let the data speak for themselves, rather than being masked and manipulated by complex methods."

FIGURE 3.1. Planning a crime spree (or graduate study) using Rational Choice Theory. Ted Rall ©2008 Ted Rall. Used by permission of Universal Press Syndicate. All rights reserved.

created to deal with it. (A sufficiently large data set can be split in two, permitting the analyst to explore one of them to his/her heart's content, and the knowledge learned applied to the other to see if the patterns hold.)

I also want to distinguish between visualizing data and visualizing the results of data analyses, which can also be helpful in understanding their import. For example, Loftus (1993) shows how figures can be more informative than tabulated hypothesis tests; Maltz and Zawitz (1998) use figures to portray the uncertainty in survey-based victimization data; Gelman et al. (2002) take statisticians to task for not employing graphs to facilitate understanding; Gelman and Hill (2007, Appendix B) make specific suggestions about visualizing the results of regression analyses; and Wainer (2009) shows the different ways that uncertainty in data can be effectively communicated using graphical methods. These uses of visualization are important and deserve consideration by all researchers; the focus of this chapter, however, is limited to the use of data visualization techniques to explore the characteristics of data, not of their analysis, and of criminal justice data in particular.

The figures in this chapter are cleaned up considerably from the original graphs I generated. For the most part, the first graphs were thrown together by transferring data to a spreadsheet and generating a quick plot by highlighting different columns and clicking on the Chart icon. If a pattern emerged, I then cleaned up the figure; if not, I continued exploring the data until a pattern emerged or until I convinced myself (whether true or not) that one was not present. In other words, as Tukey (1977) has noted, there is no set procedure for exploring data sets: just do it!

With this as prologue and rationale, we turn our attention to the various techniques that have been and can be used for data visualization in studying crime. There is a long history of using graphical methods to infer patterns from data, stretching back to the early nineteenth century, using both economic (Wainer and Spence 2005 [Playfair 1801]) and demographic data (Lexis 1880). In more recent years, the work of Cleveland (1993, 1994), Tufte (1983), Tukey (1977), Unwin et al. (2006), Wainer (1997, 2005, 2009), and Wilkinson (1999) have shown how and why graphical methods can be used in rigorous analyses of many different types of data.[4]

As will be shown, they are very useful in analyzing criminal justice data and can provide new insights that would not have been possible using standard statistical methods. Their applications include using visualization techniques to spot mistakes in the data, to find complex nonlinear relationships among variables, and to show the dynamic interactions between people and events over time.[5] In most of these cases, I use examples of my own work and techniques developed specifically for these examples. They are not unique or very complicated; others have used similar techniques for similar problems. It should be noted, however, that because different data sets have different variables and different relationships among their variables, there is no standard means of visualizing data. That is, sometimes the best visualization method is a 3-D plot, sometimes a dot plot, sometimes a longitudinal plot, sometimes a trellis plot, sometimes a network graph. This can make it difficult to promote these techniques, because there isn't a cookbook that provides a specific recipe for a specific type of data – different techniques need to be tried on a specific data set to see what technique makes the most sense, allowing the data set to tell its story. As Ripley (quoted in Unwin et al. 2006: 2) notes, "Finding ways to visualize datasets can be as important as ways to analyse them."

The advantage to using standard analytic techniques, i.e., the computer as an autopilot, is that you don't have to think too much about how to analyze the data. But that is also its disadvantage. Too often, researchers take data and perform their analyses without ever actually looking at the data.

A well-known case in point dealt with an agricultural experiment conducted in the 1930s concerning the yield of ten different varieties of barley in six different sites in Minnesota, for the years 1931 and 1932. The data were subsequently analyzed by three top statisticians: Fisher in 1971, Daniel in 1976, and Anscombe in 1981. Cleveland (1993: 5) also decided to analyze the data, but he first displayed them in a trellis plot (Fig. 3.2). When he did, he found unmistakable evidence that the 1931 and 1932 data for one of the sites had been interchanged. No one had any idea that this had occurred, because no one troubled to look at the data! And of course, it changed the conclusions that could be inferred from the data.

In this chapter, I describe a number of examples showing that plotting data in different ways permits the analyst to obtain information from the data set that would normally not be possible using standard (nonvisual) social science methods. Sections "Checking for Data Accuracy: Longitudinal Analyses" and "Checking for Data Accuracy: Scatterplots" discuss plots to determine data accuracy; section "Simple Variables and Complex Relationships"

---

[4] Those as fascinated as I am with the great variety of data visualization techniques should visit the website http://addictedtor.free.fr/graphiques/thumbs.php?sort=votes, which also includes the source code for the plots (in the computer language R). I thank Andrew Gelman for pointing out this treasure. Antony Unwin noted (personal communication) that Martin Theus developed Mondrian, an interactive graphics package that can be used for most data visualization purposes.

[5] Visualization is the key ingredient in map-based analyses as well. It is not covered in this chapter; Ratcliffe (Chap. 2) describes how it can be used to find space-time patterns in crime data.

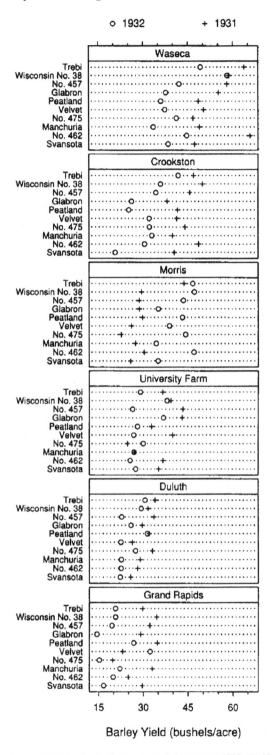

FIGURE 3.2. Yield data from a 1930s barley experiment, from Cleveland (1993: 4). Note the obvious reversal of years in the Morris data.

shows how a simple plot of victim and offender age data can tease out complex relationships between them. A more speculative use of visualization, to combine data about individuals with their geographical context, over time, is given in section "Dynamic Relationships: Animation." Section "Networks" shows how depicting networks can help in analyzing crime.

CHECKING FOR DATA ACCURACY: LONGITUDINAL ANALYSES

Crime counts

Anomalies in a set of numerical data are not easy to spot, especially when the data set is so large that visual inspection of the individual elements is out of the question. It is hard to spot anomalies even in a rather small sequence of numbers, let alone many pages of data. When this is the case, the only way to determine if the data are reliable is to plot them and see if there are any surprises. Huber (quoted in Unwin et al. 2006: 19) "found that some of the hardest errors to detect by traditional methods are unsuspected gaps in the data collection (we usually discovered them serendipitously in the course of graphical checking)." Wainer (2005: 2) noted that John Arbuthnot (1710) would have found his mistake in transcribing English birth data had he plotted them before publishing them.

This was how we dealt with determining the accuracy of crime data provided to us by the FBI (Maltz and Weiss 2006).[6] The FBI realized that some of the data they collected from police departments over the past few decades may have included errors, and we were asked to clean the data. The amount of data was prodigious: we dealt with monthly data on 7 crime types and an additional 19 subtypes (i.e., not just robbery, but robbery with a gun, with a knife, etc.) from over 17,000 police agencies, for every month from 1960–2004. For example, Fig. 3.3 shows raw data on rape for Boulder Colorado, from 1960–2004.

As can be seen, there is no doubt that one entry, 999 rapes for May 1993, is incorrect. Those who commonly use statistical packages like SPSS understand what may have happened, since 999 is often used to signify a missing datum.[7]

This error might not be normally picked up by someone working with a table of the raw data. Once it is visually detected, however, the entire data set can be inspected to see if other agencies have also used the same missing datum indicator. This is what we did in our analysis of the data; after spotting this anomaly, we then wrote a short computer algorithm to check the entire data set for 999s, 9999s, and 99999s, and determined (based on neighboring data points) whether those data points were true or missing values.

Moreover, some apparent anomalies are true values: the spike in murders in Oklahoma City in April 1995 was due to the bombing of a federal building (Fig. 3.4).

There is also a need to determine whether a zero is a true zero or a missing datum. For example, Fig. 3.5 shows the number of Index crimes[8] reported to the FBI by the Bibb County (Georgia) Police Department.

As can be seen, there are a number of times when the crime counts were zero:

---

[6] A similar strategy was used in cleaning FBI-collected arrest data (Maltz and Weiss 2007).

[7] If the field contains five characters, as it might for the crime of larceny in large cities, then the missing value might be 99999.

[8] The Crime Index is the sum of the crimes of murder, forcible rape, robbery, aggravated assault, burglary, larceny, and vehicle theft.

1. December 1960 (context: 79, 39, 45, [0], 79, 48, 52);
2. October 1962 (context: 10, 19, 11, [0], 12, 17, 10);
3. December 1964 (context: 20, 38, 33, [0], 25, 9, 6);
4. January 1966–December 1968 (context: 12, 10, 8, [36 0s], 19, 20,24);
5. July 2001 (context: 245, 281, 222, [0], 287, 307, 307); and
6. July–November 2004 (context: 194, 212, 189, [5 0s], 169).

All but the second and third zeros are obviously due to missing data. In other words, human judgment must be used to distinguish the true zeros from missing data, to reduce the number of ambiguous data to a minimum.

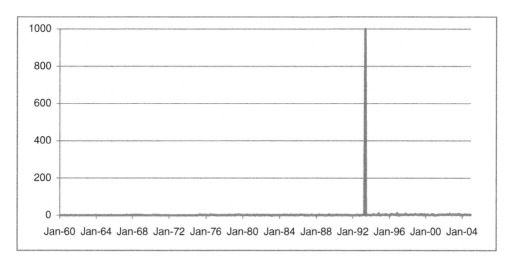

FIGURE 3.3. Raw rape data, Boulder CO Police Department, 1960–2004. The spike (999 rapes!) for May 1993 is not a valid entry: 999 was used to signify a missing datum.

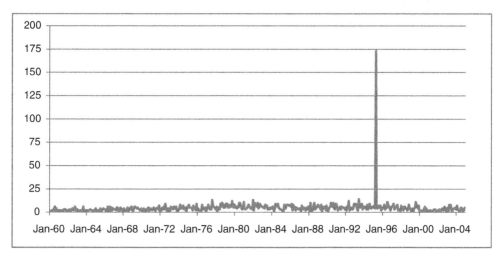

FIGURE 3.4. Raw murder data, Oklahoma City OK Police Department, 1960–2004. The spike in April 1995 (173 murders) is a valid entry: in that month a Federal building was bombed, resulting in 168 deaths.

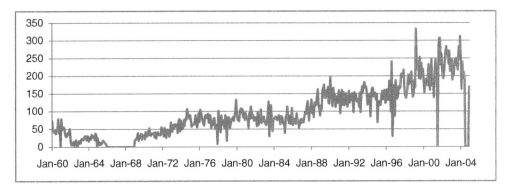

FIGURE 3.5. Raw index crime, Bibb County Police Department, 1960–2004. Note the occasional runs of zero crimes, indicating lapses in reporting crime to the FBI.

Of course, it is possible to write algorithms that attempt to identify missing data automatically, but they can get very complicated. For example, suppose (as has happened) an agency neglects to send in its data 1 month. To compensate for it, in the next month's report, the agency submits data for both that month and the missing month. In this case, both the zero and the subsequent spike are true data, although they do not reflect monthly data.

It is not that easy to write an algorithm to distinguish between true zeros and missing data. One would have to insure that the zero (followed by a higher-than normal count of crime) did not occur due to seasonality or due to secular trends – or even due to a change in policies, which can sometimes be discerned from data patterns. We found that the best way to locate these anomalies was to visually inspect the trajectories.

In general, these data "contaminants" (e.g., unexpected spikes and zeros) should not just be discarded. Like other outliers, they may contain useful information. The Oklahoma City spike is easily explained, but in some cases, a run of zeros might also be explainable and of interest to analysts. For example, it may reflect a change in administration or in reporting policies.

Dates and States

Corrections departments have to keep track of their inmates as they move through the correctional system: participating in programs, accruing "good time," credits toward early release from prison; and/or forfeiting it due to violations and infractions. They may be transferred to hospitals or other institutions, get sent to halfway houses, be placed on parole, or be released from prison without supervision. That is, prisoners move through different states (or statuses) on different dates, and the dates and states need to be recorded and retained in real time.

The system maintaining this information on prisoners can be likened to an inventory control system, where the prisoners constitute the inventory that needs to be tracked. A system like this, called a Data Warehouse, is maintained by the California Department of Corrections and Rehabilitation. In analyzing data from their Data Warehouse, we found certain anomalies due to incorrect dates. An example (based on real data) is shown in the following section in Fig. 3.6; it is exemplary of one offender's record and shows how data can be depicted to check on its validity.

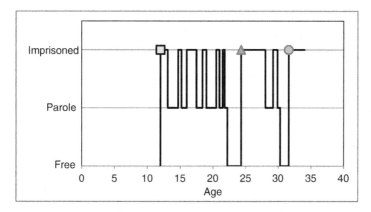

FIGURE 3.6. Hypothetical offender trajectory. The square represents a property crime, the triangle a violent crime, and the circle a drug crime. This shows that the offender was first imprisoned for a property crime, and then bounced from parole to prison five times before his first release from prison.

We developed a plotting procedure that took the movement data and focused on only certain moves – prison, parole and release – and on offenses that returned people to prison. The points with geometric shapes represent different crime types and severities, a square for property crimes, a triangle for violent crimes, a circle for drug crimes. (In the actual implementation, these shapes were colored to provide additional information for determining patterns.)

Note that the offender was first arrested at age 12, which is obviously a mistake – the Data Warehouse includes only offenders committed to adult institutions. The remaining data points seem logical – after his initial incarceration, the offender was paroled, but experienced a number of parole violations. He was free for a few years, but then returned to prison for a violent offense. Again he was released on parole, returned to prison once, and then set free from parole just after he "turned 30" (based on an incorrect date of birth). His last status was imprisonment for a drug offense.

The point of this exercise is to show how different kinds of data can be depicted in such a way to spot anomalies. Based on this data anomaly, the analyst can write an algorithm to display the trajectories that start earlier than age 15 or 16. Moreover, it is also easy to spot a trajectory where some data are missing (e.g., say date of parole completion), since the diagonal line in Fig. 3.7 would cause this trajectory to stand out from trajectories with complete data.

Summary

Two points should be noted about the way the data are plotted. First, the data are depicted longitudinally, over time; the horizontal axis is time. The UCR data sets are collected and published by the FBI annually, so stringing them together permits the analyst to see how different crimes have risen and fallen over the 45 years for which the FBI produced electronic data files. And the correctional data depict the correctional careers of individuals who have been convicted of different crimes, showing the extent to which they violate parole, are imprisoned for new crimes, or remain free of additional imprisonment. (As an aside, it may be useful

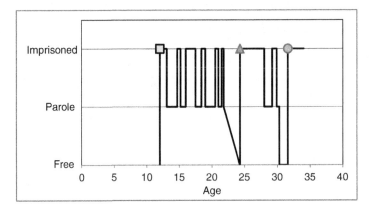

FIGURE 3.7. The same offender trajectory showing a missing date of parole completion.

to include in-prison programs in these trajectories for evaluative purposes: some programs may be better than others in keeping prisoners from violating parole or from committing new crimes.)

Second, the vertical axis can be used to depict not just standard variables (crime counts, as with the UCR data), but offenders' states as well. The correctional example above depicts three states in which an offender can be found: prison, parole, and free. Other states can be added as needed (and as data become available) – enrollment in a prison program, in a halfway house, in school; working; sought by police; in jail, etc. – which would add more complexity to the picture, but would also provide a measure of explanatory texture to the trajectory. A person viewing trajectory after trajectory of individuals about the same age, who had committed similar crimes, might be able to get a Gestalt impression of how these variables interact (which would certainly not be linearly!). That is, visualization can be used in this way to generate hypotheses that can then be tested using more formal methods.

The figures, and the means of scrolling rapidly through them, were generated by macros (tailor-made programs) embedded in Microsoft Excel, into which the data sets were ported. This is not the only software product that can be used to this end, but its advantage is that Excel is ubiquitous. The development of these macros is relatively straightforward, but does take some specialized knowledge. Those who are interested in developing similar techniques for their own use, but are not adept at computer programming, might do the following: pick out a few different examples and plot them manually; work with a programmer to develop a program to plot them; and test it on enough cases to make sure that it shows the features and patterns in which you are interested.

CHECKING FOR DATA ACCURACY: SCATTERPLOTS

When an analyst has a great deal of data at hand, it can sometimes be difficult to determine how to deal with them. This was true of an analysis we conducted of missingness in FBI-collected arrest data. Arrest data are less well-reported by police departments than are crime data (Maltz 1999), yet the level of underreporting has not been ascertained. In a study conducted for the US Bureau of Justice Statistics (BJS), we attempted to depict the extent of underreporting (Maltz and Weiss 2007), in terms of the percentage of a county's population that reported its arrest statistics, month by month from January 1980 to December 2004. Thus, we had data for the over 3,000 US counties to depict. Using a plotting strategy similar to that used by Unwin et al. (2006: 65), we produced a two-stage scatterplot (Fig. 3.8) that provides both an overview and a more detailed picture of the data.

The figure shows that, in general, the larger the county the higher the degree of arrest data reporting. Cook County, however, is an outlier that bears further examination.[9] What a figure of this nature does is, permit the analyst to find the general pattern as well as to spot the outliers and focus in on their differences with the general pattern.

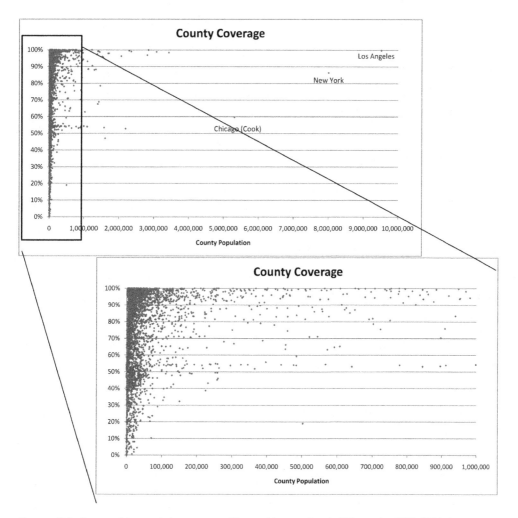

FIGURE 3.8. Percent of the population represented in monthly arrest data for US counties, 1980–2004 (*Zoom region indicated by box*). Note that the data points indicate that most county populations are small and that many counties have a high percentage of the population represented in their arrest data.

---

[9] It turns out that, for many of the years included in the study, the only police department in Cook County Illinois reporting arrest statistics to the FBI was the Chicago Police Department.

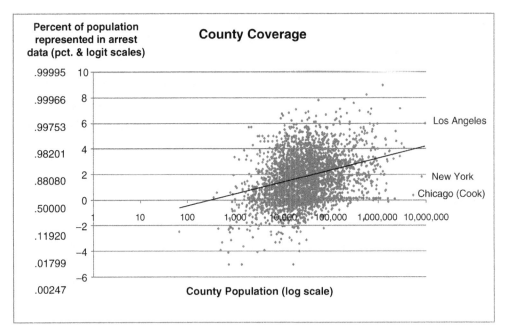

FIGURE 3.9. Percent of population represented in monthly arrest data for US counties, 1980–2004, plotting transformed data.

Note that the data clump heavily at the low end of the population scale and the high end of the percent scale. This suggests that a transformation of the data would be a productive.[10] If we exclude the (relatively few) cases of 100 percent or 0 percent reporting and plot the logit of the percent reporting against the log of the population, we end up with a relatively uniform bivariate distribution, as depicted in Fig. 3.9. This shows that, aside from the known tendency of better reporting among larger counties (indicated by the positive slope to the regression line), there are probably no (additional) obvious relationships between county population and percent reporting.

SIMPLE VARIABLES AND COMPLEX RELATIONSHIPS

What seems to be a simple picture may generate a complex picture. This was the case in a search for the relationship between victim age and offender age in homicides. In the late 1990s, I had downloaded the Supplementary Homicide Reports (SHR)[11] file to see if I could use it in a statistics class. I asked my graduate assistant, Julie Moody, to select cases with only one victim and one offender, where the ages of both were known, and do a crosstab. She then downloaded the data into a spreadsheet and made a three-dimensional plot of the data,

[10] Sometimes it takes another pair of eyes to see what may be obvious. I thank Howard Wainer for serving in that capacity.

[11] These files have been prepared by Fox (2008) for over a decade. They aggregate all of the annual SHR reports from 1976 to the most current year, and can be downloaded from the National Archive of Criminal Justice Data (http://www.icpsr.umich.edu/nacjd). The most recent version contains data from 1976 through 2005.

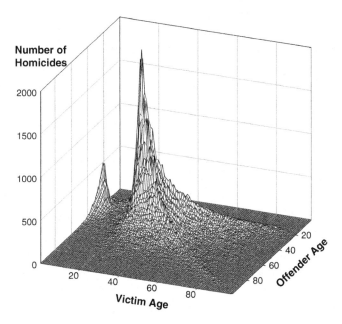

FIGURE 3.10. One-on-one homicides, raw SHR data, 1976–2005.

similar to that in Fig. 3.10. We had an "Aha!" experience when we saw that figure with all its complexity.

The *x* and *y* axes represented victim and offender ages, respectively, and the *z* axis (height) represented the number of cases for that particular combination of ages. The peak is at 19 and 20; that is, the most prevalent combination is 19-year-olds killing 20-year-olds.

A plot of the raw data shows some interesting patterns. For example, note the sawtoothed feature. When we investigated this, it turned out that there were peaks every 5 years, suggesting that when police officers filled out the SHR forms they tended to "age-heap," to round off ages (Vaupel et al. 1998: 85).

When this feature is dealt with by smoothing the data[12] (Fig. 3.11), certain patterns became even more prominent. Feature A points out something we know well, that most homicide victims and offenders are young. Feature B shows us that infanticide is not a small matter, with offenders between 15 and 40 accounting for most of the deaths of children 0–5 years old. The story of Feature C (which I call the "valley of the shadow of death") is that those between ages 6–12 are relatively safe from homicide, too old to be killed by their "caregivers," yet too young to be killed by their peers. Feature D, the diagonal ridge, indicates that even in homicide among 60- and 70-year-olds, like ages are more inclined to kill each other, which may indicate domestic homicide. And Feature E is a ridge of 20-somethings killing victims of all ages, many of which may be homicides committed during the commission of a felony.

---

[12] See Maltz (1998) for how the smoothing was accomplished.

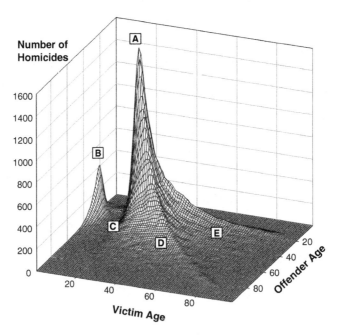

FIGURE 3.11. One-on-one homicides, smoothed SHR data, 1976–2005.

Obviously, this figure is much more informative than a simple statistical analysis of victim age and offender age – it provides food for thought rather than just a correlation coefficient or significance level.

There is no one way to display such data. In general, I display data without making any changes to it, to get an overall impression of the relationships among the variables. In this figure, for example, the sharpness of the major peak is telling, reinforcing the fact that homicide is a young person's crime.

One can drill down to another level and disaggregate the data by victim sex and offender sex (Fig. 3.12). Now, the graphical analysis is even more informative: the dominance of male-on-male homicide is very apparent, as are the opposite-sex diagonal ridges suggestive of domestic homicide. Also note that the four infanticide peaks vary more by sex of offender than sex of victim.[13] Moreover, if one factor in the presumed greater daily contact between infants and adult females than between infants and adult males, male offenders are probably strongly dominant in infanticide as well. In any event, the figure does what was intended, tell a story as well as generate hypotheses.

Additional information, however, can sometimes be gleaned by transforming the data, as was seen in Fig. 3.9. In this case, one can apply a square root transformation to the data (Fig. 3.13).[14] Its benefit is that it permits the use of the same vertical axis on all four graphs. It also highlights the diagonal "spines" in the M-on-F and F-on-M graphs, and the homicidal propensity of 20-something males.

---

[13] The peak values are indicated on the figures. Note that the scales of the male-offender and female-offender figures are not the same.

[14] Again I thank Howard Wainer for pointing this out.

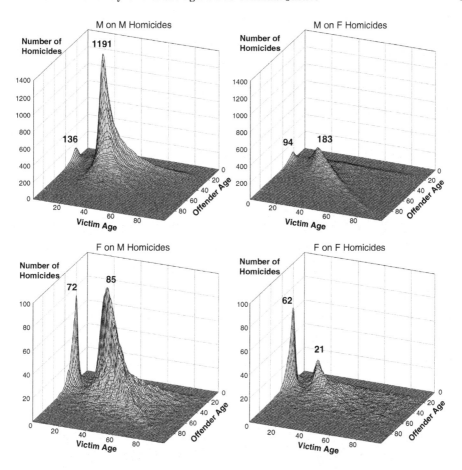

FIGURE 3.12. Smoothed SHR data, 1976–2005, disaggregated by sex of victim and sex of offender (Note: different vertical scales for male and female offenders). Heights of peaks are shown.

Multivariate Relationships

The foregoing example investigated the relationship among many variables: number of homicides, and the age and sex of victims and of offenders. Social scientists normally collect a great number of variables when investigating a phenomenon. As mentioned in the introduction, the standard way to analyze multivariate relationships is to posit a regression model, or a series of models, relating the variables to each other.

Relationships are complicated, not just those on the personal level, but in analyses as well. Most statistical techniques rely on assumptions about the variables – for example, that they are normally distributed, that the observations are independent of each other, and that the relationship between variables is linear or some variant thereof.[15] Not only are assumptions of

---

[15] A researcher might posit a log-linear or a polynomial (i.e., quadratic or cubic) relationship, but even these are linear in some sense. Assuming that something is related to (for instance) the log of family income, plus age squared, plus education level cubed is also a linear assumption: the model implicitly assumes that the factors are additive, because statistical software can handle that kind of relationship more easily.

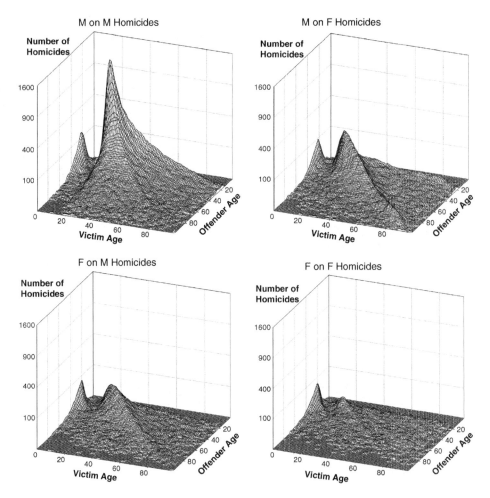

FIGURE 3.13. Smoothed SHR data, 1976–2005, disaggregated by sex of victim and sex of offender; vertical axis plotted using a square root transformation.

normality, linearity and independence rarely the case (Lieberson 1985), the standard analyses mask important insights that can be obtained by investigating outliers, those cases that are often suppressed or ignored in standard analyses. That is, most analyses focus on means: a t-test answers the question, "Is there a statistically significant difference between the mean value of this group and the mean value of that group?" But the mean, variance, kurtosis, and other standard statistics don't tell the whole story (Maltz 1994).

There are a number of ways to depict multivariate relationships graphically. Even presentations of tabular data can be improved by judicious rearranging and arraying of the data, as well as by using polygon plots and trees (Wainer 1983). (Another method, using Chernoff faces (Chernoff, 1973) is shown in section "Networks.")

Graphical models can provide insight into relationships that may elude standard statistical analyses. For example, Fig. 3.14 shows the relationship between the reported domestic

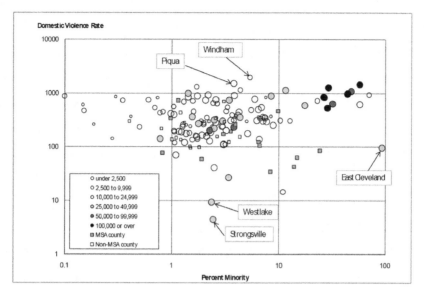

FIGURE 3.14. Domestic violence rate and percent of minorities in the population.

violence rate and percent minority population for Ohio cities and counties in 2004 that submitted crime reports through OIBRS, the Ohio Incident-Based Reporting System (Payne et al. 2007).

Note that, although there is a generally positive correlation between the two variables, there are a number of outliers. The question then becomes, why are these cities outliers? Do they have different populations, different police reporting practices, different kinds of programs for dealing with domestic violence, or some other reason for deviating from the general pattern? In other words, while most statistical analyses are designed to test hypotheses, this figure causes one to generate hypotheses.

Trellis Plots

Another way of visualizing multiple variables is to use trellis plots (called multi-way plots in Cleveland 1993). A trellis plot is a sequence of x-y plots where the sequence is ordered by another variable. It permits the user to see how the nature of the relationship between x and y changes as the third variable changes. In our analyses of UCR crime data, we found that agencies often did not report their crimes to the FBI consistently, so we plotted the distribution of length of gaps in their monthly reporting behavior to see if we could find patterns. They are shown in Fig. 3.15, plotted on linear and logarithmic scales. The peak at 5 months could indicate that agencies were aggregating data in 6-month intervals and reporting just once (inspecting the data showed that this was not the case); the next peak, at 12 months, indicates that agencies sometimes drop out of reporting for a full year.

A further analysis of the data showed additional patterns. Agencies are categorized by the FBI into groups, depending on their population and type, generally going from larger (Group 1) to smaller jurisdictions. A trellis plot of length of reporting gaps (Fig. 3.16) shows that larger agencies are more consistent in reporting crime to the FBI than are smaller agencies, which have more and longer gaps in their reporting histories.

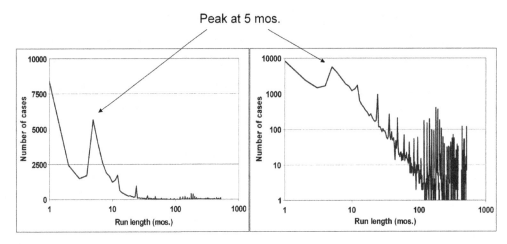

FIGURE 3.15. Size of gaps (in months) in reporting crime to the FBI. Number of cases shown on linear and logarithmic scales, run length on logarithmic scale.

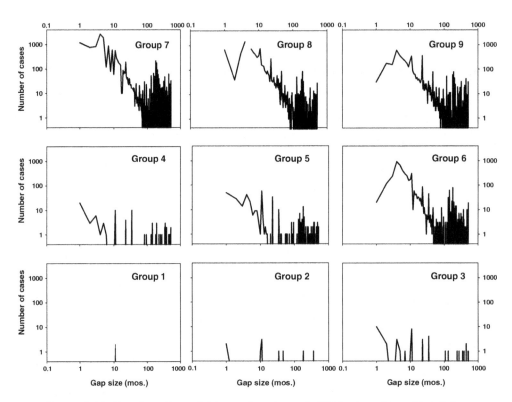

FIGURE 3.16. Size of gaps (in months) in reporting crime to the FBI, by size and type of jurisdiction.

DYNAMIC RELATIONSHIPS: ANIMATION

Kids live in neighborhoods, with their families and with other kids and their families. Not being very mobile, they interact for the most part in their neighborhoods. Taking random samples of youths to study their behavior makes it all but impossible to study these interactions. Basically it prevents one from considering the effects of what Zimring (1981) has called a "well-known secret" (see also Reiss 1986, and Reiss and Farrington 1991) – that youths start out committing crime in groups, not individually. Random sampling precludes one from investigating how the offending careers of youths interact, since it is hardly possible that all youths in a network will be in a randomly selected sample.

In addition, sampling restricts full consideration of the characteristics of the youths' neighborhoods. When a population is sampled, its subjects are drawn from many neighborhoods. Since it is difficult to give a complete description of every one of these neighborhoods, it is usually necessary to characterize them using a handful of variables. Such studies attempt to incorporate "community effects" in their analyses by including the community-level variables (percent owner-occupied housing, median income, percent on welfare, etc.).

But we know that community characteristics vary considerably, and even communities similar in terms of these standard demographic variables may have very different social ecologies. While crime mapping deals with some of these issues (see Chap. 2 in this book), the relationship between criminality and geography is complex and plays itself out over time. The difficulty is to see how it can be understood, how patterns can be teased from the data.

Suppose you had a bird's-eye view of a high-risk community and could record the physical condition of every block over time. Further, suppose you could track the offenses committed by every youth (both delinquent and nondelinquent) in the community. You would then find out where they lived, where and with whom they hung out, with whom they co-offended, and the types of offenses they committed during the observation period. If you had additional data about them (e.g., educational attainment, substance abuse, etc., and how they vary over time), you could then map them over time and show how their development affects their criminality, and vice versa. Figure 3.17 (see also Maltz 2008) shows how such information can be assembled using Chernoff faces (Chernoff 1973).

Locating the blocks and the individuals on a map, drawing lines between co-offenders, and running the relationships over time will depict how alliances form and change as people are incarcerated, move away, and move into the community. While this has been attempted to a limited extent in a static form (Maltz 1996), software tools such as Microsoft's Visio (used in the creation of Fig. 3.17) and Rosling's Gapminder (http://www.gapminder.org/) can be used to animate charts, to show how relationships change over time. An example of such an animation, showing how co-offending can be traced over time in a neighborhood, is available from the author.

Computer-based animation tools can be likened to televised weather reports. While no doubt one can develop statistical relationships among the many variables – date, time of day, latitude, longitude, altitude, precipitation, temperature, wind velocity, and barometric pressure – so as to forecast the weather in a specific location at a specific time, an animated map conveys so much more information, giving the viewer insight into how weather patterns develop and what is likely to occur in the near future.

Similarly, static individual trajectories of offending (as in Fig. 3.6) can be interleaved with other characteristics of importance. Aside from the three states shown in that figure, one can weave in personal characteristics (birth, birth of siblings, education, marriage, initiation

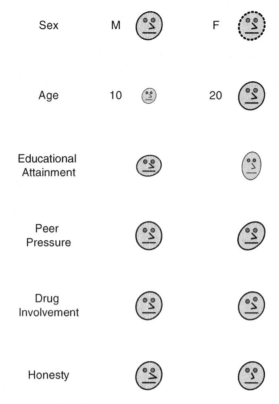

Sex

Age

Educational
Attainment

Peer
Pressure

Drug
Involvement

Honesty

FIGURE 3.17. Using Chernoff Faces to represent multivariate individual characteristics.

and termination of substance abuse, and other events of significance). Parole and probation reports often contain such information, which can be harnessed to develop graphical life course histories (Maltz 1996; Maltz and Mullany 2000).

One method of showing such life course histories is described by Francis and Pritchard (1998, 2000). As they note, a criminal career "will consist of a sequence of offences at various dates throughout the offender's life, together with information about the sentence passed for each offence, time served. Other information may also be collected relating to the personal life of the offender. For example, information on his marital history (single, cohabiting, married, divorced etc.), family history (number of children in the household) and work history (unemployment or employment, salary) might also be collected over time." The events comprising an individual's history can be using a Lexis "pencil," a multi-faceted "line" whose different facets portray different types of events. One facet might portray his/her personal events (schooling, marriage, divorce), another his/her work history, and finally his/her involvement in the criminal justice system.

These data visualizations are attempts to tell the whole story (or as much as can be gleaned from the available data) of individuals and how their environment may have shaped them. While they can never achieve the granularity of the "thick description" described by Geertz (1973), the overall goal is the same: to have a "thick data representation" provide a greater measure of understanding of how the different aspects of a person's life shape his/her trajectory.

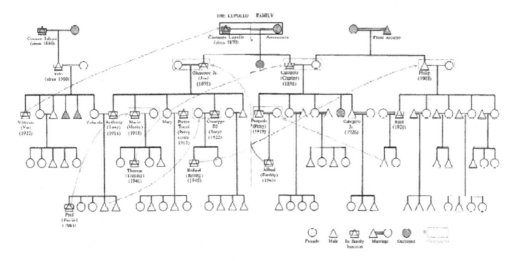

FIGURE 3.18. Godparent–Godchild relations in the Lupollo family.

NETWORKS

The shifting alliances among delinquent youths depicted in the previous section may just be a foretaste of what happens to them as they grow older. They may mature into juvenile gangs, which then become even more stable and turn into organized crime networks. Some may be based on kinship patterns, as in Fig. 3.18, depicting the "Lupollo" crime family (Ianni and Reuss-Ianni 1972); others may be based on an expanding web of contacts as an individual moves up the hierarchy, as in Fig. 3.19, and on his areas of activity, as in Fig. 3.20 (Morselli 2005).

An even more important use of network analysis in recent years is its use in tracing terrorist networks. Memon and Larsen (2006) describe how it can be used in conjunction with data mining to detail the structure and infer the hierarchy in the network associated with the destruction of the World Trade Center in New York City on 11 November 2001. Similarly, Xu and Chen (2005) apply data visualization techniques (specifically, Social Network Analysis) to the interconnections among the participants in the September 11, 2001 attacks – see Fig. 3.21.

These figures can be used to tell a story, as Morselli (2008, 37) notes:

> How is the overall network structured? Are relationships in the network dispersed, dense, or segmented? Is there a concentration of relationships around key nodes? Is there a chain-like quality to the network? Are the key nodes positioned as brokers or bridges between links in the chain? Does the network have a clustering pattern at the overall or localized level? If the graph is directional, is some level of reciprocity or asymmetry observable?

These and similar questions can help the researcher and investigator to determine the network's strong and weak points. One of the main differences between its use in terrorist networks and criminal networks is that, for criminal networks it is helpful in proving conspiracy charges in court, usually after the conspiracy has occurred. In cases of terrorist incidents, it is most important to discover them prior to their carrying it out.

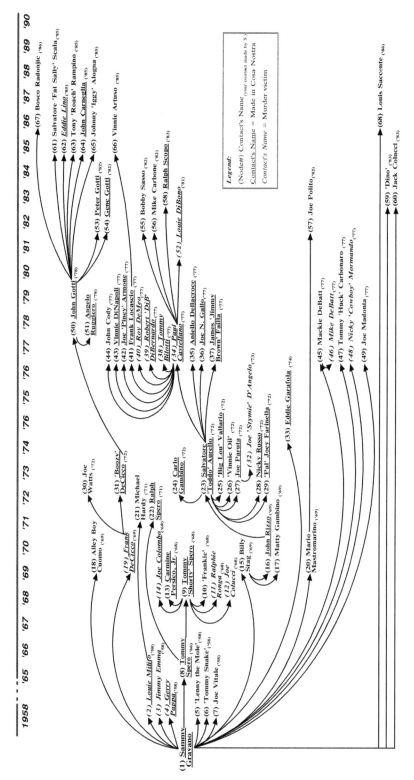

FIGURE 3.19. The Development of the Working Network of a Mafia Underboss Over time.

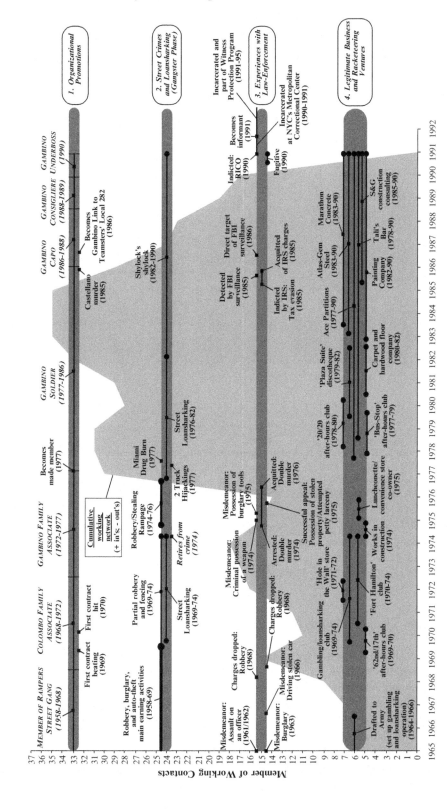

FIGURE 3.20. The Different Aspects of the Career of a Mafia Underboss.

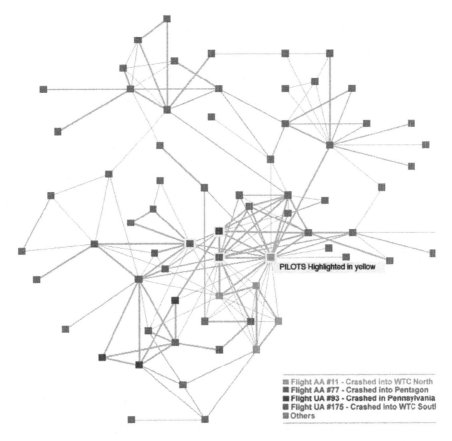

PILOTS Highlighted in yellow

Flight AA #11 - Crashed into WTC North
Flight AA #77 - Crashed into Pentagon
Flight UA #93 - Crashed in Pennsylvania
Flight UA #175 - Crashed into WTC South
Others

FIGURE 3.21. The terrorist network containing the 19 hijackers on September 11, 2001.

CONCLUSIONS AND RECOMMENDATIONS

As Loftus (1993) has noted over 15 years ago, "A picture is worth a thousand p-values." He was discussing visualization in the context of presenting results rather than as a tool in the analysis of data. This chapter has focused exclusively on its use for the latter purpose. Listed below are some suggestions for promoting such use.

Promote Data Visualization as a First Step

Rather than considering visual inspection of a data set "cheating," the analyst should consider it an imperative, to make sure that the data set does not contain mistakes or anomalies that could throw off conclusions. For example, the standard deviation in the Oklahoma City monthly murder count (1960–2004) is 7.7, including all the data. Were we to reduce the 173 (actual) murders in April 1995 by the 168 that occurred in the bombing, the SD would drop to 2.6, which is a much better indicator of the expected variation in the monthly murder count. Blindly applying statistical methods to data sets, without taking unique circumstances like this into account, can lead to inappropriate conclusions.

Similarly, visualizing the data can tease out relationships beyond the ones preprogrammed into statistical routines. As discussed earlier, for the most part the standard routines rely on assumptions about linearity, normality and/or independence that are rare in criminology and criminal justice data. Visual inspection of the data can often show whether these assumptions hold. Large datasets permit the analyst to "drill down" beyond the surface and look at subgroup characteristics directly rather than through regression coefficients or by using dummy variables.

But the first step is only the beginning. It should also be used as an intermediate step in modeling processes, to check the fit of the model to data, and as a final step as well, to display the results of the modeling process (e.g., Maltz and Zawitz 1998).[16]

Rethink Analytic Strategies and Methods

There are two primary reasons for the lack of progress in using graphical methods. First is the fact that, although the techniques for using them are well-known and accessible to the interested analyst (the books by Cleveland, Tufte, and Tukey are the most well-known), most have not yet found their way into the most commonly used statistical toolboxes – SAS, SPSS, Stata, and Systat. These programs generally assume that the analyst will be using algorithms based on standard inferential techniques, rather than slicing and dicing the data to look for patterns that may elude discovery using those techniques. Although the above-mentioned statistical programs all have graphical components, they are used primarily for presenting results rather than visually exploring the characteristics of the data. In contrast, statistical programs like Data Desk (and computer languages like S-Plus and R) are specifically designed to explore data in ways described in this chapter. But there is a new kid on the block; called Mondrian, it is freeware and available from http://rosuda.org/mondrian/.[17]

Develop Teaching Tools that Incorporate Visualization

Second, there is a lot of inertia in the academy, wherein those who teach statistics courses in criminal justice and criminology have generally been trained in statistical techniques by social scientists who learned their statistical techniques in the same manner, based on inferential statistics. And of course, familiarity with these methods means that newer methods may be ignored.

This need not be the case. Since textbooks can now be supplemented with CDs, DVDs, and even websites containing data sets (the National Archive of Criminal Justice Data, housed at the University of Michigan's Interuniversity Consortium for Political and Social Research; and StatLib, a website housed at the Carnegie Mellon Department of Statistics are notable examples), it makes teaching such a course much easier. One can develop a course that shows students how to navigate around relational databases (e.g., NIBRS), extract files from

---

[16] Gelman (2004) shows how "(a) exploratory and graphical methods can be especially effective when used in conjunction with models, and (b) model-based inference can be especially effective when checked graphically."

[17] It is limited, however, in dealing with time series. There is a very useful (but not free) book describing this package (with downloadable examples), "Interactive Graphics for Data Analysis" (Theus and Urbanek 2008).

them looking for specific characteristics (e.g., weapon use and injuries in attempted and completed robberies), and show students how to examine the relationships among the variables by a judicious choice of graphical techniques.

- - - - - - -

The examples shown in this chapter barely scratch the surface of what can be done in visualizing criminal justice data. Many of the books listed in the references section contain examples that could be adapted for use in criminal justice contexts. The increasing use of automated data capture in the criminal justice system means that the size of our datasets will continue to increase as well. Unwin et al. (2006: 5) suggest that this calls for rethinking the way we analyze our data. They go on:

> It does not take long to find out that a X^2-test will always give a significant result if only the sample is big enough, or vice versa, given a big enough dataset, there is no interaction between two categorical variables that is not significant. Unfortunately, most textbooks use examples of only a limited size. This upscaling problem can be found for many mathematical statistical tests, questioning the relevance of much of the statistical theory developed during the past century for problems that are not of small size.

The increasing proliferation of large datasets in criminal justice, therefore, requires analysts to develop new and better ways of extracting patterns from data. Fortunately for us, the increasing power of computer graphics permits analysts to develop new and innovative ways of discerning those patterns.

Acknowledgements Over the years my research has been supported by the National Institute of Justice, the Bureau of Justice Statistics, the Ohio Office of Criminal Justice Services, the California Department of Corrections and Rehabilitation, and the American Statistical Association, which I acknowledge with gratitude. I am indebted to Andrew Gelman and Howard Wainer for their comments on earlier versions.

REFERENCES

Arbuthnot J (1710) An argument for divine providence taken from the constant regularity in the births of both sexes. Phil Trans R Soc 27:186–190

Chernoff H (1973) The use of faces to represent points in k-dimensional space graphically. J Am Stat Assoc 68:342, 361–368

Cleveland WS (1993) Visualizing data. Hobart Press, Summit, NJ

Cleveland WS (1994) The elements of graphing data. Hobart Press, Summit, NJ

Cohen J (1994) The earth is round (p < .05). Am Psychol 49: 12, 997–1003

Fox JA (2008) Uniform crime reports [United States]: supplementary homicide reports with multiple imputation, cumulative files 1976–2005 [computer file]. ICPSR22161-v1. Inter-university Consortium for Political and Social Research [producer and distributor], Ann Arbor, MI, May 12, 2008

Francis B, Pritchard J (1998) Bertin, Lexis and the graphical representation of event histories. Bull Comite Francais de Cartographie 156:80–87

Francis B, Pritchard J (2000) Visualisation of criminal careers. In: Erbacher RF, Chen PC, Roberts JC, Wittenbrink CM (eds) Visual data exploration and analysis VII. Proceedings of the Society of Photo-Optical Instrumentation Engineers (SPIE), vol 3960, 96–105

Freedman DA (1985) Statistics and the scientific method. In: Mason WM, Fienberg SE (eds) Cohort analysis in the social sciences: beyond the identification problem. Springer-Verlag, New York

Geertz C (2005). Thick description: toward an interpretive theory of culture, Chap 1. In Geertz C (1973) The interpretation of cultures: selected essays. Basic Books, New York

Gelman A (2004) Exploratory data analysis for complex models (with discussion). J Comput Graph Stat 13(4): 755–779

Gelman A, Hill J (2007) Data analysis using regression and multilevel/hierarchical models. Cambridge University Press, New York

Gelman A, Pasarica C, Dodhia R (2002) Let's practice what we preach: turning tables into graphs. Am Stat 56: 121–130

Harmon RJ, Gliner JA, Morgan GA, Leech NL (2001) Problems with null hypothesis significance testing. J Am Acad Child Adolesc Psychiatry 40(2):250–252

Ianni FAJ, Reuss-Ianni E (1972) A family business: kinship and social control in organized crime. Russell Sage Foundation, New York

Lieberson S (1985) Making it count: the improvement of social research and theory. University of California Press, Berkeley, CA

Loftus GR (1993) A picture is worth a thousand p values: on the irrelevance of hypothesis testing in the microcomputer age. Behav Res Meth Ins C 25(2): 250–256

Maltz MD (1994) Deviating from the mean: the declining significance of significance. J Res Crime Delinq 31(4): 434–463

Maltz MD (1996) Criminality in space and time: life course analysis and the micro-ecology of crime. In: Eck J, Weisburd D (eds) Crime and place. Criminal Justice Press, Monsey, NY

Maltz MD (1998) Visualizing homicide: a research note. J Quant Criminol 14(4):397–410

Maltz MD (1999) Bridging gaps in police crime data, a discussion paper from the BJS Fellows Program. Bureau of Justice Statistics Report No. NCJ-1176365. Office of Justice Programs, U.S. Department of Justice, Washington, DC, September, 1999, 72 pp http://www.ojp.usdoj.gov/bjs/pub/pdf/bgpcd.pdf

Maltz MD (2006) Some p-baked thoughts (p > 0.5) on experiments and statistical significance. J Exp Criminol 1(2):211–226

Maltz MD (2008) Waves, particles, and crime. In: Bernasco W, Bruinsma G, Weisburd D (eds) Units of analysis in the study of the geography of crime. Springer, New York

Maltz MD, Gordon AC, Friedman W (1991) Mapping crime in its community setting: event geography analysis. Springer, New York. Internet version published in 2000; http://www.uic.edu/depts/lib/forr/

Maltz MD, Mullany J (2000) Visualizing lives: new pathways for analyzing life course histories. J Quant Criminol 16(2):255–281

Maltz MD, Weiss HE (2006) Creating a UCR utility, final report to the National Institute of Justice. Criminal Justice Research Center and Department of Sociology, The Ohio State University, February 23, 2006

Maltz MD, Weiss HE (2007) Analysis of FBI-collected arrest data, final report to the Bureau of Justice Statistics. Criminal Justice Research Center and Department of Sociology, The Ohio State University, December 31, 2007

Maltz MD, Zawitz MW (1998) Displaying violent crime trends using estimates from the National Crime Victimization Survey. Bureau of Justice Statistics Technical Report. No. NCJ 167881. Office of Justice Programs, U.S. Department of Justice, Washington, DC http://www.ojp.usdoj.gov/bjs/pub/pdf/dvctue.pdf

Memon N, Larsen HL (2006) Investigative data mining toolkit: a software prototype for visualizing, analyzing and destabilizing terrorist networks. In: Visualising network information. Meeting Proceedings RTO-MP-IST-063, Paper 14. RTO, Neuilly-sur-Seine, France, pp 14-1–14-24. ftp://ftp.rta.nato.int/PubFullText/RTO/MP/RTO-MP-IST-063/MP-IST-063–14.pdf

Morselli C (2005) Contacts, opportunity, and criminal enterprise. University of Toronto Press, Toronto, Ontario

Morselli C (2008) Inside criminal networks. Springer, New York

Morton S (2009) ASA president delivers NC State commencement speech. AMSTAT News July 2009, p 13

Payne D, Maltz MD, Peterson R, Krivo L (2007) Domestic violence in in Ohio 2004, a report to the State of Ohio's Office of Criminal Justice Services, Criminal Justice Research Center, The Ohio State University, March 5, 2007 http://www.ocjs.ohio.gov/research/Final%20OIBRS%20Report%203-26–07.pdf

Rall T (2008) How deterrence works. January 7, 2008. © 2008 Ted Rall, Distributed by Universal Press Syndicate, Kansas City, MO

Reiss AJ Jr (1986) Co-offending influences on criminal careers. In: Blumstein A, Cohen J, Roth JA, Visher CA (eds) Criminal Careers and career criminals, vol 2. National Academy of Sciences, Washington, DC, pp 121–160

Reiss AJ Jr (1988) Co-offending and criminal careers. In: Tonry M, Morris N (eds) Crime and justice: a review of research, vol 10. University of Chicago Press, Chicago

Reiss AJ Jr, Farrington DP (1991) Advancing knowledge about co-offending: results from a prospective survey of London males. J Crim Law Criminol 82:360–395

Stamp J (1929) Some economic factors in modern life. P. S. King, London, England

Theus M, Urbanek S (2008) Interactive graphics for data analysis: principles and examples. CRC Press, Boca Raton, FL

Tufte ER (1983) The visual display of quantitative information. Graphics Press, Cheshire, CT

Tukey JW (1977) Exploratory data analysis. Addison-Wesley, Reading, MA

Unwin A, Theus M, Hofmann H (2006) Graphics of large datasets: visualizing a million. Springer, New York

Vaupel JW, Zhenglian W, Andreev KF, Yashin AI (1998) Population data at a glance: shaded contour maps of demographic surfaces over age and time. Odense University Press, Odense, Denmark

Wainer H (1983) On multivariate display. In: Rizvi MH, Rustagi JS, Siegmund D (eds) Recent advances in statistics. Academic Press, New York

Wainer H (1997) Visual revelations: graphical tales of fate and deception from Napoleon Bonaparte to Ross Perot. Copernicus (Springer-Verlag), New York

Wainer H (2005) Graphic discovery: a trout in the milk and other visual adventures. Princeton University Press, Princeton, NJ

Wainer H (2009) Picturing the uncertain world: how to understand, communicate and control uncertainty through graphical display. Princeton University Press, Princeton, NJ

Wainer H, Spence I (2005) The commercial and political atlas and statistical breviary, by William Playfair (1801), 3rd edn. Cambridge University Press, New York

Wilkinson L (1999) The grammar of graphics. Springer, New York

Wilkinson L, the Task Force on Statistical Inference (1999) Statistical methods in psychology journals: guidelines and explanations. Am Psychol 54(8):594–604

Xu J, Chen H (2005) Criminal network analysis and visualization. Commun ACM 48(6):100–107

Zimring FE (1981) Kids, groups and crime: some implications of a well-known secret. J Crim Law Criminol 72: 867–885

CHAPTER 4

Group-Based Trajectory Modeling: An Overview

DANIEL S. NAGIN

INTRODUCTION

This chapter provides an overview of a group-based statistical methodology for analyzing developmental trajectories – the evolution of an outcome over age or time. A detailed account of the method's statistical underpinnings and a full range of applications are provided in Nagin (2005).

In this discussion, the term developmental trajectory is used to describe the progression of any phenomenon, whether behavioral, biological, or physical. Charting and understanding developmental trajectories is among the most fundamental and empirically important research topics in the social and behavioral sciences and medicine. A few prominent examples include: criminological analyses of the progression and causes of criminality over life stages or of time trends of reported crime across geographic locations, psychological studies of the course and antecedents of psychopathologies, sociological investigations into the interaction between human behavior and social context over time, and medical research on the impact of treatments on the progress of diseases.

Longitudinal data – data with a time-based dimension – provide the empirical foundation for the analysis of developmental trajectories. Most standard statistical approaches for analyzing developmental trajectories are designed to account for individual variability about a mean population trend. However, many of the most interesting and challenging problems in longitudinal analysis have a qualitative dimension that allows for the possibility that there are meaningful sub-groups within a population that follow distinctive developmental trajectories that are not identifiable *ex ante* based on some measured set of individual characteristics (e.g., gender or socioeconomic status). In psychology, for example, there is a long tradition of taxonomic theorizing about distinctive developmental progressions of these sub-categories. For research problems with a taxonomic dimension, the aim is to chart out the distinctive trajectories, to understand what factors account for their distinctiveness and to test whether individuals following the different trajectories also respond differently to a treatment such as a medical intervention or major life event such as the birth of a child. This chapter describes an approach, based upon a formal statistical model, for conducting group-based analysis with time- and age-based data.

A.R. Piquero and D. Weisburd (eds.), *Handbook of Quantitative Criminology*,
DOI 10.1007/978-0-387-77650-7_4, © Springer Science + Business Media, LLC 2010,
First softcover printing 2011

Across all application domains, this group-based statistical method lends itself to the presentation of findings in the form of easily understood graphical and tabular data summaries. In doing so, the method provides statistical researchers with a tool for figuratively painting a statistical portrait of the predictors and consequences of distinct trajectories of development. Data summaries of this form have the great advantage of being accessible to non-technical audiences and quickly comprehensible to audiences that are technically sophisticated.

AN ILLUSTRATION OF GROUP-BASED TRAJECTORY MODELING

Figure 4.1 reports a well-known application of group-based trajectory modeling that was first reported in Nagin and Tremblay (1999). It is based on the data assembled as part of a Montreal Longitudinal-Experimental Study of Boys that has tracked 1,037 males from school entry through young adulthood. Assessments were made on a wide range of factors. Among these were teacher reports of each boy's physical aggression at age 6 and again annually from age 10 to 15. The scale was based on items such as frequency of fighting and physically bullying.

The best model was found to involve four groups. A group called "lows" comprised individuals who display little or no physically aggressive behavior. This group is estimated to comprise about 15% of the sample population. A second group, comprising about 50% of the population, is best labeled "moderate declining." At age 6, boys in this group displayed a modest level of physical aggression, but by age 10 they had largely desisted. A third group, comprising about 30% of the population, is labeled "high declining." This group starts off scoring high on physical aggression at age 6 but scores far lower by age 15. Notwithstanding this marked decline, at age 15 they continue to display a modest level of physical aggression. Finally, there is a small group of "chronics," comprising less than 5% of the population, who display high levels of physical aggression throughout the observation period.

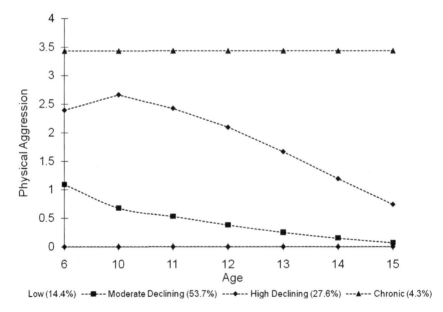

FIGURE 4.1. Trajectories of physical aggression.

Much could be said about the implications of these trajectories for the development of physical aggression but for our purposes here two implications are emphasized. One implication follows from the observation that all the trajectories are either stable or declining from the initial assessment at age 6. This implies that to understand the developmental origins of physical aggression, it is important to begin studying physical aggression at an even earlier age. A second and related observation is that the onset of physical aggression is not in adolescence as many theories of delinquent behavior suggested. See Tremblay and Nagin (2005) for a full development of these two observations.

These two points are highlighted because they illustrate the value of conducting longitudinal analysis in terms of groups. The groups can be thought of as latent longitudinal strata in the data that are composed of individuals following approximately the same development course on the outcome of interest. These strata identify distinctive longitudinal features of the data. In this application, the fact that all the trajectories are stable or declining is a feature of the data that is of great substantive significance. Further the absence of a feature, namely a trajectory reflecting the adolescent onset of physical aggression also has important substantive significance.

The group-based methodology is intended to be responsive to calls for the development of "person-based" approaches to analyzing development (Bergman 1998; Magnusson 1998). Such appeals are motivated by a desire for methods that can provide a statistical snapshot of the distinguishing characteristics and behaviors of individuals following distinctive developmental pathways. The group-based method lends itself to creating such profiles. Table 4.1 reports profiles and the characteristics of individuals following the four physical aggression trajectories shown in Fig. 4.1. As developed in Chap. 5 of Nagin (2005), the model's parameter estimates can be used to calculate the probability of an individual belonging to each of the trajectory groups. To create the profiles reported in Table 4.1, individuals were assigned to the trajectory group to which they mostly likely belonged, based on their measured history of physical aggression. The summary statistics reported in the table are simply the product of a cross-tabulation of group membership with the various individual characteristics and outcomes reported in the table.

The profiles conform to longstanding findings on the predictors and consequences of problem behaviors such as physical aggression. Individuals in the chronic aggression group tend to have the least educated parents and most frequently, score in the lowest quartile of the sample's IQ distribution. By contrast, individuals in the low aggression group are least likely to suffer from these risk factors. Further, 90% of the chronic aggression group fail to reach the eighth grade on schedule and 13% have a juvenile record by age 18. By comparison, only 19% of the low aggression group had fallen behind grade level by the eighth grade and none have a juvenile record. In between are the moderate- and high- declining groups.

TABLE 4.1. Physical aggression group profiles

Variable	Group			
	Low	Moderate declining	High declining	Chronic
Years of school – Mother	11.1	10.8	9.8	8.4
Years of school – Father	11.5	10.7	9.8	9.1
Low IQ (%)	21.6	26.8	44.5	46.4
Completed 8th grade on time (%)	80.3	64.6	31.8	6.5
Juvenile record (%)	0.0	2.0	6.0	13.3
# of sexual partners at age 17 (past year)	1.2	1.7	2.2	3.5

Table 4.1 demonstrates that trajectory group membership varies systematically with the individual's psychosocial characteristics. An important generalization of the base model that is laid out in Chap. 6 of Nagin (2005) allows for joint estimation of both the shapes of the trajectory groups and the impact of psychosocial characteristics on the probability of trajectory group membership. For example, such an analysis shows that the probability of trajectory group membership is significantly predicted by low IQ, low paternal education, and being born to a mother who began child-bearing as a teenager (Nagin and Tremblay 2001).

As noted, trajectories are not immutable. Life events or interventions may alter trajectories for the better or worse. Nagin et al. (2003) explore the effect of grade retention from age 6 to 15 on the trajectories of physical aggression shown in Fig. 4.1. They find that grade retention seems to exacerbate physical aggression in the low declining and high declining trajectory groups but has no apparent effect on the physical aggression of the extreme groups – the lows and the chronics. The model extension allowing for this sort of analysis is developed in Chap. 7 of Nagin (2005). See also Haviland et al. (2007, 2008) for a discussion of the use of propensity score matching in combination with group-based trajectory modeling in making causal inferences about the effect of life events and interventions on developmental trajectories.

A trajectory charts the progression of an outcome over age or time. The examples discussed earlier all involve the developmental course of an individual-level behavior with age. It is important to emphasize that the outcome does not have to be a behavior. Mustillo et al. (2003), for example, analyze trajectories of body mass index and van Bokhoven et al. (2005) analyze trajectories of cortisol levels. Further the unit of analysis does not have to be an individual. Weisburd et al. (2004, 2008), for example, study trajectories of reported crimes at spatial units measured at the level of the street segment. Similarly, Griffith and Chavez (2004) analyze trajectories of homicides at the level of the census track. The Weisburd et al. and Griffith and Chavez studies also demonstrate that trajectory can be measured over time as well as age. In these studies, the time metric is the calendar year. Time can also be measured relative to some fixed point in time. Christ et al. (2002) for example, measure trajectories of internet usage from the date of gaining computer access to the internet and Krishnan (2008) examine trajectories of mobile phone ring tone downloads from the date of account activation. For a recent review of studies of crime using group-based trajectory modeling, see Piquero (2008).

LIKELIHOOD FUNCTION

Group-based trajectory models are a specialized application of finite mixture models. While the conceptual aim of the analysis is to identify clusters of individuals with similar trajectories, the model's estimated parameters are not the result of a cluster analysis. Rather they are the product of maximum likelihood estimation. As such, they share the many desirable characteristics of maximum likelihood parameter estimates – they are consistent and asymptotically normally distributed (Cramèr 1946; Greene 1990; Thiel 1971).

The specific form of the likelihood function to be maximized depends on the type of data being analyzed, but all are a special form of the following underlying likelihood function: let $Y_i = \{y_{i1}, y_{i2}, \ldots, y_{iT}\}$ denote a longitudinal sequence of measurements on individual i over T periods. For expositional convenience, y_{it} will generally be described as the behavior of an individual. However, the outcome of interest doesn't have to pertain to an individual or a behavior – y_{it} can reference an entity such as a community, block face, or an organization, or it can measure a quantity such as a poverty rate or a mean salary level.

Let $P(Y_i)$ denote the probability of Y_i. As developed in Chap. 2 of Nagin (2005), for count data $P(Y_i)$ is specified as the zero-inflated Poisson distribution, for censored data it is specified as the censored normal distribution, and for binary data, it is specified as the binary logit distribution. Whatever the probability distribution, the ultimate objective is to estimate a set of parameters, Ω, that maximizes the probability of Y_i. The particular form of this parameter set is distribution specific. However, across all distributions, these parameters perform the basic function of defining the shapes of the trajectories and the probability of group membership. As in standard grow curve modeling, the shapes of the trajectories are described by a polynomial function of age or time.

If the parameters of this polynomial function were constant across population members, the expected trajectory of all population members would be identical. Neither standard growth curve methods nor the group-based method assume such homogeneity. Indeed, the assumption of homogeneity is antithetical to the objective of either approach because both aim to analyze the reason for individual differences in development. Standard growth curve modeling assumes that the parameters defining the polynomial describe only a population mean and that the trajectories of individual population members vary continuously about this mean, usually according to the multivariate normal distribution. The group-based method assumes that individual differences in trajectories can be summarized by a finite set of different polynomial functions of age or time. Each such set corresponds to a trajectory group which is hereafter indexed by j. Let $P^j(Y_i)$ denote the probability of Y_i given membership in group j, and π_j denote the probability of a randomly chosen population member belonging to group j.

If it were possible to observe group membership, the sampled individuals could be sorted by group membership and their trajectory parameters estimated with readily available Poisson, censored normal (tobit), and logit regression software packages. However, group membership is not observed. Indeed, the proportion of the population comprising each group j, π_j, is an important parameter of interest in its own right. Thus, construction of the likelihood function requires the aggregation of the J conditional likelihood functions, $P^j(Y_i)$, to form the unconditional probability of the data, Y_i:

$$P(Y_i) = \sum_j^J \pi_j P^j(Y_i) \tag{4.1}$$

where $P(Y_i)$ is the unconditional probability of observing individual i's longitudinal sequence of behavioral measurements, Y_i. It equals the sum across the J groups of the probability of Y_i given i's membership in group j weighted by the probability of membership in group j. Equation 4.1 describes what is called a "finite mixture model" because it sums across a finite number of discrete groups that comprise the population. The term "mixture" is included in the label because the statistical model specifies that the population is composed of a mixture of unobserved groups.

For given j, conditional independence is assumed for the sequential realizations of the elements of Y_i, y_{it}, over the T periods of measurement. Thus,

$$P^j(Y_i) = \prod^T p^j(y_{it}), \tag{4.2}$$

where $p^j(y_{it})$ is the probability distribution function of y_{it} given membership in group j.

The rationale for the conditional independence assumption deserves elaboration. This assumption implies that for each individual within a given trajectory group j, the distribution of y_{it} for period t is independent of the realized level of the outcome in prior periods, y_{it-1}, y_{it-2},..... Thus, $p^j\,(y_{it})$ does not include prior values of y_{it} in its specification. This assumption greatly reduces the complexity of an already complex model. Due to this reduction in complexity, most applications of finite mixture modeling with longitudinal data assume conditional independence for the sake of tractability.

On its face, the conditional independence assumption may seem implausible because it would seem to imply that current behavioral outcomes are uncorrelated with past outcomes. At the level of the group, which are not observed, this is indeed the case. For individuals within a given group j, behavioral outcomes over time are assumed not to be serially correlated in the sense that individual-level deviations from the group trend are uncorrelated. However, even with the assumption of conditional independence at the level of the latent group, there will still be serial dependence over time at the level of the population. Specifically, past outcomes will be correlated with current outcomes (e.g., across individuals body mass index at period t will be correlated with its value in subsequent periods). Such serial dependence results from the group specific specification of $p^j\,(y_{it})$. Differences in this specification across groups allow for persistent differences of the outcome variable across population members.

The conditional independence assumption is also invoked in the standard random effect model that underlies conventional growth curve models. The random effect model assumes that the sequential realizations of y_{it} are independent, conditional upon the individual's random effect. Thus, in the group-based model the conditional independence assumption is made at the level of the group, whereas in the random effect model it is invoked at the level of the individual. In this sense, the conditional independence assumption is stronger in the group-based model than in the standard random effect model. Balanced against this disadvantage is the advantage that the group-based model does not make the very strong assumption that the random effect is independently and identically distributed according to the normal distribution.

The likelihood for the entire sample of N individuals is simply the product of the individual likelihood functions of the N individuals comprising the sample:

$$L = \prod_{i}^{N} P(Y_i).$$

Intuitively, the estimation procedure for all data types identifies distinctive trajectory groups as follows. Suppose a population is composed of two distinct groups: (1) youth offenders (comprising 50% of the population) who up to age 18 have an expected offending rate, λ, of 5 and who after age 18 have a λ of 1; and (2) adult offenders, (comprising the other 50% of the population) whose offending trajectory is the reverse of that of the youth offenders – through age 18 their $\lambda = 1$ and after age 18 their λ increases to 5. Longitudinal data on the recorded offenses of a sample of individuals from this population would reveal two distinct groups: a clustering of about 50% of the sample who have had many offenses prior to 18 and relatively few offenses after age 18, and another 50% clustering with the reverse pattern.

If these data were analyzed under the assumption that the relationship between age and λ was identical across all individuals, the estimated value of λ would be a "compromise" estimate of about 3 for all ages. From this, one might mistakenly conclude that the rate of offending is invariant with age in this population. If the data were instead analyzed using the group-based approach, which specifies the likelihood function as a mixing distribution, no such mathematical "compromise" would be necessary. The parameters of one component of the mixture would effectively be used to accommodate (i.e., match) the youth offending portion of the data whose offending declines with age and another component of the mixing distribution would be available to accommodate the adult offender data whose offending increases with age.

GROUP-BASED TRAJECTORY MODELING CONTRASTED WITH STANDARD GROWTH CURVE MODELING

Hierarchical modeling (Bryk and Raudenbush 1987, 1992; Goldstein 1995), and latent curve analysis (McArdle and Epstein 1987; Meredith and Tisak 1990; Muthén 1989; Willett and Sayer 1994) are two important alternative approaches to the group-based methodology for modeling developmental processes. Like the group-based approach that is the subject of this book, these two alternatives are designed to provide a statistical tool for measuring and explaining differences across population members in their developmental course. Because all three approaches share the common goal of modeling individual-level heterogeneity in developmental trajectories, each must make technical assumptions about the distribution of trajectories in the population. It is these assumptions that distinguish the three approaches.

While the assumptions underlying hierarchical modeling and latent curve analysis differ in important respects, they also have important commonalities (MacCallum, Kim, Malarkey, and Kiecolt-Glaser 1997; Willett and Sayer 1994; Raudenbush 2001). For the purposes of this book one commonality is crucial: both model the population distribution of trajectories based on *continuous* distribution functions. Unconditional models estimate two key features of the population distribution of trajectory parameters – their mean and covariance structure. The former defines average growth within the population and the latter calibrates the variances of growth throughout the population. The conditional models are designed to explain this variability by relating trajectory parameters to one or more explanatory variables.

Modeling individual-level differences requires that assumptions be made about the distribution of trajectory parameters in the population. Both hierarchical modeling and latent curve analysis assume that the parameters are continuously distributed throughout the population according to the multivariate normal distribution. Group-based trajectory modeling takes a qualitatively different approach to modeling individual differences. Rather than assuming that the population distribution of trajectories varies continuously across individuals and in a fashion that can ultimately be explained by a multivariate normal distribution of population parameters, it assumes that there may be clusters or groupings of distinctive developmental trajectories that themselves may reflect distinctive etiologies. In some applications, the groups may be literal entities. For example, the efficacy of some drugs depends on the users' genetic make-up. However, in many other application domains, the groups should not be thought of as literally distinct entities. Rather they serve as a statistical approximation to a more complex underlying reality.

One use of finite mixture models is to approximate a continuous distribution function (Everitt and Hand 1981; Heckman and Singer 1984; McLachlan and Peel 2000; Titterington et al. 1985). Heckman and Singer (1984) built upon the approximating capability of finite mixture models to construct a nonparametric maximum likelihood estimator for the distribution of unobservables in duration models. The motivation for this seminal innovation was their observation that social science theory rarely provides theoretical guidance on the population of distribution of unobserved individual differences yet statistical models of duration data were often sensitive to the assumed form of the distribution of such differences. Their proposed estimator finessed the problem of having to specify a distribution of unobserved individual difference by approximating the distribution with a finite mixture model.

The idea of using a finite number of groups to approximate a continuous distribution is easily illustrated with an example. Suppose that Panel A in Fig. 4.2 depicts the population distribution of some behavior z. In Panel B, this same distribution is replicated and overlaid with a histogram that approximates its shape. Panel B illustrates that any continuous distribution with finite end-points can be approximated by a discrete distribution (i.e., a histogram) or alternatively by a finite number of "points of support" (i.e., the dark shaded "pillars"). A higher number of support points yields a discrete distribution that more closely approximates the true continuous distribution.

Why use groups to approximate a continuous population distribution of developmental trajectories? This brings us back to the key distinction between standard growth curve modeling and group-based trajectory modeling. Both approaches model individual trajectories with a polynomial relationship that links age to behavior. The approaches differ in their modeling strategy for incorporating population heterogeneity in the growth curve parameters (e.g., β_0, β_1, β_2, and β_3 in a cubic function of age or time). In conventional growth curve modeling, the parameters describing individual-level trajectories are assumed to be

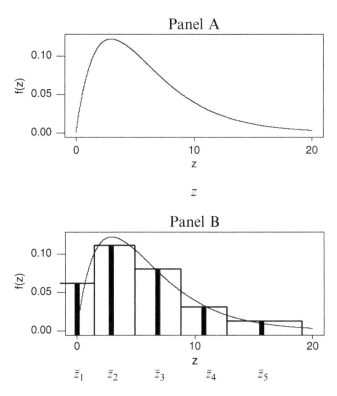

FIGURE 4.2. Using groups to approximate an unknown distribution.

distributed according to a specific function, usually the multivariate normal distribution. In the group-based trajectory model, the distribution is approximated by a finite number of trajectory groups, aka points of support.

By identifying latent strata of individuals with similar developmental trajectories, differences that may explain or at least predict individual-level heterogeneity can be expressed in terms of group differences. By contrast, a modeling strategy that assumes a continuous distribution of trajectories must explain individual level heterogeneity in terms of that distribution function. This difference has fundamental implications for the framing of the statistical analysis.

The application depicted in Fig. 4.3 may serve to illustrate the difference in approach between group-based trajectory modeling and conventional growth curve modeling. The data used in this application were also from the Montreal-based study used to estimate the trajectories of physical aggression. In this case, the trajectories are based on annual self-reports from age 11 to 17 about involvement with a delinquent gang in the past year. Application of the group-based method to this gang involvement data identified the three highly distinct groups shown in the figure (Lacourse et al. 2003). The trajectory for each group is described by the probability of gang membership at each age. One trajectory, called the never group, is estimated to comprise 74.4% of the population. This group's probability of gang membership was very small over all ages. The second group, called the childhood onset group, began at age 11 with a high probability of gang membership that modestly rises till age 14 and declines thereafter. The third group, called the adolescent onset group, had a near-zero probability of gang membership at age 11, but thereafter, the probability rose to a rate that actually exceeded that of the childhood onset group. The latter two groups are each estimated to constitute 12.8% of the sampled population.

Had standard growth curve modeling methods been applied to these data, the product of the analysis would have been entirely different. The counterpart to the results in Fig. 4.2 would have been the unconditional model which would have described the average probability trajectory of gang involvement at each age from 11 to 17 and an associated set of variance parameters measuring the population variability about this mean trajectory. Thus, the points

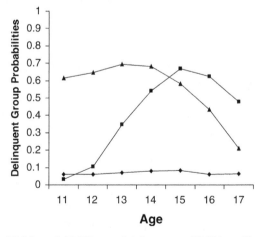

FIGURE 4.3. Trajectories of gang membership following would be the footnotes.

of departure of the two modeling approaches for drawing inferences about data are fundamentally different. The growth curve approach aims to identify the factors that account for individual variability about the population's mean trajectory of development. By contrast, the group-based approach frames questions of statistical inferences in terms of the trajectory group: what factors distinguish group membership and how do groups differ, if at all, in their response to events that might alter a trajectory?

For what types of problems is the group-based approach more appropriate than standard growth curve modeling and conversely, for what types of problems is the standard approach a better fit? This is a question without a clear answer. Still some guidelines are possible. One guideline relates to the adjective "growth" that modifies "curve modeling." The prototypical application of standard growth curve modeling involves a process in which populations members follow a common developmental pattern of either increase or decline. Raudenbush (2001) offers language acquisition as a quintessential example of such a process. Another good example is time spent with peers from childhood through adolescence (Warr 2002). Standard growth curve methods are well suited for analyzing such developmental phenomena because it is reasonable to assume that most individuals experience a common process of growth or decline, albeit at different rates. However, there are large classes of developmental phenomena for which the conception of a common growth process does not naturally fit. Raudenbush describes the population differences for this class of problems as "multinomial" and for such problems, he recommends a group-based approach as particularly appropriate. Raudenbush (2001:59) uses depression as an example. He observes: "It makes no sense to assume that everyone is increasing (or decreasing) in depression... many persons will never be high in depression, others will always be high, while others will become increasingly depressed."

The basis for Raudenbush's making a distinction between the developmental processes underlying language acquisition and depression is fundamental and cannot be overstressed. The former are appropriately analyzed by conventional analysis of variation; the latter are not. Because the vocabularies of all young children from normal populations increase with age, it is sensible to ask questions such as: What is the average growth curve of children's vocabulary over a specified age range? How large is the variation across children in their individual-level language acquisition growth curves? How do such "between person" variations relate to factors such as the child's cognitive functioning and parental education? How are "within person" changes in acquisition related to changes in interactions with primary caregivers due, for example, to parental conflict?

These questions are framed in the language of analysis of variance as reflected in the use of terms such as "within person change" and "between person change." This is only natural because standard growth curve analysis has its roots in analysis of variance. Like analysis of variance, growth curve analysis is designed to sort out factors accounting for variation about a population mean.

To meaningfully frame an analysis in the conceptual apparatus of analysis of variance requires that it be sensible to characterize population differences in terms of variation about the population mean. For processes such as language acquisition the mean trend is, in fact, a sensible statistical anchor for describing individual variability. However, for many processes evolving over time or age, it is not. For example, it makes no sense to frame a statistical analysis of population differences in the developmental progression of attention deficit disorder (ADD) in terms of variation about the mean trajectory of ADD, because ADD is the exception, not the norm, within the general population. Other examples of evolving behavioral phenomena that are not properly described in terms of variation about a population mean are most forms of psychopathology and abuse of both licit and illicit drugs. More generally, a group-based approach to analyzing longitudinal data is usefully applied to phenomena in which there may be qualitatively different trajectories of change over age or time across sub-populations that are not identifiable *ex ante* based on measured characteristics such as gender or race.

The assumption that all individuals follow a process that increases or decreases regularly within the population may also be violated because there may not be a single explanation for the differences in the developmental trajectories of subpopulation. For example, Nagin and Tremblay (2001) found that a host of predictors involving the individual's psychological make-up and family circumstances distinguished individuals following low versus high trajectories of physical aggression in childhood. However, a comparison of two distinct sub-populations of high childhood trajectories – those following a trajectory of chronic aggression versus those who started childhood with high aggression but later declined – revealed that only two maternal characteristics distinguished these groups. Using standard growth curve modeling methods, it would have been very difficult to identify this important difference in variables that distinguished among trajectories of childhood physical aggression. Identification of such differences is far easier with a methodology that clusters individuals with similar developmental trajectories.

A second guideline concerns the motivation for the analysis. One common aim of analyses of longitudinal data is to uncover distinctive developmental trends in the outcome variable of interest. For example, do sizable numbers of youths follow a trajectory of adolescent onset conduct disorder? The group-based approach is ideally suited for testing whether such distinctive patterns are present in the data. By contrast, another common aim of developmental studies is to test whether some identifiable characteristic or set of characteristics are associated with individual differences in trajectories of development. An example is whether trajectories of conduct disorder differ across sexes. For this type of problem, standard growth curve modeling provides a natural starting point for framing the statistical analysis – a comparison of the mean trajectories for boys and girls. Thus according to this second guideline, the group-based approach lends itself to analyzing questions that are framed in terms of the shape of the developmental course of the outcome of interest, whereas standard growth curve modeling lends itself to analyzing questions framed in terms of predictors of the outcome's developmental course.

A third guideline concerns the possibility of path dependencies in the response to turning point events, such as marriage, or to treatments, such as hospitalization for a psychiatric disorder. Path dependencies occur when the response to a turning point event or treatment is contingent upon the individual's developmental history. For example, Nagin et al. (2003) find that the seeming impact of grade retention on physical aggression depended upon the child's trajectory of physical aggression. The subsequent physical aggression of children who had been following trajectories of little physical aggression or of chronic physical aggression appeared to be unaffected by the event of being held back in school. By contrast, the physical aggression of individuals who had been following trajectories of declining physical aggression seemed to be exacerbated. Such path dependencies are commonplace in the literature on human development (Elder 1985). Indeed the possibility of path dependencies is a key rationale for longitudinal studies. The group-based trajectory model is well suited for identifying and testing whether the response to a turning point event or treatment is contingent upon the individual's developmental trajectory.

Laying out guidelines for the use of alternative statistical methods is a precarious exercise. Users naturally desire bright line distinctions. Yet bright line distinctions are generally not possible. The first guideline implies that developmental processes can be cleanly divided between those involving regular growth or decline and those that do not. The reality is that for many developmental processes, it is not possible to confidently make this distinction. The second guideline implies that the objective of an analysis can be classified as either identifying distinctive developmental trajectories or testing predictors of developmental trajectories. The reality is that most analyses have both objectives. Still, a further complication is that standard growth curve modeling can be used to identify distinctive developmental trajectories for *predefined* groups (e.g., races or genders) and the group-based modeling can be used to test theories about the underlying predictors and causes of population differences in developmental trajectories. The third guidelines might be interpreted as implying that it is not possible to identify path dependencies with conventional growth curve models. This is not the case. Stated differently, both methods are designed to analyze change over time. The group-based method focuses on the identification of different trajectory shapes and on examining how the prevalence of the shape and shape itself relates to predictors. By contrast, standard growth curve modeling focuses on the population mean trajectory and how individual variation about that mean relates to predictors. Thus, the alternative approaches are best thought of as complementary, not competing.

AN ALTERNATIVE CONCEPTION OF A GROUP FROM THE STRUCTURAL EQUATION MODELING TRADITION

In group-based trajectory modeling, the parameters of the polynomial function defining the mean trajectory of group j are denoted by a vector β^j. Muthén and Shedden (1999) develop an elegant and technically demanding extension of the uncensored normal model which adds random effects to the parameters, β^j, that defines a group's mean trajectory.

This extension allows the trajectories of individual-level group members to vary about the group's mean trajectory. The model for each group can be interpreted in a manner that is equivalent to that for the conventional normal-based growth curve model. The estimate of β^j defines the mean trajectory for the group and the estimate of the covariance matrix of the random effects characterizes the variation of group members' trajectories about this mean. The fundamental difference between the Muthen and Shedden model and the conventional growth curve model is that the former is comprised of multiple latent groups whereas the latter is defined by a single group.

Muthén (2001) uses the term generalized growth mixture modeling (GGMM) to label this modeling extension. The principal advantage of GGMM is that the addition of random effects may improve model fit. Balanced against this important benefit are a number of disadvantages. One is that the addition of random effects to a group-based model can result in the use of fewer trajectory groups because their addition allows for more within group heterogeneity. In group-based trajectory modeling, a group is conceptually thought of as a collection of individuals who follow approximately the same developmental trajectory. The groups correspond to the points of support in Fig. 4.2. They describe the distinctive features of the population distribution of trajectories. Population variability is captured by differences across groups in the shape and level of their trajectories. Because the trajectory groups are intended to define clusters of individuals following approximately the same developmental course, increasing within group heterogeneity can be counterproductive to this objective.

In the GGMM schema, a latent group is a population of individuals with *heterogeneous* developmental trajectories that can nonetheless be described by a single probability distribution. The population-at-large is only comprised of multiple latent groups when more than one probability distribution is required to model individual differences within the population. Stated differently, the GGMM describes population heterogeneity with multiple layers of heterogeneity. This layering of heterogeneity may serve to improve model fit but it can also result in a fundamental indeterminancy in the conception of a group because it implies that an individual belonging to group A might actually have a trajectory that more closely corresponds to the mean trajectory of group B.

The layering of heterogeneity also raises difficult issues of model identification. The challenge of identification is reflected in the work of Bauer and Curran (2003, 2004). Their analyses show that under the GGMM definition of a group, relatively modest errors in the specification of the group's probability distribution can result in mistaken inferences about the number of groups comprising the population. Specifically, one might conclude that multiple groups are required to model the population when, in fact, the population can be described by a single correctly specified probability distribution. Thus, Bauer and Curran conclude that GGMM is vulnerable to creating the illusion of groups when, in fact, there are none.

Bauer and Curran's analysis is technically sound. However, their caution about illusory groups has little relevance to the actual application of group-based trajectory modeling as developed in this chapter. In all applications of group-based modeling known to the author, the researchers are attempting to identify whether there are distinctive clusters of trajectories and, if so, whether individuals following such trajectories are distinctive in some respects. In this context, a group bears no relationship to the definition of a group analyzed by Bauer and Curran. Specifically, it is not a sub-population of *heterogeneous* individuals that can be described by a single probability distribution. Instead, it is a cluster of approximately *homogenous* individuals, in the sense that they are following about the same developmental course, who may have distinctive characteristics from other clusters of individuals following different developmental courses.

CONCLUDING REMARKS

A hallmark of modern longitudinal studies is the variety and richness of measurements that are made about the study's subjects and their circumstances. Less often acknowledged is that this abundance of information is accompanied by a difficult companion – complexity. Commonly, researchers are confronted with the dilemma of how best to explore and communicate the rich set of measurements at their disposal without becoming so bogged down in complexity that the lessons to be learned from the data are lost on them and their audience.

An important motivation for my commitment to developing and promoting the group-based trajectory method is the belief that alternative methods for analyzing development in longitudinal data sets too often leave the researcher with a Hobson's choice of balancing comprehensibility against an adequate exploration of complexity. Group-based trajectory modeling does not solve the problem of balancing comprehensibility and complexity. However, it does provide researchers with a valuable tool for identifying, summarizing, and communicating complex patterns in longitudinal data.

Summarizing data necessarily requires reduction. Reduction requires approximation. In the case of group-based models, the approximation involves the grouping of individuals who are not entirely homogenous. Balanced against this reduction error is a greatly expanded capability for creating dense, yet comprehensible, descriptions of groups of people through time.

Acknowledgement This research has been supported by the National Science Foundation (NSF) (SES-99113700; SES-0647576) and the National Institute of Mental Health (RO1 MH65611–01A2).

REFERENCES

Bauer DJ, Curran P (2003) Distributional assumptions of the growth mixture models: implications for over-extraction of latent trajectory classes. Psychol Methods 8:338–363

Bauer DJ, Curran P (2004) The integration of continuous and discrete latent variable models: potential problems and promising opportunities. Psychol Methods 9:3–29

Bergman LR (1998) A pattern-oriented approach to studying individual development: snapshots and processes. In: Cairns RB, Bergman LR, Kagan J (eds) Methods and models for studying the individual. Sage Publications, Thousand Oaks, CA

Bryk AS, Raudenbush SW (1987) Application of hierarchical linear models to assessing change. Psychol Bull 101:147–158

Bryk AS, Raudenbush SW (1992) Hierarchical linear models for social and behavioral research: application and data analysis methods. Sage Publications, Newbury Park, CA

Christ M, Krishnan R, Nagin DS, Guenther O (2002) An empirical analysis of web site stickiness. Proceedings of the 10th European conference on information systems (ECIS-02), Gdansk, Poland

Cramér H (1946) Mathematical methods of statistics. Princeton University Press, Princeton, NJ

Elder GH (1985) Perspectives on the life course. In: Elder GH Jr (ed) Life course dynamics. Cornell University Press, Ithaca

Everitt BS, Hand DJ (1981) Finite mixture distributions. Chapman and Hall, London

Goldstein H (1995) Multilevel statistical models, 2nd edn. Edward Arnold, London

Greene WH (1990) Econometric analysis. Macmillan, New York

Griffith E Chavez J (2004) Communities, street guns and homicide trajectories in Chicago, 1980–1995: merging methods for examining homicide trends across space and time. Criminology 42:941–978

Haviland A, Nagin DS, Rosenbaum PR (2007) Combining propensity score matching and group-based trajectory modeling in an observational study. Psychol Methods 12:247–267

Haviland A, Nagin DS, Rosenbaum PR, Tremblay RE (2008) Combining group-based trajectory modeling and propensity score matching for causal inferences in nonexperimental longitudinal data. Dev Psychol 44(2):422–436

Heckman J, Singer B (1984) A method for minimizing the impact of distributional assumptions in econometric models for duration data. Econometrica 52:271–320

Krishnan R (2008) Trajectories of ring tone downloads. Paper under preparation. Carnegie Mellon University, Pittsburgh, PA

Lacourse E, Nagin D, Vitaro F, Claes M, Tremblay RE (2003) Developmental trajectories of boys delinquent group membership and facilitation of violent behaviors during adolescence. Dev Psychopathol 15:183–197

MacCallum RC, Kim C, Malarkey WB, Kiecolt-Glaser JK (1997) Studying multivariate change using multilevel models and latent curve models. Multivariate Behav Res 32:215–253

Magnusson D (1998) The logic and implications of a person-oriented approach. In: Cairns RB, Bergman LR, Kagan J (eds) Methods and models for studying the individual. Sage Publications, Thousand Oaks, CA

McArdle JJ, Epstein D (1987) latent growth curves within developmental structural equation models. Child Dev 58:110–113

McLachlan G, Peel D (2000) Finite mixture models. Wiley, New York

Meredith W, Tisak J (1990) Latent curve analysis. Psychometrika 55:107–122

Moffitt TE (1993) Adolescence-limited and life-course persistent antisocial behavior: a developmental taxonomy. Psychol Rev 100:674–701

Moffitt TE (1997) Adolescence-limited and life-course-persistent offending: a complementary pair of developmental theories. In: Thornberry TP (ed) Advances in criminological theory. Transaction Publishers, New Brunswick, NJ, pp 11–54

Mustillo S, Worthman C, Erkanli E, Keeler G, Angold A, Costello EJ (2003) Obesity and psychiatric disorder: developmental trajectories. Pediatrics 111:851–859

Muthén B (1989) Latent variable modeling in heterogeneous populations. Psychometrika 54:557–585

Muthén BO (2001) Second-generation structural equation modeling with a combination of categorical and continuous latent variables: new opportunities for latent class/latent curve modeling. In: Sayers A, Collins L (eds) New methods for the analysis of change. American Psychological Association, Washington, DC

Muthén B, Shedden K (1999) Finite mixture modeling with mixture outcomes using the EM algorithm. Biometrics 55:463–469

Nagin D, Pagani L, Tremblay R, Vitaro F (2003) Life course turning points: a case study of the effect of school failure on interpersonal violence. Dev Psychopathol 15:343–361

Nagin DS (2005) Group-based modeling of development. Harvard University Press, Cambridge, MA

Nagin DS, Tremblay RE (1999) Trajectories of boys' physical aggression, opposition, and hyperactivity on the path to physically violent and nonviolent juvenile delinquency. Child Dev 70:1181–1196

Nagin DS, Tremblay RE (2001) Parental and early childhood predictors of persistent physical aggression in boys from kindergarten to high school. Arch Gen Psychiatry 58:389–394

Piquero A (2008). Taking stock of developmental trajectories of criminal activity over the life course. In: Liberman AM (ed) The long view of crime a synthesis of longitudinal research. Springer, New York, NY

Raudenbush SW (2001) Comparing-personal trajectories and drawing causal inferences from longitudinal data. Annu Rev Psychol 52:501–25

Thiel H (1971) Principals of econometrics. Wiley, New York, NY

Titterington DM, Smith AFM, Makov UE (1985) Statistical analysis of finite mixture distributions. Wiley, New York

Tremblay RE, Nagin DS (2005) Aggression in humans. In: Tremblay RE, Hartup WW, Archer J (eds) Developmental origins of aggression. Guilford, New York, NY

van Bokhoven I Van Goozen SHM, van Engeland H, Schaal B, Arseneault L Séguin JR, Nagin DS Vitaro F, abd Tremblay RE. (2005) Salivary cortisol and aggression in a population-based longitudinal study of adolescent males. J Neural Transm 112:1083–1096

Warr M (2002) Companions in crime: the social aspects of criminal conduct. Cambridge University Press, New York

Weisburd D, Bushway S, Lum C, Yang S (2004) Trajectories of crime at places: a longitudinal study of street segments in the city of Seattle. Criminology 42:283–320

Weisburd D, Morris N, Groff E (2008) Hot spots of juvenile crime: a longitudinal study of crime incidents at street segments in Seattle, Washington. Working paper. James Madison University, Fairfax, VA

Willett JB, Sayer AG (1994) Using covariance structure analysis to detect correlates and predictors of individual change over time. Psychol Bull 116:363–381

CHAPTER 5

General Growth Mixture Analysis with Antecedents and Consequences of Change

HANNO PETRAS AND KATHERINE MASYN

INTRODUCTION

Describing and predicting the developmental course of an individual's involvement in criminal and antisocial behavior is a central theme in criminological inquiries. A large body of evidence is available documenting that individual differences in levels of criminal behavior across time can effectively be described qualitatively using a discrete number of criminal career patterns which vary by age of onset, career length, as well as type and frequency of the behavior. The majority of studies, using selective offender or population-based samples, have identified offending typologies made up of four to six distinct trajectory profiles. Most of these profiles are declining and are distinguished by the level of offending at their peak and the timing of the decline (Picquero 2008). For example, Sampson and Laub (2003) identified several distinct offending trajectories patterns. One small group of individuals (3%) peaked in their offending behavior in the late 30s and declined to almost "0" at age 60 was labeled "high-rate chronics." In addition, three desisting groups were identified, who declined after middle adolescence, late adolescence, and early adulthood, respectively. Finally, a small group (8%) followed a low-rate chronic offending pattern between the ages of 19 and 39, and declined thereafter.

Childhood aggressive behavior is widely recognized as a precursor for antisocial and criminal behavior in adolescence and adulthood. Numerous prospective studies have demonstrated that conduct problems (as early as preschool) predict later delinquent behavior and drug use (Ensminger et al. 1983; Hawkins et al. 2000; Lynam 1996; McCord and Ensminger 1997; Yoshikawa 1994). Motivated by developmental research (Loeber and Hay 1997; Moffitt, 1993; Patterson et al. 1989; Patterson et al. 1998), a large body of longitudinal research has identified several developmental prototypes for individuals that vary in onset and course of aggressive behavior (Broidy et al. 2003; van Dulmen et al. 2009; Nagin and Tremblay 1999; Schaeffer et al. 2006; Petras et al. 2004; Petras et al. 2008; Shaw et al. 2003). Despite differences in terminology and emphasis, each study identifies two to five distinct patterns on youth

A.R. Piquero and D. Weisburd (eds.), *Handbook of Quantitative Criminology*,
DOI 10.1007/978-0-387-77650-7_5, © Springer Science + Business Media, LLC 2010,
First softcover printing 2011

antisocial behavior over time with different behavior trajectories, risk factors, and prognoses for desistence from antisocial behavior as adults. Each proposed typology includes one to two chronic profiles with early and persistent aggression that is likely to be related to a biological or genetic vulnerability, exacerbated by poor parenting and early school failure. Each also identifies one or two less severe profiles with antisocial behavior that starts later, is less aggressive, is more sporadic, and stems from later socialization experiences such as deviant peer affiliations in early adolescence. Implicit in each typology is also the assumption that there is at least one other profile that characterizes youth who do not exhibit problems with antisocial behaviors. Additional evidence suggests that there is also a profile characterizing the substantial proportion of those children who display high levels of aggressive behavior in childhood but who do not manifest antisocial behavior in adolescence or adulthood (Maughan and Rutter 1998).

In summary, many of the studies of youth, adolescents, and adults related to delinquent, antisocial, and criminal offending, have utilized a language of trajectory typologies to describe the individual differences in the behavioral course manifest in their longitudinal data. Although this language maps well onto some of the corresponding theories that provide the conceptual frameworks for these empirical investigations, the majority of these studies have not relied on subjective or heuristic taxonomies but instead relied on empirically-derived taxonomies based on statistical modeling techniques, analogous to clustering and, by doing so, have been able to progressively evaluate the veracity of the underlying theories themselves. The two most common statistical methods currently in use are the semiparametric group-based modeling, also known as latent class growth analysis (LCGA; Nagin and Land 1993; Roeder et al. 1999; Nagin 2005), and general growth mixture analysis (GGMA; Muthén 2001, 2004; Muthén et al. 2002; Muthén and Asparouhov 2008; Muthén and Muthén 1998–2008a; Muthén and Shedden 1999). Although there are differences in model specification and estimation (see the chapter in this handbook for more information on LCGA), both methods characterize some portion of the systematic population heterogeneity in the longitudinal process under study (i.e., between-individual variability not due to time-specific or measurement error) in terms of a finite number of trajectories groups (latent growth classes or mixture components) for which the mean or average growth within each group typifies one of the growth patterns or profiles manifest in the population. Together, the studies employing these methods have helped shift the study of antisocial and criminal behavior away from what has been termed a "variable-centered" focus, describing broad predictors of behavior variance, toward a more "person-centered" focus, emphasizing discretely distinct individual differences in development (Magnusson 1998).

In concert with the growing popularity of these data-driven, group-based methods for studying developmental and life-course behavior trajectories, have come active and spirited ontological discussions about the nature of the emergent trajectory groups resulting from the analyses (Bauer and Curran 2003, 2004; Nagin and Tremblay 2005; Sampson et al. 2004; Sampson and Laub 2005), i.e., whether the resultant trajectory typology defined by the subgroups derived from the data represent a "true" developmental taxonomy. Further debate involves whether it is reasonable to even apply these methods if there is not a true taxonomy underlying the data, under what conditions these methods should be applied, and how the results should be interpreted if we consider the fact that, for any given dataset, we cannot know the "truth" of the population distribution from which the observations were drawn. For example, we may not be able to make an empirical distinction between a sample of observations drawn from a population of values with a bimodal distribution and a sample of observations drawn from a mixture of two normally distributed subpopulations. Likewise, we may have a sample of observations for which a model that assumes a bimodal distribution is statistically indistinguishable from a model that assumes a finite mixture of two normal components. Thus, as is the case with any statistical modeling, the data can only empirically distinguish between models more or less consistent with the observations in the sample – they cannot identify the "truth" of the population between models with equivalent or nearly equivalent goodness-of-fit. Unfortunately, this issue of the *True* population distribution, i.e., the verity of the existence of latent subgroups in a given population, cannot be solved by means of replication since a new sample will give a similar distribution with similar ambiguities about the characteristics of the population distribution.

For the purposes of this chapter, we acknowledge that these debates are ongoing, but believe that the usefulness of these group-based models does not hinge on the ontological nature of the resultant trajectory groups. We presuppose that there are analytic, empirical, and substantive advantages inherent in using discrete components to (partially) describe population heterogeneity in longitudinal processes regardless of whether those discrete components are an approximation of a continuum of variability or if the components represent actual unobserved subpopulations within the larger population under study. In this chapter, we focus instead on the use of auxiliary information in terms of antecedents (predictors and covariates) and consequences (sequelae and distal static outcomes) of trajectory group membership in the GGMA framework (Muthén 2006). The use of auxiliary information, potentially derived from substantive theory, is highly relevant to determine the concurrent and prognostic validity of specific developmental trajectory profiles derived from a particular data set (Bushway et al. 1999; Heckman and Singer 1984; Kreuter and Muthén 2008). That is to say, the inclusion of auxiliary information in a growth mixture analysis is a necessary step in understanding as well as evaluating the fidelity and utility of the resultant trajectory profiles from a given study, regardless of one's beliefs about the veracity of the method itself. The remainder of the chapter is organized as follows: First, we briefly introduce the conventional latent growth curve model followed by a presentation of the unconditional growth mixture model, of which the latent growth curve model and latent class growth model are special cases. We then discuss the process for including antecedents and consequences of change in the general growth mixture analysis (GGMA) framework. We conclude this chapter with an empirical example using data from a large randomized trial in Baltimore.

THE UNCONDITIONAL LATENT GROWTH CURVE MODEL

Repeated measures on a sample of individuals result in a particular form of multilevel data, where time or measurement occasions at "Level 1" are nested within persons at "Level 2." This data can be analyzed using a multilevel modeling framework where *intraindividual* change is described as a function of time and *interindividual* differences are described by random effects and coefficients (Multilevel Linear Models – MLM or Hierarchical Linear Models – HLM; Raudenbush and Bryk 2002; Hox 2000, 2002). Alternatively, a multivariate latent variable approach can be used where the parameters of the individual growth curves are modeled as latent variables (e.g., latent intercept and slope factors), with a covariance and mean structure (Latent Growth Curve Models – LGCM, Latent Growth Models – LGM, or Latent Variable Growth Models – LVGM; Meredith and Tisak 1990; Willett and Sayer 1994; Muthén 2004). A typical unconditional linear latent growth curve model with T time points and n individuals is specified below.

Level 1:
$$y_{ti} = \eta_{0i} + \eta_{si} a_{ti} + \varepsilon_{ti},$$
Level 2:   (5.1)
$$\eta_{0i} = \alpha_0 + \zeta_{0i},$$
$$\eta_{si} = \alpha_s + \zeta_{1i},$$

where

$$\boldsymbol{\varepsilon} \sim MVN(\mathbf{0}, \boldsymbol{\Theta}),$$
$$\boldsymbol{\zeta} \sim MVN(\mathbf{0}, \boldsymbol{\Psi}),$$
$$\mathrm{Cov}(\varepsilon, \zeta) = 0.$$

Here, y_{ti} is the observed outcome y for individual i ($i = 1, \ldots, n$) at time t ($t = 1, \ldots, T$), a_{ti} is the time score for individual i at time t, η_{0i} is the random intercept factor (i.e., the "true score" value for individual i at time $a_{ti} = 0$), and η_{si} is the random linear slope factor (i.e., the expected change in y_i for a one unit increase in time, on the scale of a_t). In latent variable modeling terms, the y_t's are the *indicators* or *manifest variables* for the latent growth factors, η_0 and η_s. ε_{ti} represent measurement and time-specific error at time t and the ε_t's are usually assumed to be uncorrelated; however, that restriction can be relaxed. In the more traditional matrix notation of the latent variable framework, the equations in (5.1) can be written as

$$\mathbf{Y}_i = \boldsymbol{\Lambda} \boldsymbol{\eta}_i + \boldsymbol{\varepsilon}_i,$$
$$\boldsymbol{\eta}_i = \boldsymbol{\alpha} + \boldsymbol{\zeta}_i,$$ (5.2)

where $\mathbf{Y}_i$ is a ($T \times 1$) vector of observed scores for individual i, $\boldsymbol{\eta}_i$ is a ($p \times 1$) vector of growth factors, $\boldsymbol{\Lambda}$ is a ($T \times p$) design matrix of factor loadings with each column corresponding to specific aspects of change, and $\boldsymbol{\alpha}$ is a ($p \times 1$) vector of growth factor means. In this specification, $a_{ti} = a_t, \forall i$, but it is possible to incorporate individual-varying times of measurement within this framework by treating time measures at each occasion as a time-varying covariate with a random effect. For a linear model, $p = 2$, the loading matrix is given by

$$\begin{bmatrix} 1 & \lambda_{s1} \\ 1 & \lambda_{s2} \\ \vdots & \vdots \\ 1 & \lambda_{sT} \end{bmatrix}$$ (5.3)

where the loading values in the second column would be fixed to define the slope factor as the linear rate of change on the observed time metric; for example, $\boldsymbol{\lambda}_s = (a_1, a_2, \ldots, a_T)'$. Typically, time is centered such that the first loading, λ_{s1}, is fixed at zero so that the intercept factor can be interpreted as the response at the first time of measurement ($t = 1$). Although the above specification expresses the change in the outcome as a linear function of the time metric, it is possible (with an adequate number of repeated observations on each subject) to investigate interindividual differences in nonlinear trajectories of change. The most common approach is the use of polynomials where additional factors ($p > 2$) represent quadratic or cubic functions of the observed time metric. Nested models with increasing numbers of growth factors are assessed by chi-square difference testing as well as the use of SEM fit indices (Hu and Bentler 1999). Alternative specifications of time can also be easily accommodated, including piecewise linear growth models as well as exponential and sinusoidal models of change. Also, it is possible for the Level 1 equation in (5.1) and the residual variance/covariance structure of $\mathbf{Y}$ to

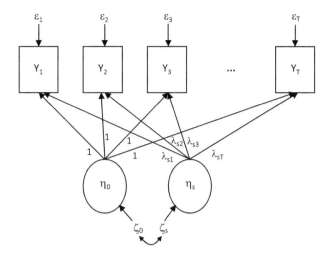

FIGURE 5.1. Path diagram for an unconditional linear latent growth curve model. Model is shown with fixed times of measurement, but individually-varying times of measurement may be specified.

be specified as a generalized linear model to accommodate binary, multinomial, ordinal, and count measures for the change process in addition to continuous measures. The path diagram for the unconditional linear latent growth curve model is shown in Fig. 5.1.

Although it is possible to specify analytically-equivalent unconditional models across the multilevel and latent variable modeling frameworks, utilizing the latent variable approach affords access to a variety of modeling extensions not as easily implemented in other frameworks, e.g., models that simultaneously include both antecedents and consequences of the changes process; higher order growth models with multiple indicators of the outcome at each assessment; multi-process and multilevel growth models; and models that employ both continuous and categorical latent variables for describing population heterogeneity in the change process (for more on growth modeling in a latent variable framework, see, for example, Bollen and Curran 2006; Duncan et al. 2006; Muthén 2000, 2001, 2004). In the next section, we describe the last extension for which the latent growth curve model serves as a foundational and restricted case in the broader category of general growth mixture models.

THE UNCONDITIONAL GENERAL GROWTH MIXTURE MODEL

General growth mixture analysis (GGMA) stands at the intersection of latent growth curve modeling and finite mixture modeling. In finite mixture modeling, rather than making the usual assumption that the observed responses in a data sample are *identically distributed*, i.e., are drawn from a singular homogeneous population, it is assumed that the data are drawn from a finite number of heterogeneous *subpopulations*. The finite mixture analysis divides the population into an unknown number of exhaustive and mutually exclusive subpopulations (or latent classes), each with its own response distribution (Muthén and Muthén 2000; Muthén and Curran 1997).

Figure 5.2 illustrates a mixture of two normally-distributed subpopulations. In the latent variable framework, the mixtures, or subpopulations, are represented by categories of a latent multinomial variable, usually termed a *latent class variable*, and the mixture components or

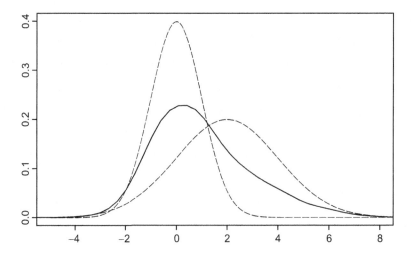

FIGURE 5.2. Illustration of a finite mixture of two normally-distributed subpopulations (*dashed lines*) and the resultant *mixed* population distribution (*solid line*).

subpopulations are referred to as *latent classes*. The distribution of an observed outcome, $\mathbf{Y}_i$, is a mixture distribution defined as

$$f(\mathbf{Y}_i) = \sum_{k=1}^{K} [\Pr(C_i = k) \cdot f(\mathbf{Y}_i | C_i = k)], \qquad (5.4)$$

where C_i represents the latent class membership for individual i, K is the total number of latent classes (subpopulations), $\Pr(C_i = k)$ is the mixing proportion for Class k, and $f(\mathbf{Y}_i | C_i = k)$ is the class-specific response distribution of $\mathbf{Y}_i$.

Latent class membership is unobserved and is determined by the class-specific model parameters. This brings us to a critical point, which we will emphasize repeatedly in this chapter: As with any latent variable, it is necessary to specify a measurement model for the latent class variable. Indicators for the latent class variable include *any* variables, observed or latent, that differ in values between individuals in the population due to latent class membership, as well as model parameters that are permitted to be class-specific, thereby designating those parameters as individually-varying or "random" effects in the given model. The latent classes are then characterized by the class-specific joint distribution of all those variables and random effects and empirically based on the overall joint distribution in the sample. Thus, the estimation of the optimal number and size of the latent classes (class proportions), as well as the corresponding model parameter estimates (class-specific and overall) and interpretation of the resultant classes, will very much depend on: (1) which variables and random effects are included as latent class indicators and (2) the specification of the within-class joint distribution of those latent class indicators. This is analogous to selecting the attribute space and the resemblance coefficient in a cluster analysis. For example, if we specified a latent class model in which the classes differed only with respect to their mean structure and assumed conditional independence of all the class indicators, we may extract different classes (number, size, and class-specific parameters estimates) than a model in which the classes differed with respect to both their mean and variance-covariance structure.

In growth mixture modeling, rather than assuming the individual growth parameters (e.g., individual intercept and growth factors) are *identically distributed*, i.e., are drawn from a singular homogeneous population, as we do in latent growth curve modeling, it is assumed that the individual growth parameters are drawn from a finite number of heterogeneous subpopulations. The growth mixture analysis divides the population into an unknown number of exhaustive and mutually exclusive latent trajectory classes, each with a unique distribution of individual growth factors. In other words, the continuous latent growth factors serve as the indicators for the K-category latent class variable, C, in a growth mixture model, as expressed below.

$$\mathbf{Y}_i = \mathbf{\Lambda}\mathbf{\eta}_i + \mathbf{\varepsilon}_i,$$
$$\mathbf{\eta}_i = \mathbf{\alpha}_k + \mathbf{\zeta}_i,$$

(5.5)

where

$$\mathbf{\varepsilon} \sim MVN(\mathbf{0}, \mathbf{\Theta}_k),$$
$$\mathbf{\zeta} \sim MVN(\mathbf{0}, \mathbf{\Psi}_k),$$
$$\Pr(C_i = k) = \frac{\exp(\pi_k)}{\sum\limits_{h=1}^{K}(\exp(\pi_h))}.$$

Here, C_i represents the latent trajectory class membership for individual i, where $C = 1, \ldots, K$. The sizes of the latent classes in the mixture, i.e., the mixing proportions, are parameterized in the model using a multinomial logistic regression, where π_k represents the log odds of membership in Class k relative to a reference class, usually Class K (and $\pi_K = 0$ for identification). Notice that the residuals (on the growth factors and observed outcomes) are all assumed to be normally distributed *within* each latent class. Thus, the normality assumption is not imposed on the overall population but merely on the subpopulations, allowing for the possibility of highly nonnormal distributions of responses at the overall population level. The path diagram for the general linear latent growth mixture model is shown in Fig. 5.3.

For a given value of K, these models can be fit using ML estimation via the EM algorithm (Muthén and Shedden 1999). Based on the model-estimated response probabilities and observed data, each individual's estimated probability of class membership, $\widehat{p}_{ik}$ (termed the *posterior class probabilities*), can be calculated using the following equation:

$$\widehat{p}_{ik} = \widehat{\Pr}(C_i = k|\mathbf{Y}_i) = \frac{\widehat{\Pr}(C_i = k)\widehat{\Pr}(\mathbf{Y}_i|C_i = k)}{\widehat{\Pr}(\mathbf{Y}_i)}.$$

(5.6)

The class-specific model parameters may include the growth factors means ($\mathbf{\alpha}_k$), the growth factor variances and covariances ($\mathbf{\Psi}_k$), and the observed outcome residual variances and covariances ($\mathbf{\Theta}_k$). However, as we mentioned before, one must give careful consideration to what is permitted to vary across the classes for it is those differences that define the classes themselves. Thus, if we wanted latent classes or mixtures that partitioned the population on the basis of differences in the systematic change process over time, i.e., mixture based exclusively on the joint distribution of latent growth factors, then we may not want to allow the outcome residual variances and covariances to be class-specific, i.e., we may want to constrain $\mathbf{\Theta}_k = \mathbf{\Theta}, \forall k$. As another example, if we changed the location of the intercept growth factor by centering the time scale at the end of the time range instead of the beginning, then the latent classes would be characterized by heterogeneity in the outcome level at the final time

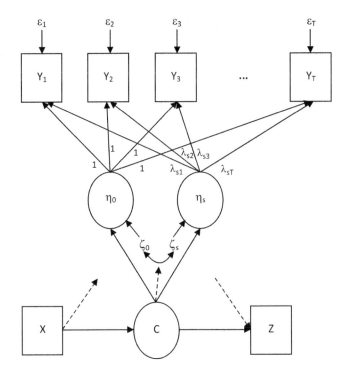

FIGURE 5.3. Path diagram for a general (*linear*) growth mixture model with observed static antecedents (X) and consequences (Z) of change.

point and the outcome change over time rather than by heterogeneity in the outcome level at the first time point and outcome change over time. Only in models with Ψ_k unstructured and unconstrained across the latent classes, the maximum likelihood value will be the same regardless of the time centering.

It is clear to see from the equations in (5.5) that the latent growth curve model described in the previous section is simply a growth mixture model with $K = 1$. Another special case is the latent class growth model developed by Nagin and colleagues (Nagin 1999; Nagin and Land 1993; Nagin 2005; Roeder et al. 1999; Jones et al. 2001) which is characterized by zero within-class growth factor variance and covariances, thus assuming homogeneity of individuals' systematic development within a particular class, i.e., $\Psi_k = \mathbf{0}, \forall k$. Not only does this stand as a special case of growth mixture modeling, it represents a very specific measurement model for the latent class variable portion such that the classes are differentiated by differences in the mean structure on the growth factors with *all* interindividual variability on the growth factors and covariance between the growth factors explained by latent class membership. Certainly, the necessary number and nature of the latent classes extracted from a given data set under this model specification will deviate from those extracted using a different measurement model specification. To be more specific, a greater number of latent classes would be needed for a model in which *all* growth factor variance and covariance had to be captured by between-class differences compared to a model in which overall growth factor variance and covariance were partitioned into inter-class and intra-class variability. Models that assign all systematic variability in growth to class membership are usually less parsimonious but are more flexible and make fewer parametric assumptions. Interestingly, although the latent class growth model may be more parameter-laden, it may be easier to estimate, i.e., converge more readily, than a less constrained model with fewer classes but an equivalent number of free parameters, especially in cases for which the overall variability in one or more of the growth factors is small. In those cases, even with fewer classes, there may not be enough overall variance to parse out across the between- and within-class differences, leading to an empirical identification problem. Unfortunately, these are not problems that can be readily foreseen ahead of the actual data analysis and must be dealt with as it arises. Models with different within- and between-class differences can be compared in terms of relative goodness-of-fit using various information indices; however, nested models that differ in the number of latent classes cannot be compared using a standard chi-squared approximation for the likelihood ratio test (LRT), as is explained in the following section on model building (although alternatives are suggested). Additionally, a K-class model with $\Psi_k = 0, \forall k$, cannot be directly compared to a K-class model with unconstrained Ψ_k using a standard chi-squared approximation for the LRT because the null hypothesis lies on the boundary of the parameter space defined by the alternative (Stram and Lee 1994).

Model Building in GGMA

Given the complexity of the model and the different measurement model specifications for the latent class variable, it is recommended that model building proceed in a systematic step-wise fashion. The first step in the process is specifying the functional form for individual change over time. Descriptive analyses at this first foray into the data can reveal commonalities across individuals and idiosyncrasies between individuals with respect to each person's pattern of growth over time. It is important to note that the shape of the mean change trajectory in the overall sample may not mirror the shape of individual trajectories within that sample. Thus, it is critical to examine smooth nonparametric as well as OLS trajectories across at least a random sample of subjects in the dataset to explore the shapes of individual change over time. In selecting a functional form, e.g., linear or curvilinear, one should consider adopting the most parsimonious choice that will adequately describe the individual trajectories, allowing for the fact that plots based on repeated measures of single subjects will reflect both systematic changes over time as well as random fluctuation due to measurement and time-specific error. (For more on this descriptive step, see, for example, Singer and Willett 2003.)

The next step in the model building process is class enumeration. All of the mixture model specifications in the previous section were predicated on a known value for K. Although we may have very compelling substantive theories, as discussed in the introduction, regarding discrete typologies of change or growth, these theories are rarely specific enough to guide a purely confirmatory model fitting process, e.g., "we hypothesize three latent trajectory classes with class-specific quadratic mean structures, class-specific growth factor variances, zero within-class growth factor covariances, and class-invariant outcome residual variances." Thus, the class enumeration process advances in a more exploratory manner while giving due consideration to *a prior* substantive hypotheses regarding the number and nature of the subpopulations that may be represented in the data. (Recall that the use of mixtures may be as much for accommodating non-normality in the overall population as uncovering "true" subpopulations.)

This step begins by considering a set of models with an increasing number of latent classes under a given measurement model. It is advisable to begin with a somewhat restricted measurement model given some of the known pitfalls in mixture model estimation. Mixture models can have difficulty with convergence and a model specification that allows the growth factor (or outcome) residual variances to differ across class results in an unbounded likelihood function which can increase the chance of nonconvergence because the candidate parameter space may include solutions with variances of zero and latent classes made up of single individuals (McLachlan and Peel 2000). This, coupled with the previous discussed motivation, suggests beginning the class enumeration process with a measurement model for which $\Theta_k = \Theta, \forall k$. We may similarly consider constraining $\Psi_k = \Psi, \forall k$ in our initial model specification as well. However, rather than assuming that the covariances between the growth factors within each latent class are the same, it may be more reasonable to start with a model that, like traditional latent class and latent profile analysis, assumes conditional independence of the class indicators, i.e., fixes the covariances of the growth factors *within* class to zero such that the growth factors are independent conditional on latent class. In such a model, the latent class variable would be designed to account for (or explain) *all* of the covariance between the growth factors in the overall population while the overall variance of the growth factors would be accounted for in part by the within-class continuous random variability on the growth factors and in part by the between-class differences in growth factor means. Thus, beginning ultimately with a measurement model where $\Psi_k = Diag(\psi_1, \ldots, \psi_p)$ and $\Theta_k = \Theta, \forall k$, with α_k free to vary across the K latent classes. This particular specification represents a probabilistic variant of a *k-means* clustering algorithm applied to the "true" growth factor values for the individuals in the sample (Vermunt and Magidson 2002). Once the class enumeration step is complete, one could theoretically use nested model tests and fit indices to investigate whether freeing the growth factor variances across the latent classes or relaxing the conditional independence assumption improves the fit of the model. However, by making such changes to the latent class measurement model specification, we should not be surprised if we see not only changes to the relative fit of the model, but also significant changes to the location, size, and substantive meaning of the latent classes. If this occurs, we may be given a cause to reevaluate the final model selection from the latent class enumeration step or, more drastically, to reconsider the model specification used for the latent class enumeration process itself, and begin again.

Mixture models are also infamous for converging on local rather than global maxima when they do converge. The use of multiple starts from random locations in the parameter space can improve the chance of convergence to global maxima (Hipp and Bauer 2006). Ideally, replication of the maximum likelihood value across a large number of random sets of start values increases confidence that the solution obtained is a global maximum.

Once a set of models, differing only in the number of classes, has been estimated, the models are then compared to make a determination as to the smallest number of classes necessary to effectively describe the heterogeneity manifest through those classes. This first step in growth mixture modeling - deciding on the appropriate number of classes - can prove the most taxing, particularly because there is no single method for comparing models with differing numbers of latent classes that is widely accepted as the best (Muthén and Asparouhov 2008; Nylund et al. 2007); but, by careful and systematic consideration of a set of plausible models, and utilizing a combination of statistical and substantive model checking (Muthén 2003), researchers can improve their confidence in the tenability of their resultant model selection. Comparisons of model fit are based primarily on the log likelihood value. The standard chi-square difference test (likelihood ratio test; LRT) cannot be used in this setting because regularity conditions of the test are violated when comparing a k-class model to a $(k\text{-}g)$-class model (McLachlan and Peel 2000). However, two alternatives, currently implemented in the Mplus V5.1 software (Muthén and Muthén 1998–2008b), are available: (1) The Vuong-Lo–Mendell–Rubin test (VLMR-LRT; Lo et al. 2001) analytically approximates the LRT distribution when comparing a k-class to a $(k\text{-}g)$-class finite mixture model for which the classes differ only in the mean structure, and (2) The parametric bootstrapped LRT (BLRT), recommended by McLachlan and Peel (2000), uses bootstrap samples (generated using parameter estimated from a $(k\text{-}g)$-class model) to empirically derive the sampling distribution of the LRT statistic. Both of these tests and their performance across a range of finite mixture models are explored in detail in the simulation study by Nylund et al. (2007). As executed in Mplus, these tests compare a $(k\text{-}1)$-class model (the null model) with a k-class model (the alternative, less restrictive model) and a statistically significant p-value suggests that the k-class model fits the data significantly better than a model with one fewer classes. In addition to these tests, likelihood-based information indices, such as the Bayesian Information Criterion (BIC; Schwarz 1978) are used in model selection. This index and similar ones (e.g., sample-size adjusted BIC) are computed as a function of the log likelihood with a penalty for model complexity (e.g., the number of parameters estimated relative to the sample size). In general, a lower value on an information criterion indicates a better model. Based on their simulation work, Nylund et al. (2007) recommend using the BIC and VLMR-LRT to trim the set of models under consideration and then including the BLRT for a smaller set of model comparisons (due to the computational demands of the BLRT).

Although the model likelihood will always improve with an increasing number of classes, sometimes none of the other fit indices reach a clear optimal value among the set of candidate model. For example, the BIC may never arrive at a single lowest value at some value for K and then begin to increase for all models with more than K classes, or the VLMR-LRT and BLRT may never return a significant p-value, favoring a $(k\text{-}1)$-class model over a k-class model, before the number of classes is increased to the point at which the model no longer converges to a proper solution or fails to converge at all. However, in these cases, we can loosely explore the diminishing gains in model fit according to these indices with the use of "elbow" plots. For example, if we graph the maximum log likelihood values models with an increasing number of classes, the addition of the second and third class may add much more information, but as the number of classes increases, the marginal gain may drop, resulting in a (hopefully) pronounced angle in the plot. The number of classes at this point meets the "elbow criterion" for that index. We could make a similar plot for BIC values. Analogous to the scree plot for principal component analysis, we could also plot the percent of total growth factor variance explained by the latent classes for each class enumeration, i.e., the ratio of the between-class growth factor variance for the total variance (Thorndike 1953). In addition to these elbow plots, graphic representations of each of the multivariate observations themselves could be used to guide in reducing the set of candidate models such as the tree plots suggested by Lubke and Spies (2008).

It can be noted that the set of the model comparisons discussed earlier are *relative* model comparisons, and evaluations of overall goodness-of-fit are conspicuously absent. For example, all of the relative comparisons may favor, say, a 3-class model over a 2-class model as a *better* fit to the data, but none of the fit indices or tests indicate whether either is a *good* fit to the data. However, depending on the measurement scale of the outcome variable and the presence of missing data, there are some model diagnostics available for overall goodness-of-fit. If the observed outcome variables are binary, ordinal, or count, it is possible to compute the overall univariate, bivariate, and multivariate model-estimated response pattern frequencies and relative frequencies for **Y**, along with the corresponding standardized

Pearson residuals. For continuous outcome variables, it is possible to compute the overall model-estimated means, variances, covariances, univariate skewness, and univariate kurtosis, along with the corresponding residuals. In each case, the overall model-estimated values are computed as a mixture across the latent classes. Additional residual graphical diagnostics designed to detect misspecification in growth mixture models regarding the number of latent trajectory classes, the functional form of the within-class growth trajectory (i.e., functional relationship between the observed outcome and time), and the within-class covariance structure are presented in a paper by Wang et al. (2005) but are not currently implemented directly in the software most commonly used by researchers in applied settings for growth mixture modeling.

In addition to the statistical criteria discussed earlier, it is also useful to assess the value and utility of the resultant classes themselves. One measure which can be used for this purpose is entropy (Ramaswamy et al. 1993). Entropy summarizes the degree to which the latent classes are distinguishable and the precision with which individuals can be placed into classes. It is a function of the individual estimated posterior probabilities and ranges from 0 to 1 with higher values indicating better class separation. Entropy is not a measure of fit, nor was it originally intended for model selection; however, if the intended purpose of the growth mixture model is to find homogeneous groupings of individuals with characteristically distinct growth trajectories, such that the between-class dispersion is much greater than the within-class dispersion, then low values of entropy may indicate that the model is not well serving its purpose (e.g., Nagin 1999).

Beyond all these measures, it is also important to make some qualitative evaluations of the usefulness and face validity of the latent class extractions by examining and interpreting the estimates and corresponding plots of the model-implied mean class trajectories for different models. If the model permits class-specific growth factor variances and covariances, it would be informative to also examine scatterplots of the estimated individual growth factor scores according to either modal latent class assignment or by pseudo-class draw (explained in a later section) since classes would be distinguished by both the mean and variance-covariance structure. It may also be worthwhile noting class size and proportions since an overextraction of classes might be revealed through particularly small and nondistinct classes emerging at higher enumerative values. Further validation of the primary candidate models can also be done. If there is an ample enough sample size, it is possible to carry out a split sample validation by conducting the exploration of latent structure on one random half of the sample and then evaluating the fit of the selected model on the second half of the sample. Additionally, auxiliary information, potentially derived from substantive theory, in the form of antecedent and consequent variables of the latent construct can be examined to evaluate the concurrent and prognostic validity of the latent structure as specified in a given model (Muthén 2003). How this auxiliary information may be included is the topic of the next section.

ANTECEDENTS AND CONSEQUENCES IN GGMA

Once an unconditional growth model has been fit to the repeated measures, and intraindividual change is appropriately modeled and marginal interindividual variability appropriately specified, the focus of the analysis usually shifts to investigating antecedents or predictors of individual differences in the change process as well as consequences or sequelae of change. For a single-class latent growth curve model, antecedents of change enter the model as predictors of the latent growth factors and sequelae of change enter the model as outcomes predicted *by* the latent growth factors as given in the equations below.

$$\mathbf{Y}_i = \mathbf{\Lambda}\mathbf{\eta}_i + \mathbf{\varepsilon}_i,$$
$$\mathbf{\eta}_i = \mathbf{\alpha}_0 + \mathbf{\Gamma}^{(\eta)}\mathbf{X}_i + \mathbf{\zeta}_i, \qquad (5.7)$$
$$\mathbf{Z}_i = \mathbf{\omega}_0 + \mathbf{\beta}\mathbf{\eta}_i + \mathbf{\xi}_i,$$

where

$$\mathbf{\xi} \sim MVN(\mathbf{0}, \mathbf{\Omega}),$$

and where the first expression associating the observed repeated measures with the growth factors is the same as for the unconditional latent growth curve model. Here, $\mathbf{X}_i$ is a $(q \times 1)$ vector of time-invariant covariate predictors of changes for individual i (although not shown here, time-varying covariates can be included in the first equation as part of the expression for $\mathbf{Y}_i$), $\mathbf{\Gamma}^{(\eta)}$ is a $(p \times q)$ matrix of regression coefficients representing the effect of $\mathbf{X}$ on $\mathbf{\eta}$, $\mathbf{\alpha}_0$ is a $(p \times 1)$ vector of regression intercepts for $\mathbf{\eta}$, $\mathbf{Z}_i$ is a $(d \times 1)$ vector of static outcomes of the change process, $\mathbf{\beta}$ is a $(d \times p)$ matrix of regression coefficients representing the effect of $\mathbf{\eta}$ on $\mathbf{Z}$, and $\mathbf{\omega}_0$ is a $(d \times 1)$ vector of regression intercepts for $\mathbf{Z}$. It is possible for the third equation in (5.7) and the residual variance/covariance structure of $\mathbf{Z}$ to be specified as a generalized linear model to accommodate not only continuous, but also binary, multinomial, ordinal, and count outcomes of changes. Notice that similar to the assumption of the unconditional single-class latent growth curve model that all individuals are drawn from a single population, the conditional model additionally assumes that predictors have the same influence on the growth factors for all individuals and that the growth factors have the same influence on subsequent outcomes for all individuals. Once we shift to a general growth mixture modeling approach, those assumptions are also relaxed by permitting predictors to influence latent class membership and then having latent class membership predict to subsequent outcomes. The standard assumptions of additive linear associations between predictors and growth factors and between growth factors and outcomes are also relaxed. The inclusion of antecedents and consequences of latent trajectory class membership also permit evaluation of the criterion-related validity for mapping the emergent classes onto theoretical developmental profiles and, ultimately, for evaluating the validity of the corresponding theory itself. For example, in Moffit's dual taxonomy, it is hypothesized that the life course persistent group consists of individuals with deficits in executive functioning (Moffitt 1993). If the probability of membership in the persistent trajectory class does not statistically differ in respect to theory driven covariates, such as executive functioning, then that particular model lacks crucial theoretical support. If there are repeated failures across various model specifications and samples to find such associations, we may begin to consider that the theory lacks critical empirical support.

Antecedents of Change

In GGMA, covariates are related to latent trajectory class membership via multinomial logistic regression, as expressed below.

$$\Pr(C_i = k | X_i) = \frac{\exp(\pi_{0k} + \mathbf{\Gamma}_k^{(C)}\mathbf{X}_i)}{\sum\limits_{h=1}^{K} \exp(\pi_{0h} + \mathbf{\Gamma}_h^{(C)}\mathbf{X}_i)}, \qquad (5.8)$$

where Class K is the reference class and $\pi_{0K} = 0$ and $\mathbf{\Gamma}_K^{(C)} = \mathbf{0}$ for identification. Here, $\mathbf{\Gamma}_k^{(C)}$ is a $(1 \times q)$ vector of logistic regression coefficients representing the effect of $\mathbf{X}$ on the log odds of membership in Class k relative to Class K, and π_{0k} is the logistic regression intercept for Class k relative to Class K. These associations between $\mathbf{X}$ and C are represented in the path diagram of Fig. 5.3 by the arrow from $\mathbf{X}$ to C.

The set of covariates may also be permitted to influence the within-class interindividual variability in the change process similar to the associations specified in the second equation of (5.7):

$$\mathbf{\eta}_i = \mathbf{\alpha}_{0k} + \mathbf{\Gamma}^{(\eta)} \mathbf{X}_i + \mathbf{\zeta}_i, \tag{5.9}$$

where $\mathbf{\Gamma}^{(\eta)}$ is a $(p \times q)$ matrix of regression coefficients representing the effect of $\mathbf{X}$ on $\mathbf{\eta}$, and $\mathbf{\alpha}_{0k}$ is a $(p \times 1)$ vector of regression intercepts for $\mathbf{\eta}$ within Class k. These possible associations are represented in the path diagram of Fig. 5.3 by a dashed arrow from $\mathbf{X}$ pointing toward the growth factors. It is also possible to allow class-specific effects of $\mathbf{X}$ on $\mathbf{\eta}$, that is,

$$\mathbf{\eta}_i = \mathbf{\alpha}_{0k} + \mathbf{\Gamma}_k^{(\eta)} \mathbf{X}_i + \mathbf{\zeta}_i, \tag{5.10}$$

where $\mathbf{\Gamma}_k^{(\eta)}$ is a $(p \times q)$ matrix of regression coefficients representing the effect of $\mathbf{X}$ on $\mathbf{\eta}$ within Class k, and $\mathbf{\alpha}_k$ is a $(p \times 1)$ vector of regression intercepts for $\mathbf{\eta}$ within Class k.

There are several critical points to which to pay attention when incorporating covariates or predictors of change into a growth mixture model. First and foremost, selection and order of covariate inclusion should follow the same process as with any regular regression model, with respect to risk factors or predictors of interest, control of potential confounders, etc. Secondly, although covariates can certainly assist in understanding, interpreting, and assigning meaning to the resultant classes, i.e., to *inform* the classes, one should exercise caution if the mixture model identification is dependent upon the inclusion of covariates or if the formation of the latent classes is sensitive to the particular subset of covariates included as predictors of class membership. On the basis of the simulation work of Nylund and Masyn (2008), misspecification of covariate effects in a latent class analysis can lead to overextraction of latent classes more often than when the latent class enumeration is conducted without covariates. Once the enumeration process is complete, covariates should first be added to the model only as predictors of the latent class variable. If the covariates are permitted to influence the change process exclusively through their effects on class membership in the model and the classes themselves change substantively in size or meaning (i.e., the class proportion or class-specific growth parameter estimates), this can signal a misspecification of the covariate associations with the latent class indicators. If that occurs, then direct effects, initially class-invariant, from the covariates to the growth factors themselves should be explored, as given in (5.9). The covariates should be centered so that there is not a radical shift in how the centroids of the latent classes are located, facilitating comparisons in class formation between the unconditional and conditional models. In the conditional model, the centroids of the latent classes, defined by class-specific growth factor mean vectors, $\mathbf{\alpha}_k$, become the center of growth factor values for the classes at $\mathbf{X} = \mathbf{0}$. Assuming correct specification of the indirect (via the latent class variable) and direct effects of the covariates on the growth factors, the resultant classes should align more closely to the classes obtained from the unconditional growth mixture model. If effects directly from the covariates to the growth factors are specified in the model, careful consideration should be given before allowing those effects to be class-varying as well, as in (5.10). Recall that any parameter that is permitted to vary across the latent classes becomes an *indicator* of that latent class variable. Thus, including class-varying covariate effects on the growth factors results in latent classes which are defined not only by heterogeneity in growth trajectories but also heterogeneity in the effect of those covariates on the growth trajectories. This is not an incorrect model specification, but it does represent what could be a significant departure from the measurement model originally intended for the latent class variable in the unconditional model. If the classes continue to change in significant ways relative to the unconditional growth mixture model with changing subsets of covariates, then careful attention should be paid to the stability of the model estimation under the original specification and to the solution sensitivity to covariate inclusion and the entire modeling approach should be reevaluated for data sample at hand.

Consequences of Change

In addition to including covariates and predictors of change, it is often of interest to relate the growth trajectories to distal outcomes or sequelae of change (depicted by the arrow from C to $\mathbf{Z}$ and the dashed arrow pointing from η toward $\mathbf{Z}$ in Fig. 5.3). This facilitates the assessment of the predictive power of class membership. While the inclusion of distal outcomes is fairly straightforward for the single class latent growth curve model, as given in the third equation of (5.7), evaluating the associations between growth mixtures and sequelae of change can pose an analytic dilemma.

There are two primary ways to frame a distal outcome of the change process when a latent class variable is involved and each way is conceptually and analytically different - the choice between them is not one that can be made by the data but must be made by the researcher with understanding of the implications for each alternative. The first way is to treat the distal outcome(s) as an additional *indicator* of the latent class variable. The second way is to treat the latent class variable and distal outcome(s) as a cause-effect pairing such that the distal outcome(s) is a true consequence of latent class membership.

For the first approach, the indicators for the measurement model of the latent class variable are made up of the latent growth factors *and* the distal outcomes (for more, see Muthén and Shedden 1999). The latent class variable is characterized by heterogeneity in *both* the change process *and* a later outcome. In other words, the latent class variable captures variability in the growth factors, variability in the distal outcomes, *and* the association *between* the growth factors and the distal outcomes. In addition to the equations in (5.5), we add the following to the measurement model for the latent class variable:

$$\mathbf{Z}_i = \omega_k + \xi_i, \tag{5.11}$$

where

$$\xi \sim MVN(\mathbf{0}, \mathbf{\Omega}_k).$$

Here, again, $\mathbf{Z}_i$ is a $(d \times 1)$ vector of static outcomes of the change process. ω_k is a $(d \times 1)$ vector of class-specific means for $\mathbf{Z}$ given membership in Class k. It is possible for (5.11) and the residual variance/covariance structure of $\mathbf{Z}$ to be specified as a generalized linear model to accommodate not only continuous, but also binary, multinomial, ordinal, and count outcomes of changes. If η and $\mathbf{Z}$ are both being used as indicators of the latent class variable, then it may be desirable to include $\mathbf{Z}$ in the class enumeration process since $\mathbf{Z}$ would be part of the measurement model for C. In this case, the residual variance/covariance matrix for $\mathbf{Z}$ could be constrained in a similar way to the one for $\boldsymbol{\eta}$, i.e., $\boldsymbol{\Omega}_k = Diag(\Omega_1, \ldots, \Omega_d)$, and $\mathbf{Z}$ and $\boldsymbol{\eta}$, as indicators for the latent class variable, could be assumed to be conditionally independent given class membership, i.e., $\text{Cov}(\boldsymbol{\Psi}_k, \boldsymbol{\Omega}_k) = \mathbf{0}$. Although it would be possible to specify and estimate a regression association within class from $\boldsymbol{\eta}$ to $\mathbf{Z}$ similar to the third equation of (5.7),

$$\mathbf{Z}_i = \boldsymbol{\omega}_{0k} + \boldsymbol{\beta}_k \boldsymbol{\eta}_i + \boldsymbol{\xi}_i, \tag{5.12}$$

this would fundamentally change the measurement model for C, where instead of just including $\mathbf{Z}$ as an indicator of C, individual heterogeneity in the association between $\boldsymbol{\eta}$ and $\mathbf{Z}$ along with the marginal distribution of $\boldsymbol{\eta}$ would characterize C. Constraining the effect of $\boldsymbol{\eta}$ on $\mathbf{Z}$ to be class-invariant would reduce the impact of this path on formation of the classes but be the equivalent of relaxing the conditional independence assumption between $\boldsymbol{\eta}$ and $\mathbf{Z}$ within class. In either case, with class-varying or class-invariant effects of $\boldsymbol{\eta}$ on $\mathbf{Z}$, the centroids of the latent classes on to the scale of $\mathbf{Z}$ will be the class-specific means of $\mathbf{Z}$ when $\boldsymbol{\eta} = \mathbf{0}$.

The second way to frame $\mathbf{Z}$ is as actual an *outcome, effect,* or *consequence* of latent class membership, rather than as an indicator of the latent class variable, C, such that C is a predictor of $\mathbf{Z}$ as given below.

$$\mathbf{Z}_i = \boldsymbol{\omega}_0 + \sum_{k=1}^{K} \left(\boldsymbol{\beta}_k^{(C)} \cdot \text{I}(C_i = k) \right) + \boldsymbol{\xi}_i, \tag{5.13}$$

where

$$\boldsymbol{\xi} \sim MVN(\mathbf{0}, \boldsymbol{\Omega}).$$

Here, $\boldsymbol{\beta}_k^{(C)}$ is a $(d \times 1)$ vector of regression coefficients for the indicator variable, $\text{I}(C_i = k)$, which is equal to unity when $C_i = k$ and zero otherwise. If we fix $\boldsymbol{\beta}_K^{(C)}$ at zero, then $\boldsymbol{\omega}_0$ represents the mean vector for $\mathbf{Z}$ among those in Class K. Then the vector of regression coefficients, $\boldsymbol{\beta}_k^{(C)}$, represents the vector of mean differences on $\mathbf{Z}$ between Class k and Class K. Alternatively, we could set $\boldsymbol{\omega}_0$ to zero so that all the $\boldsymbol{\beta}_k^{(C)}$'s are freely estimated and each represent the mean vector for $\mathbf{Z}$ given membership in Class k. In order to utilize this second approach to distal outcomes, $\mathbf{Z}$ cannot be included in the model which estimates the growth mixtures and related covariate effects. If it is included, it will automatically be treated as an indicator of the latent class variable. Instead, the growth mixture model with covariates must first be estimated without $\mathbf{Z}$. Then, the $\boldsymbol{\beta}_k^{(C)}$ parameters are estimated using what is referred to as the *pseudo-class draw* technique (see Bandeen-Roche et al. 1997; Muthén and Asparouhov 2007; Wang et al. 2005). Based on the estimated growth mixture model with covariates, the posterior latent class probability distribution, $\widehat{Pr}(C_i) = (\widehat{p}_{i1}, \widehat{p}_{i2}, \ldots, \widehat{p}_{iK})$, for each individual in the sample is computed using the estimated model and the observed data for that individual, where

$$\widehat{p}_{ik} = \widehat{\text{Pr}}(C_i = k | \mathbf{Y}_i, \mathbf{X}_i) = \frac{\widehat{\text{Pr}}(C_i = k) \widehat{\text{Pr}}(\mathbf{Y}_i | C_i = k, \mathbf{X}_i)}{\widehat{\text{Pr}}(\mathbf{Y}_i | \mathbf{X}_i)}. \tag{5.14}$$

A specified number of random draws, M, are made from the discrete posterior probability distributions for all individuals in the sample ($M = 20$ is recommended in general, see Wang et al. 2005). For example, suppose there was an individual with a posterior latent class probability distribution from a $K = 3$ class growth mixture model computed as $\widehat{\Pr}(C_i) = (\widehat{p}_{i1} = 0.80, \widehat{p}_{i2} = 0.15, \widehat{p}_{i3} = 0.05)$. Pseudo-class membership for individual i from 20 random draws might look like the following:

$$C_i^1 = 1, C_i^2 = 1, C_i^3 = 1, C_i^4 = 2, C_i^5 = 1, C_i^6 = 1, C_i^7 = 1, C_i^8 = 1,$$
$$C_i^9 = 1, C_i^{10} = 1, C_i^{11} = 1, C_i^{12} = 3, C_i^{13} = 1, C_i^{14} = 1, C_i^{15} = 3, C_i^{16} = 1,$$
$$C_i^{17} = 3, C_i^{18} = 1, C_i^{19} = 1, C_i^{20} = 1,$$

where C_i^m is the pseudo-class membership for individual i based on random draw m from the posterior distribution, $\widehat{\Pr}(C_i)$. For each pseudo-class draw, the association between $\mathbf{Z}$ and C is estimated using the pseudo-class membership and observed $\mathbf{Z}_i$ for each individual in the sample; thus, for (5.13), we would obtained $\widehat{\boldsymbol{\beta}}_k^{(C^m)}$ and $\widehat{\boldsymbol{\Omega}}^m$: the estimates for $\boldsymbol{\beta}_k^{(C)}$ and $\boldsymbol{\Omega}$, respectively, based on the mth pseudo-class draw. Consistent estimates for $\boldsymbol{\beta}_k^{(C)}$ are then obtained by averaging the $\widehat{\boldsymbol{\beta}}_k^{(C^m)}$ estimates across the M pseudo-class draws (for proof, see Bandeen-Roche et al. 1997):

$$\widehat{\boldsymbol{\beta}}_k^{(C)} = \frac{1}{M} \sum_m \widehat{\boldsymbol{\beta}}_k^{(C^m)}. \tag{5.15}$$

The asymptotic variance of the estimate can be obtained using a similar method to multiple imputations (described by Rubin 1987 and Schafer 1997). Take the simple case with a single distal outcome of interest, such that $d = 1$ and $\beta_k^{(C)}$ is a scalar quantity. Suppose that $\widehat{U}_k^m$ is the square of the standard error associated with $\widehat{\beta}_k^{(C^m)}$. Then the overall square of the standard error for $\widehat{\beta}_k^{(C)}$ is given by

$$\widehat{V} = \widehat{V}_{\mathrm{W}} + \left(1 + \frac{1}{M}\right)\widehat{V}_{\mathrm{B}}, \tag{5.16}$$

where $\widehat{V}_{\mathrm{W}}$ is the within-imputation (pseudo-class draw) variance of $\widehat{\beta}_k^{(C)}$ given by

$$\widehat{V}_{\mathrm{W}} = \frac{1}{M} \sum_m \widehat{U}_k^m,$$

and $\widehat{V}_{\mathrm{B}}$ is the between-imputation (pseudo-class draw) variance of $\widehat{\beta}_k^{(C)}$ given by

$$\widehat{V}_{\mathrm{B}} = \frac{1}{M-1} \sum_m \left(\widehat{\beta}_k^{(C^m)} - \widehat{\beta}_k^{(C)}\right)^2.$$

A significance test of the null hypothesis $\beta_k = 0$ can be performed by comparing the ratio

$$\frac{\widehat{\beta}_k^{(C)}}{\sqrt{\widehat{V}}}$$

to a Student's t-distribution with degrees of freedom

$$df = (M-1)\left(1 + \frac{M\widehat{V}_W}{(M+1)\widehat{V}_B}\right)^2.$$

In the modeling software, Mplus V5.1 (Muthén and Muthén 1998–2008b), the pseudo-class draw technique is implemented to perform Wald tests of mean differences on distal outcomes across the latent classes. A Wald test is performed separately for each outcome variable (for details, see Muthén and Asparouhov 2007). However, this pseudo-class draw technique could be expanded to include multivariate distal outcomes with other observed predictors of the distal outcomes as well as including the growth factors themselves as predictors in addition to the latent trajectory class variable, for a more complex model for sequelae of change, as given below.

$$\mathbf{Z}_i = \omega_0 + \sum_{h=1}^{K} \left(\boldsymbol{\beta}_h^{(C)} \cdot \mathbf{I}(C_i = h) \right) + \boldsymbol{\beta}^{(\eta)} \boldsymbol{\eta}_i + \boldsymbol{\beta}^{(X)} \mathbf{X}_i + \boldsymbol{\xi}_i. \qquad (5.17)$$

We now illustrate the general growth mixture modeling process from class enumeration to the inclusion of antecedents and distal outcomes of the change process using longitudinal data from a large population-based randomized trial. All analyses were conducted using the statistical modeling software, Mplus[1], V5.1 (Muthén and Muthén 1998–2008b).

DATA ILLUSTRATION: DEVELOPMENT OF AGGRESSIVE BEHAVIOR WITH CORRELATES AND CONSEQUENCES

Sample

The data come from a large randomized intervention trial consisting of two cohorts totaling 2,311 students within the 19 participating Baltimore City Public Schools in first grade (Kellam et al. 2008). Of the population, 1,151 (49.8%) were male of which 476 (41.4%) were assigned to intervention conditions not pertinent to this paper (i.e., Mastery Learning, Good Behavior Game). Of the remaining 675 control males, 53 (7.9%) had missing values on all aggression ratings and an additional 7 (1%) had missing values on the covariates. The remaining sample consisted of 615 male students who did not receive an intervention and who had at least one valid teacher rating of aggression and no missing values on the covariates. Over 60% of this sample was African-American (61.6%) and the average age in fall of first grade was 6.3 years (SD = 0.47).

Longitudinal Outcome

In fall of first grade, teacher reports of child aggressive-disruptive behavior were gathered twice during first grade and then once per year during second through seventh grade. The analyses in this chapter focus on the five teacher ratings conducted in spring of first grade to spring of fifth grade.

---

[1] Although we chose to use the Mplus modeling software, there are other software packages that can be used to estimated some (or all) of the models presented herein. Among the most prominent are: HLM (Raudenbush, Bryk, Cheong, & Congdon 2000); SAS Proc TRAJ (Jones, Nagin, & Roeder 2001); GLAMM (Rabe-Hesketh, Skrondal, & Pickles 2004); MLwiN (Rasbash, Steele, Browne, & Prosser 2004); Latent Gold (Vermunt & Magidson 2005); SuperMix (Hedecker & Gibbons 2008); and LISREL (Jöreskog & Sörbom 1996).

Teacher ratings of aggressive-disruptive behavior were obtained using the Teacher Observation of Classroom Adaptation-Revised (TOCA-R; Werthamer-Larsson et al. 1991). The TOCA-R is a structured interview with the teacher administered by a trained assessor. The level of adaptation is rated by teachers on a six-point frequency scale (1 = almost never through 6 = almost always). The analysis herein used the authority-acceptance subscale which includes the following items: (1) breaks rules, (2) harms others and property, (3) breaks things, (4) takes others property, (5) fights, (6) lies, (7) trouble accepting authority, (8) yells at others, (9) stubborn, and (10) teases classmates. For this chapter, the item-averaged summation scores are used.

Covariates

For this illustration, two covariates measured in fall of first grade were included in the analysis: (1) student ethnicity (Black = 1, non-Black = 0) and (2) standardized reading test scores from the California Achievement Test (CAT, Forms E & F). The CAT represents one of the most frequently used standardized achievement batteries (Wardrop 1989). Subtests in CAT-E and F cover both verbal (reading, spelling, and language) and quantitative topics (computation, concepts, and applications). Internal consistency coefficients for virtually all of the subscales exceed 0.90. Alternate form reliability coefficients are generally in the 0.80 range (CAT, Forms E & F). The CAT represents one of the most frequently used standardized achievement batteries (Wardrop 1989).

Consequent Outcomes

Records of violent and criminal behavior were obtained at the time of the young adult follow-up interview and repeated yearly searches were conducted thereafter. The latest search was conducted in 2007, thus covering adult arrest records up to age 25. Records of incarceration for an offense classified as a felony in the Uniform Crime Reports system (i.e., armed/unarmed robbery, assault, kidnapping, weapons, domestic offense, rape/sex offense, attempted murder, homicide) was used as an indicator of violent and criminal behavior offenses. Drug and property related offenses (i.e., drug conspiring, distribution, possession, auto theft, burglary, larceny, and motor vehicle) were coded as nonviolent offenses. Violent and nonviolent offenses were then aggregated over offenses and years such that one or more records of an arrest during that age range would result in a value of "1" on the nonviolent or the violent crime indicator. These data were obtained from the Maryland Department of Correction and are considered public record.

RESULTS

Model Building: Functional Form

Visual inspection of a plot of the sample mean trajectory shows that, on average, in spring of first grade, males start at a level of 2.2 in aggressive-disruptive behavior and tend to increase gradually toward an average level of 2.5 in spring of fifth grade (see Fig. 5.4).

Further inspection of individual trajectories makes clear that there is a tremendous variation around that mean pattern, as is evident by the random subset of observed individual trajectories plotted in Fig. 5.4. Initial descriptive analysis, as recommended in the earlier section on model building, suggested that a linear growth model was adequate to describe intra-individual change across time allowing for fluctuations due to measurement and time-specific error. Furthermore, a random intercept and a random linear slope had a reasonable fit to the first and second moments of the current data on the boys' developmental course of aggressive-disruptive behavior: $\chi^2 = 20.586$, d$f = 10$, $p = 0.0242$; CFI = 0.981; TLI = 0.981; RMSEA = 0.041. (The remaining details of this first step of data screening and descriptive analyses are omitted in the interest of space.)

Model Building: Class Enumeration

The next step in the model building process is the latent class enumeration. As explained in detail throughout the first part of this chapter, model specification at this juncture in the analysis must be purposeful in terms of how the latent classes are to be characterized. In these analyses, we follow the recommendations given earlier and begin with a set of candidate models that allow the growth factor means to vary across the latent classes, constrain the growth

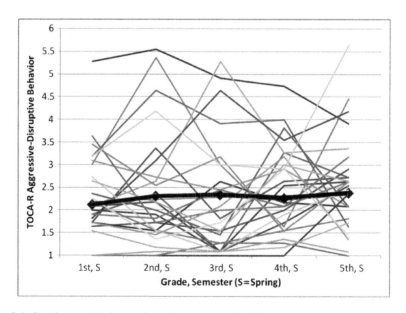

FIGURE 5.4. Sample average trajectory (*bolded*) and observed individual trajectories (random subset, $n = 25$).

factor variances and error variances to be class-invariant, and fix the growth factor covariances and error covariances to zero within-class. We also need to consider at this point the role of the distal outcomes in our analysis.

Previously, two alternative latent class measurement model specifications upon which the class enumeration can be performed were described. The first way is to treat the distal outcomes as additional indicators of the latent class variable and to therefore include the distal outcomes in the class enumeration process. The second approach treats the distal outcomes as true effects or consequences of the latent class variable and to therefore exclude them from this step in the analysis. The results of these two alternative specifications are now described in more detail.

Models with Distals-as-Class-Indicators

In Table 5.1, the aforementioned fit statistics are shown for models with an increasing number of classes. There are three 1-class models listed in the table.

The first 1-class model is the independence model for which associations between all the class indicators, growth factors and distal outcomes are fixed at zero. The second 1-class model allows the growth factors to covary but fixes associations between the distal outcomes and the distal outcomes with the growth factors to zero. The third 1-class model allows the growth factors to covary, allows the growth factors to associate with the distal outcomes, but fixes the residual covariance between the distal outcomes to zero. This third and final 1-class model is the most reasonable single-class baseline model for this class enumeration sequence since it is the model we would specify if we were working within a conventional latent growth curve framework and not considering the addition of a latent class variable. Starting with this 1-class model, the BIC decreased (indicating better fit) toward a 4-class model. However, the change in the BIC from three to four classes is much smaller than from one to two or from two to three as is evident by the "elbow" in the top BIC plot of Fig. 5.5. (A proper solution could not be obtained for a 5-class model without additional constraints, indicating problems with model identification.).

The VLMR-LRT test indicates that a 2-class model can be rejected in favor of a 3-class model ($p < 0.01$), while a 3-class model was not rejected in favor of a 4-class model. The BLRT indicates that a 4-class solution fits superior as compared to a 3-class model. Further inspection of the estimated mean trajectories reveals that the 4-class solution does not

TABLE 5.1. Fit indices for models with distals-as-class-indicators

Model	LL	# free parameters	BIC	VLMR-LRT	BLRT	Entropy	Smallest class r.f. (f)
1-class[a]	−3,435.87	11	6,942.38	n/a	n/a	n/a	n/a
1-class[b]	−3,434.65	12	6,948.36	n/a	n/a	n/a	n/a
1-class[c]	−3,368.77	16	6,840.29	n/a	n/a	n/a	n/a
2-class[a]	−3,349.88	16	6,802.50	$p < 0.0001$	$p < 0.0001$	0.73	0.21 (129)
3-class[a]	−3,309.19	21	6,753.22	$p = 0.002$	$p < 0.0001$	0.76	0.12 (77)
4-class[a]	−3,292.89	26	6,752.73	$p = 0.15$	$p < 0.0001$	01.74	0.06 (37)

[a]$Cov(\zeta) = 0$, $Cov(\zeta, \xi) = 0$, $Cov(\xi) = 0$
[b]$Cov(\zeta, \xi) = 0$, $Cov(\xi) = 0$
[c]$Cov(\xi) = 0$

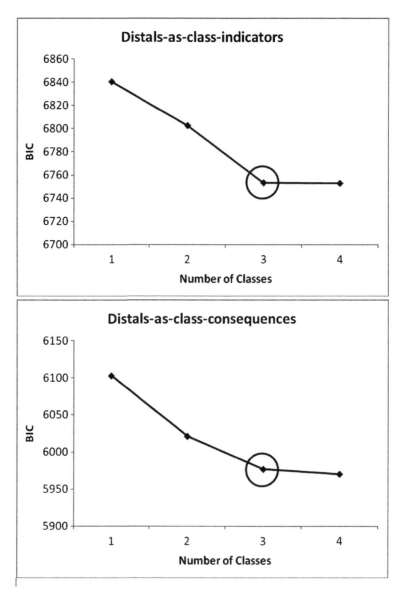

FIGURE 5.5. BIC "elbow" plots for models with distals-as-class-indicators (*top*) and with distals-as-class-consequences (*bottom*).

yield a fourth trajectory class substantively distinct from three trajectory classes derived from the 3-class solution. Given the small change in BIC, the nonsignificant VLMR-LRT, and the nondistinct fourth class, the 3-class solution was selected as the final model to carry forward to the next step of the analysis.

In the 3-class model (see top plot of Fig. 5.6), the largest class (72%) follows a low-stable development of aggression, starting at a level of "1.8" in spring of first grade. The two smaller classes are reasonable comparable in size. One of these classes (16%) starts at a similar intercept as the low-stable class, but escalates in aggression toward fifth grade. The

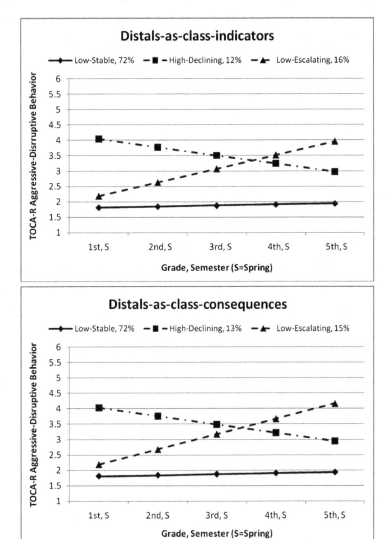

FIGURE 5.6. Model-estimated class-specific mean growth trajectory plots based on 3-class model with distals-as-class-indicators (*top*) and 3-class model with distals-as-class-consequences (*bottom*).

last class (12%) starts at a high level of aggressive behavior in spring of first grade followed by a decline toward fifth grade, which falls below the level of aggressive-disruptive behavior seen for the low-escalating class.

Models with Distals-as-Class-Consequences

In Table 5.2, the class enumeration results are shown for the models without the distal outcomes as additional class indicators.

TABLE 5.2. Fit indices for models with distals-as-class-consequences

Model	LL	# free parameters	BIC	VLMR-LRT	BLRT	Entropy	Smallest class r.f. (f)
1-class[a]	−3,019.49	9	6,096.77	n/a	n/a	n/a	n/a
1-class	−3,019.27	10	6,102.75	n/a	n/a	n/a	n/a
2-class[a]	−2,971.97	12	6,021.00	$p < 0.0001$	$p < 0.0001$	0.80	0.15 (94)
3-class[a]	−2,940.06	15	5,976.45	$p = 0.0001$	$p < 0.0001$	0.74	0.13 (78)
4-class[a]	−2,927.12	18	5,969.82	$p = 0.20$	$p < 0.0001$	0.73	0.06 (34)

[a]$Cov(\zeta) = 0$

There are two 1-class models listed in the table. The first 1-class model is the independence model for which the association between the growth factors is fixed at zero. The second 1-class model allows the growth factors to covary. This second 1-class model is the most reasonable single-class baseline model for this class enumeration sequence since it is the model we would specify if we were working within a conventional latent growth curve framework and not considering the addition of a latent class variable. Starting with this 1-class model, the BIC decreased with additional classes and reached its lowest value for a 4-class solution. However, the change in the BIC from three to four classes is somewhat smaller than from one to two or from two to three as is evident by the "elbow" in the bottom BIC plot of Fig. 5.5. (A proper solution could not be obtained for a 5-class model without additional constraints, indicating problems with model identification.) The VLMR-LRT indicates that a 2-class solution can be rejected in favor of a 3-class solution. The BLRT indicates that a 4-class solution fits superior as compared to a 3-class model. Further inspection of the estimated mean trajectories reveals that the 4-class solution does not yield a fourth latent class substantively distinct from three latent classes derived from the 3-class solution. Given the small change in BIC, the nonsignificant VLMR-LRT, and the nondistinct fourth class, the 3-class solution was selected as the final model to carry forward to the next step of the analysis. As in the first measurement model specification, the 3-class solution (see bottom plot of Fig. 5.6) yields a low-stable class (72%), a low-escalating class (15%), and a high-declining class (13%).

When comparing the results of the class enumeration process using the two alternative measurement model specification, strong similarities regarding the extracted trajectories in terms of shape and prevalence are found. Additionally, there is very little difference in estimated within-class growth factor variances: Intercept factor est. SD = 0.45, 0.47; Slope factor est. SD = 0.05, 0.08. We would expect some similarity given the overlap in information on which latent class formation is based. However, by simply comparing the estimated mean trajectories, we might incorrectly infer that the latent classes based on the two model specifications are the *same* in that the distal outcomes do not contribute to the class characterizations and that class membership at the individual level is identical across models. Although we do not directly observe latent class membership, we can explore differences in class membership by comparing modal class assignment based on the individual posterior class probabilities for each model, as shown in Table 5.3.

While 94% of individuals assigned to the low-stable trajectory class in at least one of the models were assigned to that class in both models and 96% of individuals were assigned to the high-declining class in both models, only 69% of individuals for the low-escalating class. The root of these class formation differences despite the near identical mean growth trajectories become evident in later section in which we present the class differences with respect to the distal outcomes.

TABLE 5.3. Cross-tabulation of modal latent class assignment based on model with distals-as-class-indicators versus distals-as-class-consequences

| | | Distals-as-class-consequences | | | |
		Low-stable	High-declining	Low-escalating	Total
Distals-as-class-indicators	Low-stable	442 (94.4%)	6 (1.3%)	20 (4.3%)	468
	High-declining	1 (1.4%)	66 (95.7%)	2 (2.9%)	69
	Low-escalating	22 (28.2%)	2 (2.6%)	54 (69.2%)	78
	Total	465	74	76	615

Predictors of Aggressive-Disruptive Behavior Development

Antecedents of class membership are important to further understand the profile of individuals in each class as well as to evaluate the criterion-related validity of the latent classes relative to substantive theory. For this chapter, two covariates measured in fall of first grade were included. In addition to the students' ethnicity, the results of a standardized reading test were used. As suggested by Nylund and Masyn (2008), we first compared the results of the final unconditional growth mixture model from the class enumeration step to the same model with the mean-centered covariates included as predictors of class membership, looking for any evidence of changes in the size and meaning of the classes. While the model results did not change for either of the three class solutions, the size and meaning of the extracted classes changed for the four class solutions. This level of instability indicates not only potential model misspecification of the covariate effects, but also that the three class solution is the preferred model for this sample. Given the high level of correspondence in class membership for all but the smallest trajectory class for the two alternative model specifications and the similarity in mean growth trajectories, it was not surprising to find that the covariate associations to latent class membership were similar (see Tables 5.4 and 5.5).

In both cases, Black individuals were more likely to be in the high-declining and low-escalating classes relative to the low-stable class when compared with non-Black individuals, and individuals with higher reading scores were less likely to be in the high-declining or low-escalating classes relative to the low-stable class. Neither covariate distinguished between the high-declining and low-escalating classes in either model. The most noticeable differences across the models are in the estimated size and significance of effects of race/ethnicity and reading on membership in the low-escalating class relative to the low-stable class, with the stronger effects present in the model with distals-as-class-indicators.

Distal Outcomes of Aggressive-Disruptive Behavior Development

A Department of Correction record for a violent or nonviolent crime as an adult is used as distal outcomes for aggressive–disruptive behavior trajectories in childhood. When including the distal outcomes in the class enumeration process (see Table 5.6), the high-declining and low-escalating classes were both characterized by significantly higher rates of nonviolent and violent arrests than the low-stable class. Furthermore, the low-stable class was characterized by significantly higher rates of nonviolent and violent arrests than the low-stable class. These class distinctions are similar (both for pair-wise comparisons and overall comparisons) for each arrest type.

TABLE 5.4. Latent class multinomial regression results for 3-class model with distals-as-class-indicators

Covariate	Target class	Reference class	Est.	S.E.	p-value	Est. OR[a]
Race/Ethnicity	High-declining	Low-stable	0.90	0.36	0.01	2.46[b]
	Low-escalating		1.27	0.43	0.004	3.56[b]
	High-declining	Low-escalating	−0.37	0.55	0.51	0.69[b]
Reading	High-declining	Low-stable	−0.01	0.004	<0.001	0.67[c]
	Low-escalating		−0.01	0.004	0.001	0.67[c]
	High-declining	Low-escalating	0.001	0.01	0.89	1.04[c]

[a]Odds (membership in target class): Odds (membership in reference class) among individuals in either target or reference class
[b]Calculated for Ethnicity = Black vs. Ethnicity = Non-Black
[c]Calculated for a 1 SD increase in reading score

TABLE 5.5. Latent class multinomial regression results for 3-class model with distals-as-class-consequences

Covariate	Target class	Reference class	Est.	S.E.	p-value	Est. OR[a]
Race/Ethnicity	High-declining	Low-stable	0.84	0.35	0.02	2.32[b]
	Low-escalating		0.92	0.44	0.04	2.51[b]
	High-declining	Low-escalating	−0.08	0.54	0.88	0.92[b]
Reading	High-declining	Low-stable	−0.01	0.003	<0.001	0.67[c]
	Low-escalating		−0.01	0.005	0.03	0.67[c]
	High-declining	Low-escalating	−0.001	0.005	0.78	0.96[c]

[a]Odds (membership in target class): Odds (membership in reference class) among individuals in either target or reference class
[b]Calculated for Ethnicity = Black vs. Ethnicity = Non-Black
[c]Calculated for a 1 SD increase in reading score

TABLE 5.6. Class-specific model estimated probabilities of nonviolent and violent arrests and pair-wise comparisons based on 3-class model with distals-as-class-indicators

Arrest type (Overall[a])	Target class	Reference class	Est.[b]	Est. OR[c]	p-value
Nonviolent	Low-stable	Low-stable	0.03	1.00	–
($\chi^2 = 18.69$,	High-declining		0.24	10.21	0.001
$df = 2$,	Low-escalating		0.50	32.33	< 0.001
$p < 0.001$)	Low escalating	High-declining		3.17	0.04
Violent	Low-stable	Low-stable	0.02	1.00	–
($\chi^2 = 18.10$,	High-declining		0.13	7.32	0.01
$df = 2$,	Low-escalating		0.38	30.03	< 0.001
$p < 0.001$)	Low escalating	High-declining		4.10	0.02

[a]Overall test of class differences in arrest rates
[b]Pr (arrest|membership in target class)
[c]Odds (arrest|membership in target class): Odds (arrest|membership in reference class)

By comparison, while treating the distal outcomes as consequences of trajectory class membership (see Table 5.7), membership in the high-declining and low-escalating classes is predictive of higher rates of both nonviolent and violent arrests in adulthood relative to the low-stable class; however, membership in the low-escalating class is not distinct from

TABLE 5.7. Class-specific model estimated probabilities of nonviolent and violent arrests and pair-wise comparisons based on 3-class model with distals-as-class-consequences

Arrest type (Overall[a])	Target class	Reference class	Est.[b]	Est. OR[c]	p-value
Nonviolent	Low-stable	Low-stable	0.08	1.00	–
($\chi^2 = 11.40$,	High-declining		0.21	3.06	0.01
$df = 2$,	Low-escalating		0.29	4.70	< 0.001
$p = 0.003$)	Low escalating	High-declining		1.54	0.29
Violent	Low-stable	Low-stable	0.06	1.00	–
($\chi^2 = 5.66$,	High-declining		0.14	2.55	0.06
$df = 2$,	Low-escalating		0.19	3.67	0.01
$p = 0.06$)	Low escalating	High-declining		1.44	0.37

[a]Overall test of class differences in arrest rates
[b]Pr (arrest|membership in target class)
[c]Odds (arrest|membership in target class): Odds (arrest|membership in reference class)

membership in the high-declining class relative to predicted arrest rates. However, similar to the other model, pair-wise differences due to class membership are similar across arrest type although the overall effect was stronger for nonviolent that violent arrests.

These disparities between the two model specification help explain why there were differences in class membership despite the similarity in mean class trajectories. In the model using the distal outcomes as latent class indicators, individuals placed in the low-escalating trajectory class were individuals who had *both* an aggressive–disruptive behavior trajectory resembling the low-escalating mean trajectory *and* a high probability of nonviolent and violent arrests. These individuals could very well be those who persist in their higher levels of aggressive–disruptive behavior into adolescence. For the model in which trajectory classes are based exclusively on aggressive–disruptive behavior in first through fifth grade, there is not a high level of predictive validity for adult arrest outcomes beyond that given by any deviation from the low-stable trajectory pattern, suggesting that information from later childhood and adolescence may be needed to distinguish arrest risk among those who display nonnormative behavior patterns in middle childhood.

It is important to note here that if we had used the distals-as-class-indicators specification but then *interpreted* the model results treating the distal outcomes as effects or consequences of the trajectory classes, we would have incorrectly infer that individuals in the low-escalating class were at significantly higher risk for arrest than individuals in the high-declining class. Results from the distals-as-class-consequences model showed this not to be the case.

DISCUSSION

This chapter has examined the process of including antecedents and consequences of a developmental process in a growth mixture modeling framework. We have shown that in addition to the flexibility growth mixture models offer over conventional latent growth curve models in terms of the way in which population heterogeneity in the growth process itself is characterized, there is also flexibility gained in terms of how the associations of predictors and distal outcomes with the growth process are parameterized. We have discussed the unconditional growth mixture model building process and then demonstrated the addition of covariates as predictors of the growth process and as possible means for evaluating the concurrent validity of resultant trajectory classes. We have also presented two different approaches for including distal outcomes of the growth process. In one approach, the distal outcomes are included as additional indicators of the latent class variable and, thus, resultant classes are characterized by individual response patterns on *both* growth outcomes *and* distal outcomes. We noted that if using this approach, one must be careful not to interpret the class-specific rates of the distal outcome as representing class-predicted patterns but, rather, class-defining outcome patterns. In the other approach, the distal outcomes are treated as true effects or consequences of the growth process. This approach offers the possibility of evaluating the prognostic validity of the resultant trajectory classes. Some recent work has been done to quantify the predictive validity of trajectory class membership as a screening mechanism for identifying individuals at-risk for maladaptive distal outcomes using the distal-as-class-indicator approach (Feldman et al. 2008) and this work could be extended to the distal-as-class-consequence approach. Other work has been done to examine the prediction power of trajectory class membership in one developmental period for trajectory class membership in a subsequent development period (see, for example, Boscardin et al. 2008; and for a preventive intervention settings, see, Petras et al. 2008) and this work could be extended to the models presented in this chapter where the earlier latent class variable is treated as an antecedent or the later latent class variable is treated as a consequence.

There are several interesting areas of investigation for future work. One area involves extending the distal-as-consequence model to permit more complex models for the distal outcomes. As specified in this chapter, the distal outcome is assumed to be an observed univariate or multivariate outcome. However, the distal outcome could itself be a latent variable with its own measurement model. Another area involved further exploration into the implication for model specification if the latent trajectory class membership is conceptualized as a time-invariant attribute at the individual level that merely manifests over time but it is, itself, independent of time; or if membership is conceptualized as malleable and time-dependent. A further, and much more complex, matter not dealt with in this chapter, is the collection of the antecedents, growth process, and consequences as a variable system. In both model approaches for the distal outcomes, we did not explicitly consider what the implication would be if part of the shared variance between the growth process and the distal outcomes was due to the antecedent variables. Confounding of the associations between the growth process and distal outcomes by the antecedents would have differing impact depending on how the association was modeled, i.e., distals-as-class-indicators or distals-as-class-consequences. The same is true if the growth process acted as a mediator of the antecedent effect on the distal outcome or if the antecedents acted as moderators of the associations between the growth process and the distal outcomes.

Clearly, these models hold great potential for aiding empirical investigations of developmental theories of normative and nonnormative behaviors and maladaptive outcomes across the lifespan. In no way is this more evident than in the marked increase in their use among applied researchers in criminology and other behavioral sciences. We maintain, as expounded at the beginning of this chapter, that the value and future potential of these models for examining population heterogeneity in developmental processes and correlates thereof, holds regardless of whether the resultant latent trajectory classes represent "true" subpopulations or simply reflect nonnormality in the population distribution of the growth factors. However, there is still much opportunity in the realm of methods development to capitalize on the potential of these models and extensions to better accommodate the complexities or our developmental theories. And, as with any statistical tool, the research question along with previous theoretical and empirical work, should guide these models' application in a particular study, with thoughtful and purposeful choices for model specification, selection, and interpretation.

Acknowledgement We like to thank Alex Piquero, David Weisburd, Nicholas Ialongo and Bengt Muthén for their helpful comments on a prior draft of this manuscript.

REFERENCES

Bandeen-Roche K, Miglioretti DL, Zeger SL, Rathouz PJ (1997) Latent variable regression for multiple discrete outcomes. J Am Stat Assoc 92(440):1375–1386

Bauer DJ, Curran PJ (2003) Distributional assumptions of growth mixture models: implications for overextraction of latent trajectory classes. Psychol Methods 8:338–363

Bauer DJ, Curran PJ (2004) The integration of continuous and discrete latent variable models: potential problems and promising opportunities. Psychol Methods 9:3–29

Bollen KA, Curran PJ (2006) Latent curve models: a structural equation perspective. John Wiley & Sons, Inc, Hoboken, NJ

Boscardin C, Muthén B, Francis D, Baker E (2008) Early identification of reading difficulties using heterogeneous developmental trajectories. J Educ Psychol 100:192–208

Broidy LM, Nagin DS, Tremblay RE, Bates JE, Brame B, Dodge KA, Fergusson D, Horwood JL, Loeber R, Laird R, Lyman DR, Moffitt TE, Pettit GS, Vitaro F (2003) Developmental trajectories of childhood disruptive behaviors and adolescent delinquency: a six-site, cross-national study. Dev Psychol 39:222–245

Bushway SD, Brame R, Paternoster RE (1999) Assessing stability and change in criminal offending: a comparison of random effects, semiparametric, and fixed effects modeling strategies. J Quantit Criminol 15:23–61

Duncan TE, Duncan SC, Strycker LA (2006) An introduction to latent variable growth curve modeling: concepts, issues, and applications, 2nd edn. Lawrence Erlbaum Associates, Mahwah, NJ

Ensminger ME, Kellam SG, Rubin BR (1983) School and family origins of delinquency: comparisons by sex. In: Van Dusen KT, Mednick SA (eds) Prospective studies of crime and delinquency, Kluwer-Niejhoff, Boston, pp 73–97

Feldman B, Masyn K, Conger R (2008) Assessing the quality of prediction from adolescent problem-behavior trajectories to distal categorical outcomes. Manuscript submitted for publication

Hawkins JD, Herrenkohl TI, Farrington DP, Brewer D, Catalano RF, Harachi TW, Cothern L (2000) Predictors of youth violence. Off Juv Justice Delinq Prev Bull 4:1–11

Heckman J, Singer B (1984) A method for minimizing the distributional assumptions in econometric models for duration data. Econometrica 52:271–320

Hedecker D, Gibbons RD (2008) Supermix – mixed effects models. Scientific Software International, Chicago

Hipp JR, Bauer DJ (2006) Local solutions in the estimation of growth mixture models. Psychol Methods 11(1):36–53

Hox JJ (2000) Multilevel analysis of grouped and longitudinal data. In: Little TD, Schnabel KU, Baumert J (eds) Modeling longitudinal and multiple-group data. Practical issues, applied approaches, and specific examples, Lawrence Erlbaum, Hillsdale, NJ

Hox JJ (2002) Multilevel analysis. Techniques and applications. Lawrence Erlbaum Associates, Mahwah, NJ

Hu L, Bentler P (1999) Cutoff criteria for fit indexes in covariance structure analysis: Conventional criteria versus new alternatives. Struct Equation Model 6(1):1–55

Jones BL, Nagin DS, Roeder K (2001) A SAS procedure based on mixture models for estimating developmental trajectories. Sociol Methods Res 29:374–393

Jöreskog KG Sörbom D (1996) LISREL 8: structural equation modeling. Scientific Software International, Chicago

Kellam SG, Brown CH, Poduska JM, Ialongo NS, Wang W, Toyinbo P, Petras H, Ford C, Windham A, Wilcox HC (2008) Effects of a universal classroom behavior management program in first and second grades on young adult behavioral, psychiatric, and social outcomes. Drug Alcohol Depend 95:S5–S28

Kreuter F, Muthén B (2008) Analyzing criminal trajectory profiles: bridging multilevel and group-based approaches using growth mixture modeling. J Quant Criminol 24:1–31

Lo Y, Mendell N, Rubin D (2001) Testing the number of components in a normal mixture. Biometrika 88:767–778

Loeber R, Hay D (1997) Key issues in the development of aggression and violence from childhood to early adulthood. Annu Rev Psychol 48:371–410

Lubke GH, Spies JR (2008) Choosing a "correct" factor mixture model: power, limitations, and graphical data explo-
    ration. In: GR Hancock, Samuelson KM (eds) Advances in latent variable mixture models, Information Age
    Publishing, Charlotte, NC, pp 343–361
Lynam DR (1996) The early identification of chronic offenders: who is the fledging psychopath? Psychol Bull
    120:209–234
Magnusson D (1998) The logic and implications of a person-oriented approach. In: Cairns RB, Bergman LR, Kagan
    J (eds) Methods and models for studying the individual, Sage, Thousand Oaks, CA, pp 33–64
Maughan B, Rutter M (1998) Continuities and discontinuities in antisocial behavior from childhood to adult life. In:
    Ollendick TH, Prinz RJ (eds) Advances in clinical child psychology, vol. 20. Plenum, New York, pp 1–47
McCord J, Ensminger ME (1997) Multiple risks and co-morbidity in an African-American population. Crim Behav
    Ment Health 7:339–352
McLachlan G, Peel D (2000). Finite mixture models. Wiley, New York
Meredith W, Tisak J (1990) Latent curve analysis. Psychometrika 55:107–22
Moffitt TE (1993) Adolescent-limited and life-course persistent antisocial behavior: a developmental taxonomy.
    Psychol Rev 100:674–701
Muthén B (2000) Methodological issues in random coefficient growth modeling using a latent variable framework:
    applications to the development of heavy drinking in ages 18–37. In: Rose JS, Chassin L, Presson C, Sherman
    J (eds) Multivariate applications in substance use research: new methods for new questions, Erlbaum, Mahwah,
    NJ, pp 113–140
Muthén B (2001) Second-generation structural equation modeling with a combination of categorical and continuous
    latent variables: new opportunities for latent class/latent growth modeling. In: Collins LM, Sayer A (eds) New
    methods for the analysis of change, APA, Washington, DC, pp 291–322
Muthén B (2003) Statistical and substantive checking in growth mixture modeling. Psychol Methods 8:369–377
Muthén B (2004) Latent variable analysis: growth mixture modeling and related techniques for longitudinal data.
    In: Kaplan D (ed) Handbook of quantitative methodology for the social sciences, Sage, Newbury Park, CA, pp
    345–368
Muthén B (2006) The potential of growth mixture modeling. Commentary. Infant Child Dev 15:623–625
Muthén B, Asparouhov T (2008) Growth mixture modeling: analysis with non-gaussian random effects. In: Fitzmau-
    rice G, Davidian M, Verbeke G, Molenberghs G (eds) Longitudinal data analysis, Chapman & Hall/CRC Press,
    Boca Raton, pp 143–165
Muthén B, Asparouhov T (2007) Wald test of mean equality for potential latent class predictors in mixture modeling.
    (Unpublished web note). http://www.statmodel.com
Muthén B, Brown CH, Masyn K, Jo B, Khoo ST, Yang CC, Wang CP, Kellam S, Carlin J, Liao J (2002) General
    growth mixture modeling for randomized preventive interventions. Biostatistics 3:459–475
Muthén BO, Curran PJ (1997) General longitudinal modeling of individual differences in experimental designs: a
    latent variable framework for analysis and power estimation. Psychol Methods 2:371–402
Muthén B, Muthén LK (2000) Integrating person-centered and variable-centered analyses: growth mixture modeling
    with latent trajectory classes. Alcohol Clin Exp Res 24:1–10
Muthén B, Muthén LK (1998–2008) Mplus (Version 5.1) [Computer software]. Muthén & Muthén, Los Angeles CA
Muthén LK, Muthén B (1998–2008) Mplus user's guide. 5th ed. Muthén & Muthén, Los Angeles
Muthén B, Shedden K (1999) Finite mixture modeling with mixture outcomes using the EM algorithm. Biometrics
    6:463–469
Nagin DS (1999) Analyzing developmental trajectories: a semiparametric, group-based approach. Psychol Methods
    4:139–157
Nagin DS, Land KC (1993) Age, criminal careers, and population heterogeneity: specification and estimation of a
    nonparametric, mixed Poisson model. Criminology 31:327–362
Nagin D, Tremblay RE (1999) Trajectories of boys' physical aggression, opposition, and hyperactivity on the path to
    physically violent and nonviolent juvenile delinquency. Child Dev 70:1181–1196
Nagin DS, Tremblay R (2005) Developmental trajectory groups: fact or a useful statistical fiction? Criminology
    43(4):873–903
Nagin D (2005) Group-based modeling of development. Harvard University Press, Cambridge, Massachusetts
Nylund KL, Asparouhov T, Muthén B (2007) Deciding on the number of classes in latent class analysis and growth
    mixture modeling: a monte carlo simulation study. Struct Equation Model 14:535–569
Nylund KL, Masyn KE (2008) Covariates and latent class analysis: results of a simulation study. Paper presented at
    the society for prevention research annual meeting
Patterson GR, DeBaryshe BD, Ramsey E (1989) A developmental perspective on antisocial behavior. Am Psychol
    44:329–335

Patterson GR, Forgatch MS, Yoerger KL, Stoolmiller M (1998) Variables that initiate and maintain an early-onset trajectory for juvenile offending. Dev Psychopathol 10:531–547

Petras H, Schaeffer CM, Ialongo N, Hubbard S, Muthen B, Lambert S, Poduska J, Kellam S (2004) When the course of aggressive behavior in childhood does not predict antisocial behavior: an examination of potential explanatory variables. Dev Psychopathol 16:919–941

Petras H, Kellam SG, Brown H, Muthén B, Ialongo N, Poduska JM (2008) Developmental epidemiological courses leading to antisocial personality disorder and violent and criminal behavior: effects by young adulthood of a universal preventive intervention in first- and second-grade classrooms. Drug Alcohol Depend 95:S45–S59

Petras H, Masyn K, Ialongo N (2008) The distal impact of two first-grade preventive interventions on aggressive disruptive behavior in adolescence – An application of a latent transition hybrid model. Manuscript in preparation

Picquero A (2008) Taking stock of developmental trajectories of criminal activity over the life course. In: Liberman AM (ed) The long view of crime: a synthesis of longitudinal Research, Springer Publication, New York, pp 23–70

Rabe-Hesketh S, Skrondal A, Pickles A (2004) GLLAMM Manual. U.C. berkeley division of biostatistics working paper series. Working paper 160

Rasbash J, Steele F, Browne W, and Prosser B (2004) A user's guide to MLwiN version 2.0. Institute of Education, London

Ramaswamy V, Desarbo WS, Reibstein DJ, Robinson WT (1993) An empirical pooling approach for estimating marketing mix elasticities with PIMS data. Mark Sci 12(1):103–124

Raudenbush SW, Bryk AS (2002) Hierarchical linear models: applications and data analysis methods. 2nd ed. Sage Publications, Newbury Park, CA

Raudenbush SW, Bryk AS, Cheong Y Congdon R (2000) HLM 5: hierarchical linear and nonlinear modeling. Scientific Software International, Chicago

Roeder K, Lynch, KG Nagin DS (1999) Modeling uncertainty in latent class membership: a case study in criminology. J Am Stat Asso 94:766–776

Rubin DB (1987) Multiple imputation for nonresponse in surveys. J. Wiley & Sons, New York

Sampson R, Laub J (2003) Life-course desisters? Trajectories of crime among delinquent boys followed to age 70. Criminology 41:555–592

Sampson RJ, Laub J (2005) Seductions of methods: rejoinder to Nagin & Tremblay's developmental trajectory groups: fact or fiction? Criminology 43:905–914

Sampson RJ, Laub J, Eggleston EP (2004) On the robustness and validity of groups. J Quant Criminol 20:37–42

Schaeffer CM, Petras H, Ialongo N, Masyn KE, Hubbard S, Poduska J, Kellam S (2006) A comparison of girls' and boys' aggressive-disruptive behavior trajectories across elementary school: prediction to young adult antisocial outcomes. J Consult Clin Psychol 74:500–510

Shaw DS, Gilliom M, Ingoldsby EM, Nagin DS (2003) Trajectories leading to school-age conduct problems. Dev Psychol 39:189–200

Schafer JL (1997) Analysis of incomplete multivariate data. Chapman & Hall, London

Schwarz G (1978) Estimating the dimension of a model. Ann Stat 6:461–464

Singer JD, Willett JB (2003) Applied longitudinal data analysis. Oxford University Press, New York

Stram DO, Lee JW (1994) Variance components testing in the longitudinal mixed effects model. Biometrics 40:961–971

Thorndike RL (1953) Who belong in the family? Psychometrika 18(4):267–276

van Dulmen MHM, Goncy E, Vest A, Flannery DJ (2009) Group based trajectory modeling of externalizing behavior problems from childhood through adulthood: exploring discrepancies in empirical findings. In: Savage J (ed) The development of persistent criminality. Oxford University Press, New York, NY

Vermunt JK, Magidson J (2002) Latent class cluster analysis. In: Hagenaars JA, McCutcheon AL (eds) Applied latent class analysis. Cambridge University Press, Cambridge, pp 89–106

Vermunt JK, Magidson J (2005) Technical guide for latent GOLD 4.0: basic and advanced. Statistical Innovations Inc, Belmont MA

Wang C-P, Brown CH, Bandeen-Roche K (2005) Residual diagnostics for growth mixture models: examining the impact of a preventive intervention on multiple trajectories of aggressive behavior. J Am Stat Assoc 100(3):1054–1076

Wardrop JL (1989) Review of the California achievement tests, forms E and F. In: Close Conoley, J Kramer J (eds) The tenth mental measurements yearbook, University of Nebraska Press, Lincoln, pp 128–133

Werthamer-Larsson L, Kellam SG, Wheeler L (1991) Effect of first-grade classroom environment on child shy behavior, aggressive behavior, and concentration problems. Am J Community Psychol 19:585–602

Willett JB, Sayer AG (1994) Using covariance structure analysis to detect correlates and predictors of individual change over time. Psychol Bull 116:363–81

Yoshikawa H (1994) Prevention as cumulative protection: effects of early family support and education on chronic delinquency and its risks. Psychol Bull 115:28–54

CHAPTER 6

Spatial Regression Models in Criminology: Modeling Social Processes in the Spatial Weights Matrix

GEORGE E. TITA AND STEVEN M. RADIL

A decade ago, Jacqueline Cohen and George Tita served as guest editors for a special volume of the *Journal of Quantitative Criminology* (Vol 15, #4, 1999) that was dedicated to the study of the diffusion of homicide. In their Editor's Introduction (Cohen and Tita 1999a), they concluded that the results presented in special volume,[1] along with recent work by Morenoff and Sampson (1997), clearly demonstrated that the observed patterns of violence were consistent with patterns one might expect if violence does, in fact, diffuse over space. That is, levels of violence are not randomly distributed; instead, similar rates of violence cluster together in space (i.e., violence exhibits positive spatial autocorrelation.) Furthermore, a growing number of studies began to demonstrate that even after controlling for the ecological features known to be associated with high levels of crime (e.g., poverty, population density, male joblessness, female-headed households, etc), the clustering of high values could not be explained away. These early spatial studies of diffusion helped to establish the existence of an unobserved "neighborhood effect" that seemed to be responsible for spatially concentrated high-crime areas.

    Not to diminish the contribution of these studies in advancing our understanding of crime and violence, Cohen and Tita ended their introduction by noting that there was much work to be done.[2] First, in order to understand diffusion, models needed to include a more complete accounting of temporal considerations. Though the spatial analysis of cross-sectional data is helpful in determining whether or not the initial conditions consistent with diffusion are being

---

[1] The contributors to this special issue included Cork; Mencken and Barnett; Messner, Anselin, Baller, Hawkins, Deane and Tolnay; Cohen and Tita; and Rosenfeld, Bray and Egley.

[2] Cohen and Tita neglect to address the issue of employing the appropriate spatial scale in terms of the spatial unit of analysis. Hipp (2007) and Weisburd et al. (2008) offer excellent treatment of this important topic.

A.R. Piquero and D. Weisburd (eds.), *Handbook of Quantitative Criminology*,
DOI 10.1007/978-0-387-77650-7_6, © Springer Science + Business Media, LLC 2010,
First softcover printing 2011

satisfied, without analyzing change over time one cannot capture the movement of spatial patterns over time. Second, even during the homicide epidemic of the late 1980s and early 1990s, homicide remained a rare event when compared to other types of crimes. In order to fully understand the mechanisms that drive the diffusion of violence, research needed to be conducted on nonlethal violence (as well as other types of crime.) According to the authors, however, the single most daunting challenge facing the researchers was not developing better methods or using better data in order to validate patterns of diffusion; the most important hurdle was to create models that would produce results that could be used to gain a better understanding of the "...mechanisms by which the recent homicide epidemic spread." In other words, Cohen and Tita called upon the research community to create models that would help to unlock the black box of "neighborhood effects" by explicitly modeling the processes that drive the spread of violence.

We hope to achieve several goals in this chapter. Though the term "spatial analysis" can be applied to a broad set of methodologies (e.g., hot spot analysis, journey to crime analysis, exploratory spatial analysis),[3] we wish to focus specifically on the application of spatial regression models to the ecological analysis of crime, which makes use of socio-economic data aggregated or grouped into geographic areas. To do so, however, requires an introductory discussion of the nature of spatial data and the associated exploratory analyses that are now common when using geographically aggregated data. Therefore, we begin with an overview of spatial data, with an emphasis on the key concept of spatial autocorrelation, and provide an overview of exploratory spatial analysis techniques that can assess the presence and level of spatial autocorrelation in spatial data. We then move onto a discussion of spatial regression models developed to address the presence of spatial effects in one's data. Next, we highlight some of the key findings that have emerged from the use of spatial regression in criminology and evaluate whether or not they have helped in the identification of the particular social processes responsible for the clustering and diffusion of crime. Drawing upon our own work (Tita and Greenbaum 2008; Radil et al. 2010; Tita et al. 2009), we hone in on one of the most important, though often overlooked, components of any spatial regression model – the spatial weights matrix or "W." We believe that the mechanisms and processes that drive the diffusion of crime can best be understood by "spatializing" the manner in which information and influence flows across social networks. Therefore, we examine some of the innovative ways that researchers have used to specify "W" in criminology as well as other areas of study. Keeping Cohen and Tita's (1999a, b) argument about unlocking the black box of "neighborhood effects" in mind, we conclude by emphasizing the importance of theoretically- and empirically-grounded specifications of W to this goal.

THE NATURE OF SPATIAL DATA AND SPATIAL DATA ANALYSIS

Criminology, like most social sciences, is an observational science as opposed to an experimental science. This is to say that researchers are not able to experiment with or replicate observed outcomes, which take place at specific locations at specific times. When the structure of the places and spaces in which outcomes occur is thought to affect the processes theorized

---

[3] For an introductory treatment of these methods and the manner in which they have been used in criminology and criminal justice, see Anselin et al. (2008).

to give rise to the observed outcomes (such as theorized relationships between crime and place – see Morenoff et al. 2001 or Sampson et al. 2002 for recent examples), the location of each outcome is important information for researchers. Spatial data then are those with information about the location of each observation in geographic space.

A fundamental property of spatial data is the overall tendency for observations that are close in geographic space to be more alike than those that are further apart. In geography, this tendency is referred to in "Tobler's First Law of Geography," which states that "everything is related to everything else but near things are more related than distant things" (Tobler 1970: 236). Although more of a general truism than a universal law, Tobler's "law" rightly points out that the clustering of like objects, people, and places on the surface of the earth is the norm, and such organizational patterns are of intrinsic interest to many social scientists (O'Loughlin 2003; Haining 2003). This property is called *spatial dependence* and has important implications for researchers. First, an observation at any given location can provide information about nearby locations and one can therefore make informed estimates about the level of attributes in nearby locations (e.g., spatial interpolation). Second, the tendency of data to vary together across space creates problems for classical inferential statistical models and can undermine the validity of inferences drawn from such models (Anselin 1988).

Another fundamental property of spatial data is the tendency for relationships between variables to vary from place-to-place or across space. This tendency, known as *spatial heterogeneity*, is often due to location-specific effects (Anselin 1988; Fotheringham 1997). Spatial heterogeneity has the important consequence of meaning that a single global relationship for an overall study region may not adequately reflect outcomes in any given location of the study region (Anselin 1988; Fotheringham 1997). Further, variations in local relationships can lead to inconsistent estimates of the effect of variables at global levels, if the relationship between the dependent variable of interest and the independent variables is characterized by a nonlinear function (Fotheringham et al. 2002).[4]

Both of these properties of spatial data have been at the heart of spatial data analysis, which is the development of quantitative analytic techniques that accommodate the nature of spatial data for both descriptive and inferential statistical analysis and modeling (Anselin 1988; Haining 2003; Goodchild 2004). Anselin (1998) has referred to the collection of different methods and techniques for structuring, visualizing, and assessing the presence of the degree of spatial dependence and heterogeneity as exploratory spatial data analysis, or ESDA. For Anselin (1998), the key steps of ESDA involve describing and visualizing the spatial

---

[4] We also wish to draw attention to another group of properties directly or indirectly related to how spatial data is represented, organized, and measured by researchers. While not an exhaustive list, border effects, the so-called 'modifiable areal unit problem,' and the challenges of ecological fallacy are three issues commonly encountered by researchers using aggregated spatial data (see Haining 2009). Border effects refer to the fact that the often-arbitrary boundaries of study regions may exclude information that affects outcomes within the study region (see Griffith 1983). The modifiable areal unit problem (MAUP) refers to the fact that the results of statistical analysis, such as correlation and regression, can be sensitive to the geographic zoning system used to group data by area (see Gehlke and Biehl 1934 or Robinson 1950 for classic examples of MAUP, or Openshaw 1996 for a more contemporary review). Ecological fallacy, or the difficulty in inferring individual behavior from aggregate data, is ever present in many social sciences attempting to predict individual behavior from an analysis of geographically aggregated data (see King 1997; O'Loughlin 2003) While well-established in geography, these issues tend to resurface in other disciplines as spatial analysis becomes more prevalent (for an example, see Hipp 2007). For a review of the treatment of some of these issues in the spatial analysis of crime, see Weisburd et al. (2008).

distributions of variables of interest, the identification of atypical locations (so-called "spatial outliers"), uncovering patterns of spatial association (clusters), and assessing any change in the associations between variables across space. While a comprehensive review of ESDA is beyond the scope of this chapter (see Anselin 1998, 1999), we wish to draw attention to the concept of spatial autocorrelation which is commonly present in data aggregated to geographic areal units and is therefore of relevance to criminologists that commonly use such data.

Spatial dependence in spatial data can result in the *spatial autocorrelation* of regression residuals. Spatial autocorrelation occurs when the values of variables sampled at nearby locations are not independent from each other. Spatial autocorrelation may be either *positive* or *negative*. Positive spatial autocorrelation occurs when similar values appear together in space, while negative spatial autocorrelation occurs when dissimilar values appear together. When mapped as part of an ESDA, positively spatially autocorrelated data will appear to cluster together, while a negatively spatially autocorrelated data will result in a pattern in which geographic units of similar values scatter throughout the map (see Fig. 6.1).

The presence of spatial autocorrelation may lead to biased and inconsistent regression model parameter estimates and increase the risk of a type I error (falsely rejecting the null hypothesis). Accordingly, a critical step in model specification when using spatial data is to assess the presence of spatial autocorrelation. And while different methods have been developed to address issues of spatial heterogeneity, such as identifying different spatial regimes (subregions) and modeling each separately (Anselin 1988), spatial dependence must still be addressed within distinct subregions once these have been identified.

A number of statistical methods have been developed to assess spatial autocorrelation in spatial data both globally and locally. As described in the seminal works in geography on spatial autocorrelation by Cliff and Ord (1973, 1981), the basic standard tests for spatial autocorrelation are the join count statistic, suited only for binary data, and more commonly, Moran's I and Geary's C, both suited for continuous data (Cliff and Ord 1973, 1981). Moran's I and Geary's C are global measures of spatial autocorrelation in that they both summarize the total deviation from spatial randomness across a set of spatial data with a single statistic, although they do so in different ways. Moran's I is a cross-product coefficient similar to a Pearson correlation coefficient and ranges from -1 to $+1$. Positive values for Moran's

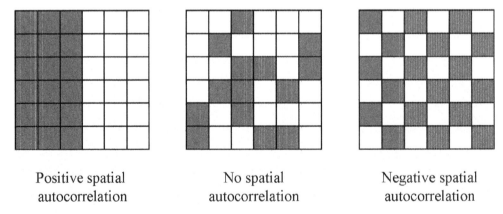

Positive spatial   No spatial   Negative spatial
autocorrelation   autocorrelation   autocorrelation

FIGURE 6.1. Spatial data may demonstrate a pattern of positive spatial autocorrelation (*left*), negative spatial autocorrelation (*right*), or a pattern that is not spatially autocorrelated (*center*). Statistical tests, such as Moran's I, should always be used to evaluate the presence of spatial autocorrelation.

I indicate positive spatial autocorrelation and negative values suggest negative spatial auto-correlation. Geary's C coefficient is based on squared deviations, and values of less than one indicate positive spatial autocorrelation, while values larger than one suggest negative spatial autocorrelation. As a counterpart to the global statistics, there are also local statistics that assess spatial autocorrelation at a specific location. These include the Getis and Ord Gi and Gi^* statistics (Getis and Ord 1992; Ord and Getis 1995) and the local Moran's I (Anselin 1995).

SIMULTANEOUS AUTOREGRESSIVE SPATIAL REGRESSION MODELS

While there are a variety of methods to address spatially autocorrelated data in regression models, we focus here on what are commonly referred to as simultaneous autoregressive (SAR) models, the standard workhorse in spatial regression in a variety of social science fields, particularly those that make use of spatially aggregated socioeconomic data (Anselin 2006; Ward and Gleditsch 2008). Spatial regression models, including SAR models, have been, in large part, developed as a response to the recognition that ignoring spatial dependence when it is present creates serious problems. As Anselin (1988) and others have demonstrated, ignoring spatial dependence in spatial data can result in biased and inconsistent estimates for all the coefficients in the model, biased standard errors, or both. Consequently, inferences derived from such models may be significantly flawed. While a thorough treatment of these models is beyond the aims of this chapter, we offer a brief summary of the main variants before moving on to offer some examples of how these models have been used in criminology.

SAR models can take three different basic forms (see Anselin 1988, 2002; Haining 2003). The first SAR model assumes that the autoregressive process occurs only in the dependent or response variable. This is called the "spatial lag" model and it introduces an additional covariate to the standard terms for the independent, or predictor variables and the errors used in an ordinary least squares (OLS) regression (the additional variable is referred to as a "spatial lag" variable which is a weighted average of values for the dependent variable in areas defined as "neighbors"). Drawing on the form of the familiar OLS regression model and following Anselin (1988), the spatial lag model may be presented as

$$Y = \rho W y + X\beta + \varepsilon,$$

where Y is the dependent variable of interest, ρ is the autoregression parameter, W is the spatial weights matrix, X is the independent variable, and ε is the error term.

The second SAR model assumes that the autoregressive process occurs only in the error term. In this case, the usual OLS regression model is complemented by representing the spatial structure in the spatially dependent error term. The error model may be presented as

$$Y = X\beta + \varepsilon, \quad \varepsilon = \lambda W \varepsilon + \mu,$$

where λ is the autoregression parameter, and ε is the error term composed of a spatially autocorrelated component ($W\varepsilon$) and a stochastic component (μ) with the rest as in the spatial lag model. The third SAR model can contain both a spatial lag term for the response variable and a spatial error term, but is not commonly used. Other SAR model possibilities include lagging predictor variables instead of response variables. In this case, another term must also appear in the model for the autoregression parameters (γ) of the spatially lagged predictors (*WX*). This model takes the form

$$Y = X\beta + WX\lambda + \varepsilon.$$

Combining the response lag and predictor lag terms in a single model is also possible (sometimes referred to as a "mixed" model).

As Anselin (1988) observes, spatial dependence has much to do with notions of relative location between units in potentially different kinds of space and, accordingly, SAR models share a number of common features with network autocorrelation models. Substantively, spatial and network approaches have been used to explore similar questions pertaining to influence and contagion effects, albeit among different units of observations (see Marsden and Friedkin 1993 for examples). In both cases, proximity or connectedness is assumed to facilitate the direct flow of information or influence across units. Individuals or organizations are also more likely to be influenced by the actions, behaviors, or beliefs of others that are proximate on different dimensions, including geographical and social space. Methodologically, the lack of independence among geographical units is identical in its content and construct to the interdependence inherent among the actors in a social network (e.g., Land and Deane 1992).[5]

EXAMPLES FROM CRIMINOLOGY

Much of the spatial analysis of crime can be traced back to the unprecedented increase in youth involved gun violence of the late 1980s' an early 1990s. Scholars and writers in the popular media were quick to start talking in terms of this being a "homicide epidemic." Within the public health framework, an epidemic is simply defined as nonlinear growth of events that typically spread within a subpopulation of susceptible individuals. Using existing data sources (SHR, Chicago Homicide Data, etc.) as well as a set of city-specific microlevel homicide data that were collected in part, or in whole, by the National Consortium on Violence Research (NCOVR)[6] in such cities as Houston, Miami, Pittsburgh, and St. Louis, it was easy for researchers to demonstrate that homicide rates did increase in a nonlinear fashion (e.g., Cohen and Tita 1999b; Rosenfeld et al. 1999; Griffiths and Chavez 2004) at the local level.

Along with these neighborhood-level studies, research at the national level (Blumstein and Rosenfeld 1998; Cork 1999) and the county level (Messner et al. 1999; Baller et al. 2001; Messner and Anselin 2004), have consistently demonstrated two things. First, the subpopulation at greatest risk of homicide victimization during the epidemic was comprised of young urban minority males. Second, homicides exhibit a nonrandom pattern as similar levels of violence cluster in space. Furthermore, the concentration of high violence areas typically occur within disadvantaged urban communities.

---

[5] In addition to the advances made by spatially oriented scholars such as Anselin (1988) and Ord (1975), much of the methodological and empirical foundation currently used in spatial analysis was developed by scholars pursuing properties of "network autocorrelation models" (Doreian and Hummon 1976; Doreian 1980).

[6] The National Consortium on Violence Research (NCOVR) at Carnegie Mellon University was supported under Grant SBR 9513040 from the National Science Foundation.

Gangs, Drugs, and Exposure to Violence

As noted above, spurred on by the youth homicide epidemic, there was a considerable increase in the number of published studies that explore the spatial distribution of violent crime, in general, and homicide, in particular. Researchers began to map homicide in an effort to identify susceptible populations, and to determine if the observed patterns of events were at least consistent with spatial diffusion/contagion. From these studies, it was concluded that homicide and violence exhibit strong patterns of spatial concentration.

The presence of positive spatial autocorrelation has been interpreted as evidence of contagion. It is generally accepted that as violence increased during the last epidemic, certain neighborhood-level social processes or "neighborhood effects" were responsible for the geographic spread and ultimately the concentration of violence in disadvantaged areas. This conclusion rests heavily upon two facts. First, even after controlling for the socioeconomic composition of place, patterns of spatial concentration remain. Second, those studies which have examined local spatial patterns of violence over time do find evidence of diffusion (Cohen and Tita's 1999b; Griffiths and Chavez 2004.) Though no definitive answer has emerged as of yet to the question of why violence displays certain spatial patterns, several explanations have been put forth. In general, researchers have focused on the impact of "exposure to violence" (including subcultural explanations) as well as the particular dynamics and structure of violence involving illicit drug markets and/or violent youth gangs.

Viewing exposure as the social process that is responsible for the spatial clustering of violence has its origins in subcultural explanations of violence. Loftin (1986) was the first to argue that the spatial concentration of assaultive violence and its contagious nature was the result of certain subcultural processes. His use of the term "subcultural" refers to a process wherein violence spreads throughout the population as the result of direct social contact. He argues that a small increase in violence can result in an epidemic in two ways. First, an epidemic results when a small increase in assaults sets off a chain reaction of events causing local individuals to enact precautionary/protective measures in hopes of reducing their chances of victimization. At the extreme, individuals take pre-emptive actions (i.e., assault others) to protect against the possibility of being the victim of an assault. As more preemptive assaults occur, even more people take preemptive actions thereby feeding the epidemic.

Secondly, Loftin argues that the very existence of the moral and social networks that link individuals together within their local environment exacerbate the epidemic. "When violence occurs it draws multiple people into the conflict and spreads either the desire to retaliate or the need for preemptive violence through the network, potentially involving ever increasing number of individuals in the fight" (Loftin 1986: 555). Loftin states this process relies upon direct social contact and implicitly suggests that the concentration of violence must be the result of the limited geographic scope of social interactions. However, one could also easily imagine instances where the victims and offenders interact at schools, entertainment districts, or possibly at the types of "staging grounds" where young men battle for respect within the realm of the "code of the streets" (Anderson 1999).

The retaliatory nature of gang violence along with the violence associated with drug markets have also been offered as explanations for spatial patterns of violence. As noted by Tita and Greenbaum (2008), these explanations are basically extensions of the above arguments in that they represent "exposure" to a particular type of violence. That is, rather than exposure to violence leading to a cultural norm that shaped individual behaviors, it was exposure to the structural features of drug markets and urban street gangs that contributed to the escalation and concentration of violence.

Several features of drug markets, especially open-air markets selling crack-cocaine, make them obvious candidates in explaining the diffusion of violence. First, guns quickly became important "tools of the trade" among urban youth dealing crack. As Blumstein (1995) hypothesized and empirically supported by Blumstein and Cork (1996), arming participants in crack markets increases the risks of violence for nonparticipants as well. Faced with increased risks to personal safety, youth outside crack markets increasingly carry guns and use them to settle interpersonal disputes, thereby spreading gun violence more broadly among the youth population. Second, drug markets often involve competition among rivals looking to increase their market share. Therefore, drug related murders are likely to be retaliatory in nature. Though these arguments are certainly plausible, the supporting evidence is mixed. Though Cork (1999) finds that the spatial and temporal patterns of the increase in violence mirror the emergence of crack-cocaine markets in various regions of the nation, studies in Pittsburgh (Cohen and Tita 1999b), and another examining both Chicago and St. Louis (Cohen et al. 1998) find little evidence that drug homicide increased levels of violence or drove local patterns of diffusion.

Two important features define gangs that make them especially suitable candidates responsible for diffusion (Decker 1996). First, they are geographically oriented. The turf or "set space" where urban street gangs come together to be a gang is a well defined, subneighborhood area that remains consistent over time (Klein 1995; Moore 1985, 1991; Tita et al. 2005). Second, urban street gangs are linked to other gangs via rivalry networks. As we note below, research has demonstrated (Tita and Greenbaum 2008; Radil et al. 2010; Tita et al. 2009) that it is precisely the geography of gangs and their social networks that present a set of structural properties researchers can exploit to better understand the spatial patterns of gang violence.

Below, we provide a brief review of the extant literature from criminology and public health that have employed spatial regression models. Though not meant to represent an exhaustive review of this burgeoning literature, these studies do represent some of the most widely cited articles in the field. After summarizing the findings and the methods, we make the case for the importance of carefully modeling processes of influence into one's spatial weights matrix (W).

Empirical Studies of Crime Employing Spatial Regression

In what is widely recognized as the first attempt to explicitly model the spatial effects inherent in the production and impact of violence, Morenoff and Sampson (1997) examine the impact of violence on residential change in Chicago. They argue that in addition to reacting to the level of violence in one's own neighborhood, residents also react to the levels of violence around them. Thus, among controlling for the socio-economic measures as well as the trends in terms of residential transition, the authors also include a spatially lagged independent variable in their model to capture the "*spatial diffusion* of homicide" (ibid: 56). Indeed, their findings show that the impact of homicide on population changes will differ in a focal tract depending upon the level of homicide in nearby tracts.

Morenoff et al. (2001) examined the spatial distribution of violence more directly. It is this work that lays out the "exposure" and "diffusion" arguments. They argue that homicide may be spatially clustered because the measures associated with violence (e.g., poverty, population density, etc.) are spatially and temporally clustered, thus exposing residents who live in close proximity to each other to the same set of conditions. Additionally, the social interactions that result in violence are likely to involve "...networks of association that follow geographical vectors" (ibid: 523) along which violence is likely to diffuse. Specifically, they mention the retaliatory nature of gang violence and the fact that homicide is likely to be committed within groups of individuals known to one another. Their final conclusion is that the spatial effects in their models are large in magnitude and that ecological models of crime that focus only on the internal characteristics of the unit of observation (census tract) are likely to suffer from misspecification. Though they find that "space" matters, and that it matters over various spatial regimes (controlling for race of a neighborhood), the precise reason it matters is less clear. As the authors note, they are "...unable to pinpoint the relative contributions of exposure and diffusion" (Ibid: 552).

Rosenfeld et al. (1999) estimated a spatial lag model to determine if the patterns of "gang-motivated" homicides differed compared to nongang youth homicides as well as homicides that involved gang members but lacked any specific gang motivation. Three separate equations are estimated using count data and also including the spatial lag of the count in surrounding census tracts as an explanatory variable. What they find is that controlling for neighborhood characteristics, only the spatial term in only the gang-motivated analysis is statistically significant. The authors see this as evidence of gang-motivated homicides being contagious in nature and that "...the spatial distribution of gang-motivated homicide may reflect intrinsic features of the phenomenon and not simply the presence of facilitating neighborhood characteristics" (Ibid: 512).

Smith et al. (2000) examine diffusion and spatial effects within the context of street robbery. Once again, we see that the amount of street robbery in neighboring areas (census block faces) impacts the level of street robbery on a focal block face. The authors conclude that the spatial effect is consistent with diffusion resulting from the spatial bounds of the "awareness space" (Brantingham and Brantingham 1981) of offenders. Drawing upon the existing "journey to crime" literature, the authors cap awareness space so that only levels of crime in block faces within 1 mile of the focal block face are accounted for in the spatial weights matrix.

Gorman et al. (2001) examine the effects of alcohol outlets on violent crime rates in Camden, New Jersey. Using census block groups at the unit of analysis, Gorman et al. make a methodological argument using a spatial regression model as they identified significant positive spatial autocorrelation in crime rates and offer two spatial models: a spatial error model and a spatial lag model. However, for the lag model, Gorman et al. produce spatial lags of the independent variables rather than of the dependent variable (crime rates). While there is little explanation offered for this modeling choice, the results of the independent variable lag model suggest to the authors that while some explanatory variables in surrounding areas had a significant impact on crime rates in a given unit, the density of alcohol outlets in neighboring areas had no significant impact on crime rates. Gorman et al. find this as evidence that the effects of alcohol outlets on violent crime are highly localized and spatially concentrated and that such effects decay quickly with distance.

Kubrin and Stewart (2006) investigated relationships between neighborhood context and recidivism rates of ex-offenders in Portland, Oregon. Although not expressly interested in spatial diffusion, Kubrin and Stewart attempted to control for spatial autocorrelation in recidivism rates across neighborhoods (measured by census tracts) by including a spatially lagged recidivism variable in their multilevel model. However, due to the limitations of incorporating spatial effects into multilevel models, they were unable to determine if the spatial dependence in the rate of recidivism is evidence of diffusion or due to other effects, such as spillovers.

Hipp et al. (2009) examine patterns of intra- and inter-group crime in an area of Los Angeles, CA that has undergone significant residential transition taking it from majority African-American to majority Latino over the last two decades. Their goal is to understand the impact of this transition on both within-group and across-group violence. To control for spatial effects, they estimate a model that includes spatially lagged predictors. Following the lead of Elffers (2003) and Morenoff (2003), they argue that explicitly modeling the spatial process through the lagged independent variables (median income, change in race/ethnicity, and income inequality between racial/ethnic groups) is theoretically superior to a spatial lag model. They contend that to "estimate a spatial lag model we would need to argue that the level of either intra- or inter-group crime in a neighboring area has a direct 'contagion' effect on crime in a focal area. We do not believe this is the case, especially with respect to inter-group crime events" (Ibid: 41). Instead, they hold that spatial impacts may best be modeled through "...the racial/ethnic composition of adjacent neighborhoods (as these group compositions could affect inter- and intra-group crime rates in the tract of interest), how that racial/ethnic composition has changed, the income level of adjacent neighborhoods (which might create additional stress or protective effects), and economic inequality in adjacent neighborhoods" (Ibid). They employ a weights matrix that captures a distance-decay functions truncated with a 2-mile cutoff. That is, the spatial effect goes to "0" for all census block groups beyond two miles. To summarize, they find that the level of income inequality in surrounding areas has a significant impact on inter-group violence in a focal tract as does the degree to which racial transitioning from African-American to Latino remains ongoing.

In contrast to the small scale studies described above, Baller et al. (2001) focused on national-level patterns of homicide aggregated to counties (see also Messner et al. 1999). Baller and his colleagues examined homicide rates against selected socioeconomic character- istics for continental U.S. counties for four decennial census years (1960, 1970, 1980, and 1990) and concluded that "homicide is strongly clustered in space" in each time period at this scale. Baller et al. also identified the southeastern US as a distinct spatial regime and interpreted a spatial lag model fit as evidence of a diffusion process in this region (the nonsoutheastern regime best fit a spatial error model, which suggested that the spatial auto- correlation in this regime was due to the presence of unmeasured variables). However, the mechanisms for such diffusion are difficult to arrive at for such macrolevel studies and as Baller et al. acknowledge, there is no a priori reason to assume spatial interaction between counties on the topic of homicide and the large amount of spatial aggregation in the data likely contributes to the perceived spatial dependence (2001: 568–569).

With the exception of Kubrin and Stewart (2006), the above studies use SAR spatial models to examine a variety of phenomena, and each time find a spatial story to the issues at hand. In these examples, spatial lag models were the most common choice but spatial error models were also occasionally fielded either as an exploratory technique (Gorman et al. 2001) or as a choice determined by model diagnostics (Baller et al. 2001). When a spatial lag model was used in these examples, the dependent variable was selected for the lag with the exception of Morenoff and Sampson (1997), Gorman et al. (2001) and Hipp et al. (2009), all of whom lagged explanatory variables instead. This overview highlights the increasing consideration of spatial effects in ecological studies of crime at different geographic scales and points to the growing (but not exclusive) use of SAR models to incorporate such effects. However, the formal model of the connection between the geographic units that underpin these and other spatial models receive little attention in some of the examples, and many of the authors use simple measures of unit contiguity or adjacency to formally model the interaction of interest. As an important but often overlooked element of spatial regression model specification we turn our attention to the spatial weight matrix, or W.

THE SPATIAL WEIGHTS MATRIX W

Both SAR and network autocorrelation models estimate parameters in the presence of presumably interdependent variables (Anselin 1988; Leenders 2002). This estimation process requires the analyst to define the form and limits of the interdependence and formalize the influence one location (or network node) has on another. In practice, this is accomplished by identifying the connectivity between the units of the study area through a $n \times n$ matrix. The matrix is usually described as a "spatial weight" or "spatial connectivity" matrix and referred to in the SAR models as "W." This W, or matrix of locations, formalizes a priori assumptions about potential interactions between different locations, defining some locations as influential upon a given location and ruling others out.

A simpler way of describing this is that W identifies, in some cases, who is a neighbor and who is not, or with whom an actor interacts. This notion of influence across space is addressed in an empirical sense by criminologists when deciding whether two geographic areal units are contiguous based upon borders or near enough for influence based on distances. However, the construction of W is more than just an empirical choice about neighbors. It is a theoretical decision regarding the processes being discussed and one that has implications for the statistical estimates generated. Whether it is geographical or network space, W is used to represent the dependence among observations in terms of the underlying social or geographic structure that explicitly links actors or geographic units with one another. As Leenders (2002: 26) notes:

> W is supposed to represent the theory a researcher has about the structure of the influence processes in the network. Since any conclusion drawn on the basis of autocorrelation models is conditional upon the specification of W, the scarcity of attention and justification researchers pay to the chosen operationalization of W is striking and alarming. This is especially so, since different specifications of W typically lead to different empirical results.

Following Leender's point, discussions about the nature of W and how different specification choices may affect regression results have indeed been underemphasized in most spatial analytic literature: the relatively few examples to the contrary include Florax and Rey (1995) and Griffith (1996). Despite these noteworthy efforts, Leenders (2002: 44) is correct in his assessment that "the effort devoted by researchers to the appropriate choice of W pales in comparison to the efforts devoted to the development of statistical and mathematical procedures." The net effect of this lack of attention is that theoretical conceptions about the role space plays in producing empirical patterns in a given dataset are often afterthoughts. Hence, the vision of a "spatially integrated social science" (Goodchild et al. 2000) for criminology remains unfulfilled, because when space is included in the analysis of crime or other social processes, it is often added in a default form without consideration of the processes in question.

Such an attention deficit is a cause for concern as the products of the SAR models are quite sensitive to the specification of W. For example, using simulated data, Florax and Rey (1995) conclude that misspecification of W can affect the outcome of spatial dependence tests, such as the commonly used Moran's I test of spatial autocorrelation, and of estimates of variables in spatial regression models. Griffith (1996), also using simulated data, reaches a similar conclusion, stressing that while assuming some connectivity is always more reasonable than assuming no connectivity, both underspecifying (identifying fewer connections between spatial units than really exist) and overspecifying (identifying more connections) W affect both regression estimates and the product of the diagnostic tests (maximum likelihood, or ML, tests) used in spatial econometrics to choose between the lag or error models.

In our review of the models used in the studies outlined above, we find that without exception, each specification of W is based either on simple contiguity, k-nearest neighbors, or the use of distance decay metrics. Although challenging, more careful modeling of spatial processes through the spatial weights matrix is of critical importance to understand the black box of neighborhood effects emphasized by Cohen and Tita (1999a). As previously described, network autocorrelation models involve a similar challenge to spatial models, and the network literature offers useful parallels to the challenge in modeling spatial dependence and interaction. In modeling dependence among nodes, social network analysts often begin with a particular social process in mind and then carefully model that process into the network autocorrelation matrix. For example, edges among nodes may be predicated upon specific social relationships (e.g., friendship, familial, or instrumental ties) or shared membership into formal/informal groups. Alternatively, one can decide that a pair of nodes is connected only when they are similar along some particular dimension such as race, sex, income or "status" (see the discussion of Mears and Bhati (2006) below). These types of important differences can lead to very different specifications of the weights matrix.

Social scientists have employed social network analysis in an effort to explain a number of social processes, most notably the diffusion of innovations, technology, and information among individuals, societies, and organizations (e.g., Coleman et al. 1966; Rogers 1983; Grattet et al. 1998). In defining underlying processes of contagion/social influence, network scientists carefully differentiate between social processes of influence that operate through direct ties or association among actors (referred to as "communication" or "structural cohesion") versus contagion that occurs among individuals who occupy shared positions within a network (referred to as "comparison" or "equivalence"). The decision to choose one process over another – communication versus comparison – is dependent upon one's chosen theory. As Leenders (2002: 26) succinctly states, "Change one's theory, change W."

To highlight the importance of specifying a W that is consistent to with the social process of choice, we draw upon a classic example from the networks literature dealing with the question of why and when certain physicians adopted a new medical innovation (tetracycline). Coleman et al. (1966) posited that peer effects mattered, and demonstrated the importance of structural cohesion or direct social ties in determining who adopted the new drug, and the order in which it was adopted. That is, once a couple of doctors of "higher status" assumed the role of "early adopters," the next wave of adopters was comprised of the initial adopters' friends. Decades later Burt (1987) offered an alternative hypothesis in which he argued that individuals are often most strongly influenced by the actions and behaviors of rivals and competitors and not by their friends. He reanalyzed the data and demonstrated that network position (as measured by "structural equivalence") was the defining predictor of adoption. Burt concluded that friendship, or any form of direct communication, had little to do with the pattern of adoption. Instead, doctors who held similarly high positions of "status" (e.g., subscribed to the multiple medical journals, were younger, made many house calls, kept up on scientific advances) within the medical community adopted earlier than did older doctors, those who spent more time with their patients than keeping up with medical advances, and who subscribed to fewer professional journals. Though neither the line of inquiry (adoption of an innovation/diffusion) nor the methodology (network autocorrelation models) ever changed, the theory employed in the research did.

MOVING BEYOND SIMPLE CONTIGUITY/DISTANCE BASED SPECIFICATIONS OF W

Recently, in order to better capture specific processes or patterns of influence, criminologists have begun to explore alternative specifications of the weights matrix that move beyond simple contiguity or distance. Mears and Bhati (2006) build off the long-standing finding that resource deprivation is positively associated with local levels of violence by asking whether the level of resource deprivation in other counties could influence violence in a focal neighborhood. In addition to controlling for the level of disadvantage in surrounding communities, the authors also construct weights matrices based upon the level of "social similarity" between places. The authors smartly point out that what happens in focal neighborhood might only influence events in other neighborhoods if there is a mixing of the population between the two places. Though the research does not actually have network data linking the friendships and communication across place, they reason on the bases of "homophily" (Blau and Blau 1982; McPherson et al. 2001) that social interactions are more likely among "similar" individuals. Using various measures of resource deprivation to construct alternative measures of W, controlling for both resource deprivation in surrounding neighborhoods (as well as controlling for spatial lags of homicide, the dependent variable), they find that geographic as well as "social proximity" to resource deprivation was associated with higher homicide rates. Furthermore, social proximity, or nearness in terms of social similarity, had a much stronger impact than did geographic proximity alone. An interesting finding from their research is that while these results held for both instrumental and expressive types of homicides, no effect was found with regard to gang-related homicides. For that insight into this finding, we turn to a recent set of studies looking specifically at gang violence.

In an effort to better understand the spatial distribution of violence involving gang members, Tita and Greenbaum (2008) and Tita et al. (2009) also examine spatially proximate effects of violence as well as violence in socially proximate communities. This body of research lays out a very clear hypothesis regarding how gang violence in an area might influence gang violence in other areas. By exploiting the spatial nature of gangs (they hang out in specific areas, known as "set space" (Tita et al. 2005)), and the social dynamics of gangs (they are linked to other gangs through a network of rivalries), they hypothesize that the violence in a focal area will have a stronger impact on violence in areas that are linked through the sociospatial dimensions of the gang rivalry network than will spatial contiguity alone. In fact, the studies in Los Angeles, CA (Tita et al. 2009) and in Pittsburgh, PA (Tita and Greenbaum 2008) both demonstrate support for this hypothesis. That is, the purely geographic nature of "diffusion" was muted when one controlled for whether or not proximate (or nonproximate) areas (block groups) were linked by containing the set space of rival gangs. The authors of both studies are careful to point out that they constructed their weights matrices with a specific process in mind – the transmission of violence through a gang rivalry network – and caution that had they been interested in looking at other types of violence (e.g., drug violence, domestic violence), their particular "social similarity matrix" would have been inappropriate.

SUMMARY

The use of spatial regression has clearly advanced our understanding of crime patterns at both the local (neighborhood) and county level. We include Table 6.1 as a summary of both the traditional and the more creative research examining spatial effects. Summarizing the table, we know that whether for recidivism, homicide, gang violence, or robbery, there is evidence for spatial dependence and possible spatial interaction processes at work. We also know that addressing the spatial autocorrelation present in most aggregated crime data offers more reliable modeling estimates and that attempting to understand the substantive sources of spatial dependence in the social processes of crime leads is a critical step in model specification. However, as Table 6.1 demonstrates, our thinking and operationalization of the spatial processes has, until recently, remained at the level of only accounting for connections between units in the simplest of geographic terms. Complex theoretical stories about the mechanisms of diffusion between places can quickly become lost in a spatial weight matrix that uses the simplest conceptions of geography (simple measures of adjacency/contiguity, or distance such as Rook/queen's contiguity, linear distance decay functions, or k-nearest neighbor) to specify the nature of interaction, including scope, direction, and intensity. As there remains no statistical method capable of estimating the "best fit" of a spatial weight matrix to one's data (Leenders 2002: 38), embodying theory into the specification of W is the only sensible recourse available.

A recent article by Sampson and Sharkey (2008) examined intra-urban movement patterns of 4,000 families in Chicago between 1994 and 2002. The take-away point of this research is that there is great disparity in the types of places that people move to, and that where people move can be explained by controlling for race and economic. While there is evidence that poor whites or poor Latinos will move into nonpoor neighborhoods that may contain sizable white populations, the mobility of blacks along all levels of income is restricted among existing predominately black neighborhoods. Nonpoor blacks rarely move into other nonpoor areas comprised of nonblacks, and while some poor blacks may move into nonpoor black communities, the vast majority of moves for poor African-Americans are into other poor black neighborhoods. We highlight this research because it provides the richness of data to truly understand the sociospatial nature of influence. From these findings, it seems evident that incidents of violence in poor black neighborhoods are far more likely to diffuse into other poor black neighborhoods than in surrounding, nonblack (poor or otherwise) neighborhoods. In this regard, it confirms the assumptions of Mears and Bhati (2006) regarding the connectivity among places based on social similarity, but the level of detail in this study far exceeds the use of resource deprivation as a proxy for social interaction.

We think that Sampson (2008) said it best noting that "The advent of GIS modeling and new data sources on social interactions and networks of spatial connection are revealing the profound spatial ordering of a bewildering array of urban phenomenon." If we want to tackle the question posed by Cohen and Tita (1999a) that motivated this chapter, researchers need to exploit these types of data sets to truly understand the processes by which violence diffuses across space.

TABLE 6.1. Summary of empirical studies using spatial regression in the study of crime

Author	Topic	Model type	Estimation	Specification of W	Conclusions
Morenoff and Sampson (1997)	Effects of violence on residential change; contagious nature of residential change	Spatially lagged dependent variable (Wy) using residential change along with spatially lagged independent variables (Wx) using homicide rate	2-stage least squares using the spatial lag of "residential change potential" (Wy) and the "homicide potential" (Wx) explanatory variables in the second-stage of estimation	Distance decay, weighted by distance from centroid	Impact of homicide on population changes will differ in a focal tract depending upon the level of homicide in nearby tracts
Morenoff et al. (2001)	Spatial distribution of homicide crime	Spatially lagged dependent variable (Wy)	Maximum-likelihood estimation using a two stage approach – Step one estimates a log-homicide rates while the second step includes a spatial lag of the estimated rate	Rook's case geographic contiguity (shared border lengths)	Spatial dependence in levels of violence persists controlling for community disadvantage as well as "collective efficacy"
Rosenfeld et al. (1999)	Spatial distribution of gang-motivated, gang-affiliated and nongang youth homicide	Spatially lagged dependent count variables (Wy)	Maximum-likelihood estimation of count models	Inverse distance across all space	Gang-motivated homicide shows greater spatial dependence, suggesting contagious nature of these types of events

(continued)

TABLE 6.1. (continued)

Author	Topic	Model type	Estimation	Specification of W	Conclusions
Smith et al. (2000)	Spatial effects of street robbery	Spatial lagged dependent variable (Wy)	Generalized negative binomial regression	K-nearest neighbor variant: sample of 20 face blocks within 1 mile radius of focal block; sample limited to only two directions (either n/s or e/w from focal block)	Street robbery in neighboring areas (census block faces) impacts the level of street robbery on a focal block face
Baller et al. (2001)	County level spatial patterns of homicide	Spatial regimes; spatial error and spatially lagged dependent variable (Wy; We)	Maximum-likelihood: Robust Lagrange Multiplier tests	K-nearest neighbor (all counties connected to exactly 10 nearest (by centroid distance) neighboring counties)	South US region shows evidence of homicide diffusion; spatial dependence in nonSouth likely due to unobserved variables
Gorman et al. (2001)	Effects of alcohol outlets on violent crime rates	Spatial error and spatially lagged independent variables (Wx, We)	Maximum likelihood	Queen's case geographic contiguity (shared border lengths and/or border points)	The density of alcohol outlets in neighboring areas had no significant impact on crime rates in focal units.

(continued)

TABLE 6.1. (continued)

Author	Topic	Model type	Estimation	Specification of W	Conclusions
Mears and Bhati (2006)	Spatial distribution of homicide, by type	Spatially lagged dependent variable (Wy); socially lagged dependent variable; Social and spatially weighted independent variables (Wx).	Negative binomial using natural log of homicide counts	Geographic space is measured using queen's case contiguity; Social space is measured by comparing measures of social similarity (including resource deprivation) between each pair of communities. The similarity matrix decays exponentially as dissimilarity increases.	With the exception of gang homicide, social similarity among geographic units is more strongly related to homicide than is geographic adjacency.
Kubrin and Stewart (2006)	Effects of neighborhood context on recidivism rates	Multilevel model (included a spatial lag variable) (Wy)	HLM with the inclusion of a spatially lagged measure of recidivism rates.	Queen's case geographic contiguity	Spatial dependence in recidivism; unable to assess evidence for diffusion

(continued)

TABLE 6.1. (continued)

Author	Topic	Model type	Estimation	Specification of W	Conclusions
Tita and Greenbaum 2008; Tita et al. 2009	Spatial distribution of gang violence	Spatially lagged dependent variable (Wy); socially lagged dependent variable	"Anselin-alternative method" using the "violence potential" as an instrumental variable in 2-stage estimation	Geographic space is measured using queen's case contiguity; Social space is constructed using the location of gangs in space, and the rivalry network that links them socially	Spatial dependence is best modeled by considering the socio-spatial distribution of gang rivalries, which extend beyond contiguous neighbors.
Hipp et al. (2009)	Intra-group and inter-group Violence	Spatially lagged independent variables (Wx)	Negative binomial with spatially lagged X's	Distance decay, 2 mile maximum	Clear evidence of income inequality and racial transition in surrounding tracts impacting inter-group violence in focal tract

REFERENCES

Anderson E (1999) Code of the street: decency, violence, and the moral life of the inner city. W. W. Norton & Company, New York

Anselin L (1988) Spatial econometrics: methods and models. Kluwer, Boston

Anselin L (2002) Under the hood: issues in the specification and interpretation of spatial regression models. Agric Econ 27(3):247–267

Anselin L (1995) Local indicators of spatial association – LISA. Geogr Anal 27(1):93–115

Anselin L (1998) Exploratory spatial data analysis in a geocomputational environment. In: Longley P, Brooks S, McDonnell R, Macmillan B (eds) Geocomputation, a primer. Wiley, New York

Anselin L (1999) Interactive techniques and exploratory spatial data analysis. In: Longley P, Goodchild M, Maguire D, Rhind D (eds) Geographical information systems. Wiley, New York

Anselin L (2006) Spatial econometrics. In: Mills TC, Patterson K (eds) Palgrave handbook of econometrics: volume 1, econometric theory. Palgrave Macmillan, Basingstoke, pp 901–941

Anselin L, Griffiths E, Tita G (2008) Crime mapping and hot spot analysis. In: Wortley R, Mazerolle L (eds) Environmental criminology and crime analysis Willan Publishing, UK, pp 97–116

Baller R, Anselin L, Messner S, Deane G, Hawkins D (2001) Structural covariates of U.S. county homicide rates: incorporating spatial effects. Criminology 39(3):561–590

Blau J, Blau P (1982) Cost of inequality: metropolitan structure and violent crime journal. Am Sociol Rev 47(1): 114–129

Blumstein Ad (1995) Youth violence, guns, and the illicit-drug industry. J Crim Law Criminol 86:10–36

Blumstein A, Cork D (1996) Linking gun availability to youth gun violence. Law Contemp Probl 59(1):5–24

Blumstein A, Rosenfeld R (1998) Explaining recent trends in us homicide rates. J Crim Law Criminol 88:1175–1216

Brantingham PJ, Brantingham PL (1981) Environmental criminology. Sage Publications, Beverly Hills

Burt R (1987) Social contagion and innovation: cohesion versus structural equivalence. Am J Sociol 92:1287–1335

Cliff AD, Ord JK (1973) Spatial autocorrelation. Pion, London

Cliff AD, Ord JK (1981) Spatial processes, models, and applications. Pion, London

Cohen J, Tita G (1999a) Editors' introduction. J Quant Criminol 15(4):373–378

Cohen J, Tita G (1999b) Diffusion in homicide: exploring a general method for detecting spatial diffusion processes. J Quant Criminol 15(4):451–493

Cohen J, Cork D, Engberg J, Tita G (1998) The role of drug markets and gangs in local homicide rates. Homicide Stud 2:241–262

Coleman J, Katz E, Menzel H (1966) Medical innovation: a diffusion study. Bobbs-Merrill, New York

Cork D (1999) Examining space–time interaction in city-level homicide data: crack markets and the diffusion of guns among youth. J Quant Criminol 15(4):379–406

Decker S (1996) Collective and normative features of gang violence. Justice Q 13:243–264

Doreian P (1980) Linear models with spatially distributed data: spatial disturbances or spatial effects? Sociol Methods Res 9:29–60

Doreian P, Hummon N (1976) Modeling social processes. Elsevier, New York

Elffers H (2003) Analyzing neighbourhood influence in criminology. J Neth Soc Stat Oper Res 57(3):347–367

Florax R, Rey S (1995) The impacts of misspecified spatial interaction in linear regression models. In: Anselin L, Florax R (eds) New directions in spatial econometrics. Springer, Berlin, pp 111–135

Fotheringham AS (1997) Trends in quantitative methods i: stressing the local. Prog Hum Geogr 21:88–96

Fotheringham AS, Charlton M, Brundson S (2002) Geographically weighted regression: the analysis of spatially varying relationships. Wiley, New York

Gehlke C, Biehl K (1934) Certain effects of grouping upon the size of the correlation coefficient in census tract material. J Am Stat Assoc 29:169–170

Getis A, Ord JK (1992) The analysis of spatial association by use of distance statistics. Geogr Anal 24:189–206

Goodchild MF (2004) GIScience, geography, form, and process Ann Assoc Am Geogr 94(4):709–714

Goodchild MF, Anselin L, Appelbaum R Harthorn B (2000) Toward spatially integrated social science. Int Reg Sci Rev 23:139–159

Gorman DM, Speer PW, Gruenewald PJ, Labouvie EW (2001) Spatial dynamics of alcohol availability, neighborhood structure and violent crime. J Stud Alcohol 62(5):628–636

Grattet R, Jenness V, Curry T (1998) The homogenization and differentiation of 'hate crime' law in the U.S., 1978–1995: an analysis of innovation and diffusion in the criminalization of bigotry. Am Sociol Rev 63:286–307

Griffith DA (1983) The boundary value problem in spatial statistical analysis. J Reg Sci 23:377–378

Griffith DA (1996) Some guidelines for specifying the geographic weights matrix contained in the spatial statistical models. In: Arlinghaus SL (ed) Practical handbook of spatial statistics. CRC Press, Boca Raton, pp 65–82

Griffiths E, Chavez JM (2004) Communities, street guns, and homicide trajectories in Chicago, 1980–1995: merging methods for examining homicide trends across space and time. Criminology 42(4):941–978

Haining R (2003) Spatial data analysis: theory and practice. Cambridge University Press, Cambridge

Haining R (2009) The special nature of spatial data. In: Fotheringham S, Rogerson PA (eds) The sage handbook of spatial analysis. Sage, Thousand Oaks, CA

Hipp JR (2007) Block, tract, and levels of aggregation: neighborhood structure and crime and disorder as a case in point. Am Sociol Rev 72:659–680

Hipp J, Tita G, Boggess L (2009) Inter- and intra-group interactions: the case of everyday violent crime as an expression of group conflict or social disorganization. Criminology 47(2):521–564

King G (1997) A solution to the ecological inference problem: reconstructing individual behavior from aggregate data. Princeton University Press, Princeton

Klein M (1995) The American street gang: its nature, prevalence and control. Oxford University Press, New York

Kubrin CE, Stewart EA (2006) Predicting who reoffends: the neglected role of neighborhood context in recidivism studies. Criminology 44:165–197

Land KC, Deane G (1992) On the large-sample estimation of regression models with spatial or network effects terms: a two-stage least-squares approach. In: Marsden P (ed) Sociological methodology 1992 Basil Blackwell, Oxford, pp 221–248

Leenders R (2002) Modeling social influence through network autocorrelation: constructing the weight matrix. Soc Networks 24:21–47

Loftin C (1986) Assultive violence as a contagious process. Bull N Y Acad Med 62:550–555

Marsden PV, Friedkin NE (1993) Network studies of social influence. Sociol Methods Res 22:125–149

McPherson M, Smith-Lovin L, Cook J (2001) Birds of a feather: homophily in social networks. Ann Rev Sociol 27:415–44

Mears D, Bhati A (2006) No community is an island: the effects of resource deprivation on urban violence in spatially and socially proximate communities. Criminology 44(3):509–548

Mencken FC, Barnett C (1999) Murder, nonnegligent manslaughter, and spatial autocorrelation in mid-south counties. J Quant Criminol 15(4):407–422

Messner SF, Anselin L (2004) Spatial analyses of homicide with areal data. In: Goodchild MF, Janelle DG (eds) Spatially integrated social science. Oxford University Press, Oxford, pp 127–144

Messner SF, Anselin L, Baller RD, Hawkins DF, Deane G, Tolnay SE (1999) The spatial patterning of county homicide rates: an application of exploratory spatial data analysis. J Quant Criminol 15(4):423–450

Moore J (1985) Isolation and stigmatization in the development of an underclass: the case of Chicano gangs in east Los Angeles. Soc Probl 33:1–12

Moore J (1991) Going down to the barrio: homeboys and homegirls in change. Temple University Press, Philadelphia

Morenoff J, Sampson RJ (1997) Violent crime and the spatial dynamics of neighborhood transition: Chicago, 1970–1990. Soc Forces 76(1):31–64

Morenoff J, Sampson RJ, Raudenbush S (2001) Neighborhood inequality, collective efficacy, and the spatial dynamics of urban violence. Criminology 39:517–560

Morenoff J. (2003) Neighborhood mechanisms and the spatial dynamics of birth weight. Am J Sociol 108:976–1017

O'Loughlin J (2003) Spatial analysis in political geography. In: Agnew JA, Mitchell K, Tuathail GÓ (eds) A companion to political geography. Blackwell Pub, Malden, MA, pp 30–46

Openshaw S (1996) Developing GIS-relevant zone-based spatial analysis methods. In: Longley P, Batty M (eds) Spatial analysis: modeling in a GIS environment. Wiley, New York, pp 55–73

Ord JK (1975) Estimation methods for models of spatial interaction. J Am Stat Assoc 70:120–126

Ord JK, Getis A (1995) Local spatial autocorrelation statistics: distributional issues and an application. Geogr Anal 27:286–306

Radil S, Flint C, Tita G (2010) Spatializing social networks: geographies of gang rivalry, territoriality, and violence in Los Angeles. Ann Assoc Am Geogr 99(2) Forthcoming

Robinson W (1950) Ecological correlation and the behavior of individuals. Am Sociol Rev 15:351–357

Rogers E (1983) Diffusion of innovations. Free Press, New York

Rosenfeld R, Bray TM, Egley A (1999) Facilitating violence: a comparison of gang-motivated, gang-affiliated, and nongang youth homicides. J Quant Criminol, 15(4):494–516

Sampson R (2008) "After school" Chicago: space and the city. Urban Geogr 29(2):127–137

Sampson R, Sharkey P (2008) Neighborhood selection and the social reproduction of concentrated racial inequality. Demography 45(1):1–29

Sampson R, Morenoff J, Gannon-Rowley T (2002) Assessing neighborhood effects: Social processes and new directions in research. Annu Rev Sociol 28:443–478

Smith WR, Frazee SG, Davison EL (2000) Furthering the integration of routine activity and social disorganization theories: small units of analysis and the study of street robbery as a diffusion process. Criminology 38:489–523

Tita G, Radil S, Flint C (2009) Modeling the spatial distribution of crime through contiguity, social influence, and status. In 2009 Crime and Place Conference, Manassas, VA, April 22, 2009

Tita G, Cohen J, Engberg J (2005) An ecological study of the location of gang 'set space'. Soc Probl 52:272–299

Tita G, Greenbaum R (2008) Crime, neighborhoods and units of analysis: putting space in its Place. In: Weisburd D, Bernasco W, Bruinsma GJN (eds) Putting crime in its place: units of analysis in spatial crime research. Springer, New York, pp 145–170

Tobler WR (1970) A computer movie simulating urban growth in the detroit region. Econ Geogr 46:234–240

Ward MD, Gleditsch K (2008) Spatial regression models. Sage, Thousand Oaks, CA

Weisburd D, Bernasco W, Bruinsma GJN (eds) (2008) Putting crime in its place: units of analysis in spatial crime research. Springer, New York

## CHAPTER 7

Mixed Method Research in Criminology: Why Not Go Both Ways?

Shadd Maruna

This chapter explores mixed method research designs that seek to combine elements of qualitative and quantitative research into a criminological investigation. This is neither a new nor a radical concept. Indeed, the differences between so-called "qualitative" methods and so-called "quantitative" methods in social science have been called "more apparent than real" (Hanson 2008: 97; see also Newman and Benz 1998; Ragin 1994). So, in a very real sense, all criminological research is "mixed methods" research. Yet, the approach remains under-appreciated and under-utilized in contemporary criminological research. The same is not true outside the discipline. First emerging as a concept around three decades ago (see esp. Brewer and Hunter 1989; Jick 1979; Fielding and Fielding 1986), "mixed methods research" has become something of a new buzzword in methodology circles with major international conferences, journals such as the *Journal of Mixed method Research, Field Methods*, and *Quality and Quantity*, and a comprehensive handbook all of its own (Tashakkori and Teddlie 2003).

Importantly, the practice of mixed method research has been around much longer than the brand name (see esp. Teddlie and Tashakkori 2003). In the early decades of social scientific research, qualitative and quantitative research coexisted far more peacefully than today, and mixed method designs were a feature of some of the most important research of the time (see e.g., Whyte's 1943 *Street Corner Society*; Roethlisberger & Dickson's 1939 "Hawthorne Effect" studies; Warner and Lunt's 1941 "Yankee City" research; and much of the Chicago School of Sociology's output). This happy mixing of qualitative and quantitative approaches to social science continued throughout what Denzin and Lincoln (2005) refer to as the "Golden Age" of qualitative research, post-World War II, with ground-breaking mixed method research such as Festinger's studies of cults (e.g., Festinger et al. 1956); Short and Strodtbeck's (1965) gang research; and Zimbardo's (1969) simulated prison studies (for a history of mixed method research in social science, see Hunter and Brewer 2003).

Like so many other methodological insights in the social sciences, the origins of the mixed method label are often attributed to Donald Campbell. Campbell and Fiske (1959) argued in favor of the use of multiple methods over "monomethod" designs on the grounds

A.R. Piquero and D. Weisburd (eds.), *Handbook of Quantitative Criminology*, DOI 10.1007/978-0-387-77650-7_7, © Springer Science + Business Media, LLC 2010, First softcover printing 2011

that getting more than one angle on a phenomenon can be a useful validity check on one's analysis. This notion later became known as the "triangulation" (Denzin 1970) of methodological perspectives, a concept that has parallels to the "long recognized natural and physical science principle of parallax" (Hanson 2008).

The idea of "triangulation" is now closely associated with mixed nomothetic-ideographic research (Fielding and Fielding 1986), yet Campbell and Fiske (1959) were instead referring to a mix of different quantitative methodologies. (Campbell, in fact, had been dismissive of qualitative research in some of his early writing). Later in his career, though, Campbell became an advocate of mixed qualitative–quantitative designs – "partly in response to growing disappointment with experimentalist research and partly in response to developments in the philosophy of science" (Howe 2004: 44). Campbell (1974: 29–30) writes:

> The polarity of quantitative-experimental versus qualitative approaches to research on social action remains unresolved, if resolution were to mean a predominant justification of one over the other. . . . Each pole is at its best in its criticisms of the other, not in invulnerability of its own claims to descriptive knowledge. . . . If we are to be truly scientific, we must reestablish the qualitative grounding of the quantitative. (cited in Howe 2004: 44).

Campbell described the isolation of quantitative and qualitative methods as an "unhealthy division of labor" (p. 13) and proceeded in later writing to strongly endorse qualitative case studies (see Campbell 1984).

So, there is nothing new or shocking about mixed method qualitative–quantitative research; in fact, methodological flexibility and efforts to "triangulate" evidence types (Denzin 1970) are broadly and noncontroversially recommended as good practice to fledgling social researchers in textbooks (e.g., Creswell 2003; Ragin 1994). Yet, because of the methodological paradigm struggles that arose in the last three decades and the lingering prejudices that resulted, the idea of combining qualitative and quantitative work has an aura of the exotic or even forbidden among criminologists today. Although one might expect that mixed quantitative–qualitative research designs might please both sides of the paradigm war, the opposite is more often the case. Hardcore advocates of either quantitative or qualitative paradigms variously dismiss mixed method research as being either "too soft" or "too positivistic," respectively. Mixed method research can therefore fall between two stools, and be difficult to place in academic journals, which are often wedded to one approach or the other.

This chapter, then, is intended to help make mixed method research more familiar and acceptable in criminology, and its simple inclusion in this Handbook is an important start. I first seek to define mixed method research and explain its purpose. In order to do this, one needs to distinguish between two types of research involved in this "mix" and explain what types of designs are included under the umbrella concept of mixed methods. I then outline some of the different types of mixed method research drawing on criminological examples. Finally, I conclude with a discussion of the major criticisms of mixed method research and attempt to briefly address these concerns.

DEFINING MIXED METHOD RESEARCH

The term "mixed method research" is used in various ways, and there are numerous, related concepts (some synonymous, others with slightly different meanings) such as "multi-method research," "mixed model research," and "mixed methodology" (see Johnson et al. 2007). Throughout this chapter, I will be using the term to refer to research that combines quantitative and qualitative research techniques and approaches into a single study (Johnson and Onwuegbuzie 2004) as in Creswell's (2003: 20) definition:

> [Mixed method research] employs strategies of inquiry that involve collecting data either simultaneously or sequentially to best understand research problems. The data collection also involves gathering both numeric information (e.g., on instruments) as well as text information (e.g., on interviews) so that the final database represents both quantitative and qualitative information (Creswell 2003: 20).

On the surface, this sounds rather clear-cut, but the definition is dependent upon some highly contested concepts (e.g., "qualitative" and "quantitative").

Distinguishing Quantitative from Qualitative

In practice, the alleged distinction between "quantitative" and "qualitative" research probably does not hold up (Bryman 1984; McLaughlin 1991). As Charles Ragin (1994: xii) argues, "All social researchers must deal with both words and quantities in some way," and it is difficult to imagine a piece of social science research that qualifies as a "pure" specimen of one type or the other. Nonetheless, in order to talk sensibly about "mixing" methods, I will need to employ the generally accepted understandings of "qualitative" and "quantitative" research in their ideal typical (or stereotypical) form.[1]

In standard criminology methods textbooks, qualitative research is defined in the following ways:

> Qualitative research is the application of observational techniques and/or the analysis of documents as the primary means of learning about persons or groups and their characteristics. Sometimes qualitative research is called fieldwork, referring to the immersion of researchers into the lives and worlds of those being studied (Champion 2000: 136).

> The phrase qualitative methodology refers in the broadest sense to research that produces descriptive data – people's own written and spoken words and observable behaviour (Taylor and Bogdan 1998: 6).

> Methods like participant observation, intensive interviewing, and focus groups that are designed to capture social life as participants experience it, rather than in categories predetermined by the researcher (Bachman and Schutt 2001: I–15).

> A qualitative approach. . . uses strategies of inquiry such as narratives, phenomenologies, ethnographies, grounded theory studies, or case studies. The researcher collects open-ended, emerging data with the primary intent of developing themes from the data (Creswell 2003).

According to these standard definitions, then, there could be said to be two core levels to this idea of qualitative methodology: (a) Data collection techniques that involve observation/participation, textual analysis, and/or open-ended interviewing; (b) An analysis involving the discovery of patterns in the textual, language-based data collected, frequently with phenomenological aims (i.e., capturing the perspectives and experiences of others with careful attention to their social context).

---

[1] I will also drop the quotation marks around the two words for clarity of presentation, although it should be remembered that the terms are being used to refer to fictional constructions.

Interestingly, it is more difficult to find a definition of quantitative research in the same sample of textbooks. When it is defined, definitions typically include the following:

> Quantitative research is the application of statistical procedures and techniques to data collected through surveys, including interviews and questionnaire administration. Quantitative interviewers are known as numbers-crunchers, since a wide variety of sophisticated statistical techniques exists to describe what they have found. By far the lion's share of articles in contemporary journals are quantitative (Champion 2000: 137).

> A quantitative approach is one in which the investigator primarily uses postpostivist claims for developing knowledge (i.e., cause and effect thinking, reduction to specific variables and hypotheses and questions, use of measurement and observation, and the test of theories), employs strategies of inquiry such as experiments and surveys, and collects data on predetermined instruments that yield statistical data (Creswell 2003: 18).

> Quantitative research refers to counts and measures of things (Berg and Lawrence 1998: 3).

> In quantitative research concepts are assigned numerical value.... This empirical orientation suggests that the same approach applicable to studying and explaining physical reality can be used in the social sciences (Hagan 1997: 14–15).

A review of these definitions suggests that so-called quantitative research usually involves the following two layers or levels: (a) Data collection from surveys or quantitative records (sometimes before-and-after some intervention as in an experimental or quasi-experimental design), (b) Analysis involving some sort of statistical analysis meant to test hypotheses in a manner similar to the physical sciences.

Methodology is, of course, about much more than mere data collection techniques (Rist 1977). To many, quantitative methods have also become synonymous with positivism, empiricism, or scientism; whereas, qualitative methods are frequently equated with interpretism, constructivism, phenomenology, or symobolic interactionism. The positivist epistemology, it is said (usually by those who do not share the position), holds that an objective reality exists that can be studied and examined (or at least approximated) objectively for law-like patterns similar to those found in the natural sciences (see Denzin and Lincoln 2005). Interpretivism, on the other hand, suggests that knowledge of the world is constituted only through people's experience of it, and therefore research should seek a contextualized understanding of the world from the point of view of the research subjects – empathic understanding rather than explanation, prediction, and control (Howe 1988). These epistemological differences in the nature of truth, reality, and the research enterprise are genuine and substantial. There may, in fact, be little common ground possible between the extreme versions of the two philosophical viewpoints (Burawoy 1998). Indeed, one advocate of interpretivism argues that "accommodation between paradigms is impossible. ... we are led to vastly diverse, disparate, and totally antithetical ends" (Guba 1990: 81).

It is possible, however, to decouple the technical differences in methodological strategies from the philosophical/epistemological assumptions that may be associated with them (Morgan 2007). Throughout this chapter, I will be using the terms "method" or "qualitative/quantitative" to refer to ways of gathering and analyzing information – the collection/analysis techniques or tools (as in the textbook definitions above), not their epistemological justifications. This decoupling of philosophy and method is not as radical as it sounds. After all, there are symbolic interactionists with phenomenological epistemologies who are perfectly comfortable utilizing quantitative methodology – including students of George Herbert Mead like Cottrell (1971) (for a discussion, see esp. Matsueda 2006). Likewise, there is a long tradition of logical positivists (or those who make the same assumptions as those labeled "positivists") employing qualitative techniques to data gathering and analysis. One of positivist sociology's great champions, Emile Durkheim utilized qualitative, anthropological findings in most of his research.

So, there is a strong correlation between epistemology and technique, but it is nothing like 100%. Denzin and Lincoln (2005: 6) write: "Qualitative research is difficult to define clearly. It has no theory or paradigm that is distinctly its own." Therefore, it is perfectly legitimate to consider the two separately as the approach here is (see Snizek 1976). Before moving on to technical issues, however, I briefly address the issue of epistemology in the section below on the rationale behind mixed method research.

The Justification for Mixed Method Research

Mixed method research, almost by definition, is more time-consuming, difficult, and complex than monomethodological studies. It can produce unwieldy findings – involving both qualitative and quantitative analyses – that are ill-suited for the standard 8,000-word limits in many criminological journals. As such, one needs a fairly compelling reason to engage in such an effort.

For most mixed method practitioners this justification is a commitment to data quality (or measurement validity) and fidelity to the phenomenon under study. Greene and colleagues (1989), for instance, outline five primary purposes of mixed method research:

(a) Triangulation: Convergence or corroboration of results via different methods.
(b) Complementarity: Elaboration, enhancement, or clarification of the results of one method through the use of another.
(c) Initiation: Seeking out contradictory findings that could help reframe the research question or model.
(d) Development: Using the findings from one type of research to inform another.
(e) Expansion: Expanding the range or breadth of the research through multiple methods.

Johnson and Turner (2003: 299) define the "fundamental principle of mixed method research" more concisely:

> *Methods should be mixed in a way that has complementary strengths and nonoverlapping weaknesses.* ... It involves the recognition that all methods have their limitations as well as their strengths. The fundamental principle is followed for at least three reasons: (a) to obtain convergence or corroboration of findings, (b) to eliminate or minimize key plausible alternative explanations for conclusions drawn from the research data, and (c) to elucidate the divergent aspects of a phenomenon (emphasis in original; see also Brewer and Hunter 1989).

To mixed methods researchers, the complementary strengths (and weaknesses) of qualitative and quantitative research are obvious. Qualitative methods involve "deep" immersion into a social scene that allows for an awareness of situational and contextual factors and concerns that are often missed in survey research. They produce "rich," "holistic" data, as opposed to the focus on "variables" (Blumer 1956), allowing for a great deal of information about very small number of cases (Ragin 1994). The research is based on the participants' own categories of meaning and captures this insider's viewpoint or "emic" (Johnson and Onwuegbuzie 2004). Qualitative research is exploratory, allowing for the discovery of new and unexpected social patterns and produces theory that is "grounded," with refutable hypotheses. In its published form, qualitative analysis provides vivid illustration of phenomena, bringing social processes "to life" for readers. Quantitative research does little of this, but has considerable strengths precisely where qualitative research is weak. Quantitative methods are transparent and do not rely on a "take my word for it" approach. This work is therefore more replicable, precise (some would say "objective"), and generalizable than qualitative research. Additionally, statistical techniques allow for the eliminating of confounding influences and better assess cause and effect relationships among variables. In published form, they produce findings that are notable for their clarity, succinctness, exactitude, and parsimony.

Mixed method research, then, requires no strict adherence to any particular epistemology. For instance, Howe (2004) argues in favor of what he calls "mixed method interpretivism" – a response to the dominant "mixed method experimentalism" (or positivist and postpositivist mixed method research), indicating that mixed method research can serve either "master" (narrative). Yet, most commonly, mixed method research is premised on neither interpretivism nor positivism, but rather the tradition of Pragmatism in social science associated with John Dewey, William James, Ludwig Wittgenstein, and Charles Sanders Pierce, among others. The Pragmatic tradition is assuredly consequence-oriented, problem-centered, and pluralistic in its approach and would reject the strict dualism of the moribund positivist–interpretivist split (Morgan 2007).

Most mixed method researchers are pragmatists with a small-"p" as well. That is, as workaday researchers, they "rarely have either the time or the inclination to assess what they do in philosophical terms" (Guba and Lincoln 1994: 117). Instead, they base their method-ological choices on the research question at hand "not on ideological commitments to one methodological paradigm or another" (Hammersley 1992: 163). For instance, Lofland and Lofland (1995) outline an impressive range of common research questions and suggest that some are better suited to quantitative research (e.g., "What is its size, strength or intensity?" or "What does it come to affect") and others more suited to qualitative research (e.g., "What are its defining features and varieties?" or "How does it operate?"). No question is seen as more important or worthy than another. Finding the "right" research question (and hence method-ological tool) is a matter of engaging with the existing literature and identifying gaps (Bayley 1978; McElrath 2001). This pragmatic dictum that problems should determine methods, not the other way around, is at the core of the mixed method approach to research.

VARIETIES OF MIXED METHOD RESEARCH

Bryman (2007) interviewed a sample of 20 UK-based social scientists who have published mixed method research and asked each to name an exemplary piece of mixed method research (presumably besides their own). He found that "virtually all" of the interviewees struggled to think of an answer. Were the same qualitative survey taken of a random sample of 20 US-based criminologists, the results would have likely differed considerably, as almost all would mention John Laub and Robert Sampson's pioneering research in this regard (Sampson and Laub 1993; Laub and Sampson 2003). Still, it is fair to assume that, beyond this ground-breaking study, examples would not come easily to most in the field.[2] This chapter, then,

---

[2] Research by Giordano et al. (2002) might be the second best-known work outside of classics like Short and Strodt-beck (1965). As Giordano's work covers similar terrain to that of Laub and Sampson, this raises the interesting question of why research on desistance from crime might be so well suited to mixed method designs (see also Burnett 2004; Farrall 2002; Maruna 2001). The answer might have something to do with the ongoing debate in that area of study regarding the relationship between subjective and objective (or cognitive and structural) changes in the desistance process (see LeBel et al. 2008).

is intended to provide some brief examples of the possibilities in mixed method research designs that are available to researchers. Some of these examples will be drawn from my own research – not because it is particularly exemplary, but simply because these examples come easily. The number of criminological examples utilizing methods such as content analysis and systematic social observations are simply too many and too rich to list in any comprehensive way here.

Methodologists have identified a wide variety of different types of mixed method research from Mayring's (2007) four types ("pre-study model," "generalization model," "enhancement model," and "triangulation model") to Tashakkori and Teddlie's (2003) nine different combinations. Although these typologies usefully seek to be comprehensive and delimit the entire range of mixed method combination possibilities, there are probably too many variations to try to keep straight or to be of much use to beginning researchers. Below, I will draw on a more parsimonious typology from my own review of this research and theory involving "sequential qual–quant designs," "sequential quant–qual designs," and "hybrid models."

Sequential Designs

Sequential designs are those in which the analysis of one type of data provides a basis for the collection of another type of data (Tashakkori and Teddlie 2003). The classic combination here involves following an exploratory qualitative investigation with a quantitative examination of the hypotheses generated. In such designs, qualitative research is considered a form of reconnaissance or "voyage of discovery" that can provide "leads" or grounded hypotheses that can then be confirmed, rejected, or qualified through quantitative testing. Mayring (2007) provides an example of this approach. He and his colleagues were interested in the construct of "coolness" among adolescents. As the concept was largely unexplored in the existing literature, they utilized a grounded theory approach involving open-ended interviews and discussions with young people about what this thing called "cool" was about. Once a theory was constructed from this exploratory research, the authors then sought to operationalize it and test it in a questionnaire study with 223 secondary school students, analyzed using LISREL.

Some advocates of qualitative research reject these designs as essentially putting the qualitative research in a subservient or auxiliary role to the quantitative: Qualitative is fine for pretest messing about, but when it is time to do the serious research, one should bring out the survey numbers. Yet, it is not immediately obvious why this should be so. Lofland (1971: 6), in fact, reverses this hierarchy, pointing out that it is the qualitative work that gets the credit for the important discoveries, the quantitative merely provides a sort of back-up: "Quantitative studies serve primarily to firm up and modify knowledge first gained in a fundamentally qualitative fashion."

Sequential research can work in the opposite fashion as well. A qualitative analysis can be used to add meaning, clarification, or illustration to a quantitative study in the same way that numbers can be used to add precision to narrative (Johnson and Onwuegbuzie 2004). For instance, Weisburd and Waring (2001) triangulate the findings from their quantitative study of white collar criminal careers with a qualitative analysis of presentence investigations for such offences. This process is described as "adding qualitative profundity to quantitative findings" (Huber 2007: 179) or more often as "humanizing" findings or bringing them "to life."

An example of this sort of design can be found in a recent study of public opinion regarding criminal justice issues in England I completed with my colleague Anna King (see Maruna and King 2004, 2009). The research began in the traditional way for public opinion research with a postal sample of randomly selected members of the British public ($n = 940$). These data were quantitatively analyzed for predictors of punitive views regarding the punishment of offenders that produced a number of interesting correlations, but raised more questions than it answered. Some of these issues were then addressed systematically in a qualitative phase of the study. The researchers sat down with 40 of the respondents to the initial survey: 20 of whom were among the most punitive in their responses to the survey, and 20 of whom were among the least punitive. Members of the two groups were chosen in an effort to insure a balance in terms of gender, geographical location, education, and other social factors thought to be associated with punitiveness. At the interviews, respondents were asked to elaborate on why they answered the survey questions in the way they did, what they "meant" by their responses, and various themes that had emerged as (statistically) significant in the quantitative analysis were probed further. In the end, the qualitative analysis did not just illustrate the findings from the survey, but rather clarified, elaborated upon, and enhanced the initial findings.

Hybrid Models

For mixed method purists, sequential designs like those outlined above certainly qualify as "triangulation," but really involve not one, but two simultaneous studies looking at the same research question. A more authentic version of mixed method research instead involves the combination of different methodological approaches at different stages of the research process for a single study. The most common example of this hybrid design is the quantification or "quantitizing" (Miles and Huberman 1984) of qualitative data.[3] These models begin with qualitative data collection techniques (e.g., ethnographic observation, open-ended interviews, documentary analysis of diaries, speeches, letters, and so forth), but analyze the data both qualitatively and quantitatively simultaneously.

CONTENT ANALYSIS.   The most common qual–quant hybrid design is probably content analysis, understood as a systematic, replicable process for compressing passages of text (or other symbols) into fewer content categories based on explicit rules of coding (Krippendorff 2004; Stemler 2001). The data for content analysis can be almost anything: political speeches by historical figures, internet chatter on discussion groups, police reports, published autobiographies, open-ended interview transcripts, presentence reports, prisoner letters – even rap lyrics (Diamond, Bermudez and Schensul 2006), political debates (Wheelock and Hartmann 2007), or televised wrestling matches (Woo and Kim 2003). The content coding can take many forms. Frequently, content analysis refers to a purely qualitative process, whereby long passages of text are sorted into smaller, more manageable thorough categories for internal qualitative analysis. Although this process can take on the shape of quantitative research, as in the "crosstabulation of qualitative themes" (Alasuutari 1995), numbers need not be involved.

---

[3] The reverse process, "qualitizing" quantitative data, is less common but is a possibility as well (see Tashakorri and Teddlie 1998). Here, presumably, the data collected is quantitative in nature (e.g., survey research), but the analysis treats these data both categorically and numerically.

At the other end of the spectrum, other forms of content analysis avoid qualitative analysis entirely and involve only word count frequencies utilizing sophisticated software. In systematically analyzing hundreds of transcripts from hospital patients, Pennebaker (2003), for instance, has found that successful recovery is associated with decreases in the use of first-person pronouns and increases in the use of causal words such as "because" and "effect." Both types of research have produced useful findings, and indeed could complement one another. That is, the same data (e.g., interview narratives) could be interrogated hermeneutically or inductively as well through a word-count analysis.

Most content analysis research, however, is pitched somewhere between these two extremes and seeks to measure the *thematic* content of qualitative materials, for example, coding for definitions favorable to crime, neutralization techniques, or attachments to informal social controls in the self-narratives of interviewees. Thematic content analysis involves "coding" or "scoring" textual material for manifest (or less often, latent) content or ideas. Some of this research draws on existing content dictionaries, and a huge number of well-validated coding schemes and content dictionaries already exist that can be utilized in this coding (see esp. Smith 1992). Other researchers create content categories de novo from the inductive analysis of qualitative materials – a process facilitated by various qualitative software packages – in order to preserve the spirit of grounded theory exploration. Other researchers combine both deductive and inductive content analysis. Once a content dictionary is established for the analysis, multiple, independent raters can be employed in the assigning of qualitative content to the selected categories or measures, and tests of inter-rater reliability can provide a sense of how replicable the methodology is.

An example of such a design can be found in my research on the self-narratives of former prisoners (Maruna 2001, 2004). A recurring theme in offender rehabilitation theory and practice is that offenders too frequently externalize or neutralize blame for their wrong-doing and need to be taught to accept responsibility for their actions in order to go straight. This belief is so widely shared among rehabilitation practitioners to be almost sacred, but appeared to be based on little or no firm research evidence. As such, I was interested in exploring the relationship between attributions of responsibility and criminality in a content analysis, with a unique sample of life story interview transcripts I had collected in working with desisting and persisting ex-offenders (Maruna 2001).

Over half of the interviewees in the study had been classified as desisting from crime, whereas the other participants self-reported on-going and active involvement in criminal pursuits. The two groups were matched case by case on a variety of background factors thought to be associated with desistance from crime. Their transcripts were content analyzed using Peterson et al.'s (1992) CAVE (Content Analysis of Verbatim Explanations) system. Based on Seligman's theory of explanatory styles, CAVE is an innovative and well-established method for measuring the cross-event consistency in the explanations that individuals provide for both positive and negative events in their lives. The CAVE system has been used in studies of depression, precursors of mental illness, and the success of presidential candidates. This previous research provides strong support for the construct validity of the CAVE technique, and coders trained by the system's authors have been able to achieve inter-rater reliability levels exceeding 0.90 (Peterson et al. 1992: 386). The coding scheme allows for the examination of the three key dimensions of causal explanations (internality–externality; stability–instability; and globality–specificity), within the everyday language and actual life stories of individuals.

Although pencil-and-paper questionnaires have also been designed to gauge these dimensions of explanatory style, narrative methodologies have certain advantages over more tightly structured questionnaire measures (Emmons 1999: 63). In particular, narrative analysis allows for a contextualization of these themes that is quite difficult to accomplish with standard screening instruments. "Idiographic research shifts attention away from abstract psychological variables and reorients it toward the lives of individuals" (Peterson 1992: 377). Further, the systematic content analysis of verbal material has the advantage of eliciting more spontaneous and less artificial responses than self-report questionnaires (Harvey et al. 1990). As such, Peterson (1992: 379) describes content analysis as a "particularly good assessment strategy, not a 'second-best' procedure" for assessing attributions and cognitive style.

> "The circumstances under which causal explanations are made without prompting are precisely those under which subjects are most likely to be mindful and thus most apt not to respond glibly or automatically as they might on a questionnaire" (ibid).

Nonetheless, the use of content analysis introduces numerous reliability problems, stemming from the multiple interpretations of subjective materials. As such, significant measures were taken in this analysis to protect against bias in the coding process. Two graduate students, blind to the hypotheses of this research, were trained in Peterson's method for extracting attributions from transcribed interview material (see Peterson et al. 1992: 383–386). Then, two different graduate students, also blind to the hypotheses of this research, coded the explanations using Peterson's content coding scheme. Because of the precautions taken in randomizing the presentation of these anonymous passages, raters were not biased by previous ratings for the same subject and would have no way of easily connecting any series of passages. Most importantly, coders had no way of knowing whether the speaker of any particular passage was an active offender or a desisting ex-offender from the information they were given. Coders rated each extracted attribution on three dimensions (internal, stable, and global) using a scale of 1 to 7, with a 7 representing the highest possible score. In all, over 1,250 separate attributions, an average of slightly more than 14 in each of the 89 interviews, were extracted and then double-coded by separate raters on all of the six key dimensions of explanatory style. This was a painstaking and highly labor-intensive process. In a measure of agreement, the two independent scorers achieved a correlation of 0.79 in their coding of these extractions. Discrepancies between raters on a particular item were worked out in a conference between the two raters and the author.

The findings, available in Maruna (2004), confirmed the earlier qualitative findings presented in Maruna (2001) and challenged some taken-for-granted assumptions in rehabilitation research.

SYSTEMATIC SOCIAL OBSERVATION. A second variety of qual–quant hybridization is the practice of systematic social observation, combining the quintessentially qualitative data collection method of ethnographic observation of field sites with sophisticated quantitative data analysis through a process of content coding similar to that of content analysis (see Mastrofski, this volume). Quantifying observational data in social science is nothing new. Some of the best known studies in the ethnographic tradition (e.g., Becker et al. 1961) have involved at least rudimentary quantification (counts, percentages, frequencies of various occurrences), and laboratory-based research (in the hard sciences as well as the social sciences) involves the systematic recording and coding of various observations. Yet, the criminologist Al Reiss (1971) is often credited with developing systematic social observation research in the early 1970s. Although the method has been "underappreciated" in recent years (Sampson and Raudenbush 1999), criminology has had a special relationship with the method ever since (see e.g., Mastrofski et al. 1995; Mazerolle et al. 1998; Taylor et al. 1985). Sampson and Raudenbush (1999) write: "In the spirit of the early Chicago school of urban sociology, we believe that direct observation is fundamental to the advancement of knowledge" (p. 606).

The potential of the method for urban studies of crime and deviance can be clearly seen in recent work by Weisburd and colleagues (2006). The researchers were interested in the question of crime "displacement" or the idea that the focusing of police resources on crime "hot spots" simply caused the criminal activity to "move around the corner" – an argument that has been made many times, but rarely tested due to the measurement problems. To rectify this situation, Weisburd and colleagues chose two areas in Jersey City, New Jersey, with high concentrations of drug crime and street-level prostitution, where intensive police interventions were being targeted, as well as two additional, neighboring areas with no equivalent police targeting. Trained observers in each neighborhood conducted more than 6,000 20-min social observations during the study period, supplemented by interviews and ethnographic field observations. The observers recorded events only on their assigned street segments (from one street corner to the next) during nine waves of social observations (one before, six during, and two after the policing intervention). Each wave was conducted over a 7-day period. These observations were then triangulated with the work of Regina Brisgone (2004), an experienced ethnographer from Rutgers University, who produced an independent report on street-level activities that played a crucial role in interpreting the quantitative findings from the observational study.

Similar methods are routinely utilized in research on police–community interactions. In so-called "ride-along studies" (e.g., Mastrofski, Worden and Snipes 1995), observers accompany police officers on their daily rounds and keep records of their interaction styles and behaviors that are later coded and quantitatively analyzed. In one such study, for instance, trained observers accompanied randomly selected police officers on 132 8-h shifts in Savannah, Georgia, to explore the question of racial bias in the determination of "suspicious" behavior (Alpert, MacDonald and Dunham 2005). Observers were trained to document the officers' interactions with citizens and a formal instrument was developed to "capture what officers were thinking and feeling" when they made decisions to stop and question individuals.

The most elaborate and sophisticated example of "ride-along" observational research in recent decades, however, is surely the Chicago neighborhood studies described by Sampson and Raudenbush (1999). For 5 months in 1995, two observers for the research project took notes of what they saw while riding in a sport utility vehicle (SUV) crawling at 5 miles per hour down every street in 196 Chicago census tracts (covering 23,815 face blocks in total). The observers, sitting each on one side of the SUV, recorded their observations of a variety of social and physical clues to neighborhood disorder and community activity, and added subjective commentary about unusual events. They were accompanied, again on each side of the SUV, by colleagues trained to take video footage of the same city scenes. The videos were coded for 126 variables measuring physical conditions, housing characteristics, business activities, and social interactions on the city streets, and the data were analyzed with tools found useful in psychometrics. The results of Sampson and Raudenbush's three-level hierarchical regression model represent an important challenge and modification of reigning ideas about disorder and "broken windows" in criminology – all the while utilizing data that "provides the sights, sounds and feels of the streets" (p. 641).

Systematic social observation has also been utilized in the courtroom as in Peter Blanck's (1987; Blanck et al. 1985) examination of judges' influence over juror decision-making. Concerned with the lack of external and ecological validity of much courtroom research (based on undergraduate students in a laboratory setting), Blanck and colleagues (1985: 107) sought to combine the "greater external validity of the observartional and field-like studies of the courtroom" with the "greater precision of the laboratory-like studies involving ratings of verbal and nonverbal behavior." They were fortunate enough to find a group of "forward-looking" California state court judges willing to allow a team of researchers into the courtrooms for systematic observations. Researchers made observations during the proceedings and took ethnographic field notes on the courtroom culture and the physical differences of each courtroom in the study. These data were triangulated with open-ended qualitative interviews and surveys with jury members. The holistic case studies produced a variety of mixed method data on courtroom culture, personal characteristics of jurors and judges, subjective views of jurors and judges, and recorded behaviors of both.

In addition, the judges in the study allowed Blanck's team to install cameras into the courtroom focused directly on the trial judge from the same angle that she/he would have been perceived by a member of the jury. The analysis involved a group of raters trained to assess the video and audio tapes for a variety of verbal and nonverbal cues from the judges' statements to the jury (e.g., warmth in tone of voice). The findings suggested that the judges were unintentionally "leaking" or signaling their views and assumptions about the case in measurable ways and that these cues had predictable influences on trial outcomes. Blanck (1987) concluded that "Only by studying judges while they presided over actual trials could we both describe judicial behavior" and that "field research – when well conducted – can employ many of the procedural safeguards associated with high internal validity (. . . precision of measurement), while yielding externally or ecologically valid results" (p. 339).

Clinical criminology is another area where mixed method research has flourished. Many clinical assessment tools with criminal justice populations involve both closed-item survey questions as well as open-ended clinical interviews that are then content coded and tested for interrater reliability (see e.g., Viljoen et al. 2006). Additionally, therapist behavior styles are often observed and coded by trained raters watching video tapes or actual therapeutic delivery styles (see e.g., Miller et al. 1993). Research using these techniques has been instrumental in classroom and business settings in demonstrating effects similar to the ones identified by Blanck in his colleagues on student and employee performance (Rosenthal 2003).

Finally, there is a long history of mixed method research in violence research, in particular (see e.g., Felson and Steadman 1983; Toch 1992), as understanding the micro-dynamics of aggression is facilitated through both observation as well as rigorous cause-and-effect analysis. Frequently, such analyses involve the content coding of crime scene narratives, as in Terance Miethe's use of Qualitative Comparative Analysis of homicide files (see e.g., Miethe and Drass 1999). Others go further afield, drawing on photographic evidence of riots, video footage of sports brawls, and the first-hand accounts of participants, as in Randall Collins (2008) important new book *Violence*. In one analysis in that work (pp. 202–204), Collins draws on an original qualitative dataset of 89 first-hand observations of violence-threatening confrontations (15 he observed first-hand, 74 based on student–observer reports) using a mixed methods approach. Collins and his students coded the field notes on factors such as whether onlookers were cheering, mixed, neutral, or uneasy/fearful, and the severity of the subsequent violence. Presenting these findings in a cross-tabular format (p. 203), Collins demonstrates empirically his grounded, inductive theory that violence is a largely staged affair with crowds playing a central role (Almost 90% of flights involving crowd cheering ending in serious violence, whereas 57% of fights in which the crowd was uneasy/fearful were aborted before anyone was hurt).

WHY GO BOTH WAYS?

The sections above focus, appropriately enough, on the strengths of mixed method research and what it has and can contribute to criminological research. For balance, in this concluding section, I contend with some of the criticisms and problems this sort of research has faced. These entail both practical failings of the research as well as theoretical/epistemological critiques. Most of these criticisms come from advocates of "pure" qualitative research, although monomethodological myopia is by no means limited to this camp. Finally, although many of these arguments are perfectly reasonable, I end by briefly attempting to respond to both with a plea for peace in the paradigm wars.

The mixed method movement has been justifiably criticized for overemphasizing technical comprehensiveness at the expense of substantive findings. Baskin (2002: 225) writes:

> Triangulation in criminological research has become increasingly common. As teachers of research methods, we begin the socialization toward triangulation early in our students' careers. Textbooks in research methods assist us by advising students that the utilization of more than one research method is optimal. ... The emphasis on technique and not on substance has left many with the impression that more is better. Thus, we have been treated to more research that uses more techniques but that produces fewer useful findings.

As a relatively "new" and exotic methodological approach, it is certainly a risk that the "mixing" becomes the central focus in mixed method designs, and researchers might lose sight of the fact that this strategy is simply a tool for getting at the real subject matter at hand. This should improve over time as the novelty of mixing methods wears off.

Another criticism of mixed method research is that it often sounds good in theory, but in practice does not live up to the hype. For instance, in an examination of 57 mixed method evaluations, Greene et al. (1989) found that only about half of the studies actually integrated findings from the two types of research. Because qualitative and quantitative researches have such different strengths and weaknesses, researchers can set off with high hopes of achieving triangulation, but instead wind up with two, quite different studies on very different aspects of a related topic. Ideally, the studies will complement each other or raise questions that can be addressed by the other wave of research. Yet, this sort of communication can be difficult, however, when the "language" of the two research types is so different.

This last point invokes an epistemological critique of mixed method research, the so-called "incompatibility thesis." This is the idea that qualitative methods and quantitative methods simply cannot be mixed because they are founded upon such contrasting, indeed conflicting, epistemological assumptions (Guba 1990; Guba and Lincoln 1994). I discuss this point in my last paragraph of chapters in depth. But, some critics legitimately see mixed method designs as a "Trojan horse for positivism" (Giddings and Grant 2007), arguing that too often the marriage of qual with quant is an imbalanced one with the qualitative work acting as mere window-dressing to what is obviously a variable-oriented, quantitative approach. It is true that too often mixeds method are utilized for purely opportunistic reasons. Hanson (2008) argues that "In [the] fight to gain credibility, and the financial and status rewards that go with it, qualitative methods have often been forced to maintain a defensive position," whereby quantification is added to a research study primarily "for status within the discipline and the attraction of research funding." As quantitative research currently holds a privileged position within US criminology (arguably the opposite is true in British and some European versions of criminology), it makes perfect sense that qualitative researchers would seek to imitate or mimic quantitative research for careerist purposes and to reach a wider audience

(DiCristina 1995). This is surely antithetical to the pragmatic motivations behind the mixed method movement though. It is hoped that as mixed method research matures, there will be greater parity of esteem for the two methodological paradigms and therefore this sort of pressure to mix methods for the wrong reasons would be reduced.

Finally, the most commonly heard critique is that quantification devalues qualitative data, reifies it, and diminishes its value. DiChristina (1995: 72) poignantly asks, "Imagine your favorite movie, a novel by Dostoevsky, or perhaps your life story being represented by a matrix of numbers. Would anything be lost?" Miller (2008) raises similar criticisms of mixed method in her essay on "The status of qualitative research in criminology" prepared for a National Science Foundation conference. Miller describes one mixed method study on the topic of desistance from crime (which shall remain anonymous in order to protect the innocent) as being "strongly influenced by positivist models":

> His discussion focuses on the use of blind coding by multiple coders (to achieve interrater reliability) of 'episodes or phrases that were extracted from the body of the larger text' (p. 170) so that the coders had no information about the broader context of the interview. These pieces of text were then applied to 'well validated' (p. 169) *a priori* coding schemes (Miller 2008: 4).

Miller argues that although the "analysis strategy was well received by quantitative scholars in criminology," it "raises vexing questions about the disciplinary push to inscribe such analytic strategies to a methodological approach whose strengths include inductive theory development and detailed attention to context, including the context of speech within the interview process" (p. 4).

DiCristina and Miller are of course absolutely right. Narrative material is rich in context, nuance, meaning, and implicit subtext. It is intended to provide research participants with a "voice" and dignifies their particular perspectives. Listen to the following excerpt from a 30-year-old, male, former prisoner from the desistance study that Miller critiqued:

> But um, all through this, all through the beatings and stuff I used to approach teachers, um, and nobody ever believed me that this was happening. Um, and I went to the Vicar once, the local Priest and nothing happened. They just all said I was a liar and stuff. I remember one day, um, (my stepfather) tried to beat me up, but he was really drunk and I'd curled up in a ball in the corner. The only piece of me that was available was the right side of me leg, and he just kicked it for about half an hour. And, er, I was in school the next day, I could hardly walk. And, I kept having to go the toilet and take me trousers down,'cause I had, er, what they call a blood bruise, where the blood's seeping through the skin, from me knee to me hip. And, me trousers kept sticking to it, so I had to keep going and wiping it with this piece of toilet paper in the toilets. And, um, one of the teachers found me, and I told them that me step-dad had done this to me. And, I remember I always used to think that "Something would get done now – they'll either take me away or take him away." But nothing, ever. I feel a bit envious now, of you know, the way social workers behave now, the way they're quite intrusive into families, and I sometimes wish like, that somebody would have done that with me. I might not have gone down the road I went down (Maruna 2001: 59–60).

How could anyone take such a remarkably revealing and honest passage and transform it into a "9" on a measure of "resentment of authority" or a "2.4" on a scale of "sense of personal agency"? Such reductionism is practically criminal in its stupidity and certainly pointless. If all one was after was a 9 or a 2.4, there are much easier ways to get it!

Yet, this is not what mixed method research does. Like most mixed method studies, the study Miller describes *did* involve inductive theory development utilizing entire, fully contextualized transcripts of interviewees that the researcher got to know personally over a series of meetings in their homes (in most cases). The narratives collected were read and re-read in their entirety, by the same person who asked the interview questions, and who experienced the full social and interactional context of the interview. Indeed, this inductive analysis is a central feature of the work. The quantification was intended to complement and supplement this qualitative analysis, providing the researcher with a sense of confidence that the patterns being observed are valid and reliable.

Of course, the quantification represents a simplification of this incredibly rich, personal material, but that is what it is supposed to be. Transforming complicated (sometimes eloquent, sometimes convoluted) qualitative material into clear, concise content codes makes the data far more manageable and the data analysis, frankly, much easier than pure qualitative analysis.[4] True, it does this through a process of data condensing (Ragin 1994) or, less charitably, reductionism. But, then, the same could be said for grounded theory – what is social science, after all, except an attempt to transform the messy complexity of lived reality into concise, parsimonious (and by nature imperfect) explanations. In his defense of mixed method research, Howe (1988) addresses this concern eloquently:

> One view seems to be quantifying over an ontologically qualitative concept objectifies it and divests it of its ontologically qualitative dimensions, that is, divests it of its value-laden and intentional dimensions. But by what sort of magic does this divestiture occur? Does changing from a pass-fail to an A–F grading scale, for instance, imply that some new, ontologically different, performance is being described and evaluated? If not, then why should the case be different when researchers move from speaking of things like critical thinking skills and cooperativeness in terms of present and absent, high and low, or good and bad to speaking of them in terms of 0–100?

Like many wars, the methodological paradigm wars in criminology (and throughout the social sciences) may be based primarily on misunderstandings of what each side is really about. Quantitative researchers are often dismissive and condescending about qualitative research (see esp. McElrath 2001). Likewise, qualitative researchers can spend a great deal of time criticizing quantitative research. Hanson (2008), in fact, argues that qualitative sociologists "may have spent more time defining quantitative methods than quantitative scholars have themselves" (see also Bryman 1984: 104). She sees this as being "analogous to the process of social construction of the Other" (p. 97) or "defining something unlike oneself in order to demarcate or reinforce one's own position" (p. 104).

Perhaps the greatest strength of mixing methods in research, then, is its ability to break down these barriers. The mixed method researcher gains great appreciation for what both sorts of methods can bring to an investigation and how much the (allegedly) different sets of strategies really have in common. Such work, then, draws on the entire body of criminological research and theory far better than monomethodological approaches can.

My prediction is that the future of criminological research (like its past) will be far more open and encouraging to mixed method research designs. Indeed, the very idea of "mixed methods" research as a special category of work – or indeed the idea of "pure" quantitative or "pure" qualitative" research – may be seen as an anachronistic oddity of a peculiar moment in the development of the social sciences. That is, when the generation that fought the "qual vs. quant" paradigm wars of the late twentieth century passes into retirement, I imagine that few of their successors will likely remember or understand what the fighting was all about. By then, perhaps all criminological research will be understood as involving "mixed methodology."

---

[4] The finding that qualitative analysis is more difficult than quantitative analyses (see e.g., Becker, 1996) is ironic considering the presumption of some quantitative practitioners that people who do qualitative research are less intelligent or otherwise inferior researchers (see McElrath, 2001, for a very honest 'confession' in this regard).

REFERENCES

Alasuutari P (1995) Beyond the qualitative-quantitative distinction: crosstabulation in qualitative research. Int J Contemp Sociol 2:251–268

Alpert G, MacDonald J, Dunham R (2005) Police suspicion and discretionary decision making during citizen stops. Criminology 43:407–434

Bachman R, Schutt RK (2001) The practice of research in criminology and criminal justice. Pine Forge, Thousand Oaks, CA

Baskin D (2002) Book review: Robert R. Weidner 'I Won't Do Manhattan': causes and consequences of a decline in street prostitution. Criminol Crim Justice 2:225–226

Bayley D (1978) Comment: perspectives on criminal justice research. J Crim Justice 6:287–298

Becker HS, Geer B, Hughes EC, Strauss A (1961) Boys in white. Chicago: University of Chicago Press

Becker HS (1996) The epistemology of qualitative research. In: Jessor R, Colby A, Shweder RA (eds) Ethnography and human development: context and meaning in social inquiry. University of Chicago, Chicago, 53–71

Berg BL, Lawrence B (1998) Qualitative research methods for the social sciences. Allyn and Bacon, Boston

Blanck PD (1987) The "process" of field research in the courtroom: a descriptive analysis. Law Hum Behav 11: 337–358

Blanck PD, Rosenthal R, Cordell LH (1985) The appearance of justice: Judges' verbal and nonverbal behavior in criminal jury trials. Stanford Law Rev 38:89–136, 157–158

Blumer H (1956) Sociolgocial analysis and the "variable". Am Sociol Rev 21(6):683–690

Brewer J, Hunter A (1989) Multimethod research: a synthesis of style. Sage, Newbury Park, CA

Bryman A (1984) The debate about quantitative and qualitative research: a question of method on epistemology? Br J Sociol 35(1):75–92

Bryman A (2007) Barriers to integrating quantitative and qualitative research. J Mixed Methods Res 1(1):8

Burawoy M (1998) The extended case method. Sociol Theory 16(1):4–33

Burnett R (2004) To re-offend or not to re-offend? The ambivalence of convicted property offenders. In: Maruna S, Immarigeon R (eds) After crime and punishment: pathways to desistance from crime. Willan, Cullompton, UK

Campbell DT (1984) Foreword to R. K. Yin's Case study research: Design and methods. Sage, Thousand Oaks, CA

Campbell DT, Fiske DW (1959) Convergent and discriminant validation by the multitrait-multimethod matrix. Psychol Bull 56(2):81–105

Champion DJ (2000) Research methods for criminal justice and criminology, 2nd Edition. Regents/Prentice Hall, Englewood Cliffs, NJ

Collins R (2008) Violence: a micro-sociological theory. Princeton University Press, Princeton

Cottrell LS (1971) Covert behavior in interpersonal interaction. Proc Am Philos Soc 115(6):462–469

Creswell JW (2003) Research design: qualitative, quantitative, and mixed method approaches. Sage, Thousand Oaks, CA

Denzin N (1970) The research act. Chicago, Aldine

Denzin NK, Lincoln YS (2005) Introduction: the discipline and practice of qualitative research. Handbook of qualitative research. Sage, Thousand Oaks, CA, pp 1–28

Diamond S, Bermudez R, Schensul J (2006) What's the rap about ecstasy? Popular music lyrics and drug trends among American youth. J Adolesc Res 21(3):269–298

DiCristina B (1995) Method in criminology: a philosophical primer. Harrow and Heston, Albany, NY

Emmons R (1999) The psychology of ultimate concerns. Guilford, New York

Farrall S (2002) Rethinking what works with offenders. Willan, Cullompton, UK

Felson R, Steadman H (1983) Situational factors in disputes leading to criminal violence. Criminology 21:59–74

Festinger L, Riecken HW, Schachter S (1956) When prophecy fails. University of Minnesota Press, Minneapolis, MN

Fielding NG, Fielding JL (1986) Linking data: the articulation of qualitative and quantitative methods in social research. Sage, Beverly Hills, CA

Giddings LS, Grant BM (2007) A trojan horse for positivism?: a critique of mixed methods research. ANS Adv Nurs Sci 30(1):52

Giordano PC, Cernkovich SA, Rudolph JL (2002) Gender, crime and desistance: toward a theory of cognitive transformation. Am J Sociol 107:990–1064

Greene JC, Caracelli VJ, Graham WF (1989) Toward a conceptual framework for mixed-method evaluation designs. Educa Eval Policy Anal 11(3):255–274

Guba EG (1990) The alternative paradigm dialog. In: Guba EG (ed) The paradigm dialog. Sage, Thousand Oaks, CA, pp 17–27

Guba EG, Lincoln YS (1994) Competing paradigms in qualitative research. In: Denzin NK, Lincoln YS (eds) Handbook of qualitative research. Sage, London, pp 105–117

Hagan FE (1997) Research Methods in Criminal Justice and Criminology (4th ed.). Boston, MA: Allyn and Bacon

Hanson B (2008) Wither qualitative/quantitative?: grounds for methodological convergence. Qual Quant 42(1): 97–111

Harvey JH, Weber AL, Orbuch TL (1990) Interpersonal accounts: a social psychological perspective. Oxford/ Blackwell, UK

Howe KR (1988) Against the quantitative-qualitative incompatibility thesis or dogmas die hard. Educ Res 17:10–16

Howe KR (2004) A critique of experimentalism. Qual Inq 10(1):42–56

Huber AA (2007) How to add qualitative profundity to quantitative findings in a study on cooperative learing. In: Mayring P, Huber GL, Gurtler L, Kiegelmann M (eds) Mixed methodology in psychological research. Sense, Rotterdam, pp 179–190

Hunter A, Brewer J (2003) Multimethod research in sociology. Handbook of mixed methods in social and behavioral research. Sage, Thousand Oaks, CA, pp 577–594

Jick TD (1979) Mixing qualitative and quantitative methods: triangulation in action. Adm Sci Q 24(4):602–611

Johnson B, Turner LA (2003) Data collection strategies in mixed methods research. Handbook of Mixed Methods in Social and Behavioral Research. Sage, Thousand Oaks, CA, pp 297–319

Johnson RB, Onwuegbuzie AJ (2004) Mixed methods research: a research paradigm whose time has come. Educ Res 33(7):14

Johnson RB, Onwuegbuzie AJ, Turner LA (2007) Toward a definition of mixed methods research. J Mixed Methods Res 1(2):112

Krippendorff K (2004) Content analysis: an introduction to its methodology. Sage, Newbury Park, CA

Laub J, Sampson R (2003) Shared beginnings, divergent lives: delinquent boys to age 70. Harvard University Press, Cambridge, MA

LeBel T, Burnett R, Maruna S, Bushway S (2008) The chicken or the egg of subjective and social factors in desistance. Eur J Criminol 5:131–159

Lofland J (1971) Analysing social settings: a guide to qualitative observation and analysis. Wadsworth, Belmont, CA

Lofland J, Lofland LH (1995) Analyzing social settings: a guide to qualitative observation and analysis. Wadsworth, Belmont, CA

Maruna S (2001) Making good: how ex-convicts reform and rebuild their lives. American Psychological Association, Washington

Maruna S (2004) Desistance and explanatory style: a new direction in the psychology of reform. J Contemp Crim Justice 20:184–200

Maruna S, King A (2004) Public opinion and community penalties. In: Bottoms T, Rex S, Robinson G (eds) Alternatives to prison: options for an insecure society. Willan, Cullompton

Maruna S, King A (2009) Once a criminal, always a criminal?: 'Redeemability' and the psychology of punitive public attitudes. Eur J Crim Policy Res 15:7–24

Mastrofski SD, Worden RE, Snipes JB (1995) Law enforcement in a time of community policing. Criminology 33:539–563

Matsueda RL (2006) Criminological implications of the thought of George Herbert Mead. Sociological theory and criminological research: views from Europe and the United States 7:77–108

Mayring P (2007) Arguments for mixed methodology. In:Mayring P, Huber GL, Gurtler L, Kiegelmann M (eds) Mixed methodology in psychological research. Sense, Rotterdam pp 1–4

Mazerolle LG, Kadleck C, Roehl J (1998) Controlling drug and disorder problems: the role of place managers. Criminology 36:371–403

McElrath K (2001) Confessions of a quantitative criminologist. ACJS Today 24(4):1–7

McLaughlin E (1991) Oppositional poverty: the quantitative/qualitative divide and other dichotomies. Sociol Rev 39(2):292–308

Miethe TD, Drass KA (1999) Exploring the social context of instrumental and expressive homicides: an application of qualitative comparative analysis. J Quant Criminol 15:1–21

Miles MB, Huberman AM (1984) Qualitative data analysis: a sourcebook of new methods. Sage, Thousand Oaks, CA

Miller J (2008) The status of qualitative research in criminology. Workshop on Interdisciplinary Standards for Systematic Qualitative Research, National Science Foundation, Washington, DC

Miller WR, Benefield RG, Tonigan JS (1993) Enhancing motivation for change in problem drinking: a controlled comparison of two therapist styles. J Consult Clin Psychol 61:455–455

Morgan DL (2007) Paradigms lost and pragmatism regained: methodological implications of combining qualitative and quantitative methods. J Mixed Methods Res 1(1):48

Newman I, Benz CR (1998) Qualitative-quantitative research methodology: exploring the interactive continuum. Southern Illinois University Press, Carbondale, IL

Pennebaker JW, Mehl MR, Niederhoffer KG (2003) Psychological aspects of natural language use: our words, our selves. Annu Rev Psychol 54(1):547–577

Peterson C (1992) Explanatory style. In: Smith CP (ed) Motivation and personality: Handbook of thematic content analysis. Cambridge, New York, pp 376–382

Peterson C, Schulman P, Castellon C, Seligman MEP (1992) The explanatory style scoring manual. In Smith CP (ed) Motivation and personality. Cambridge, New York, pp 383–392

Ragin CC (1994) Constructing social research: the unity and diversity of method. Pine Forge, Thousand Oaks, CA

Reiss A (1971) Systematic observations of natural social phenomena. In: Costner H (ed) Sociological methodology. Jossey-Bass, San Francisco, pp 3–33

Rist RC (1977) On the relations among educational research paradigms: from disdain to detente. Anthropol Educ Q 8(2):42–49

Roethlisberger FJ, Dickson WJ (1939) Management and the Worker. Cambridge, Mass.: Harvard University Press

Sampson RJ, Laub J (1993) Crime in the making: pathways and turning points through life. Harvard University Press, Cambridge, MA

Sampson RJ, Raudenbush SW (1999) Systematic social observation of public spaces: a new look at disorder in urban neighborhoods. Am J Sociol 105(3):603–651

Short JF, Strodtbeck FL (1965) Group process and gang delinquency. University of Chicago Press, Chicago

Smith CP (1992) Motivation and personality: handbook of thematic content analysis. Cambridge University Press, New York

Snizek WE (1976) An empirical assessment of sociology: a multiple paradigm science. Am Sociol 11:217–219

Stemler S (2001) An overview of content analysis. Practical Assessment, Research & Evaluation 7(17):137–146

Tashakkori A, Teddlie C (1998) Mixed methodology: combining qualitative and quantitative approaches. Sage, Thousand Oaks, CA

Tashakkori A, Teddlie C (2003) Handbook of mixed method in the social and behavioral research. Sage, Thousand, CA

Taylor RB, Shumaker SA, Gottfredson SD (1985) Neighborhood-level links between physical features and local sentiments: deterioration, fear of crime, and confidence. J Archit Plann Res 2(4):261–275

Taylor SJ, Bogdan R (1998) Introduction to qualitative research methods: a guidebook and resource. Wiley, New York

Teddlie C, Tashakkori A (2003) Major issues and controversies in the use of mixed methods in the social and behavioral sciences. Handbook of mixed methods in social & behavioral research. Sage, Thousand Oaks, CA, pp 3–50

Toch H (1992) Violent men: an inquiry into the psychology of violence revised edition. American Psychological Association, Washington

Viljoen JL, Vincent GM, Roesch R (2006) Assessing adolescent defendants' adjudicative competence: interrater reliability and factor structure of the fitness interview test–revised. Criminal Justice and Behavior 33(4):467–487

Warner WL, Lunt PS (1941) The social life of a modern community. H Milford, Oxford University Press, Oxford

Weisburd D, Waring EJ (2001) White-collar crime and criminal careers. Cambridge University Press, Cambridge

Weisburd D, Wyckoff LA, Ready J, Eck JE, Hinkle JC, Gajewski F (2006) Does crime just move around the corner? A controlled study of spatial displacement and diffusion of crime control benefits. Criminology 44:549–592

Wheelock D, Hartmann D (2007) Midnight basketball and the 1994 crime bill debates: the operation of a racial code. The Sociological Quarterly 48(2):315–342

Whyte WF (1943) Street corner society. University of Chicago, Chicago

Woo H, Kim Y (2003) Modern gladiators: a content analysis of televised wrestling. Mass Commun Soc 6(4):361–378

Zimbardo PG (1969) The human choice: individuation, reason, and order versus deindividuation, impulse, and chaos. Nebraska Symposium on Motivation 17:237–307

Part I-B
Descriptive Approaches for Research and Policy: *New Estimation Techniques for Assessing Crime and Justice Policy*

## CHAPTER 8

Estimating Costs of Crime

MARK A. COHEN AND ROGER BOWLES

INTRODUCTION

This chapter reviews the theory, methods, and evidence on estimating the costs of crime. The topic is of growing importance in the criminal justice policy world in an era when policy makers want to know more about an intervention or project: not only "does it work?" but they also want to compare the value of the crime prevented with the cost of achieving the reduction. Valuing the benefits of crime prevention requires information about the costs that would have been incurred if the crimes had taken place: Dhiri and Brand (1999).

While this chapter focuses on the underlying theory and methods for researchers who are interested in generating estimates of the costs of crime, it is also meant to be of value to "users" of costs of crime data. Since there are many different types of cost estimates in the literature – including many that are "incomplete" – it is important that users be informed about the different approaches and their limitations. This chapter is primarily limited to estimates of the cost of traditional "street crime," and largely ignores white collar, corporate, and regulatory crimes. However, many of the techniques discussed here are also appropriate to estimating the costs of these other types of crimes.

This chapter is organized as follows. First, "Theory of Crime Costs," examines the underlying theory on what costs are to be estimated. Next, "Taxonomy of Crime Costs" provides a taxonomy of crime cost types, while "Costing Methodologies" discusses the various methods used to estimate these crime costs. The section "Examples of Latest Research on Crime Costs" provides examples of cost estimates from both the U.S. and U.K., which allows for a comparison of some of the contrasting methods. Finally, "Emerging and Future Issues in Cost Estimation" concludes with some observations about outstanding issues in this evolving literature and suggestions for further research.

THEORY OF CRIME COSTS

Before one can estimate the costs of crime, it is important to start with some simple but important economic concepts. There are many types of costs in economics – private costs, taxpayer/public costs, social costs, and opportunity costs – to name only a few. A researcher who is interested in estimating the costs of crime should first identify the purpose of the

A.R. Piquero and D. Weisburd (eds.), *Handbook of Quantitative Criminology*,
DOI 10.1007/978-0-387-77650-7_8, © Springer Science + Business Media, LLC 2010,
First softcover printing 2011

costing exercise. This will dictate the type of costs to be estimated. For example, if one is only interested in the monetary burden to victims of crime, then only direct costs borne by crime victims would be included. However, for most policy purposes, the researcher is interested in a broader notion of costs – something akin to the burden on society. Economists would generally view this as the "social cost" of crime – anything that reduces the aggregate well being of society.

Economists generally start with a presumption that they want to estimate the "social costs" of harmful activities such as pollution or crime. However, (Cohen 1998) argues that the relevant concept for analysis of crime control programs is that of "external" costs. The concepts of social costs and external costs are closely related but not identical. "External costs" are simply the costs imposed by one person on another, where the latter person does not voluntarily accept this negative consequence – often termed an "externality" by economists. "Social costs" are costs that reduce the aggregate well being of society.

While oftentimes external and social costs are identical, this is not always the case. The value of stolen property is an often cited example. Some economists have argued that stolen property is an "external" but not technically a "social" cost, since the offender can enjoy the use of the stolen property. For example, Cook (1983) argues that the relevant concept should be the "social cost" which would exclude transfers of money or property. By excluding transfers, Cook (1983) considered the offender a member of society and thus worthy of inclusion in the social welfare function. In contrast, Lewin and Trumbull (1990) argue that those who violate the criminal law are not entitled to have their utility counted in the social welfare function, i.e., their gain or loss is to be ignored. Similarly, in the case of victimless crimes (e.g., drug abuse, prostitution, and gambling), one might argue that the "social costs" of these crimes are zero or small (once factoring in the welfare of the participants who enjoy these activities). Yet, as Cohen (2005) argues, these activities impose significant external costs (such as reduced quality of neighborhoods, medical costs borne by taxpayers, etc.)

Authors are not in agreement on whether or not to use external or social costs. Cohen (1988), French et al. (1991), Miller et al. (1996), Brand and Price (2000), Dubourg et al. (2005), and others have argued in favor of the external cost approach.[1] Anderson (1999) takes the opposite approach and explicitly takes transfers out of his cost estimates – although they are shown as a separate item. Whichever conceptualization of costs is ultimately adopted, it is important to be explicit about the underlying approach and, if possible, provide estimates utilizing both – i.e., identify both the full costs as well as the portion that are determined to be outside the scope of the exercise, so that the reader can make her own choice about which concept to use. Thus, if transfer payments are to be excluded from the final estimates, they should at least be identified.

Before estimating costs of crime, it is important to specify the underlying goal of the exercise – whose costs are being estimated and for what purpose? If the underlying purpose is to estimate the cost to taxpayers, that is a much different exercise than estimating the cost to victims or the cost to society as a whole. While there are certainly legitimate reasons why one might want a less than comprehensive accounting, one generally should start from the perspective of estimating the full "social costs" or "external costs" of crime. Most important, however, the analyst should explicitly state the underlying concept being estimated and the methodology. In many applications of benefit-cost analysis, several estimates are provided,

---

[1] Becker (1968) also would include property transfers, but he theorized that they approximate true social costs if the market for fencing was competitive.

so that policy makers can see the components of costs and make a determination as to which approach they want to use. For example, Aos et al. (2004) systematically analyze the costs and benefits of early prevention programs and identify both taxpayer costs and external costs.

Individual Versus Aggregate Costs

Another issue that must be decided before estimating costs is whether the goal is to understand the impact of individual crime types or crime in general. While most efforts to estimate the costs of crime focus on individual crime types, some authors (see e.g., Anderson 1999) have attempted to estimate costs from aggregate data such as the total government spending on police, courts, and the criminal justice system; private expenditures on security alarms and other precautionary expenditures. Such an approach might also look at aggregate victimization costs from government or hospital surveys. These approaches might be useful for understanding the magnitude of the crime problem relative to other measures, such as health expenditures or GDP. They are not suitable for other purposes, however, such as comparing harm by types of crimes or conducting benefit-cost analyses of programs designed to reduce certain types of crimes. Of course, some crime costs are more easily estimated on an aggregate basis (especially general government expenditures that are not targeted towards one type of crime). However, even in these cases, methodologies exist to apportion the costs by the type of crime.

Opportunity Costs

Many costs are not observable as direct monetary exchanges. Economists have long recognized the notion of "opportunity costs" as being the conceptual approach to valuing such burdens. The opportunity cost of a good or service is simply its value in the next best alternative – or put differently, what must be given up in exchange for that good or service. Thus, for example, if a victim must spend on average 10 h meeting with police, prosecutors, and attending court proceedings, it is important to include the opportunity cost of the victim's time. In this case, the opportunity cost would generally be based on the hourly earning capacity of victims. Additional opportunity costs that should be estimated include the value of pain, suffering and lost quality of life to victims, as well as fear to the public at large.

"Incidence" Versus "Prevalence"-Based Costs

The health economics literature generally distinguishes between "incidence-based" and "prevalence-based" costs. An "incidence-based" cost of crime estimate would attempt to look at each individual crime episode and identify all of the costs. An injury that is sustained today may continue to have consequences and impose costs for many years. Thus, if one is interested in the cost of crime in any 1 year, it is important to decide whether this should be defined as the costs actually *incurred* during that year ("prevalence" based costs), or the costs *imposed* that year even if they are not realized until many years down the road ("incidence" based costs). Cost estimates based on incidence count both present and future costs in the year in which the injury-cost stream began (Hartunian et al. 1981). Costs based on prevalence count all costs of injury that were incurred in a given year, regardless of when the injuries occurred. Incidence-based estimates indicate how much could be saved by preventing future incidents and are thus most relevant for criminal justice policy analysis. Prevalence-based estimates may be used to provide insight into the cost savings attainable through improved treatment of existing injuries and are of more interest to those in the public health community interested in estimating medical care needs.

Discounting Costs to Present Value

Costs incurred in the future (i.e., more than 1 year postvictimization) must be discounted to "present value." Since a dollar spent today is not the same as a dollar spent 15 years from now, future costs must be discounted to present value when compared to the costs borne today.[2] Although there is no general consensus on the appropriate discount rate for purposes of policy analysis, most "cost of crime" studies have used a rate of between 2 and 3% per year, which is consistent with the "real" (i.e., net of inflation) discount rate for worker wages over time, and the real consumer interest rate over time.[3] This discount rate is also within the range most likely to be used in the U.S. in tort awards for lost wages. Further, statistical modeling suggests workers apply a 2% discount rate when they trade off possible loss of future life years against extra earnings in the present (Moore and Viscusi 1989). Finally, the Congressional Budget Office concluded from a review of the economic evidence that the most appropriate discount rate for public decision making was 2% (Hartman 1990). A similar consensus appears to have developed around a 3% net discount rate in healthcare economics (Gold et al. 1996) and by the U.S. government (OMB 2003) when analyzing the present value of health benefits. The U.K. government uses a 3.5% discount rate for analysis of public spending projects (U.K. HM Treasury 2003) – a rate that has been used by Brand and Price (2000) and Dubourg et al. (2005) when estimating the present value costs of crime in the U.K.

TAXONOMY OF CRIME COSTS

Crime costs are pervasive in society. The two most obvious costs associated with crime are the burden imposed on victims (such as lost wages, medical costs, pain and suffering), and government expenditures on police and the criminal justice system, which are designed to capture and punish offenders. However, crime has impacts on many other segments of society – not just victims.

---

[2] The concept of "present value" is fundamental to economics and is relatively easy to understand. A dollar today is worth more than a dollar tomorrow in purchasing power due to inflation. Similarly, a dollar next year is worth less than having a dollar today, since I could just as easily take that dollar and invest it at current interest rates and have more than a dollar next year. Thus, when economists talk about the "present value" of a future income stream, they are simply computing the amount of money today that would be equivalent to the amount needed in future years, after accounting for the fact that (a) prices and wages increase over time, and (b) today's dollars can be invested and interest compounded. Except in rare circumstances, present value is always less than future value.

[3] Note that these are "net" discount rates, as they already account for inflation. Thus, for example, a 2% discount rate would be consistent with long-term cost of living increases of 4% and long-term interest rates of 6%.

Various authors have categorized the burdens of crime in slightly different – yet complementary ways. The economics of crime literature has traditionally distinguished between three types of costs (Demmert 1979: 2–5):

(1) costs caused directly by criminal behavior (i.e., external costs imposed by the offender),
(2) costs society incurs in response to crime to deter or prevent future incidents or to exact retribution, and
(3) costs incurred by the offender (such as the opportunity cost of the offender's time while either engaging in the offence or being punished, if he or she otherwise could have been employed in productive activity).

An alternative formulation by Brand and Price (2000) is:

(1) costs incurred in anticipation of crime (e.g., prevention and insurance administration)
(2) costs incurred as a consequence of crime (e.g., victimization), and
(3) costs in response to crime (e.g., criminal justice expenditures)

The Brand and Price (2000) characterization largely focuses on the first two of Demmert's crime cost types and ignores offender costs. It also ignores some of the more difficult costs that Cohen et al. (1994) identified – such as the cost to victim's families, justice or overdeterrence. While this categorization has some intuitive appeal and has been followed by subsequent Home Office reports, note that it is often difficult to sort out which category costs belong to. For example, while Brand and Price (2000) include criminal justice expenditures in their "response to crime" category, the spending may also have an "avoidance/deterrent" role. Imprisonment of an offender may be intended in part to discourage others from offending in the future. The motivation extends beyond simply punishing an offender for past wrongs into an investment in preventing future offending.

Cohen et al. (1994) and Cohen (2000, 2005) started from the Demmert (1979) list and progressively expanded it into a comprehensive taxonomy.[4] Tables 8.1 and 8.2 regroup this taxonomy into the three types of crime costs suggested by Brand and Price (2000). Thus, Tables 8.1 and 8.2 provide a comprehensive taxonomy that is consistent with the Brand and Price approach. The first table includes costs in anticipation and the consequences of crime. The second table details society's response to crime. Regardless of how these costs are grouped, it is useful to start with a comprehensive listing – which allows researchers and policy makers to understand which costs are included and which are not. Enumerating costs or benefits that are *not* monetized is a fundamental principle of benefit-cost analysis (see for example Zerbe and Bellas 2006). Tables 8.1 and 8.2 also include information on "who bears the cost" of crime.

For accounting purposes, these burdens can be divided into the following categories (see Cohen 2005):

(1) Victimization costs (including out-of-pocket losses, pain, suffering, and lost quality of life from victimization)
(2) Precautionary expenditures by individuals and business
(3) Avoidance behaviors by individuals

---

[4] See also "Mainstreaming Methodology for Estimating Costs of Crime" (www.costsofcrime.org, last accessed 11/05/09) for a detailed taxonomy and discussion of methodologies for estimating the costs of crime.

TABLE 8.1. Taxonomy of crime costs – anticipation and consequences of crime

Crime cost category	Who bears the cost
Anticipation of crime	
Precautionary expenditures	Potential victims
Avoidance behaviors	Potential victims
Fear of crime	Potential victims
Crime prevention programs	Society/government
– Government	Society/government
– Non-government agencies	Society
Consequences of crime	
Property losses	
– Losses not reimbursed by insurer	Victim
– Losses reimbursed by insurance	Society
– Administrative costs of insurance	Society
Productivity losses	
– Lost wages for unpaid workdays	Victims
– Lost productivity for paid workdays	Society/employers
Household service losses	Victims/family
Lost school days	
– Foregone wages due to lack of education	Victim
– Foregone nonpecuniary benefits of education	Victim
– Foregone social benefits due to lack of education	Society
Medical and mental health costs	
– Losses not reimbursed by insurer	Victim & family
– Losses reimbursed by insurance	Society
– Administrative costs of insurance	Society
Pain, suffering and lost quality of life	
– Pain, suffering & lost quality of life	Victim
– Loss of affection/enjoyment, trauma	Victim family
Victim support services	
– Expenses charged to victim	Victim
– Expenses paid by service agency	Society/government
Legal costs associated with tort claims	Victim/society
Long-term consequences of victimization	Victim family/Society
Offender costs	Offender

(4) Criminal justice system
(5) Government prevention and rehabilitation programs
(6) Residual effects on individuals (e.g., fear)
(7) Residual effects on community (e.g., loss of tax base)
(8) Over deterence (e.g., activities not undertaken by innocent people for fear of being accused of criminal activity)
(9) "Justice" costs (e.g., costs incurred solely to ensure that "justice" is done)
(10) Burden imposed on incarcerated offenders and their families

To tally up the value of reducing crime, it is not necessarily correct to simply add up the current costs – that is a static view. As shown in Fig. 8.1, the impact of crime induces behaviors on the part of many actors. For example, crime might induce fear on the part of the general public. But, fear induces the public to avoid certain areas of town (avoidance behavior) as well as purchase burglar alarms (precautionary expenditures). Thus, any methodology

TABLE 8.2. Taxonomy of crime costs – response to crime

Crime cost category	Who bears the cost
Response to crime	
Police	Society/government
Prosecution	Society/government
Courts	Society/government
Legal fees	
– Public defenders	Society/government
– Private lawyers	Offenders
Criminal sanctions	Society/government (sometimes offenders)
Victim and witness costs	Victim/Witnesses
Jury service	Jurors
Victim compensation	Society/government
Offender costs	
– Productivity	Offender/society
– Injury/death to offender while incarcerated	Offender/society
– Loss of freedom to offender	Offender
– Offender's family	Offender's family/society
Overdeterrence costs	
– Innocent individuals accused of offenses	Innocent "offenders"
– Restrictions on legitimate activities	Society
– Costs of additional detection avoidance by offenders	Offenders
Justice costs	Society

designed to estimate the cost of crime needs to consider these interactions and be certain that included in the value of a crime reduction (for example), are changes in avoidance behavior and precautionary expenditures.

One of the challenges in the cost of crime literature is the fact that many of the costs of crime are difficult to attribute to individual types of crime. For example, a burglar alarm in a home will help prevent home burglary as well as rape. Community policing might help reduce armed robbery as well as drug dealing and auto theft. Attributing these costs to individual crime types is thus difficult. Similarly, many of the methodologies used to estimate the intangible costs of crime such as public fear – have been unable to sort out these costs by individual crime types. For most policy analyses, it is important to have individual crime costs; hence a good deal of attention has been placed on methods that allow for individual crime type estimates.

COSTING METHODOLOGIES

"Top Down" Versus "Bottom Up" Approaches

There are two basic approaches to estimating the costs of crime. The most prevalent to date has been a "bottom up" approach that attempts to piece together the various component crime costs enumerated in Tables 8.1 and 8.2. That is the approach taken by Cohen (1988) who estimated the cost of crime to victims. Cohen et al. (1994), Brand and Price (2000) and Dubourg et al. (2005) added the cost of prevention and the criminal justice system to victim costs.

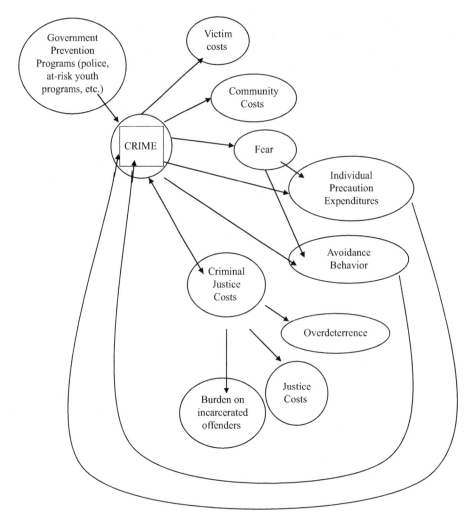

FIGURE 8.1. Interdependency of cost of crime components.

However, as noted by Nagin (2001), all of these "bottom up" approaches ignored some very important components of the costs of crime – including the "fear of crime," expenditures or actions taken by the public to avoid the risk of crime, as well as any residual loss to the community in terms of social cohesion, community development, etc. Recent papers by Dolan et al. (2005) and Moore (2006) have attempted to estimate the cost of "fear of crime," but these approaches are still being refined and still do not fully encompass all of the cost categories enumerated in Tables 8.1 and 8.2 nor the full characterization sought by Nagin (2001).

An alternative approach is thus to estimate costs from the "top down." Although there are several methodologies that can be adopted (discussed further below), these "holistic" approaches attempt to elicit information on the public's willingness-to-pay for reduced crime. Examples include Ludwig and Cook (2001), Cohen et al. (2004), and Atkinson et al. (2005).

In theory, the "top down" and "bottom up" approaches should lead to the same estimates if the latter is all inclusive. The extent to which these two approaches yield similar results has been explored by Cohen (2009), who concludes that to date, the bottom up approaches have not fully captured the costs of crime. Nevertheless, there is merit in both approaches. While the top down approach is likely to be more comprehensive, it does not allow for a disaggregation of crime cost components.

Tangible Costs of Crime

At first, it might appear that the tangible costs of crime are relatively straightforward to estimate. In fact, aside from data on direct government expenditures on the criminal justice system, this is far from the truth. For example, there is no national accounting system tallying up the out-of-pocket losses to crime victims. The only direct source of crime victim costs in the U.S. is the ongoing National Crime Victimization Survey (NCVS), which interviews households and elicits information from those who have experienced a recent criminal victimization (Bureau of Justice Statistics 2008). The NCVS includes several questions asking crime victims about their out-of-pocket losses, including an estimate of the dollar cost of medical care, lost wages, and property loss. These estimates are periodically published by the Bureau of Justice Statistics (see e.g., Klaus 1994).

Similar surveys are conducted in other countries. The British Crime Survey (BCS), conducted first in 1982,[5] asks households in England and Wales about crimes they have experienced in the previous year. It asks questions about victim loss including days lost from work, the value of damage caused to property as well as to property stolen during burglaries and, so on. Many other countries have developed their own household crime victimization surveys, although these surveys vary widely in their breadth and depth of coverage. For further discussion of the International Crime Survey conducted at intervals in various countries in the EU and further afield see Van Dijk et al. (2005), Alvazzi del Frate and Van Kesteren (2004), Mayhew and Van Dijk (1997).

Despite their official look, the crime cost estimates from many of these surveys severely understate the tangible costs of crime to victims. For example, the, reference period for the NCVS is crimes committed during the previous 6 months. Since the average crime will have occurred about 3 months prior to its being reported, any medical costs or lost wages are necessarily limited to those short-term costs. Even short-term costs are likely to be underestimated, however, since hospital bills are often sent directly to insurance companies, and may arrive months after hospitalization. In addition, some cost categories are simply excluded from NCVS. For example, respondents are not asked about mental healthcare, despite the fact that this is a significant cost of victimization (Cohen and Miller 1998). Finally, the consequences of victimization can be farreaching and beyond the scope of any government survey. Although few studies have quantified these effects, Dugan (1999) found that victims were more likely to move to a new home following victimization than their peers who were not victimized. Long term implications of victimization may also be hidden and underestimated. For example, Macmillan (2000) finds that educational attainment and lifetime earnings are lower for victims of childhood physical or sexual assault. These impacts have yet to be incorporated into cost of crime estimates that are based on victim costs.

---

[5] For a summary of the development of the BCS see Jansson (2007).

Other tangible crime costs that are relatively easier to measure include police expenditures and the criminal justice system itself. Although aggregate costs may be available from government statistics, the cost *per crime* is not always available. For some purposes, we might be interested in these costs. For example, in studying the costs and benefits of an early release program, we would want to know the cost of recidivism imposed by those who are let out of prison early. Thus, we might want the marginal cost of police resources associated with investigating a crime, as well as the marginal costs to the criminal justice system from having to reprocess a repeat offender. Such studies exist for specific jurisdictions and/or specific time frames (see e.g., Aos et al. 2004). However, these studies are not routinely updated, and the costs might vary considerably by location.

Moolenaar (2008) has estimated police costs in The Netherlands by the type of crime based on the frequency of criminal offences reported to police, assuming that the cost per reported crime, is the same across crime types. By dividing each category by the number of reported crimes an estimate is made of the cost per recorded crime. A more direct method is used by Gardlund (2008) based on data collected in Sweden by police who record their daily allocation of time by activity.

Some countries have systems for sampling and recording police time allocation, such as the Activity Based Costing (ABC) system used in England: (HM Inspectorate of Constabulary 1998). Even these systems are rarely implemented sufficiently thoroughly to support an allocation of police activity to offence types. Elsewhere one-off studies and surveys may be conducted in efforts to identify the costs of policing particular offence types. Donnelly et al. (2007) mounted a special survey of police activity in order to make estimates of the law enforcement costs associated with alcohol-related crime in New South Wales.

Finally, even potential victims suffer tangible costs of crime by taking costly preventive measures – such as purchasing and installing security systems, deadbolt locks, cell phones, guard dogs, and guns purchased for defensive protection. Although direct measures of these expenditures should be relatively easy to obtain through survey methods, one difficulty in doing so is the fact that many of these expenditures serve dual roles. The guard dog may also be a pet that provides companionship. The cell phone might provide a sense of security to a nighttime traveler, but also can be used for other purposes. Sorting out the reason for purchase and value obtained for each reason is not a trivial task.

Intangible Costs of Crime

Several different approaches have been utilized to estimate the monetary value of intangible costs. Perhaps the earliest indirect method was to infer property owners' willingness to pay for a safer neighborhood through higher property values. To the extent that home buyers take into account the risk of victimization when deciding whether or not to buy a home, we expect higher crime neighborhoods to have lower housing prices controlling for all other factors that affect house prices (Thaler 1978; Rizzo 1979; and Hellman and Naroff 1979). A statistical methodology called "hedonic pricing" has been developed to estimate the component of the housing price that is attributable to crime. The methodology developed by Thaler (1978) requires detailed location-specific housing characteristics (square feet, number of rooms, age, etc.), housing prices, crime rates and other location-specific amenities (e.g., tax rates, school quality, distance to the center of the city, etc.). Statistical techniques (e.g., multiple regression analysis) isolate the effect of crime on housing prices. The effect that crime has on housing prices can be inferred from this statistical technique (e.g., from the regression coefficient on the crime variable), and one can interpret this relationship as the marginal willingness to pay for a reduction in the crime rate. Note that this is a marginal valuation, based on the current crime rate and small changes around that rate.

Property value studies necessarily rely on important assumptions about the competitiveness of the housing market and consumer information about neighborhood crime rates. They also ignore the effect that location-specific amenities – including crime – have on local wage rates. A few researchers have estimated both the housing and wage equation in order to capture both effects (see e.g., Hoehn et al. 1987). Although these models use two equations, it remains to use them for estimating simultaneous models taking account of the interaction between housing prices and wages.

Data limitations have generally prevented these property value and/or wage rate studies from isolating the cost of any individual crime type. Since many types of crime tend to move in similar directions, it is difficult to sort out the effect that one particular crime has on wage rates or property values. Instead, studies to date have estimated the cost of an aggregate measure of crime such as the crime index. In theory, a comprehensive data set could isolate the effect of each crime type on housing prices. Bartley (2000) had some success in isolating these costs by analyzing wages and rents in cities around the country. However, even larger data sets and more fine geographic distinctions appear to be needed to fully disentangle these individual crime costs. One exception is the recent study by Linden and Rockoff (2006), who estimated the cost of a sex offence by examining housing prices nearby known sex offenders, following the passage of laws requiring the registering and public availability of information on where sex offenders live.

One of the positive features of the property value studies of crime is that they rely upon actual market transactions. Although economists tend to favor estimation procedures whereby actual market transactions (e.g., housing prices) are used, any market-based approach necessarily takes into account the wealth and income of the buyer. Thus, the fact that less wealthy individuals necessarily buy less expensive homes leads to an estimate of the value of crime that is based on "ability to pay." This concern applies to many of the methodologies discussed in this chapter. In some cases, researchers or policy makers, who want to impose a different value system, can easily adjust the estimates to "neutralize" the effect of ability to pay and instead estimate the willingness to pay for a "typical" citizen. However, this cannot be done in all cases.

The housing market is not the only place affected by crime rates. People buy handguns and security alarms, take cabs instead of walk, and other precautions are taken to avoid crimes. Although all of these expenditures can be considered part of the cost of society's response to crime, they might also be used in estimating the cost of crime itself. For example, a study of the purchase of security alarms might allow us to infer the value that consumers place on a particular reduction in the probability of being victimized. For example, if the purchase of a double bolt lock at the cost of $25 reduces the risk of being burglarized from 1 in 500 to 1 in 1,000, we could infer that the individual who purchases the lock values the reduced risk by at least that amount. Collectively, if 1,000 households were each willing to pay $25 to decrease their risk from 2 in 1,000 to 1 in 1,000 (hence preventing one burglary from occurring among this population of 1,000 individuals), this would imply a willingness to pay $25,000 to reduce one burglary ($25 \times 1,000 = \$25,000$).

Another method of estimating the nonmonetary costs of crime is to infer society's willingness to pay for reductions in crime from noncrime studies of society's willingness to pay for safety. Although there are several approaches, this growing literature primarily estimates wage rate differentials for risky jobs (Viscusi 1998, 2000). Thus, for example, if workers are paid an additional $50 wage rate premium for accepting an increased risk of death of one in 500,000, it is interpreted to mean that the collective "value of life" is $25 million ($50 × 500, 000). Now, there is an extensive literature on the statistical "value of life." Value of life estimates should not be interpreted as the value of any one particular life, but instead, as society's value of saving a "statistical" life. The first attempt to incorporate these "value of life" estimates into the cost of crime appears to be Philips and Votey (1981) who combined the "value of life" estimates and out-of-pocket costs of crime with society's perception of the seriousness of crime to arrive at crime-specific monetary estimates. However, their methodology was unable to account for the risk of injury and death for many crimes.

Cohen (1988) attempted to overcome these data limitations by combining estimates of the "value of life" with monetary estimates of the pain, suffering, and lost quality of life for nonfatal injuries. The approach used in Cohen (1988) is a hybrid of direct and indirect cost estimation. Direct costs are taken from NCVS data as well as several additional sources to augment some of the weaknesses of the government survey. Nonmonetary costs are estimated using indirect techniques. The value of life estimates were used to value the risk of being fatally injured during the commission of a crime. These include the "value of life" for fatal crimes and pain, suffering, and lost quality of life for nonfatal injuries. Risk of death is calculated directly from FBI data identifying the underlying crime in homicide cases. Risk of death probabilities are multiplied by the "value of life" to arrive at an estimate of the value of the risk of death component of each crime type.

The innovative – and most controversial – methodology introduced by Cohen (1988) was the use of jury award data to estimate the monetary value of pain, suffering, and lost quality of life for nonfatal injuries. At the time, Cohen (1988) relied upon jury awards in traditional tort cases and matched up the type and severity of injury (e.g., broken bones) found in tort cases with typical injuries identified in crime victim data through the NCVS. Juries in the U.S. are instructed to compensate victims an amount that will make them "whole" – i.e., put them back in a position prior to the incident. Although punitive damages may be added on top of the compensatory award, Cohen (1988) only included the smaller compensatory damage award. This approach implicitly assumes that identical injuries are valued the same whether caused by an auto accident or an assault. However, crime victims might endure more pain and suffering due to the psychological trauma and fear of repeat victimization. Subsequently, Miller et al. (1996) obtained data on jury awards to victims of physical and sexual assault and estimated crime costs using these court cases. These data were unavailable previously, since civil lawsuits by crime victims are a relatively new phenomenon that has grown to the point where adequate data exist. These lawsuits are generally against third parties for inadequate security, such as a parking lot owner failing to provide adequate lighting or an apartment owner not adequately securing a building.

One reason the jury award approach is controversial is the popular notion that jury awards in the U.S. are unpredictable and/or unreasonably high. Despite popular beliefs to the contrary, considerable evidence exists that jury awards are predictable in a large sample (Cohen and Miller 2003). In addition, Cohen and Miller (2003) found that the implied statistical value of life awarded by juries is very comparable to that found in studies of worker wage rate differentials. Popular press articles and calls for tort reform often focus on the outliers and punitive damage awards. Punitive damages are meant to punish the tortfeasor, not to compensate the victim; hence, they are excluded from the pain, suffering, and lost quality of life estimates. Compensatory damages (i.e., payments that are meant to compensate for out-of-pocket losses, pain, and suffering – but not to punish), however, are quite predictable, and jury awards are being used as a measure of pain and suffering in other contexts, including government regulatory agencies (e.g., Consumer Product Safety Commission). Perhaps most compelling, however, is the fact that society has placed its tort system in the hands of juries and has decided that these awards are "just compensation." Of course, these comments apply more to the U.S. than elsewhere where victim compensation seldom takes on such an expansive role.

Another source of estimates of losses is the tariff used in national schemes for compensating victims of crime. For example, individuals injured in an act of violence in England, Scotland, and Wales can make a claim (for up to half a million pounds sterling) to the Criminal Injuries Compensation Authority[6]. The tariff bears some relation to the amounts a civil court might be expected to award in cases involving a comparable injury. However, Britain, the awards exclude healthcare costs met through social insurance provision; hence they will understate the social costs of injuries.

Despite the above rationale for the use of jury awards (or other compensation mechanisms) to measure victim compensation for nonmonetary harms, this approach is theoretically not the most appropriate one for purposes of estimating the willingness to pay to reduce the risk of crime. Jury awards are *ex post* compensation designed to make a person whole. In fact, no amount of money will really make a person "whole." How many murder victims do you think would have accepted a $2 million payment in exchange for their life? Thus, the measure that we really want for determining public policy outcomes is based on the *risk of victimization*. We are all willing to trade off money for small changes in the risk of injury or death – we do it all of the time in our everyday activities by deciding whether or not to purchase a less safe car, a burglar alarm, or to take a cab at night instead of walking in an unsafe neighborhood. As discussed in the previous section, for policy purposes, the more relevant question is the "willingness to pay" (WTP) to reduce crime, which is an ex ante concept. The *ex post* compensation approach necessarily overstates the amount the public would be willing to pay to reduce the impact of crime on victims. The property value studies described above are ex ante WTP approaches, since they are based on actual market transactions taking into account the prospective risk of criminal victimization. However, as noted earlier, researchers have only been able to value an index crime using this method – not individual crime types.[7]

An alternative approach to estimating the ex ante WTP for reduced crime is to directly survey the public (i.e., potential victims). This approach, often called "contingent valuation," is a methodology developed in the environmental economics literature and has been used extensively to place dollar values on nonmarket goods such as improvements in air quality or endangered species. There have been literally hundreds of contingent valuation studies, meta-analyses and textbooks written on the subject.[8] Although there is some disagreement on the reliability of these surveys, they are continually being used in benefit-cost analysis, natural resource damages litigation, and for other purposes. A distinguished panel of social scientists, chaired by two Nobel laureates in economics (Arrow et al. 1993) was commissioned by the National Oceanic and Atmospheric Administration (NOAA) to assess the contingent valuation methodology. This panel was brought together because NOAA had drafted regulations

---

[6] www.cica.gov.uk (last accessed 11/05/09).

[7] Regardless of the theoretical concerns, Cohen (1990) finds that the jury award method yields estimates of the cost of an index crime that are consistent with the property value studies.

[8] For an overview of the contingent valuation method, see Mitchell and Carson (1989). See also Cohen (2009).

calling for the use of this methodology when estimating natural resource damages in legal proceedings involving compensation for damaged public property. The panel concluded that this is a valid approach and provided a set of guidelines for conducting a reliable contingent valuation survey. Thus, if done properly, contingent valuation surveys can be useful policy tools. Although being used in many different policy contexts, contingent valuation is only beginning to be employed in criminal justice research (see Cohen et al. 2004).

Finally, economists often rely upon indirect measurement techniques by appealing to the notions of *opportunity cost* and *revealed preference*. In some instances, this is as straightforward as identifying foregone productive opportunities, such as the time an offender spends in prison, or the time a victim spends out of work while dealing with the criminal justice process. In other instances, the costs are much more subtle. If consumers are rational and act in their own self-interest (in the jargon of economics, are "utility maximizers"), we can learn many useful things from their behavior – i.e., their "revealed preference" for one choice over another. Thus, the fact that individuals choose a leisure activity over working another hour provides us with a lower bound estimate of the value of that leisure activity. The "opportunity cost" of the time involved must be at least as much as the net income they would have earned during it. Put differently, if an individual enjoys an hour of leisure time instead of working overtime and earning $30 per hour, we can infer that the person values his/her own time by at least that amount. This notion can be used to value the cost of many preventive or avoidance activities that people take to reduce their likelihood of victimization. Examples of these time costs include the time people take to lock and unlock cars and homes and taking a long route home to avoid an unsafe neighborhood.

Some crimes with very large intangible costs like treason or crimes that betray the public trust may never be monetized. However, that does not invalidate the theory that would identify the social cost of treason to be the risk of harm to our national security or the social cost of a public betrayal of trust to be a diminution of public trust and moral behavior.

"Top Down" Approach to Crime Cost Estimation

Unlike the "bottom up" approach that attempts to estimate each component cost of crime, an alternative (or complementary) methodology is to estimate costs from the top down. Three methods have been used to date; revealed preferences, stated preferences, and life satisfaction (for details, see Cohen 2009). The revealed preference approach has generally focused on estimating differences in property values based on crime rates. As discussed in the previous section, to the extent that home buyers take into account the risk of victimization when deciding whether or not to buy a home, we expect higher crime neighborhoods to have lower housing prices controlling for all other factors that affect house prices.

While the revealed preference approach observes actual market prices and tries to infer the value of crime, stated preference methodologies ask respondents to provide their subjective evaluation of a public good. Oftentimes this is done through a public survey, where respondents are asked to state their "willingness to pay" for a reduction in crime. Studies that have utilized this approach to estimate the costs of crime include Zarkin et al. (2000), Ludwig and Cook (2001), Cohen et al. (2004), Atkinson et al. (2005), and Nagin et al. (2006).

A relatively new approach to valuing crime is to infer values from life satisfaction surveys. Like stated preferences studies, data are based primarily on respondent surveys. The surveys do not ask for valuations; instead, they ask for a subjective evaluation of the respondent's satisfaction with life. Moore (2006) analyzed the European Social Survey, which asks a question "How happy are you," based on an 11-point scale as well as a question on neighborhood safety, "How safe do you – or would you – feel walking alone in this area after dark?" Using multiple regression analysis, he is able to estimate the equivalent income required to maintain one level of "happiness" while varying levels of subjective safety. This provides an estimate of individual's value of safety from crime. Cohen (2008) conducts a similar analysis in the U.S.

EXAMPLES OF LATEST RESEARCH ON CRIME COSTS

"Top Down" Versus "Bottom Up" Estimates

There have been several attempts to build "bottom up" cost of crime estimates. Cohen (1988) started with criminal victimization data, where surveys collect information on medical costs and lost wages of victims. To estimate intangible "pain and suffering," he combined the information on the distribution of physical injuries to crime victims with jury award data for comparable physical injuries taken from road traffic and other personal injury lawsuits. In the U.S., juries are asked to award an *ex post* compensation amount that is designed to make the victim whole following the event. Hence, this approach is close to "willingness to accept" – although the decision maker is not the victim, but an outside jury. Miller et al. (1996) improved on this earlier approach by obtaining data from actual court cases involving crime victims – usually suing third parties alleging inadequate security. Cohen et al. (1994), added criminal justice costs to the cost of crime to victims. However, none of these prior studies using jury awards include more comprehensive estimates, such as fear of crime to non-victims or losses to the community.

A similar approach was utilized by Brand and Price (2000) in the U.K., when they applied estimates of the distribution of physical injuries from criminal victimization to willingness to pay estimates from road transport injuries to arrive at the intangible victim costs. Dolan et al. (2005) and Dubourg et al. (2005) also began with crime victimization data, but combined them with independent estimates of reductions in the quality of life from physical and mental injuries sustained by crime victims (as measured by the QALY index used in the healthcare literature). Like the earlier work in the U.S., these studies provide estimates of the tangible and intangible costs to crime victims, but do not include values for fear of crime to nonvictims or losses to the community.

Table 8.3 illustrates the bottom up approach for the cost of rape in England and Wales, and in the United States. The estimates have been updated for inflation from their original sources and the English data converted to US dollars for ease of comparison. It can be seen that the figures do not differ a great deal for the principal cost categories. Healthcare costs (defined to cover both physical and mental care) are somewhat higher in the US, while the reverse is true for lost output. The most important feature shared by data for both countries is that the largest single component is for pain and suffering. Improvements in the methodology of estimating the costs of crime mean that these elements, which were missing from early work on the costs of rape, for example, now play a central role. It is notable that criminal

TABLE 8.3. **Estimated costs of rape in US and UK**

Costs of rape: "Bottom up approach"		
Component	US	England
Victim		
Health care	$4,707	$3,762
Lost output	$3,820	$18,007
Pain & suffering	$141,205	$111,023
Public		
Criminal justice costs	$4,048	$1,605[a]
Avoidance costs	?	?
Fear	?	?
Community costs	?	?
Offender costs	?	?
Justice costs	?	?
Overdeterrence	?	?
Total	$153,780 plus	$134,397 plus

Notes: Victim costs for US taken from Miller et al. (1996), Table 8.2
US Criminal Justice costs taken from Cohen (1998), Table 8.3
English data based on Dubourg et al. (2005)
US costs have been updated for inflation to 2008 by the Historical
CPI-U index. English costs have been updated for inflation to 2008
by the CPI and converted to US dollars at $1.60 to the pound
[a]Criminal justice costs are not disaggregated as between rape and
other sexual offences, so this figure is an underestimate

justice related costs associated with each rape appear to be very low at around $4,000 in the US.[9] Although the average rape offender might be incarcerated for several years at a cost of $100,000 or more, the fact that so few rapists are ultimately charged, convicted, and sentenced for their crime yields a low cost per victimization. Combining these figures, the cost of a rape is estimated to be at least $153,000 in the US and $134,000 in England.

However, these totals exclude the avoidance costs by citizens at large who might buy added security equipment, taking taxis instead of walking home at night, the mental anguish and fear to the general pubic (including those nonrape victims who do walk home at night despite their perceived risk). It also excludes the cost to the community in a high crime area, cost to the offender and/or family, justice costs, and any costs of over-deterrence. Using a "top down" approach estimating the public's willingness to pay for a reduction in rape in the U.S., Cohen et al. (2004) estimated the cost of rape to be $237,000 in 2000 dollars, or approximately $300,000 in 2008 dollars – about twice the cost of rape using a bottom up approach. Cohen et al. (2004) find the ratio of willingness-to-pay to a bottom up approach to be about 2.0 for the crimes of rape, serious assaults and murder, and as much as five to ten times for armed robbery and burglary. Thus, one possible measure of the unknown costs of crime in Table 8.3 is the difference between willingness to pay and the bottom up estimates. However, this assumes that individuals who answer willingness to pay surveys understand and internalize the component costs of crime. For example, when asked whether they would be

---

[9] The figure for England is lower still, but it fails to distinguish between rape and other sexual offences, so is almost certainly an underestimate. Rape is a more serious offence than many other sexual offences, and thus will typically result in longer terms of imprisonment and thus higher costs.

willing to pay $100 annually for a 10% reduction in rape, respondents might only consider their own fear of rape, and the impact that reduced rape might have on other aspects of their life (e.g., their ability to walk in the park at night, the value of homes in their neighborhood, or the risk that their family members or friends might be victimized). They might not consider the fact that fewer rapes mean lower criminal justice costs (and potentially lower taxes or higher benefits from other government services being substituted into). Thus, future research on what respondents consider in their survey responses to these questions is needed.

EMERGING AND FUTURE ISSUES IN COST ESTIMATION

There are many issues that remain unresolved in the measurement of the costs of crime. Some of the challenges are conceptual while others are empirical. The conceptual issues include the choice between top down and bottom up measures, which we have discussed at length. The omission of fear of crime is also important, particularly in spheres such as the risk of terrorism. An important theoretical issue associated with estimating the cost of fear is the extent to which cost estimates should be based on the public's fear even if it is based on misunderstood risks or consequences. Crime survey findings demonstrate that subjective estimates of the likelihood of being victimized are a good deal higher than the objective risk of victimization, at least in relation to offences such as burglary. While estimating the willingness to pay to reduce "unwarranted fear" might be of value in understanding the potential value to the public in reducing fear, it might not be appropriate to base actual crime reduction strategies on such misplaced fears. But these policy implications are well beyond the scope of a chapter focusing on methods for estimating costs of crime.

Empirical issues arise in abundance, because estimating the costs of crime requires vast amounts of information much of which is simply not collected or is not available in suitable format. We referred above to the example of knowing how to split police time inputs across many offence types. There are countless other barriers of a similar kind. Estimating the costs to victims and healthcare agencies of injuries sustained in violent attacks, for example, requires very large victim surveys to ensure adequate coverage of the range of injuries that might result from the rarer types of violent offences. Increasing thought is being given to the methodology for making estimates in settings where data are poor and to the transferability of estimates between countries: Dubourg (2009).

Efforts to make international comparisons of the costs of crime have to be based on agreed definitions of offences. Many countries have idiosyncracies in their definitions with the result that analysts have to go back to a more disaggregated set of offence classifications and recombine elements in a new way, which is more consistent with the definitions being used by others: See further the discussion in the European Sourcebook project in Europe: http://www.europeansourcebook.org/.

For some policy purposes, it is necessary to compile "composites" of offence types which have more public resonance than legal definitions of offences, and this can challenge cost estimation. "Domestic abuse," for example, is not a unique offence type: it entails a variety of offences including violence against the person, making threats and sexual assault. In order to estimate the returns from interventions to reduce domestic abuse, it may be necessary to estimate the mix of offence types if all that is known is that some particular proportion of households has ceased to be a victim of such abuse. Another instance where the case mix has to be treated carefully before applying costs of crime is in the forensic science evaluation field. In order to evaluate a policy such as the extension of DNA testing, estimates need to be made of the change in the profile of offending, resulting before cost of crime estimates can be applied.

If DNA testing represents a more effective deterrent to some offence types than others, the evaluation design has to allow for the possibility of adjustments in the offence pattern.

We conclude by noting that a great deal of criminal justice policy discussion can be usefully illuminated with estimates of the costs of crime. Well-specified models, that embrace all relevant aspects of the costs of crime, can play a central role in articulating and comparing policy options. The significance for a government of having cost of crime estimates available is becoming increasingly evident. At project (and programme) level it can be seen in the increasing emphasis on the use of economic methods of appraisal and evaluation in the criminal justice field. At a strategic level, it can be found in a commitment to prioritize criminal justice resources explicitly on those offence types generating greatest costs to society rather than on the offence types where the volume of offences is the greatest: Bowles (2008). A final benefit from constructing cost of crime estimates using the kinds of methods outlined in this chapter is that it makes more transparent where costs fall. This can be invaluable not only in identifying the full costs of crime, but also in helping deconstruct the (budgetary and other) interests of stakeholders ranging from victims of crime to criminal justice agencies to the taxpayer and to society at large.

REFERENCES

Alvazzi del Frate A, Van Kesteren JN (2004) Criminal Victimisation in Urban Europe. Key findings of the 2000 International Crime Victims Survey. UNICRI, Turin

Anderson DA (1999) The aggregate burden of crime. J Law Econ 42:611–642

Aos S, Lieb R, Mayfield J, Miller M, Pennucci A (2004) Benefits and Costs of Prevention and Early Intervention Programs for Youth, Washington State Institute for Public Policy, Olympia, WA. www.wsipp.wa.gov/pub.asp?docid=04–07–3901 (last accessed 11/05/09)

Arrow K, Solow R, et al. (1993) Report of the NOAA panel on contingent valuation. Fed Regist 58:4601–4614

Atkinson G, Healey A, et al. (2005) Valuing the costs of violent crime: a stated preference approach. Oxf Econ Pap 57:559–585

Bartley WA (2000) A valuation of specific crime rates. Vanderbilt University, Mimeo.

Becker GS (1968) Crime and punishment: an economic approach. J Polit Econ 76:169–217

Bowles R (2008) The impact of costs of crime methodology on criminal justice policy. In: Faure M, Stephen F (eds) Essays in the Law and Economics of Regulation. Liber Amicorum Anthony Ogus. Intersentia, Antwerp

Brand S, Price R (2000) The economic and social costs of crime. Home Office, London

Bureau of Justice Statistics (2008) Criminal Victimization, 2007. U.S. Department of Justice. NCJ 224390

Cohen MA (1988) Pain, suffering, and jury awards: a study of the cost of crime to victims. Law and Society Review 22:537–55

Cohen MA (1990) A note on the cost of crime to victims. Urban Studies 27:125–32

Cohen MA (1998) The monetary value of saving a high-risk youth. J Quant Criminol 14(1):5–33

Cohen MA (2000) Measuring the costs and benefits of crime and justice. Crim Justice 4:53

Cohen MA (2005) The costs of crime and justice. Routledge, New York

Cohen MA (2008) The effect of crime on life satisfaction. Journal of Legal Studies 37:S325–53

Cohen MA (2009) Valuing crime control benefits using stated preference approaches. In: Dunworth T (ed) Cost and benefits of crime. Urban Institute, Washington, DC

Cohen MA, Miller TR, Rossman SB (1994) The Costs and Consequences of Violent Behavior in the United States, in Understanding and Preventing Violence: Consequences and Control of Violence, edited by Albert J. Reiss, Jr. and Jeffrey A. Roth, Committee on Law and Justice, Commission on Behavioral and Social Sciences and Education, National Research Council. (Washington, D.C.: National Academy Press), 4:67–166

Cohen MA, Miller TR (1998) The cost of mental health care for victims of crime. J Interpers Violence 13:93–100

Cohen MA, Miller TR (2003) 'Willingness to Award' nonmonetary damages and the implied value of life from jury awards. Int Rev Law Econ 23:165–181

Cohen MA, Rust RT, Steen S, Tidd S (2004) Willingness-to-pay for crime control programs. Criminology 42(1): 86–106

Cook PJ (1983) Costs of crime. In: Kadish SH (ed) Encyclopedia of crime and justice. Free Press, New York

Demmert HG (1979) Crime and crime control: what are the social costs? Stanford University, Hoover Institution, Center for Econometric Studies of the Justice System

Dhiri S, Brand S (1999) Analysis of costs and benefits: guidance for evaluators, Crime Reduction Programme, Guidance Note 1. Home Office, London

Dolan P, Loomes G, et al. (2005) Estimating the intangible victim costs of violent crime. Br J Criminol 45(6):958–976

Donnelly N, Scott L, et al. (2007). Estimating the short-term costs of police time spent dealing with alcohol-related crime in NSW. Hobart, Tasmania, National Drug Law Enforcement Research Fund

Dubourg R (2009) Comparisons of cost-weighted and volume-based crime measures for EU countries. Eur J Criminal Policy Res (forthcoming)

Dubourg R, Hamed J, et al. (2005) The economic and social costs of crime against individuals and households 2003/04. Home Office On-Line Report

Dugan L (1999) The effect of criminal victimization on a household's moving decision. Criminology 37(4):901–929

French MT, Rachal JV, Hubbard RL (1991) Conceptual framework for estimating the social cost of drug abuse. J Health Social Policy 2:1–22

Gardlund A (2008) Allocation of police costs in Sweden. PowerPoint presentation available at www.costsofcrime.org/Milan (last accessed 11/05/09)

Gold MR, Siegel JE, Russell LB, Weinstein MC (1996) Cost-effectiveness in health and medicine. Oxford University Press, New York

Hartman R (1990) One thousand points of light seeking a number: A case study of CBO's discount rate policy. *J Envt'l Econ & Mgt* 18:S3–S7

Hartunian NS, Smart CN, et al. (1981) The incidence and economic costs of cancer, motor vehicle injuries, coronary heart disease, and stroke: a comparative analysis. Am J Public Health. 70(12):1249–1260

Hellman DA, Naroff JL (1979) The impact of crime on urban residential property values. Urban Stud 16:105–112

Her Majesty's Inspectorate of Constabulary (1998) What price policing? A study of efficiency and value for money in the police service. HM Stationery Office, London

Her Majesty's Treasury (2003) Appraisal and evaluation in central government: "The Green Book," treasury guidance. HM Stationery Office, London

Hoehn JP, Berger MC, Blomquist GC (1987) A hedonic model of interregional wages, rents, and amenity values. J Reg Sci 27:605–620

Jansson K (2007) British crime survey: measuring crime for 25 years. Home Office, London

Klaus PA (1994) The costs of crime to victims. U.S. Department of Justice, Washington, DC

Lewin JL, Trumbull WN (1990) The social value of crime? Int Rev Law Econ 10:271–284

Linden L, Rockoff J (2006) There goes the neighborhood? Estimates of the impact of crime risk on property values from Megan's laws. NBER Working Paper, 12253

Ludwig J, Cook PJ (2001) The benefits of reducing gun violence: evidence from contingent-valuation survey data. J Risk Uncertain 22:207–226

Macmillan R (2000) Adolescent victimization and income deficits in adulthood: rethinking the costs of criminal violence from a life-course perspective. Criminology 38(2):553–588

Mayhew P, Van Dijk JJM (1997) Criminal Victimisation in eleven industrialised countries. Key findings from the 1996 International Crime Victims Survey. Ministry of Justice, WODC, The Hague

Miller T, Cohen MA, et al. (1996) Victim costs and consequences: a new look. National Institute of Justice, Washington, DC

Mitchell RC, Carson RT (1989) Using Surveys to Value Public Goods. RFF Press, Washington DC

Moolenaar DEG (2008) Jaarlijkse kosten van criminaliteit (Annual costs of crime). In:. Eggen AThJ, Kalidien SN (eds) Criminaliteit en Rechtshandhaving 2007 (Crime and law and order 2007). Boom Legal, The Hague

Moore MJ, Viscusi WK (1989) Discounting environmental health risks: New evidence and policy implications. *J Envt'l Econ & Mgt* 18:S51–S62

Moore SC (2006) The value of reducing fear: an analysis using the European Social Survey. Applied Economics 38(1):115–117

Nagin DS (2001) Measuring the economic benefits of developmental prevention programs. Crime and Justice 28: 347–384

Nagin DS, Piquero A, et al. (2006) Public Preferences for Rehabilitation versus Incarceration of Juvenile Offenders: Evidence from a Contingent Valuation Survey. Criminology & Public Policy 5(4):627

Office of Management and Budget (2003) Circular A-4 (September 17)

Rizzo MJ (1979) The cost of crime to victims: an empirical analysis. J Legal Stud 8:177

Thaler R (1978) A note on the value of crime control: evidence from the property market. J Urban Econ 5:137–145

Van Dijk JJM, Manchin R, Van Kesteren J, Nevala S, Hideg G (2005) The burden of crime in the EU. Research Report: A Comparative Analysis of the European Crime and Safety Survey (EU ICS)

Viscusi WK (1998) The value of life in legal contexts: survey and critique. Am Law Econ Rev 2:195–222

Viscusi WK (2000) The value of life in legal contexts: Survey and critique. *American Law and Economics Review* 2:195–222

Zarkin GA, Cates SC, Bala MV (2000) Estimating the willingness to pay for drug abuse treatment: a pilot study, J Substance Abuse Treatment 18(2):149–159

Zerbe RO, Jr., Bellas AS (2006) A primer for benefit-cost analysis. Edward Elgar, Cheltenham, UK

## CHAPTER 9

Estimating Treatment Effects: Matching Quantification to the Question

THOMAS A. LOUGHRAN AND EDWARD P. MULVEY

INTRODUCTION

In criminal justice as well as other areas, practitioners and/or policy makers often wish to know whether something "works" or is "effective." Does a certain form of family therapy reduce troubled adolescents' involvement in crime more than what would be seen if they were on probation? Does a jail diversion policy substantially increase indicators of community adjustment for mentally ill individuals who are arrested and processed under this policy? If so, by how much?

Trying to gauge the impact of programs or policies is eminently logical for several reasons. Obviously, this type of information is important from a traditional cost-benefit perspective. Knowing the overall impact of a program in terms of tangible and measurable benefits to some target group of interest is necessary to assess whether an investment in the program buys much. For instance, a drug rehabilitation program, which requires a large fixed cost of opening plus additional considerable operating expenses, should be able to show that this investment is worth it in terms of reduced drug use or criminal activity among its clients. Quantifiable estimates about the impact of policies or programs are also important in assessing the overall social benefit of particular approaches; it is often useful to know how much a recent change in policy has affected some subgroup in an unintended way. For instance, more stringent penalties for dealing crack, rather than powdered cocaine, appears to have provided only a marginal decrease in drug trafficking at the expense of considerable racial disparity in sentencing. Informed practice and policy rests on empirical quantifications of how much outcomes shift when certain approaches or policies are put into place.

These estimates of program or policy impact are rarely easy to obtain or to trust fully. It is often too easy to adopt a traditional empirical method of analysis (e.g., regression, odds ratios) to provide a metric of program effectiveness, without considering the limitations or restrictions of such approaches. Finding that two groups, on average, significantly differ statistically on some outcome after some statistical controls have been introduced, or that a certain group

A.R. Piquero and D. Weisburd (eds.), *Handbook of Quantitative Criminology*,
DOI 10.1007/978-0-387-77650-7_9, © Springer Science + Business Media, LLC 2010,
First softcover printing 2011

affected by an intervention, is several times more likely to have a particular outcome than a non-affected comparison group, is far from definitive proof of the intervention's effectiveness. Relying on findings like these, analysts can often provide biased estimates of success or harm, estimates of outcome effects that are irrelevant for answering the appropriate policy question at hand, or, in some cases, both. Obtaining and interpreting quantitative results about outcomes in a manner which is both correct and germane, requires delicate consideration of both the question at hand and the methods used to generate the numbers considered.

There are a variety of ways to explicitly estimate treatment effects, including several that are formally outlined within this edition. This chapter does not focus on actual estimation methods per se, but rather addresses the broader question of interpreting these effects, once estimated. We attempt to provide the reader with some clarity regarding the use and interpretation of estimates of *treatment effects*, a term which we believe is often used in too generic a manner. Specifically, we focus on understanding which type of treatment effect estimate is of interest to particular types of policy problems.

This chapter is organized as follows: Section 2 presents some definitions and two important issues that have to be addressed in any effort to estimate the impact of a practice or policy. Section 3 provides some technical notation for defining several different quantities that can be calculated, each of which is often referred to as a treatment effect. Section 4 describes the issues connected with interpreting treatment effects when the researcher is capable of experimentally manipulating treatment assignment. Section 5 introduces additional considerations regarding the interpretation of treatment effects with observational data. Section 6 concludes and offers a general discussion of inferring causality for program and policy discussions.

COMMON TERMS AND CONSIDERATIONS

We should first be clear about several terms that are used throughout the ensuing discussion. A *treatment* refers to a policy or intervention, which may be administered to (or, alternatively, withheld from) an individual in a population of interest. For instance, an offender being sent to prison or entering drug rehabilitation would constitute examples of individuals "being treated," as compared to those individuals within the same population who are not sent to prison or do not enter drug rehabilitation. We denote those in the former conditions as members of a *treatment group*; those in the latter conditions are considered members of the *comparison group*. Researchers are typically interested in estimating a *treatment effect*, that is, the effect of a policy or intervention on some related outcome of interest. For instance, criminologists are typically interested in determining the effect of being sent to prison on an individual's subsequent recidivism, or the effect of a drug rehabilitation program on the likelihood that an individual will relapse into drug use.

In a broader scientific sense, researchers in these situations are interested in determining a *causal* effect of the treatment. The effect *caused* by a treatment is a comparison of an outcome a subject reveals after involvement with some treatment the subject *actually received* with the latent, and unobserved outcome the subject *would have* exhibited under the alternative treatment. This unobservable outcome for the individual under the alternative treatment is known as a *counterfactual* outcome. However, as considered in more depth below, it can often be very difficult, if not impossible, to make a strong causal inference regarding the effect of a treatment.

There are two main impediments to coming to a strong conclusion about the size of the treatment effect, namely *selection bias* and *response heterogeneity*. These two issues take a variety of forms in evaluation designs, and there are a number of different strategies to address them. Depending on how well and appropriately they are addressed, we gain more or less confidence that we are getting a valid estimate of the desired effect of a treatment.

Selection bias (or a *selection effect*) is the result of a situation in which a subset of the population is more likely to be assigned to or select into some treatment than the rest of the population. The problem is that the factors, which make this subset more likely to select into the treatment, may also be directly influencing some outcome of interest. In this case, a comparison of treatment and control groups may be inappropriate as it involves a comparison of groups which are dissimilar in important ways *prior* to entering the treatment. It is, thus, difficult to disentangle whether differences in outcomes after treatment between the treatment and control groups are caused explicitly by the treatment, or if they may be due to these preexisting differences, between groups. Such preexisting differences which mask the true causal nature of the relationship between treatment and outcome, are often referred to as *confounders*. For example, if we are trying to determine the true causal effect of being sent to prison on an individual's subsequent criminality, the problem is made difficult by the fact that those offenders who are likely to be sent to prison are inherently likely to be more criminally active after being released than those who are not sent to prison. Inherent differences between groups bias our estimate of a true causal effect to an unknown degree, and while this problem is typically well recognized, it is not always properly controlled for in many empirical designs.

There is a second issue which is less mentioned, yet, is equally problematic for assessing treatment effects for their policy relevance. *Heterogeneity in response to treatment* among different subsets of the population presents issues when both estimating the causal impact of a treatment as well as when applying the observed effects to program or policy improvements. In some instances, even if one is able to get an unbiased estimate of the effect of a treatment on some subset of the population, it may not be generalizable to the population at large. In other words, the same treatment may have dramatically different effects on different segments of the population; that is, different subgroups may *respond* differently to exposure to the treatment. If this is the case, any attempt to generalize the effects learned from one particular segment to another may rely on extrapolation and lead to nonsensical, or even worse, harmful conclusions. For instance, suppose we find evidence that one-on-one sessions with a school psychologist greatly benefit children who follow a high, chronic trajectory of conduct problems by reducing this behavior. It is likely the case that providing the same sessions to those children who do not exhibit such intense conduct problems may not only fail to benefit these children, but may actually work to impede some of their basic school outcomes by removing them from the classroom environment.

These issues are certainly not new. Researchers address them regularly, using a variety of quantitative methods ranging from randomized treatment assignment, sophisticated statistical and econometric methods, to testing the representativeness of samples to ensure generalizability. We mention them here as a backdrop for our discussion of the more common ways that treatment effects are estimated in the literature. Carefully considering how selection bias and heterogeneity of response have been addressed in a particular approach is essential for applying findings about treatment effects to policy questions appropriately.

DEFINING TREATMENT EFFECTS

There are several specific quantities which fall under the broader rubric of "treatment effect." We use the *potential-outcomes* conceptual framework, first introduced by Neyman (1923) and later developed by Rubin (1974, 1977, and 1978), to define these different quantities.[1] Due to scope and spatial constraints, we restrict our discussion exclusively to *point-treatment* studies, where the impact of a single treatment on some later outcome in an individual is considered, and there are no multiple time-dependant states of treatment status. In other words, we only consider such cases where there is neither treatment exposure nor covariate confounding which is time-dependent.[2] This seems to us to be the most common situation encountered when practitioners and policy makers question whether there is sufficient evidence to believe that something "works."

Bodies of literature regarding specific treatments are often analyzed and summarized using *meta-analyses*, which treat separate studies of treatments as data points in an analysis of overall effectiveness of a particular approach. We do not address this technique here, as there is a separate chapter in this volume specifically devoted to this topic. The discussion here, however, raises questions that might be considered when conducting these sorts of summary analyses, especially with regard to the types of treatment effects considered to be equivalent in the consideration of a set of investigations.

Some Basic Notation

Let y_1 denote some outcome with treatment and y_0 denote the outcome without treatment. Notice that since an individual cannot be in both states of treatment simultaneously, we *cannot* observe both y_1 and y_0. Let $Z = 1$ for each subject if that subject has been treated, and $Z = 0$ if the subject is assigned to the control condition. To measure the *effect of the treatment*, we are interested in the difference in the outcomes in each treatment condition, $y_1 - y_0$.

Notice that this treatment effect cannot be calculated for individuals, since any single individual's counterfactual outcome is never actually observed. In other words, we are only able to observe an individual's outcome either under treatment or under control, but never both simultaneously. Therefore, when evaluating the effect of a treatment, we are limited to estimating the *average* effect across either some predefined population or subpopulation.

Population Average Treatment Effect

We define the *population average treatment effect (PATE)* as

$$E(y_1 - y_0)$$

The *PATE* (or, alternatively, the *average treatment effect*, or *ATE*) is the expected effect of treatment on a randomly drawn person from the population. This answers the question, if

---

[1] For a thorough overview of the framework of the Rubin Causal Model, see Holland (1986).

[2] For a discussion of these more complicated situations involving time-dependency in treatment and covariate confounding, see Robins et al. (2000) and Robins et al. (1999).

we could randomly choose someone from the entire population and treat them, what would we expect the effect to be? Conceptually, this quantity may appear to be highly attractive to researchers, since it provides an estimate of the effect of a policy across the entire population. This same reason, however, also undermines the utility of this estimate in many situations. The *PATE* is sometimes not practical because as it averages precisely across the entire population in making an estimate, it may include units never eligible for particular types of treatment in the first place.

Consider an example where we are interested in estimating the effectiveness of a technical job training program on increasing the future labor market success of those who participate as measured by future wages. There are some individuals in the population such as those with a 4-year college degree, for whom this particular type of training might have zero, or perhaps even a negative impact on their future wages. Many of these individuals would likely never enter such a training program in the first place. Therefore, the *PATE*, which takes the entire population into consideration, is often not particularly useful in evaluating the effectiveness of a specific treatment, since it gives an estimate of a treatment effect that will never happen.

The *PATE* is well suited to provide information about the possible impact of universal prevention efforts. Because the PATE estimates the effect of a treatment on a population, it provides an estimate of the overall societal cost or benefit connected with particular policies or practices. For example, exposure to lead has been shown to have an effect on the development of early antisocial behavior (Needleman et al. 1996; Nevin 2000), and subsequent estimates have been made regarding the amount of delinquency in a particular locale that can be reasonably attributed to this exposure (Wright et al. 2008). These estimates of the *PATE* indicate the expected impact across the entire population of children from lead exposure. Thus, they give policy makers an indication of the potential general payoff from a broadly implemented strategy and the concomitant benefit and cost deriving to each taxpayer.

Average Effect of Treatment on the Treated

A second quantity of interest is known as the *average effect of the treatment on the treated (ATT)*, which is defined as

$$E(y_1 - y_0 | Z = 1)$$

The *ATT* is the mean effect for those who *actually participated* in the treatment or program. It answers the question, for a random individual who *actually received the treatment*, what would we expect this effect to be? The *PATE* and *ATT* generally differ, but are equivalent in some special cases discussed below. Return to the job training example from above. A program evaluator charged with understanding the effectiveness of such a program would likely wish to know how the treatment affected those who actually underwent the training, with no concern for those who had no intention of doing so. Thus, the *ATT* is a much more appealing quantity in this case and in many others. Ridgeway (2006) provides an empirical example of *ATT* in his analysis of the role of racial biases in traffic stop outcomes, by using propensity score *weighting* (McCaffrey et al. 2004). For the purposes of estimation, Ridgeway notes that in general, propensity scores methods (chapter in edition; see also Rosenbaum and Rubin 1983) are closely linked to the potential-outcomes framework.

Within-Group Treatment Effect

It certain instances, we might be interested in how some treatment affects a certain subgroup of the population. Rather than just being concerned with how a program has an effect across the whole population or those who were enrolled in the program, we might want to know how the program affects a particular group of policy interest (e.g., females vs. males). Both the *PATE* and *ATT* can be redefined to generalize to a specific subset of the population. We may do this by simply expanding these definitions to condition on some covariate x or vector of covariates $\mathbf{x}$.

The *PATE* conditional on $\mathbf{x}$ is simply

$$E(y_1 - y_0|\mathbf{x})$$

This quantity answers the question, if we randomly treat an individual from the entire population with characteristic $\mathbf{x}$, what would we expect the effect to be? For example, consider the example of estimating the effects of lead exposure presented above. The *PATE* obtained above regarding the effects of lead exposure may be valuable for estimating the overall impact of a program limiting the use of certain materials in a community. By examining the *PATE* for those individuals living in housing projects versus the rest of the community, however, we would get a picture of the relative effect of focusing efforts at control in just those settings. The *PATE* estimates conditioned on certain individual level characteristics of a sample can thus provide guidance about ways to maximize the impact of an intervention or policy change.

Similarly, the *ATT* conditional on $\mathbf{x}$ is

$$E(y_1 - y_0|\mathbf{x}, \quad Z = 1)$$

This quantity answers the question, for a random individual with characteristic $\mathbf{x}$ who *actually received the treatment*, what would we expect this effect to be? By suitably choosing $\mathbf{x}$, we may define the *PATE* and *ATT* for various subsets of the population. This may or may not be important depending on the policy question one is interested in addressing. For example, we might be interested in how incarceration specifically affects women as opposed to men, or how a drug rehabilitation program helps chronic users as opposed to less serious users. We explore differences in these quantities and their potential utility in more detail below.

SUMMARY

Clearly there are multiple ways to represent a causal effect of treatment. The different quantities used, however, are not all the same. Each answers specific, and sometimes very different questions and they may give very different estimates under different conditions. Given this, it becomes critical to recognize precisely which of these quantities is most appropriate to the policy question of interest in any inquiry. Confusion about which of these estimates is most appropriate, or worse, generic confusion in estimation, can lead to incorrect and potentially harmful policy conclusions.

These considerations drive the remainder of the discussion in this chapter. We continue by considering the two distinct situations under which researchers must estimate and interpret effects of treatment. In one, researchers are allowed to randomly decide who receives a treatment, and, in the other, individuals are allowed to self-select into treatment through their own means or via some other, nonrandom mechanism. We consider the latter case, which is much more prevalent in the social sciences, in deeper detail.

INTERPRETING TREATMENT EFFECTS UNDER RANDOMIZATION

Causal Effects in Randomized Experiments

The universally accepted best method for determining a treatment effect is to conduct a controlled application of a treatment to two groups, composed at random, who either receive or do not receive the treatment. This strategy of *randomized controlled trials*, or *RCTs*, has been widely accepted in medicine for a long time and is currently coming more into vogue as the sine qua non of scientific proof in the social sciences (Weisburd et al. 2001; see also evidence from the Campbell Collaboration, http://www.campbellcollaboration.org/index.asp). In this approach, the researcher is conducting an *experiment* and has the power to control the assignment of the treatments to subjects. Thus, the treatment can be *randomly* assigned. This is critically important, then, as the treatment assignment will not be correlated in any way with the outcome in question. This tends to produce relatively comparable, or *balanced* treatment groups in large experiments, meaning that the treatment and control groups are similar in terms of the distribution of both *observable* and *unobservable* individual characteristics, which are set prior to the treatment. Thus, randomization essentially rules out the presence of selection biases confounding the estimated effect. Although we draw caution to some important considerations below, we cannot stress strongly enough that randomization with a sufficiently large sample is *the absolute best* condition under which to determine causal effects of treatment.

In the case of treatment randomization, the PATE can be thought of in the potential-outcomes framework as a simple difference in means of treatment and comparisons:

$$\text{PATE} = \bar{y}_1 - \bar{y}_0$$

Under randomization, this simple difference in means yields an *unbiased* and *consistent* estimate of the causal treatment effect – a very powerful result. Also note that randomization implies that all individuals within the population are equally likely to be treated (say, with probability $= .5$), and thus, the *PATE* and the *ATT* will be equivalent.

Furthermore, randomization can be applied usefully in more basic regression contexts as well. Consider the following simple regression model

$$y_i = \alpha + \beta Z_i + u_i$$

If the treatment is randomly assigned, then it is independent of all other factors, or formally, $Cov(Z, u) = 0$, meaning that, an Ordinary Least Squares (OLS) estimate of β in the above equation will too yield an unbiased and consistent estimate of the *PATE*.

While randomization is unequivocally the de facto gold standard in evaluation research for the reason described above, we still must be careful about simply generalizing this effect to a wide population. It may be that not all members of the population were equally eligible to be included in the treatment allocation process. Thus, simply because we employ randomization of treatment, this does not mean we have a universally generalizable treatment effect. If the group eligible to be selected for treatment is not the same as the population in general, then any attempt to extend the results to the population at large is potentially problematic. This is sometimes referred to as a lack of *external validity* (Shadish et al. 2001), and it can present serious complications to the conclusions, even if there is pure randomization of treatment assignment.

This issue becomes relevant when implementing "evidence based practices" in different locales. Oftentimes, researchers conduct controlled studies of a treatment program in several locales, documenting impressive treatment effects for a particular intervention approach. This treatment effect may or may not be found, however, when the intervention is then applied to locales that differ substantially from the demonstration locales (e.g., in the demographics of the adolescents/families served, the history of the individuals referred to the intervention). The generation of a treatment effect is certainly a different process than demonstrating the applicability of that effect to a broadly defined group of individuals such as serious adolescent offenders in general. While concerns such as these are most common, there are other factors with randomization, which need be considered. Heckman and Smith (1995) offer a thoughtful and detailed discussion of some other important considerations and limitations of experiments and randomization in the social sciences.

Another important caveat of randomization, which poses a potential threat to the external validity of measured treatment effects, deals with *treatment compliance*, or more precisely, the lack thereof. It cannot simply be assumed that all individuals who are randomly assigned to receive some treatment or control actually do receive it, or, in other words, *comply* with their assigned treatment status.[3] Noncompliance can occur in two general forms. First, an individual who is randomized to the treatment group can end up not receiving the treatment. This is known as *treatment dilution*. Second, some subjects who are assigned to the control group could still potentially end up receiving treatment. In this case, we have *treatment migration*. Both of these occurrences are potentially problematic, as they could possibly reintroduce selection biases into the interpretation of a randomized experiment if not properly considered.

One initial strategy to deal with noncompliance (which at first seems rather intuitively appealing) is to simply ignore those who did not properly comply, and estimate treatment effects from only those who did properly comply. However, the exclusion of noncompliant individuals will likely not be random, if the reason for noncompliance is correlated with the outcome in question. The result is a nonrandom compliance group that no longer balances overall pretreatment characteristics, and thus, might not reveal the realistic effect of the treatment. For example, consider a hypothetical therapy intervention for terminally ill cancer patients aimed at prolonging their survival time. Some of the most seriouslyill individuals might die prior to receiving treatment. This is an extreme example of noncompliance; however, by excluding these individuals from the analysis, we are, in all likelihood, limiting

---

[3] The concept of noncompliance should be thought of in a purely statistical interpretation in this case, where it literally means not adhering to the randomly assigned treatment. Often, particularly in some clinical applications, the term noncompliant can have a negative connotation, as in lack of willingness to accept a helpful therapy. Noncompliance can occur for a variety of reasons, not simply lack of insight or stubbornness, and should therefore not be thought to indicate anything negative about an individual when used in this context. For instance, if a chronic headache sufferer is randomized into the treatment group testing the effectiveness of a new drug and chooses to not take the drug for the simple reason that there is no pain at the time of treatment, then this individual is a non-complier as defined here.

the most severelyill individuals from the treatment group but not the control group (in which case, we are still capable of observing their outcome, survival time). As such, we gain a biased estimate of the treatment effect.

An alternative is to conduct an analysis based on *Intention to Treat (ITT)*, which requires the inclusion of individuals as members of the treatment group to which they are assigned, regardless of compliance or noncompliance. In contrast to the above strategy of excluding noncompliers, this approach may, at first glance, seem counterintuitive; for example, including people who refuse to be treated in a treatment group does not seem very logical. However, the ITT framework is actually critical in that it preserves randomization, which is in direct contrast to the approach of excluding those who do not comply. Also, it can be interpreted as a much more practical assessment of external validity. Assessing the size of a treatment effect in an ITT framework provides a picture of what the impact of a treatment is likely to be when the approach is implemented in the real world. It builds in the attrition that a particular intervention might precipitate into the estimate, thus, in many ways allowing for both the potentially positive and negative aspects of an intervention to be considered. Since it retains randomization, it tests whether the overall effect of the intervention is likely to be positive when it is implemented with individuals like those who are enrolled in the study.

However, there are some limitations to an ITT analysis; most notably, it may reveal a more conservative, or muted estimated treatment effect because of dilution from noncompliance. This is problematic, particularly if one wishes to test for the inequality of different treatment effects, since it will be harder to reject a null hypothesis of no difference. Also, if there is an unusually high degree of noncompliance, then it can become complicated to interpret the estimated treatment effect.

Local Average Treatment Effect

Although randomization is a powerful method to deal with selection bias, opportunities for pure experimental randomization are rare in many of the social sciences. There are, however, situations where randomization of treatment may naturally occur through some other mechanism for some segment of the population, and thus, preserve many of the benefits of experiments. Such situations, known as *natural experiments*, may be exploited in order to circumvent some issues of noncompliance as well as provide useful estimates of treatment effects when explicit randomization of treatment assignment is generally unfeasible or impossible.

In such cases, instrumental variable (IV) methods may be employed. IV methodology relies on pockets of exogenous variation which affect treatment assignment in ways otherwise unrelated to the outcome of interest. Moreover, it yields another sound solution to the problem of noncompliance. For instance, Angrist (2006) shows how IV methodology can be applied to the Minneapolis domestic violence experiment (Sherman and Berk 1984; Berk and Sherman 1988) to counteract the problems of noncompliance in arrests for domestic disputes.

When using IV to estimate causal treatment effects, however, it is important to note that we identify yet another quantity. Recall that, with IV, the source of exogenous variation critical to identification of the treatment effect, centers on individuals being induced to receive treatment based on their having different values of the instrumental variable. As such, the treatment group can be broken into two distinct categories as defined by Angrist et al. (1996): *always-takers*, or those who select into the treatment regardless of their individual value of the instrument, and *compliers*, or those individuals who would not have selected into the treatment had the instrument not induced them to do so.[4]

With the assumption of monotincity, (that is, some binary instrumental variable, D, makes everyone either more or less likely to select into some binary treatment, Z, but not both), Imbens and Angrist (1994) define what they call the *local average treatment effect (LATE)*, which can be written as:

$$\frac{E(y|D=1) - E(y|D=0)}{P(Z=1|D=1) - P(Z=1|D=0)}$$

Notice that numerator in this expression, which is commonly known as the *Wald estimator*, is the difference in outcome between the two groups split by the binary instrument, D. However, since not everyone receiving a value of $D = 1$ will also select into treatment (i.e., have $Z = 1$), this difference in outcomes for the two groups must be adjusted by the probability that individuals in each group select into treatment. As such, having a value $D = 1$ must induce some additional subset of individuals to select into treatment, $Z = 1$, than would not select in if $D = 0$, or else there will be no identification, as the denominator of this quantity would be equal to zero.

However, this identification comes at a price. Since it is identified only off of the compliers, without the very strong assumption of treatment effect homogeneity, the *LATE* will not equal either the *PATE* or *ATT*. Instead, the *LATE* estimator answers the question, what is the expected effect for the compliers, or those who received treatment explicitly because the instrument induced them to do so but otherwise would not have selected into the treatment?

For example Angrist (1990) employs IV methodology in an attempt to determine the causal effects of military service on future civilian labor market outcomes by using the Vietnam draft lottery number IV. The treatment group, that is, those who joined the military, included two distinct groups of individuals: those who would have joined the military regardless (i.e., the always-takers), and those who only joined because their low draft number induced them to do so (i.e., the compliers). Allowing that the draft number met the assumptions to be used as an instrument (i.e., it predicts military service but is otherwise random), Angrist is able to estimate the causal effect of military service on future wages in the civilian labor market, but is only able to generalize with regard to those who only joined the military *because they had a low draft number*. There is no way to estimate the effect for those who joined the military regardless of draft number (which likely includes those with the worst potential civilian labor market outcomes, an interesting subgroup in this context) This inherent inability of the *LATE* estimator to generalize to a broader set of the population is one of its main criticisms, and it has been argued that natural experiments and IV methods are best suited when the response to treatment is *homogeneous* (Heckman 1997; Angrist 2004).

There are, however, some instances where the exogenous variation exploited by an IV answers *precisely* the policy question of interest, and hence, the *LATE* estimator may actually be the most preferred method. Consider an example of two adjacent areas, say neighboring

---

[4] Angrist, Imbens and Rubin also defines a group known as *never-takers*, or those who, regardless of the instrument, never select into treatment, and therefore are not included as part of the treatment group. Furthermore, the assumption of monotonicity effectively rules out the existence of *defiers*, or those who would have selected into treatment had the instrument made them less likely to do so, but not selected into treatment had their value of the instrument made them more likely to do so.

counties, which are relatively homogenous, except that one adopts a policy lowering the legal limit of blood alcohol content for driving in hopes of deterring Driving Under the Influence (DUI)'s. Clearly, those who are the worst offenders of driving under the influence of alcohol (i.e., those who choose to drive no matter how much they have to drink) will not be deterred by such a change. Yet, such a policy is not aimed at curbing these individuals anyway, but rather, those at the margin, who may be deterred from driving given the lowered legal limit. It is the impact on these individuals that the *LATE* estimator provides, and it can be argued that in this context, the *LATE* estimate is most relevant for evaluating the effectiveness of the policy. The *ATT*, often attractive in other instances, would not be suitable here, since it would consider all drunk drivers, including those who would never respond to such a policy shift.

Summary

True randomization of treatment assignment is undoubtedly the best way to evaluate causal effects of treatments. It should be noted that no statistical or econometric methodology, no matter how sophisticated, can do better in terms of estimating treatment effects, and often-times yield substantial bias in the presence of specification errors (see LaLonde 1986, for an assessment of several nonexperimental estimators). Furthermore, even in situations where pure randomization is infeasible or impossible, pockets of exogenous variation, such as abrupt law changes or variation in policy in otherwise similar areas may present the possibility of a convincing natural experiment. This high regard for randomization or the estimation of exoge-nous effects should be tempered, however, by skepticism about whether the requirements of randomization are really met in any investigation. Randomization is often difficult to generate convincingly, and the methods used in a study to achieve randomization matter in terms of the estimate of the treatment effects. For example, Weisburd et al. (2001) compared studies involving randomized and nonrandomized interventions in the National Institute of Justice Studies, and found study design to influence its conclusions substantially. Without a demon-stration of effective randomization, the treatment effects generated in such studies should be examined closely for the possible impact of factors such as compliance on the estimates obtained.

In many situations, randomization is simply impossible. Interventions are rarely withheld at random, experiences do not occur at random to individuals, and policies are not applied to only a randomly selected subset of population. We now consider such situations, which are of much more importance to criminologists.

TREATMENT EFFECTS IN OBSERVATIONAL DATA

In most evaluation research in social science, in general, and in criminology in particular, ran-domization of treatment assignment is neither possible (e.g., incarceration) nor ethical (e.g., drug use), meaning that people may *self-select* into the treatment they wish to receive. Conse-quently, one must rely on data from an *observational study* in order to study these treatments and their effects. An observational study is an empirical analysis of treatments or policies and the effects that they cause, which differs from an experiment in that the investigator has no control over the treatment assignments (Rosenbaum 2002). As mentioned earlier, these situations involve consideration of selection effects, in which differences in outcomes between treatment and control groups may be due to preexisting differences of those who are and are not selected for treatment as opposed to an actual causal effect of the treatment. There are multiple methods that can be employed to correct for selection bias and these methods work with varying degrees of success to eliminate these effects.

As mentioned above, though, this is not the end of the story. Even in instances where we may reasonably believe we have eliminated all or most of the bias due to selection for some subgroup of the population, it still may be the case that the treatment effect we estimate is not necessarily generalizable to the population at large due to population heterogeneity in the response to treatment. While this residual bias or apparent lack of external validity may appear to be problematic on the surface, we develop an argument below as to why this is not always the case. Instead, we see this variability as an analytic opportunity. In particular, we posit several situations in which the *global treatment effect*, that is, an effect describing the treatment effect for the entire population (or treatment population) in question, is actually *less* interesting and relevant for substantive policy applications than the variable effects that might exist within subpopulations of the group examined. Before we get to an illustration of this latter point, however, we will examine the issues related to constructing valid estimates of treatment effects when confronted with observational data.

Common Support

When attempting to estimate treatment effects with observational data, it is critical to determine whether proper counterfactual outcomes can be found within the control group data. In an ideal situation, a counterfactual outcome can be generated in the control group data to directly assess the impact of the treatment in question. In many situations, though, this is impossible. Consider the example of testing the discharge practices used in a forensic psychiatric hospital. There are simply some individuals who will never be released because of the bizarre and violent nature of their crimes and their lack of responsiveness to medications. Finding the counterfactual of what would happen if a person with such a severe criminal and mental health profile were released is simply not possible.

In the absence of such counterfactual outcomes, depending on the method of estimation, we may be either estimating a biased effect, a fractional effect, which is not necessarily generalizable to the population of interest, or an extrapolated effect, which has no meaning at all. It is, therefore, necessary to assess the overall impact of these situations that cannot be represented in any control condition to determine how applicable any observed treatment effect might be to the policy in question. To do this, we may examine the conditional treatment and control group distributions over some covariate x or covariates $\mathbf{x}$ to make sure there is sufficient overlap, or *common support*. If there is a portion of treated individuals whose values of x (or vector $\mathbf{x}$) are so different that they are unlike any control individuals, then we must be cautious in how we interpret our estimated effect.

An illustration of how some situations indicating different levels of common support helps us to see the importance of this issue for later interpretation of any treatment effect generated on nonrandomized treatment and control groups. Suppose we examine frequency histograms of treatment and control group membership, based on some covariate x, which is important in treatment selection, as is done in Fig. 9.1. Note that the dimension of x may

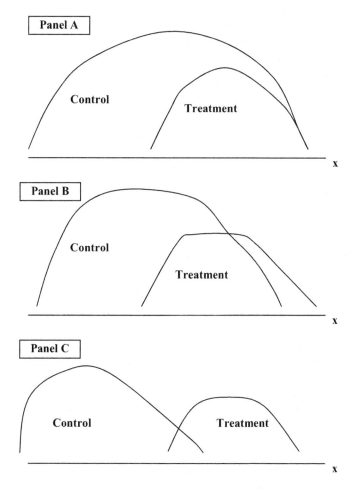

FIGURE 9.1. Some examples of common support.

be easily increased to multiple covariates important to treatment selection, in which case, the scale can then be thought of as some scalar combination of these values such as a propensity score (Rosenbaum and Rubin 1983).

First consider Fig. 9.1, Panel A. In this case, the entire distribution of the treatment group is overlapped by the distribution of controls on x. Thus, we have common support over this entire distribution of treated individuals, and hence, a proper counterfactual for inference can be generated in each case. Suppose we estimate the *ATT* in this case. We then might think of the *ATT* as a *global effect of treatment*, that is, a treatment effect which is an average of, and thus, generalizable to the entire treatment group.

Now consider Fig. 9.1, Panel B. Notice that much of the distribution of the treatment group overlaps with that of the control group on the covariate of interest, although the upper tail of the treatment distribution does not overlap. In this case, while most treated individuals do have a proper counterfactual with which to compare, some in the extreme tail do not. Screening these individuals out could potentially lead to the introduction of more bias in estimating a global *ATT*, as there are treated individuals we are not considering (Rosenbaum and Rubin 1985). However, as developed below, while it may be the case that we have a biased estimate of the global effect of treatment, in some instances, we may have a quantity which is still relevant for some specific policy of interest.

Finally, consider Fig. 9.1, Panel C, which appears to have very little overlap between the distributions of treatment and control groups. In this case, there may be very little we can infer regarding the effect of this treatment as there is simply no proper comparison in the data. In an instance such as this, we are powerless to do much. It is worth noting that this problem *may not* disappear with a larger sample size. In econometric parlance, this is what is known as a fundamental identification problem, that is to say, given the parameters of the problem, we are unable to implicitly identify the treatment effect of interest (see Manski 1995, for a general discussion of identification). Any attempt to quantify a treatment effect in such a case would need to rely on extrapolation, and by extension, be more conjecture than conclusion.

Global vs. Limited Effects

In an instances where we are not fully capable of estimating the global effect of a treatment (as in Fig. 9.1, Panel B above), it is often accepted that what we are able to estimate is merely a "biased" treatment effect and generally not applicable in an evaluation sense (Rosenbaum and Rubin 1985). However, it may be the case that the effect which we have estimated is actually interpretable and valuable, from a policy perspective, despite not being a valid estimate of the global treatment effect. For instance, if there are some individuals within the population who are likely to be treated with high probability, or probability equal to one, then the effect of the treatment on these individuals, at least in a policy evaluation sense, is generally likely to be irrelevant. The policy question is not whether it is worth treating these individuals; they are going to be treated anyway. Thus, the fact that no counterfactual exists in the data for these individuals is not necessarily problematic. We would likely be more interested in answering a policy question relating to those individuals who have some chance or none of being treated. In many instances, these are the cases falling in the area of common support, as they are the individuals "in play" in the policy sense.

Consider our earlier example of releasing individuals from a forensic psychiatric hospital. Even with variability in governing state laws and clinical practice, under which offenders get released, an individual with multiple arrests who has committed murder and does not respond to medication will not be released; that is, his probability of release is equal to 0, or conversely, the probability of being retained equal to 1. Conversely, a young individual with a strong response to treatment, a history of public nuisance crimes, and no prior arrests will be released with probability equal to 1 (again, that is, he or she will likely have no chance of being retained indefinitely in the hospital). Therefore, attempting to compute a global *PATE* or *ATT*, it can be argued, is conceptually irrelevant in a practical sense, as there will never be a situation where the laws and practice will be changed so as to release the murderer mentioned above. Again, conversely, it is also difficult to imagine a world where the laws are expanded to the point where the young, treatment-responsive misdemeanant will be retained for a long period.

In cases like this, a more relevant policy question might instead be to ask, if we redraw the line of demarcation for release from these facilities, where is the logical place to put it? Few would argue that all of the murderers portrayed above should be released. Instead if we look at the effects of release (say, on subsequent recidivism as a measure of future criminality), *only on those where there is discretion involved*, we may evaluate release policy in a more pragmatic sense. Thus, the absence of a global treatment effect in this case is not necessarily handicapping to the analysis, but instead, potentially conceptually preferable.

Global vs. Within-Group Effects

Another important instance of the potential of delimited effects occurs when we are capable of estimating a global effect, yet the particular policy problem of interest is better addressed by examining more localized, within-stratum effects. This situation occurs when one appreciates the possibilities created by the issue of heterogeneity in a global treatment effect, introduced earlier. In some instances, there may be a global null effect of a treatment, and one may be tempted to say that the treatment in question is useless. Further consideration of possible heterogeneous treatment effects, though, can lead to more focused analyses beyond the simple assessment of the overall treatment effect. It may be that there is considerable heterogeneity within various strata of the treatment group and the treatment is causing different groups to respond significantly, but in different ways.

The effects of institutional placement in juvenile justice provide relevant examples. In this area, there is often a global null effect of institutional care on the rate of rearrest in adolescent offenders. As a result, it may be tempting to dispel any consequences, positive or negative, of the use of these types of settings. It may be the case, however, that for certain subgroups within the larger population, say older, more-seasoned offenders, being placed in an institution serves no useful deterrent to future criminality. Conversely, for another subgroup, say younger, more impressionable offenders, such a placement actually exposes them to new people and situations, and thus, for such individuals, is actually criminogenic. Thus, depending on the "case mix" of the treatment group, we might see an overall null effect, even though there were actually strong opposite effects according to age group. If we feel that there is theoretical or practical heterogeneity in the treatment group, then it is possible, if not likely, that there is also heterogeneity in response to treatment. Depending on the policy question of interest, it is likely worth examining subgroup effects to focus future policy alternatives more specifically.

Summary

In the presence of observational data, it is typical of researchers to attempt to address selection, yet ignore heterogeneity, when quantifying treatment effects. We argue that both such problems are equally dangerous, and when considering them, a focus on the relevant policy problem or question should be employed to drive the analysis and results. Furthermore, often despite the efforts to control for a selection effect, in observational data, there may always be some unmeasured confounders, which we cannot account for because we have no observations of their values. If such unobservable factors exist, they may be responsible for bias but we have no knowledge of the direction or magnitude of that bias. That is why randomization is the gold standard, as it creates reasonable balance over all covariates, observable or not.

In the case of observational data, where we suspect such hidden biases may exist, it is useful to conduct a *sensitivity analysis* for hidden biases in order to address this possibility. A sensitivity analysis asks what some unmeasured covariate *would have to be like* in order to materially alter the conclusions of the study. Notice we are unable to actually prove (or disprove) the existence of such a confounder, but if our results are highly sensitive to potential hidden biases, then we may wish to reevaluate our general policy conclusions (for more information of measuring sensitivity to hidden biases, see Rosenbaum 2002). Such additional information about the robustness of treatment effects can be very informative, but is rarely provided.

CONCLUSIONS

Empirical validation of the effects of practices and policies is central to the improvement of interventions in criminal justice. The magnitude and specific effect of an intervention can tell us whether that intervention is worth continuing from a cost-benefit perspective, or whether the intervention should even be implemented in the first place. Too often, however, this question is framed in a rather general manner, with little critical examination of whether the treatment effect calculated matches the question asked about the implementation of the policy or practice. The points raised in this chapter address the nuances of the different methods for calculating treatment effects and emphasize the fact that not all treatment effects are created equal. Different policy problems and research questions require different approaches to the quantification of treatment effects.

We have discussed several quantities, all of which fall under the rubric of "treatment effect," i.e., the *PATE, ATT, LATE,* and various extensions of these quantities, which condition on a specific subset of the population. None of these quantities is necessarily "right" or "better." The main idea we stress is that the burden falls on the researcher to determine which, if any, of these quantities is most relevant for the purpose of a particular policy application, Naive use of any these quantities when another is better suited holds the potential for inappropriate conclusions.

We urge the reader to focus on two central issues, selection bias and response heterogeneity when assessing the utility of any particular treatment effect estimate.

As we note, selection bias is a common, well-recognized nemesis of the social science researcher, and we have oftentimes become somewhat complacent about documenting its effects. In the absence of a selection bias (or, alternatively, if one feels that it has been completely and properly accounted for), one is often tempted to invoke an argument of causality. Although tempting, we urge the reader to treat usage of the term "causal effect" with the same level of concern that one might adopt in handling a container of highly explosive material. Indeed, we may even have been too casual in how we discussed causality above, in the context of our examples, providing insufficient attention to the key assumption of *ignorability of treatment* in most treatment effect literature. That is, when attempting to make causal inference, we must be sure there is nothing unobservable, which is potentially biasing our estimates despite our best efforts to control for observables. This is why randomized trials, if done correctly, remain the undisputed champion for inferring causality, since they are able to rule out both observable and unobservable confounders. In the absence of randomization, our ability to completely rule out the latter is oftentimes tenuous.

Finally, we urge the reader to consider that, even in the situation where one feels most or all of the bias due to selection has been eliminated, the quantity still may not have a universal interpretation. The idea of heterogeneity of the effect of treatment is one that is given considerably less attention than the related problem of selection. It is, however, equally, if not in some cases, more important. Our position is that failure to consider the effects of heterogeneity of treatment may rob us of many opportunities to be more useful than we currently are to policy makers. The question may be posed as to whether something "works" or not, but there are multiple ways in which we can provide an answer that illuminates under what conditions and how it works best. Choosing the precise quantity for characterizing a treatment effect that is applicable to the policy question at hand is one key to making evaluation more informative in criminal justice.

REFERENCES

Angrist JD (1990) Lifetime earnings and the Vietnam era draft lottery: evidence from social security administrative records. Am Econ Rev 80:313–335

Angrist JD (2004) Treatment effect heterogeneity in theory and practice, The Royal Economic Society Sargan Lecture. Econ J 114:C52–C83

Angrist JD (2006) Instrumental variables methods in experimental criminological research: what, why, and how. J Exp Criminol 2:23–44

Angrist J, Imbens G, Rubin DB (1996) Identification of causal effects using instrumental variables. J Am Stat Assoc 91:444–455

Heckman JJ (1997) Instrumental variables: a study of implicit behavioral assumptions used in making program evaluations. J Hum Resour 32(2):441–462

Heckman JJ, Smith JA (1995) Assessing the case for social experiments. J Econ Perspect 9(2):85–110

Holland PW (1986) Statistics and causal inference. J Am Stat Assoc 81:945–960

Berk RA, Sherman LW (1988) Police response to family violence incidents: an analysis of an experimental design with incomplete randomization. J Am Stat Assoc 83(401):70–76

Imbens GW, Angrist JD (1994) Identification and estimation of local average treatment effects. Econometrica 62:467–475

LaLonde RJ (1986) Evaluating the econometric evaluations of training programs with experimental data. Am Econ Rev 76:604–620

Manski CF (1995) Identification problems in the social sciences. Harvard University Press, Cambridge

McCaffrey DF, Ridgeway G, Morral AR (2004) Propensity score estimation with boosted regression for evaluating causal effects in observational studies. Psychol Methods 9(4):403–425

Needleman HL, Riess JA, Tobin MJ, Biesecker GE, Greenhouse JB (1996) Bone lead levels and delinquent behavior. J Am Med Assoc 275(5):363–369

Nevin R (2000) How lead exposure relates to temporal changes in IQ, violent crime, and unwed pregnancy. Environ Res 83(1):1–22

Neyman JS (1923) On the application of probability theory to agricultural experiments. Essay on principles. Section 9. Stat Sci 4:465–480

Ridgeway G (2006) Assessing the effect of race bias in post-traffic stop outcomes using propensity scores. J Quant Criminol 22(1):1–29

Robins JM, Greenland S, Hu F-C (1999) Estimation of the causal effect of a time-varying exposure on the marginal mean of a repeated binary outcome. J Am Stat Assoc 94:687–700

Robins JM, Hernan MA, Brumback B (2000) Marginal structural models and causal inference in epidemiology. Epidemiology 11(5):550–560

Rosenbaum PR (2002) Observational studies, 2nd edn. Springer-Verlag, New York

Rosenbaum P, Rubin DB (1983) The central role of the propensity score in observational studies for causal effects. Biometrika 70:41–55

Rosenbaum PR, Rubin DB (1985) The bias due to incomplete matching. Biometrics 41:103–116

Rubin DB (1974) Estimating causal effects of treatments in randomized and nonrandomized studies. J Educ Psychol 66:688–701

Rubin DB (1977) Assignment to treatment groups on the basis of a covariate. J Educ Stat 2:1–26

Rubin DB (1978) Bayesian inference for causal effects: the role of randomization. Ann Stat 6:34–58

Shadish WR, Cook TD, Campbell DT (2001) Experimental and quasi-experimental designs for generalized causal inference. Houghton Mifflin, Boston

Sherman LW, Berk RA (1984) The specific deterrent effects of arrest for domestic assault. Am Sociol Rev 49(2):261–272

Weisburd D, Lum C, Petronsino A (2001) Does research design affect study outcomes in criminal justice? Ann Am Acad Pol Soc Sci 578:50–70

Wright JP, Dietrich KN, Ris MD, Hornung RW, Wessel SD, Lanphear BP, Ho M, Rae MN (2008) Association of prenatal and childhood blood lead concentrations with criminal arrests in early adulthood. PLoS Med 5:e101

CHAPTER 10

Meta-analysis

DAVID B. WILSON

Advancement in science depends on a clear understanding of what is currently known. A challenge in many areas of science, including criminology and criminal justice, is making sense of rather disparate findings across studies of a common research question and grappling with a large number of studies. Meta-analysis is a statistical method designed to tackle these problems and approaches the task of taking stock of the literature as a research endeavor in its own right. That is, meta-analysis applies the methods and logic of social science research to the task of synthesizing results across studies and exploring explanations for variability in those results.

The logic of meta-analysis is straightforward and examples date back over 100 years. Arguably, the earliest was by Karl Pearson, the developer of the Pearson's product moment correlation coefficient (Pearson 1904, as cited in Hunt (1997)). Pearson synthesized the finding from multiple studies of the effectiveness of inoculation for typhoid fever. The very idea of inoculations was controversial among the medical community at the time. When looked at individually, the results for the effectiveness of inoculation were inconsistent, with some studies finding a statistically significant effect and others not. Pearson computed the tetrachoric correlation between inoculation and mortality within each study and then averaged the correlations across studies. The average result across studies clearly supported the value of inoculations. By today's standard, this was a meta-analysis, although the term was not introduced until the 1970s (Glass 1976) and the statistical methods have undergone substantial refinement.

Meta-analysis addresses a primary complication of synthesizing results across studies: findings will differ. As an example, imagine that you are interested in the effectiveness of a new treatment program, called XYZ, for adjudicated juveniles. An evaluation randomly assigned 200 youth to either the XYZ program or a control condition and found a statistically significant lower level of postprogram delinquent behaviors in the XYZ condition relative to the control condition (43% vs. 57%, respectively). This single study is seen as a promising evidence of the effectiveness of this program. Unfortunately, a second independent evaluation with a smaller sample size, 50 in each condition, failed to find a statistically significant effect. From a traditional perspective, this second study weakens the inference that this program is effective. However, shifting the focus from statistical significance to the magnitude and direction of effect shows that the second study also observed an association between assignment to the XYZ condition and postprogram delinquency (30% vs. 45% for the XYZ

A.R. Piquero and D. Weisburd (eds.), *Handbook of Quantitative Criminology*,
DOI 10.1007/978-0-387-77650-7_10, © Springer Science + Business Media, LLC 2010,
First softcover printing 2011

and control conditions, respectively). Furthermore, the size of the effect is larger in the second study. When combined with the first study, the results from the second study strengthens the inference that the XYZ program is effective, rather than weakens it.

As seen in this example, the focus in meta-analysis shifts from statistical significance, a common emphasis in more traditional methods of reviewing studies, to the direction and magnitude of observed effects. This avoids a profound limitation of statistical significance: A statistically significant finding is a strong conclusion, whereas a statistically nonsignificant finding is a weak conclusion. Recall that null hypothesis significance testing dictates that we *fail to reject* (not *accept*) the null hypothesis when the *p*-value is not significant. A nonsignificant finding may simply reflect a lack of sufficient statistical power, a common problem in criminological and criminal justice research (Bushway et al. 2006; Lipsey et al. 1985; Weisburd et al. 2003). As such, statistical significance can be misleading when used as the basis for drawing inferences across a collection of related studies.

For meta-analysis to make sense, the collection of studies on which it is based must be estimating a common relationship of interest, such as that between program XYZ and recidivism or between race and the likelihood of arrest in a police–citizen encounter. If the studies are a collection of pure replications, then the idea of creating an overall estimate of the effect is indisputable, as long as one accepts the logic and assumptions of standard statistical practices in the social sciences. On the basis of these assumptions, we would expect some replications to *overestimate* the true population effect and other replications to *underestimate* the true population effect. The overall average should provide a more accurate and robust estimate of the true population effect.

Collections of pure replications are rare within the social sciences. More typically, studies addressing a common research question will vary with respect to the operationalization of the constructs, the implementation of any experimental manipulation, and other methodological or substantive features. For meta-analysis to be credible, one must be able to argue that the studies are at least *conceptual* replications – each is examining a common empirical relationship despite substantive and methodological variations. The greater the variability in study features, the more abstract the nature of the conceptual replication. For example, the meta-analytic work of Lipsey (e.g., Lipsey 1995; Lipsey and Wilson 1998) on the effectiveness of juvenile delinquency includes great variability in the nature of the intervention. However, at a conceptual level, all of the studies are examining the relationship between a juvenile delinquency intervention and future delinquent behavior.

The analysis of effect-sizes across a collection of pure replications focuses on estimating the common or mean effect-size. This focus shifts to an examination of the relationship between study characteristics and observed effects as the collection of studies moves from pure replications to more abstract conceptual replications. The differences between the studies, both substantive and methodological, and how these differences related to effect-sizes takes on greater meaning than simply the overall mean effect-size.

OVERVIEW OF META-ANALYTIC METHODS

There are several distinct tasks involved in conducting a meta-analysis (see Cooper 1998; Lipsey and Wilson 2001a). The first task relates to problem formulation and involves an explication of the research question(s) or objectives of the meta-analysis. Second, an explicit set of inclusion and exclusion criteria must be specified that clearly define the characteristics of studies that will be included in the meta-analysis. Third, a comprehensive search for all eligible studies, published or unpublished, is conducted. This typically involves searching multiple sources, including bibliographic databases, reference lists of prior reviews and eligible studies, Internet searches, and contacting authors active in the area (see Cooper 1998; Lipsey and Wilson 2001a; Wilson 2009). The fourth task involves the coding of eligible studies. Using a coding form similar to a survey, information about the features of the studies are captured and effect-sizes are computed. The latter represent the results or findings of the studies and are discussed in more detail below. Fifth, the effect-sizes are analyzed using statistical methods specific to meta-analysis. These may include analyses that examine the relationship between coded study features and effects sizes. And finally, the results are interpreted and written up. The focus of this chapter is on the statistical methods of meta-analysis, that is, the computation of effect-sizes and their analysis. Before introducing effect sizes, I discuss issues related to primary study design and meta-analysis.

BASIC RESEARCH DESIGNS

Meta-analysis can be applied to many different research designs. Typically, a single meta-analysis will be focused on studies that share a common research design or at least designs that are conceptually the same and lend themselves to a common effect-size index, such as experimental and quasiexperimental designs with a comparison group. Research designs can be broadly conceptualized as univariate, bivariate, and multivariate. The former are designs estimating a statistical parameter of a single variable, such as a mean or proportion. For example, with colleagues I have conducted a meta-analysis of the proportion of homicide victims testing positive for illicit drugs (Kuhns et al. 2008).

Bivariate research designs fall into two main types, those examining a correlation between naturally occurring variables and those examining the relationship between an experimental (or potentially manipulated) variable and a dependent variable. An example of the former type is a meta-analysis by Lipsey and Derzon (1998) of cross-sectional and longitudinal studies examining the correlation between risk factors and delinquent behavior. Examples of the latter are bivariate designs examining the effectiveness of correctional programs, police activities, or other policies designed to reduce crime. Lipsey and Cullen (2007) provide a recent review of such meta-analyses within criminology and criminal justice.

Multivariate research involves the examination of three or more variables. Although there are examples of meta-analyses of such research, often the focus is on a specific bivariate relationship imbedded within the multivariate context. For example, Pratt and Cullen (2000) examined the relationship between low self-control and crime from a collection of multivariate studies. Later in this chapter, I discuss complications involved in meta-analyzing multivariate research. The analysis of univariate and bivariate research designs is generally straightforward. The first step in the process is the selection of the appropriate effect-size index.

THE EFFECT-SIZE

The key building block of meta-analysis is the effect-size. An effect-size is a statistical measure of the effect of interest that can be computed and compared across studies. In this context, I am using the term *effect-size* in a generic sense – it can refer any statistical index that is aggregated across studies. Common effect-sizes include the standardized mean difference, the correlation coefficient, the odds-ratio, and the risk ratio. The choice of an effect-size type should be driven by the nature of the relationship of interest.

Most meta-analytic work in the social sciences has thus far focused primarily on bivariate relationships although examples of meta-analyses of multivariate relationships and of single variable point-estimates can be found. For a bivariate relationship, the selection of the effect-size type will depend on the nature of both the independent and dependent constructs of interest and whether these are inherently dichotomous (binary) or continuous.

The Standardized Mean Difference

The standardized mean difference (d) is applicable to research designs that involve the comparison of two groups on one or more dependent variable. These two groups may be experimental in nature, such as a treatment group vs. a control group, or naturally occurring, such as boys vs. girls. As the names implies, the effect-size is based on the difference between the means. Thus, this effect-size is best suited to a dependent variable with a continuous underlying construct that will typically be measured in a manner consistent with the computation of means and standard deviations (below I will address how to estimate a standardized mean difference from studies that measure the construct of interest dichotomously). The basic equation for the standardized mean difference (d) is

$$d = \frac{\overline{X}_1 - \overline{X}_2}{\sqrt{\dfrac{(n_1 - 1) s_1^2 + (n_2 - 1) s_2^2}{n_1 + n_2 - 2}}}, \tag{10.1}$$

where $\overline{X}_1$, s_1^2, and n_1, are the mean, variance, and sample size for group 1, and $\overline{X}_2$, s_2^2, and n_2, are the mean, variance, and sample size for group 2. The denominator of this equation is pooled within groups standard deviation and serves to standardize the difference between the means in terms of the natural variability on this dependent variable, less any variability due to the treatment or group effect. A d of 0.5 indicates that group 1 is half a standard deviation above group 2. It is this standardization that allows for comparison of effects across studies.

Hedges and Olkin (1985) showed that the standardized mean difference effect-size is upwardly biased when based on small sample sizes. While this bias is relatively small when sample sizes exceed 20 (Hedges 1981), it has become standard practice to apply this adjustment to d even if your sample sizes all exceed 20. The equation for adjusting the effect-sizes is

$$d' = \left[1 - \frac{3}{4N - 9}\right] d, \tag{10.2}$$

where d is from (10.1). This adjusted d is referred to as the *unbiased standardized mean difference* effect-size.

Not all authors report means, standard deviations, and sample sizes for all outcome measures. This necessitates computing d based on other available information. Some of these alternative formulas are algebraically equivalent to (10.1) above, whereas others provide a reasonable estimate. An algebraically equivalent equation for computing d based on a t-value is

$$d = t \sqrt{\frac{n_1 + n_2}{n_1 n_2}}, \tag{10.3}$$

where t is from an independent t test assessing the difference between two means and n_1 and n_2 are the respective sample sizes. Additional equations for computing d can be found in Borenstein (2009) and Lipsey and Wilson (2001a). A simple effect size calculator is also available at http:\\mason.gmu.edu\dwilsonb\ma.html.

Another common problem in the application of the d-type effect-size is that some of the studies will use a dichotomous indicator for the dependent variable of interest. For example, a meta-analysis of school-based bullying programs may be interested in aggression as the outcome and aggression may be measured on an interval scale in some studies and dichotomously (aggressive, not aggressive) in others. It is desirable to calculate an effect-size that is comparable across both sets of studies. There are several ways to estimate a d-type effect-size from 2 by 2 data (i.e., treatment vs. control by a dichotomous dependent variable). Computer simulations by Sánchez-Meca et al. (2003) suggest that the best method is the Cox method (Cox 1970), which is based on the logged odds-ratio. Using this method, d is estimated as

$$d = \frac{\ln(\text{OR})}{1.65}, \tag{10.4}$$

where OR is the odds-ratio (see below). This method is very similar to the Hasselblad and Hedges (1995) method which divides the logged odds-ratio by $\pi/\sqrt{3}$ or 1.81. The latter method slightly underestimates d, particularly for large values of the logged odds-ratio, although in practice the difference tends to be slight. The Cox method also produces values that are very close to the probit method.

The Correlation Coefficient

Correlational research is common in the social sciences. The correlation coefficient is a natural effect-size for literature of this type. For example, Lipsey and Derzon (1998) conducted a large meta-analysis of both cross-sectional and longitudinal predictors of delinquency. The dependent variable, delinquency, was conceptualized as continuous in nature and often, but not always, measured on a scale with a range of possible values. Similarly, the independent variables, the risk factors, were also often measured in a continuous fashion or at least in a manner consistent with the computation of a Pearson correlation coefficient.

Extracting correlation coefficients (r) from studies where the correlation is the natural effect-size is generally straightforward: the majority of studies will report the correlation coefficient. However, studies will be identified for which this is not the case. It is often possible to use other available data to compute the correlation coefficient, or at least a close approximation. For example, a study might simply report the t-value associated with a significance test of the correlation coefficient. In this case, r can be computed as

$$r = \frac{t}{\sqrt{t^2 + \text{df}}}, \tag{10.5}$$

where t is the t-value and df is the degrees of freedom. Similarly, if the study only reports the exact p-value for the t-test of the correlation, the t-value can be determined using an inverse distribution function (this is available in most all spreadsheets and statistical software packages). Other equations for computing r can be found in Borenstein (2009) and Lipsey and Wilson (2001a).

The Odds-Ratio and Risk-Ratio

Dichotomous dependent variables are common in criminology and criminal justice. Research designs that examine the relationship between a dichotomous independent variable, such as assignment to a boot-camp vs. prison, and a dichotomous dependent variable, such as arrest within 12-months of release, are well suited to the odds-ratio or risk ratio as the effect-size. Data such as this can be represented in a 2 by 2 contingency table.

The odds ratio is the odds of success (or failure) in one condition relative to the odds of success (or failure) in the other. An odds is the probability of an event relative to its complement, the probability of the absence of an event. For example, assume that 54 of 100 offenders released from a correctional boot-camp were arrested in the first 12-months. Using this data, the probability of an arrest in the boot-camp condition is 0.54 and the probability of not being arrested is 0.46. The odds of an arrest in the boot-camp condition is 0.54/0.46 or 1.17. Assume also that we have a prison condition and that 50 of 100 offenders released from prison were arrest in the first 12-months. The odds of an arrest for the prison condition is 0.50/0.50 = 1. The ratio of these two odds is the odds ratio, or 1.17/1.00 or 1.17. Thus, the boot-camp condition has a slightly higher odds of an arrest than the prison condition. If we had defined the event of interest as *not* arrest, then the odds ratio would have been the inverse of this or (0.46/0.54)/(0.50/0.50) = 0.85. An odds ratio of 1 indicates a null effect. There is a simple way to compute the odds-ratio (OR) using frequencies:

$$OR = \frac{ad}{bc}, \tag{10.6}$$

where a, b, c, and d are the cell frequencies of a 2 by 2 contingency table. As done above, the odds ratio can also be computed from the proportion exhibiting the event within each condition as

$$OR = \frac{p_1/(1-p_1)}{p_2/(1-p_2)}, \tag{10.7}$$

where p_1 is the event rate (proportion) for the first condition, and p_2 is the event rate for the second condition.

The risk ratio (also called relative risk) can also be used in the above situation and is easier to interpret as it is the ratio of the probabilities of the event, rather than the ratio of the odds of the event. For example, the probability of an arrest for the boot-camp condition is 0.54 and the probability of an arrest in the prison condition is 0.50. Thus, the risk ratio is 0.54/0.50 or 1.08. This can be interpreted as an 8% increase in the probability of arrest for the boot-camp condition. Using cell frequencies, the risk ratio (RR) can be computed as follows:

$$RR = \frac{a/(a+b)}{c/(c+d)} = \frac{p_1}{p_2}, \tag{10.8}$$

where a, b, c, and d are defined as above and p_1 and p_2 are the probability of an event for each group, respectively. Despite its intuitive appeal, the risk ratio has two statistical limitations (Fleiss and Berlin 2009). The first is that when the probability of the event is high in the comparison condition, the theoretically possible values of RR are constrained. This may produce (or add to) heterogeneity in effects across studies. The second is that the two probabilities on which it is based cannot be properly estimated in retrospective studies that select cases based on the outcome (Fleiss and Berlin 2009) (i.e., case-control studies). These designs are common in epidemiological research. A criminological example would be to obtain a sample of delinquent and nondelinquent youths and then compare these groups on past history of potential risk factors. In this design, it is not possible to estimate the probability of delinquency given the presence of the risk factor as cases were selected because they were delinquent. The odds ratio does not suffer from these weaknesses and has other advantages (see for a full discussion Fleiss and Berlin (2009) and Fleiss (1994)).

Other Effect Sizes

The standardized mean difference, correlation coefficient, odds ratio, and risk-ratio are by no means the only possible effect-sizes for meta-analysis. Any statistical parameter that is comparable across studies and reflects the direction and magnitude of the effect of interest can be used as an effect-size. It is important, however, that the statistical parameter used is *not* a direct function of sample size, such as a t-value, and that it has a computable standard error. The latter is critical for determining the inverse-variance weight used in the analysis of effect-sizes.

There are several examples of other effect-sizes that have been used in meta-analysis. One example is the unstandardized mean difference. This would be used in situations in which all of the studies of interest used the same dependent variable, such as the asocial tendencies subscale of the Jesness Inventory. In this situation, there is no need to standardize the mean difference prior to aggregation. An unstandardized mean difference may be more meaningful as it maintains the original metric of the outcome measure. The unstandardized mean difference effect-size index was used in a meta-analysis of the effectiveness of teenage pregnancy prevention programs conducted by Frost and Forrest (1995). The standardized gain score is another example of an alternative effect-size index. There are numerous examples of meta-analyses in the educational literature examining prepost gains across studies. Another example of an alternative effect-size index is a proportion or rate. With colleagues (Kuhns et al. 2008), I conducted a meta-analysis that examined the proportion of murder victims testing positive for illicit substances. For statistical reasons (see Lipsey and Wilson 2001a), the analyses were performed on the logit of the proportion, but the purpose here is simply to illustrate that the effect-size index used in a meta-analysis should fit the research question and type of research design being synthesized.

WORKING EXAMPLE

A sample of studies from a meta-analysis that I conducted with colleagues (Wilson et al. 2005) is used as a working example to illustrate the methods of meta-analysis throughout this chapter. This meta-analysis examined the effectiveness of group-based cognitive-behavioral treatment for adult offenders. Table 10.1 presents the data and odds-ratio effect-size for ten studies included in that meta-analysis. These studies evaluated either the *Moral Reconation* program, or the *Reasoning and Rehabilitation* program. Only those studies with a randomized design or with a strong quasiexperimental design are shown. The latter studies had a credible comparison group and provided evidence of the comparability of the treatment and comparison conditions. Only one effect-size per study is shown in this table. The selected effect-size was based on a decision rule that gave preference to general measures of criminal behavior that were dichotomous in nature. Furthermore, measures of arrest were preferred over measures of

TABLE 10.1. Odds-ratio effect sizes for group-based cognitive-behavioral programs for adult offenders

Author	Sample Size		% Recidivating		Odds-Ratio	Logged OR	v	w
	Treatment	Control	Treatment	Control				
Burnett (1996)	30	30	0.100	0.200	2.25	0.81	0.579	1.727
Johnson and Hunter (1995)	47	51	0.255	0.294	1.22	0.20	0.206	4.843
Little and Robinson (1989)	115	65	0.200	0.276	1.52	0.42	0.131	7.614
Little et al. (1991)	70	82	0.610	0.700	1.49	0.40	0.118	8.466
Little et al. (1994)	1,052	329	0.655	0.779	1.86	0.62	0.022	45.742
Porporino et al. (1991)	40	23	0.450	0.521	1.33	0.28	0.275	3.633
Porporino and Robinson (1995)	550	207	0.150	0.160	1.08	0.08	0.050	19.919
Robinson (1995)	1,746	379	0.212	0.248	1.25	0.20	0.018	56.895
Ross et al. (1988)	22	23	0.182	0.696	10.29	2.33	0.511	1.958

Note: These studies are a subset of studies included in Wilson et al. (2005) and represent two specific treatment programs (Moral Reconation and Reasoning and Rehabilitation) and studies that were randomized or used high quality quasiexperimental designs

conviction, and measures of conviction were preferred over measures of reinstitutionalization. The first available posttreatment effect-size was used to increase comparability across studies. This decision rule resulted in a single effect-size per study. This differs slightly from the analyses presented in Wilson et al. (2005), in which the analyses were based on a composite effect-size per study, rather than a single selected effect-size.

Examining the data for the first study listed in the table, Burnett (1996), shows that the treatment and control conditions had 30 individuals each. Only 10% of the treatment group recidivated during the follow-up period compared to 20% in the control group. Using equation 10.7, the odds-ratio is computed as

$$OR = \frac{0.10/(1-0.10)}{0.20/(1-0.20)} = 0.444.$$

In this meta-analysis, we wanted to have larger values (those greater than 1) associated with a positive treatment effect. This is accomplished easily by taking the inverse of the odds ratio. Inverting the odds ratio simply changes the direction of the effect. For the above odds ratio, the inverse is $1/0.444 = 2.25$. Thus, the treatment group had 2.25 times the odds of success as the control group. The remaining columns in Table 10.1 are discussed below.

META-ANALYSIS OF EFFECT-SIZES

In meta-analysis, the effect-size is the dependent variable and study characteristics are potential independent variables. The starting point of most meta-analyses is an examination of the central tendency of the effect-size distribution: the mean effect-size. Also of interest is the variability in effects across studies. A collection of effect-sizes might be homogeneous or heterogeneous. A homogeneous collection of effect-sizes varies no more than would be expected due to sampling error alone. Essentially, the studies in such a collection are telling a consistent story with respect to the underlying relationship of interest. A heterogeneous collection of effect-sizes reflects genuine differences in the underlying effect being estimated by the studies. More simply, there are real differences in effects across studies. These differences can be explored through moderator analyses that examine whether study characteristics are associated with effect-sizes, or stated differently, account for some of the variability in effects. A moderator analysis might simply compare the means of the effect-sizes across a categorical variable, such as program type, or may adopt a regression based approach with one or more independent variables.

There are two main statistical approaches to estimate the mean effect-size and related statistics. The first is the inverse-variance weight method developed by Hedges and Olkin (1985). This approach is widely used and is broadly applicable to a range of research questions. The second approach is the Hunter and Schmidt method (Hunter and Schmidt 1990, 2004; Schmidt et al. 2009). The Hunter and Schmidt method was developed in the context of validity generalizability research within the area of industrial–organizational psychology. The principle conceptual difference between these approaches is that the Hunter and Schmidt method corrects effects sizes for methodological artifacts, including error of measurement (unreliability) in both the independent and dependent variables, dichotomization of a continuous independent or dependent variable, measurement invalidity, and range restriction. All of these corrections increase the observed effect-size and attempt to estimate the true underlying effect-size given perfect measurement, etc. Unfortunately, in many areas of research, particularly within criminology and criminal justice, the information needed to fully implement the Hunter and Schmidt method is not available (e.g., reliability and validity coefficients), limiting the applicability of the method. However, the Hunter and Schmidt method has been widely used to synthesize psychometric research and is also popular within social psychology. Schulze (2004) provides a nice comparison of these approaches, including Monte Carlo simulations establishing the strengths and weaknesses of each. This chapter will focus on the inverse-variance weight method.

Independence of Effects

A common complication of conducting a meta-analysis is that multiple effect-sizes can be computed from an individual study. These multiple effect-sizes cannot be treated as independent estimates of the effect of interest – they are based on the same sample and as such are statistically dependent. Treating them as independent estimates would result in an overstatement of the precision of the overall meta-analytic results. Thus, it is important to maintain statistical independence among the effect-sizes included in any given analysis.

There are several methods for addressing this issue. First, distinct measurement constructs can be analyzed separately. For example, a meta-analysis of school-based drug-use prevention programs could meta-analyze the effect-sizes based on measures of knowledge, attitudes, and drug-use behavior separately. If multiple effect-sizes remain within a construct category, then there are three options (1) compute the average effect-size (or select the median) from each study, (2) select an effect-size based on a decision rule, or (3) randomly select one effect-size per study. You may also run multiple analyses based on different decision rules. The basic idea is to make sure that only one effect-size per independent sample is included in any given statistical aggregation.

Another alternative is to model the statistical dependencies directly, thus allowing for the inclusion of multiple effect-sizes per study in a given analysis. Methods have been developed for meta-analysis to do this (e.g., Gleser and Olkin 1994; Kalaian and Raudenbush 1996). Unfortunately, these methods are difficult to implement giving currently available software and generally require information not typically reported by authors, such as the correlation among different measures. However, there are situations, such as the examples provided by Gleser and Olkin (1994) and Kalaian and Raudenbush (1996), where the application of these methods is worthwhile.

Weighting of Effect Sizes

Effect-sizes based on larger samples are more precise than effect-sizes based on smaller samples, all other things being equal. For example, a correlation coefficient between impulsivity and aggressive based on a sample size of 200 is a more precise estimate of this relationship than one from a study with a sample size of 50. Intuitively, it makes sense to give greater weight to the more precise estimate. Although sample size would seem like the natural choice of a weight, and was used as a weight in many meta-analyses conducted in the late 1970s and 1980s when the statistical methods of meta-analysis were undergoing rapid development, a more precise statistical indicator of the precision of an effect-size is its standard error. The smaller a standard error, the more precise the effect-size, at least in terms of sampling error. Because greater weight is to be given to the effect-sizes with smaller standard errors, we need a value that is the inverse of the standard error. Hedges and Olkin (1985) showed, however, that the best weight from a statistical standpoint is based on the squared standard-error, or the inverse of the variance.

For some effect-size types, such as the correlation, odds ratio, and risk ratio, the effect-size must be converted into an alternate form for analysis to allow for the computation of the inverse-variance weight. For example, the correlation coefficient does not have an easily computable standard error, but a Fisher's Zr transformed correlation coefficient has an easily computable one. Thus, when analyzing correlation coefficients, the correlation is first converted into a z as follows[1]:

$$z = 0.5 \ln \left(\frac{1 + r}{1 - r} \right), \tag{10.9}$$

where r is the correlation effect-size. For values of r less than 0.30, the transformation is slight ($r = 0.30$ converts to a $z = 0.31$) but increases as the value of r approaches 1 ($r = 0.90$ converts to a $z = 1.47$). The variance of z is a simple function of sample size:

$$v_z = \frac{1}{n - 3}, \tag{10.10}$$

where n is the sample size for the correlation. The inverse of this is $n - 3$. As such, the weight for a z-transformed correlation is essentially the sample size. You can convert final

---

[1] There is debate within the meta-analytic literature on the relative merits of analyzing the correlation in its raw form or using the Fisher z transformed value (see Field 2001; Hunter and Schmidt 2004). Computer simulations have shown that the raw correlation is slightly downwardly biased but to a lesser degree than the upward bias of the z transformed value. The original purpose, however, of the z transformation was to provide a computable standard error. An alternative approach is to use the raw correlation as the effect-size and approximate the variance as $v = \left(1 - r^2\right)^2 / (n - 1)$ (e.g., Hunter and Schmidt 2004; Shadish and Haddock 2009).

meta-analytic results, such as the mean and confidence interval, back into correlations using the following formula:

$$r = \frac{e^{2z} - 1}{e^{2z} + 1}. \tag{10.11}$$

As with the correlation, the odds ratio in its raw form does not have a computable standard error. This stems from the asymmetric nature of the odds ratio. Values greater than 1 up to infinity indicate an increased odds whereas values less than 1 but greater than 0 indicate a decreased odds of the event for the target condition relative to the control condition. An odds ratio of 2 reflects the same strength of association as an odds-ratio of 0.5. Similarly, an odds ratio of 4 reflects the same strength of association as an odds ratio of 0.25. The solution to this problem is the take the natural log of the odds ratio as the effect-size (Fleiss and Berlin 2009; Fleiss 1994). This centers the effects around zero (the natural log of 1 is 0) and positive and negative effects are symmetrical (e.g., the natural log of 2 is 0.69 and the natural log of 0.5 is −0.69). The variance of the logged odds ratio is

$$v_{\ln(OR)} = \frac{1}{a} + \frac{1}{b} + \frac{1}{c} + \frac{1}{d}, \tag{10.12}$$

where a, b, c, and d are defined as above for the odds ratio. The inverse of this value is used as the weight in meta-analyses of logged odds-ratios. Final results can be converted back into odds-ratios through simple exponentiation (e.g., e^x where x is the meta-analytic mean logged odds-ratio or lower and upper bounds of the confidence interval).

The risk-ratio has the same complications as the odds-ratio with the same solution. Meta-analysis is performed on the natural log of the risk-ratio. The variance of the logged risk-ratio is

$$v_{\ln(RR)} = \frac{1 - p_1}{n_1 p_1} + \frac{1 - p_1}{n_1 p_1}, \tag{10.13}$$

where p_1 and p_2 are the proportion of positive events in groups 1 and 2, and n_1 and n_2 are the respective sample sizes (Fleiss and Berlin 2009). As with the logged odds-ratio, final results can be converted back into risk-ratios through exponentiation.

The standardized mean difference effect-size does have a computable standard error and therefore is analyzed in its raw form. The variance of the standardized mean difference is computed as

$$v_d = \frac{n_1 + n_2}{n_1 n_2} + \frac{d^2}{2(n_1 + n_2)}, \tag{10.14}$$

where d is the small sample size adjusted standardized mean difference, and n_1 and n_2 are the sample sizes for each group.

The formulas for computing the variance, and thus the inverse-variance weight, for other effect-size types can be found in Lipsey and Wilson (2001a). What should be clear at this point is that for meta-analysis to be possible on a collection of research studies of interest, an effect-size index that is comparable across studies and that has a computable variance is required. The statistical methods presented below are generic and suitable to all effect-size types. ES will be used to denote an effect-size, v the variance of the effect-size, and w the inverse-variance weight (i.e., $1/v$).

Table 10.1 presents the logged-odds ratio, variance, and inverse-variance weight for our example meta-analysis. Focusing on the first row of data, the natural log of the odds-ratio is 0.81. Note that had we left the odds-ratios in their natural direction, with values less than 1 indicating a positive treatment effect (i.e., a reduction in recidivism), then the logged odds-ratio for the calculated odds-ratio of 0.444 is −0.81. This clearly shows that taking the inverse of an odds-ratio simply changes the direction of the effect. What is critical in a meta-analysis is that you code effect-sizes so that the direction of the effect-sizes maintains a consistent meaning across studies. The variance of the logged odds-ratio is computed using (10.12). The cell frequencies of the 2 by 2 contingency table are not provided in Table 10.1. They can, however, be determined through simple algebra. For the treatment group, the number of individuals recidivating (cell a) is the sample size times the percent recidivating. The remaining cell frequencies can be found in a similar fashion. Applying (10.12) to the first row in Table 10.1 produces a variance of

$$v = \frac{1}{3} + \frac{1}{27} + \frac{1}{6} + \frac{1}{24} = 0.579.$$

The inverse-variance weight is simply the inverse of this value:

$$w = \frac{1}{0.579} = 1.727.$$

Fixed-Effects and Random-Effects Models

In conducting a meta-analysis, you must choose between a fixed- or random-effects model. The two models make very different assumptions about the data. The fixed-effects model assumes that all of the studies are estimating a common population effect-size and that the differences between the studies are simply a function of sampling error (Overton 1998; Lipsey and Wilson 2001a; Hedges and Olkin 1985). This is rarely plausible with the possible exception of a meta-analysis of pure replications. In the case of moderator analyses, the fixed-effect model assumes that any variability in effects across studies is a function of sampling error. A random-effects model assumes two sources of variability in effects, one from sampling error and one for study level differences. More specifically, the random-effects model assumes a distribution of true population effects from which the observed studies are sampled (Hunter and Schmidt 2004; Lipsey and Wilson 2001a; Overton 1998; Raudenbush 1994). The random-effects model is recommended unless you have good reason to assume a fixed-effects model. Furthermore, a random-effects model will simplify to a fixed-effects model if the variability in effects across studies is homogeneous (Overton 1998).

The Mean Effect Size and Related Statistics

As with any statistical analysis, it is wise to examine a distribution for outliers or other anomalies. Outliers may represent genuinely unusual effects, often from small sample size studies, or they may reflect a computational error; as such, it is worth verifying the calculation of extreme effect-sizes. Both histograms and stem-and-leaf plots are useful graphical methods of examining the distribution of effect-sizes. Because analyses are weighted, an effect-size that represents an outlier may have a small effect on the overall analysis if it has a small relative weight (large variance). Of greater concern is an outlier with a moderate to large relative weight. I recommend performing sensitivity analyses that include and exclude any such effect-sizes.

The mean effect size under the fixed-effects model is simply a weighted mean, computed as

$$\overline{\text{ES}} = \frac{\sum\limits_{i=1}^{k} w_i \text{ES}_i}{\sum\limits_{i=1}^{k} w_i}, \tag{10.15}$$

where w is the inverse variance weight, and ES is the effect-size. The subscript i denotes the individual effect-sizes from 1 to k, where k is the number of effect-sizes.

Applying this equation to the data in Table 10.1 produces the following:

$$\overline{\text{ES}} = \frac{55.956}{150.798} = 0.37.$$

Thus, the fixed-effects mean logged odds-ratio for these nine studies is 0.37. Taking the antilogarithm of this value converts the logged odds-ratio into a simple odds-ratio:

$$\text{OR} = e^{0.37} = 1.45.$$

The mean effect-size can be tested against the null hypothesis that the true population effect size equals zero using a z-test. To compute z, you need to compute the standard error of the mean effect-size:

$$\text{se}_{\overline{\text{ES}}} = \sqrt{\frac{1}{\sum\limits_{i=1}^{k} w}}. \tag{10.16}$$

Recall that the inverse-variance weight for an individual effect-size is based on its standard error and a standard error is a statistical index of the precision of an effect-size. Thus, it is intuitive that the precision of the mean effect-size is a function of the precision of the effect-sizes on which it is based. The standard error of the mean effect-size (logged odds-ratio) for the data in Table 10.1 is

$$\text{se}_{\overline{\text{ES}}} = \sqrt{\frac{1}{150.798}} = 0.081.$$

Using the standard error of the mean effect-size, z is computed as

$$z = \frac{\overline{ES}}{\text{se}}. \tag{10.17}$$

This tests the null hypothesis that the mean effect-size is zero. The mean effect-size is statistically significant at $p < 0.05$ if the z is greater than or equal to 1.96, assuming a two-tailed test. For a more precise p-value, consult the statistical tables in any good statistics book or use the built-in distribution functions of computer spreadsheets, mathematical programs, or statistical software packages. Applying this to the data in Table 10.1 produces

$$z = \frac{0.37}{0.081} = 4.57,$$

a z-value that is statistically significant at a conventional alpha level of 0.05. Under the assumptions of a fixed-effects model, we can clearly reject the null hypothesis that the population effect-size estimated by this collection of studies is zero.

Arguably, more informative than a significance test is a confidence interval, and in meta-analysis these are constructed in the usual manner using the standard error. The lower and upper bounds of a 95% confidence interval are computed as:

$$E S_{\text{lower}} = \overline{\text{ES}} - 1.96\text{se}, \tag{10.18}$$

$$E S_{\text{upper}} = \overline{\text{ES}} - 1.96\text{se}. \tag{10.19}$$

The 95% confidence interval for the mean effect-size for our working example is

$$\text{ES}_{\text{lower}} = \overline{0.37} - 1.96(0.081) = 0.21,$$

$$\text{ES}_{\text{upper}} = \overline{0.37} - 1.96(0.081) = 0.53.$$

We can be 95% confident that the true population effect estimated by these studies is between 0.21 and 0.53, under the assumptions of a fixed-effects model.

An important issue in meta-analysis is whether the distribution of effect-sizes is homogeneous or heterogeneous. A homogeneous distribution is one that varies no more than would be expected based on sampling error alone. In other words, the observed differences in the results across studies can be fully explained based on chance variation stemming from sampling error. A heterogeneous distribution is one that varies more than would be expected based on sampling error alone. This indicates that at least some portion of the observed differences in the effect-sizes across studies reflects true study effects. In statistical terms, there is a distribution of true population effects being estimated by these studies.

A statistical test of homogeneity is based on the chi-square distribution and is computed as

$$Q = \sum_{i=1}^{k} w_i \text{ES}_i^2 - \frac{\left(\sum_{i=1}^{k} w_i \text{ES}_i\right)^2}{\sum_{i=1}^{k} w_i}, \tag{10.20}$$

where the terms are defined as above. The degrees of freedom for Q is the number of effect-sizes (typically denoted as k) minus 1. The significance level is determined using the chi-square distribution. A statistically significant Q indicates that the distribution is *heterogeneous* and that the assumptions of the fixed-effects model are unjustified. The observed variability is greater than would be expected by chance suggesting that there are true differences across the studies.

Applying this equation to the effect-sizes in Table 10.1 is straightforward. The Q for these effect-sizes is

$$Q = 34.953 - \frac{55.956^2}{150.798} = 34.953 - 20.763 = 14.19,$$

with 8 degrees of freedom (the number of effect-sizes, k, minus 1). The p-value associated with the Q is $p = 0.077$; as such, it is not statistically significant at a conventional alpha level. We cannot reject the null hypothesis that these effect-sizes are homogeneous.

A weakness of the Q test is that it is statistically underpowered in cases where the number of studies is small, such as in this example. This often results in a failure to identify true heterogeneity. Higgins et al. (2003) have proposed an alternative index of heterogeneity, I^2, recommended for use when the number of studies is small. This index is computed as

$$I^2 = 100\% \times \frac{Q - df}{Q} \tag{10.21}$$

and ranges from 0 to 100%. If Q is less than df, then I^2 is set to 0%. The larger the value of I^2, the more heterogeneity, with the values of 25%, 50%, and 75% roughly representing low, moderate, and high levels of heterogeneity. Applying this to the effect-sizes in Table 10.1 suggests that this distribution has moderate heterogeneity:

$$I^2 = 100\% \times \frac{14.19 - 8}{14.19} = 44\%. \tag{10.22}$$

Computing the above statistics under a *random-effects* model involves first estimating the random-effects (or between study) variance component (τ^2), of which there are several estimators (see Schulze 2004; Raudenbush 2009; Viechtbauer 2005). The most commonly used one was developed by DerSimonian and Laird (1986) and is a closed-form method-of-moments estimator. Not surprisingly, it is based on the value Q, the estimate of heterogeneity. The DerSimonian and Laird formula for the random-effects variance component is

$$\tau^2 = \frac{Q - (k - 1)}{\sum w - \frac{\sum w^2}{\sum w}}, \tag{10.23}$$

where the terms are defined as above. Notice that when Q is less than $k - 1$, τ^2 becomes negative. Because it is not possible to have negative variability, negative values of τ^2 are set to zero. The expected value for a chi-square is its degrees of freedom. Hence, if Q is greater than its degrees of freedom ($k - 1$), then there is greater variability than expected under the null hypothesis, even if not statistically significantly so. A Q that is less than $k - 1$ indicates that there is less variability than expected under the null hypothesis. In this way, τ^2 reflects the excess variability in the effect-size distribution.

Under the fixed-effects model, the inverse-variance weight only reflects variability due to sampling error. The random-effects model assumes that the precision of an effect-size is a function not only of sampling error but also true variability in effects across studies in the population from which these studies were drawn. Thus, we must add this variability to the estimated sampling error variability and recompute the inverse-variance weight. The random-effects inverse-variance weight for each effect-size is defined as,

$$w_i = \frac{1}{v_i + \tau^2}, \tag{10.24}$$

where v is the appropriate formula above (i.e., (10.10), (10.12), (10.13), or (10.14)). The mean effect-size, z-test, and confidence intervals are computed using these new weights. The homogeneity test, Q, is not computed with these new weights as the excess variability is now incorporated into the model.

Most of the values needed to compute τ^2 for the data in Table 10.1 have already been computed with the exception of the sum of the squared weights. Squaring the weights and summing produces the value $63,848.51$. Using this value and those determined previously, τ^2 equals

$$\tau^2 = \frac{14.19 - (9 - 1)}{150.798 - \dfrac{5,899.210}{150.798}} = \frac{6.19}{111.669} = 0.0554.$$

This value is added to the variance estimate for each effect-size and a new inverse-variance weight is computed. Doing so for the first row in Table 10.1 produces

$$w_i = \frac{1}{0.579 + 0.0554} = 1.576. \tag{10.25}$$

For our working example, the random-effects mean is 0.40 with a 95% confidence interval of 0.14 to 0.66. The random-effects mean is slightly higher than the fixed-effects mean of 0.37 and the confidence interval is larger. The latter reflects the more conservative nature of a random-effects model when compared with a fixed-effects model. There is increased uncertainty incorporated into the model based on the variability in effect-sizes across studies.

The DerSimonian and Laird (1986) method-of-moments estimator for τ^2 is considered unbiased, but is less efficient than other estimators, such as the restricted maximum likelihood estimator. However, as discussed in Friedman (2000), Shadish and Haddock (2009), and Viechtbauer (2005), the DerSimonian and Laird method is suitable for many typical situations in meta-analysis, except when the study sample sizes are large or the heterogeneity between studies is large (greater than 3 times the degrees of freedom of Q). The maximum likelihood estimator is more efficient but negatively biased when the number of studies is small. Viechtbauer (2005) argued that the restricted maximum likelihood estimator strikes a good balance between efficiency and bias and I would recommend it, at least for situations where the DerSimonian and Laird estimator is known to be weak. Given the iterative nature of the restricted maximum likelihood estimator, I recommend relying on computer software implementations for performing analyses based on these alternative estimators of τ^2.

Moderator Analyses

Rarely is a meta-analysis focused solely on the overall mean effect-size. Frequently, one is also interested in examining the relationship between study features of the variability in results across studies. For example, you may be interested in examining whether characteristics of the studies relate to the observed effects sizes, or in a meta-analysis of a specific offender treatment program, you may be interested in examining whether some program elements are more effective than others. This is the focus of moderator analysis and there are two main analytic approaches. The first compares the means across a categorical grouping of studies, such as treatment type. The second relies on multiple regression methods to examine either a continuous moderator variable, such as program size or year of publication, or multiple moderator variables.

A SINGLE CATEGORICAL MODERATOR. Studies included in a meta-analysis can often be categorized into meaningful subgroups either on a substantive or a methodological variable, such as treatment type, restriction of the sample to high-risk offenders, etc. These categorical variables can serve as the independent variable in a moderator analysis that is analogous to a t-test when the independent variable has only two categories and a one-way analysis-of-variance (ANOVA) when the independent variable has three or more categories. Of interest is whether the means differ across the categories. Hedges and Olkin (1985) developed an analog-to-the-ANOVA that tests this hypothesis.

The analog-to-the-ANOVA partitions the total variability in effect-sizes into two portions: that between the groups and that within the groups. The Q of (10.20) represents the total variability in effect-sizes, that is, the variability of effect-sizes around the overall mean effect-size. The variability within each groups is the variability of effect-sizes around the group means. Hence, the Q_{within} is computed as

$$Q_{\text{within}} = \sum w_{ij} \left(\text{ES}_{ij} - \overline{\text{ES}_j} \right)^2, \tag{10.26}$$

where j denotes the individual groups or categories of the independent variable. Essentially, this computes a Q within each group and then sums those Qs across groups. The Q_{between} can be computed through subtraction as

$$Q_{\text{between}} = Q_{\text{total}} - Q_{\text{within}} \tag{10.27}$$

where Q_{total} is the overall Q from (10.20). Q_{between} can also be computed directly as

$$Q_{\text{between}} = \sum_{j=1}^{p} \left(\overline{\text{ES}}_j w_j \right)^2 - \frac{\left(\sum_{j=1}^{p} \overline{\text{ES}}_j w_j \right)}{\sum_{j=1}^{p} w_j}, \tag{10.28}$$

where $\overline{\text{ES}}_j$ is the mean effect-sizes for each group, and w_j is the sum of the weights within each group. The degrees of freedom for Q_{between} is the number of groups (p) minus 1, just as with the F_{between} in a one-way ANOVA. Similarly, the degrees of freedom for the Q_{within} is the number of studies (k) minus the number of groups (p). The degrees of freedom between and within should sum to the degrees of freedom total, or $k - 1$. As with Q_{total}, Q_{between} and Q_{within} are distributed as chi-squares.

A statistically significant Q_{between} is interpreted in the same way as an F from a one-way ANOVA or as an independent t-test if the independent variable has only two categories. In the latter case, a significant Q_{between} indicates that the difference between the two mean effect-sizes is statistically significant. For an independent variable with three or more groups, a significant Q_{between} indicates that the independent variable explains significant variability across the effect-sizes, or more simply that the mean effect-sizes differ across groups. Focused contrasts between means, such as pairwise comparisons, can be run to identify the source of the variability, just as with a one-way ANOVA.

Under a fixed-effects model, the Q_{within} is also meaningful, as it indicates whether the residual variability in effect-sizes remains heterogeneous after accounting for the independent variable. A statistically nonsignificant Q_{within} indicates that the moderator variable reduced the variability across effect-sizes to not more than what would be expected because of chance variation. A statistically significant Q_{within} indicates that the variability in the effect-sizes within the groups remains heterogeneous. In which case, you should consider fitting a random-effects version of the analog-to-the-ANOVA.

A random-effects analog-to-the-ANOVA is sometimes referred to as a *mixed-effects* model. This is because the categorical or independent variable is treated as fixed and the variability within the groups is treated as random. In terms of a general linear model, this would be a fixed-slopes, random-intercept model. As with the overall mean, the mixed-effects model is based on a recomputed inverse-variance weight that includes a random-effects variance component representing the variability across studies. In the case of moderator analysis, however, only the variability across studies which is *not* explained by the independent variable is used. Thus, the method-of-moments estimator for the random-effects variance component (τ^2) is based on Q_{within} rather than from Q_{total}. The denominator for τ^2 becomes more complicated and is not presented here (see Raudenbush 1994). The computer macros discussed below for SPSS, Stata, and SAS, as well as meta-analysis computer programs such as comprehensive meta-analysis (http:\www.meta-analysis.com) implement several of these methods. With the new set of inverse-variance weights, the analog-to-the-ANOVA model is refit, producing new values for $Q_{between}$, Q_{within}, and the mean effect-size and related statistics within each group. It is important to recognize that the Q_{within} produced using the random-effects weights is not meaningful, as the excess variability is now incorporated into the weights. The Q_{within} from the fixed-effects model is the correct test for whether the moderator variable accounts for the excess variability in the distribution of effect-sizes.

Figure 10.1 shows the output from a Stata macro called *metaf* available at http://mason. gmu.edu/~dwilsonb/ma.html. This moderator analysis compared the mean effect-size from studies with a randomized or true experimental design with the mean effect-size from studies with a nonrandomized or quasiexperimental design. The output shows that the test of the difference between the means was not statistically significant ($Q_{between} = 0.007$, df $= 1$, $p = 0.93$). The mean effect-size for the two design types was roughly equal (0.43 vs. 0.40, respectively). Thus, design type was not related to the observed effect-size.

```
. metaf lgor random [w=wlgor], model(mm) Version 2005.05.23 of
metaf.ado

Meta-Analytic Analog to the One-way ANOVA, Mixed Effects Model
-------------------------------------------------
  Source |          Q         df          P
-------------------------------------------------
 Between |     0.0070          1    0.93319
  Within |     8.6461          7    0.27907
-------------------------------------------------
   Total |     8.6531          8    0.37240

Descriptive Fixed Effects Meta-Analytic Results by: random
----------------------------------------------------------------------------
random  |     Mean  St. Er.  [95% Conf. Int.]         z    P>|z|         k
----------------------------------------------------------------------------
0       |   .42787   .26154  -.08475   .94048   1.6359  0.10185
4 1     |   .40181   .16799   .07255   .73107   2.3918
0.01677        5
----------------------------------------------------------------------------
Total   |   .40942   .14135   .13238   .68645   2.8965  0.00377
9

Mixed Effects Homogeneity Analysis by: random
-------------------------------------------------
  Source |         Qw         df          P
-------------------------------------------------
0        |     0.2890          3    0.98274 1             |
8.3571         4    0.12107
-------------------------------------------------
Random effects variance component (via method of moments) =
.0716085
```

FIGURE 10.1. Output from Stata showing an analog-to-the-ANOVA type moderator analysis of the relationship between design type (Random $=$ 1; Nonrandom $=$ 0) and effect size.

A CONTINUOUS MODERATOR OR MULTIPLE MODERATORS.

Continuous variables and multiple moderator variables fit naturally within a multiple regression framework. For example, it may be meaningful to examine whether the number of sessions of a cognitive-behavioral program is related to the observed reduction in reoffending or whether the year of data collection is related to the effect of race on an officer's decision to make an arrest. Additionally, it may be meaningful to examine multiple moderator variables in a single analysis given the often highly confounded nature of study characteristics. Unfortunately, standard OLS regression is not appropriate for meta-analytic data, as it produces incorrect standard errors and associated inferential statistics (Hedges and Olkin 1985). Under a fixed-effects model, it is possible to adjust the results of a standard weighted least squares regression model (see Hedges and Olkin 1985; Lipsey and Wilson 2001a). However, I recommend that you simply use the computer macros discussed in this chapter or a meta-analysis computer program that performs meta-analytic regression.

Meta-analytic regression, or meta-regression as some call it, is specifically designed for meta-analytic data. Both fixed- and random-effects regression models can be estimated. As with the analog-to-the ANOVA, two Q values are estimated, one for the model and one for the residuals. The Q_{model} is interpreted in the same fashion as the overall F from OLS regression. A statistically significant Q_{model} indicates that the linear combination of moderator variables explains significant variability in the observed effects. Under the fixed-effects model, a statistically significant Q for the residuals indicates that the residual distribution in effect-sizes remains heterogeneous, suggesting that the assumptions of a fixed-effects model are likely false and a random-effects (mixed-effects) model should be used.

Figure 10.2 shows the results of a regression analysis using data from Table 10.1. The two independent variables are a dummy code for treatment type (Moral Reconation, coded as 0, and Reasoning and Rehabilitation, coded as 1) and a dummy code reflecting whether the treatment occurred within a prison/jail or a community setting (1 = yes; 0 = no). The results show that these variables do not significantly predict the observed effect-size, either as an overall model ($Q_{model} = 1.4158$, df = 1, $p = 0.49$), or individually (both regression coefficients are statistically nonsignificant at a conventional level). It is worth noting, however, that the regression coefficients are of a meaningful size. The coefficient for treatment type

```
. metareg lgor txtype institution [w=wlgor], model(mm)
Version 2005.05.23 of metareg.ado

Meta-Analytic Random Intercept, Fixed Slopes Regression Analysis

   Source |         Q          df          P          No. of obs  =        9
----------------------------------------------------                Mean ES   = 0.4070
    Model |     1.4158          2      0.49267                       R-squared = 0.1605
 Residual |     7.4064          6      0.28489
----------------------------------------------------
    Total |     8.8222          8      0.35752


-----------------------------------------------------------------------------
 Variable |        B          SE          z       P>|z|     [95% Conf. Interval]
-----------------------------------------------------------------------------
 txtype   |   -.39058    .333902    -1.16973    0.242108    -1.04502    .263872
institution|  -.28644    .345596     -.82884    0.407195     -.963813    .390925
 _cons    |    .80564    .383221     2.10228    0.035529     .054526    1.55675
-----------------------------------------------------------------------------
Random effects variance component (via method of moments) =  .0661342
```

FIGURE 10.2. Output from Stata showing a multiple regression type moderator analysis regressing effect size on the type of program (Moral Reconation vs. Reasoning and Rehabilitation) and whether the program was in a prison or jail.

predicts a −0.391 difference in the logged odds-ratio between the treatment types, with Moral Reconation producing the larger effect. The five programs that were conducted in a prison or jail produced effects that are roughly −0.286 smaller than four programs conducted in a community setting. The small number of effect-sizes resulted in low statistical power for the moderator analysis. Clearly, these differences are worthy of future research but must be interpreted with caution. We cannot rule out sampling error as an explanation. Furthermore, with moderator analysis, it is always possible that some other feature of the studies is confounded with the moderator variable and could be responsible for the difference in effects (see Lipsey and Wilson 2001b).

Publication Bias

Publication bias is recognized as a particularly significant threat to the validity of meta-analysis (Wilson 2009). This bias stems from the well documented phenomenon that statistically significant results are more likely to be published than nonsignificant results (see Cooper 1998; Dickersin 2005; Gerber and Malhotra 2008; Lipsey and Wilson 2001a, 1993; Rosenthal 1991; Wilson 2009). There are several mechanisms for this effect. First, authors may be more likely to write-up and submit for publication results that are statistically significant. Second, peer reviewers and editors tend to be more enthusiastic about publishing statistically significant results than nonsignificant results. Third, statistically significant results are more likely to be cited by other studies making them more easily identified as part of the review process. Publication-selection bias not only affects whether an entire study is included in a meta-analysis but which outcomes and analyses are included. Primary authors are more likely to report those outcomes or statistical models that produced significant results than those that did not. There is substantial empirical evidence that publication-selection bias occurs throughout the social and medical sciences (see Dickersin 2005; Lipsey and Wilson 1993; Stern and Simes 1997). This problem affects all methods of taking stock of the research literature, whether it is through a traditional narrative review or a meta-analysis.

The first line of defence against publication-selection bias is to search for and include both published and unpublished studies that meet explicit criteria. Unpublished sources might include dissertations, technical reports, government reports, and conference presentations. A common concern that I hear when advocating for the inclusion of unpublished studies in a meta-analysis is that these studies may be of inferior quality. First, this presumes that unpublished studies are studies that were rejected by the peer review process because of methodological flaws. Many unpublished studies were never submitted to an academic journal and thus never rejected based on methodological flaws (Cooper et al. 1997). Second, much good work in criminology and criminal justice is conducted in research organizations where publishing in peer reviewed journals is less of a priority. Once a technical report is submitted to the funding agency, the authors may be too busy working on new projects to pursue publication. Finally, the peer review process does not have unique information about the methodological quality of a study. Assessments of methodological quality are based on the written manuscript as part of the peer review process and as part of a meta-analysis. The criteria for determining which studies to include and exclude should specify the necessary methodological characteristics, including any methodological flaws that would exclude a study from consideration. The nature of the research question should determine how strict or lenient these criteria are.

Assuming you have included unpublished studies in your meta-analysis, you should still examine the data for evidence of publication-selection bias. There are several ways to do this. First, you can simply examine the mean effect-size for published and unpublished studies. A large difference suggests that publication bias is likely to be present in your data. For example, four of the studies reported in Table 10.1 were peer reviewed journal articles and five were from unpublished works (two), government reports (one), and book chapters (two). The mean effect-size for the journal articles was 0.62, whereas it was 0.19 for the latter publication types, suggesting the presence of publication-selection bias. Had we only included published studies, we would have overestimated the effectiveness of these programs.

A second method is the funnel plot (Sterne et al. 2005). This is a simple scatter plot of the effect-size against the standard error of the effect-size ($se_{ES} = \sqrt{v_{ES}}$ and $v_{ES} = 1/w$). Generally, the effect-size is on the x-axis and the standard-error of the effect-size is on the y-axis. The scatter plot should look like a funnel. The logic of this is that the effect-sizes with small standard errors (large sample size studies) should vary little around the overall mean effect-size whereas study with large standard errors (small sample size studies) should vary substantially around the overall mean effect-size. Publication bias is evident when this scatter plot is asymmetric around the mean effect-size. In particular, publication bias is most evident when effects for larger standard error studies are missing near the null value (i.e., effects that would not have been statistically significant).

A third method proposed by Egger et al. (1997) and Sterne et al. (2005) examines the linear relationship between the standard normal deviate of the effect-size and its precision. The standard normal deviate is the effect-size divided by its standard error

$$z_i = \frac{ES_i}{se_i}. \tag{10.29}$$

Precision is the inverse of the standard error

$$prec_i = \frac{1}{se_i}. \tag{10.30}$$

Thus, the smaller the precision of an effect-size, the smaller the value of $prec_i$. The standard normal deviate of the effect-size is then regressed on the precision of the effect-size using OLS regression. A negative relationship between effect-size and precision is suggestive of publication bias. The logic of this method is that smaller effects will be statistically significant in larger studies and as such more likely to be observed. Unfortunately, a weakness of this method is that there are other reasons why effect-size might be related to precision. Larger studies often differ from smaller studies in important ways that might affect the observed effect. In program effectiveness research, larger studies may have more problems with the integrity of the intervention or have a more diverse and less ideally selected group of participants than a smaller study. Thus, a relationship between effect-size and precision is evidence of publication-selection bias, but there are often other plausible explanations for the relationship.

Forest-Plots

A powerful graphical representation of meta-analytic data is the forest-plot. The forest-plot presents the effect-size and 95% confidence interval for each study and typically also

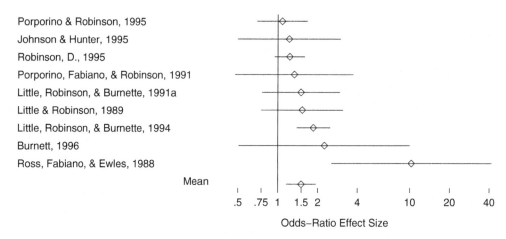

FIGURE 10.3. Forest-plot of odds-ratios and 95% confidence intervals for the effects of cognitive-behavioral programs on recidivism.

includes the overall mean effect-size and confidence interval. A forest-plot of the group-based cognitive-behavioral programs for offenders is shown in Fig. 10.3. The diamonds in this figure show the value of the odds-ratio effect-size for each study and the horizontal line through each diamond represents the 95% confidence interval. The studies are sorted by the size of the odds-ratio. We can clearly see that all of the studies observed a positive odds-ratio (i.e., odds-ratio greater than 1) and the pattern of results suggests that these programs are effective overall. The mean odds-ratio is shown at the bottom and is roughly 1.5 with a 95% confidence interval that does not include the null value of 1. As such, it is statistically significant at $p < 0.05$ and suggests a reduction in the odds of reoffending of roughly 50% attributable to the cognitive-behavioral programs.

Figure 10.3 is a "bare-bones" forest-plot. More complex forest-plots can include the sample size of the studies or the inverse-variance weights. Studies may be grouped by an important moderator variable with mean effect-sizes reported for each grouping. Another common variation is to size the diamond as a function of the inverse-variance weight. This helps visually depict the weight each effect has on the overall mean. Regardless of its complexity, forest-plots are excellent tools for communicating the results of meta-analysis to a broad audience.

Multivariate Research

The meta-analysis of multivariate research presents unique challenges. The methods discussed earlier assume a single statistical parameter of interest, based either on a single variable, such as a rate, or a bivariate relationship between two variables, as is represented in a correlation or odds-ratio. Many research questions in criminology involve multivariate statistical models and it is desirable to be able to meta-analyze collections of such studies. I will distinguish between two types of multivariate research, as the meta-analytic issues differ between them. First are basic multiple regression designs with a single dependent variable and two or more independent variables where the research focus is on one independent variable and the additional independent variables are included in the model to control for spuriousness. Second are multivariate statistical models with multiple dependent variables and independent variables, such as a structural equation model.

Multiple regression and related methods, such as logistic regression, are widely used in criminology and the social sciences more generally. This statistical method tests the effect of multiple independent variables on a dependent variable. The regression coefficient for each independent variable represents a bivariate effect-size between a specific independent variable and the dependent variable, adjusted for any confounding with the other independent variables. The standardized regression coefficient, β, from an ordinary least squares (OLS) regression model is a usable effect-size and can be interpreted as an r, adjusted for the other independent variables in the model.

There are, however, several complications in meta-analyzing standardized regression coefficients from OLS models. First, each study is likely to include a different set of independent variables. This will produce heterogeneity in the βs across studies. As such, an important theoretical question is whether these variations in the models across studies produce effect-sizes that are incommensurate. It may be possible to treat the variation in models as a moderator in the meta-analysis, depending on the amount of variation and the number of studies available for analysis. Second, not all studies will report the standardized regression coefficient, opting instead to report the unstandardized form. Given the right descriptive statistics, β can be computed as

$$\beta = B\frac{s_x}{s_y}, \tag{10.31}$$

where B is the unstandardized regression coefficient, s_x is the standard deviation for the independent variable, and s_y is the standard deviation for the dependent variable. Third, the variance or standard error for β is often not provided. The standard error of the unstandardized regression coefficient is often provided and this can be converted to the standard error of β with (10.31). Recall that the variance is simply the standard error squared. The inverse-variance weight for z (10.10) can be used but will overestimate the variance and underweight the effect-size. A better approximation is

$$se_\beta = \sqrt{\frac{1 - R_y^2}{n - p - 1}}, \tag{10.32}$$

where R_y^2 is the multiple R-squared for the regression model, n is the sample size, and p is the number of predictors. This will still overestimate the standard error but to a lesser degree than (10.10). The overestimation is a function of the degree of covariation with the other variables in the regression model, as shown by

$$\sqrt{\frac{1}{1 - R_x^2}}, \tag{10.33}$$

where R_x^2 is the variance in the independent variable of interest explained by all other independent variables in the model (Cohen and Cohen 1983).

Meta-analyzing logistic regression models is less complicated. As with OLS regression, the models are likely to include different predictors across studies, adding heterogeneity to the effect-size. However, the unstandardized regression coefficient is a logged odds-ratio and can be used directly as the effect-size. Studies reporting on the results from a logistic regression model typically provide both the unstandardized regression coefficient and its associated standard error.

Meta-analyzing truly multivariate research involving multiple dependent variables and both direct and indirect effects requires an alternative model-based approach (Becker 2009). The fundamental goal is to estimate a common correlation matrix across studies and use this synthesized correlation matrix as the basis for multivariate analysis, whether that is factor analysis, structural equation modeling, or regression analysis. This model-based approach has also been called meta-analytic structural equation modeling (Cheung and Chan 2005; Furlow and Beretvas 2005) and two-stage structural equation modeling (Cheung and Chan 2005). A restricted application of this approach includes only studies that measure all of the variables of interest. In more common usage, most studies will only estimate portions of the correlation matrix with few or no studies estimating all of the correlations. There are numerous statistical challenges in producing a synthesized correlation matrix and several methods have been developed for conducting these model-based meta-analyses (see Becker 2009; Cheung and Chan 2005). This is an area of meta-analysis with great potential given the ubiquity of multivariate models in the social sciences.

COMPUTER SOFTWARE

There are several computer programs designed specifically for meta-analysis. I am most familiar with Comprehensive Meta-Analysis[2] (http://www.meta-analysis.com). This program can perform all of the analyses discussed in this chapter and can also produce publication quality forest-plots and funnel-plots. Other similar programs include RevMan developed by the Cochrane Collaboration (http://www.cochrane.org), Meta-Analysis (Version 5.3) developed by Ralf Schwarzer (http://userpage.fu-berlin.de/~health/meta_e.htm), Meta-Win (http://metawinsoft.com), WEasyMa (http://www.weasyma.com), and DSTAT (http://www.erlbaum.com). This is by no means an exhaustive list.

An alternative to using a free-standing software program is to use macros to extend the capabilities of existing statistical software packages. For example, I have developed a set of macros for SAS, SPSS, and Stata that perform the analyses discussed in this chapter. See http://mason.gmu.edu/~dwilsonb/ma.html for more details. These macros have the advantage that you can make use of all the data manipulation capabilities of the main software program. This flexibility is useful when conducting a large meta-analysis with possibly numerous effect-sizes per study. Using standard data manipulation procedures, subsets of statistically independent effect-sizes can be generated and meta-analyzed.

CONCLUSION

Since the seminal pieces of research on meta-analysis in the mid and late 1970s (see Hunt (1997) for a discussion of the development of meta-analysis), meta-analysis has become an increasingly popular method of synthesizing the empirical evidence on a research question

---

[2] I have served as a consulted in the development of this program.

throughout the social sciences, medicine, public health, ecology, and other fields. I believe that this growth stems from the many advantages of meta-analysis over more traditional review methods.

First, the systematic review methods of meta-analysis allow for a transparency and replicability that are valued in the sciences. A properly executed meta-analysis is explicit about the study inclusion and exclusion criteria, the methods for searching for studies, the coding process, and the statistical methods. This allows for critical scrutiny by other scholars and replication. Author judgments are still a critical part of the process, such as defining the boundaries for the review, or deciding which moderator analyses to explore. However, these decisions are explicit and open to scholarly debate.

Second, the focus on the direction and magnitude of the effects across studies, rather than simply obsessing over statistical significance, provides more detailed information about the empirical findings of interest and does so in a way that allows for comparisons across studies. Statistical significance confounds sample size and the size of the empirical relationship of interest. The former is not a feature of the phenomenon under study but something under the control of the researcher. The use of effect-size appropriately shifts the focus to the direction and magnitude of effect, which is, after all, what is of greatest interest.

Third, the methods of meta-analysis allow for the exploration of variability in results across studies. In its simplest form, this illuminates whether findings are consistent or not across studies. Variation in effects across studies can be explored through moderator analyses. These analyses can assess whether substantive or methodological differences across studies explain variation in observed effects. The statistical methods also help protect against interpretation of differences across studies that may simply reflect chance variation.

Fourth, the detailed coding and comprehensive search methods that are integral to a well done meta-analysis allow for the assessment of gaps in the existing knowledge base. By carefully cataloging what is known, meta-analysis provides a firm foundation for identifying areas of needed research. A meta-analyst may also conclude that a specific research question has been adequately answered by the extant research base and that future research should focus on extending the knowledge-base in new ways.

Fifth, meta-analysis can handle a large number of studies. Although meta-analysis can be productively applied to a small number of studies (i.e., 2–10 studies), it is robust enough to handle hundreds of studies. The larger the meta-analysis, the greater the opportunity for complex moderator analyses.

The methods of meta-analysis have greatly advanced over the past 30 years and will continue to be refined and extended. An exciting area of potential advancement is in the handling of multivariate research questions. Although there is debate about the validity of specific statistical methods in meta-analysis (see, for example Berk 2007; Lipsey 2007; Shadish 2007), this approach provides a superior alternative to traditional narrative review methods that place too much emphasis on statistical significance and unusual findings that may simply be statistical outliers. The appeal of meta-analysis is spreading to disciplines beyond social science and medicine, such as ecology. I expect this trend to continue.

REFERENCES

Becker BJ (2009) Model-based meta-analysis, 2nd edn, Russell Sage Foundation, New York

Berk R (2007) Statistical inference and meta-analysis. J Exp Criminol 3:247–270, doi10.1007/s11292-007-9036-y, URL http://dx.doi.org/10.1007/s11292-007-9036-y

Borenstein M (2009) Effect sizes for studies with continuous outcome data, 2nd edn. Russell Sage Foundation, New York

Burnett WL (1996) Treating postincarcerated offenders with Moral Reconation Therapy^{TM}: A one-year recidivism study. PhD thesis, University of Phoenix

Bushway SD, Sweeten G, Wilson DB (2006) Size matters: standard errors in the application of null hypothesis significance testing in criminology and criminal justice. J Exp Criminol 2:1–22, doi: 10.1007/s11292-005-5129-7, URL http://dx.doi.org/10.1007/s11292-005-5129-7

Cheung MWL, Chan W (2005) Meta-analytic structural equation modeling: A two-stage approach. Psychol Methods 10:40–64. doi: 10.1037/1082-989X.10.1.40, URL http://search.ebscohost.com/login.aspx?direct=true&db=pdh&AN=met-10-1-40&site=ehost-live

Cohen J, Cohen P (1983) Applied multiple regression/correlation analysis for the behavioral sciences, 2nd edn. L. Erlbaum Associates, Hillsdale, NJ

Cooper HM (1998) Synthesizing research: A guide for literature reviews. Sage, Thousand Oaks, CA

Cooper HM, DeNeve K, Charlton K (1997) Finding the missing science: The fate of studies submitted for review by a human subjects committee. Psychol Methods 2:447–452. doi: 10.1037/1082-989X.2.4.447, URL http://search.ebscohost.com/login.aspx?direct=true&db=pdh&AN=met-2-4-447&site=ehost-live

Cox DR (1970) The analysis of binary data. Methuen, London

DerSimonian R, Laird N (1986) Meta-analysis in clinical trials. Control Clin Trials 7:177–88. doi: 3802833, URL http://www.ncbi.nlm.nih.gov/pubmed/3802833

Dickersin K (2005) Publication bias: recognizing the problem, understanding its origins, and preventing harm. Wiley, Chichester, pp 11–33

Egger M, Smith GD, Schneider M, Minder C (1997) Bias in meta-analysis detected by a simple, graphical test. BMJ 315:629–634, URL http://www.bmj.com/cgi/content/abstract/315/7109/629

Field AP (2001) Meta-analysis of correlation coefficients: A monte carlo comparison of fixed- and random-effects methods. Psychol Methods 6:161–180. doi: 10.1037/1082-989X.6.2.161, URL http://search.ebscohost.com/login.aspx?direct=true&db=pdh&AN=met-6-2-161&site=ehost-live

Fleiss JL (1994) Measures of effect size for categorical data. Russell Sage Foundation, New York, pp 245–260

Fleiss JL, Berlin JA (2009) Measures of effect size for categorical data, 2nd edn. Russell Sage Foundation, New York

Friedman L (2000) Estimators of random effects variance components in meta-analysis. J Educ Behav Stat 25:1–12. doi: 10.3102/10769986025001001, URL http://jeb.sagepub.com/cgi/content/abstract/25/1/1

Frost JJ, Forrest JD (1995) Understanding the impact of effective teenage pregnancy prevention programs. Fam Plann Perspect 27:188–195, URL http://mutex.gmu.edu:2112/stable/2136274

Furlow CF, Beretvas SN (2005) Meta-analytic methods of pooling correlation matrices for structural equation modeling under different patterns of missing data. Psychol Methods 10:227–254, doi: 10.1037/1082-989X.10.2.227, URL http://search.ebscohost.com/login.aspx?direct=true&db=pdh&AN=met-10-2-227&site=ehost-live

Gerber AS, Malhotra N (2008) Publication bias in empirical sociological research: Do arbitrary significance levels distort published results? Sociol Methods Res 37:3–30, doi: 10.1177/0049124108318973, URL http://smr.sagepub.com/cgi/content/abstract/37/1/3

Glass GV (1976) Primary, secondary, and meta-analysis research. Educ Res 5:3–8

Gleser LJ, Olkin I (1994) Stochastically dependent effect sizes. Russell Sage Foundation, New York, pp 339–356

Hasselblad V, Hedges (1995) Meta-analysis of screening and diagnostic tests. Psychol Bull 117:167–178. doi: 10.1037/0033-2909.117.1.167, URL http://search.ebscohost.com/login.aspx?direct=true&db=pdh&AN=bul-117-1-167&site=ehost-live

Hedges LV (1981) Distribution theory for Glass's estimator of effect size and related estimators. J Educ Behav Stat 6:107–128, doi: 10.3102/10769986006002107, URL http://jeb.sagepub.com/cgi/content/abstract/6/2/107

Hedges LV, Olkin I (1985) Statistical methods for meta-analysis. Academic, Orlando, FL

Higgins JPT, Thompson SG, Deeks JJ, Altman DG (2003) Measuring inconsistency in meta-analyses. BMJ 327:557–560. doi: 10.1136/bmj.327.7414.557, URL http://www.bmj.com

Hunt MM (1997) How science takes stock: The story of meta-analysis. Russell Sage Foundation, New York

Hunter JE, Schmidt FL (1990) Methods of meta-analysis: Correcting error and bias in research findings. Sage Publications, Newbury Park

Hunter JE, Schmidt FL (2004) Methods of meta-analysis: Correcting error and bias in research findings, 2nd edn. Sage, Thousand Oaks, CA

Johnson G, Hunter RM (1995) Evaluation of the specialized drug offender program. In: Ross RR, Ross B (eds) Thinking straight. Cognitive Center, Ottawa, ON, pp 215–234

Kalaian HA, Raudenbush SW (1996) A multivariate mixed linear model for meta-analysis. Psychol Methods 1:227–235. doi: 10.1037/1082-989X.1.3.227, URL http://search.ebscohost.com/login.aspx?direct=true&db=pdh&AN=met-1-3-227&site=ehost-live

Kuhns JB, Wilson DB, Maguire ER, Ainsworth SA, Clodfelter TA (2008) A meta-analysis of marijuana, cocaine, and opiate toxicology study findings among homicide victims. Addiction 104:1122–1131

Lipsey MW (1995) What do we learn from 400 research studies on the effectiveness of treatment with juvenile delinquents? Wiley, New York, pp 63–78

Lipsey MW (2007) Unjustified inferences about meta-analysis. J Exp Criminol 3:271–279. doi: 10.1007/s11292-007-9037-x, URL http://dx.doi.org/10.1007/s11292-007-9037-x

Lipsey MW, Cullen FT (2007) The effectiveness of correctional rehabilitation: A review of systematic reviews. Annu Rev Law Soc Sci 3:297–320, doi: 10.1146/annurev.lawsocsci.3.081806.112833, URL http://mutex.gmu.edu:2078/doi/full/10.1146/annurev.lawsocsci.3.081806.112833

Lipsey MW, Derzon JH (1998) Predictors of violent or serious delinquency in adolescence and early adulthood: A synthesis of longitudinal research. Sage Publications, Thousand Oaks, CA, pp 86–105

Lipsey MW, Wilson DB (1993) The efficacy of psychological, educational, and behavioral treatment: Confirmation from meta-analysis. Am Psychol 48:1181–1209. doi: 10.1037/0003-066X.48.12.1181, URL http://search.ebscohost.com/login.aspx?direct=true&db=pdh&AN=amp-48-12-1181&site=ehost-live

Lipsey MW, Wilson DB (1998) Effective intervention for serious juvenile offenders: A synthesis of research. Sage Publications, Thousand Oaks, CA, pp 313–345

Lipsey MW, Wilson DB (2001a) Practical meta-analysis. Applied social research methods series. Sage Publications, Thousand Oaks, CA

Lipsey MW, Wilson DB (2001b) The way in which intervention studies have "personality" and why it is important to meta-analysis. Eval Health Prof 24:236–254. doi: 10.1177/016327870102400302, URL http://ehp.sagepub.com/cgi/content/abstract/24/3/236

Lipsey MW, Crosse S, Dunkle J, Pollard J, Stobart G (1985) Evaluation: The state of the art and the sorry state of the science. New Dir Program Eval 27:7–28

Little GL and Robinson KD (1989) Treating drunk drivers with Moral Reconation therapy: A one-year recidivism report. Psychol Rep 64:960-962

Little GL, Robinson KD Burnette KD (1991) Treating drug offenders with Moral Reconation therapy: A three-year recidivism report. Psychol Rep 69:1151–1154

Little GL, Robinson KD, Burnette KD (1994) Treating offenders with cognitive-behavioral therapy: 5-year recidivism outcome data on MRT. Cogn Behav Treat Rev 3:1-3

Overton RC (1998) A comparison of fixed-effects and mixed (random-effects) models for meta-analysis tests of moderator variable effects. Psychol Methods 3:354–379. doi: 10.1037/1082-989X.3.3.354, URL http://search.ebscohost.com/login.aspx?direct=true&db=pdh&AN=met-3-3-354&site=ehost-live

Porporino FJ, Robinson D (1995) An evaluation of the Reasoning and Rehabilitation program with Canadian federal offenders. In: Ross RR, Ross B (eds) Thinking straight. Cognitive Centre, Ottawa, ON, pp 155–191

Porporino FJ , Fabiano EA, Robinson D (1991) Focusing on successful reintegration: Cognitive skills training for offenders, r19. Ottawa, Canada: Research and Statistics Branch, The Correctional Service of Canada

Pratt TC, Cullen FT (2000) The empirical status of Gottfredson and Hirschi's General Theory of crime: A meta-analysis. Criminology 38:931–964, doi: 10.1111/j.1745-9125.2000.tb00911.x, URL http://mutex.gmu.edu:2167/doi/abs/10.1111/j.1745-9125.2000.tb00911.x

Raudenbush SW (1994) Random effects models. Russell Sage Foundation, New York, pp 301–322

Raudenbush SW (2009) Statistically analyzing effect sizes: Random effects models, 2nd edn. Russell Sage Foundation, New York

Robinson D (1995) The impact of cognitive skills training on postrelease recidivism among Canadian federal offenders. Correctional Research and Development, The Correctional Service of Canada, Ottawa, ON

Rosenthal R (1991) Meta-analytic procedures for social research, Rev. ed edn. Applied social research methods series. Sage Publications, Newbury Park

Ross RR, Fabiano EA, Ewles CD (1988) Reasoning and Rehabilitation. Int J Offender Ther Comp Criminol 32:29-36

Schmidt F, Le H, Oh IS (2009) Correcting for the distorting effects of study artifacts in meta-analysis, 2nd edn. Russell Sage Foundation, New York

Schulze R (2004) Meta-analysis: A comparison of approaches. Hogrefe & Huber, Toronto

Shadish WR (2007) A world without meta-analysis. J Exp Criminol 3:281–291. doi: 10.1007/s11292-007-9034-0, URL http://dx.doi.org/10.1007/s11292-007-9034-0

Shadish WR, Haddock CK (2009) Combining estimates of effect size, 2nd edn. Russell Sage Foundation, New York

Sánchez-Meca J, Marín-Martínez F, Chacón-Moscoso S (2003) Effect-size indices for dichotomized outcomes in meta-analysis. Psychol Methods 8:448–467, URL jsmeca@um.es

Stern JM, Simes RJ (1997) Publication bias: Evidence of delayed publication in a cohort study of clinical research projects. BMJ 315:640–645

Sterne JAC, Becker BJ, Egger M (2005) The funnel plot. Wiley, Chichester, pp 75–99

Viechtbauer W (2005) Bias and efficiency of meta-analytic variance estimators in the random-effects model. J Educ Behav Stat 30:261–293. doi: 10.3102/10769986030003261, URL http://jeb.sagepub.com/cgi/content/abstract/30/3/261

Weisburd D, Lum CM, Yang SM (2003) When can we conclude that treatments or programs "don't work"? Ann Am Acad Pol Soc Sci 587:31–48, doi: 10.1177/0002716202250782, URL http://ann.sagepub.com/cgi/content/abstract/587/1/31

Wilson DB (2009) Missing a critical piece of the pie: Simple document search strategies inadequate for systematic reviews. J Exp Criminol. doi: 10.1007/s11292-009-9085-5

Wilson DB, Bouffard LA, Mackenzie DL (2005) A quantitative review of structured, group-oriented, cognitive-behavioral programs for offenders. Crim Justice Behav 32:172–204. doi: 10.1177/0093854804272889, URL http://cjb.sagepub.com/cgi/content/abstract/32/2/172

## CHAPTER 11

Social Network Analysis

Jean Marie McGloin and David S. Kirk

CHAPTER

Consideration of social networks has long been central to some of the most influential theories in criminology. For instance, in his theory of differential association, Sutherland (1947) posits that criminal behavior is learned through interaction in intimate social groups. This proposition helps explain one of the most robust findings in the field of criminology, namely that the bulk of delinquency is carried out in groups. Perhaps the most illustrative example of this familiar finding is Shaw and McKay's (1931) discovery that over 80% of the juveniles they observed, appearing before the Cook County Juvenile Court had accomplices. As Warr (2002, p. 3) argues, "[C]riminal conduct is predominantly social behavior. Most offenders are imbedded in a network of friends who also break the law, and the single strongest predictor of criminal behavior known to criminologists is the number of delinquent friends an individual has." This is but one example; social networks also play salient parts in theories of social control (Hirschi 1969), social disorganization and collective efficacy (Sampson and Groves 1989; Sampson et al. 1997), opportunity perspectives (Osgood et al. 1996), and even have the capacity to shape offender decision-making processes (Hochstetler 2001). Moreover, studying social networks can provide insight on crime patterns and criminal organizations (e.g., Finckenauer and Waring 1998; Natarajan 2006), and consequently inform and guide policy (e.g., Kennedy et al. 2001; McGloin 2005; Tita et al. 2005).

For researchers interested in social networks (or personal networks)[1], network analysis provides the leverage to answer questions in a more refined way than do nonrelational analyses. This analytic strategy has the primary purpose of determining, if there are regular patterns in social relationships and how these patterns may be related to attributes or behavior (Wasserman and Faust 1994). "One of the most important tasks of network analysis is to attempt to explain, at least in part, the behavior of the elements in a network by studying specific properties of the relations between these elements" (Sarnecki 2001, p. 5). Therefore, unlike other analytical procedures, network analysis turns attention away from individual attributes and toward the relationships among units. To be clear about the distinction between attributional and relational data, consider the following example: "...the value of goods that

---

[1] In contrast to a social network, a personal, or egocentric, network focuses on one node of interest (i.e., ego) and its alters (i.e., associates).

A.R. Piquero and D. Weisburd (eds.), *Handbook of Quantitative Criminology*,
DOI 10.1007/978-0-387-77650-7_11, © Springer Science + Business Media, LLC 2010,
First softcover printing 2011

a nation imports in foreign trade each year is an attribute of the nation's economy, but the volume of goods exchanged between each pair of nations measures an exchange relationship" (Knoke and Kuklinski 1982, p. 11).

Perhaps more so than other methods, network analysis is vulnerable to analysts plucking out certain measures and placing them under their current framework, paying little attention to the assumptions behind these measures (see Osgood 1998, for criminology's tendency to "steal from our friends"). As Wellman (1983, p. 156) contends, however, "the power of network analysis resides in its fundamental approach to the study of social structure and not as a bag of terms and techniques." Social network analysis is more than a set of methods – it is an orientation toward the understanding of human behavior that focuses on the importance of social relations, as well as the set of tools that enable the investigation of social relations and their consequence. While many methods in this text carry with them assumptions about the data at hand, this method also carries assumptions about the social world, namely the notions that: (1) people typically act in social systems that contain other actors who act as reference points for behavior, and (2) there is a systematic structure to these relationships (Knoke and Kuklinski 1982).

Network analysis is an approach to the study of social structure, with the premise that the best way to study a social system is to examine the ties among the members of the system. It is assumed that the pattern of these social relations, which we define as *social structure*, has implications for behavior. In contrast, social scientists have traditionally limited their focus to the role of actor attributes and norms as explanatory variables of behavior. The assumption with such an approach is that individuals with similar attributes (e.g., gender, socioeconomic status) or similar norms will behave similarly, and variation in behavior across individuals is therefore explained by differing attributes and norms (Wellman and Berkowitz 1988). Furthermore, most empirical explanations for behavior, including criminal behavior, rely upon statistical methods which assume that individuals are *independent*, autonomous units. From a theoretical standpoint, however, social network analysis focuses on the relations and *interdependence* between nodes, and how the constraints and opportunities derived from patterned relations ultimately influence behavior (Wellman 1983).

Network approaches are gaining popularity in criminology, but the formal use of network techniques and methods remains limited. Still, there are a number of theoretical traditions in criminology and criminal justice that draw upon social network conceptions to explain the causes and consequences of crime. For instance, investigations of social bonds, social disorganization, deviant peer effects, and some opportunity perspectives utilize relational conceptions. Social bond theory (Hirschi 1969) orients us to the quality of the relationships people have with other individuals and institutions (e.g., attachment and involvement). With an emphasis on the importance of relational networks to facilitate social control, much of the current theorizing in the social disorganization tradition has made use of the systemic model, which identifies the social organization of communities by focusing on local community networks (Kasarda and Janowitz 1974). Bursik and Grasmick (1993) argue that the density and extent of neighborhood networks and social bonds influence the neighborhood's capacity for social control. Next, studies of peer effects implicitly or explicitly are founded upon the assertion that social relations are necessary for the transmission of influence, skills, and norms. Learning theory (particularly differential association) orients us toward the importance of the following factors: (1) with whom a person associates; (2) the balance of individuals in the network (i.e., whether it is mostly deviant); (3) the transference of deviant norms through these links; and, (4) the quality or strength of the associations (i.e., more frequent associations can have a greater impact on behavior). Finally, recent conceptions of routine activities also root the construction of criminal opportunities in (unsupervised and unstructured) social networks (Osgood et al. 1996; see also Haynie and Osgood 2005).

Network analysis also holds utility outside theoretical inquiries. For instance, some authors have adopted network perspectives to address inter and intraorganizational relationships within the criminal justice system, focusing on such issues as intelligence sharing and whether network structure predicts policy adoption (Alter 1988; Curry and Thomas 1992; Gustafson 1997; Miller 1980; Sparrow 1991). Other work has used network analysis to address whether criminal networks actually exist (Coles 2001) and what delinquent and organized crime networks look like (Finckenauer and Waring 1998; Krohn and Thornberry 1993; McGloin 2005; Sarnecki 2001). Finally, another stream of the literature essentially advocates for its use in law enforcement investigations (Coady 1985; Davis 1981; Howlett 1980) and demonstrates how it can guide interventions (Braga et al. 2001).

Obviously, network analysis has broad utility for criminology and criminal justice. Yet, it unfortunately remains a relatively sporadic technique and approach. The purpose of this chapter is to provide the reader with a working knowledge of network analysis and to demonstrate its utility for researchers across a wide array of criminological interests. Specifically, it will offer a brief background of network analysis, basic knowledge of the requisite data, important points for consideration regarding data and sampling, and illustrate some basic analyses, supplemented by further examples of similar techniques in contemporary criminological research.

Background of Network Analysis

Social network analysis evolved from a number of diverse research traditions, including the fields of sociometry, mathematics, psychology, and anthropology. Sociometry is the study of social relations, with roots in the work of psychiatrist Jacob L. Moreno. Moreno and his colleagues sought to uncover how individuals' group relations shape their psychological development and well-being (Scott 2000). One of Moreno's (1934) most enduring contributions to social network analysis is the "sociogram," in which individuals are represented by points (i.e., nodes) and social relations are represented by lines between the points. Sociometrists argued that society is best understood not simply as an aggregate of independent individuals and their characteristics, but rather as a set of interdependent, interpersonal relations. Thus, from the perspective of sociometry, the best way to study society is to examine social relations, as well as the causes and consequences of social relations (as opposed to studying individuals as though they are totally independent).

The visual appeal of Moreno's sociogram to represent social relations became more formalized with the advent of graph theory in mathematics (Cartwright and Harary 1956; Harary et al. 1965). A graph is a set of lines connecting various points. Graph theory provides a vocabulary for describing a social network as well as a set of axioms and theorems, which can be used to understand the pattern of lines formed between points (Scott 2000). In the vocabulary of graph theory, social units are termed nodes or vertices, and the relations between units are termed arcs or edges. Diagrams, such as sociograms, are certainly appealing, but matrices are another useful tool to represent graphs and store data on social networks. The integration of algebraic models and statistical/probability theory further expanded the means to study, describe, and quantify relational data (Wasserman and Faust 1994).

In addition to the sociometric and graph theoretic foundations, the roots of modern network analysis are also found in the work of psychologists and anthropologists (see Scott 2000). First, during the 1930s, cognitive and social psychologists working under the gestalt paradigm researched group structure as well as the information flow among members. Second, scholars at Harvard University refined the premises of anthropologist A.R. Radcliffe-Brown by focusing on interpersonal relations and subgroups within social networks. Third, researchers at Manchester University focused on tribal societies, using these studies to further refine social theory and the study of community relations. Although Radcliffe-Brown was also the primary influence for the Manchester researchers, their studies tended to focus on conflict and change rather than cohesion, which served as the focus for the Harvard group (Scott 2000). Together, these streams of research, which led to theoretical, methodological, and analytical maturity and refinement, serve as the foundation for network analysis.

Network Data and Sampling Considerations

Network analysis requires different data than most criminologists typically employ. It may be clear by now that the unit of analysis in network studies is not the node or individual, but the tie between entities (i.e., links among the nodes). This tie or link can take many forms, such as kinship, friendship, co-membership, communication, trust, shared or exchanged goods, among many others.[2] Depending upon the nature of the links, as well as the research questions, these relational ties can be undirected or directed. Examples of undirected ties would include co-authorship, siblings, married partners, or an affiliation tie such as two individuals belonging to the same street gang. Directed links would include such relations as exporting products to another node, identifying someone as a friend, receiving a call in a wiretapping ring; the notion behind a directed tie is that there is a flow or direction to the relationship and it is considered important for the inquiry at hand. Directed data may be important for criminological questions of interest, perhaps in terms of directing policy (e.g., who is "organizing" the illegal market by initiating and handling contact and product exchange?) or stimulating research questions (e.g., is there a difference between someone who has reciprocal deviant friends and someone who is not viewed as a mutual friend by deviant peers). It is important to note that relational ties can also have value. For example, researchers may code relations according to some level of attachment or involvement (e.g., number of days per week two individuals communicate). These values may reflect a continuous measure or scale, they can be categorical, reflecting distinct relations (i.e., friends versus siblings), or some combination thereof. The latter example is also known as a multirelational network (i.e., two nodes may be tied together in multiple ways).

Knowing the requisite data for network analysis is one thing, but acquiring them is something else. A proper social network is fully complete and reflects the population of interest. In some cases, this is plausible. For example, perhaps the investigation is interested in the social network within a school or business – this is a population with defined boundaries around what constitutes the network. In other cases, however, sampling becomes a thorny issue, both conceptually and practically because the boundary of the population is unclear. If one is interested in deviant peer networks or street gangs, for example, and begins sampling people in a

---

[2] Similarly, nodes can be of many different types, including individuals, organizations, countries, and groups.

school or on the street, to complete this network, the researcher should follow-up each identified friend in what could be a never-ending snowball sample. At some point, the researcher must decide on when the boundary has been "met" and justify it accordingly. Ideally, this boundary should have conceptual merit, not simply be based on ease or previous work.

Finally, most criminological inquires wrestle with missing data and the varied techniques of how to manage it. We do not bring it up here to ruminate on this general issue, but rather to make readers aware of the domino-effect missing data can have with regard to network information. To illustrate this point, imagine a project that gathers network data on a fifth grade class, asking about friendship links among the students. The researcher is interested in drug use within the students' personal networks (i.e., "egocentric" networks). If one student was absent on the day of the survey, of course there will be no peer network data for him. Importantly, unlike with typical data, his absence can affect the degree to which other subjects have missing data. Though it arguably will not affect the structure of other students' basic networks, because they were able to identify him as a friend even though he was absent, it could impact the extent to which their peer group appears to engage in drug use. If peer drug use is based on self-reports, then if this absent student was identified as a friend in 20 networks, these 20 people now have missing data on whatever variable measures the extent of peer drug use/endorsement. Under certain circumstances therefore, the impact of missing data can quickly escalate in network studies.

A Demonstration of Network Techniques

In order to understand the utility of network analysis, even in its most basic graphical form, it is instructive to use an example dataset and carry it through the various forms of analysis and description. This chapter will use a hypothetical dataset on a supposed organized crime group, whose members are all known to police and are currently under observation through wiretapping. The nodes are therefore the individuals in this criminal group and the links are phone calls made among them.[3] In this hypothetical dataset, there are 15 individuals and the links are both directed and valued. The direction indicates who received the phone call and the value of the link indicates the number of phone calls.

After the period of observation/data collection, the data are summarized and stored in an adjacency matrix, in which the rows and columns are defined by the actors in the network and the cell values of the matrix indicate whether two actors are associated (i.e., adjacent).[4] Table 11.1 displays the hypothetical data in matrix format. For a directed network, a positive value indicates "movement" from the row to the column. A zero value in a cell indicates that the person in the relevant row did not initiate a call to the person in the relevant column. The matrix shows that person 2 called person 1, but person 1 did not ever initiate a call to person 2. In order to characterize the "value" of the link, this dataset defines the connection as a continuous variable, capturing the number of phone calls initiated by the person in the row to the person in the column. Thus, the table shows that person 9 called person 7 three times during the observation period, where as person 11 called person 3 only one time.

---

[3] This hypothetical example is similar to the work of Natarajan (2006), which used wiretapping information to study network attributes of a heroin distribution group in New York.

[4] In addition to adjacency matrices, there are also incident matrices, in which the rows are the nodes and the columns are incidents, events, or affiliations (i.e., the value in a cell would indicate whether a particular node was part of that specific incident, event, or affiliated with that specific group).

TABLE 11.1. Adjacency matrix for hypothetical dataset

	1	2	3	4	5	6	7	8	9	10	11	12	13	14	15
1		0.0	0.0	0.0	0.0	0.0	1.0	0.0	0.0	0.0	0.0	0.0	0.0	0.0	0.0
2	1.0		0.0	0.0	4.0	0.0	0.0	0.0	0.0	0.0	1.0	0.0	0.0	3.0	0.0
3	0.0	2.0		0.0	0.0	0.0	10.0	0.0	1.0	0.0	0.0	0.0	0.0	0.0	0.0
4	0.0	0.0	0.0		0.0	0.0	2.0	0.0	0.0	0.0	0.0	1.0	0.0	0.0	0.0
5	0.0	0.0	5.0	0.0		0.0	0.0	0.0	0.0	1.0	0.0	0.0	0.0	0.0	0.0
6	0.0	0.0	0.0	0.0	0.0		0.0	0.0	0.0	0.0	0.0	0.0	0.0	0.0	0.0
7	0.0	0.0	6.0	0.0	0.0	0.0		0.0	0.0	0.0	1.0	0.0	0.0	1.0	0.0
8	0.0	0.0	0.0	2.0	0.0	0.0	0.0		0.0	0.0	0.0	0.0	0.0	0.0	0.0
9	0.0	0.0	0.0	0.0	0.0	0.0	3.0	0.0		0.0	0.0	0.0	1.0	0.0	1.0
10	0.0	0.0	0.0	0.0	0.0	0.0	0.0	0.0	0.0		0.0	0.0	0.0	0.0	0.0
11	0.0	0.0	1.0	0.0	1.0	0.0	1.0	0.0	1.0	0.0		1.0	0.0	1.0	0.0
12	0.0	0.0	0.0	0.0	0.0	0.0	0.0	0.0	0.0	0.0	0.0		0.0	0.0	0.0
13	0.0	0.0	0.0	0.0	0.0	0.0	4.0	0.0	0.0	1.0	0.0	0.0		0.0	0.0
14	0.0	0.0	0.0	0.0	0.0	0.0	0.0	0.0	0.0	0.0	0.0	0.0	0.0		0.0
15	0.0	0.0	0.0	0.0	0.0	0.0	1.0	0.0	1.0	0.0	0.0	0.0	0.0	0.0	

GRAPHICAL DISPLAYS. Maltz (1998, p. 400) argues that "when shown in graph forms data are displayed without assumption." Although social patterns may be evident in smaller adjacency matrices, as the network grows, patterns may be obscured by the sheer volume of data (i.e., there are 600 possible links within a network of only 25 people). Graphs can reveal patterns that provide a more in-depth understanding of the data at hand. Of course, nuances within sociograms of very large networks may be difficult to discern, but even these graphs may provide insight (e.g., Sarnecki 2001).

As an example, Fig. 11.1 translates the matrix in Table 11.1 into graph form. Figure 11.1a is a directed graph (i.e., the arrows point to the recipient of the phone call), but not valued (i.e., the lines do not demonstrate the frequency of such phone calls). Therefore, it treats all of the values in Table 11.1 as if they were dichotomous rather than continuous. This graph highlights some interesting findings, such as person 6 appears to be "unimportant" to the criminal enterprise, at least if phone calls are the primary means of communication. It also suggests that much of the "action" is among persons 3, 7, 9, 11, and 14. For example, both nodes 7 and 11 are communicating with many people in the network, though it seems that 7 is primarily a recipient of communication, whereas 11's role is more balanced between receiving and initiating phone calls.

The graph in Fig. 11.1b incorporates the value of the associations among the actors by affecting the thickness of the links among the nodes (i.e., thicker lines indicate more frequent contact). Though Fig. 11.1a provides a sense of the individuals most enmeshed in this network, once the values are incorporated in Fig. 11.1b, it orients investigators interested in key lines of communication to persons 3 and 7, not necessarily person 11. Moreover, whereas person 5 did not "stand out" in Fig. 11.1a, this complementary figure suggests that this actor may be more embedded in the communication network than previously thought. In this way, even simple graphs can provide insight and direction into intervention techniques and prosecutorial strategies (e.g., RICO).

A number of extant investigations in criminology and criminal justice have benefited from such graphical displays. For instance, the Boston Gun Project used network analysis in its problem analysis phase when attempting to understand the local gang landscape (Kennedy et al. 1997). As part of its endeavor to study rising gang violence and

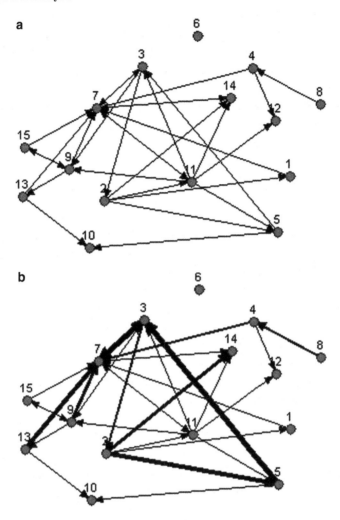

FIGURE 11.1. (a) Directed graph of the hypothetical dataset from Table 11.1. (b) Valued graph of the hypothetical dataset from Table 11.1.

youth use of firearms, the Boston Gun Project gathered data on the area gangs that were especially problematic for the local neighborhoods and the law enforcement community (Braga et al. 2001; Kennedy et al. 1996, 2001). While delineating the gangs and their respective territories, the researchers also investigated the relationships among gangs. In particular, they produced sociograms in which the gangs served as the nodes and rivalries among the gangs served as the linkages. This analysis served three important functions for the intervention. First, it allowed the stakeholders to understand why particular geographic areas were experiencing violent conflict – largely because the gangs tied to those territories were those heavily embedded in conflictual relations with other gangs. Second, it illustrated what gangs were most integral to the network – that is, the gangs that had the most connections, which nominated them for law enforcement focus and intervention. Finally, it gave insight into potential victimization on the heels of the intervention. In particular, if law enforcement directed resources at a particular gang, the rivals may take advantage of their vulnerability by engaging in aggressive dominance, leading to unintentional collateral violence. Rather than considering one gang set to the exclusion of the remainder of the land-scape – a common strategy within law enforcement (Stelfox 1996) – the knowledge of the connections among the gangs provided unique leverage when undertaking the intervention strategy (see also Tita et al. 2005)

McGloin (2005) also recently used network analysis to describe the gang landscape in Newark, New Jersey. In contrast to the Boston Gun Project, the nodes in her networks were the gang members and the links were multirelational, capturing five distinct relationships that could overlap (e.g., siblings and co-defendants). The sociograms emerging from this work demonstrate that gangs in Newark are not very cohesive, but instead are characterized by a fragmented assortment of smaller subgroups. Given this network structure, the graphs drew attention to those gang members who serve as the bridge between subgroups, since they are vital to maintaining the overall connectedness of the network. From this graphical display of the data, she asserts that removing these "cut points" through police intervention may ulti-mately fragment the overall gang (for other examples of network graphs, see Finckenauer and Waring 1998; Sarnecki 2001; Whyte 1943).

MOVING PAST GRAPHS. Although network graphs can be very informative, investi-gators often have an interest in comparing networks or nodes within networks. Relying on visual assessments for such comparisons can be quite subjective. There are various network measures, however, which provide a more quantifiable metric of key concepts and therefore allow for more ready comparison. This comparison can extend from quantitative investiga-tions focused on connections, such as those among deviant peers, to rich ethnographic work that describes social processes and interconnections. Thus, the network approach, and the measures and descriptors contained within, has the capacity to both shed insight on individual inquires, but also promote comparison and "knowledge-building" across studies (McGloin 2007).

Much of the literature investigating correlates of crime such as attachment to parents, associations with deviant peers, and the extent of neighborhood-level mutual trust and interac-tions typically utilize survey-based measures to describe the nature and importance of social networks. Still, there are formal measures used in network studies that move beyond these variables and provide greater analytic insight into some nuanced concepts important for the-ory and practice. The focus here is on these measures that derive from more precise network data, in which one has definable nodes and links (i.e., "how attached are you to your friends?" does not provide specific or precise network information). Our overview of network measures is not exhaustive; rather, we attempt to call the reader's attention to a number of measures and concepts, which are particularly useful for scholars interested in group structure and/or indi-vidual (i.e., node) positions within a network (see Wasserman and Faust 1994 for a detailed description of the many tools and techniques of network analysis).

With regard to group structure, scholars are often interested in cohesion. *Density* is a traditional measure of cohesion, which measures the proportion of ties that exist in the net-work to all possible ties. The density formula produces values ranging from 0, indicating no nodes in the network are linked, to 1, indicating that every possible tie in the network exists. The key pieces of information one needs to calculate density are the number of nodes ("g") and the number of linkages ("L") between nodes. One can determine density with the following formula:

$$2L/g(g-1)$$

This formula is applicable for networks with undirected linkages – for directed networks, as with our hypothetical example, the formula is slightly different. Because two ties can exist for each pair of nodes (i.e., a call from node 1 to node 2, and a call from node 2 to node 1), the formula is:

$$L/g(g-1)$$

Calculating the density for valued graphs can be slightly more complicated. According to Wasserman and Faust (1994), one way to measure the density of a valued network is to rely on the average value of the ties, but this has somewhat less intuitive appeal and is not held to the same traditional interpretation of density (i.e., a 0–1 range). For this reason, valued links are sometimes treated as if they were dichotomous when calculating density.[5]

Under the second density formula for directed networks, the density coefficient for our hypothetical dataset of wiretapped conversations is 0.138. There is no established threshold at which a network is considered "cohesive", but this network does not appear very dense. Indeed, less than 14% of all possible ties are present in the network. This would indicate that the criminal enterprise is not tightly organized, which also may be important as stakeholders attempt to understand and determine the most appropriate intervention and suppression strategies.

Though a person may not be able to speak in concrete terms about whether a network has passed the tipping point for being cohesive, one can certainly compare density values across networks and their impact on behavior. For example, Haynie (2001) incorporated the density of adolescent peer networks into an investigation of the criminogenic impact of deviant peers on delinquency. Unlike the previous example of a criminal enterprise network, the networks under focus in this investigation (via data from AddHealth) were egocentric (i.e., personal networks) rather than a global social network (e.g., an organized crime group). In a manner consistent with learning theory, she found that being part of dense school-based friendship networks amplified the deleterious effect of having deviant peers. A large body of work in network analysis has examined the repercussions of group cohesion on the behavior of group members, with the general conclusion that we should expect relatively greater homogeneity in behavior (e.g., delinquency) within cohesive groups. Groups are pressured toward uniformity as cohesiveness increases (see Friedkin 1984); it is harder for an individual in a dense group to break free from the group identity (i.e., by avoiding delinquency) than for individuals in less cohesive networks. Of course, criminologists working outside of a formal network framework have produced groundbreaking work on peer influence, but the focus is generally limited to the distribution of influence along a two-person dyad or from a generalized "group" of friends. A network approach, such as Haynie's, allows us to expand our focus and recognize that the connectivity and cohesiveness among one's peers may be extremely consequential to the behavior of the focal individual.

Density describes the cohesion of the entire network, but researchers may also be interesting in identifying cohesive subgroups within the larger network. For instance, research on street gangs has often noted that group organization tends to be loose, transient, and not very dense, but that pockets of intense cohesion do exist (e.g., Klein 1995; McGloin 2005). Theory and policy could arguably benefit from understanding whether these subgroups are responsible for a disproportionate amount of "gang crime" or whether the subgroup members can

---

[5] If the value of the tie does not reflect the strength of some relationship, but instead some combination of relationships (i.e., the network is multirelational), researchers also have the option of determining the density for the network across each type of relationship.

be readily distinguished from other gang members on variables of interest. A "clique" is a type of cohesive subgroup that contains at least three nodes, all of which are adjacent to (i.e., connected to) one another. Thus, cliques traditionally have a density coefficient of 1.[6]

Cliques can be difficult to identify or define in directed networks (Scott 2000). So, for illustrative purposes, the data in the hypothetical example will be recoded as dichotomous and undirected, which can be seen in Table 11.2. In this network, there are six cliques.[7] Figure 11.2 highlights one clique (in the right portion of the graph), which is comprised of nodes 3, 7, 9 and 11. This suggests that in the network, which does not have an impressively high density coefficient, there nonetheless exist collectives of interactions that are very cohesive. At first blush, therefore, though it may seem that this criminal enterprise is not well organized, it may instead be organized in a cell-like manner, in which connections are forged when and as necessary. Of course, this could prove to not be the case, but the identification of these cliques would prompt the question and facilitate a deeper understanding of the network under focus.

Researchers may also be interested in inquiries that characterize or describe the node(s). For instance, scholars can determine how embedded a person is in a social network, or how "important" s/he is to this network. There are a few ways to operationalize prominence, but one manner is to assess a node's centrality. As with density, measures of prominence can take on different calculations when the network is directed and/or valued. In an attempt to focus on basic measures and their meaning, we will focus on formulae for undirected, unvalued, graphs. Thus, the calculations here will rely on the matrix in Table 11.2. For readers interested in doing such calculations for other kinds of networks, we direct your attention to Wasserman and Faust (1994).

TABLE 11.2. Adjacency matrix with recoded data

	1	2	3	4	5	6	7	8	9	10	11	12	13	14	15
1		1.0	0.0	0.0	0.0	0.0	1.0	0.0	0.0	0.0	0.0	0.0	0.0	0.0	0.0
2	1.0		1.0	0.0	1.0	0.0	0.0	0.0	0.0	0.0	1.0	0.0	0.0	1.0	0.0
3	0.0	1.0		0.0	1.0	0.0	1.0	0.0	1.0	0.0	1.0	0.0	0.0	0.0	0.0
4	0.0	0.0	0.0		0.0	0.0	1.0	1.0	0.0	0.0	0.0	1.0	0.0	0.0	0.0
5	0.0	1.0	1.0	0.0		0.0	0.0	0.0	0.0	1.0	1.0	0.0	0.0	0.0	0.0
6	0.0	0.0	0.0	0.0	0.0		0.0	0.0	0.0	0.0	0.0	0.0	0.0	0.0	0.0
7	1.0	0.0	1.0	1.0	0.0	0.0		0.0	1.0	0.0	1.0	0.0	1.0	1.0	1.0
8	0.0	0.0	0.0	1.0	0.0	0.0	0.0		0.0	0.0	0.0	0.0	0.0	0.0	0.0
9	0.0	0.0	1.0	0.0	0.0	0.0	1.0	0.0		0.0	1.0	0.0	1.0	0.0	1.0
10	0.0	0.0	0.0	0.0	1.0	0.0	0.0	0.0	0.0		0.0	1.0	0.0	0.0	0.0
11	0.0	1.0	1.0	0.0	1.0	0.0	1.0	0.0	1.0	0.0		1.0	1.0	0.0	0.0
12	0.0	0.0	0.0	1.0	0.0	0.0	0.0	0.0	0.0	0.0	1.0		0.0	0.0	0.0
13	0.0	0.0	0.0	0.0	0.0	0.0	1.0	0.0	1.0	1.0	0.0	0.0		0.0	0.0
14	0.0	1.0	0.0	0.0	0.0	0.0	1.0	0.0	0.0	0.0	1.0	0.0	0.0		0.0
15	0.0	0.0	0.0	0.0	0.0	0.0	1.0	0.0	1.0	0.0	0.0	0.0	0.0	0.0	

[6] There are also *n*-cliques, which focus on geodesic distances (i.e., the shortest path between two nodes). A 1-clique would be a subgroup in which all geodesic distances among the members is 1 (i.e., a traditional clique). A 2-clique would be a subgroup in which nodes were connected to each other directly or indirectly through another node (thus, the largest geodesic distance is 2). For more information about n-cliques and other cohesive subgroups, see Scott (2000) and Wasserman and Faust (1994).

[7] The six cliques contain the following nodes: (1) 3,7,9,11; (2) 3,7,9,13; (3) 2,3,5,11; (4) 7,9,15; (5) 7,11,14; and (6) 2,11,14.

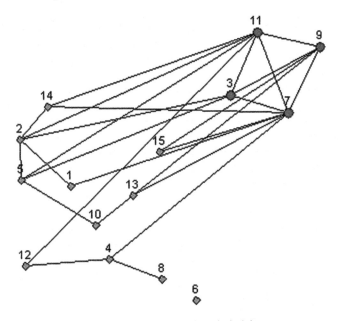

FIGURE 11.2. Cliques in the hypothetical dataset.

In its most basic form, prominence is captured as *degree centrality*. Degree refers to the number of ties connected to the node under consideration. In order to standardize this measure for comparison purposes (since degree is largely dependent on the number of nodes in the network), we divide the degree by the number of nodes in the network excluding the focal node $(g-1)$ producing, a measure of degree centrality. Thus, in the hypothetical dataset, node 8 has degree of 1, and therefore a degree centrality of 0.071 (i.e., 1/14), whereas node 7 has a degree of 8 and a degree centrality of 0.571 (i.e., 8/14). Though this is a very simple measure, it nonetheless gives a sense of embeddedness, which may be quite important to certain investigations. For example, in his investigation of unemployment, Hagan (1993, p. 468) has argued that events are "not determined solely by individual propensities or states, but more significant, by socially structured connections between individuals." Being part of a deviant peer network has the capacity to affect one's own delinquency, which in turn reduces the likelihood of legitimate employment. Additionally, one can argue that this would only further embed and constrain the person within this deviant network. Thus, researchers interested in such concepts may find utility in a measure like degree centrality.

There are also other types of centrality measures that may be of greater interest for investigators. For example, betweenness centrality captures whether a node has "some control over paths in the graph" (Wasserman and Faust 1994, p. 188). A person who lies on the shortest path between other individuals arguably can control the flow of information and resources, and therefore is central and important. In specific terms, betweenness centrality assesses the extent to which one node is on other nodes' geodesics, which is defined as the shortest path between two nodes. In our hypothetical network (Fig. 11.1a), node 4 lies on the geodesic between node 8 and node 2, and therefore may control the flow of information between these latter two nodes. Each node in a network has a probability of being on the geodesic between two other nodes, and betweenness centrality is the sum of these probabilities across all pairs of nodes in the network. As with degree centrality, it must be standardized because the size of the network can influence this value, thereby making comparisons difficult. Thus, one should divide this sum by its maximum value: $[(g-1)(g-2)]/2$. Under the standardized formula, this centrality measure ranges from 0 (indicating this person has no "control" over other nodes' geodesics) to 1.

For our hypothetical dataset (see Table 11.2), this measure of centrality could shed insight on who exerts the most control over the illegal enterprise, as measured by communication among the actors. For instance, nodes 6, 8, and 15 have betweenness centrality values of 0, which might suggest that they do not occupy essential communication positions in this criminal enterprise. Nodes 4 and 11 have values of 0.148 and 0.167, respectively, indicating that some other people in the network do have to "go through" them in order to communicate with others in the network. Finally, node 7 has a betweenness centrality value of 0.361, which is the highest for the entire network. This appears to confirm the graphical displays, highlighting node 7 as a potential person of focus for additional investigations and law enforcement attention.

Finally, there are also centrality measures that address the notion that two people in a network who have equal degree centrality measures may not actually be equivalent if the individuals to whom one is connected have differing centrality. Thus, some centrality measures weigh the node's centrality by the centrality of the other nodes to which it is tied. The Bonacich centrality measure captures this concept and has been used by many researchers who have relied on the AddHealth data (e.g., Haynie 2001; McGloin and Shermer 2009; Schreck et al. 2004).

Density, centrality, and the identification of subgroups are but a few examples of the wealth of measures available to scholars interested in social networks. Though we believe network analysis remains underused in criminology, there nonetheless are a few examples that demonstrate the broad utility of such measures across a wide variety of interests. For example, the idea of weak ties and structural holes occupies a prominent place in discussions of social networks, especially in the economic sociology literature (Burt 1992; Granovetter 1973). From this work, scholars have argued that redundant networks (i.e., networks where relationships overlap with regard to the people to whom they provide contact) constrain an individual's exposure to information, skills, and opportunities. In contrast, individuals in nonredundant networks have greater returns for social investments because they have access to more diverse skills, knowledge, and opportunities (see also Davern and Hachen 2006; Lin 1982, 1990; Podolny and Baron 1997). Morselli and Tremblay (2004) recently imported this concept to criminology, finding that offenders in less redundant networks had higher criminal earnings than did their counterparts in more redundant criminal networks (see also McGloin and Piquero 2010). Next, in Haynie's (2001) previously mentioned analysis, she also investigated the conditioning effect of popularity. By turning attention to this measure (along with centrality), she found that an individual's position within his/her friendship network, not simply the cohesion of this network, also serves to moderate the impact of having deviant peers on an individual's own level of deviance. Interestingly, Schreck et al. (2004) confirmed this conditioning impact when shifting the outcome from offending to victimization. This is only a sampling of the breadth of network measures and concepts available to criminologists.

MORE ADVANCED OPTIONS.   There is a wealth of social network measures that offer unique insight for researchers studying an array of theoretical and policy-relevant issues. There are also more advanced options, such as network autocorrelation models, often used to study diffusion of ideas and innovation. As we have noted, many empirical explanations for behavior, including criminal behavior, rely upon statistical methods, which assume that individuals are *independent* units. Multilevel modeling is one advance used to account for the interdependence among units, in this case among units within some cluster (e.g., neighborhoods and schools; also see descriptions of random and fixed effect models). The fact that social network analysis explicitly focuses on the *interdependence* among nodes has implications for inferential modeling. If there is interdependency among the behaviors of individuals in a social network, researchers necessarily need an inferential strategy, which captures the endogenous feedback effect of this undirected influence (Erbring and Young 1979). For some network studies, the extent of interdependence among subjects/nodes may be minimal and not require nontraditional modeling approaches. If individuals cannot be assumed to be independent, however, then analytic methods that assume independence may not be able to capture the true importance of group structure on behavior. Practically speaking, the interdependence among individuals' behavior leads to inconsistent OLS estimates of model parameters in a standard linear regression model.

A good example of the use of network autocorrelation models to directly model interdependence is Papachristos' (2009) investigation of gang conflict. From his analysis, Papachristos finds that the act of murder between members of rival gangs is best understood as a form of social contagion. Rather than random acts of violence, gang murders create an institutionalized, patterned network of conflict. Gangs continually battle over positions of dominance, and murder routinely results. Outside of criminology, Morris (1993) has also done work on diffusion, relying on more advanced modeling techniques. In particular, she adopts an epidemiological perspective and persuasively shows how social networks impact and shape the diffusion of HIV/AIDS. While it is out of the scope of this chapter to give full treatment to inferential statistics in social network analysis, we mention these points about inferential modeling to caution the reader to select the appropriate modeling strategy when conducting an analysis utilizing interdependent social units. For additional information on such modeling approaches, see Carrington et al. (2005), as well as Wasserman and Faust (1994).

SOFTWARE OPTIONS

A number of software package options exist for researchers to compute network measures, as well as visualize social networks. A fairly comprehensive list can be found at the website for the International Network for Social Network Analysis: http://www.insna.org/INSNA/soft_inf.html, and descriptions of many software packages can be found in Huisman and van Duijn (2005) and Scott (2000). Figures and calculations used in this chapter were produced in Netminer (www.netminer.com). Other popular software options include UCINET, Pajek, and STRUCTURE, among others. In most cases, the software allows the user to input or import data matrices, produce graphs, as well as explore and analyze the data.

CONCLUSION

In this chapter we have attempted to provide an overview of the development of network analysis, as well as a description of the distinctiveness of social network methodology, with the goal of providing researchers and practitioners with information on how to better understand their data, since it can impact both theoretical and policy growth and refinement. To reiterate several of the points made herein, social network analysis is more than a set of methods. It is an orientation toward the understanding of human behavior that focuses on the interdependency of individuals and how such interdependencies structure behavior. Alternatively, many of the statistical and methodological techniques described in chapters throughout the rest of this volume assume that social units are independent. Thus, social network analysis stands in marked contrast to many traditional statistical methods, and provides a set of analytic and methodological tools distinct from traditional social statistics, which are necessary to study social relations. In light of the key role many theories ascribe to social relations for the onset, persistence, frequency, and desistence of offending behavior, one could assert that criminology fundamentally must attend to the interdependencies among individuals.

The techniques covered in this chapter are in no way exhaustive, so we encourage aspiring network analysts to consult the references contained herein for further information on the vast possibilities for inquiry through social network analysis. As we have noted, social networks play a prominent role in many of the leading explanations of criminal behavior. Yet, the use of formal social network analysis is still quite limited in the fields of criminology and criminal justice. This is unfortunate since a network framework can help illuminate a number of key areas in criminology, whether by providing more refined measures of theoretical concepts, a more in-depth understanding of patterns in data, and/or guidance for policy decisions and evaluations. For instance, discussions about the shifts in peer associations and their relation to crime over the life course have occupied a prominent position in recent years. It would be greatly informative to understand how specific network connections and nodes in these networks shift and change over time, whether these patterns are systematically related to social factors, and how network stability and change is related to multiple contemporaneous and future offending dimensions, such as the frequency and seriousness of crime. One of the most innovative applications of SNA in recent years has been with understanding how to best model longitudinal network data (e.g., Snijders 2005) which coincides nicely with this proposed inquiry. To be sure, the implications of social network evolution for delinquent and criminal behavior are virtually unexplored.

In the end, there are a number of potentially fruitful research avenues, across a wide array of criminological interests, which could benefit from the unique insight offered by social network analysis. As Osgood (1998) has argued, one way for criminology and criminal justice to avoid insularity and stagnation is to keep abreast of work in other disciplines and integrate it as necessary. In light of arguments and examples presented here then, we would argue that it is certainly warranted for scholars to incorporate social network analysis into their analytic "tool box."

REFERENCES

Alter CF (1988) Function, form and change of juvenile justice systems. Child Youth Serv Rev 10:71–100

Braga AA, Kennedy DM, Waring EJ, Piehl AM (2001) Problem-oriented policing, deterrence, and youth violence: an evaluation of Boston's Operation Ceasefire. J Res Crime Delinq 38:195–225

Bursik RJ, Grasmick HG (1993) Neighborhoods and crime: the dimensions of effective community control. Lexington Books, New York

Burt RS (1992) Structural holes: the social structure of competition. Harvard University Press, Cambridge, MA

Carrington P, Scott J, Wasserman S (2005) Models and methods in social network analysis. Cambridge University Press, New York

Cartwright D, Harary F (1956) Structural balance: a generalisation of Heider's theory. Psychol Rev 63:277–292

Coady WF (1985) Automated link analysis – artificial intelligence-based tool for investigators. Police Chief 52:22–23

Coles N (2001) It's not what you know – It's who you know that counts. Analysing serious crime groups as social networks. Br J Criminol 41:580–594

Curry GD, Thomas RW (1992) Community organization and gang policy response. J Quant Criminol 8:357–374

Davern M, Hachen DS (2006) The role of information and influence in social networks: examining the association between social network structure and job mobility. Am J Econ Sociol 65:269–293

Davis RH (1981) Social network analysis – An aid in conspiracy investigations. FBI Law Enforc Bull 50:11–19

Erbring L, Young AA (1979) Individuals and social structure: contextual effects as endogenous feedback. Sociol Methods Res 17:396–430

Finckenauer JO, Waring EJ (1998) Russian mafia in America: immigration, culture, and crime. Northeastern University Press, Boston, MA

Friedkin NE (1984) Structural cohesion and equivalence explanations of social homogeneity. Sociol Methods Res 12:235–261

Granovetter M (1973) The strength of weak ties. Am J Sociol 81:1287–1303

Gustafson LFJ (1997) An historical and network analysis of the juvenile justice system in the Austin, Texas, metropolitan area. University Microfilms International, Ann Arbor, MI

Hagan J (1993) The social embeddedness of crime and unemployment. Criminology 31:465–491

Harary F, Norman R, Cartwright D (1965) Structural models: an introduction to the theory of directed graphs. Wiley, New York

Haynie DL (2001) Delinquent peers revisited: does network structure matter? Am J Sociol 106:1013–1057

Haynie DL, Osgood DW (2005) Reconsidering peers and delinquency: how do peers matter? Soc Forces 84: 1109–1130

Hirschi T (1969) Causes of delinquency. University of California Press, Berkeley, CA

Hochstetler A (2001) Opportunities and decisions: interactional dynamics in robbery and burglary groups. Criminology 39:737–764

Howlett JB (1980) Analytical investigative techniques: tools for complex criminal investigations. Police Chief 47: 42–45

Huisman M, van Duijn MAJ (2005) Software for social network analysis. In: Carrington PJ, Scott J, Wasserman S (eds) Models and methods in social network analysis. Cambridge University Press, New York

Kasarda JD, Janowitz M (1974) Community attachment in mass society. Am Sociol Rev 39:328–339

Kennedy DM, Braga AA, Piehl AM (1997) The (un)known universe: mapping gangs and gang violence in Boston. In: Weisburd D, McEwen T (eds) Crime mapping and crime prevention. Criminal Justice Press, Monsey, NY

Kennedy DM, Braga AA, Piehl AM, Waring EJ (2001) Reducing gun violence: The Boston gun project's operation ceasefire. National Institute of Justice, Washington, DC

Kennedy DM, Piehl AM, Braga AA (1996) Youth gun violence in Boston: gun markets, serious youth offenders, and a use reduction strategy. John F. Kennedy School of Government, Harvard University, Boston, MA

Klein MW (1995) The American street gang. Oxford University Press, New York

Knoke D, Kuklinski JH (1982) Network analysis. Sage, Thousand Oaks, CA

Krohn MD, Thornberry TP (1993) Network theory: a model for understanding drug abuse among African-American and Hispanic youth. In: De la Rosa M, Adrados JLR (eds) Drug abuse among minority youth: advances in research methodology, NIDA Research Monograph 130. Department of Health and Human Services, Bethesda, MD

Lin N (1982) Social resources and instrumental action. In: Marsden P, Lin N (eds) Social structure and network analysis. Sage, Beverly Hills, CA

Lin N (1990) Social resources and social mobility: a structural theory of status attainment. In: Breiger RL (ed) Social mobility and social structure. Cambridge University Press, New York

Maltz MD (1998) Visualizing homicide: a research note. J Quant Criminol 14:397–410

McGloin JM (2005) Policy and intervention considerations of a network analysis of street gangs. Criminol Public Policy 43:607–636

McGloin JM (2007) The organizational structure of street gangs in Newark, New Jersey: a network analysis methodology. J Gang Res 15:1–34

McGloin JM, Piquero AR (2010) On the relationship between co-offending network redundancy and offending versatility. J Res Crime Delinq

McGloin JM, Shermer LO (2009) Self-control and deviant peer structure. J Res Crime Delinq 46:35–72

Miller J (1980) Access to interorganizational networks as a professional resource. Am Sociol Rev 45:479–496

Moreno JL (1934) Who shall survive?. Beacon Press, New York

Morris M (1993) Epidemiology and social networks: modeling structured diffusion. Sociol Methods Res 22:99–126

Morselli C, Tremblay P (2004) Criminal achievement, offender networks and the benefits of low self-control. Criminology 42:773–804

Natarajan M (2006) Understanding the structure of a large heroin distribution network: a quantitative analysis of qualitative data. J Quant Criminol 22:171–192

Osgood DW (1998) Interdisciplinary integration: building criminology by stealing from our friends. Criminologist 23:1, 3–5, 41

Osgood DW, Wilson JK, O'Malley PM (1996) Routine activities and individual deviant behavior. Am Sociol Rev 5:635–655

Papachristos AV (2009) Murder by structure: dominance relations and the social structure of gang homicide in Chicago. Am J Sociol 115:74–128

Podolny JM, Baron J (1997) Social networks and mobility in the work place. Am Sociol Rev 62:673–694

Sampson RJ, Groves WB (1989) Community structure and crime: testing social disorganization theory. Am J Sociol 94:744–802

Sampson RJ, Raudenbush SW, Earls F (1997) Neighborhood and violent crime: a multilevel study of collective efficacy. Science 227:918–924

Sarnecki J (2001) Delinquent networks. Cambridge University Press, Cambridge, UK

Schreck CJ, Fisher BS, Miller JM (2004) The social context of violent victimization: a study of the delinquent peer effect. Justice Q 21:23–47

Scott J (2000) Social network analysis: a handbook, 2nd edn. Sage, London

Shaw C, McKay HD (1931) Report on the causes of crime, Volume II. U.S. Government Printing Office, Washington, DC

Snijders T (2005) Models for longitudinal network data. In: Carrington P, Scott J, Wasserman S (eds) Models and methods in social network analysis. Cambridge University Press, New York

Sparrow MK (1991) The application of network analysis to criminal intelligence: an assessment of the prospects. Soc Networks 13:251–274

Stelfox P (1996) Gang violence: strategic and tactical options. Crown, Manchester

Sutherland EH (1947) Principles of criminology, 4th edn. J.B. Lippincott, Philadelphia, PA

Tita G, Riley JK, Greenwood P (2005) Reducing gun violence: operation ceasefire in Los Angeles, Research in Brief. National Institute of Justice, Washington, DC

Warr M (2002) Companions in crime: the social aspects of criminal conduct. Cambridge University Press, Cambridge, UK

Wasserman S, Faust K (1994) Social network analysis: methods and applications. Cambridge University Press, Cambridge, UK

Wellman B (1983) Network analysis: some basic principles. Sociol Theory 1:155–200

Wellman B, Berkowitz SD (1988) Introduction: studying social structures. In: Wellman B, Berkowitz SD (eds) Social structures: a network approach. Cambridge University Press, Cambridge, UK

Whyte WF (1943) Street corner society. University of Chicago Press, Chicago

CHAPTER 12

Systematic Social Observation in Criminology

STEPHEN D. MASTROFSKI, ROGER B. PARKS, AND JOHN D. MCCLUSKEY

INTRODUCTION

Systematic social observation (SSO) came to criminology at the hand of Albert J. Reiss, Jr., who, in the 1960s, encouraged social scientists to shed some "nonsensical" views about the limits and benefits of different forms of observing social phenomena (Reiss 1968, 1971b). Reiss objected to the notion that direct observation of social phenomena in their natural setting was work for solo researchers using qualitative methods, while survey research was suitable as a group enterprise with many researchers using a systematized protocol to gather quantified data. Reiss argued that both direct social observation and survey research were in fact forms of observation that must confront the same set of challenges to produce interpretable information, that both were amenable to either solo or group practice, and that both could be used effectively for discovery or validation of propositions about social phenomena. Beyond these insights, Reiss's important contribution to criminology was the development and practice of the techniques of SSO. Acknowledging that others before him had associated social field observation with the sorts of systematic protocols that had become popular in survey research, Reiss demonstrated how SSO could be used to answer important questions about what influences police–citizen interactions, with implications for theories about police–citizen relationships and for public policies concerning justice, race relations, and crime control. Since Reiss, criminologists have expanded the application of SSO more broadly, but it is still used relatively infrequently.

In this chapter, we describe SSO, noting what distinguishes it from other forms of observation, as well as shared features. We review methodological issues and then turn to practical considerations in fielding SSO studies. We provide a brief description of SSO's contributions to the field of criminology and suggest future directions and uses for SSO.

A.R. Piquero and D. Weisburd (eds.), *Handbook of Quantitative Criminology*,
DOI 10.1007/978-0-387-77650-7_12, © Springer Science + Business Media, LLC 2010,
First softcover printing 2011

DEFINITION OF SYSTEMATIC SOCIAL OBSERVATION

> An observational method is *the selection, provocation, recording, and encoding of that set of behaviors and settings concerning organisms "in situ" which is consistent with empirical aims* (Weick 1968:360).

When the set of behaviors and settings of empirical interest are those of humans, we call this *social observation*. Social observation becomes *systematic* when

> ... observation and recording are done according to explicit procedures which permit replication and ... rules are followed which permit the use of the logic of scientific inference. The means of observation and recording, whether a person or some form of technology must be independent of that which is observed and the effects of observing and measuring must be measurable (Reiss 1971b:4)

SSO, so defined and employed, is a powerful tool for the study of human behaviors, especially human interactions, as they occur.

Of course, SSO is not the only means for observing human behaviors; certainly, it is not the most commonly employed in criminology. In institutionally structured settings, it is common to rely on the traces of behaviors captured in transactions recorded by institutional data systems. In more open settings, it is common to rely on research subjects for accounts of their past behaviors, often in structured interviews. In these methods, researchers rely on retrospective observation at second hand, accepting the observation and recording procedures employed by institutions, and hypothecating the procedures employed by their untrained subjects as observers. The power of SSO derives from its direct connection to the behaviors of empirical interest.

ORIGINS AND APPLICATIONS

In the late 1920s and early 1930s, scholars studying early childhood social development practiced systematic social observation, using methods "... designed ... to ensure consistent recordings of the same events by different observers ..." (Arrington 1943:83). Arrington's discussion of "the feasibility of systematic observation of social behavior under life conditions" (1943:89), the technology employed, and the reliability and validity of measures obtained by observation remains relevant today. Later reviews of SSO research and methods by Weick (1968), Hartmann and Wood (1982), and McCall (1984) document its spread to additional fields of inquiry and review the issues of feasibility, technology, reliability, and validity found in those fields.

In addition to early childhood development, Arrington cites systematic observation of adult factory workers in the 1930s by Thomas et al. (1933), Whitehead (1935), and Roethlisberger and Dickson (1939). Social psychologists interested in parent and child interactions employed SSO in the 1950s (e.g., Barker and Wright 1955). Boyd and Devault (1966) review SSO research in education, especially classroom behaviors, and Rosenshine and Furst (1973) discuss its application to the study of teaching. The methods of SSO were developed and applied to the study of police by Reiss (1968, 1971b) in the late 1960s, and by Sykes (1977, 1978) and Ostrom and her colleagues (Whitaker et al. 1982) in the 1970s. Mastrofski et al. (1998) further refined and applied these methods to policing in the 1990s. And a body of SSO research on controlling violence and aggression in bars and nightclubs emerged in the 1990s (Graham et al. 2000, 2004, 2005, 2006a, b; Homel and Clark 1994; Homel et al. 1997; Macintyre and Homel 1997).

Others have used SSO to study the pace of life in large U.S. cities (Levine 1997), the presence of social incivilities on residential blocks (Raudenbush and Sampson 1999; Taylor 1997; Taylor et al. 1985), the causes and effects of display of emotion by retail clerks (Rafaeli and Sutton 1989, 1990), the style of management in organizations (Mintzberg 1972; Luthans and Lockwood 1984), and many other phenomena. Recent SSO applications include measuring school environments (Wilcox et al. 2006), evaluating therapeutic communities for drug offenders (Bouffard et al. 2003), expression in service encounters (Pugh 2001), physician counseling of patients (Ellerbeck et al. 2001), the delivery of outpatient medical services (Stange et al. 1998), and evaluating iris scanning technology in three New Jersey schools (Uchida et al. 2004).

METHODOLOGICAL ISSUES AND DECISIONS

Here, we consider the suitability of SSO for the research question, sampling, instrumentation, recording observations, and dealing with various sources of error.

Suitability of SSO

What make SSO especially valuable to researchers gathering data directly in the natural setting are precision of the observations and the independence of the observer from that being observed (Reiss 1971b:4). For example, some classic qualitative field research pioneered researcher access to the police occupation (Skolnick 1966; Van Maanen 1974), but the necessarily selective samples of these solo researchers appear to have overstated the uniformity of police practice (Skogan and Frydl 2004:27). SSO researchers have observed considerable variation in the way police use their authority (Black 1980:ch. 5; Mastrofski et al. 2002; Terrill et al. 2003), and some have shown the high degree of variability that may be found with the same officer over time (Snipes and Mastrofski 1990). Precision is also accomplished through the sequencing of events and the detailing of context (Barnsely 1972:222), matters that may not be well documented by routine official records or accurately recalled by participants when interviewed – for example, how police encounters with the public escalate into rebellion or violence (Sykes and Brent 1983; Terrill 2001). Sometimes, SSO precision derives from the application of complex standards or expectations to the practices of persons with obligations to perform in particular ways: the extent to which legal actors conform to constitutional standards (Gould and Mastrofski 2004) or professional standards (Bayley and Garofalo 1989; Terrill 2003). But, SSO can also be used to determine the extent to which justice officials comply with the preferences of citizens they encounter or whether citizens comply with the preferences of justice officials (Mastrofski et al. 1996, 2000).

The observer's independence of the phenomena observed is a benefit and also a limitation of SSO, and it can be challenging to maintain. Of course, the survey interviewer is also independent of the respondent, but almost entirely dependent upon the respondent to serve as an informant. Interviewers used in victimization surveys are at the mercy of the candor and recall of their research subjects in attempting to determine the occurrence and nature of a crime. The SSO observers are not so dependent; they may rely upon what their senses tell them, recording elements of an event consistent with a protocol that examines the degree of evidence that a crime occurred.

SSO may be especially desirable when the question demands detailed knowledge of situations, conditions, or processes that are not otherwise well-illuminated or where there is reason to question the validity of knowledge based on other forms of observation. SSO may also be useful in studying people who might find it difficult to provide an objective or accurate account of what the researcher wishes to know (such as their behavior and the context of that behavior in highly emotional situations) (McCall 1984:266). Where there are strong temptations to omit, distort, or fabricate certain socially undesirable features, such as illegal, deviant, or otherwise embarrassing situations, SSO offers an independent account. This is, for example, a limitation of survey-based citizen self reports of encounters with police to deal with a problem caused by the survey respondent (Langan et al. 2001), and especially problematic if there is systematic variation in the degree of error across important subgroups within the sample, for example according to race (Engel and Calnon 2004:68).

While much of the SSO research has focused at the level of individual persons as decision makers, the 1980s saw the beginning of studies that use an ecological unit, such as the neighborhood block face, as the unit of SSO analysis. Noting that neighborhood residents find it difficult to offer accurate descriptions of their neighborhood's social and physical environment, Raudenbush and Sampson (1999), building on research by Taylor et al. (1984, 1985, Perkins et al. 1993), highlighted the value of an "ecometric" approach that uses SSO in conjunction with neighborhood survey research to more fruitfully characterize the state of neighborhood physical and social structure.

SSO may be especially well-suited to situations and events where all of the relevant actors and events pertinent to the phenomenon of interest can be observed from start to finish in a limited, well-defined time period. For example, the police decision on how to deal with a traffic violator is clearly bounded in time and place. To the extent that (as currently popular theory suggests) the decision is heavily influenced by the context of the immediate situation (e.g., the offense, the evidence, the driver's demeanor), the decision on how to treat the traffic offender lends itself to SSO (Schafer and Mastrofski 2005). However, observing behaviors relevant to a police chief's decision on establishing departmental traffic enforcement policy would require advance knowledge about when and where such activities take place, something that is seldom available.

Although some forms of large-scale human interactions would not seem so amenable to SSO, a creative approach may overcome the challenges. For example, studying the dynamics of mass protest and its potential for facilitating illegality (riots, for example), could be accomplished when researchers have sufficient advance notice of the organization of protests. Placing observers in the protest strategically, according to the dictates of one's theoretical framework, would allow SSO researchers to generate on-scene, objective accounts of whether certain presumed precursors to riot occur, when and how they occur, and the consequences.

In general, SSO lends itself to observing phenomena that occur either with high frequency, such as drivers' noncompliance with speed limits on public highways (Buckman and Lamberth 2001; Meehan and Ponder 2002; Smith et al. 2004), or at predictable times and places, such as criminal trials (Mileski 1971), field tests of prison security systems (Wilson and Mastrofski 2004), or scheduled meetings between probation officers and offenders. Events that occur less frequently, such as acts of social disorder in public places may require considerably more observation time to obtain reliable estimates (Raudenbush and Sampson 1999), or they may be so infrequent and unpredictable as to make SSO simply infeasible, such as the police use of lethal force or the life-course of criminality in a sample of individuals.

Processes, such as plea negotiations in the criminal process, may be ubiquitous, but they typically occur in ways that make it difficult for the researcher to follow negotiations in specific cases, since those negotiations do not occur at predictable times and places.

One of the most frequent uses of SSO has been investigating how criminal justice workers operate in the context of role expectations generated by their organization or profession (McCall 1984:267). Primarily focused on police, SSO research in criminology has been very concerned with how officers negotiate the tension between the formal (legal, bureaucratic, and professional) standards set for them and those that issue from the occupational culture. SSO could also be applied to role conformance in the context of informal or illegitimate organizations, such as gangs.

SSO is often used in conjunction with other forms of observation. Some studies have used SSO to measure the extent to which treatment conditions in randomized trials have been maintained (Sherman and Weisburd 1995:685). Sometimes, SSO is linked on a case-by-case basis to other forms of data collection on research subjects, such as census data (on neighborhoods), survey interviews of police officers, and follow-up interviews with citizens who were observed in encounters with police (Parks 1984; Percy 1980; Smith 1984, 1986). And sometimes, SSO is used to supply data not otherwise available, such as objective measures of the physical and social disorder in urban neighborhoods (Raudenbush and Sampson 1999).

Perhaps, the most frequent reason that criminologists have turned to SSO is their dissatisfaction with the data they could obtain by other means, such as official records and surveys of research (Buckle and Farrington 1984:63). For example, official records not only measure criminality, but may be affected by other considerations taken into account by those in the agency who record and process that information. Self-report and victim surveys, even though fairly commonplace, also have a number of biases and limitations (O'Brien 2000). As with any method, SSO has its methodological strengths and drawbacks, which will be discussed below.

Unit of Analysis and Sampling

Planning the selection of what is to be observed is often not an explicit feature of qualitative observation, but it is an essential element for SSO. Like survey interviewing, SSO requires a careful focusing of what is to be observed, and makes it possible to estimate parameters and evaluate error (Reiss 1968:357–358).

The first step is establishing the unit of analysis. Given that much SSO focuses on social interactions, there are three distinct approaches (McCall 1984:268–269). One uses a time period as the unit of analysis, observing what happens within each discrete time segment, such as what behaviors police officers show in a 15-min segment (Frank et al. 1997) or the level of social disorder on a street segment during a 1-h period (Weisburd et al. 2006). Another uses a behavior or act as the unit, tracking the sequencing of different behaviors over time, such as the behavioral transactions between officers and citizens who engage each other (Sykes and Whitney 1969). And a third approach is to socially construct an event, such as a face-to-face encounter between a police officer and citizen (Reiss 1971b) or a public meeting between police and members of a neighborhood organization (Skogan 2006).

Sometimes, defining the boundaries of an event-based unit of analysis, such as the encounter, is relatively straightforward. Noting when the parties to the encounter begin and end their interaction is not too difficult, but even here lie complexities. For example, a police officer engages two citizens in a domestic dispute and then disengages them to go to another part of the house out of sight and sound of these two to engage another citizen for several minutes – before returning to re-engage the original citizens. To determine whether this constitutes one or multiple encounters requires careful thought about what constitutes an event of interest.

Sometimes, the challenge is not definitional, but rather observational, because the event of interest does not readily manifest itself in what can be observed. Take, for example, the police decision to stop a suspicious citizen, a decision that concerns criminologists wishing to determine whether police stops are influenced by the race of the citizen. The challenge for the field observer is determining when a citizen is actually observed by the officer, and when that observation is worthy of suspicion or in fact elicits suspicion in the officer. Researchers have attempted to do this by observing the officer for outward manifestations of police suspicion (the "doubletake") and to ask observed officers as part of the research protocol to announce to the researcher when they have formed suspicion so that the observer may inquire further what the officer observed (features of the citizen versus behavior of the citizen) and what judgments were made (Alpert et al. 2005). Of concern here is the regularity and reliability with which officers provide outward manifestations of suspicion forming and the regularity and reliability with which observers will accurately note them.

Once the unit of analysis is decided, the researcher must consider the sampling frame. Of course, the same principles of sampling apply to SSO as any other data collection method, such as survey research (Reiss 1971b:9–11). The researcher must consider where and when the units of interest may be found, and determine an efficient method of capturing a representative sample. An example of a straightforward sampling strategy is an SSO study of shoplifting that randomly selected shoppers entering a store, systematically varying the location of observers among entrances to the store (Buckle and Farrington 1984).

SSO researchers often use more complex sampling strategies focusing on geographic space. We have sampled police beats and specific days and times within them, oversampling places and times where higher levels of police–citizen encounters were expected (Mastrofski et al. 1998). Some researchers rely upon the observed subjects making their own choices as to where observers conduct their observations. This makes sense when the object of study is a specific research subject, but when the object of study is the geographic entity itself, an independent sampling plan is required. For example, a study of public order in a park required researchers to conduct hourly park patrols to observe and record activities of persons by location within the park (Knutsson 1997). Some researchers have used a smaller geographic unit than a police beat or park. Several studies use the face block to apply SSO to the measurement of disorder on public streets, defined in terms of traces of physical and social disorder (trash, graffiti, loitering, public intoxication) (Taylor et al. 1985; Sampson and Raudenbush 1999). In one study, observers drove through street segments videotaping what was viewable from the vehicle (*ibid*). Others have performed live observation at the "epicenter" of each block face (best location to observe the most activity), randomly selecting short periods of time for observation from that location and recording them on check sheets (Weisburd et al. 2006). But observers could focus on single addresses, as might be done if one were interested in observing the extent of different kinds of desired and undesired social activity at crime hotspots. Even smaller spatial units have served as the sampling frame. A study of the relationship between crowding and aggression in nightclubs selected high traffic areas within the establishment (10 sq m) to observe levels of patron aggression for 30-min time periods (Macintyre and Homel 1997).

While much of the extant SSO research must develop time- or area-based sampling frames that capture stochastically-distributed events, some SSO studies have focused on scheduled events, such as the delivery of therapeutic community programs in corrections institutions (Bouffard et al. 2003) or the previously-mentioned police–community neighborhood meetings. Sampling of regularly scheduled events is common in research on educational practices and physician behavior, a practice easily replicated for certain aspects of the legal process of interest to criminologists.

Sometimes, the practicalities of conducting successful field observation make the research vulnerable to sample biases. In cases wherein consent of those to be observed must be secured, a clear bias is introduced when those who refuse to be observed differ in their behaviors from those who are willing to be observed (Fyfe 2002; Mastrofski 2004). The sheer physics of observation can introduce bias as well. For example, the observation of disorder on Chicago block faces required light that was sufficient for observation only between 7 am and 7 pm (Sampson and Raudenbush 1999), meaning that researchers were unable to measure many forms of disorder that predominantly occur in the darkness (Kelling 2001). It would also be challenging to observe many aspects of law enforcement inquiry and exchanges in the investigative and prosecutorial processes, because much of the effort is not limited to face-to-face encounters, but rather occurs through telephone and computer, modes of communication that may necessitate very different sampling frames and observational methods. Particularly challenging are studies that require a sampling of *cases* rather than individual decision-makers, inasmuch as it is difficult to track and observe the behavior of many different persons who may be involved in making decisions about a case.

Instrumentation

Principles that apply to other forms of research also apply to the creation of instruments for structuring and recording SSO (Reiss 1971b:11). Sometimes, the instrument takes the form of a tally sheet or log for recording the frequency at which phenomena were observed, such as counting disorderly elements at block faces (Sampson and Raudenbush 1999) – or the timing and duration of events, such as police presence in a hotspot (Sherman and Weisburd 1995). Often, however, the instrument takes the form of a questionnaire, in this case, directed to the observer. For example, a study of police use of force might ask a series of close-ended questions about the citizens involved in an incident (their personal characteristics, their appearance, their behavior), the behavior of police (how much force was used at which junctures), and other features of the situation (location of the event, its visibility, the presence of bystanders) (Terrill and Mastrofski 2002).

SSO instruments, which can be brief or extensive, have the desired effect of focusing observers' attention on items selected for observation. Field researchers have demonstrated a substantial capacity to recall the relevant features of long sequences of these events, given the repetitive use of the protocols. Nonetheless, greater complexity in the coding system heightens the risk of error (McCall 1984:272). The accuracy of such recall is undoubtedly variable, but we are unaware of the research that has assessed most of the correlates of recall accuracy (e.g., observer characteristics, instrument characteristics, and the observational setting).

As with any questionnaire, the selection of fixed responses requires careful consideration, and detailed instructions may be necessary to standardize the classification of what is observed. In research we have conducted, more than a page of text was required to instruct how citizens encountered by police should be sorted into four categories of wealth, based on their appearance, language, and context of the situation.

In addition to fixed-response items, SSO can be easily supplemented with open-ended items and general descriptions of events that are entered as qualitative data -- narrative accounts. Sometimes, they constitute elaborations of what has been coded on fixed-response items, such as observer commentary on unusual events (Sampson and Raudenbush 1999:616). Sometimes, they introduce other forms of observation, such as when participants are "debriefed" to an event to learn how they perceived and interpreted an event that had just transpired (Mastrofski and Parks 1990). And sometimes, observers are asked to provide lengthy and less structured descriptions of the event (Reiss 1971b:13; Mastrofski et al. 1998). These narrative accounts are used to validate the reliability of observers' classification of phenomena, to document the time sequencing of certain events that is too cumbersome to incorporate into fixed-response items, to learn more about the perceptual framework of the observer, or to capture or clarify features of the event that were not anticipated in the construction of the fixed-response part of the instrument. The risk in using these less-structured modes alone is that narratives could be sufficiently *unsystematic* that they undermine much that SSO is designed to accomplish. Our approach to this problem has focused on detailing a priori the sorts of things that should appear in observers' narrative accounts, thereby adding more structure to the qualitative data than typically occurs in ethnographies (Mastrofski et al. 1998).

Recording Observations

Two issues arise in recording of phenomena observed through SSO: (a) whether it occurs contemporaneous with the observation or later, and (b) whether technological recording devices are employed. Resolving these issues requires choosing the highest priority and what must suffer as a consequence. The more contemporaneous the recording of an observation, the less the vulnerability to recall error and various forms of bias (e.g., when coding decisions about earlier observations are influenced by what subsequently was observed to happen), but in many cases, the act of recording may increase the reactivity of the observed parties to the process of being observed, as for example, when observers posing as shoppers follow actual shoppers to observe whether they are shoplifting (Buckle and Farrington 1984, 1994). Reiss's pioneering SSO of police required observers to complete some paper-and-pencil logs in the field to record the time, location, and participants of events (for example, what might fit on a clipboard) (1971b:14), but many later researchers opted for recording the information in less structured form (in small notebooks that would fit in one's pocket). In both cases, the data encoding occurred subsequently at a separate research office (Mastrofski et al. 1998). Observers attempted to reduce any concerns felt by the observed police by making their field recorded materials available to the officers to review, and by stressing that making these notes was simply part of their job, just as the police were required to record events as part of theirs. The lower level of obtrusiveness afforded by the limited-field-note approach must be balanced with concern for the accuracy of recall, a particularly salient issue when the observations per unit are extensive or complex. Consequently, these projects imposed a number of safeguards. Observers were trained to record keywords to stimulate memory, and completion of data entry took place within hours of departure from the field setting.

Some SSO projects ban any note taking by observers on scene, instead relying entirely on memory. For example, studies of pub violence placed pairs of unobtrusive observers (posing as patrons) in drinking establishments, making visits of 2 h or more (Homel and Clark 1994; Homel et al. 1997). Observers were expected to note hundreds of items, including covering the physical environment, staff levels and characteristics, behavior of patrons and staff regarding deviance, alcohol consumption and efforts to control it and violence, forms of aggression, and the dynamics of incidents involving violence. Observers recorded their observations according to written protocols as soon as possible after leaving the pub.

Employing technological aids is usually intended to increase the accuracy or detail of observation from that which would be otherwise available. Handheld electronic recording devices have been used in observing police–public interactions (Sykes 1977) and in observing the social and physical environment of neighborhoods (Gravlee et al. 2006). Audio-taping of calls for service to police telephone operators has been used to gather data on police workload (Scott 1981). Videotaping neighborhood block faces from a slow-moving motor vehicle has been used to observe neighborhood disorder (Sampson and Raudenbush 1999). Handheld personal digital devices allow contemporaneous observation and recording of brief, frequent events and are most practical when the number of aspects to be observed per event are small in number, which minimizes the interference of recording events occurring in close succession with observing them (McCall 1984:272).

The major advantage of initially recording events electronically and then encoding those records later for analysis is not only the elimination of recall problems, but also that more detailed and accurate observations may be made, and the testing of inter-observer reliability is facilitated. Further, field researchers may in some instances feel safer when they make the initial recording of their observations from the security of a moving vehicle or when events are recorded with a remote and unobtrusive device (e.g., time-lapse photography of a street corner or address). Nonetheless, there are a number of drawbacks that have concerned other researchers. Video recordings cannot exactly replicate what all of the available senses would communicate to an observer who was there "in the moment." The use of drive-by photography can be expensive; it raises ethical concerns because denizens of the neighborhood find them intrusive and perhaps anxiety producing; it may raise legal and human subjects protection issues if alleged criminal acts are recorded; and they may cause significant reactivity among those being observed (Caughy et al. 2001; Gravlee et al. 2006; Kelling 2001; but cf Smith et al. 1975). In other instances, however, the pervasiveness of already-present surveillance technology that records observations in readily shared (digital) formats (closed circuit television in public and mass-private settings or in-car police video cameras to record traffic stops) may afford researchers a relatively unobtrusive source of data that does not encounter these problems. Dabney et al. (2004), for example, used augmented video surveillance to study shoplifters. The researchers followed a sample of drugstore customers at a single location equipped with high resolution video surveillance cameras. They were able to determine which customers engaged in shoplifting and coded data on customers' personal characteristics, as well as behavior. Increasingly, much technology-based surveillance derives its unobtrusiveness, not from its being unknown to subjects, but that it is taken-for-granted (Shrum et al. 2005:11). And with the advent of nonlinear editing packages for digital video, the data itself (traditionally analyzed in quantitative or text format) can be readily manipulated and analyzed as images (Shrum et al. 2005:5).

Dealing with Error, Reliability, and Validity

SSO data are subject to the same range of threats that befall other methods. Here we consider errors introduced by the observer, reliability, and validity issues.

OBSERVER ERROR.   Observers can introduce error intentionally (cheating) or unintentionally (bias or reactivity). Cheating is rarely reported in SSO, although its frequency is unknown. In our own experience (with approximately 100 observers covering about 15,000 h of observation across five projects), we have uncovered but one instance, a situation where the observer fabricated an excuse to switch officers so that she could accompany one in whom she had developed a romantic interest. It seems likely that most instances of SSO cheating go undetected. Detection in this case occurred because the observer carelessly recorded an account of her actions on the same medium used to submit her observation data, which one of her supervisors read when reviewing her materials.

A more subtle form of cheating, shirking, may occur in SSO if observers attempt to reduce their postobservation workload by failing to record events that would require extensive narratives and structured coding. Although there has been no direct systematic assessment of the extent and impact of this form of shirking in SSO, one researcher did examine the effects of time-on-the-job on researcher productivity. Presumably, project burnout might encourage some to engage in workload shedding as the project progresses, but the analysis showed that observers' productivity was not significantly lower late in the project, when compared with the earlier time period (Spano 2005:606–608).

One can assume that, as with any employment situation, instances of cheating are reduced to the extent that the research enterprise (a) selects as observers persons who are committed to integrity, (b) who are socialized during training to maintain it, (c) whose morale is an important concern of those running the operation, and (d) whose field work and work products are carefully monitored and given feedback at the time that researchers are in the field.

Potential sources of unintended biases in SSO are the mindset and prejudices that observers bring to the field or develop on the job, as these may affect what they observe and how they interpret it. The limited extant research exploring these issues for SSO does not offer clear and consistent findings but is dependent upon the particular information in question. Reiss (1968, 1971b:17–18) found that an observer's professional background (law student, sociology student, or police officer) did have consequences for some types of information, but not others. A later study attempted to determine whether a statistical relationship between observed police orientation to community policing and officer success in securing citizen compliance could be attributed to observers' own views on community policing (Mastrofski et al. 1996:295). A clear association was not found between the observers' attitudes and the effects that their analysis produced.

While there is no reason to expect observer bias in SSO to be any more or less a problem than in survey research, the nature of SSO does present some interesting challenges. For example, it is more difficult to check for biases in SSO, at least when the field observation cannot be directly observed, as is usually the case when observers accompany criminal justice decision makers or offenders far from a controlled or predictable setting. A significant contributor to reduction in survey interviewer bias (and shirking) in recent years has been the change from in-person interviews conducted in the field to telephone interviews by interviewers located in call centers, where close monitoring is both possible and unobtrusive.

There are, however, a number of methods for detecting biases. If other, independent sources of data are available, comparisons can be made between what SSO generated and what the observer generated. Although official crime and justice documents often fail to capture the full range of events that interest the researcher, where there is overlap, crosschecking the observations of the SSO field worker is possible, such as crime and arrest reports filed by police officers. The extensive records of officer activities captured in modern police communication systems – both voice and data – are another potential source for cross-validation. Another option is to test observers in a simulated environment, for example, having them evaluate a video of one or more situations and comparing their observations to each other or some presumed objective standard (Mastrofski et al. 1998:9). Another is to look for unexpected or unusual patterns in observer-generated data from field observations, especially when there are a sufficient number of observations to make it reasonable to expect certain sorts of observations to fall within a given range (Mastrofski et al. 1998:14). And of course, one can monitor observers by periodically surveying or debriefing them about their beliefs and perceptions or by requiring that they constantly self-observe in a diary-like format (Reiss 1971b; Spano 2005). One must remain sensitive, however, to the weak and often subtle links between observer attitudes and their observational judgments and behaviors. Well-trained and supervised observers may have or develop stronger judgments and beliefs about what they observe, but still remain true to the research protocols designed to limit the effects of personal biases.

Some types of observation judgment are undoubtedly more vulnerable to personal bias than others. For example, some research required field observers to judge whether police officers applied excessive force against citizens (Worden 1996:36). But it may prove more effective to bifurcate the process into (a) recording narrative accounts of what happened (without asking the field observer to make a judgment about excessive force), and (b) having separate, specially trained experts review these accounts and make an independent judgment about whether they constitute a violation of some standard, legal or otherwise (Gould and Mastrofski 2004).

One particular source of observer error is extended exposure to field conditions. Researchers may "go native" (adopting the perspective of their research subjects), or they may experience "burnout," cynicism about what they are observing. The closer the observer is to the phenomena observed, and the more beneficial the establishment of rapport with the research subject, the greater the risk of going native. An examination of these effects in an SSO study of police found little evidence of a significant change in attitudes toward police between the beginning and end of the study, and surprisingly found that observers who developed more positive attitudes toward the police over time were *less* likely to render assistance to police officers while observing them, albeit the relationship was not statistically significant (Spano 2005:605–606).

Of all the sources of observer error in SSO, reactivity receives the most attention. Reactivity occurs when the method of observation alters what is being observed (Kazdin 1979). In general, the less obtrusive the observation of human behavior, the lower is the risk of reactivity. Much has been written about "interviewer effects" – reactivity in survey research and ways to reduce it (Webb et al. 1981). Much less is known about reactivity in SSO. Measuring SSO's reactivity is challenging, because often SSO is the only means available to measure the object of study, and even when other methods of observation are available, they may have their own reactivity issues. It may be possible to make inferences by comparing the results of different forms of observation, some presumably more conspicuous than others (Brackett et al. 2007). But for SSO by observers who are noticeably present, the challenges of comparing behavior when observers are present to when they are not is nigh impossible unless there are other unobtrusive ways of monitoring the behavior in question both when observers are and are not present. This is rarely possible.

No responsible researcher dismisses the risks of reactivity in SSO, but a number suggest that it is dependent on the context of the observational setting and the nature of the relationship between observer and observed (McCall 1984:273–274). In SSO of police, it has been argued that reactivity to the observer can be reduced by the observer downplaying any evaluative role and emphasizing one's naivety as a "learner" (Mastrofski et al. 1998; Reiss 1968). Yet, even this approach may generate more "teaching" or show-off activity in police subjects. Observed officers who engage in such teaching have been noted to self report making contact with citizens to illustrate elements of police work to the observer (Mastrofski and Parks 1990:487). And some types of observers (for example females in the presence of male police officers), may produce more of this effect than others (Spano 2007:461).

Certainly, some types of research subject behavior are more susceptible to the presence of an observer than others; the stronger the social valence of a particular pattern, the greater the risk that behavior will be altered. Nonetheless, many well-ingrained patterns of behavior may be especially difficult to alter (Reiss 1971a), including such things as racial discrimination and violations of constitutional rights, especially if the making of this particular determination is not an obvious purpose of the research. And it has been noted that research subjects often habituate to the presence of observers over time (McCall 1984:274; Spano 2007:461). Compared to other forms of data (interviews, self-reported behavior, agency records) SSO may well be less reactive. Interview respondents can easily offer inaccurate or distorted answers that are difficult to detect. An official can easily misrepresent what he or she reports on agency records where there is a weak organizational capacity to detect it. When SSO researchers are present to observe the event, especially when the subject is engaging other people, changing his or her habitual behavior may be far more challenging (Reiss 1971b:24). Such manipulations may be especially difficult where skill levels and experience influence the research subject's course of action.

Controlling reactivity is accomplished by (a) making the observation less obtrusive, (b) making the observation less consequential, and (c) selection, training, and monitoring observers to remain within the appropriate limits of their research role (McCall 1984:275). Exposing research subjects to repeated observation facilitates the habituation effect, as does establishing rapport, although it may be difficult to know in advance how much observation is needed to reduce reactivity to an acceptable level (Barnsely 1972:227). Assurances of confidentiality (when possible) that are also reinforced by action can reduce the consequences of observing something that research subjects would regard as socially undesirable. Selecting persons willing and able to be taught to avoid comments and behaviors that provoke reactivity (e.g., the expression of judgments), and following up that training with supervision while in the field can reinforce the appropriate researcher role for a given study.

However, some of these reactivity countermeasures can suppress one kind of reactivity and stimulate others. For example, using an expert to observe the same kind of expert may make it easier for the observer to establish rapport, but it might also make it more difficult for the observer to refrain from offering an opinion or assistance, based on a claim of ignorance or inexperience. Repeatedly reminding research subjects of the project's confidentiality guarantees reminds them that they are the object of an outsider's attentions and will result in a record of their activities. And the best persons and methods for establishing rapport with a research subject may in fact also stimulate researcher involvement in activities that are decidedly beyond the research role (Reiss 1968). Clearly, some compromises must be made in drawing the line between what is and is not acceptable observer behavior in attempting to control reactivity.

RELIABILITY.   One of the distinct advantages of SSO over solo field research is that it facilitates the testing and improvement of the reliability of observations (Reiss 1968, 1971b). Early on, much attention was given to the use of multiple observers and estimating their inter-rater reliability. Where many researchers can independently observe the same phenomenon (by having multiple observers on scene or by using video recordings), the testing of inter-rater reliability is accomplished by measuring the extent of agreement among the pool of observers for the same set of events (Raudenbush and Sampson 1999:14; Homel et al. 1997:63; Wilcox et al. 2006). Sometimes, disparate independent observations of the same event are resolved by a process of discussion and negotiation (Graham et al. 2006b:284). Where multiple independent observations of the same event are not possible, and that is often the case in situations wherein having more than one observer would be too disruptive, observers might be tested by using their detailed narrative descriptions to determine (a) if they are properly classifying phenomena according to the protocol and (b) the extent of agreement among persons who use those narratives to make classifications (Reiss 1971b:22). For example, this has been done for characterizing a wide range of police and citizen behaviors in predicting citizen compliance with police requests (McCluskey 2003:60–74).

Recently, SSO researchers have broadened their reliability concerns to incorporate measurement accuracy and stability (McCall 1984:275). Raudenbush and Sampson (1999) apply psychometrics to the development of "ecometrics" to better understand the error properties of SSO data gathered from observing physical and social disorder in urban neighborhoods. They adapt three psychometric analytic strategies: item response modeling, generalizability theory, and factor analysis to illuminate the error structure of their observational data and to make judgments about the best ways to limit different sources of error in future observational studies. For example, they find that physical disorder can be more reliably measured at lower levels of aggregation than social disorder, due to the much lower frequency of the latter in their observations (Raudenbush and Sampson 1999:30).

VALIDITY.   While texts often note that field studies are less vulnerable to validity problems than surveys because the method places the observer "there" while events are unfolding (Maxfield and Babbie 1998:286), they are of course only valid insofar as they produce data that measure what the researcher intends for them to measure (McCall 1984:276). For the most part, the challenges of assessing the validity of SSO data are those common to other forms of data collection, and we will not elaborate them here. However, we will raise three points that may be useful to those contemplating the use of SSO.

First, SSO in its purest form is not well-suited for observing internal thought processes and motivations. An example is inferring the level of intent to harm someone solely from naturalistic observation of human interaction, such as might take place at school or bars (Boulton 1991; Graham et al. 2006a). Intent is a key concept in theories of aggression and violence. The search for reliable, observable cues that reveal the degree of intent is challenging, not only because the links between cues and intentions are not empirically well validated, but also because of the ambiguity of certain cues: when is a person so intoxicated that his behavior cannot have been guided by a high degree of intent to harm (Graham et al. 2006b:285)?

Observing judgments can also be challenging for SSO. Theories about the impact of procedural justice on citizen compliance and law abidingness have been expressed in terms that readily admit their testing from survey data (e.g., whether a respondent perceived a given judicial action as procedurally just) (Tyler and Huo 2002). While many social scientists have been willing to accept the respondent's answer as a valid reflection of his or her assessment, this has not been readily available to practitioners of SSO. Consequently, they have three options. One is to take whatever behavioral indicators are available and infer thoughts and feelings from them. This may be appropriate for some things (general citizen satisfaction with the police) (see McIver and Parks 1983:31), but rather risky for others (citizen judgments about specific aspects of police action). Another option is to measure procedural justice objectively from what can be observed (for example, whether the officer showed respect, explained what he was doing, referred to evidence) (Mastrofski et al. 1996; McCluskey et al. 1999). The problem is, of course, that these things may not in fact register as procedurally just for the citizen being observed. However, this objectivity does have the clear policy-relevant advantage of allowing the researcher to determine how influential a given police behavior is on a citizen's response, such as compliance. A third option is to observe events and then later debrief those involved to elicit what they were thinking and feeling at the time (Mastrofski and Parks 1990). This mixed approach to gather both objective and subjective data about an event has been used in police research (Alpert et al. 2005; Mastrofski et al. 1998), but its error and validity properties have not been explored.

A second concern with the validity of measures derived from SSO is their generalizability, especially across different cultures. For example, an SSO study that attempted to predict when police would show disrespect toward a suspect used as one predictor whether the police were disrespectful (Reisig et al. 2004). The sample of citizens was diverse in terms of race, age, and wealth, and it is conceivable that conceptions of what is disrespectful could be conditioned by those variables. That police disrespect failed to predict suspect disrespect was consistent with the researchers' theoretical expectations, but the failure to find the effect could have been due to variability in the sample of how disrespect is subjectively defined. Under these circumstances, tests of criterion validity are appropriate, but not conclusive, according to the relevant cultural classifications where differences are expected.

A third validity issue has to do, not with what the observers recorded, but what judgments are made about it. For example, SSO researchers may use experts to generate judgments about the likelihood that an observed event would be treated in a particular way – for example, the probability that an officer's behavior would be regarded in court as a violation of Fourth Amendment standards for search and seizure (Gould and Mastrofski 2004). It is appropriate to think of the constitutionality of a police action in terms of probabilities because there are many courts and many judges, and they can vary in their decision, especially in hard or borderline cases. The question is, did the researchers produce a valid assessment of what the relevant pool of judges would have produced? Unable to submit their observations to such a sample of judges, the researchers performed a sensitivity analysis to see if shifts in the scale of probabilities (more and less lenient judgments about constitutional violations) would alter results.

PRACTICAL CONSIDERATIONS

There are a number of practical issues that arise when fielding an SSO research project. Among these are matters pertaining to the research staff and matters relating to the research subjects.

Organization and Staffing of the Research

SSO typically involves the efforts of a group of researchers, and as with any group effort, organizational issues require attention. SSO researchers are often recruited from the ranks of graduate and undergraduate university students, but not always; they may come from the ranks of the persons being observed or from some other group (Reiss 1968). For example, an SSO study of shoplifters used trained psychologists experienced in observing children in classrooms. They had received additional training from store detectives on how to observe unobtrusively (Buckle and Farrington 1984:67). The complexity of the tasks required (interacting with observed research subjects and gathering/recording data) – even when the observer has experience in the role of the people being observed – will likely call for persons with a certain temperament as well as certain aptitudes and skills, especially for projects that place the observer in a participant role.

Our experience with SSO of patrol officers has shown a need for the following skills and traits to deal with the complexities of police field work and a demanding observation protocol: strong writing skills, ease with social conversation, curiosity about policing, self discipline and strong work ethic, team player, candor and integrity, and facility with word processing software. Absent from this list is expertise in policing and the law, in part because we provide researchers with the basics of what they need to know during training, and when expertise is necessary (such as judging the constitutionality of an action), we draw on a separate pool of experts *ex post facto* to code the data collected by our field staff. It is much harder to find persons who make good field researchers *and* have the requisite subject matter expertise. Where SSO projects require little or no field involvement with research subjects, we anticipate that a different set of skills and priorities would be relevant. On the other hand, we can imagine certain settings (courts) where observers with extensive legal training would be highly desired to note and interpret events. Finding the best mix of skills and traits depends upon the particulars of the job task, and innovative SSO projects may require an iteration or two in the field for the investigator to learn precisely what is most valuable in a field researcher.

Regardless of the recruitment pool, researchers who are inexperienced with SSO may underestimate the amount of time and effort it takes to train their field staff. Naturally, the more complex and elaborate the research instrument, the more training time required, and the more direct involvement or exposure the field researchers will have with the research subjects, the more training required. In our SSO of police, we have expended considerable training time on familiarizing prospective field researchers with the manners and customs of the officers and the communities where they will be observed – long before they logged any training time in the patrol car. This has included using representatives from the police organization to deliver presentations on the department.

The importance of establishing the specific role expectations for researchers cannot be overstated (McCall 1984:273; Reiss 1968, 1971b). Where to draw the lines between permissible and impermissible participation with research subjects is not only important for methodological purposes, but also for legal and ethical ones. Given that many SSO projects place observers in the field for extended time, it is important to train observers in how to maintain a professional, yet congenial relationship with research subjects, even when encouraged or pressured to engage in activities that are inappropriate. Establishing some bright lines around forbidden practices is essential.

As with survey research, quality control of SSO calls for attentive monitoring of the field researchers and their work products. Using supervisors experienced in conducting that form of SSO is a major advantage, not only because they will know more about the challenges, but also they will have greater credibility with the observers they supervise. They should meet frequently with the field researchers to discuss not only their research products, but also their feelings and state of mind. Computer software can be developed to check for logical inconsistencies in coding and to flag potential problems that deserve double checking (Mastrofski et al. 1998:14). If project resources do not allow detailed checking of each item or case, then researchers should consider sampling items or cases to catch potential problems as quickly as possible. Errors can pile up quickly, so it is valuable to give rapid feedback to field researchers.

Management of field observers goes well beyond the need to check for problems with various sources of measurement error that have already been described. There are a number of issues that will likely arise, depending upon the length and social context of the observation period. Supervisors need to be readily available to counsel people who have observed traumatic events. The daily exposure to bleak social conditions and human frailty can have significant effects on the observers' emotions and outlooks. And of course, supervisors need to monitor and manage, to some extent, relationships among the researchers themselves, some of whom will experience conflicts and crises found in any organization.

A host of other practical issues arise in fielding SSO, many of which are reviewed by Reiss (1971b:24–27) and Mastrofski et al. (1998). These include the legal liability of the observers (should their presence or action stimulate a lawsuit), the legal liability of the project's organization, and the availability of civil action to the investigator and the employees for harms that may arise in the course of the research. Of particular concern may be the risk of injury to field researchers and their vulnerability to legal action, including the subpoena of observers and their work products. In the case of protecting the confidentiality of observations, federally-sponsored research may offer some protections, but they are limited, which raises concern about the power of the research organization to compel its employees to maintain certain confidentiality guarantees in the face of legal action (Mastrofski et al. 1998:16). In general, investigators should seek the advice of qualified legal counsel to manage these risks.

Beyond that, investigators are well advised to incorporate the project's key governing policies into the terms of the field observers' contracts. Due diligence requires that this carry over to training and supervision for the SSO project. Much of the pressure for revealing protected information is delivered not through formal legal channels, but informally while researchers are in the field. Learning how to deflect these and when to summon supervisors for assistance should be part of the training. We recommend that investigators incorporate some role-playing sessions involving scenarios where observers are presented with inducements or pressure to violate policies, providing instruction and practice on how to respond to these situations.

Although SSO can be quite labor intensive, its efficiency (amount of desired data acquired per unit of cost), can be quite variable. For example, it is undoubtedly more efficient to gather data on shoplifting by surveying a sample of shoppers or gathering data from store records about shoppers and shoplifters. Indeed, one such study committed approximately 755 h of field observer time (two observers per sampled shopper) to yield only nine instances of shoplifting (Buckle and Farrington 1984). SSO studies of patrol work tend to yield on average slightly less than one police–citizen encounter per hour of field work (Parks et al. 1998:2–23). A survey researcher doing follow-up calls with citizens who have had recent contact with the police could be more efficient, but even that can be time consuming, given the difficulty of catching such persons at home and persuading them to participate. On the other hand, SSO studies that deal with how certain kinds of subjects (criminal justice officials or offenders) spend their time can be fairly efficient, since each moment of observation time yields relevant data. Of course, if electronic recordings of the phenomenon of interest are already available (for example, CCTV recordings of specific locations), costs may be limited primarily to interpreting and coding those recordings, making this method more efficient than alternatives to gathering data. Ultimately, efficiency is usually only one consideration for researchers, and so the real issue is whether there are sufficient gains in access to relevant data, and improvements in validity and reliability of those data to justify the SSO investment.

Preparing Organizations and Research Subjects for SSO

Many research subjects have some degree of familiarity with what is involved in survey research, interviews, and other forms of data gathering that involve subject interaction with researchers. But most know nothing about SSO, what it requires of the research subject, or what it requires of the researcher. Preparation of the research subjects is important, not only so that the requirements for informed human subjects research are satisfied, but so that the project is conducted with minimum error and hassle. If the research subjects work within a formal organization, advance time spent explaining the project and its methods at all levels of the organization, but especially the immediate supervisors of the persons to be observed, is time well spent. Conducting a few "demonstration" observation sessions will also help to reduce anxieties or uncover unanticipated problems that can be resolved before actual data collection is launched. Over the course of the study, frequent contact with persons at various levels within the organization is advisable, to detect and deal with problems quickly.

Among the essential elements of a good relationship with the research subjects is making clear to them how human subjects research issues will be handled. Not infrequently, research subjects are skeptical about the willingness of field researchers to maintain confidentiality guarantees, and some may go so far as to test them in subtle, as well as not-so-subtle ways. This may arise in the course of casual conversation about something that researchers may have observed previously with other research subjects who are known to both the researcher and the current research subject. Sensitizing both the researchers and the research subjects to the need to avoid discussion of these events is particularly important. On the not-so-subtle side, supervisors of research subjects (e.g., police sergeants) may exert tremendous pressure on field observers to reveal information that may be inculpatory or exculpatory for an observed subordinate. Invoking project policy and, if necessary, summoning a research supervisor may be the most effective way of avoiding unnecessary revelations of protected information.

SSO CONTRIBUTIONS TO CRIMINOLOGY AND FUTURE OPPORTUNITIES

SSO has been heavily concentrated on gathering data on two aspects of criminology: the behavior of police patrol officers and disorder in the public parts of urban neighborhoods. We offer a comprehensive review of neither body of literature, but summarize key contributions that SSO has made in advancing knowledge in each area. We then suggest a few areas that seem especially promising for future SSO applications.

SSO data have dominated the empirical research that describes and accounts for variation in the discretionary choices of officers: making stops and arrests, issuing citations, using force, assisting citizens, and displaying procedural justice (Skogan and Frydl 2004:ch. 4). One of SSO's special contributions has been the scope of explanatory elements made available for the researchers' models. These include many details of not only the officer's behavior, but also the context in which it occurs (nature of the participants, their behavior, the location, and the neighborhood). SSO has also been instrumental in detailing the nature of the *process* of police–citizen interaction, opening our eyes to the interactive quality of temporally ordered micro-transactions or stages that may occur in even a relatively short police–citizen face-to-face encounter (Bayley 1986; Sykes and Brent 1983; Terrill 2003). And SSO has also allowed researchers to observe elements of organizational control and community influence on the work of police officers. For example, we learn more about the influence of police supervisors on subordinates' practices (Engel 2000), and we learn the dynamics of police–community interaction and their consequences when police and neighborhood residents deal with each other at community problem-solving meetings (Skogan 2006).

A second area where SSO research has concentrated is the examination of neighborhood physical and social disorder. Ralph Taylor and colleagues pioneered this focus in the 1980s in Baltimore (Taylor 2001; Taylor et al. 1985), and it has been used to test the impact of police interventions in hotspots, showing that police interventions in these "micro-places" not only reduce crime and disorder, they also diffuse those benefits to nearby areas (Sherman and Weisburd 1995; Weisburd et al. 2006). The largest project in this area has focused on Chicago neighborhoods and has produced a number of insights relevant to the testing and development of theories of the role of neighborhood disorder in causing crime in urban neighborhoods (Raudenbush and Sampson 1999). Using SSO-based measures of "objective" disorder described earlier in this chapter, researchers have examined the sources and consequences of public disorder. The research has demonstrated the importance of "collective efficacy" in predicting lower crime rates and observed disorder, controlling for structural characteristics of the neighborhood (Sampson and Raudenbush 1999). Collective efficacy also predicted lower levels of crime, controlling for observed disorder and the reciprocal effects of violence. The researchers found that the relationship between public disorder and crime is spurious, with the exception of robbery, which is contrary to the expectations of the well-known "broken windows" theory of neighborhood decline.

In general, SSO has afforded precision that has in many cases shown the phenomena of interest to be more complex than other forms of data collection had indicated. For example, we have already noted that SSO researchers have found rich variation among police officers in their patterns of discretionary choice, and even noted the instability of those patterns for individual officers over time. And the independence of SSO observers from the phenomenon of interest has provided a means to understand the contributing factors to the social construction of phenomena, such as the contributions of a neighborhood's racial profile in assessing its level of disorder (Sampson and Raudenbush 2004).

Beyond the above areas of recent high visibility in criminology, there are many opportunities to expand the use of SSO to improve knowledge. Largely untapped is the observation of crime and disorder, especially at the micro-level, where observers have the opportunity to make detailed observations of offenders in the act. SSO studies of shoplifting and aggressive or disorderly behavior in bars and clubs show that this is feasible where observers can easily blend into the environment. Where that is not possible, access to unobtrusive surveillance technologies appears to offer opportunities for detailed observation that reduce reactivity concerns. Indeed, it seems highly likely that in the future, criminologists will take advantage of the ubiquity of electronic surveillance in society generally to capture events that would otherwise be costly to observe. For example, the growing sophistication of surveillance and identification technology, may make it possible to use facial identification software to gather data for a network analysis of persons who frequent hotspots. This includes not only the growing use of video recording devices by government and private sector organizations, but the now ready availability of miniaturized recording devices to the general public (through cell phone recording devices).

In searching for efficient ways to use SSO, criminologists should bear in mind the growing body of evidence about the predictability of crime and disorder occurring in small geographic spaces ("hotspots") (Weisburd 2008). Because much "street" crime is so highly concentrated in a relatively small portion of addresses or face blocks, the location of observers or observational devices can very efficiently generate lots of information on what occurs, especially in public areas. In addition, given heightened levels of obtrusive surveillance (security procedures in public places), SSO should prove an excellent way of better understanding how security and surveillance operate, why certain methods are effective, and the collateral impacts of various methods of monitoring and control designed to increase public safety.

Another venue for SSO to be used fruitfully is in experimental studies. We have already identified some field experiments that used SSO to validate the application of treatment protocols and to measure outcomes. But beyond that, SSO can be used to measure key aspects of the process that presumably operate to link treatments to outcomes. For example, if the physical redesign of bars and serving practices of bartenders is intended to reduce violence in those establishments, do patrons in fact alter their patterns of behavior in the ways that are expected to produce less violence (Graham et al. 2004)?

CONCLUSION

Four decades after Albert Reiss showed criminologists the utility of systematic social observation, it remains a method used infrequently in the discipline. This is undoubtedly due in no small part to two things. First, criminologists are rarely exposed to training and opportunities to do SSO during their course of study. Hence, they remain ignorant of its applications or unfamiliar with how to do it. This could be remedied by increasing researchers' exposure to the method in coursework and the early, formative years of their work. But doing this requires a cadre of researchers sufficiently skilled and experienced to teach it. One way to prime the pump would be holding methods workshops, sponsored by organizations such as ICPSR. Second, those who know a little about it may often expect that it requires more time and resources than they have available. This may indeed be the case, but we suspect that many projects could be taken on a smaller scale with a narrower scope of questions than the better-known, large SSO projects. Some researchers may decline to use SSO because of reactivity concerns, but the available evidence suggests that these problems are often manageable and may be no more severe in any event than found with other data gathering methods.

Increased use of SSO will undoubtedly attract and stimulate greater scrutiny of its limitations, as well as its advantages. Certainly, the error properties of most SSO data sets have been underexplored, and more attention is needed here. We expect that expanding the use of SSO and more comprehensively assessing its strengths and limits can be fruitfully combined into a more comprehensive assessment of other methods of gathering data on crime and justice phenomena.

SSO deserves the consideration of researchers because of its many advantages. For the study of crime and justice phenomena, it offers enhanced prospects of validity, and in many situations it provides for increased confidence in reliability, because of the researcher's direct access to the phenomenon of interest and greater control and transparency of data encoding. Further, it affords greater precision in capturing details of the phenomenon and its context, such as the sequencing of what happens before, during, and after those events. In many cases, it may be the least problematic method for acquiring information. Criminology, which has strong roots in the traditions and methodologies of sociological research, remains heavily reliant on the use of sample surveys and official records (McCall 1984:277; Reiss 1971b). But, as the field matures and diversifies intellectually, more of its researchers may, with justification, be inclined to make systematic social observation the method of first, not last resort.

REFERENCES

Alpert GP, Macdonald JM, Dunham RG (2005) Police suspicion and discretionary decision making during citizen stops. Criminology 43(2):407–434

Arrington RE (1943) Time sampling in studies of social behavior: a critical review of techniques and results with research suggestions. Psychol Bull 40(2):81–124

Barker RG, Wright HF (1955) The Midwest and its children. Row, Peterson, Evanston, IL

Barnsley JH (1972) The social reality of ethics: the comparative analysis of moral codes. Routledge and Kegan Paul, Boston

Bayley DH (1986) The tactical choices of police patrol officers. J Crim Justice 14:329–348

Bayley DH, Garofalo J (1989) Management of violence by police patrol officers. Criminology 27:1–25

Black D (1980) The manner and customs of the police. Academic, San Diego, CA

Bouffard JA, Taxman FS, Silverman R (2003) Improving process evaluations of correctional programs by using a comprehensive evaluation methodology. Eval Program Plann 26:149–161

Boulton MJ (1991) A comparison of structural and contextual features of middle school children's playfull and aggressive fighting. Ethol Sociobiol 12:119–145

Boyd RD, Devault MV (1966) The observation and recording of behavior. Rev Educ Res 36(5):529–551

Brackett L, Reid DH, Green CW (2007) Effects of reactivity to observations on staff performance. J Appl Behav Anal 40:191–195

Buckle A, Farrington DP (1984) An observational study of shoplifting. Br J Criminol 24(1):63–73

Buckle A, Farrington DP (1994) Measuring shoplifting by systematic observation: a replication study. Psychol Crime Law 1(2):133–141

Buckman WH, Lamberth J (2001) Challenging racial profiles: attacking Jim Crow on the interstate. Rutgers Race Law Rev 3:83–115

Caughy MO, O'Campo PJ, Patterson J (2001) A brief observational measure for urban neighborhoods. Health Place 7:225–236

Dabney DA, Hollinger RC, Dugan L (2004) Who actually steals? A study of covertly observed shoplifters. Justice Q 21(4):693–728

Ellerbeck EF, Ahluwalia JS, Jolicoeur DG, Gladden J, Mosier MC (2001) Direct observation of smoking cessation activities in primary care practice. J Fam Pract 50(8). http://www.jfponline.com/toc.asp?FID=278&issue=August%202001&folder_description=August%202001%20(Vol.%2050,%20No.%208) Accessed January 31, 2009

Engel RS (2000) The effects of supervisory styles on patrol officer behavior. Police Q 3(3):262–293

Engel RS, Calnon J (2004) Examining the influence of drivers' characteristics during traffic stops with police: results from a national survey. Justice Q 21(1):49–90

Frank J, Brandl SG, Watkins RC (1997) The content of community policing: a comparison of the daily activities of community and "beat" officers. Policing Int J Police Strateg Manage 20:716–728

Fyfe JJ (2002) Too many missing cases: holes in our knowledge about police use of force. Report prepared for the National Research Council, Committee to Review Research on Police Policy and Practices Data Collection Workshop, Washington, DC

Gould JB, Mastrofski SD (2004) Suspect searches: assessing police behavior under the constitution. Criminol Public Policy 3:316–362

Graham K, West P, Wells S (2000) Evaluating theories of alcohol-related aggression using observations of young adults in bars. Addiction 95:847–863

Graham K, Osgood D, Zibrowski E, Purcell J, Gliksman L, Leonard K, Pernanen K, Saltz R, Toomey T (2004) The effect of the Safer Bars programme on physical aggression in bars: results of a randomized controlled trial. Drug Alcohol Rev 23:31–41

Graham K, Bernards S, Osgood D, Homel R, Purcell J (2005) Guardians and handlers: the role of bar staff in preventing and managing aggression. Addiction 100:755–766

Graham K, Bernards S, Osgood D, Wells S (2006a) Bad nights or bad bars? Multi-level analysis of environmental predictors of aggression in late-night large-capacity bars and clubs. Addiction 101:1569–1580

Graham K, Tremblay PF, Wells S, Pernanen K, Purcell J, Jelley J (2006b) Harm, intent, and the nature of aggressive behavior: measuring naturally occurring aggression in barroom settings. Assessment 13(3):280–296

Gravlee CC, Zenk SN, Woods S, Rowe Z, Schulz AJ (2006) Handheld computers for direct observation of the social and physical environment. Field Methods 18:382–397

Hartmann DP, Wood DD (1982) Observational methods. In: Bellack AS, Hersen M, Kazdin AE (eds) International handbook of behavior modification and therapy. Plenum, New York, pp 109–138

Homel R, Clark J (1994) The prediction and prevention of violence in pubs and clubs. In: Clarke RV (ed) Crime prevention studies, vol 3. Criminal Justice Press, Monsey, NY, pp 1–46

Homel R, Hauritz M, Wortley R, McIlwain G (1997) Preventing alcohol-related crime through community action: The Surfers Paradise Safety Action Project. In: Homel R (ed) Policing for prevention: reducing crime, public intoxication and injury. Criminal Justice Press, Monsey, NY, pp 35–90

Kazdin AE (1979) Unobtrusive measures in behavioral assessment. J Appl Behav Anal 12:713–724

Kelling GL (2001) "Broken windows" vs. "A new look." Law Enforcement News, March 15, 9

Knutsson J (1997) Restoring public order in a city park. In: Homel R (ed) Policing for prevention: reducing crime, public intoxication and injury. Criminal Justice Press, Monsey, NY, pp 133–151

Langan PA, Greenfeld LA, Smith SK, Dunrose MR, Levin DJ (2001) Contacts between police and the public, findings from the 1999 national survey. Department of Justice, Office of Justice Programs, Bureau of Justice Statistics, Washington, DC

Levine R (1997) A geography of time. Basic Books, New York

Luthans F, Lockwood D (1984) Toward an observation system for measuring leader behavior in natural settings. In: Hunt J, Hosking D, Schriesheim C, Steward R (eds) Leaders and managers: international perspective of managerial behavior and leadership. Pergamon, New York, pp 117–141

Macintyre S, Homel R (1997) Danger on the dance floor: a study of interior design, crowding and aggression in nightclubs. In: Homel R (ed) Policing for prevention: reducing crime, public intoxication and injury. Criminal Justice Press, Monsey, NY, pp 91–113

Mastrofski SD (2004) Controlling street-level police discretion. Ann Am Acad Pol Soc Sci 593:100–118

Mastrofski SD, Parks RB (1990) Improving observational studies of police. Criminology 28(3):475–496

Mastrofski SD, Snipes JB, Supina A (1996) Compliance on demand: the public's response to specific police requests. J Res Crime Delinq 33:269–305

Mastrofski SD, Parks RB, Reiss AJ Jr, Worden RE, DeJong C, Snipes JB, Terrill W (1998) Systematic observation of public police: applying field research methods to policy issues. NCJ 172859. National Institute of Justice, Washington, DC

Mastrofski SD, Snipes JB, Parks RB, Maxwell CD (2000) The helping hand of the law: police control of citizens on request. Criminology 38:307–342

Mastrofski SD, Reisig M, McCluskey JD (2002) Police disrespect toward the public: an encounter-based analysis. Criminology 40:519–552

Maxfield MG, Babbie E (1998) Research methods for criminal justice and criminology, 2nd edn. West, Belmont, CA

McCall GJ (1984) Systematic field observation. Annu Rev Sociol 10:263–282

McCluskey JD (2003) Police requests for compliance: coercive and procedurally just tactics. LFB Scholarly Publishing LLC, New York

McCluskey JD, Mastrofski SD, Parks RB (1999) To acquiesce or rebel: predicting citizen compliance with police requests. Police Q 2(4):389–416

McIver JP, Parks RB (1983) Evaluating police performance: identification of effective and ineffective police actions. In: Bennett RR (ed) Police at work: policy issues and analysis. Sage, Beverly Hills, pp 21–44

Meehan AJ, Ponder MC (2002) Race and place: the ecology of racial profiling African American motorists. Justice Q 19(3):399–430

Mileski M (1971) Courtroom encounters: an observational study of a lower criminal court. Law Soc Rev 5:473–538

Mintzberg H (1972) The nature of managerial work. Harper Collins, New York

O'Brien RO (2000) Crime facts: victim and offender data. In: Sheley JF (ed) Criminology. Wadsworth, Belmont, CA, pp 59–83

Parks RB (1984) Comparing citizen and observer perceptions of police-citizen encounters In: Whitaker GP (ed) Understanding police agency performance. U.S. Government Printing office, Washington, DC, pp 121–135

Parks RB, Mastrofski SD, Reiss AJ, Worden RE, Terrill WC, DeJong C, Stroshine M, Shepherd R (1998) St. Petersburg project on policing neighborhoods: a study of the police and the community. Indiana University, Bloomington, IN

Percy S (1980) Response time and citizen evaluation of police. J Police Sci Adm 8(1):75–86

Perkins DD, Wandersman A, Rich RC, Taylor RB (1993) The physical environment of street crime: defensible space, territoriality and incivilities. *J Environ Psychol* 13:29–49

Pugh SD (2001) Service with a smile: emotional contagion in the service encounter. Acad Manage J 44(5):1018–1027

Rafaeli A, Sutton RI (1989) The expression of emotion in organizational life. In: Cummings LL, Staw BM (eds) Research in organizational behavior. JAI Press, Greenwich, CT, pp 1–42

Rafaeli A, Sutton RI (1990) Busy stores and demanding customers: how do they affect the display of positive emotion? Acad Manage J 33:623–637

Raudenbush SW, Sampson RJ (1999) Toward a science of assessing ecological settings, with applications to the systematic social observation of neighborhoods. Sociol Methodol 29:1–41

Reisig M, McCluskey JD, Mastrofski SD, Terrill W (2004) Suspect disrespect toward the police. Justice Q 21: 241–268

Reiss AJ Jr (1968) Stuff and nonsense about social surveys and observation. In: Becker HS, Geer B, Riesman D, Weiss RS (eds) Institutions and the person: papers presented to C. Everett Hughes. Aldine Publishing Company, Chicago, pp 351–367

Reiss AJ Jr (1971a) The police and the public. Yale University Press, New Haven, CT

Reiss AJ Jr (1971b) Systematic observation of natural social phenomena. In: Costner HL (ed) Sociological methodology. Jossey-Bass, Inc, San Francisco, pp 3–33

Roethlisberger FJ, Dickson WJ (1939) Management and the worker. Harvard University Press, Cambridge, MA

Rosenshine B, Furst NF (1973) The use of direct observation to study teaching. In: Gage NL (ed) Handbook of research on teaching, 2nd edn. Rand-McNally, Chicago, pp 122–183

Sampson RJ, Raudenbush SW (1999) Systematic social observation of public spaces: a new look at disorder in urban neighborhoods. Am J Sociol 3:603–651

Sampson RJ, Raudenbush SW (2004) Seeing disorder: neighborhood stigma and the social construction of "broken windows." Soc Psychol Q 67(4):319–342

Schafer J, Mastrofski S (2005) Police leniency in traffic enforcement encounters: exploratory findings from observations and interviews. J Crim Justice 33:225–238

Scott EJ (1981) Calls for service – Citizen demand and initial police response. NCJ 078362. Workshop in Political Theory and Policy Analysis, Bloomington, IN

Sherman LW, Weisburd D (1995) General deterrence effects of police patrol in crime "hot spots": a randomized, controlled evaluation. Justice Q 12(4):625–648

Shrum W, Duque R, Brown T (2005) Digital video as research practice: methodology for the millennium. J Res Pract 1(1):1–19. http://jrp.icaap.org/index.php/jrp/article/view/6/11

Skogan WG (2006) Police and community in Chicago: a tale of three cities. Oxford University Press, New York

Skogan W, Frydl K (eds) (2004) Fairness and effectiveness in policing: the evidence. The National Academies Press, Washington, DC

Skolnick JH (1966) Justice without trial: law enforcement in democratic society. Wiley, New York

Smith DA (1984) The organizational context of legal control. Criminology 22(1):19–38

Smith DA (1986) The neighborhood context of police behavior. In: Reiss A, Tonry M (eds) Crime and justice: a review of research. University of Chicago Press, Chicago, pp 314–332

Smith RL, Mc Phail C, Pickens RG (1975) Reactivity to systematic observation with film: a field experiment. Sociometry 38:536–550

Smith WR, Tomaskovic-Devey D, Zingraff MT, Mason HM, Warren PY, Wright CP (2004) The North Carolina highway traffic study: appendix A. National Institute of Justice, Office of Justice Programs, U.S. Department of Justice, Washington, DC. http://www.ncjrs.gov/app/Publications/Abstract.aspx?ID=204021 Accessed January 31, 2009

Snipes J, Mastrofski SD (1990) An empirical test of Muir's typology of police officers. Am J Crim Justice 14(4): 268–296

Spano R (2005) Potential sources of observer bias in police observational data. Soc Sci Res 34:591–617

Spano R (2007) How does reactivity affect police behavior? Describing and quantifying the impact of reactivity as behavioral change in a large-scale observational study of police. J Crim Justice 35:453–465

Stange KC, Zyzanski SJ, Smith TF, Kelly R, Langa D, Flock SA, Jaen CR (1998) How valid are medical records and patient questionnaires for physician profiling and health services research?: a comparison with direct observation of patient visits. Med Care 36(6):851–867

Sykes RE (1977) Techniques of data collection and reduction in systematic field observation. Behav Res Methods Instrum 9:404–17

Sykes RE (1978) Toward a theory of observer effect in systematic field observation. Hum Organ 37:148–56

Sykes RE, Brent EE (1983) Policing: a social behaviorist perspective. Rutgers University Press, New Brunswick, NJ

Sykes RE, Whitney F (1969) Systematic observation utilizing the Minnesota interaction data coding and reduction system. Behav Sci 14:167–169

Taylor RB (1997) Social order and disorder of street blocks and neighbor-hoods: ecology, microecology, and the systemic model of social disorganization. J Res Crime Delinq 34:113–155

Taylor RB (2001) Crime, grime, fear, and decline. Westview Press, New York

Taylor RB, Gottfredson SD, Brower S (1984) Block crime and fear: defensible space, local social ties, and territorial functioning. J Res Crime Delinq 21:303–331

Taylor RB, Shumaker S, Gottfredson SD (1985) Neighborhood-level links between physical features and local sentiments: deterioration of fear of crime and confidence. J Archit Plann Res 21:261–265

Terrill W (2001) Police coercion: application of the force continuum. LFB Scholarly Publishing, LLC, New York

Terrill W (2003) Police use of force and suspect resistance: the micro process of the police-suspect encounter. Police Q 6(1):51–83

Terrill W, Mastrofski SD (2002) Reassessing situational and officer based determinants of police coercion. Justice Q 19:215–248

Terrill W, Paoline EA III, Manning PK (2003) Police culture and coercion. Criminology 41(4):1003–1034

Thomas DS, Loomis AM, Arrington RE (1933) Observational studies of social behavior. Institute of Human Relations, Yale University, New Haven

Tyler TR, Huo YJ (2002) Trust in the law: encouraging public cooperation with the police and courts. Russell Sage, New York

Uchida CD, Maguire ER, Solomon SE, Gantley M (2004) Safe kids, safe schools: evaluating the use of iris recognition technology in New Egypt, NJ. 21st Century Solutions, Inc, Silver Spring, MD

Van Maanen J (1974) Working the street: a developmental view of police behavior. In: Jacob H (ed) The potential for reform in criminal justice. Sage, Thousand Oaks, CA, pp 83–130

Webb EJ, Campbell DT, Schwartz RD, Sechrest L, Grove JB (1981) Nonreactive measures in the social sciences. Houghton Mifflin, Boston

Weick KE (1968) Systematic observational methods. In: Lindsey G, Aronson E (eds) The handbook of social psychology, 2nd edn, vol 2. Addison-Wesley, Reading, MA, pp 357–451

Weisburd D (2008) Place-based policing. Ideas in Policing. Police Foundation, Washington, DC

Weisburd D, Wyckoff LA, Ready J, Eck JE, Hinkle JC, Gajewski F (2006) Does crime just move around the corner? A controlled study of spatial displacement and diffusion of crime control benefits. Criminology 44(3):549–592

Whitaker GP, Mastrofski SD, Ostrom E, Parks RB, Percy SL (1982) Basic issues in police performance. National Institute of Justice, Washington, DC

Whitehead TN (1935) Social relationships in the factory: a study of an industrial group. Hum Factor 9:381–394

Wilcox P, Augustine MC, Clayton RR (2006) Physical environment and crime and misconduct in Kentucky schools. J Prim Prev 27(3):293–313

Wilson D, Mastrofski S (2004) Final report: evaluation of the Biometric Inmate Tracking System at the Consolidated Navy Brig, Charleston, South Carolina. Report to the Space and Naval Warfare Systems Center. Center for Justice Leadership and Management, Manassas, VA

Worden RE (1996) The causes of police brutality: theory and evidence on police use of force. In: Geller WA, Toch H (eds) Police violence: understanding and controlling police use of force. Yale University Press, New Haven, pp 23–51

Part II
New Directions in Assessing Design, Measurement and Data Quality

## CHAPTER 13

Identifying and Addressing Response Errors in Self-Report Surveys

James P. Lynch and Lynn A. Addington

INTRODUCTION

Much of the data used by criminologists is generated by self-report surveys of victims and offenders.[1] Although both sources share a common reliance on responses to questions, little overlap exists between the two traditions. They have largely talked past each other, especially with regard to sharing methodological studies and findings. At first glance, this miscommunication appears a bit strange since the basic cognitive task required for both sets of respondents is the same: report on criminal activity in which they have been involved. The division between the two traditions makes greater sense upon examination of their initial motivating goals and auspices.

Self-report offending surveys originated from a desire to identify predictors of offending in order to develop and test theories to explain the differences in criminal behavior across individuals. To achieve these goals, criminologists designed survey instruments that focused on individuals and the relative volume of crime across offenders. Researchers concentrated their methodological efforts on ways to maximize information collected about criminal offenders and their social context (see Thornberry and Krohn 2000; and Junger-Tas and Marshall 1999 for discussions of these issues). In contrast, the principal purpose of victimization surveys was to estimate the level and change in the level of crime across periods of time, which included generating annual crime rates. This goal required a focus on the criminal victimization incident rather than on an individual person. As a result, researchers emphasized methodological issues that maximized the accuracy of recalling and reporting crime events.

The distinct motivations for collecting data and the primary uses of the data have contributed to different interests in locating crime events in space and time. For example,

---

[1] We use the terms "self-report offending surveys" and "offender surveys" as well as "self-report victimization surveys" and "victimization surveys" to refer to data collection efforts that rely on respondents reporting their own experiences with crime (as either an offender or victim).

A.R. Piquero and D. Weisburd (eds.), *Handbook of Quantitative Criminology*,
DOI 10.1007/978-0-387-77650-7_13, © Springer Science + Business Media, LLC 2010,
First softcover printing 2011

researchers use self-report offending surveys to identify offenders, distinguish high and low volume offenders, and understand why some people become offenders and others do not. Such concerns place less emphasis on the precise counting of crime events, whereas more on obtaining individual and contextual information to explain offending patterns. Self-report victimization surveys, on the other hand, are used to estimate crime rates. This task requires exhaustive reporting of target events and precise dating of their occurrence to ensure accurate rates. Victimization surveys also are frequently used to check crime data reported by police. This additional role requires measuring the precise location of events by jurisdiction as well as enough detail about events to reproduce common types of crime classifications used by the police.

These diverse interests and tasks across traditions produce differences in the design and emphasis among the major self-report offending and victimization surveys. Until recently these parallel worlds were able to operate separate and distinct from one another with little reason to commingle. Currently, changes in how these data are being used – especially with the self-report offending surveys – necessitate a re-examination of this division. Self-report offending data are now being used to study offending careers and career criminals using trajectory models.[2] The sophisticated statistical models used in this work assume a precision of the data and how the criminal event is reported. These new demands on self-report offending surveys are beginning to resemble the long-standing requirements of victimization surveys. For example, the use of trajectories and growth curves to distinguish the types of criminal careers now makes exhaustive reporting and the temporal placement of offenses more important (Thornberry 1989; Lauritsen 1999). In addition, the desire to separate serious from less serious crime events requires that the respondent provide more detail on the nature of offending events so that researchers can make such distinctions (Thornberry and Krohn 2000). With this increasing overlap in the need for both types of surveys to accurately locate events in time and space, the methodological work conducted in the context of victimization surveys becomes a relevant resource for self-report offending surveys. Research conducted in the victimization context can identify areas where offending surveys might not be providing enough precision and suggest ways to improve data accuracy.

In this chapter, we seek to highlight the methodological work conducted in the context of victimization surveys to suggest how this research can benefit self-report offending surveys. In this way, we can identify major response errors in both traditions. Before beginning this discussion, three caveats are important to mention.

First, our discussion is limited to response errors, that is, errors having to do with the performance of the cognitive task required of respondents and the recording of their responses. Errors resulting from sampling or nonresponse are not addressed. Our focus is restricted to response error because the cognitive task required in surveys of victimization and offending is similar. Both traditions require respondents to search their memory for crimes in which they were involved, to accurately locate these events in time, and to recount details of the event so that they can be classified. Other aspects of victim and offender surveys may vary more.

Second, our discussion reflects a reliance on a few main victimization and self-report offending surveys. One reason is practical as the number of self-report surveys of offending

---

[2] In particular, the use of sophisticated statistical tools such as latent growth curve analysis or semi-parametric group-based modeling (SPGM) of trajectories has increased dramatically in the past decade. Piquero (2008), identified over 80 studies that have employed these methods to analyze criminal activity over the life course, and many of these studies use data from self-report surveys of offending.

and victimization has exploded since the 1960s (Thornberry and Krohn 2000; Junger-Tas and Marshall 1999; Lynch 2006). Another reason is that each tradition has a handful of prominent surveys that serve as the benchmark for designing other surveys. These exemplars tend to be large-scale surveys where a great deal of time and money has been invested on design issues. As a result, the data are viewed as being of very high quality and are widely used among criminologists. For victimization surveys, our discussion relies most heavily upon the National Crime Victimization Survey (NCVS) and its predecessor the National Crime Survey (NCS) and to a lesser extent on the British Crime Survey (BCS).[3] In terms of surveys of offending, three leading surveys shape our paradigms. These include the National Youth Survey (NYS), the Cambridge Youth Study (CYS), and the Program of Research on the Causes and Correlates of Delinquency (PRCCD).

Finally, by taking this approach, we are not implying that no methodological work has been done in the self-report offending area or that victimization surveys cannot benefit from this literature. Rather we believe that communication across the two traditions is long overdue, and this chapter is a first attempt at cross-fertilization. We begin this dialog with what victimization surveys have to say to self-report offending surveys because we are more familiar with the victim survey tradition. We welcome a corresponding article that addresses the methodological work from the self-report offending tradition that can improve victimization surveys. Topics such as panel bias, use of calendrical devices, strategic response, and development of age-appropriate interviews have all received much more attention in surveys of offending than in those of victimization (Lauritsen 1998, 1999; Horney and Marshall 1992; Mennard and Elliot 1990; Thornberry 1989).

The remainder of this chapter is organized as follows. First, we identify the main sources of response errors studied in victimization surveys that are pertinent to surveys of offending. Each of these response errors is explored in turn. For each type of error, we discuss what is known about the error from the self-report victimization survey literature, we describe how surveys of offending have approached this issue, and we examine how research from self-report victimization surveys can benefit self-report offending surveys. We conclude by using the juxtaposition of the two survey traditions to suggest how to improve our understanding of response error in self-report surveys. We also recommend interim ways to address response errors based on currently available information.

SOURCES OF RESPONSE ERRORS IN VICTIMIZATION SURVEYS

The original development and subsequent redesign of the National Crime Survey (NCS) relied upon extensive methodological work concerning response and other types of survey error. In developing the NCS, two factors motivated the emphasis on and investment in methodological work. The primary reason was the federal government's reliance on victimization rates as a social indicator similar to the unemployment rate and its use of the Census Bureau to administer the survey (Biderman and Reiss 1967). As a result, survey statisticians at the Census Bureau, rather than criminologists or other social scientists, controlled the development of these surveys. As with other Census surveys, the Bureau devoted a significant amount

---

[3] Two smaller victimization surveys are of note with regard to their work on improving our understanding of recall and screening with regard to sexual assault and rape. These two surveys are the National Violence Against Women Survey (Tjaden and Thoennes 1998) and the Campus Survey of Sexual Violence (Fisher and Cullen 2000).

of attention to issues of sampling and measurement errors. Addressing these sources of error figured prominently in the NCS's design. A second reason for the emphasis on methodological work was more political. Leaders at the Census Bureau and the Justice Department had a keen interest in ensuring that the design of the NCS was defensible, since groups such as the powerful police lobbies viewed victimization surveys with suspicion.

Even after the NCS was developed, methodological work continued (Lehnen and Skogan 1981). This work combined with the National Academy of Sciences' influential publication *Surveying Crime* (Penick and Owens 1976) prompted the NCS Redesign. The Redesign constituted a multi-year, multi-million dollar effort to identify the error structure of the NCS and modify the survey's design to reduce errors (Biderman et al. 1986). The resulting changes were implemented in the National Crime Victimization Survey (NCVS). The initial development work and redesign coupled with a continuous stream of research from the Census Bureau as well as more modest efforts from the academic community generated a rich base of methodological work (Cantor and Lynch 2000). A comparable resource is not available with regard to self-report offending surveys, especially with regard to response errors. In addition to the different organizing principles mentioned earlier, the resources available to the self-report offending tradition have been more meager. In particular, the self-report offending tradition has lacked large and continuous government-sponsored national surveys.[4]

This extensive methodological research in the victimization context identified a number of response errors as well as determined the effect these errors have on estimates and the need to ameliorate the errors or adjust the results (if the errors cannot be eliminated). Three major sources of response error contribute to inaccuracies in victimization surveys: recall bias, high volume incidents, and temporal placement of events. Principal among these response errors is *recall bias* wherein respondents fail to report their involvement in a crime because either they did not understand the cognitive task or they forgot that the event occurred. Asking about and recording the number of *high volume incidents* involving the same victim or offender has also proved to be problematic in victim surveys because of the detail collected for each incident and the potential for overburdening the respondent. Problems with *temporal placement of events* constitute another well-documented issue in victimization surveys. In this case, respondents report their involvement in a crime but inaccurately date the incident, usually moving it closer to the interview than it actually was.[5] Each type of error is discussed more fully in the following section.

Recall Bias

Recalling and reporting criminal events are deceptively difficult tasks to perform. The victim survey tradition has devoted a great deal of time and attention to facilitating this task for

---

[4] In the United States, no federally-sponsored survey of offending that is comparable to the NCVS exists. The United Kingdom takes a different approach. There, the Home Office sponsors an *Offending, Crime and Justice Survey*, which was first fielded in 2003 (Budd et al. 2005).

[5] Martin et al. (1986) also identified strategic response as a problem. Here, respondents recall the event but refuse to report it because they are ashamed, embarrassed, or suspicious. This source of error is not included in our discussion here because the victim survey tradition has very little to contribute beyond that which the offender survey tradition has done already. Both types of surveys employ Computer-Assisted Self Interviewing (CASI) to reduce strategic response (Thornberry and Krohn 2000; Cantor and Lynch 2000).

respondents. Two techniques to improve the recall of particular interests are screening strategies and cues to prompt the recall of crime events and reference period length to limit memory decay and facilitate recall (Biderman et al. 1967; Reiss 1967; Dodge 1970; Turner 1972; Biderman et al. 1986; Koss 1996). Studying the effect of implementing these techniques provides estimates of the magnitude and distribution of recall bias in victimization surveys.

SCREENING STRATEGIES AND CUING FOR CRIME EVENTS. Screening questions in victimization surveys are designed to cue respondents to report whether they have experienced a particular type of victimization or not. When the NCS was designed, some debate surrounded whether screening for eligible events should be conducted in one or two steps (Biderman et al. 1967; Cantor and Lynch 2000). One-step screening identifies and classifies eligible crime events based on the response to one screening question. For example, a "yes" to the screening question would both indicate that a respondent was a victim and count the respondent as the victim of a particular crime, such as robbery if the question were designed to elicit mention of a robbery. Two-step screening, on the other hand, separates identification of an eligible event from classification of the event. The screening interview is devoted solely to prompting recall of a potential victimization event. Here, a "yes" to a screening question results in the administration of a second set of questions designed to elicit very detailed information about the event. Gathering this additional information serves two purposes. First, the information provides greater detail about the victimization. Second, the details allow out-of-scope events to be excluded from victimization estimates. An out-of-scope incident could be one that took place outside the time period of interest or is not the type of crime included in the study. In addition to gathering more detailed and accurate information, this two-step procedure is believed to be superior to the one-step approach from a cognitive perspective because it allows the respondent to focus on the recall task exclusively. Early tests of victimization surveys found that separating the screening and description tasks resulted in more exhaustive reporting of victimization events (Biderman et al. 1967). As a result, the NCS and NCVS – as well as surveys modeled after such as like the BCS – utilize a two-step procedure.

LESSONS FROM VICTIMIZATION SURVEYS. The need to improve respondents' recall was a motivating factor that prompted redesigning the NCS. During the NCS Redesign, Albert Biderman was the first to bring survey researchers and cognitive psychologists together to discuss how best to stimulate the recall and reporting of crime events (Biderman and Moore 1982). The hope was that theories of cognition would serve as a framework for screening strategies to promote more complete recall of crimes. This Cognition Workshop in 1982 served as the stimulus for more extensive collaboration between cognitive psychologists and survey researchers as well as more elaborate theories of how respondents stored and retrieved memories of crime events (Jabine et al. 1984). These theories, in turn, were the basis of survey procedures that fostered more complete reporting of crimes.

On the basis of the discussions generated by the Cognition Workshop, the failure to report crime events was attributed to conceptual failure, memory failure, response inhibition, or a combination of these (Biderman et al. 1986). *Conceptual failure* occurs when the survey instrument does not correctly convey the cognitive task concerning the detail expected, the activity or time period of interest, or the concept at issue. Respondents in victimization surveys may, for example, believe that general and approximate reporting of crime events is sufficient, when the survey actually is demanding greater specificity in reporting attributes of crime event. Alternatively, the respondent may report on crime-like events rather than actual crimes or events outside the reference period because he misunderstood his task. Another issue with conceptual failure is that the respondent's definition of crimes may differ from that used in the survey such that he omits "gray area" events such as assaults in which his brother was the offender. *Memory failure* is the inability of respondents to locate in their memory the target event when they clearly understand the nature of that event. *Response inhibition* occurs when respondents are ashamed or embarrassed to report events accurately and completely, so they fail to report or they report inaccurately.

This simple typology of why respondents do not report eligible crimes was used as the blueprint for redesigning the screening procedures in the NCVS, with the greatest emphasis given to reducing memory and conceptual failures. The principal method for reducing memory failure was to substantially increase the number of prompts given to the respondent to help them search their memory for crime events. This goal was accomplished by using a "short cue" screening interview.[6] Traditional victimization surveys (including the NCS) simply asked respondents "If they had been hit, kicked or punched?". The NCVS still asks the initial question ("Were you ever hit, kicked, or punched?"), but follows up with a number of other possible attributes of events in rapid succession. These questions are designed to cue incident attributes like weapons ("with a stick?"), known offenders, ("By a friend? By your brother?"), and locations ("At work or at school?"). Using these incident attributes as prompts sought to help the respondents locate the event in their memory. By asking the cues in rapid succession, the goal was to deliver as many as possible in a short period of time.

To take into account conceptual failures in which the respondent did not define eligible events as crimes, alternative frames of reference were added to the screener. Here as well, additional cues were added to reduce memory failure. Alternative frames of reference are important because victims may not treat the criminal act as the most salient aspect of the crime event. If the event happened at work, for example, respondents may not regard the incident as a victimization, especially for respondents who work in professions such as police officers or bouncers where crimes such as assaults may frequently occur. If respondents store memory of the assault at all, they may keep it in the "at work" memory file rather than the "victimization" memory file. By explicitly including "work" as a frame of reference, this question both signals to the respondent that these incidents are eligible events to report to the survey and it prompts him to search this part of his memory. Failures of concept were also addressed by asking explicitly about some forms of crime such as rape[7] as well as firming up "gray area" events by indicating that these events are within the scope of the surveys. Cues such as, "Sometimes people do not report attacks by people they know...", were used to prompt respondents to include events that the respondent might not classify as a victimization incident, but that the NCVS includes in its estimates.

The major contribution of the NCS Redesign was the improvement of screening procedures to reduce underreporting. Much of the increase in reporting of victimization events as a result of the redesign was due to improved screening procedures (Hubble and Wilder 1988; Persley 1995; Kindermann et al. 1997). Specifically, these strategies contributed to a 40%

---

[6] In fact, the screening interview more than doubled in the amount of time it took to administer. The screener developed for the NCVS requires about 18 minutes to complete as compared to the screener previously used in the NCS, which only took about 8 minutes.

[7] The NCS did not specifically ask about rape because of concerns that such questions were too sensitive to be asked, especially in a government-sponsored survey. During the redesign, it was determined that societal norms had changed enough to permit directly asking questions about rape and sexual assault (Rennison and Rand 2007).

increase in the reporting of victimization events (Martin et al. 1986; Hubble and Wilder 1988; Rand et al. 1997; Cantor and Lynch 2005). The research and development work on screening as well as the results of the redesign indicate that a lot of crime remains unreported both to the police and to casual crime surveys and one must work hard at screening to get the most complete reporting possible.

APPROACH IN SELF-REPORT OFFENDING SURVEYS.   In comparison, self-report surveys of offending have devoted less attention to screening. The approach taken to screening in offender surveys actually tends to be odds with the best practices identified in the self-report victimization literature. For example, self-report offending surveys generally use the one-step approach to inquiring about offending. This reliance on the one-step approach generates other screening problems including the minimal use of cues, multiple cognitive tasking, mix of screening and detail recall, and inability to exclude ineligible events. The discussion in the following section examines these problems using specific examples.

One primary problem in screening questions used in offending surveys concerns the minimal use of cues presented to stimulate recall of criminal events. The instrument used in one of the PRCCD instruments (Rochester Youth Development Study), for example, asks respondents:

> Since your last interview have you damaged, destroyed or marked up somebody else's property on purpose?

This question provides only two cues that prompt recall of the target crime: the action (destruction of property) and the victim (somebody else's property). The question fails to clarify gray areas, such as instances wherein ownership or intentionality is vague. For example, a teenage respondent's parents buy a car for his use, but he damages the car to antagonize his parents. In the respondent's mind, the car is his property and no delinquent act would be reported in response to this question. As a result, the survey would undercount these types of activities. The question also fails to use multiple frames of reference, such as school or home or certain types of leisure behavior during which the destruction took place.[8] The vandalizing of playground equipment, for example, may be so common place that it would not be singled out unless specific reference was made to this activity or location. Property damage also is common place in sibling disputes, but the incident most likely would not be recalled and reported unless some specific reference was made about the sibling. The failure to recall such an event may be due to the event being stored in a "sibling" memory file as opposed to a "property destruction" file.

A second screening problem in self-report offending surveys is that respondents often are asked to do a number of complex cognitive tasks rather than focusing on the single task of searching their memory for potentially eligible events. This "multi-tasking" requires respondents not only to find the target event in their memory, but also to identify how many times it has occurred in the past year. This problem can be illustrated by the following question on vandalism from the National Youth Survey (NYS):

> How many times in the last year have you purposely damaged or destroyed OTHER
> PROPERTY that did not belong to you, not counting family or school property?

---

[8] Other self-report offending surveys such as the NYS do screen with some reference to school, family, and other as frames of reference. However, the density of cues is more limited than in the NCVS.

Here, the question requires respondents to search for instances involving damage to property, then exclude those that did not happen in the last year as well as those that did not involve property owned by family members or the school. A significant effort is demanded from the respondent in a single operation, especially since the respondent is also expected to answer carefully and accurately.[9]

A third common problem with screening questions regarding offending is the interspersing of screening with short descriptions of events. This structure adds unnecessary complexity to the respondent's cognitive task. For example, the NYS asks the screening question:

> How many times in the Last Year have you:
>
> 226. Stolen or tried to steal a motor vehicle such as a car or motorcycle?
>
> If the respondent answers something other than "none" they are asked:
>
> 226. Thinking of the last time:
>
>   (a) What type of vehicle was it?
>
>   (b) Did you actually steal it?
>
>   (c) Who did the vehicle belong to?
>
>   (d) How did you get the vehicle started?
>
>   (e) What were you going to do with the vehicle?
>
>   (f) Were you alone or did others take part in this event?
>
>   (g) Had you been drinking or taking drugs before the incident?
>
>   (h) Did you report this same event for any other question in this set?

Here, the question requires the respondent to move between the cognitive task of recalling any events of motor vehicle theft to recalling details of the last theft. If the entire survey instrument is examined, the cognitive task is even more complicated. The next question requires the respondent to return to searching his memory to count another type of crime, such as robbery, and then provide specific details. This switching between recalling types and counts of events to recalling details of a specific event can make it more difficult for a respondent to perform either task well for that particular question. Describing the specifics of one event can make it more difficult to search one's memory for other types of crime referred to in subsequent screening questions in the survey instrument.

A fourth and final problem frequently observed in the screening questions for offending surveys concerns the failure of the follow-up questions to gather information that can be used to exclude ineligible events and that can serve as a check on the performance of the cognitive tasks required of respondents in the screening questions. This problem includes both the failure to ask any follow-up questions at all as well as the failure to ask questions that would provide these details. For example, the vandalism screening question described earlier, did not include any follow-up questions that asked respondents for the date of the event, which would ensure that the event happened during the reference period. Respondents also are not asked about ownership of the property or the intentionality of damage in the vandalism events. Asking respondents about these aspects of the event as a follow up to the screen questions would permit the exclusion of ineligible events.

---

[9] In the victimization survey context, studies have compared early surveys that asked respondents to do these complex exclusions within one question with surveys that isolated identifying potential events from exclusion of ineligible events. Respondents were more productive when asked separate questions that allowed them to identify potential events and exclude ineligible ones (Biderman et al. 1967; Reiss 1967; Cantor and Lynch 2000).

IMPLICATIONS. The evidence from victimization surveys suggests that the current screening strategies employed in self-report surveys of offending likely suffer from a mix of both underreporting due to limited cuing and complex cognitive tasks and over reporting due to the inclusion of ineligible events. While these errors may be equal and off-setting for aggregate estimates of the volume of offending, they may have serious repercussions for correlational analyses due to the selectivity of offenders and events captured by the surveys. In particular, underreporting could be very consequential especially for estimates of the offending rates of individuals in a given unit of time (also referred to as *lambda*) which is used in creating offender typologies. The effect on other analytical uses of the data is less clear since underreporting could be distributed differently across values of predictor variables. In the victimization survey context, initial assessments of the change in the NCVS design suggested that increases in reporting were greater for low risk groups than high risk groups, such as older respondents as opposed to younger and wealthy as opposed to poor respondents (Kindermann et al. 1997). This finding suggests that underreporting is not uniformly distributed across values of independent variables. Cantor and Lynch (2005) estimated models with data collected before and after the NCVS redesign and found substantial stability in the models predicting victimization. The changes in cuing had the expected effects on the level of victimization reported, and the coefficients for predictor variables had the same sign and relative magnitude before and after the redesign. The constancy of the effects of changes in the cuing strategy across predictor variables was especially the case for clearly defined crimes like robbery. This tendency was much less true for less well defined crimes like aggravated assault and simple assault because these incidents are more susceptible to interactions between design characteristics of the survey and attributes of respondents and crime events. The interactions between design changes and attributes of victims and crime events suggest that the inclusion of more extensive screening for crime events may result in quite different correlates of offending than are currently the case, at least for ill-defined types of crime like simple assault.

REFERENCE PERIOD. As discussed earlier, work done as part of the NCS Redesign identified three sources for respondents' failure to report crime: conceptual failure, memory failure, and response inhibition or distortion (Biderman et al. 1986). Of relevance to reference periods is *memory failure*, which is the inability of respondents to locate in their memory the target event when they clearly understand the nature of that event. This problem increases with the passage of time such that the longer the period between the interview and the occurrence of the crime event, the less complete the reporting. Memory decay occurs more slowly for events that have been rehearsed or that have consequences that anchor the event in memory. Cues and other memory aids can facilitate more complete recall, but the decay of memory over time is a universal in retrospective surveys.

Based on issues of memory failure, the reference period has implications for recall and the reporting of crime events. *Reference period* refers to the length of time that respondents are asked to search their memory to find eligible crimes. Longer reference periods mean more underreporting of crime events in general. The exception arises for serious criminal events, which are remembered longer and more uniformly than less serious crimes. While the effects of reference period length are reasonably consistent across both traditions, the research conducted in the victimization survey tradition employs more rigorous research designs and less highly selective populations. As a result, this research strongly suggests that shorter reference periods may change the results of analyses of self-report offending data.

LESSONS FROM VICTIMIZATION SURVEYS.   A consistent finding from both work done as part of the NCVS redesign as well as methodological studies in other retrospective surveys is that shorter reference periods produce more complete reporting (Lepkowski 1981). In theory, no point occurs at which shortening the reference period does not improve data quality (Biemer et al. 2004). One reason is that the work on victimization surveys suggests that memory decay happens very quickly so that reference periods of a few days would be optimal. In practice, however, reducing recall error is not the only concern of researchers, and a trade-off exists between reference period length and sampling error. Short reference periods require large samples to ensure including enough respondents who experienced victimization or offending in that very short span of time to provide reliable estimates.[10] In other words, reporting of crimes is more complete in a short reference period, but there will be less of it.

The issue with regard to reference periods and recall becomes one of finding the optimal balance between measurement and sampling error as well as ensuring the ability to report on an appropriate unit of time, such as a particular year or the past 12 months. The NCVS uses a 6-month reference period. Other surveys use longer periods such as the British Crime Survey, which employs a 12-month reference period. The decision to use a 6-month reference period for the NCVS was the basis of findings from randomized experiments that compared various reference period lengths and supported after the fact by analyses of recency slopes. When Census researchers compared 3-, 6-, and 12-month reference periods in the NCS, they found shorter periods resulted in significantly higher reporting rates than did longer reference periods (Bushery 1981). Biderman and Lynch (1981) obtained similar results when examining recency slopes in the NCS. Here 26% of all victimizations reported in the survey were reported in the month of the reference period most proximate to the interview and only 12% of the incidents were reported in the most distant month of the 6-month reference period. While many factors contribute to the negative relationship between recency and reporting, the most plausible explanation is memory decay.

This underreporting due to memory decay and long reference periods may vary by types of events and respondents; however, the evidence for such a conclusion is mixed. NCS reference period experiments (Kobelarcik et al. 1983) indicated that reporting is more complete for younger persons across all types of crime when shorter reference periods are employed. Minority respondents reported more violent crimes than non-minority respondents with the 3-month reference period but no differences were observed between the 6- and 12-month reference periods. On the other hand, Biderman and Lynch (1981) did not find many differences between respondents or events reported in the most proximate as opposed to the most distant months of the reference period. Younger respondents had a slight tendency to be more affected by recency bias than older respondents. The largest effect observed was in police-reported events. Here a greater proportion of the crimes reported to the survey in the most distant month of the reference were reported to the police as compared to the most proximate month of the reference period. This finding is consistent with findings that events that are rehearsed or have consequences are less subject to memory decay.

In sum, the methodological work on victimization surveys indicates the longer the reference period, the less complete the reporting of crime events. This underreporting does not seem to be correlated with attributes of respondents when reference periods of 6 months or more are compared, but there are differences in reporting when reference periods of 3 months or less are compared to longer reference periods. Even when longer reference periods are used,

---

[10] In addition, sample size, in turns, brings issues of cost into play.

crime events that result in some additional repercussion such as reporting to the police, reporting to insurance, obtaining treatment for injury are reported more completely than events without these consequences.

APPROACHES IN SELF-REPORT OFFENDING SURVEYS. Self-report offending surveys often use much longer reference periods than the NCVS's 6-month reference period. The original self-report surveys of offending were cross-sectional surveys that asked respondents to recount their offending experience over reasonably long periods of time such as 3 years (Gold 1972). No consistent reference period is used. The NYS uses a 12-month reference period. One of the interviews in the Cambridge Youth Study, however, asks its 32-year-old respondents to report on their offending since 16 years of age. Using reference periods of several years or one's lifetime will result in substantial underreporting of offending behavior. More recently, most of surveys of offending have been longitudinal panel designs that interview respondents repeatedly at intervals that allow for a reference period of a year or two at the most.

A number of studies have compared offending rates produced by prospective (longitudinal surveys) and retrospective (cross-sectional surveys) designs. These studies are essentially comparisons of different reference periods. In their comparison of different reference periods, Mennard and Elliot (1990) found longer reference periods produced much lower estimates of the incidence and prevalence of juvenile offending. They also found differences in models predicting the frequency and patterns of offending using these different reference periods. Unlike the methodological studies conducted with victimization surveys, most of the work concerning reference periods in the self-report offending tradition compares already lengthy recall periods such as 1 year, with even longer periods such as 2 or more years. This comparison almost certainly underestimates the magnitude of the reference period effect and distorts the distribution of these events across attributes of respondents and events.

In the offender survey tradition, only one comparison has included an "ultra-short" reference period. Roberts et al. (2005) found large discrepancies between a retrospective survey that employed a 1-week reference period as compared to one utilizing a 5-month reference period. The ultra-short, 1-week reference period produced much higher estimates of offending and even affected the classification of individual as high or low volume offender. The Roberts study is not very generalizable, however, for three reasons. It utilized a very small sample ($n = 75$). The sample was from a very selective population (young people admitted to an emergency room who were identified as having histories of violence). In addition, the surveys used different formats. The group with the 5-month reference period was interviewed using life events calendar while the group with the 1-week reference period was interviewed with more traditional formats with more highly structure and uniform questioning.[11] While research in the self-report offending tradition established the superiority of reference periods of a year relative to longer reference periods, no work has been done on the effects of ultra-short reference periods relative to more commonly used reference periods of a year or two.

---

[11] Life event calendars use the recounting of life events on a calendar as a means of improving recall of target events in retrospective surveys and increasing the accuracy of dating these events. For an application in offending surveys, see Horney and Marshall (1992).

IMPLICATIONS. Exploring reference periods in self-report offending surveys is particularly important due to the new use of these data in trajectory studies. These statistical methods are sensitive to data accuracy and even modest errors in recall may affect trajectory groupings (Eggleston et al. 2004; Sampson et al. 2004). In their call for more investigation of the effects of data quality, Eggleston et al. (2004) explicitly mention the length of the reference period in self-report offending surveys as a potential source of distortion. Departure from complete reporting or the inaccurate dating of crime events that can result from the use of long reference periods likely has consequences for identifying offending trajectories and for distinguishing types of trajectories.

Methodological testing in both victimization and offending survey traditions support the idea that shorter reference periods promote more complete recall and reporting than longer reference periods do. The work in victimization surveys, however, informs with regard to how best to balance the need for accuracy with the practical needs of sample size and implementation. The reference periods of 1 and 2 years that are customary in offender surveys, however, may result in substantial underreporting and perhaps even bias. The comparisons of reporting using different reference periods across offender surveys may be understating the extent and nature of under-reporting because they do not capture the steepest part of the recency slope which occurs in the days and weeks immediately after the event. Work from the victimization survey tradition suggests that self-report offending surveys could benefit from methodological studies that explored using very short (such as a month) reference periods and comparing these findings with the more commonly used annual reference period to better estimate the magnitude of underreporting and any potential bias in reporting of offenses.

High Volume Repeat Events

A second type of response error concerns high volume repeat events. These events are crimes that occur frequently in a given period of time and share many of the same characteristics, such as the type of criminal act, the same offender or the same victim. A cab driver, for example, who gets robbed every Friday night, would be experiencing high volume repeat victimization. Intimate partner violence is another example commonly associated with high volume repeat events (Dodge and Balog 1987). Here the difficulty – and potential for error – arises from how to accurately count and capture these incidents. Different techniques have arisen from the victimization and offending survey traditions.

LESSONS FROM THE VICTIMIZATION SURVEYS. Asking respondents about high volume repeat events has proven to be difficult in victimization surveys. The incident focus of the surveys required that an incident form be completed for each positive response to a screener question. In some cases, respondents, such as those experiencing domestic violence, indicate that a large number of similar events have occurred and that they cannot date them or provide distinct information on each crime. Under these conditions, the interviewer has the option of following a "series incident" procedure in which one incident form is completed on the most recent incident and the number of times this type of crime occurred in the reference period is recorded. The series incident procedure was developed to reduce the reporting burden for respondents.

While this strategy helps respondents, it introduces error into the estimates since it amounts to asking the more imprecise question of "how many times" the respondent has been victimized with no incident report requiring greater specificity. Such concerns are significant enough that the Justice Department does not include series events in the annual crime counts because it considers these counts to be unreliable. Studies examining the effects of including series counts results in annual rates that fluctuate wildly (Biderman and Lynch 1991; Planty 2007). Planty (2007), for example, estimated that in 1993, rape and sexual assault estimates would have increased 225% if series victimizations were included. This change is driven by 21 unweighted incidents with very high estimates of the number of crimes they have experienced. The maximum number of aggravated assaults reported in a series event over the period 1993–2002 ranged from 75 in 2000 to 750 in 1996. Planty (2007) also observed that estimates of the number of events in a series tended to bunch around figures that were multiples of months or weeks in the reference period. This pattern suggested that respondents were estimating the frequency of these events rather than recalling events separately. These findings indicate that very imprecise crime estimates will result from asking respondents with a lot of crime experience to report on how many crimes occurred unless these estimates are subjected to the rigor of an incident form.

The inclusion of high volume repeat events clearly has implications for estimates of crime overall, but the treatment of these experiences also affects estimates of crime across population groups. Planty (2007) found that when series victimizations were excluded from the aggravated assault rates, blacks (35) had higher rates per hundred thousand than whites (27) or Hispanics (29). When the victims' estimates of the number of events in the series were included in the rates, Hispanics became the highest risk group (77) compared to blacks (47) and whites (39).

APPROACHES IN THE SELF-REPORT OFFENDING TRADITION. Since offending surveys do not have an incident focus, they have relied almost exclusively on the respondent's estimate of "how many times" an offense has occurred. For example in the PRCCD's Rochester Youth Development Study, a screening question asks about a certain type of offending. If the answer is positive, then the respondent is asked "How many times?" The NYS employs a more elaborate procedure that asks respondents to report on how many crimes of a certain type occurred and, if over ten crimes are reported, questions are asked about the rate at which these crimes occurred such as two or three per month.

IMPLICATIONS. Asking respondents to indicate whether they were involved in a specific number of crimes of certain type yields imprecise information on the number of crimes that occurred and the nature of those crimes. When respondents are asked to report in detail about individual crimes, rather than simply reporting counts of crime, estimates of aggregate crime rates are more stable over time. The victimization survey technique of forcing respondents to recount details of specific crime events in the form of an incident report appears to encourage more reliable reporting. The instability in aggregate victimization rates when reported counts of events are included was observed when they were used for persons who reported six or more victimizations. It may be that reporting counts of crimes is accurate when a respondent only has a few crimes to report and it becomes progressively less accurate when more crimes are reported. The instability in the aggregate crime rates was similar in the NCVS trends when the series victimization procedure was used for three or more events and when it was used for six or more events (Biderman and Lynch 1991; Planty 2007). This finding suggests that after a relatively small number of events, respondents start estimating rather than recounting the number of crimes they were involved in. At minimum, the experience from victimization surveys suggests that responses to the "how many" question in screening for offenses that involve large numbers should be regarded with caution.

Temporal Placement of Crime Events

A third type of response error concerns the temporal placement of crime events. Here, the respondent is required to accurately date when the criminal incident occurred. Errors in temporal placement more often move the target events forward in time so that they are reported as closer to the interview than they actually are. This phenomenon is often referred to as "telescoping." As a result, a concern for victimization surveys is the effect this error has on annual rates and change estimates.

LESSONS FROM VICTIMIZATION SURVEYS.   Both studying the effect of and ameliorating the error generated by telescoping has been given much more emphasis in the victimization surveys than in the self-report offending tradition. One source of data on temporal placement in the victim survey tradition is reverse record checks. In these studies, a sample of crimes reported to police is taken from police records. The victims are contacted and interviewed to see if they will report the events to the survey. The date of the event as reported by the victim is compared to the date of the police report to determine the respondent's accuracy in dating the event. Several reverse-record check studies conducted prior to designing the original NCS (Dodge 1970; Turner 1972) and additional record check studies performed as part of the NCS Redesign (Miller and Groves 1986). These studies indicated a substantial amount of error in the temporal placement of crime events in retrospective surveys. Moreover, the errors in temporal placement increased as the reference period lengthened (Dodge 1970).

Another source of data on the temporal placement of crime events comes from the testing of techniques designed to reduce temporal displacement. Reducing telescoping has been a major influence on the design of victimization surveys. The NCVS, for example, employs a rotating panel design in large part to control telescoping. Respondents are interviewed seven times at 6 month intervals. The first interview is a "bounding interview" that is not used for estimation purposes but simply to bound the reference period for subsequent interviews.[12] Respondents are asked to report crime that occurred since the last interview, so the previous interview serves as a cognitive bound on the recall task. When respondents report a victimization, an incident form is administered, and as one of the first questions, respondents are asked the date of the event. This question provides another opportunity for the respondent to not report an event out of the reference period. The events reported in the incident form are checked against crimes reported in the previous interview and respondents are asked to affirm that similar events were not actually reported in the previous interviews. Respondents in unbounded interviews report about 40% more victimizations than respondents in unbounded interviews, so telescoping arguably has a considerable effect (but see Addington 2005, questioning the effect of telescoping across types of crimes). Studies of bounding also show that bounding effects vary across types of crime with property crimes being affected more than violent crimes, attempts more than completed crimes and crimes not reported to the police more than those reported (Murphy and Cowan 1984; Addington 2005).

Rotating panel designs are not the only technique to limit telescoping errors. Temporal anchors are useful, especially for cross-sectional victim surveys. Loftus and Marburger

---

[12] Three reasons have been posited for how bounding in the crime survey reduces telescoping (see, Biderman and Cantor 1984; Skogan 1981). First, the information from the bounding interview generates a reference list for the interviewer. Second, the bounding interview provides a cognitive reference point for the respondent. Third, the bounding interview educates respondents about precision expected in their responses.

(1983), as part of the NCS Redesign, demonstrated the power of temporal anchors when they interviewed persons at the Seattle Airport and asked them about their victimization experience in the past 12 months. After they responded, the interviewers asked if the incident occurred before or after the eruption of Mount St. Helens which happened exactly a year before. With this temporal anchor about 40% of the respondents allowed that the event they reported did not occur within the reference period. This finding indicates a massive amount of foreword tele-scoping and the potential of temporal anchors for more precise temporal placement. Because of the use of rotating panel designs in the major victimization surveys, the use of temporal anchors and other calendrical devices, such as life event calendars have not made their way into the major victimization surveys discussed here.

LIMITATIONS IN SELF-REPORT OFFENDING SURVEYS.   A number of studies in the self-report offending literature have examined the accuracy of respondents' dating of crime events. Like the comparable victimization studies, these analyses use comparisons both with police records and of alternative survey procedures meant to reduce temporal misplacement. The record check studies find reasonably close correspondence between the temporal location of crime events in self-report surveys and in police records. Comparisons of dating across different types of surveys find larger differences.

Record check studies conducted with offending surveys, however, are not the same as the reverse-record checks performed in the victimization survey context. The former compare counts of events reported as occurring in a specific time period while the latter compare specific incidents occurring in a particular point in time.[13] Matching overall counts of events is considerably easier than matching specific incidents. Matching counts of crimes is easier in part because one can have the same count of crimes per month in the survey and police records with each source including very different events. The police counts can be low because not all events come to the attention of the police and the police fail to record many events, while the respondents' counts can be low because of underreporting. Assessed on an event or incident basis, these two data sources would have very low correspondence, but assessed in the aggregate the correspondence is high. It is not surprising, therefore, that comparisons of survey responses and police records in the offender survey tradition find reasonably high correspondence.

Comparisons of the temporal placement of events across different survey procedures are rare, and they have usually examined the effect of reference period length on the temporal placement of crimes. Two studies are noteworthy. One is from the work conducted by Roberts et al. (2005) discussed earlier. In this study, the rate of reporting an event and placing that event in the correct month is 13.6 per hundred, while the probability of reporting an event is 43.6 per hundred. This finding suggests that a substantial number of errors occur in dating offenses in retrospective surveys and that these errors increase with the length of the reference period. The applicability of the results of the Roberts study to self-report surveys more generally is complicated by the selectivity factors in the Roberts study that were discussed in the foregoing section. A second study is that of Kazemian and Farrington (2005). Kazemian and Farrington (2005) compared a prospective survey with a 2-year reference period to a retrospective survey

---

[13] Huizinga and Elliot (1985) come the closest in the self-report offending survey tradition to an incident-based reverse record check where arrests incidents found in police records are matched on a one to one basis with reports from the self-report survey. Even in this study, the amount of information used to match is quite limited, and dates are not included.

with a reference period of approximately 16 years. In examining the time of onset of offending in prospective and retrospective surveys of offending, they found little agreement between the two procedures. Respondents in retrospective surveys typically reported the age of onset as being later, that is, they reported it closer to the interview than was the case in prospective surveys. Temporal placement errors occurred more frequently with more minor as opposed to more serious events.

Self-report offending surveys differ considerably in the procedures used to promote accurate temporal placement of events. Early cross-sectional surveys used a 3-year reference period that was not bounded in any way, although respondents were asked to date the events separately (Gold 1972). The National Youth Survey (Elliot 2008) used Christmas as a bounding event. The PRCCD's Rochester Youth Development Study (RYDS) survey asks respondents to report on offending that occurred since the last interview, usually a year or two ago.[14] The prior interview serves as the far bound of the reference period and should reduce telescoping into the reference period. While this procedure appears to be similar to the NCVS bounding method, the RYDS instrument does not give as much emphasis to minimizing telescoping as does the NCVS. For example, both the RYDS and the NCVS interviews caution the respondent about the length of the interview period and makes reference to "since the last interview." Unlike the RYDS interview, the NCVS incident form asks the respondent a second time about temporal placement when requiring the month of the criminal incident. In addition, the NCVS interviewers keep a narrative description of the crimes reported in the prior interview on the control card. When crimes are reported in the current interview, the interviewers compare the events reported in the current interview with those reported in prior interviews. If an event is similar, then respondent are asked if the current event is the same as one they reported in the previous interview. If they respond affirmatively, the event is not counted. This "unfounding" task is not done in RYDS.

IMPLICATIONS.   Research in victimization and offending survey traditions indicates that the temporal placement of events is difficult for respondents, who tend to move events forward in time both into the reference period from outside and within the reference period. The evidence for this forward telescoping is much stronger in the victimization survey tradition largely because of the need for victimization surveys to isolate and attempt to date events. The methodological testing done with victimization surveys used samples more similar to the general population than many of the analyses conducted in the self-report offending tradition. The methodological work based upon police record checks in the victimization area also compared individual events reported in the survey to events record by the police, while studies in the offending tradition compared counts of events reported in the surveys to counts of events in official records. The former provides a more stringent test of temporal placement. Evidence also suggests that bounding procedures such as those used in the NCVS reduce telescoping. Most of the major offending surveys employ substantially less extensive bounding procedures. Consequently, offending surveys likely suffer from a substantial amount of forward telescoping and this telescoping probably involves more minor crimes that are not reported to the police.

---

[14] The authors are grateful to Terry Thornberry for providing a copy of the Rochester Youth Development Study interview schedule.

DISCUSSION

As with much of the measurement error in criminological data, response error and the problems it generates do not lend themselves to quick or easy solutions. These problems are compounded by the fact that little attention has been devoted to studying measurement error let alone investigating the magnitude and direction of measurement error. In this context, our knowledge of measurement error in the self-report survey tradition is much greater than for data based on official records. Within the self-report area, more resources have been invested in understanding response error for victimization surveys than those for offending. Even for victimization surveys, the amount of existing research is much too small for us to speak definitively and specifically about the effects of response errors on various uses of these data. It is not surprising, then, that our first suggestion is for more research on this topic. Specifically, we recommend a two-prong approach of long- and short-term research, which are discussed in more detail in the following section. In the long-run, the research community needs to invest in the creation of a "gold-standard" survey. Such a project is well beyond the means of individual researchers and will require concerted efforts of teams of criminologists and other social scientists dependent upon self-report methodologies. In the short term, interim strategies can be adopted by individual researchers. In addition to strategies to reduce error, we recommend specific approaches that individual researchers can take to avoid the effects of response errors or to test for the magnitude of their effects.

The Need for a "Gold Standard" Survey

Much of the foregoing discussion is predicated on our ability to know how much crime there is and when it occurs. Talking intelligently about response errors is difficult unless some standard is available against which responses can be compared. Tests of content validity are easy to do, but are subject to substantial disagreement about what constitutes the content of the concept. Construct validity tests require robust theory and are open to debate as to the strength of the relationships among the relevant concepts. Criterion validity is more persuasive than content and construct validity as it is less subject to debate so long as an agreed upon standard exists against which ones measure of crime can be compared. Unfortunately, no gold standard exists in the area of either self-report victimization or offending. As we have seen in this chapter, the traditional criteria for establishing the accuracy in self-report surveys are official records or surveys with different (and arguably superior) methodology. Both of these criteria have their problems. Police records are highly selective and have their own error structure that lessens their ability to serve as a standard for valid reporting (Biderman and Lynch 1981; Huizinga and Elliot 1985, 1986; Miller and Groves 1986). Moreover, Biderman (1966) argued that the social organization of surveys is so different from the social organization of official record systems that they could not and should not arrive at similar counts and characterizations of crime events. Using alternative surveys as standards for judging the validity of self-report surveys would not be subject to the distortion introduced by administrative records systems. Moreover, surveys are under the control of researchers, whereas administrative record systems are not, so it is, in principle, simpler to eliminate selectivity and other sources of non-comparability across the surveys than it is when comparing survey results to administrative records (Biderman and Lynch 1991). Alternative surveys would provide a much clearer assessment of the effects of specific survey procedures.

To investigate an alternative survey strategy, the initial question is whether theories of response in self-report surveys (for either victimization or offending) are sufficiently developed to identify clearly superior methodologies for self-report surveys that can be used as "the standard" against which lesser methods can be compared. When the self-report method was first developed, this question could not be answered. In the interim, a considerable amount of progress has been made in the development of response theories, particularly in the last 25 years. Today, we are better able to identify a package of instrumentation and procedures that would provide the most complete recounting of criminal involvement possible in a self-report survey. For these reasons, we believe that the greatest advances in outlining the error structure of self-report surveys will come from studies using "best practices" surveys as their standard for accurate reporting.

Developing a "gold standard" self-reporting survey is not a far-fetched idea. From the research on victimization and offending surveys reviewed in this paper, we know that a number of substantial response errors affect estimates of the level of crime, the distribution of both victimization and offending across population groups and the temporal placement of crime events. We also know that self-report surveys employing extensive screening interviews and very short reference periods can reduce many of these response errors. In addition, requiring detailed questioning about each event identified in the screening interview will provide better estimates of the number of crimes committed, especially in the case of high volume offenders. As such, we could develop an offender survey, for example, with these design characteristics. This survey would be done purely for methodological purposes, to be used as a "gold" standard against which on-going surveys of offenders can be compared. Such a survey would be devoted entirely to getting the most complete reporting of offenses rather than gathering information on the offenders or the social context of offending. A split sample could be employed with one half receiving this "state of the art" design and the other the design currently employed in major prospective surveys of offenders. Conducting such a survey would help address whether the response errors identified in the foregoing sections affect the characterization of offending trajectories and the attributes of offenders that predict whose career will follow a specific trajectory. Research done to date in the victimization survey strongly suggests that these response errors exist and likely affect uses of data, especially with the more recent studies employing trajectory analysis. Little more can be said definitively about these response errors until more methodological work is conducted to estimate the magnitude and direction of those errors.

Interim Strategies for Estimating the Effects of Response Errors

While we await this "state of the art" survey, researchers have other means to learn more about response errors in self-report surveys of victimization and offending and to protect their substantive analysis from likely errors. The following three options suggest ways to learn more about response errors. First, researchers can look across surveys and exploit the existing variation in offender survey methodologies to learn more about the effects of survey design on the resulting responses. The NYS, for example, has much more extensive cuing in their screening procedures than other high quality offender survey. Comparing the offense distributions in the NYS to those found in the PRCCD surveys such as RYDS or PYS can provide some idea of the importance of these design differences for reporting in the surveys. These comparisons will be very blunt assessments for investigating the effects of response errors because the designs of these surveys differ in many ways, which could be offsetting. In addition to design differences, the surveys vary in the samples and populations addressed, which could affect the results as well. To minimize the effect of population and sample differences, a second option is to assess response errors within a single survey. Cuing density in the NYS may differ across the types of crime such that comparisons of reporting by cue and type of crime could reveal the effects of cuing on reporting. Similarly, changes in survey methodology over the course of these longitudinal surveys provide another opportunity to understand the effects of method on reporting. This type of quasi-experimental design has been used extensively in the NCVS to study various response errors (Biderman et al. 1985; Biderman and Cantor 1984; Reiss 1982; Addington 2005). Finally, comparisons can be made with surveys of offending other than the dominant surveys discussed in this essay. These surveys often utilize very different methodologies. The survey used by Roberts et al. (2005) that utilized a life events calendar is a good example. In addition, the distributions of offending across population subgroups in these surveys can be compared with those from RYDS, CYS, PYS or NYS to see how sensitive findings are to differences in survey methods. These interim efforts to assess the effects of response errors in self-report offending surveys are not a substitute for the "state of the art" survey, but they can keep the focus on the effects of response errors until that survey is fielded.

Avoiding and Delimiting the Effects of Response Errors

In some cases, we know enough about response errors in the self report tradition and have the requisite information to take specific steps to limit the effect of response errors on estimates. Two examples illustrate how this can be accomplished. The first example concerns responses to questions of "how many times." Here, it is well established that such questions evoke imprecise responses unless the respondent is required to recount specific incidents. Compounding this problem is the well-established effect of extreme values on most statistical methodologies. The effect of these issues on trajectory models, though, is not well understood. Researchers using such questions in trajectory models may want to examine how different treatment of extreme responses might affect their results. For example, offense counts could be treated as an ordinal variable rather than as a continuous variable.[15] Another approach could impose upper limits on responses to the how many times questions and assessing the effects on the resulting analyses.

The second example concerns the type of crime studied. Response errors are known to have greater effect on less serious crimes than more serious crime. Robbery, for example, is particularly unaffected by changes in survey methodology and this is attributed to the fact that it is the quintessential crime that involves violence, theft and occurs among strangers (Cantor and Lynch 2005; Rosenfeld 2007). Assault, on the other hand, is much more sensitive to changes in self-report survey methodology in part because it does not comport with stereotypic definitions of crime.[16] Here, researchers can restrict their analyses to more serious crimes in order to reduce the effects of response errors. Alternatively, researchers can

---

[15] The authors thank the editors for suggesting this option.

[16] Some debate exists over what "serious" means. Typically, a more serious crime means a more morally objectionable act, but these acts also are more likely to have consequences, such as being report to police or insurance companies and hospital visits, all of which make them more memorable. Still others argue that it is the unambiguous nature of certain crime events that makes them more immune to response errors.

analyze separately more and less serious crimes and to estimate the effects of response errors. If models restricted to serious crimes are different from those for less serious crime in ways that can be attributed to response errors, researchers should be cautious in relying on analyses conducted using less serious crimes as well as the conclusions that are drawn.

CONCLUSION

Self-report surveys of offending behavior were developed to identify predictors of criminal behavior as well as to distinguish high rate offenders from low rate offenders and to explain why these people offended at different rates. More recently, these data have been used with sophisticated statistical procedures to characterize offense trajectories. These methods have many features to recommend them over the relatively simple and more subjective methods of data reduction and classification previously used (Nagin 1999, 2004). At the same time, these new trajectory methods have been shown to be sensitive to the nature of the data used (Eggleston et al. 2004). Inaccurately dating an offense, for example, or substantially under-reporting the number in a given period may not have mattered when the data from offending surveys were only used to distinguish high- and low-rate offenders, but these errors may have much greater effects on trajectory analysis. Victimization surveys, in contrast, have always had high demands for exhaustive reporting of crime events and for accurate dating of these events. This chapter reviewed some of the methodological work done on self-report victimization surveys in an effort to suggest where and why self-report offending survey data may not be as complete and accurate as these new uses require. In particular, we focused on response errors introduced by recall bias, high volume crime events, and temporal placement.

Comparisons of self-report offending survey and self-report victimization survey methodology suggest that several types of response error in self-report offending surveys may affect the results obtained. Confirming these suspicions is not simple given the difficulties in validating self reports of victimization or offending. Further exploration of these sources of response error may only be possible by comparing "state of the art" survey to lesser surveys to determine the adequacy of the latter survey. The state of the art survey would employ the best procedures as defined by survey research and cognitive psychology. To the extent that the results other surveys comport with the results of the state of the art survey, they would be considered valid. In the interim, researchers can utilize existing self-report surveys to obtain a better understanding of how response errors affect crime estimates, especially for particular uses such as trajectory modeling.

REFERENCES

Addington LA (2005) Disentangling the effects of bounding and mobility on reports of criminal victimization. J Quant Criminol 23:321–343

Biderman AD (1966) Social indicators and goals. In: Bauer R (ed) Social indicators. MIT Press, Cambridge, MA

Biderman AD, Cantor D (1984) A longitudinal analysis of bounding respondent conditioning and mobility as sources of panel bias in the National Crime Survey. In: American Statistical Association 1984 proceedings of the Section on Survey Research Methods. American Statistical Association, Washington, DC

Biderman AD, Lynch JP (1981) Recency bias in data on self-reported victimization. American Statistical Association 1981 proceedings of the Social Statistics Section. American Statistical Association, Washington, DC

Biderman AD, Lynch JP (1991) Understanding crime incidence statistics: why the UCR diverges from the NCS. Springer, New York

Biderman AD, Moore J (1982) Report on the Workshop on Cognitive Issues in Retrospective Surveys. Bureau of Social Science Research and U.S. Census Bureau, Washington, DC

Biderman AD, Reiss AJ Jr (1967) On exploring the "dark figure" of crime. Ann Am Acad Pol Soc Sci 374:1–15

Biderman AD, Johnson LA, McIntyre J, Weir AW (1967) Report on a pilot study in the District of Columbia on victimization and attitudes toward law enforcement. President's Commission on Law Enforcement and Administration of Justice, Field Surveys no. 1. U.S. Government Printing Office, Washington, DC

Biderman AD, Cantor D, Reiss A (1985) A quasi-experimental analysis of personal victimization by household respondents in the NCS. Paper presented at the annual meetings of the American Statistical Association, Philadelphia

Biderman AD, Cantor D, Lynch JP, Martin E (1986) Final report of the National Crime Survey redesign. Bureau of Social Science Research, Washington, DC

Biemer PP, Groves RM, Lyberg LE, Mathiowetz NA, Sudman S (2004) Measurement errors in surveys. Wiley, New York

Budd T, Sharp C, Mayhew P (2005) Offending in England and Wales: first results of the 2003 Crime and Justice Survey. Home Office Research Study No. 275. London Home Office

Bushery J (1981) Recall bias for different reference periods in the National Crime Survey. Proceedings of the American Statistical Association Survey Methods Research Section. American Statistical Association, Washington, DC, pp 238–243

Cantor D, Lynch JP (2000) Self-report surveys as measures of crime and criminal victimization. In: Duffee D, McDowall D, Mazerolle LG, Mastrofski SD (eds) Criminal Justice 2000: measurement and analysis of crime and justice. National Institute of Justice, Washington, DC

Cantor D, Lynch JP (2005) Exploring the effects of changes in design on the analytical uses of the NCVS data. J Quant Criminol 21:293–319

Dodge R (1970) The Washington DC Recall Study. Reprinted in Robert G. Lehnen and Wesley G. Skogan (1981) The National Crime Survey: Working papers, volume 1: Current and historical perspectives. Washington, DC: U.S. Department of Justice

Dodge R, Balog F (1987) Series victimization: a report on a field test. Bureau of Justice Statistics, Washington, DC

Eggleston E, Laub JH, Sampson RJ (2004) Methodological sensitivities to latent class analysis of long-term trajectories. J Quant Criminol 20:1–42

Elliot D (2008) National Youth Survey [United States]: Wave V, 1980. [Computer File]. Inter-university Consortium for Political and Social Research, Ann Arbor, MI

Fisher BS, Cullen FT (2000) Measuring the sexual victimization of women: evolution, current controversies and future research. In: Duffee D, McDowall D, Mazerolle LG, Mastrofski SD (eds) Criminal Justice 2000: measurement and analysis of crime and justice. National Institute of Justice, Washington, DC

Gold M (1972) National Survey of Youth, 1972 [Computer file]. Inter-university Consortium for Political and Social Research, Ann Arbor, MI

Horney J, Marshall I (1992) An experimental comparison of two self-report methods for measuring lambda. J Res Crime Delinq 29:102–121

Hubble D Wilder BE (1988) Preliminary results from the National Crime Survey CATI experiment. In: American Statistical Association 1988 proceedings of the Section on Survey Research Methods. American Statistical Association, Washington, DC

Huizinga D, Elliot DS (1985) A preliminary examination of the reliability and validity of the National Youth Survey self-reported delinquency indices. National Youth Survey Project Report No. 2. Behavioral Research Institute, Boulder, CO

Huizinga D, Elliot DS (1986) Reassessing the reliability and validity of self report delinquency measures. J Quant Criminol 2:293–327

Jabine TB, Straf ML, Tanur JM, Tourangeau R (eds) (1984) Cognitive aspects of survey methodology: building a bridge between disciplines. National Academy Press, Washington, DC

Junger-Tas J, Ineke Marshall (1999) The self-report methodology in crime research. In: Tonry M (ed) Crime and Justice: a review of research, vol 25. University of Chicago, Chicago, pp 291–359

Kazemian L, Farrington DP (2005) Comparing the validity of prospective retrospective and official onset for different offending categories. J Quant Criminol 21:127–147

Kindermann C, Lynch JP Cantor D (1997) The effects of the redesign on victimization estimates. U.S. Department of Justice, Washington, DC

Kobelarcik E, Alexander C, Singh R, Shapiro G (1983) Alternative reference periods for the National Crime Survey. Proceedings of the American Statistical Association Survey Methods Section, 1983. American Statistical Association, Washington, DC

Koss M (1996) The measurement of rape victimization in crime surveys. Crim Justice Behav 23:55–69

Lauritsen J (1998) The age crime debate: assessing the limits of longitudinal self-report data. Soc Forces 77:127–155

Lauritsen J (1999) Limitations on the use of longitudinal self-report data: a comment. Criminology 37:687–694

Lehnen RG, Skogan WG (1981) The National Crime Survey: Working papers, volume 1: current and historical perspectives. U.S. Department of Justice, Washington, DC

Lepkowski J (1981) Sample design issues from the National Crime Survey. Survey Research Center, University of Michigan, Ann Arbor, MI

Loftus E, Marburger W (1983) Since the eruption of Mt. St. Helens has anyone beaten you up? Mem Cogni 11: 114–120

Lynch JP (2006) Problems and promise of victimization surveys for cross-national research. In: Tonry M (ed) Crime and Justice: a review of research. University of Chicago Press, Chicago, pp 229–287

Martin E with Groves R, Maitlin J, Miller P (1986) Report on the Development of Alternative Screening Procedures in the National Crime Survey. Bureau of Social Science Research, Inc. Washington, DC

Mennard S, Elliot D (1990) Longitudinal and cross-sectional data collection and analysis in the study of crime and delinquency. Justice Q 7:11–54

Miller PV, Groves RM (1986) Matching survey respondents to official records: an exploration of validity in victimization reporting. Public Opin Q 49:366–380

Murphy LR, Cowan CD (1984) Effects of bounding on telescoping in the National Crime Survey. In: Lehnen R, Skogan W (eds) The National Crime Survey: Working Papers, vol II. U.S. Department of Justice, Washington, DC

Nagin D (1999) Analyzing developmental trajectories: a semi-parametric group based approach. Psychol Methods 4(2):139–157

Nagin D (2004) Response to "methodological sensitivities to latent class analysis of long term criminal trajectories". J Quant Criminol 20:27–35

Penick BKE, Owens M (1976) Surveying crime. National Academy Press, Washington, DC

Persley C (1995) The National Crime Victimization Survey redesign: measuring the impact of new methods. In: American Statistical Association 1995 proceedings of the Section on Survey Research Methods. American Statistical Association, Washington, DC

Piquero AR (2008) Taking stock of development trajectories of criminal activity. In: Lieberman A (ed) The long view of crime: a synthesis of longitudinal research. Springer, New York

Planty M (2007) Series victimization and divergence. In: Lynch JP, Addington LA (eds) Understanding crime statistics: revisiting the divergence of the UCR and the NCVS. Cambridge University Press, Cambridge, UK

Rand M, Cantor D, Lynch JP (1997) Criminal victimization, 1973–95. Bureau of Justice Statistics, Washington, DC

Reiss AJ (1967) Measurement of the nature and the amount of crime: studies in crime and law enforcement in major metropolitan areas. President's Commission on Law Enforcement and Administration of Justice, vol. 1 of Field Surveys no. 3. U.S. Government Printing Office, Washington, DC

Reiss AJ (1982) Victimization Productivity in Proxy Interviewing. Institution for Social and Policy Studies, Yale University, New Haven, CT

Rennison CM, Rand M (2007) Introduction to the National Crime Victimization Survey. In: Lynch JP, Addington LA (eds) Understanding crime statistics: revisiting the divergence of the NCVS and UCR. Cambridge University Press, Cambridge, UK

Roberts J, Mulvey E, Horney J, Lewis J, Arter M (2005) A test of two methods of recall for violent events. J Quant Criminol 21:175–194

Rosenfeld R (2007) Explaining the divergence between UCR and NCVS aggravated assault trends. In: Lynch JP, Addington LA (eds) Understanding crime statistics: revisiting the divergence of the NCVS and UCR. Cambridge University Press, New York

Sampson R, Laub JH, Eggleston E (2004) On the robustness and validity of groups. J Quant Criminol 20:37–42

Skogan WG (1981) Issues in the measurement of victimization. U.S. Department of Justice, Bureau of Justice Statistics, Washington, DC

Thornberry TP (1989) Panel effects and the use of self-reported measures of delinquency in longitudinal studies. In: Klein MW (ed) Cross-national research in self-reported crime and delinquency. Kluwer, Los Angeles

Thornberry TP, Krohn MD (2000) Self-report surveys as measures of delinquency and crime. In: Duffe D (ed) Criminal Justice 2000: measurement and analysis of crime and justice. United States Department of Justice, Washington, DC, pp 33–84

Tjaden P, Thoennes N (1998) Prevalence, incidence, and consequences of violence against women: findings from the National Violence Against Women Survey. U.S. National Institute of Justice, Washington, DC

Turner A (1972) San Jose Methods Test of Known Crime Victims. U.S. Department of Justice, Law Enforcement Assistance Administration, National Institute of Law Enforcement and Criminal Justice, Washington, DC

CHAPTER 14

Missing Data Problems in Criminological Research

ROBERT BRAME, MICHAEL G. TURNER, AND RAY PATERNOSTER

INTRODUCTION

Missing data problems are a ubiquitous challenge for criminology and criminal justice researchers (Brame and Paternoster 2003). Regardless of whether researchers are working with survey data or data collected from official agency records (or other sources), they will inevitably have to confront data sets with gaps and holes. As a result, researchers who design studies must take whatever steps that are feasibly and ethically possible to maximize the coverage and completeness of the data they will collect. Even with the best planning and implementation, however, nearly all studies will come up short. Records will be incomplete, targeted survey participants will not be located, some who are located will not participate, and some who participate will not participate fully. These common pitfalls result in a problem most researchers face, in that we want to use the data sets we collect to form inferences about an entire target population – not just the subset of that population for whom valid data are available.

Unfortunately, for the field of criminology and criminal justice, there is little advice and guidance on this issue that is available and accessible to applied researchers (see Allison 2002 for a notable exception). Most discussions of missing data issues are presented as statistical problems with examples from a wide range of fields. It is left to criminology and criminal justice researchers to identify appropriate analogies for the problems they encounter. Further complicating matters, most discussions about missing data are pitched in highly technical language and terminology that is outside the training of most criminology and criminal justice researchers. From the vantage point of most criminologists, serious treatments of missing data issues require significant investments of time and effort to identify appropriate analogies and methods (largely from other fields) or technical assistance by individuals who are already acquainted with these issues. To make matters worse, criminologists may be tempted to "solve" their missing data problems by blindly applying missing data routines now available in canned statistical packages.

A.R. Piquero and D. Weisburd (eds.), *Handbook of Quantitative Criminology*,
DOI 10.1007/978-0-387-77650-7_14, © Springer Science + Business Media, LLC 2010,
First softcover printing 2011

We, of course, will not resolve the problems identified above with a single essay. Instead, our goal for this essay is to provide a systematic primer of the key missing data issues arising in crime research and a conceptual-level discussion of how these issues can be addressed. In the next section, we discuss some different types of missing data problems that typically arise in the kinds of research projects often conducted by criminologists. Next, in section "Analytic Difficulties," we turn our attention to the specific types of analytic difficulties that are presented by various kinds of missing data problems, while section "Methods for Addressing Missing Data Problems" considers some methods that have been devised to deal with these problems. Finally, in section "Conclusions," we offer some closing thoughts and recommendations for how individual researchers and the field as a whole can make systematic progress in dealing with missing data problems.

TYPES OF MISSING DATA PROBLEMS

A wide range of different types of missing data problems routinely arise in criminology and criminal justice research. In this section, we survey the types of problems that most commonly present themselves and provide some examples of each problem. We specifically address six broad categories of missing data problems in this section: (1) missing administrative and official record data, (2) missing survey data, (3) incomplete responses among survey participants, (4) attrition or loss of cases in longitudinal studies, (5) experimental attrition, and (6) planned nonresponse or incomplete data. While we make no claim that these categories are exhaustive, we do think they cover the broad range of missing data problems that are typically encountered by criminologists.

Missing Administrative and Official Record Data

Major data sources such as the FBI Uniform Crime Reports (UCR), the National Incident Based Reporting System (NIBRS), the Supplemental Homicide Reports (SHR), and data sources used in specific research projects such as arrest, court, prison, probation, and parole records, all suffer from a range of difficulties associated with missing data. For example, the UCR, SHR, and NIBRS programs all depend on voluntary participation by law enforcement agencies, and each year – for a variety of reasons – some fraction of agencies choose not to participate in the program (Maltz and Targonski 2002). For example, it is almost always a bad idea to compare UCR-based crime rate estimates for different jurisdictions because the UCR only measures "crimes known to the police." One basic issue that bedevils such comparisons is that victims in some jurisdictions may be more or less likely to report crimes to the police than victims in other jurisdictions, which itself is a missing data problem. In these instances, inferences about crime rate differences among the jurisdictions will be misleading (i.e., whether one city is "safer" than another).

The problem of missing data also arises in court-related research. For example, in a capital punishment study conducted by Paternoster et al. (2003), the authors relied on data maintained in prosecution and court records for each of the death-eligible offenders. Despite a gubernatorial order granting the researchers direct access to the file folders and case records of each offender, the authors reported substantial amounts of missing data on a number of important characteristics, such as the socioeconomic status of the victim.

Correctional studies are not immune from these problems either. For example, the Bureau of Justice Statistics has conducted two major studies of criminal recidivism among offenders released from prisons in over a dozen states in 1983 (Beck and Shipley 1989) and then again in 1994 (Langan and Levin 2002). In each study, the goal was to take the cohort of offenders released from prison and follow each of them for 3 years to measure recidivism rates in arrest, court, and correctional files. Each of these studies reported nontrivial missing data problems in terms of both the background characteristics and post-release experiences of the offenders.

The use of administrative or official record data is often attractive because of the uniformity of data collection procedures and the standardized recording of events and the dates on which those events occurred. Yet, in criminal justice settings, it is almost inevitable that there will be difficult missing data problems lurking within official record databases. Sometimes, these problems are obvious (e.g., an item is left blank on a rap sheet), and sometimes, they are more subtle (e.g., police can only know about crimes if they witness them or if someone reports them). Nevertheless, researchers working with officially recorded data must always be vigilant to try to think about how missing data problems might be affecting their results.

Missing Survey Data

For the last half century, criminologists have increasingly relied on survey research to study a wide range of crime-related phenomena. In fact, some of the earliest interview studies in criminology challenged longstanding assumptions about the relationship between social class and criminality, which themselves were based on officially recorded data (Nye 1958; Williams and Gold 1972; Tittle et al. 1978; Elliott and Ageton 1980; Hindelang et al. 1981). The power of survey research lies in the insights that intensive detailed study of a relatively small group of people can provide about much larger, interesting populations. Yet, survey research – whether focused on samples drawn from the general population or special populations, or on the study of offending or victimization – must confront the problem of non-response.

Researchers must make decisions about the boundaries of the sampling frame (i.e., who has a chance of being selected to receive a survey). Specifically, if the sample is drawn exclusively from certain subpopulations, then consideration must be given to what is lost by excluding other subpopulations. If the sample is drawn by quota, convenience, purposive, or other nonprobability sampling methods, then consideration should be given to the effects of those sampling designs on both external validity (i.e., to what extent do the results generalize to the entire population of interest?) and internal validity (i.e., are the comparisons within the study fair and reasonable?). The basic problem is that studies that systematically exclude or underrepresent individuals in the target population *may* yield invalid results.

Additionally, researchers must obtain voluntary, informed consent from the individuals they seek to interview. Individuals targeted for survey participation have no obligation to make themselves available to researchers or participate in the research. Thus, survey researchers will always have to deal with two sets of difficult nonresponse problems: (1) some individuals who are targeted for the study can be contacted to determine whether they are willing to participate, while some cannot and (2) among those who are successfully contacted, some will agree to participate, and others will not. Virtually, all survey studies in the criminology literature suffer from nonresponse because of both these issues.

Incomplete Responses Among Survey Participants

If the plan for drawing the sample of survey participants is reasonable and there is no systematic omission of individuals from the study either by failure to contact or refusal to participate, the participants may, nevertheless, not answer some of the questions on the survey (Brame and Paternoster 2003). Sometimes, this type of nonresponse is planned and intentional. An example of planned partial nonresponse would be the use of so-called "gateway questions" or "filter questions" wherein the answer to a certain question dictates whether certain subsequent questions will be skipped. An example would be the question, "Have you used marijuana in the past 12 months?" Those replying "No" to this gateway question would not be asked to respond to the follow-up questions pertaining to the location, social circumstances, and perceived effects of marijuana use. Gateway questions are designed to make the survey more sensible for the respondent, and if planned carefully, they can be helpful for survey researchers. But the use of gateway or contingency questions can present risks for the research when people "skip out" of questions wherein they could have provided useful information. Also, in panel studies, there is a risk of so-called "testing effects" when respondents learn that they can shorten the interview if they answer gateway questions in certain ways.

Leaving aside the issue of gateway questions, respondents are routinely told by researchers – for ethical reasons – that they can refrain from answering questions they don't want to answer. So, respondents can answer some questions but not others. For some items in the survey, the respondent may be able to provide valid data, but, for other items, the respondent may be indistinguishable from individuals who could not be contacted or refused to participate in the survey. A related issue arising in survey research is the proper handling of "don't know" responses or Likert-format "neither agree nor disagree" responses. In this case, researchers cannot categorize their responses into meaningful areas, since respondents lack knowledge of how to respond or have not formed an opinion about the particular subject under investigation.

Attrition in Longitudinal Studies

The criminology literature is increasingly populated by various types of studies with a longitudinal component. In some cases, these studies involve the study of a small number of highly aggregated units over time (time-series studies). In other cases, researchers repeatedly follow the same large group of individuals over time (panel studies). Some studies are also able to follow a large number of units over very long periods of time (pooled cross-sectional time-series studies). Regardless of whether the study is focused on changes in crime rates as neighborhood dynamics unfold within a city or whether the study examines how criminal behavior develops and evolves for individuals over the life span, attrition or drop-out is always a potential threat to the study's validity (Brame and Paternoster 2003).

In fact, different kinds of attrition can cause problems for researchers. Cases may be present at the beginning of a study and then drop out; or they may drop out and then drop back in. Individuals die or become incapacitated, new schools open and old schools close, and neighborhoods emerge and then vanish. In other words, one of the hazards of studying cases over time is that the population of cases that is *relevant* for the study and the population of cases *available* for study are both subject to change while a longitudinal study is underway. And, of course, since study participation is voluntary, prior study participants can change their mind about whether they want to continue participating in a study (also generally an ethical requirement). An interesting and useful feature of studies suffering from attrition is that some information is usually known about the cases that drop out – as distinguished from many missing data problems wherein little or nothing may be known about missing cases (see e.g., Brame and Piquero 2003). The advantage of this is that, sometimes, it is possible to make inferences about the missing data based upon information that is available about the cases.

Attrition in Experimental Studies

Attrition is often viewed as a problem with longitudinal studies, but it is an equally important problem in criminal justice field experiments. As an example, consider the experimental studies in the Spouse Assault Replication Program (see e.g., Sherman and Berk 1984; Hirschel and Hutchison 1992). In these studies, misdemeanor domestic violence cases were randomly assigned to arrest and nonarrest treatment conditions. An important outcome measure in these experiments is information about future victimization obtained from victim interviews. The problem is that many of the victims – for a variety of reasons – could not be interviewed. Even though the cases in the different treatment groups are comparable to each other because of the experimental design, it does not follow that the subsample of interviewed cases in the different treatment groups are comparable to each other.

Table 14.1 presents a concrete example of this important problem from the Charlotte Spouse Abuse Experiment (Brame 2000). In this study, only about half of the victims participated in the 6-month follow-up interviews. Within this subsample of interviewed cases, approximately 60% of the victims reported that they had been revictimized. What the observed victim interview data cannot tell us is whether the revictimization rates are higher, lower, or about the same for the noninterviewed cases. Another, more complicated, issue is whether these differences vary in important ways between the different treatment groups. In sum, if the revictimization rates vary in some systematic way for the missing and observed cases, we will have problems obtaining a valid estimate of the treatment effect.

It is fair to point out that this problem is not unique to experimental designs. But the purpose of conducting an experiment is to ensure that comparisons of different groups are, in fact, apples-to-apples comparisons. If interview nonresponse or some other form of attrition leaves us with groups that are not comparable or attrition biases that cause other problems,

TABLE 14.1. Prevalence of victim interview-based recidivism by treatment

| Victim interview-based recidivism | Assigned Treatment Group | | | |
	Arrest	Citation	Separate/advise	Total
No subsequent assaults	46	43	41	130
At least one subsequent assault	66	81	61	208
Number interviewed	112	124	102	338
Total number of cases	214	224	212	650
Proportion of cases interviewed	0.500	0.554	0.481	0.520
Proportion of interviewed cases with new victimization	0.589	0.653	0.598	0.615

the additional effort and expense that often go into planning and implementing an experiment might not be worthwhile. In these instances, it may be preferable to conduct a well-controlled observational study.

Planned Nonresponse or Incomplete Data

In some situations, nonresponse or the acquisition of incomplete information is actually formally built into a study's research design. The classic example of this situation is the United States Census Bureau's long and short forms used in conducting the decennial census of the population (which criminologists often analyze) (Gauthier 2002:137). While the Census Bureau attempts to collect certain pieces of information from the entire U.S. population, a more detailed database of information is collected on a probability sample of the population. On the basis of the information provided by the probability sample, it is possible to form inferences about the more detailed information on the long form for the entire population. In this type of situation, planned nonresponse provides a way to make research, data collection, and analysis activities more efficient and economically feasible.

Other types of nonresponse and incomplete data problems, while not built formally into the design, are anticipated with certainty by the research team. For example, a typical recidivism study must pick a date (or dates) on which to conduct follow-up record searches to identify those who recidivated and individuals who did not. One problem is that the status of nonrecidivist is subject to change each and every day. If an individual is a nonrecidivist at the time the records are searched but then recidivates the next day, that individual is counted as a nonrecidivist for purposes of the study. This is also referred to as "right censored data" or "suspended data" (Maltz 1984; Schmidt and Witte 1988). The term "right censored" indicates that the events of interest (i.e., committing new offenses) could have occurred to the right of the last data collection point and therefore go unobserved if subsequent data collections are not administered.

Another type of censoring problem is known as "interval censored data" wherein the analyst does not know the exact time an event occurred, but only that it did, in fact, occur. An example of interval censored data is when individuals are assessed every 6 months and asked to self-report their involvement in criminal activity. At the time of the assessment, it is only determined that the individual did or did not recidivate. If a unit did recidivate, it is not known precisely when the new offense occurred, but only that a failure (a new offense) did indeed occur; instead of an exact time to failure, the analyst would only be in a position to record that the failure occurred between, for example, the third and fourth data collection interval. A special case of interval censored data is referred to as "left censored data" wherein the failure occurred between time zero and a particular inspection time. To continue with the example above, left censoring would be present if a failure occurred prior to the first assessment; the specific time after release before which the event occurred is unknown.

The provisional nature of outcomes, as illustrated above, is not a purely criminological problem. In fact, researchers in other fields such as engineering, medicine, psychology, sociology, and economics often study outcomes that are subject to change after the study has ended (Maltz 1984). As discussed above, generally, researchers refer to this problem as "censoring," and data with provisional outcomes are called "censored." Studies can always be lengthened or extended, so updating can occur, but unless the study is carried out over very long periods of time (sometimes requiring multiple generations of researchers), with very specific documentation in detailing the time in which an event occurred, the problem of censoring will always be present and require attention.

A different but related issue arises when cases are only observed when they exhibit certain characteristics or behaviors and those characteristics or behaviors are actually part of the outcome measure. For example, suppose we wish to study variation in the frequency of offending, only individuals who offend at least one time are observed. In these situations, we say the sample is "truncated." Truncation is different from censoring. When data are censored, we actually get to see characteristics of individuals who are censored – what we can't see is their final status; only their provisional status can be seen. When data are truncated, we only get to see the characteristics of individuals who score above the lower limit and below the upper limit of truncation; for other cases, we know nothing about the variables of interest. Thus, censoring is actually more of a problem of incomplete, but partially observed, data, while truncation is actually a problem of completely missing data for cases outside the limits of inclusion in the sample.

Overall, what planned nonresponse, censoring, and truncation all have in common is that they can be anticipated ahead of time by researchers, and analytic methods for addressing them can be planned in advance of data collection efforts (Maddala 1983). Planning for other types of missing data problems will usually be more speculative until the study is underway or concluded.

ANALYTIC DIFFICULTIES

Up to this point, we have been discussing specific kinds of missing data problems without saying much about the difficulties and consequences they create. In this section, we will consider how some of these problems correspond and relate to terminology used by statisticians to describe various missing data problems. We then consider the consequences of different types of missing data problems for the kind of inferential work usually conducted by criminologists. Although the problems discussed in this section are not necessarily mutually exclusive or exhaustive, we think the labels we use and the problems we describe will be recognizable to most criminologists as the most prevalent problems in the field.

Missing Units

This is perhaps the most basic type of missing data problem. It occurs when cases that should have been included in the study (to support the study inferences) are not included. The problem of missing units can occur for a variety of reasons: data were not available, potential participants could not be located or refused to participate, or potential participants were not included in the sampling frame. The researcher may be aware of which cases are missing and know some things about those cases, or the researcher may be oblivious to the existence of those cases. The consequences of missing units can range from simply reducing statistical efficiency of parameter estimates (i.e., increasing the size of the standard errors) to severely biased and misleading parameter estimates.

Missing Items on Otherwise Observed Units

This problem arises when some data are available but other data is missing for certain cases. Items could be missing from administrative data sources because of data recording or data entry problems, individuals may respond "don't know" or prefer not to answer some questions, they may not have seen the question or some variation of planned non-response such as censoring, truncation, or a mixture of simple surveys combined with intensive surveys on a sample may be the source of partially observed data. Attrition from longitudinal studies can also be viewed as a special case of the problem of partially observed data; at some time points, a case supplies data, while at other time points, that case is missing. The range of consequences for this problem is similar to that of the missing units problem: a loss of statistical efficiency and power but no bias to severely biased and misleading parameter estimates.

Missing Completely at Random

According to Little and Rubin (1987), units which are not observed or only partially observed may be missing completely at random. Allison (2002: 3) writes that the data on some measured variable Y are said to be missing completely at random (MCAR) "if the probability of missing data on Y is unrelated to the value of Y itself or to the values of any other variables in the data set." If $p(x|y) = p(x)$, we say that x and y are independent of each other. Using the notation of Little and Rubin (1987), MCAR implies that

$$p(M|x_{\mathrm{o}}, x_{\mathrm{m}}) = p(M) \tag{14.1}$$

where M is a variable which indicates whether individuals have missing data or not and x_{o} and x_{m} refer to observed and missing data. If missingness is independent of both the observed and missing data, we say that the data are missing completely at random.

Oftentimes, this is a desirable result because it means that the observed sample is a representative sample of the target population. In other words, on average, missing and observed cases do not differ systematically from each other. A violation of the MCAR assumption would occur if, say, those who fail to provide responses to self-reported offending items on a questionnaire were also on average lower in self-control than those who supplied complete information. However, as we will argue below, even if the missing data on one variable is unrelated to missing data on others, it does not prove that the data are missing completely at random.

The main consequence of MCAR is a loss of efficiency. That is, parameter estimates obtained from MCAR samples will have larger standard errors (owing to smaller sample sizes) than estimates obtained from samples with no missing data at all. But estimator properties of unbiasedness or consistency (bias tends to zero as sample size increases) will still hold in MCAR samples.

Unfortunately, while the MCAR assumption can be called into question by identifying differences between missing and observed cases on characteristics that are observed for all cases, it is a very strong assumption and can never be proven or empirically demonstrated to be true. Even if missing and observed cases look similar to each other on characteristics observed for both groups, there may not be many characteristics on which to compare them; even if there are more than a few characteristics on which to compare them, it is always possible that the groups look different on factors that can only be seen in the observed cases, or that the groups differ with respect to factors that are unobserved for everyone. If a researcher wishes to assert MCAR (which is often a hazardous exercise), the strongest case is showing that observed and missing cases are comparable to each other on a wide range of characteristics (that can be seen for both groups), and a plausible narrative about why the process producing the missing data is likely to operate in a way that will lead to no systematic differences between observed and missing cases.

Missing at Random

According to Little and Rubin's (1987) taxonomy of missing data, cases are missing at random (MAR) when the missing and observed cases are similar to each other after conditioning the analysis on measured variables for the observed cases. They note that the data are missing at random when

$$p(M|x_o, x_m) = p(M|x_o) \tag{14.2}$$

which implies that the missing data patterns are not completely random, but that they are random after conditioning on the observed data. If the probability model for the missing data is $p(M)$ or $p(M|x_o)$, then the missing data mechanism is "ignorable."

This assumption is weaker than MCAR, which requires missing and observed cases similar to each other *without conditioning* on any variables – measured or unmeasured. In our previous example, the self-reported offending data would be missing at random if the probability of missing self-report data depended upon a person's level of self-control, but within every level of self-control, the probability of an individual missing data on self-reported offending was unrelated to one's level of self-reported offending.

Similar to MCAR, the validity of the MAR assumption cannot be tested. Clearly, it is not possible to know whether conditioning on measured variables for observed cases is a sufficient adjustment for biases caused by unmeasured variables. In other words, because we do not observe the missing data on self-reported offending, we cannot compare the level of self-control for those with and without self-reported offending data. Thus, the validity of MAR is asserted – but cannot be demonstrated by the researcher, and the assertion is generally accompanied by a narrative about why it is reasonable to think that conditioning on measured variables for the observed cases is sufficient to remove bias caused by missing data. Most formal adjustments for missing data in the criminology and criminal justice literature invoke – either implicitly or explicitly – the MAR assumption.

Nonignorable Nonresponse

According to Little and Rubin (1987) and Allison (2002), the MCAR and MAR assumptions imply that the "missing data mechanism" (i.e., the process which determines which cases are observed and which are missing) is ignorable. In these situations, it will be possible to obtain a point estimate and a measure of uncertainty for that point estimate (i.e., a standard error). However, in some situations, the MCAR and MAR assumptions will not be plausible. For example, it may be that there are simply not many variables measured even for the observed cases, or that variables which could help build a convincing case for MAR are not measured. The basic problem here is that conditioning on measured variables for the observed cases is not sufficient to ensure that the missing and observed cases are equivalent on variables where there is missing data. Little and Rubin (1987) note that nonignorable missing data exists when:

$$p(M|x_0, x_m) \qquad (14.3)$$

and is not equal to either $p(M)$ or $p(M|x_0)$.

As noted by Little and Rubin (1987), nonignorable missing data models generally imply the use of a sensitivity analysis of some sort. More specifically, nonignorable models require the researcher to formally characterize or specify the process by which some cases have observed data and other cases have missing data in order to arrive at satisfactory parameter estimates. Since the process generating the missing data is not generally well understood and the data contain no information about what is driving the process, it is advisable for the researcher to consider a number of different possible missing data mechanisms. This type of analysis, then, allows the researcher to consider the sensitivity of the final analysis results to variation in untestable assumptions about the missing data mechanism. Little and Rubin (1987) and Rubin (1987) also discuss how this approach can be implemented within a Bayesian framework where the goal is to estimate the posterior distribution of the parameter of interest after specifying appropriate prior distributions for the missing data mechanism and the parameters of substantive interest. In one respect, nonignorable analyses are attractive because they allow us to relax some of the restrictive assumptions on which MCAR and MAR analyses depend. But, these models will also require the researcher to tell a more complicated story about the findings and how sensitive the findings are to different sets of untestable assumptions. These models also tend to be more difficult to estimate and often require specialized computer programming and software development.

Sample Selection Bias

One special class of missing data problems arising in criminology and criminal justice research is the problem of studying individuals who are observed because some event has occurred (i.e., a selected sample) (Glynn et al. 1986). For example, if we study decisions to imprison offenders, we must bear in mind that individuals who could be imprisoned (or placed on probation) must first be convicted of a crime. To obtain valid parameter estimates of the effects of covariates on sentencing outcomes, it would be necessary to properly adjust for the selection process. A widely used approach is the Heckman (1976) two-stage procedure wherein one initially estimates the selection process before obtaining estimates of the substantive process of interest.

Ideally, one would simultaneously estimate models of both the conviction process among all charged offenders and the sentencing process among the convicted offenders. A problem that arises in this literature is the need for valid exclusion restrictions. An exclusion restriction is a variable that is assumed to have important effects on the selection variable (first stage) but no effect on the substantive outcome variable (second stage). If this assumption can be justified theoretically, then it is possible to jointly model the processes governing sample selection and the substantive outcome. If the assumption cannot be justified, then the statistical model depends on untestable assumptions about the bivariate distribution of the error terms of the selection and substantive equations; this is a condition that Smith and Paternoster (1991) and Smith et al. (1989) referred to as "weak identification."[1] Little and Schenker (1995) go even further, concluding that "the approach cannot be generally recommended." A recent discussion of this estimator by Bushway et al. (2007) appears in the criminology literature and offers detailed consideration of the advantages, disadvantages and difficulties involved in implementing this estimator.

METHODS FOR ADDRESSING MISSING DATA PROBLEMS

In this section, we discuss the various methodological strategies researchers could employ when faced with missing data problems. In so doing, we offer some thoughts about the kinds of issues researchers should consider when making decisions about how to proceed when missing data is a problem. Inevitably, many of these decisions are predicated on the assumptions about the types of missing data discussed above.

Listwise Deletion of Missing Cases

One simple option is to drop cases on any observations that have missing data for any variable that will be included in the model to be estimated and then proceed with a conventional analysis. When the researcher believes the data are MCAR, no further adjustments are necessary for valid analyses, since the sample based upon the listwise deletion will be a random sample of the original. As noted above, however, MCAR is a strong assumption and should be accompanied by a discussion as to why it is plausible in any particular study. Further, if the data are MAR and not MCAR, then parameter estimates will be biased. Allison (2002: 6) notes that listwise deletion of missing data is the method that is the most robust to violation of the MAR assumption among the independent variables in a regression analysis. In other words, if the probability of missing data on any of the independent variables is not related to the dependent variable, then obtained regression estimates will be unbiased. Cases with missing data are also dropped in some other kinds of analyses – particularly when weights for nonresponse are used. But most efforts to weight do not invoke the MCAR assumption. In these instances, missing cases are dropped, but the assumption underlying the weights is that the data are MAR or that the missing data mechanism is nonignorable.

Pairwise Deletion of Missing Cases

Some multivariate analyses – such as factor analysis, linear regression analysis, and structural equation modeling – are capable of generating solutions and estimates based exclusively on correlation or covariance matrices involving two or more variables (some of which may have missing data). Observations with missing data can be deleted before estimating these matrices (listwise deletion) or each of the individual correlations or covariances can be estimated on the

---

[1] In effect, a well-justified exclusion restriction allows for the estimation of a MAR model; in the absence of a well-justified exclusion restriction, the only alternative is to impose constraints on the bivariate distribution of the error term. Any constraint imposed would be an example of a nonignorable missing data model.

cases that have valid data on which the correlation can be estimated (pairwise deletion). Some software packages provide researchers with the option of selecting listwise or pairwise (also known as available case analysis) deletion of missing data. As Little and Schenker (1995:45) note, an important problem with correlation or covariance matrices estimated after pairwise deletion is not always positive definite (which implies noninvertability). This problem is more likely to arise when there is a good deal of variation in the rates of missing data for the variables included in the matrix.

Dummy Coded Missing Data Indicators

Sometimes, when missing data exists for an independent or control variable, X, in a regression analysis, researchers can create a dummy variable D, coded 1.0 if the variable has missing data and 0.0 otherwise (Cohen and Cohen 1983). Another variable X^* is also created such that

$$X^* = X \text{ when data are not missing on } X$$
$$X^* = Z \text{ when data are missing on } X$$

where Z can be any constant, though for interpretational purposes Z is usually the mean of X among those cases without missing data. This technically allows each case to contribute information to the analysis. This can be done for any number of right-hand-side variables that have missing data. Then, X^*, D and other variables can be included in the estimated regression model. In this instance, the coefficient for D is the predicted value of the dependent variable for those with missing data on X minus the predicted value of Y for those at the mean of Y, controlling for other variables in the model. The estimated coefficient for X^* is the effect of X among those that have observed data on X.

While this type of analysis will provide parameter estimates, the estimator does have two important shortcomings. First, the coefficient estimates are biased (Allison 2002: 11). Second, the missing dummy variables only allow researchers to see whether rates of missing data vary for different groups within the sample under study. They do not tell us anything about the true unobserved values of the variables that are missing. Other approaches that rely on imputation and weighting attempt to overcome this problem.

Model-Based Imputation

Another method for keeping cases with missing observations in the analysis is to impute or "plug" missing values with some guess about what the value of the variable would have been if it had been observed, and the analysis then proceeds as if there were no missing data (Little and Rubin 1987). The basis for this guess or prediction is the imputation model. In the simplest case, an analyst could simply substitute a mean or median to fill in the missing data. This method, mean substitution, is known to produce biased estimates of the variances and covariances. The analyst might also estimate a regression model on the nonmissing cases wherein the dependent variable, Y, is the variable with missing data and the independent variables are the other relevant variables in the data set thought to be related to Y. Then, the model is used to estimate predicted values of the missing variable for the cases with missing data. These predictions could be plugged in directly or they could be drawn from a probability distribution for that variable. Rubin (1987) has suggested that only three to ten imputations are likely to be needed in most applications. He has shown (1987: 114) that the efficiency of an estimate based on m imputations can be determined as

$$\left(1 + \frac{\gamma}{m}\right)^{-1} \tag{14.4}$$

where γ is the proportion of missing data.

Unless there is a large proportion of missing data, there is little computational advantage in producing more than five imputations. While there are different methods to impute the missing data, all suffer from the same problem that they produce coefficient standard errors that are smaller than what they should be, leading to biased hypothesis tests.

When conducting a final analysis with imputed data, it is important to adjust the standard errors for the uncertainty or sampling variation that is created by the fact that the imputed values are not known. Since they are estimated, they create additional variation that must be taken into consideration. Therefore, standard error formulas that ignore the imputation of the missing data will generally be biased toward zero. Imputations can be based on nonignorable models, or they can assume MAR.

Hot Deck Imputation

Hot deck imputation, used frequently by the U.S. Census Bureau to impute missing values in public-use data sets, differs from model-based imputation insofar as the basis for the imputation is not a statistical model but a "donor" case with valid data (Heitjan and Little 1991). First, the researcher identifies a case with missing data on a variable but has some observed characteristics. Next, the researcher looks for a donor case with valid data and a similar set of observed characteristics. The donor's value on the missing variable is then used as the basis for imputing data for the case with missing information on that variable. Generally, the donor's value would not be directly imputed but would first be perturbed and then imputed. As in model-based imputation, formulas that take the uncertainty of the imputation into account in calculating standard errors must be used in the final analysis.

Weighting

One of the most common methods of adjusting for missing data involves the construction of sampling weights. In general, a sampling weight is the inverse of the probability of being selected for the sample. The problem with missing data is that the self-weighted sample represents only the nonmissing cases. The goal of weighting estimators to adjust for missing data is to ensure that the weighted sample appropriately represents both the missing and the nonmissing cases. One way to construct the sampling weights, then, is to identify the individuals with valid data who look very much like the individuals with missing data on characteristics that are observed for all cases. In the final weighted analysis, these individuals will receive more weight. On the other hand, observed individuals who look less like the missing cases on observed characteristics will tend to receive less weight. Although the goal of weighting the sample is to ensure that both observed and missing cases are adequately represented in the final analysis, the success of that effort cannot be rigorously tested. Thus, weighted estimators share some of the same ambiguities that confront other approaches to missing data; ultimately, if the data are missing, there will be some conjecture about whether corrective measures produce valid inferences.[2]

EM Algorithm

Tanner (1996) is one of many careful discussions about the expectation–maximization (EM) algorithm (see also, McLachlan and Krishnan 1997). The principle behind the algorithm is to iterate to a final solution by imputing or estimating data (either imputation or certain statistics) (the E or expectation step) and then maximizing the log-likelihood function (the M or maximization step). Each of the iterations consists of one E-step and one M-step. Once improvement in maximizing the log of the likelihood function becomes very small, the algorithm is said to have converged. As Tanner (1996:64) notes, the EM algorithm allows researchers to address missing data problems by substituting a single, complex analysis with "a series of simpler analyses." A number of computer programs are now available for estimating models via the EM algorithm. Schafer (1997, 1999) has made available the NORM program that does the EM algorithm and is free to users at: http://www.stat.psu.edu/~jls/misoftwa.html. SPSS version 16 also contains a missing data procedure that does an EM algorithm. Nevertheless, the EM algorithm is a more advanced topic and expert assistance should be sought when trying to implement it in applied settings.

Mixture Models

Another advanced approach to dealing with missing data is to view the entire population as a mixture of two subpopulations (observed and missing cases). The overall inference is based on averaging the parameters for the two groups where the weight of each group is directly proportional to the percentage of the population in that group (Holland 1986:150). Glynn et al. (1986) and Holland (1986) discuss this model as an alternative to traditional sample selection models. According to these authors, the mixture parameterization is more transparent than the sample selection model. In fact, mixture models show clearly how inferences about the entire population are sensitive to the specification of the model that corresponds to the missing observations. The implication of this work is that the identification of both mixture and selection models depends on strong assumptions that may be too strong for ignorable analyses. Sensitivity analysis may be the best way to proceed.

CONCLUSIONS

Missing data problems are a nearly ubiquitous feature of criminology and criminal justice research projects. Whether the research is focused on the analysis of administrative records within a criminal justice agency or direct interviews with offenders or crime victims, missing data is almost certain to create ambiguity and difficulties for analysts. There are reasons

---

[2] Additionally, weighted estimators require specialized formulas for calculating variances and standard errors, which are available in some but not all software packages.

to believe that the problem of missing data in criminal justice research may become more pronounced in years to come. For example, in criminal justice field research settings, it is becoming increasingly common for Institutional Review Boards (IRB's) to require researchers to be more comprehensive in their consideration and description of risks to study participants. As researchers begin to emphasize the risks of research to potential study participants, they may begin to withhold their consent at higher rates. Additionally, in an era of increased reliance on cell phones and decreased reliance on landline telephones, it is rapidly becoming more difficult to track individuals down and contact them to participate in research studies. This problem is compounded in longitudinal studies as contact information may change over the course of the study. Despite the regularity with which incomplete data and nonresponse occur, however, the issue has received relatively little attention within the field.

Fortunately for the field, a wide range of tools have been emerging which should lead us to more principled treatments of missing data problems. These treatments range from the use of selection and mixture models to imputations and nonresponse weighting. Commonly used statistical software packages such as SAS, R, and Stata have all seen major improvements to their ability to handle missing data in more rigorous ways in recent years. What is needed now is more intensive training of researchers in the thoughtful use of these tools. This will require criminologists and criminal justice researchers to actively engage with professional statisticians and methodologists about the interesting and difficult missing data problems that commonly arise in our field.

Among the most pressing needs is for criminology and criminal justice researchers to become aware of the distinctions between different types of missing data, how missing data problems threaten the validity of commonly used research designs in the field, and the best ways of addressing the uncertainty missing data creates. In particular, we think the field would benefit by thinking more carefully about including sensitivity analysis in studies with missing data. While sensitivity analysis may not be the most prominent feature of our data analysis efforts, it should probably be present most of the time and be discussed in the appendices and footnotes of our research papers. Ultimately, missing data implies that uncertainty and more systematic, careful consideration of missing data problems will be a step in the right direction.

REFERENCES

Allison PD (2002) Missing data. Sage, Thousand Oaks, CA

Beck AJ, Shipley BE (1989) Recidivism of prisoners released in 1983. Bureau of Justice Statistics, Special Report. U.S. Department of Justice, Bureau of Justice Statistics, Washington, DC

Brame R (2000) Investigating treatment effects in a domestic violence experiment with partially missing outcome data. J Quant Criminol 16:283–314

Brame R, Paternoster R (2003) Missing data problems in criminological research: two case studies. J Quant Criminol 19:55–78

Brame R, Piquero AR (2003) Selective attrition and the age-crime relationship. J Quant Criminol 19:107–127

Bushway SD, Johnson BD, Slocum LA (2007) Is the magic still there? the use of the Heckman two-step correction for selection bias in criminology. J Quant Criminol 23:151–178

Cohen J, Cohen P (1983) Applied multiple regression/correlation analysis for the behavioral sciences, 2nd edn. Lawrence Erlbaum Associates, New York

Elliott DS, Ageton SS (1980) Reconciling race and class differences in self-reported and official estimates of delinquency. Am Sociol Rev 45:95–110

Gauthier JG (2002) Measuring America: The Decennial Census From 1790 to 2000. U.S. Department of Commerce, Washington, DC

Glynn RJ, Laird NM, Rubin DB (1986) Selection modeling versus mixture modeling with nonignorable nonresponse. In: Wainer H (ed) Drawing inferences from self-selected samples. Springer, New York, pp 115–142

Heckman J (1976) The common structure of statistical models of truncated, sample selection and limited dependent variables, and a simple estimator of such models. Ann Econ Soc Meas 5:475–492

Heitjan DF, Little R (1991) Multiple imputation for the fatal accident reporting system. Appl Stat 40:13–29

Hirschel D, Hutchison IW (1992) Female spouse abuse and the police response: The Charlotte, North Carolina Experiment. Journal of Criminal Law and Criminology 83:73–119

Holland PW (1986) A comment on remarks by Rubin and Hartigan. In: Wainer H (ed) Drawing inferences from self-selected samples. Springer, New York, pp 149–151

Hindelang MJ, Hirschi T, Weis JG (1981) Measuring delinquency. Sage, Beverly Hills, CA

Langan PA, Levin DJ (2002) Recidivism of prisoners released in 1994. Bureau of Justice Statistics Special Report. U.S. Department of Justice, Bureau of Justice Statistics, Washington, DC

Little RJA, Rubin DB (1987) Statistical analysis with missing data. Wiley, New York

Little RJA, Schenker N (1995) Missing data. In: Arminger G, Clogg CC, Sobel ME (eds) Handbook for statistical modeling in the social and behavioral sciences. Plenum, New York, pp 39–75

Maddala GS (1983) Limited-dependent and qualitative variables in econometrics. Cambridge University Press, New York

Maltz MD (1984) Recidivism. Academic, New York

Maltz MD, Targonski J (2002) A note on the use of county-level UCR data. Journal of Quantitative Criminology 18:297–318

McLachlan GJ, Krishnan T (1997) The EM algorithm and extensions. Wiley, New York

Nye F (1958) Family relationships and delinquent behavior. Wiley, New York

Paternoster R, Brame R, Bacon S Ditchfield A (2003) An empirical analysis of Maryland's Death Sentence System with respect to the influence of race and legal jurisdiction. Unpublished manuscript. University of Maryland, College Park, MD

Rubin DB (1987) Multiple imputation for nonresponse in surveys. Wiley, New York

Schafer JL (1997) Analysis of incomplete multivariate data. Chapman & Hall, London

Schafer JL (1999) Multiple imputation: a primer. Stat Methods Med Res 8:3–15

Sherman LW, Berk RA (1984) The specific deterrent effects of arrest for domestic assault American Sociological Review 49(2):261–271

Schmidt P, Witte AD (1988) Predicting recidivism using survival models. Springer, New York

Smith DA, Paternoster R (1991) Formal processing and future delinquency: deviance amplification as selection artifact. Law Soc Rev 24:1109–1131

Smith DA, Wish ED, Jarjoura GR (1989) Drug use and pretrial misconduct in New York City. J Quant Criminol 5:101–126

Tanner MA (1996) Tools for statistical inference: methods for the exploration of posterior distributions and likelihood functions, 3rd edn. Springer, New York

Tittle CR, Villemez WJ, Smith DA (1978) The myth of social class and criminality: an empirical assessment of the empirical evidence. Am Sociol Rev 43:643–656

Williams JR, Gold M (1972) From delinquent behavior to official delinquency. Soc Probl 20:209–229

CHAPTER 15

The Life Event Calendar Method in Criminological Research

JENNIFER ROBERTS AND JULIE HORNEY

The life events calendar (LEC), used in a number of fields for collecting retrospective data on one or more aspects of individuals' lives, has been variously referred to as the "life history calendar," "event history calendar," "life chart interview," "calendar method," "calendar interviewing," and "timeline followback" method. Regardless of the name, the method capitalizes on what is known about the storage of autobiographical memory and involves entering key time markers on a calendar in order to facilitate the recall of events and life circumstances.

With increased use of the LEC across a variety of disciplines, more attention has been focused on this method and on the quality of data resulting from its use. Early reviews of the method and its utility were provided by Freedman et al. (1988) and by Caspi et al. (1996). More recently, Belli and colleagues have written extensively about the method's theoretical foundations and have conducted important research comparing the LEC to more traditional methodological approaches (Belli 1998; Belli et al. 2001, 2007, 2009).

In this chapter, we update information on the LEC methodology and its utility while focusing on applications in criminology. We start by describing the theoretical underpinnings of the LEC methodology, and then we elaborate on the varied ways calendars are employed by providing detailed criminological examples. We then move to a discussion of practical design and implementation issues, following with a review of studies on the quality of calendar data. Finally, we discuss future directions for LEC research.

THEORETICAL UNDERPINNINGS OF THE LEC

In all of its various forms, the LEC facilitates recall through processes that capitalize on the sequential and hierarchical storage of memory (Caspi et al. 1996; Belli 1998). Sequential storage was emphasized by Bradburn et al. (1987), who used the term "autobiographical sequences" to refer to linked sets of events that are remembered together. They gave the example of a person remembering a visit to the dentist "as part of an extended temporal-causal unit beginning with a toothache, continuing with an initial appointment, and finishing with the last of a series of dental visits (p. 158)."

A.R. Piquero and D. Weisburd (eds.), *Handbook of Quantitative Criminology*,
DOI 10.1007/978-0-387-77650-7_15, © Springer Science + Business Media, LLC 2010,
First softcover printing 2011

Other theorists (Barsalou 1988; Brewer 1986; Conway 1996; Linton 1986) have emphasized the hierarchical structure of stored memories. Belli (1998) summarized this literature, describing three types of hierarchically organized memories. At the top of the hierarchy are extended events – those that last for relatively long periods of time, have distinctive starting and stopping points, and are relatively easily remembered. Extended events typically represent some phase of a person's life, such as a first marriage, working in a particular factory, or serving a prison sentence. These events tend to be the basic building blocks for organizing memory, and they serve as useful cues for events lower in the hierarchy. In the middle of the hierarchy are summarized events, which have common themes and last for time periods generally shorter than those occupied by extended events. These might include periods of hanging out regularly in bars or using drugs heavily. At the bottom of the hierarchy are specific events, such as burglaries, domestic violence victimizations, or arrests, that can be pinpointed to short, distinctive time periods.

In facilitating recall, the LEC method capitalizes on the structure of memory storage in three distinct ways (Barsalou 1988; Belli 1998; Caspi et al. 1996; Conway 1996). First, in order to tap into memories stored in autobiographical sequences, interviewers use sequential cuing, generally by tracking a particular domain for the entire calendar period before moving to another domain. For example, by entering all residences for the calendar period, an interviewer takes advantage of a respondent's memory of a sequence of moves (such as moving from the apartment on Main Street where the respondent lived with friends to the house on Fifth Avenue, where he moved in with a romantic partner). The interviewer might then proceed to the domain of employment, where the respondent might rely on linked memories to report that he moved from the assembly line job to a supervisor's position, and so on.

Second, parallel cuing encourages respondents to tap into cross-domain associations. A respondent who is struggling to remember precisely when he started a particular job can be prompted by asking whether the job coincided with residence X or Y, or relationship X or Y. Finally, top-down cuing capitalizes on the hierarchical structure of memory by using the extended events at the top of the hierarchy to cue the recall for summarized events and specific events that are nested within those broader life periods. Thinking about a period when living with friends, for example, can help a respondent remember periods in which he was going out to bars several nights a week. These memories, in turn, can facilitate the memory of specific events, such as bar fights, that occurred during that time.

Through all these cuing processes the LEC "contextualizes events by connecting them to other events; less-easily remembered events may then be more reliably recalled when connected to other more memorable life events" (Caspi et al. 1996, p. 104). These more memorable events have been referred to as time markers or cognitive "landmarks" (Loftus and Marburger 1983; Belli 1998) in the storage of memories. A blank calendar can provide dates that frame a reference period, but research has shown the importance of salient events and life circumstances in improving recall. A classic study by Loftus and Marburger (1983) found that survey respondents given time markers as cues (e.g., "Since the first major eruption of Mt. St. Helens, has anyone beaten you up?") were less likely to telescope forward their recall of victimizations compared to survey respondents in the traditional condition (e.g., "In the past 6 months, did anyone beat you up?").

VARIETIES OF LEC APPLICATION

In some studies, the LEC has been used primarily as a visual cue to frame a reference period and enhance the recall of events or behavior elicited through traditional survey questions. In the RAND Second Inmate Survey (Peterson et al. 1982), for example, a calendar was used to frame the 24-month period for which researchers wanted to measure the rates of criminal offending. In group administered surveys, prison inmates were instructed to mark pre-printed calendars to show the months during which they were "on the street" before their most recent incarceration. They were then asked a series of questions about their life circumstances during the reference period, including where and with whom they were living. Although these circumstances were not entered on the calendar, their recall was intended to help respondents answer questions about the number of crimes committed during the reference period.

In most criminological applications, the LEC has been used as a tool for collecting time-based data as well as a tool for stimulating memory. As Schubert et al. (2004) observed regarding juvenile offenders, collecting time-based data is challenging because their "lives often are chaotic and unstable, with frequent changes in residence, education, employment, and interpersonal relationships" (p. 7). These problems apply widely to the subjects of criminological research, and they make the use of the LEC appealing.

LEC designs for collecting time-based data have ranged from the simplest paper calendars with check lists of a few basic life circumstances to complex computerized calendars designed to chart numerous domains in great detail. The calendars have been designed to address recall periods that are relatively short (e.g., 6 months) while others span entire lifetimes. They have been used to collect data on specific incidents, key life transitions, and spells of continuing activities. Here, we describe several versions of the LEC that have been used to collect time-based data of interest to criminologists.

Simple Checklist Calendar

In one of the simplest applications of the LEC, Horney and Marshall (1991, 1992), in a methodological elaboration of the RAND study with Nebraska inmates, used two paper calendars with basic checklists to collect monthly data on life circumstances and on offending (see crime calendar in Fig. 15.1). Interviewers questioned respondents about their lives and their criminal involvement for a period preceding their most recent arrest and placed checks on the calendar to capture the timing of these circumstances. The data were analyzed to study the correspondence between local life circumstances and criminal involvement (e.g., offending during periods of living with a wife) over a period between 25 and 36 months (Horney et al. 1995). Versions of these simple calendars were later used to study male and female probationers (MacKenzie and Li 2002; Li and MacKenzie 2003) and female jail inmates (Griffin and Armstrong 2003; Armstrong and Griffin 2007).

Grid Calendar with Multiple Domains

Whereas the LEC applications described earlier involved one-time surveys, the LEC has also been used in conjunction with prospective longitudinal studies in order to provide a more complete account of the time between the waves of data collection. In their New Zealand birth

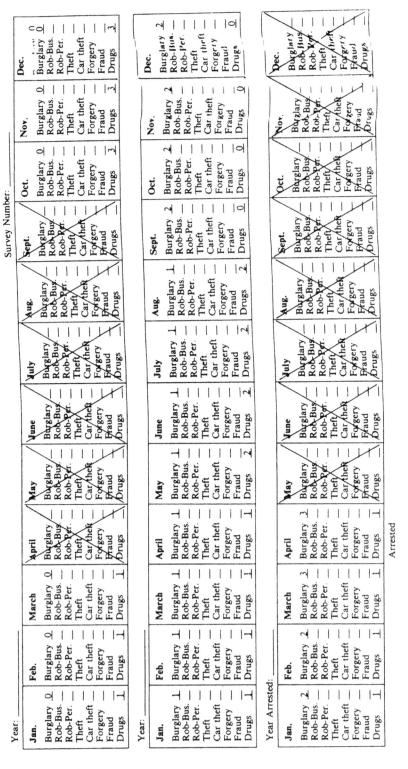

FIGURE 15.1. "Checklist Crime Calendar," originally published in Horney and Marshall (1991: Fig. 3).

cohort study, Caspi, et al. (1996) used a more elaborate paper LEC to provide continuous, monthly data about residential patterns, spouses and partners, children, education, work, arrests, incarceration, victimization, disability, and deaths for the period that had elapsed since their 21-year-old respondents had last been interviewed. They noted that the LEC allows for the collection of "continuous rather than static information about life events" in contrast with longitudinal studies that typically "yield only sequential snapshots of individual lives" because they fail to ask about conditions during the times between assessment periods (p. 102).

Figure 15.2 shows the Caspi et al. calendar covering a 5-year period, along with their techniques for marking events and the duration of life circumstances. In recording with whom the respondent was living, for example, the interviewer marked an X in the month in which the respondent began living with a partner, drew a line through succeeding months in which the cohabitation continued, and then entered another X for the final month in which the respondent lived with that partner. This method provides a strong visual image for the respondent that establishes contextual cues for the questions that follow.

Computerized Calendars

The paper calendars described earlier rely on a grid format that allows recording events in a number of domains. With either larger numbers of domains or more detail within domains, a paper calendar quickly becomes cumbersome. In a second Nebraska inmate study, Horney (2001) used a computerized LEC programmed with Microsoft Access that facilitated the retrospective collection of highly detailed monthly data on numerous domains including: incarceration and correctional supervision, residence, employment, income, school, military service, living relationships, intimate partnerships, gang membership, routine leisure activities, stress, gun possession and carrying, alcohol and substance use, and criminal involvement. The calendar was also used to record violent and avoided violent events in which the respondent was involved. A version of this calendar has also been used with prison inmates in Ohio (Bellair and Sutton 2006).[1]

As seen in Figs. 15.3 and 15.4, the computerized calendar forms described by Horney (2001) were limited to specific life domains (employment forms shown here). The interviewer began the time-based data collection for each domain by eliciting information about the last month on the calendar (Fig. 15.3). If the respondent reported any changes during the preceding months of the reference period, the second screen (Fig. 15.4) appeared and, working backwards, the interviewer entered all employment sequences. In Fig. 15.4, the first 16 of the 36 calendar months are shown. It can be seen that the respondent worked 40 h a week as a welder (a job to which he was committed) for the first 5 months, at which point he was

---

[1] In the interest of facilitating the collection of data on the situational aspects of violence, the National Consortium on Violence Research (NCOVR) funded three projects to adapt the Nebraska computerized calendar for use in new data collection efforts. One project focused on validation of the calendar method with a group of mental patients with a history of violence (Roberts et al. 2005). In a second project the calendar developed for male inmates was adapted for use in the Women's Experience of Violence (WEV) study (Principal investigators Julie Horney, Rosemary Gartner, Candace Krutschnitt, and Sally Simpson), in which jailed women in three cities were interviewed. In the third NCOVR-funded project, an adaptation of the calendar was used by Richard Trembley and his colleagues in The Quebec Longitudinal Study of Kindergarten Children (QLAKC) when their respondents were age 20 in order to capture details about respondents' lives for the 5-year period since the previous wave of data collection.

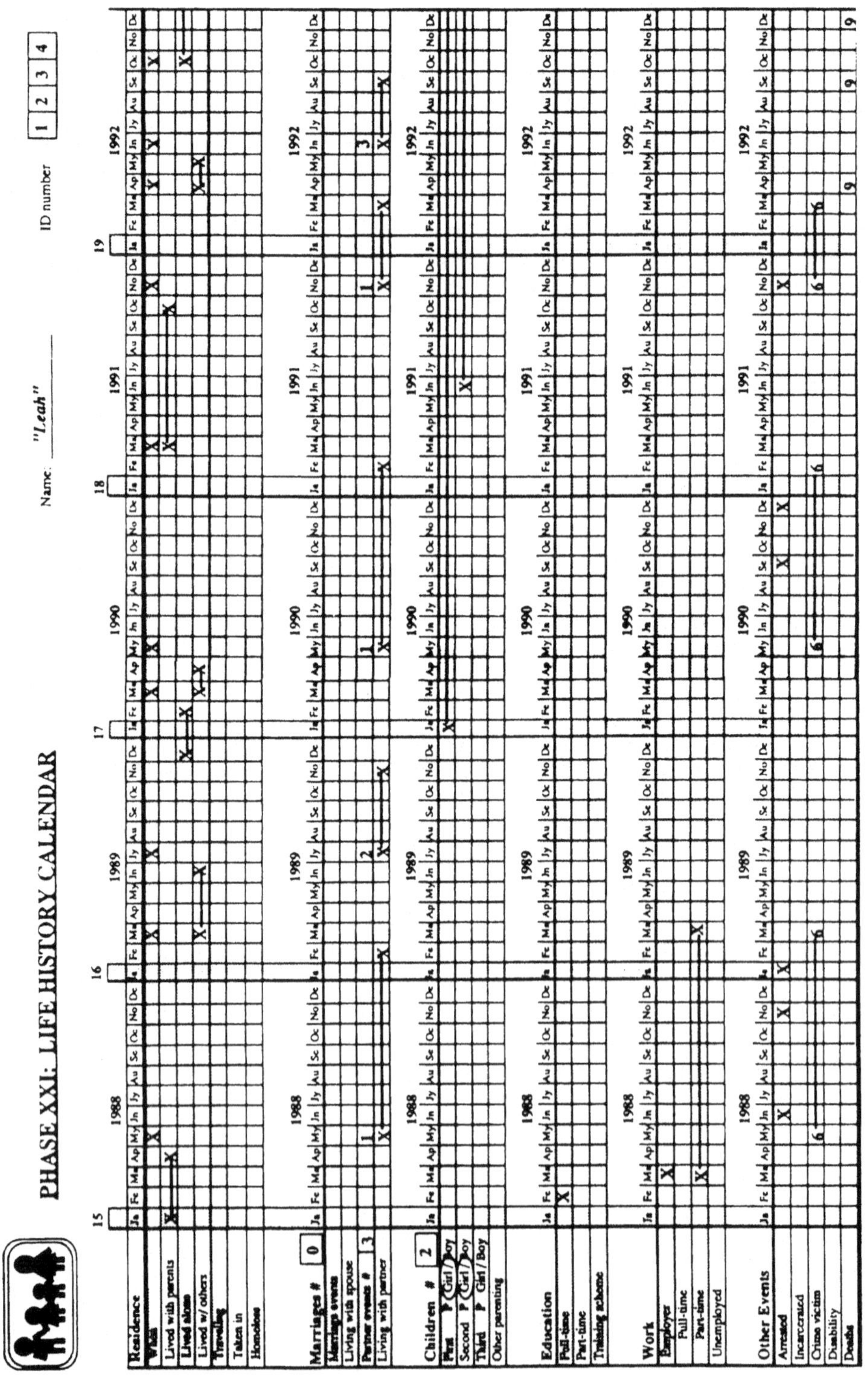

FIGURE 15.2. "Grid Calendar with Multiple Domains," originally published in Caspi, et al. (1996: Fig. 1).

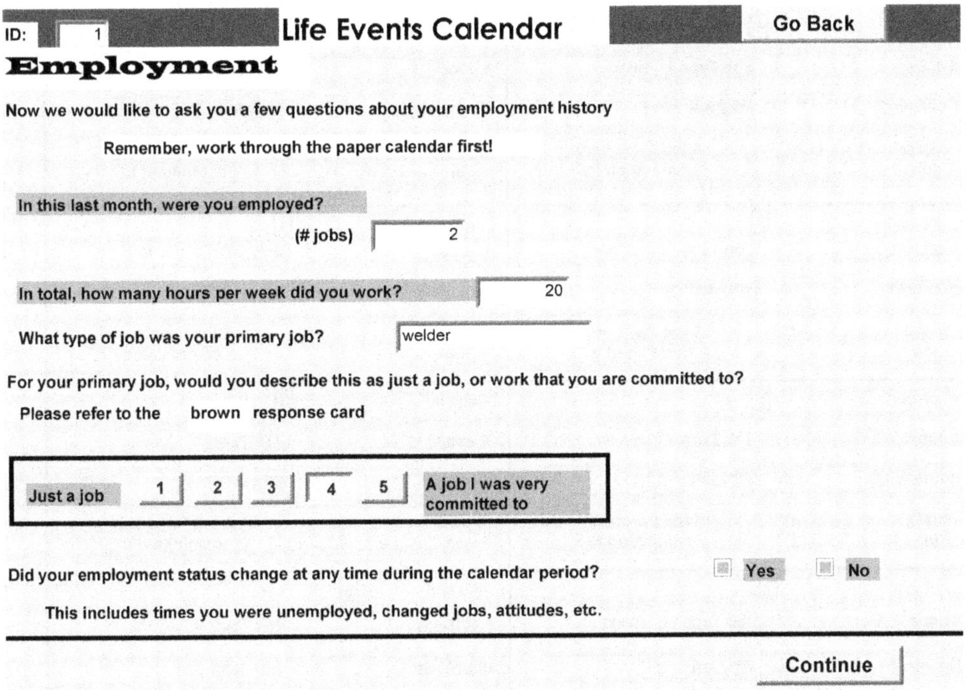

FIGURE 15.3. "'Last Month' Employment Questions, Computerized Calendar".

dismissed from his job (code 3 for "why left"). In the sixth month, he started working 40 h a week on a road construction job to which he had little commitment. He continued working on roads through month 14, when he was laid off (code 2 for "why left"). In month 15, the respondent again obtained work as a welder (along with another unspecified job) but for fewer hours, and was again committed to the job. The computerized calendar format allowed a similar level of detail to be recorded for each of the domains of life circumstances, but it did not provide a visual calendar display with multiple domains. In order to provide visual cues, interviewers entered particularly salient information on a paper calendar that was placed before the respondents throughout the interview. Respondents were also encouraged to use it to make any notes they thought would be helpful.

A different design was used in creating a computerized calendar for the *Pathways to Desistance* study of juvenile offenders in Philadelphia and Phoenix (Schubert et al. 2004). In this study, interviews were conducted every 6 months during the first 3 years of the study and then yearly for the fourth through seventh year of the study. As can be seen in Fig. 15.5, which shows the screen for recording data on schooling, this LEC format differs considerably from the calendar used by Horney (2001). Across the top of the screen are a series of tabs corresponding to the different life domains included in their study, arrayed so that the interviewer can easily move from one to the other. Above the spaces for entering school data, information already gathered on major life events and respondent's residence is displayed to facilitate recall for the questions about schooling. The format allows for visual calendar cues to be present throughout the collection of extensive details of the respondents' lives.

☐ job end	**1**		☐ job end	**2**	

# Jobs	1	Job Type	welder
Hours/wk	40	Why left	0

Just a job	1 2 3 **4** 5	A job I was very committed to

# Jobs	1	Job Type	welder
Hours/wk	40	Why left	0

Just a job	1 2 3 **4** 5	A job I was very committed to

☐ job end	**3**

# Jobs	1	Job Type	welder
Hours/wk	40	Why left	0

Just a job	1 2 3 **4** 5	A job I was very committed to

☐ job end	**4**

# Jobs	1	Job Type	welder
Hours/wk	40	Why left	0

Just a job	1 2 3 **4** 5	A job I was very committed to

☑ job end	**5**

# Jobs	1	Job Type	welder
Hours/wk	40	Why left	3

Just a job	1 2 3 **4** 5	A job I was very committed to

☐ job end	**6**

# Jobs	1	Job Type	roads
Hours/wk	40	Why left	0

Just a job	1 **2** 3 4 5	A job I was very committed to

☐ job end	**7**

# Jobs	1	Job Type	roads
Hours/wk	40	Why left	0

Just a job	1 **2** 3 4 5	A job I was very committed to

☐ job end	**8**

# Jobs	1	Job Type	roads
Hours/wk	40	Why left	0

Just a job	1 **2** 3 4 5	A job I was very committed to

☐ job end	**9**

# Jobs	1	Job Type	roads
Hours/wk	40	Why left	0

Just a job	1 **2** 3 4 5	A job I was very committed to

☐ job end	**10**

# Jobs	1	Job Type	roads
Hours/wk	40	Why left	0

Just a job	1 **2** 3 4 5	A job I was very committed to

☐ job end	**11**

# Jobs	1	Job Type	roads
Hours/wk	40	Why left	0

Just a job	1 **2** 3 4 5	A job I was very committed to

☐ job end	**12**

# Jobs	1	Job Type	roads
Hours/wk	40	Why left	0

Just a job	1 **2** 3 4 5	A job I was very committed to

☐ job end	**13**

# Jobs	1	Job Type	roads
Hours/wk	40	Why left	0

Just a job	1 **2** 3 4 5	A job I was very committed to

☐ job end	**14**

# Jobs	1	Job Type	roads
Hours/wk	40	Why left	2

Just a job	1 **2** 3 4 5	A job I was very committed to

☐ job end	**15**

# Jobs	2	Job Type	welder
Hours/wk	20	Why left	0

Just a job	1 2 3 **4** 5	A job I was very committed to

☐ job end	**16**

# Jobs	2	Job Type	welder
Hours/wk	20	Why left	0

Just a job	1 2 3 **4** 5	A job I was very committed to

FIGURE 15.4. "Computerized Employment Calendar".

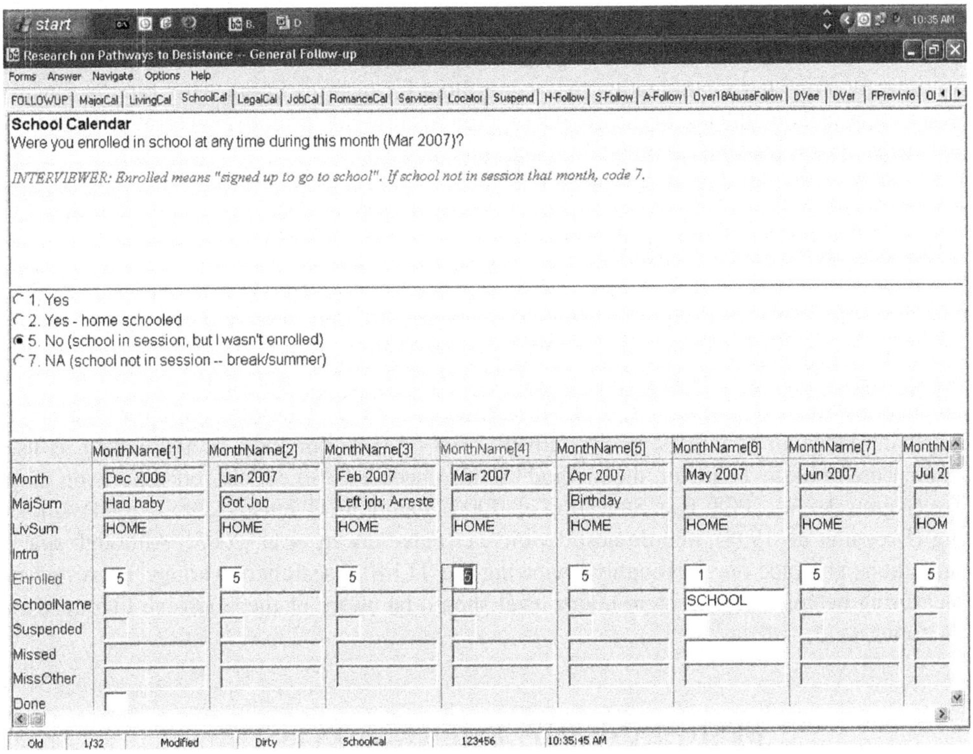

FIGURE 15.5. "Computerized School Calendar".

Lifetime Calendars

Although most of the criminological applications of the LEC have used the technique to collect time-based data for a relatively short recall period, others have employed the LEC in order to obtain lifetime accounts of the life events of interest. For example, Yoshihama and her colleagues (see Yoshihama et al. 2002, 2006; Yoshihama 2009) have used the LEC methodology to facilitate women's recall of lifetime experience of intimate partner violence (IPV). Yoshihama (2009) explained how the study of IPV is especially challenging methodologically:

> Because an intimate partner has ongoing access to the woman, IPV is often recurrent and can last for a considerable portion of the woman's life. Recurrence can be episodic (with varying interval lengths) or ongoing (e.g., every day or week). It is also possible (and quite common) that a woman is abused by more than one partner at different periods over her life course. (p. 136)

The LEC is well suited to facilitating the recall and structuring the recording of such complex data. In addition, as Yoshihama et al. (2002) observed, the very events that are expected to serve as effective memory cues are also likely to be correlated with IPV and women's health. Thus the "method by design obtains information on the occurrence and timing of not only domestic violence but also events that affect the relationship between domestic violence and women's well-being" (p. 301).

Whereas Yoshihama and colleagues focused on domestic violence, Wittebrood and Nieuwbeerta (2000) studied lifetime occurrences of a number of categories of victimization.

They analyzed data collected with the LEC method in face-to-face interviews with a nationally representative sample of 1,939 Dutch respondents in order to determine the impact of prior victimization on later victimization risk, controlling for patterns in other life circumstances. They suggested that the use of the life history approach could "provide powerful insights into the causal process behind criminal victimization" (p. 117).

Timeline Followback Methods

In contrast to calendars used to measure events over a lifetime, a version of LEC methodology developed to measure alcohol use focuses on daily changes in behavior. This method has been referred to as the timeline followback (TLFB) method (see Sobell and Sobell 1992, for an overview of the approach). The TLFB method uses days as the time units for measuring a specific behavior of interest over relatively brief reference periods. In addition to its use to measure drinking behavior, the method has also been used to collect self-reports on drug use (Agrawal et al. 2008; Fals-Stewart et al. 2000), gambling (Weinstock et al. 2004), smoking (Brown et al. 1998), and domestic violence (Fals-Stewart et al. 2003). Although space limitations preclude our thoroughly reviewing the TLFB, researchers who are interested in measuring behavior at this more micro level should be aware of the extensive literature on the topic.

DESIGN AND IMPLEMENTATION ISSUES

In describing the varied approaches to the LEC in criminological studies, we touched on differences in calendar design and differences in how interviewers use the LEC. Here, we discuss in more detail a number of practical design and implementation issues that researchers need to address when planning an LEC study.

Time Units and Reference Periods

In order to use the LEC to collect time-based data, researchers must determine the length of both the time unit of measurement and the overall reference period for the study. We have described studies with reference periods as brief as 2 months to studies of entire lifetimes, with time units ranging from 1 day to 1 year. The choice of both reference period and time unit obviously depend on the purpose of the research. As Caspi et al. (1996) observed, one important consideration is "whether the designated time unit is fine-grained enough to measure with precision the sequence and interrelation of different events" (p. 107). A common problem in prospective longitudinal studies has been the inability to sort out the sequences of events, such as onset of alcohol consumption and delinquent activity, when surveys at fairly widely spaced intervals have simply asked whether each occurred during the period since the last interview. Because a major goal of using the LEC is to establish accurate sequencing of events, the choice must consider how quickly the events and transitions of interest are believed to occur.

The length of reference periods and time units will generally be inversely related. With time units as long as a year, data might be collected for periods as long as a lifetime, whereas with daily or monthly accounts there will be serious limits on the period of time for which such detailed memory will be reliable. Little research has addressed the question of how data quality is affected by choice of either the time unit of measurement or the entire reference period in calendar research. We see a need for much more research on both topics in order to determine the limits of human memory when using the LEC to collect retrospective data.

Split Time Units

Regardless of the particular time unit chosen for a study, researchers must make decisions about how to classify a time unit that is "split." For example, presume the calendar month is the time unit. If a respondent reports living in jail *and* living out on the street in a particular month, how is this coded? Researchers could mark the month as being split or they could mark the month according to where the subject spent the majority of the month. These kinds of decisions will likely be driven by the research question at hand but should be thought through during the planning stage.

Time Markers

Most researchers using the LEC start by entering extended events such as where the respondent was living and with whom, and whether and where the respondent was working, as well as easily remembered specific events, such as marriages and births of children. For criminologists, periods of incarceration are often among the first entries on the LEC. All of these time markers can then serve as anchoring points to stimulate memory and to help pinpoint dates of less salient events (Belli 1998).

Some researchers have used "respondent-generated landmarks" (Yoshihama 2009) to facilitate recall. With this technique, in addition to the structured questions about standard life circumstances that are asked, respondents are asked to report significant events that have occurred in their lives during the reference period (Yoshihama 2009). Events such as hospitalizations, special awards, or deaths of loved ones might be entered on the calendar. In our pre-tests with groups of male prison inmates, one respondent suggested that we should ask for information on what cars respondents were driving at different times throughout the reference period because this would help the men to recall other events.

Some studies have shown such personal events to be more effective in cuing recall than public events (e.g., presidential elections), because memory for public events is poorer in terms of occurrence, detail, and timing (see for example, Rubin and Kozin 1984; Shum 1998). However, contrary results were found by Axinn et al. (1999), who used preliminary interviews with members of their study population to identify public events of particular salience. In their study of families in south-central Nepal, the first democratic election held in Nepal and a major earthquake that had occurred in the area served as notable cognitive landmarks for most respondents, stimulating recall of the personal events of interest. Public events that are effective as time markers may be generated by individual respondents when using an approach like that reported by Yoshihama (2009), but then these markers could not be pre-printed on calendars. The approach used by Axinn et al. (1999) would probably be most useful when researchers want to establish the same historical reference period for all respondents.

Yoshihama (2009) has provided interesting data on the relative utility of different time markers for enhancing recall. She asked respondents to rate how helpful events in other domains were to them in recalling their experiences with intimate partner violence. Respondents gave higher ratings to residence, partner names or initials, and respondent-generated landmarks. We believe it would be fruitful to expand this line of research by explicitly examining the relative effectiveness of different kinds of time markers in improving the validity of retrospective data gathered with the LEC. Such research may need to be specific to particular populations of interest.

Moving Through the Calendar

As noted earlier, in collecting time-based data, interviewers typically inquire about one calendar domain at a time in order to focus on the streams of events and tap into the sequential storage of memories. However, different approaches have been taken to move through time within a particular domain. Caspi, et al. (1996, p. 109) report moving forward from the beginning of the calendar period to the end. Thus, they started collecting residential data by saying to the respondent "To start with, please tell me each of the places you have lived since your 15th birthday and how long you lived there. Where were you living when you turned 15?" After recording the initial information, the interviewer would ask "Until what date did you live at that same address?" followed by "Then where did you live?"

In the Horney (2001) study of incarcerated offenders, the interviewer always started with the last month on the calendar (the month of the arrest that led to the respondent's incarceration). As shown in Fig. 15.3, a number of questions were asked about employment in the last month. As responses were keyed in for each variable, the program automatically entered the values in a data table for the last calendar month and all preceding months. Next, the interviewer asked if any features of employment had changed during the calendar period. If the respondent answered "yes," the program went to the calendar screen (Fig. 15.4), and the interviewer asked him to indicate the most recent preceding month in which there had been a change. The change was then entered and that value was back-filled for all preceding months. This process of entering changes continued until data were entered for every month on the calendar.

We are unaware of any research directly comparing the different approaches to moving through the LEC, but Bradburn et al. (1987) report that "experiments on autobiographical memory show that people achieve better levels of recall if they are required to begin with the most recent item in a series and work backward than if they must begin at the beginning" (p. 210). Belli et al. (2001) have proposed that interviewers should consider respondents' preferences for moving through time, perhaps using different approaches for different domains. They consider such flexibility an important feature of the LEC.

Paper versus Computerized Calendar

The choice of whether to employ a paper or a computerized calendar depends on the purpose of the calendar and on its complexity. If the LEC is intended primarily as an aid to recall, the paper calendar with checklists or with blank space for entry of salient life circumstances is easy to construct and use. The key concern is to have the entire calendar period laid out in a format that makes it a strong visual cue for the respondent. If the calendar is to be used for the collection of time-based data, the choice of paper or computer calendar will depend on both the breadth and detail of the questions to be asked as well as on the length of the reference period. A paper calendar can quickly become unwieldy when many time units are involved or when the domains of life circumstances of interest include many categories and sub-categories.

With complex data collection, the computerized calendar has a number of advantages:

1. Electronic entry of data. When data are entered on a paper calendar, an extra step is needed for entering the data into an electronic database in order to make them available for analysis. This step can be costly and also introduces another stage at which errors can be made. With a computerized calendar, the extra step and additional errors are avoided as the program can be directly linked to a database. Data can be immediately transferred from the laptops of interviewers to centralized databases, and in some multi-site studies, this has facilitated the sharing of data across sites, allowing for "ongoing monitoring of the psychometric properties of the measures, identification of inconsistencies or problems with the data, and detection of study-wide and site-specific trends in the data as they emerge" (Schubert et al. 2004, p. 7).

2. Automatic cross-referencing. Computerized calendars can be programmed to check for consistency in answers and raise flags for the interviewer. As Schubert et al. (2004) noted, cross-referencing can allow for "identification of significant status changes (e.g., whether the person who is identified as having raised the adolescent in the current interview is the same person named in prior sections or interviews)" and "(E)rror messages can be built in to alert the interviewer to these inconsistencies" (p. 7).

3. Facilitation of skip patterns and accurate interviewing. Computerized calendars can be programmed to make it easy for an interviewer to follow complex skip patterns in questioning. In an inmate survey, for example, once a respondent has identified months of incarceration in the reference period, the program can automatically enter a "not applicable" code for those months for irrelevant questions (e.g., whether the respondent was living with wife or children). Certain computer forms can be skipped altogether when answers to screen questions make them irrelevant. For example, if a respondent reports that he did not possess any guns in a particular month, the screen asking about the types of guns and how they were obtained would not appear.

4. Visual interest. Although both paper and computerized calendars are intended to provide visual cues that aid in recall, a computerized calendar can be programmed to make it visually interesting and even entertaining. In very long interviews, screens that change in appearance and different visual formats keyed to different kinds of questions can help in motivating respondents to remain attentive.

Schubert et al. (2004) point out that one potential disadvantage of computerized calendars is that "a major investment must be made in programming and software testing before data collection can begin" (p. 7). However, they report reducing development time by using commercially available software for constructing interviews. In their *Pathways to Desistance* study, Mulvey and colleagues tried several software packages before settling on Blaise software (Mulvey, personal communication, October 15, 2008). Some of the software they initially tried would not support their calendar instrument because of its size. The Microsoft Access program developed by Horney (2001) has been used by a number of other researchers who have adapted it to their own needs, but at least some minimal programming costs have been involved. As more computerized calendars come into use, the initial programming costs are likely to be substantially reduced.

A second disadvantage of computerized calendars is that it is more difficult to display the entire calendar so that the respondent has constant visual cues for time markers that have been entered. As shown earlier in Fig. 15.5, however, the calendar developed for the *Pathways to Desistance* project (Schubert et al. 2004) provides a display of some basic time markers on every screen. Horney (2001) dealt with this problem by entering key information on a paper calendar that was placed before the respondent throughout the interview.

Working Together on a Complex Task

The completion of the LEC can seem a daunting task. In our experience, respondents are at first skeptical that they will be able to remember the details and timing of their life circumstances but are usually surprised at how well the technique helps them to construct the past. We found by accident, during pre-testing our instrument, that having the interviewer and respondent sit side-by-side viewing the computer screen is a very good arrangement (Horney 2001). Schubert et al. (2004) and Caspi et al. (1996) also report using the side-by-side approach. We believe this arrangement, whether used in conjunction with a paper or a computerized calendar, accomplishes several things:

1. It creates a sense of two people working together to solve a complex puzzle, which provides additional motivation to the respondent. We found that respondents frequently asked the interviewer to go back and make changes when they realized that they had made mistakes, such as having been wrong about the month in which an event occurred.
2. It fosters a sense of trust in the interviewer. Instead of sitting across the table from an interviewer and wondering what he or she is actually writing down, the respondent sees all the information that is entered into the computer or onto the paper calendar.
3. It reinforces the assurances of confidentiality. The respondent sees that his/her name is not recorded anywhere and that most data entries are simply checks or numbers or letter codes and not anything that reveals of the respondent's identity.

Training Interviewers

Even experienced survey interviewers may be largely unfamiliar with calendar interviewing. Thus, they should be trained not only in the "how to's" of the method but also in the theoretical underpinnings. Understanding the principles of sequential and parallel cuing can help interviewers get the maximum benefit from the LEC. In our use of the LEC with prison inmates (Horney 2001), we found practice interviews with all other interviewers observing, were particularly helpful. We started with interviewers practicing with other students who simulated answers that might be given by an inmate, and then we conducted test interviews with inmates in a prison setting similar to the one to be used in the actual interviews. In initial practice sessions, one interviewer asked all the questions, but all of the interviewers observed and individually recorded the information. Interviewers were encouraged to ask questions to clarify specific issues that arose.

The initial interviews were followed by one-on-one practice interviews. These steps allowed the interviewer to gain comfort with the instrument and work on interviewing technique as well (e.g., probing for more information, using the calendar elements to enhance subject recall). Such training is a critical component of any project using the LEC, and the more complex the instrument, the more extensive the training will need to be. Especially with computerized calendars, the practice sessions are important not only to ensure the skill and comfort of the interviewer but also to ensure that all bugs in the computer program have been detected.

From the discussion above, it is clear that designing a calendar study requires synthesizing good survey methodology with a number of pragmatic considerations. In deciding whether to employ the LEC in any particular study, the researcher will want to weigh the costs involved in the method against the benefits to be obtained from its use. An important part of that assessment is the quality of the data obtained with the LEC, which we address in the next section.

QUALITY OF LEC DATA

Several approaches have been used to assess the quality of data obtained through the use of the LEC. Most have involved comparing the data collected retrospectively with the LEC to data obtained through another source. In some cases, that other source is a self-report by the same respondent that was given at a time closer to the status or event in question and is therefore assumed to be more accurate than a more distant report. In other cases, official records provide the alternative source for the data. In most assessments, the LEC has been evaluated as the only retrospective method, either focusing on the absolute accuracy of the data, or comparing LEC accuracy under differing conditions, such as the length of the recall period. A few studies, however, have directly compared the accuracy of data collected with the LEC to data collected through more traditional survey methods, with the strongest of these studies using randomized experimental designs.

Comparisons of Retrospective LEC Data to Earlier Self-Reports

Both Freedman et al. (1988) and Caspi et al. (1996) employed the LEC in the context of ongoing prospective longitudinal studies and were thus able to compare the retrospective accounts respondents gave for a particular time period using the LEC with the same respondents' reports given previously at that actual time period. Freedman et al. as part of a panel study of mothers and their children in Detroit, employed the LEC to interview approximately 900 23-year olds to obtain month-by-month retrospective accounts of key features of their lives back to the time they were 15 years old. These same young adults had been interviewed at the age of 18, at which time they described their current status on a number of dimensions. To assess the quality of the LEC data, Freedman et al. compared the LEC reports (1985) for the month in which the respondents had been interviewed in 1980 with the original reports for that month.

At least 90% of the respondents gave the same date for marriages and births, 87% gave identical responses as to whether they were attending school full-time, part-time, or not at all, and 72% gave the same classification in describing their employment as full-time, part-time, or no employment. Freedman et al. suggested that memory for employment was somewhat less accurate than for schooling because at age 18 employment was generally changing more frequently.

Caspi et al. (1996) also reported on LEC data quality in the context of a prospective longitudinal study. Like Freedman et al. (1988), they assessed the accuracy of retrospective reports on schooling and employment. In addition, they considered reports on whether or not the respondent was living with parents, cohabiting with a partner, serving as a primary caregiver for a child, and involved in job training. Caspi et al. used the LEC to obtain month-by-month accounts of the respondents' life circumstances between age 15 and 21. In order to assess the quality of the retrospective data, they compared the LEC reports for the month in 1990 when the respondents, then age 18, had last been interviewed to the reports given at that earlier time. Complete data for both reporting periods were available for 951 persons. With a 3-year retrospective recall period, they found that "(o)ver 90% of the reports about each of the seven different content domains were reported in the exact month on both occasions" (p. 105).

As Caspi et al. (1996) noted, the validity data in their study as well as the Freedman et al. (1988) study were limited to sociodemographic variables. A very different focus is found in the study by Roberts et al. (2005), who assessed the quality of LEC data on involvement in violent events. In a prior study[2] researchers identified, through a validated screening process, a group of individuals admitted to a psychiatric center emergency room who were expected to be repeatedly involved in violence when they were released back into the community. Subjects who were enrolled in the study were interviewed in the community once a week for 6 months and asked about their drinking, drug use, relationship quality, general living situation, and involvement in violence during the previous week.

For the Roberts et al. (2005) project, 75 of the 132 participants in the original study were interviewed using the LEC at times that were 1, 2, or 3 plus years after their first interview in the original study. The recall period for the LEC overlapped with the period during which they had participated in weekly interviews and thus allowed a comparison of retrospective accounts of events with accounts given almost concurrently. The correspondence in reporting violent events was considerably lower than those found in the studies of sociodemographic variables. Retrospective reports of whether or not violence occurred in specific months matched reports from the weekly interviews in 59% of the cases, but most of the matches were for reports of no violence. Using the LEC, respondents retrospectively reported violence in only 18% of the months in which violence had been originally reported. Violence was more likely to be reported when the violent events were serious rather than minor (reported in 14% of the months in which serious violence was previously reported compared to 5% of the months with minor violence). Surprisingly, the length of the recall period was unrelated to concordance between the retrospective and weekly reports.

The Roberts et al. study represents an especially rigorous test of the LEC methodology. The sample was not only diagnosed as suffering from various mental health disorders, but was, in addition, screened into the original study based upon significant histories of substance use and violence. The respondents' mental health status, their use of prescribed medications, and their additional substance use were likely to make the recall task especially problematic. In addition, the screening for involvement in violence means that such events were probably more frequent and therefore less salient for this group than they would be for a general popu-lation. Although this sample shares some characteristics with a sample of criminal offenders, it may be even more extreme in terms of problems that would affect memory. An important

---

[2] "Intensive follow-up of violent patients," funded by the National Institute of Mental Health (NIMH); Edward Mulvey, Ph.D. and Charles W. Lidz, Ph.D., co-principal investigators.

question not addressed by the Roberts et al. study is whether, under these challenging circumstances, the quality of data obtained with the LEC was different from what would have been obtained with a traditional questionnaire method.

Comparisons of Retrospective LEC Data to Records Data

The criterion data compared to LEC data in the three studies described previously were earlier reports given by the same individuals at or very close to the time of the life circumstances in question. Other studies have assessed LEC data quality by comparing them to external records. For example, Morris and Slocum (forthcoming), Roberts and Wells (2009), and Mulvey and Schubert (personal communication, October 15, 2008) compared offenders' self-reports of arrests to official records. In the Morris and Slocum study (Women's Experience of Violence data), almost 88% of the jailed women correctly reported whether they had been arrested during the reference period. Roberts and Wells (Second Nebraska Inmate Study data) found that 74% of the male inmates gave accurate reports as to whether they had been arrested, and that they reported roughly 51% of the officially recorded arrests.

In both studies, reports on the timing of arrests in specific months produced the least concordance with official records. Morris and Slocum found that 24% of the calendar months with an official arrest were accurately reported as an "arrest month" using the LEC, while Roberts and Wells reported correct identification in only 14.5% of the official arrest months. Both studies additionally found that those individuals who reported the highest number of offenses had the greatest numbers of errors in reporting. Results using officially recorded arrests as criteria for evaluating the quality of self-reports should be interpreted cautiously, as prior researchers have commented on the ambiguous nature of the arrest incident (see for example, Rojek 1983; Weis 1986; Johnson et al. 2002). Incarcerated individuals have likely had numerous contacts with criminal justice officials, and accurately distinguishing an arrest from another form of criminal justice contact may be difficult for these offenders.

Roberts and Wells also examined the self-reports of adult jail and prison terms against official records and found that recall of these events was much better than the recall of arrests. Fifty-seven percent of the respondents accurately reported their frequency of adult jail terms, and 90% accurately reported frequency of adult prison terms. Similarly, Mulvey and Schubert (personal communication) found 92% agreement between the self-reported occurrence and timing of juvenile facility placement and official records of these incarceration periods.

Roberts and Mulvey (2009), in additional analyses of the LEC reports of released mental patients, compared the self-reports of mental health hospitalizations against hospital intake records, and found that 63% of the respondents accurately reported the total number of hospitalization months. As with jail and prison terms, accuracy with respect to timing was much lower. Their respondents accurately reported 19% of the officially recorded "hospitalization months" as such using the LEC.

Better recall of jail and prison terms and hospitalizations than of arrests is to be expected. A jail/prison stay or stay in a mental hospital has an impact on many aspects of a person's life, including living arrangements, employment status, and significant relationships. This change across life domains naturally makes these events memorable, and also makes the LEC methodology especially likely to facilitate recall. In contrast, an arrest, which might only inconvenience a person for a few hours or days, is less likely to be tied to other domains on the LEC, and therefore will be harder to remember. In addition, jail terms, prison terms, and hospitalizations occurred relatively infrequently during the short reference periods used in these studies, and were therefore more likely to stand out in memory.

Direct Comparisons of the LEC to Traditional Methods

All of the assessments of data quality described above compared reports obtained through LEC methodology with either earlier self-reports or with official records data in order to determine the accuracy of LEC retrospective reports. Although useful in assessing absolute level of accuracy, these studies have not determined whether using the LEC methodology leads to improvement over traditional methods of collecting retrospective accounts. Direct comparisons of the LEC to traditional methods are especially important.

Yacoubian (2000, 2003) assessed the impact in two Arrestee Drug Abuse Monitoring (ADAM) Program sites of adding a calendar component to the standard ADAM interview used to question arrestees about their recent drug use. Arrestees' reports of drug use during the 30 days previous to their arrest are typically compared to urinalysis results to assess validity. Yacoubian compared the correspondence of self-reports to urinalysis results in 1999, when standard survey methodology was used, to results obtained in 2000, when a calendar component was added to the interview, for Oklahoma City (Yacoubian 2000) and Portland (Yacoubian 2003). The kappa statistics computed to measure the extent of agreement between self-reports and urinalysis results for marijuana, crack cocaine, powder cocaine, and heroin were substantially the same for 1999 and 2000, indicating no improvement in the self-reports with introduction of the calendar methodology. It is important to note that the recall period in this study was 30 days, a period for which recall would be assumed to be relatively easy. Yacoubian did not describe the calendar employed except to say that "the assumption is that the reporting of personal drug use, treatment history, and criminal justice involvement will be enhanced when recalled in conjunction with more personal events (e.g., birthdays, anniversaries, and holidays)" (2003, p. 28). It seems likely that the calendar was designed to improve the memory of life circumstances occurring over a longer term rather than specifically to cue recall of events in the last 30 days. The finding of no difference thus would not be surprising.

Yoshihama et al. (2005) compared two studies in which they obtained women's accounts of their lifetime experience with intimate partner violence (IPV). They compared a small methodological study, in which they employed the LEC, to a larger epidemiological study (the Mothers' Well-Being Study (MWS), in which they used traditional survey methods. Both studies used the same sampling frame and the same sampling criteria. For the comparisons, they selected a subset of the sample from the larger study who matched the race and county of residence of the smaller sample in the LEC study.

Interviewers in the LEC study used women's reports of their experiences in a number of domains to enter timing and duration data on a pre-printed calendar that the women then referred to when they were questioned about IPV. Calendar entries were made for residence, schooling, employment, births of children, receipt of public assistance, relationship history, pregnancy outcomes, as well as other particularly memorable life events that the women identified.

There were no criterion data available against which to compare the reports gathered by the two methods. Instead, the researchers hypothesized several results that should follow if the LEC led to more accurate reporting. They predicted that the calendar method should lead to more reports of IPV over the life course, that it should lead to more reports especially in more distant time periods, and that the differences between the two methods should be greater for recall of far distant periods than of recall for the past year. They found, as predicted, that the women in the LEC study were more likely to report having experienced IPV, reported that the first IPV occurred at an earlier age, and had a higher estimated cumulative probability of experiencing IPV by age 50. They tested their second hypothesis by comparing women in different age groups and found differences between the two studies. Women in the LEC study reported similar patterns of IPV regardless of age group, whereas women in the traditional method study reported patterns that varied by age group, with younger women reporting more and earlier IPV. Finally, as predicted, they found no difference between the two study samples in their reports of IPV experience in the previous 12 months.

Although the previous two studies directly compared the LEC methodology with traditional survey methodology, neither employed an experimental design to make that comparison. We now turn to three important studies in which respondents were randomly assigned to be interviewed either by the LEC method or by traditional methods.

Comparisons of Interviewing Methods Through Randomized Experiments

Belli et al. (2001, 2005, 2007) have employed randomized experimental designs to compare the quality of self reports of various life-events obtained using the LEC to reports obtained with more traditional survey methodologies. Their experimental comparisons involved randomly selected subsets of respondents from the Panel Study on Income Dynamics (PSID) whose responses could be compared to their reports in earlier waves of that survey.

Belli et al. (2001, 2005) randomly assigned participants to be interviewed by telephone in 1998 either with LEC methodology or with traditional survey questions, covering the same domains about which they had been questioned in the 1997 PSID (asking mostly about 1996 life circumstances). The smallest time units used with the LEC were a third of the month (respondents were asked whether events occurred, started, or stopped near the beginning, in the middle, or at the end of a month). The reference period was 1 year and it ranged between 1 and 2 years before the date of the experimental interviews.

The LEC approach produced higher quality data in a number of domains. Belli et al. found overall higher levels of agreement and less underreporting for reported moves; smaller differences in mean absolute error for weeks away from work for illness of self or other; and significantly larger correlation coefficients for income, weeks unemployed, weeks away from work because of illness and weeks away from work for other reasons. In contrast, standard survey techniques produced less over-reporting of numbers of jobs and of others moving into the residence. There were no consistent over- or under-reporting biases with either method for the continuous measures, and no data quality differences between the two methods with regards to whether the respondent received AFDC/Food stamps, whether household members had left the residence, and the number of weeks per year that the respondent was working, out of the labor force, or on vacation.

In contrast to the previous study, which covered a 1-year recall period, Belli et al. (2007) compared the quality of data produced by the LEC and by standard survey methods when asking respondents about the 30-year period during which PSID data were collected annually (between 1968 and 1997). This study also employed a computerized LEC rather than the paper and pencil version.

In 2002, a subset of PSID respondents were randomly assigned to LEC or standard survey methodologies and were interviewed by telephone, using questions that referred to their entire lifetimes. Domains covered included residence, marriage, cohabitation, employment, and smoking. Their reports for each year were compared to reports obtained during the original panel study. The results indicated that correspondence to earlier reports was significantly better for those in the LEC condition for cohabitation, employment, amount worked, and smoking. The improvement achieved with the LEC for employment reports was even greater for the more distant reporting periods. The standard methodology produced greater agreement for one domain – marriage, although the data quality was high for both methods. There were no statistically significant differences between the two conditions in reporting of residential changes.

The two randomized experiments conducted by Belli and colleagues represent an important advance in determining the value of the LEC methodology. Both found generally greater agreement between retrospective reports and earlier reports from the same individuals when the LEC was used, but the differences between methods were not overwhelming for the most part, and they were not always in favor of the LEC. It is important to note that both studies were conducted using telephone interviews, and, therefore, one very important feature of the LEC – it's serving as a visual aid to facilitate the respondent's recall – was missing from these tests. The *interviewers* were able to take advantage of the visual aid (either in the form of the paper calendar or the computerized version) to spot inconsistencies in the respondent's reports, but the *respondents* had no record of responses to stimulate sequential or parallel (cross-domain) cuing of memory. We might thus expect these studies to underestimate the benefits of the LEC over traditional methods.

Telephone interviewing was also used in a randomized experiment conducted by Van der Vaart and Glasner (2007), but it was supplemented by a calendar mailed to respondents in advance of the interview. In this study, 233 clients registered with Dutch opticians were questioned about their purchases of eyeglasses for a 7 year time frame; their reports gathered either with the LEC or with a standard interview were compared to opticians' records. Before the scheduled interview, respondents in the LEC condition were sent a calendar with instructions for entering monthly information about age, residence, domestic situation, jobs, schooling, and personal landmarks. During the interview in the LEC condition, respondents were asked to mark any purchases of a pair of glasses on the calendar and to refer to the calendar as they were asked questions about the purchase price and date of purchase for the most recently purchased pair of eyeglasses.

The researchers found that, for price and date of purchase of the last pair of eyeglasses, errors were significantly smaller in the LEC condition than in the standard survey condition. Errors in total number of glasses purchased were also smaller in the LEC condition, but the difference was not significant, a result the authors attributed to "the fact that 91% of all the respondents had bought two pairs of glasses, at most" (p. 233).

The researchers hypothesized that there would be greater reduction in errors in the LEC condition relative to the standard condition when the task was more difficult, as when the purchase was less salient (glasses were less expensive) or less recent. Their hypotheses were supported. The reduction in recall error using the LEC was 25% with higher priced glasses and 61% with the less expensive glasses. Similarly, the LEC method led to a 32% reduction in error with recently purchased glasses (the last $2^1/_2$ years) and a 55% reduction in error with those purchased from $2^1/_2$ to 7 years earlier.

Conclusions on LEC Data Quality

Several general conclusions can be drawn from these studies of the quality of LEC data. First, across the studies, data obtained with LEC methods are more frequently of higher quality than data obtained with standard survey methods. In some cases, there is little difference between the methods, but the standard methods are rarely more effective than the LEC.

Second, the LEC appears to have greater benefits over traditional methods when the task places a heavier burden on recall, as when the events to be recalled are less salient, more frequent, or more distant. For very recent events or major events such as marriages and births, the two methods are likely to produce similarly high quality recall data.

Third, even when the LEC is used, the difficulty of the task or the characteristics of the respondents may seriously limit the accuracy of recall. The lowest levels of accuracy were reported for respondents with serious mental health problems, problems of substance abuse, and high rates of involvement in violence, who were asked to recall specific violent events in which they were involved over 1–3 years earlier. We do not know, however, how accurate their recall would have been with traditional survey methods.

CONCLUSIONS AND FUTURE DIRECTIONS

As the research on LEC data quality indicates, the calendar methodology has the potential to improve individual recall of life circumstances, events, and behavior. While many questions remain about the limits of the method, the potential benefits for capturing time-based data are considerable. The LEC is particularly well suited to capturing data applicable to questions about the sequencing of events or about the correspondence of events in time. Researchers, of course, have to consider the costs of the approach. Costs of instrument development depend on the complexity of the instrument. The simplest paper calendars involve very low development costs, whereas computerized calendars can require substantial investments in programming. Those costs, however, are likely to decrease significantly as more calendars are developed and shared with other researchers.

The costs of using the LEC must always be assessed against alternatives. If the LEC allows the retrospective collection of high quality data that could otherwise only be gathered through costly prospective studies, savings can be substantial. If used in conjunction with prospective longitudinal research to produce more detail on events and behavior during the periods between waves of data collection, the marginal cost of the LEC may be quite small.

In order for the costs and benefits to be more adequately understood, further methodological research on the LEC is needed. The only randomized experiments conducted to date compared LEC telephone interviews with more traditional questioning and, therefore, evaluated the LEC without the visual calendar cues that many consider a critical feature for cuing recall. Randomized experiments with face-to-face interviews will be important for assessing the full potential of the LEC.

Research on design and implementation details is also needed. More research on the length of reference periods and on the interaction between time units and reference periods is necessary for establishing reasonable limits for producing valid data with the LEC. Research to determine the impact of different approaches to moving through time with the LEC (forward, backward, or mixed) will help researchers get the maximum benefit from the methodology.

New ways of enhancing the LEC should also be explored. We described earlier the Van der Vaart and Glasner study which supplemented a telephone-administered LEC with a calendar mailed in advance to respondents. In typical face-to-face LEC interviews, entering life circumstances on the calendar can be quite time consuming. Providing calendars in advance and asking respondents to enter some of the basic data could save on interview time and might also improve recall by giving respondents more time to think about what was going on during a certain period of their lives.

Besides research on the basic elements of the LEC, there is also a need for research specific to the populations in which criminologists are interested. Many of these populations present serious challenges for researchers collecting retrospective data. The challenges arise because respondents in criminological studies often are educationally and economically disadvantaged, report substantial histories of drug and alcohol use/abuse, and have higher rates of mental illness than the general population (see for example, Beck et al. 1993; Teplin 1994). These conditions make them likely to have memory problems that decrease the accuracy of their retrospective accounts. In addition, their memory for offending and victimization may be less clear because of their more frequent involvement. These challenges, although making the LEC, with its built-in cues for recall, a particularly attractive technique, also call for attending to special needs of these populations when designing the LEC.

We suggest that more research is needed to enhance the LEC effectiveness for these populations and to determine its limits. Population-specific research to determine what events serve best as time markers, for example, could improve the LEC cuing of recall. Individuals for whom arrests or violent events occur with some frequency may not find such things effective in aiding their memory, but researchers may find that they have in common other kinds of events that serve well as cognitive landmarks. Researchers might consider obtaining consent to access respondents' official records (e.g., arrest, court, prison, and mental health) prior to the interviews so that key events could be entered on the calendar in advance of the interview.

With more theoretical and empirical interest in the timing, duration, and interconnectedness of events, self-report methods like the LEC will play an increasingly important role in criminology. With more attention to fine-tuning the method for use with special populations, we see great promise in the LEC for producing useful, high-quality data on the lives of the individuals we study.

REFERENCES

Agrawal S, Sobell M, Sobell L (2008) The timeline followback: a scientifically and clinically useful tool for assessing substance use. In: Belli R, Stafford F, Alwin D (eds) Calendar and time diaries: methods in life course research. Sage, Los Angeles, CA. pp 57–68

Armstrong GS, Griffin ML (2007) The effect of local life circumstances on victimization of drug-involved women. Justice Q 24:80–105

Axinn WG, Pearce LD, Ghimire D (1999) Innovations in life history calendar applications. Soc Sci Res 28:243–264

Barsalou LW (1988) The content and organization of autobiographical memories. In: Neisser U, Winograd E (eds) Remembering reconsidered: ecological and traditional approaches to the study of memory. Cambridge University Press, New York

Beck A, Gilliard D, Greenfeld L, Harlow C, Hester T, Jankowski L, Snell T, Stephan J, Morton D (1993) Survey of state prison inmates, 1991. Bureau of Justice Statistics, Washington, DC

Bellair PE, Sutton J (2006) Test-retest reliability of self-reports among prison inmates, Paper presented at the meetings of the American Society of Criminology. Los Angeles, CA

Belli RF (1998) The structure of autobiographical memory and the event history calendar: potential improvements in the quality of retrospective reports in surveys. Memory 6:383–406

Belli RF, Shay WL, Stafford FP (2001) Event history calendars and question list surveys: a direct comparison of interviewing methods. Public Opin Q 65:45–74

Belli RF, Shay WL, Stafford FP (2005) Errata. Public Opin Q 69:172

Belli RF, Smith LM, Andreski PM, Agrawal S (2007) Methodological comparisons between CATI event history calendar and standardized conventional questionnaire instruments. Public Opin Q 71:603–622

Belli RF, Stafford FP, Alwin D (eds) (2009) Calendar and time diaries: methods in life course research. Sage, Los Angeles, CA

Bradburn NM, Rips LJ, Shevel SK (1987) Answering autobiographical questions: the impact of memory and inference on surveys. Science 236:157–162

Brewer WF (1986) What is autobiographical memory? In: Rubin, DC (ed) Autobiographical Memory. Cambridge University Press, New York, pp. 25–49

Brown RA, Burgess ES, Sales SD, Whiteley JA, Evans DM, Miller IW (1998) Reliability and validity of a smoking timeline follow-back interview. Psychol Addict Behav 12:101–112

Caspi A, Moffitt TE, Thornton A, Freedman D, Amell JW, Harrington H et al (1996) The life history calendar: a research and clinical assessment method for collecting retrospective event-history data. Int J Methods Psychiatr Res 6:101–114

Conway MA (1996) Autobiographical knowledge and autobiographical memories. In: Rubin DC (ed) Remembering our past: studies in autobiographical memory. Cambridge University Press, New York, pp 67–93

Fals-Stewart W, Birchler G, Kelley M (2003) The timeline followback spousal violence interview to assess physical aggression between intimate partners: reliability and validity. J Fam Violence 18:131–142

Fals-Stewart W, O'Farrell T, Freitas T, McFarlin S, Rutigliano P (2000) The timeline followback reports of psychoactive substance use by drug-abusing patients: psychometric properties. J Consult Clin Psychol 68:134–144

Freedman D, Thornton A, Camburn D, Alwin D, Young-DeMarco L (1988) The life history calendar: a technique for collecting retrospective data. Sociol Methodol 18:37–68

Griffin ML, Armstrong GS (2003) The effect of local life circumstances on female probationers' offending. Justice Q 20:213–239

Horney J (2001) Criminal events and criminal careers: an integrative approach to the study of violence. In: Meier R, Kennedy L, Sacco V (eds) The process and structure of crime: criminal events and crime analysis. Transaction Publishers, New Brunswick, NJ, pp 141–168

Horney J, Marshall I (1991) Measuring lambda through self reports. Criminology 29:471–495

Horney J, Marshall I (1992) Risk perceptions among serious offenders: the role of crime and punishment. Criminology 30:575–594

Horney J, Osgood W, Marshall I (1995) Criminal careers in the short-term: intra-individual variability in crime and its relation to local life circumstances. Am Sociol Rev 60:655–673

Johnson BD, Taylor A, Golub A, Eterno J (2002) How accurate are arrestees in reporting their criminal histories?: concordance and accuracy of self-reports compared to official records. US Department of Justice, Washington DC

Li SD, MacKenzie DL (2003) The gendered effects of adult social bonds on the criminal activities of probationers. Crim Justice Rev 28:278–298

Linton M (1986) Ways of searching and the contents of memory. In: Rubin, DC (ed) Autobiographical memory. Cambridge University Press: New York, pp. 50–67

Loftus E, Marburger W (1983) Since the eruption of Mt. St. Helens, has anyone beaten you up? Improving the accuracy of retrospective reports with landmark events. Mem Cognit 11:114–120

MacKenzie DL, Li SD (2002) The impact of formal and informal social controls on the criminal activities of probationers. J Res Crime Delinq 39:243–276

Morris N, Slocum L (Forthcoming) The validity of self-reported prevalence, frequency and timing of arrest: an evaluation of data collected using a life event calendar. J Res Crime Delinq

Peterson MA, Chaiken JM, Ebener PA, Honig PA (1982) Survey of prison and jail inmates: background and methods. Rand Corporation, Santa Monica, CA

Roberts J, Mulvey E (2009) Reports of life events by individuals at high risk for violence. In: Belli R, Stafford F, Alwin D (eds) Calendar and time diaries: methods in life course research. Sage, Los Angeles, CA. pp 191–206

Roberts J, Wells W (2009) The validity of criminal justice contacts reported by inmates: a comparison of self-reported data with official prison records, unpublished manuscript

Roberts J, Mulvey EP, Horney J, Lewis J, Arter ML (2005) A test of two methods of recall for violent events. J Quant Criminol 21:175–193

Rojek DG (1983) Social status and delinquency: do self-reports and official reports match? In: Waldo GP (ed) Measurement issues in criminal justice. Sage, Beverly Hills, pp 71–88

Rubin DC, Kozin M (1984) Vivid memories. Cognition 16:81–95

Schubert CA, Mulvey EP, Cauffman E, Steinberg L, Hecker T, Losoya S, Chassin L, Knight G (2004) Operational lessons from the pathways to desistance project. Youth Violence Juv Justice 2:237–255

Shum MS (1998) The role of temporal landmarks in autobiographical memory processes. Psychol Bull 124:423–442

Sobell LC and Sobell MB (1992) Timeline follow-back: a technique for assessing self-reported alcohol consumption. In: Litten R, Allen J (eds) Measuring alcohol consumption. Humana, Totowa, NJ, pp 41–72

Teplin LA (1994) Psychiatric and substance abuse disorders among male urban jail detainees. Am J Public Health 84:290–293

Van der Vaart W, Glasner T (2007) Applying a timeline as a recall aid in a telephone survey: a record check study. Appl Cognit Psychol 21:227–238

Weinstock J, Whelan JP, Meyers AW (2004) Behavioral assessment of gambling: an application of the timeline followback method. Psychol Assess 16:72–80

Weis JG (1986) Issues in the measurement of criminal careers. In: Blumstein A, Cohen J, Roth JA, Visher CA (eds) Criminal careers and "career criminals". National Academy Press, Washington, DC, pp 1–51

Wittebrood K, Nieuwbeerta P (2000) Criminal victimization during one's life course: the effects of previous victimization and patterns of routine activities. J Res Crime Delinq 37:91–122

Yacoubian GS (2000) Assessing the efficacy of the calendar method with Oklahoma City arrestees. J Crime Justice 26:117–131

Yacoubian GS (2003) Does the calendar method enhance drug use reporting among Portland arrestees? J Subst Use 8:27–32

Yoshihama M (2009) Application of the life history calendar approach: understanding women's experiences of intimate partner violence over the life course. In: Belli R, Stafford F, Alwin D (eds) Calendar and time diaries: methods in life course research. Sage, Los Angeles, CA, pp 135–155

Yoshihama M, Clum K, Crampton A, Gillespie B (2002) Measuring the lifetime experience of domestic violence: application of the life history calendar method. Violence Vict 17:297–317

Yoshihama M, Gillespie B, Hammock AC, Belli RF, Tolman R (2005) Does the life history calendar method facilitate the recall of domestic violence victimization? Comparison of two methods of data collection. Soc Work Res 29:151–163

Yoshihama M, Hammock AC, Horrocks J (2006) Intimate partner violence, welfare receipt, and health status of low-income African American women: a lifecourse analysis. Am J Community Psychol 37:95–108

CHAPTER 16

Statistical Power

Chester L. Britt and David Weisburd

INTRODUCTION

Criminal justice researchers have placed a premium on statistical inference and its use in making decisions about population parameters from sample statistics. In assessing statistical significance, the focus is on the problem of Type I, or alpha (α), error: the risk of falsely rejecting the null hypothesis. Paying attention to the statistical significance of a finding should keep researchers honest because it provides a systematic approach for deciding when the observed statistics are convincing enough for the researcher to state that they reflect broader processes or relationships in the general population from which the sample was drawn. If the threshold of statistical significance is not met, then the researcher cannot reject the null hypothesis and cannot conclude that a relationship exists.

Another type of error that most criminal justice researchers are aware of, but pay relatively little attention to, is Type II, or beta (β), error: the risk of falsely failing to reject the null hypothesis. A study that has a high risk of Type II error is likely to mistakenly conclude that treatments are not worthwhile or that a relationship does not exist when in fact it does. Understanding the risk of a Type II error is crucial to the development of a research design that will give the researcher a good chance of finding a treatment effect or a statistical relationship if those effects and relationships exist in the population. This is what we fundamentally mean by statistical power – given the current design of a study, does it have the ability (i.e., power) to detect statistically significant effects and relationships?

Although researchers in criminal justice have placed much more emphasis on statistical significance than on the statistical power of a study, research in fields, such as medicine and psychology routinely report estimates of statistical power (see, e.g., Maxwell et al. 2008). Funding agencies (e.g., National Institutes of Health) are increasingly likely to require research proposals to estimate how powerful the proposed research design will be. The purpose of this chapter is to present the key components in an assessment of statistical power, so that criminal justice researchers will have a basic understanding of how they can estimate the statistical power of a research design or to estimate the size of sample necessary to achieve a given level of statistical power. Toward that end, our discussion is organized as follows. The next two sections present the basic and conceptual background on statistical power and the three key components to statistical power, respectively. We then focuses on the computation of statistical power estimates, as well as estimates of sample size, for some of the most common

A.R. Piquero and D. Weisburd (eds.), *Handbook of Quantitative Criminology*,
DOI 10.1007/978-0-387-77650-7_16, © Springer Science + Business Media, LLC 2010,
First softcover printing 2011

types of statistical tests researchers will confront.[1] Finally, we conclude by noting some of the more recent developments and future directions in estimating statistical power in criminology and criminal justice.

STATISTICAL POWER

Statistical power measures the probability of rejecting the null hypothesis when it is false, but it cannot be measured directly. Rather, statistical power is calculated by subtracting the probability of a Type II error – the probability of falsely failing to reject the null hypothesis – from 1:

$$\text{Power} = 1 - \text{Probability}(\text{Type II error}) = 1 - \beta.$$

For many sample statistics, the Type II error can be estimated directly from the sampling distributions, commonly assumed for each statistic. In contrast to a traditional test of statistical significance, which identifies the risk of stating that factors are related when they are not (i.e., the Type I error), for the researcher statistical power measures how often one would fail to identify a relationship that in fact does exist in the population. For example, a study with a statistical power level of 0.90 has only 10% probability of falsely failing to reject the null hypothesis. Alternatively, a study with a statistical power estimate of 0.40 has 60% probability of falsely failing to reject the null hypothesis. Generally, as the statistical power of a proposed study increases, the risk of making a Type II error decreases.

Figure 16.1 presents the relationship between Type I and Type II errors graphically. Suppose that we are interested in a difference in groups means, say between a control and treatment group in a criminal justice experiment, and based on prior research and theory, we expect to find a positive difference in the outcome measure. We would test for a difference in group means using a one-tailed t-test. If we have 100 cases in each group, then the critical t-value is 1.653 for $\alpha = 0.05$. The distribution on the left side of Fig. 16.1 represents the t-distribution – the sampling distribution – under the null hypothesis, with the significance level (α) noted in the right tail of the distribution – the vertical line represents the critical

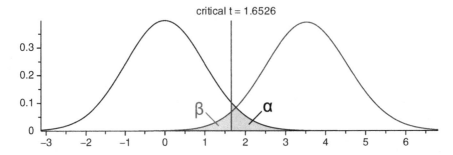

FIGURE 16.1. Graphical representation of Type I and Type II errors in a difference of means test (100 cases per sample).

---

[1] Since the actual computation of statistical power varies with the sample statistic being tested, there is voluminous literature on how to compute statistical power for a wide range of statistical models and our discussion is necessarily limited.

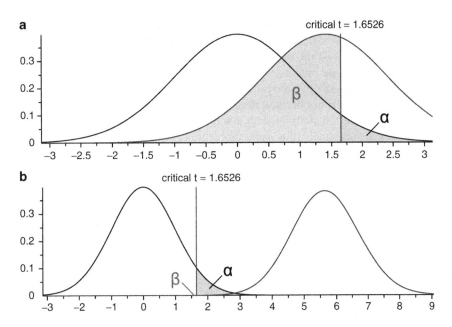

FIGURE 16.2. Graphical representation of Type I and Type II errors in a difference of means test – changing the difference in mean values. (**a**) smaller difference in means – fixed sample size. (**b**) larger difference in means – fixed sample size.

value. The distribution on the right side of Fig. 16.1 represents the hypothesized sampling distribution based on prior research and theory and our expectations for differences in the two group means. The probability of making a Type II error (β) is the cumulative probability in the figure on the right, which represents the chances of finding a difference in the two group means that is less than the critical value. The power of the difference of means test is represented in the figure by the area under the curve on the right that falls to the right of the critical value – the difference between 1 and β.

It is important to note that our estimate of β is fully dependent on our estimate of the magnitude of the difference between the two groups. Figure 16.2 illustrates the differences for alternative effect sizes, assuming that the sample sizes remain fixed at 100 cases per group. For example, if we expect the difference of means to be smaller, we would shift the hypothesized sampling distribution to the left, increasing our estimate of β (see Fig. 16.2a). If we expect a large difference, we would shift the hypothesized sampling distribution to the right, reducing the estimate of β (see Fig. 16.2b).

If the statistical power of a research design is high and the null hypothesis is false for the population under study, then it is very likely that the researcher will reject the null hypothesis and conclude that there is a statistically significant finding. If the statistical power of a research design is low, it is unlikely to yield a statistically significant finding, even if the research hypothesis is in fact true. Studies with very low statistical power are sometimes described as being "designed for failure," because a study that is underpowered is unlikely to yield a statistically significant result, even when the outcomes observed are consistent with the research hypothesis (Weisburd 1991).

Consider the implications for theory and practice in criminal justice of a study that has low statistical power. Suppose that a promising new program has been developed for dealing with offender reentry to the community following incarceration. If that program is evaluated with a study that has low statistical power, then the research team will likely fail to reject the null hypothesis based on the sample statistics, even if the program does indeed have the potential for improving the outcomes of offenders after release from prison. Although the research team is likely to say that the program does not have a statistically significant impact on offender reentry, this is not because the program is not an effective one, but because the research team designed the study in such a way that it was unlikely to be able to identify program success. Conceptually, this same problem occurs in the analysis of other types of data when trying to establish whether a relationship exists between two theoretically important variables. Although the relationship may exist in the population of interest, a study with low statistical power will be unlikely to conclude that the relationship is statistically significant.

One might assume that researchers in criminal justice would work hard to develop statistically powerful studies, because such studies are more likely to support the research hypothesis proposed by the investigators. Unfortunately, statistical power is often ignored altogether by criminal justice researchers, resulting in many criminal justice studies having a low level of statistical power (Brown 1989; Weisburd 1991).

Setting the Level of Statistical Power

What is a desirable level of statistical power? There is no single correct answer to this question, since it depends on the relative importance of Type I and Type II errors for the researcher. That said, one of the more common suggestions in the statistical power literature has been that studies should attempt to achieve a power level of 0.80, meaning the chances of a Type II error are $\beta = 0.20$. In many ways, this is an arbitrary threshold. At the same time, it implies a straightforward gauge for the relative importance of both types of error. If we use a conventional level of statistical significance ($\alpha = 0.05$) and statistical power (0.80, $\beta = 0.20$), it implies that the researcher is willing to accept a risk of making a Type II error that is four times greater than the risk of a Type I error:

$$\beta/\alpha = 0.20/0.05 = 4.0.$$

If the target level of statistical power is 0.90, then $\beta = 0.10$, and the ratio of probabilities decreases to $0.10/0.05 = 2.0$. Consequently, for a fixed level of statistical significance (α), increasing the level of statistical power reduces the chances of a Type II error (β) at the same time that the ratio of β/α moves closer to 1.0, where the chances of both types of error are viewed as equally important.

What happens if we reduce the desired level of statistical significance? For example, suppose we were particularly concerned about our chances of making a Type I error and reduced α from 0.05 to 0.01. For a statistical power level of 0.80, this would imply that we are willing to accept a probability of making a Type II error that is 20 times greater than the probability of a Type I error. If we simultaneously increase the level of statistical power to 0.90 at the same time we reduce the significance level, the β/α ratio decreases to 10, but it still implies a much greater likelihood of a Type II error. If we want to maintain the ratio of error probabilities at 4.0, we need a study with a power level of 0.96 ($=1-4(\alpha) = 1 - 0.04$). Intuitively, this makes good sense though: if we are going to make it more difficult to reject the null hypothesis by reducing α, we will simultaneously increase our chances of our failing to reject a false null hypothesis, unless we have a more powerful study.

COMPONENTS OF STATISTICAL POWER

The level of statistical power associated with any given test of a sample statistic is influenced by three key elements:

- Level of statistical significance, including directional tests when appropriate
- Sample size
- Effect size

The level of statistical significance and sample size are within the control of the researcher, while the estimated effect size is not. The following discussion briefly highlights the links between each element and the statistical power of any given test.

Statistical Significance and Statistical Power

The most straightforward way to increase the statistical power of a test is to change the significance level used. As we reduce the chances of making a Type I error by reducing the level of statistical significance from 0.10 to 0.05 to 0.01, it becomes increasingly difficult to reject the null hypothesis. Simultaneously, the power of the test is reduced. A significance level of 0.05 results in a more powerful test than a significance level of 0.01, because it is easier to reject the null hypothesis using more lenient significance criteria. Conversely, a 0.10 level of significance would make it even easier to reject the null hypothesis.

As a simple illustration, Table 16.1 presents z-scores required to reject the null hypothesis for several levels of statistical significance using a two-tailed test. It would take a z-score greater than 1.645 or less than -1.645 to reject the null hypothesis with $p = 0.10$, a z-score greater than 1.960 or less than -1.960 with $p = 0.05$, and a z-score greater than 2.576 or less than -2.576 for $p = 0.01$. Clearly, it is much easier to reject the null hypothesis with a 0.10 significance threshold than with a 0.01 significance threshold.

This method for increasing statistical power is direct, but it means that any benefit we gain in reducing the risk of a Type II error is offset by an increase in the risk of a Type I error. By setting a more lenient significance threshold, we do indeed gain a more statistically powerful research study. However, the level of statistical significance of our test also declines. Since a 0.05 significance level has become the convention in much of the research in criminology and criminal justice, it is important for authors to note why a more (or less) restrictive level of statistical significance is used.

DIRECTIONAL HYPOTHESES. A related method for increasing the statistical power of a study is to limit the direction of the research hypothesis to either a positive or negative outcome, which implies the use of a one-tailed statistical test. A one-tailed test will provide greater statistical power than a two-tailed test for the same reason that a less stringent level of statistical significance provides more power than a more stringent one. By choosing

TABLE 16.1. z-Scores needed to reject the null hypothesis in a two-tailed test of statistical significance

α	0.20	0.10	0.05	0.01	0.001
z-score	± 1.282	± 1.645	± 1.960	2.576	3.291

TABLE 16.2. *z*-Scores needed to reject the null hypothesis in one-tailed and two-tailed tests of statistical significance

α	0.20	0.10	0.05	0.01	0.001
z-score (1-tail test)	−0.842 or 0.842	−1.282 or 1.282	−1.645 or 1.645	−2.326 or 2.326	−3.090 or 3.090
z-score (2-tail test)	±1.282	±1.645	±1.960	2.576	3.291

a one-tailed test, the researcher reduces the absolute value of the test statistic needed to reject the null hypothesis by placing all of the probability of making a Type I error in a single tail of the distribution.

We can see this in practice again with the z-test. Table 16.2 lists the *z*-scores needed to reject the null hypothesis in one- and two-tailed tests for five different levels of statistical significance. (For the sake of simplicity, we assume in the one-tailed test that the outcome will be positive.) At each level, as in other statistical tests, the test statistic required to reject the null hypothesis is smaller in the case of a one-tailed test. For example, at $p = 0.05$, a *z*-score greater than or equal to 1.960 or less than or equal to −1.960 is needed to reject the null hypothesis in the two-tailed test. In the one-tailed test, the *z*-score need only be greater than or equal to 1.645. When we reduce the significance level to $p = 0.01$, a *z*-score greater than or equal to 2.576 or less than or equal to −2.576 is needed to reject the null hypothesis in the two-tailed test, but in the one-tailed test, the *z*-score need only be greater than or equal to 2.326.

Although the researcher can increase the statistical power of a study by using a directional, as opposed to a nondirectional, research hypothesis, there is a price for shifting the rejection region to one side of the sampling distribution. Once a one-directional test is defined, a finding in the direction opposite to that originally predicted cannot be recognized. To do otherwise would bring into question the integrity of the assumptions of the statistical test used in the analysis.

Sample Size and Statistical Power

The method used most often to change the level of statistical power in social science research is to vary the size of the sample. Similar to specifying the level of statistical significance, sample size can be controlled by the researcher. Modifying the size of the sample is a more attractive option for increasing statistical power than modifying the level of statistical significance, since the risk of a Type I error remains fixed – presumably at the conventional $p = 0.05$.

The relationship between statistical power and sample size is straightforward. All else being equal, larger samples provide more stable estimates of the population parameters than do smaller samples. Assuming that we are analyzing data from random samples of a population, the larger sample will have smaller standard errors of the coefficients than will the smaller sample. As the number of cases in a sample increases, the standard error of the sampling distribution (for any given statistical test) decreases. For example, it is well known that the standard error (*se*) for a single-sample *t*-test is computed as:

$$se = \frac{sd}{\sqrt{N - 1}}.$$

TABLE 16.3. Number of statistically significant outcomes expected in 100 two-sample *t*-tests for four scenarios

Scenario	Sample size (per group)	$\mu_1 - \mu_2$	σ	Expected significant outcomes
1	35	0.2	1	13
2	100	0.2	1	29
3	200	0.2	1	51
4	1,000	0.2	1	99

As N gets larger, irrespective of the value of the standard deviation (*sd*) itself, the standard error of the estimate gets smaller. As the standard error of a test decreases, the likelihood of achieving statistical significance grows, because the test statistic for a test of statistical significance is calculated by taking the ratio of the difference between the observed statistic and the value proposed in the null hypothesis (typically 0) to the standard error of that difference. If the difference is held constant, then as the sample size increases, the standard error decreases, and a larger test statistic is computed, making it easier to reject the null hypothesis.

The effect of sample size on statistical power for a *t*-test of the difference of two independent sample means is illustrated in Table 16.3. The last column of Table 16.3 indicates the number of statistically significant outcomes expected in 100 two-sample *t*-tests in which there is a mean difference of two arrests between groups ($\sigma = 1$) is examined for four different scenarios (using a 5% significance threshold and a two-tailed test). In the first scenario, the sample size for each group is only 35 cases; in the second scenario, the sample size is 100; in the third, 200; and in the fourth, fully 1,000. Table 16.3 shows that the likelihood of rejecting the null hypothesis changes substantially with each increase in sample size, even though all other characteristics are held constant across the four scenarios. Under the first scenario, we would expect only about 13 statistically significant outcomes in 100 tests. In the second scenario, 29 significant outcomes would be expected; and in the third, 51. In the final scenario of samples of 1,000, nearly every test (99 out of 100) would be expected to lead to a significant result.

Sample size is often a primary concern in statistical power analysis because (1) it is directly related to statistical power, (2) it is a factor usually under the control of the researcher, and (3) it can be manipulated without altering the criteria for statistical significance of a study.

In most cases, researchers maximize the statistical power of a study by increasing sample size. The concern with sample size is also reflected in the number of publications focused on advising researchers on how to determine the appropriate sample size for a proposed research study (see, e.g., Dattalo 2008; Kraemer and Thiemann 1987; Murphy and Myors 2003).

Although sample size should be under the control of the researcher, it is important to be aware of the unanticipated consequences of simply increasing sample size may have on other factors that influence statistical power, particularly in evaluation research (Weisburd 1991). For example, suppose a researcher has developed a complex and intensive method for intervening with high-risk youth. The impact of the treatment is dependent on each subject, receiving the "full dosage" of the treatment for a 6-month period. If the researcher were to increase the sample size of this study, it might become more difficult to deliver the treatments in the way that was originally intended by the researcher. More generally, increasing the sample size of a study can decrease the integrity or dosage of the interventions that are applied and result in the study showing no effect of the treatment. Increasing the size of a sample may also affect the variability of study estimates in other ways. For example, it may become more difficult to monitor implementation of treatments as a study grows. It is one thing to make sure that 100 subjects receive a certain intervention, but quite another to ensure consistency of interventions across hundreds or thousands of subjects. Also, studies are likely to include more heterogeneous groups of subjects, as sample size increases. For example, in a study of intensive probation, eligibility requirements were continually relaxed in order to meet project goals regarding the number of participants (Petersilia 1989). As noted earlier, as the heterogeneity of treatments or subjects in a study grows, it is likely that the standard deviations of the outcomes examined will also get larger. This, in turn, leads to a smaller effect size for the study and thus a lower level of statistical power.

Effect Size and Statistical Power

Effect size (ES) is a component of statistical power that is unrelated to the criteria for statistical significance used in a test. Effect size measures the difference between the actual parameters in the population and those hypothesized in the null hypothesis. In computing effect size, it is important to take into account both the raw differences between scores and the degree of variability found in the measures examined. Taking into account variability in effect size is a method of standardization that allows for the comparison of effects across studies that may have used different scales or slightly different types of measures. It has also allowed for the standardization of estimates of statistical power across a wide range of studies and types of analyses.

Generally, effect size (ES) is defined as:

$$ES = \frac{Parameter - H_0}{\sigma}$$

The relationship between effect size and statistical power should be clear. When the standardized population parameters differ substantially from those proposed in the null hypothesis, the researcher should be more likely to observe a significant difference or effect in a particular sample. Effect size is dependent on two factors: (1) the difference between the actual parameter and the hypothesized parameter under the null hypothesis and (2) the variability (i.e., standard error) in the measure examined. Effect size will increase when the difference between the population parameter and the hypothesized parameter increases and the standard error is held constant or when the difference is held constant and the standard error is decreased, perhaps through the use of a larger sample of cases.[2]

A difference of means test for two independent samples provides a simple illustration for these relationships. In the difference of means test, effect size would be calculated by first subtracting the population difference as stated in the null hypothesis ($H_0\mu_1 - H_0\mu_2$) from the difference between the true means in the population ($\mu_1 - \mu_2$). When comparing these two

---

[2] Effect size can also be calculated for observed differences in a study. This is a common approach in meta-analysis, where a large group of studies are summarized in a single analysis. For example, in calculating effect size for a randomized experiment with one treatment and one control group, the researcher would substitute the outcome scores for both groups in the numerator of the *ES* equation and the pooled standard deviation for the two outcome measures in the denominator. For a more detailed discussion of effect size and its use generally for comparing effects across different studies, see Lipsey and Wilson (2001) and Rosenthal (1984).

populations, variability is defined as the pooled or common standard deviation of the outcome measures in the two populations (σ). Consequently, ES would be computed as:

$$ES = \frac{(\mu_1 - \mu_2) - (H_0\mu_1 - H_0\mu_2)}{\sigma}.$$

Since the null hypothesis for a difference of means test is ordinarily that the two population means are equal (i.e., $H_0\mu_1 - H_0\mu_2 = 0$), we can simplify this formula and include only the difference between the actual population parameters:

$$ES = \frac{(\mu_1 - \mu_2)}{\sigma}.$$

Thus, ES for a difference of means test may be defined simply as the raw difference between the two population parameters, divided by their common standard deviation. To reiterate an earlier comment, when the difference between the population means is greater, the ES for the difference of means will be larger. Also, as the variability of the scores of the parameters grows, as represented by the standard deviation of the estimates, the ES will get smaller.

Table 16.4 presents a simple illustration of the relationship between effect size and statistical power in practice. The last column of Table 16.4 presents the number of statistically significant outcomes expected in 100 t-tests (using a 0.05 significance threshold and a nondirectional research hypothesis, resulting in a two-tail test), each with 100 cases per sample, under six different scenarios. In the first three scenarios, the mean differences between the two populations are varied and the standard deviations for the populations are held constant. In the last three scenarios, the mean differences are held constant and the standard deviations differ.

As Table 16.4 shows, the largest number of statistically significant outcomes is expected in either the comparisons with the largest differences between mean scores or the comparisons with the smallest standard deviations. As the differences between the population means grow (scenarios 1, 2, and 3), so too does the likelihood of obtaining a statistically significant result. Conversely, as the population standard deviations of the comparisons get larger (scenarios 4, 5, and 6), the expected number of significant outcomes decreases.

As this exercise illustrates, there is a direct relationship between the two components of effect size and statistical power. Studies that examine populations in which there is a larger

TABLE 16.4. **Number of statistically significant outcomes expected in 100 two-sample t-tests for six different scenarios (100 cases in each sample)**

Scenario	μ_1	μ_2	σ	Expected significant outcomes
(a) means differ; standard deviations constant				
1	0.3	0.5	2	10
2	0.3	0.9	2	56
3	0.3	1.3	2	94
(b) means constant; standard deviations differ				
4	0.3	0.5	0.5	80
5	0.3	0.5	1	29
6	0.3	0.5	2	10

effect size will, all else being equal, have a higher level of statistical power. Importantly, the relationship between effect size and statistical power is unrelated to the significance criteria we use in a test. In this sense, effect size allows for increasing the statistical power of a study (and thus reducing the risk of Type II error) while minimizing the risk of Type I error (through the establishment of rigorous levels of statistical significance).

Although effect size is often considered the most important component of statistical power, it is generally very difficult for the researcher to manipulate in a specific study (Lipsey 1990). Ordinarily, a study is initiated in order to determine the type and magnitude of a relationship that exists in a population. In many cases, the researcher has no influence at all over the raw differences, or the variability of the scores on the measures examined. For example, a researcher who is interested in identifying whether male and female police officers have different attitudes toward corruption may have no idea prior to the execution of a study the nature of these attitudes or their variability. It is then not possible for the researcher to estimate the nature of the effect size prior to collecting and analyzing data – the effect size may be large or small, but it is not a factor that the researcher is able to influence.

In contrast, evaluation research – in which a study attempts to assess a specific program or intervention – the researcher may have the ability to influence the effect size of a study and thus minimize the risk of making a Type II error. There is growing recognition, for example, of the importance of ensuring the strength and integrity of criminal justice interventions (Petersilia 1989). Moreover, many criminal justice evaluations fail to show a statistically significant result simply because the interventions are too weak to have the desired impact or the outcomes are too variable to allow a statistically significant finding (Weisburd 1991).

Statistical power suggests that researchers should be concerned with the effect size of their evaluation studies if they want to develop a fair test of the research hypothesis. First, the interventions should be strong enough to lead to the expected differences in the populations under study. Of course, the larger the differences expected, the greater the statistical power of an investigation. Second, interventions should be administered in ways that maximize the homogeneity of outcomes. For example, interventions applied differently to each subject will likely increase the variability of outcomes and thus the standard deviation of those scores. Finally, researchers should recognize that the heterogeneity of the subjects studied (and thus the heterogeneity of the populations to which they infer) will often influence the statistical power of their tests. Different types of people are likely to respond in different ways to treatment or interventions. If they do respond differently, the variability of outcomes will be larger, and thus the likelihood of making a Type II error will grow.

ESTIMATING STATISTICAL POWER AND SAMPLE SIZE FOR A STATISTICALLY POWERFUL STUDY

A number of texts have been written that provide detailed tables for defining the statistical power of a study (Cohen 1988; Kraemer and Thiemann 1987; Lipsey 1990; Murphy and Myors 2003). All of these texts also provide a means for computing the size of the sample needed to achieve a given level of statistical power. In both cases – the estimation of statistical power or the estimation of necessary sample size – assumptions will need to be made about effect size and level of statistical significance desired. The following discussion provides a basic discussion for how to compute estimates of statistical power. (The computations reported in the following discussion have been performed with a variety of statistical software tools, several of which are freely available to interested researchers. A later section of the chapter highlights several easily accessible resources that that will perform the power estimates reported in this chapter.)

The most common application of statistical power analysis in criminology and criminal justice research has been to compute the sample size needed to achieve a statistically powerful study (generally at or above 80%). As noted above, we need to be cautious about simply increasing the size of the sample, since a larger sample can affect other important features of statistical power. Thus, in using increased sample size to minimize Type II error, we must consider the potential consequences that larger samples might have on the nature of interventions or subjects studied, particularly in evaluation research. Nonetheless, sample size remains the tool most frequently used for adjusting the power of studies, because it can be manipulated by the researcher and does not require changes in the significance criteria of a test.

To define how many cases should be included in a study, we must conduct power analyses before the study is begun, generally referred to as prospective or a priori power analysis, and where our attention is focused in this chapter. Some authors have advocated the use of power analysis to evaluate whether studies already conducted have acceptable levels of statistical power, based on the sample statistics, referred to as retrospective or post hoc power analysis. Although there is much agreement about the utility of prospective power analysis, there is little consensus about the appropriateness of retrospective power analysis (see, e.g., Hayes and Steidl, 1997; Thomas 1997). The widespread use of secondary data sources in the study of crime and criminal justice further complicates the interpretation of results from a statistical power analysis. Since it is not possible for researchers to augment the original study's sample, results from a power analysis will still be informative in the sense that the results will indicate to the researchers using these data sources what the archived dataset can and cannot tell them about the statistical relationships they may be most interested in.

To define the sample size needed for a powerful study, we must first clearly define each of the components of statistical power other than sample size. These include:

1. The statistical test
2. The significance level
3. The research hypothesis (whether directional or nondirectional)
4. The effect size

The first three of these elements should be familiar, since they are based on common assumptions made in developing any statistical test. The statistical test is chosen based on the type of measurement and the extent to which the study can meet certain assumptions. For example, if we want to compare three sample means, we will likely use analysis of variance as our test. If we are comparing means from two samples, we will likely use a two-sample t-test. If we are interested in the unique effects of a number of independent variables on a single interval-level dependent variable, we will likely use OLS regression and rely on t-tests for the individual coefficients and F-tests for either the full regression model or a subset of variables from the full model.

To calculate statistical power, we must also define the significance level of a test and its research hypothesis. By convention, we generally use a 0.05 significance threshold, and thus we are likely to compute the statistical power estimates based on this criterion. The research hypothesis defines whether a test is directional or nondirectional. When the statistical test allows for it, we will typically choose a nondirectional test to take into account the different types of outcomes that can be found in a study (Cohen 1988). If we were evaluating an existing study, we would use the decisions as stated by the authors in assessing that study's level of statistical power.

The fourth element, defining effect size, is more difficult. If we are trying to estimate the magnitude of a relationship in the population that has not been well examined in the past, how can we estimate the effect size in the population? It may be useful to reframe this criterion. The purpose of a power analysis is to see whether our study is likely to detect an effect of a certain size. Usually, we define that effect in terms of what is a meaningful outcome in a study. A power analysis, then, tells us whether our study is designed in a way that is likely to detect that outcome (i.e., reject the null hypothesis on the basis of our sample statistics). This is one of the reasons why the statistical power is sometimes defined as the design sensitivity (Lipsey 1990). It assesses whether our study is designed with enough sensitivity to be likely to reject the null hypothesis if an effect of a certain size exists in the population under study.

The task of defining the effect size has been made easier by identifying broad categories of effect size that can be compared across studies. Cohen's (1988) suggestions have been the most widely adopted by other researchers and simply refer to classifying effect sizes as small, medium, and large. The specific value of an effect size classified as small, medium, or large, is contingent on the specific statistical test being considered. For example, if our focus is on a difference of means test for two independent samples, the standardized effect size estimate is known as d (explained below) and is considered to be a small effect if it is 0.2, a medium effect if it is 0.5, and a large effect if it is 0.8. In contrast, if we are considering the statistical power of an OLS regression model, the standardized effect size estimate is known as f^2 and is considered to be a small effect if it is 0.02, a medium effect if it is 0.15, and a large effect if it is 0.35. Other authors have followed suit and attempted to define similar types of standardized effects for more complex statistical models not addressed in Cohen's (1988) work. For example, Raudenbush and Liu (2000) develop criteria for defining small, medium, and large standardized effects in hierarchical linear models.

The following discussion turns to the computation of statistical power for several common situations in criminology and criminal justice research: difference of means test, ANOVA, correlation, and OLS regression. Of course, there are a variety of other statistical models used in criminological research. In some cases, there are well-developed means for determining statistical power. In other applications, there are no clear guidelines for estimating the statistical power, and it is up to the researcher to conduct simulation studies to estimate the level of statistical power for a given model and sample. For example, structural equation models are notoriously complex, and with slight changes to the model being estimated, the statistical power estimates can be wildly different and necessitate the use of simulations to estimate power (see, e.g., Muthén and Muthén 2002).

The computation of statistical power estimates requires the comparison of a sampling distribution under the null hypothesis with a sampling distribution under the alternative or research hypothesis (see again Fig. 16.1, above). The sampling distribution under the research hypothesis is referred to as a noncentral distribution. For example, in Fig. 16.1, the sampling distribution under the null hypothesis is the t-distribution, while the sampling distribution under the research hypothesis is the noncentral t-distribution.

The noncentral sampling distribution is computed based on a "noncentrality" parameter, which in all cases, is a function of the standardized effect for the statistical test under consideration. For each of the statistical tests discussed below, we describe both the standardized effect and the noncentrality parameter and explain how to use these values to estimate the statistical power of a sample as well as the size of sample needed to meet a target level of statistical power.

Difference of Means Test

Throughout this chapter, we have pointed to the difference of means test as an example for many of the points we wanted to make about statistical power. More directly, the standardized effect size d is

$$d = \frac{\mu_1 - \mu_2}{\sigma},$$

which is identical to the equation noted earlier for computing a standardized difference of means for two independent samples. Recall that σ represents the pooled, or common, standard deviation for the difference of means.

The noncentrality parameter δ for the t-distribution is

$$\delta = d \sqrt{\frac{N}{4}},$$

where $N = n_1 + n_2$ when there are equal numbers of cases in each group (i.e., $n_1 = n_2$). For the situation where $n_1 \neq n_2$, the noncentrality parameter δ is

$$\delta = d \sqrt{\frac{N_H}{2}}, \quad \text{where} \quad N_H = \frac{2n_1 n_2}{n_1 + n_2}.$$

To illustrate the computation of a statistical power estimate, suppose that we want to assess the effectiveness of a treatment program for property offenders. Our design calls for random assignment of 100 cases to each group. We expect the program to be effective at reducing recidivism in the treatment group, and so can assume a one-tailed t-test with a significance level of 5%. What is the statistical power of our design for detecting standardized effects at the small ($d = 0.2$) at the medium ($d = 0.5$), and at the large ($d = 0.8$) levels?

For all three scenarios, the critical t-value will be 1.653, based on a one-tailed test with a significance level of 0.05 and $df = N - 2 = 198$. For a small effect, the noncentrality parameter δ is 1.414 $\left(= 0.2 \times \sqrt{(200/4)}\right)$. This provides us with an estimate for risk of making a Type II error of $\beta = 0.593$, suggesting that we have a probability of 59.3% of making a Type II error and fail to reject the null hypothesis when it is false. The corresponding estimate of statistical power is $1 - 0.593 = 0.407$. Substantively, this result suggests that if we have only 100 cases in each group, our probability of rejecting the null hypothesis when it is false is only about 40.7%. In regard to a medium effect size, $\delta = 3.536$, $\beta = 0.030$, and power $= 0.970$. For a large effect size, $\delta = 5.657$, $\beta < 0.0001$, and power >0.9999. Putting these results together indicates that our design with 100 cases assigned to each group provides a high level of statistical power for detecting medium effects and larger, but an inadequate level of power for detecting small effects.

Alternatively, we may be interested in determining the sample size needed to provide us with a statistical power estimate of 80% for each of the three effect sizes: small, medium, and large. In the case of a small effect, we find that we need a total sample of 620 cases – 310 in each group – to assure us that we will be able to reject the null hypothesis when it is false about 80% of the time. To achieve a power estimate of 80% for a medium effect, we only need 102 cases (51 in each group). For a large effect, the sample size drops to 40 (20 in each group).

ANOVA

For a simple ANOVA, where we are looking only at fixed effects and assume equal sample sizes across groups, the standardized effect size f is defined as

$$f = \frac{\sigma_m}{\sigma},$$

where $\sigma_m = \sqrt{\sum_{i=1}^{k} \frac{(m_i - m)^2}{k}}$, k is the number of groups, m is the grand mean, and m_i represents each of the group means with $n_1 = n_2 = \ldots = n_k$.

The noncentrality parameter λ for the F-distribution is

$$\lambda = f^2 N,$$

where f^2 refers to the square of the standardized effect size (f) and N refers to the total sample size.

As an illustration of the calculation of statistical power estimates for a fixed-effects ANOVA model, assume that we have three groups, each with 100 cases participating in an experiment aimed at reducing recidivism among violent offenders: a control group and two different kinds of treatment groups. Assume that the significance level has been set at 5%. What is the level of statistical power of our design for detecting standardized effects at the small ($f = 0.1$), at the medium ($f = 0.25$), and at the large ($f = 0.4$) levels?

For each of the three scenarios, the critical value of the F-statistic is 3.026 ($df_1 = 2$, $df_2 = 297$). For a small effect, the noncentrality parameter λ is 3 (=$0.1^2 \times 300$). This provides us with an estimate for risk of making a Type II error of $\beta = 0.681$, suggesting that we have a probability of 68.1% of making a Type II error and fail to reject the null hypothesis when it is false. The corresponding estimate of statistical power is $1 - 0.681 = 0.319$, meaning that we have only a 31.9% chance of rejecting the null hypothesis when it is false. For the medium effect size, $\lambda = 18.75$, $\beta = 0.022$, and power $= 0.978$. The large effect size has $\lambda = 48$, $\beta < 0.0001$, and power >0.9999. Similar to the previous situation with only two groups, our research design with 100 cases assigned to each of three groups provides a high level of statistical power for detecting medium and large effects, but an inadequate level of power for detecting small effects.

If our concern is focused on the size of the sample needed for a power level of 80% for each of the three effect sizes – small, medium, and large – then we would again proceed in the same way as in the two-sample t-test. To have an 80% chance of detecting a small effect ($f = 0.10$), we would need a sample of 969 cases (323 in each group). For the medium effect, we would need only 159 cases (53 in each group) and for the large effect, only 66 cases (22 in each group).

Correlation

To test the statistical power of a correlation coefficient, we can use either the correlation coefficient (r) or the Fisher r-to-Z transformation of the correlation coefficient (r_Z) as the standardized effect size. Although the estimates of statistical power will not be identical, they will tend to be very close, typically differing only at the second or third decimal.

The noncentrality parameter δ for the correlation coefficient is:

$$\delta = \sqrt{\frac{r^2}{1 - r^2} \times N},$$

where r is either the sample correlation coefficient (r) or the transformed (r_Z) and N is the sample size.

We can again illustrate the calculation of statistical power for correlations by assuming that we have 100 observations that would allow us to compute a correlation between two variables. For example, suppose we interview a random sample of police officers and are interested in the correlation between the number of years on the police force and a scale that measured hostility toward judges. We might expect that more years on the police force will have a positive correlation with hostility toward judges, implying that we can conduct a one-tailed t-test of statistical significance. As with the preceding examples, assume that the level of statistical significance is 5%. What is the level of statistical power of our design for detecting standardized effects at the small ($r = 0.1$), at the medium ($r = 0.3$), and at the large ($r = 0.5$) levels?

The critical t-value for all three scenarios is 1.661, based on $df = N - 2 = 98$. For a small effect size ($r = 0.1$), the noncentrality parameter is $\delta = 1.005$. This provides us with an estimate for risk of making a Type II error of $\beta = 0.741$, suggesting that we have a probability of 74.1% of making a Type II error and would fail to reject the null hypothesis when it is false. The corresponding estimate of statistical power is 0.259, indicating that we would only reject the null hypothesis when it was false about 26% of the time. The statistical power analysis of the medium effect indicates that $\delta = 3.145$, $\beta = 0.070$, and power $= 0.930$. The large effect shows an even greater level of statistical power, where $\delta = 5.774$, $\beta < 0.0001$, and power >0.9999.

The sample size required to detect each of the three effect sizes – small, medium, and large – with a statistical power of 80% again requires the use of the t-distribution. To achieve a power level of 80% for a small effect ($r = 0.1$), a sample of 614 cases would be needed. For the medium effect ($r = 0.3$), the required number of cases drops to 64, while for the large effect ($r = 0.5$), only 21 cases are required to have an 80% chance of rejecting the null hypothesis when it is false.

Least-Squares Regression

The statistical power analysis of least-squares regression can take two different, but related, forms. One question asks about the ability to detect whether a regression model – a single dependent variable and two or more independent variables – has a statistically significant effect on the dependent variable. This means that the null hypothesis is focused on whether the regression model in its entirety has an effect on the dependent variable. A second question asks about the ability to detect the effect of a single variable or subset of variables added to a regression model. This addresses the more common substantive question in much of the published research: once the other relevant independent and control variables have been taken into account statistically, does variable X add anything to the overall model?

Whether we are analyzing the full model or a subset of the full model, the standardized effect size (denoted as f^2) is based on either the R^2 for the full model or the partial R^2 for the subset of variables we are interested in analyzing. Specifically,

$$R^2 = f^2(1 + f^2).$$

Cohen's (1988) recommendations for small, medium, and large standardized effect sizes are 0.02, 0.15, and 0.35, respectively. To provide some context to these values, an f^2 value of 0.02 corresponds to an R^2 of 0.02, while $f^2 = 0.15$ implies that $R^2 = 0.13$, and $f^2 = 0.35$ implies that $R^2 = 0.26$. Statistical power analysis for least squares regression uses the F-distribution.

As noted in the discussion of statistical power analysis for ANOVA models, the noncentrality parameter λ for the F-distribution is

$$\lambda = f^2 N.$$

To assess the statistical power for the full regression model consider the following simple example. Suppose that we are interested in the effects of various case and defendant characteristics on the amount of bail required by a court. Typical analyses of bail decisions would consider some of the following characteristics (as well as others not listed): (1) severity of the prior record, (2) severity of the current offense, (3) number of counts of the current offense, (4) type of attorney, (5) whether the defendant was under criminal justice supervision at the time of the current offense, (6) age of the defendant, (7) race of the defendant, and (8) gender of the defendant. This provides us with a regression model with eight independent and control variables.

As a point of illustration, we may want to estimate the statistical power of the regression model assuming that we have a sample of only 100 cases and have set a significance level of 5%. For the small effect size ($f^2 = 0.02$), we have noncentrality parameter $\lambda = 2.0$ (=0.02× 100). We then find $\beta = 0.876$, meaning that with only 100 cases, we have a probability of making a Type II error of just under 88%. Alternatively, the estimate of statistical power is 0.124, meaning that we have a probability of only 12.4% of rejecting the null hypothesis when it is false. For the medium effect ($f^2 = 0.15$), $\lambda = 15.0$, $\beta = 0.242$, and power = 0.758, which is still an inadequate level of power, although it is much closer to the target of 80%. For the large effect ($f^2 = 0.35$), $\lambda = 35.0$, $\beta = 0.007$, and power = 0.993, which is well beyond the desired level of 80%.

For a regression model with eight independent and control variables, what sample size is required to achieve a statistical power level of 80% for detecting effects at the small ($f^2 = 0.02$), at the medium ($f^2 = 0.15$), and at the large ($f^2 = 0.35$) levels? For the small effect, we would require a sample of 759 cases to achieve a power level of 80%. For the medium and large effects, we would require samples of 109 and 52 cases, respectively. The number of cases required to detect a statistically significant effect at either the medium or the large effect level may strike many readers as small. It is important to keep in mind that we have only been assessing the full model – the number of cases required for detecting individual effects will tend to be different than the number of cases required for detecting whether the full model is significant.

The assessment of statistical power for a single independent variable or a small subset of independent variables proceeds in much the same way as the analysis for the full model. The key difference is in the degrees of freedom required for the F-distribution. In the case of a single independent variable, the numerator $df = 1$, while the denominator df remains the same as in the full model. For a subset of independent and/or control variables, the numerator $df =$ the number of variables in the subset (the denominator df remains the same).

If we return to the bail example above, the analysis of statistical power for any one of the independent and control variables will be identical. We continue to keep the sample size at 100 cases, the level of statistical significance at 5%, and the definition of small, medium, and large effects the same as before. For the small effect ($f^2 = 0.02$), $\lambda = 2.0$, $\beta = 0.712$, and power $= 0.288$, meaning that we would only be able to reject the null hypothesis of no relationship between the independent and dependent variables about 28.8% of the time. For the medium effect ($f^2 = 0.15$), $\lambda = 15.0$, $\beta = 0.031$, and power $= 0.969$, while for the large effect ($f^2 = 0.35$), $\lambda = 35.0$, $\beta < 0.0001$, and power > 0.9999.

Similarly, we may be interested in assessing the statistical power of a subset of variables. For example, in the bail example, the subset of demographic characteristics (age, race, and gender) may be important to testing some aspect of a theory predicting differential treatment of defendants within the courts. We find a similar pattern to the results. For the small effect ($f^2 = 0.02$), $\lambda = 2.0$, $\beta = 0.814$, and power $= 0.186$, again indicating a low level of statistical power for detecting a statistically significant relationship between demographic characteristics and bail amount. For the medium effect ($f^2 = 0.15$), $\lambda = 15.0$, $\beta = 0.095$, and power $= 0.905$, while for the large effect ($f^2 = 0.35$), $\lambda = 35.0$, $\beta = 0.001$, and power $= 0.999$.

Sample size calculations work in the same way as for the full model. If we hope to achieve a power level of 80%, what size sample is necessary to detect small, medium, and large effects for either single variables or subsets of variables? Continuing the bail example, we assume that there are eight independent and control variables. For the single variable, the number of cases required to detect a small effect with a probability of 80% is 395. A medium effect requires only 55 cases, while a large effect requires only 26 cases. It is worth noting that sample size calculations for single variable effects are not affected by the number of variables included in the full regression model

In practice, many of the individual effects that researchers are trying to assess in their multivariate models will tend toward the small effect size. For example, much survey research aimed at trying to explain attitudes toward a particular topic will incorporate 10 to 20 independent and control variables and have a full model R^2 typically between 0.15 and 0.20. This implies that many of the individual-variable effects will tend to be quite small in magnitude and in order for an analysis to detect a statistically significant relationship, a large sample becomes necessary.

Statistical Software

There are a variety of software packages available for computing statistical power as well as a number of websites that host power calculators for a wide range of statistical tests. All of the analyses presented in this chapter were performed with two different software packages: (1) G*Power (version 3.0.10) and (2) the `pwr` library available for the R system. G*Power 3 is freely available to download from the Institut fur Experimentelle Psychologie at Universitat Dusseldorf (http://www.psycho.uni-duesseldorf.de/abteilungen/aap/gpower3/). G*Power 3 is a specialized package devoted to statistical power estimation and offers a wide range of tests beyond those discussed here. G*Power 3 also features the simple creation of powerful graphs that will plot power estimates across a range of sample sizes, effect sizes, and statistical significance levels. All of the figures presented in this chapter were produced with G*Power 3. Faul et al. (2007) provide a useful overview of the capabilities of G*Power 3.

The R system is a comprehensive mathematical and statistical package that is modeled on S-Plus (R Development Core Team 2009). R can be freely downloaded from the Comprehensive R Archive Network website (http://cran.r-project.org/). The pwr library (Champely 2007) is a user-contributed set of routines that computes the basic estimates of statistical power discussed in this chapter and is based on Cohen's 1988) work. The R system also includes a powerful set of graphics routines and libraries. Although not as user-friendly for computing complicated graphs of power estimates as G*Power 3, every graph produced in this chapter can be reproduced in the R system.

Power and Precision v. 2.0 (Borenstein et al. 2001) is a commercially available software package designed to compute power estimates for a wide range of statistical models in a user-friendly environment. Its range of capabilities is greater than G*Power 3. A particularly useful feature is that all of the output – text and graphs – can be easily exported to other programs.

In addition to the software options noted above, more widely available all-purpose statistical packages – SAS, SPSS, and Stata – also include routines for estimating statistical power. For readers interested in pursuing the estimation of statistical power with one of these three packages, consult the appropriate software websites.

For the reader who simply wants to compute a small number of power estimates without bothering to learn a new software package, a reasonably comprehensive list of web-based power calculators can be found at http://statpages.org/#Power. The list of web sites hosting power calculators is categorized by the type of statistical test that the user is searching for – one-sample t-test, two-sample t-test, correlation, regression, and so on.

Finally, it is worth noting that there will be slight differences across statistical software packages and power calculators in the estimated sample sizes needed to achieve a given level of statistical power. The primary reason for this appears to be focused on rounding the estimated sample size to an integer, since we cannot sample a fraction of a case in any research study. Some packages round up, so that the estimated statistical power as always at least as great as the target entered into the computation. Other packages and calculators will round to the closest integer (regardless of whether it is larger or smaller), so the overall estimate of statistical power may be slightly less than the initial target.

SUMMARY AND CONCLUSION

The focus of this chapter has been the presentation of the key components and the rationale underlying the computation and the estimation of statistical power and sample size. Due to the wide range of statistical models used in the study of crime and criminal justice, our discussion necessarily touched on a limited number of more common situations. That said, the key components of statistical power – level of statistical significance, size of sample, and effect size – apply to estimating statistical power across all types of linear models, regardless of the specific form that a model may take. The manner in which statistical power is computed may vary widely by the type of model, but the components of statistical power remain the same.

Beyond the issues discussed in this chapter, there are four other important issues that we wish to highlight. First, in recent years, there has been a significant growth in the computation of statistical power for a much wider range of statistical models. For example, multilevel models that involve the analysis of clustered data raise a number of issues related to statistical power: How many groups? How many observations within each group? What are the estimates of statistical power, given different configurations for the number of groups (at different levels of aggregation) and the number of individual observations? Raudenbusch and Liu's (2000) simulation study focusing on multilevel models is a nice example for how power estimates vary across a range of small, medium, or large effects that they tried to make comparable to Cohen's (1988) recommendations.

In a similar way, the complexity of structural equation models makes the computation of statistical power estimates that much more challenging. Muthén and Muthén (2002) illustrate the application of simulation studies to structural equation models as a means for estimating statistical power. In general, simulation studies will likely grow in their use, as researchers confront increasingly complex multivariate models and are either unsure about the sampling distributions of the statistics being tested or are attempting to measure the sampling distribution. Using a similar approach, Kleiber and Zeileis (2008) provide an example for how to compute the power of the autocorrelation coefficient in an autoregression model.

Second, much of the written work on tests of statistical power notes that we make important assumptions about the sampling distributions for the statistics we estimate. Since the assumptions for many of the statistical models used by researchers in criminology and criminal justice are often violated, it is not clear that the assumed sampling distributions remain appropriate. Bootstrapping techniques offer a way around assuming a specific sampling distribution for a test statistic by allowing the researcher to generate an empirical sampling distribution through resampling the current sample data and performing the same statistical analysis (see, for example, Efron and Tibshirani (1993) and Dattalo (2008)). The empirical sampling distribution can then be used to provide a better sense of the statistical power of a study, since it will be based on the data, methods, and models used by the researcher.

Third, Maltz (1994) noted several years ago that the expanded use of archival datasets in criminology and criminal justice resulted in many researchers analyzing populations, rather than samples. The increased frequency with which populations are analyzed calls into question many of the assumptions about performing tests for statistical significance. Put simply, the analysis of population data implies no need for statistical significance testing, since the researcher is not trying to generalize from a sample to a population. Clearly, issues of statistical power are not relevant when we analyze a population: setting a significance level makes little sense, the number of cases in the dataset is as large as it possibly can be, and the effect size is simply what is observed (excluding measurement error).

Finally, we think it is important for all researchers to be sensitive to issues of statistical power. Although much of the research published in criminology and criminal justice journals relies on secondary data sources, we think that researchers analyzing these datasets will still benefit from thinking through issues of statistical power prior to setting off on a complicated analysis. Clearly, researchers cannot alter the size of the sample in a secondary dataset. At the same time, the use of the techniques discussed in this chapter and elsewhere should provide researchers with a better sense of the potential findings from any given dataset, which in the long run should improve the quality of the research enterprise.

REFERENCES

Borenstein M, Rothstein H, Cohen J (2001) Power and precision. Biostat, Inc., Englewood, NJ
Brown SE (1989) Statistical power and criminal justice research. J Crim Justice 17:115–122
Champely S (2007) pwr: Basic functions for power analysis. Rpackage version 1.1.

Cohen J (1988) Statistical power analysis for the behavioral sciences, 2nd edn. Lawrence Erlbaum, Hillsdale, NJ

Dattalo P (2008) Determining sample size. Oxford University Press, New York

Efron B, Tibshirani RJ (1993) An introduction to the bootstrap. Chapman & Hall, New York

Faul F, Erdfelder E, Land AG, Buchner A (2007) G*Power 3: a flexible statistical power analysis program for the social, behavioral, and biomedical sciences. Behav Res Methods 39:175–191

Hayes JP, Steidl RJ (1997) Statistical power analysis and amphibian population trends. Conserv Biol 11:273–275

Kleiber C, Zeileis A (2008) Applied econometrics in R. Springer, New York

Kraemer HC, Thiemann S (1987) How many subjects: statistical power analysis in research. Sage, Newbury Park, CA

Lipsey MW (1990) Design sensitivity: statistical power for experimental research. Sage, Newbury Park, CA

Lipsey M, Wilson D (2001) Practical meta-analysis. Sage, Thousand Oaks, CA

Maltz MD (1994) Deviating from the mean: the declining significance of significance. J Res Crime Delinq 31:434–463

Maxwell SE, Kelley K, Rausch JR (2008) Sample size planning for accuracy in parameter estimation. Annu Rev Psychol 59:537–563

Murphy KR, Myors B (2003) Statistical power analysis, 2nd edn. Lawrnce Erlbaum, Mahwah, NJ

Muthén LK, Muthén BO (2002) How to use a monte carlo study to decide on sample size and determine power. Struct Equ Model 9:599–620

Petersilia J (1989) Randomized experiments: lessons from BJA's intensive supervision project. Eval Rev 13:435–458

Raudenbusch S, Liu X (2000) Statistical power and optimal design for multisite randomized trials. Psychol Methods 5:199–213

R Core Development Team (2009) R: a language and environment for statistical computing. http://www.R-project.org

Rosenthal R (1984) Meta-analytic procedures for social research. Sage, Beverly Hills

Thomas L (1997) Retrospective power analysis. Conserv Biol 11:276–280

Weisburd D (1991) Design sensitivity in criminal justice experiments. Crim Justice 17:337–379

CHAPTER 17

Descriptive Validity and Transparent Reporting in Randomised Controlled Trials

AMANDA E. PERRY

INTRODUCTION

The validity of any research is key in addressing the inferences or conclusions that stem from a study (Campbell 1957). Such issues of validity have been central to the develop-ment of research design within criminology since the early 1950s, when two famous social scientists researched the validity of experiments in social settings. This work conducted by Campbell (1957) and Campbell and Stanley (1963) proposed four distinct categories of valid-ity. These included internal validity, (i.e., whether the intervention did cause a change in the outcome) statistical conclusion validity, (i.e., whether the cause and effect were related), construct validity (i.e., the measurement of the theoretical constructs that underlay the inter-vention and outcome), and external validity (i.e., the representative or generalisability of causal relationships across populations, type of treatment, or intervention).

While these forms of validity have been around for a number of decades, more recent forms of validity, such as descriptive validity, have been developed to enhance the reporting of trial information (e.g., Farrington 2003). In criminology, descriptive validity was first noted as important because of its role in systematic reviews. Most commonly reported studies in systematic reviews are those using either quasi-experimental or experimental study designs, which are often combined to provide an overall effect of treatment. The combining of studies through meta-analytical techniques is often completed on the assumption that such studies are similar on a number of different measures. Such measures include the inferences that can be drawn with respect to the internal and external validity of the study. In all studies, the judgement upon which this inference is drawn is based upon the availability of information reported by the authors of the study, or what we refer to as descriptive validity.

Descriptive validity is, therefore, inextricably linked to the concept of internal and external validity and relies upon the transparent reporting of information. As a result, a well-conducted study will only have high descriptive validity if the authors of the study fully describe the details of the study at all stages (e.g., identification and selection of participants

A.R. Piquero and D. Weisburd (eds.), *Handbook of Quantitative Criminology*,
DOI 10.1007/978-0-387-77650-7_17, © Springer Science + Business Media, LLC 2010,
First softcover printing 2011

through to interpretation of the results). Authors who conduct sound studies, but who provide poor descriptions about how the experiment was conducted, would, therefore, have low descriptive validity.

In healthcare, such concerns about the transparent reporting of Randomised Controlled Trials (RCTs) brought about the development of the Consolidated Standards of Reporting Trials (CONSORT) Statement, which was specifically devised to assess the extent to which authors reported transparent information within RCTs (e.g., Altman 2001). For these reasons, we are particularly interested in the issue of descriptive validity and its importance for criminologists with RCTs. This is not to say that descriptive validity is not important with other types of study designs, but the preponderance of evidence in other discipline areas has concentrated on RCTs because of their use and influence in conclusions drawn from meta-analyses.

As a result, this chapter will consider the emergence of descriptive validity in criminology and the application of the CONSORT Statement to criminal justice trials. In particular, the chapter refers to two studies, which help us to identify poor descriptive validity in criminology and provide some examples of best practice guidance.

Descriptive Validity in Criminology

General validity issues within criminology have been debated by researchers for many decades and include the development of mechanisms for reporting the internal and external validity of study information (e.g., Farrington 2003; Lösel and Köferl 1989; Sherman et al. 2002). However, descriptive validity in criminology is rarely reported, but has shown to be of great importance in RCTs conducted in healthcare. (e.g. Moher et al. 1998). Researchers have been keen to emphasize the extent to which a report provides information about the design, conduct, and analysis of the trial and its methodological quality (Moher et al. 1995). Equally as important are findings, which demonstrate the link between poor reporting of information and biased trial results (e.g. Hewitt et al. 2005).

In criminology, descriptive validity was first formally recognised by Farrington (2003), and more recently by Perry and Johnson (2008) and Perry et al. (in press). Descriptive validity in criminology is a critical concern for criminologists as they seek to develop evaluation studies of the highest standard (Perry et al. in press). For criminologists, the explicit reporting of study details are important because such information helps to maintain the methodological rigour and quality of reporting trial information. Farrington's recognition of descriptive validity was noted in his methodological evaluation of criminal justice research where he defines descriptive validity as "the adequacy of the presentation of key features of an evaluation in a research report" (p. 56). Farrington in his assessment of descriptive validity maintains that descriptive validity is important because without such key information it is difficult to assess the appropriateness of combining the results of trials or quasi-experimental studies in systematic reviews or meta-analyses where studies may differ in their methodological quality (see also Boruch 1997; chap. 10).

One other important element of descriptive validity is how descriptive validity is measured to provide an accurate picture of the adequacy of reporting within a particular study. Farrington suggests his 14 item checklist as one mechanism for studies within criminology (Farrington 2003). The 14 different elements include the design of the study, a description of the characteristics of the experimental units and setting, information on sample sizes and attrition rates, hypotheses to be tested and the theories from which it was derived. Other factors for consideration also include operational definitions of the intervention and details about how it was implemented and a description of what the control and treatment group received. The final elements noted relate to the definition, reliability and validity of the outcome, the study follow up period, the reporting of effect sizes, confidence intervals and statistical significance levels, a description of how independent and extraneous variables were controlled for knowledge of the intervention and finally any conflict of interest issues, including the independence of the researchers and how the research was funded.

In healthcare, a widely accepted measurement of descriptive validity is the CONSORT Statement.

Measuring Descriptive Validity

In healthcare, the CONSORT Statement was published in 1996 to aid the transparent reporting of information in trials. Since its first publication, the CONSORT Statement has evolved with a number of subsequent revisions in 2001 and the Statement currently consists of two sections. Section one contains 22 items (Altman 2001; Moher et al. 2001b), which cover all aspects of reporting, including information across the title and abstract, introduction and background, methods (participants, interventions, objectives, outcomes, sample size, randomisation, blinding, and statistical methods), results (participant flow, recruitment, baseline data, numbers analysed, outcomes and estimation, ancillary analyses, and adverse events), interpretation, generalisability and overall evidence of a trial (see http://www.consort-statement.org/). Table 17.1 provides a detailed description of each checklist item.

The second section of the CONSORT Statement is a flow diagram. The CONSORT flow diagram is used to show the progression of participants through a trial and offers the authors an opportunity to standardise the methodology for the preparation of trial findings. At each stage in the trial (e.g., enrolment, intervention allocation, follow-up, and analysis) information is gathered for the purpose of transparency. Figure 17.1 shows the flow diagram outline, which allows readers to critically appraise and interpret the trial findings allowing the reader to assess the number of participants who did and did not complete the study enabling an assessment of the trial analysis (i.e., intention to treat or per protocol).

Although this concept is familiar to researchers in healthcare, there has been little use of the CONSORT Statement in criminology. As a consequence, we know little about the descriptive validity of criminal justice trials and can identify only two recent studies addressing this issue (Perry and Johnson 2008; Perry et al. in press). These two studies applied the CONSORT Statement to a number of RCTs reporting on aspects of good and poor descriptive validity in criminology. We use the findings of these two studies to identify areas of weak descriptive validity and examples of best practice from a range of criminal justice trials, which demonstrate how descriptive validity can be improved.

The first study of these two studies reports on the descriptive validity of a selection of RCTs focusing on the provision of mental health services for juvenile offenders (Perry and Johnson 2008). The second provides the results of a comprehensive evaluation of 83 criminal justice trials across a range of different areas of crime and justice (Perry et al. in press).

TABLE 17.1. The CONSORT checklist

CONSORT checklist item	CONSORT item	CONSORT checklist description
Title and abstract	1	How participants were allocated to interventions
Introduction and Background	2	Scientific background and explanation of the rationale
Methods Participants	3	Eligibility criteria for participants and settings and locations of the data collection.
Interventions	4	Details of the interventions intended for each group, and how and when they were administered.
Objectives	5	Specific objectives and hypotheses
Outcomes	6	Clearly defined primary and secondary outcome measures and methods used to enhance the quality of measurement.
Sample size	7	How the sample size was determined and when applicable an explanation of any interim analyses and stopping rules.
Randomisation	8	Method used to generate the random allocation sequence including any details of restrictions.
Sequence allocation and allocation concealment	9	Methods used to implement the random allocation sequence.
Implementation	10	Who enrolled participants and who assigned participants to their groups
Blinding	11	Whether or not participants, those administering the interventions, and those assessing the outcomes were blinded to group assignment. When relevant, how the success of blinding was evaluated.
Statistical methods	12	Statistical methods used to compare groups for primary outcome. Methods for additional analyses such as subgroup analyses and adjusted analyses
Results Participants flow	13	Flow of participants through each stage of the trial from enrolment to follow up
Recruitment	14	Dates defining the periods of recruitment and follow up
Baseline data	15	Baseline demographics and clinical characteristics of each group
Numbers analysed	16	Number of participants in each group included in each analysis and whether the analysis was by intention to treat.
Outcome and estimation	17	For each primary and secondary outcome a summary of results for each group and the estimated effect size and its precision
Anicillary analyses	18	Reports on any other adjustments performed, including subgroup analyses and adjusted analyses indicating those pre-determined and those exploratory analyses.
Adverse events	19	All important adverse events or side effects in each intervention group
Discussion Interpretation	20	Interpretation of results, taking into account study hypotheses, potential sources of bias and dangers associated with multiplicity of analyses and outcomes.
Generalisability	21	The external validity and generalisability of the trial results
Overall evidence	22	General interpretation of the results in the current context of evidence.

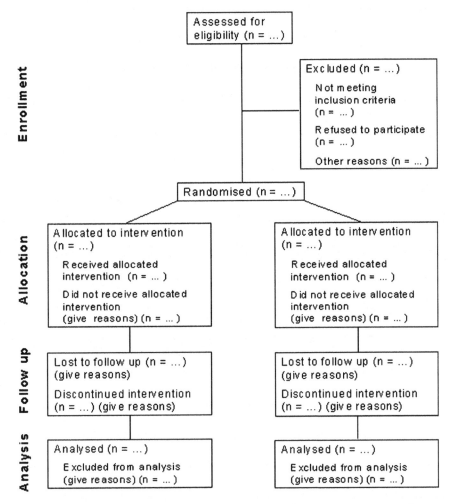

FIGURE 17.1. CONSORT flow diagram. Source: (see http://www.consort-statement.org/).

Using CONSORT to Measure Descriptive Validity in Criminology

The first study examined the application of the CONSORT Statement in a group of RCTs identified from a systematic review of mental health provision for juvenile offenders (Perry and Johnson 2008). This study applied the CONSORT Statement to a selection of RCTs to assess their descriptive validity, and the extent to which journal editors referenced the CON-SORT Statement in the "instructions to authors" section when submitting articles to journals for publication.

The study identified a selection of 17 trials published between January 2001 and December 2006. These were identified using a total of 13 electronic databases,[1] grey literature databases

[1] PsychINFO, Applied Social Sciences Index and Abstracts, International Bibliography of the Social Sciences, Social Policy and Practice, Social Services Abstracts, Sociological Abstracts, ERIC, Criminal Justice Abstracts, PAIS International, C2 SPECTR, Swets-Wise, DARE and Cochrane Database of Systematic Reviews.

(SIGLE, Index of Theses and ZETOC) and ten key websites.[2] In addition, the Journal of Adolescence, and the Child and Adolescent Mental Health Journal were hand-searched for relevant papers which formed the basis of a larger systematic review, focusing on the provision of mental health services for juvenile offenders (Perry et al. 2008).

The study used two independent reviewers to extract relevant data systematically from each study using a modified version of the CONSORT Statement. The modified version was used to ensure that multiple aspects of single items on the CONSORT Statement were listed separately for the purpose of data extraction. This process resulted in a 42 item checklist. Each item on the CONSORT Statement was then rated as either "yes" (information reported) or "no" (no information reported).

The findings of the study identified studies with both high and low descriptive validity. Items of high descriptive validity generally included the less technical aspects of the study for example, reporting of the sample demographics at baseline. Other more technical aspects of descriptive validity were poorly reported. These included sample size estimations, outcome measures, effect sizes, and blinding. The study also revealed that 18% of the editors' instructions for authors contained details about the CONSORT Statement. This somewhat encouraging finding is particularly important especially considering that the CONSORT Statement has been rarely mentioned in criminology, and comparable findings have been identified in healthcare (Altman 2005).

The authors of the study do note a number of limitations with the study findings, which have an impact on how descriptive validity may be presented within criminology. Firstly, the selection of 17 trials represent only a small percentage of all trials conducted in the criminal justice system. Because of this reason, we cannot be sure that the trials are representative of other criminal justice trials conducted in the area. Secondly, the endorsement of the CONSORT Statement by journal editors in this specific sample of trials may be an artefact of the journals themselves. For example, many of the journals reported on both health and criminal justice issues and such journal may not be representative of trials published in criminology more broadly (e.g., in the courts, police, and prisons). As a consequence, these recognised limitations could affect how we draw conclusions about what this tells us about descriptive validity in criminal justice trials (e.g., external validity). In order to address these difficulties, the second study reports on the findings from a large-scale evaluation of descriptive validity in a representative sample of criminal justice trials (Perry et al. in press).

Descriptive Validity Across a Representative Sample of Criminology Research

The second study is aimed to explore the application of descriptive validity using the CONSORT Statement in a representative sample of RCTs. Three further objectives of the study assessed; (1) changes in reporting of transparent information over time, (2) the impact of sample size in relation to the number of CONSORT items reported, and (3) an assessment of the differences between the transparent reporting of information in trials with different types of interventions.

---

[2] Department of Health, Department of Education and Skills, Ministry of Justice, Joseph Rowntree Foundation, Royal College of Psychiatrists, Youth Justice Board, Policy Studies Institute, Mental Health Foundation, Young Minds and NACRO.

These three areas of interest were chosen because of previous evidence demonstrating that these factors have an impact on descriptive validity (e.g., Emerson et al. 1990). For our first issue, the idea of progression is thought to stem from the fact that methodological advances in writing and reporting of scientific manuscripts have improved naturally over time as standards of journals demand the highest quality research. As such, researchers anticipated that some improvement in the transparent reporting of trial information would be identified through the evaluation. (Graf et al. 2002; Prady et al. 2008; Shea et al. 2006).

Our second issue of sample size suggests that trials of larger sample sizes demonstrate greater descriptive validity with a general progression over time (e.g., Ioannidis et al. 1998; Kjaergard et al. 2001). This finding may be an artefaxt of the article length which will vary depending upon the type of publication (e.g., journal article or government report). Other differences have been found with different types of interventions. Reasons for such differences point towards the suggestion that some interventions may be easier to blind than others, and as a consequence, the reporting of some items (e.g., blinding and how it was achieved) may be easier to achieve in some studies than others. The final aspect of the study compared the reporting of descriptive validity in criminal justice and healthcare trials. This element of the study was used to assess whether the descriptive validity of criminal justice trials faired better or worse than those conducted in healthcare.

The study used a group of RCTs identified from a previous study conducted by Farrington and Welsh (Farrington and Welsh 2005). The 83 trials were published between 1982 and 2004 and were identified using four key criteria. The key criteria included: (1) studies where units (persons or places) were randomly assigned, (2) studies with conditions with at least 100 units assigned to two experimental groups, (3) studies reporting on measures of offending, and (4) studies published in English. Trials were grouped into different sections of the criminal justice system and included policing, prevention, corrections, courts and, community interventions.

Using similar methodology to the first study, each RCT was assessed using two independent reviewers and the CONSORT Statement was modified so that multiple items were listed separately. In this second study, the modification process also incorporated some additional aspects of Farrington's 14 item validity checklist (Farrington 2003). This was to ensure that any absent information (not present in CONSORT), but covered in the 14 questions was added to the tool. This process resulted in a 54 item coding tool. Additionally, the scoring key in the first study was expanded to include the "partial" reporting of information. This addition was necessary because some, but not all, information was often reported on each item of the CONSORT Statement. The additional "partial" scoring key therefore recorded instances where some aspects of the CONSORT Statement were reported.

In preparation for the analysis of the findings the items were divided into a number of different domains. These domains included a description of the study background and introduction (items, 1, 2a, 2b, 8 and 9), participant details (items, 3a, 3b, 13, 26, 31 and 32), data collection information (items, 4a, 4b, 4c, 29, 30 and 12), intervention and control group descriptions (items, 5a, 5b, 6a, 6b, 7a and 7b), the randomisation methodology (items, 16, 17, 18, 19, 20, 21, 22 and 23), information on outcome measures (items, 10, 11, 24, 25, 35, 36 and 38), the statistical analysis (items, 14, 15, 27, 28, 33, 34a, 34b, 37a and 37b), and study findings (items, 39, 40, 41, 42, 43, 44 and 45).

Figure 17.2 shows the overall results of each item reported for the relevant domain. Overall, the results of the study found similar findings to those presented in the first study with some areas being relatively well reported. For the background and introduction domain, all but two items scored above 50%. A similar pattern is shown in the participant and data collection domains. The remaining five domains demonstrate generally poor descriptive validity

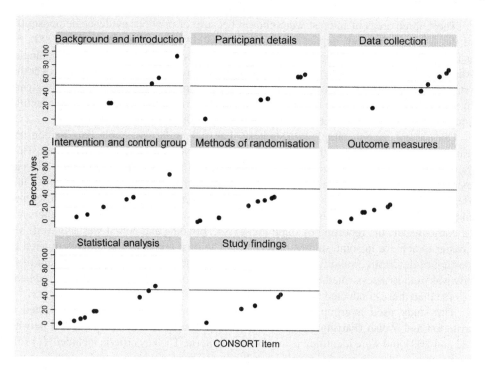

FIGURE 17.2. Findings of CONSORT in themed areas.

with nearly all items being reported in less than 50% of cases. Only two items on the intervention and control domain and one item on the statistical analysis domain report above the 50% threshold.

Contrary to other research evidence, the results of this study did not show a significant improvement in reporting over time (Prady et al. 2008; Shea et al. 2006). This is perhaps surprising given the expectation that methodological advances in other scientific discipline areas have shown improvement. (e.g., Graf et al. 2002).

The second evaluation assessed the impact of sample size and trial outcome. Previous research in this area has shown mixed results with some larger trials showing better reporting of trial information (e.g., Kjaergard et al. 1999), whilst other researchers have shown no association between sample size and trial outcome (e.g., Jüni et al. 2002). The findings from our evaluation of criminal justice trials therefore supports the latter of these two findings suggesting that there is no evidence to substantiate the relationship between the sample size of the trial and reporting on the CONSORT Statement.

The third evaluation assessed the impact of intervention differences on the application of the CONSORT Statement. The findings of our study revealed no significant differences between the different intervention types (although the policing interventions do far better than the others). The authors note this finding could be due to the fact that the same authors tend to report on their areas of research interest, and have a particular writing style and type of publication (e.g., journal article publications vs. reports for government). This effect may consistently have an impact on the quality and amount of information reported within a study design.

The final analysis of this second study compared the application of the CONSORT Statement to a range of other healthcare trials. Because the CONSORT Statement has been used for a number of decades in healthcare, the authors anticipated that the criminal justice trials may fair worse in comparison. Surprisingly, the results of the study showed that the reporting of descriptive validity was comparable with some items in criminal justice trials fairing better than healthcare (e.g., random allocation concealment). Other items were, however, significantly worse (e.g., blinding and the reporting of attrition). In conclusion, the authors of this study suggested that there was still room for overall improvement in the transparent reporting of information in criminal justice trials. Generally, the reporting of descriptive validity in criminal justice studies were found to be behind those conducted in healthcare in most areas of the CONSORT Statement, though in some aspects (e.g., random allocation) they seemed to fair better. The results from this study demonstrate how the reporting of descriptive validity in criminal justice trials information varies across the application of the CONSORT Statement. Such variability may be due to a number of different reasons. Firstly, the CONSORT Statement was initially developed for use with medical trials, and therefore aspects of its endorsement may not be applicable for research conducted in criminology. Secondly, these results may reflect a lack of attention paid by criminologists to the issue of descriptive validity. As a result, the quality of reporting information and hence the descriptive validity fall significantly behind those researchers who conduct medical trials in healthcare.

In summary, the evidence from these two studies seemed to suggest that criminologists report fairly well on some aspects of descriptive validity. Such areas tend to be the less technical aspects of the paper (e.g., study recruitment and aim of the study). Where criminologists faired significantly worse were on aspects of statistical information. The following section of this Chapter extends our review of this evidence to concentrate on examples of poor descriptive validity identified by the two previous studies (Perry and Johnson 2008; Perry et al. in press). Furthermore, it considers whether this lack of reporting is due to issues relating specifically to the study of criminology or whether such reporting is because the issue of descriptive validity is relatively new to criminologists.

Application of the CONSORT Statement in Criminal Justice Trials

The findings from the two criminology studies of descriptive validity provide some indication of which elements of descriptive validity are poorly endorsed by criminologists on the CONSORT Statement. As noted earlier, this may be for a number of different reasons. Firstly, the CONSORT Statement was originally developed for use in healthcare trials; it is, therefore, perhaps not surprising that none of the trials reviewed in the two studies reported on all items on the Statement. This concern leads to the question of whether the CONSORT Statement needs to be refined for use with evaluations of descriptive validity in criminal justice trials and/or whether criminologists need to improve the standard of reporting information to enable the accurate assessment of descriptive validity.

In both studies similar poorly endorsed items of descriptive validity were identified. These included the reporting of adverse events, blinding, reporting of primary and secondary outcome measures, descriptions about how the results were analysed (including intention to treat and per protocol approaches), reporting of information relating to the number of participants processed throughout the trial and details about the control group.

The following section of this chapter considers these poorly reported items of descriptive validity in more detail and evaluates whether these findings are an artefact of the type of research conducted in criminology or whether the lack of emphasis on descriptive validity in criminology has resulted in researchers whose reporting of descriptive validity should be improved.

Descriptive Validity in Criminology and Reporting of Adverse Events

Unintended and often undesirable effects are rarely noted in criminology, but form an important element of the CONSORT Statement. The Statement advocates that authors examining the results of trial information need to be aware that an intervention can harm participants as well as providing benefits. In healthcare, anticipated adverse effects are most commonly associated with the side effects of taking a newly prescribed drug. In criminology, the concept of an adverse event is therefore somewhat different as few trials are interested in reporting on the impact of prescribed drugs. Instead, an adverse event in criminological research may focus on an increase (as apposed to a decrease) in recidivism rates following the delivery of an intervention.

Examples of such adverse events can be identified from the criminological literature with one of the most famous examples being the "Scared Straight" evaluation. The findings of this study resulted in an increase in the likelihood of criminal activity following young people being exposed to the program (Petrosino et al. 2002). Other considerations of adverse effects in criminology may also consider whether a particular intervention is deemed ethical, acceptable, and is of benefit to those undergoing the intervention.

Within our discussion of the two papers, few examples of adverse events were noted. This could be because the majority of these trials showed positive results, or it may suggest that adverse events are either not widely published by journal editors and/or considered by criminology researchers as important. There is, of course, the tendency for publishers to consider trials with positive results more favourably than those with negative results, and this has certainly been evidenced in healthcare (e.g., Egger and Smith 1998). This phenomenon is often referred to as publication bias where the published literature presents the findings of a particular perspective. Although we have no evidence for this in criminology, it could explain why a few researchers have addressed the issue of adverse events.

We did, however, find one trial which describes the unexpected findings of an intervention group experiencing higher recidivism rates than the control (see Table 17.2: Peters et al. 1997). An acceptance of such important negative findings should encourage criminologists and journal editors alike to present the findings of their research, which acknowledge the presence of any adverse events. The consequence of not reporting such information increases the risk of wasting valuable resources on unethical interventions, which have undesired effects on society.

Descriptive Validity in Criminology and the Reporting of Blinding and Masking

Our second area of poor descriptive validity in criminology is that of blinding or masking participants. In RCTs the term "blinding" refers to keeping the study participants, administrators delivering the intervention, and those collecting and analysing the data unaware of the assigned intervention (Boutron et al. 2005). This ensures that individuals are not unduly influenced by the knowledge of who is receiving the intervention. For descriptive validity, the reporting of blinding should recognise who was blinded (for example participants,

TABLE 17.2. Examples of descriptive validity and adverse events in criminology

CONSORT item number	CONSORT item description	Example from the literature
19	All important adverse events or side effects in each intervention group.	"In Cleveland, the question that must be asked is, why did the experimental groups do worse? This question calls for further investigation and leads to the second point: the findings presented here are from interim reports. The groups included in this study must be tracked for a longer period of time. It is entirely plausible that the control group in Cleveland will, over time, experience a recidivism rate comparable to that of the experimental group". (Peters et al. 1997).

TABLE 17.3. Examples of descriptive validity and blinding in criminology

CONSORT item number	CONSORT item description	Example from the literature
11a	Blinding or Masking: whether or not participants, those administering the interventions and those assessing the outcomes were blinded to group assignment	"The research design is a double-blinded baseline study. The program participants were divided into three groups; an experimental group which received acupuncture on a regular basis, a control group which did not receive acupuncture, and a placebo group which received an acupuncture-like simulation. It should be noted that initially all cases referred to the program were given the acupuncture treatment. Once the acupuncture study began, offenders were randomly placed into one of the three groups listed above. Neither staff nor clients were aware of group placement" (Latessa and Moon 1992).
11b	If blinding was done, how was the success of the blinding evaluated	"To evaluate participant blinding, a questionnaire asked participants which treatment they believed they had received. . .they were asked to indicate what led to this belief" (Adapted from Lao et al. 1999).

evaluators, or data analysts), and the mechanism of blinding. Blinding is, however, not always possible, but, a lack of blinding does not prevent authors from explaining why participants, administrators of the intervention or evaluators were not blinded.

Where blinding has been implemented the reporting of descriptive validity should also include information about whether such blinding was successful. In principle, if blinding was successful, the ability of participants to accurately guess their group assignment should be not better than chance. Our examples (see Table 17.3) provide a description of a double-blind study of acupuncture treatment for a group of offenders (Latessa and Moon 1992) and an evaluation of blinding using a questionnaire where participants were asked which treatment they believed they had received (Lao et al. 1999).

The standard expectation of "double blinding" occurs when both the evaluator and the participant are blind to the intervention, allocation, and assessment. Evidence from a systematic review assessing methods of blinding across different trials reports that blinding in the literature was most commonly represented in three different categories (Boutron et al. 2006). These categories included; (1) blinding with patients and care providers, (2) the maintenance of blinding, and (3) whether assessors were blind to the main outcomes. The results of the study revealed that blinding of outcome assessors depended upon the primary outcome. For example, where mortality was the primary outcome, there was little point in blinding the outcome assessor. In other situations, they argue that blinding the outcome assessor should be possible with a centralized assessment of complementary investigation. Some examples of this blinding show how this is possible to achieve in different types of interventions (Boutron et al. 2006; Francis et al. 2003; Fiorucci et al. 2004).

In summary, blinding in criminal justice trials at least at the level of the outcome assessor should be feasible in all trial situations. This was certainly not something that was reported by criminologists. Other levels of blinding may be more difficult (that is not to say impossible) and innovative ideas about blinding in criminology research should be encouraged. This is particularly pertinent given that research from other areas shows how an absence of blinding can threaten the internal validity of a trial and its results (Boutron et al. 2005).

Descriptive Validity in Criminology and the Reporting of Primary and Secondary Outcome Measures

In criminological research most trials have several outcomes. Specifying which of these outcomes is the primary outcome of interest is not common place. However having more than one or two outcomes can incur problems of interpretation associated with multiplicity of analyses (see also CONSORT items 18 and 20).

Other information recorded about the outcome measures should include how they were measured and whether any steps were taken to increase the reliability of the measurements. This is often referred to as "enhancing the quality of the outcome measures". Such measures are more likely to be free from bias if the participant and assessor are blinded to group assignment, or where additional data is collected to support or corroborate other evidence (e.g., official data from criminal records is obtained to check self-report measurement of crime). Examples from two trials (see Table 17.4) provide some evidence to demonstrate the use of primary outcome measures and the enhancement of their quality in two criminal justice trials (Rhodes and Gross 1997; Robinson 1995).

Whilst these examples are found in the criminological literature, such examples are not in plentiful supply. In comparison, medical trials have well established protocols that require

TABLE 17.4. Examples of descriptive validity and primary and secondary outcome measures in criminology

CONSORT item number	CONSORT item description	Example from the literature
6a	Clearly defined primary and secondary outcome measures	"While recidivism remains the primary outcome measure in studies of program effectiveness, the impact of program participation on the granting of conditional release is also of interest" (Robinson 1995)
6b	When applicable enhance the quality of outcome measures	"Outcomes were evaluated using formal assessment instruments to measure self-reported behaviour at baseline and again at 3 and 6 months. Independent data from criminal justice and drug treatment systems were analysed to gauge the validity of these self reports" (Rhodes and Gross 1997).

pre-determined primary outcome measures to be specified in the trial protocol prior to commencement of the analysis (Freemantle 2001). Such specification seeks to ensure a reduction in a number of potential biases. Type I error is one particular problem for trials which include many outcome measures because there is an increased possibility of the results occurring simply by chance. Pre-determined outcome measures also reduce the temptation for researchers to potentially "trawl" for positive results when these are not indicated by the initial analysis (see Freemantle 2001 for further discussion).

In contrast, criminological studies tend to clearly state the outcome measures, but do not make the distinction between primary and secondary outcomes. For example, a trial conducted by Needles and colleagues reports on a range of outcome measures (including self-reported drug use, cocaine and hair test results, marijuana hair test results, physical and social problems relating to alcohol or drug use, participation in drug treatment programmes and sexual behaviour) without specifically listing the primary and secondary measures (Needles et al. 2005). Such reporting of outcomes in criminology is common and many studies evaluate the impact of multiple outcome measures and analyses running the risk of introducing Type I error.

In conjunction with the primary outcome measure is the calculation of the sample size. Many trials in healthcare and education have been noted as being too small to be able to detect differences between the intervention and control groups (Torgerson and Elbourne 2002). In order to estimate the sample size in a trial, a number of different elements are required. These include (1) the estimated outcomes in each group, (2) the alpha (type I) error level, (3) the statistical power (type II) error, and (4) for continuous outcomes (e.g. mean number of offences), the standard deviation or standardised effect size of the measurements.

Sample size estimates are important in trial design because a study needs to be large enough to have high probability (power) of detecting a statistically significant difference of a given size (e.g., the anticipated percentage reduction in the number of reconvictions). The size of the effect is related to the size of the sample, so large samples are necessary to detect small differences and vice versa. In criminology, the reporting of sample size calculations are rare. This may be because such calculations are not conducted by researchers or that such methodological requirements are not commonly considered important enough by criminologists to report. Either way, criminologists should include sample size calculations within their study descriptions. Such calculations when conducted prior to the start of the study should help identify those studies, which may be inadequately powered from the outset.

Descriptive Validity in Criminology and the Reporting of Statistical Analyses

The reporting of statistical analyses was generally poor across the two criminological studies. Basic information about the number of participants in each group or arm of a trial provides important information about why individuals may fail to complete an intervention and what may bias the results of the trial. Primarily, two approaches to the analysis of trial information are taken. Intention To Treat (ITT) analysis includes all the study participants regardless of whether they "crossed over" into another intervention or did not complete the intervention. Supporters of this view argue that this methodology provides a conservative estimate of the results by truly reflecting what happens to individuals receiving a treatment or intervention in practice (Torgerson and Torgerson 2008). The logic of this argument suggests that by including all participants (and not just necessarily those who are most likely or most highly

TABLE 17.5. Examples of descriptive validity and intention to treat analyses in criminology

CONSORT item number	CONSORT item description	Example from the literature
16	Number of participants (denominator) in each group included in each analysis and whether the analysis was by "intention to treat".	"An intent-to-treat analysis plan was followed in which each individual who participated in the follow up was analyzed according to his or her original per-school ($N = 104$) or school-age group ($N = 95$) random assignment, regardless of the length of exposure. This has the advantage of increased stringency while increasing detection power by increasing the number of individuals available for analysis. Post hoc analyses were then conducted with data from five individuals originally assigned to the pre-school treatment group removed from the sample." (Campbell et al. 2002)

motivated to complete treatment) in the analysis this method reduces any possibility of bias. In contrast, some trialists try to correct for non-adherence by using a per protocol analysis. This method can produce a biased estimate of effect as participants not complying with the treatment protocol are excluded from the analysis. An example of an ITT description from criminology (see Table 17.5) shows a trial of school children (Campbell et al. 2002).

The fundamentals of this analysis are central to the design of a trial and are equally apparent regardless of whether the trial is conducted in healthcare or criminology. This lack of transparent reporting in criminological trials may therefore suggest an inherent flaw of this important element of trial design. This is therefore something that criminologists need to pay greater attention to in the reporting of trial information.

Descriptive Validity in Criminology and the Reporting of Participant Numbers

The number of participants who started and finished a trial in each arm of the design provides important information on how many people were used in the data analysis. This information is important because participants who were excluded after allocation are unlikely to be representative of all participants in the study. For example, participants who do not complete all the data evaluation points may do so because they may be less motivated or could be distinctly different (i.e., commit different sorts of crimes) than those that do not. For healthcare, this is usually represented by using the CONSORT flow chart (see Fig. 17.1). The Statement advocates that for each group authors should report the number of participants randomly assigned, receiving intended treatment, completing the study protocol and analysed for the primary outcome.

Only 2 of our 83 criminal justice trials used any form of this flow chart. This is perhaps not surprising since the CONSORT Statement in criminology has not been widely disseminated, nor has it been adopted by the majority of journal editors as a requirement of authors' submission of research reports for publication. Researchers reporting on the findings of trials in criminology should therefore be encouraged to be more transparent about the reporting of participants throughout all stages of their trials.

Descriptive Validity in Criminology and the Reporting of Control Group Information

Our final area of concern in the reporting of descriptive validity in criminology relates to the description of the intervention and control group(s). In both the control and intervention group(s) it is important to provide information on the details of the intervention received. These details should include information about who administered the intervention. For example, with cognitive behavioural interventions it may be necessary to describe the number, training and experiences of the staff. Additionally, the details of the timing and duration of both the intervention and control groups are required. This is particularly important if the intervention has multiple components as it allows the study to be replicated (e.g. a therapeutic community, followed by aftercare in the community and a work release program). The four examples (see Table 17.6) provide information about an intervention group receiving multi-systemic therapy in comparison to a group of offenders receiving individual therapy (Borduin et al. 1995). The final example provides information about the timing and duration of a Big Brother Big Sister evaluation (Grossman and Tierney 1998).

TABLE 17.6. Examples of descriptive validity and the reporting of control and intervention information in criminology

CONSORT item number	CONSORT item description	Example from the literature
4	The precise details of the interventions intended for each group and how and when they were actually administered	"Therapeutic interventions were based on the multisystemic approach to the treatment and prevention of behavior problems. . . Using interventions that are present-focused and action orientated, MST directly addresses intrapersonal and systemic factors that are known to be associated with adolescent antisocial behavior. . .." (Borduin et al. 1995).
		"All offenders in this condition received individual therapy that focused on personal, family and academic issues. . . . Their theoretical orientations were an eclectic blend of" . . .. . . (Borduin et al. 1995).
		"MST (multisystemic therapy) was provided by three female and three male graduate students (ages ranged from 23 to 31 years, $M = 26$) in clinical psychology. One of the therapists was Native American, and the others were white. Each had approximately 1.5 years of direct clinical experience with children or adolescents before the study. The six therapists served in the study for an average of 16 months (range 12–24 months). Therapist supervision was provided by Charles M. Borduin in a 3-h weekly group meeting and continued throughout the course of the investigation. During these meetings..." (Borduin et al. 1995).
		"The average length of match for those treatments who had been matched was almost 12 months, with white girls having met with a Big Sister for the longest period (12.4 months) . . ..Little Brothers and little Sisters met with their Big Brother and Big Sister on a regular basis. More than 70% of the youths met. . . at least three times a month, and approximately 45% met one or more times per week. An average meeting lasted 3.6 h" (Grossman and Tierney 1998).

These examples demonstrate best practice evidence giving the amount of detail that should be reported on both the intervention and control groups. In the majority of criminal justice trial information was lacking about the control group. Often, for example, phrases were used that included "care as usual", without describing what this meant and how much was received by the control group.

SUMMARY

Descriptive validity and validity more broadly is one of the most important aspects of research design as it ensures the implementation of sound methodology from which conclusions can be drawn and generalised to other research findings (Campbell 1957; Perry et al. in press). In criminology, the concept of descriptive validity has been around for a few years (e.g., Farrington 2003), but has received greater recognition in healthcare (e.g., Altman 2005). The key driving force for this interest in healthcare was the development of the CONSORT group and subsequently the CONSORT Statement in 1996 (Altman 2001). Since then, the CONSORT Statement has been internationally adopted by many journal editors and evaluations of the CONSORT Statement have shown how it has improved the quality of reporting in RCTs over time (e.g., Plint et al. 2006).

The impact of poor descriptive validity has been conducted on three key areas of interest. These include an assessment of whether the introduction of the CONSORT Statement has increased the reporting of transparent information (e.g., Moher et al. 2001a), the extent to which journal editors have adopted the CONSORT Statement (e.g., Devereaux et al. 2002), the relationship between the impact of transparent reporting on allocation concealment in the randomization process (Hewitt et al. 2005), selection bias (Moher et al. 1998), performance bias (Jüni et al. 2000), blinding (Schulz et al. 1995), sample size (Ioannidis et al. 1998), and different types of interventions (Emerson et al. 1990). The CONSORT Statement in healthcare is therefore an established fundamental and credible tool that is used to assess the extent of transparent reporting in trials.

In criminal justice trials, the reporting of descriptive validity varies across the CONSORT Statement. The majority of CONSORT items cover the essential requirements of trial design, methodology, results, and trial findings common to all RCTs regardless of the subject matter. Other aspects of the CONSORT Statement may need some adaptation (e.g. the impact of adverse events). Indeed adoption of the CONSORT Statement in discipline areas has occurred in education (Torgerson et al. 2005) and non-pharmocological trials (Boutron et al. 2005). There is therefore no reason to suggest that the CONSORT Statement cannot be used (with some minor amendments) with trials conducted in the criminal justice field.

The other assumption that can be drawn from these findings is that criminology and the reporting of descriptive validity has not been acknowledged and as a consequence, the transparent reporting of trial information appears to be worse than in other disciplines such as healthcare. Use of a CONSORT like Statement in criminology would provide a useful framework for researchers not only in the reporting of good descriptive validity, but also in the best practice methodology for trial design. Any such adoption of the CONSORT Statement by criminal justice researchers is likely to enhance the quality of reporting information of trials and should be used to aid the interpretation of evidence.

Our discussions surrounding the application of the CONSORT Statement in criminology raise a number of issues. The central question to the adoption of a CONSORT-like Statement in criminology is whether such a tool would increase the transparent reporting of trial information. Evaluations to assess whether the CONSORT Statement has improved the reporting of trial information over time have been systematically reviewed in an evaluation of studies that compared CONSORT-adopting and non-adopting journals after the publication of CONSORT; CONSORT adopters before and after the publication of CONSORT, or a combination of both the listed criteria (Plint et al. 2006). The results of the systematic review showed that journals endorsing the CONSORT Statement reported significantly more information about methods of sequence allocation, allocation concealment, and the overall number of CONSORT items than did journal editors who had not endorsed the Statement.

Overall, the results of the study concluded that the CONSORT Statement was associated with some improvements in the reporting of transparent information although, clear endorsement of the Statement by journal editors in the "instructions to authors" has shown more varied results (Altman 2005; Hopewell et al. 2008).

Other researchers have also investigated the impact of reporting transparent information on different aspects of the CONSORT Statement. Research evaluating specific aspects of descriptive validity have found mixed results. For example, researchers evaluating the impact of reporting inadequate details of allocation concealment found exaggerated intervention effects compared with trials reporting adequate allocation concealment (Moher et al. 1998, 1999; Schulz et al. 1995).

Further work on this issue was also conducted by Juni and colleagues (2001) who showed that trials with inadequate or unclear concealment produced odds ratios that were, on average, 30% lower (more beneficial) than those with adequate methodology (combined odds ratio 0.70, 95% CI: 0.62–0.80). However, other researchers have found no association between reported allocation concealment and intervention effects (Emerson et al. 1990).

Other debates in the literature around validity and reporting bias include the impact of trial size and trends in the improvement of reporting methodology over time. The size of the trial has shown discrepancies between the results of several small trials in meta-analyses (e.g., Ioannidis et al. 1998). Reasons for such differences point towards the fact that small trials are more likely to be published if they show a statistically significant intervention effect. In such cases, these discrepancies may be due to publication bias (e.g., Egger and Smith 1998). Other researchers have shown how trials with greater sample sizes show greater descriptive validity (Kjaergard et al. 1999; Prady et al. 2008; Shea et al. 2006). This effect does, however, seem to be specific to the type of intervention. For example, Jürgen and colleagues in 2002 found improvement in trials with mortality outcomes whereas surrogate outcome trials did not demonstrate an improvement in methodological quality over time.

To summarise, use of the CONSORT Statement in healthcare has generally improved the descriptive validity of trials. Specific evaluations of different aspects of the CONSORT Statement have revealed mixed results which may or may not demonstrate specific links between descriptive validity and bias within trial interpretation and design. Several aspects of the CONSORT Statement have, however, been used in groups of educational trials and has recently been referred to in criminology (Perry et al. in press; Torgerson et al. 2005).

For criminologists, descriptive validity is an important concept because it ensures that the methodological rigour and reporting of trial information is of the highest standard. As a consequence, one of the limitations of descriptive validity is its reliance upon an accurate and full description of the trial details (Moher et al. 2005). This is particularly important with the increasing use of meta-analytical techniques and systematic review evidence which seeks to synthesise different studies together to ascertain an overall effect. Without this information, a well conducted RCT or quasi-experimental study may have low descriptive validity because the authors have provided a poor description.

Research investigating the use of the CONSORT Statement in criminology found mixed results with some aspects of reporting highly endorsed but others severely lacking in the criminological literature. To some extent, it is difficult to ascertain why such differences might occur and suggestions for these differences might include an inability to acknowledge the importance of descriptive validity in criminological literature. This lack of acknowledgement does not, however, excuse the poor aspects of reporting on many of the more technical aspects of study design (e.g., calculation of sample sizes). What faces criminologists is a challenge to raise their game in the reporting of full transparent and accurate information, thus increasing the standard of research within the discipline. The transparent reporting of information does not stop at studies only using RCT designs, and such issues are equally of concern for quasi-experimental and observational study designs. Whilst the CONSORT Statement has been specifically designed to focus on aspects of trial design (e.g., random allocation), other aspects of the CONSORT Statement are also applicable to other types of study designs (e.g., the aim and recruitment of participants into the study).

It is crucial that RCTs are reported in a transparent manner to ensure that judgements can be made about the internal and external validity of the study. We would therefore recommend that the concept of descriptive validity be supported by journal editors and researchers within criminology to ensure that methodological rigour is upheld to the highest standards in RCTs and other quasi-experimental study designs.

REFERENCES

Altman DG (2001) The revised CONSORT Statement for reporting randomized trials: explanation and elaboration. Ann Intern Med 134:663–694

Altman DG (2005) Endorsement of the CONSORT statement by high impact medical journal: a survey of instructions for authors. Br Med J 330:1056–1057

Borduin CM, Mann BJ, Cone LT, Henggeler SW, Ficci BR, Blaske DM et al. (1995) Multisystemic treatment of serious juvenile offenders: long term prevention of criminality and violence. J Consult Clin Psychol 63:569–578

Boutron I, Moher D, Tugwell P, Giraudeau B, Poiraudeau S, Nizard R, Ravaud P (2005) A checklist to evaluate a report of a nonpharmacological trial (CLEAR NPT) was developed using consensus. J Clin Epidemiol 58(10):1233–12240

Boutron I, Estellat C, Guittet L, Dechartres A, Sackett DL, Hróbjartsson A et al. (2006) Methods of blinding in reports of randomised controlled trials assessing pharmacologic treatments: a systematic review. PLoS Med 3(10):1931–1939

Boruch RF (1997) Randomized field experiments for planning and evaluation: a practical guide. Sage Publications, Newbury Park, CA

Campbell DT (1957) Factors relevant to the validity of experiments in social settings. Psychol Bull 54:297–312

Campbell DT & Stanley JC (1963) Experimental and quasi-experimental designs for research on teaching. In: Gage NL (ed) Handbook of research on teaching. Chicago, Rand McNally, 171–246

Campbell FA, Ramey CT, Pungello E, Sparling J, Miller-Johnson S (2002) Early childhood education: young adult outcomes from the Abercedarian project. Appl Dev Sci 6:42–57

Devereaux PJ, Manns BJ, Ghali WA, Quan H, Guyatt GH (2002) The reporting of methodological factors in randomized controlled trials and the association with a journal policy to promote adherence to the Consolidated Standards of Reporting Trials (CONSORT) checklist. Control Clin Trials 23:380–388

Egger M, Smith GD (1998) Bias in location and selection of studies. Br Med J 316:61–66

Emerson JD, Burdick E, Hoaglin DC, Mosteller F, Chalmers TC (1990) An empirical study of the possible relation of treatment differences to quality scores in controlled randomized clinical trials. Control Clin Trials 11:339–352

Farrington DP (2003) Methodological quality standards for evaluation research. Ann Am Acad Pol Soc Sci 587:49–68

Farrington DP, Welsh BC (2005) Randomized experiments in criminology: what have we learned in the last two decades? J Exp Criminol 1(1):9–38

Fiorucci S, Mencarelli A, Lechi A, Renga B et al. (2004) Co administration of nitric oxide aspirin prevents platelet and monocyte activation and protects against gastric damage induced by aspirin in humans. J Am Coll Cardiol 44:635–641

Francis CW, Berkowitz SD, Comp PC, Lieberman JR Ginsberg JS et al. (2003) Comparison of ximelagatran and warfarin for the prevention of venous thromboembolism after total knee replacement. N Engl J Med 349: 1703–1712

Freemantle N (2001) Interpreting the results of secondary end points and subgroup analyses in clinical trials: should we lock the crazy aunt in the attic? Br Med J 322(7292):989–991

Graf J, Doig GS, Cook DJ, Vincent JL, Sibbald WJ (2002) Randomized controlled trials in sepsis: has methodological quality improved over time? Crit Care Med 30(2):461–472

Grossman JB, Tierney JP (1998) Does mentoring work? An impact study of the Big Brothers Big Sisters Program. Eval Rev 22:403–426

Hewitt C, Hahn S, Torgerson DJ, Watson J, Bland MJ (2005) Adequacy and reporting of allocation concealment: review of recent trials published in four general medical journals. Br Med J 330:1057–1058

Hopewell S, Altman DG, Moher D, Schulz KF (2008) Endorsement of the CONSORT statement by high impact factor medical journals: a survey of journal editors and journals 'Instructions to Authors'. Trials 9:20

Ioannidis JP, Cappelleri JC, Lau J (1998) Issues in comparisons between meta-analyses and large trials. JAMA 279:1089–1093

Jüni P, Altman DG, Egger M (2001) Assessing the quality of controlled clinical trials. In: Egger M, Davey-Smith G, Altman DG (eds) Systematic reviews in health care: meta-analysis in context, 2nd ed. BMJ Books, London

Jüni P, Holenstein F, Sterne J, Bartlett C, Egger M (2002) Direction and impact of languate bias in meta analyses of controlled trials: empirical study. International Journal of Epidemiology 31:115–123

Jüni P, Tallon D, Egger M (2000) 'Garbage in – garbage out'? Assessment of the quality of controlled trials in meta-analyses published in leading journals. In: Proceedings of the 3rd symposium on systematic reviews: beyond the basics. St. Catherines College, Centre for Statistics in Medicine, Oxford

Kjaergard LL, Villumsen J, Gluud C (1999) Quality of randomised clinical trials affects estimates of intervention efficacy. In: Proceedings of the 7th Cochrane Colloquium. Universitia S. Tommaso D'Aquino Rome. Milan, Centrro Cochrane Italiano, poster B10

Kjaergard LL, Nikolova J, Gluud C (1999) Reported methodological quality and discrepancies between large and small randomized trials in meta-analyses. Ann Intern Med 135:982–989

Kjaergard LL, Villumsen J, Gluud C (2001) Reported methodological quality and discrepancies between large and small randomized trials in meta-analyses. Annals of Intern Medicine 135:982–989

Lao L, Bergman S, Hamilton GR, Langenberg P, Berman B (1999) Evaluation of acupuncture for pain control after oral surgery. Arch Otolaryngol Head Neck Surg 125:567–572

Latessa E, Moon (1992) The effectiveness of acupuncture in an outpatient drug treatment program, Journal of Contemporary Criminal Justice 8(4):317–331

Lösel F, Köferl P (1989) Evaluation research on correctional treatment in West Germany: a meta-analysis. In: Wegener H, Lösel F, Haisch J (Eds) Criminal behavior and the justice system: psychological perspectives. Springer-Verlag, New York, pp 334–355

Moher D, Jadad AR, Nichol G Penman M, Tugwell M, Wash S (1995) Assessing the quality of RCT: an annotated bibliography of scales and checklists. Control Clin Trials 16:62–73

Moher D, Pham B, Jones A, Cook DJ, Jadad AR, Moher M, Tugwell P, Klassen TP (1998) Does quality of reports of randomized trials affect estimates of intervention efficacy reported in meta-analyses? Lancet 352:609–613

Moher D, Cook DJ, Jadad AR, Tugwell P, Moher M, Jones A, et al. (1999) Assessing the quality of reports of randomised trials: implications for the conduct of meta-analyses. Health Technol Assess 3(i–iv):1–98

Moher D, Schulz KF, Altman D, for the CONSORT Group (2001a) The CONSORT Statement: revised recommendations for improving the quality of reports of parallel-group randomized trials. JAMA 285:1987–1991

Moher D, Jones A, Lepage L (2001b) Use of the CONSORT statement and quality of reports of randomized trials: a comparative before and after evaluation. JAMA 285:1992–1995

Moher D, Altman D, Schulz K, for the CONSORT Group. The CONSORT statement: revised recommendation for improving the quality of reports of parallel-group randomized trials [Chinese]. Chin J Evid-Based Med 2005; 5(9):702–707

Needles K, James-Burdumy S, Burghardt J (2005) Community case management for former jail inmates: its impacts on re-arrest, drug use and HIV risk. J Urban Health 82(3):420–431

Perry AE, Johnson M (2008) Applying the Consolidated Standards of Reporting Trials (CONSORT) to studies of mental health provision for juvenile offenders: a research note. J Exp Criminol 4:165–185

Perry AE, Gilbody S, Akers J, Light K (2008) Access and provision of services for young people with mental health needs. Youth Justice Board, England and Wales

Perry AE, Weisburd D, Hewitt C (in press) Are criminologists reporting experiments in ways that allow us to assess? J Exp Criminol

Peters M, Thomas D, Zanberlon C (1997) Boot camps for juvenile offenders. Office of Juvenile Justice and Delinquency Prevention (Program Summary, Washington, DC

Petrosino A, Turpin-Petrosino C, Buehler J (2002) Scared straight and other juvenile awareness programs for preventing juvenile delinquency: a systematic review of randomized experimental evidence. Campbell Collaboration, USA

Plint AC, Moher D, Morrison A, Schulz K, Altman D, Hill C, Gaboury I (2006) Does the CONSORT checklist improve the quality of reporting randomized controlled trials? A systematic review. Med J Aust 185(5):263–267

Prady SL, Richmond SJ, Morton VM, MacPherson H (2008) A systematic evaluation of the impact of STRICTA and CONSORT recommendations on quality of reporting for acupuncture trials. PLos One 3(2):1–10

Rhodes W, Gross M (1997) Case management reduces drug use and criminality among drug-involved arrestees: an experimental study of an HIV prevention intervention (PDF Version). Washington, D.C.: National Institute of Justice, U.S. Department of Justice

Robinson D (1995) The impact of cognitive skills training on post release recidvisim among Canadian federal offenders. Correctional Service of Canada, Ottowa, Research Report R-41

Schulz KF, Chalmers I, Hayes RJ, Altman DG (1995) Empirical evidence of bias: dimensions of methodological quality associated with estimates of treatment effects in controlled trials. JAMA 273:408–412

Shea B, Boers M, Grimshaw JM, Hamel C, Bouter LM (2006) Does updating improve the methodological and reporting quality of systematic reviews? BMC Med Res Methodol 6:27

Sherman LW, Farrington DP, Welsh BC, Mackenzie DL (eds) (2002) Evidence-Based Crime Prevention. Routledge, London

Torgerson CJ & Elbourne D (2002) A systematic review and meta analysis of the effectiveness of information and communication technology (ICT) on the teaching of spelling. J Res Read 35:129–143

Torgerson CJ, Torgerson DJ, Birks YF, Porthouse J (2005) A comparison of RCTs in health and education. Br Educ Res J 31(6):761–785

Torgerson CJ, Torgerson DJ (2008) Designing and running randomised trials in health and the social sciences, Palgrave, MacMillan

## CHAPTER 18

Measurement Error in Criminal Justice Data

JOHN PEPPER, CAROL PETRIE, AND SEAN SULLIVAN

INTRODUCTION

While accurate data are critical in understanding crime and assessing criminal justice policy, data on crime and illicit activities are invariably measured with error. Measurement errors occur to some degree in nearly all datasets, but are arguably more severe in surveys of illicit activities. Some individuals may be reluctant to admit that they engage in or have been victims of criminal behaviors, whereas others may brag about and exaggerate accounts of illicit activities. Administrative data on arrests or reported crimes are likewise susceptible to systematic recording errors and misreporting. The utility of data on illicit behavior is reduced when variables are measured with error.

In this chapter, we discuss the implications of measurement error when drawing inferences on crime and justice policy. We take as given that even the best-designed surveys of illicit activities are apt to suffer extensive and systematic data errors.[1] In light of this problem, we review the consequences of measurement error for identification and inference, and document key issues that should be addressed when using potentially mismeasured data.

We begin, in section "Background and Evidence," with a brief review of several important measurement problems in data on crime and illicit behavior. We consider three related, but conceptually different, forms of data error: response error, proxy error, and imputation error. Response errors arise when variables of interest are observed, but possibly reported with error. This type of error is thought to be pervasive in self-report surveys on illicit activities, but can also be problematic in administrative data, such as the Uniform Crime Reports. Proxy errors arise when unobserved variables are replaced by related variables. An example is the use of the fraction of suicides committed with a firearm as a proxy measure for the rate of firearm ownership (Azrael et al. 2001). Finally, imputation errors arise when missing data are replaced

---

[1] An extensive literature attempts to document the validity and reliability of criminal justice data (Lynch and Addington 2007; Mosher et al. 2002). In this chapter, we make no attempt to fully summarize this literature and offer no specific suggestions for modifying surveys to improve the quality of collected data.

A.R. Piquero and D. Weisburd (eds.), *Handbook of Quantitative Criminology*, DOI 10.1007/978-0-387-77650-7_18, © Springer Science + Business Media, LLC 2010, First softcover printing 2011

by imputed values. A prominent example is the practice of imputing missing observations in the Uniform Crime Reports.

In sections "The Convolution Model" and "The Mixture Model," we formalize a number of statistical models to illustrate the impact of measurement error on inference. Repeatedly, we observe that data errors lead to fundamental identification problems, and therefore have important consequences when drawing informative inferences.

Section "The Convolution Model" concentrates on the case where mismeasured variables follow a convolution generating process, such that errors are approximated by additive unobserved random terms. Using a bivariate mean regression model, we first review the implications of the classical errors-in-variable model, where measurement errors are assumed to be mean zero and exogenous. In this classical model, the ordinary least squares estimator is downwardly inconsistent, and without additional data or assumptions, the mean regression can only be partially identified. Though a useful starting point, we argue that classical assumptions are frequently inappropriate for the study of crime and justice data, where errors are likely to be systematic and related to activities and policies of interest. When classical model assumptions are relaxed, the asymptotic properties of the ordinary least squares estimator cannot be easily characterized and, without additional data or assumptions, the mean regression is not identified.

Section "The Mixture Model" argues that for crime data, where outcomes are often discrete and only some observations are in error, a mixing model may be an appropriate framework for thinking about the effects of measurement error. Combined with fairly weak assumptions about the degree and nature of data errors, we show that the mixing model can be used to partially identify parameters of interest. Under weak assumptions, however, we observe that even small amounts of measurement error can lead to high degrees of ambiguity. Stronger assumptions on the unobserved error process lead to sharper inferences, but may not be credible in many cases.

Section "Conclusion: The Law of Decreasing Credibility" concludes with a discussion on the law of decreasing credibility (Manski 2007). Agnostic models will often lead to indeterminate conclusions, while models imposing strong and potentially inaccurate assumptions lead to less credible inferences. Throughout this chapter, we suggest situations in which apparent middle grounds may be available. In a variety of cases, one can draw informative inferences without imposing untenable assumptions.

BACKGROUND AND EVIDENCE

The fundamental challenge of measuring crime is starkly illustrated by comparing different sources of crime data for the United States. The two most important sources are the uniform crime reports (UCR) and the National Crime Victimization Survey (NCVS). For almost eight decades, the Federal Bureau of Investigation (FBI) has compiled the UCR by collecting information on arrests and crimes known to the police in local and state jurisdictions throughout the country. The NCVS, which began in 1973, is a general population survey conducted by the Bureau of Justice Statistics; it is designed to discover the extent, nature, and consequences of criminal victimization in the United States.

Table 18.1 displays a time-series of the rates (per 1,000) of rape, robbery, aggravated assault, and property crime in the United States in 1990, 2000, and 2005, as reported in the official annual summaries of the UCR (US Department of Justice 2008) and NCVS (US

TABLE 18.1. UCR and NCVS annual crime rates (per 1,000) in the United States: 1990, 2000 and 2005[a]

Crime survey	Rape		Robbery		Assault		Property crime	
	UCR	NCVS	UCR	NCVS	UCR	NCVS	UCR	NCVS
1990	0.4	1.7	2.6	5.7	4.2	9.8	50.7	348.9
2000	0.3	0.6	1.5	3.2	3.2	5.7	36.2	178.1
2005	0.3	0.5	1.4	2.6	2.9	4.3	34.3	154.0
% Change[b]	−22.6	−70.6	−45.1	−54.4	−31.2	−56.1	−32.4	−55.9

[a]UCR estimates come from the US Department of Justice (2008), and NCVS estimates from the US Department of Justice (2006)
[b]Percentage Change from 1990 to 2005

Department of Justice 2006). Comparison of these two surveys reveals major differences in estimated crime rates and crime trends (see, for example, Blumstein and Rosenfeld 2009; Lynch and Addington 2007; McDowall and Loftin 2007; NRC 2003, 2008). Crime rates estimated from the NCVS are always substantially greater than those from the UCR. Although trends move in the same direction over this period, the estimated percentage drop in crime is notably more pronounced in the NCVS. For example, data from the UCR imply that the annual rate of aggravated assaults fell from 4.2 in 1990 to 2.9 in 2005 – a 31% drop – while data from the NCVS indicate that the annual rate fell from 9.8 in 1990 to 4.3 in 2005 – a 56% drop.

Such discrepancies are largely attributable to basic definitional and procedural differences between the two surveys (US Department of Justice 2004; Lynch and Addington 2007). The two datasets measure different aspects of crime, with the UCR aiming to provide a measure of the number of crimes reported to law enforcement authorities, and the NCVS aiming to measure criminal victimization, including crimes not reported to authorities. These surveys also differ in the way they measure criminal behavior: the UCR is administrative data collected from individual criminal justice agencies (e.g. police departments), whereas the NCVS is a large-scale social survey that relies on self-reports of victimization.

Both methods of collecting data give rise to a number of response error concerns, including the potential for false reporting, nonstandard definitions of events, and general difficulties associated with collecting information on sensitive topics and illegal behavior. In the NCVS, for example, self-reports by respondents who are concerned with the consequences of truthful admissions may yield a number of inaccurate reports. Likewise, police discretion in whether and how to record incidents may lead to substantial errors in the measurement of reported crimes in the UCR (Mosher et al. 2002, 84–86). In fact, Black (1970) observes that about one-quarter of reported felonies and just under one-half of reported misdemeanors are never formally recorded by the police.

In this section, we review several examples of measurement errors that are thought to confound inference on crime and criminal justice policy. Three related types of data errors are illustrated: response errors, proxy errors, and imputation errors.

Response Errors

Response errors arise when survey respondents misreport information. In the NCVS, for example, some respondents may misreport the incidence of crime; in the UCR, some police may fail to report, or misclassify reported crimes. Although there is much indirect evidence of response errors in survey data on illicit behavior, there is almost no direct evidence – especially for the basic crime data collected in the UCR and NCVS. An exception is a series of validation studies that evaluate the incidence of illicit drug use by comparing self-reports to laboratory tests on hair, blood and urine. These validation studies suggest nontrivial and systematic self-reporting errors, but only apply to select populations (NRC 2001).

INDIRECT EVIDENCE ON RESPONSE ERRORS.   Indirect evidence on response error is often framed in terms of disparate findings between apparently similar surveys. A striking example is found in the literature examining the incidence of rape. A number of surveys reveal that between 20 and 25% of American women have been victims of completed or attempted rape at some point over their lifetime (Koss 1993, Table 1); yet, NCVS data – which measure yearly, not lifetime, victimization – indicate that less than 0.1% of women experience a rape or attempted rape (Koss 1996). Similarly, divergent conclusions can be found in the most widely cited studies of the incidence of defensive gun use. Using data from the 1993 National Self-Defense Survey (NSDS), Kleck and Gertz (1995) estimate over 2 million defensive gun uses per year; yet, the NCVS data from 1992 and 1994 reveals just over one-hundred thousand defensive gun uses per year (McDowall et al. 1998).

These large differences have been attributed to the use of different survey questions, to sampling variability, and to response errors. As discussed in NRC (2005) and Tourangeau and McNeeley (2003), the surveys are structurally different, covering different populations, interviewing respondents by different methods, using different recall periods, and asking different questions. While the surveys attempt to study common topics, the particular measurements taken are different. Moreover, because rape and defensive gun use are sensitive, stigmatized and difficult to define, small differences in survey methods may lead to large differences in the quality of the self-reported data on these topics (NRC 2003). Although response errors almost certainly affect these data, the extent of such errors is unknown.

DIRECT EVIDENCE ON RESPONSE ERRORS.   In contrast to the previous examples, a number of validation studies provide direct evidence on the direction and magnitude of response errors in self-report data on illicit drug use. As summarized by NRC (2001) and Harrison and Hughes (1997), report-validation studies have been conducted on arrestees, addicts in treatment programs, employees, and persons in high-risk neighborhoods. Some of the most detailed and important validation studies were conducted with data from the arrestee drug abuse monitoring (ADAM)/drug use forecasting (DUF) survey of arrestees, which elicits self-reports of drug use and also conducts urinalysis tests. Comparing self-reports of marijuana and cocaine use during the past three days to urinalysis tests for the same period, Harrison (1995) finds evidence of substantial and systematic response errors. In particular, she finds between 15 and 30% of respondents give inaccurate answers, with typically higher rates of false negatives than false positives. In the 1989 ADAM/DUF survey, for example, Harrison (1995) finds that 24.7% of respondents falsely deny using cocaine in the past three days, while 2.3% provide false positive reports. For marijuana use, 11.0% of responses are false negatives and 11.3% are false positives.

These validation studies provide some of the only direct evidence we have about the degree and nature of misreporting in surveys of illicit behaviors – we are not aware of similar direct evidence on response errors in other surveys of crime and victimization. Moreover, these studies provide only limited evidence about misreporting in national surveys on illicit drug use. The current validation studies examine particular subpopulations of individuals who have much higher rates of drug use than the general population. Response rates in the validation studies are often quite low, and respondents are usually not sampled randomly from a known population.

Proxy Variable Errors

In studies of illicit activities, it is often costly or impossible to directly measure variables of interest. In these cases, researchers may decide to use measurable variables as stand-ins or "proxies" for the unobserved variables. A proxy variable may be closely related to the unobserved variable of interest, but it is not a measurement of that variable. As a result, using a proxy in place of an unobserved variable can introduce substantial measurement error.

An important example is the use of UCR data on reported crime to act as a stand-in for the actual incidence of crime. A central but often overlooked problem is that many crimes are not reported to the police. The propensity of individuals to report crimes may be influenced by a variety of factors including the actual crime rate, the way victims are treated, community policing efforts, police manpower, and so forth (Rand and Rennison 2002). It is therefore possible for crime reported to police, as measured by the UCR, to rise or fall independent of changes in actual crime. In this case, UCR data may result in misleading conclusions about crime trends and the impact of criminal justice policies on crime.

A number of other proxy variables are used in crime and justice research. For example, ecological studies evaluating the relationship between access to firearms and crime frequently rely on proxy variables for the rate of gun ownership (NRC 2005). Proxies employed in the literature include the fraction of homicides committed with a firearm, the fraction of suicides committed with a firearm, and subscription rates to *Guns & Ammo* magazine (Azrael et al. 2001). Similarly, without access to information on the quantity of illicit drugs consumed, attempts to evaluate the demand for illicit drugs often rely on proxy variables. A common proxy for the actual quantity of drugs consumed is an indicator of whether an individual has used an illegal drug in a specified period of time. The accuracy of this proxy is unknown (NRC 2001).

Imputation Errors

In nearly every survey, some members of the surveyed population choose not to respond to particular questions. This missing data problem is often addressed using imputation procedures that fill in missing data using values from complete records in the same dataset. Imputation errors arise when the values of imputed data differ from the true values of the underlying variable. Importantly, this measurement problem is conceptually different from the response and proxy variable problems. With imputation errors, the fraction of nonrespondents is known, and the survey often identifies records with imputed values. This contrasts with response and proxy variable problems, where the fraction of observations measured with error is generally unknown. Thus, in principle, we can learn much more about the implications of imputation error than response and proxy variable errors.

An important example of this type of error in criminal justice research involves the imputation of missing values in UCR data. These data are compiled through the voluntary reporting of local agencies. Some agencies neglect to provide information as called for in the reporting protocol, while others fail to report altogether (Maltz 1999; Maltz and Targonski 2002).

In 2003, for example, over one-third of agencies filed incomplete monthly reports (Lynch and Jarvis 2008). A higher frequency of nonresponding agencies come from small jurisdictions, so that the agencies with missing data serve just over 12% of the population.

The FBI uses a simple procedure to impute the values of crime data for nonresponding agencies. Missing values for agencies reporting three or more months of crime data are replaced by the agency-average crime rate over observed months. For agencies reporting two or fewer months, crime rates from agencies of similar size and location are used (for details, see Maltz 1999).

Surprisingly, little research has been aimed at examining the inferential implications of imputed response problems in the UCR. Maltz and Targonski (2002) argue that imputation methods are likely to bias estimates of crime rates and program evaluation at the county level, but may be benign for analyses at higher geographic aggregations. Lynch and Jarvis (2008), however, find that the imputations can have a large impact on estimates of national trends in crime: from 1992 to 1993, UCR data without imputed values indicate a 4.7% drop in the volume of offenses, whereas this drop is only 1.9% when imputed values are included in the data.

THE CONVOLUTION MODEL

Because data used to monitor crime and evaluate crime policy are invariably measured with error, it is important to understand how such errors may impact inferences, and whether anything can be done to credibly mitigate negative effects. Exactly how data errors affect statistical inference depends heavily on the specifics of the problem: critical details include the type of model being estimated, the way measurement errors enter the model, and the joint distribution of the observed and unobserved random variables.

In this section, we use a convolution model, where errors are approximated by unobserved additive random terms, to focus on the problem of drawing inferences on a bivariate mean regression model. This model of data errors can be used to formalize the effects of response errors, and with minor modifications can also be generalized to accommodate proxy variable errors. Imputation errors, where only a known fraction of observations may be in error, are probably better addressed by the mixing model considered in section "The Mixture Model." Consider the bivariate mean regression model

$$y^* = \alpha + x^*\beta + \varepsilon, \tag{18.1}$$

where y^* and x^* are scalars and ε is an unobserved random variable distributed according to some probability distribution F_ε, mean independent of x^*: formally, we assume

[A1] $E[\varepsilon|x^*] = 0$.

Assumption A1 is the standard mean independence requirement for linear regression models. Given a random sample on (y^*, x^*), one can consistently estimate (α, β) using the ordinary least-squares estimator.

In the presence of data errors, however, x^* and y^* may not be revealed by the sampling process. Rather, the convolution error model assumes observable data are imperfect reflections of the true variables of interest: $x = x^* + \mu$ and $y = y^* + \nu$, with unobserved measurement errors, μ and ν, randomly distributed according to probability distributions F_μ and F_ν

respectively. The sampling process does not reveal the joint distribution of the variables of interest, (x^*, y^*), but it does reveal that of (x, y). Specifically, we assume an observable random sample of size N: $\{(x_i, y_i)\}_{i=1}^{N}$.[2]

What can this sampling process reveal about the parameters of interest, namely (α, β)? Under various assumptions on the characteristics of the error distributions, F_μ and F_ν, we explore the effects of measurement error on the probability limit of the least squares slope estimator, and suggest potential solutions to the inferential problems caused by data errors. We first review the classical errors-in-variables model, and then motivate and consider several nonclassical variations on this model. Finally, we discuss complications introduced by measurement error in regressions on differenced panel data. These examples are by no means exhaustive, but help give a taste for important considerations and implications when using error-ridden measurements in statistical analysis.[3] In particular, we observe the following:

(a) The "classical" generating processes, where errors are assumed to be mean zero and exogenous, is unlikely to apply in many of the important data error problems in criminal justice research

(b) Outcome-variable errors, ν, impact inferences on the mean regression in (18.1) and, in particular, can bias inferences on crime levels and trends

(c) Regressor errors, μ, do not always result in attenuation bias

(d) In panel data models, the impact of measurement error can be exaggerated by differencing or the inclusion of fixed effect terms.

In the following, let $\sigma_{x^*}^2$ denote the population variance of x^*, with similar notation for other variables, and let $\sigma_{x^*, \mu}$ and $\rho_{x^*, \mu}$ denote the population covariance and correlation of x^* and μ with similar notation for other pairwise combinations of variables. In regression models, we adopt the terminology that y^* is the "outcome variable" while x^* is the "regressor." Finally, let $\hat{\beta}_{y,x}$ be the ordinary least squares (OLS) slope estimator from a sample regression of y on x.

Classical Assumptions

The classical measurement error model supposes that the additive error terms μ and ν are mean zero, uncorrelated with the true values of all variables in the model, and uncorrelated with each other. In the present model, classical measurement error assumptions may be stated as follows:

[A2] $E[\mu] = E[\nu] = 0$

[A3] $\sigma_{x^*, \nu} = \sigma_{\mu, \nu} = \sigma_{\varepsilon, \nu} = 0$

[A4] $\sigma_{x^*, \mu} = 0$

[A5] $\sigma_{\varepsilon, \mu} = 0.$

---

[2] To accommodate proxy errors, this model has often been generalized by including a factor of proportionality linking the observed and true variables. For example, $y = \delta y^* + \nu$, where δ is an unknown parameter. For brevity, we focus on the pure measurement model without an unknown factor of proportionality. Including a scaling factor of unknown magnitude or sign induces obvious complications beyond those discussed here. For additional details, see Wooldridge (2002, 63–67) and Bound et al. (2001, 3715–3716).

[3] The interested reader should consult more detailed presentations in Wooldridge (2002), Wansbeek and Meijer (2000) and Bound et al. (2001).

Assumption A2 implies that the measurement errors, μ and ν, are mean zero, while the remaining assumptions restrict errors to be uncorrelated with each other, with the outcome variable, and with the regressor. In particular, assumption A3 implies that the error in the outcome variable, ν, is uncorrelated with the other measurement error, μ, with the regressor x^*, and with the outcome variable y^*. Assumptions A4 and A5 restrict the error in the regressor, μ, to be uncorrelated with the true value of the regressor, x^*, and with the outcome, y^*.

Under A1–A5, it is well known that the probability limit of the OLS slope parameter is proportional to the true value β in the following way (Wooldridge 2002):

$$\text{plim}_{N \to \infty} \hat{\beta}_{y,x} = \beta \frac{\sigma_{x^*}^2}{\sigma_{x^*}^2 + \sigma_{\mu}^2}. \tag{18.2}$$

Two important conclusions may be drawn from (18.2). First, measurement error in the outcome variable does not affect the consistency of $\hat{\beta}_{y,x}$: the slope coefficient from a sample regression of y on x^* is a consistent estimator of β.[4] Second, classic measurement error in the regressor causes the sample regression slope parameter to be an inconsistent estimator of β such that asymptotically $\hat{\beta}_{y,x}$ has the same sign as β but is closer to zero. This effect is generally termed "attenuation bias." The presence of measurement error in the regressor dilutes the apparent strength of the relationship between x^* and y^*, causing the estimated slope parameter to understate the magnitude of the true effect. While we focus on the OLS estimator of the slope parameter, the estimator of the constant term, α, is also inconsistent when the regressor is measured with error.[5]

With access to auxiliary data or model structure, the parameters (α, β) may be point identified.[6] For example, one common approach is to exploit an instrumental variable, z, that is known to be independent of all of the unobserved error terms, (μ, ν, ε), but is also correlated with the regressor, x^*. In particular, assume that

[A6] $\sigma_{z,x^*} \neq 0$
[A7] $\sigma_{z,\mu} = \sigma_{z,\nu} = 0$
[A8] $\sigma_{z,\varepsilon} = 0$.

In this case, the instrumental variable (IV) estimator is consistent for β:

$$\text{plim}_{N \to \infty} \hat{\beta}_{y,x(z)}^{IV} = \beta. \tag{18.3}$$

---

[4] When the available measurement of y^* is a proxy variable of the form $y = \delta y^* + \nu$, the probability limit of $\hat{\beta}_{y,x^*}$ is $\delta \beta$. If δ is known in sign but not magnitude, then the sign, but not scale, of β is identified.

[5] Although a full treatment of the effects of measurement error in multivariate regression is beyond the scope of this chapter, several general results are worth mentioning. First, measurement error in any one regressor will usually affect the consistency of all other parameter estimators. Second, when only a single regressor is measured with classical error, the OLS estimator of the coefficient associated with the error-ridden variable suffers attenuation bias in the standard sense (see, for example, Wooldridge 2002, 75). In general, all other OLS parameters are also inconsistent, and the direction of inconsistency can be asymptotically signed by the available data. Finally, with measurement error in multiple regressors, classical assumptions imply that the probability limit of the OLS parameter vector is usually attenuated in an average sense, but there are important exceptions (Wansbeek and Meijer 2000, 17–20).

[6] A number of possible strategies are available, and the interested reader should consult the discussions in Wansbeek and Meijer (2000) and Bound et al. (2001).

It is often observed that alternative measurements of x^* may serve as instrumental variables satisfying these conditions. For example, suppose a researcher has access to an alternative measurement $x' = x^* + \eta$ with η randomly distributed according to some probability distribution F_η. If error in the alternative measurement, η, is classical and uncorrelated with μ, then $z = x'$ satisfies A6–A8 and a consistent point estimator of β is available even in the presence of classical measurement error.[7]

In the absence of auxiliary data or structure, point identification of β is impossible. Under classical assumptions, however, the sampling process places bounds on the true value of β (Frisch 1934). Part of the work is already done: with classical measurement error in the outcome variable, (18.2) shows that probability limit of $\hat{\beta}_{y,x}$ is closer to zero than is the true value of β, so that $|\hat{\beta}_{y,x}|$ is an estimable lower bound on the magnitude of β.

Now, consider a new estimator of β constructed from the reverse regression of x on y. Specifically, define the new estimator of β as the inverse of the ordinary least squares estimator of the slope from a regression of x on y: $\hat{\beta}_{x,y}^{-1}$. Under A1–A5, the probability limit of this new estimator is

$$\text{plim}_{N\to\infty}\hat{\beta}_{x,y}^{-1} = \beta + \frac{\sigma_\varepsilon^2 + \sigma_\nu^2}{\beta\sigma_{x^*}^2}. \tag{18.4}$$

Like the usual slope estimator from a regression of y on x, the probability limit of $\hat{\beta}_{x,y}^{-1}$ has the same sign as β. Unlike the usual slope estimator, however, the probability limit of $\hat{\beta}_{y,x}$ is farther from zero than is the true value of β.

This means that in the presence of classical measurement error, data on x and y alone can be used to provide informative bounds on the set of possible values of β. When $\beta > 0$, $\hat{\beta}_{x,y}^{-1}$ and $\hat{\beta}_{y,x}$ are asymptotic upper and lower bounds on the true value of the slope parameter:

$$\text{plim}_{N\to\infty}\hat{\beta}_{y,x} < \beta < \text{plim}_{N\to\infty}\hat{\beta}_{x,y}^{-1} \tag{18.5}$$

and inequalities reverse when $\beta < 0$.[8]

Problems with Classical Assumptions

In any analysis with imperfectly measured data, the researcher should carefully consider whether classical assumptions are appropriate. Trivial examples which give rise to classical conditions are the cases where errors are generated by random clerical mistakes in data entry or by sampling variation when x^* and y^* represent population averages (Bound et al. 2001). In general, however, classical measurement error assumptions are inappropriate. Failure of any one of the assumptions has implications for drawing inferences on the regression parameters (α, β).

---

[7] Of the required conditions for using a second measurement as an instrumental variable, the assumption that the two errors are uncorrelated, $\sigma_{\eta,\mu} = 0$, may be the most difficult to satisfy in practice. Even if both errors are classical in other regards, errors in different measurements of the same variable may be expected to correlate so that $\sigma_{\eta,\mu} > 0$. When covariance between μ and η is nonzero, the IV slope estimator is no longer a consistent point estimator of β, though it may still provide an informative bound on β under certain circumstances (see, for example, Bound et al. 2001, 3730; Black et al. 2000).

[8] Klepper and Leamer (1984) suggest a similar strategy for the case where multiple regressors are measured with error. The general approach is described by Bound et al. (2001, 3722–3723).

To evaluate these problems, we present two illustrations where nonclassical measurement errors are likely to confound inference: these are the common monitoring problem of inferring levels and trends in crime rates, and the problem of inferring how expected crime rates vary with illicit drug use. In each situation, we argue that various classical assumptions are unlikely to hold. We then derive formal results to illustrate the implications of alternative assumptions on the measurement error process.

ILLUSTRATION 1: CRIME LEVELS AND TRENDS.   Perhaps, the most central function of the data on crime is to monitor levels and trends in crime rates. Level estimates from the UCR and NCVS, however, are thought to be downwardly biased. This violates assumption A2, because measurement errors are not mean zero.

As estimated crime rates are perceived to be systematically biased, trend estimates are often argued to be more reliable than levels. An example is the study of differences in crime statistics between the UCR and NCVS; these two crime series differ systematically in levels, with the NCVS always estimating a higher rate of crime than the UCR (see Table 18.1). Despite obvious level differences, some researchers suggest that the two series are comparable in terms of long-term time trends (US Department of Justice 2004). On this topic, McDowall and Loftin (2007, 96) argue that studies attempting to reconcile differences between the UCR and NCVS crime rates might want to focus on differences in trends as a less demanding standard of comparability than differences in levels.

Similar sentiments have been expressed in the context of survey data on illicit drug use. To the extent that survey respondents may be reluctant to admit engaging in illegal and socially unacceptable behavior, it seems likely that drug use data may suffer from a systematic, negative bias. On the basis of the premise that measurement errors are constant over time, Johnston et al. (1998, 47–48) argue that measurements of drug use trends should be robust to the presence of measurement error. Anglin et al. (1993, 350) take a similar stance, claiming "[I]t is easier to generate trend information... than to determine the absolute level."

Under what conditions might one consistently estimate trends, even if the level estimates are systematically biased? Let x^* be an indicator function measuring two distinct time periods, say 2009 and 2010, and suppose the noisy reflection of the crime rate satisfies $y = y^* + v$. Assume that the measurement error, v, is uncorrelated with the time period so that $\sigma_{x^*, v} = 0$, but allow for the possibility of nonzero expected errors (e.g., $E[v] < 0$). That is, maintain assumption A3 but relax A2 to allow for nonzero mean errors. In this case, with only the outcome variable measured with error, the OLS estimator of the slope parameter from a regression of y on x^* is a consistent estimator of β (see (18.2)) but the estimator of α is generally inconsistent:

$$\text{plim}_{N \to \infty} \hat{\alpha}_{y, x^*} = \alpha + E[v]. \tag{18.6}$$

Thus, even when the available measurement of y^* is systematically biased, we can consistently estimate the trend, β, but not the level of $E[y^*|x^*]$.

The result that trends are robust to biased measurements of the outcome variable is critically dependent on the assumption that measurement error is uncorrelated with the observed regressor: assumption A3. The reason results depend so heavily on this condition is easily seen in terms of general conditional expectations of y at arbitrary values $x^* = x_a^*$ and $x^* = x_b^*$. For any given value of x^* – say, $x^* = x_a^*$ – the expected value of y is

$$E[y|x^* = x_a^*] = E[y^*|x^* = x_a^*] + E[v|x^* = x_a^*] \tag{18.7}$$

and the difference in conditional expectations is

$$E[y|x^* = x_a^*] - E[y|x^* = x_b^*] = (E[y^*|x^* = x_a^*] - E[y^*|x^* = x_b^*])$$
$$+ (E[v|x^* = x_a^*] - E[v|x^* = x_b^*]). \qquad (18.8)$$

Thus, the observed level is equal to the true level only when $E[v|x^*] = 0$, which is violated in this example. The observed difference, on the other hand, is equal to the true difference under the weaker condition that $E[v|x^*] = E[v]$ for all x^*. Intuitively, if the expected measurement error is mean independent of the conditioning variable, then the bias terms cancel out so that changes in conditional expectations of y are the same as changes in the conditional expectation of y^*.

As previously asserted, the critical assumption is that measurement errors in y are unrelated to the conditioning variable x^*. This assumption is particularly questionable when x^* represents time. Consider measurement errors in self reports of illicit drug use: changes over time in the social and legal stigma of drug use seem likely to correlate with response errors (see Pepper 2001). Similarly, for crime rate data in the UCR, the frequency and quality of reporting seems likely to vary over time in response to changes in laws, social attention to crime, and the crime rate itself (Mosher et al. 2002; Rand and Rennison 2002).

Nonclassical measurement errors in the outcome variable are also likely to impact numerous program evaluation studies of criminal justice policy. Consider, for example, the problem of assessing the impact of the police-force size or policing practices on crime, or the impact of restrictive firearms policies on crime. In these cases and many others, errors in measuring crime are likely to be associated with effects of the policies of interest.

When measurement errors in crime data are associated with the conditioning variable, analysis in trends or marginal changes is not clearly preferable to that in levels. Comparing bias terms in (18.7) and (18.8), the absolute magnitude of $E[v|x^*]$ may be greater than that of $E[v|x_a^*] - E[v|x_b^*]$, but relative to $E[y^*|x^*]$ and $E[y^*|x_a^*] - E[y^*|x_b^*]$, the impact of the bias term in changes may well exceed that in levels. Certainly, the claim that crime data are biased in levels but not trends cannot generally be supported.

ILLUSTRATION 2: DRUGS AND CRIME. In many cases, concerns over errors in the regressor may also play an important role in inference. As an example, suppose a researcher sought to measure the effect of drug use on the propensity to engage in criminal behavior (Bennett et al. 2008; Chaiken and Chaiken 1990). Assume the bivariate mean regression model in (18.1), where x and y are indicator functions for self reports of drug use and criminal activity, respectively. To properly interpret the slope parameter from a sample regression of y on x, a detailed understanding of the sources of measurement error is required. Far from random clerical errors or sampling variability, measurement errors in this model potentially violate classical assumptions A3–A5.

Take assumption A3, which requires measurement error in the outcome variable to have zero covariance with both the true value of the regressor and the measurement error in this variable. If individuals who falsely deny engaging in one of the activities are likely to falsely deny engaging in both (with similar logic for false positives), then measurement errors in self reports of x^* and y^* will positively correlate in the population: $\sigma_{v,\mu} > 0$. Likewise, errors in reporting criminal activity, v, are arguably related to whether the respondent actually used illicit drugs, x^*.

Because x^* is a binary variable in this model, assumption A4 is violated by definition. To see why, note that when $x^* = 0$ any error must be a false positive, and when $x^* = 1$ any error must be a false negative. As such, errors in the regressor exhibit negative correlation with true values of the variable, violating assumption A4.[9] Of course, assumption A4 can also be violated in cases where x^* is not binary. Suppose binary reports were replaced by state-level aggregates of self-reported drug use and criminal behavior. If the negative stigma of drug use decreases as drug use becomes more mainstream, then errors in the state-level statistics should again negatively correlate with actual aggregate drug use: $\sigma_{x^*,\mu} < 0$.

Finally, assumption A5 fails when measurement error in the regressor is correlated with unobserved random variable, ϵ, in the population regression. An active police presence in the community may tend to reduce the likelihood that an individual would actually commit a crime and at the same time make individuals less likely to truthfully admit illicit drug use, leading to negative covariance between measurement error in the regressor, μ, and the regression error term, ε. A similar story can be told at the state level. Violence and other criminal behavior in areas with higher-than-average crime rates may desensitize these populations to the negative stigma associated with admitting drug use, again leading to negative covariance between drug use statistics and the error term in the population model: $\sigma_{\mu,\varepsilon} < 0$.

NonClassical Assumptions

As the previous illustrations demonstrate, classical assumptions may be invalid in many important applications. Although the effects of measurement error on the consistency of the OLS slope estimator were simple to characterize under classical errors-in-variables assumptions (A2–A5), relaxing these assumptions leads to a less parsimonious probability limit:

$$\text{plim}_{N\to\infty}\hat{\beta}_{y,x} = \frac{\sigma_{x^*,v} + \sigma_{\mu,v}}{\sigma_{x^*}^2 + \sigma_\mu^2 + 2\sigma_{x^*,\mu}} + \beta\frac{\sigma_{x^*}^2 + \sigma_{x^*,\mu}}{\sigma_{x^*}^2 + \sigma_\mu^2 + 2\sigma_{x^*,\mu}} + \frac{\sigma_{\mu,\varepsilon}}{\sigma_{x^*}^2 + \sigma_\mu^2 + 2\sigma_{x^*,\mu}}.$$

$$(18.9)$$

Each term on the right-hand side of (18.9) corresponds to the failure of one of the classical assumptions: A3–A5.[10] The first term is nonzero when errors in the outcome are related to the true value of the regressor or its measurement error, so that assumption A3 is not satisfied. The second term differs from the classical result when errors in the regressor are related to the true value of the regressor, $\sigma_{x^*,\mu} \neq 0$, so that assumption A4 is not satisfied. The third term is nonzero when the errors in the regressor are related to the regression residual, so that assumption A5 does not hold.

In this more general setting, the two central lessons of the classical errors-in-variables model no longer apply: data errors in the outcome variable have consequences for inference, and measurement errors x^* in the regressor need not bias the OLS estimator toward zero. In particular, because the first term in (18.9) is unrestricted in both size and sign, the failure of A3 alone is a sufficient condition for $\hat{\beta}_{y,x}$ to be potentially inconsistent for both the sign and magnitude of the true slope parameter. Likewise, the failure of assumption A5 – where the error in the regressor, μ, is related to the regression error, ε – leads to an additive term which is unrestricted in size and sign. Failure of A5 is also sufficient to cause general inconsistency of the OLS estimator of β.

---

[9] Similar logic suggests violation for any discrete variable, and any continuous but bounded variable.
[10] Failure of assumption A2 affects inference regrading α, but not β (see, for example, Illustration 1).

Even if A3 and A5 hold, so that the only deviation from classical assumptions is nonzero covariance between the true value of the regressor and its measurement error, attenuation bias is not guaranteed. If $\sigma_{x^*,\mu} > 0$, then $\hat{\beta}_{y^*,x}$ is consistent for the sign of β and indeed suffers from attenuation bias. However, when $\sigma_{x^*,\mu} < 0$, as might be the case in a study of the impact of illicit drug use on crime, nonclassical error in the regressor may lead to arbitrary inconsistencies. Depending on the relative variance and correlation of x^* and μ, the probability limit of the OLS slope estimator may have the incorrect sign, or may artificially amplify (rather than attenuate) the strength of the relationship between the outcome variable and regressor.

As should be clear at this point, nonclassical measurement error is a more insidious concern than classical error. Without auxiliary data or structure, the sampling process places no restrictions on the true value of β, and the prospects for identification and estimation of β are grim.

Under certain restrictions, however, it may still be possible to construct informative bounds on β. For example, consider the situation where the only deviation from classical assumptions is a negative covariance between the regressor and its measurement error; $\sigma_{x^*,\mu} < 0$. Thus, assumptions A2, A3 and A5 are assumed to hold, but assumption A4 does not. Assume for simplicity that $\beta > 0$. As long as x^* and μ are not too highly correlated, the OLS estimator still acts as an asymptotic lower bound on β, and under fairly weak conditions the IV estimator using an alternative measurement of x^* is an asymptotic upper bound on the true slope parameter (Black et al. 2000).[11] Thus, the value of β can be bounded in a manner similar to the case for the classical errors-in-variables model:

$$\text{plim}_{N \to \infty} \hat{\beta}_{y,x} < \beta < \text{plim}_{N \to \infty} \hat{\beta}^{IV}_{y,x(x')} \tag{18.10}$$

and inequalities reverse when $\beta < 0$.

Panel Data Models

Up to this point, we have maintained assumption A1 so that OLS estimators of (α, β) would be consistent if x^* and y^* were observable in the data. In many cases, however, this assumption is likely to be violated. A common example is the situation where multiple observations are collected on each sampling unit: for example, let i index a county and let t index the year of the observation. Let the unobserved regression error contain unit-specific effects, α_i, so that $\varepsilon_{i,t} = \alpha_i + \omega_{i,t}$ where α_i is potentially correlated with $x^*_{i,t}$ and $\omega_{i,t}$ is an unobserved random variable distributed according to some probability distribution F_ω, mean independent of x^*. To simplify discussion, suppose $y^*_{i,t}$ is measured accurately, $x_{i,t} = x^*_{i,t} + \mu_{i,t}$ is an imperfect measurement of $x^*_{i,t}$, classical measurement error assumptions hold, and all variables have stationary variance and covariance across counties and time.[12]

We assume access to a panel-data sample of two years worth of data: $\{\{(x_{i,t}, y_{i,t})\}^2_{t=1}\}^N_{i=1}$. Denote by $\hat{\beta}_{y,x}$ the OLS slope estimator from regression of $y_{i,t}$ on

---

[11] Bollinger (1996) and Frazis and Loewenstein (2003) derive bounds when a binary regressor is measured with error.

[12] With panel data, assumptions A1–A5 must account for correlations in both the cross-section and the time series dimension. For detailed examples, see Wooldridge (2002) and Griliches and Hausman (1985).

$x_{i,t}$ which does not account for variation in α across counties. As should be expected, $\hat{\beta}_{y,x}$ is an inconsistent estimator of β:

$$\text{plim}_{N \to \infty} \hat{\beta}_{y,x} = \beta \frac{\sigma_{x*}^2}{\sigma_{x*}^2 + \sigma_\mu^2} + \frac{\sigma_{x*,\alpha} + \sigma_{\mu,\alpha}}{\sigma_{x*}^2 + \sigma_\mu^2}. \tag{18.11}$$

The first term in (18.11) is just the classical attenuation bias observed in the linear regression models without unobserved effects. The second term comes from failure to account for unobserved county-specific effects: these terms end up in a composite regression-error term which correlates with x_i^*, effectively violating the assumption of conditional mean zero regression errors (assumption A1) and resulting in an additional source of inconsistency.

To avoid problems caused by ignoring time-constant unobserved effects, the researcher may exploit the panel structure of the collected data. For example, a first difference (FD) estimator eliminates any time-constant terms while leaving β estimable:

$$\Delta y_i^* = \Delta x_i^* \beta + \Delta \varepsilon_i, \tag{18.12}$$

where $\Delta y_i^* = y_{i,2}^* - y_{i,1}^*$ with similar notation for other variables, and where $\Delta \alpha_i = 0$ by definition. With an accurate measurement of x_i^* available to the researcher, OLS performed on Δy_i^* and Δx_i^* would provide a consistent estimator of β.

Since x_i^* is not observed, let $\hat{\beta}_{\Delta y^*, \Delta x}$ denote the slope parameter from a sample regression of Δy_i^* on Δx_i. Under classical assumptions, $\hat{\beta}_{\Delta y^*, \Delta x}$ suffers from standard attenuation bias:

$$\text{plim}_{N \to \infty} \hat{\beta}_{\Delta y^*, \Delta x} = \beta \frac{\sigma_{\Delta x*}^2}{\sigma_{\Delta x*}^2 + \sigma_{\Delta \mu}^2}. \tag{18.13}$$

At first glance, (18.13) would seem an improvement upon (18.11), with consistency of $\hat{\beta}_{\Delta y^*, \Delta x}$ only limited by attenuation bias due to the presence of measurement error in x_i. While the FD estimator does eliminate inconsistency due to the presence of time-constant unobserved variables, it may also exacerbate attenuation bias due to measurement error. More extreme attenuation bias results if the true regressor exhibits relatively strong serial correlation while measurement error does not.[13]

Switching from levels to differences is not uniformly preferable when the regressor is measured with error. On one hand, working with differences allows the researcher to eliminate inconsistency due to the presence of time-constant unobserved effects. On the other hand, differencing and related approaches may tend to increase the magnitude of measurement error bias when true values of the regressor exhibit strong serial correlation and measurement errors do not. For a detailed discussion of related panel data models and solutions when more than two periods of data are available, see Griliches and Hausman (1985).

THE MIXTURE MODEL

The previous section presented textbook results for several chronic errors-in-variables models, where the observable variable, y, is the noisy reflection of the true variable of interest, y^*,

---

[13] Note that the variance of Δx_i^* is smaller when x_i^* has positive autocorrelation: $\sigma_{\Delta x*}^2 = 2\sigma_{x*}^2 (1 - \rho_{x_2^*, x_1^*})$. To see why the relative strength of serial correlation is a concern, suppose that $\rho_{x_2^*, x_1^*} > 1/2$ while random measurement errors exhibit no autocorrelation. This implies $\sigma_{\Delta x*}^2 < \sigma_{x*}^2$ while $\sigma_{\Delta \mu}^2 = 2\sigma_\mu^2$, so attenuation bias will be greater after first differencing the data.

such that $y = y^* + v$. In many settings, this model of chronic errors may be inappropriate. When considering imputation errors in the UCR, for example, we know that some observations are imputed while others are not. Likewise, when focusing on invalid response problems regarding victimization in the NCVS or illicit drug use in the National Survey of Drug Use and Health (NSDUH), it seems likely that some respondents report accurately while others may not.

In light of these concerns, a growing body of literature conceptualizes the data error problem using a mixture model in which the observed outcome distribution is a mixture of the unobserved distribution of interest, and another unobserved distribution. See, for example, Horowitz and Manski (1995), Lambert and Tierney (1997), Dominitz and Sherman (2004), Mullin (2005) and Kreider and Pepper (2007, 2008, forthcoming). In this setting, the observed random variable, y, is viewed as a contaminated version of the variable of interest, y^*. In particular, the observed variable is generated by the mixture:

$$y = y^* z + \widetilde{y}^*(1 - z), \tag{18.14}$$

where z indicates whether the observed outcome, y, comes from the distribution F_{y*} or some alternative distribution, $F_{\widetilde{y}*}$.

In this environment, the "contaminated sampling" model pertains to the case in which the mixing process, z, is known to be statistically independent of sample realizations from the distribution of interest, y^*. The more general "corrupted sampling" model pertains to the case where nothing is known about the pattern of data errors.

Using nonparametric methods, Horowitz and Manski (1995) derive sharp bounds on the distribution of y^* under both corrupt and contaminated sampling models. Hotz et al. (1997), Kreider and Pepper (2007), Kreider and Hill (2009), and Kreider et al. (2009) use this framework to derive bounds on the mean regression model when a regressor, x^*, is measured with error.

To illustrate how these bounds work, we focus on the important and relatively simple example of a binary outcome variable which may in some cases be misclassified.[14] To simplify the exposition, regressors are assumed to be accurately measured and are left implicit; in any of the following, one can condition the results on the observed regressors, x^*. Although our focus is on identification, the actual estimation strategy is very simple. Given a random sample from the joint distribution of (y, x^*), the derived identification bounds can be consistently estimated by replacing population probabilities with their sample analogs.

In this context, we first present the corrupt and contaminated sampling bounds, and then apply these methods to a couple of important questions in criminal justice research. These examples are by no means exhaustive, but help give a taste for important considerations and implications when using error-ridden measurements in statistical analysis. Most notably, we observe that small amounts of measurement error can lead to substantial ambiguity about the true mean regression. Stronger assumptions on the unobserved error process can lead to sharper inferences, but may not be credible in many applications.

---

[14] As discussed is the previous section, when a variable with bounded support is imperfectly classified, it is widely recognized that the classical errors-in-variables model assumption of independence between measurement error and true variable cannot hold. Molinari (2008) presents an alternative and useful conceptualization of the data error problem for discrete outcome variables. This "direct misclassification" approach allows one to focus on assumptions related to classification error rates instead of restrictions on the mixing process.

Mixture Model Bounds

Let y^* be an indicator function for self-reported drug use, and suppose one is interested in making inferences on the rate of illicit drug use: $P(y^* = 1) = E(y^*)$. Some unknown fraction of respondents, $P(y = 1, z = 0)$, inaccurately admit to using drugs (false positives) while another fraction, $P(y = 0, z = 0)$, inaccurately deny using drugs (false negatives). The relationship between the true and reported rates of drug use is as follows:

$$P(y^* = 1) = P(y = 1) + P(y = 0, z = 0) - P(y = 1, z = 0). \tag{18.15}$$

If the fraction of false negatives exactly offsets the fraction of false positives, then the reported rate of use equals the true rate of use: $P(y^* = 1) = P(y = 1)$. Unfortunately, the data alone only identify the fraction of the population that self-reports use: $P(y = 1)$. The sampling process cannot identify the fraction of false negatives or false positives.

A common starting point in this literature is to assume a known lower bound v on the fraction of cases that are drawn from the distribution of interest:[15]

$$P(z = 1) \geq v. \tag{18.16}$$

A particular lower bound restriction may be informed by a validation study of a related population (e.g., Harrison 1995) or the known fraction of responses that are imputed. Moreover, by varying the value of v, we can consider the wide range of views characterizing the debate on inaccurate reporting. Those willing to assume fully accurate reporting can set $v = 1$, in which case the sampling process identifies the outcome probability. Those uncomfortable with placing any lower bound on the fraction of accurate responses can set $v = 0$, in which case the sampling process is uninformative. Middle ground positions are evaluated by setting v somewhere between 0 and 1.

Given the restriction that no more than some fraction, $1 - v$, of the population misreport, we know from (18.15) that in the case of corrupt sampling, bounds are as follows:

$$\max\{P(y = 1) - (1 - v), 0\} \leq P(y^* = 1) \leq \min\{P(y = 1) + (1 - v), 1\}. \tag{18.17}$$

Under contaminated sampling, where we are willing to assume that y^* and z are statistically independent, the bounds are different:

$$\max\{[P(y = 1) - (1 - v)]/v, 0\} \leq P(y^* = 1) \leq \min([P(y = 1)/v], 1). \tag{18.18}$$

These bounds are derived by Horowitz and Manski (1995, Corollary 1.2), and are referred to as the corrupt and contaminated sampling bounds, respectively.

Several features of these bounds are important. First, the bounds are sensitive to the upper bound misreporting rate, $1 - v$. Identification of $P(y^* = 1)$ deteriorates rapidly with the allowed fraction of misclassifications; so small amounts of error can have large effects on inferences. Second, the contaminated sampling bounds are narrower than the corrupt sampling bounds. Whether the independence assumption is valid, however, depends on the application:

---

[15] This type of restriction is used in the literatures on robust statistics (Huber 1981) and data errors with binary regressors (see, e.g., Bollinger 1996 and Frazis and Loewenstein 2003).

it seems unlikely, for example, that the misreporting of illicit drug use is independent of actual drug use status or that the true crime rate is independent of whether an observation must be imputed. Finally, without additional assumptions, we cannot point identify the mean regression. Rather, all we can conclude is that the true outcome probability lies within some upper and lower bound.

Mixture Model Applications

To illustrate how the mixture model might be applied in practice, we consider two important questions in criminal justice research where nonclassical measurement errors are likely to confound inference: these are the problem of using data from the NSDUH to infer the rate of illicit drug use, and using data from the UCR to infer the aggravated assault rate. In the former case, the data are contaminated from response errors; some respondents do not provide accurate reports of drug use. In the latter case, the data are contaminated from imputation errors; about one-third of all reporting agencies, representing over 10% of the population, have imputed crime data.

ILLUSTRATION 3: ILLICIT DRUG USE.   To illustrate the implications of data errors using the mixing model approach, consider using data from the NSDUH to draw inferences on the true rate of illicit drug use. While there is very little information on the degree of data errors in this survey, there are good reasons to believe that the errors are extensive and systematic. Respondents concerned about the legality of their behavior may falsely deny consuming illicit drugs, while the desire to fit into a deviant culture or otherwise be defiant may lead some respondents to falsely claim to consume illicit drugs (Pepper 2001). Thus, ignoring these errors may be problematic and the classical errors-in-variables model is inappropriate.

Instead, Kreider and Pepper (2009) consider using the mixing model to address the problem of drawing inferences on the rate of marijuana use in the presence of nonrandom reporting errors. The 2002 NSDUH reveals that 54% of 18–24 year-olds claimed to have consumed marijuana within their lifetime, with 30% reporting use during the last year (Office of Applied Studies 2003). To draw inferences about true rates of illicit drug use in the United States, one must combine these self-reports with assumptions about the nature and extent of reporting errors. As noted above, Harrison (1995), who compares self-reported marijuana use to urinalysis test results among a sample of arrestees, finds a 22% misreporting rate for marijuana consumption. Arguably, the accurate reporting rate, z, in the general noninstitutionalized population exceeds that obtained in the sample of arrestees studied by Harrison (1995). Arrestees have a relatively high incentive to misreport (Harrison 1995; Pepper 2001). Under this restriction alone, the corrupt sampling bounds reveal much uncertainty about the true rates of drug use. For example, we only learn that between 32% ($=54 - 22$) and 76% ($=54 + 22$) of the young adult population has ever used marijuana. Importantly, this uncertainty reflects the identification problem caused by data errors; these bounds do not reflect the presence of additional uncertainty due to sampling variability.

Under the contaminated sampling assumption, the bounds narrow considerably. The bounds on lifetime marijuana use, for example, narrow from [32%, 76%] to [41%, 69%], a 36% reduction in bound width. When Kreider and Pepper impose the additional assumption that all draws from the alternative distribution, $\widetilde{y}^*$, are in error (i.e., the response error model), the lifetime marijuana use rate is nearly point-identified, lying in the narrow range

[54%, 57%]. These latter findings, however, rest on the implausible contaminated sampling assumption that drug use rates are identical among accurate and inaccurate reporters. More realistically, the rate of illicit drug use is higher among inaccurate reporters. Under this restriction, the lifetime rate of marijuana use is bounded to lie within [54%, 76%].

A useful practical feature of mixing model results is that we can assess the sensitivity of the bounds to variation in v. After all, Harrison's estimates might not accurately reflect misreporting rates in the general population. Figures 18.1 and 18.2 display bounds on the lifetime and past year marijuana use rates, respectively, under the corrupt sampling, contaminated sampling, and response error models considered by Kreider and Pepper (forthcoming). The vertical axis measures the outcome probability, $P(y = 1)$, and the horizontal axis represents the lower bound fraction of responses known to come from the distribution of interest, v.

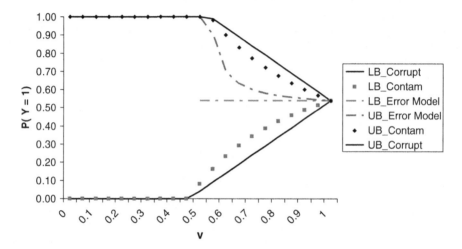

FIGURE 18.1. Bounds on lifetime marijuana use given response error $[P(y^* = 1) = 0.54]$.

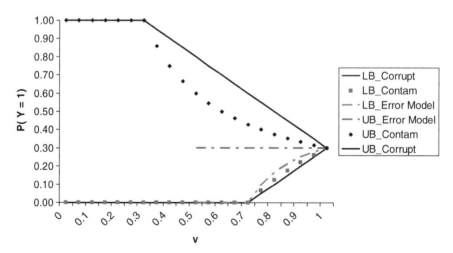

FIGURE 18.2. Bounds on past year marijuana use given response errors $[P(y^* = 1) = 0.30]$.

The diagonal lines converging at $P(y = 1) = P(y^* = 1)$ when $v = 1$ depict the Horowitz and Manski corrupt sampling bounds. For any v, $P(y = 1)$ must lie within the vertical interval between these diagonal lines. The lower bound is uninformative for $v \leq 1 - P(y^* = 1)$, while the upper bound is uninformative for $v \leq P(y^* = 1)$. Thus, for lifetime use, the bounds are uninformative unless we know that over 50% of responses are valid; for past year use, the lower bound is uninformative unless we know that over 30% of responses are valid. What is most striking about these corrupt sampling bounds is that even with fairly small degrees of reporting error, there is much ambiguity in the prevalence rate of marijuana use. If, for example, we know that only 10% of all reports may be misclassified, then the lifetime use rate can only be restricted to lie within a 20 point range: [0.44, 0.64]. Without richer information on the nature and degree of reporting errors in the NSDUH, the only way to draw tighter inferences is to impose additional assumptions.

It is tempting to address the data error problem with strong, but possibly flawed, modeling assumptions. The contaminated sampling models, for example, substantially narrow the corrupt sampling bounds (see Figs. 18.1 and 18.2). As discussed earlier, however, these models are untenable in this setting. In this case, stronger assumptions do not resolve the ambiguity reflected in the corrupt sampling bounds – they simply replaced uncertainty over data errors with uncertainty over the model.

There may be other assumptions that can be credibly applied. Pepper (2001), for example, assumes the fraction of false negatives exceeds the fraction of false positives, in which case the reported lifetime rate of 0.54 serves as a lower bound for all v. Thus, if no more than 10% of respondents are misclassified, the lifetime prevalence rate is bounded to lie with [0.54, 0.64]. Kreider and Pepper (forthcoming) formalize the assumption that the rate of illicit drug use is higher among inaccurate reporters. While these assumption narrow the bounds, there remains much uncertainty about the rates of use and, as shown in Pepper (2001), identifying trends in use can be even more problematic.

ILLUSTRATION 4: THE AGGRAVATED ASSAULT RATE.   Mixing models of measurement error are also a natural way to address imputation errors in UCR reported crime figures. While most police agencies provide UCR data to the FBI, Maltz and Targonski (2002) and Lynch and Jarvis (2008) find that a nontrivial and nonrandom portion of UCR data are imputed. Consider, for example, the problem of inferring the 2005 aggravated assault rate in the United States from the rate of 0.0029 in the UCR (see Table 18.1).[16] Without additional information, the corrupt sampling bounds reveal that violent crime rates lie between zero and the imputation rate. So, for example, if crime rates are imputed for 5% of the population, then the 2005 aggravated assault rate is only known to lie between [0, 5%]. Information identifying which records are imputed may narrow these bounds, but not by an appreciable amount.

By contrast, information on the direction of the imputation bias might be informative. Maltz and Targonski (2002) argue, for example, that nonresponse is likely to occur in periods where there is little reported crime. If so, this would lead to an upward imputation bias, so that the observed rate of 0.0029 serves as an upper bound on the 2005 aggravated assault rate. Unfortunately, this assumption seems unsubstantiated. Arguably, some police departments do

---

[16] In this discussion, we are concerned with drawing inferences on the true rate of aggravated assault reported to the police. Inferences regarding the overall rate of aggravated assault – known and unknown to the police – are complicated by the proxy variables problem discussed previously.

not respond (or under-report) in periods where crime rates are inflated, in which case there would be a downward imputation bias (Mosher et al. 2002).

Maltz and Targonski (2002) have argued that imputation errors may bias conclusions drawn from analyses conducted at fine geographic levels, such as counties, but will be less important for inferences about state and national-level crime rates. The data alone do not support this conclusion. Unless one is willing to make strong and seemingly unsubstantiated assumptions, even small amounts of imputation errors can lead to substantial uncertainties about true crime rates and trends.

CONCLUSION: THE LAW OF DECREASING CREDIBILITY

Measurement errors continue to frustrate attempts to draw credible inferences from data used to track the extent and expression of crime in the United States. Lack of detailed information on the degree and nature of measurement errors in major national crime datasets, namely the UCR and NCVS, is especially troubling. In the absence of direct information on these errors, inferences on crime rates and trends, and on the impact of policy on crime, are largely speculative. Although it might be – as some have suggested – that misreporting rates are stable over time and unrelated to policies of interest, this conjecture seems implausible and is unsupported by evidence. Either way, measurement errors are likely to be both substantial and systematic in survey data on crime and illicit behavior.

Though these problems do not imply that the data are completely uninformative, they do imply that researchers must choose between the unpleasant alternatives of either tolerating a certain degree of ambiguity in inference, or imposing strong assumptions about unobserved measurement errors. The problem, of course, is that weak assumptions may lead to indeterminate conclusions, whereas strong assumptions may be inaccurate and yield flawed conclusions (Pepper 2001; Manski 2007; Manski et al. 2002). Manski (2007) refers to this fundamental trade-off as the *Law of Decreasing Credibility*: stronger assumptions yield sharper but less credible inferences.

This trade-off should not be easily dismissed. Imposing convenient assumptions does not resolve the measurement error problem, but simply exchanges uncertainty over unobserved errors with uncertainty over the accuracy of the model. Assumptions that data errors are exogenous or "classical," for example, are in many applications untenable. As we have noted in this chapter, relaxing the central assumptions of the classical errors-in-variable model has substantive implications for the conclusions we might draw from the data. Inferences are highly sensitive to even small amounts of measurement and modeling errors.

There are practical solutions to this predicament. If stronger assumptions are not imposed, the way to resolve an indeterminate finding is to collect richer data. More detailed information on the nature of data error problems might supplement the existing data and help to suggest credible assumptions about error processes. Alternatively, efforts to increase the valid response rate may directly reduce the potential effects of these problems. Even with the best survey sampling methods, however, researchers must confront the fact that data on such sensitive topics as crime and victimization will always be subject to poorly behaved measurement errors, and inferences drawn using these data will be impacted by such errors. Failure to seriously address data error problems can only lead to decreased credibility and potentially costly mistakes in drawing inferences relevant to crime policy.

Acknowledgments We thank Stephen Bruestle, Alex Piquero, and David Weisburd for their helpful comments. Pepper's research was supported, in part, by the Bankard Fund for Political Economy.

REFERENCES

Anglin MD, Caulkins JP, Hser Y (1993) Prevalence estimation: policy needs, current status, and future potential. J Drug Issues 23(2):345–360

Azrael D, Cook PJ, Miller M (2001) State and local prevalence of firearms ownership: measurement structure and trends, National Bureau of Economic Research: Working Paper 8570

Bennett T, Holloway K, Farrington D (2008) The statistical association between drug misuse and crime: a meta-analysis. Aggress Violent Behav 13:107–118

Black D (1970) Production of crime rates. Am Sociol Rev 35:733–48

Black DA, Berger MC, Scott FA (2000) Bounding parameter estimates with nonclassical measurement error. J Am Stat Assoc 95(451):739–748

Blumstein A, Rosenfeld R (2009) Factors contributing to U.S. crime trends, in understanding crime trends: workshop report Goldberger AS, Rosenfeld R (eds) Committee on Understanding Crime Trends, Committee on Law and Justice, Division of Behavioral and Social Sciences and Education. The National Academies Press, Washington, DC

Bollinger C (1996) Bounding mean regressions when a binary variable is mismeasured. J Econom 73(2):387–99

Bound J, Brown C, Mathiowetz N (2001) Measurement error in survey data. In: Heckman J, Leamer E (eds) Handbook of econometrics, 5, Ch. 59:3705–3843

Chaiken JM, Chaiken MR (1990) Drugs and predatory crime. Crime Justice: Drugs Crime, 13:203–239

Dominitz J, Sherman R (2004) Sharp bounds under contaminated or corrupted sampling with verification, with an application to environmental pollutant data. J Agric Biol Environ Stat 9(3):319–338

Frazis H, Loewenstein M (2003) Estimating linear regressions with mismeasured, possibly endogenous, binary explanatory variables. J Econom 117:151–178

Frisch R (1934) Statistical confluence analysis by means of complete regression systems. University Institute for Economics, Oslo

Griliches Z, Hausman JA (1985) Errors in variables in panel data: a note with an example. J Econom 31(1):93–118

Harrison LD (1995) The validity of self-reported data on drug use. J Drug Issues 25(1):91–111

Harrison L, Hughes A (1997) Introduction – the validity of self-reported drug use: improving the accuracy of survey estimates. In: Harrison L and Hughes A (eds) The validity of self-reported drug use: improving the accuracy of survey estimates. NIDA Research Monograph, vol 167. US Department of Health and Human Services, Rockville, MD, pp 1–16

Horowitz J, Manski C (1995) Identification and robustness with contaminated and corrupted data. *Econometrica*, 63(2):281–302

Hotz J, Mullins C, Sanders S (1997) Bounding causal effects using data from a contaminated natural experiment: analyzing the effects of teenage childbearing. Rev Econ Stud 64(4):575–603

Huber P (1981) Robust statistics. Wiley, New York

Johnston LD, O'Malley PM, Bachman JG (1998) National survey results on drug use from the monitoring the future study, 1975–1997, Volume I: Secondary school students. NIH Publication No. 98-4345. National Institute on Drug Abuse, Rockville, MD

Kleck G, Gertz M (1995) Armed resistance to crime: The prevalence and nature of self-defense with a gun. J Crim Law Criminol 86:150–187

Klepper S, Leamer EE (1984) Consistent sets of estimates for regressions with errors in all variables. Econometrica 52(1):163–183

Koss M (1993) Detecting the scope of rape: A review of prevalence research methods. J Interpers Violence 8:198–222

Koss M (1996) The measurement of rape victimization in crime surveys. Crim Justice Behav 23:55–69

Kreider B, Hill S (2009) Partially identifying treatment effects with an application to covering the uninsured. J Hum Resour 44(2):409–449

Kreider B, Pepper J (2007) Disability and employment: reevaluating the evidence in light of reporting errors. J Am Stat Assoc 102(478):432–441

Kreider B, Pepper J (2008) Inferring disability status from corrupt data. J Appl Econom 23(3):329–349

Kreider B, Pepper J. (forthcoming). Identification of expected outcomes in a data error mixing model with multiplicative mean independence. J Business Econ Stat

Kreider B, Pepper J, Gundersen C, Jolliffe D (2009) Identifying the effects of food stamps on children's health outcomes when participation is endogenous and misreported. Working Paper

Lambert D, Tierney L (1997) Nonparametric maximum likelihood estimation from samples with irrelevant data and verification bias. J Am Stat Assoc 92:937–944

Lynch JP, Addington LA (eds) (2007) Understanding crime statistics: revisiting the divergence of the NCVS and UCR. Cambridge University Press, Cambridge

Lynch J, Jarvis J (2008) Missing data and imputation in the uniform crime reports and the effects on national estimates. J Contemp Crim Justice 24(1):69–85. doi:10.1177/1043986207313028

Maltz M (1999) Bridging gaps in police crime data: a discussion paper from the BJS Fellows Program Bureau of Justice Statistics, Government Printing Office, Washington, DC

Maltz MD, Targonski J (2002) A note on the use of county-level UCR data. J Quant Criminol. 18:297–318

Manski CF (2007) Identification for prediction and decisions. Harvard University Press, Cambridge, MA

Manski CF, Newman J, Pepper JV (2002) Using performance standards to evaluate social programs with incomplete outcome data: general issues and application to a higher education block grant program. 26(4), 355–381

McDowall D, Loftin C (2007) What is convergence, and what do we know about it? In Lynch J, Addington LA (eds) Understanding crime statistics: revisiting the divergence of the NCVS and UCR, Ch. 4: 93–124

McDowall D, Loftin C, Wierseman B (1998) Estimates of the frequency of firearm self-defense from the redesigned national crime victimization survey. Violence Research Group Discussion Paper 20.

Molinari F (2008) Partial identification of probability distributions with misclassified data. J Econom 144(1):81–117

Mosher CJ, Miethe TD, Phillips DM (2002) The mismeasure of crime. Sage Publications, Thousand Oaks, CA

Mullin CH (2005) Identification and estimation with contaminated data: When do covariate Data Sharpen Inference?" J Econom 130:253–272

National Research Council (2001) Informing America's policy on illegal drugs: what we don't know keeps hurting us. Committee on Data and Research for Policy on Illegal Drugs. In: Manski CF, Pepper JV, Petrie CV (eds) Committee on Law and Justice and Committee on National Statistics. Commission on Behavioral and Social Sciences and Education. National Academy Press, Washington, DC

National Research Council (2003) Measurement problems in criminal justice research: workshop summary. Pepper JV, Petrie CV. Committee on Law and Justice and Committee on National Statistics, Division of Behavioral and Social Sciences and Education. The National Academies Press, Washington, DC

National Research Council (2005) Firearms and violence: a critical review. Committee to improve research information and data on firearms. In: Wellford CF, Pepper JV, Petire CV (eds) Committee on Law and Justice, Division of Behavioral and Social Sciences and Education. The National Academies Press, Washington, DC

National Research Council (2008) Surveying victims: Options for conducting the national crime victimization survey. Panel to review the programs of the bureau of justice statistics. In: Groves RM, Cork DL (eds). Committee on National Statistics and Committee on Law and Justice, Division of Behavioral and Social Sciences and Education. The National Academies Press, Washington, DC

Office of Applied Studies. (2003). Results from the 2002 National Survey on Drug Use and Health: summary of national finding, (DHHS Publication No. SMA 03-3836, Series H-22). Substance Abuse and Mental Health Services Administration, Rockville, MD

Pepper JV (2001) How do response problems affect survey measurement of trends in drug use? In: Manski CF, Pepper JV, Petrie C (eds) Informing America's policy on illegal drugs: What we don't know keeps hurting us. National Academy Press, Washington, DC, 321–348

Rand MR, Rennison CM (2002) True crime stories? Accounting for differences in our national crime indicators. Chance 15(1):47–51

Tourangeau R, McNeeley ME (2003) Measuring crime and crime victimization: methodological issues. In: Pepper JV, Petrie CV (eds) Measurement Problems in Criminal Justice Research: Workshop Summary. Committee on Law and Justice and Committee on National Statistics, Division of Behavioral and Social Sciences and Education. The National Academies Press: Washington, DC 0

U.S. Department of Justice (2004) The Nation's two crime measures, NCJ 122705, http://www.ojp.usdoj.gov/bjs/abstract/ntmc.htm.

U.S. Department of Justice (2006) National Crime Victimization Survey: Criminal Victimization, 2005. Bureau of Justice Statistics Bullentin. http://www.ojp.usdoj.gov/bjs/pub/pdf/cv05.pdf

U.S. Department of Justice (2008) Crime in the United States, 2007-+. Federal Bureau of Investigation, Washington, DC. (table 1). http://www.fbi.gov/ucr/cius2007/data/table_01.html

Wansbeek T, Meijer E (2000) Measurement error and latent variables in econometrics. Elsevier, Amsterdam

Wooldridge JM (2002) Econometric analysis of cross section and panel data. MIT Press, Cambridge, MA

## CHAPTER 19

Statistical Models of Life Events and Criminal Behavior*

D. Wayne Osgood

The goal of developmental and life course criminology is to understand patterns of crime and delinquency over the life course. To date, research in this field has devoted a great deal of attention to describing patterns of change in the dependent variable over different ages, often in the form of trajectories or growth curves of offending in relation to age (LeBlanc and Loeber 1998; Piquero et al. 2007). Closely tied to such studies is a sizable body of research investigating potential predictors of differences in trajectories (e.g., Nagin et al. 1995; Nagin and Tremblay 1999, 2005).

Focusing on growth curves or trajectories has often been associated with an emphasis on the role of early experience and personality traits in shaping the course of development of crime. According to Laub and Sampson (2003), however, criminologists need to balance such work with greater attention to the connections between crime and later events in people's lives. Indeed, the longitudinal data used to study trajectories is equally suitable for this purpose as well. Furthermore, both traditional and developmental/life course theories of crime hypothesize a wide variety of effects on crime from life events, which recent studies have begun to test (for a review, see Siennick and Osgood 2007). For instance, both traditional (Hirschi 1969) and age-graded (Sampson and Laub 1993) versions of social control theory predict that changes in social bonds will affect offending (King et al. 2007; Sampson et al. 2006), social learning theories (Akers 1977; Sutherland and Cressey 1955) predict that offending will increase after a switch to a more delinquent peer group (Warr 1993), and generalized strain theory (Agnew 1992) predicts that experiencing stressful events will promote offending (Slocum et al. 2005).

The aim of this chapter is to facilitate research on life events and crime by presenting a set of statistical tools for analyzing the relationship between events in people's lives and changes in their levels of offending. The presentation will concentrate on events that constitute a categorical change in one's life, such as marriage, gaining employment, or entering a treatment or service program. For the most part, however, these methods apply equally well to

---

*A version of this chapter was presented at The Social Contexts of Pathways in Crime: Methods and Analytical Techniques, The Second Annual SCoPiC Conference, Cambridge, UK, June 2005.

A.R. Piquero and D. Weisburd (eds.), *Handbook of Quantitative Criminology*,
DOI 10.1007/978-0-387-77650-7_19, © Springer Science + Business Media, LLC 2010,
First softcover printing 2011

studying changes of degree in more continuous variables such as marital commitment or job satisfaction, which are also central to the study of crime over the life course (e.g., Sampson and Laub 1993).

The statistical approach I present is meant for analyzing longitudinal panel data with repeated measures of both crime and a time-varying explanatory variable reflecting the event of interest (e.g., not married versus married). This research design is typically "observational" in the sense that it captures only naturally occurring variation in the explanatory variable, in contrast to a study in which the variation comes from random assignment or is affected by a strictly exogenous source, such as a policy change. Though the techniques presented here are also useful for longitudinal studies with random assignment (Esbensen et al. 2001; Osgood and Smith 1995), I will give special attention to issues of causal inference that arise with observation data. Observational research designs can never yield definitive proof of causality, but the tools presented here offer means of ruling out several important types of competing explanations and thereby strengthening the plausibility of a causal interpretation.

AN INITIAL MODEL OF THE EFFECTS OF EVENTS

The key feature that distinguishes these statistical models is the *time varying covariate*, which is simply an explanatory variable that can vary over time for a person. The idea of a time varying covariate implies a longitudinal research design that follows a sample of individuals through multiple measurements over some period. We study the effects of events by analyzing how the outcome of interest, crime, relates to change over time in a variable reflecting the event of interest, such as whether or not the respondent is married.

The most basic model for accomplishing this is simply:

$$Y_{ti} = \beta_0 + \beta_1 X_{ti} + e_{ti} \tag{19.1}$$

Equation (19.1) looks very much like a standard bivariate regression equation, but there is one subtle difference. In the standard version, variables have just one subscript, but here they have two, i and t. The additional subscript means that we are differentiating observations not just in terms of the person being studied (i), but also in terms of the occasion or time of measurement (t). Thus, (19.1) specifies that both the outcome variable, Y, and the explanatory variable, X, are measured for each wave of data that a person contributes to the analysis, and that their values can vary within individuals over time.

Straightforward interpretations for the regression coefficients of (19.1) follow from coding the explanatory variable as a dummy variable equaling 0 before the event occurs (e.g., unmarried) and 1 after it has occurred (e.g., married). In this case, β_0 will reflect the mean of the outcome variable before the event (the crime rate when respondents are not married), and β_1 will capture its difference from the mean of the outcome after the event. Thus, a large negative value for β_1 would indicate considerably less crime among married respondents than among unmarried respondents.

STATISTICAL CONCERNS

The focus of this chapter is on variations of (19.1) that flexibly capture potential patterns of change associated with events and that rule out important alternative interpretations of the relationships between events and outcomes. Before turning to these matters, it is important to consider some technical issues that mean (19.1) must be estimated using specialized statistical techniques. Because these issues are not the focus of this chapter, this section only briefly explains the main concerns and their standard solutions, referring the reader to other sources for more thorough discussions.

Basic statistical models, such as ordinary least squares regression (OLS), assume independence among observations. For (19.1), this assumption implies that there should be no systematic relationships among the residuals, e_{ti}, for different observations, so that knowing the value e for any one observation should be of no help for predicting its value for any others. Data from longitudinal panel studies almost always violate this assumption in two ways. First, even modest stability in individual behavior means that people are generally more similar to themselves across different occasions than they are to most other people. Second, individual change over time tends to be at least somewhat gradual rather than totally haphazard, with the result that observations from the same individual that are closer to each other in time are, on average, more similar than are observations that are farther apart. The residuals, e_{ti}, would be independent only if a regression model fully accounted for these response patterns, and it would be inappropriate to assume in advance that it did. Thus, analyzing longitudinal panel data requires a statistical model that takes into account dependence among observations that arises from both individual differences in average response levels and serial correlation.

One can allow for dependence among observations due to individual differences in average response level by dividing the original residual term, e_{ti}, into two components, one capturing that consistency across time for each person, u_i, and the other the time-specific variation around that average level, r_{ti}. It is then plausible to assume that the u_i residuals are independent across individuals and that the r_{it} residuals are independent within each individual over time (ignoring serial correlation for the moment). This division of e_{ti} changes (19.1) to (19.2):

$$Y_{ti} = \beta_0 + \beta_1 X_{ti} + u_i + r_{ti} \tag{19.2}$$

An alternative way of representing consistent individual differences that are not accounted for in the model is to make the intercept term unique to each person by adding the subscript i, yielding β_{0i}. Equation (19.3) illustrates this conception of the problem:

$$Y_{ti} = \beta_{0i} + \beta_1 X_{ti} + r_{ti} \tag{19.3}$$

Equation (19.4) shows that the two approaches are mathematically equivalent, and thus the difference between (19.2) and (19.3) is a matter of notation rather than substance.

$$\beta_{0i} = \beta_0 + u_i \tag{19.4}$$

There are two widely available methods for estimating this statistical model. The fixed effects[1] approach directly estimates a separate intercept, β_{0i}, for each individual. This method, in effect, adds to (19.1) a separate dummy variable for each person, resolving the dependence among repeated observations by fully removing all individual differences in average response

---

[1] The name "fixed effects" is unfortunate because it is used for many other purposes in statistics as well. For instance, it should not be confused with the use of the term "fixed effect" to refer to the regression coefficients estimated for explanatory variables in random effects models (as in printout from the HLM program).

levels. The alternative is the random effects approach, which instead estimates the variance of the residuals u_i and uses that estimate to adjust the regression coefficients and their standard errors.

Both of the methods are quite useful, and each has advantages and disadvantages. Overall, the fixed effects method requires fewer assumptions, while the random effects method provides greater statistical power and is applicable to a broader range of problems. For more detailed comparisons of the two approaches, see Allison (2005), Johnson (1995), and Peterson (1993). Both methods can be found in advanced statistical software such as STATA and LIMDEP, and the random effects model can be estimated through multilevel regression programs such as MLwiN, HLM, and SAS PROC MIXED.

Even after addressing dependence due to individual differences in average responses, some dependence is likely to remain among the residuals r_{ti} because observations that are closer in time will be more similar than those that are more widely separated. There are several ways to tackle this serial correlation. The typical growth curve modeling approach is to expand the random effects model just described with additional residual variance terms that allow for variation across individuals in the relationship of age or time to the outcome (Bryk and Raudenbush 1987). This more elaborate version is referred to as a random coefficient model as opposed to a random intercept model. Following the tradition of time series research, one could instead directly model the serial dependence, and the most common means of doing so is by estimating the autocorrelation between the residual terms of adjacent time points. A final option is simply to estimate and adjust for all of the across-wave correlations of the residuals. Though this last approach is guaranteed to fit the data well, it is less useful when there are many observations per person or the timing of observations is highly variable. All three approaches for addressing serially correlated error have been implemented for both multilevel regression models (Raudenbush 2001b) and structural equation models for latent growth curves (Curran and Bollen 2001; Rovine and Molenaar 2001). Raudenbush's (2001b) discussion of serially correlated error in analyses of longitudinal panel data will prove useful for readers who would like to know more about the topic.

Measures of crime and deviance usually have highly skewed and discrete distributions that violate other assumptions of standard statistical models such as homogeneity of residual variance and consistency between fitted values and actual means (Osgood and Rowe 1994). For cross-sectional data, generalized linear models, such as logistic and Poisson regression, will usually resolve these problems. These generalized models are also available within multilevel regression (e.g., Raudenbush and Bryk 2002; Snijders and Bosker 1999), providing a flexible framework for analyzing longitudinal panel data on crime and deviance that is suitable for all of the models presented in this chapter. Readers seeking additional background on generalized linear models should see sources such as Agresti (2007) or Long (1997).

In sum, the statistical issues that arise from a longitudinal research design and from the nature of measures of crime and deviance require the use of specialized statistical methods briefly discussed here. The remainder of the chapter omits these elements from the models presented, however, to reduce complexity not directly relevant to issues being discussed.[2]

---

[2] For instance, I will present models with the standard residual term e_{ti}, though the reader should assume that these terms are not independent, and that in actual data analysis, they would be replaced by more complex composite residuals, such as $e_{ti} = u_{0i} + u_{1i} \text{ Age} + r_{ti}$.

FOCUSING ON CHANGE

In (19.1), our initial model, the regression coefficient β_1 indexes the association of the event variable with the outcome of interest. For the example of marital status and crime, this coefficient will contrast the mean of the crime measure for all observations of married people with its mean for all observations of unmarried people. Unfortunately, the difference between these means will reflect not only the impact of the event of interest, but also any preexisting differences in offense rates that are associated with the event variable. For instance, a person who never marries contributes only to the mean for the unmarried status, while a person who was married for the entire study contributes only to the mean of the married status. Thus, much like a cross-sectional analysis, β_1 from (19.1) is an undifferentiated amalgam of within-person change associated with the event and preexisting differences between people who do and do not experience the event.

If we are interested in the impact of an event, then we would like to eliminate the contribution of prior differences and focus instead on the association between within-individual change on the event variable and within-individual change in offending (Horney et al. 1995). One way to accomplish this would be to reformulate our regression equation as follows:

$$\left(Y_{ti} - \overline{Y}_{\bullet i}\right) = \beta_1 \left(X_{ti} - \overline{X}_{\bullet i}\right) + e_{ti} \tag{19.5}$$

Equation (19.5) eliminates all stable individual differences on both the event variable and the outcome by subtracting each individual's mean across time from his or her scores for both X and Y from each wave of data.[3] Thus, β_1 will reflect only the within-individual association between X and Y, contrasting each person's offense rate when married with his or her offense rate when unmarried, and pooling that information across the sample. People who never marry or who are always married will not contribute to β_1 because, for them, the transformed explanatory variable, $(X_{ti} - \overline{X}_{\bullet i})$, has a constant value of zero.

There are several straightforward ways to obtain estimates of within-individual relationships that are equivalent to (19.5). The first is through the fixed effects approach to addressing dependence due to stable individual differences, discussed above. The dummy variables for every person in the analysis fully account for all individual differences in average response, restricting the estimates of relationships for time-varying explanatory variables to within-individual change over time. For examples of criminological studies using this approach to obtaining within-person estimates, see Osgood et al. (1996) and Paternoster et al. (2003). Another approach is to subtract the individual means of the explanatory variable (also known as group mean centering), as was done by Horney et al. (1995):

$$Y_{ti} = \beta_0 + \beta_1 \left(X_{ti} - \overline{X}_{\bullet i}\right) + e_{ti} \tag{19.6}$$

In this case, the explanatory variable has a mean of zero for each person, so it cannot explain differences between people, but rather only within-individual variation in the outcome. A third approach is to add the individual mean on X as an additional explanatory variable:

$$Y_{ti} = \beta_0 + \beta_1 X_{ti} + \beta_2 \overline{X}_{\bullet i} + e_{ti} \tag{19.7}$$

---

[3] Note that (19.5) has no constant term, β_0. None is needed because subtracting the individual means constrains both the left- and right-hand sides of the equation to have means of zero.

This approach capitalizes on a basic principle of regression analysis that the coefficient for each variable is determined entirely by the portion of its variance that is independent from the other variables in the model. The variance in X that is independent of individual means over time would be within-individual change in X. These three strategies will produce logically equivalent and (with reasonably large samples) nearly identical estimates of the effects of the time-varying explanatory variable (Allison 2005; Bushway et al. 1999; Raudenbush and Bryk 2002).

Taking these simple steps to focus the analysis on within-individual change over time has enormous methodological importance. As Allison (1990) has shown, this strategy is a much more effective means of adjusting for prior differences than is treating earlier measures of the outcome as covariates. Analysis of within-individual change totally eliminates the possibility that any stable individual characteristic can account for the estimated effect of the time-varying explanatory variable, without measuring that characteristic and including it in the analysis. No stable factor such as gender, IQ, or self-control can possibly account for a lower rate of crime when people are married compared to their own rates of crime when they were not married.[4] Thus, this approach precludes a broad class of potential selection effects, which is why methodologists view it as one of the most powerful tools for studying causal processes using nonexperimental data (Allison 2005; Greene 2000; Winship and Morgan 1999).[5]

It may appear that controlling for unmeasured variables in this fashion gains us something for nothing, but that is not the case. Rather, this strategy is only possible because of strength inherent in the longitudinal panel research design, which enables us to use "subjects as their own controls," in the old terminology of experimental design. The limits of this design mean that two key explanations remain as competing alternatives to a causal interpretation of the estimates from (19.5) to (19.7). First, these within-person estimates control only for stable unmeasured characteristics, but not for other time-varying variables. Thus, these estimates are potentially subject to omitted variable bias due to any time-varying variables omitted from the model that have a causal impact on the outcome and are correlated over time with the variable of interest. For instance, an apparent effect of marriage might be partly or entirely due to an uncontrolled variable such as parenthood or income. Second, this within-person analysis does not preclude the possibility that some or all of the estimated effect of the event on crime is actually due to an influence of crime on the event, which would be a form of simultaneity bias.

MATURATION AND EFFECTS OF EVENTS

The next issue we need to consider in assessing effects of events on crime is the threat to validity that Campbell and Stanley (1966) labeled maturation. Maturation threatens validity when the apparent effect of an event may be due merely to similar age trends for both the event and the outcome. As Raudenbush (2001a: 523) pointed out, longitudinal analyses must take into account that people are naturally growing or changing apart from the effects of the

---

[4] Of course this reasoning only applies to the extent that a variable really is stable over time. Thus, this approach would not control for effects of changes in self control, if self control varied meaningfully over time, contrary to Gottfredson and Hirschi's claim (Hay and Forrest, 2006).

[5] As Allison (1990) pointed out, true experiments with random assignment are an exception for which this approach is not optimal. In that case, prior differences are attributable to chance rather than genuine group differences, and limiting the analysis to within-individual change unnecessarily sacrifices statistical power.

variables of interest. For instance, because rates of marriage increase with age from the late teens into middle adulthood while rates of crime decrease, there may be a negative association between the two, even if marriage has no impact on crime. Similarly, parental supervision could be associated with delinquency from preadolescence through middle adolescence only because the former decreases while the latter increases over that period. Though such similarities in age trends no doubt spark life course scholars' interest in potential explanatory variables, they also mean that we must construct our analyses to insure that estimated effects of those variables are not merely an artifact of that similarity.

Age is, of course, a time-varying variable, and thus maturation constitutes a potential omitted variable bias for analyses of the effects of events. As with other relevant but omitted variables, the straightforward way to address maturation as an alternative explanation is to incorporate the age trend in the regression model, such as:

$$Y_{ti} = \beta_0 + \beta_1 X_{ti} + \beta_2 \text{Age}_{ti} + \beta_3 \text{Age}_{ti}^2 + \beta_4 \overline{X}_{\bullet i} + e_{ti} \tag{19.8}$$

The two new terms in (19.8) allow for a quadratic age trend, thereby combining a growth curve model with (19.7). The quadratic trend will be appropriate for some problems, too complex for some, and too simple for others. Because developmental trends are rarely linear over extended periods, it is important to be sure that the form of the age trend in the model is well suited to the data, as reflected in a close match between the fitted age trend and age-specific means. Several sources provide useful guidance for specifying this aspect of the model (e.g., McClendon 1995; Raudenbush and Bryk 2002; Singer and Willett 2003).

Adding age trends to the analysis also provides a vehicle for assessing whether an event accounts for some, or all, of the age trend in offending, which is one of the most central topics of the study of crime and the life course (Osgood 2005). Hirschi and Gottfredson's (1983) influential paper on age and crime claimed that social variables cannot account for the dramatic changes in rates of offending over the life course. Since that time, developmental and life course criminologists have offered many theories that attempt to do so (e.g., Moffitt 1993; Sampson and Laub 1993; Thornberry and Krohn 2005), but there have been surprisingly few empirical tests of the success of those theories in this regard (but see Osgood et al. 1996; Warr 1993).

To determine how well the event variable, X, accounts for age trends in offending, results for (19.8) can be compared to those for a reduced form model that excludes that variable:

$$Y_{ti} = \beta_0 + \beta_2 \text{Age}_{ti} + \beta_3 \text{Age}_{ti}^2 + e_{ti} \tag{19.9}$$

An event such as marriage will account for the average age trend in offending to the degree that it is strongly associated with offending and that its age trend matches the age trend in offending (Hirschi and Gottfredson 1985). This will be reflected in reductions of the coefficients for Age and Age^2 between (19.8) and (19.9). Because the age trend is curvilinear, the extent of mediation is more easily seen in a graph such as Fig. 19.1 than in the coefficients themselves. The more that the explanatory variable accounts for the age trend, the flatter the age trend after adjusting for that variable, in comparison to the original or overall trend. A useful basis for judging the proportion of the age trend that has been explained is to compute fitted values based on age from (19.8) and (19.9) (by applying the coefficients for age to the values of age in the dataset) and compare the resulting standard deviations (Osgood et al. 1996).

Time-varying explanatory variables such as marriage, employment, or peer relations not only have the potential to explain the average age trend in offending, but also to account for

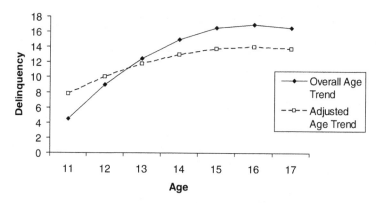

Figure 19.1. Illustration of explaining a portion of the age trend by controlling for a time varying covariate.

individual differences in patterns of change over time, as they are reflected in individual trajectories or growth curves. In growth curve models, those individual differences are expressed in the variance components for the polynomial terms for age. Accordingly, an event such as becoming a parent succeeds in explaining how people differ in their offending trajectories to the degree that adding it to the model reduces those variance components (i.e., (19.9) versus (19.8)). For an illustration, see Jacobs and colleagues' (2002) analyses of self-concepts and values concerning achievement.

Studying More Complex Patterns of Change

The models discussed so far assume that the effect of an event takes a specific, simple form. This section of the chapter explains several ways to expand the basic model in order to capture more complex patterns of change. As before, some of these variations will also prove useful for ruling out alternative explanations, thereby increasing the plausibility of viewing results as reflecting a causal effect of the variable of interest.

The preceding regression equations index the effect of an event as a mean difference between observations before the event and those after it. When applied to metric (rather than dichotomous) time-varying explanatory variables, the results will reflect the difference in means between data points that differ by one unit on that variable. As such, these models imply that the effect of the event or change on X is immediate, that it is constant over age and time, and that it applies equally to different subgroups. Figure 19.2 presents hypothetical data to illustrate the assumed pattern for two individuals, one with a higher initial offense rate who experiences the event of interest at age 21 and the other with a lower initial offense rate who experiences it at age 26. The solid lines represent the patterns of change over time accounted for by a model that focuses on within-individual change and adjusts for the overall age trend. The lines dip when the event occurs, indicating that it is associated with a decline in offending. The dashed lines show the pattern of change due to maturation that would be expected if the event did not occur. The difference between dashed and solid lines reflects the impact of the event, which corresponds to β_1 in the above regression equations. As required by these

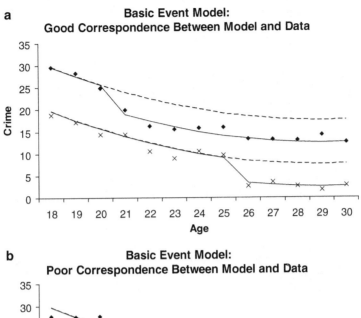

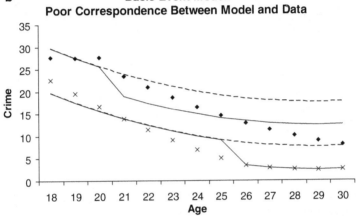

FIGURE 19.2. The form of change inherent in the basic event model, (**a**) good correspondence, (**b**) poor correspondence.

regression models, this difference is immediate, permanent (as long as X stays at 1 rather than 0), and applies equally to both individuals.

The separate points shown in Fig. 19.2 represent the hypothetical raw data, which would be the amount of offending observed for each person, each year. Figure 19.2a illustrates a good correspondence between the model and the data. The data points fall close to the solid lines, and it would be hard to discern any coherent pattern in the discrepancies between the data points and the fitted line from the model. In Fig. 19.2b, however, the discrepancies between the model and the data are systematic and suggest coherent patterns of change inconsistent with the constraints of the statistical model. These systematic departures illustrate some of the limitations of the basic model. For the person with the higher crime rate, the raw data suggest that the event's impact is not immediate and constant, but rather is initially small and grows over time. The effect of the event appears illusory for the person with the lower rate of crime. His or her offending after the event is consistent with the trend in offending before the event, not a departure from it.

Before turning to ways of modifying our basic model in order to capture patterns such as these, it is worth considering advantages that will be lost in more complex models. Because this initial model uses a single parameter to summarize the time-varying covariate's impact across several time points, it has greater statistical power than most other alternatives. It also expresses the relationship in a simple form that is easy to explain, namely, the mean change in the outcome upon the occurrence of the event (or per unit of change in a metric variable such as hours per week spent with spouse). Furthermore, the model's data requirements are so minimal that it is applicable to the simplest of longitudinal studies, even those with only two waves of data. More complex alternatives will require additional data.

AGE VARYING EFFECTS OF EVENTS

First, consider the possibility that the effect of an event might vary with age, which would be inconsistent with the constraints illustrated in Fig. 19.2. Age differences of this sort are a core feature of Thornberry's interactional theory (1987; Thornberry and Krohn 2005), which specifies that variables such as parental attachment and peer delinquency have a greater impact during the developmental periods in which they are most prominent. Indeed, age differences in influences on behavior are central concerns of developmental and life course perspectives.

For regression models of the sort considered here, age variation in effects corresponds to interactions between age and the time-varying explanatory variable. A basic form of this model would be:

$$Y_{ti} = \beta_0 + \beta_1 X_{ti} + \beta_2 \text{Age}_{ti} + \beta_3 X_{ti} \times \text{Age}_{ti} + \beta_4 \overline{X}_{\bullet i} + \beta_5 \overline{\text{Age}_{\bullet i}} + \beta_6 \overline{(X_{ti} \times \text{Age}_{ti})}_{\bullet i} + e_{ti}$$

(19.10)

The new coefficient β_3 will reflect change in the effect of X per unit of age. Jang (1999) used models in this form to test interactional theory's main hypotheses about age varying effects. This specific interaction term constrains the effect of X to change by a constant value each year, which may or may not be a good match to the data. One can capture other patterns through interaction terms with age coded in other ways, such as a polynomial or a categorical classification (e.g., 14–18 versus 19–22).

As discussed above, estimates of the effects of events should be restricted to within-individual change in order to reduce the possibility of spurious results due to selection effects. Equation (19.10) accomplishes this by also including terms for the individual means of all time-varying variables, including the interaction term. The alternative strategy of subtracting individual means from the event variables (as in (19.6)) would not require this second version of the interaction term, and thus it is somewhat simpler in this regard. To simplify the presentation in the rest of this chapter, the remaining equations will omit the extra elements needed to limit the analysis to within-individual change.

Figure 19.3 illustrates the consequences of allowing a time varying effect in (19.10). Figure 19.3a shows an effect of parental supervision that is constant across ages (as in (19.8)), which is reflected in the unchanging difference between the higher rate of delinquency for adolescents who receive little supervision in comparison to the lower rate for adolescents who are highly supervised. In Fig. 19.3b, adding the interaction between parental supervision and age allows the effect of supervision to progress from quite sizable at age 11 to minimal at age 19. Figure 19.3b would be consistent with the impact of parental supervision declining with age, perhaps due to norms that parents should grant increasing autonomy to their children as they near the age of home-leaving.

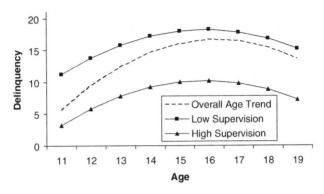

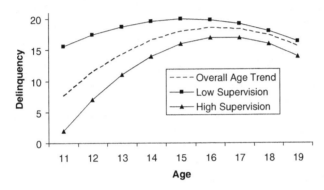

FIGURE 19.3. Illustration of time varying effects of an event, (**a**) effect independent of age, (**b**) effect varying with age.

Figure 19.3 also reflects the relationship between a time-varying explanatory variable and the overall age trend, which appears as a dashed line. The overall trend always falls between the trends for adolescents receiving the two levels of supervision. At younger ages, the overall trend is closer to the line for more highly supervised youth because high supervision predominates. Most parents want to keep close track of where their 11 year old children go and what they do. By age 19, however, few youth are so closely supervised, and accordingly, the average rate of supervision is quite close to the other line. The degree to which parental supervision can explain the age trend is readily apparent in Fig. 19.3a from the steeper slope of the overall age trend relative to the age trends given specific levels of supervision. How well supervision explains the age trend is less apparent from Fig. 19.3b because the trend differs with the level of supervision.

THE TIMING OF AN EVENT'S EFFECTS

Many interesting research questions concern patterns of change inconsistent with the basic model's assumption that an event's effect is immediate and constant over time. For instance, we might hypothesize that the impact of family poverty grows with the length of time the family is poor, that the benefits of a marriage or job emerge gradually (Laub and Sampson 2003; Sampson and Laub 1993), or that the beneficial effect of a treatment program grows during participation in the program and decays after finishing (Osgood and Smith 1995).

To address such possibilities, our model must incorporate information about the timing of an observation relative to the event of interest.

$$Y_{ti} = \beta_0 + \beta_1 X_{ti} + \beta_2 \text{Time}(X)_{ti} + \beta_3 \text{Age}_{ti} + e_{ti} \qquad (19.11)$$

Equation (19.11) does so by adding a variable, $\text{Time}(X)_{ti}$, that indexes the time elapsed since the event occurred. $\text{Time}(X)_{ti}$ would equal zero from the start of the study until the observation at which the event occurred. It would change to one at the subsequent time point, two at the next time point, three at the time point after that, and so forth. With the data in this form, β_1 will now reflect the average instantaneous change upon the occurrence of the event and β_2 will indicate the amount of increase or decrease in that change per unit of time (relative to the baseline age trend). Another way of putting this is that β_1 is a change in level associated with the event, and β_2 is a change in the slope over time. When the event occurs, the intercept changes from β_0 to $\beta_0 + \beta_1$ and the slope for age changes from β_3 to $\beta_2 + \beta_3$. Osgood and Smith (1995) explain the application of this general modeling strategy to topics in program evaluation.

Examples of the patterns of change possible in (19.11) appear in Fig. 19.4. First, employment brings about an immediate reduction in crime that stays constant over the years in Fig. 19.4a. This pattern corresponds to a change in level (β_1) of -4 combined with 0 change in slope (β_2), in which case (19.11) reduces to the more restrictive basic model of (19.8). In contrast, in the example of Fig. 19.4b, employment brings no immediate crime reduction ($\beta_1 = +1$) but instead carries a gradually increasing benefit ($\beta_2 = -1.2$) that eventually results in a very low crime rate. This pattern could reflect processes such as growing social control from increasing commitment to the job or gradual socialization toward conventional values from time spent with fellow employees who are more prosocial. Finally, in Fig. 19.4c, employment has a large immediate beneficial impact on offending ($\beta_1 = -8$), but that benefit decays over time ($\beta_2 = 1.2$) as the crime rate gradually returns to the baseline.

Timing of Effects and Causal Interpretation.

The timing of effects is also relevant to determining whether or not findings are consistent with a causal interpretation. If the change in offending precedes the event, then it is hard to argue that the event caused that change. In contrast, a lag between the event and change in the outcome is often seen as evidence that the effect is causal. Yet, the relevance of such a lag depends on the processes thought to explain offending. For instance, the socialization and accumulation of experience prominent in social learning theory should take time, which would be consistent with delayed effects. We could incorporate this delay in our statistical model if the theory made clear just how long the delay should be, but theories in social and behavioral science rarely have this level of precision. Furthermore, many theories imply relatively instantaneous effects, such as the situational explanation of routine activity theory (Felson 2002; Osgood et al. 1996) or social control theory's emphasis on current bonds to conventional people and institutions (Hirschi 1969). In these cases, a delay between a change in the explanatory variable and a change in the outcome would actually weigh against the theory. Unfortunately, it is especially difficult to distinguish an instantaneous effect of an event on crime from a reverse effect of crime on the event.

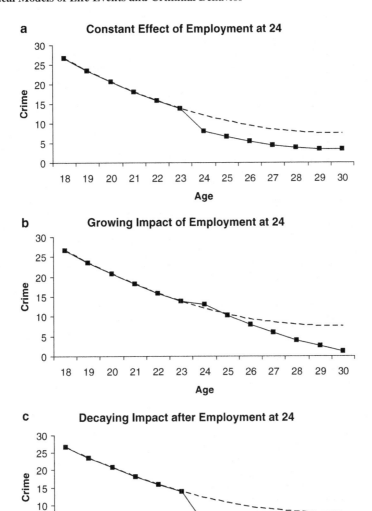

FIGURE 19.4. Effects of events on both levels and slopes, (**a**) constant effect, (**b**) growing impact, (**c**) decaying impact.

Regardless of the theory, however, a closer examination of the timing of the relationship between changes in the explanatory variable and changes in offending would be useful for determining whether the data are consistent with viewing the event as a cause of crime. One simple way of doing this is to compare results across three analyses: (a) the first based on the current value of the explanatory variable, X_t, in order to capture the simultaneous relationship (as in (19.8)), (b) the second substituting its earlier value, X_{t-1}, to capture the lagged or delayed relationship, and (c) the third using its later value, X_{t+1}, so that the outcome measure precedes the event. Figure 19.5 shows these three possibilities. A stronger relationship of

Lagged Effects of Events

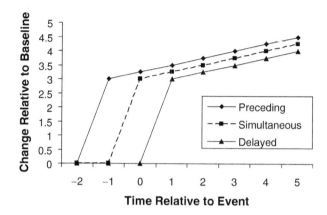

FIGURE 19.5. Lagged effects of events.

offending to the subsequent value of X suggests that the "effect" precedes its supposed cause, so the relationship is likely to be spurious rather than causal.[6]

This strategy is simple, applies to both events and metric (i.e., nondichotomous) time-varying explanatory variables, and is suitable to all of the models discussed so far. It does not provide a very precise picture of the timing of changes in the outcome, however, so it can easily yield ambiguous findings in which there are minimal differences among the three specifications of the timing of X.

For an explanatory variable reflecting an event, we can gain a more precise understanding of the timing of changes in the outcome by following Laub et al.'s (1998) strategy of further reducing constraints on the form of the effect over time. Equation (19.8) assumed the effect was instantaneous and constant over time by representing the event through a single dummy variable indicating its presence or absence. Equation (19.11) allowed the effect to evolve by adding an index of time since the event occurred, but this model still limits the effect to growing or declining in a uniform progression. Laub and colleagues' (1998) approach removes that constraint by representing time in relation to the event through a series of dummy variables, as illustrated in (19.12):

$$Y_{ti} = \beta_0 + \sum_{j=-2}^{5} \alpha_j T_{jti} + \beta_2 \text{Age}_{ti} + e_{ti} \tag{19.12}$$

The dummy variables T_{jit} indicate the timing of each observation t relative to the occurrence of the event for individual i. The index j calibrates this timing, so the variable T_{-1ti} is zero unless this observation is one time unit before the event, in which case, it equals one, T_{2ti} indicates whether this observation is two time units after the event in the same fashion, and so forth. Accordingly, the coefficients α_j will reflect the within-person change (relative to the baseline age trend) for various time points before and after the event.

---

[6] This reasoning would not apply to cases where it is plausible that a causal effect would precede the measured event. For instance, for marriage this pattern might be interpreted as indicating that the important event is the onset of a committed romantic relationship rather than its culmination in marriage.

Year-by-Year Examination of Change

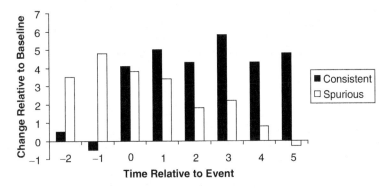

FIGURE 19.6. More detailed examination of timing of effects.

Figure 19.6 illustrates potential results from such an analysis. In one case, the findings are consistent with a causal interpretation because there is no systematic change in the outcome until the event occurs, after which there is a fairly consistent difference from the baseline. In the second case, the major change precedes the event, so we would likely have to judge that any association between the event and offending was spurious rather than causal.

Results from (19.12) may also be useful in guiding the specification of a more parsimonious model. For instance, a chart of the timing of changes such as Fig. 19.6 would be helpful for deciding whether the initial change in level is simultaneous or delayed (guiding whether to use X_{ti} or X_{t-1i} in the model), whether there is merely a change in level or in both level and slope (e.g., whether to use (19.8) or (19.11)), and whether any change in slope is likely linear or curvilinear (i.e., how to code Time$(X)_{ti}$ in (19.11)).

The utility of the model of (19.12) depends on the number and spacing of observations in the study. This approach would be most useful with many observations close in time, such as the event calendar approach developed by Horney and colleagues (see Chap. 15), which has often been used to gather 36 monthly observations for each respondent. In contrast, a panel study with only two or three time points could distinguish few time lags, and a study with observations spaced years apart is uninformative about the timing of any causal process operating on shorter time scales.

DIFFERENTIAL EFFECTS OF EVENTS

Criminologists also have offered many interesting hypotheses in which the effect of an event depends on some other variable that does not change over time. For instance, Moffitt (1993) argued that role transitions such as marriage and employment would have a greater impact for late onset offenders than for early onset offenders (a topic investigated in terms of propensity toward crime by Ousey and Wilcox 2007, and Wright et al. 2001). In this case, the impact of the event depends on an aspect of the individual's personal history. Differential effects could also arise in relation to other stable characteristics such as demographic variables or personality traits. A similar possibility is that the impact of an event might depend on some attribute of that event. That attribute could be some quality of the event, such as Sampson and Laub's (1993) argument that only high quality marriages and jobs will serve as turning points that reduce offending, or it could be the timing of the event, such as Uggen's (2000) finding that gaining employment brings crime reductions for older offenders but not younger offenders.

The general form of models that allow such differences in the effects of events is:

$$Y_{ti} = \beta_0 + \beta_1 X_{ti} + \beta_2 Z_i + \beta_3 X_{ti} \times Z_i + \beta_4 \text{Age}_{ti} + \beta_5 Z_i \times \text{Age}_{ti} + e_{ti} \qquad (19.13)$$

Z_i represents a time constant variable, which lacks the time-varying index t because it varies across people but not time. The parameters β_2 and β_5 allow for differences in the overall level and baseline age trend related to this variable, while β_3 captures variation in the effect of the event.[7]

Figures 19.7 and 19.8 illustrate the additional possibilities that arise in this model. Fig. 19.7 shows a hypothetical pattern of gender differences in the impact on crime of becoming a parent. As one would expect, the baseline age trends differ considerably between males and females, with males having a higher offense rate that declines more rapidly. If Z were coded as zero for females and one for males, then this pattern would correspond to a positive value for β_2 and a negative value for β_5. Because women typically bear the larger share of responsibilities for child-rearing, we might expect parenthood to have a greater impact on their lives, as shown here. With this coding for gender, the sizable decline in offending for females upon becoming a parent matches a large negative value for β_1, while the small decline in offending for males matches a positive value for β_3 (because they decline less than females).

Figure 19.8 shows a more complex example with differential change on both levels and slopes. In this case, the time constant variable is the age at which employment begins, and the figure indicates that years of full time employment brings less benefit to the earnings of people who begin full time employment younger rather than older. As we will see below, adjusting age trends for the occurrence or timing of the event has other useful implications.

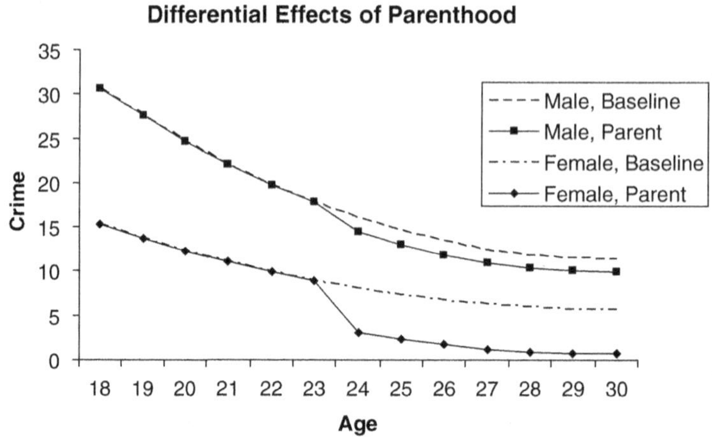

FIGURE 19.7. Differential effects of parenthood for males and females.

---

[7] To maintain a consistent focus on the relationships of events to within-individual change, it is necessary either to include the individual mean of the interaction term in the model as well, or else to subtract the individual mean from the event variable before forming its interaction with the time-constant variable.

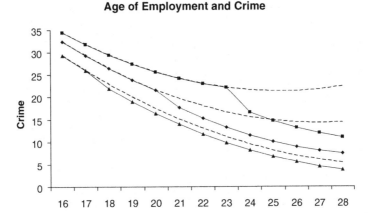

Age of Employment and Crime

FIGURE 19.8. Both effect and baseline varying by the age at which the event occurs: the effect of employment on crime.

Addressing the Possibility of Differing Age Trends

As discussed in an earlier section, models of the impact of events should allow for overall age trends in order to insure that results cannot be explained by the typical pattern of maturation. Analyses of differential effects based on (19.13) take this theme one step farther by allowing the age trends to differ in relation to the time stable variable of interest, such as the different baseline trends for males and females in Fig. 19.7. Doing so seems prudent in that it compares each individual to others who are more similar to themselves. Yet this also raises the broader question of what constitutes an appropriate baseline age trend for estimating the impact of an event.

It is useful to think of this issue in terms of the counter-factual model that dominates current thinking on causal inference (e.g., Winship and Morgan 1999). In this framework, the causal effect for each person is defined by the difference between the value of the outcome variable in the presence of the cause and its value in the cause's absence. The difficulty of causal inference is that we can never have the data needed to make this comparison. Because the cause cannot be simultaneously present and absent for the same person, at any given time we observe only one state of affairs or the other. Random assignment solves this problem by guaranteeing that, in the absence of a causal effect, the distributions of the outcome variable in the two conditions would differ only by chance.

For studying the effects of events, I have recommended that researchers routinely limit their analyses to within-person change and control for the overall age trend, each of which yields a considerable improvement over the basic regression model of (19.1). First, analyzing within-individual change narrows the comparison for observations in the presence of the cause to observations for the same person in its absence. Second, adjusting for the typical change between ages further refines the comparison to implicitly reflect a "difference in differences" comparing change for people who experience the event with change over the same ages for people who do not. Given the limitations of nonexperimental research designs, this is a relatively strong strategy because it rules out broad classes of plausible alternative explanations of findings. Specifically, the estimated effect cannot be due to any unchanging personal characteristics (whether measured or not) or to the typical pattern of maturation.

Of course, given an observational research design, even comparing people to themselves can never fully resolve the counterfactual dilemma. The data before and after the event are necessarily obtained at different ages and under different life circumstances, and we have no basis for arguing that at those occasions the outcome has identical distributions. As noted above, this leaves open the possibility of spurious effects due to omitted time-varying variables that could also contribute to differences in the outcome between the two time points, as well as the potential for reverse causality. These possibilities must be addressed by measuring and including the omitted variables most likely to be correlated with the event of interest and also to influence crime and by closely examining the timing of the effect of the event of interest (as in Fig. 19.6).

An additional challenge to causal inference when using this analytic approach is establishing an appropriate expectation for the change that would occur in the absence of the potential causal event, which is an essential component of its implicit counterfactual comparison. The models I have presented to this point largely rely on the overall pattern of maturation or change for this purpose, but we also need to address the possibility that people experiencing the event would not, on average, have followed this pattern. To date, the issue has received little attention, and it is an important direction for future methodological development. In the remainder of this section I offer some thoughts about the nature of this problem and potential strategies for addressing it.

The essence of the issue is the possibility that underlying developmental trends differ across individuals in such a way that the pattern of change for people who experience the event would be different from that of people who do not, even in the absence of the event. If not incorporated in the analysis somehow, this difference would create a bias in our estimate of the events' effect.

One possibility for addressing such differences in age trends is through interactions between age and individual characteristics. Equation (19.13) includes such an interaction to allow the underlying age trend to differ in terms of gender, and adding additional interactions with age would permit age trends to depend on a larger set of predictors. Suppose that these additional terms explained all of the reliable variation in age trends (evidenced by reduction in random variance components for the age trend), while there was little change in the estimated effect of the event. This pattern would enhance the plausibility of a causal effect by demonstrating that the result does not appear to be a spurious result of an undifferentiated specification of the baseline age trend that is inaccurate for this subpopulation.

A simpler and perhaps more effective means of establishing an appropriate baseline of expected change would be to focus more directly on who does and does not experience the event, and who does so earlier versus later. This strategy enhances the likelihood of taking into account the individual differences in patterns of developmental change that are most relevant to this event. Figure 19.8 illustrates this approach by making the baseline age trends (shown by the dashed lines) specific to people who experience the event at the same age.

A model to differentiate among people who experienced the event for longer and shorter periods of time would have some interesting and familiar features. The individual mean over time of the event variable, $\overline{X}_{\bullet i}$, indexes this variation, for instance, reflecting the proportion of time an individual was employed (to use the example of Fig. 19.8). Equation (19.14) allows age trends to depend on this variable:

$$Y_{ti} = \beta_0 + \beta_1 X_{ti} + \beta_2 \overline{X}_{\bullet i} + \beta_3 \text{Age}_{ti} + \beta_4 \overline{X}_{\bullet i} \times \text{Age}_{ti} + e_{ti} \qquad (19.14)$$

Earlier in this chapter, a main effect for $\overline{X}_{\bullet i}$ appeared in (19.7), and in that case, it served to restrict the estimate of the event's effect to within-individual change by making that estimate independent from individual differences in average response level. Equation (19.14) adds the interaction of this variable with age as a way to make the estimated effect of the event independent from individual differences in the rate of age related change.[8]

To gain perspective on the causal model implicit in the data analysis approach presented in this chapter, it is useful to consider the multiple sources of information that contribute to the baseline of expected change. People who experience the event contribute to the overall baseline age trend through their waves of data before the event occurs. Individuals observed for at least two waves prior to the event provide information about the rate of age related change prior to the event (Bryk and Weisberg 1977). Using this information as the baseline of expected change entails projecting the trend beyond the available data. In the absence of other supporting information, such projections are always risky, and they are especially risky when projecting far into the future and when the trend is curvilinear, as age trends so often are.

People who do not experience the event provide a second source of information about expected age trends. Information from this group has the advantage that it extends throughout the period of study, including time during which others experience the event. Thus, it is free from the problem of projection beyond the data. The corresponding disadvantage of relying on this group as a baseline for change is that their age trend may differ from that of people who do experience the event.

The plausibility of viewing estimates from these models as causal effects will be considerably stronger if these two sources of information are in agreement about the expected pattern of change. Equation (19.14) provides a convenient vehicle for assessing whether they converge. For individuals who will experience the event, change over time before the event occurs is $\beta_3 \text{Age}_{ti} + \beta_4 \overline{X}_{\bullet i} \times \text{Age}_{ti}$, while for other individuals, change over time is $\beta_3 \text{Age}_{ti}$. Thus, β_4 captures the difference in age trend, and if its value is zero, then the baseline pattern of change does not depend on whether and for how long the event is experienced.[9]

What if β_4 is not close to zero, thus indicating differences in baseline age trends for people who do and do not experience the result? A causal interpretation of the effect of the event may still be plausible if allowing the baseline age trend to depend on the mean of the event variable does not alter the estimate of the effect (i.e., β_1 is little changed upon adding $\overline{X}_{\bullet i} \times \text{Age}_{ti}$ to the model). This pattern would suggest that, though baseline age trends are related to experiencing the event, they do not differ in a way that would account for the relationship between the event and the outcome variable.

The case for interpreting the estimated relationship as a causal impact of the event is weaker if adding this interaction alters the estimate. This pattern of findings would indicate that the estimated effect is sensitive to the set of individuals included in the analysis, which

[8] Halaby (2003) recommended using this interaction as a means for resolving a correlation between a time-varying covariate and a random effect for age, and I am suggesting that including it also enhances causal inference by adjusting for differing underlying age trends in relation to the event variable of interest. This is a close parallel to what is gained when we include the main effect for the individual mean on the event variable, as in (19.7). Doing so solves a technical statistical problem by removing any correlation between the time-varying covariate and the residual term for varying intercepts, while it serves the important methodological role of limiting the analysis to within-individual change.

[9] Data with curvilinear patterns of change would require the same comparisons for additional interactions of $\overline{X}_{\bullet i}$ with polynomial terms for age.

suggests that it would be wise to limit the analysis to the individuals for whom such comparisons are most justified. It would be plausible to do so through matching or weighting cases in terms of their propensity for experiencing the event (Rosenbaum and Rubin 1983), as several authors have recently pursued in studying relationships of events to crime (Haviland et al. 2007; King et al. 2007; Sampson et al. 2006).

In addition to these two sources of information, the baseline age trend is also affected by other constraints inherent in a specific statistical model. For instance, in most models I have discussed (including (19.14)), the event affects only the level of the outcome, and not its slope over time. This constraint implicitly assumes that the age-related change after the event follows the same pattern as that of people who either never experience the event or experienced it at a younger age. Accordingly, this constraint means that these postevent age trends also contribute to the baseline or expected age trend, while they would not (or at least would contribute less), if we removed the constraint by allowing the event to affect the slope (as in (19.11) and Figs. 19.4 and 19.8). Because such constraints bring more information to bear in estimating the effect of an event, they tend to increase statistical power and also provide a broader base for causal inference. At the same time, applying such constraints will distort the estimated effects if they are inconsistent with the data. Thus, it would be appropriate to test them by means such as assessing whether effects of events vary with age ((19.10)) or duration of the event ((19.11)).

CONCLUSION

In sum, the statistical models I have discussed provide flexible tools for using longitudinal data to examine the effects of events on crime. First, these models allow us to examine in detail the timing of these effects and to study differences in effects across groups of people and types of events. Furthermore, the models offer means of either testing for or eliminating many alternative explanations that compete with a causal interpretation of the estimated effect of the event. They allow us to address preexisting individual differences, overall developmental trends, the possibility that the supposed cause actually precedes the event, and the appropriateness of the baseline age trend as a basis for estimating the effect of the event.

One should not forget, however, that the basic longitudinal panel study has a passive observational research design, and it can never prove causality. Even so, this research design provides a great deal of information useful for eliminating or testing competing explanations, and thereby strengthening the plausibility of a causal interpretation of results. The techniques described in this chapter are meant to help researchers make the most of the information inherent in this research design. Successful application of this analytic approach has the potential to narrow the plausible alternative explanations to reverse causality and to other time-varying variables that are correlated with the one of interest. Controlling for time-varying variables and careful examination of the timing of the effect, as in Fig. 19.6, may provide evidence against those alternative interpretations as well.

There are, of course, other valuable approaches for studying causal effects, most notably, random assignment experiments, instrumental variable analyses (especially those using natural experiments or exogenous events as instruments), and propensity analyses (Winship and Morgan 1999). I suspect that life course criminologists will find the approach presented here especially useful, because they are most likely to find appropriate data on relevant topics in longitudinal panel studies (for examples, see Liberman 2007). Even so, confirmation of findings across methods would be especially valuable, and I encourage life course criminologists to be watchful for diverse opportunities to investigate effects of life events on crime.

REFERENCES

Agnew R (1992) Foundation for a general strain theory of crime and delinquency. Criminology 30:47–87

Agresti A (2007) An introduction to categorical data analysis, 2nd edn. Hoboken, NJ, Wiley

Akers RL (1977) Deviant behavior: a social learning perspective. Belmont, CA, Wadsworth

Allison PD (1990) Change scores as dependent variables in regression analysis. Sociol Methodol 20:93–114

Allison PD (2005) Fixed effects regression methods for longitudinal data using SAS. SAS Institute Inc, Cary, NC

Bryk A, Raudenbush SW (1987) Application of hierarchical linear models to assessing change. Psychol Bull 101:147–158

Bryk A, Weisberg H (1977) Use of the nonequivalent control group design when subjects are growing. Psychol Bull 84:950–962

Bushway S, Brame R, Paternoster R (1999) Assessing stability and change in criminal offending: a comparison of random effects, semiparametric, and fixed effects. J Quant Criminol 15:23–61

Campbell DT, Stanley JC (1966) Experimental and quasi-experimental designs for research. Chicago, Rand McNally

Curran PJ, Bollen KA (2001) The best of both worlds: combining autoregressive and latent curve models. In: Collins LM, Sayer AG (eds) New methods for the analysis of change. American Psychological Association, Washington, DC, pp 105–135

Esbensen F-A, Wayne Osgood D, Taylor TJ, Peterson D, Freng A (2001) How great is G.R.E.A.T.?: results from a longitudinal quasi-experimental design. Criminol Public Policy 1:87–115

Felson M (2002) Crime and everyday life: insights and implications for society, 3rd edn. Pine Forge Press, Thousand Oaks, CA

Greene WH (2000) Econometric analysis. Prentice Hall, Upper Saddle River, NJ

Halaby CN (2003) Panel models for the analysis of change and growth in life course studies. In: Mortimer JT, Shanahan MJ (eds) Handbook of the life course. Kluwer, New York, pp 503–527

Haviland A, Nagin DS, Rosenbaum PR (2007) Combining propensity score matching and group-based trajectory analysis in an observational study. Psychol Methods 12:247–267

Hay C, Forrest W (2006) The development of self-control: examining self-control theory's stability thesis. Criminology 44:739–774

Hirschi T (1969) Causes of delinquency. University of California Press, Berkeley, CA

Hirschi T, Gottfredson M (1983) Age and the explanation of crime. Am J Sociol 89:552–584

Hirschi T, Gottfredson M (1985) All wise after the fact learning theory, again: reply to baldwin. Am J Sociol 90:1330–33

Horney J, Osgood DW, Marshall IH (1995) Criminal careers in the short-term: intra-individual variability in crime and its relation to local life circumstances. Am Sociol Rev 60:655–73

Jacobs JE, Lanza S, Osgood DW, Eccles JS, Wigfield A (2002) Changes in children's self-competence and values: gender and domain differences across grades one through twelve. Child Dev 73:509–527

Jang SJ (1999) Age-varying effects of family, school, and peers on delinquency: a multilevel modeling test of interactional theory. Criminology 37:643–685

Johnson DR (1995) Alternative methods for the quantitative analysis of panel data in family research: pooled time-series methods. J Marriage Fam 57:1065–1077

King RD, Massoglia M, MacMillan R (2007) The context of marriage and crime: gender, the propensity to marry, and offending in early adulthood. Criminology 45:33–65

Laub JH, Nagin DS, Sampson RJ (1998) Trajectories of change in criminal offending: good marriages and the desistance process. Am Sociol Rev 63:225–238

Laub JH, Sampson RJ (2003) Shared beginnings, divergent lives: delinquent boys to age 70. Harvard University Press, Cambridge, MA

LeBlanc M, Loeber R (1998) Developmental criminology updated. In: Crime and justice: a review of research, vol 23. pp 115–198

Liberman AM (ed) (2007) The long view of crime: a synthesis of longitudinal research. Springer, New York

Long JS (1997) Regression models for categorical and limited dependent variables. Sage, Thousand Oaks, CA

McClendon MJ (1995) Multiple regression and causal analysis.Peacock Publishers, Itasca, IL

Moffitt TE (1993) Adolescence-limited and life-course-persistent antisocial behavior: a developmental taxonomy. Psychol Rev 100:674–701

Nagin DS, Farrington DP, Moffitt TE (1995) Life-course trajectories of different types of offenders. Criminology 33:111–139

Nagin DS, Tremblay RE (1999) Trajectories of boys' physical aggression, opposition, and hyperactivity on the path to physically violent and non-violent juvenile delinquency. Child Dev 70:1181–1196

Nagin DS, Tremblay RE (2005) What has been learned from group-based trajectory modeling? examples from physical aggression and other problem behaviors. Ann Am Acad Pol Soc Sci 602:82–117

Osgood DW (2005) Sense of crime and the life course. Ann Am Acad Pol Soc Sci 602:196–211

Osgood DW, Rowe DC (1994) Bridging criminal careers, theory, and policy through latent variable models of individual offending. Criminology 32:517–554

Osgood DW, Smith G (1995) Applying hierarchical linear modeling to extended longitudinal evaluations: the boys town follow-up study. Eval Rev 19:3–38

Osgood DW, Wilson JK, Bachman JG, O'Malley PM, Johnston LD (1996) Routine activities and individual deviant behavior. Am Sociol Rev 61:635–655

Ousey GC, Wilcox P (2007) The interaction of antisocial propensity and life-course varying predictors of delinquent behavior: differences by method of estimation and implications for theory. Criminology 45:313–354

Paternoster R, Bushway S, Brame R, Apel R (2003) The effect of teenage employment on delinquency and problem behaviors. Soc Forces 82:297–335

Peterson Trond (1993) Recent advances in longitudinal methodology. Annu Rev Sociol 19:425–454

Piquero AR, Farrington DP, Blumstein A (2007) Key issues in criminal career research: new analyses of the cambridge study in delinquent development. Cambridge University Press, Cambridge, UK

Raudenbush SW (2001a) Comparing personal trajectories and drawing causal inferences from longitudinal data. Annu Rev Psychol 52:501–525

Raudenbush SW (2001b) Toward a coherent framework for comparing trajectories of individual change. In: Collins LM, Sayer AG (eds) New methods for the analysis of change,American Psychological Association, Washington, DC, pp 33–64

Raudenbush SW, Bryk AS (2002) Hierarchical linear models, 2nd edn. Sage, Newbury Park, CA

Rosenbaum PR, Rubin DB (1983) The central role of the propensity score in observational studies for causal effects. Biometrika 70:41–55

Rovine MJ, Molenaar PCM (2001) A structural equations modeling approach to the general linear mixed model. In: Collins LM, Sayer AG (eds) New methods for the analysis of change, American Psychological Association, Washington, DC, pp 65–96

Sampson RJ, Laub JH (1993) Crime in the making: pathways and turning points through life. Harvard University Press, Cambridge, MA

Sampson RJ, Laub JH, Wimer C (2006) Does marriage reduce crime? A counterfactual approach to within-individual causal effects. Criminology 44:465–508

Siennick SE, Osgood DW (2007) A review of research on the impact on crime of transitions to adult roles. In: Liberman AM (ed) The long view of crime: a synthesis of longitudinal research, Springer, New York, pp 161–190

Singer JD, Willett JB (2003) Applied longitudinal data analysis. Oxford University Press, New York

Slocum LA, Simpson SS, Smith DA (2005) Strained lives and crime: examining intra-individual variation in strain and offending in a sample of incarcerated women. Criminology 43:1067–1110

Snijders TAB, Bosker R (1999) Multilevel analysis: an introduction to basic and advanced multilevel modeling. Sage, Thousand Oaks, CA

Sutherland EH, Cressey DR (1955) Principles of criminology, 5th edn. J. B. Lippincott, Philadelphia

Thornberry TP (1987) Toward an interactional theory of delinquency. Criminology 25:863–891

Thornberry TP, Krohn MD (2005) Applying interactional theory to the explanation of continuity and change in anti-social behavior. In: Farrington DP (ed) Integrated developmental and life course theories of offending. Advances in criminological theory, vol 14. Transaction, Piscataway, NJ, pp 183–210

Uggen C (2000) Work as a turning point in the life course of criminals: a duration model of age, employment, and recidivism. Am Sociol Rev 67:529–546

Warr M (1993) Age, peers, and delinquency. Criminology 31:17–40

Winship C, Morgan SL (1999) The estimation of causal effects from observational data. Annu Rev Sociol 25:659–707

Wright BRE, Caspi A, Moffitt TE, Silva PA (2001) The effects of social ties on crime vary by criminal propensity: a life-course model of interdependence. Criminology 39:321–348

Part III-A
Estimation of Impacts and Outcomes of Crime and Justice: *Topics in Experimental Methods*

## CHAPTER 20

An Introduction to Experimental Criminology

LAWRENCE W. SHERMAN

Experimental criminology is scientific knowledge about crime and justice discovered from random assignment of different conditions in large field tests. This method is the preferred way to estimate the average effects of one variable on another, holding all other variables constant (Campbell and Stanley 1963; Cook and Campbell 1979). While the experimental method is not intended to answer all the research questions in criminology, it can be used far more often than most criminologists assume (Federal Judicial Center, 1981). Opportunities are particularly promising in partnership with criminal justice agencies.

The highest and best use of experimental criminology is to develop and test theoretically coherent ideas about reducing harm (Sherman 2006, 2007), rather than just "evaluating" government programs. Those tests, in turn, can help to accumulate an integrated body of grounded theory (Glaser and Strauss 1967) in which experimental evidence plays a crucial role. When properly executed, randomized field experiments provide the ideal tests of theories about both the prevention and causation of crime.

The advantages of experimental methods help explain why this branch of criminology is growing rapidly (Farrington 1983, Farrington and Welsh 2005), with its first journal (*Journal of Experimental Criminology*) and a separate Division of Experimental Criminology of the American Society of Criminology established just since 2005. Yet these advantages depend entirely on the capability of the experimenters to insure success in achieving the many necessary elements of an unbiased comparison. Many, if not most, randomized field experiments in criminology suffer flaws that could have been avoided with better planning. The lack of such planning, in turn, may be due to the scant attention paid to field experiments in research methods' texts and courses. Even skilled, senior researchers can make basic mistakes when conducting field experiments, since experiments require a very different set of skills and methods than the "normal science" of observational criminology. As in any complex work, the value of 10,000 hours of practice can make an enormous difference in its success (Gladwell 2008).

The goal of this chapter is to help its readers improve the design and conduct of criminological experiments. The chapter's method is to describe the necessary steps and preferred decisions in planning, conducting, completing, analyzing, reporting, and synthesizing high-quality randomized controlled trials (RCTs) in criminology. The evidence for the

A.R. Piquero and D. Weisburd (eds.), *Handbook of Quantitative Criminology*,
DOI 10.1007/978-0-387-77650-7_20, © Springer Science + Business Media, LLC 2010,
First softcover printing 2011

chapter comes from both the authors' experience in conducting such experiments, as well as from published literature: on statistics (especially biostatistics), systematic and nonsystematic reviews of research in criminology, and reports on experiments in criminology. The chapter defines the concept of "experimental method" broadly, so as to embrace the social processes, infrastructure, and personal skills needed to conduct field experiments successfully.

Metaphors for experiments. The success of experimental criminology may depend on choosing the right metaphor. For researchers who are used to finding and analyzing an existing data set, the most tempting metaphor may be a recipe for "baking": mix ingredients, put in the oven, remove data when ready, and then analyze. No metaphor could be further from the mark. More appropriate metaphors for experiments might be found in raising children, governing a small village, or chairing a university department. The most useful metaphor, however, is constructing a building. Construction is a job, like all group life, that requires careful attention every day. But it also has a set of finite features that are much like a randomized experiment: finding money, drawing up and negotiating blueprints, buying land, hiring contractors, and then putting the building up in a controlled sequence of steps.

This chapter is organized around the sequence of steps required to complete a successful field experiment in crime and justice. These steps are conceptual, social, and methodological. The recurrent metaphor of constructing a building helps to illustrate the order of steps to take for best results. The property must be chosen before design can even begin. A building's foundation must be laid before the frame goes up, and the frame must be finished before the roof is installed. Some steps may be arranged in less rigid order, such as whether to install a staircase banister before or after installing the roof. Yet even in that case, evidence can indicate a preferred sequence: the lack of banisters may increase the risk of injury to workers who fall off stairs, for example. What is a "successful" building may thus be seen to have more dimensions than whether the building remains standing (or falls down – as parts of many cathedrals have done).

The steps presented in this introductory chapter begin with the intellectual property of every experiment: formulating the research question. We also consider the social foundation of a randomized experiment: choosing and developing the field research "station," as the science of agriculture describes it. In criminology, a field station can comprise many different kinds of settings, but all of them must (by definition) have some agents actively delivering some treatment(s) that will have hypothesized effects on crime or justice outcomes. Once a partnership is established between these agents and the experimenters (who could even be the same people), the next step is developing a research "blueprint" for building the experiment, known as the research protocol. This step may include a "dry run" of treating cases that will not be included in the final experiment, because the evidence from such pretest cases may prompt a change in experimental design. Other decisions must be made at that stage to address the issues described in the following sections, including the requirements of the CONSORT statement about reporting randomized trials in all fields of study.

Once a protocol is agreed and approved, the experimenters (like builders) must find and "contract" with a wide range of agents and others to construct and sustain the experiment in the most favorable way possible. Sustainability depends on well-planned and responsive management of the experiment, covering each of the following steps: supplying cases, screening for eligibility, randomly assigning treatments, delivering treatments consistently, measuring treatments delivered, and measuring outcomes.

When and if all these steps are completed, the experiment will be ready for analysis. The basic principles of experimental analysis are partly addressed in the general literature on data analysis, but several principles unique to experiments are widely violated. The chapter briefly maps out those principles and the arguments for and against fundamentally different analytic approaches in experimental criminology (EC). A separate section addresses the communication of the results of experiments to both professional and lay audiences. The penultimate section addresses the synthesis of experiments into more general knowledge, including the benefits of designing experiments as prospective meta-analyses, or "REX-Nets," and some examples of them in EC. The chapter concludes with reflections on the personal skills, training, and apprenticeships needed to practice EC, in light of the many tasks required to complete experiments successfully.

The chapter is intentionally "front-loaded," concentrating far more on the early stages of an experiment than on its final phases. The latter are far more extensively covered in standard research methods texts. Sadly, even the best research methods cannot make up for failings in research design. Because those failings are best avoided by better strategic planning at the beginning of an experiment, this chapter invests most where it may do the most good. Appendix 1 distills much of the planning needed into a protocol, which we have named the Crim-PORT or Criminological Protocol for Operating Randomized Trials. We invite anyone who is launching a randomized trial in experimental criminology to use the Crim-PORT in designing it. Even better, we invite them to register their trial protocols at the Cambridge Criminology Register of Randomized Controlled Trials (http://www.crim.cam.ac.uk/experiments).

INTELLECTUAL PROPERTY: FORMULATING THE RESEARCH QUESTION

The mere formulation of a problem is often more essential than its solution, which may be merely a matter of mathematical or experimental skill.

—Albert Einstein and Leopold Infeld
([1938] 1971: 92)

What is "merely" a matter of experimental skill is the subject of this entire chapter and of thousands of books. The subject of the present section of this mere chapter is the skill required in formulating testable questions. That skill begins with a conceptual appreciation of what questions are theoretically important. But it also includes a technical appreciation of what hypotheses are testable. Finally, it includes a utilitarian conception of how important a question is from a cost–benefit perspective. These considerations provide the basis for laying the intellectual foundations of a great experiment.

Great experiments in criminology are arguably based on these three criteria:

1. They test theoretically central hypotheses.
2. They eliminate as many competing explanations as possible.
3. They show one intervention to be far more cost effective than others.

Putting these three criteria together in the formulation of an experimental research question may seem to be more a matter of "art" than of science. But such a judgment would demean the importance of intuition, inspiration, and insight in science, as in many fields involving complex decisions (Gladwell 2005). What will always distinguish great from routine science is the capacity of a given contribution to make a major leap forward in understanding (with theory), intervention (with public benefits), or both.

Testing Theoretically Central Hypotheses

Better theory is the initial goal of all science; public benefit is arguably the ultimate value of any theory. Public benefits may (or may not) follow from better theory, sooner or later – and sometimes much, much later. James Lind's experiments in the prevention and treatment of scurvy on long sea voyages led to the British Navy issuing citrus fruit to all their sailors – hence the term "limies" – which saved thousands of lives. Yet the time between research results and policy change was substantial: it took over four decades for the Navy to act on the experimental results (Tröhler 2003). Ignaz Semmelweis showed in a nearly randomized experiment that gynecologists could reduce death in childbirth by washing their hands before examining new mothers, but half a century elapsed before the findings were widely accepted in the medical profession (Loudon 2002).

Neither Lind nor Semmelweis conducted experiments that were seen as critically important to a current theoretical debate, which may enhance the speed with which the findings are accepted (Tilley 2009). But that does not mean that the experiments failed to make major contributions to theory. To the contrary, the fact that Lind's and Semmelweis's experiments are still celebrated today shows just how important they were in the long run, theoretically as well as in terms of public benefit. Lind laid the foundation for theories of the immune system, while Semmelweis offered crucial evidence for the germ theory of disease.

In criminology, the deterrence doctrine has been central to both theory and policy for over two centuries. Yet few unbiased tests of that doctrine have been conducted. The lack of definitive experiments has limited the development of deterrence as a formal theory that specifies the conditions under which punishment or its threat prevents crime (Gibbs 1975). Great experiments in criminology have begun to advance that theory in predicting effects of legal sanctions on the criminal behavior of punished individuals, their communities, and their nations (Sherman 1993). They could also create great public benefit, limiting the harm of punishment under guidance of experimentally supported theory.

The promise of experimental criminology (EC) is equally great for understanding other social responses to crime, such as the engagement of schools and families in the prevention of serious delinquency (Multisite Violence Prevention Project 2008). Large-scale, multidisciplinary research on such questions can identify differential effects of similar responses on different kinds of people or communities. Of special theoretical importance is any finding of opposite effects of identical programs on different kinds of people, especially low-risk vs. high-risk persons (Erwin 1986; Sherman and Smith 1992; Hanley 2006; Multisite Prevention Project 2008). Experiments designed to test for such differential effects help advance theory by showing the interactions among the multiple causes of crime.

When experimental criminologists are asked to help evaluate innovations or programs intended to reduce crime or injustice, they are rarely asked if the innovations make any sense in terms of theory. Rather, the question is baldly put to them: does this program work? Often the best response is not empirical, but theoretical: why should it work? What is the theory of cause and effect implicit in the design of the program, and what prior evidence (if any) is consistent with that theory?

Experimentalists can do the most good for science when they are the most focused on the theoretical implications of their experiments. Evaluation research methods often assume – or require – a passive role for an "evaluator" in the design of a program, in order to keep the evaluation "independent" and free from conflict of interest (Eisner 2009). Yet society's limited resources for research are better served when experimental criminologists actively help to reshape a program before it is tested, in order to make a better contribution to theory. That is a role many experimenters have played without deriving any financial benefit from the design or success of the program (Sherman and Strang 2010).

The author was fortunate to have been asked to design repeated RCTs (14 completed) of the globally influential theory of reintegrative shaming (Braithwaite 1989). The first four of these experiments (Sherman et al. 2000) allowed more detailed measures of the constituent elements of the theory, which led to the theory's revision (Braithwaite 2002). More important for experimental criminology, the theory itself was adapted into a program (restorative justice) supported by a social movement that has welcomed the RCT evidence as a tool for helping to transform contemporary justice. It has also become a prime example of how RCTs can generate evidence on cost effectiveness (Shapland et al. 2008).

In their most theoretical posture, experimental criminologists have designed field experiments for the sole purpose of testing theories of crime *causation*. Farrington and Knight (1980), for example, randomly assigned the characteristics of potential crime victims to determine the effects of those characteristics on decisions of potential offenders to commit crime in an anonymous urban setting. Their findings put substantial empirical flesh on the bones of routine activities theory, which hypothesizes that a potential victim's "suitability" is a central condition for crime to occur.

There are always limits, of course, to how well theory can be tested in collaboration with governmental agencies wielding the power to manipulate variables of theoretical interest (Farrington 2003). Ariel (2009), for example, proposed theoretically coherent versions of letters that a tax agency could send to taxpayers. After negotiations for a large-sample experiment were concluded, the experiment had a sample of over 16,000 cases randomly assigned to receive different letters, with direct measurement of taxes subsequently paid. The content of the letters, however, was altered substantially by the agency for administrative reasons, thus limiting somewhat the theoretical payoff from an experiment of great policy significance. The experiments were an excellent test of the specific text of the letters. But because the government did not allow the text to be stated in a way that would tap the key theoretical questions about compliance with law, the results could not be directly incorporated into a grounded theory of tax compliance or broader theory of social control.

Whatever the practical limits to theory testing may be in an experimental design, the only way to find them is to push for as much theoretical benefit as possible. As Ariel (2008) observed, his experiment consisted of "three years of negotiation and one day of random assignment." The value of clear testing of a theory justified every day of those 3 years as a fight for strong theoretical implications of the results. For in theory as in policy, unambiguous results have the capacity to move discussion forward. It is the capacity to limit ambiguity by eliminating competing explanations that makes EC so important to criminological theory.

Eliminating Competing Explanations

"…when you have excluded the impossible, whatever remains, however improbable, must be the truth."
—Sherlock Holmes, *The Adventure of the Beryl Coronet*, by Arthur Conan Doyle[1]

---

[1] See http://www.online-literature.com/doyle/adventures_sherlock/11/, downloaded on July 24, 2009.

The reason that experimental criminology can make major advances in theory is the strong internal validity of the RCT design (Campbell and Stanley (1963). Internal validity is the extent to which a research design can eliminate competing explanations of a correlation. The more "plausible rival hypotheses" about a correlation that a study can eliminate, the more likely it becomes that the surviving explanation is the "true" cause of the observed correlation. Assume, for example, that you are taller than your father and that you drank more orange juice while growing up than he did. A theory to explain your height difference might then be that orange juice caused it – or at least some of it. But many other factors could also have caused your difference in height. The only way we can be confident about a causal impact of orange juice intake is to eliminate all (or most) other possible explanations for a height difference. While it is arguably impossible to assess causation just for you and your father – i.e., in a single, anecdotal comparison – we can learn, on average, what difference orange juice intake may cause across a large group of people.

One way to isolate the independent effects of orange juice – perhaps the best way – would be a prospective, longitudinal experiment that manipulated the amount of orange juice a large sample of people drank while they were growing up. To use this ethically unimaginable example as a hypothetical, we could randomly assign 2,000 children into two groups. We could pay 1,000 of them to drink 12 ounces of free orange juice daily and pay the other 1,000 *not* to drink more than 3 ounces of orange juice a day. Everything else about growing up would remain the same – varying from one child to the next, but with the averages and percentages of almost everything from their television watching to their cigarette smoking being almost identical in each group. Why? *Because random assignment makes it so.*

The "magic" of random assignment is that, with large enough samples, it almost always yields similar distributions in two different groups of the potential causes of any future behavior by the members of those groups. This should mean that the only average difference between the groups is the one that the experimenter has *independently* manipulated: independent, that is, of the normal preferences and habits in drinking orange juice across 2,000 children. In our orange juice example, any difference in average height between the two groups (the *dependent variable)* could then be attributed to the difference in (measured) intake of orange juice, on average, between the two groups (the *independent* variable).

EC thus shares the common distinction between experimental and nonexperimental branches of all fields of science: it tests causation by *systematically altering* variables in the units of study, as well as by *observing* those units over time. All empirical science systematically observes phenomena, but only experiments intentionally (or "independently") manipulate one or more of those variables. The power to independently modify variables under observation is so important that some statisticians have suggested that it is essential to understanding cause and effect (Salsburg 2001: 181–194), using the adage:

"No causation without manipulation."

Criminology graduate students are usually trained, improperly, to "control" for mere correlations using statistical equations in multivariate analysis in the hope that observational controls will identify causal pathways. This may imply that they are "manipulating" the variables with statistics.

They are not.

They cannot.

Manipulation means actually *changing* a factor in real life, *doing* something to someone or something. Merely selecting cases or writing equations is not manipulation. Nor does statistical "control" demonstrate causation with the same strong internal validity as random assignment to experimental and control groups.

The reason that observations alone fail to eliminate competing explanations is that they require data analysts to be too smart and too lucky. Unless analysts are both *smart* enough to think up (or "specify") every variable that needs to be held constant and *lucky* enough to have a data set in which all possible conditions of all relevant variables have enough cases for analysis of the primary causal hypothesis, statistical controls are not enough. Causation cannot be *strongly* inferred without being sure that you were both smart and lucky. Sadly, there is little way to tell without stronger research designs. Not all of these designs entail randomized experiments (see other chapters in this volume), but they all entail more than multiple regression.

NATURAL AND RANDOMIZED EXPERIMENTS. Sometimes this problem can be largely solved by an experiment of nature, in which the observer must merely document a process that was independently manipulated by factors outside the phenomenon under study (or an "instrumental variable"; see Angrist et al. 1996; Angrist 2006). That is exactly what David Kirk (2009) did with Hurricane Katrina, as a test of the well-developed and data-grounded theory that criminals are more likely to desist from crime if they succeed in "knifing off" their contact with the social networks that have supported and encouraged them in criminal activity (Laub and Sampson 2003). This theory had been tested by prospective, life-course measurement in a number of settings prior to Hurricane Katrina. But none of those tests could rule out competing explanations that were also correlated with the result, such as making more use of the educational benefits made available to World War II veterans.

It was only the hurricane that could provide an *independent* manipulation that "knifed off" prior friendships. The manipulation was independent – or random, in the statistical sense – because the hurricane was not influenced by social factors related to crime. What Kirk (2009) knew was that some New Orleans residents who came out of prison could not return home after Hurricane Katrina wiped out some, but not all, high crime neighborhoods. When he compared those "homeless" offenders to those who *could* return home, he found the now-homeless offenders were much less likely to be sent back to prison. In general, those now-homeless who resettled farthest from their last address before entering prison were the least likely to be reincarcerated for a new crime.

This evidence is more convincing than previous tests because the hurricane was disconnected from other factors embedded in the life course of the offenders. But did it eliminate all competing explanations? Arguably not, as Kirk (2009) carefully observes. Nor would anyone build a crime prevention policy that relied upon hurricanes.

More important is the theoretical nature of the intervention. Moving people from one community to another is itself theoretically ambiguous. Even if the intervention were designed as an RCT, it would not be easy to eliminate all competing explanations. One competitor, for example, is that when offenders move to different cities (or even neighborhoods) they are not as well known to police. Nor do the usual police informants know them or hear rumors about their criminal activities. Thus rather than committing fewer crimes (desisting) because they have "knifed off" their prior relationships, a competing explanation for lower reincarceration rates is a detection hypothesis. Offenders who change locations, it could be argued, commit just as many or more crimes than they did in their old neighborhood. They are simply less likely to be detected, arrested, convicted, and reincarcerated where they are unknown than where they grew up.

The point of considering the Kirk (2009) Katrina study, in this context, is to illustrate the process of designing a great experiment in criminology. Kirk's study was a brilliant formulation of a research question about a natural experiment. What it implies for EC is the development and testing of a *program* designed on the *theory* associated with "knifing off" in the life course (Laub and Sampson 2003). This could involve subsidizing offenders' moves to new (and distant) communities, with more support and integration into a community. Unlike a natural experiment that destroyed old neighborhoods, it would require measurement of the rate at which offenders give up on the new community and move back to their old one (measurement of treatment condition). It could also require measurement of the extent to which offenders stay in touch with old contacts.

Whatever an RCT design does to build on Kirk's natural experiment, its success will depend on its ability to rule out, or at least test, competing explanations. Thus if reentering offenders have less reincarceration when they are randomly assigned to move far away, the key question will be whether they are really desisting from crime. The experiment must therefore build in one or several strong tests of the detection hypothesis. Self-reported offending, DNA checks of crime scenes, or even efforts to make local police aware that the offenders have moved in – these and other strategies could help address a competing explanation.

COMPETING EXPLANATIONS OF A GOOD RESULT.   In the absence of such tests of competing explanations, even positive results from one or more RCTs may fail to convince the prime audience for the experiments: theorists and policymakers. A prime example of this is the hot spots policing experiments. Ever since Sherman and Weisburd (1995) demonstrated that extra patrols suppressed crime and disorder in 55 Minneapolis hot spots (compared to 55 controls), some police and crime theorists have remained skeptical of the result. They point to the competing explanation that hot spot policing simply "pushes crime around the corner."

In a series of subsequent studies, Weisburd refuted the displacement hypothesis by demonstrating that crime actually declines in the immediate vicinity of areas targeted with extra patrol – a finding for which he won the 2010 Stockholm Prize in Criminology. Yet many police and criminologists remain unconvinced. Weisburd has even demonstrated that once drug markets were shut down in Jersey City, they did not pop up in other parts of the city. But skeptics suggested that the markets could have moved to another nearby jurisdiction.

One reason for continued skepticism is the impact of extra policing on the individual offenders who were committing crime in the hot spots. No published evidence to date has tested the hypothesis that when crime goes down in one location the offenders simply move to other locations, perhaps at some distance, within the same metropolitan area. That is one reason why the Greater Manchester Police are now working with the present authors to conduct a new hot spots patrol experiment that would track offenders' arrests across the 500 square-mile area of their jurisdiction, in contrast to the 15 square miles of land in Jersey City (or even the 300 square miles of land in New York City). By testing for displacement across such a broad catchment area, a Greater Manchester experiment could falsify the individual offender displacement hypothesis more convincingly than previous tests – assuming it finds a reduction in offender frequencies of arrest or convictions. Such a finding would be predicted by routine activities theory; its converse would falsify the theory and support the "hydraulic pressure" displacement espoused by so many police and theorists.

No matter what the results are, the point of formulating the right research questions is to *anticipate* competing explanations for any test of a theory. As the Katrina and Manchester examples suggest, anticipating rival explanations may require enormous work in finding the right places to do the experiment. Yet that work is well worth the investment. The more competing explanations an RCT design can rule out, the more convincing the results will be to Sherlock Holmes and his numerous followers.

Demonstrating Cost Effectiveness

The greatest advertisement for EC is research demonstrating the cost effectiveness of one strategy over another. In recent years, rising interest in this principle alone has done more to encourage evidence-based government than any other. From the creation of the Washington State Public Policy Institute (http://www.wsipp.wa.gov/) to President Obama's 2009 Inaugural address and from the UK's National Institute for Health and Clinical Excellence (http://www.nice.org.uk/) cost-effectiveness standards for medical treatments to the "evidence help desk" established by the Bush administration in the US Office of Management and Budget with support from the Jerry Lee Foundation (http://evidencebasedpolicy.org/wordpress/), the cost effectiveness of government programs is attracting more analysis than ever. At the same time, these developments favor the use of experimental evidence over research designs with less internal validity.

These developments notwithstanding, EC is still more focused on theory and explanation than it is on cost effectiveness. The plea by Welsh et al. (2001) that experimentalists should monetize the benefits found in crime prevention experiments has barely been heeded. A review of articles in the *Journal of Experimental Criminology* since its founding in 2005 shows that very few authors report their effects in financial terms – including the present author! Instead, there is a clear emphasis on reporting effect sizes as standardized mean differences or Cohen's D. While that statistic offers the mathematical appeal of making effect sizes more comparable across experiments, it is impossible to derive much policy or political appeal from purely mathematical formulae. This, however, is *mostly* matter of presentation and not a fundamental problem of shaping a research question.

The framing of research questions for great experiments in criminology must do two things to capture cost effectiveness. One is that experiments must be planned to measure the costs of delivering programs, both in a start-up (developmental) phase and in a "rollout" model with perhaps more efficiencies from mass production. Without gathering measures of personnel time, travel costs, or equipment in delivering a treatment during the course of the experiment, it is often impossible to compare costs of treatment and control conditions. The same is true for the dependent variables. Offense-specific measures of crime, as distinct from counts of crimes or even mere prevalence of repeat offending, can say much more about the benefits of crime reduction. Yet it is common for many experiments to limit their measurement to counting any crimes rather than recording the *types* of crime committed. Once those types are known, a far more precise – if not perfect – assessment of the costs of crimes prevented can be calculated. These calculations can use recent average costs tracked in national samples. The costs of crime are increasingly available in standardized estimates, such as the UK's Home Office (2005) calculations for England and Wales.

The second requirement is far more important and less technical than the first. The requirement is simple: *test the most expensive strategies*. Frame experiments in ways that address major questions of cost and harm, where the payoff of the research can become a big "win" for experimental criminology. Showing how prison populations can be reduced or prisons actually closed (at US$40,000 or more per year per inmate), for example, without increasing crime, could appeal to all shades of politics. Showing how murders can be prevented, at US \$2 million per murder (Home Office 2005), might have far greater cost-effectiveness value than showing how auto theft can be reduced. In short, when framing the research question for an experiment, look for ways to test not just important theories, but ways to reduce major economic and social costs allocated to crime responses.

One way to do this is for experimental populations to be selected on the basis of Pareto's principle of the "power few" (Sherman 2007). By focusing on the small proportion of offenders (or of victims or street corners) that produce the most crime, experiments have the greatest potential to demonstrate large differences in cost effectiveness of two policy choices. The "million dollar blocks" of big cities generate enough prison inmates to cost US \$1 million per year. The high cost of these blocks has become the basis for an entire – but as yet unevaluated – strategy called "justice reinvestment." The strategy illustrates a "power few" approach that could readily become the basis for random assignment of a standard intervention across high-inmate-cost residential street blocks.

SOCIAL FOUNDATION: DEVELOPING A "FIELD STATION"

The least appreciated requirement for doing EC is its social foundation. You cannot (usually) just walk into an agency and propose an experiment. Even if the agency agrees, the experiment is likely to fail without constructing firm social capital at the outset. The foundation of social capital is the set of human relationships and social networks linking what we call the "experimenters" and those who control the resources to be allocated by random assignment. The experimenters are criminologists trained in experimental design. The people who control the resources can be called research partners, such as leaders and middle managers of police agencies, schools, courts, probation agencies, prisons, social service agencies, and parole boards.

This task is getting more complex as "evidence-based" or "data-driven" practices become more fashionable. That fashion has led to in-house hiring of research staff who may actively resist external research collaborations. What was once a bilateral relationship between external experimenters and internal operating personnel is more often a trilateral relationship between external and internal researchers and the operating personnel. Sometimes this may simply block experiments from ever getting started. In other cases, the experiments proceed, but with structural tensions involving the research roles more than the operating roles.

Even the bilateral relationships of operators and experimenters can deteriorate into a mutually suspicious, us-vs.-them antagonism. This has been especially likely when experimenters were brought into a relationship with partners as "evaluators," when an evaluation was required by a third party, such as a program funder. Increasingly, however, EC has solved this problem by abandoning long-term relationships with *funders* in favor of long-term relationships with operating agencies. These agencies, in turn, are increasingly willing to invest their own funds in the conduct of randomized experiments.

A long-term social foundation for EC can support many more than one experiment. That multitest approach to a single site helps to earn back the heavy initial costs for experimenters in learning how the partner agency operates. It also helps the partner agencies to earn back the time they have invested in teaching the experimenters what they need to learn to do just one experiment; for the same "sunk" costs, the partnership can do 2, 3, 5, or 10 experiments – or more, if they take the long view.

Field Stations in Experimental Field Sciences

The history of experimental field science shows many examples of research centered in what looks much like an indoor laboratory – but with a crucial difference. Any "field" science, by definition, studies questions that cannot be answered in a laboratory. How do infections actually spread in populations of humans or of cows? How cost effective is the addition of fertilizer to crops? How many geese will fly south from Canada to the US next year? Not all of these questions require experimental methods (only the fertilizer test does). But none of them can be answered in a laboratory, at least not directly.

Field research stations have collected various kinds of observational data systematically in the same places for at least 300 years, ever since a network of weather stations was set up across Italy (Bradley and Jones 1992: 144). Experimenters have conducted various experiments in field settings for at least two centuries, at least since Benjamin Franklin went to the belfry of Christ Church in Philadelphia to fly a key from a kite in a thunderstorm to see if he could attract lightning to it (he did).

What was perhaps the first *experimental* field site was the Rothamsted Agricultural Experimental Station established in 1843 by Sir John Bennet Lawes, owner of the estate and its fertilizer factory (also the first such factory in the world). In a 57-year partnership with chemist Joseph Henry Gilbert as the "experimenter," Lawes established a program of "classical experiments" in how to increase crop production, largely through fertilizers. Some of these experiments are still being conducted.[2] Even more important was the intellectual product of the Rothamsted Station at the end of its first century: the classic treatise on the design of RCTs by Sir Ronald Aylmer Fisher (1935).

Many other experimental field stations have been established around the world since 1843. Under the 1862 Morrill Act in the US, every state was entitled to establish a land-grant agricultural school, most of which established experimental field stations to test farming practices on large samples of fields or grazing animals. By the 1950s, hospitals associated with medical schools took on the same character as field stations, linking teaching and research with a large number of clinical RCTs. These "power few" hospitals developed the greatest concentrations of research grants and researcher–practitioners. While it took a half-century from the call by the great medical educator, Sir William Osler, for research universities to "invade the hospitals" (Bliss 1999), the growth of medical experimentation was clearly advanced by its concentration in teaching hospitals with a strong empirical ethos of testing every practice possible.

Field "Stations" in Experimental Criminology

From at least the 1960s, similar concentrations of field experiments have been found in the criminal justice system. The Vera Institute of Justice in New York appears to have been the first center of repeated experiments in criminology, launching its first RCT in October 1961. Comparing money bail to release (without cash) on recognizance in the 1960s, Vera literally changed the world with its conclusion that showed how to reduce jail populations without

---

[2] See http://www.rothamsted.bbsrc.ac.uk/corporate/Origins.html, downloaded on July 26, 2009.

increasing crime (Ares et al. 1963). Vera went on to treat all five boroughs in New York as one large field station, conducting repeated RCTs (and observational studies) in New York's prisons, courts, prosecutors' offices, and police agencies.

In the same year that Vera began randomized experiments in New York, the California Youth Authority (CYA) began a long program of RCTs on the other side of the US. This "field station" thrived until it was pushed aside by the "just deserts" model of sentencing, which denied the relevance of "what works" in reducing repeat offending as a morally unacceptable question (Palmer and Petrosino 2003). But just as the CYA's research culture was dying out, the Police Foundation launched a series of RCTs and quasiexperiments with police departments around the country, culminating in the random assignment of arrest in 1981–1982 with the unanimous approval of the Minneapolis City Council (Sherman and Berk 1984). Of all the police agencies with which the Police Foundation collaborated, the Kansas City (Mo) PD became the most like a field station, with repeated research grants and quasiexperiments (Sherman 1979; Sherman and Rogan 1995a, b) and with multiple researchers (Sherman 1979; Sherman and Rogan 1995a, b). Other police agencies have played similar roles, including Jersey City and San Diego.

It is arguable whether such "hot spots" of Experimental Criminology should be called "field stations," using the same terminology as experimental agriculture. Many officials prefer the image of a teaching or research hospital, if only because medicine is generally more prestigious than farming. Both fields are quite scientific, however, and the science of policing is spatial in much the same way as the treatment of fields in agriculture. But marketing brand names aside, the concept of a field station where data are recorded and experiments can last for many decades is an explicit vision for how to conduct experiments in criminology. Any investment in EC is best directed to such locations. Anyone leading an experiment is well advised to study the histories of previous such sites, with as many case studies as possible (Sherman 1992, Appendix 2; Sherman and Strang 2010).

The Social Elements of Experiments

The key to holding an experiment together is understanding a cognitive map of its social elements. These elements include (1) the funders, (2) the executive leadership of an operating agency, (3) the mid-level operating liaison person(s), (4) the agents delivering treatments, and (5) (where necessary) the agents providing cases.

1. The *funders* vary widely in their previous experience with EC or with randomized experiments in any field. In some instances, grant managers may know more about randomized experiments than the principal investigators. In other cases, the funding organization has unrealistic expectations of how quickly or feasibly an experiment can be accomplished. The latter problem is especially likely to arise when the funding staff members attempt to design an experiment in the abstract, without being grounded in the daily operations of a particular agency which can carry out an experiment. In one case, a senior prosecutor designed an experiment with 37 criteria for which cases were ineligible – leaving only 15 cases out of over 5,000 that were eligible when the criteria were finally applied in the field. No one in the funding agency ever thought to check the eligibility criteria against field data before the experiment was funded; they did not hesitate, however, to blame the problem on the research team that was awarded the contract to implement (and "evaluate") the funder's design.

Whatever the funder's background, however, a candid and constructive relationship is an insurance policy against the many predictable problems of constructing experiments. Frequent communication and warnings of delays may help pave the way for funder's support for extensions of time or additional resources. These can often be justified on the basis of achievements in the first phases of the experiments, including substantial numbers of cases randomly assigned with a high level of integrity.

2. The *agency executive* is someone who should strongly support the experiment from the first day of planning and then be left alone unless a critical problem requires intervention that no one else can provide. Ideally, the principal investigator should be able to communicate directly with the executive, providing progress reports in writing or in person once or twice a year. This privilege should be used as little as possible, however, especially in very large organizations. Only with a strong preexisting relationship is frequent contact likely to be welcomed. A large program of experiments at any one time would also create a firmer basis for more frequent contacts. Where the executive is frequently replaced during the course of an experiment – as occurred five times in 5 years with our Canberra experiments – a legally binding contract with the agency signed at the outset can keep the experiment going until completion.

3. The *operating liaison* is the most critical player after the principal investigator. A skilled leader such as Lt. Dean Collins in Milwaukee can make a better case for random assignment than any researcher; Collins presented the design to the City Council, which voted unanimously to approve it (Sherman 1992). Lt. Anthony Bacich, also in Milwaukee, selected and led a team of 36 officers who delivered the tightest implementation of random assignment in the history of police experiments. In contrast, the refusal of the Canberra police to designate a permanent liaison for the life of the experiments led to much less consistency and fidelity in the implementation of the experimental protocol.

4. The *agents delivering treatments* should arguably be as few in number as possible and preferably invited to serve in the experiment on a voluntary basis. A labor-intensive experiment that requires all operating personnel to participate, such as the Minneapolis Hot Spots patrol experiment (Sherman and Weisburd 1995), raises far more issues of compliance with random assignment than develop along with a small voluntary team. A smaller team can also become more committed to the experiment by knowing that their names will be on the final report, by attending monthly briefing sessions, by attending a 1–3 day conference at the outset of the experiment, and other means of fostering team spirit. The more effort experimenters can put into such relationships, the more likely the treatments are to be delivered as the protocol specifies.

5. The *agents providing cases* may be entirely different people from those delivering the treatments. Sometimes they may seem almost invisible, such as the dispatcher referring domestic disturbance calls to a small portion of the patrol force who have been designated to conduct the experiment. Ignore them at your peril, since they can choke off the sample size needed for statistical power.

Some will always be more responsive than others, as persistent attempts to win them over may discover. Dispatchers can be visited, briefed, and cosseted. Magistrates' courts clerks in England, however, may smile, attend meetings and luncheons, promise to help, and then refuse to do what even the head of the nation's judiciary asks them to do in person. In that example, their opposition was more to the substance of the intervention being tested than to the idea of experimentation.

No matter what the reason, a failure to persuade those providing cases is the number one source of experiments failing to reach sample size goals. The wary may choose to refuse an experiment in which the sources of cases may oppose their referrals. The bold may choose to forge ahead, as Sarah Bennett, Nova Inkpen, and Dorothy Newbury-Birch did in England. After repeated trial and error with multiple targets for extracting cases prior to sentencing, they discovered a year later that what the courts denied us (same-day notice of guilty pleas), probation departments were willing to supply.

BLUEPRINTS: DECIDING ON THE EXPERIMENTAL PROTOCOL

In the long history of real-world field experimentation, as in building construction, formal blueprints are a recent arrival. Most cathedrals were built without the modern equivalent of architectural plans, yet most are still standing. Medical research rarely required protocols, even when patients were dying (as in the first patient treated with penicillin). Careful records were often kept, tracking fast-moving innovations in finding a better way to carry out tests. Initial plans were often subject to change.

All this has been changed in the modern US university environment of Institutional Review Boards (IRBs), where a formal research protocol is a legal requirement. Any major change in that protocol needs to be reviewed and approved by IRBs in advance of implementation. The negative effect of this requirement on EC is hard to overstate, as we have learned by operating experiments in England without legal requirements for such protocols. We can say that our eight UK experiments would have been virtually impossible to do with constant delays of 2 months or longer, each time we decided to alter a protocol for case referrals or types of offenses eligible. Yet the future is clear: experimental criminology will need to design blueprints and stick to them, absent approval from oversight bodies.

On balance, it can be argued that EC will be substantially improved by wider use of experimental protocols. One reason is that there have been so many RCTs in criminology that either violated good design standards or failed to report fundamental information (Weisburd 1993). The 1996 publication of the first CONSORT statement – the CONsolidated Standards On Reporting of Trials – was prompted by a similar concern in medicine, after surveys documented the common gaps in reporting on medical trials (e.g., Pocock et al. 1987). The elements in the CONSORT statement are an extremely valuable guide to reporting RCTs in any field, not just medicine. But as late as 2009, many leading criminologists and experimenters had never heard of the CONSORT statement (http://www.CONSORT-Statemen.org). Wider knowledge of the statement may lead to more complete reporting of EC. But more important is that it can lead to better planning of experiments with protocols that anticipate these reporting requirements.

The checklist of CONSORT's 22 reporting elements includes the following outline of a final report:

1. Title & Abstract
2. Background
3. Participants
4. Interventions
5. Objectives
6. Outcomes
7. Sample size

8. Randomization – Sequence Generation
9. Randomization – Allocation Concealment
10. Randomization – Implementation
11. Blinding (masking)
12. Statistical Methods
13. Participant Flow
14. Recruitment
15. Baseline Data
16. Numbers Analyzed
17. Outcomes and Estimation
18. Ancillary Analyses
19. Adverse Events
20. Interpretation
21. Generalizability
22. Overall Evidence

Any experimental criminologist reading this list will question the sequence and logic of the items. They may also question the relevance if items such as "blinding" of participants to the treatment they are receiving – a difficult task in criminal justice research when, for example, people are being arrested (or not). But the adoption of at least the CONSORT caseflow diagram could lead to far greater transparency in EC, if not all of its elements (Fig. 20.1).

A flow diagram is an excellent tool for depicting what happened across all randomly assigned cases in an experiment. An illustration of such a diagram above comes from an RCT in Philadelphia comparing low intensity probation with standard intensity (Barnes et al. 2010). It shows the pipeline of cases flowing into the experiment, which was a repeated batch design. It also illustrates what happened to cases after random assignment – showing that all cases were analyzed as if they had been treated as they were randomized, regardless of what actually happened (often due to offender behavior which led to their attrition from probation supervision). Knowing that such a chart is required may insure that the data are gathered as the RCT progresses.

Yet CONSORT alone is not enough. A reporting system does not tell you how to design a protocol for an experiment before it starts. It only tells you what readers need to know after it is finished. There are many essential things you must do to make experiments succeed that the reader has little need to know. These are not only the *formal* elements of a protocol, such as informed consent and statistical power. They are, more importantly, the managerial elements of delivering the experiment as desired. And perhaps because there are so many differences across research fields, there is no consolidated statement for the development of RCT protocols. It is therefore incumbent on experimental criminology to develop its own standard.

For this and other reasons, we include in this chapter the first version of a standard protocol format for experiments in criminology. Appendix 1 lays out the elements of the protocol, with more detailed instructions to be posted on the Web site. The Web site is provided for the dual purpose of (1) helping experimenters to design better trials and (2) providing a public registry where protocols can be posted in advance of a trial starting. Such registries have become essential in medicine to combat the "file-drawer problem": the systematic bias that comes from not reporting tests in which no statistically significant differences were found or differences were found in the opposite direction from where it was anticipated (or hoped).

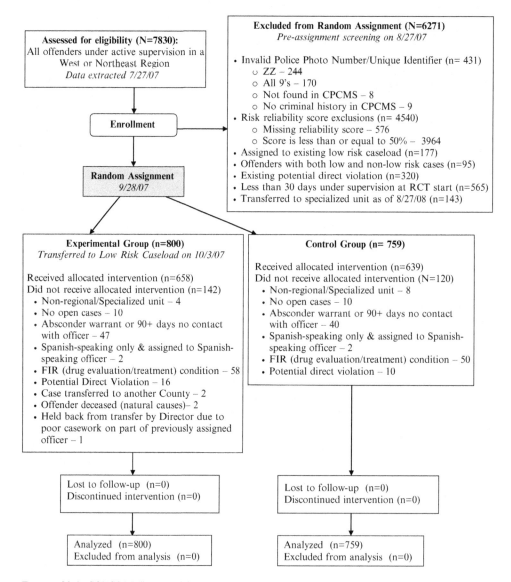

FIGURE 20.1. CONSORT diagram of the Philadelphia low-intensity probation RCT (source: Barnes et al. 2010).

The file-drawer problem is a major obstacle to systematic reviews of the literature that are essential to science (see section "Synthesizing Results"). If for no other reason than to reduce the potential bias in reporting the results of research, a registry of randomized trials is needed in criminology to encourage all tests to be made transparent by design and not by results. Once such a registry (or registries) exists, then criminology journals can do what medical journals have recently done. They can require that no publication will be allowed unless a trial was registered publicly in advance of its implementation.

* * * * * * * * *

This section closes our discussion of the "front end" of experimental criminology. The remainder of this chapter is a brief overview of each of the key issues and arguments that a protocol can anticipate and plan for. Anyone using our Crim-PORT in Appendix 1 may find the next 12 sections especially useful.

"CONTRACTS": RECRUITING, CONSULTING, AND TRAINING KEY PEOPLE

Using the construction metaphor, experiments must be built by contractors (who may also have been the architect) who know how to "contract" with the right people (for money or *pro bono* love of the research). The person in the metaphorical role of building contractor in an experimental criminology is the principal investigator.

Principal investigators in experimental criminology will generally be PhD-level academics. While Jonathan Shepherd and others have espoused a practitioner–investigator model as a means of building a research culture in criminal justice agencies, the current structure of these agencies militates against that model. Anyone in a position to launch a controlled experiment in, for example, a police agency is unlikely to have the time to design an experimental protocol. Nor are they likely to benefit as much in their police careers from publishing a research project as any academic would – unlike doctors in academic medicine. Thus we write the Crim-PORT with an academic experimenter in mind, even as we look to the day when experimenters will be found within crime prevention and justice agencies.

The experimental criminologist – or "random assigner," as Carol Weiss ironically calls all experimentalists – serving as principal investigator should be supported and held accountable as the primary leader of the experiment. While in some experiments an independent evaluator is assigned to measure the results of the experiments (e.g., Shapland et al. 2008), even then the directors of the RCTs must take responsibility for making things happen. When there is no person clearly in that role, the chances of a major failure may increase. In one police experiment, for example, the data were all to be analyzed by a researcher who rarely visited the project site. The research coordinator on the ground was not a PhD and had little status as a temporary employee of the police department. More important, the coordinator had not been hired by the data analyst and had no prior relationship. During the experiment, independent audits of the data showed that there was systematic misrecording of results and ways by which the officers could learn of random assignment in advance of declaring cases eligible.

As this case illustrates, experiments cannot just be "put in the oven and removed when fully baked." They must be steered every moment like an automobile. Alternatively, they must be managed like a construction site. Academics who work at arms length from the randomly assigned operations cannot know what problems exist in the field or how to interpret the data. They need to have an independent source of intelligence on the ground.

Field Coordinators

A field coordinator or manager is the eyes and ears of a distant academic. Only by constant communication with a field coordinator can the principal investigator be sure that the right decisions are taken as crises or routine problems arise. Just as an architect needs to have a good working relationship with a contractor, a principal investigator needs a high level of skill – and trust in – the field coordinator.

This principle is so important that a major foundation recently insisted on giving a leading academic more money than requested to run an experiment at a great distance. The foundation insisted that the academic either hire a competent field coordinator to work daily within the experimenting agency or receive no grant at all. The academic accepted the extra funding, and the experiment was a success.

Other Key Roles

The field coordinator can often be hired with local knowledge about key actors. This helps the academic investigator to do a better job at recruiting key staff and partners. The field coordinator must also be at the center of all social networks connected to the experiment, such as the *agency liaison* and any oversight groups. Some may have a PhD, some may be working on a PhD, and some may not aspire to a PhD. But all should be emotionally and politically intelligent, pragmatic problem solvers of the highest integrity. The same can be said for the *data manager*, who is best kept off-site from the experiment. By reporting independently to the principal investigator, the data manager becomes a second source of check and balance on the experiment. Contacts with the *agents supplying the cases*, in particular, can provide important clues to the progress of the experiment.

Even before recruiting key agency and research people for an experiment, a principal investigator can consult widely among local VIPs to seek advice about who to recruit for key roles. Often the agency liaison can recommend a local research coordinator. Even if advertising is the only source of candidates, enlisting the agency liaison to help choose a field coordinator can help build commitment to the experiment. The same is true for selecting operating agents to apply the treatment to the extent that they can be limited to volunteers. In one relatively small experiment, Minneapolis Police Chief Anthony Bouza let Lawrence Sherman (as principal investigator) choose the entire 5-police officer team for the 2-year experiment. The team included the sergeant in command, who became the primary agency liaison. The team then worked closely with the (local) research coordinator (Dr. Michael Buerger) and the (distant) data manager (Dr. Patrick Gartin), both of whom were doctoral students at the time. All showed sustained commitment to the experiment, from start to finish.

BUILDING: STARTING AND SUSTAINING THE EXPERIMENT

How an experiment begins depends on how it must be designed. There is nothing easier than launching a "batch" random assignment project and nothing harder than launching a "trickle-flow" random assignment project. While months or years of preparation may be required for batch random assignment, they sometimes offer a capacity to literally push a button that will launch the experiment. Random assignment of thousands of letters to taxpayers is a prime example of the batch model.

Trickle-flow experiments, in contrast, may require the cooperation of hundreds of people to supply eligible cases for random assignment. It may be essential to reach them with as much publicity as possible. A press conference, assembly in-person of large groups of agency staff, letters sent to all agents, a launch party with good food and drink, an overnight planning conference at a resort venue, and many other methods have all been used with varying degrees of success. Anything possible that alerts people with access to the raw materials of the experiment is worth trying to encourage them to make "donations" of cases to the cause.

Once the experiment is launched, the even greater challenge with trickle-flow experiments is to sustain the caseflow. The key method is to keep reminding agents who can supply cases to do so. In Sherman's Minneapolis and Milwaukee domestic violence experiments, monthly meetings with the research team kept caseflow moving at a steady pace. In Strang and Sherman's Canberra restorative justice experiments, the local police would not allow us to hold meetings with agents who could supply cases. We could only use informal contacts in police agencies where restorative justice meetings were held to remind officers to call our 24-h phone line to refer any eligible cases they encountered. Despite a steady decline in the rate of case referrals, we nonetheless managed to recruit some 1,400 cases over 5 years.

Even batch designs, however, face challenges in launching and sustaining the experiments. In the Minneapolis hot spots experiment (Sherman and Weisburd 1995), the research team spent months checking the units of analysis for eligibility (Buerger et al. 1995). The result was an extremely clean set of visually independent units of analysis. The major challenge was in sustaining a consistent difference in the delivery of the patrol treatment between experimental and control locations over an entire year. The trickle flow in this case was not of new *cases* into the experiment, but of daily treatment dosage into the units of analysis.

Even the selection of batch assignment cases can be problematic if not all the information is available on record. In the Philadelphia Low-Intensity Probation Experiment (Barnes et al. 2010), there was a substantial rate of error in the data entry on characteristics that were keys to the eligibility of probationers for the experiment. Even though the experimenters who checked the eligibility requirements followed all rules precisely, the errors in the data they examined were not made apparent until after random assignment, when treatment modifications were attempted.

Finally, the Philadelphia experiment also illustrates a repeated batch design. This procedure is necessary if the cases age out of the treatment condition as their probation sentences expired, but a certain ratio of offenders to probation officers was part of the definition of the experimental treatment. In order to keep the ratio constant over time, new cases that were not included in the experimental analysis had to be assigned each month or so to the probation officers.

SUPPLYING: OBTAINING CASES

The biggest challenge in trickle-flow experiments is to find and extract the cases that are "leaking" out of the experimental sample. Increasingly, information technology applications can be used to identify the missed cases and the agents who could have referred them to the experimenters. If the agency strongly supports the experiment, there may be ways to encourage agents who do not refer the cases to start doing so. But if the agency will not, or cannot, attempt to persuade those who can contribute cases to an experiment, the only tool left is the ingenuity of the site coordinator or principal investigator.

In Northumbria, for example, neither the Crown Prosecution Service nor the Court Service referred cases to a national government experiment, despite promising to do so. But Dr. Newbury-Birch, the site coordinator, negotiated with the Probation service to have them fax to our research office a copy of any request from the court for a presentence report. That allowed us to directly approach the offenders who had pled guilty in order to seek their consent to be randomly assigned to a restorative justice conference.

SCREENING FOR ELIGIBILITY

"If you break it, you own it," as Colin Powell famously said about the US-led invasion of Iraq in 2003. The same can be said for random assignment of cases that were not eligible for the experiment. Once a case is randomly assigned within a sequence of random numbers, it cannot be deleted without introducing selection bias – exactly the kind of bias random assignment is designed to control.

There is a widespread, mistaken assumption by economists and other analysts that ineligible cases can simply be deleted after random assignment. Samples "corrected" in this way cannot then be analyzed as if the random assignment had never occurred. The only honest correction is to specify a multivariate model that considers both intention-to-treat (ITT) and treatment received (TR), along with any variables that might predict a gap between those two conditions (Piantadosi 1997: 276–282). Taking this path, however, entails the same requirement to be smart and lucky, that is the reason to conduct a randomized trial. Despite advances in statistical thinking about what is called "instrumental variables" to help strengthen causal inference (Angrist 2006), sample sizes large enough to use this approach are in short supply in criminology.

The best solution to the problem of including ineligible cases is to prevent it prior to random assignment. Like so many problems in randomized field experiments, this one can be minimized by better planning and protocols. Hence the best time to exclude ineligible cases is when writing the *budget*: making sure that you spend enough money to have an independent check on the eligibility of cases.

In our Canberra restorative justice experiments (Sherman et al. 2000), the budget included the research team staffing a 24 h a day, 365 days a year telephone hotline for police to call in eligible cases. The first thing staff members did when they answered the phone was to run through a checklist of eligibility requirements. While this rarely detected ineligible cases, it did detect some that were never randomly assigned. The only ineligible cases that slipped through the screening process were those in which police provided inaccurate data: offender's date of birth or other pending charges, for example. The budget for the eligibility screening was also justified by an even more important element of protocol planning: an independent process of random assignment.

RANDOMLY ASSIGNING TREATMENTS

Sherman's first randomized experiment (Sherman and Berk 1984) produced a major finding: saving money on random assignment costs is penny wise and pound foolish. Sherman designed the experiment so that all random assignment sequences were given in advance, without allocation concealment, to each of the agents referring cases and delivering treatments. In that experiment, they were the same people, all Minneapolis patrol officers. This procedure saved money on staffing costs to answer the telephone. But it also allowed officers to selectively include cases when they knew they had an arrest up next in their sequence.

As Gartin (1992) has shown, at least some of the experimental officers in Minneapolis apparently held on to their arrest cases until they encountered a suspect they did not like – or perhaps already knew. In any case, the cases "randomly" assigned to arrest, in proper sequence, for some reason had higher levels of prior arrests than the offenders randomly assigned to nonarrest alternatives. This fact did not alter the substantive conclusion that arrest deterred repeat offending relative to other treatments. Prior arrests predict a higher likelihood of recidivism. But the group that had lower recidivism had more prior arrests. This means that all the officers did was to cause an underestimate of the deterrent effect of arrest in Minneapolis, not an overestimate.

This question never arose in Milwaukee, in which Sherman had a larger budget for random assignment. The chance for biased selection of eligible cases was virtually eliminated by having research staff answer the phone by a secure computer, take the identifying details of the officers and the suspects, and then open a numbered envelope sealed with red sealing wax. Close supervision each day ensured that no envelopes were opened in advance. Analytic checks for prior record and other differences across treatment groups found no significant variation in proportions of such baseline characteristics.

Yet even after Minneapolis, other arrest experiments saved money on random assignment costs by delegating the job to police dispatchers. The theory was that the call record would create transparency about what was known prior to random assignment. What a dispatch center call record would not reveal, however, was the cases that were left out if the dispatcher told the police what assignment was next on an open list. One experiment solved this problem by having a computerized random assignment program programmed right into the dispatch system, so that treatment instructions would not be generated until the identifying case details were registered. Even then, the credibility of an independent random assignment system is well worth the increased budget. A complete firewall of social relations between the operating agents applying treatments and the staff applying random assignments is a policy above suspicion. In our UK restorative justice experiments (Sherman et al. 2005), we even put the random assignment computer and staff on another continent.

Far worse systems of random assignment have been employed. Tossing coins, using dates of birth or days of the week (odd or even dates) – these are all systems that appear to have sufficient integrity to create equal probability of assignment. The general experience is that such systems, like Sherman's in Minneapolis, are more likely to produce differences in case characteristics between randomly assigned groups. Such differences can always happen by chance, of course, especially in a relatively smaller sample. But they are easily prevented by designing a protocol that separates random assignment from operating staff.

DELIVERING TREATMENTS CONSISTENTLY

A great body of literature discusses the role of heterogeneity in the statistical power of experiments. The more differences within groups, the less power there is in the test (Weisburd 1993). This applies to both cases and treatments. Anything that creates differences within the units of analysis, or in the way treatments are delivered, can cause a misleading result: no significant difference despite a "true," underlying difference. While eligibility criteria can limit the differences in cases (for example, in age or prior record), it is much harder for a protocol to insure consistency in the treatment.

The importance of this issue depends in part on the subtlety of the treatment being tested. Something quite blunt, like a decision to arrest, may be full of subtlety (see Paternoster et al. 1997). But the major feature of treatment is taking someone to jail. That is a transparent and easily auditable feature of treatment. Analysts can readily compare cases in which arrest did or did not happen.

In longer and complex treatments, auditing is much harder to attain. Treatments requiring repeated contact can count the number of contacts attained. But they are unlikely to be able to audit the number of minutes the contact lasted, what was discussed, whether participants cried or got angry, or whether their feelings toward treatment staff improved or worsened (Sherman and Strang 2004). All of these things may be important theoretically. If they are – as they were in our Canberra restorative justice experiments – the best plan is to invest heavily in measurements, such as observations and interviews. Even then, however, it is much harder to *deliver* consistency than to *measure* consistency.

What we learned by repeating our Canberra experiments in England was that the protocol mattered. In Canberra, the first police chief was committed to a "generalist" view of policing, in which restorative justice is a skill every police officer should have. At his request, we saw that over 400 officers were trained in the method, and most of the treatments were delivered by officers who delivered them only once. By contrast, the English experiments provided enough funding to have fulltime specialists delivering the same treatment. Even though the same trainers were used to train restorative justice staff in both Canberra and England, the consistency was far higher in England. What created consistency was a specialized unit of "professional" restorative justice facilitators, all of whom having extensive practice. In contrast, delivery of a complex treatment by a "volunteer" created well-documented inconsistency.

MEASURING TREATMENTS DELIVERED

The failure to measure treatment delivery is one of the most common in experimental criminology. Numerous experiments assume that once treatment is assigned it will be delivered. Yet when budgets are invested in measuring delivery, the research shows at least some portion of cases in which delivery did not occur.

The rapid development of information technology will help to lower the costs of treatment measurement. In the Minneapolis Hot Spots patrol experiment, Sherman and Weisburd (1995) invested large sums of National Institute of Justice funds in trained observers with stop watches observing street corners. Their job was to count the number of minutes that police officers were present at each street corner, with arrival and departure times for each "presence," as well as to count crimes and disorders observed.

As we now redesign the experiment with police in Greater Manchester (England), we can save great sums by using two kinds of electronic data. One is the Automatic Radio Locator System (ARLS) that will record where each and every police officer is at all times. This will produce exact counts of minutes that their radio (which they keep on their person at all times for safety reasons) is located at each point in the jurisdiction, by GPS (Global Positioning Satellite) transmissions. The other technology is CCTV cameras, which are trained on many hot spots and can record what happens 100% of the time. High-speed coding software can review the videos of human behavior in high-crime hot spots, thereby saving even data entry costs.

Police presence, however, is a fairly blunt treatment. More subtle treatments will be harder to measure with electronic technologies. The Police Foundation's experiment in counseling officers who were frequently subject to complaints (Pate et al. 1976) entailed discussions behind closed doors with older officers who were allegedly "reformed" from their "cowboy" days on the street. The discussions were supposed to encourage younger officers to keep their tempers and to let insults pass without response. When the experiment backfired – with "counseled" officers suffering more rather than fewer complaints than uncounseled officers – the explanation could not be extracted from the data. The reason was because there were no data. The counseling officers had insisted on no independent observations of the counseling sessions. The result was a classic black box. And the value of the experiment from the standpoint of police service delivery was nil.

The main conclusion that can be derived from such experiments is that investment in treatment measurement is well worth the cost. Without knowing what the treatment truly comprises, there is no way to build upon the results of the experiment. One word for this idea is "descriptive validity," a useful concept for considering the budget issues in every protocol.

MEASURING OUTCOMES

Experimental criminology is blessed with a plethora of official records about crime, as well as growing emphasis on medical records (from emergency rooms), victim interviews, offender self-reports, and observational measures such as CCTV. The challenge is to make sense of them. Several principles may help.

Choose Universal Measures Over Low Response Rate Measures

In studies with two competing measures, findings of each are often given equal weight. This equality may be fine if both are universal measures, such as hospital records and arrest records. They are universal because everyone in the jurisdiction is subject to the record keeping, whatever limitations that may entail. This is true both before and after random assignment, which is unlikely to affect the data collection. But if one measure depends on interviews, it cannot be universal. All interviews are subject to sampling biases from nonresponse. And unlike the universal measures, these biases may be reactive to randomly assigned differences in treatments.

In our Canberra experiments, we had differential response rates from interviews of offenders receiving different treatments. We learned much about offender perceptions of treatments by conducting the interviews, despite the response rate issues. But as measure of repeat offending, we relied more heavily on the universal measures. Whatever biases they suffered, there was far less suggestion of reactivity to treatment.

Choose Crime Frequency Over Prevalence

Crime prevention experiments are ultimately aimed to reduce the crime problem in communities. When individual offenders are the unit of analysis, the best measure of their effect on community crime is the frequency and seriousness of their offending. Yet by tradition, many government agencies are locked into a precomputer definition of "recidivism" as the *prevalence* of repeat offending: what percentage of offenders in each group had one or more arrest or conviction during the follow-up period. We know many instances in which the findings showed no differences in prevalence, but with large differences in frequency. The UK Home Office only used prevalence criteria for many years to judge any program a success. Only when Shapland and her colleagues (2008) discovered that our restorative justice experiments had reduced the frequency of crime (but not its prevalence) did the policy of exclusive focus on prevalence change. As an indicator of how much crime occurs in the community in response to treatments, frequency seems to be the far more sensitive and reliable indicator.

Choose a Seriousness Index Over Categorical Counts

The larger problem with measuring community benefit in criminology is the general failure to weight the seriousness of crimes. Crimes vary widely in their costs or perceived seriousness. On this measure, in fact, we have had our greatest success, with the cost effectiveness of our UK experiments showing a significant 9 to 1 return on investment (Shapland et al. 2008). But this too has not been a traditional measure of success, even though the UK has some of the best-developed measures of the average costs of crime of any country.

Choose One Measure as Primary at the Outset

The best way to avoid arguments at the end of an experiment is to agree at the outset what the primary outcome measure will be. Had we agreed on cost effectiveness based on seriousness and frequency of crime as the key criterion for a US $10 million set of experiments, the public would have been better served in its investment in testing restorative justice. But even this is an elusive goal, since funding personnel changed so often in the course of the 5-year project. What may matter most in the long run is a development of consensus within professional groups, such as the Campbell Collaboration. Financial agencies of governments, such as the US Office of Management and Budget or the Treasury in the UK, could also support a greater focus on cost effectiveness rather than the kind of bean-counting of prevalence (or even frequency) that Sherman and other experimentalists have done in the past.

Perhaps the best reason to pick a primary measure in advance is the frequent debate about whether data analysts "fished" for a significant result, highlighting one significant difference in a long procession of null findings. Gorman and Huber (2009) have recently demonstrated that even a program widely believed (on the evidence) to be ineffective (DARE) can be shown to be effective by the same analytic methods used to report programs widely believed to "work." Advance registration of a protocol following the Crim-PORT would prevent this problem before an experiment even begins.

ANALYZING RESULTS

Many statistics textbooks address this question. We have two comments to supplement those texts. The first is to seek simplicity in analysis. Experiments are elegant in their simplicity. They can also be analyzed that way. The simpler the analysis, the more people will be able to grasp the meaning of the results. Cost effectiveness is attractive on these grounds as well as on the substantive grounds of public benefit. Complex statistical models and uninterpretable effect sizes are not.

The second comment is to test policies, not treatments. This means, in general, that Intention-To-Treat (ITT) analysis makes the most sense in keeping the analysis simple. Experiments in criminology will always feature complexity of how people deliver treatments and react to them. But testing a decision to follow one *policy* to attempt one treatment or another with each case does not require that the treatment actually occurs. What happens after the attempt-to-treat begins is actually an answer to the question posed by the experiment. That question can be answered just fine by ITT analysis. So can the question about what effect the policy had on outcomes. What the experiment cannot answer – absent near-perfect delivery of the treatment – is what effect the treatment had.

Why is policy more important than treatment? In the long run, treatment delivery could be improved and policies of offering it could have very different effects. If that happened, then new experiments would be needed to test the effect of the treatment-enriched policies. Thus as long as the experiment is limited to the random assignment of policy and cannot control treatment, the honest thing to do is to analyze the effects of policy.

COMMUNICATING RESULTS

Simplicity is also a great virtue in communicating results. Academics inclined to making fine distinctions are often impatient with simplicity. But they lack evidence to support the claim that complexity will lead to better policymaking or even better science. We know few academics who can recall the details of any particular study unless it directly pertains to their own research of the moment. The error rate in print in describing our own research is also very high, even among distinguished scholars. Those who attack simple conclusions, like saying something "works" or not, may be praised for their lofty aspirations for the future of human intelligence.

SYNTHESIZING RESULTS

The best reason for doing experiments is that they have value far beyond the era in which they are completed and reported. This value is sometimes limited to the single experiment. More often, however, the value of each experiment grows as replications and related research accumulates (Sherman and Strang 2004a). And as experimental criminology has grown, so too has the related field of research synthesis.

The goal of research synthesis is to draw conclusions from a universe of all tests of a single hypothesis. The Campbell Collaboration is promoting this task in crime and justice, as well as in other social policy areas. Randomized experiments are especially valuable for systematic reviews and meta-analysis of accumulated tests of a program or policy. Even those who are generally critical of the statistical basis of meta-analysis are ready to endorse its use when only randomized experiments are included in the calculations (Berk 2005).

There is all the more reason, then, to plan experiments well, to minimize alternative explanations, and to report all the items needed for others to include your results in research syntheses. The experimenter's prime audience is no longer the scholars and leaders of the day. A much larger audience will use solid research results for many decades to come.

BECOMING A RANDOM ASSIGNER

We conclude our introduction to experimental criminology with a recruitment poster. Do you have what it takes to become what Weiss (2002) calls a "random assigner"? Can you tell by now what personal qualities are needed to do this well? Can you tell how the personal experience of experimental criminologists differs from the daily life of other field researchers and from people who analyze existing data?

In our view, experimental criminology requires a more extroverted personality than is needed for scholarship in general. Like experimental physics, EC needs large teams of people to cooperate. Leadership skills are essential to fostering that cooperation. Someone who would enjoy being a university department chair would probably enjoy and do well at EC. But such people are generally rare in academic life.

Experimental criminology may also require a greater readiness to accept the big problems that cannot be changed quickly, in order to attack smaller problems that can be. Social and economic injustice has deep roots and structural support. But much of what we do about it may only make things worse. Experimentalists can at least find better ways to do no harm and perhaps more good.

The best experimental criminology will feature the best traits of scholarship in general: erudition, broad theoretical vision, a nuanced grasp of causal inference, and abiding curiosity. The "sacred spark" that drives all scholarship is especially needed to persevere in the face of the many setbacks that EC suffers. Even Einstein might see it as a field involving more than "mere experimental skill."

So think it over. Experimental criminology is looking for a few good women.

And men.

Further Readings: Boruch, 1997; Gottfredson et al., 2006; Sherman, 2009.

REFERENCES

Angrist JD (2006) Instrumental variables methods in experimental criminological research: What, why and how. J Exp Criminol 2(1):23–44

Angrist J, Imbens G, Rubin D (1996). J Am Stat Assoc 91:444–455

Ares CE, Rankin A, Sturz H (1963) The Manhattan Bail Project: an interim report on the use of pre-trial parole. N Y Univ Law Rev 38:67–95

Ariel B (2008) Seminar presented to the Jerry Lee Centre for Experimental Criminology, Institute of Criminology, University of Cambridge, October

Ariel B (2009) Taxation and compliance: an experimental study. Doctoral Dissertation, Hebrew University of Jerusalem, Israel

Barnes G, Ahlman L, Gill C, Kurtz E, Sherman L, Malvestuto R (2010) Low-intensity community supervision for low-risk offenders: a randomized, controlled trial. Journal of Experimental Criminology, forthcoming

Berk RA (2005) Randomized experiments as the bronze standard. J Exp Criminol 1(4):417–433

Bliss M (1999) William Osler: a life in medicine. University of Toronto Press, Toronto

Boruch RF (1997) Randomized experiments for policy and planning. Sage, Newbury Park, CA

Bradley RS, Jones PD (1992) Climate since A.D. 1500. Routledge, London

Braithwaite J (1989) Crime, Shame and Reintegration. Cambridge: Cambridge University Press

Braithwaite J (2002) Restorative Justice and Responsive Regulation. NY: Oxford U. Press

Buerger M, Cohn E, Petrosino A (1995) Defining the "hotspots of crime": operationalizing theoretical concepts for field research. In: Eck JE, Weisburd D (eds) Crime and place. Crime Prevention Studies, vol 4. Police Executive Research Forum. Criminal Justice Press, Monsey, NY

Campbell DT, Stanley JC (1963) Experimental and quasi-experimental designs for research. Rand-McNally, Chicago, IL

Cook TD, Campbell DT (1979) Quasi-experimentation: design and analysis issues for field settings. Rand-McNally, Chicago

Einstein A, Infeld L ([1938] 1971) The evolution of physics, 2nd edn. Downloaded at Google Books on 12 July 2009

Eisner MP (2009) No effects in independent prevention trials: can we reject the cynical view? J Exp Criminol 5(2):163–183

Erwin BS (1986) Turning up the heat on probationers in Georgia. Fed Probat 50:17–24

Farrington DP (1983) Randomized experiments on crime and justice. In: Tonry M, Morris N (eds) Crime and justice: an annual review of research, vol 4. University of Chicago Press, Chicago, IL

Farrington DP (2003) British randomized experiments on crime and justice. Ann Am Acad Polit Soc Sci 589:150–169

Farrington DP, Knight BJ (1980) Stealing from a "Lost" letter: effects of victim characteristics. Crim Justice Behav 7:423–436

Farrington DP, Welsh BC (2005) Randomized experiments in criminology: what have we learned in the last two decades? J Exp Criminol 1(1):9–38

Federal Judicial Center (1981) Experimentation in the law. Federal Judicial Center, Administrative Office of the US Courts, Washington, DC

Fisher RA (1935) The design of experiments. Oliver and Boyd, Edinburgh

Gartin PR (1992) A Replication and Extension of the Minneapolis Domestic Violence Experiment. PhD. Dissertation, University of Maryland

Gibbs JP (1975) Crime, punishment and deterrence. Elsevier, New York

Gladwell M (2005) Blink: the power of thinking without thinking. Little, Brown, Boston, MA

Gladwell M (2008) Outliers: the story of success. Little, Brown, Boston, MA

Glaser BG, Strauss AL (1967) The discovery of grounded theory: strategies for qualitative research. Aldine Publishing Company, Chicago, IL

Gorman DM, Huber JC (2009) The social construction of "evidence-based" drug prevention programs: a reanalysis of data from the Drug Abuse Resistance Education (DARE) Program. Eval Rev 33:396–414

Hanley D (2006) Appropriate services: examining the case classification principle. J Offender Rehabil 42:1–22

Home Office (2005) The economic and social costs of crime against individuals and households 2003/04. Home office on-line report 30/05 downloaded on 26 July, 2009 from http://www.homeoffice.gov.uk/rds/pdfs05/rdsolr3005.pdf

Kirk DS (2009) A natural experiment on residential change and recidivism: lessons from hurricane Katrina. Am Sociol Rev 74(3):484–504

Laub J, Sampson R (2003) Shared Beginnings, Duivergent Lives. Cambridge: Harvard University Press

Loudon I (2002) Ignaz Phillip Semmelweis' studies of death in childbirth. The James Lind Library (http://www.jameslindlibrary.org). Accessed FxTuesday 4 August 2009

Palmer T, Petrosino A (2003) The "experimenting agency". The California Youth Authority Research Division. Eval Rev 27:228–266

Pate T, McCullough JW, Bowers R, Ferra A (1976) Kansas City Peer Review Panel: An Evaluation Report. Washington, DC: Police Foundation

Paternoster R, Brame R, Bachman R, Sherman L. (1997) Do fair procedures matter? The effect of procedural justice on spouse assault. Law Soc Rev 31(1):163–204

Piantadosi S (1997) Clinical trials: a methodologic perspective. Wiley, New York

Pocock SJ, Hughes MD, Lee RJ (1987) Statistical problems in the reporting of clinical trials. A survey of three medical journals. N Engl J Med 317:426–432

Salsburg D (2001) The lady tasting tea: how statistics revolutionized science in the twentieth century. Henry Holt, New York

Shapland J, Atkinson A, Atkinson H, Dignan J, Edwards L, Hibbert J, Howes M, Johnstone J, Robinson G, Sorsby A (2008) Does restorative justice affect reconviction? The fourth report from the evaluation of three schemes. Ministry of Justice Research Series 10/08, June. Ministry of Justice, London

Sherman LW (1979) The case for the research police department. Police Mag 2(6):58–59

Sherman LW (1992) Policing Domestic Violence: Experiments and Dilemmas. NY: Free Press

Sherman LW (1993) Defiance, deterrence and irrelevance: a theory of the criminal sanction. J Res Crim and Delin 30:445–473

Sherman LW (2006) To develop and test: the inventive difference between evaluation and experimentation. J Exp Criminol 2:393–406

Sherman LW (2007) The power few: experimental criminology and the reduction of harm. The 2006 Joan McCord Prize Lecture. J Exp Criminol 3(4):299–321

Sherman LW (2009) Evidence and liberty: the promise of experimental criminology. Criminol Crim Justice 9:5–28

Sherman LW, Berk RA (1984) The specific deterrent effects of arrest for domestic assault. Am Sociol Rev 49:261–271

Sherman LW, Rogan DP (1995a) Effects of gun seizures on gun violence: "hot spots" patrol in Kansas city. Justice Q 12(4):673–693

Sherman LW, Rogan DP (1995b) Deterrent effects of police raids on crack houses: a randomized controlled experiment. Justice Q 12(4):755–781

Sherman LW, Strang H (2004a) Verdicts or inventions? Interpreting randomized controlled trials in criminology. Am Behav Sci 47(5):575–607

Sherman LW, Strang H (2004b) Experimental ethnography: the marriage of qualitative and quantitative research. In: Anderson E, Brooks SN, Gunn R, Jones N (eds) Annals of the American academy of political and social science, vol 595, pp 204–222

Sherman LW, Strang H (2010) Doing experimental criminology. In: Gadd D, Karstedt S, Messner S (eds) Handbook of criminological research methods. Sage, Thousand Oaks, CA

Sherman LW, Weisburd D (1995) General deterrent effects of police patrol in crime hot spots: a randomized, controlled trial. Justice Q 12(4):635–648

Sherman LW, Smith DA, Schmidt J, Rogan DP (1992) Crime, punishment and stake in conformity: legal and informal control of domestic violence. Am Sociol Rev 57:680–690

Sherman LW, Strang H, Woods D (2000) Recidivism patterns in the Canberra reintegrative shaming experiments (RISE). Downloaded on 5 August 2009 at http://www.aic.gov.au/criminal_justice_system/rjustice/rise/aspx

Sherman LW, Strang H, Angel C, Woods D, Barnes G, Bennett S, Rossner M, Inkpen N (2005) Effects of face-to-face restorative justice on victims of crime in four randomized controlled trials. J Exp Criminol 1(3):367–395

The Multisite Violence Prevention Project (2008) Impact of a universal school-based violence prevention program on social-cognitive outcomes. Prev Sci 9(4):231–244

Tilley N (2009) Sherman vs Sherman: realism vs rhetoric. Criminol Crim Justice 9(2):135–144

Tröhler U (2003) 'James Lind and Scurvy: 1747 to 1795.' The James Lind Library (http://www.jameslindlibrary.org). Downloaded 4 August, 2009

Weisburd D (1993) Design sensitivity in criminal justice experiments. Crime and Justice 17:337–379

Weiss C (2002) What to do until the random assigner comes. In: Mosteller F, Boruch R (eds) Evidence matters. Brookings Institution, Washington, DC

Welsh BC, Farrington DP, Sherman LW (2001) Costs and benefits of preventing crime. Westview Press, Boulder, CO

Appendix 1

CRIM-PORT 1.0:

Criminological Protocol for Operating Randomized Trials

@ 2009 by Lawrence W. Sherman and Heather Strang

INSTRUCTIONS: Please use this form to enter information directly into the WORD document as the protocol for your registration on Cambridge University's Jerry Lee Centre of Experimental Criminology's *Registry of EXperiments in Policing Strategy and Tactics* (REX-POST) or the separate *Registry of Experiments in Corrections Strategy and Tactics* (REX-COST) at http://www.crim.cam.ac.uk/experiments.

CONTENTS:

1. Name and Hypotheses
2. Organizational Framework
3. Unit of Analysis
4. Eligibility Criteria
5. Pipeline: Recruitment or Extraction of Cases

6. Timing
7. Random Assignment
8. Treatment and Comparison Elements
9. Measuring and Managing Treatments
10. Measuring Outcomes
11. Analysis Plan
12. Due Date and Dissemination Plan

1. Name and Hypotheses

A. **Name of Experiment**_____

B. Principal Investigator
   (Name)_____
   (Employer)_____

C. 1st Co-Principal Investigator
   (Name)_____
   (Employer)_____

D. 2d Co-Principal Investigator (Name)_____
   (Employer)_____

E. **General Hypothesis**: (Experimental or Primary Treatment) _____ causes (less or more) _____ (crime or justice outcome) _____ than (comparison or control treatment) _____.

F. **Specific Hypotheses**:

   1. List all variations of treatment delivery to be tested.
   2. List all variations of outcome measures to be tested.
   3. List all subgroups to be tested for all varieties of outcome measures.

2. Organizational Framework: Check only one from a, b, c, or d

A. **In-House** delivery of treatments, data collection and analysis ___

B. **Dual Partnership**: Operating agency delivers treatments with independent research organization providing random assignment, data collection, analysis ___

   Name of Operating Agency_____
   Name of Research Organization_____

C. **Multi-Agency Partnership**: Operating agencies delivers treatments with independent research organization providing random assignment, data collection, analysis

   Name of Operating Agency
   1_____
   Name of Operating Agency
   2_____
   Name of Operating Agency
   3_____
   Name of Research
   Organization_____

D. **Other Framework** (describe in detail).

3. Unit of Analysis
Check only one

__A. People (describe role: offenders, victims, etc.)_____
__B. Places (describe category: school, corner, face-block, etc.)_____
__C. Situations (describe: police-citizen encounters, fights, etc.)_____
__D. Other (describe)_____

4. Eligibility Criteria

A. **Criteria Required** (list all)
B. **Criteria for Exclusion** (list all)

5. Pipeline: Recruitment or Extraction of Cases (answer all questions)

A. Where will cases come from?
B. Who will obtain them?
C. How will they be identified?
D. How will each case be screened for eligibility?
E. Who will register the case identifiers prior to random assignment?
F. What social relationships must be maintained to keep cases coming?
G. Has a Phase I (no-control, "dry-run") test of the pipeline and treatment process been conducted? If so,

- How many cases were attempted to be treated
- How many treatments were successfully delivered
- How many cases were lost during treatment delivery

6. Timing: Cases come into the experiment in (check only one)

A. A trickle-flow process, one case at a time____
B. A single batch assignment____
C. Repeated batch assignments____
D. Other (describe below)____

7. Random Assignment

A. How is random assignment sequence to be generated?
(coin-toss, every Nth case, and other nonrandom tools are banned from CCR-RCT).
Check one from 1, 2 or 3 below

1. Random numbers table → case number sequence → sealed envelopes with case numbers outside and treatment assignment inside, with 2-sheet paper surrounding treatment____
2. Random numbers case–treatment generator program in secure computer____
3. Other (please describe below)____

B. Who is entitled to issue random assignments of treatments?
Role:
Organization:
C. How will random assignments be recorded in relation to case registration?
Name of data base:
Location of data entry:
Persons performing data entry:

8. Treatment and Comparison Elements

A. Experimental or Primary Treatment

    1. What elements must happen, with dosage level (if measured) indicated.
      Element A:
      Element B:
      Element C:
      Other Elements:
    2. What elements must *not* happen, with dosage level (if measured) indicated.
      Element A:
      Element B:
      Element C:
      Other Elements:

B. Control or Secondary Comparison Treatment

    3. What elements must happen, with dosage level (if measured) indicated.
      Element A:
      Element B:
      Element C:
      Other Elements:
    4. What elements must not happen, with dosage level (if measured) indicated.
      Element A:
      Element B:
      Element C:
      Other Elements:

9. Measuring and Managing Treatments

A. Measuring

    1. How will treatments be measured?
    2. Who will measure them?
    3. How will data be collected?
    4. How will data be stored?
    5. Will data be audited?
    6. If audited, who will do it?
    7. How will data collection reliability be estimated?
    8. Will data collection vary by treatment type?
      If so, how?

B. Managing

    1. Who will see the treatment measurement data?
    2. How often will treatment measures be circulated to key leaders?
    3. If treatment integrity is challenged, whose responsibility is correction?

10. Measuring and Monitoring Outcomes

A. Measuring

    1. How will outcomes be measured?
    2. Who will measure them?

3. How will data be collected?
4. How will data be stored?
5. Will data be audited?
6. If audited, who will do it?
7. How will data collection reliability be estimated?
8. Will data collection vary by treatment type?
   If so, how?

B. Monitoring

1. How often will outcome data be monitored?
2. Who will see the outcome monitoring data?
3. When will outcome measures be circulated to key leaders?
4. If experiment finds early significant differences, what procedure is to be followed?

11. Analysis Plan

A. Which outcome measure is considered to be the primary indicator of a difference between experimental treatment and comparison group?
B. What is the minimum sample size to be used to analyze outcomes?
C. Will all analyses employ an intention-to-treat framework?
D. What is the threshold below which the percent Treatment-as-Delivered would be so low as to bar any analysis of outcomes?
E. Who will do the data analysis?
F. What statistic will be used to estimate effect size?
G. What statistic will be used to calculate P values?
H. What is the magnitude of effect needed for a $P = 0.05$ difference to have an 80% chance of detection with the projected sample size (optional but recommended calculation of power curve) for the primary outcome measure.

12. Dissemination Plan

A. What is the date by which the project agrees to file its first report on CCR-RCT? (report of delay, preliminary findings, or final result).
B. Does the project agree to file an update every 6 months from date of first report until date of final report?
C. Will preliminary and final results be published, in a 250-word abstract, on CCR-RCT as soon as available?
D. Will CONSORT requirements be met in the final report for the project? (See http://www.consort-statement.org/)
E. What organizations will need to approve the final report? (include any funders or sponsors)
F. Do all organizations involved agree that a final report shall be published after a maximum review period of 6 months from the principal investigator's certification of the report as final?
G. Does principal investigator agree to post any changes in agreements affecting items 12A to 12F above?
H. Does principal investigator agree to file a final report within 2 years of cessation of experimental operations, no matter what happened to the experiment?

(e.g., "random assignment broke down after 3 weeks and the experiment was cancelled" or "only 15 cases were referred in the first 12 months and experiment was suspended").

An Introduction to Experimental Criminology: Lawrence W. Sherman

Background   Experimental criminology (EC) is scientific knowledge about crime and justice discovered from random assignment of different conditions in large field tests.

1. This method is the preferred way to estimate the average effects of one variable on another, holding all other variables constant
2. While the experimental method is not intended to answer all research questions in criminology, it can be used far more often than most criminologists assume

   - Opportunities are particularly promising in partnership with criminal justice agencies

   Note: The goal of this chapter is to help its readers improve the design and conduct of criminological experiments. This chapter's method is to describe the necessary steps and preferred decisions in planning, conducting, completing, analyzing, reporting, and synthesizing high-quality randomized controlled trials (RCTs) in criminology.

EC use   The highest and best use of experimental criminology is to develop and test theoretically coherent ideas about reducing harm (Sherman 2006, 2007), rather than just "evaluating" government programs.

- Those tests, in turn, can help to accumulate an integrated body of grounded theory in which experimental evidence plays a crucial role.
- The advantages depend entirely on the capability of the experimenters to insure success in achieving the many necessary elements of an unbiased comparison:

1. Many randomized field experiments in criminology suffer flaws that could have been avoided with better planning.

Metaphors for experiments   The success of experimental criminology may depend on choosing the right metaphor.

- The most useful metaphor is constructing a building.
- The recurrent metaphor of constructing a building helps to illustrate the order of steps to take for best results.
- The steps presented in this chapter begin with the intellectual property of every experiment: formulating the research question.
- Once a protocol is agreed and approved, the experimenters (like builders) must find and "contract" with a wide range of agents and others to best construct and sustain the experiment.
- When and if all these steps are completed, the experiment will be ready for analysis.
- This chapter briefly maps out those principles and the arguments for and against fundamentally different analytic approaches in EC.

Part 1: Intellectual Property: Formulating the Research Question

Great experiments   Great experiments in criminology are arguably based on three criteria:

1. They test theoretically central hypotheses – experimentalists can do the most good for science when they are the most focused on the theoretical implications of their experiments.
2. They eliminate as many competing explanations as possible – it is the capacity to limit ambiguity by eliminating competing explanations that makes EC so important to criminological theory.
3. They show one intervention to be far more cost effective than others – rising interest in this principle alone has done more to encourage evidence-based government programs than any other.

   - Experiments must be planned to measure costs of delivering programs, both in a start-up phase and in a "rollout" model with perhaps more efficiencies from mass production.

Note: Putting these criteria together in the formulation of an experimental research question may seem to be more a matter of "art" than of science. Such a judgment would demean the importance of intuition, inspiration, and insight in science, as in many fields involving complex decisions.

Part 2: Social Foundation: Developing a "Field Station"

Field stations   The history of experimental field science shows many examples of research centered in what looks much like an indoor laboratory – but with a crucial difference – studies consider questions that cannot be answered in a laboratory

   - Field research stations have collected various kinds of observational data systematically in the same places for at least 300 years.

- By the 1950s, hospitals associated with medical schools took on the same character as field stations, linking teaching and research with a large number of clinical randomized controlled trials (RCT)
- From at least the 1960s, similar concentrations of field experiments have been found in the criminal justice system
- The concept of a field station where data are recorded and experiments can last for many decades is an explicit vision for how to conduct experiments in criminology

Social elements   The key to holding an experiment together is understanding a cognitive map of its social elements which include the funders, the executive leadership of an operating agency, the mid-level operating liaison person, the agents delivering treatments, and where necessary the agents providing cases.

Part 3: Deciding on the Experimental Protocol

Experiment blueprints

The future is clear: experimental criminology will need to design blueprints and stick to them, absent approval from oversight bodies.

- It can be argued that EC will be substantially improved by wider use of experimental protocols.
- One reason is so many RCTs in criminology have either violated good design standards or failed to report fundamental information.
- CONSORT – CONsolidated Standards On Reporting of Trials can lead to better planning of experiments with protocols that anticipate reporting requirements.
- The CONSORT checklist includes 22 reporting elements

Title & Abstract	Background	Participants
Interventions	Objectives	Outcomes
Sample size	Sequence generation	Allocation Concealment
Implementation	Statistical Methods	Participant flow
Recruitment	Baseline data	Numbers analyzed
Outcomes & estimation	Ancillary analyses	Adverse events
Interpretation	Generalizability	Overall evidence
Blinding (Masking)		

Note: CONSORT alone is not enough. A reporting system does not tell you how to design a protocol for an experiment before it starts. It only tells you what readers need to know after it is finished. Included in this chapter is the first version of a standard protocol format for experiments in criminology. The appendix lays out the elements of the protocol.

Part 4: "Contracts": Recruiting, Consulting, and Training of Key People

Contracts Using the construction metaphor, experiments must be built by contractors (who may also have been the architect) who know how to "contract" with the right people (for money or *pro bono* love of the research).

- Principal investigators in experimental criminology will generally be PhD-level academics.
- The experimental criminologist – or "random assigner," serving as principal investigator should be seen supported and held accountable as the primary leader of the experiment
- Other key roles are the field coordinator, the agency liaison, the data manager, and the agent supplying the cases

Part 5: Starting and Sustaining the Experiment

Design   How an experiment begins depends on how it must be designed.

- There is nothing easier than launching a "batch" random assignment project, and nothing harder than launching a "trickle-flow" random assignment project.

    1. While months or years of preparation may be required for batch random assignment, they sometimes offer a capacity to literally push a button that will launch the experiment.
    2. Trickle-flow experiments, in contrast, may require the cooperation of hundreds of people to supply eligible cases for random assignment – After launch, the even greater challenge with trickle-flow experiments is to sustain the case flow.

Part 6: Supplying: Obtaining Cases

Supplying cases   The biggest challenge in trickle-flow experiments is to find and extract the cases that are "leaking" out of the experimental sample.

- Increasingly, information technology applications can be used to identify the missed cases and the agents who could have referred them to the experimenters.
- If the agency strongly supports the experiment, there may be ways to encourage agents who do not refer the cases to start doing so.
- But if the agency will not, or cannot, attempt to persuade those who can contribute cases to an experiment, the only tool left is the ingenuity of the site coordinator or principal investigator.

Part 7: Screening for Eligibility

Avoiding ineligible cases   The best solution to the problem of including ineligible cases is to prevent it prior to random assignment.

- The best time to exclude ineligible cases is when writing the *budget*: making sure that you spend enough money to have an independent check on the eligibility of cases.

Part 8: Assigning Treatments

Assignment system   Saving money on random assignment costs is penny wise and pound foolish.

- The chance for biased selection of eligible cases can be virtually eliminated by having research staff answer the phone by a secure computer, take the identifying details of the officers and the suspects, and then open a numbered envelope sealed with red sealing wax
- The credibility of an independent random assignment system is well worth the increased budget.
- It is important to design a protocol that separates random assignment from operating staff.

Part 9: Delivering Treatments Consistently

Protocol matters

Anything that creates differences within the units of analysis, or in the way treatments are delivered, can cause a misleading result: no significant difference despite a "true," underlying difference.

- While eligibility criteria can limit the differences in cases (for example, in age or prior record), it is much harder for a protocol to insure consistency in the treatment
- The best plan is to invest heavily in measurements, such as observations and interviews – even then, however, it is much harder to *deliver* consistency than to *measure* consistency
- Repeating experiments done in Canberra Australia and then again in England showed that protocol matters and that as a result, consistency was far higher in England.

Part 10: Measuring Treatments Delivered

Failure to measure

The failure to measure treatment delivery is one of the most common in experimental criminology.

- Numerous experiments assume that once treatment is assigned it will be delivered; yet when budgets are invested in measuring delivery, it shows at least some portion of cases in which delivery did not occur.
- Great sums can be saved by using two kinds of electronic data:
  1. One is the Automatic Radio Locator System (ARLS) that will record where each and every police officer is at all times.
  2. The other technology is CCTV cameras, which are trained on many hot spots and can record what happens 100% of the time.

Part 11: Measuring Outcomes

Principles Several principles can help in measuring outcomes.

- Choose universal measures over low response rate measures
- Choose crime frequency over prevalence
- Choose a seriousness index over categorical counts
- Choose one measure as primary at the outset

Part 12: Analyzing Results

Analysis issues

There are two issues to supplement what textbooks say on analysis of results.

1. The first is to seek simplicity in analysis.
2. The other is test policies, not treatments – in general, Intention-To-Treat analysis makes the most sense in keeping the analysis simple.

   - As long as the experiment is limited to the random assignment of policy and cannot control treatment, the honest thing to do is to analyze the effects of policy.

Part 13: Communicating Results

Avoid   Simplicity is also a great virtue in communicating results.
complexity

- Academics inclined to making fine distinctions are often impatient with simplicity, but they lack evidence to support the claim that complexity will lead to better policymaking or even better science.

Part 14: Synthesizing Results

The goal of   The goal of research synthesis is to draw conclusions from a universe of all
synthesis   tests of a single hypothesis.

- Randomized experiments are especially valuable for systematic reviews and meta-analysis of accumulated tests of a program or policy.
- Even those who are generally critical of the statistical basis of meta-analysis are ready to endorse its use when only randomized experiments are included in the calculations

Part 15: Becoming a Random Assigner

Recruitment   Who makes the best random assigner?

- Experimental criminology requires a more extroverted personality than is needed for scholarship in general.
- Experimental criminology may also require a greater readiness to accept the big problems that cannot be changed quickly, in order to attack smaller problems that can be.
- The best experimental criminology will feature the best traits of scholarship in general: erudition, broad theoretical vision, a nuanced grasp of causal inference, and abiding curiosity.

Appendix   The appendix contains a Criminological Protocol for Operating Randomized Trials.

This information map was prepared with the support of the Jerry Lee Foundation and the assistance of Herbert Fayer.

CHAPTER 21

Randomized Block Designs

BARAK ARIEL AND DAVID P. FARRINGTON

INTRODUCTION

In randomized controlled trials, the experimental and control groups should be relatively balanced. This balance is achieved through a process of random assignment of study participants into treatment and control groups because the researcher can control for any preexisting differences between the two groups. Because participants are assigned to groups by chance, the likelihood that the experimental group will turn out to be different from the control group is significantly minimized when compared with a nonrandom assignment procedure.

But while this simple random assignment procedure is likely to provide an overall balance, it does not guarantee that there will be complete balance on any particular trait (see Altman et al. 2001; Berger and Exner 1999; Proschan 1994; Senn 1989, 1994; Wei and Zhang 2001; Weisburd and Taxman 2000). Unbalance is usually associated with a lower statistical power of the research design (see Lipsey 1990; Weisburd and Taxman 2000). So, interpreting the results from an unbalanced trial may lead to reaching biased conclusions about the true outcome effect of the tested intervention (Torgerson and Torgerson 2003). When the researcher anticipates that the groups may be unbalanced, certain measures should be taken.

It was (and perhaps still is) commonly assumed that increasing the size of the sample is associated with more balance and, in turn, with higher statistical power. But, as Weisburd et al. (1993) have shown, there is in practice little relationship between sample size and statistical power. Larger samples are likely to include a wider diversity of participants than smaller investigations. Because it is necessary to establish very broad eligibility requirements in order to gain a larger number of cases, large trials attract a more diverse pool of participants. This increases the variability in the data as there is more "noise," which makes it difficult to detect the effect of the treatment. Therefore, the design benefits of larger trials may be offset by the implementation and management difficulties they present.

Clinicians and statisticians have developed different research designs to more adequately handle unbalanced groups or high variability, such as the randomized block design (RBD). Generally speaking, if we know before we administer the treatment that certain participants may vary in significant ways, we can utilize this information to our advantage. We should use a statistical design in which participants are not simply randomly allocated directly into experimental and control groups. Instead, they are randomly allocated into groups within blocks, in a design commonly referred to as the RBD.

A.R. Piquero and D. Weisburd (eds.), *Handbook of Quantitative Criminology*,
DOI 10.1007/978-0-387-77650-7_21, © Springer Science + Business Media, LLC 2010,
First softcover printing 2011

Though generally ignored in criminal justice, variations of this design were implemented in some of the most influential studies in recent years, such as the Minneapolis Hot-Spots Experiment (Sherman and Weisburd 1995), the Jersey City Drug Market Experiment (Weisburd and Green 1995), the Jersey City Problem-Oriented Policing Experiment at violent places (Braga et al. 1999) and others. Recently, Weisburd et al. (2008) have used this design in an experiment on the effects of Risk-Focused Policing at Places (RFPP) approach to preventing and reducing juvenile delinquency. Before administering the treatment, they found a considerable variability in the characteristics of violent places selected for the study. This variability jeopardized the statistical power of the evaluation. For example, if we assume that police are more likely to be successful in addressing problems in the school domain than they are in the community domain, then by using simple randomization, the experimental group comprised of places in which this approach is implemented may result in more places with high risk factor scores in the school domain by chance alone. In this case, observation of treatment impacts will be more difficult to detect when there is a large variability or "noise" in the assessment of study outcomes. The data were thus more adequately managed under a RBD.

In the Jersey City Drug Market Experiment, Weisburd and Green (1995) tested the effects of a drug enforcement strategy developed for the drug market in Jersey City. The researchers identified 56 places of increased drug activity, which were then randomized in statistical blocks to experimental and control conditions. This, as well as other hot-spot experiments (e.g., Sherman et al. 1989; Sherman and Weisburd 1995), benefit from a RBD because it decreases the variations that characterize places, such as in terms of the drug activity, structural and cultural characteristics in the identified hot spots. An examination of the distribution of arrest and call activity in the hot-spots before the experiment revealed that the places sample falls into four distinct groups: very high arrest and call activity, and the high, medium, and low activity. Therefore, hot spots were randomly allocated to experimental and control conditions within each of these four groups.

RBDs can also be used in non place-based experiments. For example, similar issues arise in analyses of individuals in schools, prisons and other environments, that can also be regarded as blocks, for the purpose of the analyses (such as in Farrington and Ttofi, 2009). A large randomized controlled trial was conducted in order to test the hypothesis that differences in wording of letters sent to taxpayers in Israel would affect various aspects of their taxpaying behavior, such as how much money they are willing to report and pay to the tax authority (Ariel 2008). Nearly 17,000 taxpayers were randomly assigned to different groups, each receiving a different type of letter. However, a large sample of taxpayers introduced high variability. For example, the sample included very poor taxpayers as well as very rich taxpayers. The size of the sample also increased the likelihood that in one of the study groups, there would be a disproportionally larger number of extremely rich taxpayers, so their effect on the results could skew the conclusion. Therefore, the sample was divided, before random assignment, into blocks of income levels. Within each of these income-level blocks, the participants were then randomly allocated into the different letter groups. Therefore, this procedure allows for measurement of not only the overall effect of letters, but also of specific effects within the blocks (i.e., effect of letters on participants with different income levels) the data can then be analyzed using an ordinary analysis of variance and other commonly used statistics. However, over the years more complex methods have been suggested for analyzing these designs (see Chow and Liu 2004; Dean and Voss 1999; Friedman et al. 1985; Lachin 1988b; Matts and Lachin 1988; Schulz and Grimes 2002; Yusuf et al. 1984), but these go beyond the scope of this chapter.

In this chapter, we will explore the RBD. We will briefly review some the threats that cannot be adequately resolved when using the simple randomization procedure, but can be when using RBD. We will then show how the design works, and introduce four particular models of this design. Each type is more adequate for certain test conditions. We will conclude by discussing more general issues related to the design, particularly why the benefits of using it are too large to ignore.

LIMITATIONS OF SIMPLE RANDOMIZATION DESIGNS

The simple, or complete, randomization design (CRD) is the most prevalent method of random assignment in criminal justice research (Ariel 2009). Under CRD, a randomly chosen subset of units n_a out of n units is assigned to treatment a and $n_b = n - n_a$ units are assigned to treatment b. In this way, the experimental and control groups should be equivalent, in all measured and unmeasured extraneous variables.

But as we have reviewed in the introduction, CRDs are less adequate to deal with certain statistical threats, such as high variability between the participants in the study, or when the researcher anticipates that the groups will be unbalanced. When the data are indeed character-ized by high variability or imbalance, it decreases the ability of the researcher to determine the true effects of the intervention. There is a large body of literature which discusses the reasons for, as well as the adverse implications of, this threat (Kernan et al. 1990: 20, Lachin 1988a, b; Palta and Amini 1982; Lachin et al. 1988; Pocock 1979). Some of these studies further show that CRDs are less adequate to deal with certain practical constraints, such as those asso-ciated with the studies in which eligible participants are assigned to either treatment(s) or no-treatment in a sequential order (Pocock and Simon 1975; Proschan 1994). In light of these and other limitations of the simple randomization technique, alternative random allocation procedures have emerged.

The Randomized Complete-Block Design

The Randomized Complete-Block Design (RCBD), sometimes referred to as the simple complete-block design, is a frequently used experimental design in biomedical research (Cochran and Cox 1957; Lagakos and Pocock 1984; Abou-El-Fotouh 1976; see also Hill 1951; Fisher 1935; Ostle and Malone 2000: 372), but it is quite rare in criminal jus-tice research (Ariel 2009). It is often adequate when there are "several hundred participants" or less (Friedman et al. 1985: 75). The experiments reviewed in the introduction are all examples of this design.

The RCBD is used in order to decrease the variance in the data (Lachin 1988a). Unlike CRDs, where units are unrestrictedly distributed at random to either treatment or control (or more than two groups, as the case may be), under the RCBD model, units are allocated randomly to either treatment or control within pre-identified blocks. The blocking process is established based on a certain criterion which is intended to divide the sample, prior to assignment, into subgroups that are intended to be homogeneous (Hallstrom and Davis 1988; Simon 1979). Then, within blocks, units are randomly assigned to either treatment or control conditions.

It is important that the administration of the treatment in terms of potency, consistency and procedures, is identical in each block. This means that the overall experimental design is replicated as many times as there are blocks, and each block can be viewed as a disparate yet identical trial within the overall study (Rosenberger and Lachin 2002). If the administration of the treatment is different in each block, it becomes rather difficult to analyze the treatment effect (see Ostle and Malone 2000; Matts and Lachin 1988; Rosenberger and Lachin 2002).

THE HYPOTHETICAL CASE OF A RCBD: THE DRUG TREATMENT EXPERIMENT.

Consider the following hypothetical trial, as a way to show the benefits of blocking. Imagine a trial with one experimental group consisting of 52 drug-addicted offenders, treated in an antidrug program. Another group of 48 drug-addicted offenders serve as the control group, receiving no drug treatment. The allocation to treatment and control is done randomly. The experiment is conducted in order to evaluate the merits of the program, where success is nominally defined by a decrease in drug use (on a scale of 1–8, 8 being the highest and 1 being lowest). However, unlike other drug treatment programs, this particular treatment is very costly. Therefore, unless very high success rates are registered, the facilitators will be unlikely to recommend its implementation in the future. All eligible participants selected for this trial are known to be drug abusers before entering the program. Prior to the treatment, the drug use level was not statistically different between the two groups (both averaging about 5.85 on the said scale). At the 6-month follow-up period, drug use was measured again for both groups. Results show that the program was successful: there was an overall 30% reduction in the treated experimental group, when compared with the untreated control group. A visual depiction is presented in Fig. 21.1. At the same time, considering the costs of the program, the policy implication is to not recommend further implementation of the program.

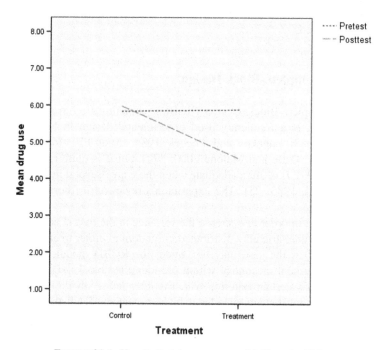

FIGURE 21.1. Hypothetical drug treatment trial: Phase I – CRD.

However, a closer look at the distribution of the pre-test scores indicates that the sample is comprised of drug abusers of four different types of drugs (with no crossovers): marijuana, MDMA, alcohol, and heroin. Generally speaking, it could be hypothesized that drug abusers of these different drugs are not addicted in the same way (based on both pharmacological and psychobiological qualities of these substances). Therefore, the prospective success rate of the drug intervention program is also hypothesized to be disparate for each subgroup; it is likely that getting clean from a heroin addiction or alcohol addiction is more difficult than from marijuana or MDMA. Thus, dividing the overall sample based on the type of drug should produce more homogeneous subgroups, whose chance to get clean is inevitably different across these subgroups. Even if the strength of the effect within each block is similar, blocking should give better estimates of the treatment effect, because of the decreased intrablock variance, or noise. Thus, a second experiment is conducted.

In the second experiment, the treatment is delivered in the very same intensity and method it was delivered when a complete randomization design was used. Nor do we make any modifications to the sampling of participants. Assuming that a similar group of participants was randomly selected, the overall 30% difference is also expected to be registered. However, because the treatment estimate is also comprised of the variability, the effect is larger within each block. In other words, the intrablock variance of the prognostic outcome is now less than the variability across the blocks, which makes it easier to detect stronger treatment effects. This is depicted in Fig. 21.2.

As can be seen, the treatment-to-control magnitude of difference is the same across blocks, but the intrablock difference is different, because there is less variance in the data. Furthermore, this disaggregation of the data into blocks indicates that the Heroin Block is less receptive to the treatment (6% decrease in drug use), as arguably expected from this

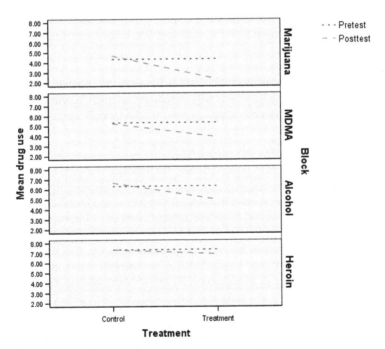

FIGURE 21.2. Hypothetical drug treatment trial: Phase II – CRBD.

subgroup, compared for example to the Marijuana Block or the MDMA Block (51% and 34% decrease, respectively). Therefore, the policy implication could then be to continue using the program for certain addictions in light of the high success rate, but not for others with a lower success rate.

This hypothetical trial was meant to show the conceptual groundwork for the RCBD. It shows how the researcher can benefit from blocking the data before random assignment, in a way that does not alter in any way the intervention or the actual allocation of participants to treatment or nontreatment. By blocking the participants, the potency of the drug program did not change. However, because the data are now classified in a way that homogenizes participants based on a qualitative criterion (type of drug), the variance within each block is smaller than the variance across the overall study.

Analyzing Randomized Block Designs

ORDINARY RBD.   There are different models of RBDs. In each one, there is a particular kind of statistical analysis that is most adequate. In this section, we introduce one that is commonly used in medical research: the ordinary RBD model. Here, we analyze the data by looking at effects caused by the treatment factor, by the blocking factor, or by the interaction between the treatment factor and the blocking factor. This design is particularly adequate when we believe that there is some sort of association between the trait which is used as a criterion for the blocks (e.g., crime level) and the trait(s) of the treatment condition (e.g., hotspot policing). There are cases when this assumption of association between the treatment and the blocking is not necessary, and therefore is ignored in the statistical analysis. But these scenarios are arguably more complex than the scope of this chapter, so specialized references should be consulted (see Canavos and Koutrouvelis 2008; Gacula 2005; Hoshmand 2006: 14; Hinkelmann and Kempthrone 1994; Kepner and Wackerly 1996; Liebetrau 1983; Matts and Lachin 1988; Milliken and Johnson 1996; Mottonen et al. 2003; Ostle and Malone 2000; Rosenberger and Lachin 2002).

One common method to analyze the RBD is by using an ordinary two-way ANOVA, or through a general linear model which will include an interaction term between the fixed treatment factor(s) and a random blocking factor term. The model can therefore be described as follows:

$$Y_{ijk} = \mu + \tau_i + \beta_j + (\tau\beta)_{ij} + \varepsilon_{ijk}$$

In this equation, Y_{ijk} represents any observed value for treatment factor (i), the blocking factor (j), and any additional effect that may exist because of the interaction between these two factors (k). The model can be, at least in theory, extended to account for an endless number of treatments and blocks. However, there is a limited number of interventions one research project can study, and naturally the number of blocks is directly affected by the number of variables on which the data can be blocked. In practice, however, it is usually the case that only one blocking factor will be used and it is often recommended that the number of blocks should not exceed the number of treatments (Gill 1984; Matts and Lachin 1988). There are also those who recommend to use only one treatment and one control conditions in each block, because the test statistic is considered more "stable" with two groups (see Canavos and Koutrouvelis 2008; Gacula 2005; Ostle and Malone 2000). Most importantly, however, is that each block will contain all treatments and that each treatment occurs an equal number of times in each block – hence the "completeness" characteristic of this design (Chow and Liu 2004: 136–140). Many of the experiments on policing crime in places are constructed this way, such as the ones reviewed in the introduction.

This notwithstanding, there are cases when more than one treatment factor or blocking factor should be used when there is good theoretical basis for further division of the sample. In a study of defiance, for example, it would be reasonable to block the data on several blocking factors, such as (a) categories of criminal background, (b) categories of psychological variables, and also (c) the amount of legitimacy the sanctioned offender ascribes to the sanctioning agent's behavior (Sherman 1993). But, how many blocking factors should be allowed before the design becomes too "messy" (see Milliken and Johnson 1996: 259)? Friedman et al. (1985: 69) claim that, for studies of 100 participants, blocking using up to 3 factors is still considered manageable. Pocock and Simon (1975) make a similar argument, showing that beyond three factors, imbalances can result in incomplete filling of blocks, which complicates the analysis.

Going back to the equation, μ signifies a grand mean, derived by the values of all units in the study and is considered a constant. The effect of the treatment is marked by τ_i, and the β_j element marks the blocking variable effect. The possible interaction between these two is shown as $(\tau\beta)_{ij}$.

Lastly, the error is represented by the ε_{ijk} term, which includes the two sources of residual variance that were not explained by the model. First, there is variance related to random and normally distributed differences in the sample or the population from which the sample was selected. These differences are assumed to equal out when the data are aggregated. Second, there is variance the researcher did not identify, but that has a systematic impact on the relationship between the treatment and the effect. The consequence of these errors is loss of statistical power of the test. So, researchers should try to avoid them as much as possible, for example by anticipating them in advance and creating better or more blocks (see Dean and Voss 1999: 299–301).

RANDOMIZED INCOMPLETE BLOCK DESIGNS.   The RCBDs described earlier are characterized by "completion," in the sense that each block is complete, including all treatments and all control slots. However, there are instances when it may not be possible to apply all treatments in every block. This is particularly the case when there are many treatments tested in one trial, or with many replications. On the one hand, a larger number of replications is usually a good thing because it translates into greater precision of the treatment effect estimate. However, this is not always feasible. For example, in a trial testing the effect of various prison-based treatments for sexual offenders, because of their level of perverted sexual cognition, some offenders may not be capable of entering the various programs offered, after the stage of random assignment. Another example may be a trial on the effect of intensive police patrols on crime reduction in a certain metropolitan city. The police may be unable to allocate enough police patrol units to the intensified crime hot-spots because of some other major police activity (such as patrolling in the Olympics). These examples can be better handled through a design that takes into account this incompleteness.

If all possible comparisons between different treatments are seen as important for the researcher, then each pair of treatments must appear together in a block the same number of times, and each treatment must be observed the same number of times in a block. Otherwise, it becomes difficult to analyze the effect of each treatment.

One way to somewhat circumvent this problem is by implementing an intent-to-treat (ITT) approach, which works by "ignoring empty cells," under a relatively relaxed assumption that missing data are proportionally distributed across study groups or blocks. However, ITT would usually mean that the effects of the treatment *policy* are tested, rather than the effects of the treatment *per se* (Lachin 2000). But, when a threat such as having incomplete blocks is

TABLE 21.1. Matrix of possible treatment pairings in a 12-participant X 4 treatments X 2-treatments-per-block study

Treatment type	Trial blocks					
	1	2	3	4	5	6
I	X	X	X			
II	X			X	X	
III		X		X		X
IV			X		X	X

known in advance, the overall design can and in fact should be modified. Otherwise, there is the risk that the analysis will be misleading.

One of the solutions suggested in the literature, which dates back to Yates (1936), is to use a balanced *in*complete block design, or BIBD (see Federer and Nguyen 2002; Fisher and Yates 1963; Milliken and Johnson 1996; Robinson 1972). In a BIBD, not all treatments occur in every block. However, all pairs of treatments (e.g., intervention and nonintervention) occur equally often in the same block. In this way, there are pairs of treatments that the researcher can compare: hence the "balance." The trick is to create enough blocks, so that all combination pairs will occur and thus be compared. Therefore, the number of blocks that are necessary for creating this treatment balance will be determined based on the number of treatments which can be administered in a single block.

The balance is guaranteed by the following procedure. We denote a as the number of treatments, and r as the number of times all treatments are tested in the trial. Therefore, $N = (a) \times (r)$. k is used to indicate the number of treatments that occur per block, and b is the number of blocks. Therefore, b can be calculated by N/k. Put together, these parameters should satisfy $(b) \times (k) = (a) \times (r)$.

Assume for example that there are 12 observations in a trial, with 4 possible treatments throughout the study. However, we know that only 2 treatments can occur in each block (that is, $k = 2$) because it would be too expensive, for example, to have all treatments running in all blocks. Therefore, this design is incomplete. The number of times each treatment should be run in the trial can be extracted by converting the above formula, such that $r = N/a$. Because there are 12 observations and each 2 treatments can occur only once in each block, then $b = 6 (=12/2)$. The number of pairs in each block of our hypothetical trial is 1, as signified by "λ," which is extracted using the following formula (see Ryser 1963):

$$\lambda = \frac{r(k - 1)}{(a - 1)}$$

Thus, the only possible matrix, in which each pair of treatments appears simultaneously within a block exactly once, is the one presented in Table 21.1. Each pairs of treatments is then analyzed.

PERMUTED BLOCK RANDOMIZATIONS. The two designs presented earlier (complete and incomplete) aim to reduce variance in the data caused by certain prognostic or other general variables. However, these models are less useful to address time-related biases created by sequential assignment of units. There are times when the researcher needs to achieve near-equality in the number of units assigned in each block to different treatments, at any stage of the recruitment process, not only at the end of the study. A special type of block randomized design is called for.

Suppose that a care-provider cannot wait for more victims of a similar type to surface, in order to provide victims with much-needed services at the same time. The treatment must be delivered as soon as possible for each individual victim. Such is also the case in deferred enrolment designs, where participants may be rejected at one point but then enrolled at a different point in time when more appropriate participants surface for a particular treatment (e.g., finish their prison sentence, become legally fit for a rehabilitation program, graduate from a training program, etc.). However, when using a CRD to evaluate this or similar treatments, the random assignment procedure could be threatened with several possible biases, such as selection bias and chronological bias. These and other threats, which stem from changes that occur in participants' characteristics across time (or even from chance variation alone), are more likely to take place in a complete randomization design (Devereaux et al. 2005; Kao et al. 2007: 364).

First introduced by Hill (1951; see Armitage 2003), the permuted-block randomization design, or PRBD, was developed in order to deal with these trial conditions. Over the years, PRBD has become the most frequently employed design in clinical trials (Abou-El-Fotouh 1976; Cochran and Cox 1957; Lagakos and Pocock 1984; Matts and Lachin 1988; Rosenberger and Lachin 2002: 154). However, in criminology, it is quite rare (Ariel 2009).

Consider the following permutational sequence with four participants in each block (Beller et al. 2002). Here, this means that the block size, or length, is 4, with one treatment group (T) and one control group (C). Deductively, this means that in each block, there are only six possible arrangements of the treatment and control: CCTT, TTCC, CTTC, TCCT, TCTC, and CTCT. Randomization is applied in order to select a particular block out of the six possible combinations, therefore setting the allocation sequence for the first four participants. This process is then repeated, depending on the number of participants participating in the study.

The PRBD is most appropriate when there is a strong need for both periodic and final balance in the number of participants assigned to each study group in each block. This is the case, for example, in small studies, or studies with many small subgroups (Rosenberger and Lachin 2002). It is therefore useful when the study incorporates interim analyses, as in studies with increased time lags between one recruitment stage and the next, or with a longitudinal design (Kernan et al. 1999). This deals with the problem which was best described as the "time-heterogeneity bias within blocks," created by changes that occur in participants' characteristics and responses with time of entry into the trial (see Rosenberger and Lachin 2002: 41–45). The PRBD model works to correct for this (Matts and Lachin 1988).

A WORD OF CAUTION.   One of the drawbacks of using a PRBD is the risk caused by the very nature of the design, namely "forcing equality" within the blocks (Schulz and Grimes 2002; see also Efron 1971; Lachin 1988b). Creating a known combination of allocation in advance jeopardizes the unpredictability of treatment assignments, which in turn may lead to intentional or unintentional unmasking of the allocation sequence, as well as prediction of future allocation, even though the blocks are selected at random.

When the size of the block is fixed and known, and the study is not double-blind (which is usually the case), this allows unmasking. It is caused by the imposition of periodic balance at the end of each successive block (Berger 2005a; Doig and Simpson 2005; Proschan 1994). Since the allocation process as well as administration of the treatment become constant over time, it is possible to know to which group the next participant will be allocated. This is particularly the case when the block size is small, with "six participants or less" (Schulz and Grimes 2002).

One worrying outcome of knowing future allocation is the increased likelihood of a selection bias. This bias implies that the outcome differences may be explained as a result of something else other than the treatment per se. While selection bias exists in all types of trials, it is more of an issue in permuted block randomization designs because, as stated, the random assignment structure is predetermined. It can lead to artificially low p values, artificially large estimated magnitudes of benefit, and artificially narrow confidence intervals (Berger 2006). The overall validity of the conclusions is also jeopardized, as well as the integrity of the trial (and possibly that of the experimenter). Therefore, the best way to decrease the likelihood of this bias would be to keep the researcher(s) implementing the trial and those controlling the random allocation sequence separate.

A CLOSER LOOK AT THE BLOCKING CRITERION

As we have tried to show, blocking on key variables is expected to create subgroups of participants which are more similar to one another than in the generally heterogeneous random sample. Whichever type of RBD is being used, this criterion can be established based on either the characteristics of the experiment (e.g., time, measurement instrument, consignment, etc.), or those of the participants (e.g., income, age, criminal background, psychological variables, or even the level of the dependent variable at pre-test, baseline level etc.). The variance between participants within blocks is then expected to become smaller than the overall variance (Abou-El-Fotouh 1976; Armitage 2003: 926; Fisher 1935). When the data are properly blocked, the estimates of the treatment effect will become more accurate because the overall power of the test statistic is increased, thus enabling the researcher to detect smaller differences between treatment means (Ostle and Malone 2000; Rosenberger and Lachin 2002).

In certain cases, it is immediately obvious that blocking should be utilized for the purposes of reducing experimental error resulting from lower variance. Blocking the data according to type of drug use, as in the hypothetical drug treatment trial presented above, is very clear. But there are other instances when the advantages of blocking are not so obvious.

Because the decision to block the data is usually based on qualitative grounds,[1] there is always the risk that the researcher has made a poor decision. In a scale-level variable, for example, this means that the cutting-points of the data might be misplaced, therefore implementing a grouping criterion that creates blocks in which the units within each block do not share common characteristics. In a study of tax evasion, for example, blocking the data according to income levels in a way that is intended to divide the sample into disparate socioeconomic backgrounds could go wrong if the researcher mistakenly categorizes participants so the blocks do not contain taxpayers with similar socioeconomic attributes. Thus, if the blocking is wrong, the block design will not only be disadvantageous compared with using an ordinary complete randomization design, it could be counterproductive and increase the error rate.

---

[1] Recently, Haviland and Nagin (2005: 2007) have proposed group-based trajectory modelling, which tests for treatment effects within trajectory groups. Their procedure can empirically and effectively cluster together groups that have similar baseline characteristics, for the purpose of then comparing them at the postrandomization stage.

Was the Blocking Efficient?

In order to quantify the improvement of using a blocked design over a complete randomization design, Relative Efficiency (RE) is calculated (Yates 1936). RE is a way to answer the question: how much have we gained by using a blocked design rather than a complete randomization design, with the same number of experimental units? (Hinkelmann and Kempthrone 1994: 260). Formally, RE compares the variance estimate of a blocked design with a counterfactual variance estimate of a complete randomization model. The larger the RE, the more effective the blocking has been. There are different ways to measure RE. However, the best way is to look at the estimated ratio of improvement in the context of the estimation of treatment comparisons, which heavily relies on the variance of each design:

$$\text{RE } (D_1 \text{ to } D_2) = \frac{\text{Efficiency } D_1}{\text{Efficiency } D_2} = \frac{\text{Var}_{D_1}}{\text{Var}_{D_2}}$$

Where D_1 and D_2 are the two designs.

Of course, the *true* ratio is not known, because we only have the true variance for the blocked design that is found in the observed data, not that which exists in the counterfactual CRD. Therefore, we use an *estimated* RE. The sources of data for the RE formula are taken from the mean square of the error term and the blocking term. Using the same terms discussed thus far (*a* being the treatment factor; *b* representing the blocking factor), Hinkelmann and Kempthrone (1994) suggest the following equation, referred to as the Expected Mean Squares for Treatment and Error approach, as a way to calculate RE:

$$\text{RE } (D_1 \text{ to } D_2) = \frac{(b-1)(\text{MS}_{\text{block}}) + b(a-1)\text{MS}_{\text{error}}}{(ba-1)\text{MS}_{\text{error}}}$$

In the numerator, the degrees of freedom of the blocking factor $(b-1)$ are multiplied by their respective mean squares, which are then added to the number of blocks used, multiplied by the product of the degrees of freedom of the treatment factor and the mean squares of the error term. In the denominator, we see that the mean squares of the error term are multiplied by the degrees of freedom of the total variance. If the ratio is larger than 1, we can say that the blocking factor was efficient. Hinkelmann and Kempthrone (1994) further suggest a criterion, where it may be advisable to consider a blocked design with RE larger than 1.25 as "better" than the comparable, counterfactual complete randomization model (p. 262). The question remains, however, what to do when RE is smaller than 1, or when it is clear from the data that blocking was counterproductive?

The Case of Unsuccessful Blocking

One way to understand the problem of poor blocking is to observe the relationship between the error term of the model and the degrees of freedom (see Ahamad 1967; Weisburd and Taxman 2000). As we explained earlier, the residual variance includes the degrees of freedom which were unaccounted by the model. These degrees of freedom stem from both random as well as systematic residual variance. In a nonblocked design, the residual variance term will include both the ordinary unexplained variance as well as the blocking variance. Likewise, the degrees of freedom that "belong" to the systematic variance that actually exists between blocks of data are also located in this residual variance error term. Therefore, as Cochran and Cox (1957) described it, "blocking takes away degrees of freedom from the estimate of the error variation." This is why, as briefly discussed above, poor blocking translates into lower precision in the estimate of error variability.

An operational dilemma soon emerges: when in reality, there are no real differences between the blocks – or when RE is smaller than 1 – how should the researcher best deal with the degrees of freedom of the blocking factor in the statistical analysis? One approach argues that these degrees of freedom should *not* be included in the residual variance because it rewards the researcher who has ineffectively blocked the sample. Therefore, the blocking variable, with its respective degrees of freedom, must be taken into account. Under this approach, conservative statisticians would most likely suggest that, once an experiment has been conducted in a RBD, the blocks cannot be ignored in the analysis and the degrees of freedom should not be included in the residual variance term (see in Devereaux et al. 2005; Hinkelmann and Kempthrone 1994: 260; see review in Lachin 1988a).

However, we believe that this conservative approach is too stringent. A more practical approach to deal with this situation would be to ignore the blocking factor and analyze the data, *ex ante,* without it. We are not alone in this approach. Matt and Lachin (1988b) suggest that, when the blocking factor is ignored, the degrees of freedom would then go into the residual variance term. Disregarding the blocking effect is acceptable, because ignoring this factor should only result in a more conservative statistical test (Friedman et al. 1985). In turn, pooling the degrees of freedom may reward the researcher who has ineffectively blocked the data, but the overall variance in a poorly blocked study should in theory be equal to the overall variance of an unblocked study (Matts and Lachin 1988).

Thus, ignoring the blocking factor in the analysis is likely to result in similar outcomes as if the blocking was considered – particularly when the participants were sampled from a homogeneous population (Lachin et al. 1988). Analyzing the data this way will "simply" mean that we sacrifice both power and precision, but not the overall integrity of the study as long as the researcher implicitly reports this procedure. (Note, that this dilemma and how to solve it is only raised in relation to a design that has no intrablock treatment replication. In more complex designs, which allow for such replication, then the analysis *must* take into account the interaction between the treatment factor and the blocking factor. Therefore, the blocking criterion cannot be ignored in these cases).

Blocking *Ex Ante* Vs. Blocking *Ex Post*

The last issue we wish to consider in regard to these designs is whether prerandom blocking is at all necessary. As we have tried to show, one of the major objectives of RBDs is to decrease the variance of the data, by subdividing the sample according to key criteria. In this way, the researcher can decrease the Type I error rate as well as increase precision and statistical power. This is achieved by the prerandomization blocking procedure. However, ordinary post hoc subgroup analyses, that are generally used in analyses of variance procedures (such as Tukey's *HSD, Scheffe, Bonferroni* and the like), are used for the same reason. These analyses allow the researcher to evaluate the treatment effect on particular groups or subgroups of participants. But in this context, they can also be used to theoretically homogenize the data according to certain key variables, much like a blocking procedure. We have covered quite a few operational as well as statistical problems in RBDs, particularly when dealing with an incomplete block. Therefore, should the researcher implement an ordinary complete randomization design instead of the relatively complex blocked design, and deal with the categorization of the data at the post hoc stage of the statistical analyses? Should certain covariates be treated *ex post* instead of *ex ante*?

Subgroup analyses are customarily viewed as a natural step that comes after testing for main effects. These analyses can provide valuable information about both planned and unanticipated benefits and hazards of the intervention. At the very least, researchers use them in order to establish treatment benefits in subsets of participants. It makes sense to first assess the treatment by comparing *all* experimental units with *all* control units (or before–after, depending on the design) and then to account statistically for any covariates or other baseline variables. It seems that most clinicians agree with this rationale as 70% of clinical trial reports include treatment outcome comparisons for participants subdivided by baseline characteristics at the postrandomization stage (Assmann et al. 2000).

At the same time, however, as logical as subgroup analyses may be in theory, it is well established now that they are often misleading (Lee et al. 1980; Moye and Deswal 2001; Peto et al. 1995). In fact, the medical community often rejects such findings (Moye and Deswal 2001), as the methods and procedures implemented are commonly misused (Assmann et al. 2000). Among some of the concerns raised against subgroup analyses, Moye and Deswal (2001) emphasize that "lack of prospective specification, inadequate sample size, inability to maintain power, and the cumulative effect of sampling error" complicate their interpretation. Some go as far as saying that the most reliable estimate of the treatment effect for a particular subgroup is the *overall* effect rather than the observed effect in that particular group (Schulz and Grimes 2005). Therefore, using subgroup analysis instead of blocking of the data before random assignment may actually be ill-advised.

Moreover, because virtually any covariate can be used to cluster units into subgroups, it allows, at least from a technical standpoint, the ability to generate multiple comparisons. This is a source of concern, because it increases the probability of detecting differences simply by chance alone (Type I error). It is not uncommon for researchers to be tempted to look for statistically significant, often publishable, differences between subgroups. It is therefore recommended that, without proper planning and sound rationale for conducting the analysis, subgroup analyses should not be considered as a replacement for prerandomization blocking. Subgroup analyses should be justified on theoretical grounds *a priori*, in order to avoid the appearance of improper data-mining. As described by Weisburd and Britt (2007: 320), "this is a bit like going fishing for a statistically significant result. However, sometimes one or another of the pairwise comparisons is of particular interest. Such an interest should be determined before you develop your analysis… if you do start off with a strong hypothesis for a pairwise comparison, it is acceptable to examine it, irrespective of the outcomes of the larger test. In such circumstances, it is also acceptable to use a simple two-sample t-test to examine group differences." Schulz and Grimes (2005: 1658) further develop this argument, by emphasizing that "seeking positive subgroup effects (data-dredging), in the absence of overall effects, could fuel much of this activity. If enough subgroups are tested, false-positive results will arise by chance alone… Similarly, in a trial with a clear overall effect, subgroup testing can produce false-negative results due to chance and lack of power."

In summary, subgroup analyses can be misleading because they focus on the heterogeneity of the intervention effect among the blocks. However, this heterogeneity is not always the question that the study is addressing (Yusuf et al. 1991). Ordinarily, hypotheses tested in the trial investigate an overall direction of the treatment effect in the study population, whereas there is no assumption of homogeneity of effect across subgroups. As shown by Adams (1998: 770), subgroups are created from the original study population, *ex post*, which may have unknown imbalances in baseline characteristics (e.g., risk factors) that cannot be adjusted for and can influence outcomes outcome. Thus, subgroup analyses oftentimes do not reveal the truth about the relationship in the larger population. The interpretation of their results should be seen as exploratory because they can suggest but not confirm a relationship in the population at large (Moye and Deswal 2001).

Despite the reservations that we just reviewed, subgroup analyses should not be completely neglected. There are times when they can in fact replace prerandomization blocking designs. This, however, should be done with caution. When the researcher specifies at the beginning of the trial that the efficacy of the treatment for a particular subgroup or a particular block is of particular interest and part of the research goals, then subgroup analyses can be considered. When this is the case, there are good strategies that can be used to estimate the effect size in subgroups created after random assignment (see Moye and Deswal 2001). These are strategies that rely primarily on the use of prospective devices to improve safeguard from sampling error. At the same time – and however promising – they are quite underused in medical research (Assmann et al. 2000) and are rarely used in criminal justice trials. The threats which arise in such an approach may somewhat cancel out the benefits.

CONCLUSIONS

Under certain conditions, RBDs are more useful when compared with ordinary completely randomized allocation procedures. They allow the researcher flexibility and control over the number of conditions assigned to the participants, as well as the number of blocks that are used to homogenize the data. By reducing the intrablock variance, the treatment estimates are more accurate because of the increased statistical power and precision of the test statistics.

The various statistical models designed to accommodate the different types of blocking techniques provide the researcher with accuracy that is generally superior to that which can be obtained using the non-blocked randomization designs. This is particularly the case when the trial is small – several hundred or less – or when the blocking criterion is "good." Unlike the complete randomization design, these blocking procedures can deal with certain shortcomings that cannot be eliminated by randomization theory: increased data variance, outliers, time heterogeneity due to sequential assignment, missing data and covariance imbalance.

In this chapter, we reviewed some common types of the randomized blocked designs. Perhaps deterred by their complexity, the majority of criminologists have failed to use these designs. However, there are instances when they are better equipped to explore the treatment effect. *Post hoc* subgroup analyses, which are generally utilized in the simple randomization model, are for the most part not good replacements for prerandomization allocation through blocking. Blocking procedures create a more powerful treatment estimate – not by altering the effect of the treatment, which is held constant – but by decreasing the variance. This leads to more efficient estimates. Thus, these designs should be implemented in criminology more fully in the future.

Figure 21.3 aims to assist in identifying the best randomization design (CRD or RBD) for RCTs in criminology. Before selecting a complete randomization design or a RBD, the researcher should answer four interconnected questions (that appear in Fig. 21.3 as diamonds at the top of the page), all of which should be addressed at the planning stage of the experiment:

1. Is the number of participants expected to be assigned to treatment groups smaller than "a few hundred"?

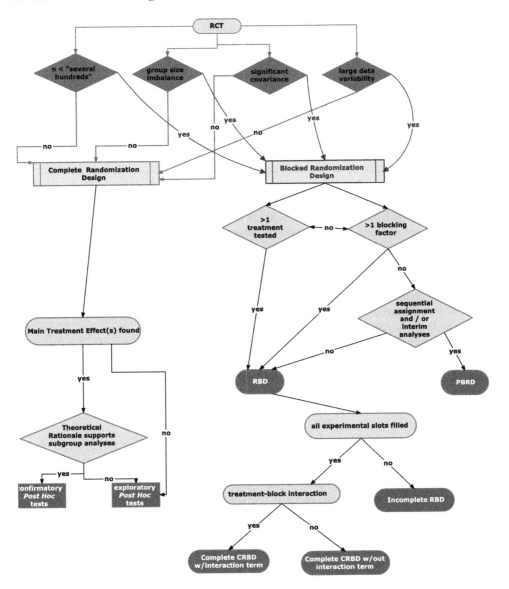

FIGURE 21.3. Identifying the best randomization design to fit the trial.

2. Is an imbalance in group-size expected?
3. Are there known covariates that are likely to have an effect on the data?
4. Are the data characterized by variance, especially that which will have a systematic impact on the distribution of the responses to the treatment?

If the answer to this entire set of questions is no, then the researcher is likely to benefit from a simple randomization design. In such a case, the treatment(s) effect should be analyzed using the statistical model which is the most useful for the nature of the data collected in the course of the experiment. *Post hoc* subgroup analyses can then be conducted, depending on whether there is a good *a priori* theoretical reasoning to justify this analysis. If not, or when main effects were not detected, then the findings of such *post hoc* tests should be viewed as exploratory, helping to generate hypotheses for future empirical exploration. Alternatively, when there is a good reason to do them, then *post hoc* tests may be considered confirmatory, but only under certain conditions.

However, even if only one of the four questions is answered yes, this would provide justification for using a RBD. In this case, if there is only one blocking factor and only one treatment, and the researcher anticipates sequential assignment, then the design which is likely to be most useful will be the permuted block randomization design. Otherwise, the more general simple RBD is better.

The next step would be to ask whether all experimental slots are likely to be filled. This is particularly relevant when there are several treatments tested together, or when it will be too expensive to have every single slot in every block filled. In cases where all slots are not filled, the complete RBD should be used. In the more likely scenario, where every slot will in fact be filled, the researcher should then ask whether an interaction is expected between the blocking variable and the treatment variable. If so, a CRBD with an interaction term should be used. If not, a CRBD without an interaction term model should be preferred. Either way, the statistical analysis, as presented above, is usually straightforward and supported by most statistical software packages. For the most part analysis of variance procedures are most common. Other test statistics can be better, depending on the type of outcome measures assessed though these are beyond the scope of this chapter.

There have been a few RBDs in criminology, and researchers have learned about how to use the simplest type of RBDs. The time is ripe for researchers to experiment with more complicated designs, building on knowledge gained in medical research.

REFERENCES

Abou-El-Fotouh HA (1976) Relative efficiency of the randomized complete block design. Exp Agric 12:145–149
Adams K (1998) Post hoc subgroup analysis and the truth of a clinical trial. Am Heart J 136(5):753–758
Ahamad B (1967) An analysis of crimes by the method of principal components. Appl Stat 16(1):17–35
Altman DG, Schulz KF, Moher D, Egger M, Davidoff F, Elbourne D, Gøtzsche PC, Lang T (2001) The revised CONSORT statement for reporting randomized trials: explanation and elaboration. Ann Intern Med 134:663–694
Ariel B (2008) The effect of written notices on taxpayers' reporting behavior – a blocked randomized controlled trial. Presented at the third annual conference on randomized controlled trials in the social sciences: methods and synthesis, York University, UK (October)
Ariel B (2009) Systematic review of baseline imbalances in randomized controlled trials in criminology. Presented at the communicating complex statistical evidence conference, University of Cambridge, UK (January)
Armitage P (2003) Fisher, Bradford Hill, and randomization: a symposium. Int J Epidemiol 32:925–928
Assmann S, Pocock S, Enos L, Kasten L (2000) Subgroup analysis and other (mis)uses of baseline data in clinical trials. Lancet 355(9209):1064–1069
Beller EM, Gebski V, Keech AC (2002) Randomization in clinical trials. Med J Aust 177:565–567
Berger VW, Exner DV (1999) Detecting selection bias in randomized clinical trials. Control Clin Trials 20:319–327
Berger VW (2005a) Is allocation concealment a binary phenomenon? Med J Aust 183(3):165
Berger VW (2006) Varying the block size does not conceal the allocation. J Crit Care 21(2):299
Braga A, Weisburd D, Waring E, Mazerolle LG, Spelman W, Gajewski F (1999) Problem-oriented policing in violent crime places: a randomized controlled experiment. Criminology 37:541–580
Canavos G, Koutrouvelis J (2008) Introduction to the design and analysis of experiments. Prentice Hall, Elk Grove Village, IL
Chow S-C, Liu J-P (2004) Design and analysis of clinical trials: concepts and methodologies. Wiley-IEEE, Taiwan
Cochran WG, Cox GM (1957) Experimental designs. Wiley, New York
Dean A, Voss D (1999). Design and analysis of experiments. Springer Science, New York

Devereaux PJ, Bhandari M, Clarke M, Montori VM, Cook DJ, Yusuf S, Sackett DL, Cina CS, Walter SD, Haynes B, Schunemann HJ, Norman GR, Guyatt GH (2005) Need for expertise based randomized controlled trials. Br Med J 7482:330–388

Doig GS, Simpson F (2005) Randomization and allocation concealment: a practical guide for researchers. J Crit Care 20:187–191

Efron B (1971) Forcing a sequential experiment to be balanced. Biometrika 58:403–417

Farrington DP, Ttofi MM (2009) Reducing school bullying: Evidence-based implications for policy. In M. Tonry (Ed.) Crime and Justice 38:281–345. Chicago: University of Chicago press

Federer W, Nguyen N-K (2002) Incomplete block designs. In: El-Shaarawi A, Piegorsch W (eds) Encyclopedia of environmetrics, Vol. 2. Wiley, Chichester, pp 1039–1042

Fisher RA (1935). The design of experiments. Oliver and Boyd, Edinburgh

Fisher RA, Yates F (1963) Statistical table for biological agricultural and medical research, 6th edn. Hafner, New York

Friedman LM, Furberg CD, DeMets DL (1985) Fundamentals in clinical trials, 2nd edn. PSG Publishing Company, Littleton, MA

Gacula M (2005) Design & analysis of sensory optimization. Blackwell, Australia

Gill JL (1984) Heterogeneity of variance in randomized block experiments. J Anim Sci 59(5):1339–1344

Hallstrom A, Davis K (1988) Imbalance in treatment assignments in stratified blocked randomization. Control Clin Trials 9(4):375–382

Haviland MA, Nagin SD (2005) Causal inference with group-based trajectory models. Psychometrika 70:1–22

Haviland MA, Nagin SD (2007) Using group-based trajectory modeling in conjunction with propensity scores to improve balance. J Exp Criminol 3:65–82

Hill AB (1951) The clinical trial. Br Med Bull 7:278–282

Hinkelmann K, Kempthrone O (1994) Design and analysis of experiments: introduction to experimental design. Wiley, New York

Hoshmand R (2006) Design of experiments for agriculture and the natural sciences. Chapman & Hall, Florida

Kao L, Tyson J, Blakely M, Lally K (2007) Clinical research methodology I: introduction to randomized trials. J Am Coll Surg 206(2):361–369

Kepner J, Wackerly D (1996) On rank transformation techniques for balanced incomplete repeated-measures designs. J Am Stat Assoc 91(436):1619–1625

Kernan WN, Viscoli CM, Makuch RW, Brass LM, Horwitz RI (1999) Stratified randomization for clinical trials. J Clin Epidemiol 52:19–26

Lachin JM (1988a) Properties of simple randomization in clinical trials. Control Clin Trials 9:312–326

Lachin JM (1988b) Statistical properties of randomization in clinical trials. Control Clin Trials 9:289–311

Lachin JM (2000) Statistical considerations in the intent-to-treat principle. Control Clin Trials 21(3):167–189

Lachin JM, Matts JP, Wei LJ (1988) Randomization in clinical trials: conclusions and recommendations. Control Clin Trials 9:365–374

Lagakos SW, Pocock SJ (1984) Randomization and stratification in cancer clinical trials: An international survey. In: Buyse ME, Staquet MJ, Sylvester RJ (eds) Cancer clinical trials, methods and practice. Oxford University Press, New York, pp 276–286

Lee KL, McNeer F, Starmer CF, Harris PJ, Rosari RA (1980) Clinical judgment and statistics: lessons from a simulated randomized trial in coronary artery disease. Circulation 61:508–515

Liebetrau A (1983) Measures of association. Sage, Thousand Oaks, CA

Lipsey MW (1990) Design sensitivity: statistical power for experimental research, Sage, Newbury Park, CA

Matts JP, Lachin JM (1988) Properties of permuted-block randomization in clinical trials. Control Clin Trials 9:327–344

Milliken AG, Johnson DE (1996) Analysis of messy data. Van Nostrand Reinhold, New York

Mottonen J, Husler J, Oja H (2003) Multivariate nonparametric tests in a randomized complete block design. J Multivar Anal 85:106–129

Moye L, Deswal A (2001) Trials within trials: confirmatory subgroup analyses in controlled clinical experiments. Control Clin Trials 22(6):605–619

Ostle B, Malone L (2000) Statistics in research: basic concepts and techniques for research workers. Iowa State University Press, Wiley-Blackwell

Palta M, Amini SB (1982) Magnitude and likelihood of loss resulting from non-stratified randomization. Stat Med 1(3):267–275

Peto R, Collins R, Gray R (1995) Large-scale randomized evidence: large, simple trials and overviews of trials. J Clin Epidemiol 48:23–40

Pocock SJ, Simon R (1975) Sequential treatment assignment with balancing for prognostic factors in the controlled clinical trial. Biometrics 31:103–115

Pocock SJ (1979) Allocation of patients to treatment in clinical trials. Biometrics 35:183–197

Proschan M (1994) Influence of selection bias on type i error rate under random permuted block designs. Stat Sin 4:219–231

Robinson J (1972) The randomization model for incomplete block designs. Ann Math Stat 43(2):480–489

Rosenberger W, Lachin JM (2002) Randomization in clinical trials: theory and practice, Wiley, New York

Ryser HJ (1963) Combinatorial Mathematics. Cambridge Mathematical Monographs No. 14. The Mathematical Association of America. John Wiley and Sons.

Schulz KF, Grimes DA (2002) Generation of allocation sequences in randomized trials: chance, not choice. Lancet 359:515–519

Schulz KF, Grimes D (2005) Multiplicity in randomized trials II: subgroup and interim analyses. Lancet 365(9471):1657–1661

Senn JS (1989) Covariate imbalance and random allocation in clinical trial. Stat Med 8:467–475

Senn JS (1994) Testing for baseline balance in clinical trials. Stat Med 13(17):1715–1726

Sherman WL (1993) Defiance, deterrence, and irrelevance: a theory of the criminal sanction. J Res Crime Delinq 30:445–473

Sherman L, Weisburd D (1995) General deterrent effects of police patrol in crime hot spots: a randomized controlled trial. Justice Q 12:625–648

Sherman L, Gartin P, Buerger M (1989) Hot spots of predatory crime: routine activities and the criminology of place. Criminology 27:27–56

Simon R (1979) Restricted randomization designs in clinical trials. Biometrics 35:503–512

Torgerson JD, Torgerson CJ (2003) Avoiding bias in randomized controlled trials in educational research. Br J Educ Stud 51(1):36–45

Wei L, Zhang J (2001) Analysis of data with imbalance in the baseline outcome variable for randomized clinical trials. Drug Inf J 35:1201–1214

Weisburd D, Britt C (2007) Statistics in criminal justice. Springer, New York

Weisburd D, Green L (1995) Policing drug hot spots: the Jersey City DMA experiment. Justice Q 12:711–736

Weisburd D, Morris N, Ready J (2008) Risk-focused policing at places: an experimental evaluation. Justice Q 25(1):163–200

Weisburd D, Petrosino A, Mason G (1993) Design sensitivity in criminal justice experiments. Crime Justice 17(3):337–379

Weisburd D, Taxman FS (2000) Developing a multicenter randomized trial in criminology: The case of HIDTA. J Quant Criminol 16(3):315–340

Yates F (1936) A new method of arranging variety trials involving a large number of varieties. J Agric Sci 26:424–455

Yusuf S, Collins R, Peto R (1984) Why do we need some large, simple randomized trials? Stat Med 3(4):409–420

Yusuf S, Wittes J, Probstfield J, Taylor HA (1991) Analysis and interpretation of treatment effects in subgroups of patients in randomized clinical trials. J Am Med Assoc 266:93–98

## CHAPTER 22

Construct Validity: The Importance of Understanding the Nature of the Intervention Under Study

John S. Goldkamp

Constructs are the central means we have for connecting the operations used in an experiment to the pertinent theory and to the language communities that will use the results to inform practical action. To the extent that experiments contain construct errors, they risk misleading both theory and practice. (Shadish et al. 2002:65)

INTRODUCTION: EXPLICATION OF CONSTRUCTS AS PROBLEMATIC

Commonly researchers address construct validity by asking whether the sample selected permits a fair examination of the effects of an intervention or phenomenon of interest. The nature of the intervention itself is described and the authors certify that a particular operationalization of the intervention to be used in the study is a "good example" of the intervention and therefore offers a "fair test." In criminology, examples of interventions can include a gamut of programs, strategies, and innovations in procedure in many arenas from courts, prosecution, policing, and corrections. With positive results from early evaluative studies of a particular innovation, a case is sometimes rapidly built for wide adoption of the intervention and related policies, so great a thirst there is for "things that work" in crime prevention or reduction.[1]

Consideration of construct validity is basically made up of two components, explication and measurement (see, e.g., Shadish et al. 2002:66). Without dealing with "explication," that is, having a clear grasp of the key or "prototypical" functions or concepts that serve as the essential constructs underlying a phenomenon, it is difficult to address the concerns associated with the second and more commonly raised part of the construct validity problem: how well measures of the underlying constructs really capture their essence in the research operation. In fact, construct validity considerations in evaluation research are often treated as routine or

---

[1] See Sherman and Berk (1984) for a famous example.

A.R. Piquero and D. Weisburd (eds.), *Handbook of Quantitative Criminology*,
DOI 10.1007/978-0-387-77650-7_22, © Springer Science + Business Media, LLC 2010,
First softcover printing 2011

given short shrift, as studies move quickly to discussions of designs, analyses, and findings – where controversies are more often addressed. Assessment of a study's construct validity, however, goes directly to the strength of the theoretical and conceptual foundation, upon which the research is based and, therefore, may have important implications for interpreting the findings produced.

This discussion focuses on explication, the first component of the construct validity consideration, because of its below-the-radar status and its potential significance in policy evaluation. Although this paper focuses on the drug court literature as an example, the issues and approaches suggested may apply equally to other examples of policy relevant criminological study. As the drug court innovation has evolved to the status of a movement based on its claim of reducing drug-related crime, the research has proceeded largely without settling clearly on the nature of the intervention by identifying the essential operating constructs underlying the various applications of the drug court innovation.

Oversimplifying for the purposes of illustrating the explication issue, the question for drug court research is "what is a drug court?" (see Goldkamp 1999) As applied to the widely popular drug court phenomenon, this oversight in clearly identifying and explicating the drug court's underlying constructs has opened the door to all sorts of construct validity problems that may undermine the confidence one can have in accepting the favorable inferences of impact being drawn from the growing body of empirical literature on drug courts. This chapter discusses the construct validity issue as applied to drug courts through the author's work with colleagues[2] in this area over the decade of their establishment. This chapter not only describes the problem, but also how various steps were taken to address it. Though the approach evolved from drug court research, the lessons identified – or at least the questions asked – can be extended to study of other crime prevention or justice innovations, from targeted policing to therapeutic communities in prisons.

CONSTRUCT VALIDITY AND THE EXAMPLE OF DRUG COURT RESEARCH

Reviews of drug court evaluations (e.g., Wilson et al. 2006; Cissner and Rempel 2005; GAO 1995, 1997, 2005; Belenko 1998, 1999, 2001) suggest that drug courts can produce lower rates of reoffending among participants than among nonparticipant comparison groups. This does not mean to suggest that there was a consensus among studies in finding a crime-reduction effect (GAO 1995), nor a consistency in the effect sizes when effects were found, for example, in a meta-analysis of drug court impact (Wilson et al. 2006). The favorable state of the findings has led some observers (including the current author) to conclude that, based on the overall body of the evidence, however, drug courts "work," or at least can work.

This favorable generalization about the impact of drug courts on drug offenders has in fact become a widely accepted "conventional wisdom" – notwithstanding a full array of caveats and methodological concerns concerning the research that produced these favorable findings, including problems of sampling, dissimilar design and reliance on mostly nonexperimental approaches (but see, e.g., Marlowe et al. 2003a, b, 2005, 2006; Gottfredson and

---

[2] These colleagues included Michael White, Jennifer Robinson, Doris Weiland, and James Moore, variously contributing to research initiatives in Miami, Philadelphia, Las Vegas, Portland, Reno, San Francisco, Brooklyn, San Bernardino.

Exum 2002; Gottfredson et al. 2003, 2005, 2006) and great diversity in the examples of drug courts and settings studied. This chapter poses the basic question of whether these findings provide sufficiently strong evidence of the innovation's favorable impact without the research having fully investigated and clarified what a drug court "is" in the first place (Goldkamp 1999). The conceptual framework serving as a framework for drug court evaluations – as in the case of other evaluations – is often merely implicit, or flexibly or incompletely discussed or even just absent, making it quite difficult to draw inferences about how the various findings should be interpreted and raising questions about external validity, among other issues.

Setting aside some of the design and analytic issues characterizing the evaluative literature, taken as a whole, drug court research has skirted the conceptually prior problems of core constructs and construct validity by failing to resolve the serious underlying theoretical and empirical question of what a drug court "is." What may appear to some as an obvious or merely academic issue to some is, this chapter argues, so basic that the growing body of favorable findings from the drug court literature may suffer from overconfidence, tantamount to growing a large tree without strong roots. As noted above, this practice is not unique to the investigation of drug court impact, but may also characterize evaluations of many other justice innovations, from policing to correctional strategies.

Admittedly, given the extraordinary expansion of the drug court movement (now celebrating its 20th year since the first drug court was established in Miami), this question may seem strangely belated – but, this chapter suggests, nevertheless it provides an excellent illustration of the fact that the diffusion of an innovation can take on life of its own, regardless of the soundness of its footing. Without having identified and tested the constructs underlying a drug court's impact – that, is reaching agreement on how drug courts work – how confidently can one accept the conclusion that the many favorable findings generated by an enthusiastic literature really show that drug courts "work"? What factors, moving parts or operations, account for the positive findings? Practitioners' assumptions and conventional wisdoms aside, what has the empirical literature learned about the underlying causal mechanism that makes a drug court a "drug court" and accounts for its impact? One could even argue that drug courts should not be assessed on the basis of their crime reduction impact at all, and that, instead, the driving constructs should be understood as the introduction of a different justice value – some sort of helping or therapeutic orientation – under which measurable "results," such as crime reduction impact, might not be appropriate or at least determinative. (This reasoning is similar to acknowledging that one would not understand the contribution of just deserts punishment through assessing its crime reduction impact – or, in a different way, to arguing that the point is to set in place a helping-oriented court-based approach, whether or not help is actually accepted by participants. The end is to achieve a change in orientation, with secondary outcomes.)

In addition to assessing the comparative impact of the new and developing innovation, the body of (the author's) research used in this critical analysis sought to develop a preliminary model of underlying causal factors to allow impact findings ("do drug courts work?") to be understood in the context of a conceptual framework ("how they work"). The preliminary model produced was meant to provide a reasonable common starting point for further testing and refinement of an understanding of what a drug court "is" for the purpose of research, if not for informing conventional wisdom. This chapter reviews the method employed by the author in the evolving body of research to develop a model representing underlying constructs and discusses its implications for assessing construct validity in drug court research.

If drug courts work, how do they work? If a working model of the underlying factors responsible for their impact can be identified, should not such a causal mechanism be evident from example to example, as the innovation has been implemented so widely across the nation and elsewhere? Put another way, and more fundamentally, if there is no common underlying model explained by key constructs, what sense can be made of evidence from the many different studies of many different drug courts in diverse settings across the land? How can replications be implemented that accurately adopt or, hopefully, improve upon the drug court model?

THE DRUG COURT INNOVATION BRIEFLY DESCRIBED

The nature of the drug court innovation has been well-described elsewhere (see e.g., Goldkamp 1994a, b, 1999, 2000; Hora et al. 1999; Nolan 2001). However, because drug courts have taken on different forms and shapes, it may be useful to provide a brief sketch of the innovation before moving to discussion of underlying constructs and construct validity. For an innovation with such potential for changing existing practices in criminal courts, the original idea was reasonably simple, at least as first conceived in Miami, and was driven by extremely pressing practical problems. Basically, the drug cases in Miami and across the country had become the "tail that wagged the dog" not only in the court system, but also in law enforcement and corrections. The overcrowding caused by these cases in the prisons and jails also translated into an overburdening and clogging of the criminal courts and a rapid burning out of law enforcement, as officers were deployed in the endless search for drug offenders.

This was particularly true in the reaction to the cocaine epidemic of the 1980s in which Miami was a gateway location for Latin American trafficking. In this drug "explosion," the Miami system can be compared with the "canary in the coal mine" in serving as one of the first and hardest hit of American jurisdictions. After trying many other ideas for managing the growing and overwhelming drug caseload in the courts, jails and prisons (including devising an earlier form of drug court that was intended to segregate and process all drug cases faster), the proposed court program in Miami sought to provide drug treatment to the huge volume of seriously charged (i.e., felony-level) substance abusing defendants in a criminal court context. The aim was to reduce the volume of drug offenders swamping the courts, jails and prisons (Goldkamp 1994a, 1999, 2000), and to stop what is seen as the endless recycling of drug offenders in and out and back into the justice system.

The Miami drug court offered felony defendants the opportunity to participate in a several stage, roughly year-long program of judicially supervised and intensive treatment in exchange for withdrawal of charges for successful participants or, later, even expunging of the original arrest charges. Successful participants could leave the justice system without a criminal record and the undesirable collateral consequences that followed. In the original design of drug court, which relied on the participants' frequent attendance in the drug court courtroom, the court leadership insisted on strict accountability to control participating defendants and made clear that the drug court's operations were a criminal justice function, occurring from within the boundaries of the justice system and involving possible criminal justice consequences.

Although the core aim was to provide treatment to substance abusing defendants under a judge's watchful eye, methods encouraging participant accountability were central to the drug court approach and ranged, for example, from drug testing, to open discussion of treatment progress before the judge and public embarrassment before a full courtroom of other addicts in treatment, to selective use of confinement – what Janet Reno referred to as "motivational jailing"(Goldkamp 1994a) – during the treatment process and, finally, to termination of consistently noncompliant defendants. Under the Miami model, the worst penalty for non-compliance was termination from the program and return of the defendant's criminal case to the regular criminal calendar to be adjudicated in the normal fashion. The original version of the drug court – the "Miami model" – was modified in many ways as the "idea" of drug court was adapted in many different settings. Any one sketch of a drug court will not work to cover the many modifications adopted as the innovation traveled to different locations across the United States and abroad (see Vilcica et al. 2009). The extent to which the "idea" traveled, was altered and became popular in so many settings underscore the difficulty involved in agreeing upon "the" underlying (causal) mechanism defining the drug court and, hence, in interpreting the findings from the many supportive drug court studies.

GETTING TO A CAUSAL MODEL: BEGINNING WITH THE NATION'S FIRST DRUG COURT

At the outset, the problems involved in trying to identify the underlying constructs from the Miami court were tantamount to trying to understand the first and "one real" example of the original innovation. It seemed an easy assignment to understand one program, but it nevertheless proved to be much more difficult, as it involved a rapidly evolving program. The task was to try to learn from officials first-hand, through interview and observation what they were trying to do in creating the first drug court, to describe that and then to try to test outcomes, comparing participants with nonparticipants to assess the innovation's impact (Goldkamp 1999). When there was no movement and only one court to study, the task of understanding the theory and operation of the drug court seemed self-evident. "Drug court" was defined as whatever the Miami officials meant for it to be or, if that was not clear, by whatever the Miami drug court actually "did" in operation. One had merely to describe it, infer underlying constructs and key mechanisms and then assess outcomes.

However, even at this first stage, the task of developing the underlying model was not so straightforward, for one, because the method of developing the drug court by officials in Miami was improvisational. Elements of the court program, such as the procedural steps, the nonadversarial style in the courtroom, what was viewed as "treatment," the link between the treatment clinic and the court, the use of acupuncture (Goldkamp 1994a), were all elements set in motion as building blocks and then adjusted along the way by the leadership group.[3] Several apparent key constructs, for example, concerning the symbolic and instrumental role of the

---

[3] The "inventors" of the drug court, including Miami's judicial leadership (Hon. Gerald Wetherington), State's Attorney (Hon. Janet Reno), Defender (Hon. David Weed), Office of Substance Abuse Control Director (Timothy Murray), and other administrators had mainly practical aims behind their innovation in the court system. They were guided in developing their approach to treatment – which relied heavily on outpatient treatment and acupuncture – by Dr. Michael Smith of Lincoln Hospital in the Bronx, whose experience was based on years of work among heavily addicted heroin abusers. How and why this improvisation might work was assumed to be commonsensical; "theory" explaining the operation of drug courts was implicit, its explication was not an initial priority. The designers were trying to address urgent practical problems and were not attempting to implement and test theory in crafting the drug court.

judge and the role of the criminal courtroom itself, an adapted version of substance abuse treatment, and participant monitoring and supervision, were implicit in the court's creation and operation. Even the use of acupuncture, not picked up in many of the later drug courts, appeared to be a key element as well.

The need to think more thoroughly about the key elements responsible for producing favorable drug court outcomes became more pronounced, however, with the rapid development of the later drug courts, which benefitted from the lessons and adaptations of the first generation courts. From the point of view of identifying a sound underlying model, however, the task became trickier, as the one interesting court innovation somehow transformed into a "movement." By 1993, for example, a first national meeting of drug courts and sites interested in developing drug courts was organized in Miami by Timothy Murray, Director of Miami's Office of Substance Abuse Control and key leader in designing Miami's drug court. That meeting, revealing then 25 drug courts in operation across the country, showed already that the original and pioneering Miami version of drug court (Goldkamp 1994b) had begun to be widely emulated and, in each new site, modified in specific ways to fit the needs, politics, and circumstances of the different settings. In fact, individual drug courts from the first generation changed in emphasis and procedure over time, even within a single jurisdiction. Thus, by then, four short years after the original court was "invented" in Miami, there were already variations across the courts in what was viewed as "a drug court."

From that meeting, at which now Attorney General Janet Reno keynoted,[4] several important results followed: first, the community of court jurisdictions that were struggling with the same drug-crime problems began to coalesce and launched a common discussion about substance abuse and the role of courts that has continued until this day (Goldkamp 1994b). Second, as a result of the Miami gathering, a formal, professional organization (National Association of Drug Court Professionals) was created to serve as a leadership and lobbying organization for the drug court movement. Third, Janet Reno was convinced to set up the Drug Court Program Office in the Department Justice (to which Timothy Murray was named as first Director). And fourth, the stage was set to provide federal funds for the development of drug courts, to be supervised by the Drug Court Program Office. With the rapid proliferation of the idea and its stimulation of other special court adaptations (community courts, domestic violence courts, mental health courts), the task of identifying the real and critical causal elements in the production of drug court impact on drug crime became more pressing. Yet, in a sense, the task became "easier" because of the many more examples of the innovation there were to consider (Goldkamp 1994b, 1999, 2000): the task was not only to identify their common elements, but ultimately to identify the common elements that were responsible for the advertised impact.

Thus, under the auspices of the general drug court "idea," many versions of the drug court were developed and adopted. Many departed considerably and even philosophically from the original and ongoing (and continually developing) Miami version itself. Observation by the author of many of the new courts revealed not only the growing diversity of the new drug courts, but also the fact that some so-called "drug courts" did not seem to be drawing on many of the original values, procedures, or operating philosophies that were assumed to be essential among the earliest versions of drug courts (Goldkamp 1999).

---

[4] She was State Attorney in Miami and had been centrally involved in the development of the nation's first drug court before moving to her new post as Attorney General of the United States.

With all these differences, there were certainly common themes. For example, the role of the judge at the center of the process (the fact that participants could appear before the judge many times while in the drug court) was a key common element. Distinguishing between an underlying construct (e.g., judicially supervised treatment), a theme (the pervasive role of the judge), and appropriate measures (frequency of courtroom appearance before the judge, content of judicial interactions) influential in producing outcomes became a more challenging, but key research task, if the impact and ultimate contribution of the drug court were to be well understood.

The center-stage role of the judge stands out as the possibly critical feature, tapping an underlying construct in the drug court. Observation of drug courts by the author during the first decade showed that the drug court "revolves" around the role of the judge and the judge's fairly unrestrained exercise of discretion in the name of accomplishing treatment aims. Certainly, the development of the drug court concept was largely – but certainly not exclusively – a judicially led and piloted innovation. It follows then that the investigation of the role of the judge in the drug court should reveal a really critical underlying element (construct) in terms of impact. If this is so, why and how is its role explained? If not, however, how can the central judicial role be understood? Did the central position of the judge in the innovation evolve as a way to ensure judicial control or to draw in broader political and operational support that judges could provide? Or, was the judge's role in drug court seen as a vehicle for reclaiming judicial discretion lost in the movement toward determinate sentencing structures during the 1970s and 1980s (Goldkamp et al. 2000). From the perspective of identifying key constructs or elements essential in a causal drug court model, how could the impact of the judicial role be measured? Was it necessary for participants to appear so frequently before the judge has became common in many drug courts (Marlowe et al. 2005)? Did the drug court require a dedicated, single judge to operate the court with effective results, or could a number of judges be used in rotation (Goldkamp et al. 2001b)? Could a probation officer produce the same results as a judge? If so, would that finding not raise questions about whether the judge's role represented an underlying construct?

Other elements of the drug court apparatus, certainly, also suggested themselves as key constructs and could have benefitted from empirical testing: To what extent does the use of sanctions generally, or jail in particular, play a key part in producing the sought after results? What impact does the widespread adoption of drug testing contribute to outcomes? Should acupuncture be routinely employed? How important is the courtroom environment in producing the posited drug court "effect"? What parts of the courtroom experience are essential? Is it critical to have drug court transactions carried out publicly before a large audience of other participants? If so, are there ways this should or should not be orchestrated? What ingredients of drug court treatment are essential (detoxification, outpatient, in-patient, group therapy)? Should methadone be employed for heroin abusers in the court? Or, should all substance abusing participants be treated the same? Is addiction the same for the heroin addict and the marijuana user? Does the context of the drug court – its institutional, legal, justice system, social or geographic context – play a critical role in producing the drug court effect? And, finally, how could these possible constructs be measured?

These questions illustrate potential constructs, the elements of the drug court approach that are posited or assumed in one way or the other to be instrumental in the drug court's capacity to bring about the desired change in substance abusing criminal defendants and offenders who participate in the drug court process. Can all of these be important? Do any really play a role in bringing about positive drug court impact or are they ideas or values that advocates wished to introduce into the justice processing of substance abusing offenders? What others should be considered? Can they all be equally important in producing the drug court effect? How would they work together in a causal model that explained drug court impact? Findings from identifying and testing underlying drug court constructs could change the nature of one's understanding the drug court innovation significantly. Imagine if certain assumed key elements (e.g., the judge's role) were not found to play a role in producing an effect. What if certain other elements (jail) wielded a much larger impact on final outcomes than previously believed? To what extent should such findings have implications for replication and expansion of the innovation itself?

THE WHY OF THE HOW: EXPLORING THEORETICAL CONTEXT

The identification of underlying drug court constructs involves two components: (1) agreement on select core working elements of the drug court innovation, and (2) recognition of some theoretical or at least conceptual explanation of *how* these elements appeared to work together to produce the advertised results (i.e., that they at least reduced drug crime via encouraging desistance of substance abuse among offenders). Themes or core elements, such as those noted above, stand out to the observer of drug courts. However, unfortunately, they may stand out differently depending on the observer and the example of drug court being observed.

In fact, only a small number of studies have examined the role of selected aspects of drug court functioning, moving the research focus from, whether, to how drug courts work.

Several researchers or observers of drug courts have posited theoretical perspectives, which were thought to provide good understandings of the drug court innovation (see, e.g., Goldkamp and Weiland 1993, 1994a, b, 1999, 2000; Goldkamp et al., 2001c; Hora et al. 1999; Longshore et al. 2001; Marlowe et al. 2003a, b, 2005; Nolan 2001; Miethe et al. 2000; Senjo and Leip 2001.) A smaller number tested aspects of their theoretical perspectives related to identifying drug court constructs (e.g., Senjo and Leip 2001; Miethe et al. 2000; Marlowe and Kirby 1999; Marlowe et al. 2005, 2006). Drug courts were viewed as an illustration of therapeutic jurisprudence in action by several authors (Hora et al. 1999; Nolan 2001; Senjo and Leip 2001), adapted from Wexler and Winnick (1991), emphasizing the use of court procedures for therapeutic reasons rather than being merely adjudicative or punitive. These authors did not draw on this explanatory perspective to develop a drug court causal model to explain how impact was produced, nor test such a model, rather therapeutic jurisprudence was used to explain philosophical underpinnings of the helping-oriented, mostly nonadversarial drug court approach, contrasting it with normal court proceedings. In Nolan's striking critique, he portrays drug courts as the most recent example of therapeutic jurisprudence (to him not necessarily a positive development). Senjo and Leip tested what they believed was a drug court function that illustrated its therapeutic jurisprudential qualities, finding that defendants experiencing favorable interactions with judges fared better than those experiencing unfavorable interactions. The therapeutic jurisprudence discussions (favorable in Hora et al. 1999; negative in Nolan 2001) captured a flavor of the emphasis on treatment over adversarial procedure or punitive aims, but were not intended to help identify key underlying constructs, compatible as drug court proceedings may be with that perspective.

Due to the practice in some drug courts, of transacting status reviews openly in front of a full courtroom of participants, Miethe et al. 2000) treated the drug court as an opportunity to test what they saw as an example of Braithewaite's reintegrative shaming theory. For example, when a participant was berated by a judge for using drugs or missing treatment sessions, this would occur in full view of other participants seated in the courtroom awaiting their appearance before the judge in the Clark County (Las Vegas) Drug Court and, together with the supportive elements of the drug court process, this was thought to lead to reduced recidivism. In testing whether this perspective explained favorable outcomes, Miethe, Lu and Reese did not find the predicted positive effect with findings that failed to support the theory.

Longmire et al. (2001) did not identify a theoretical perspective explaining the drug court effect, but did identify five dimensions characterizing drug courts intended to be directly measurable. (They did not test the influence these dimensions may have had using drug court data.) The five dimensions of drug courts included: (1) leverage over court participants, (2) population severity, (3) predictability of court response to participant behavior, (4) program intensity and (5) rehabilitation emphasis. The Longmire et al. five dimensions did not derive from a theoretical understanding of the drug court mechanism, but rather seemed to identify candidate constructs as a "mixed bag" of related explanatory perspectives that can be inferred as having to do with affecting drug court outcomes. Leverage may reflect a version of partially incapacitative functions (the restrictiveness of supervision and monitoring). Population severity may reflect the fact that different courts accept different categories of substance abusing defendants or offenders, a construct not tied to a theoretical explanation. Predictability may reflect a behaviorist or deterrent theme, for example, such as the impact of a particular method of using sanctions and rewards. Program intensity may have to do with the extent of involvement, attendance, and participation in various activities (treatment) required of drug court participants. This dimension can be seen as a court or programmatic attribute or, confusingly, as an outcome reflecting participant behavior. Rehabilitation emphasis appears be a characterization of the extent to which helping and facilitation of personal change is emphasized over threat of punishment in delivering services to participants. This dimension seems to be an attribute asking an observer to rate the extent to which treatment is featured, one supposes, over punitive interventions. Overall, some of these dimensions may be suggestive of constructs, even though they are not tied together theoretically or conceptually. One critical problem is that these dimensions do not necessarily distinguish a drug court from other kinds of treatment-related innovations, which one would think would be a critical requirement of a typology useful in suggesting drug court constructs.

Sponsored by the U.S. Department of Justice, Bureau of Justice Assistance, the drug court professional association (NADCP 1997) posited "key elements" of drug courts:

1. Drug courts integrate alcohol and other drug treatment services with justice system processing.
2. Using a nonadversarial approach, prosecution and defense counsel promote public safety while protecting participants.
3. Eligible participants are identified early and promptly placed in the Drug Court program.
4. Drug Courts provide access to a continuum of alcohol, drug, and other related treatment and rehabilitation services.
5. Abstinence is monitored by frequent alcohol and other drug testing.
6. A coordinated study governs drug court responses to participants' compliance.
7. Ongoing judicial interaction with each Drug Court participant is essential.
8. Monitoring and evaluation measure the achievement of program goals and gauge effectiveness.
9. Continuing interdisciplinary education promotes effective Drug Court planning implementation and operations.

10. Forging partnerships among Drug Courts, public agencies, and community-based organizations generates local support and enhances Drug Court effectiveness.

Most of these "key components" appear to represent descriptive themes, aims, or values, as opposed to presenting an overall theoretical perspective. However, by drawing main concepts out of the statements that are written in aspirational or "standards-like" language, several could be interpreted as suggestive of operations or measures possibly representative of constructs. Components #1 and # 2 suggest a new integration and method of justice processing, one characterized by a more blended incorporation of treatment services into processing using nonadversarial technique. Early eligibility in #3 might mean that immediate intervention is an effective construct likely to affect participant outcomes (e.g., those who enter the program immediately are more successful than those who enter later) or monitoring through drug testing might be representative of close supervision with consequence (as deterrence theory would suggest). This could be rather easily measurable. Ongoing interaction with judges (#7) certainly can be measured and tested in a number of ways (frequency, duration, substance, timing) and could be seen to reflect the judge's central role, again in as part of a possible deterrent scheme. Components 6, 9, and 10, though, would seem more difficult to tie directly to constructs that explain impact. Hiller et al. (2009) in a very recent, as yet unpublished article, attempt to translate the drug court professional organization's credo-like key components into measurable operations.

In several experimental studies, Marlowe and various colleagues (Marlowe and Kirby 1999; Marlowe et al. 2003a, 2005, 2006) have employed what Marlowe has described[5] as a behaviorist perspective (though one that could also be seen as deterrence based), focusing on drug court impact (participant outcomes) as a function of the impact of sanctions and positive rewards, including the effect of varied schedules before the judge and various varied forms and schedules of sanctions and rewards.[6] Their conclusions suggest that manipulation of sanctions, including appearances before the judge, are instrumental in producing drug court outcomes, and that overuse of negative sanctions ultimately appears to have a negative effect on participant behavior. The Marlowe studies do point to the use of sanctions and the role of the judge as probably important drug court constructs and further provide some evidence relating to how variations in their use affect participant outcomes. Thus, Marlowe and associates evoke an overall theoretical perspective (behaviorist-deterrence oriented) that seems both intuitively sensible and supported by some of their findings.

Taken together, the work reviewed above offers themes that contribute to explaining some aspects of drug court operations and their impact on participant outcomes and, indirectly, contribute to the aim of identifying constructs and an underlying model of drug court impact.

BUILDING AND TESTING A DRUG COURT CAUSAL MODEL FROM MULTIPLE STUDIES FOR ADDRESSING CONSTRUCT VALIDITY

In identifying underlying drug court constructs for developing eventual tests of a causal model, explaining the widely advertised crime reduction impact of drug courts, one might

---

[5] Comments made in a presentation at the meetings of the World Criminology Congress, August 9, 2005.
[6] Rewards, such as lessening required tasks or paying financial rewards for compliance were effective; enhanced reward schedules were more effective than just lessening of court requirements of nonfinancial rewards.

have considered three basic methods. First, if the drug court were a well-established inter-vention, one could merely draw on the constructs already agreed upon in the literature and use them to guide causal models to be tested on data from multiple drug court sites. Sec-ond, one could posit a model based on a particular theoretical perspective, operationalize it using reasonable measures given available findings, and then test it on drug court data. And/or, third, one could begin with a grounded approach building on observation, interview and preliminary descriptive studies to formulate a reasonable causal model reflecting an hypothesized theoretical explanation of how it works and then test and adjust the model and its rationale, depending on what data subsequently suggest. As there was little if any previ-ous research in the drug court field when our research team first began, the first approach was, of course, not available to us. Several authors reviewed above (e.g., Nolan 2001; Miethe et al. 2000; and Marlowe and Kirby 1999) adopted theoretical perspectives and, in the case of Miethe and Marlowe, then sought to test selected elements of drug court operations to deter-mine whether these elements acted as the theory would predict. Longmire et al. (2001) used a version of the third approach in identifying five dimensions proposed to represent constructs likely to central to producing drug court impact; however, they did not draw on a unifying theoretical perspective to explain their "dimensions."

Questions about what a drug court "is" first faced our research approach at the very begin-ning of the drug court movement, starting with the nation's first nationally funded evaluation of the nation's first drug court in Miami (Goldkamp and Weiland 1993). The goal of formu-lating a causal model was pursued in stages in successive evaluation studies of drug courts to understand and evaluate the impact and operation of drug courts through the 1990s (Gold-kamp 1999). Our approach drew not only on observation of many of the courts developed during that decade but also, in a more focused way, on the author's own experience in evaluat-ing the Miami, Philadelphia, Las Vegas, and Portland drug courts during the formative years of the drug court movement. The Miami, Las Vegas and Portland drug courts were among the first generation of drug courts – with the Miami court establishing the first example ever in 1989, then the Portland court following in 1991 and the Las Vegas becoming operational in 1993. The Philadelphia court, first operating in 1995, was a "second generation" (postfed-eral funding) court. The first courts relied heavily on their own creativity and their mission of problem-solving, including finding treatment resources and meeting costs, because there were no earlier examples to draw on. Later courts, such as Philadelphia's, differed in that by then they had many examples of courts from which to borrow and adapt and also in having federal funding available for planning, training and, in many cases, for their first years of operation.

Using observation and interview during the first half of the 1990s, accommodating the growing diversity of drug courts, the first task for the author and colleagues was to develop a working typology of drug courts (Goldkamp 1994a, 1999, 2000). The aim in developing the working typology of drug courts was, using a grounded approach, to draw on observations and interviews to provide a conceptual frame of reference, which identified key commonal-ties in courts (that were also essential ingredients) despite their variations. Once these classes of attributes describing drug courts were identified, they were considered as suggestive of underlying drug court constructs. Next, measures were adopted to serve as indicators of the constructs in formulating a drug court causal model. Using contemporaneous data from two sites (Portland and Las Vegas), the preliminary model was then tested empirically for confir-mation that the candidate constructs actually played significant roles in producing drug court outcomes. With this as a first step, then, ideally the model could be tested and further refined in subsequent and more specifically focused drug court studies.[7]

A REHABILITATION-DETERRENCE EXPLANATION

From observation, interview, and preliminary drug court studies, the preliminary causal models inferred that drug courts operated under a dual theoretical perspective, similar to the one reflected later in Marlowe et al.'s (2005, 2006) work. The proposed models were hypothesized (Goldkamp 2000; Goldkamp et al. 2001c) to operate based on rehabilitation (specific deterrence) and general deterrence. It was argued that rehabilitation, a long-standing justice aim particularly dominant during the first half of the twentieth century, alone did not fully capture the operations of the drug court. There were many aspects of the drug court that appeared clearly rehabilitative (as in their "let's-treat-them-rather-than-just-punish-and-recycle them" orientations) (see Nolan 2001). Although not viewed as sufficient as a total overall guiding explanation for the drug court model, rehabilitation explained much of the language and emphasis on traditional forms of treatment characteristic in drug courts. Observation and interview suggested, however, that the drug court could not simply be explained as a sort of rehabilitation redux, the treatment ethic long dormant, but now reemerging. Moreover, in addition to the features seemingly compatible with a rehabilitation framework, other aspects of drug courts were not well accounted for by this perspective, including the increasingly complex use of sanctions and jailing. While some might debate that rehabilitation includes specific deterrence and that a reading of Bentham (1781, reprint ed., 1988) would show elaborate use of sanctions and rewards; in a noticeable sense, the treatment emphasis in observed drug courts was carefully circumscribed by more traditional criminal justice boundaries, on the other side of which more punitive aims were still in the waiting. The court brought the coercive powers of punishment strongly to bear on the rehabilitative practices that were otherwise evident.

General deterrence complemented specific deterrence functions, as individual transactions in the drug court were used for dual purposes: first to instruct the individual him/herself in the process of self-change (specific), and, second, as a public lesson for other drug court participants advertising consequences that lay in wait when noncompliance occurred (general). Individual treatment was greatly supplemented by group treatment. Individual level actions (favorable and unfavorable to treatment progress) were advertised publicly in court. A defendant who missed treatment or used drugs would be addressed loudly and publicly in front of all the other participants seated in the courtroom awaiting their own turns to face the judge. When the judge heralded a participant's success, this also was absorbed by the audience, providing examples of how one should act to receive positive outcomes. When a participant transgressed, various sanctions would be imposed publicly, ranging from rather minor but embarrassing sanctions (sitting in the jurors box observing court for a few days) to rather severe sanctions (such as being sent back to earlier treatment phases, being sent to jail for a few days, or, worse being terminated from the program and sentenced to a punitive term). The use of jail as a sanction among the unconvicted participants in drug court seemed particularly deterrence-based and was widely perceived by participants as the most undesirable action a judge could take in response to their noncompliance. In contradiction to those who have argued that confinement coming at the end of an often long adjudicative process served

---

[7] As of this date, to the author's knowledge, this has not occurred in the available literature.

as a poor deterrent, drug court participants themselves reported that the immediate and unconstrained use of jail in the drug court communicated the threat of punishment quite effectively (Goldkamp et al. 2001a).

IDENTIFYING CONSTRUCTS USING A WORKING TYPOLOGY

The drug court working typology was structured in two parts, the first characterized the drug court on a general level to help distinguish drug courts from other more traditional court proceedings, and the second outlined seven more specific dimensions that were descriptive and pointed to essential elements of drug courts that posited underlying constructs (Goldkamp 1994b, 1999).

Part one of the typology identified three core attributes that characterized drug courts in broad terms, including: (1) a new substantive focus on treatment with goals, values, and methods that are non-traditional for the criminal court; (2) a new judicial role and new related roles for other players; and (3) a newly defined working relationship between treatment and criminal courts (and between drug court and other social services), basically rejecting the "refer out through probation" hands-off judicial approach.

The second and more substantively specific part of the typology identified seven dimensions, which courts shared in common but along which they varied:

1. *Target problem*: Each drug court was created in response to a particular local drug-crime problem. In more general terms, this dimension recognized that the context within which courts operated was key in understanding their impact. Drug courts differed, sometimes dramatically, in the nature of the drug-crime problem, motivating the development of a drug court in a jurisdiction. While all jurisdictions shared in common a major drug-crime orientation, the nature of that problem differed from site to site as did the particular part of that overall problem that the drug court approach was intended to address. Depending on the site and its local drug-crime issues, drug court planning, for example, may have been spurred in response drug-related property crimes, prostitution, drug-related homelessness, drug gang violence, perhaps the effects of a recent heroin epidemic, or other aspects of a drug-crime problem affecting a specific geographic area of the drug court jurisdiction.

2. *Target population*: Having determined that a certain slice of the drug-crime problem was the main issue to be addressed by a drug court, each drug court next translated this problem orientation into a decision to deal with a certain part of the entering criminal justice population that would be its specific and accessible target most closely related to the problem. Not only could a given court consider a variety of target populations that might help address the local drug-crime problem, but target populations also differed considerably from court to court, as the drug court approach grew. Some courts dealt with a mixed array of substance abusing criminally charged defendants, while others selected first time marijuana users or mainly heroin abusers. Some limited their scope to a felony population, believing that the greatest crime reduction impact could be achieved by addressing the more seriously involved highest risk participants, while others chose to deal with high-volume categories of misdemeanor substance abusers. The targeted populations might further have been limited by the stage of processing at which a drug court was designed to operate and the agreement of key justice actors on what they thought was appropriate. The research also suggested that in focusing on certain target populations, the drug court was implicitly also dealing with the settings

from which the target population came – and these were often specific, identifiable parts of town.

3. *Court processing focus and adaptations*: Drug courts varied dramatically in how they fit into the existing criminal process. Some intervened from the very first postarrest stage of criminal process, while others focused at postplea or postconviction, or the sentencing stages. Reentry drug courts, for example, dealt with the release-from-confinement stage. In addition, drug courts created new review stages, proceedings, status hearings, intake procedures, and nonadversarial methodologies. Some courts created an "orientation" stage at which all potentially eligible defendants were required to attend in advance of normal court proceedings (even before first appearance). These varied notably by setting.

4. *Identifying, screening, and evaluating candidates*: Courts differed in the kinds of methods employed to identify and enroll candidates for the drug court, ranging from the use of rough and readily available indicators such as criminal charge, prior criminal and substance abuse history criteria that would allow quick sorting of candidates from each batch of new arrestees to more extensive and time-consuming substance abuse treatment evaluation procedures borrowed from traditional drug treatment programs that would require identifying candidates more slowly as their cases advanced into the normal adjudication process. In some cases, nearly immediate screening and enrollment occurred, while other courts followed the original Miami idea that arrest is an optimal point for intervention (when the substance abuser reaches "rock bottom" and is most open to being helped), while other courts did not consider a candidate until the sentencing stage, potentially many months after arrest and many other criminal processing stages.

5. *Structure and content of treatment*: Drug courts differed considerably in what they employed as "treatment." Treatment may include a variety of procedures, from detoxification to outpatient and residential treatment. Others have blended court appearances, judicial intervention, and interaction with treatment of different types, such as various degrees of drug testing and treatment or group session attendance. Drug testing, acupuncture, and other activities have been adapted to the drug court treatment regimen. Drug courts varied in the nature, substance, and frequency of treatment as well. They also differed in the extent to which they adopted procedures borrowed directly from traditional behavioral healthcare practices or improvised and adapted court-based procedures (involving court appearances, judicial interaction, rewards, and sanctions), with selected traditional treatment practices. After an initial pilot, for example, the Miami court dropped traditional practices built on residential treatment and exclusionary procedures followed by private providers to instead design its own special treatment regimen emphasizing outpatient treatment and acupuncture in its own clinics.

6. *Responses to performance: client accountability:* Many courts have organized treatment into successive stages through which participants must progress and which employ various schedules of rewards and sanctions. In fact, the judge's announcement of a participant's advancement from one stage to the next or return to an earlier stage of treatment is conceived of as a response to a participant's positive or negative performance in the drug court. Rewards and sanctions include a wide variety of measures in different courts, including not only promotion to the next stage of treatment, but also being berated or congratulated by the judge in front of the full courtroom, being made to sit in the jury box to observe proceedings for successive sessions, writing and

reading essays to the court on self-improvement, or, in a worst case, being ordered to jail for short periods of reassessment.

7. *Extent of system support and participation*: Another key element of the drug court typology on which courts differed reflects the internal (court or justice system) or external context (other social services, laws, crime picture) surrounding the operation of the drug court. This dimension presents a wide range of possible measures that could get at this dimension, reflecting a variety of aspects. For example, internally, the large court systems viewed and supported drug courts very differently – and this has changed over time. In some courts, the drug court was permitted as the special interest of one particular judge who supervised the court in his or her own time on a part-time basis and after normal judicial duties were accomplished. Other systems rotated judges as part of normal criminal assignments. Still other systems integrated judicial drug court duties into the larger court system in a municipality or even state-wide, in effect institutionalizing the drug court as a "normal" part of the court system.

Externally, drug courts also varied in the extent to which other justice agencies participated, supported or merely "put up with" the drug court. Often the prosecutor played a central role in determining the ultimate scope and power of the drug court. In some jurisdictions, like Miami and Portland, the prosecutor was a major force behind the drug court. In others, the prosecutor supported only very narrow and restricted versions of drug court by restricting the eligibility criteria of potential candidates they would accept (e.g., when participants had pleaded guilty or even been sentenced). Courts also differed in the legal contexts within which they operated (different kinds of drug laws, for example) and in the extent to which other social service systems cooperated or played central or partnership roles in providing services.

TESTING OPERATIONAL MEASURES OF CONSTRUCTS

The ultimate way this body of research could be applied to the problem of addressing construct validity in drug court research was to construct a conceptual model showing how key elements of the drug court innovation could produce its crime reduction impact. As a point of departure, Fig. 22.1 represents a general conceptual scheme positing that the generation of positive outcomes (e.g., treatment success, less reoffending, less absconding, less termination, lowered

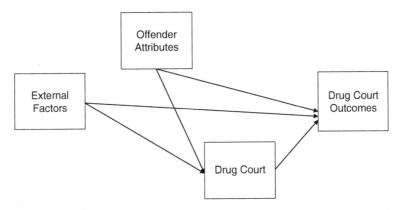

FIGURE 22.1. Drug court causal model: underlying constructs producing outcomes.

costs, etc.) were affected by: (1) external factors representing the immediate and larger context of the drug court's operation (e.g., laws and policies, administrative practices, the geography of treatment and crime), (2) participant attributes (e.g., a priori risk, drug habits, treatment history, etc.), and (3) elements of the drug court itself (judge behavior, appearance in drug court, social interactions with peers, treatment, sanctions, etc.). According to this conceptualization of a drug court causal model, the drug court produces its outcomes (of which public safety is given the greatest emphasis) only after taking into account the direct, indirect, and/or mediating effects of external factors and participant attributes. These are included in the conceptual model not only in the sense of "controls," but also because no drug court operates in a vacuum and their contexts are not only influential, but they are likely to differ considerably.

At this preliminary stage of model formation, the next step was to select and test operational measures of the concepts represented in the model (both external and internal to the courts themselves) using data generated in the national evaluation of the drug courts in Las Vegas and Portland (Goldkamp et al. 2000, 2001b). As a means of testing, the plausibility of the constructs represented in the conceptual model, the research examined: (1) the possible importance of contextual factors (external and internal to the courts) in shaping drug court participant outcomes using interrupted time series analysis and (2) the contributing roles of drug court functions, to the extent we had reasonable measures of them, in separate individual-level analyses. (External influences examined using time series included enactment of state laws affecting drug penalties, state laws affecting eligibility and costs of behavioral health care, jail crowding litigation and emergency releases, changes in court and prosecutorial policy relating to drug court (see Goldkamp et al. 2001d). Other contextual measures, geography of neighborhoods and clinics (represented as distance measures), and different judicial assignment approaches, were tested in individual level analyses. Tests of the more obvious candidate drug court elements (treatment, appearances in court, sanctions) were examined using logistic regression with controls for offender risk attributes (see Goldkamp et al. 2001c).

Times series analyses underscored the importance of external factors in affecting the function of drug courts over time, as measured by orientations of candidates and enrollments over time in Portland (1991–1997) and Las Vegas (1993–1997). Court and prosecutorial policies had major impacts on the courts in both sites, respectively. In Portland in 1995, a new much less tolerant, punitive approach to noncompliance was adopted, resulting in more court failures. In Las Vegas at roughly the same time, a new prosecutor implemented a policy that nearly ended use of drug court at the preconviction stage and implemented instead an approach aimed at the postconviction, sentencing stage, which had an important effect on court function and outcomes. Other factors such as changes in law (lowering penalties for drugs in Nevada, affecting behavioral health care eligibility in Oregon), and jail crowding interventions as well as other external factors also had an effect (Goldkamp et al. 2001d). Geography appeared to be important (statistically significant) in producing outcomes in both sites, net of controls, but in marginal ways, when measured as distance from residential neighborhoods (for non-whites) to drug court or treatment clinic site. Judicial assignment, which was testable only in Portland where various approaches to drug court assignment was attempted, had a statistically significant, nonmarginal but complex effect on drug court participant outcomes (Goldkamp et al. 2001b, 2001c).

Having established evidence of the potential importance of contextual factors in affecting drug court outcomes through time series, the analysis of factors representing drug court constructs turned to individual level analysis of the relative contributions of drug court elements on participant outcomes using the Portland and Las Vegas drug court data summarized in Table 22.1. Surviving until the final stages of multivariate analyses were measures of judge

TABLE 22.1. Modeling the effects of drug court treatment variables on later offender behavior (rearrest within 1 year; graduation within 2 years) among drug court participants in Multnomah county (1991–1997) and Clark county (1993–1997)

Multnomah variable	Any rearrest	Drug rearrest	Non-drug rearrest	Graduation w/in 2 years	Clark variable	Any rearrest	Drug rearrest	Non-drug rearrest	Graduation w/in 2 years
Risk variables					*Risk variables*				
Race (white/non-white)	0.324 (0.138)	0.706 (0.002)	0.113 (0.622)	−0.428	Prior arrests in last 3 years	0.7278 (0.0087)	0.7517 (0.0200)	0.7310 (0.0084)	0.2026 (0.5743)
Alias	−0.943 (0.000)	−0.784 (0.001)	−0.527 (0.018)	0.145 (0.553)	Prior drug arrests	0.6276 (0.0227)	0.3129 (0.2745)	0.6080 (0.0211)	−0.3627
Prior arrest in last 3 years	0.603 (.007)	−0.022 (0.929)	1.075 (0.000)	−0.078 (0.790)	Prior FTAs	0.0758 (0.7767)	0.5395 (0.0508)	−0.0656 (0.7979)	−0.4406 (0.1986)
Pending arrest charge	0.164 (0.652)	0.194 (0.589)	0.221 (0.523)	−0.856					
Treatment/sanction variables					*Treatment/sanction variables*				
Time in TX (<50%, 50% or more)	−0.209 (0.515)	−0.286 (0.411)	0.032 (0.927)	1.187 (0.002)	Time in TX (<50%, 50% or more)	−0.4122 (0.2928)	−0.9256 (0.0171)	−0.2850 (0.4477)	3.2540 (0.0020)
No. of TX contacts (30 or less, 30>)	−0.248 (0.429)	−0.012 (0.973)	−0.543 (0.100)	0.491 (.242)	No. of TX contacts (30 or less, 30>)	−1.1790 (0.0078)	−0.2304 (0.5652)	−0.9692 (0.0189)	0.4461 (0.7647)
Any sanctions	0.637 (0.203)	0.449 (0.524)	0.894 (0.101)	−0.937 (0.048)	Any sanctions	1.2867 (0.0000)	0.9898 (0.0131)	0.8947 (0.0036)	−1.5957 (0.0000)
Any jail sanctions	1.026 (0.025)	1.430 (0.024)	0.491 (0.315)	−0.476 (0.298)	Any jail sanctions	0.7029 (0.0059)	0.4279 (0.0955)	0.4830 (0.0445)	−1.4584 (0.0000)
No. of court appearances (8 or less, 8>)	−0.147 (0.588)	0.345 (0.239)	−0.138 (0.618)	3.515 (0.001)	No. of court appearances (8 or less, 8>)	1.0547 (0.0096)	0.4866 (0.1703)	1.0288 (0.0049)	2.0081 (0.0318)

(continued)

TABLE 22.1. (continued)

Multnomah county

Model statistics	Any rearrest	Drug rearrest	Non-drug rearrest	Graduation w/in 2 years
Log likelihood	148.59	488.071	526.122	363.299
Goodness of fit	4.405	3.945	3.089	7.107
GF significance	0.819	0.786	0.929	0.525
Chi square	148.59	92.539	108.574	183.421
DF	9	9	9	9
Significance	0.000	0.000	0.000	0.000
N	547	547	547	405[a]

Clark county

Model statistics	Any rearrest	Drug rearrest	Non-drug rearrest	Graduation w/in 2 years
Log likelihood	451.972	404.029	476.109	291.912
Goodness of fit (H&L)	18.4032	9.7041	4.7604	8.8744
GF significance	0.0184	0.2864	0.7828	0.3530
Chi square	110.714	70.963	75.663	220.978
DF	8	8	8	8
Significance	0.0000	0.0000	0.0000	0.0000
N	407	407	407	407

Note: These analyses are based on unweighted data. Parameter estimates and significance are indicated from logistic regression analysis
Source: Goldkamp et al. (2001c)
[a]Includes 1991–1996 defendants only in Multnomah County

(number of court appearances), treatment (time in treatment, number of treatment contacts), and use of sanctions (any sanctions, jailing).[8] The finding that the factors that surfaced as statistically significant, net of the effects of controls, differed in the two sites (i.e., by location) and by time period underscored the importance of this kind of exploratory analysis searching for underlying constructs. In Portland in final analyses of potential indicators reflecting key constructs, only use of jail as a sanction appeared to be related to reoffending when the outcome was measured as any rearrests or as drug rearrests within 2 years of drug court entry. However, the use of jailing *increased* the participants' chances of reoffending, net of controls. Other key measures relating to court, judge, and treatment functions were not found to be related to explaining reoffending outcomes in the Portland drug court data. In the Las Vegas drug court data, more of the assumed key elements were significantly (statistically and meaningfully) related to reoffending outcomes; however, court appearances, the use of sanctions, and the use of jail as a sanction each *increased* the prospects of participant reoffending during the follow-up period rather than decrease the chances as the model would have predicted. Yet, the number of court contacts and length of time in treatment were related to reoffending in the expected direction, i.e., the more contacts and the longer in treatment, the lower the probability of reoffending.

When the measures representing possible underlying constructs were used to predict programmatic outcomes (successful graduation from drug court), the findings differed from the analysis of reoffending. In Portland, net of controls, increasing time in treatment, and greater number of court appearances were related to graduating successfully from the drug court, thus supporting the predicted relationship. The use of any sanctions was related in the sense that having sanctions applied was related to failure to graduate. The Las Vegas results were very similar.

These findings raised several questions about the nature of underlying constructs and what a reasonable first approximation of the drug court causal model should include. First, contextual factors, both "external" and internal to the court system, itself seemed to play important roles in influencing court functioning (and, to the extent that court functioning affected participants outcomes, these contextual factors influenced the drug courts' productivity). The impact of contextual factors and the finding of differences across jurisdictions demonstrate both their importance in modeling drug court impact and the difficulty that would result in attempting to interpret analyses of drug court outcomes without taking these context measures into account (which no other studies have). The individual-level findings also pose challenges for identifying the drug court's underlying constructs, especially when considering the replication of drug courts across the nation. The key factors – representing treatment, the judge/court role, jailing, and sanctions in general – seemed to predict program outcomes (i.e., graduation vs. termination) better than public safety outcomes. What it takes to predict program graduation is quite different from what it takes to predict (or prevent) reoffending. This finding throws into question the crime reduction effectiveness of what are assumed to be the key elements of the drug court innovation. Because the drug court program was designed to reduce offending, one would expect the factors shaping participants' progress through the program to graduation to correspond to factors related to prevention of reoffending. One would also expect such factors to be representative of the constructs underlying by the drug court approach.

---

[8] Interactions between court, treatment and jailing were also tested but not presented here. Some statistically significant results were found. See Goldkamp et al. (2001c).

Not only did the indicators showing significant and meaningful relationships with the probability of reoffending differ by site (in two of the nation's most recognized drug courts), but, moreover, interpretation of the nature of their relationships was not self-evident. The fact that the use of jail appeared to be the only significant indicator of reoffending in Portland might suggest that the Portland drug court mainly achieved its results by coercively brandishing the use of jail. One might infer that the Portland approach was primarily deterrence-driven in the most punitive sense. In fact, however, our observation of that court in comparison with the many other courts we observed at the time led us to conclude that the Portland court was distinguished by the fact that it used jailing less frequently than most other courts. Without digressing at too great a length here, possibly the role of jailing was found to be influential because of its highly selective rather than common application.[9]

In Las Vegas, the number of court appearances (one of the measures used to tap the construct involving the judicial role in drug court) was significant in predicting reoffending, but in a positive direction: that is, the greater the number of appearances a participant made in court, the higher the probability of reoffending, net of the effects of participant risk. This finding would call into question one of the drug court movement's key assumptions that frequent appearances before the judge is an important vehicle in reducing reoffending. According to the Las Vegas results, either frequent court appearances contributed to reoffending or mainly served as an indicator of outcome mirroring reoffending (that is, people who were rearrested were also likely to be people who were in court frequently). The positive relation between any sanction use (including jailing) and reoffending in Las Vegas, net of risk, raises another dilemma for the conventional wisdom of drug court practitioners: On the one hand, yes, the use of sanctions played an important role in producing reoffending outcomes; but, on the other hand, they apparently increased the prospects of reoffending as more jailing led to, greater prospects of reoffending. Or, again, perhaps their application should be viewed more as an outcome (a dependent variable) itself. Persons who were sanctioned also were people who were rearrested during follow-up.

From any perspective, these findings are troublesome for the drug court assumptions that appearances and jailing are important deterrent vehicles in preventing later reoffending. The problem concerning the direction of the sanctioning relationships with reoffending outcomes could even lead to an interpretation that the drug courts mainly applied punishments to drug offenders who were likely to reoffend in the end anyway. Extended further, these findings may lead to questions about whether the sanction-oriented innovation is delivering punishment that otherwise might not have been applied in some of the participants' cases – in other words, not serving as an alternative to normal punishment as advertised. These admittedly preliminary or exploratory steps to develop a drug court causal model reflecting the constructs underlying the drug court idea and operation do not necessarily support the conventional wisdom concerning drug court impact. Constructing models of drug court impact is both more complex (involving multiple aspects) and variable over time and site than conventional wisdom has assumed.

WHAT DRUG COURT CONSTRUCT VALIDITY PROBLEM?

Good construct explication is essential to construct validity. (Shadish et al. 2002:69)

---

[9] Bentham's (1781) discussion of deterrence emphasizes that the deterrent impact of a sanction is enhanced by its very selective application and that overuse weakens its effect.

The logical method illustrated in this research, from the steps of observation, interview, consideration of theoretical rationale, to typology development and empirical testing, has not resulted in identification of a clearly supported set of constructs that either comport with the conventional wisdom or with other explanations of the drug court effect. Oddly, the obvious drug court functions explained participant success in the drug court program (i.e., in reaching "graduation") much better than they accounted for the probability of reoffending. This can be taken to mean that practitioners are reasonably consistent in applying several basic themes to shape the drug court's programmatic operation (concerning judge, court appearance, treatment, sanctions, jailing), but that the factors governing programmatic operation do not clearly relate to crime reduction. The search for an underlying model is made further difficult by the finding that the factors surviving controls varied by site (and within site by time period, though time-specific findings are not discussed here).

Based on this body of research, then, how do the findings regarding underlying constructs raise issues of construct validity? The first implication is a negative: how can we be assured that the drugs courts, which have been studied for impact, are consistent in approach (i.e., are based on a reasonably similar drug court "engine"), despite diversity in certain areas (structure, target populations, treatment content)? It follows then that, despite widespread replication of the drug court modality, it is uncertain whether the operation and impact of drug courts are explained by the same underlying mechanism – or even if some of the underlying constructs (e.g., sanctions) might operate in a manner opposite to that assumed.

Many issues of construct validity can be raised when the underlying constructs are uncertain. This problems falls under what Shadish et al. (2002:73) classify as "inadequate explication of constructs." It is not surprising that an innovation that became so rapidly popular proceeded without much empirical verification of its assumptions; in fact, it is probably normal. But the great number of drug court outcome studies that support the notion that drug courts are effective crime reduction tools, "movement" enthusiasm aside, should at least be considered with some caution. In short, not only are the studies based on widely different examples of the innovation, with different target populations and procedures and occurring in different settings, but the body of supportive outcome studies to date also implicitly assumes that the operation of certain underlying constructs explains the results. A reading of the findings from the author's research journey discussed above suggests that this may not be a sound assumption.

Shadish et al. also discuss "construct confounding" as an example of a construct validity problem. The assumption of an implicitly or explicitly accepted drug court "model" and the related evaluation research may also suffer from confounding the notions of treatment, sanctions, jail, and judicial supervision. Interviews by the author over the decade showed that all of these were rationalized as "treatment." In fact, frequent court attendance, jailing, and other sanctions may be perceived as or may operate as punishments, or as threats of punishment, and had the opposite than intended effect on participants in the area of reoffending.[10] Confounding levels of constructs may also pose a challenge for construct validity in testing the impact of drug courts on crime. An example might be that, while participants are assumed to be "substance abusers." However, their drug problems could differ a great deal: some could have alcohol problems, be recreational marijuana users, or be highly addicted to methamphetamine or heroin; others could suffer from serious undiagnosed mental health problems

---

[10] The confounding of constructs parallels the conceptual difficulty, for example, already existing in distinguishing between specific deterrence and rehabilitation, with the Sechrest et al. (1979) seeing the distinction hinging on the use of fear or intimidation (not in rehabilitation but implicitly in specific deterrence).

in addition to their drug addiction. Thus, an important differentiator in outcome may be participant risk. Usually, though, drug courts put all new comers through a program with similar behavioral requirements for graduation, despite important differences. To the extent that addiction may be an underlying construct (or if addiction is related to participant risk), failure to account for levels or qualitative differences in addiction/risk raises problems of construct validity in looking at the body of findings from studies showing drug court impact on crime.

CONCLUSION: IMPLICATIONS OF CONSTRUCT EXPLICATION, CONSTRUCT VALIDITY FOR THE INTERPRETATION OF EVALUATIVE FINDINGS

This chapter has selected the extraordinary growth of drug courts and its associated evaluative literature to illustrate a facet of construct validity issues that is undoubtedly relevant to many other studies of policy relevant innovations. The dramatic growth of the drug court movement and the supportive evaluative literature serve as illustrations of how these issues in construct validity – in this case focusing on explication or identification of clear theoretical and operational understanding of "what a drug court is" – could have a potentially major impact, as implementation of policy innovation quickly outpaces the soundness of findings emerging in the trailing evaluative research.

At various levels of depth, rigor, and quality, evaluations of drug court impact have followed the innovation since its early days. Plenty of evidence from this rapidly growing body of evaluative literature prove that "drug courts work." This literature has been seen as useful to the drug court movement and government funders in supporting the institutionalization of the now highly transformed innovation. Once the premise that "drug courts work" is accepted as conventional wisdom based on the collective weight of the evidence, then the problems of identifying and considering the implications of underlying causal constructs can somehow now seem unnecessary, self-evident or merely academic. One could argue, to the contrary, however, that this absence in the growing body of drug court studies, the failure to examine and sort through problems of underlying constructs and construct validity, takes on increasing importance, given that the magnitude of the adoption or emulation of the drug court innovation.

Admittedly the lessons drawn from this author's research experience examining the development of drug courts are best understood as preliminary or exploratory and are discussed here for the purposes of issue-raising. This chapter has described a logical method – or at least a sequence or collection of steps – for moving research beyond the "whether it works" question to scrutiny of "how" it works. The result of raising these construct questions, however, is unsettling. Perhaps the most unsettling implication of this analysis is that the supportive body of findings from evaluative drug court studies is to such an extent based on "apples and oranges," on different studies of different programs in different settings with different populations in different time periods (etc.), that a reasonable case can be made that findings are, on the whole, not comparable. Add to that uncertainty about which particular core causative factors are essential to a drug court and the confidence with which one can generalize about their crime reduction capacity diminishes. The drug court "impact machine" is: (1) dependent on context, (2) participant attributes (risk), and (3) aspects of what drug courts do – some of which appears to generate an effect opposite to the one presumed and widely heralded.

The fact that widespread replication has proceeded without a solid empirical understanding of the elements of the court-based justice reform is not surprising from many perspectives. Perhaps it is commonplace among innovations in any field. However, without a grasp of the underlying constructs, the validity of the replications and the research that has followed them can be called into question – or at least the sweeping inferences drawn from the research can. In the health field, one may assume that a new vaccine being introduced involves the same amount of the same substance in whatever settings it is applied. In the area of social problems and social justice, certainly, innovations are not exact and cannot applied or reapplied in a manner that is exactly the same across settings. Even so, if the supportive evaluation literature and the grand claims of substance abuse and crime reduction are not supported by a literature based on studies that have systematically examined the innovation and its impact, one could conclude that these claims require further and more careful scrutiny – contrary to the popular view.

That the value of impact studies is greatly heightened by a specific understanding of the constructs and mechanisms at work, that is, by reference to a common understanding of the elements of the "impact machine," should be obvious. First, an agreed upon model allows the research to examine overall impact as well as contributions of specific elements. Using the drug court example, "When a drug court works, why does it work?" is closely mirrored by – but is not the same as – the question, "When a drug court doesn't work, why doesn't it work?"

Second, making sense of impact findings (positive or negative) is difficult to do meaningfully without a frame of reference, without an understanding of what is being measured. Replication – the validation of findings through the repetition of studies of the innovation across different settings – does not necessarily cure this problem. Repeating an apples and oranges approach may add to the number of positive findings on which policymakers draw as showing evidence of the innovation's success, but it does not necessarily contribute to the knowledge of the innovation's impact.

Perhaps, most critically, if the aims of the innovation involve crime prevention, or improved public and personal health, then public policy has an interest in being guided by knowledge of how to adjust or improve the particular strategy. With an agreed upon underlying model of the innovation's operation and impact, research can test the innovation's impact on specific populations or the relative roles of different elements in affecting particular outcomes or particular outcomes on specific populations. Replication can be valuable in taking into account the innovation's underlying mechanism while varying elements, population, and settings, and, thus helping to building an increasingly informative general and specific body of evidence of its effects.

The discussion presented in this chapter underscores the potential importance and of one often neglected aspect of construct validity – explication of a construct or, put another way, a clear understanding of the nature of the innovation under study. The context of this discussion is informed by the attempt of the author and his colleagues to understand the nature and impact of the drug court innovation from the inside-out, as it was unfolding, growing, shape-changing, and transforming into one of the most dramatic justice innovations in its scope in recent memory. The discussion was framed not only to use the drug court innovation as an example of the challenges faced by research attempting to evaluate a new social policy phenomenon with possibly majors implications. In addition, it sought to illustrate how, in addition to responding to evidence of the impact of a rapidly unfolding policy innovation, the paper aimed to underscore the foundational importance of the need in evaluative research to know what the "it" this is. The decade long research approach sought to contribute "immediate" evidence of the impact of the drug court innovation, at times clamored for by government officials and funders, while at the same time developing a model or framework that contributed a firm grounding in what the innovation really involved. The effort to identify the underlying constructs drew on observation, interview, exploratory research, development of a typology and, finally, development of an empirically testable drug court causal model and, ultimately, called into question assumptions made by advocates that undergirded informing the drug court mythology.

With successful (favorable) results to report, why should the research community care about these abstract notions of construct explication and construct validity? Ignoring questions of identifying underlying constructs and of construct validity as studies accumulate may not necessarily be a fatal flaw, at least at first. It may be common, in fact, first to look for an effect and then, if one is indeed found, to try to explain the effect produced through careful causal model testing in a next phase of research. One could argue, for example, that it is not productive to test for underlying causal constructs and to worry about issues of construct validity when no effect is found. Given the belief among drug court practitioners that drug court practices are strongly validated by research findings, a poor job of addressing construct concerns "up front" can contribute to a stampede to adopt new practices that may, under closer scrutiny, not deliver on widely advertised promises – with implications for public safety, resource allocation and the nature of justice produced.

REFERENCES

Belenko S (1998) Research on drug courts: a critical review. Natl Drug Court Inst Rev 1(1):1–42

Belenko S (1999) Research on drug courts: a critical review, 1999 update. Natl Drug Court Inst Rev 2(2):1–58

Belenko S (2001) Research on drug courts: a critical review: 2001 update. National Center on Addiction and Substance Abuse, Columbia University, New York

Bentham J (1781, reprint ed. 1988) The principles of morals and legislation. Prometheus Books, New York

Cissner A, Rempel M (2005) The state of drug court research: moving beyond. "Do they work?" Center for Court Innovation, New York

Goldkamp J (1994a) Miami's treatment drug court for felony defendants: some implications of assessment findings. Prison J 73:(2), 110–166

Goldkamp J (1994b) Justice and treatment innovation: the drug court movement (a working paper of the First National Drug Court Conference). U.S. Department of Justice, Office of Justice Programs, National Institute of Justice, and State Justice Institute, Washington, DC

Goldkamp J (1999) When is a drug court not a drug court? In: Terry C (ed) The early drug courts: case studies in judicial innovation. Sage, Thousand Oaks, CA

Goldkamp J (2000) The drug court response: issues and implications for justice change. Albany Law Rev 63:923–961

Goldkamp J, Weiland D (1993) Assessing the impact of Dade County's felony drug court. National Institute of Justice, Washington, DC

Goldkamp J, White M, Robinson J (2000) Retrospective evaluation of two pioneering drug courts: phase I findings from Clark County, Nevada, and Multnomah County, Oregon. Crime and Justice Research Institute, Philadelphia

Goldkamp J, White M, Robinson J (2001a) An honest chance: findings from drug court participant focus groups in Brooklyn, Las Vegas, Miami, Portland, San Bernardino, and Seattle. Electronic Publication by the Office of Justice Programs (NCJ 193403). http://www. ncjrs.org/html/bja/honestchance/

Goldkamp J, White M, Robinson J (2001b) From whether to how drug courts work: retrospective evaluation of drug courts in Clark County (Las Vegas) and Multnomah County (Portland): Final Report. Crime and Justice Research Institute, Philadelphia

Goldkamp J, White M, Robinson J (2001c) Do drug courts work? Getting inside the drug court black box. J Drug Issues 31(1):27–72

Goldkamp J, White M, Robinson J (2001d) Context and change: the evolution of pioneering drug courts in Portland and Las Vegas (1991–1998). Law Policy 23(2):143–170

Gottfredson D, Exum M (2002) The Baltimore City Drug Court: one year results from a randomized study. J Res Crime Delinq 39(2):33–356

Gottfredson D, Najaka S, Kearly B (2003) Effectiveness of drug treatment courts: evidence from a randomized trial. Criminol Public Policy 2(2):171–196

Gottfredson DK, Najaka S, Rocha C (2005) The Baltimore City Drug Treatment Court: 3-year self-report outcome study. Eval Rev 29(1):42–64

Gottfredson D, Najaka S, Kearley B, Rocha C (2006) Long-term effects of participation in the Baltimore City drug treatment court: results from an experimental study. J Exp Criminol 2:67–98

Government Accountability Office (1995) Drug courts: information on a new approach to address drug-related crime: report to congressional committees. Government Accountability Office, Washington, DC

Government Accountability Office (1997) Drug courts: overview of growth, characteristics and results: report to congressional committees. Government Accountability Office, Washington, DC

Government Accountability Office (2005) Adult drug court: evidence indicates recidivism reductions and mixed results for other outcomes. Report to congressional committees. Government Accountability Office, Washington, DC

Hiller M, Belenko S, Saum C, Taxman F, Young D, Perdoni M (2009) A brief measure of drug court structure and operations: key components and beyond. Crime and Delinquency (in press)

Hora P, Schma W, Rosenthal J (1999) Therapeutic jurisprudence and the drug court movement: revolutionizing the criminal justice system's response to crime and drug abuse in America. Notre Dame Law Rev 74:439–538

Longshore D, Turner S, Wenzel S, Morral A, Harrell A, McBride D, Deschenes E, Iguchi M (2001) Drug courts: a conceptual framework. J Drug Issues 31:7–25

Marlowe D, Kirby K (1999) Effective use of sanctions in drug courts: lessons from behavioral research. Natl Inst Drug Courts Rev 2:1

Marlowe D, DeMatteo D, Festinger D (2003a) The role of judicial status hearings in drug court. Offender Subst Abuse Rep 3:33–46

Marlowe D, DeMatteo D, Festinger D, Schepise M, Hazzard J, Merrill J, Mulvaney F, McClellan T (2003b) Are judicial status hearings a key component of drug court? Crim Justice Behav 30:141–162

Marlowe D, Festinger D, Dugosh K, Lee P (2005) Are judicial status hearings a key component of drug court? Six and 12 month outcomes. Drug Alcohol Depend 79:145–155

Marlowe D, Festinger D, Lee P, Dugosh K, Benasutti K (2006) Matching judicial supervision to client' risk status in drug court. Crime Delinq 52(1):52–76

Miethe T, Lu H, Reese E (2000) Reintegrative shaming and recidivism risks in drug court: explanations for some unexpected findings. Crime Delinq 46(4):522–541

National Association of Drug Court Professionals (NADCP) (1997, reprinted in 2004) Defining drug courts: the key components. Bureau of Justice Assistance, United States Department of Justice, Washington, DC

Nolan J (2001) Reinventing justice: the American Drug Court Movement. Princeton University Press, Princeton, NJ

Sechrest L, White S, Brown E (eds) (1979) The rehabilitation of criminal offenders: problems and prospects. Panel of research on rehabilitative techniques. National Research Council: Washington, DC

Senjo S, Leip LA (2001) Testing therapeutic jurisprudence theory: an empirical assessment of the drug court process. Western Criminology Review 3(1)

Shadish W, Cook T, Campbell D (2002) Experimental and quasi-experimental designs for generalized causal inference. Houghton Mifflin Co, New York

Sherman L, Berk R (1984) The specific deterrent effects of arrest for domestic assault. Am Sociol Rev 49:261–272

Vilcica ER, Belenko S, Hiller M, Taxman F (2009) Exporting court innovation from the United States to continental Europe: compatibility between the drug court model and the inquisitorial justice system. International Journal of Comparative and Applied Criminal Justice. In press

Wexler DB, Winick BJ (1991) Therapeutic jurisprudence as a new approach to mental health law policy analysis and research. University of Miami Law Review 979

Wilson D, Mitchell O, Mackenzie D (2006) A systematic review of drug court effects on recidivism. J Exp Criminol 2(4):459–487

CHAPTER 23

Place Randomized Trials*

ROBERT BORUCH, DAVID WEISBURD,
AND RICHARD BERK[1]

BACKGROUND AND RECENT HISTORY

An important and emerging vehicle for generating dependable evidence about what works or what does not work falls under the rubric of place randomized trials. In criminology, for instance, such a trial might involve identifying a sample of high crime hot spots and then *randomly* allocating the hot spots, the *places*, to different police or community interventions. The random assignment assures a fair comparison among the interventions, and when the analysis is correct, a legitimate statistical statement of one's confidence in the resulting estimates of their effectiveness. See, for example, Weisburd et al. (2008) for illustrations of such trials and other references in what follows.

This chapter provides basic definitions and practical counsel, with illustrations from criminology, education sciences, and health and welfare research. The problems of generating dependable evidence about what works in crime prevention to detection transcend conventional academic disciplines. Their potential solutions do so. This is a reason for depending on work from different areas. The chapter also identifies issues, ideas, and challenges that might be addressed in further research, such as recent efforts to enhance the quality of reporting and in designing place randomized trials. We also discuss the special analytic difficulties that may occur in the development of place randomized trials as opposed to more traditional trials, in which individuals are the units of random allocation and analysis.

*Research and development work on this topic has been supported by the Rockefeller Foundation and done pro bono under the auspices of the Campbell Collaboration. We are grateful to Dorothy de Moya for assistance and intellectual support.

[1] Robert Boruch is University Trustee Chair Professor at the University of Pennsylvania's Graduate School of Education and Statistics Department of the Wharton School, co-directs Penn's Center for Research and Evaluation in Social Policy, and is a member of Penn's Graduate Group in Criminology. David Weisburd is Chair Professor at the George Mason University and Hebrew University of Jerusalem, and directs the Center for Evidence Based Crime policy at GMU. Richard Berk is Professor of Statistics at the Wharton School and Professor of Criminology, School of Arts and Sciences, at the University of Pennsylvania.

A.R. Piquero and D. Weisburd (eds.), *Handbook of Quantitative Criminology*,
DOI 10.1007/978-0-387-77650-7_23, © Springer Science + Business Media, LLC 2010,
First softcover printing 2011

In the vernacular here, we use the phrase "place randomized trial." In related statistical and social science literature, phrases such as "cluster randomized trial," and "group randomized trial" are used and they mean the same thing *at times*. References are given below. "Place randomized trial" is used because the term is becoming common in the criminological literature and is used in some welfare and education reports on impact evaluations. More importantly, perhaps, the phrase is likely to be better understood by nonresearchers than are other technical and less transparent phrases.

PLACES THAT ARE RANDOMIZED: THEORY AND THE UNITS OF RANDOMIZATION

Place randomized trials depend on a clear understanding of the role of place. On the one hand, a place can be an entity unto itself. For example, business establishments have a legal status separate from their owners and employees and relevant outcomes such as profit and loss can be analyzed as such even though the thousands of individuals may work in the establishments or be their customers. In many cases, schools, police departments, and neighborhoods have the same properties. Measures of such places can have little to do with the smaller units within them, e.g., the market share of a retail establishment, arrest rates in bars, or reputation of a neighborhood.

On the other hand, a place can be primarily an organizational convenience for smaller units within it. Schools can be construed as a good example. One may care about schools because they educate the young and because they provide employment for teachers and administrators. Further, when one asks, for instance, whether a school is "good," attention is often directed to the average academic performance of students at the school level as well as to performance of students (and teachers) within the schools.

Whether the place in place-based randomized trials is an entity in itself or little more than a receptacle for lower level observational units, such as people within the units, can affect dramatically how a randomized trial is designed and analyzed. For instance, the policy maker's goal may be to change how a place functions or to change the way the people within a place function. Sometimes the two are linked. However, the key definitional point in this chapter's context is that in place randomized trials, the random assignment is by place. One important implication is that the methodological benefits of random assignment adhere primarily to places, not the units within them. It follows that statistical analyses at the level of places conform to well understood and widely accepted statistical practice. It also follows that statistical analyses at the level of the units within randomized places, when units are nonrandomized, can be difficult and subject to controversy.

In statistical parlance, the "units of randomization," in a place randomized trial are the places. These units may vary considerably. Weisburd and Green's (1994) study, for instance, focused on drug crime hot spots, street segments, as opposed to specific institutions such as housing developments, schools, or business units. The broad theory underlying the trial posited that focusing police and other resources intensively on hot spots will reduce crime. This is in counterpoint to a theory that says such a focus will not have an effect, and a possible further theory that focusing police resources on hot spots will lead to migration of criminal activity to neighboring areas. Earlier, hot spot trials had been undertaken by Sherman and Weisburd (1995) in Minneapolis, where the unit of analysis was the single street segment from intersection to intersection. The earliest related precedent appears to have been the Kansas

City police patrol experiment (Kelling et al. (1974) where whole police beats were randomly allocated. See Braga (2001) for a review of nine related studies covering five such trials on policing crime hot spots.

Other places have been targeted for different kinds of interventions, such as saloons in the context of preventing violence (Graham et al. 2004) and preventing glassware-related injuries (Warburton and Sheppard 2000). Private properties, including apartment houses and businesses, have been targeted in a study on the effects of civil remedies and drug control (Mazzarole et al. 2000). Housing projects were randomized in a study on preventing elder abuse (Davis and Taylor 1997). Convenience stores, crack houses, and other entities have also been randomly allocated to different interventions.

In health research and evaluation, place randomized trials are usually called "cluster randomized trials." They are becoming frequent as researchers recognize the need to change entire healthcare institutions, or subunits of them, in the interest of enhancing peoples' health. For instance, Grimshaw et al. (2005) randomly allocated medical family practices to different interventions. Each cluster was a medical practice, with physicians, staff, and patients nested within this practice. Leviton and Horbar (2005) randomized tertiary care facilities and neonatal intensive care units within hospitals to different interventions. They did so in order to learn whether better practices in perinatal and neonatal medicine could be deployed well in multiple facilities and would have a statistically dependable effect on patient outcomes. Donner and Klar (2000) give illustrations of such trials in health research reported between the 1950 and the late 1990s.

Sikkema (2005) randomly allocated entire public housing developments to different regimens to learn whether a particular opinion leader-based intervention, tested earlier in other trials and sustained by coherent theory, produced a detectable and substantial effect on women's health behavior. Although their particular focus was AIDs prevention, health-related work has been done in other arenas, in which brothels, bars, and other entities have been the units of random allocation and analysis. For instance, hospital/clinic catchment areas were the units of allocation in rolling out Mexico's place randomized trials on the effects of universal health insurance programs for the rural poor (Imai et al. 2009).

In the Jobs Plus trials, Bloom (2005) and Bloom and Riccio (2005), and their colleagues also randomized housing developments to different interventions just as Sekkema et al. did, but they did so for an entirely different purpose. It was to understand the effects of a particular form of development-wide approach to increasing social capital, including increases in wage and employment rates, and other outcomes. Sekkema et al. depended on theoretical and empirical research on the effects of diffusion strategies, including opinion leader approaches in the health sector. Bloom and Riccio depended on what could be construed as a theory of developing human capital. A theory of diffusion of innovation and change is implicit, rather than explicit, in their work.

Brian Flay is among the first social scientists to have succeeded in randomizing entire schools to different health risk reduction interventions (Flay and Collins 2005). In the US and Canada, Flay, and Botvin et al. (2000), and others have advanced theories of change so as to develop better interventions, and tested theories which posit how changing individual behavior depends on changing school conditions, including group processes within the school. The outcome variables in prevention trials usually include substance abuse and, at times, other behaviors. This, of course, impinges on work by criminologists dealing with juveniles and adults.

Entire villages containing low income families were the targets in Progresa/Oportunidades in Mexico, reported by Parker and Teruel (2005), Gulematova-Swan (2009),

Schultz (2004), and others. In this randomized trial, the theory was that changing village behavior, notably through conditional financial incentives (conditional cash payments to mothers), would increase the rate at which children stayed in schools rather than working in the fields. Further, the theory posited that such an intervention would build social capital at the regional and country level. A main outcome variable was children dropping out of school, which has implications not only for human capital development but also for juvenile and adult crime. A partial replication of this conditional income transfer program is being undertaken in New York City.

The United States Department of Education has, since 2001, sponsored testing of curriculum packages and other interventions in multiple places as well as trials involving random allocation of individuals to different interventions. The place randomized trials involve entire school districts, or schools, or classrooms as the entities that are randomly assigned to different interventions. Nearly 100 randomized education trials were mounted from 2002 to 2009. For instance, in one place randomized trial, Merlino (2009) engaged nearly 200 schools to understand the effects of different approaches to enhancing children's understanding of science. The different approaches exploited theory from the cognitive sciences to augment commercial curriculum packages being used in the schools. See Garet et al. (2008) and Porter et al. (2005) for examples of place randomized trials involving large numbers of schools in the context of testing the effects of school based professional teacher development programs.

Each of these examples educates us and invites basic questions. How and why can such trials be deployed well? Can we develop better theory about what should happen as a consequence of an intervention at high levels of the units: province or county, city or village, institution or housing development, hospital catchment area or crime hot spot? Can theories be developed to guide thinking about change or rate of change at the primary aggregate level – the places-and below it. What new statistical problems emerge from randomization of places? Each also invites a question about how to learn about other trials of this sort, involving yet other units of allocation and analysis.

RELATIONSHIPS AND AGREEMENTS

How have people gotten place randomized trials off the ground? Part of the answer to the question lies in agreements between the trialist's team and the prospective partners in the place based trial. "Partners" here mean individuals or groups whose cooperation and experience are essential in deploying both the intervention and the trial.

In dealing with tests of prevention programs in schools, for instance, Flay et al. (2005) emphasized written agreements signed by people who are authorized to sign such agreements. In Flay's case, this includes not only a school principal but also the school superintendent. Given the mobility (turnover) of school administrators and teachers in parts of the US, one or the other signatory might disappear before the end of the trial. Having both kinds of people as signatories helps reduce the obstacles to running a fair trial to completion. Elsewhere, Slavin (2006) and colleagues took a similar tack when they required that most teachers in a school sign on to testing the Success for All program at one point in time; new people would presumably sign on as they move into the system. The education sector in the US requires formal agreements that are localized at the school or school district level rather than at the state or federal levels.

In some areas of the health sector, agreements have been able to depend on an overarching theme and organization. Leviton and Horbar (2005) work, for instance, depended partly on the Vermont Oxford Network. Healthcare institutions in such a network commit, in advance, to be willing to engage in research, including perhaps, randomized trials in the interest of contributing to the cumulation of knowledge about what works. Part of the Grimshaw et al. (2005) work also depended on formal networks of people and institutions whose interests lay in collaborating on studies that help us understand what works better.

The trials on Jobs Plus, reported by Bloom (2005) and Bloom and Riccio (2005), depended on identifying entities and people who wanted to improve employment prospects for people in public housing projects and were willing to participate in an experiment to generate evidence on the effects of the intervention. The process, of identifying prospective partners, inviting proposals, and reaching agreement on willingness and capacity to participate, which the authors describe is instructive. The relationships were formalized through written agreements at the level of agencies within the city, such as state and municipal departments responsible for public housing, as well as with the federal entities responsible for regulations. Reaching agreements requires time, talent, and industry.

In the crime research context, for instance, Weisburd (2005) emphasizes the need to develop personal relationships that lead to trust and willingness to experiment on innovations that might work better than conventional practice. In his Jersey City experiment, for instance, the strong involvement of a senior police commander as principal investigator in the study, played a crucial role in preventing a break-down of the experiment after 9 months. In the Jersey City experiment, on the other hand, the Deputy Chief who administered the interventions was strongly convinced of the failure of traditional approaches and the need to test new ones.

The commander took personal authority over the narcotics unit and used his command powers to carefully monitor the daily activities of detectives in the trial. This style of work suggests the importance of integrating "clinical" work and research work in criminal justice, much as they are integrated in medical experiments (see Shepherd 2003). It also reinforces the importance of practitioner "belief" in the importance and necessity of implementing a randomized study. The Kingswood experiment described by Clarke and Cornish (1972) illustrates how doubts regarding the application of the experimental treatment led practitioners to undermine the implementation of the study

Developing relationships in place randomized trials as in many other kinds of field research, depends of course on reputation. The topic invites attention to questions for the future. How do we develop better contracts and agreements with networks of organizations, public and private, ones that permit us to generate better evidence about the effects of an innovation? And how do we develop and publish "model" contracts and memorandums of understanding (MOUs) and make them available to other trialists and their potential collaborators so that they, and we, can learn?

JUSTIFICATIONS FOR A PLACE RANDOMIZED TRIAL

For many social scientists, an important condition for mounting a randomized trial on any innovative intervention that is purported to work is that (a) the effectiveness of conventional practice, policy, or program is debatable, and (b) the debates can be informed by better scientific evidence. In the crime sector, cops, of course, are local theorists, and they disagree about what could work better. Crime experts have also disagreed about what might work in high crime areas. More generally, of course, people disagree with one another about what might work in the policy sector and there is, at times, some agreement that better evidence would be helpful. Berk et al. (1985) took this position in the context of a MacArther Foundation initiative and it has been independently taken by others.

Weisburd's (2003) position, for instance, accords with the justifications for trials in the medical arena: disagreement among experts about the effectiveness of an intervention. This is an important factor in justifying a randomized trial using places or individuals as the units of random allocation. For instance, neither the Salk trials on polio vaccine nor trials on streptomycin for treating tuberculosis would have been mounted had not the purported effects of conventional treatments been suspect. See, for instance, Evans et al. (2006), and the references therein for contemporary history of medical trials and their scientific and ethical justifications and limits. For Leviton and Horbar (2005), the "quality chasm" between what constitutes good healthcare, based on dependable evidence and contemporary medical practice in hospital units, constituted is a major justification for running a trial. Ditto for Grimshaw et al. (2005).

In considering the prospects of a conditional income transfer program in Mexico that Parker and Teruel (2005), Schultz (2004), and others describe, economists disagreed that the effects of an incentive program, such as Progresa/Oportunidades would keep Mexican children away from working in the agricultural fields and increase the likelihood that the children would stay in schools. The economists' disagreements were important in making plain the uncertainty in outcomes. The place randomized trial was mounted partly for this reason.

The United States has a history of attempting to reduce poverty and poverty's consequences. Many of these efforts depend on community-wide or organization-wide efforts in many places. Judging by the Jobs Plus effort described by Bloom and Riccio (2005), for instance, the incentive for people in local departments of housing and other government agencies to participate in the trial include their interest in reducing the problem in a way that introduces good evidence in a sometimes politically volatile context. In a classic paper, Gueron (1985) made a similar point. She reiterated the interest of some public servants and elected officials in discovering how to do better, in the context of employment and training programs and trials on them during the 1970s and early 1980s.

In place based trials of a teacher development program that Porter et al. (2005) described, the broad justifications for the research were U.S. interests in improving mathematics and science education in the middle school grades, especially in large urban school districts. It lay also in the fact that, prior to the Porter et al. work, no sizeable controlled trials on the effects of any teacher professional development had ever been run. More recent trials, undertaken by Garet et al. (2008) at the American Institutes for Research, have involved over 90 schools with similar justification in recruiting schools into the study and in securing funding for the trial.

The scientific justification for place randomized trials is, of course, the assurance that, if the trial is carried out properly, there are no systematic differences between groups of places randomized, which in turn carries a guarantee of statistically unbiased estimates of the intervention's effect. It also assures that chance and chance imbalances can be taken into account and that a legitimate statistical statement of one's confidence in the results can be made. Further, Weisburd (2005) in criminology, Gueron (1985) in labor and welfare economics, Boruch (2007) in education and social sciences, and others have pointed out that the simplicity and transparency of the idea of fair comparison through a randomized trial has strong appeal for policy people and decision makers who cannot understand and do not trust complex model-based analyses of data from nonrandomized studies. For the abiding statistician, the crucial aspect of simplicity is that the statistical inferences as to the effect's size relative to chance need not depend on econometric or statistical or mathematical models. The randomization feature permits and invites less dependence on such speculation, and modern computing methods permit the use of randomization tests.

The empirical evidence on the vulnerability of evidence from nonrandomized trials, in comparison to the evidence from randomized trials, has been building since at least the late 1940s. Assuring that one does not depend on weak and easily assailable evidence when stronger evidence can be produced is an incentive at times in parts of the policy community. Assuring that one does not needlessly depend on heroic assumptions to produce good estimates of effect, assumptions often required in the nonrandomized trials, is an incentive for the scientific and statistical community. See references to recent papers by Deeks on healthcare, Glazerman and others on trials on employment and training, and Duflo and Kraemer on economics that are summarized by Boruch (2007). See also Kunz and Oxman (1998).

Shadish et al. (2008) provided a persuasive illustration that is especially compelling because comparisons between a randomized experiment and an observational study were anticipated as part of their study's design and before the data were collected. Their results suggest comparability, as opposed to major differences, if the quasi-experiment is designed well in a particular domain. Theirs is an interesting and potentially important specific case. More generally, the biases in estimating an intervention's effect, based on the quasi-experiments can be very large, small, or nonexistent (see Lipsey and Wilson (1993) and Weisburd et al. (2001) for instance). The variance in estimates of effects appears to be typically larger in the quasi-experiments than in the randomized tests. So far, and with some narrow exceptions, there is no way to predict the directionality or magnitude of such biases, or in the variances of the estimates, of the intervention's effect, based on a nonrandomized trial.

Studies of whether and by how much estimates of the effect of a nonrandomized trial differ from those of a randomized trial, when *individuals* are the units of random assignment and analysis (as in most medical trials), are important. It remains to be seen whether similar methodological studies on aggregate level analyses using randomized versus nonrandomized places, clusters of individuals, or groups yield similar results, i.e., uncover serious biases in estimating effects or the variance of the estimates, or both. It is however, reasonable to expect biases here also. Bertrand et al. (2002), for instance, focused on biases in estimates of the standard error of effects, assuming no effect at all using conventional different in differences methods, and found Type I error rates that were nine times the error rate presumed (0.05) in using conventional statistical tests. This was partly on account of serial correlation. More methodological research, however, needs to be done on the quasi-experimental approaches to aggregate level units so as to understand when the biases in estimates of effect appear, when the biases in estimates of their standard errors appear, and how large the mean square error is, relative to place randomized trials.

It is important to identify dependable scenarios in which bias and variance of estimates generated in non-randomized trials are tolerable. Doing so can reduce the need for randomized trials (Boruch 2007; Heinsman and Shadish 1998). It is also not easy, as yet, to identify particular scenarios in which bias in estimates of effect or variance will be small, as was the case in some work by Shadish et al. (2008) and Cook et al. (2008). See Berk (2005) for a more general handling of the strengths and weaknesses of randomized controlled trials at the individual level. This kind of work is pertinent to the analysis of data generated in place randomized trials as well. Concerns about the generalizability of results from trials, about attrition and missing data especially across arms of randomized or non randomized trial, and others are important. Further, if the treatment to which a given unit is assigned affects the response of another unit, there is an interference that can bias average treatment effect estimates, and, at a deeper level, implies that an average treatment effect is not even defined. This can be a serious problem in place-based studies when effects on the units nested within the paces are of interest.

The scientific justifications that are identified here are important in the near term. In the long term, it would be good to understand what the other incentives are and to make these explicit at different levels, e.g., policy, institution (agencies), and individual service-provider levels. Incentives for better evidence may differ depending on whether the stakeholders are members of the police force at different levels, the mayor's office, and the community organizations that have a voice, and so on. Many police executives, for instance, want to improve policing and produce evidence on whether things do improve, and also usually want to keep their jobs. The two incentives may not always be compatible if a city council or mayoral preferences are antagonistic toward defensible evidence generated in well-run field tests. Sturdy indifference to dependable evidence of any kind is, of course, a problem in some policy sectors.

DEPLOYING THE INTERVENTION

Implementation, Dimensionalization, and Measurement

Justifications and incentives are essential for assuring that places, and the influential people in them, are willing to participate in a randomized trial. Understanding how to deploy a new program or practice in each place requires more. It requires expertise at ground level and at others.

The Drug Market Analysis Program, which fostered a series of randomized experiments on crime hot spots, suggests that "ordinary" criminal justice agencies can be brought on board to participate in experimental study if there is strong governmental encouragement and financial support that rewards participation (see Weisburd et al. 2006). A similar experience in the Spouse Assault Replication Program (SARP) reinforces these observations. Joel Garner, who served as program manager for SARP, noted that he knew that the program was a success the "day that we got 17 proposals with something like 21 police agencies willing to randomly assign offenders to be arrested" (Weisburd 2005, p. 232)

Understanding how to implement an intervention at the place level in multiple places is no easy matter, one that is apart from the challenge of executing the randomized trial in which the places are embedded. Jobs Plus, for instance, required research teams to engage and guide coordination of the local housing authority, welfare department, workforce development agency, and public housing residents within each site of many sites (Bloom 2005; Bloom and Riccio 2005). The challenge of getting these agencies to work together more closely than any had in the past was piled on top of other challenges to implementation, including getting housing development residents involved as partners despite their inexperience or distrust among themselves and of government agencies, integrating services across providers (so as to meet housing needs and encourage employment in complex welfare environments), and generating job search and acquisition process that fit the place.

For school based trials that aim to test the effect of a program designed to affect the achievement of children, the implementation challenges vary: school bureaucracies differ from bureaucracies in housing, labor/employment, and so on. Nonetheless, Porter et al. (2005) advance the state of the art by developing indices of people's participation in meetings and teams that were major ingredients for change. For these trials, one simple index set includes counting training sessions in which at least one team member participated, computing the average number of participants per session, the proportion of sessions to which local leaders (school principals) contributed, and consistency of people's participation over time. This also included qualitative reconnaissance on factors that impede participation, such as the limited time that schools allow for teachers to meet during work hours.

The challenges to Sikkema et al. (2005), in deploying an AIDS risk reduction program to women in the U.S. housing developments, is similar to others in some respects but differs in others. She and her team developed three different intervention approaches prior to the trial. They used focus groups to reconnoiter the virtues and vulnerabilities of each intervention, relative to local standards of acceptability. The strategy involved identifying opinion leader cadres within housing developments, selecting them, and providing workshops to support participants. Sikkema as others did relied on basic count data, to index level of participation in workshops, and community events. As in the Jobs Plus effort, learning how to negotiate agreements with different influential entities in housing developments, and documenting this, was an essential part of implementation. Sikkema et al relied on explicit and tentative theory of change, as did Flay.

The reports on deploying programs that appear in papers published in peer reviewed journals can be excellent, but they are typically brief. This sparceness of information invites broad questions about how the authors' experience *in detail* can be shared with others, e.g., web based journals, or reports without page limits, workshops, and so on. It invites more scientific attention to the question of how one can dimensionalize implementation and the engineering questions of how to measure implementation level inexpensively and how to establish a high threshold condition for implementation and how to achieve it.

RESOURCES FOR THE TRIAL'S DESIGN, STATISTICAL PROBLEMS, AND SOLUTIONS

Some of the important technical references for trial design and model based data analysis include Donner and Klar (2000) on cluster randomized trials, a fine summary that considers the basic technical ideas and approaches and examples from different countries, mainly in the health arena. The resources include Murray's (1998) book on group randomized trials which is more detailed, focuses more on individuals within groups, considers diverse applications in the U.S. Bloom's (2005) monograph, and is excellent on account of its clarity and use of economic examples in the US. Bryk and Raudenbush's (2002) text, a tour de force, directs attention to model-based statistical analyses of multi-level data that may or may not have been generated by randomized trials. The models are complex and entail assumptions that the analyst may not find acceptable.

In the context of place randomized, cluster randomized, or group randomized trials, we have discovered no books that cover the simplest and *least* model dependent approaches to analyzing data from such a trial. Such approaches fall under the rubric of randomization tests or permutation tests, for which Edgington and Onghena's (2007) book is pertinent. A simple randomization test, for instance, involves computing all possible outcomes of the trial, ignoring the actual allocation to intervention or control conditions, and then making a probabilistic judgment about the dependability of the effect detected, based on the distribution of possible outcomes so generated. There is no dependence on linear or other explicit models.

Given the relatively small sample sizes involved in place randomized trials (less than 200, typically) and contemporary computing capacity, generating the distribution of possible outcomes in these approaches is relatively straightforward. The basic ideas were promulgated by Sir Ronald Fisher in the 1950s for trials in which individuals or plants, for instance, were the independent units of random allocation and analysis. But the idea is directly relevant to trials in which places are randomly allocated and inferences are made about the effects of intervention at the place level. Kempthorne's (1952) classic volume describes the matter better than his mentor (Fisher) did, and Neter et al. (2001) do even better. But their handling of the topic is very brief and does not take into account complex trial designs for which model based approaches are nowadays in common use.

The Campbell Collaboration organized conferences on place randomized trials in 2001 (Bellagio) and 2002 (New York). A special issue of the *Annals of the American Academy of Political and Social Sciences*, covering different social sciences came of this initiative (Volume 599, 2005). After 2002, the William T. Grant Foundation, under Robert Granger's leadership, initiated efforts to enhance the technical capacity of researchers to design such trials and to analyze results through workshops and in other ways described below. During 2002–2009, the Institute for Education Sciences, under the leadership of the IES Director Grover (Russ) Whitehurst and Commissioner Lynn Okagaki, committed funding to institutes and pre- and post-doctoral training programs on designing and executing such trials in education. We are aware of no similar efforts sponsored by the National Institute of Justice or private foundations in the criminological arena.

A major scientific issue in designing place randomized trial, one that is important in policy also, is assuring that the size of the sample of places that are randomized is large enough to permit one to detect relative effects of interventions with some statistical confidence. Put in other words, the concern is that the number of places assigned to different interventions will be sufficient to discern an important effect (or minimally detectable effect size) if, in fact, it occurs. A statistical power analysis, informing us of how many places are needed, is an essential planning device. Such an analysis, however, usually depends on informed speculation about the expected effect size (or the minimum detectable effect size), the randomization, and on particular statistical tests of hypotheses and related procedures. The power analysis may entail assumptions about an underlying model that would be employed in analyzing data from the trial. The models, of course, can be suspect in a variety ways, important and otherwise. User friendly software for estimating the model-based statistical power of a trial under various assumptions about sample size and other factors are accessible on the William T. Grant Foundation's web site (http://www.wtgrantfdn.org). The mathematical underpinnings of the software are based on Raudenbush (1997) and more other papers referenced in Spybrook (2008).

The aforementioned resources are basic but will change as the technology changes. The statistical issues that place randomized trials have uncovered over the last decade, and their resolutions, are also important. Some advances in the area are described below, along with pertinent source references.

In a simple two-level scenario, the number of places that are randomized is generally crucial for assuring statistical power, rather than the number of individuals or other units within the places. This is regardless of whether the approach is based on statistical models or based on inference directly from randomization (Small et al. 2008; Raudenbush 1997). In the past, and at worst, researchers have often wrongly employed the number of people in places for statistical power analysis and statistical hypothesis testing rather than the number of places that were randomly allocated to different interventions. In the Kansas City

Preventive Patrol Experiment, for example, the researchers analyzed survey data obtained at the level of individuals rather than police beats, beats being the units of randomization. Although there are model-based methods for analyzing "nested" units within places (Bryk and Raudenbush 2002), the most dependable (least ambiguous) units of analysis in place based trials for estimating effects are the places that were randomized.

The data generated in place randomized trials are often analyzed using regression models of various kinds rather than randomization tests that are not model dependent. In particular, because of the random assignment, it is commonly assumed that the usual regression models are necessarily correct. Nonetheless, there is usually no explicit justification for the regression model. For a place randomized trial in which the units analyzed are not the ones randomized, of course, the model based assumptions are not necessarily true; the models must be justified.

Even when the analysis is based on outcomes for the places randomized, simply assuming that the regression model is appropriate for analysis can be wrong. In particular, within the Neyman–Rubin framework of randomized trials, each observational unit has a fixed *potential* response under each treatment and control condition. The *actual* response observed depends on the condition to which that unit has been randomly assigned. Because that assignment is by chance mechanism, the observed response, not the potential response is a random variable. The uncertainty then stems solely from the random assignment process and this uncertainty also has clearly defined statistical properties.

When data from randomized trials are analyzed with linear regression, a very different framework is imposed. The uncertainty is represented by the unobservable "disturbances," i.e., the error terms in the regression model. For the regression model to perform as advertised, these disturbances must have certain properties. For instance, each disturbance is characterized by a single common variance, but when the uncertainty is, in fact, a function of the random assignment mechanism, these "certain properties" do not hold. The regression model is automatically wrong in some cases. See Freedman (2006, 2008a, b). The question then is how misleading the results of a regression analysis are likely to be relative to straightforward randomization tests. Empirical answers are very difficult to generate. With large samples, the bias in estimated average treatment effects will be small, but in place randomized trials, the number of randomized units is often modest. Even with very large samples, the standard errors can be systematically too small or too large (Freedman 2006, 2008a). Analyses based on regression models with categorical, count, or time-to-failure outcomes create additional problems (Freedman 2008b), and there are alternatives such as a simple t test for mean differences (which is tantamount to a regression with only one or more indicator variables for the intervention) or Fisher's exact test for proportions. The problems with conventional regression materialize when covariates are included in the model, and, in the case of hierarchical modeling, the problems may materialize in other ways.

Confusion often arises regarding the number of cases that are employed for statistical analysis. For instance, place base trials often involve the study of people within places, and thus, one may have a relatively small number of units at the randomized place level and a very large number of units at the nested individual level. For example, the Redlands Valley Risk Focused Policing Experiment randomized 26 census block groups for intervention, with 13 block groups assigned to each arm of the trial. The research included 800 individuals who were studied within the block groups (Weisburd et al. 2008). Simply including all individuals in an analysis that ignored the place level random assignment would have led to an underestimation of the standard error of the intervention's effects, and (consequently), a positively biased test of statistical significance.

A key issue in this scenario is that the individuals or other units within a place were not assigned to treatment or control conditions. Indeed, all individuals within each place are automatically assigned the same condition, either treatment or control, for instance, in a place randomized trial. This scenario does not mean that one cannot analyze data on individuals or entities within places that are randomized in a place randomized trial but as suggested above, the analysis is riskier (Bloom and Riccio 2005; Bryk and Raudenbush 2002; Spybrook et al. 2004). In the Redlands study, the main research question focuses on examining the impact of the Redlands intervention on individual level outcomes. In analyzing the data, the researchers acknowledged and took into account the fact that although treatment was assigned and administered at the block group level, the study was intended to examine individual level outcomes. They could be fairly certain that pre-existing differences between the treatment and control block groups in the study were not systematic due to the matching and subsequent randomization process. However, they could not make the same claim regarding individuals who reside within the treatment and control block groups because the individuals were not randomly assigned to condition. In turn, when the researchers examined the effects of the treatment on individuals, unmeasured characteristics of the groups could, of course, influence estimates of individual level effects.

Prior techniques for clustered data involved either aggregating all information to the group level (e.g., block group level) as in a straight up randomization test or t test of mean differences, or disaggregating all block group level traits to the individual, which involves assigning all block group level traits to the individual (e.g., including a dummy variable for each individual for membership in a specific census block group). For Bryk and Raudenbush (2002), the problem with the first method is that all within group information is wasted and omitted from the analysis and this can be as much as 80–90% of the total variation. The problem with the second method is that the observations are no longer independent, as we know that all individuals within a certain block group will have the same value on a certain variable. Specifically, individuals from different block groups are independent, but individuals within the same block groups will share values on many more variables, some of which will be observed and some, not observed. The effects of the omitted or unobserved variables are absorbed by the error term in a linear regression model, resulting in the correlation between individual level error terms. To account for the dependence that arises when using samples of individuals nested within block groups, Weisburd et al. (2008) used several statistical methods that attempt to correct for clustering, such as hierarchical linear modeling techniques (i.e., HLM) and generalized least squares estimation techniques with robust standard errors. These techniques are discussed in more detail in other parts of the volume.[2]

Clearly, one can properly analyze place-based randomized experiments in a manner that is largely model free. Small et al. (2008), for instance, emphasize randomization/permutation tests with different kinds of adjustments for covariates, none relying on any form of HLM. Imai et al. (2009) advance the state of the art by showing how pair-wise matching in place randomized trials can often enhance precision in estimates of the effects of interventions, increase statistical power of analysis in detecting effects, and better assure unbiasedness of the estimates of variability of the effect with a relatively small number of places (clusters, in their vernacular).

---

[2] In the Redlands study the researchers also conducted aggregate level (block level) post test analyses to assess aggregate level delinquency and substance abuse differences between experimental and control block groups. Results from this set of analyses closely mirror results generated using the HLM approach.

In criminological and other trials that are place based, matched pairs designs can be used that build on a large number of recent developments (Greevy et al. 2004). But the analysts concern has usually been that the matching may unnecessarily reduce degrees of freedom, and thus, the statistical power of the studies. There is a loss of one degree of freedom for each restriction (pair or block) in a study design.

The Redlands Valley Risk Focused Policing Experiment, for instance, used the matched pairs approach, but it is often not possible to define clearly in crime and justice work, the relationship between "blocking" or matching variables and the outcomes observed. In the Minneapolis Hot Spots Experiment (Sherman and Weisburd 1995) and the Jersey Drug Hot Spots Experiment (Weisburd and Green's 1994), for instance, subjects were classified into broad groups ("blocks"), and then randomization was carried out within the groups or blocks (see chapter on Block Randomized Trials). This approach allowed the researchers to decrease heterogeneity within the groups but led to a loss of only a few degrees of freedom in the study design. A fully matched pair design will provide benefit over a partially blocked design where there is strong knowledge that allows careful distinctions of place units in terms of the impacts of the blocking factors.

As a practical matter, the Imai et al. (2009) work shows that the number of units within a place (cluster) are an important matching variable per se, and that using it can reduce costs and increase statistical power of the trial. That is, when the numbers of units within randomized places vary, the numbers can be exploited in a matching process to produce a better trial design.

Imai et al. (2009) work updates and generalize earlier methodological work done mainly in health and in education where schools or classrooms are the units of randomization. Data on students at the schools level may be used to enhance precision in estimates, i.e., covariates at the place level. Within-school level data can be used to model speculated processes at the student level within school. Schochet (2009) reviews such work upto about 2008, provides numerous references, and attend to different experiment designs involving data at school, district, classroom, and student levels. Konstantopoulos (2009) incorporates cost consideration into power analysis of three level designs. Spybrook (2008) considers power reporting issues in funded federal projects in education.

Bloom and Riccio (2005) advanced the state of the art in another important respect. They couple conventional comparison of randomized places with time series analyses of data from the places. This approach permits one to also take into account the changing composition of individuals and conditions across the places (housing developments). The idea of coupling randomized trials and nonrandomized approaches to estimating effects of interventions is not new in the sense that others have done conceptual work on it. But actualizing the ideas and being thorough in the design and analysis is unusual.

Since about 2005, the idea of "step wedge" and "dynamic wait list" designs has emerged as an interesting addition to the trialists' armamentarium in estimating short term effects of interventions. The most familiar variation on this idea is a wait list design in which a random half sample of the eligible places are assigned to the intervention for some period of time. The remaining half sample receives the intervention after this period is ended. The critical policy presumption is that all units will eventually receive the intervention. The important assumption for some statistical analyses is that the time delay is inconsequential for simple comparisons. Put in other words, the policy presumption is usually based on political or ethical concerns that all places should eventually receive a purportedly desirable intervention, or on logistical concerns about the need to stage an intervention's deployment to a large number of units. The import of the statistical assumption regarding inconsequential effect of delay in an intervention is often unclear.

The general design approach in such trials is to plan how to randomly deploy the intervention to subsets of the target sample of places periodically and over some specified period of time, so as to achieve a given level of precision in estimating an effect of a specified size. A set of 32 places, for instance, might be divided randomly into eight sets of four places. Each set is then randomly subjected sequentially to the intervention at eight time points. The earliest set so assigned then receives the intervention for the longest period of time. Relevant advances in this kind of experimental design here have been health related. For instance, Brown et al. (2006) develop and illustrate dynamic wait list designs and apply the analytic work in the context of a suicide prevention program in Atlanta schools. Their paper shows how statistical power is enhanced over a simple two-group delayed intervention design and that power increases with the number of times a new subset is introduced to the intervention, using count data (incidence) as the outcome variable. In a related stream of work, Hussey and Hughes (2006) develop the idea of step wedge designs, the "steps" being the point at which a subset of places (clusters) is randomly assigned to the intervention, and apply the ideas to a trial in the state of Washington. For these authors, the design is an expansion of cross over designs. They too show how increasing the number of steps can enhance statistical power of a formal test of hypothesis, conditional on a statistical model of how nature works, and how effect size attributable to increasing exposure to the intervention can be taken into account in modeling the underlying processes. De Allegri et al. (2008) provide an illustration in the context of deploying a community based health insurance intervention in West Africa.

More generally, the Cochrane Collaboration's methods group served as the auspices for a systematic review of recent applications of the step wedge design (Brown and Lilford 2006). The step wedge and dynamic wait list designs are innovative and have very attractive features. But the power analyses and data analyses, to date, have relied on hierarchical linear models with unusual assumptions that are not always testable. There may be alternatives that are far less model dependent.

REGISTERS OF RANDOMIZED TRIALS AND STANDARDS OF REPORTING

Learning about place randomized trials, whether completed or underway, can be difficult. The authors of studies cited here, for instance, have contributed to place randomized trials in China, Canada, England, the United States, Kenya, Peru, Mexico, Colombia, Thailand, and elsewhere. Their reports have been published in a variety of scientific journals that differ, sometimes remarkably, from one another, e.g., in criminology, education, prevention science, medicine, and so on. This variety is a challenge for searchers of published and unpublished literature. Further, relying on web based searches such as ERIC and PsychInfo have not fared well relative to hand searches of the research literature, at least in regard to locating randomized trials in the social sector (Turner et al. 2003). More recently, Taljaard et al. (2009)

Found that fewer than 50% of published cluster randomized trials in health are appropriately classified as cluster trials in titles or abstracts, contrary to classification recommendations by the 2004 CONSORT statement. They had to rely on over 50 search terms for "places" to locate relevant reports. Even in the health sector then, electronic searches of electronic databases are likely to be a challenge despite advances in machine based approaches.

The difficulty in identifying randomized trials was reduced with the creation of the international Cochrane Collaboration in healthcare in the early 1993 and the international Campbell Collaboration in 2000. Both organizations, which rely heavily on voluntary participation, developed registers on randomized trials that could be accessed through their web sites. Both organizations relied heavily on hand searches (full text readings) of peer reviewed journals rather than on conventional machine based (key word, abstract, title) searches.

For instance, between 2002 and 2005, the Campbell Collaboration Social, Psychological, Educational, and Criminological Trials Register (C-SPECTR) contained about 13,000 entries on randomized and possibly randomized trials and included references to about 200 reports on place randomized trials. In C2 SPECTR, one could find entries on place randomized trials involving schools and classrooms in Kenya, El Salvador, and India, brothels in Thailand, factories in Russia, barrios (impoverished neighborhoods) in Colombia, and *lins* (neighborhoods) in Taiwan, among others. Unfortunately, the SPECTR registry has not received continued support and its operation was suspended. The Cochrane Collaboration library, on the other hand, has been supported and is routinely updated. It contains over 500 references to such trials to judge from our search based on the phrase "cluster randomized" in 2009.

In the United States, one can learn about trials in the health sector, including place randomized trials, from http://www.clinicaltrials.gov. It is a resource that criminologists and others may find helpful at times, when the interventions being tested or the outcome variables being examined are pertinent, or when information about the place trial's design can be exploited. In 2007, David Greenberg and Mark Shroder developed a new register of randomized trials, oriented toward tests of economic interventions under the auspices of the Social Science Research Network (SSRN). Their Randomized Social Experiments Abstracts are given at ERN@publish.ssrn.com.

Standards for reporting on randomized trials that involve individuals as the unit of random allocation and analysis are a product of the late 1990s. See an illustration and references to early work in Boruch (1997). More recently, the CONSORT statement provided guidance on the ingredients that a good report on a randomized trial in the health arena should contain (Moher et al. 2001). The CONSORT statement has been modified to include standards for reporting on place/group/cluster randomized trials. This extension, given in Campbell et al. (2004), covers important topics embedded in a place randomized trial. These include, for instance, consideration of the rationale for this research design and the fact that there are often at least two levels of sampling and inference: the cluster (place) level and the individual (person within place) level, different rates of attrition and measurement at each level, and so on. For instance, an experiment that involves bar rooms (places) as the primary unit of random allocation in a study of an intervention to reduce violence, may also obtain information on the individuals within bars who are a party to violence. The randomized bar room level of analysis can produce unbiased estimates of the intervention's effects. The within bar data may help to speculate about the estimates of effect and inform secondary analyses that aid in the interpretation of effects. Standardized reporting at each level, and perhaps others, is important for scientific understanding.

As of this writing, there are no uniform standards for reporting on randomized trials in crime and justice or related areas. This problem has been raised by Perry in this volume. Empirical work on the problem is reported by Perry and Johnson (2008), by Perry et al. (2009), and by Gill (2009) who assessed reporting methods in crime and justice journals. Farrington (2003) and, much earlier, Loesel and Koferl (1989), noted the lack of reporting standards. Farrington coined the term "reporting validity" to emphasize that such standards are critical for developing an experimental science in criminology.

The lack of clear and uniform standards for reporting on results of trials in criminology and in related disciplines means that valid reanalysis of experimental studies is difficult, and often impossible. Further, and as important, there are no professional standards for assuring access to the original data used in a published report on results of a trial, place randomized or not. Reanalysis at the report level or micro-record level, for instance, is often essential for verifying an original analysis, testing new hypotheses, or exploring new theories or assumptions. Dozens of reanalyses of data from Progresa/Oportunidades, for instance, have been reported in published papers, dissertations, and research monographs. These reports are on diverse topics, such as verifying the apparent equivalence of the randomized groups and conventional intent to treat impact analyses, and examining many, often elaborate structural modeling efforts that get at different aspects of the program's impact on outcomes. These have made the trial famous in the world of economics of education.

Some funding agencies in the US, such as the National Institute of Justice and the National Science Foundation, have tried to make policy to assure that independent analysts have access to micro record data generated in the research that they sponsor, including data from controlled trials. The Institute of Education Sciences policy on this is unclear as of this writing. Regardless of clarity of policy, the actualization of the intent – to make micro-records accessible – seems uneven. Given the intellectual and financial investment in the production of such data, it seems sensible to try to improve independent researchers' access to it for secondary analysis. Regardless of the question of access to micro-records, criteria like those produced by the CONSORT statement for uniform reporting on randomized trials are critical for advancing experimental criminology.

ETHICS AND LAW

As of this writing, no professional society or government agency has promulgated explicit statements about the ethical propriety of place randomized trials. Contemporary rules and ethics statements, for instance, attend to the rights and well being of individuals, rather than places, groups, or entities that are engaged in a trial. The earliest fundamental statements on research ethics, such as the Helsinki Statement and the Belmont Report direct attention to individuals' rights. Contemporary government regulations regarding human subjects research in the US, Canada, the UK, and other countries also do not consider place/cluster/group trials explicitly.

Applying contemporary standards to place randomized trials can be awkward and imperfect. See, for instance, the report of the Planning Committee on Protecting Student Records and Facilitating Education Research (2009) and Boruch's (2007) attempt to the Federal Judicial Center's guidelines to understand the ethical justification for the Progresa/Oportunidades place randomized trial.

At times, contemporary professional standards of ethics and governmental regulations are not clearly relevant to place randomized trials. At other times, standards and regulations may be only partially relevant. This invites exploration. Taljaard et al. (2008, 2009) have taken the lead in an effort based at University of Ottawa, to understand and explicate the ethics issues engendered by place/cluster/group randomized trials. They attend mainly to health and risk reduction in health and school based risk prevention settings. Sabin et al. (2008) took another approach in exploring the ethics of cluster trials in the context of drug testing in health plans. The issues that Taljaard et al. (2008, 2009) and Sabin et al. (2008) confront are likely to be relevant to criminological place randomized trials.

To illustrate one issue, the commonly used phrase "human subjects" is arguably inappropriate in settings in which a city's crime hot spots are the targets for random allocation and the interventions are approved by a city council or police department under their administrative authority. The target of research is jurisdictions in which people happen to commit crime, reside, or do business. A recent Institute of Medicine Report has taken issue with the use of the phrase, "human subjects" for different reasons, maintaining that the word "participant" is arguably more accurate and less rebarbative.

The concerns of an institutional review board (IRB) may be moot when the law determines actual random allocation of places to different interventions and the individual's rights are entrained in the determination or, the IRB's concern may be pertinent in that the trialist may seek detailed information which goes beyond that obtained in conventional administrative/police record systems, such as attitudes, beliefs, wages, etc. Most importantly, perhaps, the matter of whose consent ought to be sought in place randomized trial is not easily resolved. It may be the "agent" responsible for the place, such as a police chief or director of a health plan, or it may be individuals within the place such as teachers within schools that are testing curriculum packages, or it may be both, and the responsibility may lie with entirely different agents.

Boruch et al. (2004) suggested that it may be possible to avoid some ethical and moral dilemmas commonly associated with experimentation by randomly allocating at the organizational or place level, rather than randomly allocating individuals. At first glance, one might question why the change in unit of analysis should affect ethical concerns. Why should it matter, for example, whether students in a specific school are allocated to treatment and control conditions versus all students in specific schools? The end result is the same. Some individuals will gain treatment and others will not. However, where individuals do not experience the inequality of treatment directly (e.g., by seeing other students in their school being treated differently), ethical issues may just not be raised.

The general proposition that place based studies are likely to be faced with relatively few ethical objections is illustrated by both the Minneapolis Hot Spots Experiment (Sherman and Weisburd 1995) and the Jersey City Drug Hot Spots Experiment (Weisburd and Green's 1994). City officials in these studies did not raise significant ethical concerns during negotiations over randomly allocating either crime hot spots or drug markets to intervention and control conditions. Sherman, for example, notes that "no one ever raised ethical objections" to the Minneapolis Hot Spots Experiment (Weisburd 2005, p. 233). Moreover, as neither study collected information directly from individuals within hot spots (human subjects), but relied rather on official police data and observations of the sites, they were not subject to significant human subject review. This contrasts strongly with controversies often surrounding the random allocation of individuals to different interventions in some criminal justice settings.

While common ethical objections to random allocation did not surface in the police hot spots studies, different types of objections were raised by citizens and the police. The objections are suggestive of more serious problems that might develop. These objections can be construed as a part of a political or institutional ethic concerning group rights, as opposed to an ethic that concerns individual rights. For example, in Minneapolis, the City Council was asked to approve the reallocation of police resources in the hot spots experiment. One city councilman in a low crime area would not give his approval unless "an early warning crime trend analysis plan" would monitor burglary trends and send more patrols back into his neighborhood if "burglary rashes developed" (Weisburd 2005). Monitoring did not reveal such increases in burglary, and thus, the experiment was not affected.

In the Jersey City experiment, when a citizens group in one area of Jersey City found out that their neighbors were getting extra police attention, they demanded to be made part of the hot spots study. The police convinced the citizens group that they continued to get good police service, but that their problem (to their benefit) was not sufficiently serious to make them eligible to join the experiment. In Jersey City, all of the drug areas that showed consistent and serious activity were included in the study. This coverage, combined with the equality of "service" (this was a treatment and "comparison" group design in which some type of treatment was delivered to every site) in the experimental and control areas made it possible to avoid objections that some serious drug markets were receiving more police attention than others. Nonetheless, the rule that "(e)xperiments with lower public visibility will generally be easier to implement" (Weisburd 2005, p. 186) appears particularly relevant to place randomized trials.

A more complex problem was raised by police officers participating in the Minneapolis study. Many patrol officers objected to the hot spots approach of "sitting" in or riding through specific areas. While researchers tried to draw support from rank and file police officers for the experiment through briefings, pizza parties, and the distribution of t-shirts bearing the project logo ("Minneapolis Hot Spot Cop"), many officers argued that the hot spots approach was unethical and violated their obligations to protect the public. In particular, the officers argued that the intensive approach to handling crime hot spots allowed crime to shift to around the corners from the hot spots. The officers' theory is important. In fact, and in opposition to the theory, there were no wide scale attempts by officers to undermine the experiment and no displacement of crime activity from one area to another in this trial (Weisburd et al. 2006). But the early objections by officers, in this instance, are similar to the practitioners' concerns that undermined the Kingswood study that forms the basis for Clarke and Cornish's (1972) well known critique of experimentation in the Home Office.

Regardless of the ethical dilemmas engendered by place based trials over the last decade, there appear to have been no serious challenges in the US courts to the conduct of place randomized trials. For instance, the former director of the Institute for Education Sciences (IES), Russ Whitehurst, reported in a personal communication (2008), that he had encountered no court challenges as a consequence of the IES's sponsoring many such trials in education during 2002–2008. Similarly, we are aware of no judicial challenges in the context of place randomized trials in the crime sector, such as the trials on crime hot spots, bar room violence, convenience store vulnerability to hold ups, and so on.

CONCLUSIONS AND IMPLICATIONS FOR THE FUTURE

Place randomized trials have become important in criminology, health, education, prevention research, and other sectors. This is because they employ substantive theory about the effects of intervention at the place level, which is different from theory that is focused on individuals. It is because the statistical technology for designing such trials has advanced remarkably since the late 1990s. Their importance has increased because the resources and capacity for mounting such trials have increased.

The interest in place randomized trials transcends academic disciplines. Such trials are being mounted in the health sector to understand how hospital units can be encouraged to change practice in the interest of enhancing people's health or reducing costs of healthcare. They have been mounted in the education sector to judge the effectiveness of curriculum packages in elementary, middle, and high schools, and to evaluate risk prevention programs that focus on substance abuse and non-criminal disorder. They have, of course, been employed in criminological research to understand how to reduce crime or prevent it. One implication for the future is that cross discipline work will enhance understanding: the problems of engaging places in a trial, assuring ethical propriety and good statistical design and analysis transcend discipline. For instance, criminological place randomized trials, with few exceptions, have not attended to health (injury) outcomes as a variable, nor have health trials paid much attention to crime interventions. Prevention research that is school based is a remarkable exception in cutting across disciplines.

The statistical armamentarium for design and analysis of place randomized trials is fundamental. Its origins lie in the simple idea of randomization and permutation tests that do not depend on complex statistical models. The statistical models and methods that get beyond a basic test of the statistical dependability of the intervention's effects in a place randomized trial has also developed apace. Statistical theory and the development of relevant software for power analysis and data analysis have improved and are accessible on account of some private foundation and US federal agency efforts. Specialized institutes for advanced study have become more common over the last decade. For the criminological community, it is a fine prospect to look to other advances in training and in statistical design and analysis of such trials.

The experience of people who have been involved in the design, execution, and analysis of place randomized trials is an important source of intellectual and social capital. Part of the future lies in exploiting and building on this capital, in graduate and post graduate education, for instance. The future lies also in producing published documentation on negotiated agreements, MOUs, "model agreements," etc., among criminologists, police, and other stakeholders, such as community groups that have agreed to participate in such trials.

Ethics in a place randomized trial are important. The ethical issues in such a trial arguably differ from those encountered in a trial in which individuals, rather than entities, are randomly allocated to different interventions. The advanced thinking lies in exploring the implications of randomization of entire counties, businesses, schools, and crime hot spots to different interventions when the expected effects of the interventions' effects are in "equipoise." The issues remain unclear until colleagues who are doing advanced work on the ethics of cluster/place/group randomized trials in health make their empirical findings and intellectual understandings known.

Standardized reporting on the design, execution, and analysis of the data from place randomized trials has become improved in health research and in education research. Reporting has not been standardized in criminological research and related social research sectors, including social services. Criminology's future lies partly in developing better and uniform reporting standards. In addition, learning how to assure better access to well documented microdata stemming from randomized trials will be important for reanalysis and secondary analysis, especially in controversial studies.

Walter Lippmann, an able social scientist and newspaper writer, had a strong interest in cops, and crimes by adults and adolescents, and was familiar with political ambivalence about or opposition to sound evidence. He was a street level criminologist, remarkable writer, and good thinker. In the 1940s, Lippmann (1963) said: "The problem is one for which public remedies are most likely to be found by choosing the most obvious issues and tackling them experimentally... the commissions of study are more likely to be productive if they can study the effects of practical experimentation." Nowadays, trialists in criminology would have little difficulty in subscribing to Lippmann's counsel.

REFERENCES

Berk R (2005) Randomized experiments as the bronze standard. J Exp Criminol 1(4):417–433

Berk R, Boruch R, Chambers D, Rossi P, Witte A (1985) Social policy experimentation: a position paper. Eval Rev 9(4):387–430

Bertrand M, Duflo E, Mullainathan S (2002) How much should we trust differences in differences estimates? Working Paper 8841. National Bureau of Economic Research, Cambridge, MA.

Bloom HS (2005) Learning more from social experiments: evolving analytic approaches. Russell Sage Foundation, New York

Bloom HS, Riccio JA (2005) Using place random assignment and comparative interrupted time-series analysis to evaluate the jobs-plus employment program for public housing residents. Ann Am Acad Pol Soc Sci 599:19–51

Boruch RF (1997) Randomized experiments for planning and evaluation. Thousand Oaks, California, Sage Publications

Boruch RF (2007) Encouraging the flight of error: ethical standards, evidence standards, and randomized trials. New Dir Eval 133:55–73

Boruch RF, May H, Turner H, Lavenberg J, Petrosino A, deMoya D, Grimshaw J, Foley E (2004) Estimating the effects of interventions that are deployed in many places. Am Behav Sci 47(5):575–608

Botvin G, Griffin K, Diaz T, Scheier L, Williams C, Epstein J (2000) Preventing elicit drug use in adolescents. Addict Behav 25(5):769–774

Braga A (2001) The effects of hot spots policing on crime. In: Farrington DF, Welsh BC (eds) What works in preventing crime? Special issue. Ann Am Acad Pol Soc Sci, vol 578, pp 104–125

Brown CH, Wyaman PA, Guo J, Pena J (2006) Dynamic wait-listed designs for randomized trials: new designs for prevention of youth suicide. Clinical Trials 3:259–271

Brown C, Lilford R (2006) The step wedge trial design: a systematic review. BMC Med Res Methodol 6:54. Available at: http://www.biomedcentral.com/info/1471-2288/6/54

Bryk AS, Raudenbush SW (2002) Hierarchical linear models. Sage, Thousand Oaks, CA.

Campbell MK, Elbourne DR, Altman DG (2004) CONSORT statement: extension to cluster randomized trials. BMJ 328:702–708

Clarke RV, Cornish D (1972) The controlled trial in institutional research: paradigm or pitfall for penal evaluators. London, Her Majesty's Stationary Office

Cook T, Shadish W, Wong V (2008) Three conditions under which experiments and observational studies produce comparable causal estimates: new findings from within study comparisons. J Policy Anal Manage 27(4): 724–750

Davis R, Taylor B (1997) A proactive response to family violence: the results of a randomized experiment. Criminology 35(2):307–333

De Allegri M et al (2008) Step cluster randomized community-based trials: an application to the study of the impact of community health insurance. Health Res Policy Syst 6:10. Available at: http://www.health-policy-systems.com/content/6/1/10

Donner A, Klar N (2000) Design and analysis of cluster randomized trials in health research. Arnold, London

Evans I, Thornton H, Chalmers I (2006) Testing treatments: better research for healthcare. British Library, London

Edgington E, Onghena P (2007) Randomization tests (Fourth Edition), New York, Chapman and Hall/CRC

Farrington DP (2003) Methodological standards for evaluation research. Ann Am Acad Pol Soc Sci 587(1):49–68

Flay BR, Collins LM (2005) Historical review of school based randomized trials for evaluating problem behavior prevention programs. Ann Am Acad Pol Soc Sci 599:115–146

Freedman DA (2006) Statistical models for causation: what inferential leverage do they provide. Eval Rev 30(5): 691–713

Freedman DA (2008a) On regression adjustments to experimental data. Adv Appl Math 40:80–193

Freedman DA (2008b) Randomization does not justify logistic regression. Stat Sci 23:237–249

Garet M et al (2008) The impact of two professional development interventions on early reading instruction and achievement. Institute for Education Sciences, US Department of Education and American Institutes for Research, Washington DC

Gill C (2009) Reporting in criminological journals. Report for seminar on advanced topics in experimental design. Graduate School of Education and Criminology Department, University of Pennsylvania, Philadelphia, PA

Graham K, Osgood D, Zibrowshi E, Purcell J, Glicksman K, Leonared K, Perneanen K, Alitz R, Toomey T (2004) The effect of the safer bars programme on physical aggression in bars: results of a randomized trial. Drug and Alcohol Review 23:31–41

Greevy R, Lu D, Silber JH, Rosenbaum P (2004) Optimal multivariate matching before randomization. Biostatistics 5(2):263–275

Grimshaw J, Eccles M, Cambpell M, Elbroune D (2005) Cluster randomized trials of professional and organizational behavior change interventions in health settings. Annals of the American Academy of Political and Social Science 599:71–93

Gulematova-Swan M (2009) Evaluating the impact of conditional cash transfer programs on adolescent decisions about marriage and fertility: the case of oportunidades. PhD Dissertation, Department of Economics, University of Pennsylvania

Gueron JM (1985) The demonstration of state/welfare initiatives. In: Boruch RF, Wothke W (eds) Randomization and field experimentation. Special issue of new directions for progam evaluation. Number 28. Jossey Bass, San Francisco, pp 5–14

Heinsman D, Shadish W (1998) Assignment methods in experimentation: when do nonrandomized experiments approximate answers from randomized experiments? Psychol Methods 1(2):154–169

Hussey M, Huges J (2006) Design and analysis of stepped wedge cluster designs. Contemporary Clinical Trials, doi: 1.1016/j.cct2006.05.007

Imai K, King G, Nall C (2009) The essential role of pair matching in cluster randomized experiments, with application to the Mexican universal health insurance evaluation. Stat Sci 24(1):29–53

Kelling G, Pate A, Dieckmann D, Brown C (1974) The Kansas city preventive police patrol experiment. Washington DC, The Police Foundation

Kempthorne (1952) The design and analysis of experiments. New York: Wiley, and Malabar Florida: Robert E. Krieger Publishers (Reprint 1983)

Konstantopoulos S (2009) Incorporating cost in power analysis for three-level cluster-randomized designs. Eval Rev 33(4):335–357

Kunz R, Oxman A (1998) The unpredictability paradox: review of the empirical comparisons of randomized and non-randomized clinical trials. BMJ 317:1185–1190

Leviton LC, Horbar JD (2005) Cluster randomized trials for evaluation of strategies to promote evidence based practice in perinatla and neonatal medicine. Annals of the American Academy of Political and Social Science 599:94–114

Lippmann W (1963) The young criminals. In: Rossiter C, Lare J (eds) The essential Lippmann. Random House, New York, Originally published 1933

Lipsey M, Wilson D (1993) The efficacy of psychological, educational, and behavioral treatment: confirmation from meta-analysis. Am Psychol 48:1181–1209

Loesel F, Koferl P (1989) Evaluation research on correctional treatment in West Germany: a meta-analysis. In: Wegerner H, Loesel F, Haisch J (eds) Criminal behavior and the justice system: psychological perspectives. Springer, New York, pp 334–355

Mazzarole L, Price J, Roehl J (2000) Civil remedies and drug control: a randomized trial in Oakland California. Eval Rev 24(2):212–241

Merlino J (2009) The 21st century research and development center on cognition and science instruction. Award from the Institute of Education Sciences, U.S. Department of Education. Award Number R305C080009. Author, Conshahocken, PA

Moher D, Shulz KF, Moher D, Egger M, Davidoff F, Elbourne D et al (2001) The CONSORT statement: revised recommendations for improving the quality of reports on parallel group randomized trials. Lancet 387: 1191–2004

Murray D (1998) Design and analysis of group randomized trials. Oxford University Press, New York

Neter J, Kutner M, Nachtsheim C, Wasserman W (2001) Applied linear statistical models. McGraw Hill, New York

Parker SW, Teruel GM (2005) Randomization and social program evaluation: the case of progresa. Annals of the American Academy of Political and Social Science 599(May):199–219

Perry AE, Johnson M (2008) Applying the Consolidated Standards of Reporting Trials (CONSORT) to studies of mental health for juvenile offenders: a research note. J Exp Criminol 4: 165–185

Perry AE, Weisburd D, Hewitt C (2009) Are criminologists reporting experiments in ways that allow us to access them? Unpublished Manuscript/Report. Available from the Authors: Center for Evidence Based Crime Policy (CEBCP), George Mason University, Virginia US

Planning Committee on Protecting Student Records and Facilitating Education Research (2009) Protecting student records and facilitating education research. National Academy of Sciences, Washington DC

Porter AC, Blank RK, Smithson JL, Osthoff E (2005) Place randomized trials to test the effects of instructional practices of a Mathematics/Science professional development program for teachers. Annals of the American Academy of Political and Social Science 599:147–175

Raudenbush S (1997) Statistical analysis and optimal design for cluster randomized trials. Psychol Methods 2(2): 173–185

Sabin JE, Mazor K, Metereko V, Goff SL, Platt R (2008) Comparing drug effectiveness at health plan: the ethics of cluster randomized trials. Hastings Cent Rep 35(5):39–48

Schochet P (2009) Statistical power for random assignment evaluations of education programs. J Educ Behav Stat 34(2):238–266

Schultz TP (2004) School subsidies for the poor: evaluating the Mexican Progresa poverty program. J Dev Econ 74:199–250

Shadish WR, Clark MH, Steiner PM (2008) Can nonrandomized experiments yield accurate answers? A randomized experiment comparing random and nonrandom assignments. J Am Stat Assoc 103(484):1334–1356

Shepard J (2003) Explaining feast or famine in randomized field experiments: medical science and criminology compared. Evaluation review 27:290–315

Sherman LW, Wesiburd D (1995) General deterrent effects of police patrol in crime "Hot spots." A Randomized Controlled Trial. Justice Quarterly 12:626–648

Sikkema KJ (2005) HIV prevention among women in low income housing developments: issues and intervention outcomes in a place randomized trial. Ann Am Acad Pol Soc Sci 599:52–70

Slavin R (Oct 6 2006) Research and Effectiveness. Education Week

Small DS, Ten Have TT, Rosenbaum PR (2008) Randomization inference in a group-randomized trial of treatments for depression: covariate adjusted, noncompliance, and quantile effects. J Am Stat Assoc 103(481):271–279

Spybrook J (2008) Are power analyses reported with adequate detail? J Res Educ Eff 1:215–235

Taljaard M, Grimshaw J, Weijer C (2008) Ethical and policy issues in cluster randomized trials: proposal for research to the CIHR. Authors: University of Ottawa, Ottawa, Canada

Taljaard M, Weijer C, Grimshaw J, Bell Brown J, Binik A, Boruch R, Brejhaut J, Chaudry S, Eccles M, McRae A, Saginur R, Zwarenstein M, Donner A (2009) Ethical and policy issues in cluster randomized trials: rational and design of a mixed methods research study. Trials 10:61

Turner H, Boruch R, Petrosino A, Lavenberg J, de Moya D, Rothstein H (2003) Populating an international web based randomized trials register in the social, behavioral, criminological, and education sciences. Ann Am Acad Pol Soc Sci 589:203–225

Warburton AL, Sheppard JP (2000) Effectiveness of toughened glass in terms of reducing injury in bars: a randomized controlled trial. Inj Prev 6:36–40

Weisburd D (2003) Ethical practice and evaluation of interventions in crime and justice: the moral imperative for randomized trials. Eval Rev 27(3):336–354

Weisburd D (2005) Hot spots policing experiments and lessons from the field. Ann Am Acad Pol Soc Sci 599: 220–245

Weisburd D, Green L (1994) Defining the drug market: the case of the Jersey city DMA system. In McKenzie DL, Uchida CD (eds) Drugs and crime: evaluating public policy initiatives. Thousand Oaks California, Sage Publications

Weisburd D, Lum C, Petrosino A (2001) Does research design affect study outcomes? Ann Am Acad Pol Soc Sci 578:50–70

Weisburd D, Wycoff L, Ready J, Eck JE, Hinkle JC, Gajewski F (2006) Des crime move around the corner? A controlled study of spatial displacement and diffusion of crime control benefits. Criminology 44(3):549–591

Weisburd D, Morris N, Ready J (2008) Risk focused policing at places: an experimental evaluation. Justice Q 25(1):200

## CHAPTER 24

Longitudinal-Experimental Studies

DAVID P. FARRINGTON, ROLF LOEBER, AND BRANDON C. WELSH

More than two decades ago, the book *Understanding and Controlling Crime: Toward a New Research Strategy* (Farrington et al. 1986a), argued as follows:

1. The most important information about the development, explanation, prevention, and treatment of offending has been obtained in longitudinal and experimental studies.
2. New studies are needed in which these two methods are combined by embedding experimental interventions in longitudinal studies.

At the time, this book was quite influential; for example, it won the prize for distinguished scholarship awarded by the American Sociological Association Criminology Section.

While a great deal of effort and money have been expended on both longitudinal and experimental research in the ensuing two decades, no prospective longitudinal study of offending has yet been conducted containing several years of developmental data collection, an experimental intervention, followed by several more years of developmental data collection. Why has such a study not been undertaken so far? This chapter reviews the advantages and problems of longitudinal surveys, randomized experiments, and longitudinal-experimental designs, in attempting to answer that question. It also reviews the advantages and problems of quasi-experimental analyses (compared with experimental interventions) in longitudinal surveys, and concludes by assessing (in light of developments in the ensuing two decades) whether the recommendations in the 1986 book are valid.

There have been a number of longitudinal-experimental studies in criminology in which persons who did or did not receive an experimental intervention were followed up for several years (for reviews, see Farrington 1992, 2006; Loeber and Farrington 1994, 1995, 1997, 2008). It is not controversial to argue for the desirability of adding a long-term follow-up to a randomized experiment. What is much more controversial is the desirability of embedding an experiment within an ongoing prospective longitudinal survey, essentially because of concerns that the experiment might interfere with the aims of the longitudinal survey, such as documenting the natural history of development. This is a key issue that is addressed in this chapter.

A.R. Piquero and D. Weisburd (eds.), *Handbook of Quantitative Criminology*, DOI 10.1007/978-0-387-77650-7_24, © Springer Science + Business Media, LLC 2010, First softcover printing 2011

PROSPECTIVE LONGITUDINAL SURVEYS

Advantages

Prospective longitudinal surveys involve repeated measures of the same people. Therefore, they involve at least two data collection points. The word "prospective" implies risk and promotive/protective factors that are measured before outcomes. Risk factors predict a high probability of an undesirable outcome such as offending, whereas promotive factors predict a low probability. Where a variable is nonlinearly related to offending, there can be promotive effects in the absence of risk effects or vice versa (see Loeber and Farrington 2008, Chap. 7). Protective factors predict a low probability of offending in the presence of risk, so they interact with and nullify risk factors.

The most important prospective longitudinal surveys focus on community samples of hundreds of people, with repeated personal interviews spanning a period of at least 5 years (Farrington 1979b; Farrington and Welsh 2007). We focus on community surveys (as opposed to surveys of offenders) because they are needed to study the natural history of offending and the effects of risk/promotive/protective factors and life events. In order to avoid retrospective bias, it is important to measure risk and promotive/protective factors before the development of offending and to calculate prospective probabilities. We require interview data because we believe that official record data cannot provide adequate information on offending, risk and promotive/protective factors, and life events. We set a minimum of a 5-year time period because we think that at least this period is required to provide minimally adequate information about the natural history of development of offending. Of course, many prospective longitudinal surveys of offending extend for much longer, for 30–40 years or more (e.g., Farrington 2009; Laub and Sampson 2003).

In criminology, the main advantage of these longitudinal surveys is that they provide information about the development of offending over time, including data on ages of onset and desistance, frequency and seriousness of offending, duration of criminal careers, continuity or discontinuity of offending, and specialization and escalation. They also provide information about developmental sequences, within-individual changes, effects of life events, and effects of risk and promotive/protective factors at different ages on offending at different ages (Farrington 2003a; Loeber and Farrington 1994). A great advantage of longitudinal surveys when compared with cross-sectional surveys is that longitudinal surveys provide information about time ordering, which is needed in trying to draw conclusions about causes.

Problems

While prospective longitudinal surveys have many advantages, they also have problems. The main challenge is to draw convincing conclusions about causal effects (see Murray et al. 2009). Because of their focus on naturalistic observation, longitudinal surveys find it difficult to disentangle the impact of any particular variable from the effects of numerous others. It is particularly difficult to rule out selection effects; for example, child abuse may predict delinquency because antisocial parents tend to abuse their children and also tend to have delinquent children, without there being any causal effect of child abuse on delinquency. Few researchers have tried to study the effects of life events by following up people before and after in within-individual analyses. The best method of establishing causal effects is to carry out a randomized experiment (Robins 1992).

Other problems can be overcome more easily. Attrition is a problem in some longitudinal surveys, but others have very high response rates (Farrington 2003b; Farrington 2006). The infrequency of data collection often makes it difficult to pinpoint causal order, although some studies (e.g., the Pittsburgh Youth Study: see Loeber and Farrington 2008) have many years of repeated assessments. Testing effects can also be problematic, but they can often be estimated (Thornberry 1989). The length of time before key results are available is sometimes a problem, as is the confounding of aging, period and cohort effects, but these difficulties can be overcome by following up multiple cohorts in an accelerated longitudinal design.

As an example of such a design, Tonry et al. (1991) proposed that seven cohorts, beginning at birth and at ages 3, 6, 9, 12, 15, and 18, should be followed up by annual assessments for 8 years. These seven cohorts were indeed followed up in the Project on Human Development in Chicago Neighborhoods, but only three waves of data were collected (in 1994–1997, 1997–1999, and 2000–2001) with an average interval of 2.5 years between interviews (see e.g., Gibson et al. 2009; Kirk 2006; Sampson and Sharkey 2008).

RANDOMIZED EXPERIMENTS

Advantages

An experiment is a systematic attempt to investigate the effect of variations in one factor (the independent or explanatory variable) on another (the dependent or outcome variable). In criminology, the independent variable is often some kind of intervention and the dependent variable is some measure of offending. Most criminological experiments are pragmatic trials designed to test the effectiveness of an intervention rather than explanatory trials designed to test causal hypotheses (Schwartz et al. 1980). The independent variable is under the control of the experimenter; in other words, the experimenter decides which persons receive which treatment (using the word "treatment" very widely to include all kinds of interventions).

The focus here is on randomized experiments where people are randomly assigned to different treatments. The unique advantage of randomized experiments is their high internal validity. Providing that a large number of people are assigned, randomization ensures that the average person receiving one treatment is equivalent (on all possible measured and unmeasured extraneous variables) to the average person receiving another treatment, within the limits of small statistical fluctuations. Therefore, it is possible to isolate and disentangle the effect of the independent variable (the intervention) from the effects of all other extraneous variables (Farrington 1983; Farrington and Welsh 2005, 2006). However, it is also desirable to investigate the intervening mechanisms or mediators (e.g., Harachi et al. 1999).

Because of our concern with internal validity, we focus on relatively large-scale experiments in which at least 100 persons or other units are randomly assigned to experimental or control conditions. This excludes the vast majority of experiments in which schools are randomly assigned (e.g., Metropolitan Area Child Study Research Group 2002; Petras et al. 2008), although we will describe two large studies (Fast Track and Z-PROSO: see later) in which over 50 schools were randomly assigned to conditions. A power analysis should be carried out before embarking on any longitudinal or experimental study, to assess whether the likely relationships or effects can be statistically detected, bearing in mind the sample size.

Problems

Many problems arise in randomized experiments on offending. For example, it is difficult to ensure that all those in an experimental group actually receive the treatment while all those in a control group do not. Manipulation checks and studies of implementation are desirable. Also, differential attrition from experimental and control groups can produce noncomparable groups and lead to low internal validity (Farrington and Welsh 2005). There is often some blurring of the distinction between experimental and control groups (treatment crossovers), leading to an underestimation of the effect of the treatment. Angrist (2006) has described a method of correcting this. Another difficulty is that participants and treatment professionals can rarely be kept blind to the experiment, and knowledge about participation in the experiment may bias outcomes or outcome measurement.

Typically, it is only possible to study the effect of one or two independent variables in an experiment at two or three different levels (different experimental conditions). Few of the possible causes of offending could be studied experimentally in practice, because few of the important variables could be experimentally manipulated (but see Farrington 1979a, 2008, for experiments on causes of offending). Experiments are usually designed to investigate immediate or short-term causal effects only. However, some interventions may have long-term rather than short-term effects, and in some cases the long-term effects may differ from the short-term ones. More fundamentally, researchers rarely know the likely time delay between cause and effect, suggesting that follow-up measurements at several different time intervals are desirable. A longitudinal-experimental study deals with many of these problems.

Many ethical, legal, and practical issues arise in randomized experiments. For example, Farrington and Jolliffe (2002) carried out a study on the feasibility of evaluating the treatment of dangerous, severely personality-disordered offenders, using a randomized controlled trial. They found that all the clinicians were opposed to such a trial because they thought that everyone should be treated and that no one should be denied treatment. However, where the number who need or want treatment exceeds the number who can be treated (in light of available resources), random assignment may be the fairest way to select people for treatment. Cook and Payne (2002) have answered many objections to randomized experiments, while Boruch (1997) has provided detailed practical advice about how to mount such experiments successfully.

LONGITUDINAL-EXPERIMENTAL RESEARCH

Advantages

Strictly speaking, every experiment is prospective and longitudinal in nature since it involves a minimum of two contacts or data collections with the participants: one consisting of the experimental intervention (the independent variable) and one consisting of the outcome measurement (the dependent variable). However, the time interval covered by the typical experiment is relatively short. Farrington et al. (1986a) argued that longitudinal-experimental studies were needed with three elements: (1) several data collections, covering several years; (2) the experimental intervention; and (3) several more data collections, covering several years afterwards. No study of this kind has ever been carried out on offending using interview data. A few experiments collected official record data retrospectively for a few years before an intervention and prospectively for a few years after the intervention (e.g., Empey and Erickson 1972), but these did not assess the effect of the intervention on criminal career trajectories or developmental sequences of offending. In the Montreal longitudinal-experimental study (see later), Vitaro et al. (2001) and Lacourse et al. (2002) pioneered the method of studying the effects of the intervention on subsequent offending trajectories.

An important advantage of a combined longitudinal-experimental study in comparison with separate longitudinal and experimental projects is economy. It is cheaper to carry out each of the studies with the same individuals than with different individuals. For example, the effect of interventions and the effect of risk/promotive/protective factors on the same people can be compared. The number of individuals and separate data collections (e.g., interviews) is greater in two studies than in one (other things being equal).

More fundamentally, the two types of studies have complementary strengths and weaknesses, and a combined longitudinal-experimental study could build on the strengths of both. For example, the longitudinal survey could provide information about the natural history of development, while the experiment could yield knowledge about the impact of interventions on development. Even if the experimental part could not be carried through successfully (e.g., because of case flow problems or implementation failure), the longitudinal-experimental study would yield valuable knowledge about the natural history of development, and quasi-experimental research on the impact of risk/promotive/protective factors and life events would still be possible. Therefore, longitudinal-experimental research is arguably less risky than experimental research.

Experiments are designed to test hypotheses. In the combined project, causal hypotheses could be generated in the longitudinal study from risk/promotive/protective factors and life events and then tested on the same individuals in the experimental study. Experiments are the best methods of testing the effects of variations (between individuals) in an independent variable on a dependent one, whereas the longitudinal study can investigate the effect of changes (within individuals) in an independent variable on a dependent one. Therefore, the combined project can compare the impact of variation with the impact of change, to see if the same results are obtained with the same individuals. This is an important issue, because most findings on risk/promotive/protective factors for offending essentially concern variations between individuals, whereas most theories and interventions refer to changes within individuals (Farrington 1988; Farrington et al. 2002). The longitudinal and experimental elements are also complementary in that the experiment can demonstrate (with high internal validity) the effect of only one or two independent variables, whereas the longitudinal study can demonstrate (with somewhat lower internal validity in quasi-experimental analyses), the relative effects of many independent variables.

It might be thought that an experimental study with a single pretest measure and a single posttest measure of offending would have many of the advantages of a longitudinal-experimental study, for example, in permitting the comparison of changes within individuals and variation between individuals. However, Fig. 24.1 illustrates some of the advantages of the longitudinal-experimental study in comparison with the simple pretest-posttest design. In this figure, 1–8 are observation points, and X indicates the experimental intervention. The simple pretest-posttest design would have only observations 4 and 5, whereas the longitudinal-experimental study could have 1–8. The lines indicate the values of some outcome variable over time (e.g., frequency of offending).

First of all note that, in all cases except line C, the change between observations 4 and 5 is the same. Hence, the simple pretest-posttest design would not distinguish between cases A, B, D, E, F, and G. However, as the longerterm series of observations show, these cases

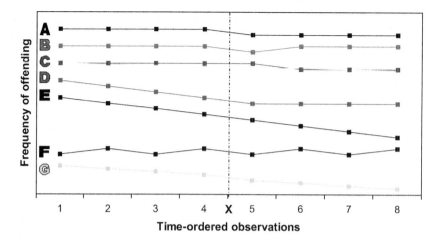

FIGURE 24.1. Advantages of longitudinal-experimental studies. *Source*: Farrington (2006).

differ in very important respects. Line A shows an immediate lasting effect of the intervention, while line B shows an immediate but short-lived effect, and line C shows a delayed lasting effect. Line D shows a delayed undesirable effect of the intervention on a pre-existing trend; note that, without the pretest series of observations, the desirable effect in case A and the undesirable effect in case D could not be distinguished. Line E shows no effect of the intervention because of the pre-existing trend, and similarly line F shows no effect of the intervention because of the haphazard oscillation. Finally, line G shows a discontinuity in a pre-existing trend that might be attributable to the intervention. Many other lines could be shown, but the main point is that false conclusions would be drawn only from observations 4 and 5 (the pretest and posttest).

The main advantages of longitudinal-experimental research have been summarized by Blumstein et al. (1988). The impact of interventions can be better understood in the context of pre-existing trends or developmental sequences, which would help in assessing maturation, instability, and regression effects in before and after comparisons. Prior information about participants would help to verify that comparison groups were equivalent so as to set baseline measures, to investigate interactions between types of persons (and their risk/promotive/protective factors and prior histories) and types of treatments, to establish eligibility for inclusion in the experiment, and to estimate the impact of differential attrition from experimental conditions. The long-term follow-up information would show effects of the intervention that were not immediately apparent, facilitate the study of different age-appropriate outcomes over time, make it possible to compare short-term and long-term effects and to investigate the developmental sequences linking them. The experimental intervention could help to distinguish causal or developmental sequences from different age-appropriate behavioral manifestations of the same underlying construct.

Problems

A major problem centers on the extent to which the experiment might interfere with the goals of the longitudinal study. In a simple experiment, some of the samples will be ineligible, some will be in the experimental group, and the remainder will be in the control group. After the experimental intervention, it might be inadvisable to draw conclusions about the natural history of offending from the experimental group, since it would have been treated in an unusual way. The experiment may increase or decrease attrition (or cause differential attrition) from the longitudinal study. Therefore, in drawing conclusions about the whole sample, results obtained with the ineligibles, experimentals, and controls might have to be treated differently.

It is less obvious that experimental persons would have to be eliminated in investigations of impact questions using quasi-experimental analyses. If the experimental intervention could be viewed as just another independent variable impinging on them, investigations of the effect of nonmanipulated independent variables could be based on the whole sample. Of course, it might be interesting to investigate whether the impact of one independent variable differed at different levels of another independent variable (e.g., in experimental and control groups).

It could be argued that each person should receive only one experimental treatment, because of the likely effect of the treatment in making the person different from a control or an ineligible. However, there may be good reasons to investigate the interactive effect of two consecutive treatments. The analysis of the data needs to mirror the factorial nature of the design. If the controls received a special treatment (e.g., being denied something that was usually available in the community), then it might even be argued that they also should not be included in a subsequent experiment.

The passage of time will inevitably cause problems. An experiment that was desirable and feasible at one time (e.g., at the start of a longitudinal study) may be less desirable and feasible some years later because of the changes in theory or policy concerns, in methodology, or in practical constraints (e.g., a change in a "gate-keeper" such as a police chief). Also, the participants in a longitudinal study will move around, and it may be that an experiment can only be conducted in a specific location. Possibly, only those who are residentially stable (at least in staying the same metropolitan area) may be eligible to participate in the experiment. For a number of reasons, the eligibility of participants could change over time, as their personal circumstances changed.

Since it is likely that attrition will increase with the length of the follow-up, differential attrition could prove to be one of the greatest problems that need to be overcome in a longitudinal-experimental study (Farrington and Welsh 2005). It is important to use methods that minimize attrition and to conduct research on this topic. For example, Farrington et al. (1990) described the methods of tracing and securing cooperation used in the Cambridge Study in Delinquent Development. Famous longitudinal researchers like Robins (1966) and McCord (1979) were able to locate and interview high percentages of their samples over follow-up periods of 30 years or more.

KEY LONGITUDINAL-EXPERIMENTAL STUDIES IN CRIMINOLOGY.   Undoubtedly, the best known and most famous longitudinal-experimental studies in criminology are those by McCord (1978), Tremblay et al. (1996), Schweinhart et al. (2005), and Olds et al. (1998). All these studies essentially added a long-term follow-up to a randomized experiment. The first two studies have provided a great deal of information about both the effects of the intervention and the development of offending, while the second two have focused more on the effects of the intervention. There are many other important longitudinal-experimental studies where the participants were not strictly randomly assigned to interventions (e.g., Hawkins et al. 2003, 2005; Raine et al. 2003; Reynolds et al. 2004), but we do not review these here. Similarly, we do not review longitudinal-experimental studies that do not include measures of offending (e.g., McCarton et al. 1997; Olds et al. 2004).

McCord (1978) carried out the most important pioneering longitudinal-experimental study. In the Cambridge-Somerville study in Boston, the experimental boys received special counseling help between the average ages of 10 and 15, and over 500 boys in both experimental and control groups were then followed up for over 30 years afterwards, in records and through questionnaires and interviews (McCord 1990). The treatment was ineffective in preventing offending since about a quarter of both groups were known to have committed crimes as juveniles, while about two-thirds of both groups had been convicted as adults. Significantly more of the experimental boys had two or more convictions. Other undesirable effects of this treatment were reviewed by McCord (2003).

The Montreal longitudinal-experimental study (Tremblay et al. 1995) is also very well known. Initially, over 1,000 Montreal boys in 53 schools were rated by teachers on their disruptive behavior at age 6, and of these 319 scoring above the 70th percentile were randomly assigned to experimental or control groups. The experimental boys received skills training and parent training between ages 7 and 9. The results of the intervention showed that the experimental boys committed less delinquency (according to self-reports) between ages 10 and 15. The experimental boys were less likely to be gang members, to get drunk or take drugs, but they were not significantly different from the controls in having sexual intercourse by age 15 (Tremblay et al. 1996). Interestingly, the differences in antisocial behavior between experimental and control boys increased as the follow-up progressed. A later follow-up showed that fewer experimental boys had a criminal record by age 24 (Boisjoli et al. 2007).

Another extremely influential experiment with a long-term follow-up is the Perry Preschool Project in Ypsilanti, Michigan (Schweinhart et al. 2005). This was essentially a "Head Start" program targeted on disadvantaged African-American children. The experimental children attended a daily preschool program backed up by weekly home visits, usually lasting 2 years, and covering ages 3 and 4. The aim of the program was to provide intellectual stimulation, to increase cognitive (thinking and reasoning) abilities, and to increase later school achievement.

An important feature of this project is that its true significance became apparent only after long-term follow-ups at ages 15 (Schweinhart and Weikart 1980), 19 (Berrueta-Clement et al. 1984), 27 (Schweinhart et al. 1993) and 40 (Schweinhart et al. 2005). As demonstrated in several other Head Start projects, the experimental group initially showed higher intelligence at age 4–5, but was no different from the control group by age 8–9 (Schweinhart and Weikart 1980). This led to the argument that compensatory education was ineffective. However, by age 27, the experimental group had accumulated only half as many arrests as the controls – an average of 2.3 as against 4.6 arrests for the controls. Also, they had significantly higher earnings and were more likely to be home owners. A cost-benefit analysis showed that for every $1 spent on the program, $7 were saved in the long term (Barnett 1996). At age 40, 91% of the participants were interviewed (112 out of the original 123), and it was estimated that $13 were saved for every $1 spent on the program (Belfield et al. 2006).

Another famous experiment was conducted by Olds et al. (1998) on the effects of home visiting. In Elmira (NY), 400 pregnant women were randomly assigned to receive home visits by nurses during pregnancy and for the first 2 years of their child's life, or to receive visits only during pregnancy, or to receive no visits. The nurses visited every 2 weeks and gave advice on child-rearing, infant nutrition, infant development, substance use avoidance, and maternal life-course development (family planning, educational achievement, and participation in the workforce). Fifteen years later, it was found that the women who had received visits during pregnancy and infancy had fewer substantiated reports of child abuse and neglect, and their children's infancy had fewer arrests and convictions, when compared with the control group (Olds et al. 1997, 1998).

Several other experiments have been conducted with long follow-up periods (at least 5 years) but with few developmental analyses. In the Carolina Abecedarian Project, 111 children aged 3 were randomly assigned either to receive full-time preschool child care (concentrating on the development of cognitive and language skills) or not. At age 21, 104 were interviewed, and fewer of the experimental participants (but not significantly so) reported being convicted or incarcerated (Campbell et al. 2002). Significantly fewer of the experimental participants were regular smokers or marijuana users, significantly more had attended college or university, and had higher status jobs.

In another preschool experiment, Mills et al. (2002) in Washington State randomly assigned 206 children (average age 5) to either a cognitively oriented or a direct instruction preschool program. The cognitively oriented program emphasized the development of thinking and problem-solving processes and did not include formal instruction in reading, math, and language skills, unlike the direct instruction program. At age 15, 171 children were reinterviewed and their self-reported delinquency was measured. The researchers found that the experimental and control participants did not differ significantly in their delinquency.

Several experimental studies based on offenders have included a follow-up in criminal records of at least 5 years (e.g., Berntsen and Christiansen 1965; Bottcher and Ezell 2005; Jesness 1971; Ortmann 2000). Schaeffer and Borduin (2005) followed up 176 youths, who had been randomly assigned either to multisystemic therapy (MST) or individual therapy for 14 years afterwards. The results (using survival analysis) showed that the experimental offenders had fewer arrests and fewer days of confinement in adult facilities. The authors concluded that over $50,000 had been saved for each youth on average, compared with the MST program costs of $4,000–$6,000 per youth.

Kling et al. (2005) evaluated the impact of the Moving to Opportunity program in five cities in the United States, in which vouchers were randomly assigned to low socioeconomic status (often minority) families to enable them to move to better areas. The effects of this move (and, hence, of different neighborhoods) on the offending of their children aged 15–20 were investigated. At least 5 years after the move, 1,807 youth were surveyed, and 3,079 were searched in arrest records. The researchers found that there was little effect of the move on the prevalence of arrests overall, but there were desirable effects in reducing the number of arrests of females for violent and property crimes and undesirable effects in increasing the number of arrests of males for property crimes.

Several experimental studies now under way may eventually publish long-term longitudinal-experimental data on offending. One of the most famous of these is the Fast Track prevention trial, implemented by the Conduct Problems Prevention Research Group (2002, 2004). At four sites, children were identified as high-risk or moderate-risk and randomly assigned by matched sets of schools to experimental or control conditions. The experimental children received a "cutting-edge" program in grades 1–5 including home visiting, parent training, social skills, and anger control training. By grade 9, the high-risk experimental children (only) were lower on conduct disorder, attention deficit-hyperactivity disorder, and self-reported delinquency (CPPRG 2007).

Ambitious longitudinal-experimental studies have recently begun in Germany and Switzerland. In the Erlangen–Nuremberg Development and Prevention Study (Lösel and Beelman 2003), 675 kindergarten children aged 3–6 were randomly assigned to receive either parent training, child skills training, both, or neither, and all children were followed up. In the

Zurich Project on the Social Development of Children (Z – PROSO; Eisner and Ribeaud 2005, 2007), 1,378 children aged 7 in 56 elementary schools were randomly assigned to Triple-P parent training (Sanders et al. 2000), the PATHS skills training program used in Fast Track, both, or neither (14 schools in each condition). All children are being followed up to age 11.

Other ambitious experimental studies that may eventually have long-term follow-up data on offending include Raising Healthy Children (Catalano et al. 2003), Focus on Families (Catalano et al. 2002) and Preparing For the Drug Free Years (Mason et al. 2003). While there have been a number of longitudinal-experimental studies, surveys with several years of interview data before and after an intervention have not yet been conducted in criminology.

QUASI-EXPERIMENTAL ANALYSES

While well-conducted randomized experiments yield more convincing evidence of causal and intervention effects, it is easier to carry out quasi-experimental analyses within prospective longitudinal surveys than to implement experimental interventions. A quasi-experimental analysis tries to isolate the impact of a naturally occurring presumed causal factor (e.g., getting married or joining a gang) by treating it as though it was experimentally manipulated and then trying to eliminate plausible alternative explanations of observed effects (or threats to internal validity; see Farrington 2003c; Shadish et al. 2002). Experimental and quasi-experimental analyses do not always yield the same results, and often quasi-experimental analyses indicate stronger effects of interventions (Weisburd et al. 2001).

Almost all studies of the causes of offending have carried out analyses between individuals showing, for example, that unemployed people commit more crimes than employed people and that this relationship holds after controlling for measured extraneous variables. However, analyses within individuals are more relevant to the concept of cause, which suggests that changes within individuals in a causal factor (e.g., from employment to unemployment) tend to be followed by changes within individuals in offending (Farrington 1988). Similarly, analyses within individuals are more relevant to prevention or treatment research (which requires within-individual change). Quasi-experimental analyses within individuals control for individual factors that do not change over time (e.g., gender and race).

Quasi-experimental analyses within individuals have been carried out in the Cambridge Study. For example, getting convicted led to an increase in self-reported offending, and a plausible intervening mechanism was increased hostility to the police (Farrington 1977). Males committed more offenses during periods of unemployment than during periods of employment, but only for crimes of financial gain, such as theft, burglary, robbery, or fraud (Farrington et al. 1986b). Getting married was followed by a decrease in offending, while separating from a wife was followed by an increase (Farrington and West 1995).

In the Pittsburgh Youth Study, there were changes in individuals' offending as a result of entering or subsequently leaving a gang (Gordon et al. 2004), and starting or stopping drug dealing (Van Kammen and Loeber 1994). It is important in all these analyses to control selection effects. For example, in the Gordon et al. (2004) study, boys who joined gangs were more delinquent before entering the gang than those who did not join.

One currently popular method of controlling for selection effects is to use propensity scores. For example, Theobald and Farrington (2009) investigated the effect of marriage on offending in the Cambridge Study. They calculated propensity scores indicating the probability of getting married, and matched married and unmarried men both on these and on prior offending. They found that convictions decreased after marriage, but only for men who married at earlier ages (under age 25). Just as randomization equates the probability of each person receiving a treatment, matching on propensity scores aims to equate treated and untreated persons on their prior probability of receiving the treatment (here, marriage).

We are aware of only one report in criminology that compared whether causes identified in within-individual analyses were similar to or different from causes identified in between-individual analyses (see Verthein et al. 1997 for an example in medicine). Farrington et al. (2002) examined the course of offending of 506 boys in the oldest sample of the Pittsburgh Youth Study over seven data waves between ages 14 and 18 on average. Risk factors were only examined if they were available at each data wave. These risk factors were HIA problems (hyperactivity-impulsivity-attention problems), low school achievement, depressed mood, poor parental supervision, low parental reinforcement, poor parent–boy communication, low involvement of the boy in family activities, low SES, poor housing, and peer delinquency. The between-individual correlations were computed for each wave and then averaged across the seven waves. In contrast, the within-individual correlations were calculated for each boy (on the basis of seven waves), resulting in 370–380 correlations for boys who had admitted at least one delinquent act, and averaged over boys.

All ten variables were significantly correlated with delinquency in the between-individual analyses. The within-individual correlations with delinquency were on average lower, and statistically significant for only four variables: peer delinquency, poor parental supervision, low involvement in family activities, and poor parent–boy communication. To test whether the associations held prospectively, subsequent analyses investigated whether variables in one wave predicted delinquency in the next wave. Only poor parental supervision, low parental reinforcement, and low family involvement predicted within individuals, and not peer delinquency. We concluded that although peer delinquency is correlated with offending between individuals, it is not a within-individual cause of offending. However, poor parental supervision, low involvement in family activities, and low parental reinforcement appeared to be causes in that, as they increased or decreased over time, the delinquency of most participants would subsequently rise and fall as well. Thus, temporal covariation between risk factors and offending suggests a causal influence.

It should be mentioned that multilevel statistical techniques (e.g., HLM and MLWIN) could make it possible simultaneously to study between-individual and within-individual causes of offending. However, we are not aware that these techniques have yet been used to compare within-individual and between-individual causes.

CONCLUSIONS

Is it better to keep longitudinal and experimental studies separate, or should new longitudinal-experimental research, with survey data before and after an intervention, be implemented to advance knowledge about the development, causes, prevention, and treatment of offending? Such research has many advantages (specified above). However, the fact that such a project has not yet been carried out suggests that it is difficult. For example, Tonry et al. (1991) proposed experimental interventions in their accelerated longitudinal design, but no interventions were included when the design was implemented as the Project on Human Development in Chicago Neighborhoods. Indeed, it is difficult enough to conduct separate longitudinal and experimental studies; only about 50 large-scale longitudinal studies and about 100 large-scale randomized experiments have been carried out in criminology (Farrington and Welsh 2006, 2007).

And yet, it is not clear that adding an experiment would interfere with the goals of a longitudinal survey, or that those who receive an intervention should be deleted from developmental analyses. For example, most of McCord's (1979, 1982) analyses of the childhood antecedents of adult criminal behavior were carried out with the experimental group, because more extensive information was collected about these boys than about the control group. As mentioned, an experimental intervention could be viewed as one of many interventions that impinge on all persons over time.

There is, however, at least one finding in the literature that suggests that relationships between risk factors and offending might differ in experimental and control groups. In analyses of the effect of the Olds nurse home visiting program, Eckenrode et al. (2001) found that child maltreatment predicted early onset problem behaviors of the children in the control group only. They concluded that the home visits had reduced the impact of this risk factor in the experimental group.

Existing longitudinal-experimental studies (in which persons were followed up after an experiment) should be reanalyzed to investigate whether development is different in experimental and control groups, and whether risk/promotive/protective factors and life events have different effects in experimental and control groups. It would also be important to investigate whether long-term attrition is different in experimental and control conditions. In addition, it would be valuable in randomized experiments to analyze official offending data for several years before and after the intervention, to investigate the effects of the intervention on trajectories of offending and developmental sequences.

Very little is known about the advantages and problems of longitudinal-experimental studies with several years of survey data before and after an intervention. In light of the advantages, a great deal could be learned by mounting such a study. Two decades ago, Farrington et al. (1986a) recommended following up four cohorts from birth to age 6, age 6 to age 12, age 12 to age 18, and age 18 to age 24, with interventions at ages 3, 9, 15, and 21. They suggested preschool and parent training interventions in infancy and childhood, peer and school programs at age 15, and employment and drug programs at age 21.

In our opinion, it would be highly desirable to mount new longitudinal-experimental studies that have at least 3 years of personal contacts with the subjects before and after an intervention, and that also have repeated, frequent data collection from a variety of sources. Large samples (e.g., 500 persons) would be needed to have sufficient statistical power to investigate risk/promotive/protective factors, criminal career features, and the effects of interventions on offending. These kinds of studies would not be cheap, although one way of minimizing the cost might be to add an experimental intervention to an existing longitudinal study. However, they could lead to significant advances in knowledge about the development, explanation, prevention, and treatment of offending and antisocial behavior.

REFERENCES

Angrist JD (2006) Instrumental variables methods in experimental criminological research: what, why and how. J Exp Criminol 2:23–44

Barnett WS (1996) Lives in the balance: age-27 benefit-cost analysis of the high/scope Perry Preschool Program. High/Scope, Ypsilanti, MI

Belfield CR, Nores M, Barnett S, Schweinhart L (2006) The High/Scope Perry preschool program: cost-benefit analysis using data from the age-40 follow-up. J Hum Resour 51:162–190

Berntsen K, Christiansen KO (1965) A resocialization experiment with short-term offenders. In: Christiansen KO (ed) Scandinavian studies in criminology, vol. 1. Tavistock, London

Berrueta-Clement JR, Schweinhart LJ, Barnett WS, Epstein AS, Weikart DP (1984) Changed lives: the effects of the Perry Preschool Program on youths through age 19. High/Scope, Ypsilanti, MI

Blumstein A, Cohen J, Farrington DP (1988) Longitudinal and criminal career research: further clarifications. Criminology 26:57–74

Boisjoli R, Vitaro F, Lacourse E, Barker ED, Tremblay RE (2007) Impact and clinical significance of a preventive intervention for disruptive boys. Br J Psychiatry 191:415–419

Boruch RF (1997) Randomized experiments for planning and evaluation. Sage, Thousand Oaks, CA

Bottcher J, Ezell ME (2005) Examining the effectiveness of boot camps: a randomized experiment with a long-term follow-up. J Res Crime Delinq 42:309–332

Campbell FA, Ramey CT, Pungello E, Sparling J, Miller-Johnson S (2002) Early childhood education: young adult outcomes from the Abecedarian project. Appl Dev Sci 6:42–57

Catalano RF, Haggerty KP, Fleming CB, Brewer DD, Gainey RD (2002) Children of substance-abusing parents: current findings from the Focus on Families project. In: McMahon RJ, Peters RD (eds) The effects of parental dysfunction on children. Kluwer/Plenum, New York, pp 179–204

Catalano RF, Mazza JJ, Harachi TW, Abbott RD, Haggerty KP, Fleming CB (2003) Raising healthy children through enhancing social development in elementary school: results after 1.5 years. J School Psychol 41:143–164

Conduct Problems Prevention Research Group (2002) Evaluation of the first 3 years of the Fast Track Prevention Trial with children at high risk for adolescent conduct problems. J Abnorm Child Psychol 30:19–35

Conduct Problems Prevention Research Group (2004) The effects of the Fast Track program on serious problem outcomes at the end of elementary school. J Clin Child Adolesc Psychol 33:650–661

Conduct Problems Prevention Research Group (2007) Fast Track randomized controlled trial to prevent externalizing psychiatric disorders: findings from grades 3 to 9. J Am Acad Child Adolesc Psychiatry 46:1250–1262

Cook TD, Payne MR (2002) Objecting to the objections to using random assignment in educational research. In: Mosteller F, Boruch RF (eds) Evidence matters. Brookings Institution Press, Washington, DC, pp 150–178

Eckenrode J, Zielinski D, Smith E, Marcynyszyn LA, Henderson CA, Kitzman H, Cole R, Powers J, Olds DL (2001) Child maltreatment and the early onset of problem behaviors: can a program of nurse home visitation break the link? Dev Psychopathol 13:873–890

Eisner M, Ribeaud D (2005) A randomized field experiment to prevent violence: the Zurich Intervention and Prevention Project at Schools, ZIPPS. Eur J Crime, Crim Law Crim Justice 13:27–43

Eisner M, Ribeaud D (2007) Conducting a criminological survey in a culturally diverse context: lessons from the Zurich Project on the Social Development of Children. Eur J Criminol 4:271–298

Empey LT, Erickson ML (1972) The Provo experiment: evaluating community control of delinquency. D.C. Heath, Lexington, MA

Farrington DP (1977) The effects of public labelling. Br J Criminol 17:112–125

Farrington DP (1979a) Experiments on deviance with special reference to dishonesty. In: Berkowitz L (ed) Advances in experimental social psychology, vol. 12. Academic Press, New York, pp 207–252

Farrington DP (1979b) Longitudinal research on crime and delinquency. In: Morris N, Tonry M (eds) Crime and justice, vol. 1. University of Chicago Press, Chicago, pp 289–348

Farrington DP (1983) Randomized experiments on crime and justice. In: Morris N, Tonry M (eds) Crime and justice, vol. 4. University of Chicago Press, Chicago, pp 257–308

Farrington DP (1988) Studying changes within individuals: the causes of offending. In: Rutter M (ed) Studies of psychosocial risk: the power of longitudinal data. Cambridge University Press, Cambridge, pp 158–183

Farrington DP (1992) The need for longitudinal-experimental research on offending and antisocial behavior. In: McCord J, Tremblay RE (eds) Preventing antisocial behavior: interventions from birth through adolescence. Guilford, New York, pp 353–376

Farrington DP (2003a) Developmental and life-course criminology: key theoretical and empirical issues. Criminology 41:221–255

Farrington DP (2003b) Key results from the first 40 years of the Cambridge study in delinquent development. In: Thornberry TP, Krohn MD (eds) Taking stock of delinquency: an overview of findings from the contemporary longitudinal studies. Kluwer/Plenum, New York, pp 137–183

Farrington DP (2003c) Methodological quality standards for evaluation research. Ann Am Acad Pol Soc Sci 587: 49–68

Farrington DP (2006) Key longitudinal-experimental studies in criminology. J Exp Criminol 2:121–141

Farrington DP (2008) Criminology as an experimental science. In: Horne C, Lovaglia M (eds) Experiments in criminology and law. Rowman and Littlefield, Lanham, MD, pp 175–179

Farrington DP, Jolliffe D (2002) A feasibility study into using a randomized controlled trial to evaluate treatment pilots at HMP Whitemoor. London Home Office (Online Report 14/02; see www.homeoffice.gov.uk)

Farrington DP, Pulkkinen L (2009) Introduction: the unusualness and contribution of life span longitudinal studies of aggressive and criminal behavior. Aggress Behav 35:115–116

Farrington DP, Welsh BC (2005) Randomized experiments in criminology: what have we learned in the last two decades? J Exp Criminol 1:9–38

Farrington DP, Welsh BC (2006) A half-century of randomized experiments on crime and justice. In Tonry M (ed) Crime and justice, vol. 34. University of Chicago Press, Chicago, pp 55–132

Farrington DP, Welsh BC (2007) Saving children from a life of crime: early risk factors and effective interventions. Oxford University Press, Oxford

Farrington DP, West DJ (1995) Effects of marriage, separation and children on offending by adult males. In: Hagan J (ed) Current perspectives on aging and the life cycle, vol. 4: delinquency and disrepute in the life course. JAI Press, Greenwich, CT, pp 249–281

Farrington DP, Ohlin LE, Wilson JQ (1986a) Understanding and controlling crime: toward a new research strategy. Springer, New York

Farrington DP, Gallagher B, Morley L, St Ledger RJ, West DJ (1986b) Unemployment, school leaving, and crime. Br J Criminol 26:335–356

Farrington DP, Gallagher B, Morley L, St Ledger RJ, West DJ (1990) Minimizing attrition in longitudinal research: methods of tracing and securing cooperation in a 24-year follow-up study. In: Magnusson D, Bergman LR (eds) Data quality in longitudinal research. Cambridge University Press, Cambridge, pp 122–147

Farrington DP, Loeber R, Yin Y, Anderson SJ (2002) Are within-individual causes of delinquency the same as between-individual causes? Crim Behav Ment Health 12:53–68

Farrington DP, Coid JW, Harnett L, Jolliffe D, Soteriou N, Turner R, West DJ (2006) Criminal careers up to age 50 and life success up to age 48: new findings from the Cambridge study in delinquent development. Home Office (Research Study No. 299), London

Gibson CL, Morris, SZ, Beaver KM (2009) Secondary exposure to violence during childhood and adolescence: does neighborhood context matter? Justice Q 26:30–57

Gordon RA, Lahey BB, Kawai E, Loeber R, Stouthamer-Loeber M, Farrington DP (2004) Antisocial behavior and youth gang membership: selection and socialization. Criminology 42:55–87

Harachi TW, Abbott RD, Catalano RF, Haggerty KP, Fleming CB (1999) Opening the black box: using process evaluation measures to assess implementation and theory building. Am J Community Psychol 27:711–731

Hawkins JD, Smith BH, Hill KG, Kosterman R, Catalano RF, Abbott RD (2003) Understanding and preventing crime and violence: findings from the Seattle Social Development Project. In: Thornberry TP, Krohn MD (eds) Taking stock of delinquency: an overview of findings from contemporary longitudinal studies. Kluwer/Plenum, New York, pp 255–312

Hawkins JD, Kosterman R, Catalano RF, Hill KG, Abbott RD (2005) Promoting positive adult functioning through social development intervention in childhood. Arch Pediatr Adolesc Med 159:25–31

Jesness CF (1971) Comparative effectiveness of two institutional treatment programs for delinquents. Child Care Q 1:119–130

Kirk DS (2006) Examining the divergence across self-report and official data sources on inferences about the adolescent life-course of crime. J Quant Criminol 22:107–129

Kling JR, Ludwig J, Katz LF (2005) Neighborhood effects on crime for female and male youth: evidence from a randomized housing voucher experiment. Q J Econ 120:87–130

Lacourse E, Cote S, Nagin DS, Vitaro F, Brendgen M, Tremblay RE (2002) A longitudinal-experimental approach to testing theories of antisocial behavior development. Dev Psychopathol 14:909–924

Laub JH, Sampson RJ (2003) Shared beginnings, divergent lives: delinquent boys to age 70. Harvard University Press, Cambridge, MA

Loeber R, Farrington DP (1994) Problems and solutions in longitudinal and experimental treatment studies of child psychopathology and delinquency. J Consult Clin Psychol 62:887–900

Loeber R, Farrington DP (1995) Longitudinal approaches in epidemiological research on conduct problems. In: Verhulst FC, Koot HM (eds) The epidemiology of child and adolescent psychopathology. Oxford University Press, Oxford, pp 309–336

Loeber R, Farrington DP (1997) Strategies and yields of longitudinal studies on antisocial behavior. In: Stoff DN, Breiling J, Maser JD (eds) Handbook of antisocial behavior. Wiley, New York, pp 125–139

Loeber R, Farrington DP (2008) Advancing knowledge about causes in longitudinal studies: Experimental and quasi-experimental methods. In: Liberman A (ed) The long view of crime: a synthesis of longitudinal research. Springer, New York, pp 257–279

Loeber R, Farrington DP, Stouthamer-Loeber M, White HR (2008) Violence and serious theft: development and prediction from childhood to adulthood. Routledge, New York

Lösel F, Beelman A (2003) Early developmental prevention of aggression and delinquency. In: Dunkel F, Drenkhahn K (eds) Youth violence: new patterns and local responses. Forum Verlag, Monchengladbach, Germany

Mason WA, Kosterman R, Hawkins JD, Haggerty KP, Spoth RL (2003) Reducing adolescents' growth in substance use and delinquency: randomized trial effects of a parent-training prevention intervention. Prev Sci 4:203–212

McCarton CM, Brooks-Gunn J, Wallace IF, Bauer CR, Bennett FC, Bernbaum JC, Broyles RS, Casey PH, McCormick MC, Scott DT, Tyson J, Tonascia J, Meinert CL (1997) Results at age 8 years of early intervention for low-birth-weight premature infants. J Am Med Assoc 277:126–132

McCord J (1978) A thirty-year follow-up of treatment effects. Am Psychol 33:284–289

McCord J (1979) Some child-rearing antecedents of criminal behavior in adult men. J Personality and Social Psychology 37:1477–1486

McCord J (1982) A longitudinal view of the relationship between paternal absence and crime. In: Gunn J, Farrington DP (eds) Abnormal offenders, delinquency, and the criminal justice system. Wiley, Chichester, pp 113–128

McCord J (1990) Crime in moral and social contexts – the American Society of Criminology 1989 Presidential Address. Criminology 28:1–26

McCord J (2003) Cures that harm: unanticipated outcomes of crime prevention programs. Ann Am Acad Pol Soc Sci 587:16–30

Metropolitan Area Child Study Research Group (2002) A cognitive-ecological approach to preventing aggression in urban settings: initial outcomes for high-risk children. J Consult Clin Psychol 70:179–194

Mills PE, Cole KN, Jenkins JR, Dale PS (2002) Early exposure to direct instruction and subsequent juvenile delinquency: a prospective examination. Except Child 69:85–96

Murray J, Farrington DP, Eisner MP (2009) Drawing conclusions about causes from systematic reviews of risk factors: the Cambridge Quality Checklists. J Exp Criminol 5:1–23

Olds DL, Eckenrode J, Henderson CR, Kitzman H, Powers J, Cole R, Sidora K, Morris P, Pettitt LM, Luckey DW (1997) Long-term effects of home visitation on maternal life course and child abuse and neglect. J Am Med Assoc 278:637–643

Olds DL, Henderson CR, Cole R, Eckenrode J, Kitzman H, Luckey D, Pettitt L, Sidora K, Morris P, Powers J (1998) Long-term effects of nurse home visitation on children's criminal and antisocial behavior: 15-year follow-up of a randomized controlled trial. J Am Med Assoc 280:1238–1244

Olds DL, Kitzman H, Cole R, Robinson J, Sidora K, Luckey DW, Henderson CR, Hanks C, Bondy J, Holmberg J (2004) Effects of nurse home visiting on maternal life course and child development: age 6 follow-up results of a randomized trial. Pediatrics 114:1550–1559

Ortmann R (2000) The effectiveness of social therapy in prison: a randomized experiment. Crime Delinq 46:214–232

Petras H, Kellam SG, Brown CH, Muthen BO, Ialongo NS, Poduska JM (2008) Developmental epidemiological courses leading to antisocial personality disorder and violent and criminal behavior: effects by young adulthood of a universal preventive intervention in first and second grade classrooms. Drug Alcohol Depend 95S:S45–S59

Raine A, Mellingen K, Liu J, Venables PH, Mednick SA (2003) Effects of environmental enrichment at ages 3–5 years on schizotypal personality and antisocial behavior at ages 17 and 23 years. Am J Psychiatry 160:1627–1635

Reynolds AJ, Ou S-R, Topitzes JW (2004) Paths of effects of early childhood intervention on educational attainment and delinquency: a confirmatory analysis of the Chicago Child-Parent Centers. Child Dev 75:1299–1328

Robins LN (1966) Deviant children grown up. Williams and Wilkins, Baltimore, MD

Robins LN (1992) The role of prevention experiments in discovering causes of children's antisocial behavior. In: McCord J, Tremblay RE (eds) Preventing antisocial behavior: interventions from birth through adolescence. Guilford, New York, pp 3–18

Sampson RJ, Sharkey P (2008) Neighborhood selection and the social reproduction of concentrated racial poverty. Demography 45:1–29

Sanders MR, Markie-Dadds C, Tully LA, Bor W (2000) The Triple P-Positive Parenting Program: a comparison of enhanced, standard and self-directed behavioral family intervention for parents of children with early onset conduct problems. J Consult Clin Psychol 68:624–640

Schaeffer CM, Borduin CM (2005) Long-term follow-up to a randomized clinical trial of multisystemic therapy with serious and violent juvenile offenders. J Consult Clin Psychol 73:445–453

Schwartz D, Flamant R, Lelouch J (1980) Clinical trials. Academic Press, London

Schweinhart LJ, Weikart DP (1980) Young children grow up: the effects of the Perry Preschool Program on youths through age 15. High/Scope, Ypsilanti, MI

Schweinhart LJ, Barnes HV, Weikart DP (1993) Significant benefits: the High/Scope Perry Preschool Study through age 27. High/Scope, Ypsilanti, MI

Schweinhart LJ, Montie J, Zongping X, Barnett WS, Belfield CR, Nores M (2005) Lifetime effects: the High/Scope Perry Preschool Study through age 40. High/Scope, Ypsilanti, MI

Shadish WR, Cook TD, Campbell DT (2002) Experimental and quasi-experimental designs for generalized causal influence. Houghton-Mifflin, Boston

Theobald D, Farrington DP (2009) Effects of getting married on offending: results from a prospective longitudinal survey of males. Eur J Criminol 6:496–516

hornberry TP (1989) Panel effects and the use of self-reported measures of delinquency in longitudinal studies. In: Klein MW (ed) Cross-national research in self-reported crime and delinquency. Kluwer, Dordrecht, Netherlands, pp 347–369

Tonry M, Ohlin LE, Farrington DP (1991) Human development and criminal behavior: new ways of advancing knowledge. Springer, New York

Tremblay RE, Pagani-Kurtz L, Mâsse LC, Vitaro F, Pihl RO (1995) A bimodal preventive intervention for disruptive kindergarten boys: its impact through mid-adolescence. J Consult Clin Psychol 63:560–568

Tremblay RE, Mâsse LC, Pagani L, Vitaro F (1996) From childhood physical aggression to adolescent maladjustment: the Montreal prevention experiment. In: Peters RD, McMahon RJ (eds) Preventing childhood disorders, substance use, and delinquency. Sage, Thousand Oaks, CA, pp 268–298

Van Kammen WB, Loeber R (1994) Are fluctuations in delinquent activities related to the onset and offset of juvenile illegal drug use and drug dealing? J Drug Issues 24:9–24

Verthein U, Köhler T (1997) The correlation between everyday stress and angina pectoris: a longitudinal study. J Psychosom Res 43:241–245

Vitaro F, Brendgen M, Tremblay RE (2001) Preventive intervention: assessing its effects on the trajectories of delinquency and testing for mediational processes. Appl Dev Sci 5:201–213

Weisburd D, Lum CM, Petrosino A (2001) Does research design affect study outcomes in criminal justice? Ann Am Acad Pol Soc Sci 578:50–70

## CHAPTER 25

Multisite Trials in Criminal Justice Settings: Trials and Tribulations of Field Experiments

FAYE S. TAXMAN AND ANNE GIURANNA RHODES

Researchers have choices to make regarding the design of any experiment including the type of design (randomized or quasi-experimental design) and the number of sites to include in a study. The latter decision is one that few have paid significant attention to. As previously argued by Weisburd and Taxman (2000), there are advantages to multicenter trials. Multicenter trials are familiar in medical settings where they provide the opportunity to test a new protocol or innovation within various settings. No decision rules exist as to when a single or multisite trial should occur. Single site trials provide a starting point to test out the feasibility of a new innovation, but multisite trials have a clear advantage in testing the innovation under various operating conditions. In some ways, the multisite trial offers the potential to accumulate knowledge more quickly by using each site as a laboratory for assessing the characteristics or factors that affect the question of "value added" or improved outcomes. The multisite trial creates the opportunity to simultaneously test the innovation as well as learn from these sites about the parameters that affect outcomes. The prospect of doing a multisite trial is more complicated than a single site trial because it requires attention to both the design and the management of the study. It is through multisite trials that we can learn about areas where "drift" may occur, whether it is in the innovation, the management of the study, external factors that affect the innovation, or the inability of the environment to align to the innovation.

This paper is designed to provide insight into the complexity of a multisite trial, and how different design, site preparation, and research management affect the integrity of the experiment. We use case studies of two recently completed multisite trials that involve complex innovations, or innovations that involve more than one operating agency. Unlike other documented work on describing the management problems associated with multicenter trials (a multisite trial with one lead investigator but other site investigators, see Friedman et al. 1985; Pocock 1983), this paper highlights the continuing need to consider implementation issues that affect the integrity of the experiment. In these case studies, we use the various types of threats to internal validity as a conceptual framework to illustrate the decisions that

A.R. Piquero and D. Weisburd (eds.), *Handbook of Quantitative Criminology*,
DOI 10.1007/978-0-387-77650-7_25, © Springer Science + Business Media, LLC 2010,
First softcover printing 2011

researchers must make in a study. The case studies serve to provide a discussion of issues regarding the design and conduct of multisite trials. We conclude by providing lessons learned in conducting or being involved in multisite trials.

THE MULTISITE TRIAL

While randomized control trials are the "gold-standard" of research, they are often plagued by design and implementation issues. Adding diverse sites complicates matters, particularly when the goal is to develop a standardized protocol across sites, and the study sites have a wide range of expertise and resources. These issues can be even more pronounced in criminal justice settings, where design considerations are often impacted by the structure and administration of local, state and federal agencies. While there has been a push for more trials in the criminal justice field (Weisburd 2003), the number of randomized studies (especially those that are multisite) remains low.

An important first step in multicenter trials is the development of the study protocol. The protocol should have the following: (1) the rationale for the study, (2) a description of the intervention, (3) a list of the procedures to implement the study, (4) copy of the instruments and key measures, and (5) human subject procedures including consent forms and certificates of confidentiality. This protocol is needed to provide the guidance in terms of implementation of the study in the real-world settings with the myriad of organizations, both research organizations and agencies where the innovation is going to be fielded (Chow and Liu 2004). The protocol manual should also consider the unique characteristics of the sites involved, particularly if these characteristics are likely to impact findings or can influence the degree to which the innovation is likely to be delivered. Up front analyses of these issues, often through pipeline or feasibility analyses or piloting of procedures, will ensure that the trial is uniformly conducted across study sites. The goal is to mitigate differences and to reduce the need to control for these issues during the analytic stage. The issues to be addressed in the protocol are:

Rationale for the Study. Every trial has a purpose that should be specified in study aims and hypotheses. The rationale provides a guidebook as to why the trial is necessary and what we will learn from the trial.

Theoretical Foundation and How it Informs the Innovation. Trials are essentially about innovations, either an introduction of a new idea or a change in an existing procedure or process. The innovation should be guided by theory which should help explain why the new or revised procedure or process is likely to result in improvements in the desired outcomes. And, the theory should be articulated into the procedures that will be tested. It is important to ensure that each component of the procedure is theoretically based to provide an explanation of why the component is needed as part of the innovation.

Defining the Study Population. Based on the study aims, the nature of the study population should be defined. The criteria for inclusion and exclusion should be specified to ensure that the innovation is reaching the appropriate target population. Generally, inclusion criteria relate to traits of the individual or setting. But, in the real-world criminal justice settings, other selection forces may be present that may be a function of the process or environment. Researchers may not have access to the full base population, which can potentially bias results. For example, in recruiting at a prison or jail, wardens or correctional officers may decide that offenders under certain security restrictions are ineligible for study participation. Selection forces can vary between study sites because of factors that are often not evident. Also, sites may operationalize selection criteria differently. A recent article on multisite trials in health services research by Weinberger et al. recommended that the lead center develop selection criteria that allow each site to operationally define these criteria given the local environment (Weinberger et al. 2001).

Defining the Intervention. The innovation that is being tested should, by definition, be different than traditional practice. As discussed above, the intervention needs to be outlined in detail, including theoretical rationale, dosage and duration, procedures essential to implementation, and core components that will be tracked using fidelity measures (Bond et al. 2000). Most interventions consist of different components that are combined together to produce the innovation. It is also important to specify who will implement the intervention (the provider) and how they will become proficient in the skills needed to deliver the intervention. In an experiment, it is important to clearly delineate how the innovation will be integrated into the existing infrastructure of an organization and what potential issues are expected to occur and how these will be handled.

Defining the Control Group(s) or Practice As Usual. The main purpose of the control group in an RCT is to have a contrast to the innovation. The control group generally represents practice as usual, and allows the ability to distinguish subject outcomes. The control group is expected to have the same distribution of other factors that could potentially affect outcomes as the treatment group, and thus, avoids the possibility of confounding. To achieve this goal, randomization gives each eligible subject an equal chance of being assigned to either group in a two-armed design. Blinding, in conjunction with randomization, ensures equal treatment of study groups. In general, the services received by the control group should follow the principle of equipoise, meaning that there should be uncertainty about whether the control or the experimental condition is a better option (Djulbegovic et al. 2003).

Measurement and Observations. Another important component of a study is how effects of the intervention will be determined, i.e., what instruments will be used to measure outcomes and how and when these instruments will be used. Dennis outlines four types of variables to be collected: design variables (sites, study condition, weights, etc.), other covariates (demographics, diagnoses, etc.), pre- and post-randomization intervention exposure, and pre- and post-dependent variables (Dennis et al. 2000). Most experiments have multiple waves of data collection where the same data is collected at baseline and at specified follow-up points. Outcome measurements can be subject to a number of different biases, including recall bias for self-report measures, sensitivity and specificity issues (biomedical tests), and rater error (file reviews). The types of data to be collected should be based on the hypotheses to be tested and the availability and cost of data. For the main outcomes, it is often recommended to have multiple sources of measurement, such as self-report and urine-testing for drug outcomes. These can be put together to create combined measures (Dennis et al. 2004).

Quantitative Analysis. The analysis of multisite trial data is dependent on the types of measures collected and the format of the outcome and independent variables. While the trial is ongoing, interim analyses may be conducted, mainly for data monitoring purposes. Some trials in the justice system may require oversight from a data and safety monitoring board (DSMB) who will run reports on a regular basis to determine if subject flow and follow-up are adequate and if treatment effects are observed in the data. These interim data runs often use t-tests, ANOVAs, or effect sizes (Cohen 1988). For more formal analyses, multivariate models are used to account for the repeated measures and multisite designs. With repeated measures data, hierarchical models can be used, which nest observations within person over time (Raudenbush 2001). Different types of models are available including latent growth models (LGM), which captures individual differences in change trajectories over time (Meredith and Tisak 1990). With multiple assessment points, LGM tests for both linear and nonlinear growth through the use of specified growth functions and additional growth factors (e.g., quadratic, piecewise linear models). LGM also allows for an examination of what factors predict changes in outcomes over time, controlling for both measured and unmeasured stable individual-level characteristics (Bollen and Curran 2006).

To an extent, a multisite trial allows for the ability to pool the overall impacts of treatment and the specific impacts of treatment within separate sites in the context of a single statistical model. The sites in a multicenter trial can be seen in this context as building blocks that can be combined in different ways by the researchers. The separate randomization procedures allow each center to be analyzed as a separate experiment as well as combined into an overall experimental evaluation where the researcher is able to identify direct and interaction effects in a statistically powerful experimental context. If the researcher was to identify subjects from all sites and then randomly allocate subjects to treatment and control conditions (without reference to site), then any statistical analysis of the impacts of site on outcomes would be nonexperimental and subject to the same threats to internal validity due to omitted variables common in nonexperimental research (see Smith 1990).

There is a cautionary note in analyzing multisite studies. A multisite study is not really a multicenter study where there is a random sample of sites themselves. Without a random sample of sites, a number of restrictions must be placed on the generalizations that can be made and the type of statistical models that can be estimated. Site must be defined as a fixed factor in the statistical models employed, because of the possible variation in the context of the sites. It is important to consider that the generalizability of these effects is limited and cannot be applied to the larger population. In the mixed effects model, a hypothesis about the average treatment effect of the population refers to the population of sites from which the sample of sites is drawn.

Weisburd and Taxman (2000) recommend a statistical process for using mixed effects model in analyzing multisite studies. A model for this example is presented in (25.1) below. This provides a technique for dealing with the multisite issues.

$$Y = \mu + S_i + T_j + ST_{ij} + O_{k(i,j)} + e_{k(i,j)} \tag{25.1}$$

where T_j is the larger population of centers for the mixed effects model; S_i is the average impact of a site (or center) on outcomes, averaged over treatments; ST_{ij} is the interaction effect between treatment and site, once the average impacts of site variation and treatment variation have been taken into account; and $O_{k(i,j)}$ is nested within a site by treatment combination.

TOOLS TO MONITOR IMPLEMENTATION: CONSORT FLOW CHARTS IN CJ SETTINGS

Understanding the flow of subjects through the different phases of an experiment is an important task to manage the quality and integrity of the experiment. In multisite trials, subject flow may be influenced by facets of the particular criminal justice system, the behavior of study subjects, or factors that are difficult to identify. In 2001, the Consolidated Standards of Reporting Trials (CONSORT) statement was issued as a way to improve the reporting of information from trials (Moher et al. 2001). The CONSORT flow chart illustrates how to

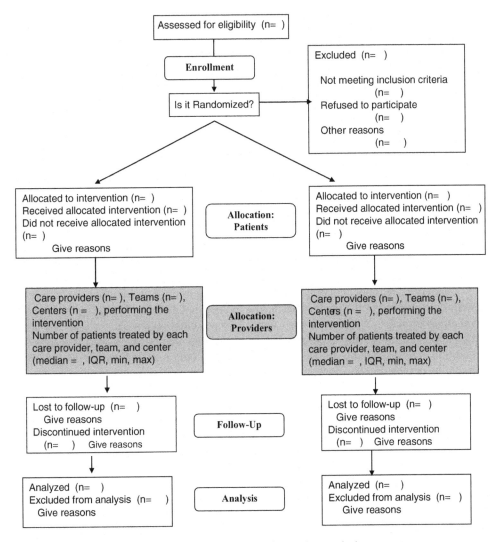

FIGURE 25.1. Sample consort flowchart for nonpharmacologic treatments.

report subjects through each trial phase; the flow chart was amended in 2008 to specifically address issues related to nonpharmacologic treatments (such as different types of therapy or different modes of sanctions). A copy of the amended chart is in Fig. 25.1 (Boutron et al. 2008). The CONSORT chart provides documentation for each phase of the experiment, and provides sufficient information to assess the quality of the implementation of the experiment.

This section describes the CONSORT flow chart for nonpharmacologic treatments (Fig. 25.1), as it relates to implementing trials in criminal justice settings. The unique challenges presented by these settings include not only the target population as potentially vulnerable to coercion and exploitation, but also reflects the difficulties of work in settings that are, by their nature, authoritarian and often not amenable to the rigors of randomized trials.

The first section concerns eligibility. Most trials involve decisions about specific inclusion and exclusion criteria that should be in place for the trial so that the results can be generalizable to the appropriate population. The identification of people that fit the desired criteria may involve a multistep process. For example, a specific protocol may require the exclusion of sex offenders. This will require the research project to define the term "sex offenders" and then develop specific criteria to meet this term. In practice, researchers will generally need to conduct a prior chart review of offenders to make a determination of which offenders might meet the eligibility criteria. This screening often occurs before the research interview or consent is given. Other types of frequent eligibility criteria are offense specific, geographical areas, age or gender issues, language, or other characteristics. In general, screening criteria should be geared towards obtaining a study population that would be appropriate for the intervention that will be tested. The question for the CONSORT chart is how many subjects meet the criteria, and what process is used to identify the target population. This defines the intent to treat group.

Prior to randomization, subjects may be dropped from the study because they fail to meet screening criteria or refuse to participate in the study. Once they are randomized, they may either receive their allocated intervention (control or treatment) or they may not receive it for a variety of reasons including not meeting the eligibility criteria when they are interviewed, dropping out of the study, transferring to another CJ facility, or having a change in criminal justice status. All of these are examples of postchart review factors that may affect participation in a study. The randomization process is such that once a subject is assigned to a condition, they are eligible for follow-up even if they only receive a partial dosage of the intervention or they do not complete the period of time devoted to the intervention.

The provider allocation section of the CONSORT chart was added in 2008 and reflects the need to characterize the settings where the treatment(s) take place. The researcher needs to identify all of the potential settings that might be involved in the experiment. For example, the range of settings could be treatment, criminal justice, courts, or other areas. To be documented is the number of providers, teams, and/or centers and the number of subjects in each area. In criminal justice settings, it will often be the specific organization that is of interest such as the parole office or prison where the trial may be implemented. Each organization will have different characteristics, and these require documentation.

A key issue is the follow-up rates for subjects in all arms of the study. The documentation should include the number that have been followed-up and the reasons for missed follow-ups. Reasons for attrition from a study are critical to ensure the study has sufficient power for the analyses. It is important to document follow-up rates at each wave, along with reasons for exclusions of any cases.

The last component of the CONSORT documentation is the result from the final outcome variables that relate to the study aims and the timing of all variables. The researcher is also required to document any assumptions that were made about the data.

Some criticisms have been made of the lack of detail present in the CONSORT chart (Mayo-Wilson 2007), specifically the lack of information on implementation details. As our case studies will demonstrate, the CONSORT chart does not capture a number of issues that can present threats to the internal validity of a multisite trial. Other scales and checklists have been developed to measure the quality of randomized trials, including the Balas Scale for health services research (Balas et al. 1995) and the Downs scale for public health research (Downs and Black 1998). A review of these scales found little widespread use of them and also found that most had not been tested for construct validity or internal consistency (Olivo et al. 2008).

CASE STUDIES OF RCTS IN CRIMINAL JUSTICE SETTINGS

The following sections present case studies of two RCTs that were implemented in criminal justice settings as part of the Criminal Justice Drug Abuse Treatment Studies (CJ-DATS1), a 10-center research cooperative sponsored by the National Institute on Drug Abuse from 2002 to 2008. Part of the objective of CJ-DATS was to use rigorous scientific methods to conduct studies in criminal justice settings. In all, six randomized trials were done in CJ-DATS. The purpose of the studies was to conduct studies at the point where offenders transit from incarceration to the community, referred to as the structured release or reentry process. The studies involved numerous agencies including prison, probation/parole agencies, prison or community treatment providers, and nonprofit agencies.

The case studies are presented to illustrate the issues regarding study design and management. We use as the conceptual framework for this analysis the threats to internal validity that are specified in many textbooks on conducting social experiments (Campbell and Stanley 1966). By examining these issues, as well as looking at how the researchers managed the study, we can learn about the issues inherent in implementing multisite trials.

THREATS TO INTERNAL VALIDITY

Confounding. The degree to which a third variable, which is related to the manipulated variable, is detected. The presence of spurious relations might result in a rival hypothesis to the original causal hypothesis that the researcher may develop.

Selection (bias). Both researchers and study participants bring to the experiment many different characteristics. Some of these characteristics, which may not have been included in the eligibility criteria, may influence those who participate in an experiment. These factors may influence the observed outcomes. The subjects in both groups may not be alike in regard to independent variables.

History. Study participants may be influenced by events outside of the experiment either at the onset of the study or between measurement periods. These events may influence attitudes and behaviors in such a way that it might be detectable.

Maturation. During the experiment, subjects may change and this change may result in how the study participants react to the dependent variable.

Repeated testing. Conducting multiple measures over periods of time may result in bias on the part of the study participants. These impacts may occur from the failure to recall correct answers, or the prospects of being tested.

Instrument change. An instrument used during the experimental period could be altered.

Mortality/differential attrition. Study dropouts may be the result of the person, the experiment, or the situation. An understanding of the reasons for the attrition and the differential rates of attrition can address the issue of whether the attrition is natural or due to some other factors.

Diffusion. The experimental category should be different than traditional practice, and movement from the experimental to control group or vice versa may pollute the assigned conditions.

Compensatory rivalry/resentful demoralization. The control group behavior could be tainted by the result of being in the study.

Experimenter bias. The researcher or research team may inadvertently affect the experiment by their actions.

1. *Step'N Out.* An RCT at six Parole Offices in five States

Step'N Out tested an integrated system of establishing target behaviors for offenders on parole, collaborative behavioral management (CBM). CBM requires the parole officers and treatment counselors to work together with offenders over a 12 week period, using a system of graduated sanctions and incentives. A more detailed description of the study can be found in Friedmann et al. (2008).

Theoretical Intervention. CBM has three major components. First, it explicitly articulates parole and treatment staff roles as well as the offenders' and the expectations of each party (role induction theory). Second, a behavioral contract defines the consequences if offenders meet or fail to meet those expectations. The behavioral contract specifies concrete target behaviors in which the offender is expected to engage on a weekly basis; these target behaviors include requirements of supervision and formal addiction treatment, and involvement in behaviors that compete with drug use (e.g., getting a job; enhancing nondrug social network) (behavioral targeting). Third, it regularly monitors adherence to the behavioral contract, and employs both reinforcers and sanctions to shape behavior. The motto is "Catching People Doing Things Right," which is to say, the intervention creates the conditions to notice and reward offenders for achieving incremental prosocial steps as part of normal supervision (contingency management). CBM establishes a systematic, standardized, and progressive approach to reinforcement and sanctioning to ensure consistency and fairness.

The CBM contract specifies expectations in terms of concrete target behaviors that the offender must meet before the next weekly session. Examples of target behaviors include producing a negative urine specimen; attending supervision and counseling sessions; and completing incremental steps toward getting a job or finding drug-free housing. These target behaviors are managed using a computer program, the Step'N Out COmputerized INput Environment (SNOCONE). The contract is printed out with copies for all three parties to sign and keep for their records. This process is completed weekly as part of standard parole conditions. The CBM contract is monitored weekly to expedite identification and reinforcement of compliance and sanction of noncompliance, and then the contract is renegotiated and printed for the following week. Compliance with the contract earns points and, when pre-established milestones are reached, material and social rewards.

Control Condition. Offenders were supervised by the assigned parole officer in the manner that is used by that jurisdiction. As shown in Table 25.1 below, each site had different standards for parole visits and drug testing based on standard practice.

Study Sites. Five CJ-DATS centers participated in Step'N Out – the University of Delaware (Wilmington parole office), Brown University/Lifespan Hospital (Providence parole office), UCLA (Portland, OR parole office), CT Department of MHAS (Bridgeport and Hartford parole offices), and George Mason University (Richmond parole office). All sites except Connecticut had one parole officer and one treatment counselor assigned to the CBM condition at their sites. In Connecticut, two or three officers were trained in CBM at each site, with one counselor also trained at each office.

Site Preparation. The initial two-and-half-day training for the Step'N Out teams occurred in December, 2004. This training brought together parole officer and addiction counselor teams and their supervisors. The training began with lecture presentation of the theoretical model and rationale for the intervention, research evidence for its components, and an outline of key elements. Training staff then demonstrated the key components of CBM. The remainder of the training focused on having the teams practice skills in case-based role plays with

TABLE 25.1. RCT implementation issues for Step'N Out

Issue	BP/HT	DE	OR	RI	VA
Place of randomization	Parole office	Halfway house	Parole office, switched to prison	Prison	Parole office
Selection bias	BP – 2 persons randomized but did not make initial parole session (CBM = 1, control = 1); HT – 2 persons (CBM = 1, control = 1)	85 offenders were not released to parole CBM = 42, control = 43	3 offenders not released (all control)	1 offender not released in CBM	Gang members were excluded
History	An event occurred (a parolee committed homicide) that resulted in a crackdown on parolees which increased violations			Recruitment was suspended in 2005. All subjects recruited were dropped from the study. Recruitment began again in July 2006 with offenders placed on electronic monitoring	
Maturation – time to touch base session	6.1 days (0–27 days) CBM = 5.9 vs. control = 6.2 for Bridgeport 7.7 days (2 to 25) for Hartford CBM = 7.4 vs. control = 12	68.3 days (0 to 470 days) CBM = 47 vs. control = 92.8	51.6 days (0 to 175 days) CBM = 51.2 vs. control = 52.1	17.1 days (5 to 69 days) CBM = 9.8 vs. control = 20.4	10.7 days (0 to 78 days) CBM = 10.4 vs. control = 10.9
Mortality/ differential attrition – 3 month FU	3M FU BP: CBM = 100% Control = 100% 3M FU HT: CBM = 100% Control = 95.7%	3M FU: CBM = 98.9% Control = 97.9%	3M FU: CBM = 79.4% Control = 87.5%	3M FU CBM = 100% Control = 85.7%	3M FU CBM = 79.5% Control = 91.3%
Mortality/ differential attrition – 9 month	9M FU BP: CBM = 97.2% Control = 97.2% 9M FU HT: CBM = 92.3% Control = 82.6%	9M FU BP: CBM = 97.2% Control = 97.2% 9M FU HT: CBM = 92.3% Control = 82.6%	9M FU: CBM = 73.5% Control = 90.6%	9M FU: CBM = 88.2% Control = 78.6%	9M FU: CBM = 64.1% Control = 78.3%
Selection-maturation interaction (average)	Control group saw parole officers once a month	Control group saw parole officers once a week	Control group saw parole officers two times a month	Control group saw parole officers once a week	Control group saw parole officers once a month
Diffusion		Possibly in group SA sessions since treatment sessions for control and CBM at parole office			Possibly in group SA sessions as treatment for both control and CBM was at parole office

(continued)

TABLE 25.1. (continued)

Issue	BP/HT	DE	OR	RI	VA
Compensatory rivalry		Anecdotal stories of resentment by control subjects of material and social rewards given to CBM			
Experimenter bias	Had a number of POs implementing CBM at each site; may have been differential implementation by PO. PO had few CBM clients, may have diluted effects	Changed CBM POs part way through the study, may have had different implementation styles	Changed CBM counselor part way through process, may have different implementation styles		CBM PO felt isolated, also had substantial non-CBM clients, may have diluted effects

reinforcement and corrective feedback. A checklist of the key elements for fidelity to the protocol guided the role plays and feedback. The teams were encouraged to negotiate roles with regards to initiating the role induction discussion, establishing goals and setting target behaviors, but the protocol recommends that the PO take primary responsibility for rewards and sanctioning and the counselor for problem-solving.

Additional on-site trainings were also scheduled due to the lag time between the initial training and the time that sites began recruitment, the addition of new sites, and staff turnover. A 2-day booster training session in September, 2006, focused on enhancing both the fidelity and finesse with which teams delivered the intervention.

Parole officers were also asked to tape random sessions. Feedback on the sessions was to be given on a monthly basis to build the skills of the officers in using the contingency management procedure.

Study Implementation. Table 25.2 outlines the issues encountered in implementing the study across the fives sites. One of the first challenges was the point of randomization. Because those who were randomized to the CBM condition had to be assigned to a specific parole officer (the one who had received the CBM training), randomization had to be done at a point where parole officer assignment had not yet been done. This point varied from site to site, with some assigning officers prior to an offender's release from prison, while others assigned the officer once the offender appeared at the parole office. While the ideal situation was to randomize at the parole office where the intervention was occurring, this was not possible at all sites, particularly in Delaware and Rhode Island. At those two sites, the agency practice was to assign the officer prior to an offender's release. In these sites, screening and randomization were done while the offender was still incarcerated; this allowed the offender who was randomized to CBM to be assigned to the CBM officer. In Oregon, randomization began at the parole office, but recruitment was very slow in the initial months of the study and it was determined that the research staff had a better working relationship at the prisons; thus, recruitment was moved to the prison after 6 months of commencing the experiment. In the end, half of the sites were randomizing in prison and half were randomizing at the parole office.

TABLE 25.2. RCT implementation issues in HIV/HEPC study

Issue	DE	KY	VA
Place of randomization	Halfway house	Prisons (2 male, 1 female)	Local jail
Start of follow-up	Randomization	Release date	Release date
Selection bias	Unknown selection forces for initial groups – had 406 randomized but only 391 released (96.3%)	Unknown selection forces for initial groups – had 184 randomized but only 125 released (67.9%)	Unknown selection forces for initial groups – had 113 randomized but only 67 released (59.2%)
History	A confidentiality breach in DE on a different project shut down interviewing and recruiting until new processes were put in place	KY was unable to recruit in the men's prisons	Jail staffing issues and changes in security procedures affected recruitment; suspended for 2 months
Maturation		Longer time between randomization and follow-up than DE because of release dates	Longer time between randomization and follow up than DE because of release dates
Repeated testing			
Mortality/Differential Attrition	30 Day FU: Std = 98%, NIDA = 100%, DVD = 99%; 90 Day FU: Std = 98%, NIDA = 98%, DVD = 96%	30 Day FU: Std = 100%, NIDA = 76%, DVD = 92%; 90 Day FU: Std = 100%, NIDA = 85%, DVD = 92%	30 Day FU: Std = 90%, NIDA = 73%, DVD = 94%; 90 Day FU: Std = 75%, NIDA = 60%, DVD = 88%
Selection–maturation interaction			
Diffusion	All arms of the study were all housed in the same facility for a period of time. Those in the intervention arms could share information with those in the control arms	All arms of the study were all housed in the same facility for a period of time. Those in the intervention arms could share information with those in the control arms	All arms of the study were all housed in the same facility for a period of time. Those in the intervention arms could share information with those in the control arms
Experimenter bias	Changed DVD interventionist part way through the study, also changed NIDA standard interventionist. Occasionally had same person do both arms		

A consequence of the place of assignment in these studies at the "transition" point is that not all randomly assigned subjects were exposed to the intervention. A substantial portion of those who were randomized in prison never made it to the parole office. In Rhode Island, this was due to the fact that many offenders "flattened" in prison, or served out their parole sentences in prison, because of the unavailability of space in halfway houses where offenders were supposed to go upon release. In Delaware, many offenders committed violations in the halfway house that resulted in them being returned to prison before they could begin their parole sentence. This group of "postrandomization dropouts" was problematic, because they were technically part of the study population to be followed, yet they were not exposed to the intervention or any study activities. Many had no time in the community, postrandomization. Rhode Island dropped their initial cases and changed their recruiting practices so that all of their cases were to be placed on electronic monitoring after release. Delaware also changed their recruiting to make their screening closer to the initial parole session. These measures drastically reduced postrandomization dropouts. The final CONSORT chart for Step'N Out is given in Fig. 25.2 (note that when the study was done, the revised CONSORT for nonpharmacological interventions had not yet been published). There were a total of 93 postrandomization dropouts, with the majority ($n = 85$) from the Delaware site.

Having randomization occur in two different places (depending on the sties) meant that this needed to be accounted for in the analysis. The place of randomization has to be controlled

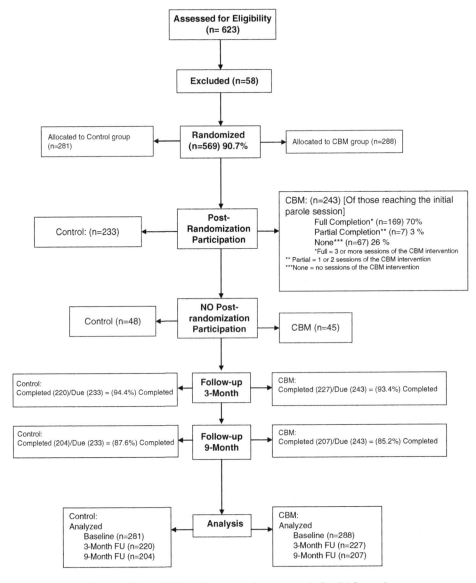

FIGURE 25.2. CONSORT flowchart of participants in Step'N Out study.

for when running statistical analyses and differences have been found in outcomes, according to this variable (Rhodes et al. 2009). Also, as is shown in Table 25.1, other selection forces also occurred during the study at different sites. In Virginia, gang members were never sent to the research interviewer for screening because a special program for gang members was being conducted with an assigned parole officer.

Another important site difference in implementation was the time it took for a person to begin the intervention after randomization. In some of the sites, those in the CBM group were able to begin parole services sooner than those in the control group, perhaps, due to the availability of a dedicated parole officer for the CBM intervention who did not have the same large caseloads as other officers. In both Delaware and Rhodes Island, it took about half the time for those in CBM to begin parole services as compared to those in the control group. This could lead to instrumentation issues, since the results from CBM, such as positive results, could indicate simply that those who begin parole sooner have different outcomes than those who started later (MacKenzie et al. 1999), as better outcomes could be a function of the timing rather than the superiority of the CBM intervention attributes.

Timing of instrumentation also affected the study. The follow-up clock for Step'N Out began with the date of the first parole session (the "touch base" session). Because the time to the touch base session was longer for some subjects than for others, the time to the follow-up interviews also varied. In some cases, the 3 month follow-up, occurred about 3 months after randomization (when randomization occurred close to the first parole session), but in other cases, there was over a year of time between randomization and the first parole session resulting in over 15 months between baseline and the 3 month follow-up. While the follow-up was generally capturing the first 3 months on parole, there was a wide variation in how much time had elapsed since randomization for each subject. It was also complicated since some sites (Delaware) also tended to have differential timing between follow-up periods.

An attrition-related issue involved missed follow-ups. The Delaware center, which had the largest number of clients in Step'N Out, had some staffing issues during the project and missed the 3 month follow-up window for a number of subjects. Because the main outcomes relied on data from the 3 month interview, provisions were made to obtain these data at a later date. Basically, at the 9 month interview, a full timeline follow back was completed which included all time back to the initial parole session. The prospects for historical and maturation issues increased by this procedure, especially with the different timeframes for data collection across the various sites. The strategy allowed for the study to obtain needed outcome data, but it also created potential recall issues, where subjects were asked to recall drug use, arrest, crime, and living situation data on a daily basis up to 18 months after it occurred. The varying lengths of the follow-up period may have affected the integrity of the data.

An issue that was inherent to the specific criminal justice systems in each state was the status of the control group. Because this group received parole and treatment services "as usual" in each state, the services received by the control group were not uniform across all sites, as shown Table 25.1. In some sites, parole officers met with subjects once a month; in others, once a week. These were due to standard conditions of parole but other variations could be due to the individual offenders who have different conditions which require different schedules for parole. The same issues applied to substance abuse treatment. While the screening instrument used to assess eligibility ensured that those in the study had substance abuse dependency issues, it was not necessarily required that members of the control group would receive treatment since this decision depended upon the parole recommendations or was a decision of the local parole officer. Not all parole officers recommended their clients for treatment. Thus, variations occurred in the conditions under which the control group was supervised both within site and across sites.

2. The HIV/HEPC Study: A 3-Armed RCT at three Centers

This RCT was designed to test the efficacy of a criminal justice based brief HIV/HCV intervention administered during the reentry period of incarceration. Rates of both HIV and Hepatitis C are disproportionately high for those involved in the criminal justice system (Hammett et al. 2002), and the reentry period has been found to be a particularly risky time for offenders (Arriola and Braithwaite 2008). This study was a three-group randomized design, with (1) current practice, a group of offenders who saw an HIV awareness video shown as part of group sessions in the facilities during the pre-release process; (2) the NIDA Standard Version 3 HIV/HepC prevention intervention delivered by a health educator via cue cards in a one-on-one didactic setting and (3) the CJ-DATS Targeted, a near-peer facilitated intervention that used an interactive DVD format with gender/race congruent testimonials, also in one-on-one setting. Participants in all three groups were offered HIV and HCV testing. The full study design has been described elsewhere (Inciardi et al. 2007). The study was conducted by three CJ-DATS centers, the University of Delaware (Lead Center), the University of Kentucky, and George Mason University. The main purpose of the study was to test the interactive DVD method to determine if those who were exposed to a gender and culturally specific message had greater reductions in risky behaviors than those that receive the NIDA standard and current practice arms of the study. Follow-ups for this study were done at 30 and 90 days after either randomization or the date of release from the prison.

Theoretically Driven Intervention. Based on focus groups with offenders, the study team developed a DVD that addressed issues related to reducing risky behaviors that involve the transmission of HIV/Hep C. The messages were then developed to be consistent with the gender and ethnicity (i.e. Caucasian, African-American) of the offender. The theory was that the same messages delivered in a gender-culturally specific manner would result in greater compliance. The DVD arm of the study was administered by a near-peer, usually a former addict and/or someone with HIV or HCV. There were four separate DVDs, based on race/gender combinations (black male, black female, white male, white female) and they included testimonials from former offenders and persons infected with HIV and HCV discussing their situations. Peer facilitators have been found to be effective in reducing HIV risk behaviors in needle sharing populations (Latkin 1998).

Control Conditions. In this study, two control conditions were used: (1) traditional practices, where a group of offenders are shown a HIV awareness video as part of group sessions in the facilities in the prerelease process; and, (2) the NIDA Standard Version 3 HIV/HepC prevention intervention delivered by a health educator via cue cards in a one-on-one didactic setting (National Institute on Drug Abuse 2000). These represent two different conditions that reflect the variety of practice that might be used.

Study Recruitment. Potential participants were shown a video on HIV prevention in a group setting while still incarcerated (see section on setting by site), and were given information about the study and asked if they would like to participate. If they said yes, they were then screened individually to determine eligibility, and if eligible, they went through the informed consent process and were randomized into one of the three arms of the study. Testing for HIV and HCV was done at baseline and was voluntary and did not affect participation in the rest of the study. The main point of the study was to provide information on HIV and HCV prevention to offenders just prior to their release.

Implementation. Table 25.2 presents some of the implementation issues of this study. Most of the challenges resulted from the varied settings where the intervention took place. For Delaware, the study was implemented in a halfway house facility, a place which ensured an adequate flow of subjects and continuous access to subjects. This site selection was convenient but in many ways altered the original intent of the study, as the offenders at this facility were already at risk in the community since they reside in the halfway house but still can spend time in the community. In Kentucky, the study was implemented at a men's prison and a women's prison, while in Virginia, it was implemented at a local jail. Because the point of the follow-up period was to obtain information on risky behaviors in the community, the start of the follow-up clock was different according to site. For Delaware, because subjects were already at risk at the time of randomization, the follow-up clock started at the randomization date. In both Kentucky and Virginia, the follow-up clock did not start until the subject was released from the institution. This situation created a number of problems including the fact that the type of site (prison, jail, halfway house) was completely nested within state, and that the time at risk was not comparable among all subjects. Those in Delaware may have had some time at risk prior to being enrolled in the study. While baseline behavior data were gathered for the period prior to the last incarceration, the follow-up data collected may not reflect the same period of initial risk for those in Delaware as for those just released from prison and jail in Kentucky and Virginia.

Another issue that may have affected implementation was the initial selection of the group of offenders to watch the video at each site. Generally, these groups were gathered by personnel at the facilities who were given the criteria for the study (offenders had to be within 60 days of release, speak English, and not have cognitive impairments). Researchers were not often privy to the decisions about the type of offenders that participated in the sessions. It may be that different types of groups were selected for inclusion at the different sites.

Since follow-up was dependent on release in both Kentucky and Virginia, a substantial percentage of those randomized were ineligible for follow-up because they were not released during the time frame of the study. While those randomized were initially scheduled for release within 60 days of randomization, the release date often changed because of pending charges or other issues that occurred in the facility. In Kentucky, 33% of the randomized population was never released and in Virginia, 41% of the randomized population was not released during the timeframe of the study. This issue had the potential to create selection bias and differential attrition. The final CONSORT chart for this study is given in Fig. 25.3. Note that a good number of those assessed were lost both prior to completing the baseline and also postrandomization, because of prison release issues.

Finally, in one site, the same interventionist, a peer counselor, administered the NIDA arm and DVD arm for a period of time. Bias should have been minimized, since the interventionists could also do the testing for those in the control arm. There is a potential that the interventionists provided information to that group that was specific to their arm of the study. The interventionists were not blind to the study allocation of the subjects.

DISCUSSION

Multisite trials are important tools to accomplish scientific goals of (1) testing the efficacy of an innovation; (2) simultaneously "replicating" the study in multiple sites to determine the robustness of the innovation; and (3) allowing the unique characteristics of agencies,

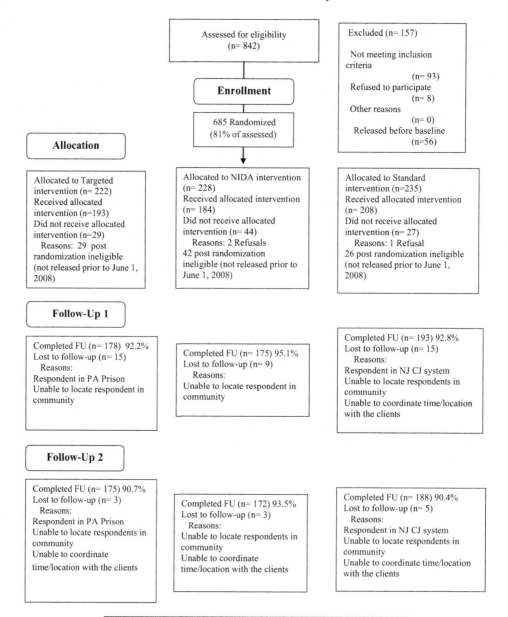

FIGURE 25.3. CONSORT flowchart of participants in HIV/HEPC study.

communities, and/or target populations to be concurrently examined in the test of an innovation to specify acceptable parameters. The trials represent the science of conducting field experiments but the process also reveals that there is an art in the process of conducting randomized trials. It is the art – the crafting of the experiment, the mechanisms to conduct the experiment, and the daily decisions regarding the handling of "real world" situations – that determines whether the experiment achieved the goal of testing the theoretically based innovation.

The analysis in this paper presented the art in terms of issues that have been identified as threats to internal validity, threats also identified by others (Dennis et al. 2000). We used these as tests of internal validity to demonstrate how experimental processes and research designs affect the integrity of an experiment, and the findings from the experiment. These two experiments allow us to draw lessons about study management to reduce the degree to which the threats affect the dependent variables:

1. *Confounding*. An important step in reducing the influence of third variables is to conduct three pipeline flows: (1) the research process in each participating site; (2) the core components of the innovation should be outlined to determine what other factors affect the independent variable; and (3) the potential mediators or moderators that may affect the independent variable. All three of these pre-experimental processes are important to minimize extraneous variables. The CONSORT flow chart with the suggested new modifications provides a tool that is useful to complete at each site to raise questions about the influence of other factors or variables. That is, the researcher might consider the CONSORT flow chart as an implementation chart that can be used at all stages of the experiment to proactively identify potential issues that the researchers should explore and examine how they will impact study processes and findings.

2. *Selection Bias*. The inclusion and exclusion criteria of an experiment are critical in assessing potential sources of bias. But, more important than simply analyzing these a priori decisions, is to map these criteria to the study population to ensure that the research processes are not enhancing or affecting selection bias. For example, in the Step'N Out experiment, the researchers in one study site were unaware that the agency did not release offenders without the use of extra controls (e.g., electronic monitoring). Yet, in the early stages of the experiment, when this was discovered, it resulted in consideration of new eligibility criteria. Maps of the system would assist in this process. The two multisite trials analyzed here had other selection biases that crept into the study such as the use of different types of recruitment sites in the HIV/HEP C study. While this variation was useful in assessing the elasticity of the innovation across different correctional settings (prison, work release, jail), it introduced new problems, including a large population of postrandomization ineligibles, who were not released from the prison/jail within the study period of 12 months. This created a potential bias because it affects the intent to treat group, and the differences in releases versus detainees must be assessed to determine the degree to which the study protocol affected study outcomes. The use of a historical control group can mitigate issues with selection bias for this part of the population and can also reduce other biases, including diffusion, compensatory rivalry, and experimenter bias. In this case, the researcher must usually rely on records to obtain data for the historical group, but this strategy is useful, especially when the experimental condition appears to be clearly superior to the treatment as usual and denying it to a portion of the current population would be unethical. Another related issue is to have a historical control group that could define the base rates for the dependent variables. A historical control group can then help determine whether the inclusion and exclusion criteria affect the dependent variable(s).

3. *History.* The impact of events outside of the experiment, either at the onset of the study or between measurement periods, may influence attitudes and behaviors in such a way that it might be detectable. In Step'N Out, a crackdown on parolees in Connecticut occurred during the follow-up period, resulting in a higher number of parole violations than would have otherwise occurred. While it was felt that this event did not differentially affect the study groups, it was presumed that the overall number of parole violations was higher in the study than it normally would have been. This information is important to know and to report with all analyses of the study, especially as parole violations were considered a main outcome and ended up being much lower for the CBM group than the control group. It is important to be aware of events that occur that may affect the study outcomes.

4. *Maturation.* During the experiment, subjects may change and this change may result in how the study participant reacts to the dependent variable. In both studies, some sites had longer times between randomization and the follow-ups because of timing and release issues and some subjects also had longer times until their follow-ups were completed. In these cases, it is difficult to determine if the intervention caused positive changes or if more time in the community and exposure to other factors could be a possible cause. Future studies could focus on ensuring that randomization and followup schedules are implemented so that there is little room for variance and that research interviewers are trained to understand the importance of completing followups in the given time windows. For example, studies that focus on the release period could delay randomization until an offender is released to avoid the uncertainty associated with release dates.

5. *Mortality/differential attrition.* Study drop-outs may be the result of the person, the experiment, or the situation. In a couple of sites in Step'N Out, the CBM group had lower follow-up rates at both 3 and 9 months, indicating that offenders may have found it more difficult to complete the CBM intervention in these sites and to stay connected with the parole office. The implementation of the intervention at these sites should be explored to determine how it differed from other sites. In Oregon, for example, those participating in CBM, had to attend parole sessions at a different office, located at the treatment center, which may have been inconvenient for them. In another site, the CBM officer was required to also maintain a caseload of regular parole clients, and she often had scheduling conflicts with her CBM clients. These issues provide insight into how implementation can affect participation. One suggestion for future iterations of Step'N Out was to have it be an office-based, rather than officer-based intervention, where the entire parole office practiced CBM.

6. *Diffusion.* The experimental category should be different than traditional practice and movement from the experimental to control group or vice versa may pollute the assigned conditions. While there was no known crossover from one study condition to another, there was potential in both studies for offenders from different conditions to mix with each other and share information. In Step'N Out, one site had a control group that was not extremely dissimilar to the CBM group, as the study was implemented at a parole site where specialized parole services were already offered and officers met with their clients weekly. These officers often used novel methods of sanctions and rewards. In these cases, it is difficult to determine the explicit effects of the intervention under study, as: (1) the control group may have been influenced by the intervention and (2) the control group may not reflect current practice accurately. For multisite trials, this variation among current practice at sites is an issue that is

often raised. An initial feasibility study at each site should identify potential issues and provide insights on how each site works. Each study protocol should have some flexibility so that it can be adapted to multiple sites, but also must specify minimum conditions for the control group that must be met in order for the site to participate.

7. *Compensatory rivalry/resentful demoralization.* The control group behavior could be tainted by the result of being in the study. This is more of a possibility in longer lasting interventions where the treatment under study appears as a "better" alternative to those who are targeted for treatment. In Step'N Out, there was some evidence that persons wanted to be in the CBM condition (often asking for this at randomization) and felt those in CBM were getting an "easy ride." This could lead to resentment from the control group, especially if they were aware that the CBM group would receive material rewards for good behavior and they would not. This could create a disincentive for good behavior for those in the control group and study results could be biased upward, with results better than they should be under normal circumstances. Researchers should also be careful in using language to describe the study conditions to ensure that the experimental condition is not seen as highly preferable to the current practice and should also work with staff at the agencies to train them not to present the intervention as an improvement or something better, as staff attitudes are usually quickly conveyed to offenders.

8. *Experimenter bias.* The researcher or research team may inadvertently affect the experiment by their actions. Both of the studies we examined here had interventionists on-site at justice agencies who were not blinded to the study condition assignment of the offenders. Blinding cannot be done for the interventionist in these types of studies as they must know what condition a person is in so that they can deliver the correct intervention to them. While a number of measures were in place to ensure fidelity (tapes in Step'N Out, checklist in HIV), there were concerns that parole officers may have implemented CBM differently at different sites and even at the same site, based on the person involved. The same is true for the health educator and peer interventionist in HIV, especially the peer counselor who had less of a script to work with and used more of her own experience in working with her clients. While the tapes were a good idea in Step'N Out, they were not used effectively as a feedback tool, as there was a long delay in coding and providing feedback to the parole officers. Because delivery of the intervention is such a key component of the study, researchers should make provisions for ongoing and timely fidelity monitoring of the intervention, with a clear plan on how fidelity will be tracked, how feedback will be provided, and how corrective actions will be taken (Carroll et al. 2007).

The multisite trial also affords the opportunity to assess issues of external validity or the generalizability of the study. The simultaneous replication of an innovation in various settings, that are defined by sociopolitical environments that affect both the innovation and the research processes, allows the innovation to be tested for its elasticity or "fit" in various environments. It is these "tests" of the sociopolitical environments, not just the innovation itself, that demonstrate that the innovation has both internal and external validity. An innovation that cannot be implemented in a myriad of research settings is unlikely to be useful in practice, since research prototypes are seldom fully employed in practice. Alignment to an environment accounts for the acceptability of an innovation. It is important in experiments to identify the factors that affect innovation rejection or the characteristics or features when the organism is unable to be accepted by the existing body. The multisite trial offers the ability to assess these issues.

If, however, the political or organizational practices make it impossible to implement the intervention, no information can be gained from the effort (Rossi et al. 1999).

Another important area in trials, especially in justice settings, is the potential impact of the consent process on the study. Prisoners are considered a vulnerable population and while not all justice research is done with prisoners, all populations in this arena should be considered vulnerable and precautions should be taken to ensure human subjects protection. Research center Institutional Review Boards (IRBs), as well as IRB for justice agencies, should adhere to the following, as outlined by the Office of Human Research Protections (OHRP) in part 46 subpart C pertaining to prisoners in research:

- A majority of the IRB (exclusive of prisoner members) will have no association with the prison(s) involved, apart from their membership on the IRB.
- At least one member of the IRB must be a prisoner, or a prisoner representative with appropriate background and experience to serve in that capacity, except that where a particular research project is reviewed by more than one IRB, only one IRB has to satisfy this requirement.

When going through the informed consent process with offenders, the following points should be stressed (1) Participation or nonparticipation will not affect their legal status; (2) Individual or identifiable data collected in the study will not be made available to criminal justice authorities; (3) Choosing to participate or not participate will not affect their length of stay in the criminal justice system; (4) Their criminal justice records will not mention their choice to participate or not participate in a study protocol and this decision will not be a part of any official record on file. But this process can result in some selection bias in that some subjects may elect not to participate in the study based on the consenting process. This may or may not impact the study.

As a researcher considers validity threats to a multisite experiment, they should ask themselves the following five questions and to carefully consider how the decisions made affect the experiment:

1. How does the issue affect the flow of subjects on the CONSORT chart?
2. How does the issue affect inclusion and exclusion (selection forces)?
3. Does the issue disrupt the theory underlying the intervention? Or does it disrupt the treatment as usual?
4. How might the issue affect the dependent variable(s)?
5. How might the issue affect possible confounders?

CONCLUSION

Field experiments are well known to test an innovation as well as the environment where an innovation can be offered. In addition, the field experiment requires the researcher and/or research team to be sensitive to the impact of design and implementation decisions on the integrity of the experiment, as well as the generalizability to the wider target population. This article has been designed to help researchers think about the issues related to internal validity threats, and how decisions that are made about the target population, eligibility processes, intervention design and processes, and instruments. In addition, attention to attrition during waves of follow-up is critical to assess the quality of the experiment. Managing one study site presents sufficient challenges while managing more than one study site requires the researchers and investigator(s) to be cognizant of how each decision might affect whether the goals of the study can be obtained. In both case studies, we have examples where practical realities crept into the experiment. More work will need to be done to determine the impact on the outcome variables. In the end, it is apparent that scientists must also be good research administrators to ensure the one or more study sites uphold the experimental design, and that each decision is weighed against the concern about the integrity of the design. Research requires an attention to methodological details from design to each phase of data collection to analysis. These details are the cornerstone of whether a study answers the questions it was designed to address.

Acknowledgements This study was funded under a cooperative agreement from the U.S. Department of Health and Human Services, Public Health Service, National Institutes of Health, National Institute on Drug Abuse (NIH/NIDA) to George Mason University (Grant U01 DA016213–01, Action Research to Advance Drug Treatment in the CJS). The funding for this cooperative agreement was supplemented by the Center for Substance Abuse Treatment, Bureau of Justice Assistance, Centers for Disease Control and Prevention, and National Institute on Alcohol Abuse and Alcoholism. The authors acknowledge the collaborative contributions by federal staff from NIDA and the other nine Research Center grantees of the NIH/NIDA CJ-DATS Cooperative. The contents are solely the responsibility of the authors and do not necessarily represent the official views of NIH/NIDA or other participants in CJ-DATS.

REFERENCES

Arriola KRJ, Braithwaite R (2008) Male prisoners and HIV prevention: a call for action ignored. Am J Public Health 98(9 Suppl):S145

Balas EA, Austin SM, Ewigman BG, Brown GD, Mitchell JA (1995) Methods of randomized controlled clinical trials in health services research. Med Care 33(7):687–699

Bollen KA, Curran PJ (2006). Latent curve models: a structural equation perspective. Wiley Interscience, Hoboken, NJ

Bond G, Evans L, Saylers M, Williams J, Kim H (2000) Measurement of fidelity in psychiatric rehabilitation. Ment Health Serv Res 2(2):75–87

Boutron I, Moher D, Altman DG, Schulz KF, Ravaud P (2008) Extending the CONSORT statement to randomized trials of nonpharmacologic treatment: explanation and elaboration. Ann Intern Med 148(4):295–309

Campbell DT, Stanley JC (1966) Experimental and quasi-experimental designs for research. Houghton Mifflin, Boston

Carroll C, Patterson M, Wood S, Booth A, Rick J, Balain S (2007) A conceptual framework for implementation fidelity. Implementation Science 2:40–48

Chow SC, Liu JP (2004) Design and analysis of clinical trials, 2nd edn. Hoboken, NJ: Wiley Interscience

Cohen J (1988) Statistical power analysis for the social sciences, 2nd edn. New York: Lawrence Erlbaum Associates

Dennis ML, Perl HI, Huebner RB, McLellan AT (2000) Twenty-five strategies for improving the design, implementation and analysis of health services research related to alcohol and other drug abuse treatment. Addiction 95:S281–S308

Dennis M, Godley SH, Diamond G, Tims FM, Babor T, Donaldson J et al. (2004) The cannabis youth treatment (CYT) study: main findings from two randomized trials [Abstract]. J Subst Abuse Treat 27(3):197–213

Djulbegovic B, Cantor A, Clarke M (2003) The importance of the preservation of the ethical principle of equipoise in the design of clinical trials: relative impact of the methodological quality domains on the treatment effect in randomized controlled trials. Account Res: Policies Qual Assur 10(4):301–315

Downs S, Black N (1998) The feasibility of creating a checklist for the assessment of the methodological quality both of randomised and non-randomised studies of health care interventions. J Epidemiol Community Health 52(6):377–384

Friedman L, Furberg C, DeMets D (1985). Fundamentals of clinical trials. PSG Publishing Company, Inc., Littleton, MA

Friedmann PD, Katz EC, Rhodes AG, Taxman FS, O'Connell DJ, Frisman LK, et al. (2008) Collaborative behavioral management for drug-involved parolees: rationale and design of the step'n out study. J Offender Rehabil 47(3;3): 290–318

Hammett TM, Harmon MP, Rhodes W (2002) The burden of infectious disease among inmates of and releasees from US correctional facilities, 1997. Am J Public Health 92(11):1789–1794

Inciardi JA, Surratt HL, Martin SS (2007) Developing a multimedia HIV and hepatitis intervention for drug-involved offenders reentering the community. Prison J 87(1):111–142

Latkin C (1998) Outreach in natural settings: the use of peer leaders for HIV prevention among injecting drug users' networks. Public Health Rep 113(Suppl 1):151

MacKenzie D, Browning K, SKroban S, Smith D (1999) The impact of probation on the criminal activities of offenders. J Res Crime Delinq 36(4):423–453

Mayo-Wilson E (2007) Reporting implementation in randomized trials: proposed additions to the consolidated standards of reporting trials statement. Am J Public Health 97(4):630–633

Meredith W, Tisak J (1990) Latent curve analysis. Psychometrika 47:47–67

Moher D, Schulz KF, Altman DG (2001) The CONSORT statement: revised recommendations for improving the quality of reports of parallel-group randomised trials. Lancet 357(9263):1191

National Institute on Drug Abuse (2000) The NIDA community-based outreach model: a manual to reduce the risk of HIV and other blood-borne infections in drug users No. (NIH Pub. No. 00-4812). National Institute on Drug Abuse, Rockville, MD

Olivo SA, Macedo LG, Gadotti IC, Fuentes J, Stanton T, Magee DJ (2008) Scales to assess the quality of randomized controlled trials: a systematic review. Phys Ther 88(2):156–175

Pocock S (1983) Clinical trials: a practical approach. Wiley, New York

Raudenbush SW (2001) Comparing personal trajectories and drawing causal inferences from longitudinal data. Annu Rev Psychol 52:501

Rhodes A, Taxman F, Rose JR, Friedmann P (2009) Rapport between parole officers and offenders: a mediation analysis. Unpublished manuscript

Rossi P, Freeman H, Lipsey MW (1999) Evaluation: a systematic approach, 6th edn. Sage Publications, Thousand Oaks, CA

Smith JK (1990) Alternative research paradigms and the problem of criteria. In E. G. Guba (Ed.), The paradigm dialog (pp. 167–187). Newbury Park, CA: Sage

Weinberger M, Oddone EZ, Henderson WG, Smith DM, Huey J, GiobbieHurder A, et al. (2001) Multisite randomized controlled trials in health services research: scientific challenges and operational issues. Med Care 39(6): 627–634

Weisburd D, Taxman FS (2000) Developing a multicenter randomized trial in criminology: The case of HIDTA. Journal of Quantitative Criminology 16(3):315–340

Weisburd D (2003) Ethical practice and evaluation of interventions in crime and justice: the moral imperative for randomized trials. Eval Rev 27(3):336–354

Part III-B
Estimation of Impacts and Outcomes of Crime and Justice: *Innovation in Quasi -Experimental Design*

## CHAPTER 26

Propensity Score Matching in Criminology and Criminal Justice

ROBERT J. APEL AND GARY SWEETEN

INTRODUCTION

Researchers in the discipline of criminology have long been interested in the "treatment effect" of discrete events on an individual's delinquent and criminal behavior. Is stable employment associated with less delinquency and crime? What is the effect of marriage to a noncriminal spouse on desistance? Is high school dropout related to a higher rate of offending? Notice the conspicuous absence of explicitly causal terminology in the way that these questions are posed. Criminological research is typically reliant on nonexperimental data, or data in which the treatment of interest (e.g., employment, marriage, dropout) is often not randomized for ethical or practical reasons. Yet this creates a situation known as the selection problem – a situation in which individuals are free to exercise some degree of discretion or choice with regard to the event(s) that they experience. The selection problem arises when there is something peculiar to the choice set, the choice maker, or some combination thereof, which partially determines the individual's choice as well as his or her behavioral response to that choice. Moreover, researchers are rarely privy to all of the relevant factors that go into the choice-making process.

In the absence of randomization, researchers interested in point identification of causal effects are forced to approximate the conditions of a controlled experiment. The evaluation literature is replete with examples of different quasi-experimental techniques, so called because they attempt to create a situation in which treatment is "as good as randomly assigned." In this chapter, we are interested in a procedure generally known as matching, which is a kind of *selection on observables* approach to causal effect estimation (see Heckman and Hotz 1989). Matching refers to a broad class of techniques that attempts to identify, for each individual in a treatment condition, at least one other individual in a comparison condition that "looks like" the treated individual on the basis of a vector of measured characteristics that may be relevant to the treatment and response in question. Matching is not new to criminology. For example, Glueck and Glueck (1950) matched each institutionalized youth in their classic study to a

A.R. Piquero and D. Weisburd (eds.), *Handbook of Quantitative Criminology*,
DOI 10.1007/978-0-387-77650-7_26, © Springer Science + Business Media, LLC 2010,
First softcover printing 2011

school-going youth on the basis of age, ethnicity, intelligence, and neighborhood socioeco-nomic status. Widom (1989) matched each youth who was abused or neglected as a child to an officially nonabused youth by age, gender, race, and neighborhood socioeconomic status. These two prominent studies are examples of *covariate matching*, *categorical matching*, or *exact matching* (there are several naming conventions) on the basis of a handful of observed characteristics.

Exact matching, however, can become intractable as the list of measured characteris-tics grows, a problem known as the "curse of dimensionality." Fortunately, within the larger class of matching methods exists a technique known as *scalar matching* or *propensity score matching*. This is a data reduction technique that has the advantage of allowing researchers to match treated and comparison individuals on a very large number of measured characteris-tics, including pretreatment outcomes. In the remainder of this chapter, we will be specifically concerned with the details of propensity score matching. First, we will introduce the coun-terfactual framework on which the method is based. Second, we will turn to technical issues that arise in the use of propensity scores in applied research. Third, we will provide an empir-ical example of our own and describe other studies in criminology that employ the propensity score methodology. Finally, we will close the chapter with an outline to guide practice and some concluding comments.

PROPENSITY SCORE MATCHING IN THEORY

An understanding of propensity score matching is aided by familiarity with the language and logic of counterfactual estimation, known also as the analysis of *potential outcomes* (see Rubin 1974, 1977).[1] According to this framework, the causal effect of a binary treatment is the difference between an individual's value of the response variable when he or she is treated and that same individual's value of the response variable when he or she is not treated. Under this definition of causality, then, each individual experiences a response under *two simultaneous conditions*. As a straightforward example, consider the question of the effect of marriage on crime. For each individual, one must imagine outcomes under two alternate states: Crime patterns when an individual is married, and crime patterns when that individual is simultaneously not married.[2] The treatment effect of marriage is the difference between the crime outcomes for the same individual in these two simultaneous states. The "fundamental problem of causal inference" (Holland 1986) is that, for each individual, only one of the two potential outcomes is observed at any given time. The other is purely hypothetical, making direct estimation of the causal effect of treatment impossible.

To formalize the counterfactual approach to treatment effect estimation, suppose that all individuals in a target population have information on Y_i^1, their potential outcome under treatment; Y_i^0, their potential outcome under non-treatment; and T_i, their assigned treatment status that takes the values of 1 and 0, respectively, when treatment either is or is not received.

---

[1] Readers desiring a more thorough survey of the counterfactual framework generally and the propensity score method specifically are referred to Cameron and Trivedi (2005: chap. 25), Imbens (2004), Morgan and Harding (2006), and Wooldridge (2002: chap. 18).

[2] Notice that the counterfactual definition of causality requires that the individual occupy two states at the same time, not two different states at two different times. If the latter condition held, panel data with a time-varying treatment condition would suffice to estimate a causal effect of treatment. In the marriage example, the period(s) in which the individual is not married would be the counterfactual for the period(s) in which the same individual is married.

Treatment is defined generally as any form of intentional intervention. For each individual, the causal effect of treatment is computed as $Y_i^1 - Y_i^0$. Aggregating across the target population, the *average treatment effect* (ATE) is defined as the expected effect of treatment on a randomly selected person from the target population:

$$\text{ATE} = \text{E}\left(Y_i^1 - Y_i^0\right)$$
$$= \text{E}\left(Y_i^1\right) - \text{E}\left(Y_i^0\right) \tag{26.1}$$

Note that ATE may also be written as a function of two other types of treatment effects. The *average treatment effect on the treated* (ATT) is defined as the expected effect of treatment for those individuals actually assigned to the treatment group, or the "gain" from treatment among those in the treated group:

$$\text{ATT} = \text{E}\left(Y_i^1 - Y_i^0 \,\middle|\, T_i = 1\right)$$
$$= \text{E}\left(Y_i^1 \,\middle|\, T_i = 1\right) - \text{E}\left(Y_i^0 \,\middle|\, T_i = 1\right) \tag{26.2}$$

Although rarely of policy interest, it is also possible to determine the *average treatment effect on the untreated* (ATU), defined as the expected effect of treatment for those individuals assigned to the non-treatment (i.e., control or comparison) group:

$$\text{ATU} = \text{E}\left(Y_i^1 - Y_i^0 \,\middle|\, T_i = 0\right)$$
$$= \text{E}\left(Y_i^1 \,\middle|\, T_i = 0\right) - \text{E}\left(Y_i^0 \,\middle|\, T_i = 0\right) \tag{26.3}$$

Collecting terms, ATE can be rewritten as a weighted average of ATT and ATU:

$$\text{E}\left(Y_i^1 - Y_i^0\right) = \Pr\left(T_i = 1\right)\text{E}\left(Y_i^1 - Y_i^0 \,\middle|\, T_i = 1\right) + \Pr\left(T_i = 0\right)\text{E}\left(Y_i^1 - Y_i^0 \,\middle|\, T_i = 0\right) \tag{26.4}$$

The first term on the right-hand side is ATT, weighted by the probability of treatment, and the second term is ATU, weighted by the probability of nontreatment.[3]

The obvious problem for causal identification under this framework is that only one of the two potential outcomes is observed for all individuals in the target population. The rule for determining which potential outcome is observed for any given individual is written as:

$$Y_i = \begin{cases} Y_i^1 & \text{if} \quad T_i = 1 \\ Y_i^0 & \text{if} \quad T_i = 0 \end{cases}$$

where Y_i represents the observed (as opposed to potential) outcome and T_i represents the observed treatment.

The potential outcomes framework reveals that treatment effect estimation represents, fundamentally, a missing data problem. The problem can be illustrated more clearly by decomposing ATE in terms of the known factuals and unknown counterfactuals. Inserting (26.2) and (26.3) into (26.4) yields:

$$\text{E}\left(Y_i^1 - Y_i^0\right) = \Pr\left(T_i = 1\right)\left[\text{E}\left(Y_i^1 \,\middle|\, T_i = 1\right) - \text{E}\left(Y_i^0 \,\middle|\, T_i = 1\right)\right]$$
$$+ \Pr\left(T_i = 0\right)\left[\text{E}\left(Y_i^1 \,\middle|\, T_i = 0\right) - \text{E}\left(Y_i^0 \,\middle|\, T_i = 0\right)\right]$$

---

[3] In this chapter, we will be mostly concerned with estimation of ATE rather that its constituents, ATT and ATU.

The unknown quantities, or counterfactuals, are $E\left(Y_i^1 \mid T_i = 0\right)$ and $E\left(Y_i^0 \mid T_i = 1\right)$. These are, in words, the potential outcome under treatment for individuals in the untreated sample, and the potential outcome under non-treatment for individuals in the treated sample, respectively. The goal of treatment effect estimation is the imputation of a hypothetical value or range of values for these missing counterfactuals.

The underlying issue for estimation of the causal effect of treatment is *balance*, or ensuring that treated individuals are statistically equivalent to untreated individuals on all background factors that are relevant for estimating the causal effect of interest. To the extent that balance is achieved, treatment is said to be exogenous or *ignorable*, meaning that treatment assignment is independent of the potential outcomes. The selection problem, of course, arises when treatment is endogenous or non-ignorable. In the case of the marriage-crime relationship, for example, individuals who get married might be endowed with a variety of other characteristics that are correlated with low crime, such as higher education and income, better long-term employment prospects, and no arrest history. They might also differ in ways that are challenging to observe and measure, for example, their intelligence, orientation to family, desire for children, career ambition, and ability to delay gratification. The goal of treatment effect estimation is to confront this endogeneity in a tractable and compelling manner.

Randomization of treatment ensures that treatment assignment is independent of potential outcomes (formally, $Y_i^1, Y_i^0 \perp T_i$), rendering the treatment assignment process ignorable. By virtue of its design, randomization also achieves balance (in expectation) on all potential confounding variables, observed and unobserved.[4] Consequently, the control group can be used as a valid counterfactual source for the experimental group.[5] Because the experimenter exercises *physical control* over the treatment conditions that participants experience, adjustment for additional covariates is technically unnecessary because the selection problem is eliminated (although covariate adjustment is still good practice, even in an experiment). Returning to the marriage-crime example, to the extent that a researcher can assign individuals to marriage and non-marriage with the flip of a fair coin, for instance, the treatment effect of marriage on crime can be readily estimated.[6] The average treatment effect is simply the mean of the response variable for the treated (married) less the mean of the response variable for the untreated (unmarried).

---

[4] Because it renders treatment ignorable, randomization is sufficient to identify the average treatment effect in the following manner:

$$ATE = E\left(Y_i^1 \mid T_i = 1\right) - E\left(Y_i^0 \mid T_i = 0\right)$$
$$= E\left(Y_i \mid T_i = 1\right) - E\left(Y_i \mid T_i = 0\right)$$

Notice that this is simply the mean difference in the outcome for treated and untreated individuals in the target population, as the potential outcomes notation in the first equality can be removed. The second equality necessarily follows because treatment assignment independent of potential outcomes ensures that:

$$E\left(Y_i^1 \mid T_i = 1\right) = E\left(Y_i^1 \mid T_i = 0\right) = E\left(Y_i \mid T_i = 1\right)$$

and

$$E\left(Y_i^0 \mid T_i = 1\right) = E\left(Y_i^0 \mid T_i = 0\right) = E\left(Y_i \mid T_i = 0\right)$$

As an interesting aside, in the case of a randomized experiment, it is also the case that ATT and ATU are equivalent to ATE by virtue of these equalities.

[5] To be perfectly accurate, randomization may in fact produce imbalance, but the imbalance is attributable entirely to chance. However, asymptotically (i.e., as the sample size tends toward infinity) the expected imbalance approaches zero.

[6] Aside from ethical and practical concerns, this experiment would be unable to assess the effect of marriage as we know it, as marriages entered into on the basis of a coin flip would likely have very different qualities than those freely chosen.

In observational studies, on the other hand, the researcher exercises no physical control over the treatment status. In this setting, the researcher strives to achieve *statistical control* over treatment assignment in a way that approximates the conditions of randomization. In the case of marriage and crime, the challenge is to identify one or more unmarried individuals that may serve as a counterfactual source for each married individual. One method of doing so is to choose, as a counterfactual source, a group of untreated individuals who most closely resemble the individuals in the treatment group as measured by a large number of potential confounding variables. If this requirement is satisfied, treatment is then said to be independent of potential outcomes, conditional on the confounding variables, a situation known as the *conditional independence assumption*, a scenario that can be formalized as $Y_i^1, Y_i^0 \perp T_i \mid x_i$. In other words, balance is achieved (i.e., treatment assignment is ignorable) once the relevant covariates are properly controlled. Rosenbaum and Rubin (1983) additionally show that conditional independence, given a vector of covariates, implies conditional independence, given a particular function of the covariates known as a propensity score, to which we now turn.

PROPENSITY SCORE MATCHING IN PRACTICE

In evaluation practice, it is often the case that a comparatively small proportion of the target population is treated relative to the proportion of individuals who are not treated. In addition, not all untreated individuals are equally desirable comparisons for treated individuals, as they may be quite different with respect to background characteristics, and thus, altogether inappropriate as a counterfactual source. Propensity score matching offers a way to select a subsample of treated and untreated cases that are observationally equivalent (or at least observationally similar) so that valid treatment effect estimates may be obtained. Rooted in the work of Rosenbaum and Rubin (1983, 1984, 1985), a propensity score is defined as "the conditional probability of assignment to a particular treatment, given a vector of observed covariates" (Rosenbaum and Rubin 1983: 41). It is equivalent to a *balancing score*, whereby, the conditional distribution of the covariates, given the propensity score, is the same for treated and untreated respondents. With the demonstration of balance, a researcher then has a stronger case for assuming that treatment is "as good as randomly assigned," at least with respect to the variables included in the estimation of the propensity score.

Propensity score matching is similar to standard regression in that it is assumed in both cases that selection into treatment is random conditional on observed characteristics ("selection on observables"). However, propensity score matching differs from regression techniques in two key respects. First, it does not rely on a linear functional form to estimate treatment effects. Although propensity scores are typically estimated using a parametric model, once these are obtained, individuals are usually matched nonparametrically. Second, propensity score matching highlights the issue of common support. It reveals the degree to which untreated cases actually resemble the treated cases on observed characteristics. Standard regression (known as covariate adjustment), on the other hand, obscures this issue, and can, in some situations, extrapolate treatment effect estimates, based solely on functional form when treated and untreated groups are actually not comparable at all. In many applications, only a subset of the treated and untreated populations will be useful (read, valid) for estimating treatment effects.

In practice, propensity score matching involves at least three steps. First, the propensity score must be estimated. Second, the conditional independence assumption must be evaluated by demonstrating balance on potential confounders. Third, the treatment effect of interest (ATE, ATT, or ATU) must be estimated. Each step is considered in more detail below.

Estimation of the Propensity Score

Propensity score matching begins with the formal specification and estimation of a treatment status model. At this stage, great care must be taken to choose a specification that fully characterizes the treatment assignment mechanism with respect to variables that potentially confound the relationship between treatment status and the outcome variable. The goal is to model the non-random elements of the selection process using observed information.[7] A propensity score, $P(x_i)$, is defined as the probability of treatment, conditional on a vector of k observed confounders. [8] In most applications, it is conveniently estimated by way of the logistic distribution function:

$$P(x_i) = \Pr(T_i = 1 \mid x_i)$$
$$= \frac{\exp(\beta_0 + \beta_1 x_{i1} + \beta_2 x_{i2} + \cdots + \beta_k x_{ik})}{1 + \exp(\beta_0 + \beta_1 x_{i1} + \beta_2 x_{i2} + \cdots + \beta_k x_{ik})}$$

The key output from the treatment status model is the predicted probability of receiving treatment, which is the propensity score. With the propensity score in hand, treatment status is presumed to be independent of potential outcomes conditional on the propensity score – this is the conditional independence assumption.

Once the propensity score is obtained, an important consideration is *common support*. This concerns the distribution of propensity scores for treated individuals versus the distribution for untreated individuals. Common support exists where the propensity score distributions for the two groups overlap. "Off-support" cases will typically be found in the tails of the propensity score distribution, since untreated individuals will tend to have a low probability of treatment, whereas treated individuals will have a comparatively high probability of treatment. Another support problem concerns those cases within the range of common support for which no comparable matches can be found due to a sparse propensity score distribution.

Absence of common support is valuable information, as it reveals conditions under which individuals *always* or *never* receive the treatment of interest within the sample (not necessarily within the population). There is some discretion in how many of the off-support cases to include in treatment effect estimates through the use of a bandwidth (or caliper), which is employed in several different kinds of matching protocols. The bandwidth specifies how far away a potential match can be on the propensity score metric and still be used as a counterfactual.[9]

---

[7] Researchers differ in their preferences for how exhaustive the treatment status model should be. In a *theoretically informed model*, the researcher includes only a vector of variables that are specified a priori in the theory or theories of choice. In a *kitchen sink model*, the researcher includes as many variables as are available in the dataset. In our view, a theoretically informed model is appealing only to the extent that it achieves balance on confounders that are excluded from the treatment status model but would have been included in a kitchen sink model.

[8] Some researchers also include functions of the confounders in the treatment status model, for example, quadratic and interaction terms.

[9] A useful sensitivity exercise is to estimate treatment effects using a number of different bandwidths to determine stability of the estimates. With smaller bandwidths, common support shrinks and fewer cases are retained. This

Demonstration of Covariate Balance

Once propensity scores have been estimated and support issues resolved, there are a number of ways in which one can test whether or not balance has been achieved. That is, whether conditioning on the propensity score makes treatment appear random, providing evidence for the validity of the conditional independence assumption. A common first step is to stratify the sample into equally-sized bins, based on the propensity score, and then test differences in both propensity scores and other independent variables between treated and untreated cases within bins, using independent samples t-tests (Dehejia and Wahba 1999, 2002).

Another very flexible way to assess balance is through estimation of the standardized bias (SB). This method, first described by Rosenbaum and Rubin (1985: 36), is equivalent to Cohen's d (Cohen 1988), a common measure of effect size. In order to assess balance, two SBs are to be computed: One before matching (unadjusted SB) and one after matching (adjusted SB). The degree to which the SB is attenuated by conditioning on the propensity score provides some indication of the degree to which the conditional independence assumption is satisfied. The formula for the SB is as follows:

$$ SB = 100 \times \frac{\bar{x}_i - \bar{x}_{i,j}}{\sqrt{\left(s_i^2 + s_j^2\right)/2}} $$

The means are indexed by i and i, j, signifying the mean of x for treated individuals less the mean for their matched, untreated counterparts. However, in the denominator, the variances are indexed by i and j, denoting the variance of x for all treated individuals and the variance of x for all untreated individuals, whether they are matched or not. Following convention (Cohen 1988; Rosenbaum and Rubin 1985), the rule of thumb used to judge whether the SB is substantively large – that is, whether the covariate in question is imbalanced – is $|SB| \geq 20$.[10]

The SB is also a useful metric to assess balance across several matching methods by comparing the percent of potential confounders balanced under each method. Typically, the choice of a propensity score model and the assessment of balance is an iterative process. If treated and untreated cases are imbalanced, the initial propensity score model is modified to include more variables, or to include interaction or squared functions of key predictors until balance is achieved. Additionally, imbalanced covariates (if any) may be directly adjusted even after their inclusion in the treatment status model.

Estimation of Treatment Effects

The most common type of treatment effect is the average treatment effect (ATE), representing the average difference in potential outcomes across the entire population. Under other circumstances, however, the researcher may be concerned exclusively with the effect of a particular treatment only within that segment of the population who actually experienced the

---

alters the nature of the estimated treatment effect, particularly if a large number of cases are excluded. This can be dealt with by simply acknowledging that the estimated effect excludes certain kinds of cases, and these can be clearly described since the dropped cases are observed.

[10] Where substantive significance is as important as statistical significance, the standardized bias formula can also be used to estimate an effect size for the treatment effect estimate (see Cohen, 1988).

treatment. This is known as the average treatment on the treated (ATT). Alternately, one may be interested in estimating the average treatment on the untreated (ATU). It should be clear that ATE is simply a weighted average of ATT and ATU, as shown earlier. There are three conventional methods for estimating any of these treatment effect parameters: Regression, stratification, and matching.

The *regression method* involves controlling for the propensity score in a model that also includes the treatment status indicator (a dummy variable). The coefficient on this indicator provides an estimate of the ATE. This method represents a control function approach to treatment effect estimation. The regression model is specified as follows:

$$Y_i = \alpha + \beta T_i + \gamma P(x_i) + e_i$$

From this model, the ATE is, quite simply, β, the coefficient conforming to the treatment status indicator.[11] The regression method has the advantage of making it easy to adjust directly for covariates that remain imbalanced after conditioning on the propensity score. However, unlike other methods, this method relies on a specific functional form for assessing treatment effects. Also, to avoid extrapolating off-support, common support conditions should be imposed prior to employing the regression method.

The *stratification method* proceeds by dividing the sample into subclasses or strata of approximately equal size. This method groups several treated and untreated individuals within a common range of the propensity score. Since Cochran (1968) demonstrated that stratification into five subclasses removes approximately 90% of bias due to the stratifying variable (see also Rosenbaum and Rubin 1984), the accepted practice is to divide the sample into quintiles on the propensity score, although more strata may be used as sample size permits. A stratum-specific treatment effect is derived as the mean difference in the response variable between treated and untreated individuals in each stratum. The ATE is simply the weighted average of the stratum-specific treatment effects, where the weights are defined as the proportion of the sample in each stratum. Using S_i to index the propensity score stratum in which each individual is classified, ATE can be recovered from:

$$\text{ATE} = \sum_{S} \frac{N_s}{N} \left(\frac{1}{N_{1,s}} \sum_{i \in (T=1)} Y_i - \frac{1}{N_{0,s}} \sum_{i \in (T=0)} Y_i \right)$$

where N is the total number of individuals in the sample, N_s is the number of individuals in stratum s, $N_{1,s}$ is the number of treated individuals in stratum s, and $N_{0,s}$ is the number of untreated individuals in stratum s. By conditioning on the propensity score strata, the stratification method has the advantage of ensuring closer correspondence between treated and untreated cases within each subclass. Yet, even within strata, the cases may still be poorly matched.

The *matching method* involves selecting from the pool of all untreated individuals only those who closely resemble the treated individuals on the propensity score. This method is explicit about estimating the counterfactual response from a subset of the untreated sample.

---

[11] In practice, Wooldridge (2002) recommends augmenting the regression model in the following way:

$$Y_i = \alpha' + \beta' T_i + \gamma' P(x_i) + \delta' T_i \left[P(x_i) - \bar{P}(x_i) \right] + e_i'$$

where $\bar{P}(x_i)$ represents the mean propensity score for the target population and ATE is estimated the same way, but by using β' in place of β.

With suitable matches between treated and untreated individuals, then, it is possible to estimate ATE as follows:

$$\text{ATE} = \frac{1}{N} \sum_{i \in (T=1)} \left[Y_i - \sum_{j \in (T=0)} \omega_{i,j} Y_j \right]$$

where i indexes treated individuals, j indexes untreated individuals, and $\omega_{i,j}$ is an arbitrary "weight" assigned to the response of each untreated individual that is subject to the constraint that $\sum \omega_{i,j} = 1 \forall i \in (T = 1)$. The latter criterion means that for each treated individual, the weights for all of his or her matched untreated subjects sum to unity. Note that, for untreated individuals who are poor matches, the weight may be zero. Importantly, all matching methods may be characterized as weighting functions, with a variety of algorithms available that define match suitability in different ways.

The simplest form of matching involves nearest available matching or *nearest neighbor matching*, in which the untreated case with the closest propensity score to a treated case is used as the counterfactual. In this case, $\omega_{i,j} = 1$ for all matched untreated respondents, a scenario known as single-nearest-neighbor or one-to-one matching. Treated individuals may also be matched to multiple nearest neighbors, known as many-to-one matching, in which case, $\omega_{i,j} = 1/J_i$ where J_i is the number of matched untreated cases for each treated individual i, with a maximum number of matches selected by the researcher (e.g., 2-to-1, 3-to-1, and so on). With multiple nearest neighbors, the mean of several untreated individuals serves as the counterfactual. There is a tradeoff between using single and multiple nearest neighbors (see Smith and Todd 2005). Using multiple nearest neighbors decreases variance at the cost of increasing potential bias because matches are less accurate. On the other hand, single nearest neighbor matching decreases bias but increases variance. A variation on nearest neighbor matching is *caliper matching*, which selects the specified number of untreated cases from within a maximum distance or tolerance known as a caliper. If no untreated subjects lie with the chosen caliper, the treated subject is unmatched.[12]

A more complicated weighting protocol is *kernel matching*, which provides a means of differential weighting of untreated cases by their distance from the treated subjects.[13] Kernel matching allows for finer distinctions in weighting compared to other methods. With this method, the researcher must decide which kernel function and bandwidth to use. Any finite probability distribution function may be used as a kernel, but the three most common kernels used in practice are the uniform, the Gaussian, and the Epanechnikov. A uniform kernel

---

[12] Nearest neighbor matching can be done with or without replacement. *Matching without replacement* means that once an untreated case has been matched to a treated case, it is removed from the candidates for matching. This may lead to poor matches when the distribution of propensity scores is quite different for the treated and untreated groups. Matching without replacement also requires that cases be randomly sorted prior to matching, as sort order can affect matches when there are cases with equal propensity scores. *Matching with replacement* allows an untreated individual to serve as the counterfactual for multiple treated individuals. This allows for better matches, but reduces the number of untreated cases used to create the treatment effect estimate, which increases the variance of the estimate (Smith and Todd 2005). As with the choice of the number of neighbors, one has to balance concerns of bias and efficiency.

[13] When there are many cases at the boundaries of the propensity score distribution, it may be useful to generalize kernel matching to include a linear term; this is called local linear matching. Its main advantage over kernel matching is that it yields more accurate estimates at boundary points in the distribution of propensity scores and it deals better with different data densities (Smith and Todd 2005).

assigns a weight of $1/J_i$ to each of the J_i matched untreated cases within a chosen radius. What makes this different from matching with multiple nearest neighbors or caliper matching is simply that all available matches within the specified radius are used, rather than the pre-specified number of matches.

A Gaussian kernel matches all untreated individuals to each treated individual, with weights assigned to untreated cases that are proportional to the well-known normal distribution. One can imagine a normal curve centered above each treated case on the propensity score continuum, with its kurtosis (i.e., the sharpness of the distribution's peak) determined by the size of the bandwidth. Each untreated case which lies beneath this curve (which, under a normal curve, is *all* untreated cases), receives a weight proportional to the probability density function of the normal curve evaluated at that point. In effect, this accords the greatest importance to counterfactual cases that are the closest on the propensity score metric. An Epanechnikov kernel matches all untreated individuals within a specified bandwidth of each treated individual, but unlike the Gaussian kernel, assigns zero weight to untreated cases that lie beyond the bandwidth.

Each of these propensity score methods described above has particular advantages and disadvantages, and is useful under different circumstances. If, for example, there are numerous treated and untreated cases throughout the propensity score distribution, then the nearest neighbor matching without replacement may be the best option. However, if the distributions are quite different, then kernel matching may be preferred. There are no foolproof rules for implementing propensity score matching. Rather, one must carefully consider each research situation, preferably implementing at least a few different matching protocols (if appropriate) in order to assess sensitivity of the estimates to the matching method.

AN EMPIRICAL ILLUSTRATION OF THE RELATIONSHIP BETWEEN ADOLESCENT EMPLOYMENT AND SUBSTANCE USE

To provide a step-by-step example of propensity score matching, we examine the relationship between youth employment and substance use. This is a question that has been of longstanding interest to developmental psychologists and criminologists.[14] Three decades of research leaves little doubt – with a few notable exceptions – that employment during adolescence is positively correlated with the use of a wide variety of illicit substances, including cigarettes, alcohol, marijuana, and hard drugs. In particular, research demonstrates that employment which is of "high intensity" – referring to a work commitment that is over 20 h per week, generally the median work intensity among adolescents – and which takes place during the school year, is most strongly correlated with substance use.

The data chosen for this example are from the National Longitudinal Survey of Youth 1997, which is a nationally representative survey of 8,984 youth born during the years 1980 through 1984 and living in the United States during the initial interview year in 1997. The data

---

[14] Apel et al. (2006, 2007, 2008); Bachman et al. (1981, 2003); Bachman and Schulenberg (1993); Gottfredson (1985); Greenberger et al. (1981); Johnson (2004); McMorris and Uggen (2000); Mihalic and Elliott (1997); Mortimer (2003); Mortimer et al. (1996); Paternoster et al. (2003); Ploeger (1997); Resnick et al. (1997); Safron et al. (2001); Staff and Uggen (2003); Steinberg and Dornbusch (1991); Steinberg et al. (1982, 1993); Tanner and Krahn (1991).

were collected to document the transition from school to work in a contemporary sample of adolescents. There is thus rich information on individual work histories, in addition to a variety of other indicators of health and wellbeing, including delinquency and substance use. For this illustration, we select the subsample of youth in the 12- to 14-year-old cohorts. Exclusion of those who worked in a formal ("paycheck") job prior to the first interview or with missing information at the second interview yields a sample of 4,667 youth. Propensity score matching is then used to estimate the average treatment effect (ATE) of high-intensity work during the school year on illicit substance use.

The key independent variable – the "treatment" – is a binary indicator for employment in a formal job of at least 15 h per week during the school year between the first and second interviews. A 15-h threshold is chosen because this represents the median number of hours worked per week during the school year among the workers in this sample. Just under one-quarter of the sample, 23.0% ($N = 1,073$), are employed during the school year, and 11.8% ($N = 550$) are employed at high intensity during the school year. The dependent variable – the "response" – is a binary indicator for the use of cigarettes, alcohol, marijuana, or other hard drugs between the first and second interviews. Almost half the sample, 49.4% ($N = 2,304$), reports such use.

The National Longitudinal Survey of Youth 1997 also has available a wide variety of background variables measured from the first interview that may be used to model the probability of high-intensity work at the second interview. Because this analysis is intended to be little more than an illustration of the propensity score approach, we limit our attention to 18 variables, listed in Table 26.1. These include measures of individual demographics (gender, race/ethnicity, age), family background (intact family, household size, mobility, income, socioeconomic status, disadvantage), family process (parental attachment, parental monitoring), school engagement (test scores, attachment to teachers, homework), and miscellaneous risk indicators (antisocial peers, delinquency, arrest), including prior substance use.

Estimation of the Propensity Score and Evaluation of Covariate Balance

The probability of intensive employment during the school year – the propensity score – is estimated from the logistic regression model, shown in Table 26.1. The pseudo R-square from the model is 0.187, meaning that the model explains 18.7% of the variation in intensive work.[15] The mean propensity score for treated youth is 0.25 (median = 0.25) and for untreated youth is 0.10 (median = 0.06). The model findings indicate that minorities are significantly less likely to work intensively, while youth who are older at the first interview are significantly more likely to be intensively employed. Youth who are from highly mobile households are also more likely to be intensively employed, as are youth from high-SES households (higher values on the low-SES index indicate lower SES). Youth who have higher test scores (as measured by the Peabody Individual Achievement Test) are more likely to work intensively, as are youth who have more antisocial peers and who use a wider variety of illicit substances.

The distributions of the propensity scores for treated and untreated youth are displayed in Fig. 26.1. As a measure of covariate balance, we rely on the standardized bias (SB)

---

[15] If we select the sample treatment probability as the classification threshold, 71.8 percent of the sample is correctly classified from the model shown in Table 26.1.

TABLE 26.1. Descriptive statistics, propensity score model, and balance diagnostics

Variable	Mean (S.D.)	Logit model of intensive work b (S.E.)	Balance diagnostics: standardized bias (SB)	
			Before matching	After matching
Demographics				
Male	50.7%	0.135 (0.105)	3.0	4.0
Minority	47.9%	−0.364 (0.117)**	−11.9	−1.5
Age	13.8 (0.9)	1.377 (0.077)***	104.5	−1.8
Family background				
Both biological parents	49.9%	−0.087 (0.140)	−13.2	5.7
Household size	4.6 (1.5)	0.040 (0.036)	−4.4	−2.0
Residential mobility	0.5 (0.4)	0.320 (0.157)*	−20.5	1.2
Family income ($10K)	4.5 (4.1)	−0.014 (0.018)	−2.4	1.4
Low SES index	0.9 (1.1)	−0.119 (0.063)+	−10.5	1.4
Disadvantage index	1.7 (1.5)	0.053 (0.054)	3.7	−0.0
Family processes				
Attachment to parents	4.0 (1.3)	−0.025 (0.041)	−17.1	−0.7
Monitoring by parents	1.7 (1.1)	−0.004 (0.052)	−13.9	1.2
School engagement				
P.I.A.T. percentile (÷10)	4.9 (3.4)	0.030 (0.017)+	1.6	−0.8
Attachment to teachers	5.1 (1.5)	−0.029 (0.034)	−22.8	0.2
Hours of homework	2.0 (3.1)	0.012 (0.021)	−3.2	0.7
Risk indicators				
Antisocial peer affiliation	1.2 (1.5)	0.072 (0.036)*	50.8	3.7
delinquency variety	0.9 (1.3)	0.032 (0.043)	30.5	−4.8
Arrested	5.4%	0.187 (0.193)	24.2	−3.3
Substance use variety	0.7 (1.0)	0.117 (0.056)*	45.3	−7.2

Note: $N = 4{,}667$. Estimates are unweighted. All variables are measured at the first (1997) interview. Means of binary variables are presented as percentages. Descriptive statistics and balance diagnostics are estimated from cases with valid data. Pseudo R-square for the logit model is 0.187, with a correct classification rate of 71.8%. The post-matching standardized bias is based on single-nearest-neighbor matching with no caliper.
+ $p < 0.10$, * $p < 0.05$, ** $p < 0.01$, *** $p < 0.001$ (two-tailed tests).

(Rosenbaum and Rubin 1985). Recall that variables with $|SB| \geq 20$ are considered imbalanced. By this criterion, seven variables are imbalanced prior to matching – age, mobility, teacher attachment, and all four of the risk indicators.[16] If a stricter criterion of ten is chosen instead, 12 variables are imbalanced prior to matching. After matching, however, no variable is imbalanced irrespective of whether 20 or 10 is chosen as the balance threshold. Notice also that, in all but one case (gender), the SB becomes smaller in absolute magnitude when matching is performed. The variable with the largest SB after matching is prior substance use $(SB = -7.2)$.

---

[16] The sign of the standardized bias is informative. If positive, it signifies that treated youth (i.e., youth who work intensively during the school year) exhibit more of the characteristic being measured than untreated youth. Conversely, if negative, it means that treated youth have less of the measured quality than untreated youth.

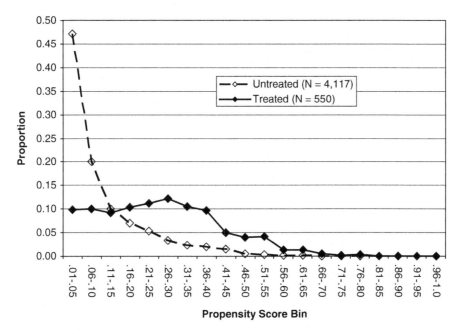

FIGURE 26.1. Propensity score distribution, by treatment status. Note: The sample includes 4,667 youth who were non-workers at the initial interview. "Treated" youth are those who report working at high intensity (more than 15 h per week) on average during the school year (September-May) between the first and second interviews. "Untreated" youth are those who report working at low intensity (15 or fewer hours per week) on average during the school year, or who report not working during the school year at all.

Estimation of the Average Treatment Effect

In Table 26.2, we provide estimates of the average treatment effect (ATE) from a variety of model specifications. In the first two rows (panel A), we perform standard regression adjustment, in which we regress substance use on intensive work. With no control variables, youth who work intensively during the school year are significantly and substantially more likely to engage in substance use. Specifically, their probability of substance use is 18.6 points higher than youth who work only moderately during the school year (15 or fewer hours per week) or who do not work during the school year at all. When the control variables from Table 26.1 are included, the ATE is attenuated but is still statistically significant, implying that intensively employed youth have a substance use likelihood that is 5.1 points higher. Thus, when traditional methods are used to establish the relationship between intensive work and substance use, the findings from previous research are replicated.[17] Specifically, high intensity during the school year appears to "cause" substance use.

In the remainder of Table 26.2, a variety of propensity score methods are employed – regression, stratification, and matching. Each method conditions on the propensity score in a slightly different way. First, in panel B, the regression method is used, in which substance use

---

[17] If a logistic regression model of substance use is estimated instead, the coefficient for intensive work with no control variables is 0.77 (odds ratio = 2.16), and with control variables is 0.28 (odds ratio = 1.33). Both coefficients are statistically significant at a five-percent level.

TABLE 26.2. Average treatment effect of intensive work
on substance use

Model	ATE (S.E.)
A. Standard regression adjustment	
No control variables	0.186 (0.023)***
All control variables	0.051 (0.021)*
B. Propensity score model: regression	
No trimming	0.054 (0.026)*
Trim upper and lower 10%	0.074 (0.030)*
C. Propensity score model: stratification	
Five strata	0.057 (0.037)
Ten strata	0.028 (0.030)
D. Propensity score model: matching	
Nearest neighbor matching	
1 Nearest neighbor, no caliper	0.029 (0.045)
1 Nearest neighbor, caliper = 0.01	0.029 (0.045)
1 Nearest neighbor, caliper = 0.001	0.035 (0.036)
1 Nearest neighbor, caliper = 0.0001	0.024 (0.042)
3 Nearest neighbors, no caliper	0.032 (0.041)
3 Nearest neighbors, caliper = 0.01	0.032 (0.040)
3 Nearest neighbors, caliper = 0.001	0.050 (0.034)
3 Nearest neighbors, caliper = 0.0001	0.017 (0.041)
5 Nearest neighbors, no caliper	0.038 (0.040)
5 Nearest neighbors, caliper = 0.01	0.038 (0.040)
5 Nearest neighbors, caliper = 0.001	0.047 (0.036)
5 Nearest neighbors, caliper = 0.0001	0.016 (0.046)
Kernel matching	
Uniform kernel	0.029 (0.045)
Gaussian kernel	0.029 (0.045)
Epanechnikov kernel	0.029 (0.045)

Note: $N = 4,667$. Estimates are unweighted. For the propensity
score regression and matching models, bootstrapped standard errors
with 100 replications are provided.
$^+ p < 0.10$, $^* p < 0.05$, $^{**} p < 0.01$, $^{***} p < 0.001$ (two-tailed
tests).

is regressed on intensive work, controlling only for the propensity score. In the first model,
the entire sample is retained, while in the second model, only the middle 80% of the sample is
retained. In both cases, the ATE of intensive work on substance use is positive and statistically
significant. The results from propensity score regression thus harmonize with the results from
standard regression adjustment.[18]

Next, in panel C, the sample is classified on the basis of the estimated propensity score
into equal-sized intervals of five strata (quintiles) and ten strata (deciles). In both cases, the
ATE is positive but no longer statistically significant. Notice also that, as the sample is classified into more strata – guaranteeing more homogeneous matches between the treated and

---

[18] Notice that the ATE from standard regression in panel A ($b = 0.051$) is very similar to the ATE from propensity
score regression with no trimming in panel B ($b = 0.054$). The similarity is not coincidental. The discrepancy is
only due to the fact that the propensity score was estimated from a logistic regression model at the first stage. Had
a linear regression model been used instead, the two coefficients would be identical, although the standard errors
would differ.

untreated in each stratum vis-à-vis the probability of intensive work – the ATE is halved. The results from propensity score stratification conflict with the foregoing models, and indicate that the positive correlation between intensive work and substance use is a selection artifact.

Finally, in panel D, a variety of matching protocols are employed.[19] We use single and multiple (three, five) nearest neighbors as matches within several calipers (none, 0.01, 0.001, 0.0001). We also employ kernel matching with three different kernels (uniform, Gaussian, Epanechnikov). In virtually all cases, the ATE is consistently in the neighborhood of 0.030, with a range of ATEs from 0.016 to 0.050. However, these estimates do not even approach statistical significance. The results from propensity score matching thus provide strong evidence that the relationship between intensive work and substance use is attributable to selection rather than causation.

To summarize, propensity score methods that ensure some degree of homogeneity between treated and untreated cases – stratification and matching, in particular – demonstrate that the positive correlation between intensive school-year employment and substance use is due to the fact that intensive workers differ in some fundamental way prior to their transition to work. Their higher substance use risk is, thus, due to self-selection rather than to the causal impact of their work involvement. In this application, regression-based methods – standard regression adjustment and propensity score regression – perform poorly because they fail to achieve a true "apples-to-apples" comparison between treated and untreated individuals.[20]

Other Examples of Propensity Score Matching in Criminology and Related Disciplines

The foregoing illustration represents a traditional application of propensity score methods to the study of individual-level treatment effects – in this case, of intensive school-year employment on substance use during adolescence. There are a number of other examples of this more traditional approach to treatment effect estimation in criminology, for example, arrest and wife battery (Berk and Newton 1985), court disposition and recidivism risk (Banks and Gottfredson 2003; Blechman et al. 2000; Caldwell et al. 2006; Krebs et al. 2009), youth employment and delinquency (Brame et al. 2004), exposure to community violence and perpetration of violence (Bingenheimer et al. 2005; Molnar et al. 2005), school sector and juvenile misbehavior (Mocan and Tekin 2006), marriage and crime (King et al. 2007), incarceration and crime (Sweeten and Apel 2007), and child maltreatment and adolescent weapon carrying (Leeb et al. 2007). In these studies, treatment status is modeled from as few as two covariates (Caldwell et al. 2006) to as many as 153 covariates (Bingenheimer et al. 2005). There are applications of regression (Banks and Gottfredson 2003; Berk and Newton 1985; Caldwell et al. 2006; Mocan and Tekin 2006; Molnar et al. 2005), stratification (Bingenheimer et al. 2005; Blechman et al. 2000; Brame et al. 2004; Leeb et al. 2007), and matching (King et al. 2007; Krebs et al. 2009; Sweeten and Apel 2007).

---

[19] We employ the user-written Stata protocol -psmatch2- to estimate average treatment effects from the matching models (see Leuven and Barbara 2003). To obtain the standard error of the ATE, we perform a bootstrap procedure with 100 replications.

[20] As a further test of sensitivity, we estimated the ATE of intensive employment on substance use for subsamples with different substance use histories. For this test, we employed single-nearest-neighbor matching with no caliper, although the findings were not sensitive to this choice. Among the 2,740 youth who, at the initial interview, reported never having used illicit substances, ATE = 0.084 (S.E. = 0.060). Among the 1,927 youth who reported having used at least one type of illicit substance prior to the initial interview, ATE = −0.019 (S.E. = 0.046).

There have also been recent applications of the propensity score methodology in criminology that extend the method in appealing ways. One extension is the use of generalized boosted regression (GBR) in the construction of the propensity score, providing a more flexible model of treatment assignment compared to standard logistic regression, using higher-order polynomials and interaction terms. McCaffrey et al. (2004) applied the method to the study of the effect of a community-based, residential drug treatment program on alcohol and marijuana use among juvenile probationers (see Ridgeway 2006, for an application of GBR to racial bias in citation rates, search rates, and stop duration in police traffic stops). They found that GBR was superior to the standard logit model as determined by pre-treatment balance in the confounders, prediction error in the propensity scores, and the variance of treatment effect estimates.

A second extension is the application of the propensity score methodology to the study of aggregate-level treatment effects, such as at the level of neighborhoods. Tita and Ridgeway (2007) were interested in the impact of gang formation on 911 call volume (calls for service) among Pittsburgh census block groups. They employed a technique known as propensity score weighting that involves weighting untreated cases by the odds of treatment (as predicted by the treatment status model) such that the distribution of covariates is balanced between treated and untreated cases (see Hirano et al. 2003; Robins et al. 1992; Robins and Rotnitzky 1995; see McNiel 2007, for an application of weighting to the study of the effect of mental health courts on recidivism).

A third extension is the estimation of treatment effects when the treatment, outcome, and confounders are all time-dependent. Sampson et al. (2006) estimated the treatment effect of marriage on official criminal behavior through middle adulthood (ages 17–32) and later adulthood (ages 17–70) among men institutionalized in a Boston-area reform school as boys (see Glueck and Glueck 1950). They employed a variation on propensity score weighting known as inverse probability-of-treatment weighting (IPTW) that involves adjusting treatment effect estimates by a time-varying propensity score incorporating cumulative treatment exposure (see Robins 1999; Robins et al. 2000). Similarly, Nieuwbeerta et al. (2009) estimated the time-dependent treatment effect of incarceration on recidivism in a Dutch conviction cohort, but in the context of a discrete-time event history model. This approach is referred to as risk set matching (see Li et al. 2001; Lu 2005).

A fourth extension is the integration of propensity scores into the group-based trajectory methodology of Nagin (2005). In a series of papers, Haviland and Nagin (2005, 2007; Haviland et al. 2007) were interested in the effect of joining a gang on youth violence. Youth were first classified into trajectory groups on the basis of finite mixture models of prior violence throughout early adolescence. Within trajectory groups, propensity scores were then estimated using information from background covariates. Using this two-step approach, Haviland and Nagin demonstrated balance not only on potential confounders but also on prior realizations of the response variable.

DISCUSSION OF GOOD RESEARCH PRACTICE

Before closing this chapter, we would like to offer some of our own thoughts on what we regard as good research practice with the use of propensity scores.

(1) *Have a clear, unambiguous definition of treatment, preferably the first experience of treatment.* The propensity score methodology is best conceived as an observational

analog to a randomized experiment involving a novel treatment. Otherwise, the right-hand side of the treatment status model should account for state dependence effects, that is, the cumulative experience of the treatment state. Moreover, in these instances, it might be fruitful to match directly on individuals' cumulative treatment status in addition to the propensity score.

(2) *Be thoughtful about the specification of the treatment status model.* A concise, theoretically informed model of treatment status is not necessarily desirable, simply because criminological theory is not as explicit as other disciplines about relevant confounders in the treatment–response relationship. In the case of propensity score models, parsimony is not necessarily a virtue. Parsimonious models are only appropriate to the extent that balance can be demonstrated on confounders that are not included in the treatment status model. The researcher should make the case that any nonrandom sources of selection into treatment are fully captured by the treatment status model. Failure to do so, or to do so convincingly, renders the propensity score method no better than standard regression adjustment.

(3) *Include confounders that are temporally prior to treatment in the treatment status model.* The treatment status model should necessarily include predictors that are realized prior to treatment assignment. This should include pretreatment outcomes when they are available. Temporal priority of confounders vis-à-vis treatment implies that panel data are preferable to crosssectional data, because potential confounders at one time period can be used to model treatment status at the next time period. Modeling treatment status from crosssectional data is potentially problematic because some of the confounders in the prediction model could actually precede treatment status in time. A possible exception to this guideline is when the confounders refer to behavior prior to the interview, while treatment refers to behavior at the time of the interview, or even perhaps to expected behavior.

(4) *Demonstrate that the support condition is satisfied.* At a minimum, this should entail displaying the propensity score distributions for treated and untreated cases to ensure that there is sufficient overlap between them. This is especially important if the propensity score is used as a control variable in a regression model, in which case, results can be misleading if there are unmatched or poorly matched cases, as in the empirical example we provided earlier.

(5) *Demonstrate balance on confounders that are included in the treatment status model, as well as balance on confounders that are not included in the treatment status model, if available.* The latter criterion increases confidence that the conditional independence assumption has been satisfied. The most useful balance diagnostics include t-tests and estimates of the standardized bias (SB). Confounders in the treatment status model that remain imbalanced should be adjusted directly in the estimate of the treatment effect.

(6) *Employ multiple propensity score methods as tests of robustness.* Generally speaking, we would advise against using propensity score regression, simply because our experience is that conclusions from these models rarely differ from standard regression adjustment. However, using propensity score stratification, this guideline means assessing the sensitivity of estimated treatment effects to the number of strata. If using propensity score matching, this means testing sensitivity to the specific matching protocol employed. Ideally, estimates from multiple methods will agree in substance. However, applied research settings are rarely ideal, and it is not uncommon for two

propensity score methods to lead to different inferences. In such instances, the relative merits of the two models should be closely evaluated before a decision is made about which set of results to report.

(7) *Think carefully about what type of treatment effect is relevant for the study.* For basic social scientific questions, the typical parameter of interest is the average treatment effect (ATE), which we estimated in our empirical example. However, in many policy applications, the average treatment effect on the treated or the untreated (ATT or ATU) may actually be more relevant. Consider, for example, an evaluation of a targeted after-school program for delinquency prevention. Program stakeholders and potential adopters of the program are clearly interested in ATT: "What effect did the program have on those individuals who participated in the program?" However, if one were interested in expanding the target population for the program, ATU may be the more relevant consideration. For example, consider the question of the effect of net-widening criminal justice policies such as the use of mandatory arrest: "What effect would the program have on those individuals who are not the usual targets of the intervention?"

CONCLUDING REMARKS

Propensity score matching has emerged as an important tool in the program evaluator's toolbox. Criminology is no exception to this trend, as indicated by the growing number of studies that employ the method. In fact, of the two dozen or so criminological studies reviewed earlier, all but one have been published since 2000. While propensity score matching is by no means a panacea to the pernicious problem posed by selection bias (what quasi-experimental method is?), it does have several advantages to recommend its use in causal effect estimation, as we have attempted to outline in this chapter. We would encourage researchers who are interested in applying the method to their specific question to think very carefully about the issues we have discussed here.

REFERENCES

Apel R, Bushway SD, Brame R, Haviland AM, Nagin DS, Paternoster R (2007) Unpacking the relationship between adolescent employment and antisocial behavior: a matched samples comparison. Criminology 45:67–97

Apel R, Bushway SD, Paternoster R, Brame R, Sweeten G (2008) Using state child labor laws to identify the causal effect of youth employment on deviant behavior and academic achievement. J Quant Criminol 24:337–362

Apel R, Paternoster R, Bushway SD, Brame R (2006) A job isn't just a job: the differential impact of formal versus informal work on adolescent problem behavior. Crime Delinq 52:333–369

Bachman JG, Johnston LD, O'Malley PM (1981) Smoking, drinking, and drug use among American high school students: correlates and trends, 1975–1979. Am J Public Health 71:59–69

Bachman JG, Safron DJ, Sy SR, Schulenberg JE (2003) Wishing to work: new perspectives on how adolescents' part-time work intensity is linked to educational disengagement, substance use, and other problem behaviors. Int J Behav Dev 27:301–315

Bachman JG Schulenberg JE (1993) How part-time work intensity relates to drug use, problem behavior, time use, and satisfaction among high school seniors: are these consequences or merely correlates? Dev Psychol 29:220–235

Banks D, Gottfredson DC (2003) The effects of drug treatment and supervision on time to rearrest among drug treatment court participants. J Drug Issues 33:385–412

Berk RA, Newton PJ (1985) Does arrest really deter wife battery? An effort to replicate the findings of the Minneapolis spouse abuse experiment. Am Sociol Rev 50:253–262

Bingenheimer JB, Brennan RT, Earls FJ (2005) Firearm violence exposure and serious violent behavior. Science 308:1323–1326

Blechman EA, Maurice A, Bueckner B, Helberg C (2000) Can mentoring or skill training reduce recidivism? Observational study with propensity analysis. Prev Sci 1:139–155

Brame R, Bushway SD, Paternoster R, Apel R (2004) Assessing the effect of adolescent employment on involvement in criminal activity. J Contemp Crim Justice 20:236–256

Caldwell M, Skeem J, Salekin R, Rybroek GV (2006) Treatment response of adolescent offenders with psychopathy features: a 2-year follow-up. Crim Justice Behav 33:571–596

Cameron AC, Trivedi PK (2005) Microeconometrics: methods and applications. Cambridge University Press, New York

Cochran WG (1968) The effectiveness of adjustment by subclassification in removing bias in observational studies. Biometrics 24:295–313

Cohen J (1988) Statistical power analysis for the behavioral sciences, 2nd edn. Lawrence Erlbaum, Hillsdale, NJ

Dehejia RH, Wahba S (1999) Causal effects in nonexperimental settings: reevaluating the evaluation of training programs. J Am Stat Assoc 94:1053–1062

Dehejia RH, Wahba S (2002) Propensity score-matching methods for nonexperimental causal studies. Rev Econ Stat 84:151–161

Glueck S, Glueck E (1950) Unraveling juvenile delinquency. The Commonwealth Fund, Cambridge, MA

Gottfredson DC (1985) Youth employment, crime, and schooling: a longitudinal study of a national sample. Dev Psychol 21:419–432

Greenberger E, Steinberg LD, Vaux A (1981) Adolescents who work: health and behavioral consequences of job stress. Dev Psychol 17:691–703

Haviland AM, Nagin DS (2005) Causal inferences with group based trajectory models. Psychometrika 70:1–22

Haviland AM, Nagin DS (2007) Using group-based trajectory modeling in conjunction with propensity scores to improve balance. J Exp Criminol 3:65–82

Haviland AM, Nagin DS, Rosenbaum PR (2007) Combining propensity score matching and group-based trajectory analysis in an observational study. Psychol Methods 12:247–267

Heckman JJ, Joseph Hotz V (1989) Choosing among alternative nonexperimental methods for estimating the impact of social programs: the case of manpower training. J Am Stat Assoc 84:862–874

Hirano K, Imbens GW, Ridder G (2003) Efficient estimation of average treatment effects using the estimated propensity score. Econometrica 71:1161–1189

Holland PW (1986) Statistics and causal inference. J Am Stat Assoc 81:945–960

Imbens GW (2004) Nonparametric estimation of average treatment effects under exogeneity: a review. Rev Econ Stat 86:4–29

Johnson MK (2004) Further evidence on adolescent employment and substance use: differences by race and ethnicity. J Health Soc Behav 45:187–197

King RD, Massoglia M, MacMillan R (2007) The context of marriage and crime: gender, the propensity to marry, and offending in early adulthood. Criminology 45:33–65

Krebs CP, Strom KJ, Koetse WH, Lattimore PK (2009) The impact of residential and nonresidential drug treatment on recidivism among drug-involved probationers. Crime Delinq 55:442–471

Leeb RT, Barker LE, Strine TW (2007) The effect of childhood physical and sexual abuse on adolescent weapon carrying. J Adolesc Health 40:551–558

Leuven E, Barbara S (2003) PSMATCH2: Stata module to perform full Mahalanobis and propensity score matching, common support graphing, and covariate imbalance testing. Available online: http://ideas.repec.org/c/boc/bocode/s432001.html

Li YP, Propert KJ, Rosenbaum PR (2001) Balanced risk set matching. J Am Stat Assoc 96:870–882

Lu B (2005) Propensity score matching with time-dependent covariates. Biometrics 61:721–728

McCaffrey DF, Ridgeway G, Morral AR (2004) Propensity score estimation with boosted regression for evaluating causal effects in observational studies. Psychol Methods 9:403–425

McMorris BJ Uggen C (2000) Alcohol and employment in the transition to adulthood. J Health Soc Behav 41:276–294

McNeil DE, Binder RL (2007) Effectiveness of a mental health court in reducing criminal recidivism and violence. Am J Psychiatry 164:1395–1403

Mihalic SW Elliott DS (1997) Short- and long-term consequences of adolescent work. Youth Soc 28:464–498

Mocan NH, Tekin E (2006) Catholic schools and bad behavior: a propensity score matching analysis. J Econom Anal Policy 5:1–34

Molnar BE, Browne A, Cerda M, Buka SL (2005) Violent behavior by girls reporting violent victimization: a prospective study. Arch Pediatr Adolesc Med 159:731–739

Morgan SL, Harding DJ (2006) Matching estimators of causal effects: prospects and pitfalls in theory and practice. Sociol Methods Res 35:3–60

Mortimer JT (2003) Working and growing up in America. Harvard University Press, Cambridge, MA

Mortimer JT, Finch MD, Ryu S, Shanahan MJ, Call KT (1996) The effects of work intensity on adolescent mental health, achievement, and behavioral adjustment: new evidence from a prospective study. Child Dev 67:1243–1261

Nagin DS (2005) Group-based modeling of development. Harvard University Press, Cambridge, MA

Nieuwbeerta P, Nagin DS, Blokland AAJ (2009) Assessing the impact of first-time imprisonment on offenders' subsequent criminal career development: A matched samples comparison. J Quant Criminol 25:227–257

Paternoster R, Bushway S, Brame R, Apel R (2003) The effect of teenage employment on delinquency and problem behaviors. Soc Forces 82:297–335

Ploeger M (1997) Youth employment and delinquency: reconsidering a problematic relationship. Criminology 35:659–675

Resnick MD, Bearman PS, Blum RW, Bauman KE, Harris KM, Jo J, Tabor J, Beuhring T, Sieving RE, Shew M, Ireland M, Bearinger LH, Richard Udry J (1997) Protecting adolescents from harm: findings from the national longitudinal study of adolescent health. J Am Med Assoc 278:823–832

Ridgeway G (2006) Assessing the effect of race bias in post-traffic stop outcomes using propensity scores. J Quant Criminol 22:1–29

Robins JM (1999) Association, causation, and marginal structural models. Synthese 121:151–179

Robins JM, Rotnitzky A (1995) Semiparametric efficiency in multivariate regression models with missing data. J Am Stat Assoc 90:122–129

Robins JM, Mark SD, Newey WK (1992) Estimating exposure effects by modeling the expectation of exposure conditional on confounders. Biometrics 48:479–495

Robins JM, Hernán MÁ, Brumback B (2000) Marginal structural models and causal inference in epidemiology. Epidemiology 11:550–560

Rosenbaum PR, Rubin DB (1983) The central role of the propensity score in observational studies for causal effects. Biometrika 70:41–55

Rosenbaum PR, Rubin DB (1984) Reducing bias in observational studies using subclassification on the propensity score. J Am Stat Assoc 79:516–524

Rosenbaum PR, Rubin DB (1985) Constructing a control group using multivariate matched sampling methods that incorporate the propensity score. Am Stat 39:33–38

Rubin DB (1974) Estimating causal effects of treatments in randomized and nonrandomized studies. J Educ Psychol 66:688–701

Rubin DB (1977) Assignment of treatment group on the basis of a covariate. J Educ Stat 2:1–26

Safron DJ, Schulenberg JE Bachman JG (2001) Part-time work and hurried adolescence: the links among work intensity, social activities, health behaviors, and substance use. J Health Soc Behav 42:425–449

Sampson RJ, Laub JH, Wimer C (2006) Does marriage reduce crime? A counterfactual approach to within-individual causal effects. Criminology 44:465–508

Smith JA, Todd PE (2005) Does matching overcome lalonde's critique of nonexperimental estimators? J Econom 125:305–353

Staff J Uggen C (2003) The fruits of good work: early work experiences and adolescent deviance. J Res Crime Delinq 40:263–290

Steinberg L Dornbusch S (1991) Negative correlates of part-time work in adolescence: replication and elaboration. Dev Psychol 17:304–313

Steinberg L, Fegley S, Dornbusch S (1993) Negative impact of part-time work on adolescent adjustment: evidence from a longitudinal study. Dev Psychol 29:171–180

Steinberg LD, Greenberger E, Garduque L, Ruggiero M, Vaux A (1982) Effects of working on adolescent development. Dev Psychol 18:385–395

Sweeten G, Apel R (2007) Incapacitation: revisiting an old question with a new method and new data. J Quant Criminol 23:303–326

Tanner J, Krahn H (1991) Part-time work and deviance among high-school seniors. Can J Sociol 16:281–302

Tita G, Ridgeway G (2007) The impact of gang formation on local patterns of crime. J Res Crime Delinq 44:208–237

Widom CS (1989) The cycle of violence. Science 244:160–166

Wooldridge JM (2002) Econometric analysis of cross section and panel data. MIT Press, Cambridge, MA

## CHAPTER 27

Recent Perspectives on the Regression Discontinuity Design

Richard Berk

INTRODUCTION

The regression discontinuity design has a long and complex history. It was originally proposed by psychologists Thistlewaite and Campell in 1960 (Thistlewaite and Campbell 1960). The design became widely known with the publication of the justly famous *Experimental and Quasi-Experimental Designs for Research* by Campbell and Stanley (Campbell and Stanley 1963) and was later elaborated by Trochim (1984, 2001). In 1972, the design was independently rediscovered by econometrician Arthur Goldberger (Goldberger 1972).

Even in these early formulations, the design was simple and powerful. However, there were few applications and apparently only four published studies with significant crime and justice content (Berk and Rauma 1983; Berk and de Leeuw 1999; Chen and Shapiro 2007; Berk et al. 2010). Over the past 15 years, a number of economists have extended the design (Imbens and Lemieux 2008b; Imbens and Kalyanaraman 2009) and applied it in a wide variety of settings (Imbens and Lemieux 2008a; Lee and Lemieux 2009). An account of how and why interest in the regression discontinuity design has varied over the years can be found in recent paper by Thomas Cook (Cook 2008).

In this chapter, the fundamentals of the regression discontinuity design are considered. Some recent advances are highlighted. The discussion begins with brief introduction to the ways in which statisticians think about causal inference. Then, the classic regression discontinuity design is examined. Newer material follows.

THE BASIC REGRESSION DISCONTINUITY DESIGN

The regression discontinuity (RD) design has many of the assets of a randomized experiment, but can be used when random assignment is not feasible. Typically, the goal is to estimate the causal effect of an intervention such as gate money for prison inmates, anger management for troubled teens, or changes in police patrolling practices. In the simplest case, there is an experimental and comparison group with assignment fully determined by an explicit and

A.R. Piquero and D. Weisburd (eds.), *Handbook of Quantitative Criminology*,
DOI 10.1007/978-0-387-77650-7_27, © Springer Science + Business Media, LLC 2010,
First softcover printing 2011

observable rule. For example, whether community policing is introduced in a neighborhood depends on whether the crime rate is above a specific threshold. Neighborhoods falling above that threshold get community policing. Other neighborhoods get business as usual. A relatively simple and compelling analysis can follow. In some circles, the RD design is called a "quasi-experiment."

One appeal of the RD design is "political." If the assignment rule represents need, either empirically or morally, one can sometimes more easily garner the support of stakeholders. Cooperation from study subjects can also follow more easily. For example, it might seem to just make good sense to assign a policing innovation to high crime neighborhoods. The technical complication is that neighborhoods assigned to the treatment condition will not be comparable on the average to neighborhoods assigned to the alternative. Indeed, systematic selection is explicitly built into the design. How the potential biases can be overcome in practice is a key theme in the material that follows.

To appreciate the underlying machinery of the RD design requires some familiarity with the way causal inference has come to be formulated by most statisticians. The framework was proposed by Neyman in 1923 and later extended by Rubin (1974) and Holland (1986). These days, it is sometimes called the "Rubin Causal Model."

In its most simple form, there are observational units: people, neighborhoods, police departments, prisons or other entities. There is a binary intervention. Some of the units are exposed to one "arm" of the intervention, and the other units are exposed to the alternative "arm" of the intervention. There is an interest in the intervention's causal effect. For example, one might want to learn how intensive parole supervision, when compared with conventional parole supervision, affects recidivism.

Each *unit* is assumed to have two *potential* outcomes, one if exposed to the treatment and one if exposed to the alternative. These outcomes are hypothetical and can vary across units. Thus, a given parolee would have one response if placed under intensive supervision and another response if placed under the usual supervision. Another parolees would also have two potential responses, which could differ from those of the first parolee.

Following Imbens and Lemieux (2008b), let $Y_i(1)$ denote the outcome if unit i is exposed to the treatment, and $Y_i(0)$ denote the outcome if unit i is exposed to the alternative condition. Interest centers on a comparison between $Y_i(1)$ and $Y_i(0)$, often their difference. An example is the number of failed urine tests should a given parolee be placed under intensive supervision minus the number of failed unit tests should that same parolee be placed under supervision as usual.

In practice, however, one can never observe both $Y_i(1)$ and $Y_i(0)$. A given unit will only experience the treatment or the alternative. Let $W_i = 1$ if unit i is actually exposed to the treatment, and $W_i = 0$ if unit i is actually exposed to the alternative. The *observed* outcome is then

$$Y_i = (1 - W_i) \cdot Y_i(0) + W_i \cdot Y_i(1). \tag{27.1}$$

Both Y_i and W_i can be observed. For the basic RD design, one also has a single observed covariate X_i that fully determines whether unit i is exposed to the treatment or the alternative. In the simplest case, X_i is a continuous covariate with an imposed threshold. A unit that falls on one side of the threshold or right on it is assigned to the treatment condition. A unit that falls on the other side of the threshold is assigned to the comparison condition.

X can be associated with the potential outcomes. For example, X may be a measure of parole risk. A parolee who scores on or above some threshold is assigned to intensive supervision. If that parolee scores below the threshold, assignment is to conventional supervision.

The risk measure is by design associated with the potential outcome of reoffending. This may seem curious, but it will soon be clear that possible biases can be addressed, at least in principle.

There can be other observed covariates Z. In some cases, they are used to define a multivariate assignment rule. For example, parolees who are younger than 21 and who have more than two prior convictions for a violent crime may be assigned to intensive supervision. In other cases, the Z play no role in the assignment, but are related to the potential outcomes. For now, there is no need to consider either complication.

Because by definition a causal effect, $[Y_i(1) - Y_i(0)]$, is unobservable in practice,[1] there is a shift to the group level. Interest centers on the observed *average* response of the units exposed to the treatment when compared with the observed *average* response of the units exposed to the alternative. We seek the average treatment effect. Given the assignment rule, however, there is the possibility that the units exposed to the treatment will differ systematically from the units exposed to the alternative. And, those systematic differences can be related to the potential outcomes. There is the risk of building in selection bias.

Under certain assumptions, there is a solution. Consider Fig. 27.1. On the horizontal axis is the assignment variable X. On the vertical axis is the response (outcome) variable Y. Units scoring at or above 5 on X are exposed to the intervention. Units scoring below 5 on X are exposed to the alternative. The higher line (dotted below the threshold of 5 and solid on or above the threshold of 5) represents the average potential response for different values of the assignment variable when a unit is exposed to the intervention. The lower line (solid below the threshold of 5, and dotted on or above the threshold of 5) represents the average potential response for different values of the assignment variable when a unit is exposed to the alternative. The solid parts of each response function represent the potential responses

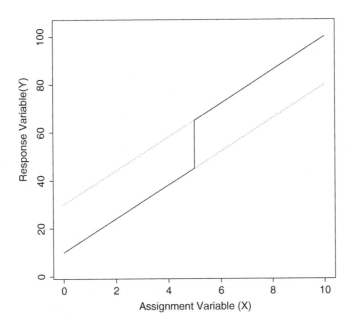

FIGURE 27.1. Conventional linear case.

---

[1] Sometimes the ratio rather than the difference is used, but that too is unobservable.

actually observed under the assignment rule. The vertical solid line at $X = 5$ represents the causal effect of the intervention.

Figure 27.1 shows the theory required for the basic RD design, and there is a lot going on. For both groups, the relationship between X and Y is positive. The larger the value of X, the larger the value of Y tends to be. If one just compared the observed mean of the group receiving the intervention (i.e., with $X \geq 5$) with the observed mean of the group receiving the alternative (i.e., with $X < 5$), as one might do in a randomized experiment, an estimate of the average treatment effect could be substantially biased. In this illustration, the group exposed to the treatment has by design larger values for X, which imply larger values of Y regardless of the treatment. Analogous risks follow if the relationship between X and Y is negative.

However, note that the relationship between the assignment variable and the response variable is for both groups assumed to be linear. This is true for potential responses that are observed (i.e., the solid lines) and potential responses that are not observed (i.e., the dotted lines). The linearity is a very restrictive but very convenient. Note also that the linear relationships are assumed to be parallel. This too is very restrictive but very convenient. One has a strong two-part theory about how the assignment variable is related to the response: the two response functions can differ only by a constant. That constant is the treatment effect.

If the relationships shown in Fig. 27.1 are a good approximation of reality, a very simple and effective analysis can follow. The difference between the vertical placement of the linear relationship for the units exposed to the intervention and the vertical placement of the linear relationship for the units exposed to the alternative can provide an estimate the average treatment effect.

More specifically, let

$$Y_i = \beta_0 + \beta_1 W_i + \beta_2 X_i + \varepsilon_i. \tag{27.2}$$

Equation (27.2) is a conventional regression expression representing the way the values of the response variable are generated. All of the observables are defined as before, and ε_i is the usual regression disturbance. When $W_i = 0$, the conditional expectation of (27.2) gives the linear relationship between X and Y for the group exposed to the alternative. When $W_i = 1$, the conditional expectation of (27.2) gives the linear relationship between X and Y for the group exposed to the treatment. β_2 is the common slope of the two response functions. β_0 is the intercept of the response function for the group exposed to the alternative. β_1 is the vertical distance between the two estimated response functions, which quantifies how much the response function for the treatment group is shifted up (i.e., $\beta_1 > 0$) or down (i.e., $\beta_1 < 0$) because of the intervention. In Fig. 27.1, the length of the vertical line at $X = 5$ is equal to the value of β_1. If the intervention has no effect, $\beta_1 = 0$, and the two lines collapse into one.

It is important to appreciate that (27.2) is not a causal model. It is a summary of the *association* of the assignment and intervention variables with the response variable. Although the intent is to estimate an average treatment effect, no claims are made that the two regressors can account for all of the systematic variation in the response or that if the assignment variable is manipulated, β_2 shows how the response will be altered. Equation (27.2) is no more than a way to estimate the average treatment effect. It is rather like the differences between the mean of the experimental group and the mean of the control group in a randomized experiment. There is no causal model there either.

In practice, one can use the data on hand and ordinary least squares to estimate the parameters of (27.2). If the two linear relationships are at least nearly linear and parallel, $\hat{\beta}_1$ is an unbiased estimate of the average treatment effect. A key is that the true selection mechanism is known and can be accurately represented by a threshold on X. The usual hypothesis test is that $\beta_1 = 0$; there is no treatment effect.

An obvious question is how one would determine in practice whether the two relationships are linear and parallel. A good way to start is to construct a scatterplot of Y against X. On each side of the threshold, one should see a truncated version of the idealized elliptical scatterplot. If there is a treatment effect, the plotted points should be shifted up or down in the region to the right of the threshold (where the units are exposed to the intervention). An example is discussed later.

A useful second step is to examine a scatterplot constructed from the residuals and fitted values of (27.2). When the residuals are plotted against the fitted values, one should see with no dramatic patterns. In particular, there should be no evidence that the assumed linear and parallel regression response functions are something else. It can also be useful to consider whether the usual assumption of a constant residual variance is credible. In short, one should examine the results from (27.2) as one would the results from any regression analysis. Graphical methods can be especially instructive and are less constrained by the untestable assumptions that test-based diagnostic methods require (Freedman 2008). An excellent discussion of a number of useful diagnostic methods can be found in the text by Cook and Weisberg (1999).

What can go wrong if proper diagnostic methods are not employed? Figure 27.2 provides a simple illustration. The two response functions for the potential outcomes are not parallel. The response function for the treatment group is much steeper. (The solid part of the line is

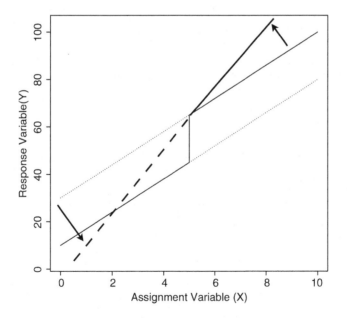

FIGURE 27.2. The conventional linear case gone wrong.

observed and the dashed part of the line is unobserved.) In this particularly perverse example, the gap at the threshold between the observed outcomes for the group exposed to the treatment and the observed outcomes for the group exposed to the alternative just happens to be the same as the treatment effect when the assumption of parallel response functions is met. But, this gap is not caused by a discontinuity. There is no evidence of a treatment effect.

It is certainly possible to alter (27.2) allowing for linear response functions that are not parallel. Looking again at Fig. 27.2, however, one would have to know about the nonparallel response functions in advance. One cannot determine from the data alone whether the response functions are not parallel or whether the intervention altered the slope and intercept of the treatment group.

This can lead to an identification problem. Suppose one were prepared to bet that the two response function were linear but not parallel. Then, β_1 combines the intercept of the response function for the treatment group in the absence of the intervention with a new intercept for the treatment group, should the intervention shift the treatment group response function. Because there are no observations for the treatment group in the absence of the intervention, the confounding cannot be disentangled, and the basic regression discontinuity design fails.

Suppose one were prepared to assume that the two response functions are linear and parallel before the intervention, but that after the intervention, the slope and intercept are altered. By including $(W_i \times X_i)$ as new regressor in the (27.2), the intervention-altered linear relationship for those exposed to the treatment can be identified, and the linear relationship for those exposed to the alternative can be identified. One has specified an interaction effect between W_i and X_i for certain values of X_i.

But, there is an important complication. The size of the gap between the response function of the treatment group and the response function of the comparison group depends on the value of X. Indeed, the treatment effect may be positive for some values of X and negative for other values of X. Although this is statistically acceptable, constructing a coherent substantive explanation can be challenging. One simplification is to focus only on the estimated average treatment effect in the immediate neighborhood of the threshold although important external validity questions can be raised. The estimate only applies to case in the neighborhood of the threshold. Nevertheless, this is an approach to which we return shortly.

There is nothing in the RD design precluding other kinds of interaction effects that are more easily interpreted. One can subset the data by values of covariates Z_i and consider whether there are different average treatment effects. Or, one can respecify (27.2) so that interaction effects are represented. For example, an intervention may be more effective for women than for men. One way to explore this would be to do one RD analysis for men and another RD analysis for women. Alterations in (27.2) would depend on the precise form the interaction effect takes. For instance, one might include a binary variable for gender and the product of the intervention variable and gender. That would allow for different intercepts and difference in average treatment effects for men and women.

Some of lessons from the linear case carry over to the nonlinear case. If the two response functions are nonlinear but parallel, one can in principle estimate a shift resulting from an intervention. However, it is not clear what a change in slope means if the response functions are not linear. The nonlinear case is discussed a more later.

THE GENERALIZED REGRESSION DISCONTINUITY DESIGN

One problem with the basic RD design is that the response is assumed to be quantitative. In many applications, the response is categorical or a count. An example of the former is whether a parolee reoffends. An example of the latter is the number of crimes the parolee commits.

The basic RD design is easily extended to include formulations from the generalized linear model. Logistic regression and Poisson regression are two common illustrations. Consider, for instance, a binary response.

We can proceed initially as before. Equation (27.3) is the same as (27.2) except that the quantitative response Y_i^* is now completely unobserved regardless of whether a unit falls above or below the threshold. For example, Y_i^* may be the proclivity of a prison inmate to engage in some form of serious misconduct, and no measures of this proclivity are available. As before, we let

$$Y_i^* = \beta_0 + \beta_1 W_i + \beta_2 X_i + \varepsilon_i. \tag{27.3}$$

We now hypothesize a second kind of threshold. If an inmate's proclivity toward misconduct exceeds a certain value, an act of misconduct is observed. If that threshold is not exceeded, no act of misconduct is observed. Suppose this outcome is coded so that "1" denotes an observed act of misconduct, and "0" denotes no observed act of misconduct.

Drawing on a common motivation for logistic regression (Cameron and Trivedi 2005: Sect. 14.4), the probability P_i of observing a "1" depends on the probability that Y_i^* will exceed the misconduct proclivity threshold. If one then assumes that ε_i has a logistic distribution, (27.4) can follow directly:

$$\log\frac{P_i}{1 - P_i} = \gamma_0 + \gamma_1 W_i + \gamma_2 X_i, \tag{27.4}$$

where γ_0 through γ_2 are new regression coefficients. In other words, the systematic part of the formulation is the same as in (27.2), but the response is now in units of log-odds (also called "logits"). Figure 27.3, therefore, is analogous to Fig. 27.1.

If (27.4) is solved for P_i, the result is shown in Fig. 27.4. Note that in Fig. 27.3 when the response is in logit units, the two response functions are linear and parallel. But when in Fig. 27.4 the response is in probability units, the two response functions are neither linear nor parallel. This is not a problem as long as, consistent with (27.4), the estimated treatment effect is reported in logit units or as an odds multiplier. If stakeholders want the story told in probability unit, however, the complications introduced by nonparallel response functions reappears. The good news is that there is no identification problem. The bad news is that the average treatment effect depends on the value of the assignment variable. In addition, any regression diagnostics should be applied to the log-odds form of the model as well. In the logit metric, there are many graphical diagnostic procedures for logistic regression. Again, a good reference is Cook and Weisberg (1999).

Berk and de Leeuw (1999) provide an instructive application. In their study, the outcome was misconduct in prison. Misconduct could include minor but common infractions such as failing to report for a work assignment or rare but serious infractions that would be felonies if committed on the outside. The assignment covariate was a risk score computed at intake for each inmate. The intervention was the highest level security placement with the alternative any lower placement. Placement was determined by a threshold on the risk score; scoring about the threshold led to a high security placement. The empirical question was whether a high security placement reduced prison misconduct. It did, but not dramatically.

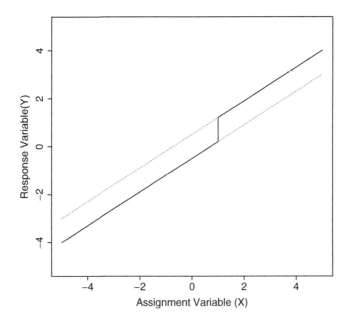

FIGURE 27.3. The log odds representation of the logistic case.

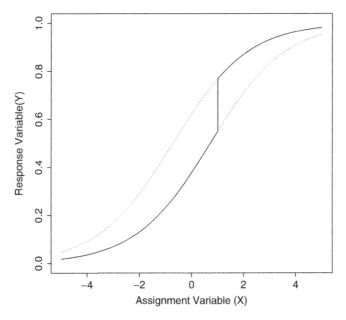

FIGURE 27.4. The generalized linear case.

Analogous issue arise if the response variable is a count. The canonical mean function is not the log of the odds, but the natural logarithm of the count. The generalized RD design still applies and can easily be employed.

MATCHING STRATEGIES

From the issues just discussed, it should be clear that the credibility of the basic and generalized RD design depends on the assumptions one makes about the two response functions linking X to Y. Both designs respond to the same fundamental problem: the observed responses of the group exposed to the treatment and the observed responses of the group exposed to the alternative reside in disjoint regions of the assignment variable. There are no values of X at which one can observe responses for both groups. Therefore, all comparisons necessarily depend on extrapolations, which in turn, depend on the functional forms assumed.

An alternative strategy is to focus on the observed responses on either side of the threshold and very close to it. If this region, often called a "window," is sufficiently narrow, the values of X within it are likely to be very similar. Because Y is a function of X, this suggests a matching strategy comparing the average observed response of the units just to the right of the threshold to the average observed response of the units just to the left of the threshold. The difference between the two averages can serve as an estimate of the average treatment effect. The same rationale applies if the response variable is categorical and one is comparing proportions.

An important assumption is that the small piece of the response function just to the right of the threshold and the small piece of the response function just to the left of the threshold are linear and parallel to each other. To the degree that this assumption is violated, the size of the possible bias increases. For example, if both are linear and parallel but with a positive or negative slope, the absolute value of the difference between the two averages will be larger than the absolute value of the gap size at the threshold.[2] The hope is that if the window can be made sufficiently narrow, this bias will be negligible. Ideally, therefore, the matching strategy can provide useful estimates of average treatment effects with far less reliance on assumed functional forms over the entire length of the response functions.

Figure 27.5 illustrates the general idea. The two response functions are neither linear nor parallel. And these would likely be unknown in any case. If within the shaded region the two functions were linear and flat, the difference between the two averages would be the same as the treatment effect at the threshold. In this illustration, the estimated treatment effect would be a bit too large. The gap would have been larger then had the two functions been linear and flat.

It follows that a critical feature of the window approach is the width of the shaded area (Imbens and Kalyanaraman 2009). How wide should the shaded area be? If the shaded area is more narrow, the true causal effect often can be better approximated. But, there will be fewer observations with which to estimate the average treatment effect. With less information, there will be more uncertainty in the estimate. The tension is an example of the well-known bias-variance tradeoff (Hastie and Tibshirani 1990, 40–42). To consider the implications of this tradeoff, we turn to the way one can estimate the average treatment effect. In this context, the terms "bandwidth" or "span" are sometimes used instead of the term "window."

Perhaps, the simplest estimator of the average treatment effect within the window is the difference between the mean of the responses to the right of the threshold and mean of the responses to the left of the threshold (Imbens and Lemieux 2008b, 623–624). Sometimes, a better approach is to use an explicit kernal function (Hastie and Tibshirani 1990, 18–19), the

---

[2] One can construct special cases in which the assumptions are violated, and there is no bias. But in practice, such scenarios would be extremely rare.

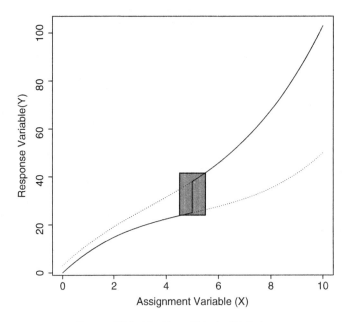

FIGURE 27.5. Matching within the RD design.

impact of which can be to weight observations so that those closer to the threshold are given more weight when the means are computed. Values of Y closer to the threshold will often provide more accurate information about the value of Y at the threshold.

Different weighting schemes can be used. For example, when a linear kernel is used, weights decline linearly with distance from the threshold. When a Gaussian kernel is used, the weights decline as a function of the normal distribution centered on the threshold. In practice, all of the common weighting functions that decline with distance from the threshold usually give very similar results. In fact, there is often not much difference between the estimated treatment effect using any of the common weighting functions and the estimated treatment effect using no weighting at all (i.e., all cases get the same weight).

In contrast, the size of the window can have a dramatic effect. Therefore, a criterion is needed that strikes a useful balance between the bias and the variance. One popular criterion when the response variable is quantitative is the mean squared error: the mean of the squared disparities between the fitted values $\hat{Y}_i$ and the observed values of Y_i. If a window size can be chosen to minimize the mean squared error, the sum of the variance and the bias squared will be minimized as well (Hastie et al. 2009, Sect. 7.7). In this sense, minimizing the mean squared error provides a good way to define an appropriate balance between the variance and the bias.

Several procedures can be used as an operational stand-in for the theoretical mean squared error. Cross-validation is a useful option and with modern computers, the calculations can be done very quickly. Other options include the generalized cross-validation statistic, AIC, BIC, and Mallows Cp. Imbens and Kalyanaraman (2009) provide a very interesting advance on this theme. In practice, each of these approaches usually will lead to the same results, and many work well if the response variable is a count or is categorical. An excellent discussion of the underlying issues can be found in the book by Hastie and his colleagues (2009, Chap. 7).

The comparison between means within the window can be generalized. Suppose that within the window the two unknown response functions are linear, but not necessarily flat or even and parallel. Then, one can often obtain a more accurate estimate of the treatment effect by employing two linear regressions within the window, one on each side of the threshold (Imbens and Lemieux 2008, 624–625). Each is a form of local linear regression. The sole regressor is the distance from the threshold. More specifically, we assume that

$$Y_{iL} = \delta_{0,L} + \delta_{1,L}(X_{iL} - T) + \varepsilon_{iL}, \qquad (27.5)$$

and

$$Y_{iR} = \delta_{0,R} + \delta_{1,R}(X_{iR} - T) + \varepsilon_{iR}, \qquad (27.6)$$

where within the window, L denotes the left side of the threshold, R denotes the right side of the threshold, T is the value of X at the threshold, X_i is the value of X for given observations, and ε_{iL} and ε_{iR} are conventional regression disturbances. Because $\delta_{1,L} \neq \delta_{1,R}$, the linear response functions do not have the same slope.

At the threshold, $(X_i - T) = 0$. Therefore, the average treatment effect at the threshold is $\delta_{0,R} - \delta_{0,L}$. With data for Y and X, one can estimate the values of the parameters from both equations and obtain an estimate of the treatment effect at the threshold by computing the difference between the two intercepts. That is, the estimate of the average treatment effect is $\hat{\delta}_{1,L} - \hat{\delta}_{1,R}$. The same logic can apply for the entire generalized linear model although some of the details will necessarily differ.

Although (27.5) and (27.6) have much the same structure as (27.2), their purpose is rather different. The goal is to estimate the difference between the response functions at the threshold. Therefore, despite the use of regression, the matching logic still prevails. If the regression model is approximately correct, there should be gains by the mean squared error criterion. In addition, the usual statistical inference undertaken with linear regression can apply although sometimes robust standard errors are desirable (Cameron and Trivedi 2005, Sect. 4.4.5).

In principle, the regression estimate can be improved upon in two ways. First, one can employ a kernel weighting scheme so that when the regression coefficients are estimated, observations closer to the threshold are given greater weight. In practice, the mean squared error gains are usually modest at best. Second, one can assume that $\hat{\delta}_{1,L} = \hat{\delta}_{1,R}$ and re-estimate the values of $\hat{\delta}_{0,L}$ and $\hat{\delta}_{0,R}$. In other words, one proceeds as if the two linear response functions are parallel. There can be small but noticeable gains by the mean squared error criterion if the equivalence is approximately true. Once again, regression diagnostics can be very instructive.

There can be substantial bias in the estimated average treatment effect at the threshold if regression diagnostics indicate that the response functions are not linear. One possible remedy is to replace the local linear regression with local polynomial regression (Fan and Gijbels 1996) or an even more flexible smoother such as found in the generalized additive model (Hastie and Tibshirani 1990). But, the moment one opens the door to nonparametric regression, there may be no longer a need to stay within the window, and a wide variety of tools are in play. Regression splines and regression smoothers, for instance, can be very effective (Berk 2008a, Chap. 2; Bowman et al. 2004). The task at hand can be reformulated as function estimation problem, with the amount of smoothing replacing the size of the window as a key matter for tuning. The result can be

$$Y_i = \beta_0 + \beta_1 W_i + f(X_i - T) + \varepsilon_i, \qquad (27.7)$$

where $f(X_i - T)$ is determined empirically. Equation (27.7) is easily extended to the generalized linear model so that binary and count response variables can be analyzed.

One interesting feature of (27.7) is that if the fitting procedure for $f(X_i - T)$ is made sufficiently flexible, there may be no need to include W_i as a regressor. Should there be an important change in the response function in the neighborhood of the threshold, the nonparametric regression procedure is likely to find it. The size of the neighborhood will be determined as well. At the very least, this suggests first using a very flexible nonparametric regression procedure as an exploratory technique to help in the specification of (27.7). The risk is that statistical inference can be invalidated (Leeb and Pötscher 2006; Berk et al. 2009) and that any findings may be the result of overfitting. Neither problem is unique to the analysis of RD designs, however.

SOME EXTENSIONS NOT ADDRESSED

The RD design may be extended further, but space limitation preclude more than a very brief discussion. One easy and direct extension is to have a deterministic assignment rule constructed from more than one covariate. If there are two such covariates, for example, the threshold is a line not a point. The various estimation procedures can be altered accordingly. Likewise, it is relatively easy to have a proper RD design with more than one intervention, much in the spirit of factorial designs in true experiments.

A more complicated extension addresses the problem of compliance. Just as in randomized experiments, study subjects do not always comply with the treatment or alternative condition assigned. Then, one might be interested in trying to estimate the impact of the intervention assigned (i.e., an "intention-to-treat" analysis) or the impact of the intervention received. The former can be estimated with the procedures we have described. The latter requires more complicated and fragile procedures. A possible approach is using the treatment assigned, conditional on the assignment variable, as an instrumental variable. These and other alternatives are discussed by Imbens and Lemieux (2008b).

EXTERNAL VALIDITY

The results from an RD design raise the same external validity issues as those from a randomized experiment and more. If the study subjects are probability sample from a well-defined population, generalizations to that population can be appropriate. If the study subjects are not selected by probability sampling, generalizations beyond the study subjects must rely on theory or replications. However, any estimates using the matching approach can restrict generalizations further. The relevant units are now only those that fall in the window or for some procedures, only at the threshold. For data that are a proper probability sample, generalizations can now only be to elements in the population that would fall within the window or at the threshold, respectively. When the data are not a proper probability sample, generalizations based on theory or replications must also take these restrictions into account.

In short, the basic and generalized RD design has the same kinds of external validity constraints as randomized experiments. The external validity constraints can be far more binding if a matching estimation approach is used. The tradeoff is that the matching approach's internal validity may be stronger.

POWER

To the degree that the assignment variable is correlated with the treatment indicator there is, other things equal, a reduction in statistical power. However, other things are not always equal. A possible compensating factor is the strength of the association between the assignment variable and the response. With a larger correlation, there can be an increase in power. It is in practice difficult to determine before the data are collected how strong these two correlations will be. Consequently, conventional power analyses risk being driven very substantially by assumptions that may well prove wrong. The problems are even more serious if one attempts a post hoc power analysis after average treatment effects have been estimated. As a formal matter, post hoc power analyses are difficult to justify (Hoenig and Heisey 2001) and probably should not be taken seriously.

The safest strategy is work with large samples whenever that is possible (e.g., samples of 500 or more). When the data come from existing data sets or administrative records, the costs of large samples may be no more than the costs of small samples.

AN ILLUSTRATION

We turn now to an illustration. The intent is to provide an overview of how some of the procedures described earlier can be used in practice. Space limitation preclude an in-depth discussion using several different data sets with varying properties.

A good way to begin the analysis of data from any RD design is to examine a scatterplot of the response variable against the assignment variable. Figure 27.6 is just such a plot for some fictitious data. There are 1,000 observations. The true relationship between X and Y is a fourth degree polynomial. This implies that the relationship on either side of the threshold between the response and the assignment variable is the same. Also by construction, the threshold is at 0.0, and the treatment effect equals 10.0. It is readily apparent that there is a discontinuity at the threshold. For real data, evidence of a treatment effect is usually not so easily discovered.

One would normally not know that the relationship between X and Y was a fourth degree polynomial. But it would likely be empirically apparent that the two response functions were approximately linear and flat over much the range of X, at least where there are data. Except for a few observations at the tails, two linear parallel response functions might seem to be a sufficiently good approximation for the RD analysis.

Table 27.1 shows some results. Its four columns contain in order the kind of estimator, the average treatment effect estimate, the standard error and the proportion of the deviance that is accounted for by the estimator.[3] The proper results would be in the first row if the correct relationship between X and Y were known. This is the estimation gold standard. The estimated treatment effect is 10.4, the standard error is 0.37 and about 83% of the deviance is accounted for. The estimate is about one standard error from the truth of 10.0. One would not reject the null hypothesis that the treatment effect is 10.0.[4]

---

[3] Fit quality was evaluated using the AIC, but the adjusted proportion of deviance accounted for by the model is reported for ease of exposition.

[4] The treatment effect estimate is not exactly 10.0 because of random sampling error.

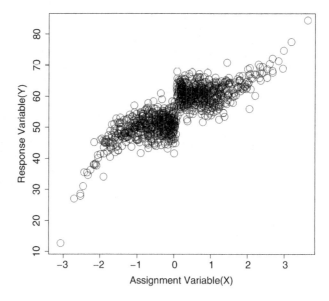

FIGURE 27.6. A scatter plot for some fictitious data ($N = 1,000$).

TABLE 27.1. Estimates of the RD average treatment effect for fictitious data – true treatment effect = 10.0

Model	Estimate	SE	Fit
Correct model	10.4	0.37	0.83
Linear model	6.3	0.37	0.74
Difference in means ($N = 400$)	9.8	0.31	0.72
Regression splines ($k = 3$)	6.16	0.37	0.75
Regression splines ($k = 5$)	11.8	0.43	0.82
Regression splines ($k = 7$)	9.97	0.51	0.83

The second row contains the results if the basic RD design is assumed and the linear model is applied. The estimate of the average treatment effect is now 6.3, a reduction of about a third. The standard error has not changed (up to two decimal places), but the fit drops from 0.83 to 0.74. In this case, if after looking at the scatterplot, a researcher decided that the linear model was good enough, the results would not be grievously wrong. The linear fit is not terribly far from the ideal fit: 0.83 vs. 0.74 (although the ideal fit would not be known) because where most of the data are, the linear model is about right. Whether the size of the treatment effect underestimate is large enough to matter would depend on context. In many policy settings, underestimating an average treatment effect by a third can transform a cost-effective intervention into one that is not cost-effective.

The third row shows the results for the difference between means in the region immediately on either side of threshold. The region was defined by the X between -1 and 1. Four hundred observations are contained between these two boundaries. The estimated average treatment effect is 9.8, the standard error is 0.31 and about 72% of the deviance for the 400 observations is accounted for. The reduction in the standard error despite the smaller sample size results from a substantial decrease in the variance of the response variable once the more extreme values of X are trimmed. Similar improvements in fit may or may not be found for other data.

Overall, these are all very good results. A key reason is that within the window, the response functions are close to linear and flat. A close look at Fig. 27.6, makes this clear. Enlarging or shrinking the region by as much as 25% does not materially change the results. Had the relationship not been approximately flat, a very different causal effect estimate could have resulted.

Rows four through six contain the results for a particular form of nonparametric regression: regression splines. In effect, the procedure seeks to fit the response function inductively (Berk 2008a, Chap. 2). A single functional form with a possible offset is assumed, just as in (27.7). And the entire dataset is used.

A key tuning parameter determines the amount of smoothing. Here, that tuning parameter is the number of "knots" (k). The larger the number of knots, the more flexible the fitting function, and the less smooth the fitted values will be. Results when $k = 3$, suggest that the fitted values are not flexible enough. The story is about the same as for the linear model. When $k = 5$, the fit improves dramatically, but the estimated average treatment effect is a bit too large. When $k = 7$, the fit of the fourth degree polynomial is improved a bit more, and the estimated average treatment effect is almost perfect. Also, the quality of the fit is virtually the same as for the gold standard in the first row.

From the sequence of results, there are several lessons. To begin, the key to obtain the useful estimates of the average treatment effect is to first arrive at good approximation of the relationship between X and Y. To this end, no single method dominates over the variety of scatterplot patterns one is likely to find in practice. In this illustration, all of the estimates obtained were positive, some very close to the truth. In each case, one would easily reject the null hypothesis that the average treatment effect is zero.

With real data, it will often make sense to proceed in the following steps.

1. Construct and examine a scatterplot of Y against X. The goal is to obtain some initial hunches about how Y is related to X and whether there may be a discontinuity at the threshold.

2. Apply the difference in means estimator with several different window sizes. A key factor will be the number of observations within the window. If there are too few, estimated average treatment effect will be very unstable. But enlarging the window may introduce additional bias. One can use a goodness-of-fit measure such as the generalized cross-validation statistic to help determine the best window size. But new proposals have been appearing with some regularity (e.g., Imbens and Kalyanaraman 2009). The goal is to obtain an instructive initial sense of what impact the intervention may be having.

3. Apply a smoother such as lowess or regression splines to the data ignoring the W. Set the tuning parameters so that a very flexible fitting function is applied and then try several different values of these tuning parameters. An overlay of the fitted values on the scatter plot will help to reveal how Y is related to X and what sharp shifts up or down may be apparent for different values of X. Ideally, there will be only one, and it will be located at the threshold. If there are large discontinuities elsewhere, it may lead to suspicions about the one found at the threshold.

4. Apply a form of nonparametric regression with X and W as predictors. Vary the tuning parameters and use a measure like the cross-validation statistic to pick the best model. If the number of observations is relatively large, any of the common fit measures will likely lead you to the same models. In addition, examine the usual regression diagnostics to provide additional information about model quality. It will

often turn out that two or three models are about equally good. Then, the results for all three should be reported. For example, the last two estimates in Table 27.1 are reasonable.

Given all of the data "snooping," p-values will likely be biased downward. False power will result. It can make sense, therefore, to discount p-values by the Bonferroni method (Westfall and Young 1993, Sect. 2.3.1). For example, the 0.05 level might be represented by a probability 0.005. However, the problems are actually much deeper (Leeb and Pötscher 2006; Berk 2008b), and it can be useful to randomly partition the data into a training dataset and a test dataset (Berk et al. 2009). All of the model building is done with the training dataset. At the end, the model is evaluated with the test dataset. A useful discussion of how to use training data and test data can be found in Hastie et al. (2009, 219–223). If the sample is too small to effectively partition, the best advice may be to interpret any tests judiciously and require that large and substantively sensible treatment effect estimates materialize in addition to "statistical significance."

CONCLUSIONS

When the RD design can be implemented properly, it has the same capacity as randomized experiments to obtain unbiased estimates of the average treatment effect. Why then has it not been more widely used? Perhaps, the most important reason is that researchers have too often failed to appreciate that a wide variety of social interventions are delivered conditional on some explicit and deterministic rule. Another reason may be that because of the correlation between X and W, the RD design can sometimes deliver less precise estimates than randomized experiments with the same number of subjects. However, another factor is the relationship between the response and the assignment variable, which in some circumstances may be strong enough to effectively compensate. Moreover, when an RD design is built into the way one or more social interventions are delivered, it is often easy to obtain a very large sample at little additional expense. The bulk of the costs associated with data collection are born by the organization that is responsible for the intervention. In short, the RD design can be a very useful tool that should be far more widely exploited in crime and justice settings.

Acknowledgments Work on this paper was funded by a grant from the National Science Foundation: SES-0437169, "Ensemble methods for Data Analysis in the Behavioral, Social and Economic Sciences."

REFERENCES

Berk RA (2008a) Statistical learning from a regression perspective. Springer, New York

Berk RA (2008b) Forecasting methods in crime and justice. In: Hagan J, Schepple KL, Tyler TR (eds) Annual review of law and social science. Annual reviews, Palo Alto

Berk RA, de Leeuw J (1999) An evaluation of California's inmate classification system using a generalized regression discontinuity design. J Am Stat Assoc 94(448):1045–1052

Berk RA, Rauma D (1983) Capitalizing on nonrandom assignment to treatments: a regression discontinuity evaluation of a crime control program. J Am Stat Assoc 78(381):21–27

Berk RA, Brown L, Zhao L (2009) Statistical inference after model selection. Journal of Quantitative Criminology, forthcoming, University of Pennsylvania, Department of Statistics, Working Paper (under review)

Berk RA, Barnes G, Ahlman L, Kurtz E (2010) When second best is good enough: a comparison between a true experiment and a regression discontinuity quasiexperiment. University of Pennsylvania, Department of Statistics. Working Paper

Bowman AW, Pope R, Ismail B (2004) Detecting discontinuities in nonparametric regression curves and surfaces. Stat Comput 16:377–390

Cameron AC, Trivedi PK (2005) Microeconometrics: methods and applications. Cambridge University Press, Cambridge

Campbell DT, Stanley JC (1963) Experimental and quasi-experimental designs for research. Houghton Miffin, Boston

Chen MK, Shapiro JM (2007) Do harsher prison conditions reduce recidivism? A discontinuity-based approach. Am Law Econ Rev 9(1):1–29

Cook TD (2008) 'Waiting for life to arrive:' A history of the regression-discontinuity design in psychology, statistics, and economics. J Econom 142:636–654

Cook RD, Weisberg S (1999) Applied regression analysis including computing and graphics. Wiley, New York

Fan J, Gijbels I (1996) Local polynomial regression modeling and its applications. Chapman & Hall, London

Freedman DA (2008) Diagnostics cannot have much power against general alternatives. http://www.stat.berkeley.edu/ freedman/

Goldberger AS (1972) Selection bias in evaluating treatment effects: some formal illustrations. Madison, WI. Unpublished manuscript

Hastie TJ, Tibshirani RJ (1990) Generalized additive models. Chapman and Hall, New York

Hastie TJ, Tibshirani R, Friedman J (2009) The elements of statistical learning, 2nd edn. Springer, New York

Holland P (1986) Statistics and causal inference. J Am Stat Assoc 8:945–960

Hoenig JM, Heisey DM (2001) The abuse of power: the pervasive fallacy of power calculation for data analysis. Am Stat 55:19–24

Imbens G, Kalyanaraman K (2009) Optimal bandwidth choice for the regression discontinuity estimator. Harvard University, Department of Economics, Working Paper

Imbens G, Lemieux T (2008a) Special issue editors' introduction: The regression discontinuity design – theory and applications. J Econom 142:615–635

Imbens G, Lemieux T (2008b) Regression discontinuity designs: a guide to practice. J Econom 142:611–614

Lee DS, Lemieux T (2009) Regression discontinuity designs in economics. National Bureau of Economic Research: working paper #14723

Leeb H, Pötscher BM (2006) Can one estimate the conditional distribution of post-model-selection estimators? Ann Stat 34(5):2554–2591

Neyman J (1923) Sur Les Applications de la Thorie des Probabilits aux Experiences Agricoles: Essai des Principes. Roczniki Nauk Rolniczych10:151. In Polish

Rubin D (1974) Estimating causal effects of treatments in randomized and nonrandomized studies. J Educ Psychol 66:688–701

Thistlewaite DL, Campbell DT (1960) Regression-discontinuity analysis: an alternative to the ex-post facto design. J Educ Psychol 51:309–317

Trochim WMK (1984) Research design for program evaluation. Sage Publications, Beverly Hills

Trochim WMK (2001) Regression discontinuity design. In: Smelser NJ, Bates PB (eds) International encyclopedia of the social and behavioral sciences, vol 19. 12940–12945, Elsevier, New York

Westfall PH, Young SS (1993) Resampling based multiple testing. Wiley, New York

Testing Theories of Criminal Decision Making: Some Empirical Questions about Hypothetical Scenarios

M. LYN EXUM AND JEFFREY A. BOUFFARD

Elsewhere, we have argued that empirical tests of deterrence/rational choice theory should recognize the physiological and psychological conditions in which criminal decision making commonly occurs (Assaad and Exum 2002; Bouffard 2002a, 2002b; Bouffard et al. 2000; Exum 2002). For example, periods of "hot" emotional states may undermine "cold" deliberative processes by making the actor more present-oriented and inwardly focused. Similarly, psychopharmacological agents such as alcohol may short-circuit otherwise rational thought by disrupting the ability to problem-solve and assess risk. Although offending commonly occurs during these hot and altered states-of-mind, empirical tests of criminal decision making are largely based on data from participants in more cool, clear-headed conditions. This, in turn, raises questions about the generalizability of the studies' findings.

Such concerns notwithstanding, in this chapter we critically examine a commonly used method to collect decision making data: the hypothetical scenario method (HSM). We begin by discussing the evolution of the HSM, and then identify two potential criticisms of the technique. First, we consider whether self-reported intentions to offend are valid proxies for real-world criminal behavior. Second, we explore the possibility that researchers are inadvertently influencing perceptions of the costs and benefits of crime by providing participants with a pre-determined list of consequences to consider. We assess the merits of each criticism based on findings from both existing research as well as original datasets collected with these two concerns in mind. Finally, we offer recommendations for future research on criminal decision making.

A.R. Piquero and D. Weisburd (eds.), *Handbook of Quantitative Criminology*,
DOI 10.1007/978-0-387-77650-7_28, © Springer Science + Business Media, LLC 2010,
First softcover printing 2011

DECISION MAKING THEORIES AND THE DEVELOPMENT
OF THE HSM

In criminology, deterrence and rational choice theories are the principal frameworks for examining criminal decision making. These theories assert that human beings freely choose whether to engage in crime after considering the consequences of the act. To empirically test this assertion, measures of the formal costs of crime (deterrence theory) or the formal/informal costs and benefits of crime (rational choice theory) are used to predict offending behavior. Initial tests of deterrence theory examined "objective deterrence" by comparing aggregate-level indicators of punishment to aggregate crime rates (e.g., Tittle 1969; Chiricos and Waldo 1970; Logan 1972). In response, some scholars (e.g., Gibbs 1975) argued that the decision to offend is not based on the objective reality of punishment but is instead shaped by the individual's *perceptions* of its certainty and severity. This contention prompted research on "perceptual deterrence" in which individuals' subjective estimates of punishment are used to predict their involvement in crime.

Tests of perceptual deterrence have often utilized cross-sectional surveys. In these studies, participants' perceptions of the punishment are used to predict (prior) self-reported offending (Erickson et al. 1977; Paternoster 1987). To avoid the problems of temporal ordering incumbent with such methods, other studies have used panel designs to determine the impact of current perceptions of consequences on future criminal activities (Saltzman 1982). Yet, despite this methodological advantage, longitudinal studies are nonetheless limited in that they do not easily permit researchers to capture participants' perceptions of punishments *at the moment* they engage in the decision making process. Instead, perceived consequences are recorded at only the baseline and follow-up periods, which commonly have 12–24 month intervals.

To better study participants' thought processes at the moment they decide to engage in (or refrain from) crime, researchers began asking hypothetical offending questions, such as "Would you intentionally inflict physical injury on another person?" (e.g., Grasmick and Bursik 1990; Grasmick and Green 1980). Participants' responses to these questions were then treated as proxies for behavior. Still, other scholars argued that such simple hypothetical questions failed to import adequate context for the decision maker (Klepper and Nagin 1989b). In other words, measurement error may be introduced if different respondents infer unique circumstances surrounding the hypothetical offense they are asked to contemplate, such as the relationship with the victim, the location of the assault, the availability of a weapon, and so forth. In response, Klepper and Nagin (1989b) suggested that detailed hypothetical *scenarios* be provided to respondents to improve the reliability of participants' responses. This, in turn, has given rise to the use of the hypothetical scenario method.

In a typical HSM study, the researcher presents participants with a vignette describing a hypothetical offense and asks participants to indicate their likelihood of engaging in the behavior. Participants are also queried about their perceptions of the certainty and severity of a set of potential consequences of interest to the researcher (e.g., Klepper and Nagin 1989b), which are then used to predict the participants' self-reported likelihood of offending. In some HSM studies, the researcher manipulates (often experimentally) various circumstances that are presented to the respondent within the scenario itself (e.g., Paternoster and Simpson 1996). For instance, two versions of the offending scenario may be offered to randomly assigned participants, one suggesting that the probability of punishment is low, while the other suggesting that the probability is high. Self-reported offending probabilities are compared across these conditions to determine how the certainty/severity of punishment influences offending.

EMPIRICAL SUPPORT GENERATED FROM THE HSM

Over the past two decades, more than 30 published studies of illegal/imprudent decision making have used the HSM. The technique has been used to investigate such behaviors as academic cheating (Tibbetts 1999), drunk driving (Bouffard 2007), physical assault (Exum 2002), sexual assault (Bachman et al. 1992), and white collar crime (Piquero et al. 2005). Generally speaking, such studies find that offenders are dissuaded/persuaded to offend on the basis of their subjective assessments of the costs/benefits of crime.

Three consequences have been frequently shown to have significant deterrent effects: *formal legal sanctions* (Bachman et al. 1992; Higgins et al. 2005; Klepper and Nagin 1989b; Nagin and Pogarsky 2001; Paternoster and Simpson 1996; Pogarsky 2002; Pogarsky and Piquero 2004; Strelan and Boeckmann 2006), *feelings of immorality* (Bachman et al. 1992, Carmichael and Piquero 2004; Exum 2002; Nagin and Paternoster 1994; Paternoster and Simpson 1996; Piquero and Tibbetts 1996; Strelan and Boeckmann 2006; Tibbetts 1999; Tibbetts and Herz 1996; Tibbetts and Myers 1999), and *negative emotional states* (Higgins et al. 2005; Nagin and Paternoster 1993; Piquero and Tibbetts 1996; Tibbetts 1999; Tibbetts and Herz 1996; Tibbetts and Myers 1999; Wolfe et al. 2007). Other informal sanctions – such as family, peer, school and/or professional problems – have also been found to have significant deterrent effects when examined individually (Bachman et al. 1992; Higgins et al. 2005) or as part of a global measure of informal costs (Carmichael and Piquero 2004; Loewenstein et al. 1997; Nagin and Paternoster 1993; 1994; Paternoster and Simpson 1996; Pogarsky and Piquero 2004). Regarding the benefits of crime, both perceived fun/thrill (Carmichael and Piquero 2004; Loewenstein et al. 1997; Nagin and Paternoster 1993; 1994; Paternoster and Simpson 1996; Piquero and Tibbetts 1996; Tibbetts 1999; Tibbetts and Myers 1999), and the utility of the criminal act (Exum 2002; Nagin and Paternoster 1993; Paternoster and Simpson 1996) have been found to increase the probability of offending. Thus, based on the wealth of HSM studies published to date, considerable evidence supports the basic assumptions of deterrence and rational choice theory.

CRITICISMS OF THE HSM

Despite the methodological advantages of the HSM and the empirical support it has generated for deterrence/rational choice theory, this line of research is subject to various criticisms. For example (and as noted earlier), most HSM studies of decision making do not consider the impact of hot and altered states-of-mind. Additionally, there is some concern regarding how well the samples typically used in HSM studies (university students) represent the population of offenders or even the general population as a whole (see Decker et al. 1993, and Bouffard et al. 2008 for some exceptions). In this chapter, however, we focus on two additional criticisms: one concerning the HSM's dependent variable and another concerning its independent variables. First, we examine whether self-reported "intentions to offend" are valid indicators of future behavior. Next, we examine whether the implementation of the HSM imposes too much artificial structure on the decision process, thereby biasing what we know about the decision to offend.

CRITICISM #1: ARE INTENTIONS TO OFFEND PROXIES FOR ACTUAL CRIMINAL BEHAVIOR?

Recall that the dependent variable in HSM studies is not actual behavior but is instead the self-reported intent to behave. The practice of using intentions as proxies for real-world behavior is grounded in the theory of reasoned action (Ajzen and Fishbein 1980; Fishbein and Ajzen 1975), and through its subsequent elaboration, the theory of planned behavior (Ajzen 1991). Both theories were developed to predict and explain human behavior. Both theories assume that human beings are rational and make behavioral decisions on the basis of the information that is available. Both theories assume that the results of hypothetical decisions would be similar to the results of real-world situations, so long as the circumstances surrounding each decision are similar. Finally, both theories emphasize the role of behavioral "intention" (see Fig. 28.1), which is an indicator of how much energy and effort individuals are willing to exhaust in the pursuit of the behavior (Ajzen 1991).

Predicting human behavior with these theories is reportedly very easy, because "...barring unforeseen events, a person will usually act in accordance with his or her intention" (Ajzen and Fishbein 1980: 5). Thus, the most effective way to forecast future behavior is to ask individuals their subjective probability of performing the act. *Explaining* human behavior is far more difficult and, however, requires an understanding of the factors that influence

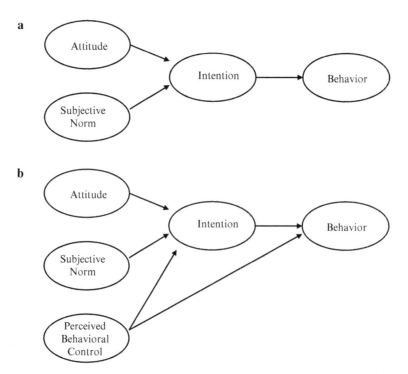

FIGURE 28.1. The theory of reasoned action (**a**), and the Theory of Planned Behavior (**b**). Figures A and B are based on the theoretical path models found elsewhere in Ajzen (1991), Ajzen and Fishbein (1980), Armitage and Conner (2001), Armitage et al., (1999), Beck and Ajzen (1991), Fishbein and Ajzen (1975), and Madden, Ellen and Ajzen (1992). For simplicity, additional exogenous variables, correlations among exogenous variables, and feedback loops are not shown.

intentions to perform. These factors include the person's attitude regarding behavior performance (either favorable or unfavorable), subjective norms, and – in the theory of planned behavior – perceived behavioral control (Ajzen 1991). An in-depth discussion of these theories is beyond the scope of this chapter. Instead, we focus on the ability of self-reported intentions to empirically predict actual behavior.

Although the theory of reasoned action and the theory of planned behavior both assert there is a strong, positive correlation between intentions (I) and behaviors (B), both theories also recognize that additional factors can influence the magnitude of this IB relationship. For example, the degree to which intentions and behaviors correspond in their "levels of specificity" will influence the correlation between the two (Fishbein and Ajzen 1975: 369). Stated more simply, if you want to predict if a person will run on the treadmill at the gym tomorrow morning at 10:00 AM, you should ask them "How likely are you to run on the treadmill at the gym tomorrow morning at 10:00 AM?" rather than "How likely are you to exercise?."

Additionally, the magnitude of the IB correlation is dependent upon the stability of the intention (Fishben and Ajzen 1975). If intentions change between the time they were measured and when behaviors are recorded, the IB correlation will naturally be impacted. Furthermore, the IB correlation is influenced by the actor's volitional control over the act (see Ajzen 1991). If an actor lacks the ability to complete the behavior or must rely upon the cooperation of others to successfully complete the task, the IB relationship may begin to breakdown. From a statistical standpoint, even the base rate of the predicted behavior can also influence the IB correlation. When the target behavior occurs extremely often or extremely infrequently, a few instances of incongruence between intentions and behavior can substantially weaken their statistical correlation. For behaviors with a more moderate base rate, however, occasional incongruence will have more negligible impacts (Fishbein and Ajzen 1975).

Despite the various methodological/statistical concerns that can plague the IB correlation, the relationship between the two remains quite strong (Ajzen 1988; Ajzen and Fishbein 1980; Armitage and Conner 2001; Sheppard et al. 1988). In a meta-analytic review of 87 studies examining the theory of reasoned action, the average IB correlation was 0.53 but had a 95% confidence interval ranging from 0.15 to 0.92 (Sheppard et al. 1988). Upon closer examination, IB correlations were found to be slightly higher when the measure of intention captured one's likelihood of *attempting* the behavior (e.g., trying to lose weight) rather than one's expectation of *accomplishing* the behavior (e.g., actually losing weight). Similarly, these correlations were slightly higher when the measure of behavior captured a specific *action* (e.g., taking diet pills) versus a specific *goal* (e.g., losing weight).

It is worth noting, however, that many of these IB correlations are based on studies examining conventional activities such as eating at a restaurant, voting, watching television, and going to church. When studying conventional behavior, participants generally have little reason to conceal their intentions to engage in the behavior or their actual involvement in the behavior. Yet, when the targeted behavior is imprudent/illegal, participants' level of social desirability may motivate them (consciously or unconsciously) to underreport their intentions and/or behaviors, thereby weakening the IB correlation.

To examine the role of social desirability on the IB relationship, Beck and Ajzen (1991) used the theory of planned behavior as the basis for studying three dishonest acts: cheating on a test/exam, shoplifting, and lying. During the baseline phase of the study, self-reported intentions to engage in these behaviors were collected from a sample of 146 college students. Approximately 6 months later, 34 participants completed a follow-up questionnaire and self-reported their dishonest acts. The IB correlations were 0.65, 0.48, and 0.30, respectively, and suggest little impact of social desirability. However, with such small sample sizes, these correlations are likely to be volatile and should be interpreted cautiously. In a similar study (with a larger sample size), Armitage et al. (1999) found the IB correlation for cannabis use to be 0.47. At first glance, this finding suggests that intentions can predict illegal behaviors at least reasonably well. However, rather than measuring cannabis use as a dichotomy (used vs. did not use), Armitage et al. provided participants with a seven-point Likert scale to rate statements such as "I used cannabis in the last week". The end result is an IB correlation that is fundamentally difficult to interpret.

In sum, while the extant research suggests at least a moderately strong IB relationship for *conventional* behaviors, much less is known about the accuracy of self-reported intentions to engage in *deviant* activities. To examine this issue further, we present findings from an original study that sought to compare participants' intentions to engage in music piracy with their actual attempts to download music files illegally (Exum et al. 2007).

STUDY #1

Sample, Materials and Procedure

A sample of 240 university students completed a survey addressing various aspects of digital technology usage. As part of the survey, all participants received a hypothetical scenario; however, unlike the vignettes used in traditional HSM studies, this study used a bogus newspaper article to describe a hypothetical offending opportunity (music piracy). Note that participants were led to believe the article was real and had recently appeared in the local newspaper. Pilot testing revealed that the article was seen as highly authentic.

The fictitious article described a (real) doctoral student in the university's Public Policy program (henceforth referred to as "John Doe," our research confederate), who is reportedly emailing illegal music files for free to anyone with an email account ending in ".edu." In the article, Doe acknowledges that distributing/downloading copyright protected files is illegal, but in an attempt to avoid punishment, he has raised a yet-to-be resolved legal challenge against the university's access to student e-mail accounts. Doe states that he will continue to distribute illegal files until a court finally orders him to stop. The article included Doe's email address as well as the date of the pending court case, which was reported to be approximately 2 months from the time of the study. This provided participants with an 8-week window of opportunity to contact Doe and request illegal files.

After reading the bogus newspaper article, participants were asked to complete a series of questions modeled after those commonly used in tests of rational choice theory, including one that asked participants to report their likelihood of contacting Doe and requesting illegal music files. Unbeknownst to participants (but with approval from the University's Institutional Review Board), the questionnaires contained hidden identifiers that could be used to identify the students by name. With these names in hand, participants' self-reported intentions to offend could be linked to any emails they sent to Doe. Approximately 4 weeks after the last surveys were administered, all participants were contacted again in order to be debriefed to the true nature of the study. (Note that no illegal music files were distributed as part of this study.)

TABLE 28.1. Self-reported intentions to offend, by all participants and current music downloaders only

Self-reported intention to offend	Total sample ($N = 240$)	Active downloaders ($N = 142$)
0–No chance	68.8%	64.1%
10	11.7%	14.1%
20	4.2%	5.6%
30	3.3%	2.8%
40	2.1%	2.1%
50	3.3%	3.5%
60	0.4%	0.0%
70	0.4%	0.7%
80	2.9%	3.5%
90	0.8%	1.4%
100–Definitely would	2.1%	2.1%
Mean value (SD)	11.21 (23.44)	12.68 (24.75)

Findings

Table 28.1 summarizes participants' self-reported intentions to offend. Results are shown for the entire sample ($n = 240$) and for those who indicated they downloaded music files on an on-going basis ($n = 142$). Regardless of the group, intentions to request pirated music from Doe are highly skewed, with approximately two-thirds of participants reporting "no chance." Among those expressing a nonzero probability of offending, most indicated that there was less than a 50% chance of requesting illegal files. Approximately, 8% of participants reported a greater than 50% change of offending, with five participants reporting they "definitely would" contact Doe.

The values in Table 28.1 summarize participants' intentions. In actuality, *none* of the participants emailed Doe to request music files. The absence of attempted music piracy does not appear to be (fully) attributable to the participants' skepticism over the authenticity of the newspaper article. As mentioned earlier, pilot testing suggested the article was highly believable. Additionally, one participant in the study found the article believable enough to email the investigators a complaint about Doe's blatant disrespect for the law. Finally, although none of the research participants contacted Doe to request illegal copies of music, Doe did receive one email request from a student who did not take part in the study. We can only speculate that this person learned about the newspaper article from a participant in the study.

Conclusion

Approximately 60% of the sample stated they would not contact Doe, and no one from that 60% actually did. At the same time, those participants who self-reported *some* likelihood of contacting Doe (any non-zero probability), those reporting a *strong*-likelihood (values greater than 50%) and even those who were *certain* they would contact Doe (value of 100%) also refrained. Collectively, these findings suggest that self-reported intentions to refrain from crime are more accurate predictors of behavior than are self-reported intentions to engage in crime. In other words, the self-reported intentions to offend have strong specificity (all negatives were true) but weak sensitivity (all positives were false). Given that the focus of HSM studies is on offending rather than abstention, the findings from the current study raise questions about how well self-reported intentions to offend approximate real-world deviance.

CRITICISM #2: ARE RESEARCHERS BIASING PARTICIPANTS' VIEWS OF CONSEQUENCES?

The rational choice perspective implicitly recognizes that decision making is both inherently natural and highly individualized. When faced with a criminal opportunity, potential offenders are presumed by their human nature to deduce a series of risks and rewards to contemplate (Bentham 1789/1970). Furthermore, these costs and benefits are assumed to vary from person-to-person in their number, kind and intensity (Bentham 1789/1970; Brezina 2002). However, in their attempts to model the hedonic calculus, rational choice scholars have generally allowed criminal decision making to be neither natural nor individualized.

When using the HSM, rational choice scholars have traditionally asked participants to consider a common set of consequences predetermined by the researcher (e.g., Paternoster and Simpson 1996; Pogarsky and Piquero 2004) rather than permitting participants to deduce their own set of personally relevant costs and benefits. Although participants are typically given the freedom to differentially rate the certainty and severity of these consequences, they generally have little-to-no opportunity to amend the list of costs and benefits to make them more personally-relevant (but see Wolfe et al. 2007). As a result, only those consequences provided by researchers are included in statistical models of decision making. There is evidence to suggest that forcing such artificial structure on the otherwise natural and individualized decision process impacts the research findings.

As early as the 1920s, researchers have known that the same question written in either open- or closed-ended format can produce vastly different results (Converse 1987). Perhaps, the most methodologically rigorous examples of studies comparing fixed choice (closed-ended) and free elicitation (open-ended) questions are the Schuman and Presser (1979) split-ballot experiments. Cross-sectional samples from Detroit and from the general US population were asked either open- or closed-ended questions about the job feature they valued most, the most important problem facing the country, and the quality that is most important for children to learn. Respectively, "importance of the work" (59.1%), "crime" (34.9%) and "thinking for themselves" (61.5%) were endorsed most often by participants completing closed-ended questions. In contrast, these same responses had endorsement rates of only 21.3%, 15.7%, and 4.6% (respectively) when the questions were left open-ended. Furthermore, the response sets for closed-ended questions commonly failed to include the opinions of a sizeable minority – or perhaps even the majority – of the sample. For example, among those completing the open-ended job quality question, 50.3% of the sample endorsed "novel" characteristics that did not correspond to any of the response options listed in the closed-ended question.

Thus, prior empirical research shows that survey results are influenced by the question format (e.g., open- versus closed-ended). This methodological artifact appears to stem from the distinct thought processes associated with each question type. From a cognitive standpoint, the difference between open- and closed-ended questions is a matter of recall versus recognition (respectively). Whereas recall techniques provide participants with an outlet for the responses that are most salient to them, recognition techniques tend to activate the participants' memory in order to determine the "best" response (Schwarz and Hippler 1991). In other words, closed-ended questions force participants to remember opinions they may had forgotten or thought too trivial to mention. This then has the effect of increasing participants' endorsements of opinions that are relatively inconsequential. In contrast, open-ended questions tend to capture the stronger opinions that are actively present in conscious thought (see also Schwarz and Oyserman 2001).

If open- versus closed-ended questions can produce vastly different results in the participants' endorsement rates, then does the typical HSM practice of providing participants with a predetermined set of costs and benefits (rather than allowing respondents to freely elicit their own) artificially inflate the empirical support for these specific consequences? There is indirect evidence from existing studies that suggest so. For example, Bouffard (2002a, 2007, Bouffard et al. 2008) presented participants with a hypothetical offending scenario and then asked them to freely elicit all the costs and benefits they might experience by engaging in the criminal act. Findings from this research reveal that many of the consequences commonly included in traditional HSM studies are mentioned infrequently during free elicitation. Furthermore, many consequences the participants did endorse are costs/benefits that traditional HSM studies have failed to present to participants.

Such research offers indirect evidence to suggest that findings obtained through HSM studies substantially differ from those obtained through the free elicitation technique (particularly in terms of the types of consequences which are deemed relevant to the decision when each technique is used). With some support for the notion that free elicitation may provide a more accurate assessment of the consequences that each individual actually considers, we now turn to a further examination of potential bias introduced when the traditional HSM is used. Specifically, we compared whether and to what extent the HSM and free elicitation methodologies produce differing results with respect to the endorsement of consequences and their ability to shape decision making.

STUDY #2

Sample, Materials and Procedure

A sample of 208 undergraduate students completed a self-report survey containing a hypothetical shoplifting scenario. After reading the scenario, participants were asked to rate their likelihood of taking some batteries without paying for them. The survey also included one of two different sets of questions designed to assess the perceived consequences associated with shoplifting. We refer to these two techniques as the "researcher-generated consequence" (RGC) and the "subject-generated consequence" (SGC) methods. Students were randomly assigned to receive one of these versions of the survey.

In the RGC method, the survey included a predetermined set of consequences for participants to assess. The list of RGCs was based on the types of costs and benefits traditionally included in prior rational choice research (e.g., Exum 2002; Loewenstein et al. 1997; Nagin and Pogarsky 2001; Piquero and Tibbetts 1996). They included seven negative outcomes associated with shoplifting: "Legal problems (such as getting arrested)," "Immorality (feeling that it is morally wrong to steal things)," "Emotional costs (such as you feel guilty or shame)," "Family Problems (such as your parents getting mad)," "Social Problems (such as your reputation is ruined)," "School Problems (such as being expelled)," and "Professional Problems (such as getting fired from a job)." Also included were four benefits: "Have fun or get a kind of 'sneaky thrill'," "Feeling good about myself (such as pride)," "Friends would think I was 'cool'," and "Have the batteries that I need" (i.e., a measure of the crime's utility). Participants rated their perceived certainty and severity of each consequence using a continuous 0- to 100-point scale.

In the SGC method, the survey did not provide participants with a set of traditionally-examined consequences, but instead presented a series of blank lines and the following instructions:

> Please fill in as many of the following blank lines as possible with a list of the negative ("bad") things that might happen to you if you took the batteries under the circumstances in the story.

A similar set of blank lines and instructions were included that asked participants to list "...the positive ('good') things that might happen to you if you took the batteries." After listing their self-generated costs and benefits, participants rated the certainty and severity of each consequence using the same 0–100 metric as in the RGC method. We then reviewed and coded the subject-generated costs and benefits into thematic groups that could be matched (where possible) to the traditionally-presented consequences used in the RGC method. This allowed us to compare the endorsement rates of identical consequences across the two experimental groups.

Findings

By design, SGC participants are asked to list only those consequences with a nonzero certainty value. We therefore examined whether the types and number of consequences listed by the SGC group differed from those endorsed by the RGC group. Note that "endorsed RGCs" are defined as those consequences that received a nonzero certainty rating by RGC participants. Table 28.2 summarizes the findings.

As seen in the table, the method through which costs and benefits are assessed greatly influences the type and number of consequences endorsed. With the exception of "legal problems," traditional costs and benefits were significantly more likely to be endorsed by the RGC group than the SGC group. For example, virtually all of RGC participants (99%) endorsed immorality, whereas only 2.9% of the SGC group did so. Furthermore, as shown at the bottom of the table, RGC participants endorsed an average of 6.18 (out of 7) traditional costs and 2.12 (out of 4) traditional benefits. In contrast, SGC participants endorsed just 1.88 and 0.78, respectively. These findings therefore indicate that when participants are given a set of consequences to evaluate, they are more likely to view these consequences as possible outcomes than when they are allowed to report their own set of relevant consequences.

Additional analyses (not shown) revealed that the certainty and severity of traditionally examined costs are perceived rather equivocally across RGC and SGC participants. However, certainty ratings for the four traditional benefits were typically (and significantly) higher among the SGC group. Thus, when SGC participants endorse a benefit they tend to do so with greater conviction. Similar results were found when comparing severity scores across experimental conditions. Finally, through a series of regression analyses we find greater support for the traditionally examined consequences when examining RGC participants. When data from SGC participants are analyzed, the traditional consequences matter very little. Instead, "novel" benefits identified by SGC participants (e.g., save money, save time, have the item, nobody is hurt) were the best overall predictors of offending intentions.

TABLE 28.2. Endorsement of traditional consequences, by experimental condition[a]

	RGC Group ($N = 105$)	SGC Group ($N = 103$)	
Traditional costs: percentage endorsing...			
Legal problems	95.2%	94.2%	
Immorality	99.0%	2.9%	***
Emotional costs	99.0%	52.4%	***
Family problems	93.3%	9.7%	***
Social problems	79.0%	24.3%	***
School problems	70.5%	1.0%	***
Professional problems	81.9%	3.9%	***
Traditional benefits: percentage endorsing...			
Fun/Sneaky thrill	63.8%	9.7%	***
Feeling good about self	30.5%	3.9%	***
Friends think I was cool	39.0%	3.9%	***
Have batteries	79.0%	60.2%	**
Mean (SD) number of endorsements among...			
Traditional costs (SD)	6.18 (1.33)	1.88 (0.89)	***
Traditional benefits (SD)	2.12 (1.43)	0.78 (0.67)	***

[a] Asterisks signify statistically significant differences in the rate of endorsement across experimental conditions.
* $p < 0.05$; ** $p < 0.01$; *** $p < 0.001$

Conclusion

This study's results do not question the fundamental assumptions of rational choice theory (that offending is rooted in hedonism and is related to anticipated pains and pleasures); however, they do question whether the traditional HSM accurately captures the number and types of pains and pleasures that matter, particularly as these relate to the factors included in statistical models of the hedonic calculus. Future research comparing the RGC and SGC method is needed in order to determine if our findings can be replicated among larger samples and using other offense types. In so doing, researchers will be better able to assess the nature of any methodological artifacts within the typical HSM procedures for testing rational choice theory. While these results await replication and extension to other offenses, and among larger and more diverse samples, we nevertheless believe our research begs for caution in the assessment of the extant rational choice literature. Quite simply, the factors we *think* influence criminal decision making may not be the factors that *actually* influence such decisions.

FUTURE DIRECTIONS

In his Sutherland Address to the American Society of Criminology, Nagin (2007) stated that much can be learned about the causes of crime through increased attention to the role of choice in criminological theorizing. Given the central role of choice as the foundation for the modern criminal justice system, Nagin argued that insufficient theoretical attention to the concept fosters an important disconnect between theory and practice. Finally, Nagin proposed that the benefits of increased attention to the notion of choice are there for the taking, if only a new generation of young researchers will "pick this low-hanging fruit" (p 262). We agree that our understanding of crime and crime-control policy will be greatly enhanced as more scholars consider the role of choice in offending. We also believe, however, that the techniques used to study decision making – especially the use of hypothetical scenarios – should be critically evaluated in order to better assess the validity of choice-based research.

The HSM has become one of the most common ways to assess criminal decision making. The technique has many advantages, including its ability to: (1) provide all participants with a common context in which to consider (hypothetical) offending, (2) avoid the type of mis-specified temporal order that plagues cross sectional studies, and (3) collect subjective perceptions of consequences concurrent with the decision to offend/abstain. Despite these advantages, important criticisms of the HSM remain. In particular, there remains a need to fully understand the relation between intentions and actual offending, as well as the impact of possible question presentation effects on participants' responses.

Additional research is needed to assess the IB correlation for *unconventional* activities. This will require researchers to design studies that capture not only participants' self-reported intentions to offend but also their actual offending behavior. However, it is important that the measure of actual behavior closely corresponds to the hypothetical behavior under which participants expressed their intentions. In other words, it is insufficient compare participants' hypothetical likelihood to shoplift inexpensive batteries out of necessity (a commonly used hypothetical scenario) to real-world acts of stealing expensive merchandise for utilitarian gains, because such a comparison lacks the necessary "level of specificity" (Fishbein and Ajzen 1975: 369).

Collecting hypothetical and real-world behaviors with specificity presents certain ethical challenges. For example, researchers will need to make participants believe they have the opportunity to engage in a criminal act (such as that described in our fictitious newspaper article), and then record the participants' behavioral responses to this opportunity (e.g., emails sent to John Doe). At the same time, researchers have an ethical obligation to ensure that their research does not foster real-world illegal activity (no illegal music files were sent in our study), and also fully inform participants about the true purpose of the research (i.e., debrief them). With careful planning and appropriate human subjects protection, this type of research can be approved by Institutional Review Boards.

Additional research is also needed to examine question presentation effects on participants' responses. As we have described here, supplying participants with a list of consequences to consider (rather than allowing them to self-identify consequences) may undermine the participants' natural decision making process. Free elicitation is arguably the best way to record such consequences, but such highly individualized, qualitative data can be cumbersome to code/analyze. Some scholars have instead adopted a "blended" approach by presenting a standard set of researcher-generated consequences but then asking participants to self-generate additional consequences that are relevant to them (e.g., Higgins et al. 2005; Wolfe et al. 2007). Unfortunately, participants typically fail to utilize the "other" option (Converse 1987; Schuman and Presser 1981). We therefore suggest an alternative strategy – one in which participants freely elicit consequences in a pilot study and then these very same consequences are compiled into a list that can be presented to participants in a subsequent study.

Research examining criminal decision making has evolved from early tests of the objective qualities of punishments, to cross-sectional (and panel) studies of the perceived consequences of actual crime, to studies of perceived consequences of hypothetical crime. Each evolutionary stage comes with its own advantages and disadvantages. A more thorough examination of the hypothetical scenario method is needed in order to better understand the role of choice in offending, and to better inform crime control policy. We hope the criticisms raised here and the research findings we presented will help to shape the ongoing evolution of the hypothetical scenario method.

REFERENCES

Ajzen I (1988) Attitudes, personality, and behavior. Dorsey Press, Chicago

Ajzen I (1991) The theory of planned behavior. Organ Behav Hum Decis Process 50:179–211

Ajzen I, Fishbein M (1980) Understanding attitudes and prediction social behavior. Prentice-Hall, Englewood Cliffs, NJ

Armitage CJ, Conner M (2001) Efficacy of the theory of planned behavior: a meta-analytic review. Br J Soc Psychol 40:471–499

Armitage CJ, Conner M, Loach J, Willetts D (1999) Different perceptions of control: applying and extended theory of planned behavior to legal and illegal drug use. Basic Appl Soc Psych 21:301–316

Assaad JM, Exum ML (2002) Understanding intoxicated violence from a rational choice perspective. In: Piquero AR, Tibbetts SG (eds) Rational choice and criminal behavior: recent research and future challenges, Routledge, New York, pp 65–84

Bachman R, Paternoster R, Ward S (1992) The rationality of sexual offending: testing a deterrence/rational choice conception of sexual assault. Law Soc Rev 26:343–372

Beck L, Ajzen I (1991) Predicting dishonest actions using the theory of planned behavior. J Res Pers 25:285–301

Bentham J (1789/1970) An introduction to the principles of morals and legislation. Oxford University Press, New York.

Bouffard JA (2002) Methodological and theoretical implications of using subject-generated consequences in tests of rational choice theory. Justice Q 19:747–771

Bouffard JA (2002) The influence of emotion on rational decision making in sexual aggression. J Crim Justice 30:121–134

Bouffard JA (2007) Predicting differences in the perceived relevance of crime's costs and benefits in a test of rational choice theory. Int J Offender Ther Comp Criminol 51:461–485

Bouffard JA, Bry J, Smith S, Bry R (2008) Beyond the "science of sophomores": does the rational choice explanation of crime generalize from university students to an actual offender sample? Int J Offender Ther Comp Criminol, 52: 698–721.

Bouffard J, Exum ML, Paternoster R (2000) Whither the beast? The role of emotions in a rational choice theory of crime. In: Simpson SS (ed) Crime and criminality: the use of theory in everyday life, Pine Forge Press, Thousand Oaks, pp 159–178

Brezina T (2002) Assessing the rationality of criminal and delinquent behavior: a focus on actual utility. In: Piquero AR, Tibbetts SG (eds), Rational choice and criminal behavior, Garland, New York.

Carmichael S, Piquero AR (2004) Sanctions, perceived anger, and criminal offending. J Quant Criminol 20:371–393

Chiricos TG, Waldo GP (1970) Punishment and crime: an examination of some empirical evidence. Soc Probl 18(2):200–217

Converse JM (1987) Survey research in the united states: roots and emergence 1890–1960. University of California Press, Berkeley

Decker S, Wright R, Logie R (1993) Perceptual deterrence among active residential burglars: a research note. Criminology 31(1):135–147

Erickson ML, Gibbs JP, Jensen GF (1977) The deterrence doctrine and the perceived certainty of legal punishments. Am Sociol Rev 42(2):305–317

Exum ML (2002) The application and robustness of the rational choice perspective in the study of intoxicated and angry intentions to aggress. Criminology 40:933–966

Exum ML, Turner MG, Hartman JL Testing rational choice theory with a behavioral measure of offending. (2007) Presented at the annual meetings of the American society of criminology, Atlanta, GA

Fishbein M, Ajzen I (1975) Belief, attitude, intention and beahvior: an introduction to theory and research. Additon-Wesley, Reading, MA

Gibbs JP (1975) Crime, punishment, and deterrence. Elsevier, Amsterdam, The Netherlands

Grasmick HG, Bursik RJ (1990) Conscience, significant others and rational choice: extending the deterrence model. Law Soc Rev 24:837–861

Grasmick HG, Green DE (1980) Legal punishment, social disapproval and internalization as inhibitors of illegal behavior. J Criminol Crim Law 71:325–335

Higgins GE, Wilson AL, Fell BD (2005) An application of deterrence theory to software piracy. J Crim Justice Pop Cult 12:166–184

Klepper S, Nagin D (1989b) The deterrent effect of perceived certainty and severity of punishment revisited. Criminology 27:721–746

Loewenstein G, Nagin D, Paternoster R (1997) The effect of sexual arousal on expectations of sexual forcefulness. J Res Crim Delinq 34:443–473

Logan CH (1972) General deterrent effects of imprisonment. Soc Forces 51:63–72

Madden TJ, Ellen PS, Ajzen I (1992) A comparison of the theory of planned behavior and the theory of reasoned action. Pers Soc Psychol Bull 18:3–9

Nagin D (2007) Moving choice to the center stage in criminological research and theory: the American society of criminology 2006 Sutherland address. Criminology 45:259–272

Nagin DS, Paternoster R (1993) Enduring individual differences and rational choice theories of crime. Law Soc Rev 27:467–496

Nagin DS, Paternoster R (1994) Personal capital and social control: the deterrence implications of a theory of individual differences in criminal offending. Criminology 32:581–606

Nagin DS, Pogarsky G (2001) Integrating celerity, impulsivity, and extralegal sanction threats into a model of general deterrence: theory and evidence. Criminology 39:865–889

Paternoster R (1987) The deterrent effect of the perceived certainty and severity of punishment: a review of the evidence and issues. Justice Q 4(2):173–217

Paternoster R Simpson S (1996) Sanction threats and appeals to morality: testing a rational choice model of corporate crime. Law Soc Rev 30:549–583

Piquero NL, Exum ML, Simpson SS (2005) Integrating the desire-for-control and rational choice in a corporate crime context. Justice Q 22:252–280

Piquero A, Tibbetts SG (1996) Specifying the direct and indirect effects of low self-control and situational factors in offenders' decision-making: toward a more complete model of rational offending. Justice Q 13:481–510

Pogarsky G (2002) Identifying "deterrable" offenders: implications for research on deterrence. Justice Q 19:431–452

Pogarsky G, Piquero AR (2004) Studying the research of deterrence: can deterrence theory help explain police misconduct? J Crim Justice 32:371–386

Saltzman L (1982) Deterrent and experiential effects: the problem of causal order in perceptual deterrence research. J Res Crim Delinq 19(2):172–189

Schuman H, Presser S (1979) The open and closed question. Am Sociol Rev 44:692–712

Schwarz N, Hippler H (1991) Response alternatives: the impact of their choice and presentation order. In: Biemer PP, Groves RM, Lyberg LE, Mathiowetz NA, Sudman S (eds) Measurement errors in surveys, John Wiley & Sons, Inc, New York

Schwarz N, Oyserman D (2001) Asking questions about behavior: cognition, communication, and questionnaire construction. Am J Eval 22:127–160

Schuman H, Presser S (1981) Questions and answers in attitude surveys. New York: Academic Press

Sheppard BH, Hartwick J, Warshaw PR (1988) The theory of reasoned action: a meta-analysis of past research with recommendations for modifications and future research. The Journal of Consumer Research 15:325–343

Strelan P, Boeckmann RJ (2006) Why drug testing in elite sports does not work: perceptual deterrence theory and the role of personal moral beliefs. J Appl Soc Psychol 36:2909–2934

Tibbetts SG (1999) Differences between women and men regarding decisions to commit test cheating. Res Higher Educ 40:323–342

Tibbetts SG, Herz DC (1996) Gender differences in factors of social control and rational choice. Deviant Behav Interdiscipl J 17:183–208

Tibbetts SG, Myers DL (1999) Low self-control, rational choice and student test cheating. Am J Crim Justice 32:179–200

Tittle CR (1969) Crime rates and legal sanctions. Soc Probl 16:409–423

Wolfe SE, Higgins GE, Marcum CD (2007) Deterrence and digital piracy: A preliminary examination of the role of viruses. Soc Sci Comput Rev XX:1–17

## CHAPTER 29

Instrumental Variables in Criminology and Criminal Justice

SHAWN D. BUSHWAY AND ROBERT J. APEL

INTRODUCTION

Instrumental variable techniques have become a core technique for empirical work in economics (Angrist and Krueger 2001; Angrist and Pischke 2008). The technique is used to estimate the local average treatment effect in experiments with noncompliance, deals with endogenous independent variables and measurement error, and creates consistent estimates in the presence of omitted variables. Although it is not a core technique in criminology, there are now examples where the technique has been imported into criminology for each of these applications. For example, Angrist (2006) and Kilmer (2008) estimate the local average treatment effect in the presence of non-compliance in criminological experiments of police response to domestic violence and drug testing, respectively. Jones and Gondolf (2002) model the endogeneity of program completion in a model of batterer recidivism and treatment, and Apel et al. (2008) generate a new estimate of the relationship between work intensity and delinquency in adolescence after documenting legitimate concerns about selection bias. Finally, Tita et al. (2006) use instrumental variable methods to deal with measurement error concerns in their model of the impact of crime on housing prices.

Beyond documenting this growing use of instrumental variables in criminology, the goal of this chapter is to provide an accessible introduction to the technique. We start the next section by describing the problems in criminological research, which instrumental variable techniques can help address, before describing the technique and providing a simple example where we use the technique to solve a selection bias problem. Readers of this chapter who decide that they want to conduct research with instrumental variable techniques should progress to one of the following excellent technical treatments of instrumental variable methods, which are specifically written for non-economists (Angrist and Krueger 2001; Angrist 2006; Angrist and Pischke 2008).

A.R. Piquero and D. Weisburd (eds.), *Handbook of Quantitative Criminology*,
DOI 10.1007/978-0-387-77650-7_29, © Springer Science + Business Media, LLC 2010,
First softcover printing 2011

THE PROBLEM

Gottfredson and Hirschi's General Theory was built on the empirical fact that stable individual factors are associated with both crime and other aspects of a person's life that can be thought to cause crime. Gottfredson and Hirschi (1990) acknowledge that those who get married or those who are employed are less involved in crime than those who are not, but they argue that these people are different on other important dimensions before they get married or become employed. Therefore, they assert, the observed correlation between marriage or employment and crime is a spurious result of the selection of certain types of people into marriage and employment (in their case, those with high self-control). This claim is the essence of selection bias. Much of the recent research in life-course criminology can be seen as an attempt to respond to Gottfredson and Hirschi's challenge by utilizing new statistical techniques to better control selection bias in causal models of crime (e.g. Brame et al. 2005; Sampson et al. 2006).

The same pattern of using improved statistical techniques to deal with selection bias can be seen in other areas, including sentencing, where large initial race effects were questioned on the grounds of omitted variables bias because researchers failed to take into account legal factors that could vary across race. Zatz (1987) documents four waves of research in sentencing that she characterizes as having increasing methodological sophistication to deal with selection or omitted variables bias. Paternoster et al. (2003) and Apel et al. (2007, 2008) use a variety of statistical techniques to control selection bias in studies of the impact of intensive employment during adolescence on antisocial behavior. These models show that failure to control selection bias leads to misleading conclusions about the criminogenic effect of adolescent work. The rise of experimental criminology in the last 10 years can be attributed to the growing focus on the need to causally identify the impact of programs on crime in the face of selection bias. It is a fact that program participation is correlated with reduced crime in most policy settings (e.g. Wilson et al. 2000), but, absent additional controls for omitted variables, it is not possible to know if the effect is caused by the program participation or by the self-selection of motivated participants in the programs. Randomized trial experiments can be effective at dealing with this threat to internal validity (Berk 2005), but instrumental variables are also an attractive alternative in the absence of experimental variation.

The problem of simultaneity has also been a major fact of life in criminology, especially with respect to the study of deterrence. At the time of Daniel Nagin's first review of the empirical deterrence literature (Nagin 1978), the problem of simultaneity was not well understood. People generally interpreted the positive relationship between prison or police levels and crime in cross-sectional analysis as evidence that prison/police did not lead to a decrease in crime. But, Nagin (1978) noted that while prison and police have a potentially negative impact on crime, crime has a potentially positive impact on the levels of police and prisons, as policymakers invest in the criminal justice system in an attempt to combat crime.[1] The net canceling out of these two effects leads to confusion when trying to estimate the causal impact of prisons/police on crime. This problem has slowly become an accepted fact in criminology over the last 30 years, and researchers are now squarely focused on the need to deal with simultaneity when looking at the causal impact of prison/police on crime (Spelman 2008; Committee to Review Research on Police Policy and Practices 2004). Experiments and instrumental variable techniques are offered as the best approaches to deal with this problem.

---

[1] See also a review piece by Cook (1980) which makes an argument for empirical research which can deal with this simultaneity problem.

For example, Spelman concludes that "if we are to learn anything further about the relationship between crime and prison, we need to focus on identifying appropriate instruments, not denying the need for them (Spelman 2008, p 175)."

The last problem for which instrumental variables is used – measurement error – is no less ubiquitous, but is perhaps less recognized as a problem that can lead to biased results in causal models. Measurement error in criminology is usually viewed as a construct or measurement problem, and therefore it is not a direct problem for internal validity. Measurement error in a dependent variable is generally viewed as less problematic than measurement error in a regressor or independent variable. But, as criminologists become more willing to explore the impact of crime on other sociological phenomenon, the use of crime as an independent variable raises the more persistent spectre of bias. Tita et al. (2006) demonstrate the potential for bias in their study of the impact of crime on housing prices. They use instrumental variables to demonstrate that measurement error in crime leads to the dramatic understatement of the causal impact of crime on housing prices.

Despite the differences between each of the aforementioned problems, in each case, instrumental variable techniques are attempting to do the same thing – render the independent variable uncorrelated with the error term. An independent variable that is uncorrelated with the error term is exogenous. In contrast, an independent variable that is correlated with the error term is considered to be endogenous. Endogeneity is a major violation of the key assumptions of the ordinary least squares regression model. Selection bias, simultaneity, and measurement error in the independent variable are all problems of endogeneous regressors. Any design or statistical fix, whether it be an experiment, instrumental variable model, or fixed-effects model, strives to remove the correlation between the error term and the regressor of interest, in effect making it an exogenous regressor.

To make this point more clearly, consider a simple ordinary least square regression such as the one given in (29.1):

$$Y_i = \alpha + \beta X_i + \varepsilon_i \tag{29.1}$$

We create an estimate of β, b_{OLS}, using ordinary least squares regression. One of the key assumptions of ordinary least squares is that the covariance of X_i and ε_i must be zero. If it is not zero, then the expected value of the ordinary least square estimator b_{OLS} is not β, which means that b_{OLS} would be both biased and inconsistent, as displayed in (29.2).

$$E(b_{OLS}) = \beta + \mathrm{Cov}(X, \varepsilon)/\mathrm{Var}(X) \tag{29.2}$$

On the other hand, if the independent variable and the error are uncorrelated, then we have an unbiased (and therefore consistent) estimator for β. This assumption is sometimes called the exogeneity assumption. When there is a violation of the exogeneity assumption, we say that the independent variable is endogenous. Fortunately, we can often "sign the bias" if we can characterize the nature of the correlation between X and the error.

There are three standard problems or cases when we generally worry about the exogeneity assumption. The first is the case where there is simultaneous causation between X and Y. In this case, not only does X cause Y, but Y also causes X. The simultaneous relationship between the price of a good and the quantity sold in the market in economics is the classic case of simultaneity, and the problem that led to the first use of instrumental variables by economists.[2] In an economic market, the fact that quantity sold is a function of the interaction

---

[2] For a concise history, see Angrist and Kreuger (2001).

between supply and demand is recognized by the specification of two simultaneous equations, one for supply and one for demand. Producers will agree to produce a certain amount of the good conditional on a variety of factors, including the price of the good. Consumers will agree to purchase a certain amount of the good, conditional on a number of factors including the price of the good. In equilibrium, the quantity produced is equal to the quantity demanded.

Price is the mechanism by which the market reaches its equilibrium. For example, suppose that initially producers produced more than was demanded by the market. The only option is for producers to lower the price, at which point more will be sold. As such, price depends on quantity demanded and supplied, and vice versa. In economic language, price is endogenous, determined by the system of equations. In contrast, other factors are exogenous, meaning they exist outside the system and do not depend on what happens as the system arrives at an equilibrium. A drought that affects the production of corn is an example of an exogenous shock to the market. The drought affects the price only because it affects the quantity supplied to the market.

In terms of (29.1), let us assume that quantity of corn brought to market by producers is Y and the price of corn is the X or independent variable. Since this is the producer or supply equation, we expect the coefficient, β, to be positive. Higher price leads to more corn being brought to the market. But shocks to Y that show up in the error term, such as a shortage of corn due to the drought, will be negatively correlated with the observed price of corn because the shortage of corn leads to an increase in price in the market. The net result of the endogeneity of price is that we will have a negatively biased coefficient on the price of corn in the corn supply equation. Because the coefficient should be positive, the negative bias means that the coefficient will not be as far away from zero as it should be, and we will conclude that price has a smaller effect on quantity supplied than it really does.

Thinking about simultaneous equations has been essential to the way economists approach the study of crime. The key variables in the crime system are not quantity and price but crime and the crime prevention measures taken by the criminal justice system as well as potential victims. Crime is dependent on, among other factors, the crime prevention measures taken in the social system. But, these measures are in turn dependent on the amount of crime in the system, among other things. That means that crime prevention is endogenous, i.e., crime and crime prevention are simultaneously determined. This fact is perhaps the biggest hurdle to models that attempt to study the deterrent impact of prison and police. In this case, crime is the dependent variable Y, and the number of police (or prison beds) is the independent variable X. Places that have a lot of crime are also likely to have a lot of crime prevention. This induces a positive correlation between the error term of crime and crime prevention policies like the number of police, when theoretically we expect that crime prevention should have a negative relationship with crime. As in the corn supply case, we can "sign the bias". To be specific, we expect a negative coefficient that is positively biased towards zero. This fundamental insight forms a key part of Nagin's (1978) paper on deterrence and is a major hurdle to any empirical estimation of deterrence – without a way to deal with endogeneity we predict that the estimated relationship will be closer to a null or weak relationship than it is in reality.

Within this framework, the fact that researchers typically find no or only a small relationship between crime prevention techniques and crime is not surprising, and at least to economists, not definitive evidence that crime prevention does not work. At the close of 1970's, Cook (1980) authored an important review paper in *Crime and Justice*, suggesting a new way forward for economic research on deterrence. He urged the empirical tests of policy interventions with special attention to the problem of endogeneity between actors in what some might consider the market for crime (see also Cook 1986).[3]

This analogy of a market for crime, which has never become embedded in criminological thought, has value in its identification of interacting parties (most prominently, potential offenders on one hand, and the criminal justice system and potential victims on the other) who simultaneously affect each other's behavior. Estimates of the impact of policies that fail to take into account the endogeneity of these policies and the response of the potential offenders (e.g., displacement) to these policies are fundamentally flawed.

But, this endogeneity is not just a statistical problem – it is a substantive problem that fundamentally frames the economist's approach to the study of crime since the criminal justice system, potential victims, and offenders are reacting to each other's action (or non-action). A standard critique from economists of an analyst's policy recommendation is that the author has failed to take into account the feedback loop between the actions of the system and would-be offender. For example, economist Steven Raphael (2006) pointed out that a policy that encourages reintegration may reduce barriers to reentry but it also simultaneously lowers the punishment cost of an arrest and conviction.

It is important to note that the simultaneity problem does not always mean that the coefficient will be biased towards zero. Consider for example the relationship between unemployment and crime, where unemployment is the independent variable X and crime is the dependent variable Y. Most people believe that unemployment leads to crime as people become stressed or encounter lower opportunity costs for crime (which means that β is positive). It is also true that crime can lead to unemployment, if for example, people stop shopping at night to avoid becoming victimized. In this case, the error term on crime will be positively correlated with unemployment. This means that we would predict that the positive coefficient on unemployment will be positively biased away from zero, or, alternatively, that the estimated coefficient will be bigger than it is supposed to be. Yet, in the unemployment-crime literature, most people find, at most, a weak positive relationship between unemployment and crime (Chiricos 1987). Simultaneity is *not* a good explanation for why researchers have not found a particularly strong relationship between unemployment and crime.

A second major case where endogeneity arises is the problem of omitted variable bias. Here, the problem is that there is another variable W which is not included in the model, and it is correlated with both X and Y. One example is the study of work intensity (the number of hours worked per week) and crime for adolescents, where the number of hours worked is the independent variable X and the amount of crime is the dependent variable Y. Among adults, researchers typically find a negative relationship between hours worked and crime, but for adolescents, the opposite is true, leading some scholars to argue that work has an adverse causal relationship with crime for adolescents, perhaps by drawing youth away from prosocial activities like school. But, what if youth who are disaffected with school are more likely to work long hours compared to other youth, and are also more likely to engage in crime? Furthermore, we do not have a measure for school disaffection. This is classic omitted variables bias, and in this case, we will observe a positive correlation between work intensity and disaffection, and between disaffection and crime. This set of correlations means that there

---

[3] In this notional market, the "demand for crime" is the inverse of the "demand for safety." As the price of safety rises, the demand for crime will increase.

will be a positive bias on the negative coefficient on work. Paternoster et al. (2003) and Apel et al. (2007) used stronger controls for unobserved heterogeneity to demonstrate how omitted variables bias could lead to misleading positive coefficients on work intensity.

The classic case of selection or omitted variables bias comes in the case of program participation or treatment, where program participation is the independent variable and crime is the dependent variable. For example, it is easy to show that work-related programs in prison are correlated with a roughly 20-percent decline in recidivism when comparing non-participants with participants (Wilson et al. 2000). But, it is also not hard to think about factors such as motivation which are unobserved and positively correlated with program participation, and negatively correlated with crime. In this case, the error term and program participation will be negatively correlated, and we will have a coefficient on program participation that is more negative than it *should* be. The accepted solution to this problem is random assignment, which in the case of perfect compliance leads to a situation where the omitted variable is uncorrelated (in expectation) with the independent variable X. In other words, random assignment is designed explicitly to overcome the endogeneity problem by forcing a situation where the error term is uncorrelated with program participation. As a result, it is generally accepted that random assignment will result in effect sizes that are smaller than the effect sizes found with less rigorous designs (Farrington and Welsh 2005).

The final class of cases where we would have the endogeneity problem is the case where there is measurement error on the independent variable X. In the classic case, when the error is random (meaning that the error has a zero mean and is uncorrelated with X), it can be shown that measurement error it will attenuate the coefficient, meaning that the bias will always be toward zero. So, if β is positive, the correlation between the error and X will be negative, and if β is negative, the correlation between the error and X will be positive. Intuitively, this should make sense. If we see a bigger X than is truly there, we will think there has been more of a change in the independent variable than has truly occurred, and we will underestimate the change that would occur if X truly did change by that same amount. And, if we see a smaller X than what is truly there, we will see more movement in Y than we expected. We might expect to see this kind of problem in the study of the relationship between perceived sanction threat and subsequent criminal behavior. At the very least, sanction threat is perceived with a lot of noise (Kleck et al. 2005), and this noise in the independent variable will lead to attenuation bias at best.

The more problematic situation occurs if the measurement error is not "classic," but is systematically different than the true value of the variable. In this case, it is difficult to sign the bias, and we expect that the bias will propagate to other coefficients as well. Unfortunately, this is likely to be the case in the study of crime, because we are using measures like arrest to capture the construct crime. Usually, we believe that arrests will understate the true amount of crime, and this measurement error can create unpredictable bias in the coefficient, depending on the relationship between the measurement error and the dependent variable of interest. For example, in the study of the deterrent effect of police, we might have systematic overestimates of the true "police presence" on the streets if we use the number of police officers on the force, and we might also have measurement error in the number of arrests through, for example, the use of drug stings to increase arrest measures.

THE INSTRUMENTAL VARIABLE SOLUTION

Better research design is the best and first solution to each of these problems. Use of experiments and better measurement can solve simultaneity, omitted variables, and measurement error problems and create exogenous right-hand-side variables. Yet, experiments and better measurement are not always possible. The use of an instrumental variable is a post hoc approach that can be helpful in dealing with these types of problem. Specifically, instrumental variables are used to identify exogenous variation in the independent variable, which can then be studied to look at the causal link between the independent and dependent variable. Only that variation in X that can be argued to be exogenous is entered into the model, therefore eliminating the endogeneity problem. This comes at a cost of increasing the size of the standard error of the coefficient, because only part of the total variation in X is used.

More formally, an excluded instrumental variable is a variable Z that is correlated with Y, but only through its relationship with X. So, we can imagine another set of equations, (29.3), where we model both Y and X. The key for identification is the exclusion of Z in the equation for Y, but the inclusion of Z in the equation for X. Other variables can exist that cause both Y and X, but Y cannot be directly caused by Z. In English, the excluded instrumental variable must have a strong impact on X, *and* only impact Y through its impact on X. This basic condition of instrumental variables is true whether we are dealing with omitted variables, simultaneity, or measurement error. Intuitively, by excluding Z from the equation of Y, we are going to estimate the relationship between Y and X using only the variation in X that can be attributed to Z. In the simplest two-stage least squares method, we literally only include the part of X that can be predicted by the model where Z is the independent variable in the equation for X. In other words, we don't regress Y on X, but rather Y on predicted X, where predicted X comes from a model with an instrumental variable that is not included in the model for Y. As a result, the variation in X will no longer be correlated with the error term. Instrumental variable estimates will remain biased, but will be consistent. "Consistency" is an econometric term meaning that the bias disappears as N gets large.

$$X_i = \delta + \gamma Z_i + v_i$$
$$Y_i = \alpha + \beta X_i + \varepsilon_i \tag{29.3}$$

One of the first uses of instrumental variable techniques to study crime was a paper in which Steven Levitt used legally mandated reductions in prison capacity to estimate the impact of incarceration on crime (Levitt 1996). His claim was that the court decisions that reduced incarceration were not caused by crime, but were caused by larger societal forces that had nothing to do with the crime generation process. As a result, this variation is essentially random with respect to crime and therefore is not correlated with the error term in Y. If this is true, he can use this random variation in incarceration to study the impact of incarceration on crime at the state level. Specifically, he ran a first-stage regression of incarceration on the court rulings that led to reductions in incarceration. Then, he predicted the level of incarceration from this regression, and used the predicted value in the second stage regression with crime as the dependent variable.

It is important to realize that the claim that the court rulings are not correlated with the crime error term is not the same thing as saying that the court decisions are uncorrelated with crime. *A common misconception is that the instrumental variable, in this case the court decision, must be uncorrelated with crime. An instrument that is uncorrelated with the dependent variable is a useless instrumental variable, guaranteed to produce a finding that*

$b_{IV} = 0$. Levitt shows clearly that the court decisions are in fact correlated with crime rates. The key assumption of instrumental variables is that the *only* way the instrumental variable is correlated with the dependent variable is through the independent variable (in this case, incarceration rates). In arguing for the validity of his instrument, Levitt needed to argue that the only reason that the court decisions are correlated with crime is because the court decision affects incarceration rates, which then affect crime. There is no way to prove this assumption with statistics, although it is possible to test this assumption if one has another instrumental variable which one can use as part of a test of overidentifying restrictions. However, the validity of the test depends on the untestable assumption that the other instrument is in fact valid. The untestability of the fundamental assumption of instrumental variables might be viewed as a problem; but the fact that the researcher must rely on substantive and theoretical arguments about the underlying causal processes is a plus, not a negative. This fact puts a premium on substance and theory, and prevents instrumental variables from being just another econometric magic trick that people do not really understand. However, it does mean that researchers *must* report the first stage, and they must go into some detail to defend their claim of exogeneity. Papers that simply state that they are going to use an instrumental variable without going into detail about the exogeneity of the instrument cannot make a contribution to the literature.

Another interesting and high-profile paper on crime-related topics, which makes use of the instrumental variable technique to deal with simultaneity, is a paper by Evans and Owens (2007), which uses federal COPS spending as an instrument to generate additional estimates of the impact of policing on crime. In this paper, as in the Levitt paper, the instrumental variable method leads to estimates that are much larger than those found with standard OLS analysis. Although these two examples are in economics journals, Spelman (2008) makes a strong argument in the *Journal of Quantitative Criminology* for the use of instrumental variable techniques to deal with the simultaneity between prison and crime. The same argument can be made for any crime prevention approach with aggregate data (see also Nagin 1998).

The instrumental variable technique is also used to deal with selection bias. Again, the goal is to find an instrumental variable Z that is correlated with Y only through its relationship with X. Using only the predicted value of X in the second stage guarantees the covariance between X and the error term is zero as N gets large, provided the exclusion restriction is valid. This basic approach has been used in a number of economics papers on crime, including a paper by Jacob and Lefgren (2003), which uses teacher conference days to estimate the impact of mandatory school attendance on the crime distribution in the larger community. Just using holidays or weekends and comparing the crime distribution during those days with crime during school days is problematic because of the many omitted variables that are correlated with both whether a day is a holiday or a school day and crime. But by using teacher service days as the comparison group, it is at least plausible to argue that the only meaningful difference is the fact that kids are not in school, and nothing else, which could explain the increase in crime in a given place. This is especially convincing when other local school districts have school on the same day.

In another example, Kling (2006) uses random assignment of cases to judges as instrumental variables to study the impact of sentence length on employment outcomes. Selection bias is the major problem with studying the impact of sentence length or sentence type on recidivism or other outcomes like employment. Sentences are not assigned randomly, and even the best sentencing dataset does not contain all of the relevant variables which might affect the sentence given by the judge. And these omitted variables could be correlated with both the outcomes, such as recidivism, and the original sentence (e.g., Spohn and Holleran 2002). But, in some jurisdictions, judges are assigned randomly to cases. And, we know that there is variation across judges in their use of discretion (Gottfredson 1999). Because of the random assignment to cases, the variation in sentence length that is due to judge preference should be uncorrelated with anything that happens at the individual level. Using that variation in the first stage to model exogenous variation in sentence length will allow us to causally identify the impact of sentence length on subsequent outcomes. The basic logic underlying this idea explains why adding observable variables reduces the relationship between sentence length and recidivism, for example (Gottfredson 1999). And, Kling (2006) found that sentence length was no longer related to employment outcomes once the instrumental variable was used to model sentence length.

A similar logic underlies Apel et al.'s (2008) study of youth employment. Prior research with the same dataset had demonstrated the existence of selection bias in studies looking at the relationship between work intensity and crime (Paternoster et al. 2003; Apel et al. 2007). Apel et al. decided to look at the variation in work hours caused by state laws about work for teenagers. At age 15, all respondents are under a uniform child labor regime monitored by the federal government. At age 16, however, the federal regime expires and is replaced by non-uniform state child labor regimes. All respondents experience a change in the prevailing child labor regime during the 15-to-16 transition, although the nature of the change varies across states. Apel et al. (2008) argue that these work rules are only indirectly related to crime through their impact on adolescent work, which makes the work rules a valid instrument for work.

Therefore, the first stage of the instrumental variable model is simply the regression of the change in work hours on the change in work rules and other observable variables. The fitted values from this model are then substituted into the second-stage model looking at how change in work intensity might be correlated with the change in delinquency. We estimated the model using two-stage least squares on first differences (fixed effect instrumental variables). In this model, identification of the "work effect" is predicated on the exogenous within-individual change in work involvement that can be attributed to the easing of child labor restrictions as youth age out of the federal child labor regime governing 15-year-old employment and into different state child labor regimes governing 16-year-old employment. It is important to point out that the fixed effect instrumental variable model does not avail itself of all of the available within-individual variation in employment, but only that portion that is explained by change in child labor laws, which they argue is plausibly exogenous.

In the first stage, we find that the more lenient work rules are correlated with more hours worked among those who entered the work force at age 16, and furthermore, that this variation induced by the different work rules was causally connected with both more dropout from school (Rothstein 2007) and less delinquency in the second stage. This finding of a causal link showing more hours and less crime is consistent with the relationship typically found for adults, but contradicts prior research arguing for, at minimum, a null relationship between work hours and crime. This change in the direction of the coefficient on work hours is exactly what we would expect if the more delinquent youth work earlier and at higher intensity than other youth (i.e., that selection bias makes it look as though the relationship is positive).

The exact same logic can be applied to randomized trials with non-compliance. Experiments are typically conducted because of concerns about selection bias, and the randomization is done to break apart the correlation between the treatment and the error term. But, in most experiments, there is non-compliance, meaning some people who were assigned to the treatment group do not actually receive treatment. The resulting experimental analysis must be an "intent-to-treat" analysis, where the research compares all those in the treatment group to all those in the control group, regardless of whether the people in the treatment group got the treatment. This by definition will lead to smaller coefficients than what would be expected from the average treatment effect, because some members of the treatment group do not actually receive the treatment. The problem with simply doing an analysis with program participation as the independent variable is the standard selection bias problem – those in the treatment group who were supposed to get the treatment but did not, for whatever reason, are in all likelihood different from those who did in fact get the treatment. For example, in the Moving to Opportunity experiment, many of the families who were offered the voucher that allowed them to move to the suburbs did not actually use the voucher. These "non-compliers" may have less family support, for example, and this lack of family support could affect both the decision to accept the voucher and other observed outcomes. If a researcher wants to study the impact of the treatment per se, the researcher needs again to find an instrumental variable that can identify exogenous variation in the participation in treatment.

Of course, in an experiment, people are randomly assigned to treatment, and in some cases, only get access to the treatment if they were randomly assigned to the treatment group. This provides the perfect instrument variable, where random assignment is included in the first-stage model predicting program participation. Program participation in the second stage is then exogenous because of the random assignment, and we end up with local average treatment effect of program participation.

This approach has recently been applied by Beau Kilmer (2008) in an experimental analysis of the impact of drug testing on parolee behavior. In the intent-to-treat analysis, Kilmer found that those assigned to drug testing were 11 percent less likely than those in the control group to be unemployed and out of school one month after release on parole. However, there was significant non-compliance, as about 30 percent of those assigned to receive drug testing were not tested in the first month. When assignment to treatment is used as an instrumental variable (because it is randomized), Kilmer finds that those who are tested (and would not otherwise have been without random assignment) were actually 22 percent less likely than those who were not tested to be unemployed and out of school one month after release. At least for the group that was influenced by the random assignment, the instrumental variable approach gives us a good estimate of the affect of drug testing. The estimate in this case is technically known as a local average treatment effect. Angrist (2006) has another excellent example in criminology based on the well-known Minneapolis domestic violence experiment.

The final class of cases where the instrumental variable technique is useful is the situation where there is measurement error in the independent variable. Again, the problem is that the independent variable X is correlated with the error term. And again, the solution is to find a variable Z that directly causes X but not Y. A recent paper by Tita et al. (2006) uses this technique to estimate the relationship between crime and housing prices. In the standard OLS model looking at the causal impact of crime on housing prices, they found a null effect, and in low-income neighborhoods, they actually found a positive relationship between violent crime and housing prices. One problem, however, is that crime is typically underreported, and the underreporting is the highest in the poorest places. They attempted to solve this problem by using murder, one of the best measured crimes, as an instrument for all violent crime. They then use the predicted crime from the first-stage model in the model of housing prices. Unlike OLS, in the IV model, crime is now negatively correlated with housing prices, as expected, especially in low-income neighborhoods. This paper by Tita et al. (2006) provides an excellent example of the power of instrumental variables. Without instrumental variables, we would either conclude that violent crime is not correlated with housing prices, or that somehow violent crime makes housing prices go up! Yet the variation in violent crime that is correlated with murder is in fact negatively correlated with housing prices, as predicted by virtually any theoretical model of crime.

CONCERNS ABOUT INSTRUMENTAL VARIABLES

Instrumental variable models are not always appropriate, and they can occasionally cause more problems than they solve. For example, see the discussion of the instrumental variable approach by Levitt (1996) in Spelman's (2008) paper on the causal impact of prisons on crime. The biggest problem is that the researcher must identify and defend a good instrumental variable. This is not a statistical exercise, but rather a substantive one in which the researcher must demonstrate a good conceptual grasp of the causal process generating the dependent variable of interest. This is easier said than done, and this problem represents the key difficulty with this method. Instrumental variable methods cannot be implemented like a fixed-effects model or propensity scores by simply implementing a statistical model. First and foremost, researchers need to identify a variable that can serve as good instrument. The model starts (and stops) with the quality of this variable. If it is not plausibly exogenous, than the researcher should stop and think harder. It makes little sense to proceed with an instrumental variable for which the author cannot make a strong substantive or theoretical argument for its exogeneity.

A recent paper by David Kirk (2009) makes these issues clear. He is interested in the impact of neighborhoods on the offending behavior of parolees. There are clear theoretical reasons why neighborhoods might affect the offending behavior of individuals, and these reasons are heightened in the case of people recently released from prison. In general, researchers can show that the highest recidivism rates occur in the worst neighborhoods. However, there is a substantial problem with selection, since people self-select into neighborhoods. A good instrument would solve this problem if it affected neighborhood choice, but did not affect criminal behavior, except through its impact on neighborhood choice.

Kirk focuses on the impact of Hurricane Katrina for parolees from Louisiana, particularly in New Orleans, where whole communities became uninhabitable. Parolees who came from New Orleans would plausibly be expected to return to New Orleans, but Kirk shows that residential choices change after Katrina. So far so good – Katrina is an exogenous event that had a major impact on the housing choice of many people. But, we also need to be able to claim that the only way Katrina will affect the criminal behavior of parolees is through its effect on neighborhood choice.

This claim is not plausible, since Katrina was like a nuclear bomb that affected all aspects of life in Louisiana, including the criminal justice system. However, Kirk does not need this to be strictly true for the instrument to work; rather, he needs it to be true net of the control variables. Therefore, he attempts to control for other factors that were affected by Katrina, and makes the argument that, net of these controls, the only way Katrina can affect crime is through neighborhood selection. The validity of the claim can be evaluated by the readers, and is typical of models that rely on natural disasters or policy changes (for a similar claim, see Apel et al. 2008 or Levitt and Miles 2006). All these models include control variables that attempt to control for other mechanisms by which the instrument could affect the primary dependent variable (or at least be correlated); that is, variables other than the endogenous regressor of interest through which the instrument might be indirectly related to the dependent variable.

Of course, even if the variable is plausibly exogenous, it might only be a weak instrument. A weak instrument is a good (meaning exogenous) instrument that only has a small relationship with X. These estimators will have large standard errors, and might be centered on the ordinary least squares estimator (Angrist and Krueger 2001). In other words, a weak instrument might be worse than no instrument at all, given that it will give the same answer as OLS with larger standard errors. A good instrument must both be exogenous and have a strong impact on the endogenous variable of choice before it will provide a truly valid answer. All of the examples described in this chapter can be described as strong instruments.

Unfortunately, it is easier to think of weak instruments than strong ones. The good news is that the weakness of the instrument, unlike its exogeneity, can be evaluated statistically by looking at the goodness of fit in the first stage-regression. There are rules of thumb about the necessary power that can be found in more detailed treatments of instrumental variables models. For this chapter, it is enough to note that it is critically important to examine the power of the instrument in the first stage when evaluating instrumental variables.

A discussion of the limitations of instrumental variables should not lead to overt pessimism about the prospect of identifying good instruments in criminology. The economics literature is full of great instrumental variables that are only obvious after someone else identifies them (Angrist and Krueger 2001). For example, consider the impact of children on women's labor supply. This is a thorny empirical problem because of the endogeneity of children with respect to labor market outcomes. Women may participate less in the labor market after having children, but women who are less involved in the labor market might also be more willing to have children. This endogeneity will lead to a negatively biased coefficient for the effect of children on labor supply. The solution to the problem is to identify exogenous variation in the number of children. Of course, this sounds impossible – randomly assigning births to women sounds as absurd as randomly assigning people to prison.

But, Angrist and Evans (1998) ingeniously speculated that women who have two children of the same sex (particularly two girls) are more likely to have a third child than are women who have a boy and girl. Anyone who has ever had two children of the same sex can attest to the fact that even strangers ask if one is going to "go for a boy (girl)".[4] Since the sex of the first two children is random (and not determined by labor supply), it can serve as an instrument for the number of children. After implementing this instrumental variable approach, Angrist and Evans (1998) found that children had a still negative but much smaller impact on labor supply than in competing models using ordinary least squares.

The random assignment of judges (and other criminal justice actors) to cases is an example in criminology where we might be able to find random variation in something like sentence length that would be hard to achieve using experiments. There are almost certainly others, but they need to be found by hard-working criminologists who understand the causal processes that generate meaningful variation in the independent variables of interest.

Of course, even if we find a good instrument, the estimated effect does have some limitations. The model estimates the local average treatment effect rather than the global average treatment effect. The local average treatment effect is the treatment effect of the variable reflected by the variation in the instrument. Typically, we are interested in the global average treatment effect, which is the average effect for the entire population. The local average treatment effect need not be the same as the average treatment effect.

---

[4] Indeed, that is how the authors identified this instrumental variable – one of the authors (Evans) had two boys.

In the Angrist and Evans (1998) paper, for example, the estimated effect is only valid for women who have two children, and may not generalize to those with none, or even one child. This occasionally can be a crippling limitation if the variation is arcane or hard to characterize. For example, in the case of random assignment to judges, the variation due to judicial discretion may very well not have the same impact on behavior as systematic and well publicized changes in sentencing guidelines. After all, why would a rational defendant change his future behavior on the basis of a past outcome that he knew was the outcome of random chance?

But in other cases, the local average treatment effect is exactly what we care about. For example, Apel et al. (2008) used the variation in state laws about adolescent work to study the impact of work intensity on crime. This means that Apel et al. (2008) only identified the impact of work intensity on crime for those people who increased their work hours as a result of the work laws. But, this is highly meaningful variation, and exactly the variation that should be studied if we are going to use the results from this study to make policy recommendations about laws governing adolescent work.

A SIMPLE EXAMPLE

In the following section, we will provide a simple example for an instrumental variable analysis to deal with selection bias using the *ivreg* command in the software package Stata.[5] Instrumental variable models can be estimated in SAS using *Proc Syslin*, and the command *2SLS* in both SPSS and Limdep.[6] The example is based on our previous work on adolescent work and crime, although it is substantively different.[7] We will ask whether working in a formal, "paycheck" job during adolescence has an impact on the prevalence of self-reported crime. We will use all available individuals ($N = 8,368$) from the second wave of the National Longitudinal Survey of Youth 1997. Over half (52.6%) of the sample work in a formal paycheck job between the first and second interviews, and just under one-third (31.9%) report committing a delinquent act during the same period. In this simple model, both the independent and dependent variable are dichotomous. Although not a standard practice in criminology, this is an econometrically valid model. We confirm our results using a non-linear instrumental variable model (*ivprobit*).

In Model A of Table 29.1, we estimate a linear probability model of the impact of adolescent work on delinquent behavior. This is from a standard regression of delinquency on employment. The coefficient on work is positive and significant, suggesting that working in the past year leads to an increase in the probability of delinquency of 2.6 percentage points, on average. This is a modest effect of about 8 percent from the mean level of delinquency, but is consistent with what is generally reported in the literature on the criminogenic impact of work (Steinberg and Cauffman 1995). The problem, from a substantive point of view, is selection

---

[5] The example is taken from a short course in instrumental variables developed by Robert Apel.

[6] We have a strong preference for the procedure in Stata because of its range of post-estimation commands, and the existence of other routines for the estimation of non-linear models such as *ivtobit* and *ivprobit*, as well as instrumental variable models for panel datasets, *xtivreg*. In our experience, it is also the program most often used by economists, and it is well supported both by the company and the online user community.

[7] In our paper (Apel et al. 2008), we use an instrumental variable on panel data, focusing on change as young people age from 15 to 16. In this case, we are using a simple cross section of all youth. In that sense, it is similar to work by Tyler (2003) using a cross-sectional analysis to look at the impact of high-school work on school performance.

TABLE 29.1. Comparative models of the effect of adolescent work on delinquent behavior

	Model A: Least squares b (s.e.)	Model B: First stage b (s.e.)	Model C: Two-stage least squares b (s.e.)
Dependent variable	Delinquency	Employment	Delinquency
Endogenous regressor			
Worked in a formal job	0.026 (.010)*		−0.074 (.028)**
Instrumental variables			
State child labor law allows 40 + h/Week		0.069 (.015)***	
No child labor law restriction in place		0.382 (.011)***	
Diagnostic statistics			
F-Test for instruments		626.6	
R-Square for instruments		0.130	
Overidentification test			0.509
Durbin-Wu-Hausman test			−3.80

Note: $N = 8,368$. Estimates are unweighted. All variables are dichotomous. The reference group for the instrumental variables is residing in a state that limits youth work involvement to fewer than 40 hours per week. The overidentification test is distributed chi-square with one degree of freedom. The Durbin-Wu-Hausman test is a z-test.
* $p < .05$, ** $p < .01$, *** $p < .001$ (two-tailed tests)

bias. Individuals who work during adolescence are not a random sample of all adolescents, and it is entirely possible that those who are more delinquent are also more likely to work. For example, these individuals may be less attached to school, and therefore, they are both more likely to work and more likely to commit crime. Alternatively, socioeconomically disadvantaged youth may be both more likely to resort to crime to meet their economic needs as well as to work.

The most obvious response to this problem is to include some control variables. In a model that is not shown, we thus add control variables for gender, race/ethnicity, fertility, dropout status, family structure, family size, urbanicity, dwelling characteristics, school suspension, county unemployment, and residential mobility. As expected, the coefficient drops from 2.6 percentage points to 1.3 percentage points, and the coefficient is no longer statistically significant. However, it is not hard to argue that there are many other variables not included which could affect both work and crime. Moreover, this result is still different than what is generally found for older samples, where employment is significantly and negatively correlated with crime. A priori, it is hard to understand why work should be prophylactic for adults and have no effect or even be criminogenic for adolescents. While it is possible to develop theoretical explanations for an age-graded effect of work, it is also possible to explain this contradiction through selection bias. There could be factors which are positively correlated with both work and crime that we are unable to account for, and these factors could introduce a positive bias in the coefficient on work.

One solution to this selection bias problem would be to conduct an experiment. Another would be to find an instrumental variable. In this case, we argue that state child labor laws governing adolescent employment constitute a plausible source of exogenous variation in youth work. The argument starts with the claim that state work rules should affect the work behavior of adolescents. Prior to age 16, all youth are under strict work rules imposed by the federal government, which limit how much an individual can work. At age 16, the federal work rules expire and youth are governed by the federal laws concerning adults, unless states have restrictions on the employment of those under the age of 18. For this illustration, we focus on state child labor laws governing the number of hours that teenagers may work per week during the school year. Four in ten (39.6%) youth in our sample reside in states that give 16 and 17 year olds unlimited discretion over the number of hours that they work per week while school is in session. One in seven (14.2%) live in states that impose some limit on their work involvement, yet still allow them to work 40 or more hours per week. The remainder (46.2%) are residents of states that limit work involvement to fewer than 40 hours per week.

Next, we will argue (but can't show directly) that the only way in which the state labor laws affect crime is through their impact on working behavior. On its face, this seems very reasonable. State labor laws have been in place for a long time and therefore seem unlikely to be related to crime rates. In fact, they are more related to the history of the state, and its reliance on farming (and youth workers). However, state labor laws could in fact be correlated with other things, such as drinking ages, driving rules, and criminal justice policies that might have a direct impact on crime. For example, conservative states might be more likely to have harsh prison sentences and less restrictive work rules. In a complete model, it would be important to control these other factors. In what follows, we will report the results without the controls for other state level factors that might be correlated with both state labor laws and crime (for results with these controls, and for a more detailed defense of this instrument, see Apel et al. 2008).

In Model B of Table 29.1, we show the first-stage regression of adolescent employment on the aforementioned state child labor laws. For ease of interpretation, the laws are dummy coded, and the coefficients represent contrasts relative to residence in states that limit the work involvement of teenagers to fewer than 40 h per week while school is in session. Both coefficients are positive and statistically significant, meaning that youth who live in states with more liberal child labor laws have a higher probability of being employed. This model fits extremely well – the F-statistic is 626.6, and the R-square is 0.130. The minimum F statistic for a first stage model is 10. Very clearly, work rules have a strong impact on the work behavior of youth. Just to make this substantively clear, youth who live in states in which there are no work rules governing the number of hours per week have a work probability that is 37 percentage points higher than youth who live in states in with work rules limiting employment to fewer than 40 hours per week. The inclusion of control variables at the first stage does little to change the results.[8]

The results from the second-stage or structural model are provided in Model C of Table 29.1. This is the two-stage least squares (2SLS) model. The results are striking – the coefficient for the effect of employment on crime prevalence is now negative and significant, while in the OLS regression the same effect was positive and significant. Moreover, the effect is substantively much larger, with youth who work 7.4 percentage points less likely to commit a delinquent offense, a 21-percent reduction in delinquency (compared with an 8-percent increase in the OLS model). Inclusion of control variables yields a work effect of 6.1 percentage points. It is hard to overstate the nature of this result. When we use 2SLS, we find not that working leads to increased crime, but rather that working actually prevents crime, at least for youth whose employment is influenced by state child labor laws.

---

[8] Control variables are also considered instrumental variables; they are just "included instruments" rather than "excluded instruments." This means that they are to be included in both the first- and second-stage models.

Another feature of instrumental variables that is worth noting is the size of the standard errors in the two models – the standard errors in 2SLS models will always be larger than the standard errors in OLS models. In this case, the standard error is almost three times larger, and it is not unusual to see cases where it is ten times larger. The difference is directly related to the strength of the instruments in the first-stage model. The stronger the instrumental variable(s), the smaller the increase in the standard errors in 2SLS relative to OLS.

Having estimated the substantive models, it is now possible to perform some routine diagnostics. We have two excluded instruments, when we technically need only one to estimate the model. An exactly identified model will need one instrument for every endogenous variable. Therefore, we can do a test of overidentifying restrictions. In this test, we look to see if the residual in the 2SLS regression is correlated with the instrumental variables. If the instruments are truly exogenous, they should be uncorrelated with the second-stage residual. Yet it is important not to act as if this is the definitive test of a "good" instrument. Weak instruments will pass this test (they are not correlated with anything), and bad instruments can negatively influence the test – the individual test of each instrument separately depends on the assumption that the other instruments in the model are valid instruments. Nonetheless, it still provides a good test for the value of an instrument. We jointly and separately pass the overidentification tests generated by Stata (using the – *overid* – command after estimating the 2SLS model).

It is also possible to compare the results from 2SLS with OLS in the form of a Durbin-Wu-Hausman (DWH) test for the endogeneity of the problem regressor. This is a straightforward z-test comparing the coefficients and standard errors from the two competing models. The null hypothesis is that both OLS and 2SLS are consistent, but OLS is efficient (smaller standard errors, which is true by definition). The alternative hypothesis is that only 2SLS is consistent. The null will be rejected when the difference between the coefficients is large relative to the difference between the standard errors. In this case, our DWH test statistic is -3.80, which leads us to reject the null hypothesis at a five-percent significance level. We conclude that the OLS estimate of the "work effect" is inconsistent, and we should therefore prefer the 2SLS estimate.

Although this is a simple example, we want to assure the reader that this result is substantively meaningful and robust. We conducted the same analysis using the non-linear instrumental variable model for a probit regression, *ivprobit*, and once again flipped the coefficient from positive and significant in the standard probit model to negative and significant in the instrumental variables probit model. This literature tends to focus on work hours rather than simply working, and our basic result holds when we focus on a continuous measure of work hours as well as a dichotomous indicator of "intensive work," measured as more than 20 hours of work per week. As in Apel et al. (2008), we have convincing evidence that employment does indeed prevent adolescent offending (as for adults) once we effectively deal with selection bias.

CONCLUSION

The goal of this chapter has been to provide a crime-centered introduction to the use of instrumental variables. We believe there are many empirical questions central to criminology which could be aided with the application of good instrumental variable methods. There are already good examples of this technique being applied profitably in the criminological literature. Moreover, we believe that the substantive and theoretical conversations that are generated by the search for good instruments will enrich the discipline. Therefore, we want this valuable technique to be applied thoughtfully in criminology by criminologists.

We are also aware, however, that there are some challenges to the insightful application of instrumental variable techniques. Instrumental variable techniques are not an add-on that can be discussed in two paragraphs at the end of the paper. The instruments need to be described and defended in detail – the substance is the thing. It is crucial to remember that the instrument must be correlated with the dependent variable of interest, but the researcher must argue on substantive and theoretical grounds that this correlation is indirect through the independent variable of interest. This claim can never be proven statistically, although tests can be conducted that support the claim. Failure to defend the instrument substantively represents a failure of the method.

The other major problem with instruments involves the use of weak instruments. The power of the instrument to explain the independent variable of interest must be demonstrated and discussed (the first stage in 2SLS). Weak instruments are almost more dangerous than bad instruments. Weak instruments by definition, will not generate an answer that is any different than the answer provided by the OLS model, yet it will pass all post hoc tests. The researcher will then naively conclude that there is no selection bias (or simultaneity or measurement error), when in fact she has shown no such thing. Weak instruments are like experiments in which no one complies with the treatment. The conclusion should be that the experiment did not work, not that the substantive problem has been solved. In the same way that an experiment that fails to report treatment compliance is a bad experiment, instrumental variable studies that do not report the first stage are poor studies. It is essential to evaluate the power of the instrument before one makes substantive conclusions based on the instrument.

Researchers interested in applying instrumental variables should pay particular attention to the treatment of instrumental variables by economists, where it represents a core tool in the statistical toolbox. Good technical (but accessible) treatments include Angrist and Krueger (2001) and Angrist and Pischke (2008). Researchers should also read empirical papers by economists to observe the care with which (a) the exclusion restriction is defended and (b) the first stage is presented. This care should be the standard that we as criminologists choose to import into criminology when we import this method.

REFERENCES

Angrist J (2006) Instrumental variables methods in experimental criminological research: what, why, and how. J Exp Criminol 2:23–44

Angrist JD, Evans WN (1998) Children and their parents' labor supply: evidence from exogenous variation in family size. Am Econ Rev 88:450–77

Angrist JD, Krueger AB (2001) Instrumental variables and the search for identification: from supply and demand to natural experiments. J Econ Perspect 15:69–85

Angrist JD, Pischke J-S (2008) Mostly harmless econometrics: an empiricist's companion. Princeton University Press, Princeton, NJ

Apel R, Bushway SD, Paternoster R, Brame R, Sweeten G (2008) Using state child labor laws to identify the causal effect of youth employment on deviant behavior and academic achievement. J Quant Criminol 24:337–362

Apel R, Brame R, Bushway S, Haviland A, Nagin D, Paternoster R (2007) Unpacking the relationship between adolescent employment and antisocial behavior: a matched samples comparison. Criminology 45:67–97

Berk R (2005) Randomized experiments as the bronze standard. J Exp Criminol 1:417–33

Brame R, Bushway S, Paternoster R, Thornberry T (2005) Temporal linkages in violent and nonviolent criminal activity. J Quant Criminol 21:149–174

Chiricos T (1987) Rates of crime and unemployment: an analysis of aggregate research evidence. Soc Probl 34: 187–212

Committee to Review Research on Police Policy and Practices (2004) Fairness and effectiveness in policing: the evidence. Skogan W, Frydl K (eds) National Research Council

Cook P (1980) Research in criminal deterrence: laying the groundwork for the second decade. In: Morris N, Tonry M (eds) Crime and justice: a review of research, vol 2. University of Chicago, Chicago

Cook P (1986) The demand and supply of criminal opportunities. In: Morris N, Tonry M (eds) Crime and justice: a review of research, vol 7. University of Chicago, Chicago

Evans WN, Owens E (2007) COPS and crime. J Publ Econ 91:181–201

Farrington D, Welsh B (2005) Randomized experiments in criminology: what have we learned in the last two decades? J Exp Criminol 1:9–28

Gottfredson DM (1999) Effects of judges' sentencing decisions on criminal careers. National Institute of Justice, Washington, DC

Gottfredson M, Hirschi T (1990) A general theory of crime. Stanford University Press, Stanford, CA

Jacob B, Lefgren L (2003) Are idle hands the devil's workshop? Incapacitation, concentration and juvenile crime. Am Econ Rev 93:1560–1577

Jones AS, Gondolf EW (2002) Assessing the effect of batterer program completion reassault: an instrumental variable analysis. J Quant Criminol 18:71–98

Kilmer B (2008) Does parolee drug testing influence employment and education outcomes? Evidence from a randomized experiment with non-compliance. J Quant Criminol 24:83–123

Kirk D (2009) A natural experiment on residential change and recidivism: lessons from Hurricane Katrina. Am Sociol Rev 74:445–464

Kleck G, Sever B, Li S, Gertz M (2005) The missing link in general deterrence research. Criminology 43:623–660

Kling J (2006) Incarceration length, employment and earnings. Am Econ Rev 96:863–876

Levitt SD (1996) The effect of prison population size on crime rates: evidence from prison overcrowding litigation. QJ Econ 111:319–351

Levitt S, Miles T (2006) Economic contributions to the understanding of crime. Annu Rev Law Soc Sci 2:147–164

Nagin DS (1978) General deterrence: a review and critique of the empirical evidence. In: Deterrence and incapacitation: estimating the effects of criminal sanctions on crime rates. National Academy of Sciences, Washington, DC

Nagin DS (1998) Criminal deterrence research at the outset of the twenty-first century. Crim Justice A Rev Res 23:1–42

Paternoster R, Bushway S, Brame R, Apel R (2003) The effect of teenage employment on delinquency and problem behaviors. Social Forces 82:297–335

Raphael S (2006) Should criminal history records be universally available? Criminol Publ Pol 5(3):515–522

Rothstein DS (2007) High school employment and youths' academic achievement. J Hum Res 42:194–213

Sampson R, Laub J, Wimer C (2006) Does marriage reduce crime? A counterfactual approach to within-individual causal effects. Criminology 44:465–508

Spelman W (2008) Specifying the relationship between crime and prisons. J Quant Criminol 24:149–178.

Spohn C, Holleran D (2002) The effect of imprisonment on recidivism rates of felony offenders: a focus on drug offenders. Criminology 40:329–357

Steinberg L Cauffman E (1995) The impact of employment on adolescent development. Ann Child Dev 11:131–166

Tita GE, Petras TL, Greenbaum RT (2006) Crime and residential choice: a neighborhood level analysis of the impact of crime in housing prices. J Quant Criminol 22:299

Tyler JohnH (2003) Using state child labor laws to identify the effect of school-year work in high school achievement. J Labor Econ 21: 81–408

Wilson DB, Gallagher CA, MacKenzie DL (2000) A meta-analysis of corrections-based education, vocation, and work programs for adult offenders. J Res Crime Delinquency 37:347–368

Zatz M (1987) The changing forms of racial/ethnic bias in sentencing. J Res Crime Delinquency 24:69–92

Part III-C
Estimation of Impacts and Outcomes of Crime and Justice: *Non-Experimental Approaches to Explaining Crime and Justice Outcomes*

CHAPTER 30

Multilevel Analysis in the Study of Crime and Justice

Brian D. Johnson

"The most pervasive fallacy of philosophic thinking goes back to neglect of context"
(John Dewey, 1931)

Neither criminal behavior nor society's reaction to it occurs in a social vacuum – for this reason, criminology, as a discipline, is inherently a multilevel enterprise. Individual criminal behavior is influenced by larger social, political, and environmental factors, as are the decisions of various actors in the criminal justice system. Classroom and school characteristics affect adolescent development, misconduct and delinquency (Beaver et al. 2008; Osgood and Anderson 2004; Stewart 2003). Family and neighborhood characteristics influence the likelihood of victimization and offending, as well as postrelease recidivism and fear of crime (Nieuwbeerta et al. 2008; Wilcox et al. 2007; Lauritsen and Schaum 2004; Kubrin and Stewart 2006; Wyant 2008; Lee and Ulmer 2000). Police department, precinct, and neighborhood factors affect police arrest practices, use of force, and clearance rates (Smith 1986; Sun et al. 2008; Lawton 2007; Pare et al. 2007; Eitle et al. 2005; Terrill and Reisig 2003). Judge characteristics and court contexts affect individual punishment decisions (Britt 2000; Ulmer and Johnson 2004; Johnson 2006; Wooldredge 2007), and prison environments are tied to inmate misconduct, substance use, and violence (Camp et al. 2003; Gillespie 2005; Huebner 2003; Wooldredge et al. 2001). Although these examples cover a diverse array of criminological topics, they all share a common analytical quality – each involves data that are measured across multiple units of analysis. When this is the case, multilevel models offer a useful statistical approach for studying diverse issues in crime and justice. As Table 30.1 demonstrates, recent years have witnessed an abundance of multilevel studies across a variety of topics in criminology and criminal justice.

This chapter provides a basic introduction to the use of multilevel statistical models in the field. It begins with a conceptual overview explaining what multilevel models are and why they are necessary. It then provides a statistical overview of basic multilevel models, illustrating their application using punishment data from federal district courts. The chapter concludes with a discussion of advanced applications and common concerns that arise in the context of multilevel research endeavors.

A.R. Piquero and D. Weisburd (eds.), *Handbook of Quantitative Criminology*,
DOI 10.1007/978-0-387-77650-7_30, © Springer Science + Business Media, LLC 2010,
First softcover printing 2011

TABLE 30.1. Recent examples of multilevel studies published in *Criminology* from 2005 to 2008

References	Topic
Xie and McDowall (2008)	Victimization and residential mobility
Schreck et al. (2008)	Violent offender and victim overlap
Johnson et al. (2008)	Federal guidelines departures
Xie and McDowall (2008)	Residential turnover and victimization
Mears et al. (2008)	Social context and recidivism
Zhang et al. (2007)	Crime reporting in China
Kreager (2007)	School violence and peer acceptance
Wilcox et al. (2007)	Guardianship and burglary victimization
Chiricos et al. (2007)	Labeling and felony recidivism
Osgood and Schreck (2007)	Stability and specialization in violence
Rosenfeld et al. (2007)	Order-maintenance policing and crime
Bernburg and Thorlindsson (2007)	Community structure and delinquency
Warner (2007)	Social context and calls to police
Hay and Forrest (2006)	The stability of self-control
Doherty (2006)	Self-control, social bonds, and desistence
Griffin and Wooldredge (2006)	Sex disparities in imprisonment
Sampson et al. (2006)	Marriage and crime reduction
Ulmer and Bradley (2006)	Trial penalties
Johnson (2006)	Judge and court context in sentencing
Kubrin and Stewart (2006)	Neighborhood context and recidivism
Simons et al. (2005)	Collective efficacy, parenting and delinquency
Slocum et al. (2005)	Strain, offending and drug use
Wright and Beaver (2005)	Parental influence and self-control
Bontrager et al. (2005)	Race and adjudicated guilt
Kleck et al. (2005)	Perceptions of punishment
Johnson (2005)	Sentencing guidelines departures

CONCEPTUAL OVERVIEW

Multilevel statistical models are necessitated by the fact that social relationships exist at several different levels of analysis that jointly influence outcomes of interest. Smaller units of analysis are often "nested" within one or more larger units of analysis. For instance, students are nested within classrooms and schools, offenders as well as victims are nested within family and neighborhood environments, and criminal justice personnel are nested within larger community and organizational contexts. In each of these cases, the characteristics of some larger context are expected to influence individual behavior. This logic can be extended to any situation involving multiple levels of analysis including, but not limited to, individuals, groups, social networks, neighborhoods, communities, counties, states, and even countries. Moreover, longitudinal research questions often involve multilevel data structures, with repeated measures nested within individuals or with observations nested over time (e.g., Horney et al. 1995; Slocum et al. 2005; Rosenfeld et al. 2007). Other common applications of multilevel analysis include twin studies with paired or clustered sibling dyads (e.g. Wright et al. 2008; Taylor et al. 2002) and meta-analyses that involve multiple effect sizes nested within the same study or dataset (e.g. Raudenbush 1984; Goldstein et al. 2000). Regardless of the level of aggregation or "nesting," though, the important point is that criminological enterprises often involve data that span multiple levels of analysis. In fact, given the complexity of our social world, it can be difficult to identify topics of criminological interest that are not characterized by multiple spheres of social influence. When these multiple influences are present, multilevel statistical models represent a useful and even necessary tool for analyzing a broad variety of criminological research questions.

A Model by any Other Name?

Given the complexity surrounding multilevel models, it is useful to distinguish up front what can sometimes be a confusing and inexact argot. Various monikers are used to describe multilevel statistical models (e.g. multilevel models, hierarchical models, nested models, mixed models). Although this nomenclature is often applied interchangeably, there can be subtle but important differences in these designations. Multilevel modeling is used here as a broad, all-encompassing rubric for statistical models that are explicitly designed to analyze and infer relationships for more than one level of analysis.[1] The language of multilevel models is further complicated by the fact that there are various different software packages that can be used to estimate multilevel models, some of which are general statistical packages (e.g. SAS, STATA) while others are specialized multilevel programs (e.g. HLM, MLwin, aML).[2]

Additional confusion may derive from the fact that scholars often use terminology, such as ecological, aggregate, and contextual effects, interchangeably despite important differences in their meaning. *Ecological effects*, or group-level effects, can refer to any group-level influence that is associated with the higher level of analysis. Group-level effects can take several forms. First, *aggregate effects* (sometime referred to as *analytical* or *derived* variables) are created by aggregating individual level characteristics up to the group-level of analysis (e.g., percent male in a school). These are sometimes distinguished from *structural effects* that are also derived from individual data but capture relational measures among members within a group (e.g., density of friendship networks) (see Luke 2004: 6). To complicate matters, when individual-level data are aggregated to the group-level, they can exert two distinct types of influence – first, they can exert *compositional effects*, which reflect group-differences that are attributable to variability in the constitution of the groups – between-group differences may simply reflect the fact that groups are made up of different types of individuals. Second, they can exert *contextual effects*, which represent influences above and beyond differences that exist in group composition. Contextual effects are sometimes referred to as *emergent properties* because the collective exerts a synergistic influence that is unique to the group aggregation

---

[1] Hierarchical or nested models, for instance, technically refer to data structures involving exact nesting of smaller levels of analysis within larger units. Multilevel data, however, can also be nonnested, or "cross-classified", in ways that do not follow a neat hierarchical ordering. Data might be nested within years and within states at the same time, for example, with no clear hierarchy to "year" and "state" as levels of analysis (Gelman and Hill 2007: 2). Similarly, adolescents might be nested within schools and neighborhoods with students from the same neighborhood attending different schools, or convicted terrorists might be nested both within terrorist groups and the district courts in which they are punished. Although these cases clearly involve multilevel data, they are not hierarchical in a technical sense. Similarly, "mixed models" technically refer to statistical models containing both "fixed" and "random" effects. Although this is often the case in multilevel models, it is not necessarily so; the broader rubric multilevel modeling is preferred, therefore, to capture the variety of models designed to incorporate data across multiple units of analysis.

[2] A useful and detailed review of the strengths and limitations of numerous software programs that provide for the estimation of multilevel models is provided by the Centre for Multlevel Modeling at the University of Bristol at http://www.cmm.bris.ac.uk/learning-training/multilevel-m-software/index.shtml.

and is not present in the individual constituent parts.[3] Although the term "contextual effect" is sometimes used as a broader rubric for any group-level influence, the narrower definition provided here is often useful for distinguishing among types of ecological influences that can be examined in multilevel models. Finally, *global effects* refer to structural characteristics of the collective itself that are not derived from individual data, but rather reflect measures that are specific to the group (e.g., physical dilapidation of the school). These and other commonly used terms in multilevel analysis are summarized in Table 30.2.[4]

Theoretical Rationales for Multilevel Models

The need for multilevel statistical models is firmly rooted in both theoretical and methodological rationales. Multilevel models are extensions of traditional regression models that account for the structuring of data across aggregate groupings, that is, they explicitly account for the nested nature of data across multiple levels of analysis. Because our social world is inherently multilevel, theoretical perspectives that incorporate multiple levels of influence in the study of crime and justice are bound to improve our ability to explain both individual criminal behavior and society's reaction to it.

Figure 30.1 presents a schematic of a hypothetical study examining the influence of low self-control on delinquency in a sample of high school students. Imagine that self-control is measured at multiple time points for the same sample of students. In such a case, multiple measures of self-control would be nested within individual students, and individual students would be nested within classrooms, which are nested within schools. The lowest level of analysis would be within-individual observations of self-control, and the highest level of analysis would be school-level characteristics. Ignoring this hierarchical data structuring, then, is likely to introduce omitted variable bias of a large-scale theoretical nature.

Moreover, many theoretical perspectives explicitly argue that micro-level influences will vary across macro-social contexts. For instance, racial group threat theories (Blumer 1958; Liska 1992) predict that the exercise of formal social control will vary in concert with large or growing minority populations. Testing theoretical models that explicitly incorporate variation in micro-effects across macro-theoretical contexts, therefore, offers an important opportunity to advance criminological knowledge. Assuming that theoretical influences operate at a single level of analysis is likely to provide a simplistic and incomplete portrayal of the complex criminological social world.

Moreover, inferential problems can emerge when data are used to draw statistical conclusions across levels of analysis. For instance, in his classic study of immigrant literacy,

---

[3] Philosophical discourse on emergent properties dates all the way back to Aristotle, but was perhaps most lucidly applied by John Stuart Mill. He argued that the human body in its entirety produces something uniquely greater than its singular organic parts, stating that "To whatever degree we might imagine our knowledge of the properties of the several ingredients of a living body to be extended and perfected, it is certain that no mere summing up of the separate actions of those elements will ever amount to the action of the living body itself" (Mill 1843). Contextual effects models have long been applied in sociology and related fields (e.g., Firebaugh 1978; Blalock 1984), but these applications differ from multilevel models in that the latter are more general formulations that specifically account for residual correlation within groups and explicitly provide for examination of the causes of between-group variation in outcomes.

[4] Table 30.2 is partially adapted from Diez Roux (2002), which contains a more detailed and elaborate glossary of many of these terms.

TABLE 30.2. Glossary of multilevel modeling terminology

Terminology	Definition
Aggregate variable	Ecological variable created by aggregating the individual properties of lower level measures up to the group level of analysis. Sometimes also referred to as "Derived" or "Analytical" variables.
Atomistic fallacy	The fallacy, also referred to as the Individualistic Fallacy, that results when faulty inferences for macro-level group relationships are drawn using micro-level individual data. See Ecological fallacy
Compositional effects	Between group differences in outcomes that are attributable to differences in group composition, or in the different individuals of which the groups are composed
Contextual analysis	Early analytical approach designed to investigate the effects of aggregate characteristics of the collective by including aggregate variables along with individual variables in traditional regression models.
Contextual effects	Macro-level influences exerted by aggregate variables above and beyond those attributable to compositional differences in groups, but sometimes the term is used to refer to any group level effects.
Contextual effects model	Statistical model that include individual characteristics and the aggregates of the individual characteristics in the same model in order to assess the influence of contextual effects on individual outcomes.
Cross-level interaction	A statistical interaction between higher and lower order variables, usually attempting to explain variation in the effects of lower level measures across higher level groupings.
Cross-classified model	A multilevel statistical model for analyzing data that is cross-nested in two or more higher levels of analysis which are not strictly hierarchical in structure. Also referred to as cross-nested models.
Ecological fallacy	The fallacy that results when faulty inferences for individual level relationships are made using group level data. See Atomistic fallacy.
Ecological variable	A broad term for any higher order group level variable, including aggregate, structural, and global measures. Sometimes referred to as a Group Level, Macro Level, or Level 2 variable.
Empirical bayes estimates	Estimates for group level parameters that are optimally weighted to combine information from the individual group itself with information from other similar groups in the data.
Fixed effects	Regression coefficients (or intercepts) that are not allowed to vary randomly across higher level units. These are sometimes referred to as fixed coefficients. See Random effects.
Fixed effects models	Statistical models in which all effects or coefficients are fixed. Often this refers to the case where a dummy variable is included for each higher level unit to remove between-group variation in the outcome.
Global variable	A group level variable that unlike aggregate variables has no individual analogue. Global (or integral) variables refer to characteristics that are uniquely defined at the higher level of analysis.
Group level variable	An alternative name for ecological variables that measure any group level characteristic. Sometimes referred to as Level 2 variables. See Individual level variable.
Hierarchical (linear) model	A multilevel model for analyzing data that is nested among two or more hierarchies. Hierarchical models technically assume that data are strictly nested across levels of analysis, although this term may refer to multilevel models generally.
Individual level variable	A variable that characterizes individual attributes or refers to individual level constructs. Sometimes referred to as Level 1 variables. See Group level variable.

(continued)

TABLE 30.2. (continued)

Terminology	Definition
Intraclass correlation	The proportion of the total variance in the outcome that exists between groups or higher level units rather than within groups or higher level units.
Mixed model	A multilevel model containing both fixed and random coefficients. Some regression coefficients are allowed to vary randomly across higher level units while other regression coefficients are specified as fixed coefficients.
Multilevel analysis	An analytical approach for simultaneously analyzing both individual and group level effects when data is measured at two or more levels of analysis with lower level (micro) observations nested within higher level (macro) units.
Multilevel model	A statistical model used in multilevel analysis for analyzing data that is measured at two or more levels of analysis, including but not limited to hierarchical linear models, hierarchical nonlinear models, and cross-classified models.
Population average estimates	Estimates for nonlinear multilevel models that provide the marginal expectation of the outcome averaged across all random effects rather than after controlling for random effects. See Unit-specific estimates
Random coefficient model	A multilvel statistical model in which the individual level intercept and regression coefficients are allowed to have randomly varying effects across higher level units of analysis. See Random intercept model.
Random effects	Regression coefficients (or intercepts) that are allowed to vary randomly across higher level units. These are sometimes referred to as random intercepts or random coefficients. See Fixed effects.
Random intercept model	A multilevel statistical model in which the individual level intercept is allowed to vary randomly across higher level units of analysis, but the individual level coefficients are assumed to have constant effects. See Random coefficient model.
Unit-specific estimates	Estimates for nonlinear multilevel models that are conditional on higher level random effects. Unit-specific models provide individual estimates controlling for rather than averaging across random effects. See Population average estimates.
Variance components	Model parameters (sometimes referred to as random effects) that explicitly capture both within-group and between-group variability in outcomes. Each level of analysis in a multilevel model has its own variance component.

Robinson (1950) examined the correlation between aggregate literacy rates and the proportion of the population that was immigrant at the state level. He found a substantial positive correlation between percent immigrant and the literacy rate ($r = 0.53$). Yet, when individual level-data on immigration and literacy were separately examined, the correlation reversed and became negative ($r = -0.11$). Although individual immigrants had lower literacy, they tended to settle in states with high native literacy rates, thus confounding the individual and aggregate relationships. This offers an example of the *ecological fallacy*, or erroneous conclusions involving individual relationships that are inferred from aggregate data. As Peter Blau (1960: 179) suggested, aggregate studies are limited because they cannot "separate the consequences of social conditions from those of the individual's own characteristics for his behavior, because ecological data do not furnish information about individuals except in the aggregate."

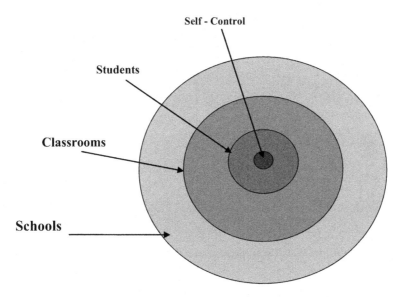

FIGURE 30.1. The hierarchical nature of multiple units of analysis in multilevel models.

The same mistake in statistical inference can occur in the opposite direction. The *atomistic (or individualistic) fallacy* occurs when aggregate relationships are mistakenly inferred from individual-level data. Because associations between two variables at the individual level may differ from associations for analogous variables at a higher level of aggregation, aggregate relationships cannot be reliably inferred from individual-level data. For instance, social disorganization theory would predict that crime rates across neighborhoods are related to mobility rates because high population turnover reduces informal social control at the neighborhood level. Because this prediction refers to neighborhoods as the unit of analysis, though, one would risk serious inferential error testing this group-level hypothesis with individual-level data. For instance, one could not test the theory by examining whether or not individuals who move residences have higher criminal involvement. To do so would be to commit the atomistic fallacy. This reflects the fact that variables aggregated up from individual-level data often have unique and independent *contextual* effects. Moving to a new residence represents a different causal pathway than living in a neighborhood with high rates of residential mobility.[5]

Because of the inherent difficulties in making statistical inferences across different levels of analysis, a preferred approach is to use multilevel analytic procedures to simultaneously incorporate individual- and group-level causal processes. Multilevel models explicitly provide for this type of statistical analysis. The difficulty is in distinguishing among the different types of individual and ecological influences that are of theoretical interest and then specifying the statistical model to properly estimate these effects.

---

[5] Two related, but distinct problems of causal inference are the *psychologistic fallacy*, which can occur when individual level data are used to draw inferences without accounting for confounding ecological influences, and the *sociologistic fallacy*, which may arise from the failure to consider individual level characteristics when drawing inferences about the causes of group variability. The pyschologistic fallacy results from a failure to adequately consider *contextual effects*, whereas the sociologistic fallacy results from a failure to capture *compositional effects*.

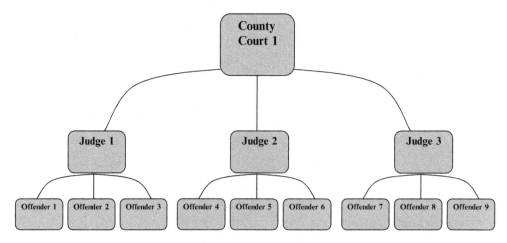

FIGURE 30.2. The nesting of multilevel data across levels of analysis.

Multilevel Modeling and Hypothesis Testing

There are also persuasive statistical reasons for engaging in multilevel modeling such as providing improved parameter estimates, corrected standard errors, and conducting more accurate statistical significance tests. Utilizing traditional regression models for multilevel data presents several problems. Figure 30.2 presents a second example of hierarchical data where individual criminal offenders are nested within judges and county courts. Because several offenders are sentenced by the same judge and several judges share the same courtroom environment, statistical dependencies are likely to arise among clustered observations. When individual data is nested within aggregate groups, observations within clusters are likely to share unaccounted-for similarities. If, for instance, some judges are "hanging judges" while others are "bleeding-heart liberals," then offenders sentenced by the former will have sentences that are systematically harsher than offenders sentenced by the latter. Statistically speaking, the residual errors will be correlated, systematically falling above the regression line for the first judge and below it for the second. Because one of the assumptions of ordinary regression models is that residual errors are independent, such systematic clustering would violate this core model assumption. The consequence of this violation is that standard errors will be *underestimated* by the ordinary regression model. Statistical significance tests will therefore be too liberal, risking Type I inferential errors in which the null hypothesis is falsely rejected even when true in the population. Multilevel statistical models are needed to account for statistical dependencies that occur among clusters of hierarchically organized data.

A related problem is that statistical significance tests in ordinary regression models utilize the wrong degrees of freedom for ecological predictors in the model. Traditional regression models fail to account for the fact that hierarchically structured data are characterized by different sample sizes at each level of analysis. For example, with data on 1,000 students nested within 50 schools, there would be an individual-level sample size of 1,000 observations, but a school-level sample size of only 50 observations. This means that statistical significance tests for school-level predictors need to be based on degrees of freedom that reflect the number of schools in the data, not the number of students. Statistical significance tests in ordinary regression models fail to recognize this important distinction. The consequence is that the amount of statistical power available for testing school-level predictors will be exaggerated. The number of degrees of freedom for statistical significance tests needs to be adjusted for the number of aggregate units in the data – multilevel models provide these adjustments.

A third advantage of multilevel models over ordinary regression models is that they allow for the modeling of heterogeneity in regression effects. The single-level regression model assumes *de facto* that individual predictors exert the same effect in each aggregate grouping. Multilevel models, on the other hand, explicitly allow for variation in the effects of individual predictors across higher levels of analysis. Ulmer and Bradley, (2006), for instance, have argued that the effect of trial conviction on criminal sentence varies across courts. This proposition is illustrated in Fig. 30.3, using federal punishment data for a random sample of eight district courts. The ordinary regression model would constrain the effect of trial conviction to be uniform across courts, but Fig. 30.3 clearly suggests intercourt variation in this effect. Multilevel analysis allows for this type of variation to be explicitly incorporated into the statistical model, providing the researcher with a useful tool for better capturing the real-world complexity that is likely to characterize individual influences across criminological contexts.

Other advantages that also characterize multilevel models are that they provide for convenient and accurate tests of cross-level interactions, or moderating effects that involve both individual and ecological variables. For example, the influence of individual socioeconomic status on delinquency might depend on the socioeconomic composition of the school. This conditional relationship could be directly investigated by specifying a cross-level interaction between an individual's SES and the mean SES at the school level.

One final statistical advantage of multilevel models is that they are able to simultaneously incorporate information both within and between groups in order to provide optimally weighted group-level estimates. This is accomplished by combining information from the group itself with information from other similar groups in the data, and it is particularly useful when some groups have relatively few observations. Because groups with smaller sample sizes will have less reliable group means, some regression to the overall grand mean is expected. Utilizing a Bayesian estimation approach, the multilevel model shifts the within-group mean toward the mean for other groups. The more reliable the group mean, the more heavily it is weighted; the less reliable (and the less variability across groups), the more the estimate is shifted toward the overall grand mean for all groups in the data. Thus, estimates for specific groups are based not only on their own within-group data, but also on data from other groups. This process is sometimes referred to as "borrowing power" because within-group estimates benefit from information on other groups, and the estimates themselves are sometimes called "shrinkage estimates" because they "shrink" individual group means toward the grand mean for all groups. The end result is that group-level estimates are optimally weighted to reflect information both within and between groups in the data.[6]

---

[6] The following equation provides the formula for this weighting process (Raudenbush and Bryk 2002: 46):

$$\hat{\beta}_j^* = \lambda_j \bar{Y}_{\bullet j} + (1 - \lambda_j)\hat{\gamma}_{00}$$

where $\hat{\beta}_j^*$ is the group estimate, which is a product of the individual group mean $\bar{Y}_{\bullet j}$ weighted by its reliability λ_j, plus the overall grand mean $\hat{\gamma}_{00}$ weighted by the complement of the reliability $(1 - \lambda_j)$. If the reliability of the group mean is one, the weighted estimate reduces to the group mean; if it is zero, it reduces to the grand mean. The more reliable the group mean, the more it counts in the multilevel estimate. When the assumptions of the multilevel model are met, this provides the most precise and most efficient estimator of the group mean.

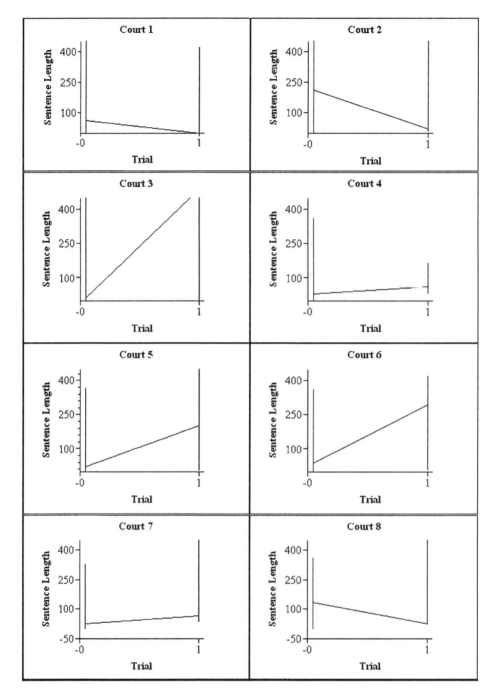

FIGURE 30.3. Variation in trial penalties across federal courts.

Multilevel models, then, provide numerous analytical and statistical advantages over ordinary regression approaches when data are nested across levels of analysis. By providing for the simultaneous inclusion of individual- and group-level information, they better specify the complex relationships that often characterize our social world, and they help overcome common problems of statistical inference associated with reliance on single-level data. Moreover, multilevel models correct for the problematic clustering of observations that may occur with nested data, they provide a convenient approach for modeling both within and between group variability in regression effects, and they offer improved parameter estimates that simultaneously incorporate within and between group information. The remaining discussion provides a basic statistical introduction to the multilevel model along with examples illustrating its application to the study of criminal punishment in federal court.

STATISTICAL OVERVIEW

Multilevel models are simple extensions of ordinary regression models, which account for the nesting of data within higher-order units. It is therefore useful to begin with an overview of the basic regression model in order to demonstrate how the multilevel adaptation builds upon and extends it to the case of multilevel data. For illustrative purposes, examples are provided using United States Sentencing Commission (USSC) data on a random sample of 25,000 convicted federal offenders nested within 89 federal district courts across the US.[7]

From Ordinary Regression to Multilevel Analysis

When faced with multilevel data (e.g. lower-level data that is nested within some higher-level grouping), ordinary regression approaches can take three basic forms. First, individual data can be pooled across groups and analyzed without regard for group structure. This approach ignores important group-level variability and often violates key assumptions of OLS regression such as independent errors. Second, separate unpooled analyses can be conducted within each group. This approach can be useful for examining between-group variability, but it requires relatively large samples for each group and it is cumbersome when the number of groups becomes large. Third, aggregate analysis can also be conducted at the group level alone, but this approach ignores within-group variability and requires a relatively large number of groups for analysis. In each of these cases, traditional regression approaches are unable to incorporate the full range of information available at both the individual and group level of analysis and they may violate important assumptions of the single-level ordinary regression model.

For illustrative purposes, the ordinary regression model is presented in (30.1):

$$Y_i = \beta_0 + \beta_1 X_i + r_i \tag{30.1}$$

where Y_i is a continuous dependent variable, β_0 is the model intercept, β_1 is the effect of the independent variable X_i for individual i, and r_i is the individual-level residual error term. Two key assumptions of the linear regression model are that the relationship between X_i and Y_i can be summarized with a single linear regression line and that all of the residual error terms for individuals in the data are statistically independent of one another. Both of these

---

[7] These data are drawn from fiscal years 1997 to 2000 and are restricted to the 89 federal districts and 11 circuit courts within the US, with the District of Columbia excluded because it has its own district and circuit court. For more information on the USSC data see Johnson et al. (2008).

assumptions are likely to be violated with multilevel data, the first because the effect of X_i on Y_i might vary by group and the second because individuals within the same group are likely to share unaccounted-for similarities.

Failure to account for the nesting of observations can result in "false power" at both levels of analysis. False power occurs because there is typically less independent information available when observations are clustered together. Consider the difference between (a) data from 50 schools with 20 students each, versus (b) data from 1,000 schools with one student each. The number of students is the same, but if students share similarities within schools, each student provides less unique information in the first sample than in the second. Moreover, there is more unique school-level data in the second sample than in the first. Because ordinary regression models ignore the clustering of individuals within schools, they treat both samples as equivalent. The consequence of this is that the amount of statistical power for the first sample is artificially inflated at both the individual and school level of analysis. Moreover, standard errors for the first sample will be underestimated and significance tests will be too liberal if there are unaccounted-for similarities among students within schools.

The multilevel solution is to add an additional error parameter to the ordinary regression model in order to capture group-level dependencies in the data. The multilevel model is represented by a series of "submodels" that model between-group variation in individual-level parameters as a function of group level processes. A basic two-level random intercept model is presented in (30.2):

$$\begin{aligned} \text{Level 1} \quad & Y_{ij} = \beta_{0j} + \beta_{1j} X_{ij} + r_{ij} \\ \text{Level 2} \quad & \beta_{0j} = \gamma_{00} + u_{0j} \end{aligned} \tag{30.2}$$

where the level one intercept β_{0j} is modeled as an outcome in the level 2 portion of the model. The γ_{00} parameter represents the Level 2 intercept (gammas are substituted for betas at Level 2 for notational convenience) and the u_{0j} parameter represents the new group-level error term, which accounts for group-level dependence. The two-level model specification is presented for simple notational convenience and can be combined into an equivalent single-level model by substituting the Level 2 model in for β_{0j} at Level 1. Doing so produces the combined model in (30.3):

$$Y_{ij} = \gamma_{00} + \beta_{1j} X_{ij} + r_{ij} + u_{0j} \tag{30.3}$$

On comparing (30.3) with (30.1), it becomes clear that the only difference between the ordinary regression model and the multilevel model is the additional group-level error term u_{0j}. The basic multilevel model, then, is nothing more than an ordinary regression equation that includes an additional group-level error parameter to capture group-level dependencies.

The addition of the group-level error term explicitly models variation among group means in the data. For example, if the outcome is the mean sentence length given to offenders across federal district courts, the group-level error term allows for mean sentence length to vary by federal district, thus capturing potentially important district-level differences in average punishment severity. These differences are illustrated in Fig. 30.4, where Panel A shows the mean sentence length pooled across a sample of 10 federal districts, and Panel B shows the mean sentence length disaggregated by federal district. The figure indicates that average punishments vary across federal courts. For instance, the mean sentence length in the Northern District of Florida is about twice the average sentence in the District of Delaware. Important differences in variability in punishment also exist across federal districts, with the standard deviation in the Western District of Oklahoma being more than twice that in the Southern District of California. These group-level variations are captured by the incorporation of the group-level error term in the multilevel statistical model, resulting in standard

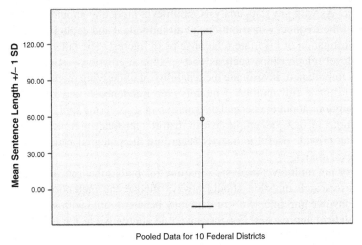

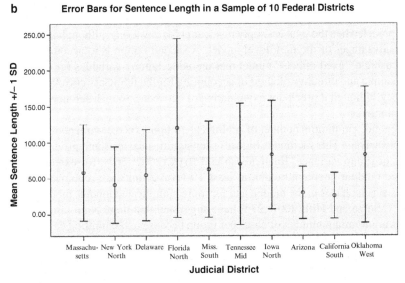

FIGURE 30.4. Variation in sentence lengths across federal courts. Panel (a): pooled data for sample of 10 districts. Panel (b): disaggregated data for sample of 10 districts.

errors and statistical significance tests that are properly adjusted for the nesting of individual cases within aggregate district court groupings.

Building the Multilevel Model

Despite its conceptual simplicity, multilevel analysis adds a layer of analytical complexity that can quickly become cumbersome when applied to research questions involving multiple predictors across multiple levels of analysis. For this reason, it is essential to thoroughly conduct exploratory data analysis and to carefully build the multilevel model from the ground up. Model misspecifications at one level of analysis can bias parameter estimates across levels of inference. As with any data analysis, multilevel modeling should begin with a careful investigation of the frequency distributions of all individual and ecological variables, as well as detailed investigation of bivariate relationships of interest. The latter should include analysis of cross-level relationships such as unit-specific regressions estimated for all level 2 units. It is also important to investigate the tenability of underlying model assumptions before attempting to estimate full multilevel models (see Raudenbush and Bryk 2002: 255). For instance, assumptions about the normal distribution of error terms apply to each level of analysis and violations of these assumptions can distort statistical inferences. These initial data explorations can provide useful indicators regarding the potential benefits and necessity of using a multilevel model.

Whether or not multilevel analysis is required is both a theoretical and empirical question. First, the research question should always dictate the methodology. Some research questions that involve multiple levels of data may be answerable with simpler and more parsimonious analytical approaches. For instance, one alternative to the multilevel model is to estimate an ordinary regression model along with robust standard errors that are adjusted to account for the clustering of observations within level 2 units. For example, STATA provides a "cluster" command option that adjusts standard errors for residual dependency. This can be a useful approach when the goal is simply to account for clustering, although it does not provide the other advantages of the multilevel model. A second option is to account for group-level variation using a "fixed effects" model that includes dummy variables for each level 2 unit. This is a simple and effective method of accounting for the intraclass correlation due to group dependency, although it precludes examination of between-group differences that are often of theoretical interest.

In general, a minimum number of ecological groupings is recommended before turning to multilevel analysis. This facilitates higher order significance tests and produces more precise estimates of group variance. Raudenbush and Bryk (2002: 267), for example, suggest that for a basic random-intercept model, at least 10 level 2 units are required for each level 2 variable that is included in the model, and for more complicated models more level 2 units are required. Gelman and Hill (2007: 275) have suggested that there is no minimum number of groupings or minimum number of cases per group because in the limiting case (e.g., with only one group or when between-group variances are zero), the multilevel model will reduce to the ordinary regression equation. Although this is technically true, in practice at least a dozen or so clusters is recommended for multilevel modeling in order to satisfy model assumptions regarding a randomly drawn sample and the normal distribution of level 2 error terms. One strength of the multilevel model is that it can handle unbalanced sample designs involving variation in the number of observations per cluster, even when some clusters contain single observations.[8] Ultimately, the researcher must weigh the added complexity introduced by the multilevel model against its analytical advantages for any given research question.

---

[8] In some research applications, such as couple or twin studies, research designs are routinely constrained to have only 2 observations per grouping. This is not a problem for multilevel modeling. As with ordinary regression, though, small sample sizes (at both level 1 and level 2) can result in low statistical power. Statistical power in multilevel models is more complicated than for ordinary regression models because it is a product of several factors, including the number of clusters, the number of observations per cluster, the strength of the intraclass correlation and the effect sizes for variables in the model. One useful optimal design software program for conducting power analysis with multilevel data is available at: http://sitemaker.umich.edu/group-ased/optimal_design_software.

Before turning to multilevel analysis, it is also useful to begin by testing for the presence of correlated errors. This can be done by estimating an ordinary regression, saving the residuals, and then conducting an analysis of variance to investigate whether or not the residuals are significantly related to group membership. Significant results provide evidence that the ordinary regression assumption of independent errors is violated by the nested structure of the data. Once the decision is made to use a multilevel model, then, there are several types of models that can be estimated. These include (1) unconditional models, (2) random intercept models, (3) random coefficient models, and (4) cross-level interaction models – each adds an additional layer of complexity and provides additional information in the multilevel analysis.

THE UNCONDITIONAL MODEL. The necessity of multilevel analysis can be further investigated through the *unconditional or null model*. This model is referred to as "unconditional" because it includes no predictors at any level of analysis, so it provides a predicted value for the mean, which is not conditional on any covariates. It is summarized in (30.4):

$$\text{Level 1} \quad Y_{ij} = \beta_{0j} + r_{ij}$$
$$\text{Level 2} \quad \beta_{0j} = \gamma_{00} + u_{0j} \tag{30.4}$$

where Y_{ij} is a continuous outcome for individual i in group j, estimated by the overall intercept β_{0j} plus an individual-level error term, r_{ij}. At level 2 of the model, the intercept β_{0j} is modeled as a product of a level 2 intercept γ_{00} plus a group-level error term, u_{0j}. The unconditional model decomposes the total variance in the outcome into two parts – an individual variance, captured by the individual-level error term, and a group variance, captured by the group-level error term. The unconditional model is therefore useful for investigating the amount of variation that exists within versus between groups. One way to quantify this is to calculate the intraclass correlation coefficient (ICC), which represents the proportion of the total variance that is attributable to between-group differences. The ICC is represented by (30.5):

$$\rho = \frac{\tau_{00}}{(\sigma^2 + \tau_{00})} \tag{30.5}$$

where τ_{00} is the between-group variance estimated by the u_{0j} parameter and σ^2 is the within-group variance estimated by the r_{ij} parameter in (30.4). The intraclass correlation is the ratio of between group variance to total variance in the outcome. Larger ICCs indicate that a greater proportion of the total variance in the outcome is due to between-group differences.[9] It is important to begin any multilevel analysis by estimating the unconditional model. It provides an assessment of whether or not significant between-group variation exists – if it does not, then multilevel analysis is unnecessary – and it serves as a useful baseline model for evaluating explained variance in subsequent model specifications.

Table 30.3 presents the results from an unconditional model examining sentence length for a random sample of federal offenders nested within U.S. district courts. The results are broken into two parts, one for the "fixed effects", which report the unstandardized regression coefficients, and one for the "random effects", which report the variance components for the model. The overall intercept is 52.5 months indicating that the average federal sentence in

---

[9] It is common in multilevel analysis for between-group variation to represent a relatively small proportion of the total variance, however, as Liska (1990) argues, this does not indicate that between group variation is substantively unimportant.

TABLE 30.3. Unconditional HLM model of federal sentence lengths

Sentence length in months					
Fixed effects	b	S.E.	df	p-value	
Intercept (γ_{00})	52.5	1.8	88	0.00	
Random effects	s^2	S.D.	df	p-value	ρ
Level 1 (r_{ij})	4,630	68			
Level 2 (u_{oj})	267.1	16.3	88	0.00	0.055
Deviance $= 282,173.7$					
Parameters $= 2$					
$N = 25,000$					

this sample is just under 5 years. The level 1 variance provides a measure of within-district variation in sentence lengths and the level 2 variance provides an analogous measure for between-district variation. The significance test associated with the level 2 variance component indicates there is significant between-district variation in sentences – sentence lengths vary significantly across federal district courts. Notice that the significance test uses degrees of freedom for the number of level 2 rather than level 1 units; it provides preliminary evidence that districts matter in federal punishment, although as Luke (2004) points out, significance tests for variance components should always be interpreted cautiously.[10]

In order to get a sense of the magnitude of interdistrict variation in punishment, the intraclass correlation coefficient (ICC) can be calculated and the random effects can be assessed in combination with the fixed effects in Table 30.3. The level 2, or between group, variance is $\tau_{00} = 267.1$ and the within-group, or individual variance is $\sigma^2 = 4,630$. Plugging these values into (30.5) gives an ICC equal to 0.055. This indicates that 5.5% of the total variation in sentence length is attributable to between-district variation in sentencing. Similarly, the standard deviation for the between group variance component can be added and subtracted to the model intercept to provide a range of values for average sentences among districts. Adding and subtracting 16.3 months gives a range between 36.2 and 68.8 months, so the average SENTENCE varies between 3 years and 5 $3/4$ years for one standard deviation (i.e., about two-thirds) of federal district courts. The significance test, intraclass correlation and range of average sentences all suggest important between-group variation, indicating that multilevel analysis is appropriate in this instance.

THE RANDOM INTERCEPT MODEL. The second type of multilevel model adds predictor variables to the unconditional model and is referred to as a random intercept model because it allows the intercept to take on different values for each level 2 unit in the data. There are three types of random intercept models – models that include only level 1 predictors, models that include only level 2 predictors, and models that include both level 1 and level 2 predictors. In the first model, the focus of the multilevel analysis is on controlling for statistical dependence in clustered observations. In the second, the focus is on estimating variation in group means as a function of group-level predictors, and in the third, the focus in on estimating the joint influence of both level 1 and level 2 predictors. The type of random

---

[10] Variances are bounded by zero so they are not normally distributed and they are usually expected to take on nonzero values anyway, so it is not always clear what a significant variance means. Although significance tests for variance components can provide a useful starting point, then, they should be used judiciously. It is much more useful to interpret the substantive magnitude of the variance component rather than just its statistical significance.

intercept model will depend on the research question of interest, but it is often useful to begin by estimating the model with only level 1 predictors. This model is presented in (30.6):

$$\begin{array}{ll} \text{Level 1} & Y_{ij} = \beta_{0j} + \beta_{1j} X_{ij} + r_{ij} \\ \text{Level 2} & \beta_{0j} = \gamma_{00} + u_{0j} \end{array} \tag{30.6}$$

where X_{ij} represents an individual-level predictor added to the unconditional model in (30.4). Again, the level 2 equation models the level 1 intercept β_{0j} as a product of both the overall mean intercept, γ_{00}, and a unique level 2 error term, u_{0j}. Substantively, this means that the model intercept is allowed to vary randomly across level 2 units; each level 2 unit in the sample has its own group-specific intercept, just as if separate regressions were estimated for each group in the data.

Table 30.4 presents the results from a model examining the impact of the severity of the offense on the final sentence. In this model, offense severity is centered around its grand mean (see discussion of centering below) and added to the level 1 portion of the model as a predictor of sentence length. β_{1j} in (30.6) represents the effect of offense severity, X_{ij}, on the length of one's sentence in federal court. It is interpreted just as it would be in an ordinary regression model – each one unit increase in offense severity increases one's sentence length by 5.56 months. The average sentence is also allowed to vary by federal district, however. This is reflected by the level 2 variance component u_{0j} in Table 30.4. Both variance components now represent residuals, or left-over variation that is unaccounted for by the model. Notice that the deviance statistic is reduced from the unconditional to the conditional model, indicating increased model fit.[11] To better quantify the model fit, it is often useful to calculate

TABLE 30.4. **Random intercept model of federal sentence lengths**

Sentence length in months				
Fixed effects	*b*	*S.E.*	*df*	*p-value*
Intercept (γ_{00})	51.0	1.1	88	0.00
Severity (β_1)	5.6	0.2	24,998	0.00
Random effects	s^2	*S.D.*	*df*	*p*-value
Level 1 (r_{ij})	2,228.7	47.2		
Level 2 (u_{oj})	93.2	9.7	88	0.00
Deviance = 263,875.9				
Parameters = 2				
N = 25,000				

[11] The deviance statistic is equal to -2 times the natural log of the likelihood function and serves as a measure of lack of fit between the model and the data – the smaller the deviance the better the model fit. The inclusion of additional predictors will decrease the model deviance, and although the deviance is not directly interpretable, it is useful for comparing alternative model specifications to one another (Luke 2004). The difference in deviance statistics for two models is distributed as a chi-square distribution with degrees of freedom equal to the difference in the number of parameters in the two models. Multilevel models are typically fit with maximum likelihood estimation, but this can be done using either full maximum likelihood (ML) or restricted maximum likelihood (REML). Both estimators will produce identical estimates of the fixed effects, but REML will produce variance estimates that are less biased than ML when the number of level 2 units is relatively small (see Kreft and DeLeeuw 1998: 131–133; Snidjers and Bosker 1999: 88–90). REML is useful for testing two nested models that differ only in their random effects (e.g., an additional random coefficient in the model), but ML must be used to compare models that also differ in their fixed effects (e.g. an additional predictor variable). All example models herein are estimated with REML.

proportionate reduction of error (PRE) measures that approximate R^2 statistics for explained variance at each level of analysis. Equation (30.7) provides the formulas for these calculations:

$$R^2_{\text{Lev1}} = \frac{\sigma^2_{\text{unc}} - \sigma^2_{\text{cond}}}{\sigma^2_{\text{unc}}}$$

$$R^2_{\text{Lev2}} = \frac{\tau_{\text{unc}} - \tau_{\text{cond}}}{\tau_{\text{unc}}}$$

(30.7)

where explained variation at level 1 is calculated by examining the reduction in level 1 variance relative to the total variance from the unconditional model reported in Table 30.3. The unconditional estimate of level 1 variance was 4,639 and the conditional (i.e., controlling for offense severity) estimate is 2,228.7. This difference (2,401.3) divided by the total unconditional variance (4,630) provides an R^2 estimate of 0.519, so offense severity explains over 50% of the variance in sentence lengths among federal offenders.

The inclusion of level 1 predictors can also explain between-district variation at level 2 of the analysis. This is because there may be important differences in offense severity across districts, with some districts systematically facing more serious crime than others. Explained variation at level 2 is calculated by examining the reduction in level 2 variance from the unconditional to the conditional model. The unconditional estimate for between-district variation was 267.1 and the conditional estimate is 93.2. The difference (173.9) divided by the total (267.1) provides an estimate of explained variation at level 2 equal to 0.651. This indicates that 65% of inter-district variation in sentences is due to the fact that districts vary in the severity of the crimes they face, or 65% of district variation is attributable to *compositional* differences in offense severity.[12]

The random intercept model can be expanded to also include a level 2 predictor as in (30.8):

Level 1 $Y_{ij} = \beta_{0j} + \beta_{1j} X_{ij} + r_{ij}$

Level 2 $\beta_{0j} = \gamma_{00} + \gamma_{01} W_j + u_{0j}$

(30.8)

Group mean differences in the intercept, β_{0j}, are now modeled as a product of a group-level predictor, W_j, with γ_{01} representing the effect of the level 2 covariate on the outcome of interest. Level 2 predictors can take several forms including aggregate, structural, or global measures (see Table 30.2). Results for the model including the individual level 1 predictor (offense severity) and the level 2 predictor (Southern location) are presented in Table 30.5. The effect of offense severity remains essentially unchanged, but districts in the South sentence offenders to an additional 7.1 months of incarceration. Although level 1 variables can explain variation at both levels of analysis, level 2 variables can only explain between-group variation at level 2. Accordingly, the level 2 predictor South does not alter the level 1 variance estimate but it does reduce the level 2 variance from 93.2 to 82.4. This is a reduction of 11.6% so Southern location accounts for just under 12% of the residual level 2 variance after controlling for offense severity. Equation (30.8) includes only one level 1 and one level 2 predictor, but the model can be easily expanded to include multiple predictors at both levels of analysis.

---

[12] These basic formulas for explained variance are simple to apply and often quite useful, but in some circumstances it is possible for the inclusion of additional predictors to result in smaller or even negative values for explained variance (Snijders and Bosker 1999: 99–100). Slightly more complicated alternative formulas are also available that include adjustments for the average number of level 1 units per level 2 unit (see e.g. Luke 2004: 36). Total explained variance at both levels of analysis can be computed using the combined formula: $R^2_{\text{Total}} = \frac{(\sigma^2_{\text{unc}} + \tau_{\text{unc}}) - (\sigma^2_{\text{cond}} + \tau_{\text{cond}})}{\sigma^2_{\text{unc}} + \tau_{\text{unc}}}$

TABLE 30.5. Random intercept model of federal sentence length

Sentence length in months				
Fixed effects	*b*	*S.E.*	*df*	*p-value*
Intercept (γ_{00})	50.9	1.0	87	0.00
South (γ_{01})	7.1	2.3	87	0.00
Severity (β_1)	5.6	0.2	24,997	0.00
Random effects	s^2	*S.D.*	*df*	*p*-value
Level 1 (r_{ij})	2,228.7	47.2		
Level 2 (u_{oj})	82.4	9.1	87	0.00
Deviance $= 263,860.9$				
Parameters $= 2$				
$N = 25,000$				

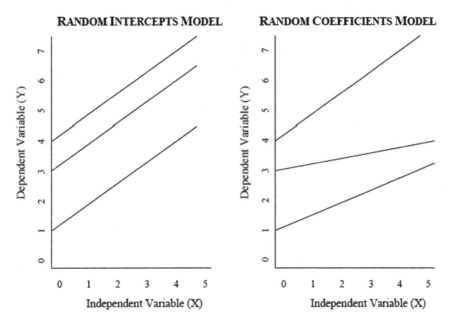

FIGURE 30.5. Comparison of random intercept and random coefficient models.

Although the random intercept model allows the group means to vary as a product of level 2 predictors, it assumes that the effects of the level 1 predictors are uniform across level 2 units. This assumption can be investigated and if it is violated then a random coefficient model may be more appropriate.

THE RANDOM COEFFICIENT MODEL. The random coefficient model builds upon the random intercept model by allowing the effects of individual predictors to also vary randomly across level 2 units. That is, the level 1 slope coefficients are allowed to take on different values in different aggregate groupings. The difference between the random intercept and random coefficient model is graphically depicted in Fig. 30.5, where each line represents the effect of some X on Y for three hypothetical groupings. In the random intercept model, the slopes are constrained to be the same for all three groups, but the intercepts are allowed to be different. In the random coefficient model, both the intercepts and slopes are allowed to differ across the three groups – the effect of X on Y varies by group. Mathematically, the random coefficient model (with a single level 1 predictor) is represented by (30.9):

$$
\begin{aligned}
\text{Level 1} \quad & Y_{ij} = \beta_{0j} + \beta_{1j} X_{ij} + r_{ij} \\
\text{Level 2} \quad & \beta_{0j} = \gamma_{00} + u_{0j} \\
& \beta_{1j} = \gamma_{10} + u_{1j}
\end{aligned}
\tag{30.9}
$$

where the key difference from (30.6) is the addition of the new random error term u_{1j} associated with the effect of X_{ij} on Y_{ij}. That is, the β_{1j} slope coefficient is modeled with a random variance component, allowing it to take on different values across level 2 units. For instance, the treatment effect of an after-school delinquency program might vary by school context, being more effective in some schools than others (Gottfredson et al. 2007). The random coefficient model can capture this type of between-group variation in the effect of the independent variable on the outcome of interest.

The decision to specify random coefficients should be based on both theory and empiricism. Regarding federal sentencing data, it might make theoretical sense to investigate variations in the effect of offense severity across courts because some literature suggests perceptions of crime seriousness involve a relative evaluation by court actors (Emerson 1983). Definitions of "serious" crime might be different in different court contexts. To test this proposition, the deviance statistics can be compared for two models, one with offense severity specified as a fixed (i.e., nonvarying) coefficient as reported in Table 30.4 and one with it specified as a random coefficient as in Table 30.6. The deviance for the random intercept model is 263,876 and the deviance for the random coefficient model is 262,530. The difference produces a chi-square statistic of 1,346 with 2 degrees of freedom, which is highly significant.[13] The null hypothesis can therefore be rejected in favor of the random coefficient model.

TABLE 30.6. **Random coefficient model of federal sentence length**

Sentence length in months				
Fixed effects	*b*	*S.E.*	*df*	*p-value*
Intercept (γ_{00})	49.7	1.0	88	0.00
Severity (β_1)	5.7	0.1	88	0.00
Random effects	s^2	*S.D.*	*df*	*p-*value
Level 1 (r_{ij})	2,098.7	45.8		
Level 2 (u_{oj})	78.7	8.9	88	0.00
Severity (u_{1j})	1.4	1.2	88	0.00
Deviance = 262,530.1				
Parameters = 4				
N = 25,000				

---

[13] The difference in the number of parameters is equal to 2 because the addition of the random coefficient introduces both an additional variance component and an additional covariance component to the model:

$$
\mathrm{Var}\begin{bmatrix} u_{0j} \\ u_{1j} \end{bmatrix} = \begin{bmatrix} \tau_{00} & \tau_{01} \\ \tau_{10} & \tau_{11} \end{bmatrix}
$$

where τ_{11} is the new variance associated with the random coefficient β_{1j}. Because the models only differ in their random components, REML estimation is used for this comparison.

Additional evidence in support of the random coefficient model is provided by the highly significant p-value for the u_{1j} parameter in Table 30.6. This suggests there is significant variation in the effect of offense severity across district courts. To quantify this effect, the standard deviation (S.D. $= 1.2$) for the random effect can be added and subtracted to the coefficient ($b = 5.7$) for offense severity. This suggests that each unit increase in offense severity increases one's sentence length between 4.5 and 6.9 months for one standard deviation (i.e., about two-thirds) of federal district courts. One final diagnostic tool for properly specifying fixed and random coefficients is to compare differences between model-based and robust standard errors.[14] Discrepancies between the two likely indicate model misspecification, such as level 1 coefficients that should be specified as random rather than fixed effects.

To demonstrate, Table 30.7 provides a comparison of an OLS, random intercept and random coefficient model, along with a pictorial representation of each. As expected, the standard errors in the OLS model are underestimated. The standard error for the model intercept, for instance, increases from 0.30 to 1.10 from the OLS to the random intercept model. Examining the robust standard errors in the random intercept model suggests there may be a problem – the robust standard error for offense severity is more than 6 times as large as its model-based standard error. This is consistent with earlier results that suggested significant variation exists in the effect of offense severity across districts. Allowing for this variation in the random coefficient model produces model-based and robust standard error estimates for offense severity

TABLE 30.7. Comparison of OLS, random intercept and random coefficient models

OLS regression			Random intercept			Random coefficient		
Without robust errors			*Without robust errors*			*Without robust errors*		
	b	S.E.		b	S.E.		b	S.E.
Intercept	47.9	0.30	Intercept	51.0	1.10	Intercept	49.7	1.02
Offense severity	5.6	0.03	Offense severity	5.6	0.03	Offense severity	5.7	0.13
			With robust errors			*With robust errors*		
				b	S.E.		b	S.E.
			Intercept	51.0	1.06	Intercept	49.7	1.01
			Offense severity	5.6	0.19	Offense severity	5.7	0.13

	Deviance $= 263,875.9$	Deviance $= 262,530.1$
	Parameters $= 2$	Parameters $= 4$

[14] Robust standard errors are standard errors that are adjusted to account for possible violations of underlying model assumptions regarding error distributions and covariance structures (see Raudenbush and Bryk 2002: 276). In the case of multilevel models, these violations can lead to misestimated standard errors that result in faulty statistical significance tests. Robust standard errors provide estimates that are relatively insensitive to model misspecifications, but because the calculation of robust standard errors relies on large sample properties, they should only be used when the number of level 2 units is relatively large.

TABLE 30.8. Random coefficient model with level 2 predictor of federal sentence length

Sentence length in months				
Fixed effects	*b*	*S.E.*	*df*	*p-value*
Intercept (γ_{00})	49.6	1.0	87	0.00
South (γ_{01})	3.4	1.4	87	0.02
Severity (β_1)	5.7	0.1	88	0.00
Random effects	s^2	S.D.	df	*p*-value
Level 1 (r_{ij})	2,098.6	45.8		
Level 2 (u_{oj})	71.6	8.5	87	0.00
Severity (u_{1j})	1.5	1.2	88	0.00

that are identical. Large differences in robust standard errors can serve as a useful diagnostic tool for identifying misspecification in the random effects portion of the multilevel model.

These diagnostic approaches, along with theoretical considerations, should be used to gradually build the random effects portion of the random coefficient model. Ecological predictors can also be included at level 2 of the random coefficient model. Table 30.8 reports the results for the random coefficient model adding Southern location as a level 2 predictor. Notice that the estimated effect of South is less in the random coefficient model in Table 30.8 than it was in the random intercept model in Table 30.5. This highlights the importance of properly specifying the random effects portion of the multilevel model – changes in the random effects at level 1 can alter the estimates for both level 1 and level 2 predictors.

Often times the final multilevel model will include a mixture of fixed and random coefficients, which is why it is sometimes called the "mixed model." Equation (30.10) provides an example of a mixed model with two level 1 predictors and 1 level 2 predictor:

$$\begin{aligned}
\text{Level 1} \quad & Y_{ij} = \beta_{0j} + \beta_{1j} X_{1ij} + \beta_{2j} X_{2ij} + r_{ij} \\
\text{Level 2} \quad & \beta_{0j} = \gamma_{00} + \gamma_{01} W_j + u_{0j} \\
& \beta_{1j} = \gamma_{10} + u_{1j} \\
& \beta_{2j} = \gamma_{10}
\end{aligned} \tag{30.10}$$

In this mixed model, the effect of the first independent variable X_{1ij} is allowed to have varying effects across level 2 units because its coefficient β_{1j} in level 2 of the model includes the random error term u_{1j}. It is this error variance that allows the effect of X_{1ij} to take on different values for different level 2 units. The effect of the second level 1 predictor X_{2ij}, however, does not include a random error variance. Its effect is therefore constrained to be "fixed" or constant across level 2 units. Although measures of explained variance can be calculated for random coefficient and mixed models, these calculations do not account for the additional variance components introduced by the random effects, so it is advisable to perform these calculations on the random intercept only model (see e.g. Snijders and Bosker 1999: 105).

THE CROSS-LEVEL INTERACTION MODEL. Like ordinary regression models, multilevel models can be further expanded to include interaction terms. These can be incorporated in three basic ways. Individual interactions can be included from cross-product terms for individual-level predictors. For instance, victim race and police officer race might be interacted in a study of police use of force (Lawton 2007). Ecological interactions can also be included using level 2 predictors. Ethnic heterogeneity could be interacted with low socioeconomic conditions at the neighborhood level, for instance, in a study of risk of victimization

(Miethe and McDowall 1993).[15] Finally, cross-level interactions can be included that specify cross-product terms across-levels of analysis. For instance, the effects of parental monitoring on problem behavior at the individual level might be expected to vary among neighborhoods with different levels of collective efficacy (Rankin and Quane 2002). This type of interaction is unique to multilevel analysis so it deserves additional explanation. Equation (30.11) specifies a cross-level interaction model with 1 individual predictor, 1 ecological predictor and the cross level interaction between them:

$$\begin{aligned}
\text{Level 1} \quad & Y_{ij} = \beta_{0j} + \beta_{1j} X_{1ij} + r_{ij} \\
\text{Level 2} \quad & \beta_{0j} = \gamma_{00} + \gamma_{01} W_j + u_{0j} \\
& \beta_{1j} = \gamma_{10} + \gamma_{11} W_j + u_{1j}
\end{aligned} \quad (30.11)$$

This model adds the level 2 predictor W_j to the level 2 equation for β_{1j}, so W_j is now being used to explain variation in the effect of β_{1j} across level 2 units, with the new parameter γ_{11} representing the cross-level interaction between X_{1ij} and W_j. Cross-level interactions are useful for answering questions about *why* individual effects vary across level 2 units; they explicitly model variation in level 1 random coefficients as a product of level 2 group characteristics.[16] Table 30.9 provides results from a cross-level interaction model examining the conditioning effects of Southern court location on the individual effect of offense severity for federal sentence lengths. The positive interaction effect indicates that offense severity has a stronger effect on sentence length in Southern districts than it does in non-Southern districts. As with other multilevel models, cross-level interaction models can easily be extended to the case of multiple predictors at both the individual and group levels of analysis, although care should be taken when including multiple interactions in the same model.

TABLE 30.9. Cross-level interaction model of federal sentence length

Sentence length in months					
Fixed effects	*b*	*S.E.*	*df*	*T-ratio*	*p-value*
Intercept (γ_{00})	49.6	1.0	87	49.14	0.00
South (γ_{01})	6.3	2.0	87	3.37	0.02
Severity (β_1)	5.7	0.1	88	42.45	0.00
South*severity (γ_{11})	0.6	0.3	87	2.07	0.04
Random effects	s^2	S.D.	df	χ^2	*p*-value
Level 1 (r_{ij})	2,098.6	45.8			
Level 2 (u_{oj})	70.2	8.4	87	1130.14	0.00
Severity (u_{1j})	1.4	1.2	88	1644.40	0.00
Deviance = 262,519.3					
Parameters = 4					
N = 25,000					

---

[15] Depending on the statistical program used, these interactions may or may not be able to be created in the multilevel interface. With HLM, both individual interactions and ecological interactions must be created and all centering adjustments must be made before importing them into the HLM program.

[16] Although conceptually the goal of cross-level interactions is usually to explain significant variation in the effects of level 1 random coefficients across level 2 units, there are instances when theory may dictate examining cross-level interactions for fixed coefficients at level 1 as well. Significant cross-level interactions may emerge involving fixed level 1 coefficients because the significance tests for the cross-level interactions are more powerful than the significance tests produced for random coefficient variance components (Snijders and Bosker 1999: 74–75).

ADDITIONAL CONSIDERATIONS

The preceding examples offer only a rudimentary introduction to the full gamut of multilevel modeling applications, but they provide a basic foundation for doing more complex multilevel analysis. The multilevel model can be further adapted to account for additional data complexities that commonly arise in criminological research, including centering conventions, nonlinear dependent variables, and additional levels of analysis. These issues are briefly highlighted below although interested readers should consult comprehensive treatments available elsewhere (e.g., Raudenbush and Bryk 2002; Luke 2004; Goldstein 1995; Snidjers and Bosker 1999; Kreft and de Leeuw 1998; Gelman and Hill 2007).

Centering in Multilevel Analysis

In multilevel models, the centering of variables takes on special importance. Centering, or reparameterization, involves simple linear transformations of the predictor variables by subtracting a constant such as the mean of X or W. Centering in the multilevel framework is no different than in ordinary multiple regression, but it offers important analytical advantages, making model intercepts more interpretable, making main effects more meaningful when interactions are included, reducing collinearity associated with polynomials and interactions, facilitating model convergence in nonlinear models, and simplifying graphical displays of output. Estimates of variance components may also be affected by the centering convention because random coefficients often involve heteroskedastic error variances that depend on the value of X at which they are evaluated (Hox 2002).

In general, three main centering options are available: no centering, grand-mean centering and group-mean centering. No centering leaves the variable untransformed in its original metric. Although this can be a reasonable approach depending on how the variables are measured, it is usually advisable to employ a centering convention in multilevel analyses for the reasons stated above. The simplest centering convention is grand-mean centering, which involves subtracting the overall mean, or the pooled average, from each observation in the data. The subtracted mean, then, becomes the new zero point so that positive values represent scores above the mean and negative values represent scores below the mean. Grand mean centering is represented as $(X_{ij} - \overline{X}_{..})$, where X_{ij} is the value of X for individual i in group j and $\overline{X}_{..}$ is the grand mean pooled across all observations in the data. Grand mean centering is often useful and rarely detrimental so it offers a good standard centering convention. It only affects the parameter estimates for the model intercept, making the value of the intercept equal to the predicted value of Y when all variables are set to their means. This allows the intercept in a grand-mean centered model to be interpreted as the expected value for the "average" observation in the data.

The alternative to grand mean centering is group mean centering, represented as $(X_{ij} - \overline{X}_{.j})$, where X_{ij} is still the value of X for individual i in group, j but $\overline{X}_{.j}$ is now the group-specific mean, so individuals in different level 2 groups have different values of $\overline{X}_{.j}$ subtracted from their scores. Group-mean centering is more complicated than grand-mean centering because it fundamentally alters the meaning and interpretation of both the parameter estimates and the variance components in the multilevel model. Group-mean centering can be a useful diagnostic tool and it is appropriate for many research questions, but in general it should be used selectively. Luke (2004: 52), for instance, recommended that "one should use group-mean centering only if there are strong theoretical reasons to do so."[17]

In general, centering is always a good idea when a variable has a nonmeaningful zero point. For example, it would make little sense to include the UCR crime rate as a predictor variable without first centering it. Otherwise, the model intercept would represent the predicted value of Y when the crime rate was equal to 0, which is clearly unrealistic. Even when variables do have meaningful zero points, it is often useful to center them. For instance, often times it is even useful to center dummy variables. Adjusting for the grand mean essentially removes the influence of the dummy variable so that the model intercept represents the expected value of Y for the "average" of that variable rather than for the reference category. Similar centering rules apply for ecological variables as for individual level variables, but the important point is that centering decisions should be made *a priori* based on theoretical considerations regarding the desired meaning of model parameters. A number of more detailed treatments offer further detail on the merits and demerits of grand-mean and group-mean centering conventions for multilevel analysis (e.g., Kreft 1995; Kreft et al. 1995; Longford 1989; Raudenbush 1989; Paccagnella 2006).

Generalized Multilevel Models

The examples up to this point all assume a normally distributed continuous dependent variable. Often times, however, criminological research questions involve nonlinear or discrete outcomes, such as binary, count, ordinal, or multinomial variables. When this is the case, the multilevel model must be adapted by transforming the dependent variable. For example, dichotomous dependent variables are common in research on crime and justice; whether or not an offender commits a crime, the police make an arrest, or a judge sentences to incarceration, all involve binary outcomes (e.g. Eitle et al. 2005; Griffin and Armstrong 2003; Johnson 2006). In these cases, the discrete dependent variable often violates assumptions of the general linear model regarding linearity, normality, and homoskedasticity of level 1 errors (Raudenbush and Bryk 2002). Moreover, because the outcome is bound by 0 and 1, the fitted linear model is likely to produce nonsensical and out of range predictions.

None of these issues are unique to multilevel analysis and the same adjustments used in ordinary regression can be applied to the multilevel model, although some important new issues arise in the multilevel context. Collectively, these types of models are labeled generalized hierarchical linear models (GHLM) or just generalized multilevel models, because they provide flexible generalizations of the ordinary linear model. The basic structure of the multilevel model remains the same, but the sampling distribution changes. For illustrative purposes, the case of multilevel logistic regression with a dichotomous outcome is illustrated. Equation

---

[17] Some exceptions to this general rule include growth curve modeling with longitudinal data, where the focus is often on separating within and between group regression effects, or research questions involving "frog pond" effects, where the theoretical interest is on individual adaptation to one's specific environment rather than the average effects of individual predictors on the outcome of interest.

(30.12) provides the formula for the unconditional two-level multinomial logistic model using the binomial sampling distribution and the logit link function:[18]

$$\text{Logit Link Function} \quad \eta_{ij} = \ln\left(\frac{p}{1-p}\right)$$
$$\text{Level 1} \quad \eta_{ij} = \beta_{0j}$$
$$\text{Level 2} \quad \beta_{0j} = \gamma_{00} + u_{0j}$$

(30.12)

In this formulation, p is the probability of the event occurring and $(1 - p)$ is the probability of the event not occurring. p over $(1 - p)$, then, represents the *odds* of the event and taking the natural log provides the *log odds*. The dependent variable for the dichotomous outcome is therefore the log of the odds of success for individual i in group j, represented by η_{ij}. The multinomial logistic model is probabilistic, capturing the likelihood that the outcome occurs. Whereas the original binary outcome was constrained to be 0 or 1, p is allowed to vary in the interval 0 to 1, and η_{ij} can take on any real value. In this way, the logistic link function transforms the discrete outcome into a continuous range of values. The level 2 model is identical to that for the continuous outcome presented in (30.4), but γ_{00} now represents the average log odds of the event occurring across all level 2 units. Equation (30.13) provides the random coefficient extension of the multilevel logistic model with one random level 1 coefficient and one level 2 predictor:

$$\text{Level 1} \quad \eta_{ij} = \beta_{0j} + \beta_{1j} X_{1ij}$$
$$\text{Level 2} \quad \beta_{0j} = \gamma_{00} + \gamma_{01} W_j + u_{0j}$$
$$\beta_{1j} = \gamma_{10} + u_{1j}$$

(30.13)

where η_{ij} still represents the log of the odds of success and all the other parameters are the same as previously described.

Notice that in both (30.12) and (30.13), there is no level 1 variance component included in the multilevel logistic model. This is because the level 1 variance is heteroskedastic and completely determined by the value of p, it is therefore unidentified and not included in the model. This means that the standard formulas for the intraclass correlation and explained variance at level 1 cannot be directly applied to the case of a binary dependent variable.[19] Also, most software packages do not provide deviance statistics for nonlinear multilevel models. This is because generalized linear models typically rely on "penalized quasi likelihood" (PQL), rather than full or restricted maximum likelihood. This involves a double-iterative process that provides only a rough approximation to the likelihood function on which the deviance is based. In most cases, this means that other methods, such as theory, significance tests for

---

[18] The "link function" can be thought of as a mathematical transformation that allows the nonnormal dependent variable to be linearly predicted by the explanatory variables in the model.

[19] The level 1 variance in the case of a logistic model is equal to $p(1 - p)$ where p is the predicted probability for the level 1 model. The level 1 variance therefore varies as a direct product of the value of p at which the model is evaluated. Although multilevel logistic models do not include a level 1 variance term, some alternatives approaches are available for estimating intraclass correlations. For example, Snijders and Bosker, (1999: Chap. 14) discuss reconceptualizing the level 1 model as a latent variable $Z_{ij} = \eta_{ij} + r_{ij}$, in which the level 1 error term is assumed to have a standard logistic distribution with a mean of 0 and variance of $\pi^2/3$. In that case, the intraclass correlation can be calculated as $\rho = \tau_{00}/(\tau_{00} + \pi^2/3)$. This formulation requires the use of the logit link function and relies on the assumption that the level 1 variance follows the logistic distribution. Alternative formulations have also been discussed for the probit link function using the normal distribution (see e.g. Gelman and Hill 2007: 118).

variance components, and robust standard error comparisons must be relied on to properly specify random coefficients in level 1 of the multilevel logistic model.[20]

A third complication involving multilevel models with nonlinear link functions is that two sets of results are produced, one labeled "unit-specific" results and one labeled "population-average" results. Unit-specific results are estimated holding constant the random effects in the model, whereas population-average results are averaged across all level 2 random effects (see Raudenbush and Bryk 2002: 301). This means that unit-specific estimates model the dependent variable conditional on the random effects in the model, which provide estimates of how the level 1 and level 2 variables affect outcomes *within* the level 2 units. Population-average estimates, provide the marginal expectation of the outcome averaged across the entire population of level 2 units. If you wanted to know how much an after-school program reduces delinquency for one student compared to another in the same school, then the unit-specific estimate would be appropriate. If you wanted to summarize the average effect of the after-school program on delinquency across all schools, then the population-average estimate would be preferred. In short, which results to report depends on the research question at hand.[21] For example, work on racial disparity in sentencing typically reports unit-specific estimates because the focus is on the effect of an offender's race relative to other offenders sentenced in the same court (e.g., Ulmer and Johnson 2004). Recent work integrating routine activities and social disorganization theory, on the other hand, reports population average estimates because in the words of the authors "our research questions concern aggregate rates of delinquency and unstructured socializing" among all schools (Osgood and Anderson 2004: 534).

Table 30.10 reports the unit-specific results with robust standard errors for a random coefficient model examining the likelihood of imprisonment in federal court. The level 1 predictor is the severity of the offense and the level 2 predictor is Southern location. Offense severity exerts a strong positive effect on the probability of incarceration. The coefficient of 0.26 represents the change in the log odds of imprisonment for a one-unit increase in severity. To make this more interpretable, it is useful to transform the raw coefficient into an odds ratio.

TABLE 30.10. **Multilevel logistic model of federal incarceration**

Prison vs. no prison (unit-specific model with robust standard errors)					
Fixed effects	*b*	*S.E.*	*df*	*p-value*	*Odds ratio*
Intercept (γ_{00})	2.80	0.08	87	0.00	
South (γ_{01})	0.07	0.11	87	0.53	1.07
Severity (β_1)	0.26	0.01	88	0.00	1.29
Random effects	s^2	S.D.	df	*p*-value	
Level 2 (u_{0j})	0.41	0.64	87	0.00	
Severity (u_{1j})	0.004	0.06	88	0.00	

---

[20] PQL estimates are usually sufficient, but tests for random effects based on the PQL likelihood function in models with discrete outcomes may be unreliable, especially for small samples. Alternative full maximum estimators, such as Laplace estimation, are available in some software packages and can be used to test for random effects using the deviance, but this can be computationally intensive.

[21] These estimates are often similar, but their differences will widen as between-group variance increases and the probability of the outcome becomes farther away from.0.50 (Raudenbush and Bryk, 2002: 302). In the case of continuous dependent variables, the unit-specific and population estimates are identical so this distinction only arises in the case of nonlinear dependent variables.

Because the left-hand side of (30.13) represents the log of the odds, we obtain the odds by taking the antilog, in this case $e^{0.256} = 1.29$. For each unit increase in the severity of the crime committed, the odds of incarceration increases by a factor of 0.29 or 29%.[22] The coefficient for South in this model is not statistically significant, suggesting there is no statistical evidence that offenders are more likely to be incarcerated in Southern districts. Turning to the random effects, the level 2 intercept indicates that significant interdistrict variation in incarceration remains after controlling for severity and Southern location, and that significant variance exists in the effect of offense severity across districts. Adding the standard deviation to the fixed effect for severity provides a range of coefficients between 0.20 and 0.32. Transformed into odds ratios, this means that the effect of offense severity varies between 1.22 and 1.38, so offense severity increases the odds of incarceration between 22% and 38% across one standard deviation (i.e., about two-thirds) of federal districts.

As with linear multilevel models, generalized multilevel models can be easily extended to the case of multiple predictors at both levels of analysis. In general, similar transformations can be applied for multilevel Poisson, binomial, ordinal, and multinomial models by simply applying different link functions to different sampling distributions (see e.g., Raudenbush and Bryk 2002: Chap. 10; Luke 2004: 53–62).[23] In this way, the basic linear multilevel model can be easily generalized to address a variety of criminological research questions involving different types of discrete dependent variables.

Three-Level Multilevel Models

The basic two-level multilevel linear and generalized models can also be extended to incorporate more complicated data structures that span three or more levels of analysis.[24] The basic logic of the multilevel model is the same, but additional error variances are added for each additional level of analysis. The three-level unconditional model for a linear dependent variable is presented in (30.14):

$$
\begin{aligned}
\text{Level 1} \quad & Y_{ijk} = \pi_{0jk} + e_{ijk} \\
\text{Level 2} \quad & \pi_{0jk} = +\beta_{00k} + r_{0jk} \\
\text{Level 3} \quad & \beta_{00k} = \gamma_{000} + u_{00k}
\end{aligned}
\tag{30.14}
$$

The i subscript indexes level 1 (e.g., students), the j subscript indexes level 2 (e.g., classrooms), and the k subscript indexes level 3 (e.g. schools). Now level 1 coefficients are represented with π's, level 2 coefficients with β's and level 3 coefficients with γ's, but the three-level structure is purely notational convenience, so it can be simplified through substitution to produce the equivalent, but simpler, combined model in (30.15):

$$
Y_{ijk} = \gamma_{000} + e_{ijk} + r_{0jk} + u_{00k}
\tag{30.15}
$$

---

[22] The individual probability of incarceration for individual i in court j can be calculated directly using the formula: $p_{ij} = \frac{e^{\gamma_{00} + \gamma_{01} W_j + \gamma_{10} X_{ij}}}{(1 + e^{\gamma_{00} + \gamma_{01} W_j + \gamma_{10} X_{ij}})}$, so with grand-mean centering the mean probability of incarceration is $\bar{p}_{ij} = \frac{e^{\gamma_{00}}}{(1 + e^{\gamma_{00}})}$.

[23] Some important differences emerge in these other contexts, for example, overdispersion frequently occurs in Poison models for count data, so it is common to incorporate an additional overdispersion parameter in the level 1 model for this type of generalized linear model (see Raudenbush and Bryk 2002: 295; Gelman and Hill 2007: 114).

[24] Some software packages, such as, HLM are currently limited to three levels of analysis, but other programs (e.g., WLwiN) can analyze up to 10 separate levels of analysis.

TABLE 30.11. Three-level unconditional model of federal sentence length

Sentence length in months					
Fixed effects	b	S.E.	df	p-value	
Intercept (γ_{000})	52.5	3.2	10	0.00	
Random effects	s^2	S.D.	df	p-value	ρ
Level 1 (e_{ijk})	4,630.1	68.0			
Level 2 (r_{0jk})	172.5	15.2	78	0.00	0.035
Level 3 (u_{00k})	85.2	9.2	10	0.00	0.017

Equations (30.14) and (30.15) are substantively identical and it becomes clear in the combined model that the outcome Y_{ijk} is modeled as a simple product of an overall intercept γ_{000} plus three different error terms, one for each level of analysis. As in the case of the two-level unconditional model, the three-level model parcels the variation in the outcome across levels of analysis. Similar estimates can therefore be calculated for intraclass correlation coefficients, but in the case of the three-level model, there are separate ρ coefficients for level 2 and level 3 of the analysis.[25]

In the federal court system, cases are nested within district courts, but district courts are also nested within circuit courts, which serve as courts of appeal and play an important role in establishing federal case law. Table 30.11 provides the results from a three-level unconditional model examining federal sentence lengths for the same random sample of 25,000 cases, nested within 89 federal districts, and within 11 federal circuits. The level 2 and level 3 variance components are highly significant, indicating that federal sentences vary significantly across both district and circuit courts. The intraclass correlation coefficients suggest that about 3.5% of the total variation sentencing is between federal districts with another 1.7% between circuit courts. Notice that some of the between-district court variation from the two-level model in Table 30.3 is now being accounted for by level 3 of the analysis.

As with the two-level model, predictors can be added at each level of analysis. That is, individual predictors can be added at level 1, district court predictors can be added at level 2, and circuit court predictors can be added at level 3. Similar steps can then be taken to identify random coefficients as with the two-level model, but care should be exercised in this process because error structures for three-level models can quickly become complicated. This is because Level 1 variables can be specified as random coefficients at *both* level 2 *and* level 3 of the analysis. Moreover, Level 2 coefficients can also be specified as random effects at level 3 of the analysis. Cross-level interactions can occur between levels 1 and 2, levels 1 and 3, or levels 2 and 3. The various possible model specifications can quickly become unwieldy, so it is particularly important in three-level models to exercise care in first identifying the hypothesized effects of interest and then properly specifying the model to capture them.

---

[25] The formula for the level 2 intraclass correlation is $\rho_{\text{Level 2}} = \tau_\pi / (\sigma^2 + \tau_\pi + \tau_\beta)$, where σ^2 is the level 1 variance, τ_π is the level 2 variance, and τ_β is the level 3 variance. The formula for the level 3 intraclass correlation is $\rho_{\text{Level 3}} = \tau_\beta / (\sigma^2 + \tau_\pi + \tau_\beta)$ (see Raudenbush and Bryk 2002: 230).

Equation (30.16) provides an example of a basic three-level mixed model with one level 1 predictor, Z_{ijk}, specified as randomly varying a cross both level 2 and level 3, one level 2 predictor, X_{jk}, fixed at level 3, and no level 3 predictors:

$$
\begin{aligned}
\text{Level 1} \quad & Y_{ijk} = \pi_{0jk} + \pi_{1jk} Z_{ijk} + e_{ijk} \\
\text{Level 2} \quad & \pi_{0jk} = \beta_{00k} + \beta_{01k} X_{jk} + r_{0jk} \\
& \pi_{1jk} = \beta_{10k} + r_{1jk} \\
\text{Level 3} \quad & \beta_{00k} = \gamma_{000} + u_{00k} \\
& \beta_{01k} = \gamma_{010} \\
& \beta_{10k} = \gamma_{100} + u_{10k}
\end{aligned} \qquad (30.16)
$$

The subscripts and multiple levels can easily become confusing, so it is often useful to examine the combined model, substituting levels 2 and 3 into the level 1 equation. Equation (30.17) provides this reformulation with the fixed effects, or regression coefficients, isolated with parentheses and the random effects, or error variances, isolated with brackets:

$$
Y_{ijk} = (\gamma_{000} + \gamma_{100} Z_{ijk} + \gamma_{010} X_{jk}) + [e_{ijk} \mid r_{0jk} + u_{00k} + r_{1jk} Z_{ijk} + u_{10k} Z_{ijk} +] \quad (30.17)
$$

γ_{000} is the overall model intercept, and γ_{100} and γ_{010} are the regression effects for the level 1 and level 2 predictors. As in the unconditional model, e_{ijk}, r_{0jk}, and u_{00k} are the level 1, 2, and 3 error variances, and the new error terms, $r_{1jk} Z_{ijk}$ and $u_{10k} Z_{ijk}$, indicate that the effect of the level 1 variable, Z_{ijk}, is allowed to vary across both level 2 and level 3 units.

Estimating this model with data on federal sentence lengths produces the output in Table 30.12. These results report model-based rather than robust standard errors because the highest level of analysis includes only 11 circuit courts. The effect of offense severity is essentially the same, increasing sentence length by about 5.7 months, but the effect for Southern location has been attenuated and is now only marginally significant. This likely reflects the fact that some of the district variation is now being accounted for by the circuit level of analysis. The random effects in Table 30.11 support this interpretation. The level 2 variance component is smaller than it was in the two-level model reported in Table 30.8. Notice also that there are two variance components associated with offense severity because its effect is allowed to vary both across district and circuit courts. The magnitude of these variance components indicates there is more between-district than between-circuit variation in the effect of offense severity, but both are highly significant. Although conceptually the

TABLE 30.12. Three-level mixed model of federal sentence length

Sentence length in months				
Fixed effects	*b*	*S.E.*	*df*	*p-value*
Intercept (γ_{000})	48.6	1.6	10	0.00
South (β_{01k})	2.8	1.7	87	0.10
Severity (π_{1jk})	5.7	0.2	10	0.00
Random effects	s^2	S.D.	df	*p*-value
Level 1 (e_{ijk})	2,098.6	45.8		
Level 2 (r_{0jk})	53.6	7.3	77	0.00
Severity (r_{1jk})	1.1	1.1	78	0.00
Level 3 (u_{00k})	17.6	4.2	10	0.00
Severity (u_{10k})	0.3	0.5	10	0.00

three-level multilevel model represents a straightforward extension of the two-level model, in practice care needs to be exercised to avoid exploding complexity (for recent examples using 3 level models see Duncan et al. 2003; Johnson 2006; Wright et al. 2007).

SUMMARY AND CONCLUSIONS

Multilevel models represent an increasingly popular analytical approach in the field of criminology. According to a recent analysis by Kleck et al. (2006), between 5% and 6% of empirical research papers in top criminology journals utilize multilevel modeling, but given the prevalence of multilevel research questions, their use is likely to continue to gain prominence in the field. Because multilevel models provide a sophisticated approach for integrating multiple levels of analysis, they represent an important opportunity to expand theoretical and empirical discourse across a variety of criminological domains. Multilevel models have already been used to study a rich diversity of topics, from examinations of self-control (Hay and Forrest 2006; Doherty 2006; Wright and Beaver 2005) and strain theory (Slocum et al. 2005) to life course perspectives (Horney et al. 1995; Sampson et al. 2006) and analyses of violent specialization (Osgood and Schreck 2007) – from crime victimization (Xie and McDowall 2008; Wilcox et al. 2007), policing (Rosenfeld et al. 2007; Warner 2007), and punishment outcomes (Kleck et al. 2005; Bontrager et al. 2005; Johnson 2005; 2006) to postrelease recidivism (Kubrin and Stewart 2005; Chiricos et al. 2007; Mears et al. 2008) and program evaluations (Gottfredson et al. 2007; Esbensen et al. 2001) – across a broad range of criminological topic areas, multilevel models have proven to be invaluable tools.

Despite their many applications, though, the old adage that "A little bit of knowledge can be a dangerous thing" applies directly to multilevel modeling. Modern software packages make estimating multilevel models relatively simple, but the fully specified multilevel model often contains complicated error structures that can easily be misspecified. Moreover, these complexities can sometimes result in instability in parameter estimates. This is particularly the case for ecological predictors and for three-level and generalized linear models. For instance, it is common for ecological predictors to have shared variance (Land et al. 1990), so inclusion or elimination of one predictor can often affect the estimates for other predictors in the model. It is therefore essential that the final model be carefully constructed from the ground up, performing model diagnostics to test for misspecification, investigating problematic collinearity and examining alternative models to ensure that the final estimates are robust to minor alterations in model specification.

Although this chapter provides a basic overview of multilevel models, it is important to note that it does not cover many of their advanced applications such as longitudinal data analysis, growth-curve modeling, time series data, latent variable analysis, meta-analytical techniques, or analysis of cross-classified data. Beyond situations where individuals are influenced by social contexts, multilevel data commonly characterizes these and many other criminological enterprises. As a discipline, we are just beginning to incorporate the full range of applications for multilevel statistical models in the study of crime and punishment. The goals of this chapter were simply to introduce the reader to the basic multilevel model, to emphasize the ways in which it is similar to and different from the ordinary regression model, to provide some brief examples of different types of multilevel models, and to demonstrate how they can be estimated within the context of jurisdictional variations in federal criminal punishments across court contexts.

Acknowledgment The author would like to thank and acknowledge the very valuable comments provided by D. Wayne Osgood on an earlier draft of this chapter.

REFERENCES

Beaver KM, Wright JP, Maume MO (2008) The effect of school classroom characteristics on low self-control: a multilevel analysis. J Crim Justice 36:174–181

Bernburg JG, Thorlindsson T (2007) Community structure and adolescent delinquency in Iceland: a contextual analysis. Criminology 45(2):415–444

Blalock HM (1984) Contextual-effects models: theoretical and methodological issues. Annu Rev Sociol 10:353–372

Blau PM (1960) Structural effects. Am Sociol Rev 25:178–193

Blumer H (1958) Race prejudice as a sense of group position. Pacific Sociol Rev 1:3–7

Bontrager S, Bales W, Chiricos T (2005) Race, ethnicity, threat and the labeling of convicted felons. Criminology 43(3):589–622

Britt CL (2000) Social context and racial disparities in punishment decisions. Justice Q 17(4):707–732

Camp S, Gaes G, Langan N, Saylor W (2003) The influence of prisons on inmate misconduct: a multilevel investigation. Justice Q 20(3):501–533

Chiricos T, Barrick K, Bales W, Bontrager S (2007) The labeling of convicted felons and its consequences for recidivism. Criminology 45(3):547–581

Diez Roux AV (2002) A glossary for multilevel analysis. J Epidemiol Community Health 56:588–594

Doherty EE (2006) Self-control, social bonds, and desistance: a test of life-course interdependence. Criminology 44(4):807–833

Duncan TE, Duncan SC, Okut H, Strycker LA, Hix-Small H (2003) A multilevel contextual model of neighborhood collective efficacy. Am J Community Psychol 32(3):245–252

Eitle D, Stolzenberg L, D'Alessio SJ (2005) Police organizational factors, the racial composition of the police, and the probability of arrest. Justice Q 22(1):30–57

Emerson RM (1983) Holistic effects in social control decision-making. Law Soc Rev 17(3):425–456. oHol

Finn-Aage E, Wayne Osgood D, Taylor TJ, Peterson D (2001) How great is G.R.E.A.T.? Results from a longitudinal quasi-experimental design. Criminol Public Policy 1(1):87–118

Firebaugh G (1978) A rule for inferring individual-level relationships from aggregate data. Am Sociol Rev 43: 557–572

Gelman A, Hill J (2007) Data analysis using regression and multilevel hierarchical models. Cambridge University Press, New York

Gillespie W (2005) A multilevel model of drug abuse inside prison. Prison J 85(2):223–246

Goldstein H, Yang M, Omar R., Turner R, Thompson S (2000) Meta-analysis using multilevel modelswith an application to the study of class size effects. Appl Stat 49:399–412

Goldstein H (1995) Multilevel statistical models. 2nd edn. Wiley, New York

Gottfredson DC, Cross A, Soule DA (2007) Distinguishing characteristics of effective and ineffective after-school programs to prevent delinquency and victimization. Criminol Public Policy 6(2):289–318

Griffin ML, Armstrong GS (2003) The effect of local life circumstances on female probationers' offending. Justice Q 20(2):213–239

Griffin T, Wooldredge J (2006) Sex-based disparities in felony dispositions before versus after sentencing reform in Ohio. Criminology 44(4): 893–923

Hay C, Forrest W (2006) The development of self-control: examining self-control theory's stability thesis. Criminology 44(4):739–774

Horney J, Osgood DW, Marshall IH (1995) Criminal careers in the short-term: intra-individual variability in crime and its relation to local life circumstances. Am Sociol Rev 60(4):655–673

Hox J (2002) Multilevel analysis: techniques and applications. Lawrence Erlbaum Associates, Inc. Publishers, Mahwah, NJ

Huebner BM (2003) Administrative determinants of inmate violence: a multilevel analysis. J Crim Justice 31(2): 107–117

Johnson BD (2005) Contextual disparities in guidelines departures: courtroom social contexts, guidelines compliance, and extralegal disparities in criminal sentencing. Criminology 43(3):761–796

Johnson BD (2006) The multilevel context of criminal sentencing: integrating judge- and county-level influences. Criminology 44(2):259–298

Johnson BD, Ulmer JT, Kramer JH (2008) The social context of guidelines circumvention: the case of federal district courts. Criminology 46(3):737–783

Kleck G, Sever B, Li S, Gertz M (2005) The missing link in general deterrence research. Criminology 43(3):623–660

Kleck G, Tark J, Bellows JJ (2006) What methods are most frequently used in research in criminology and criminal justice? J Crim Justice 36(2):147–152

Kreager DA (2007) When it's good to be "bad": violence and adolescent peer acceptance. Criminology 45(4):893–923

Kreft IGG (1995) The effects of centering in multilevel analysis: is the public school the loser or the winner? A new analysis of an old question. Multilevel Modeling Newsletter 7:5–8

Kreft IGG, De Leeuw J, Aiken LS (1995) The effect of different forms of centering in hierarchical linear models. Multivariate Behav Res 30(1):1–21

Kreft IGG, De Leeuw J (1998) Introducing multilevel modeling. Sage Publications, Thousand Oaks

Kubrin CE, Stewart EA (2006) Predicting who reoffends: the neglected role of neighborhood context in recidivism studies. Criminology 44(1):165–197

Land KC, McCall PL, Cohen LE (1990) Structural covariates of homicide rates: are there any invariances across time and social space? Am Sociol Rev 95(4):922–963

Lauritsen JL, Schaum RJ (2004) The social ecology of violence against women. Criminology, 42(2):323–357

Lawton BA (2007) Levels of nonlethal force: an examination of individual, situational and contextual factors. J Res Crime and Delinq 44(2):163–184

Lee MS, Ulmer JT (2000) Fear of crime among Korean Americans in Chicago communities. Criminology 38(4):1173–1206

Liska AE (1990) The Significance of aggregate dependent variables and contextual independent variables for linking macro and micro theories. Soc Psych Q 53:292–301

Liska AE (1992) Social threat and social control. SUNY Press, Albany

Longford NT (1989). To center or not to center. Multilevel Modelling Newsletter 1(2):7–11

Luke DA (2004) Multilevel modeling. Sage Publications, Thousand Oaks

Mears DP, Wang X, Hay C, Bales WD (2008) Social ecology and recidivism: implications for prisoner reentry. Criminology 46(2):301–340

Miethe TD, McDowall D (1993) Contextual effects in models of criminal victimization. Soc Forces 71(3):741–759

Mill, John S. (1843). A system of logic, ratiocinative, and inductive. Longmans, Green, Reader, and Dyer. (8th edn, 1872) or "Harrison & Co." for 1st edn

Nieuwbeerta P, McCall PL, Elffers H, Wittebrood K (2008) Neighborhood characteristics and individual homicide risks: effects of social cohesion, confidence, in the police, and socioeconomic disadvantage. Homicide Studies 12(1):90–116

Osgood DW, Anderson AL (2004) Unstructured socializing and rates of delinquency. Criminology 42(3):519–550

Osgood DW, Schreck CJ (2007) A new method for studying the extent, stability, and predictors of individual specialization in violence. Criminology 45(2):273–312

Paccagnella O (2006) Centering or not centering in multilevel models? The role of the group mean and the assessment of group effects. Eval Rev 30(1):66–85

Pare P-P, Felson RB, Ouimet M (2007) Community variation in crime clearance multilevel analysis with comments on assessing police performance. J Quant Criminol 23(3):243–258

Rankin BH, Quane JM (2002) Social contexts and urban adolescent outcomes: the interrelated effects of neighborhoods, families, and peers on African-American youth. Soc Probl 49(1):79–100

Raudenbush SW (1984) Magnitude of teacher expectancy effects on pupil IQ as a function of credibility of expectancy induction: a synthesis of findings from 18 experiments. J Educ Psychol 76(1):85–97

Raudenbush SW (1989) "Centering" predictors in multilevel analysis. Choices and consequences. Multilevel Modeling Newsletter 1:10–12

Raudenbush SW, Bryk AS (2002) Hierarchical linear models: applications and data analysis methods, 2nd edn. SAGE Publications Inc

Robinson WS (1950) Ecological correlations and the behavior of individuals. Am Sociol Rev 15:351–357

Rosenfeld R, Fornango R, Rengifo AF (2007) The impact of order-maintenance policing in New York City homicide and robbery rates: 1988–2001. Criminology 45(2):355–384

Sampson RJ, Laub JH, Wimer C (2006) Does marriage reduce crime? A counterfactual approach to within-individual causal effects. Criminology 44(3):465–508

Schreck CJ, Stewart EA, Wayne Osgood D (2008) A reappraisal of the overlap of violent offenders and victims. Criminology 46(4):871–906

Simons RL, Simons LG, Burt CH, Brody GH, Cutrona C (2005) Collective efficacy, authoritative parenting and delinquency: a longitudinal test of a model integrating community- and felony-level processes. Criminology 43(4):989–1029

Slocum LA, Simpson S, Smith DA (2005) Strained lives and crime: examining intra-individual variation in strain and offending in a sample of incarcerated women. Criminology 43(4):1067–110

Smith D (1986) The neighborhood context of police behavior. Crime Justice 8:313–341

Snidjers T, Bosker R (1999) Multilevel models: an introduction to basic and advanced multilevel modeling. Sage Publications, Thousand Oaks

Stewart EA (2003) School social bonds, school climate, and school misbehavior: a multilevel analysis. Justice Q 20(3):575–604

Sun IY, Payne BK, Yuning W (2008) The impact of situational factors, officer characteristics, and neighborhood context on police behavior: a multilevel analysis. J Crim Justice 36(1):22–32

Taylor J, Malone S, Iacono WG, McGue M (2002) Development of substance dependence in two delinquency subgroups and nondelinquents from a male twin sample. J Am Acad Child Adolesc Psychiatry 41(4):386–393

Terrill W, Reisig MD (2003) Neighborhood context and police use of force. J Res Crime Delinq 40(3):291–321

Ulmer JT, Bradley MS (2006) Variation in trial penalties among serious violent offenses. Criminology 44(3):631–670

Ulmer JT, Johnson BD (2004) Sentencing in context: a multilevel analysis. Criminology 42(1):137–178

Warner BD (2007) Directly intervene or call the authorities? A study of forms of neighborhood social control within a social disorganization framework. Criminology 45(1):99–129

Wilcox P, Madensen TD, Tillyer MS (2007) Guardianship in context: implications for burglary victimization risk and prevention. Criminology 45(4):771–803

Wooldredge J, Griffin T, Pratt T (2001) Considering hierarchical models for research on inmate behavior: Predicting misconduct with multilevel data. Justice Q 18(1):203–231

Wooldredge J (2007) Neighborhood effects on felony sentencing. J Res Crime Delinq 44(2):238–263

Wright JP, Beaver KM (2005) Do parents matter in creating self-control in their children? A genetically informed test of Gottfredson and Hirschi's theory of low self-control. Criminology 43(4):1169–1202

Wright JP, Beaver KM, Delisi M, Vaughn M (2008) Evidence of negligible parenting influence on self-control, delinquent peers, and delinquency in a sample of twins. Justice Q 25(3):544–569

Wright DA, Bobashev G, Folsom R (2007) Understanding the relative influence of neighborhood, family, and youth on adolescent drug use. Subst Use Misuse 42:2159–2171

Wyant BR (2008) Multilevel impacts of perceived incivilities and perceptions of crime risk on fear of crime: isolating endogenous impacts. J Res Crime and Delinq 45(1):39–64

Xie M, McDowall D (2008) Escaping crime: the effects of direct and indirect victimization on moving. Criminology 46(4):809–840

Xie M, McDowall D (2008) The effects of residential turnover on household victimization. Criminology 46(3):539–575

Zhang L, Messner SF, Liu J (2007) An exploration of the determinants of reporting crime to the police in the city of Tianjin, China. Criminology 45(4):959–984

## CHAPTER 31

Logistic Regression Models for Categorical Outcome Variables

CHESTER L. BRITT AND DAVID WEISBURD

INTRODUCTION

The study of crime and criminal justice often results in the researcher being confronted with an outcome variable measured by two or more categories. In many applications, the variables are unordered, such as, arrested vs. not arrested, convicted vs. not convicted, or type of case disposition (e.g., acquittal, guilty plea conviction, or trial conviction). Other outcome variables of interest may be measured with ordered categories, such as type of punishment (e.g., probation sentence, jail sentence, or prison sentence), self-reported delinquent acts (e.g., none, one, or two or more), and many attitudinal items, which are commonly measured on ordinal scales that use categories ranging from Strongly Agree to Strongly Disagree. Much of the published criminological research confronted with categorical outcome variables has taken one of three approaches: (1) To collapse some number of categories on a polytomous (multicategory) outcome variable to create a binary measure, and use binary logistic regression models to analyze the data, (2) to treat an ordinal measure as if it were unordered and use multinomial logistic regression models, or (3) to treat an ordinal measure as if it were continuous, and use OLS regression to analyze the data. The first two approaches effectively throw away information about the distribution of cases on the dependent variable, while the third approach assumes that too much information is contained in the ordinal variable, consequently making all three approaches less than satisfactory.

The primary focus of this chapter is a discussion on the type of logistic regression model best suited to an analysis of categorical outcome variables. Toward that end, we discuss binary logistic regression models for situations where the dependent variable has only two categories, multinomial logistic regression for situations where the dependent variable has three or more unordered categories, and ordinal logistic regression models for situations where the dependent variable has at least three ordered categories. Interestingly, and despite the relative ease of use of ordinal logistic regression models, their use in the analysis of crime and criminal justice data is relatively rare. In an attempt to address concerns about analyzing ordinal data appropriately, we place greater emphasis on the use and interpretation of ordinal logistic regression models in this chapter.

A.R. Piquero and D. Weisburd (eds.), *Handbook of Quantitative Criminology*,
DOI 10.1007/978-0-387-77650-7_31, © Springer Science + Business Media, LLC 2010,
First softcover printing 2011

The discussion is organized as follows: "Binary Logistic Regression" will present the key elements for the binary logistic regression model, since the application and interpretation of this model is foundational to the application of both multinomial and ordinal logistic regression models discussed later in this chapter. Readers who are familiar with the binary logistic regression model may skip "Binary Logistic Regression" and move on directly to "Multinomial Logistic Regression", which will present the application and interpretation of the multinomial logistic regression model. Finally, "Ordinal Logistic Regression" will then discuss two different logistic regression models for ordinal outcome variables: The proportional odds model and the partial proportional odds model. The general approach in the discussion of each model will be to highlight some of the key technical details of the model, and then to emphasize the application and the interpretation of the model. Readers who are interested in more in-depth technical discussions will be referred to the appropriate sources.

BINARY LOGISTIC REGRESSION

Preliminaries: Odds and Odds Ratios

The use of binary logistic regression models in criminology is common because of the dichotomous nature of many key outcome variables in criminology: Arrest vs. no arrest, delinquency vs. no delinquency, or incarceration sentence vs. no incarceration sentence. The following discussion of binary logistic regression models is brief and intended as a starting point (or review) for the discussion of multinomial and ordinal logistic regression models. There is an extensive literature on the use of binary logistic regression models, and readers who are less familiar with this model are encouraged to consult these sources for comprehensive and accessible treatments of binary logistic regression (Hosmer and Lemeshow 2000; Menard 2002; Pampel 2000).

We begin by assuming that we have a binary outcome variable, arbitrarily assigned the values of "1" for the category of primary theoretical or research interest and "0" for the reference category (i.e., the comparison outcome). We can define the odds of one outcome relative to the other outcome as follows:

$$\text{Odds} = \frac{P(Y = 1)}{P(Y = 0)} = \frac{P(Y = 1)}{1 - P(Y = 1)}$$

where $P(Y = 1)$ refers to the probability that the outcome variable (Y) takes on the value "1" (the category of primary interest), and $P(Y = 0)$ refers to the probability that the outcome variable takes on the value "0" (the reference category). We can compute the odds from sample data using the proportion of cases that fall into each category. For example, if 60% of cases fall into category 1 and 40% into category 0, then the odds would be $0.60/0.40 = 1.5$, meaning that category "1" is 1.5 times more likely to be observed than category "0".

Since we are typically interested in how the odds of a particular outcome differ for different groups of cases, such as males and females or treatment and control groups, we can use the odds for each group to construct an odds ratio:

$$\text{Odds ratio} = \frac{\left(\dfrac{P(Y = 1)}{1 - P(Y = 1)}\right)_{\text{group 1}}}{\left(\dfrac{P(Y = 1)}{1 - P(Y = 1)}\right)_{\text{group 2}}}$$

In practice, the odds ratio provides a measure of strength of association between the outcome variable and the independent variable. For example, in the assessment of the effectiveness of a treatment program, a researcher may compute the odds of success for individuals in the control and the treatment groups. If the treatment was effective, then there would presumably be different odds of success for each group of individuals. The magnitude of this difference would then appear in the odds ratio.

Suppose, for instance, the researcher found that 70% of the individuals in the treatment group and 50% of the individuals in the control group were classified as a "success."

The odds of success for the treatment group would be:

$$\text{Odds} = \frac{P(Y = 1)}{P(Y = 0)} = \frac{0.70}{1 - 0.70} = 2.33$$

The odds of success for the control group would be:

$$\text{Odds} = \frac{P(Y = 1)}{P(Y = 0)} = \frac{0.55}{1 - 0.55} = 1.22$$

The odds ratio comparing the odds for the two groups would be:

$$\text{Odds ratio} = \frac{\left(\dfrac{0.70}{1 - 0.70}\right)_{\text{treatment}}}{\left(\dfrac{0.55}{1 - 0.55}\right)_{\text{control}}} = \frac{2.33}{1.22} = 1.91$$

The odds ratio indicates that the odds of a success are 1.91 times larger for the treatment group than the odds of a success for the control group.

Binary Logistic Regression Model

Information about the odds is used as a fundamental component of the binary logistic regression model. The "logit" is defined as the natural logarithm of the odds:

$$\text{Logit} = ln\left(\frac{P(Y = 1)}{1 - P(Y = 1)}\right)$$

The logit is then used as the dependent variable in a linear model that includes k independent variables:

$$\text{Logit} = ln\left(\frac{P(Y = 1)}{1 - P(Y = 1)}\right) = b_0 + b_1 X_1 + \cdots + b_k X_k$$

Using the logit equation, we can rewrite the equation for $P(Y = 1)$, which turns out to be the logistic distribution function:

$$P(Y = 1) = \frac{1}{1 + \exp(-Xb)}$$

The logistic distribution function is then used to estimate the model coefficients through a maximum likelihood procedure in a wide range of statistical software packages. It is important to note that other probability functions, such as the Normal or the Gompertz, may also be used to calculate $P(Y = 1)$. The focus in this chapter is on the use of the logistic regression models because of the relative ease of interpreting the coefficients from these models over those that rely on an alternative probability distribution. Readers interested in the application of the Normal Distribution, known as the probit model, are encouraged to read Pampel (2000) for a comprehensive, and accessible discussion.

Interpreting the Coefficients

The coefficients estimated from a binary logistic regression model (the b_k) can be interpreted directly in the context of a one unit change in the independent variable: For a one unit change in the independent variable, the log of the odds is expected to change by b_k, controlling for all other independent variables included in the model. Since the "log of the odds" does not have intuitive meaning for most people, we can transform the estimated coefficients by exponentiating each coefficient (i.e., $\exp(b) = e^b$), which then estimates the odds ratio for a single one unit change in the independent variable.

For example, suppose $b = 0.2$, we could interpret this coefficient directly to mean that for each one unit increase in the independent variable, the log of the odds increases by 0.2 units, controlling for all other variables in the statistical model. Alternatively, if we take the antilog of b, we see that the odds ratio has a value of 1.22 ($e^{0.2} = 1.22$). Substantively, this tells us that for a one unit change in the independent variable, the odds of outcome $Y = 1$ increase by a factor of 1.22, controlling for all other variables in the model.

It is important to keep in mind that the odds ratio is not a linear function of the independent variables in a binary logistic regression model, which means that we cannot discuss linear changes in the odds ratio in response to changes in the independent variable. If we are interested in determining how much the odds change in response to more than a one unit change in the independent variable, we multiply that value (ΔX) by the coefficient (b) and exponentiate this quantity (i.e., $e^{\Delta X b}$). If we again use $b = 0.2$, but are interested in the change in the odds for a 5-unit change in the independent variable, then we calculate $e^{5*0.2} = e^1 = 2.72$, which means that the odds increase by a factor of 2.72 for a 5-unit increase in the independent variable.

Model Assessment

There is no single best measure for statistically assessing the quality of a binary logistic regression model. Perhaps the most common means for assessing whether a model has a statistically significant effect on the dependent variable is to use a likelihood-ratio test that compares two models. The first model constrains all coefficients for the independent variables and estimates only the model intercept (the null model), while the second model estimates coefficients for all the independent variables (the full model). Since maximum likelihood estimation techniques are used to estimate the coefficients, one of the pieces of information produced in the process of estimation is the value of the likelihood function (essentially a probability estimate). Taking the natural logarithm of this value, and then multiplying by -2 produces a value that is useful for hypothesis testing of one or more coefficients in a binary logistic regression model. The value $-2*$ log-likelihood is typically written as $-2LL$.

The hypothesis test for whether all coefficients in a model are equal to zero is given by the difference in the $-2LL$ values for the null model and the full model.

$$\text{LR test statistic} = (-2LL_{\text{null model}}) - (-2LL_{\text{full model}})$$

The LR test statistic is distributed as a chi-square statistic with degrees of freedom equal to the number of coefficients estimated in the model. This same test can also be used to test the statistical significance of individual coefficients or subsets of coefficients from the full regression model. For a single coefficient, the degrees of freedom would be $df = 1$, while for the subset of coefficients, the degrees of freedom would be equal to the number of coefficients in the subset. Conceptually, the likelihood-ratio test for the full logistic regression model or for a subset of coefficients works in much the same way as an F-test in the typical ordinary least squares regression model.

In addition to likelihood-ratio tests, there are a number of alternative means for overall model assessment of a binary logistic regression model. Two of the more commonly reported measures are the percent of observations correctly classified by the model and the pseudo-R^2 value. Both of these tests are limited in their ability to assess model quality and will tend to be more suggestive than conclusive. However, when used in conjunction with each other and the likelihood-ratio test, a reasonably clear picture of the model's effectiveness should emerge.

The percent of observations correctly classified uses the predicted value of the dependent variable based on the hypothesized logistic regression model, and compares it to the observed distribution of the dependent variable. The predicted value of the dependent variable is usually based on the category that has the highest predicted probability of occurring. In other words, if $P(Y = 1) > 0.5$, then the predicted value of the dependent variable is estimated as category "1"; $P(Y = 1) < 0.5$, means the predicted value of the dependent variable will be estimated as "0". The percent of observations correctly classified as a "0" or a "1" is then a simple percentage:

$$\text{Percent correctly classified} = \frac{\text{Number of observations correctly placed}}{\text{Total number of observations}} \times 100\%$$

One of the primary limitations of the percent of observations correctly classified is that it is dependent on the original distribution of observations. Consequently, if the original distribution has a relatively small percentage of cases in one of the two categories (say, less than 10%), the percent correctly classified will tend to be quite large, because most (or all) of the observations will be predicted to fall in the category with the most cases. Consider the somewhat common situation in the study of crime and delinquency, where 90% of the observations fall into one category, likely no delinquency or no arrest. It is also then quite common for all sample observations to be predicted to fall into the modal category of the dependent variable, which would then result in the percent correctly classified having a value of 90%, even though the model did nothing to discriminate cases and make predictions about which cases would fall into the other category.

Pseudo-R^2 measures are based on comparing values of the $-2LL$ values for the null and full models. Intuitively, this makes sense, because the $-2LL$ value provides an approximation for how close the predicted data represent the observed data. Perhaps the most commonly reported pseudo-R^2 measure is Cox and Snell's R^2:

$$R^2 = 1 - e^{-[(-2LL_{\text{null model}}) - (-2LL_{\text{full model}})]/N},$$

where N is the size of the sample. All pseudo-R^2 values are then interpreted as rough approximations of the proportion of variation in the dependent variable that is explained by the full model. It is important to note, however, that all pseudo-R^2 measures assume a hypothetical dependent variable that is continuously distributed and are then interpreted as an indicator of explained variance. Again, these kinds of model assessment measures should be viewed as suggestive, rather than conclusive.

Statistical Significance of Individual Coefficients

As noted above, the test of statistical significance for a single coefficient in a regression model could be conducted with a likelihood-ratio chi-square test and one degree of freedom. An alternative is to use a z-statistic or a Wald statistic (W). The z-statistic is simply the ratio of the logistic regression coefficient (b) to its standard error ($SE(b)$). The Wald statistic is the squared value of the z-statistic:

$$z = \left(\frac{b}{SE(b)} \right)$$

$$W = \left(\frac{b}{SE(b)} \right)^2 = z^2.$$

Substantively, the z-statistic, the Wald statistic, and the likelihood-ratio test will tend to give the same substantive answer in regard to the statistical significance of an individual coefficient.[1] For large samples, the results will be nearly identical. To the extent that the results differ for the likelihood-ratio compared to the z-statistic or the Wald statistic, it will be due to the values of z and W being more sensitive to small sample sizes, implying that the likelihood-ratio test will tend to give a more accurate assessment of statistical significance, regardless of the size of the sample (Long 1997).

An Example: Fayetteville Youth Project

The following analysis of data from the Fayetteville Youth Project (FYP) is intended to illustrate some of the key points in the preceding discussion, as well as the material to follow. Briefly, the FYP data were collected with a self-report survey administered in 1997 to students in the 9th, 10th, and 11th grades at Fayetteville High School (Arkansas). The Fayetteville sample was drawn from the 1,782 students enrolled in the 9th through 11th grades in the spring of 1997. The final sample consists of 1,130 student respondents, of which 489 are white males, 69 are black males, 83 are black females, and 489 are white females, generally reflecting the demographic composition of the school.

The dependent variable in the following analysis is self-reported theft of an item valued at \$2 to \$50 (Yes = 1, No = 0). The independent variables include age (in years), sex (Male = 1, Female = 0), race (White = 1, Nonwhite = 0), grade point average (rounded to

---

[1] Software packages differ in the default results that are reported. For example, SAS and SPSS report the Wald statistic, while Stata and LIMDEP report the z-statistic. Practically, it makes no difference which statistic (W or z) is reported, since the observed significance level of the coefficient will be the same.

nearest integer, range is 0 to 4), whether any of the respondent's friends had been picked up by the police (Yes = 1, No = 0), whether the respondent's parent(s) knew where the respondent was while away from home (Agree and Strongly Agree = 1, Undecided, Disagree, and Strongly Disagree = 0), and three items that assessed the respondent's beliefs about theft and breaking the law (all three coded as Agree and Strongly Agree = 1, Undecided, Disagree, and Strongly Disagree = 0). Descriptive statistics for these variables are presented in Table 31.1.

The logistic regression model can be represented in equation form as

$$\text{Logit (Theft)} = b_0 + b_1 \text{age} + b_2 \text{sex} + b_3 \text{race} + b_4 \text{GPA} + b_5 \text{friends picked up}$$
$$+ b_6 \text{parents know} + b_7 \text{get ahead} + b_8 \text{around the law}$$
$$+ b_9 \text{OK to take}$$

The results of the logistic regression analysis appear in Table 31.2, which reports the coefficient value, the standard error, the z-score, and the odds ratio for each coefficient. We can see from the results that all of the independent variables are statistically significant, except for the age and the sex of the respondent. More directly, and to highlight a few results, we observe the following:

- Whites have odds of self-reported theft that are exp(−0.52) = 0.59 times smaller than the odds of self-reported theft for nonwhites, controlling for all other variables in the model.

TABLE 31.1. Descriptive statistics for Fayetteville youth study ($N = 1,056$)

Variable	Mean	Standard deviation
Age	15.74	0.99
Male	0.49	0.50
White	0.87	0.33
GPA	3.04	0.92
Friends picked up by the police	0.59	0.49
Parents know where youth is while away	0.61	0.49
Have to do some things that are not right to get ahead	0.27	0.45
OK to get around the law if you could get away with it	0.27	0.45
OK to take things from big business	0.14	0.35

TABLE 31.2. Binary logistic regression results for Fayetteville youth study

Variable	Coefficient	SE	z-Score
Age	−0.04	0.08	−0.52
Male	0.29	0.16	1.89
White	−0.52	0.22	−2.43
GPA	−0.36	0.09	−4.21
Friends picked up by the police	1.17	0.17	6.81
Parents know where youth is while away	−0.66	0.16	−4.24
Have to do some things that are not right to get ahead	0.41	0.18	2.33
OK to get around the law if you could get away with it	0.53	0.18	2.94
OK to take things from big business	0.88	0.22	3.98
Intercept	0.52	1.32	0.40

- As GPA increases, the odds of self-reported theft decrease. For example, a one-unit increase in GPA reduces the odds of self-reported theft by a factor of $\exp(-0.36) = 0.69$, controlling for all other variables in the model.
- Respondents who have had friends picked up by the police have odds of self-reported theft that are about $\exp(1.17) = 3.21$ times greater than the odds of self-reported theft for those youth who have not had a friend picked up by the police, controlling for all other variables in the model.
- Youth who agreed that their parent(s) generally knew where they were when away from home had odds of self-reported theft that were $\exp(-0.66) = 0.52$ times smaller than the odds of self-reported theft for those youth who were undecided or disagreed that their parents generally knew where they were, controlling for all other variables in the model.
- Youth who agreed that one had to do some things that were not right to get ahead had odds of self-reported theft that were $\exp(0.41) = 1.51$ times higher than the odds of self-reported theft for the youth who were undecided or disagreed, controlling for all other variables in the model.
- Youth who agreed that it was okay to get around the law if one could get away with it had odds of self-reported theft that were $\exp(0.53) = 1.70$ times higher than the odds of self-reported theft for the youth who were undecided or disagreed, controlling for all other variables in the model.
- Youth who agreed that it was okay to take things from big business had odds of self-reported theft that were $\exp(0.88) = 2.41$ times higher than the odds of self-reported theft for the youth who were undecided or disagreed, controlling for all other variables in the model.

The model assessment statistics show the likelihood-ratio test ($\chi^2 = 277.34$, $df = 9$, $p < 0.001$), the pseudo-R^2 (0.20), and percent correctly classified (79.4%) values collectively suggest a model with a modest ability to predict self-reported theft.

MULTINOMIAL LOGISTIC REGRESSION

Multinomial Logistic Regression Model

Multinomial logistic regression is used to examine problems where there are three or more unordered categories in the dependent variable. There are many situations in the study of crime and criminal justice in which dependent variables include multiple unordered categories. For example, the type of case disposition may be measured as acquittal, guilty plea conviction, or trial conviction; type of crime committed by offenders may be measured as violent, property, or drug offenses; and, pretrial release decisions in a court may be measured as released on recognizance, released with supervision, released on bail, and denied release.

Multinomial logistic regression is conceptually a straightforward extension of the binary logistic regression model.[2] Recall that in the binary logistic regression model, we designated one of the two outcome categories as the presence of a given trait and the second as the

---

[2] Readers interested in more detailed and technical treatments of multinomial logistic regression should consult Agresti (2002), Long (1997), and Menard (2002).

absence of that trait. For example, in the analysis of the FYP data, we compared those who had self-reported theft ($Y = 1$) to those who did not report any theft ($Y = 0$) by estimating the logit of Y:

$$\text{Logit}(Y) = \ln\left(\frac{P(Y=1)}{P(Y=0)}\right) = b_0 + b_1 X_1 + \cdots + b_k X_k$$

The logit of Y in the equation requires that there be only the absence ($Y = 0$) or the presence ($Y = 1$) of a characteristic. What happens when the outcome variable has more than two categories? The problem here is that we do not have a simple change in the odds for one outcome compared to one other outcome, as we did with the self-reported theft example. In an outcome variable with three or more unordered categories, we have to take into account the changes in the odds of multiple outcomes, which then leads to multiple comparisons.

Suppose, for example, that our outcome variable has three categories (C1, C2, and C3) with the number of observations in each being represented by N_{C1}, N_{C2}, and N_{C3}. We could begin by estimating three binary logistic regression models that would allow for all possible comparisons of the outcome categories – the logits for C1 and C2, C2 and C3, and C1 and C3. The logit of Y for each regression could be written simply as

$$\ln\left(\frac{P(Y=C1)}{P(Y=C2)}\right), \quad \ln\left(\frac{P(Y=C2)}{P(Y=C3)}\right), \quad \text{and} \quad \ln\left(\frac{P(Y=C1)}{P(Y=C3)}\right)$$

for each comparison, respectively.[3]

If we were to estimate these three separate logits, the coefficients from each equation would be interpreted in the same way as we described in the discussion of the binary logistic regression model. While this approach would allow us to make comparisons of the likelihood of subjects falling in each of the three categories examined as compared to each other, it would require us to run three separate logistic regressions. Moreover, and more importantly from a statistical point of view, we would likely be working with three completely different samples in each of the three analyses: (1) $N_{C1} + N_{C2}$, (2) $N_{C2} + N_{C3}$, and (3) $N_{C1} + N_{C3}$. This is because the cases on the dependent variable are unlikely to be distributed evenly. For example, if we were studying case dispositions among criminal defendants – acquittal/dismissal, guilty plea conviction, or trial conviction – we would not expect the type of disposition for the sample of defendants to be distributed equally across each possible outcome. Consequently, each of our comparisons would be based on different samples. In comparing defendants who had only outcomes C1 and C2, our analyzable sample would be $N_{C1} + N_{C2}$. The sample size would not reflect the defendants that had outcome C3 (i.e., N_{C3}), since they would have been excluded from the comparison. But what we are really interested in is the choice among the three outcomes and how this choice is distributed in our entire sample. The statistical problem here is that the varying sample sizes would then result in incorrect standard errors for the coefficients, leading to inaccurate tests of statistical significance – the absolute values of the coefficients are not affected by the order of the comparisons. The multinomial logistic

---

[3] These three logits can be linked in an identity equation that illustrates how knowledge of any two logits can produce the values of the third. The identity equation can be stated as

$$\ln\left(\frac{P(Y=C1)}{P(Y=C2)}\right) + \ln\left(\frac{P(Y=C2)}{P(Y=C3)}\right) = \ln\left(\frac{P(Y=C1)}{P(Y=C3)}\right).$$

regression model simultaneously accounts for these different sample sizes, ensuring a more valid estimate of significance levels. It also has the benefit of allowing us to conduct our analysis using a single regression equation.

An important step in a multinomial regression is the definition of the "reference category." This is necessary because we need to decide which category we want to use as a baseline for all comparisons. It is an arbitrary decision about which category is designated the reference category, but to the extent that we can make a choice that has some theoretical relevance or makes the interpretation of the results simpler, that would be the preferred choice. For the case disposition example above, suppose that we choose dismissal as the reference category, which then allows us to make two comparisons between a type of conviction – guilty plea or trial – and dismissal. More directly, our multinomial logistic regression results will indicate (1) the relative likelihood of a guilty plea conviction compared to a dismissal and (2) the relative likelihood of a trial conviction compared to a dismissal. The one comparison not mentioned was the relative likelihood of a guilty plea conviction compared to a trial conviction. In the multinomial logistic regression model, this comparison is not directly estimated, but as will be illustrated shortly, the results can be obtained very simply from the results for the comparison of each conviction type to a dismissal.

The multinomial logistic regression model can be written as either a probability model or an odds ratio model. As a probability equation, the multinomial logistic equation is

$$P(Y = m) = \frac{\exp{(Xb_m)}}{\sum_{j=1}^{J} \exp{(Xb_j)}}.$$

In this equation, m refers to the outcome category of interest and has values ranging from 1 to J (the last category). The numerator to the equation tells us to exponentiate the value of Xb for category m. The denominator, in turn, tells us that we need to exponentiate the value of Xb for all categories, and then sum these values together. Since there is a redundancy built into the values of the coefficients in a multinomial logistic model, the coefficient values for the reference category ($b1$) are set at 0. The constraining of one set of coefficients to 0 results in the identification of the system of logistic regression equations, which allows for the estimation of unique coefficient estimates for the $J - 1$ logits.[4]

For the three-category case disposition variable, $m = 1$, 2, or 3. Writing out the probability equations for each outcome leads to the following formulations of the probability of each of the three outcomes in our example. For $m = 1$, $b_1 = 0$ and

$$P(Y = 1) = \frac{\exp{(X0)}}{\exp{(X0)} + \exp{(Xb_2)} + \exp{(Xb_3)}} = \frac{1}{1 + \exp{(Xb_2)} + \exp{(Xb_3)}}$$

For $m = 2$ and $m = 3$, we have

$$P(Y = 2) = \frac{\exp{(Xb_2)}}{1 + \exp{(Xb_2)} + \exp{(Xb_3)}}$$

$$P(Y = 3) = \frac{\exp{(Xb_3)}}{1 + \exp{(Xb_2)} + \exp{(Xb_3)}}$$

---

[4] As noted previously, the choice of the reference category is arbitrary. All possible comparisons of the outcome categories can be made based on single set of $J - 1$ logits.

The multinomial logistic regression model can also be written as an odds ratio equation comparing the probabilities for any two outcomes m and n on the dependent variable:

$$\text{OR}_{m|n} = \frac{P(Y = m)}{P(Y = n)} = \frac{\frac{\exp(Xb_m)}{\sum_{j=1}^{J} \exp(Xb_j)}}{\frac{\exp(Xb_n)}{\sum_{j=1}^{J} \exp(Xb_j)}} = \frac{\exp(Xb_m)}{\exp(Xb_n)}.$$

If we are interested in computing the odds ratio for a comparison between any category (m) and the reference category ($m = 1$), where $b_1 = 0$, we obtain

$$\text{OR}_{m|n} = \frac{P(Y = m)}{P(Y = 1)} = \frac{\exp(Xb_m)}{\exp(X0)} = \exp(Xb_m)$$

This result also indicates how we should interpret the coefficients from the multinomial logistic regression model. Since the coefficients for the reference category have been fixed at 0, the coefficients for each of the remaining outcome categories will compare the relative likelihood of that category to the reference category.[5]

In practice what these equations tell us is that we will have $J - 1$ sets of coefficients from a multinomial logistic regression model that can be interpreted in the same way as binary logistic coefficients, where we compare each outcome (m) to the reference category ($m = 1$) for the outcome variable. In our example for case disposition, where we have designated dismissal as the reference category, one set of coefficients will give us the log of the odds or the odds ratios comparing the likelihood of a guilty plea conviction relative to a dismissal, while the second set of coefficients will give us the log of the odds or the odds ratios comparing the likelihood of a trial conviction relative to a dismissal.

An Example: Pretrial Release Status in California

The State Court Processing Statistics database includes information on random samples of individuals arrested for felony offenses in the largest court districts in the United States. To illustrate the application of the multinomial logistic regression model, the following example will use a random sample of 6,606 felony arrestees in California in the 1990s. A question of both policy and theoretical relevance is the study of the factors that affect the defendant's pretrial release status: Nonfinancial release, financial release, held on bail, or denied bail. Table 31.3 presents the coding and descriptive statistics for all the variables included in the multivariate model.

Table 31.4 presents the results from our application of the multinomial logistic regression model. Since there are four categories to the dependent variable, there are three sets of coefficients presented in the three columns of results. Each column in Table 31.4 represents a comparison of nonfinancial release (the reference category) with each of the other three financial release categories: financial release (column 1), held on bail (column 2), and denied bail (column 3).

The first column of results shows that defendants who are older, black or Hispanic (rather than white), used a public defender, and were charged with a drug or a property crime (rather than "other" crime) were less likely to have a financial release than a nonfinancial release.

---

[5] It is worth pointing out that the binary logistic regression model presented above is a special case of the multinomial logistic regression model, where $m = 2$.

TABLE 31.3. Variable coding and descriptive statistics for pretrial release in California ($N = 6,606$)

Variable	Mean	Standard deviation
Age (years)	29.94	8.87
Male (1 = male, 0 = female)	0.83	0.37
Black (1 = black, 0 = non-black)	0.25	0.44
Hispanic (1 = Hispanic, 0 = Non-Hispanic)	0.46	0.50
Under criminal justice supervision (1 = yes, 0 = no)	0.48	0.50
Represented by public defender (1 = yes, 0 = no)	0.75	0.43
Represented by private attorney (1 = yes, 0 = no)	0.15	0.35
Charged with violent crime (1 = yes, 0 = no)	0.22	0.42
Charged with property crime (1 = yes, 0 = no)	0.31	0.46
Charged with drug crime (1 = yes, 0 = no)	0.39	0.49
Number of prior felony arrests	4.06	5.88
Number of prior violent convictions	0.14	0.59

TABLE 31.4. Multinomial logistic regression results for pretrial release in California

	Coefficients for logits:		
Variable	Financial vs. non-financial release	Held on bail vs. non-financial release	Denied bail vs. non-financial release
Age	−0.01	−0.02	−0.02
Male	0.08	0.76	0.65
Black	−0.31	0.11	0.10
Hispanic	−0.09	0.79	−0.24
Under criminal justice supervision	0.23	0.95	1.94
Represented by public defender	−0.19	0.36	−0.39
Represented by private attorney	0.97	−0.22	−0.61
Charged with violent crime	0.43	0.93	0.72
Charged with property crime	−0.43	−0.03	−0.97
Charged with drug crime	−0.52	−0.45	−0.95
Number of prior felony arrests	0.03	0.10	0.12
Number of prior violent convictions	0.18	0.50	0.63
Intercept	0.10	−0.66	−2.07

Conversely, defendants who were male, under criminal justice supervision at the time of arrest, had a private defense attorney, were charged with a violent crime, had more prior felony arrests, and more prior convictions for violent crimes were more likely to have a financial release than a nonfinancial release. As in the previous section, we can also interpret each of these coefficients more directly as odds ratios. (Recall from the previous section that the exponentiation of the coefficient provides us with the odds ratio given a one-unit change in the independent variable.)

- If age is increased by 1 year, the odds of a financial release versus a nonfinancial release decrease by a factor of $\exp(-0.010) = 0.990$, controlling for all other variables in the model.
- The odds of a financial release versus a nonfinancial release are $\exp(0.077) = 1.080$ times greater for male than for female defendants, controlling for all other variables in the model.

- The odds of a financial release versus a nonfinancial release are exp(−0.313) = 0.731 times smaller for black than for white defendants, controlling for all other variables in the model.
- The odds of a financial release versus a nonfinancial release are exp(−0.091) = 0.913 times smaller for Hispanic than for white defendants, controlling for all other variables in the model.
- The odds of a financial release versus a nonfinancial release are exp(0.227) = 1.255 times greater for defendants under criminal justice supervision than for defendants not under supervision at the time of arrest, controlling for all other variables in the model.
- The odds of a financial release versus a nonfinancial release are exp(−0.190) = 0.827 times smaller for defendants with a public defender than for defendants with self or other representation, controlling for all other variables in the model.
- The odds of a financial release versus a nonfinancial release are exp(0.969) = 2.636 times greater for defendants with a private defense attorney than for defendants with self or other representation, controlling for all other variables in the model.
- The odds of a financial release versus a nonfinancial release are exp(0.426) = 1.531 times greater for defendants charged with a violent crime than for defendants with an "other" offense, controlling for all other variables in the model.
- The odds of a financial release versus a nonfinancial release are exp(−0.428) = 0.652 times smaller for defendants charged with a property crime than for defendants with an "other" offense, controlling for all other variables in the model.
- The odds of a financial release versus a nonfinancial release are exp(−0.519) = 0.595 times smaller for defendants charged with a drug crime than for defendants with an "other" offense, controlling for all other variables in the model.
- If the number of prior felony arrests is increased by one, the odds of a financial release versus a nonfinancial release increase by a factor of exp(0.028) = 1.028, controlling for all other variables in the model.
- If the number of prior convictions for violent crimes is increased by one, the odds of a financial release versus a nonfinancial release increase by a factor of exp(0.183) = 1.200, controlling for all other variables in the model.

We can similarly interpret the results in columns 2 and 3, which compare held on bail and denied bail to nonfinancial release, respectively. Note that the effects of each of the independent variables are not necessarily constant across the three different comparisons – the effect of sex or race, for example, varies by the specific comparison. These kinds of variable effects of independent variables are to be expected and reinforce the rationale for using a multinomial logistic regression model. If the dependent variable had been collapsed into two categories, say nonfinancial release versus all other pretrial statuses, then many of the interesting effects of both legal and extra-legal characteristics on pretrial release status would have been missed.

The Missing Coefficients

As noted earlier, when we estimate a multinomial logistic regression model, the coefficients for the reference category are fixed at 0, and we estimate coefficients for comparisons of all other categories with the reference category. Clearly, there are a number of other comparisons that may be of substantive interest, but are not directly estimated. For example, in our analysis of pretrial release status, we may be interested in comparing those defendants denied release to those held on bail. Based on the identity relationship of multiple logits described above, for all possible comparisons of the outcome categories, the most direct way of obtaining the missing coefficients is to simply subtract one set of coefficients from another set of coefficients. In Table 31.4, the results in column 2 represent the logit for held on bail and nonfinancial release, while those in column 3 represent the logit for denied bail and nonfinancial release. The following discussion illustrates how to compute this specific comparison, as well as highlight the general process for computing comparisons of outcome categories not directly estimated in a multinomial logistic regression model.

We start by reconsidering the logit equation for the estimated results. Since the logarithm of a fraction can be rewritten as the subtraction of the logarithm of the denominator from the logarithm of the numerator, the logits can be rewritten as

$$\ln\left(\frac{P(Y = \text{held on bail})}{P(Y = \text{nonfinancial release})}\right) = \ln\left(P(Y = \text{held on bail})\right)$$
$$-\ln\left(P(Y = \text{nonfinancial release})\right)$$

and

$$\ln\left(\frac{P(Y = \text{denied bail})}{P(Y = \text{nonfinancial release})}\right) = \ln\left(P(Y = \text{denied bail})\right)$$
$$-\ln\left(P(Y = \text{nonfinancial release})\right)$$

By performing simple subtractions of the logits, we can generate additional contrasts between the outcome categories. To obtain the missing coefficients for the comparison of denied bail to held on bail, we subtract the logit for held on bail and nonfinancial release from the logit for denied bail and nonfinancial release:

$$\ln\left(\frac{P(Y = \text{denied bail})}{P(Y = \text{nonfinancial release})}\right) - \ln\left(\frac{P(Y = \text{held on bail})}{P(Y = \text{nonfinancial release})}\right)$$

$$= [\ln\left(P(Y = \text{denied bail})\right) - \ln\left(P(Y = \text{nonfinancial release})\right)]$$
$$- [\ln\left(P(Y = \text{held on bail})\right) - \ln\left(P(Y = \text{nonfinancial release})\right)]$$

$$= \ln\left(P(Y = \text{denied bail})\right) - \ln\left(P(Y = \text{held on bail})\right)$$

$$= \ln\left(\frac{P(Y = \text{denied bail})}{P(Y = \text{held on bail})}\right)$$

What this algebraic manipulation of logits shows us is that we can obtain the coefficients for the omitted contrast simply by subtracting one set of coefficients from another set of coefficients. If we wanted the inverse of this comparison – the logit of held on bail to denied bail – all we would need to do is alternate the order of subtraction.

When applied to the coefficients for the pretrial release status example, we obtain the results presented in Table 31.5. To highlight a few of the findings:

- The odds of being denied bail versus being held on bail are exp(0.990) = 2.691 times greater for defendants under criminal justice supervision than for defendants not under criminal justice supervision at the time of arrest, controlling for all other variables in the model.

- The odds of being denied bail versus being held on bail are exp(−0.204) = 0.815 times smaller for defendants charged with a violent crime than for defendants with an "other" offense, controlling for all other variables in the model.
- If the number of prior convictions for violent crimes is increased by one, then the odds of being denied bail versus being held on bail increase by a factor of exp(0.135) = 1.145, controlling for all other variables in the model.

A second way to obtain the coefficients for the comparison of being denied bail to being held on bail, would be to redefine the statistical model so that held on bail was chosen as the reference category and re-estimate the multinomial model. Upon rerunning the multinomial logistic regression model with held on bail used as the reference category, we obtain the results presented in Table 31.6. In regard to the comparison of being denied bail to being held on bail (see column 3), note that the results are identical to those presented in Table 31.5, based

TABLE 31.5. Results for logit comparing held on bail to denied bail

Variable	Held on bail vs. denied bail
Age	0.00
Male	0.11
Black	0.01
Hispanic	1.03
Under criminal justice supervision	−0.99
Represented by public defender	0.75
Represented by private attorney	0.39
Charged with violent crime	0.21
Charged with property crime	0.94
Charged with drug crime	0.50
Number of prior felony arrests	−0.02
Number of prior violent convictions	−0.13
Intercept	1.41

TABLE 31.6. Multinomial logistic regression results for pretrial release in California (denied bail as reference category)

Variable	Coefficients for logits:		
	Non-financial release vs. denied bail	Financial release vs. denied bail	Held on bail vs. denied bail
Age	0.02	0.01	0.00
Male	−0.65	−0.57	0.11
Black	−0.10	−0.42	0.01
Hispanic	0.24	0.15	1.03
Under criminal justice supervision	−1.94	−1.71	−0.99
Represented by public defender	0.39	0.20	0.75
Represented by private attorney	0.61	1.58	0.39
Charged with violent crime	−0.72	−0.30	0.20
Charged with property crime	0.97	0.54	0.94
Charged with drug crime	0.95	0.43	0.51
Number of prior felony arrests	−0.12	−0.09	−0.02
Number of prior violent convictions	−0.63	−0.45	−0.13
Intercept	2.07	2.17	1.41

on subtracting the coefficients from the original analysis in Table 31.4. Overall, the results in Table 31.6 will lead us to the same substantive conclusions as the results in Table 31.4, with the only difference being an alternative reference category for interpretation. What this indicates is that the selection of reference categories is arbitrary and that correctly interpreted results will lead to the same substantive conclusions.

Statistical Inference

SINGLE COEFFICIENTS.   The results from a multinomial logistic regression analysis complicate tests of statistical significance slightly. Since we now have multiple coefficients representing the effects of each independent variable on the dependent variable, there are questions about how to discern whether an independent variable has an effect on the dependent variable. Specifically, there are two issues of statistical inference that are important for interpreting the results from a multinomial logistic regression analysis. For each coefficient we can (1) estimate the statistical significance of each category compared to the reference category, and (2) estimate the overall significance of the independent variable in predicting the multi-category dependent variable.

To test the effect of each individual coefficient in comparison to the reference category, we would again use the Wald or the z-statistic described above. Table 31.7 presents the multinomial logistic coefficients from the original model, along with the standard errors (SE) of the coefficients and the z-scores.

We can see that criminal justice supervision at the time of offense and the number of prior felony arrests have statistically significant effects on all three pairs of outcomes. The number of prior convictions is statistically significant for the comparisons of financial release and held on bail to nonfinancial release, but not for the comparison of denied bail to nonfinancial release. Type of legal representation and type of offense also have variable effects across the three comparisons. In regard to defendants' demographic characteristics, age is the only variable that has statistically significant effects on all three comparisons. Defendants' sex has statistically significant effects on all pairs, except for that between financial and nonfinancial release, while the effects of race – measured with dummy variables for black and Hispanic – vary across all three comparisons.

MULTIPLE COEFFICIENTS.   Note that in Table 31.7 there are three coefficients for each independent variable. As we noted above, the number of coefficients from a multinomial logistic regression model for each independent variable will be one less than the number of categories on the dependent variable (i.e., $J - 1$). How do we assess the overall effect of each independent variable on all of the categories of the dependent variable simultaneously? There are two key ways of doing this – one is the likelihood ratio test and the other test is an extension of the Wald test – discussed above. Regardless of the statistical software package one uses to estimate a multinomial logistic regression model, both of these methods will be available as either default or requested output.

Recall that the likelihood ratio test involves estimating two different models. One model is viewed as the "full" model (i.e., it contains all the coefficients to be estimated in that specific model) and the other model is viewed as the "reduced" model (i.e., one or more coefficients

TABLE 31.7. Multinomial logistic regression results for pretrial release in California (coefficients, standard errors, and z-scores)

Variable	Financial vs. non-financial release			Held on bail vs. non-financial release			Denied bail vs. non-financial release		
	Coefficient	SE	z-Score	Coefficient	SE	z-Score	Coefficient	SE	z-Score
Age	−0.01	0.005	−2.22	−0.02	0.004	−4.65	−0.02	0.007	−2.21
Male	0.08	0.098	0.78	0.76	0.087	8.75	0.65	0.177	3.66
Black	−0.31	0.108	−2.89	0.11	0.092	1.20	0.10	0.145	0.71
Hispanic	−0.09	0.094	−0.96	0.79	0.081	9.78	−0.24	0.150	−1.58
Under criminal justice supervision	0.23	0.090	2.53	0.95	0.072	13.19	1.94	0.141	13.79
Represented by public defender	−0.19	0.129	−1.48	0.36	0.108	3.35	−0.39	0.167	−2.33
Represented by private attorney	0.97	0.145	6.67	−0.22	0.139	−1.59	−0.61	0.234	−2.61
Charged with violent crime	0.43	0.181	2.35	0.93	0.157	5.91	0.72	0.223	3.23
Charged with property crime	−0.43	0.168	−2.55	−0.03	0.142	−0.19	−0.97	0.220	−4.38
Charged with drug crime	−0.52	0.160	−3.23	−0.45	0.137	−3.24	−0.95	0.210	−4.53
Number of prior felony arrests	0.03	0.011	2.43	0.10	0.009	10.75	0.12	0.011	10.68
Number of prior violent convictions	0.18	0.156	1.17	0.50	0.123	4.02	0.63	0.139	4.53
Intercept	0.10	0.261	0.38	−0.66	0.227	−2.91	−2.07	0.394	−5.25

have been excluded from the full model). The likelihood ratio test statistic is the difference in the $-2LL$ function for each model and is distributed as a chi-square statistic with degrees of freedom equal to the number of coefficients constrained to be zero (i.e., eliminated from the full model). As a test for the statistical significance of an independent variable in a multinomial logistic regression model, the likelihood ratio test refers to estimating the full multinomial logistic regression equation with all variables, and then estimating reduced models that eliminate one independent variable ($J - 1$ coefficients) from each analysis. The difference in the $-2LL$ function for each equation will then allow for the test of each independent variable with $df = J - 1$.

For example, in the analysis of the pretrial release status data, the value of $-2LL$ for the full model is 13194.994. When we estimate the same model, but eliminate the variable age from the analysis, the value of the $-2LL$ increases to 13216.834. The difference of the two log-likelihood functions is $13216.834 - 13194.994 = 21.840$. By eliminating the variable age, we have removed three coefficients from the analysis. The corresponding degrees of freedom for the test will be $df = J - 1 = 3$ to reflect the removal of the three coefficients. Table 31.8 presents the results of the LR test for all the independent variables included in the model. Note that all of the independent variables have statistically significant effects on pretrial release status well below conventional levels of significance.

An alternative test of each independent variable is to use the Wald statistic. Up to this point, we have used the Wald statistic to test the statistical significance of a single coefficient,

TABLE 31.8. Likelihood ratio and Wald statistic results for the overall effect of each independent variable

Independent variable	df	LR test statistic	Wald
Age	3	21.70	21.84
Male	3	90.80	89.38
Black	3	17.78	17.56
Hispanic	3	177.32	173.90
Under criminal justice supervision	3	327.31	303.86
Represented by public defender	3	40.14	41.16
Represented by private attorney	3	99.48	91.59
Charged with violent crime	3	36.38	37.39
Charged with property crime	3	28.91	30.54
Charged with drug crime	3	23.80	23.39
Number of prior felony arrests	3	198.92	163.80
Number of prior violent convictions	3	32.18	26.78
Intercept	3	36.31	35.29

but it can also be used to test the group of coefficients representing the effect of any given independent variable. Recall that the Wald test statistic for a single coefficient is computed by dividing the coefficient by its standard error and then squaring this value. The Wald statistic for a group of coefficients involves an analogous calculation, but requires using matrix algebra. Many statistical software packages (e.g., SAS and SPSS) will report the results for the Wald test as part of the standard output. In most applications, the value of the Wald statistic will be very similar to the value of the LR test, unless a small sample is being analyzed. To test the overall effect of an independent variable with the Wald statistic, we continue to use a chi-square distribution with degrees of freedom equal to the number of coefficients being tested (i.e., $df = J - 1$).

The values of the Wald test for each of the independent variables included in our analysis of pretrial release status are presented in the last column of Table 31.8. All of the independent variables have statistically significant effects on pretrial release status. As expected, the values of the Wald statistic are not identical to those of the likelihood ratio test, but the substance of these results is identical to that using the LR test.

How should we address mixed results? For example, it is not uncommon for a researcher to find that the overall effect of an independent variable is not statistically significant, but one of the individual coefficients does have a significant effect on a comparison of two outcome categories. Alternatively, the likelihood ratio or the Wald test for the overall effect of an independent variable may show it to have a statistically significant effect, but there may be individual coefficients representing the effect of that independent variable on a specific comparison that are not statistically significant.

This kind of difficulty is illustrated in the results presented in Tables 31.7 and 31.8. The overall effect of the number of prior convictions is statistically significant, but the individual coefficient for the number of prior convictions on the comparison between financial release and nonfinancial release is not statistically significant. The best approach in this type of situation is to note the significance of the overall effect of the independent variable, but to explain clearly the pattern of results for the individual coefficients. In this case, our model suggests that the number of prior convictions has an overall impact on pretrial release status, but despite this, the results do not allow us to conclude, that the number of prior convictions has a significant effect on receiving a financial release as opposed to a nonfinancial release. In multinomial logistic regression, a large number of coefficients are estimated and caution should be exercised so as not to draw selectively from the results.

OVERALL MODEL. To assess the statistical significance of the full multinomial regression model, we compute a model chi-square statistic that is identical in form to that used for the binary logistic regression model previously discussed. The model chi-square is computed as:

$$\text{Model chi-square} = (-2LL_{\text{null model}}) - (-2LL_{\text{full model}})$$

For our pretrial release status analysis, the $-2LL_{\text{null model}} = 15249.398$ and the $-2LL_{\text{full model}} = 13194.994$, resulting in a model chi-square of $15249.398 - 13194.994 = 2054.404$. The $df = 36$ for the model (3 coefficients for each of 12 independent variables), indicating that the model is statistically significant ($p < 0.001$) well beyond conventional levels of significance.

A Concluding Observation about Multinomial Logistic Regression Models

In our example using data on pretrial release in California, the dependent variable had four categories, representing a total of six different possible contrasts. Realistic applications of multinomial logistic regression models with more than four categories can quickly become unwieldy in regard to the number of contrasts that are being analyzed. For example, if we had a dependent variable with five categories, we would have four sets of coefficients to represent a total of ten different contrasts. As a way of addressing the complexity of multinomial logistic regression results, there have been some attempts to graph the coefficients (Long 1987, 1997) or plot the expected probabilities (Fox and Andersen 2006) in ways that clarify the effects of the independent variables on the dependent variable. Thus far, these methods have not been used very often in criminology and criminal justice. In turn, the complexity of results from multinomial logistic regression models has likely limited its published applications to all but the simplest results.

ORDINAL LOGISTIC REGRESSION

Thus far, the discussion has focused on logistic regression models for nominal dependent variables with two categories (binary logistic regression) and three or more categories (multinomial logistic regression). How should we analyze an ordinal dependent variable? Historically, the analysis of ordered dependent variables in criminology has tended to treat the ordinal variable either as nominal and used multinomial logistic regression or as interval and used OLS regression. Although the use of multinomial logistic regression models provides a solution to the important problem of analyzing multiple category dependent variables, it is not able to use information about the ordering of the categories, which may be theoretically and substantively important. The use of OLS regression to analyze an ordered dependent variable may not be problematic if the variable has a relatively large number of categories (Fox 2008). For an ordered dependent variable with a modest number of categories, say less than seven, the use of OLS techniques will likely be inappropriate. For example, if we examine responses to a survey question about fear of crime that was measured as a series of categories from "very fearful" to "not fearful at all," it is difficult to assume that there are equal intervals between these qualitative responses. Ordinal logistic regression models offer a means for explicitly taking into account an ordered categorical dependent variable using the logistic distribution function. A growing body of literature on ordinal logistic regression models is available to readers interested in more comprehensive treatments (e.g., Agresti 1984; Clogg and Shihadeh 1994; Long 1997; O'Connell 2006).

In order to set up the application and interpretation of the ordinal logistic regression model, we need to reconsider what a variable measured at the ordinal level represents. Ideally, an ordinal variable has ranked categories that represent an underlying continuum that cannot be directly observed and measured. For example, when respondents to a survey are presented with a statement that has response choices Strongly Agree, Agree, Disagree, and Strongly Disagree, the variable is assumed to represent an underlying continuum of agreement–disagreement with some issue. Yet, we know that however an individual responds to the question, any two individuals falling in the same category may not mean exactly the same thing. For example, if we randomly selected two individuals who had responded Strongly Disagree with a policy statement, and we were able to ask more in-depth follow-up questions, we would likely discover that there were degrees of how strongly each disagreed. The same concern would apply to comparisons within any response category.

If we assume that an ordinal variable's categories represent an underlying continuum, we can think of thresholds as those points on the continuum where an individual may move from one ordinal category to another (adjacent) category. In the example above, we could make a note of the thresholds between Strongly Agree and Agree, Agree and Disagree, and Disagree and Strongly Disagree. Figure 31.1 illustrates the link between the underlying continuum and the variable measured at the ordinal level. In Fig. 31.1, each dot represents the "true value" for an individual's attitudes about a given issue – but this true value cannot be measured directly, and we are left with the four response choices indicating degree of agreement or disagreement.[6] Each of the vertical lines marks the point between one of the possible response choices and indicates the threshold for each response category.

Proportional (Cumulative) Odds Model

The most common type of ordinal logistic regression model is known as the proportional (or cumulative) odds model. The proportional odds model represents something of a hybrid of the binary logistic and the multinomial logistic regression models. Similar to the multinomial logistic regression model's estimation of multiple model intercepts, the proportional odds model estimates multiple intercepts that represent the values of the thresholds (see again Fig. 31.1). Comparable to the binary logistic model, the proportional odds model estimates one coefficient for the effect of each independent variable on the dependent variable. In part, this is due to the added information contained in an ordinal variable, rather than a multi-category nominal variable. The interpretation of the results from the proportional odds model is also potentially much simpler than the results from the multinomial logistic model.

---

[6] The vertical spread of the dots is simply a convenience to illustrate the placement of cases along the Agreement–Disagreement continuum.

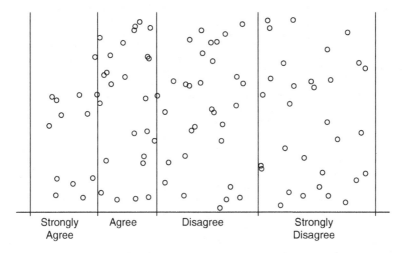

Continuum of Agreement-Disagreement

FIGURE 31.1. Hypothetical ordinal variable and underlying continuum.

One of the key differences between the proportional odds model and other logistic models is that rather than estimating the probability of a single category as in the binary and multinomial logistic regression models, this model estimates a cumulative probability (and hence the basis for its alternative name): the probability that the outcome is equal to or less than the category of interest. In equation format,

$$P(Y \le m) = \sum_{j=1}^{m} P(Y = j),$$

where m is the category of interest and can take on values ranging from 1 to $J - 1$, while j denotes each individual category and J the total number of categories. For example, using the four response categories for agreement–disagreement above would mean that $J = 4$, and we could compute a total of $J - 1 = 4 - 1 = 3$ cumulative probabilities. If we define a Strongly Agree response as 1 and Strongly Disagree response as 4, we could then compute probabilities for $P(Y \le 1)$, $P(Y \le 2)$, and $P(Y \le 3)$, representing $P(Y \le$ Strongly Agree$)$, $P(Y \le$ Agree$)$, and $P(Y \le$ Disagree$)$, respectively. We would not include the final category (i.e., $P(Y \le 4)$ or $P(Y \le$ Strongly Disagree$)$), since it would have to be equal to 1 (or 100%) – all possible values have to fall in one of the four response categories.

Using the cumulative probabilities, we can then compute odds ratios to represent the effects of the independent variables on the dependent variable. There is an important difference in the construction and interpretation of the odds ratios, since we are now using cumulative probabilities:

$$OR_m = \frac{P(Y \le m)}{1 - P(Y \le m)} = \frac{P(Y \le m)}{P(Y > m)}$$

Substantively, the odds ratio using cumulative probabilities indicates the odds of an outcome less than or equal to category m versus the odds of a category greater than m. In the context of our four response choices, the three odds ratios that we could make reference to would be the following:

- Odds of a Strongly Agree response versus the combined outcomes of Agree, Disagree, and Strongly Disagree response.
- Odds of the combined outcomes of Strongly Agree and Agree response versus the combined outcomes of Disagree and Strongly Disagree response.
- Odds of the combined outcomes of Strongly Agree, Agree, and Disagree response versus Strongly Disagree response.

Similar to the development of the binary and multinomial logistic regression models, we can use this equation for the odds ratio and rewrite it as a linear model:

$$OR_m = \frac{P(Y \leq m)}{P(Y > m)} = \exp(\tau_m - Xb).$$

The general form for this equation is very similar to that of either the binary or multinomial logistic model, except that we have introduced a new term (τ_m) and now have a negative sign to the left of Xb. The (τ_m) represent the threshold parameters, which function as intercepts in the linear model and will take on values for $j = 1$ to $J - 1$.

By taking the natural logarithm of the odds ratio equation, we produce the logit equation:

$$\ln\left(\frac{P(Y \leq m)}{P(Y > m)}\right) = \ln[\exp(\tau_m - Xb)] = \tau_m - Xb,$$

which forms the basis for estimating the proportional odds model.

Interpretation of Ordinal Logistic Regression Coefficients

In our discussion of the binary logistic regression model, we illustrated how a one-unit increase in the independent variable would modify the odds of the different outcomes by a factor of $\exp(b)$. Since the equation for the proportional odds model takes a slightly different form, we cannot simply exponentiate b to obtain the effect of the independent variable.

To illustrate the modification, suppose we have two values of X: x and $x + 1$. The odds ratio for x and $x + 1$ would be

$$\frac{OR_m(X+1)}{OR_m(X)} = \frac{\exp(\tau_m - (X+1)b)}{\exp(\tau_m - Xb)} = \exp([X - (X+1)]b) = \exp(-b).$$

Thus, to interpret the effect of a one-unit change in the independent variable in the proportional odds model, we will need to exponentiate the *negative* value of the estimated coefficient. We can then interpret the coefficient as indicating the odds of an outcome less than or equal to category m versus the odds of a category greater than m for a one-unit change in the independent variable.

TABLE 31.9. **Proportional odds model results for Fayetteville youth study**

Variable	Coefficient	Standard error	z-Score
Age	−0.06	0.074	−0.76
Male	0.28	0.147	1.93
White	−0.48	0.193	−2.49
GPA	−0.40	0.078	−5.12
Friends picked up by the police	1.13	0.167	6.77
Parents know where youth is while away	−0.68	0.148	−4.61
Have to do some things that are not right to get ahead	0.40	0.163	2.42
OK to get around the law if you could get away with it	0.57	0.168	3.41
OK to take things from big business	1.03	0.193	5.34
tau-1	−0.87	1.231	
tau-2	0.94	1.229	
tau-3	2.00	1.231	

An Example: Fayetteville Youth Project

Returning to the FYP data, we use the same model for self-reported theft as we used in the section on binary logistic regression, except that the dependent variable is kept in its original ordinal level of measurement: Never, Once or twice, Several times, and Many times. Table 31.9 presents the results for the ordinal logistic regression model; included in the table are the coefficient estimates, standard errors, and z-statistics to assess the statistical significance of the individual coefficients.

INTERPRETING THE COEFFICIENTS.   While the proportional odds model accounts for the fact that the categories in the dependent variable are ranked, for example in our case from no self-reported theft to frequent self-reported thefts, the interpretation of the coefficients is similar to that used in multinomial regression. In this case, we can compare lower categories to the categories ranked above them. Since we have four ordered categories, there are three comparisons we can make: (1) no theft (i.e., Never) to one or more thefts, (2) no theft and once or twice to several and many times, and (3) no theft, once or twice, and several times to many times. In all cases, the exponent of the negative of the coefficient provides the odds ratio for change from a category indicating less delinquency to a category indicating more delinquency. Overall, the pattern of results in Table 31.9 indicates that youth who were male, non-white, younger, had lower GPAs, had friends picked up by the police, were not well supervised by their parents, and felt that it was okay to break the law or to take things were more likely to self-report higher levels of theft. The following discussion is intended to illustrate the direct interpretation of several of these coefficients.

We see that the coefficient for male is 0.283. By exponentiating the negative of 0.283 ($\exp(-0.283) = 0.754$), we see that males are likely to self-report more frequent theft than females, controlling for the other independent variables in the model. More concretely, we can state the following about the self-reported theft of male youth:

- The odds of self-reporting no theft versus at least one theft are 0.754 times smaller for males than for females, controlling for all other variables in the model.
- The odds of self-reporting theft as never and once or twice versus self-reporting theft as several times and many times are 0.754 times smaller for males than for females, controlling for all other variables in the model.

- The odds of self-reporting theft as never, once or twice, and several times versus self-reporting theft as many times are 0.754 times smaller for males than for females, controlling for all other variables in the model.

The effect of race on self-reported theft is $\exp(-(-0.482)) = 1.619$. Writing out direct interpretations of this coefficient leads to the following statements:

- The odds of self-reporting no theft versus at least one theft are 1.619 times greater for whites than for non-whites, controlling for all other variables in the model.
- The odds of self-reporting theft as never and once or twice versus self-reporting theft as several times and many times are 1.619 times greater for whites than for non-whites, controlling for all other variables in the model.
- The odds of self-reporting theft as never, once or twice, and several times versus self-reporting theft as many times are 1.619 times greater for whites than for non-whites, controlling for all other variables in the model.

The effect of having one or more friends picked up by the police is $\exp(-1.132) = 0.322$, indicating that youth who have had at least one friend picked up tend to self-report higher levels of theft. The direct interpretations are:

- The odds of self-reporting no theft versus at least one theft are 0.322 times smaller for youth who have friends picked up by the police than those who have had none picked up by the police, controlling for all other variables in the model.
- The odds of self-reporting theft as never and once or twice versus self-reporting theft as several times and many times are 0.322 times smaller for youth who have friends picked up by the police than those who have had none picked up by the police, controlling for all other variables in the model.
- The odds of self-reporting theft as never, once or twice, and several times versus self-reporting theft as many times are 0.322 times smaller for youth who have friends picked up by the police than those who have had none picked up by the police, controlling for all other variables in the model.

The coefficient for GPA is -0.402. Since GPA is measured at the interval level of measurement, we would note that for a one-unit increase in GPA, the odds ratio changes by a factor of $\exp(-(-0.402)) = 1.495$, controlling for the other variables in the model. We can write out the interpretations as follows:

- The odds of self-reporting no theft versus at least one theft increase by a factor of 1.495 for a one-unit increase in GPA, controlling for all other variables in the model.
- The odds of self-reporting theft as never and once or twice versus self-reporting theft as several times or many times increase by a factor of 1.495 for a one-unit increase in GPA, controlling for all other variables in the model.
- The odds of self-reporting theft as never, once or twice, and several times versus self-reporting theft as many times increase by a factor of 1.495 for a one-unit increase in GPA, controlling for all other variables in the model.

Note, too, that there are three threshold parameters representing the threshold points between each of the ordered categories (i.e., never, once or twice, several times, and many times).

Table 31.9 also reports the values of the z-statistic for each independent variable. Note that the only coefficient not statistically significant at a level of 5% is the effect of age. The statistical significance of the overall model is based on a model chi-square statistic that is also computed and interpreted in exactly the same way as for the binary logistic and multi-nomial logistic regression models. In our example, the $-2LL_{\text{null model}} = 1968.274$ and the $-2LL_{\text{full model}} = 1646.683$, resulting in a model chi-square of $1968.274 - 1646.683 = 326.591$. Since there are 9 coefficients that have been estimated (one for each independent variable), the degree of freedom value for this test is equal to 9, resulting in a model that has a high level of statistical significance ($p < 0.001$), which means that the overall model has a statistically significant effect on self-reported theft.

Parallel Slopes Tests

As we noted earlier, the proportional odds model assumes that the effects of the independent variables are constant across all categories of the dependent variable, which is analogous to our interpretation of coefficients in a multivariate linear regression model. Regardless of the level (or category) of the dependent variable, we expect the independent variable to exert a constant (i.e., proportional) effect on the dependent variable. The constant effect of each independent variable should have also been clear in the direct interpretations of the coefficients noted in the previous section. This is known more generally as the parallel slopes assumption. Most statistical packages include a score test of this assumption that informs the user regarding the appropriateness of the ordinal logistic model. Somewhat less common is the Brant Test, which tests for parallel slopes in the overall model and in each independent variable.

SCORE TEST. Conceptually, the parallel slopes score test is based on the idea that we could estimate a series of $J - 1$ binary logistic regression models (i.e., one model less than the number of ordered categories in the dependent variable) of the form $P(Y \leq m)$ that allowed the effects of all K independent variables to vary by outcome category on the dependent variable. The test would then focus on whether a single coefficient or multiple coefficients best represented the effects of the independent variables on the dependent variable. Technically, the score test uses information about the log-likelihood for the ordinal logistic regression model, and assesses how much it would change by allowing the coefficients for all the independent variables to vary by the outcome category on the dependent variable. The degree of change in the likelihood function then indicates whether the parallel slopes assumption is met. The null hypothesis of the score test is parallel (equal) slopes. The research hypothesis is that the slopes are not parallel (equal). The value of the score test (reported in most statistical software) is distributed as a chi-square with $K(J - 2)$ degrees of freedom.

For our self-reported theft example, we have $K = 9$ (i.e., nine independent variables) and $J = 4$ (i.e., four outcome categories on the dependent variable). The corresponding degrees of freedom for our score test is equal to $9(4 - 2) = 18$. The value of the score test for our model is 16.217 ($p = 0.577$), which indicates that we should not reject our null hypothesis of parallel slopes and conclude that our model does indeed meet the parallel slopes assumption.

BRANT TEST. Similar to the Score Test, the Brant Test (Brant 1990) is a Wald test that assesses whether all the coefficients in a proportional odds model satisfy the parallel slopes assumption. The computation of the Brant Test is based on the values of the coefficients and their respective variances. Readers interested in a step-by-step presentation of the computation

TABLE 31.10. Brant test results for Fayetteville youth study

Variable	χ^2	df	p
Overall	14.57	18	0.691
Age	0.22	2	0.894
Male	4.87	2	0.087
White	1.59	2	0.452
GPA	0.60	2	0.742
Friends picked up by the police	1.16	2	0.561
Parents know where youth is while away	0.63	2	0.731
Have to do some things that are not right to get ahead	0.00	2	0.999
OK to get around the law if you could get away with it	1.33	2	0.514
OK to take things from big business	1.80	2	0.406

of the Brant Test should consult Long (1997).[7] In addition to providing an overall test for the parallel slopes assumption, the Brant Test can be decomposed into values for each of the independent variables in the ordinal logistic regression model.

The Brant Test for the overall model will be distributed as a chi-square with $K(J-2)$ degrees of freedom (same as in the Score Test). The test statistic of each independent variable is distributed as a chi-square with $J-2$ degrees of freedom.

The results of the Brant Test for the self-reported theft example appear in Table 31.10. The overall test again indicates that the parallel slopes assumption is satisfied for the model (chi-square $= 14.57$, $df = 18$, $p = 0.691$). Similarly, each of the independent variables in the model also satisfies the parallel slopes assumption.

Partial Proportional Odds

Although the parallel slopes assumption was satisfied in the preceding example, it is quite common for the assumption not to be met in practice. Historically, researchers confronted with results from the Score Test indicating the model failed to satisfy the parallel slopes assumption were left with a choice of fitting the proportional odds model and violating assumptions or fitting a multinomial logistic regression model by ignoring the ordinal nature of the dependent variable and then complicating the interpretation of the results through the increased number of coefficients. Recently, a class of models referred to as partial proportional odds or generalized ordinal logistic regression models has received increasing attention (Fu 1998; Lall et al. 2002; O'Connell 2006; Peterson and Harrell 1990; Williams 2005). The logic to the partial proportional odds model is to allow some or all of the coefficients of the independent variables to vary by the level of the dependent variable, much like what we see in the application of multinomial logistic regression, but to constrain other coefficients to have a single value, as in the proportional odds model.

---

[7] Long and Freese (2006) have written a procedure for Stata to compute the Brant Test.

We obtain the partial proportional odds model by generalizing the proportional odds equation from Sect. "Proportional (Cumulative) Odds Model" to allow the coefficients (the b_m) to vary by the level of the dependent variable (m):

$$\ln\left(\frac{P(Y \le m)}{P(Y > m)}\right) = \ln\left[\exp\left(\tau_m - Xb_m\right)\right] = \tau_m - Xb_m.$$

Without any further constraints on the coefficients, the total number of coefficients estimated will be identical to that obtained from a multinomial logistic regression analysis. It is important to note, however, that the coefficients do not mean the same thing. Recall that the multinomial logistic regression coefficients refer to comparisons between a given category and the reference category. As noted in the equation above, the logit in the partial proportional odds model is identical to that in the proportional odds model and refers to the odds of a category less than or equal to m versus a category greater than m.

Due to the large number of coefficients in a fully generalized ordinal logit model, most researchers will want to limit the number of variables with nonconstant effects. The results from the Brant Test are useful for determining which, if any, independent variables appear to have varying effects on the different categories of the dependent variable (i.e., the effects are not parallel). If the overall Brant Test result is not statistically significant, it implies that the parallel slopes assumption is met for the full model. In this case, there is likely little to be gained by relaxing the parallel slopes assumption for a single variable. In those cases where the overall Brant Test result is statistically significant, then the Brant Test results for individual variables will point to those variables with the greatest divergence from the parallel slopes assumption and the best candidates for allowing the effects to vary across the different ordinal logits.

All other features of the partial proportional odds model – tests for statistical significance, interpretation of the coefficients, and the like – are the same as found in the proportional odds model.

AN EXAMPLE: SENTENCING DECISIONS IN CALIFORNIA. In our discussion of multinomial logistic regression, we presented the results from an analysis of data from California pretrial release decisions in the 1990s. These same data can be used to illustrate the application and interpretation of the partial proportional odds model. The following example uses the same data, but restricts it to those cases where the offender was ultimately convicted of a crime and sentenced to probation, jail, or prison ($N = 4,765$). The independent variables used in this example include a similar set of offender and case characteristics: age, sex, race, whether the offender had a private attorney, type of offense charged, total number of charges, whether the offender was under supervision at the time of the offense, the number of prior felony arrests, and the number of prior violent convictions. Descriptive statistics for this sample of offenders appear in Table 31.11.

Table 31.12 presents the results for the proportional odds model (column 1) and the Brant Test (column 2). We see from the values of the coefficients appearing in column 1 that offenders who were male, younger, charged with a violent crime, under criminal justice supervision at the time of the offense, and did not have a private attorney were more likely to receive more severe forms of punishment (jail and/or prison). In a similar way, as the total number of charges, prior felony arrests, and prior violent convictions increased, offenders were increasingly likely to receive jail and/or prison sentences rather than probation sentences.

TABLE 31.11. Variable coding and descriptive statistics for sentencing decisions in California ($N = 4{,}765$)

Variable	Mean	Standard deviation
Age (years)	31.15	9.05
Male (1 = male, 0 = female)	0.81	0.40
Black (1 = black, 0 = non-black)	0.44	0.50
Hispanic (1 = Hispanic, 0 = non-Hispanic)	0.04	0.21
Under criminal justice supervision (1 = yes, 0 = no)	0.51	0.50
Represented by private attorney (1 = yes, 0 = no)	0.17	0.38
Total number of charges	2.30	1.66
Charged with violent crime (1 = yes, 0 = no)	0.21	0.41
Charged with property crime (1 = yes, 0 = no)	0.34	0.47
Charged with drug crime (1 = yes, 0 = no)	0.38	0.48
Number of prior felony arrests	4.91	6.64
Number of prior violent convictions	0.17	0.67

TABLE 31.12. Proportional odds model and Brant test results for sentencing in California

Variable	Coefficient (SE)	Brant test χ^2 (p-value)[a]
Age	−0.01 (0.003)	8.38 (0.004)
Male	0.53 (0.074)	0.47 (0.491)
Black	0.07 (0.060)	0.10 (0.756)
Hispanic	−0.27 (0.140)	1.98 (0.160)
Under criminal justice supervision	0.70 (0.061)	5.73 (0.017)
Represented by private attorney	−0.18 (0.078)	0.67 (0.414)
Total number of charges	0.03 (0.018)	0.54 (0.461)
Charged with violent crime	0.39 (0.122)	0.57 (0.449)
Charged with property crime	0.14 (0.115)	0.59 (0.441)
Charged with drug crime	0.06 (0.114)	7.11 (0.008)
Number of prior felony arrests	0.07 (0.005)	16.20 (<0.001)
Number of prior violent convictions	0.63 (0.072)	6.66 (0.010)
Overall ($df = 12$)		90.74 (<0.001)

[a] Individual coefficient tests based on $df = 1$.

The results from the Brant Test in Column 2 show that the overall model fails to satisfy the parallel slopes assumption ($\chi^2 = 90.74$, $df = 12$, $p < 0.001$).[8] When the overall value is decomposed into the effects for each of the independent variables, we see that the coefficients for age, drug charge, under criminal justice supervision, the number of prior felony arrests, and the number of prior violent convictions do not satisfy the parallel slopes assumption, while those for all other independent variables do.

Table 31.13 presents the results from a partial proportional odds model where all coefficients are allowed to have different effects on the two ordinal logits:

$$\ln\left(\frac{P(Y \leq 1)}{P(Y > 1)}\right) = \ln\left(\frac{P(Y = \text{probation})}{P(Y = \text{jail or prison})}\right) = \tau_1 - Xb_1$$

---

[8] The Score Test similarly indicates a failure of the full model to satisfy the parallel slopes assumption ($\chi^2 = 81.39$, $df = 12$, $p < 0.001$).

TABLE 31.13. Partial proportional odds model for sentencing in California – all coefficients allowed to vary

Variable	Probation vs. jail and/or prison Coefficient (SE)	Probation and/or jail vs. prison Coefficient (SE)
Age	−0.02 (0.004)	−0.01 (0.004)
Male	0.51 (0.094)	0.60 (0.098)
Black	0.06 (0.087)	0.10 (0.070)
Hispanic	−0.08 (0.187)	−0.48 (0.194)
Under criminal justice supervision	0.57 (0.087)	0.81 (0.070)
Represented by private attorney	−0.23 (0.102)	−0.14 (0.097)
Total number of charges	0.02 (0.024)	0.04 (0.020)
Charged with violent crime	0.28 (0.167)	0.43 (0.138)
Charged with property crime	0.19 (0.158)	0.09 (0.132)
Charged with drug crime	0.30 (0.156)	−0.09 (0.132)
Number of prior felony arrests	0.04 (0.008)	0.07 (0.006)
Number of prior violent convictions	0.45 (0.099)	0.62 (0.073)
Constant (τ)	1.25 (0.232)	−2.17 (0.211)

and

$$\ln\left(\frac{P(Y \leq 2)}{P(Y > 2)}\right) = \ln\left(\frac{P(Y = \text{probation or jail})}{P(Y = \text{prison})}\right) = \tau_2 - Xb_2.$$

Since there are two different ordinal logits being estimated, there are two full sets of unique coefficients to interpret that illustrate the different effects the independent variables have on the two different ordered logits. To highlight a few of the findings in Table 31.13:

- Age:
  - The odds of probation versus jail or prison increase by a factor of $\exp(-(-0.02)) = 1.020$ for a one-unit increase in age, controlling for all other variables in the model. For a 10 year increase in age, the odds of probation versus a jail or prison sentence increase by a factor of $\exp(-10 \times -0.02) = 1.221$, controlling for all other variables in the model.
  - The odds of probation or jail versus prison increase by a factor of $\exp(-(-0.007)) = 1.007$ for a one-unit increase in age, controlling for all other variables in the model. For a 10 year increase in age, the odds of probation versus a jail or prison sentence increase by a factor of $\exp(-10 \times -0.007) = 1.073$, controlling for all other variables in the model.

- Drug charge:
  - The odds of probation versus jail or prison are $\exp(-0.305) = 0.737$ times smaller for offenders charged with a drug offense than for offenders charged with a miscellaneous offense, controlling for all other variables in the model.
  - The odds of probation or jail versus prison are $\exp(-(-0.092)) = 1.097$ times greater for offenders charged with a drug offense than for offenders charged with a miscellaneous offense, controlling for all other variables in the model.

TABLE 31.14. **Partial proportional odds model for sentencing in California – selected coefficients allowed to vary**

Variable	Constrained Coefficient (SE)	Probation vs. jail and/or prison Coefficient (SE)	Probation and/or jail vs. prison Coefficient (SE)
Age		−0.02 (0.004)	−0.01 (0.004)
Male	0.55 (0.075)		
Black	0.09 (0.061)		
Hispanic	−0.27 (0.143)		
Under criminal justice supervision		0.57 (0.087)	0.80 (0.070)
Represented by private attorney	−0.18 (0.079)		
Total number of charges	0.04 (0.018)		
Charged with violent crime	0.39 (0.121)		
Charged with property crime	0.13 (0.114)		
Charged with drug crime		0.30 (0.128)	−0.09 (0.119)
Number of prior felony arrests		0.04 (0.007)	0.07 (0.006)
Number of prior violent convictions		0.43 (0.100)	0.63 (0.072)
Constant (τ)		1.19 (0.196)	−2.10 (0.191)

- CJ supervision:
  - The odds of probation versus jail or prison are $\exp(-0.575) = 0.563$ times smaller for offenders under criminal justice supervision at the time of offense than for offenders not under supervision, controlling for all other variables in the model.
  - The odds of probation or jail versus prison are $\exp(-0.807) = 0.446$ times smaller for offenders under criminal justice supervision at the time of offense than for offenders not under supervision, controlling for all other variables in the model.

Table 31.14 presents the results for the partial proportional odds model, where the only coefficients allowed to vary across the two ordinal logits are those identified through the Brant Test as not satisfying the parallel slopes assumption: age, drug charge, criminal justice supervision, prior felony arrests, and prior violent convictions. Note that the coefficients are virtually identical to those appearing in Table 31.13. Limiting the discussion to the effects of prior felony arrests and violent convictions, we see the following:

- Number of prior felony arrests:
  - The odds of probation versus jail or prison decrease by a factor of $\exp(-0.038) = 0.963$ for a one-unit increase in the number of prior felony arrests, controlling for all other variables in the model.
  - The odds of probation or jail versus prison decrease by a factor of $\exp(-0.070) = 0.932$ for a one-unit increase in the number of prior felony arrests, controlling for all other variables in the model.

- Number of prior violent convictions:
  - The odds of probation versus jail or prison decrease by a factor of $\exp(-0.432) = 0.649$ for a one-unit increase in the number of prior violent convictions, controlling for all other variables in the model.

– The odds of probation or jail versus prison decrease by a factor of $\exp(-0.631) = 0.532$ for a one-unit increase in the number of prior violent convictions, controlling for all other variables in the model.

Substantively, and consistent with much prior research, these findings indicate that as the severity of the offender's prior record increases, the likelihood of a prison sentence increases over the chances of a probation or a jail sentence.

Note on Statistical Software

Statistical software packages vary in their ability to estimate the models discussed in this chapter. All of the results presented in this chapter were estimated with multiple software packages, including LIMDEP (Greene 2008), R (R Development Core Team 2003), SAS (SAS Institute 2009), SPSS (SPSS Inc 2007), and Stata (Stata Corporation 2009). Of the commercially available software packages, Stata offers the widest range of procedures in a user-friendly environment that includes both command-line driven analysis and drop-down menus (which in turn generate the command-line syntax). The R system is an open source program. Various packages within the R system offer a wider selection of statistical procedures than is available in Stata, but the learning curve may be too steep for the preferences of some potential users. LIMDEP, SAS, and SPSS easily estimate the binary logit, multinomial logit, and proportional odds models. With additional syntax, it is possible to estimate the partial proportional odds model in SAS and SPSS (see O'Connell 2006 for examples).

SUMMARY AND DIRECTIONS FOR FUTURE APPLICATIONS

The focus of this chapter has been the application and the interpretation of logit models for variables with categorical dependent variables. For those situations where we have measured the dependent variable as a dichotomy, we can apply binary logistic regression. When the dependent variable has three or more categories, we need to consider the level of measurement: Are the categories ordered or unordered? If the categories are not ordered, then the application of a multinomial logistic regression model is most appropriate. The primary caution to the analyst is to watch the number of categories – too many categories can result in an unwieldy set of coefficients to interpret. If the categories are ordered, then an ordinal logit model is most appropriate. Key to the application and interpretation of the ordinal logit model is the satisfaction of the parallel slopes assumption. When the parallel slopes assumption is satisfied, then the proportional odds model provides the most parsimonious way to assess the effects of the independent variables on the dependent variable since the effects of the independent variables are constrained to be the same across all of the ordinal logits. When the parallel slopes assumption is not satisfied, the partial proportional odds model is a more effective choice, but the researcher will need to consider whether to allow all coefficients to vary across all the ordinal logits or to allow only individual variables that fail the parallel slopes assumption to vary.

In this chapter, there are several issues that were mentioned in passing that provide a basis for future applications of logit models in criminology and criminal justice. First, the presentation of results from multinomial logistic and ordinal logistic (proportional or partial proportional odds) models remains a challenge, due to the large number of coefficients. A description of the findings, as in this chapter, necessarily limits the amount of information that can be conveyed to the reader and tends to result in a more superficial discussion of the findings. The suggestions for more comprehensive interpretations of the results from these models have relied on the use of effects displays. Long (1997, 1987), for example, has proposed a graphical method for presenting coefficients from multinomial logit models that conveys information about statistical significance as well as information about the magnitude of the effects for all possible comparisons. Fox (2003, 2008) and Fox and Andersen (2006) have proposed a more general framework for effects displays that are applicable to all generalized linear models. Although these methods offer a way of simplifying the presentation and interpretation of numerous coefficients and of highlighting interesting findings in an analysis, they have not yet been widely used in criminology and criminal justice.

Second, research on crime and the criminal justice system is often confronted with a dichotomous outcome variable that occurs infrequently. For example, studies of self-reported delinquency will find a small number of cases of self-reported sexual assault. Similarly, a study of sentencing decisions within a single state may find few offenders who receive a sentence of death or life without parole. When the distribution of cases for an outcome variable shows less than about 5% of the observations in the category of interest, the coefficients from a binary logistic regression will be biased toward under-predicting the outcome of interest. King and Zeng (2001a, b) have proposed a "rare events" logistic regression model that is essentially a corrective procedure that adjusts the values of the coefficients and their standard errors to account for the bias in the coefficients. King and Zeng (2001a, b) also explain that the same corrective procedure can be used in the logistic regression analysis of small samples (<200 cases) with less skewed distributions on the dependent variable.[9] Aside from Piquero et al.'s (2005) application of the rare events logistic regression procedure to the analysis of homicide victimization and violent offending, the rare events procedure has not been widely used in criminology and criminal justice.

Third, conditional logit models (McFadden 1973) offer a potentially interesting approach to studying crime and the criminal justice system ((Long 1997) and Maddala (1983) also present brief discussions of this model). Conceptually, conditional logit models assume that an individual is confronted with a number of choices and picks one. Each choice has a set of attributes or unique characteristics that affect its probability of selection. Individual characteristics also affect the probability of selection, but these are invariant across the number of possible choices. The conditional logit model takes both choice attributes and individual characteristics into account.[10] With the exception of Phillips's (2003) application of the conditional logit model to the study of interpersonal violence, this model has not been used in criminology and criminal justice. In large part, the difficulty researchers will confront – especially those using secondary data sources – when trying to use this model is the lack of information on the attributes of the possible choices. For example, conditional logit models could be used to study the types of offenses individuals commit, but this would require a much better understanding of the costs and the benefits of each type of offense (i.e., the attributes of the choices) than is found in the typical analysis of offending patterns.

---

[9] King and Zeng (2001a, b) also note that their corrective procedure is not applicable to situations where the researcher is studying a rare event in a small sample.

[10] Through some algebraic manipulation, the conditional logit model can be shown to be equivalent to the multinomial logistic regression model (see, for example, Long 1997).

Finally, nested logit models (McFadden 1978, 1981) may offer an important avenue for understanding sequences of decisions involved in making a choice. Similar to the conditional logit model, the nested logit model assumes that an individual is confronted with a set of possible choices, each choice having a unique set of attributes that affect its probability of selection, along with the characteristics of the individual making the choice. Where nested logit models differ from conditional logit models is the assumption that the set of choices can be grouped into some smaller set of choices that essentially represent stages in a decision. For example, demographers have used nested logit models to study the resolution of a pregnancy (e.g., Plotnick 1992; South and Baumer 2001). The first stage represents whether the individual becomes pregnant and the second stage is how the pregnancy is resolved (i.e., abortion, birth, or some other form of involuntary termination).

Although nested logit models have not yet been used in the study of crime and criminal justice, there would seem to be a number of potentially relevant applications. The analysis of sentencing decisions provides an interesting possibility. A first stage may be the decision by the judge on whether or not to incarcerate an offender. Following that decision, the judge has a different set of choices that are contingent on the first choice. For those offenders being incarcerated, there may be a choice of whether to incarcerate the offender in a jail or in a prison. For those offenders not being incarcerated, there are again several choices available to many judges: probation, fine, community service, drug treatment, or some other form of therapy or intervention. Thus far, researchers who have tried to separate the various choices (probation, jail, prison) have treated all of the decisions as if they were simultaneous possibilities (e.g., Holleran and Sphon 2004) when there are clear contingencies on the final decision of the judge. Nested logit models may offer an important means for gaining a better understanding of not only the decision-making process involved in the sentencing of convicted offender, but a wide range of other criminal justice decisions as well as the choices made by offenders.

In light of the many qualitative outcome measures in the study of crime and the criminal justice system, logit models should be an important tool for criminological researchers. This chapter has outlined the primary logit models that most researchers will want to consider using in their analyses. Important to all of these applications, however, is sensitivity to the nature of the data and the research question motivating the analysis.

REFERENCES

Agresti A (1984) Analysis of ordinal categorical data. Wiley, New York

Agresti A (2002) Categorical data analysis, 2nd ed. Wiley, New York

Brant R (1990) Assessing proportionality in the proportional odds model for ordinal logistic regression. Biometrics 46:1171–1178

Clogg C, Shihadeh E (1994) Statistical models for ordinal data. Sage, Thousand Oaks, CA

Fox J, Andersen R (2006) Effect displays for multinomial and proportional-odds logit models. Sociol Methodol 36:225–255

Fox J (2003) Effect displays in R for generalised linear models. J Stat Softw 8:1–27

Fox J (2008) Applied regression analysis and generalized linear models, 2nd ed. Sage, Thousand Oaks, CA

Fu V (1998) Estimating generalized ordered logit models. Stata Technical Bulletin 8:160–164

Greene W (2008) LIMDEP 9.0 Econometric modeling guide, volumes 1 and 2. Econometric Software, Plainville, NY

Holleran D, Sphon C (2004) On the use of the total incarceration variable in sentencing research. Criminology 42:211–240

Hosmer, and Lemeshow 2000. Applied logistic regression, 2nd ed. Wiley, New York

King G, Zeng L (2001a) Explaining rare events in international relations. International Organization 55:693–715

King G, Zeng L (2001b) Logistic regression in rare events data. Polit Anal 9:137–163

Lall R, Walters SJ, Morgan K, MRC CFAS Co-operative Institute of Public Health (2002) A review of ordinal regression models applied on health-related quality of life assessments. Stat Methods Med Res 11:49–67

Long JS (1987) A graphical method for the interpretation of multinomial logit analysis. Sociological Methods and Research 15:420–446

Long JS (1997) Regression models for categorical and limited dependent variables. Sage, Thousand Oaks, CA

Long JS, Freese J (2006) Regression models for categorical dependent variables using Stata, 2nd ed. Stata, College Station, TX

Maddala GS (1983) Limited-dependent and qualitative variables in econometrics. Cambridge University Press, New York

McFadden D (1973) Conditional logit analysis of qualitative choice behavior. In: Zarembka P (ed) Frontiers of econometrics. Academic, New York, pp 105–142

McFadden D (1978) Modelling the choice of residential location. In: Karlquist A, et al. (eds) Spatial interaction theory and residential location. North-Holland, Amsterdam, pp 75–96

McFadden D (1981) Econometric models of probabilistic choice. In: Manski CF, McFaden D (eds) Structural analysis of discrete data: with econometric applications. MIT, Cambridge, MA

Menard S (2002) Applied logistic regression analysis, 2nd ed. Sage, Thousand Oaks, CA

O'Connell AA (2006) Logistic regression models for ordinal response variables. Sage, Thousand Oaks, CA

Pampel F (2000) Logistic regression: a primer. Sage, Thousand Oaks, CA

Peterson B, Harrell FE (1990) Partial proportional odds models for ordinal response variables. Appl Stat 39:205–217

Phillips S (2003) Social structure of vengeance: a test of Black's model. Criminology 41:673–708

Piquero AR, MacDonald J, Dobrin A, Daigle LH, Cullen FT (2005) Self-control, violent offending, and homicide victimization: assessing the general theory of crime. J Quant Criminol 21:55–71

Plotnick RD (1992) The effects of attitudes on teenage premarital pregnancy and its resolution. Am Sociol Rev 57:800–811

R Development Core Team (2003) R: A language and environment for statistical computing. http://www.R-project.org (accessed 16 November 2009)

SAS Institute (2009) SAS 9.2. SAS Institute, Cary, NC

South S, Baumer E (2001) Community effects on the resolution of adolescent premarital pregnancy. J Fam Issues 22:1025–1043

SPSS Inc (2007) SPSS 16.0 for Windows. SPSS, Chicago

Stata Corporation (2009) Stata 10. Stata Corporation, College Station, TX

Williams R (2005) Gologit2: a program for generalized logistic regression/partial proportional odds models for ordinal variables. http://www.nd.edu/~rwilliam/gologit2/gologit2.pdf, Accessed April, 2009

CHAPTER 32

Count Models in Criminology

JOHN M. MACDONALD AND PAMELA K. LATTIMORE

INTRODUCTION

Crime can be measured in many metrics, including occurrence (yes/no), seriousness (e.g., felony/misdemeanor), and frequency or rate. Frequency can be considered in two analogous ways – how soon until an occurrence (the rate) or how many occurrences per unit such as weeks, months, or years (counts). We can also look at frequency with respect to other units such as population groups or areal units like neighborhoods or counties.

Count models, including the basic Poisson regression model and its various approximations, are now extremely popular in criminology. For example, Gardner et al. (1995) showed the use of count models for predicting violent incidents in the community involving 797 individuals who were evaluated in an emergency room of a psychiatric hospital and tracked in the community for 6 months. Sampson and Laub (1996) relied on Poisson regression and its variant of negative binomial regression for assessing the effects of military experience on subsequent offending. Paternoster et al. (1997) used Poisson regression formulations to assess the effects of perceived fairness in arrest interactions for domestic violence on recidivism. Lattimore et al. (2004) estimated two types of Poisson regression models to examine the relationship of covariates on the average count of re-arrest and its variance on released California Youth Authority parolees. Osgood and Chambers (2000) examined county-level factors associated with counts for juvenile arrests for FBI index offenses using Poisson formulations. Parker (2004) similarly relied on count models to estimate changes in racially disaggregated counts of homicides in cities. Braga (2003) relied on the negative binomial version of the Poisson regression model to estimate changes in the counts of arrests among youth gun offenders in Boston over time. Lattimore et al. (2005) looked at the effects of substance abuse treatment on the count of rearrests among drug-involved probationers in Florida.

More generally, the importance of modeling criminal behaviors as counts has long been recognized (Blumstein et al. 1986; Greenberg 1991) and several decades of research in criminology has been devoted to studying the rate of crime among offenders according to a criminal career paradigm (see Piquero et al. 2003 for a review). Scholars of this perspective often refer to their interest in understanding Lambda (λ), the Greek symbol used in statistics to refer to an expected count or rate from a Poisson distribution. In some statistical texts, Lambda (λ) is simplified to the standard mean notation (denoted by the Greek symbol mu, μ) (see

A.R. Piquero and D. Weisburd (eds.), *Handbook of Quantitative Criminology*,
DOI 10.1007/978-0-387-77650-7_32, © Springer Science + Business Media, LLC 2010,
First softcover printing 2011

Agresti 2007). We will be consistent with notation from statistics and will use the standard mean notation conditional on the Greek symbol λ to denote the expected average count or rate of crimes from a Poisson distribution.

Rates are an expression of counts according to some defined denominator (e.g., time or population) and, as such, the two are completely interchangeable. A number of approaches have been developed over the years for estimating counts that can be usefully applied to criminology. Today, statistical software programs allow us to compute most of the elegant solutions from statistics with ease. Caution is advised, however, and before using these methods, it is useful to understand the basic assumptions of each method. To this end, we will explain both the basic notation and methods for estimating regression models on count data and then provide a case study example from data collected on two samples of paroled offenders from the California Youth Authority in the 1980s.

WHY COUNT MODELS?

The nature of criminal behavior is such that for individuals or larger aggregations like neighborhoods, cities, or counties, the counts we observe are often small (even zero) for many units and occasionally large for a few units. Some of these findings are due to only observing these events when they are reported either in official crime records or self reports; however, many crimes like homicide are simply rare. In either case, the result is that when the average counts are small (e.g., less than 5), the distribution of outcomes is skewed to the right. A skewed distribution is problematic for ordinary least squares (OLS) regression analysis that assumes normal distribution in errors around the expected average ($E(Y = \mu)$). In this case, a method that relies on another distribution may be more appropriate. The Poisson distribution is unimodal and skewed to the right taking on values 0, 1, 2 .... The Poisson distribution is represented by a single parameter $\lambda > 0$, so its mean and variance are identical ($E(Y) = \text{Var}(Y) = \lambda$) (see Agresti 2007). The skewed nature of the Poisson distribution makes it an attractive probability distribution when one wants to estimate skewed crime counts.

It is important to note that as the number of counts gets larger, the distribution becomes more normally distributed (Agresti 2007). In other words, OLS is fine with count outcomes when the mean gets large (e.g., ≥ 20). So, although currently there seems to be some confusion in criminology journals that count data require a Poisson distribution, when the average counts are large, all else equal, it is better to estimate crime outcomes using OLS because the squared standard deviations from the mean are always the minimum estimator. As Angrist (2006) notes "You cannot improve on perfection" (p. 35). However, in many studies, the observed crime counts have an average low count of incidents and a skewed outcome distribution that presents real challenges for OLS estimations.

Statisticians, over a hundred years ago, recognized the problem when attempting to describe the probability of rare event counts and developed the Poisson probability distribution as an extension of a series of Bernoulli trials or binary events with probabilities of an event equal to p_i or no event equal to $(1 - p_i)$, where each event is assumed to occur independently of the next. As Good (1986, p. 160) notes, "Poisson's Law of Large Numbers stated that in a long sequence of trials the fraction of successes will very probably be close to the average of the "chances" for the individual trails even when the average does not tend to limit." There are a number of early examples of statisticians using the Poisson distribution, including the examination of Prussian soldiers that were kicked to death by horses (see Stigler 1986). For criminologists, the event of interest is often a crime, an arrest, a conviction, etc.

The basic formulation for the Poisson distribution is:

$$\Pr(Y|\lambda) = \frac{e^{-\lambda}\lambda^Y}{Y!} \quad \text{for } Y = 0, 1, 2, 3\ldots \tag{32.1}$$

In (32.1), Y is the outcome represented by a count (e.g., count of crimes) and λ is a parameter representing the expected probability of the count according to a Poisson distribution.

For criminologists, one wants to know what predicts the number of crime counts assuming the probability of outcomes occurs via a Poisson distribution (Berk and MacDonald 2008). For example, in a simple experiment comparing the probability of committing future crimes for those randomly assigned to some treatment, one could compare the probability of crime counts for the treatment versus control condition. If arrests are a relatively rare outcome event that occurs independently of each other, then the Poisson distribution may be well suited.

However, criminology is typically focused on observational studies where there are a number of predictors and few well-controlled experiments. A solution to this situation was proposed by econometricians who expanded the Poisson probability distribution into the set of generalized linear models (GLM). These GLM are particularly useful for criminology when we are (1) trying to explain the expected response variable as counts ($E(Y = $ crime counts$|\lambda)$) by a set of independent variables (X') and (2) for point of convenience and parsimony want to assume a linear relationship between outcomes and predictors or $E(Y|\lambda = x'\beta)$ (Greene 1997). Linear relationships are easier to visualize and provide a simplified method for explaining the expected distribution of crime counts at various units (e.g., individuals or places) and may provide an appropriate first-order approximation in the complex world of human behavior. The GLM transforms (32.1) to show that conditional on a set of independent variables (X') and a parameter μ that captures the distribution of observed outcomes (Y) that remains Poisson (Cameron and Trivedi 1998), as shown in (32.2).

$$\Pr(Y|X', \mu) = \frac{e^{-\mu}\mu^Y}{Y!} \quad \text{for } Y = 0, 1, 2, 3\ldots \tag{32.2}$$

Readers interested in a more thorough coverage of GLM should consult approachable texts like Cameron and Trivedi (1998), Agresti (2007), and Long (1997).

In the remaining sections of this chapter, we will focus on the main GLM Poisson regression model and the regression variants of the negative binomial (NB) and zero-inflated Poisson (ZIP).

BASIC ASSUMPTIONS OF COUNT MODELS

Before demonstrating some applications of count models to criminology, we first discuss the basic assumptions of each approach. The Poisson regression and its variants are a form of regression analysis that models the expected rate, $E(\lambda)$ of observed crime outcomes (Y) according to a Poisson distribution. As discussed earlier, the Poisson probability distribution is skewed to the right. As a result, the logarithm of the Poisson probability distribution should be approximately linear. One can see this graphically in Fig. 32.1, where a distribution of observations is highly skewed to the right and the logarithmic smoother fits an almost straight line to the distribution. To get the expected count conditioned on $\lambda(E(\mu|\lambda))$ into linear form,

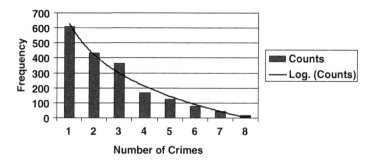

FIGURE 32.1. Distribution of crime counts.

Poisson regression relies on the canonical log-link function that provides the approximation between the linear predictors variables (denoted by X_k) and the mean of the expected distribution of counts (Cameron and Trivedi 1998). In other words, the Poisson regression model is a member of a class of log-linear models (Agresti 2007).

POISSON REGRESSION

The Poisson regression model can be expressed as the logarithm of the expected count outcome according to the following form:

$$\log(E(\mu|\lambda)) = \alpha + x'\beta \tag{32.3}$$

In (32.3), the expected average count of crime, μ, conditioned on λ is denoted by $(E(\mu|\lambda))$, which is a function of the intercept (α) plus a set of linear predictor variables (X'). Unlike in the OLS regression model that assumes predicted values follow a normal distribution defined by an expected average (μ) and a variance (σ^2), the Poisson distribution is defined by a single parameter, μ, where $E(Y) = \mu$ and var $(Y) = \mu$. Note for the Poisson regression this refers to the expected mean for outcomes and variance from the model – not the unconditional mean of the outcome and its variance. A number of criminology related articles express this assumption by simply examining the mean of the outcome and its variance. What one wants to see is whether the estimated mean from the regression model equals the variance.

The assumption that the conditional mean and variance are equal is rarely met with observational data in criminology. Instead, the variance is either less than or greater than the mean. When the conditional variance is less than the conditional mean, this is referred to as underdispersion. When the conditional variance is greater than the conditional mean, this is referred to as overdispersion. These terms simply mean that the model fit to the observed data has less or more variation than is expected according to the Poisson model. Underdispersion is often observed when estimating extremely rare counts of outcomes (e.g., arrests for murder in which the observed average of the outcome is zero and there are few observations with high counts). Overdispersion often occurs in count data with greater numbers of observations with more than fifty counts. One estimation solution for under or overdispersion is to correct by including a variance parameter in the estimating equation. Most statistical software packages that estimate Poisson regression set the variance parameter equal to 1 so that the conditional mean and variance are equal by default. These packages also generally provide tests of this assumption that the variance parameter equals 1. We discuss two examples of dispersion corrections – the negative binomial and zero-inflated Poisson – below.

NEGATIVE BINOMIAL REGRESSION

The negative binomial is the most commonly used correction for overdispersion. Osgood (2000) provides an excellent review of the negative binomial model and its application to aggregate crime counts, while Berk and MacDonald (2008) review the necessary assumptions for the negative binomial and how these assumptions may not be plausible in many circumstances. The basic formulation for the negative binomial is discussed in a number of statistical texts and posits that at different values of the observed outcome (Y = crime counts) one has a mixture of Poisson and gamma distributed data. The resulting distribution is one whose expected average outcome follows a Poisson distribution ($\lambda = \mu$) but whose variance follows a gamma distribution (var $\lambda = \mu^2/k$). A subset or marginal of a gamma mixture of Poisson distributions yields the negative binomial distribution (Agresti 2007). The negative binomial distribution, therefore, incorporates both distributions such that the expected mean of the outcome of counts (Y) follows a Poisson distribution and the variance is equal to the Poisson and gamma distribution, as shown in (32.4).

$$E(Y) = \mu, \quad \text{var}(Y) = \mu + \mu^2/k^{-1} \tag{32.4}$$

The parameter $k > 0$ describes the shape of the gamma distribution which is skewed to the right. It, therefore, follows that when $k = 0$, one returns to the original Poisson formulation because the expected mean and variance will be equal. The greater that k gets from zero, the greater the amount of overdispersion. For example, if the expected mean $\mu = 4$ and $k = 3$, the expected variance will equal 52. When $k < 0$, this is evidence of underdispersion because the expected variance will be less than the expected mean (e.g., expected mean $\mu = 4$ and $k = -3$ the expected variance will equal -44).

The basic extension of the Poisson Generalized Linear Model (GLM) to test for over- or under-dispersion is accomplished by adding a variance parameter (denoted by D^2)

$$\log(E(\mu|\lambda)) = \alpha + x'\beta + D^2 \tag{32.5}$$

When one rejects the null hypothesis that D^2 equals 1, this suggests that there is either under- or over-dispersion (see Agresti 2007). When D^2 equals 1 the model remains the standard Poisson GLM.

ZERO INFLATED POISSON REGRESSION

A potential problem with the standard Poisson regression analysis framework is that the counts may be extremely low such that most observations have values of zero and a few observations to the right-hand-side of the distribution drive the parameter estimates. As a result, one may have less variation (under-dispersion) than is captured in the expected mean when the zeros exceed what would be expected from a standard Poisson distribution. One way to deal with low counts within the Poisson framework is the zero-inflated Poisson (ZIP) model. The ZIP model works by combining the likelihood functions from the probit or logit and the Poisson regression models such that:

$$\log E(\mu|\lambda) = (1 - \omega)^* \alpha + x'\beta \qquad (32.6)$$

Where ω captures the influence of covariates from extra zeros according to a logit model ($E(\omega) = \log(p_i/(1 - p_i)) = x'\beta$). These models are less common in criminology, because criminology seems to more often confront cases where the counts on the right-end of an observed distribution exceed what one would expect from a simple Poisson process, hence there is greater variability than expected. However, as criminologists increasingly examine rare event outcomes, ZIP and other related models will increasingly be used.

A NOTE OF CAUTION

Before one abandons standard Poisson regression models and turns to other variants, we would like to caution readers against assuming that rejection of the null hypothesis that the variance parameter equals 1 provides prima fascia evidence that the Poisson model estimated is wrong. Having less or more variation than the expected average of the counts only implies that the Poisson regression model is the incorrect model if one assumes that the estimated model includes the correct predictors and the correct specification of the functional form. Alternatively, the "excess" variation may simply indicate that one has omitted an important variable or failed to incorporate relevant interactions between predictor variables that capture important heterogeneity between observations. Relying on theory and close scrutiny of the data in developing the model is essential, correcting the disturbance term is less important. After all, the model should describe the process that generated the data, rather than the data describing the process that generated the model. We refer readers to an article by Berk and MacDonald (2008) that has several illustrations of these points.

EXPRESSING COUNTS AND CALCULATING RATES

The Poisson regression model relies on the log-link function to provide a simple expression of the linear relationship between the predictor variables on the right hand side of (32.1) and the expected count. The expected count is obtained by exponentiating both sides of the equation. By taking the exponent of both sides of the equation, one obtains the expected average count, as demonstrated in (32.7).

$$\text{Exp}(\log(E\mu|\lambda)) = \text{Exp}\left(\alpha + x'\beta\right) = E(\mu|\lambda) = e^\alpha + e^{x'\beta} \qquad (32.7)$$

The exponential values for the parameters β_k are referred to as multipliers or incidence ratios (IR), since they multiply the expected count or incidence of the outcome by a function of the predictor variable (x). The exponential values of the parameters times the predictors $(e^{x'\beta})$ are typically what is of interest to criminologists since one wants to know how much a predictor variable increases the expected count or incidence of crime. For example, if the expected count is multiplied by 1.0, this means that the variable has no effect. If the expected count is multiplied by 1.5, this means that the expected count increases by a factor of 1.5. If the multiplier is 0.5, then one reduces the expected count by 0.5. Analysts often use relative percentage terms to interpret the multipliers, such that 1.7 would be interpreted as increasing the expected count by 70%, and 0.6 would be interpreted as reducing the expected count by 40%. If you are used to thinking of things in terms of relative ratios, then the IR expression may be more intuitive than percentage changes.

Poisson regression can also be used to describe expected rates, when the rate is a count of crimes divided by a specific unit of exposure (e.g., population, time, etc.). In the context of crime counts, the rate could be an expression of crimes per unit of time. A criminologist, for example, may be interested in modeling the expected number of crimes committed per week or month or number per neighborhood or city population. In Poisson regression, estimating the rate is handled by adding an "offset term" (log* exposure) to the right-hand-side of the equation, with the parameter estimate constrained to equal 1 – so that it doesn't get absorbed into the intercept and predictors (Maddala 1983). Offset simply means that the measure is treated differently from the "set" of explanatory variables on the right hand side of the equation. By constraining the estimated offset term to equal 1 gives the equivalent of a rate (Maddala 1983). Equation (32.8) shows that the addition of this offset term results in a model modification to (32.7).

$$\log (E(\mu|\lambda)) = \log (\text{exposure}) + \alpha + x'\beta \qquad (32.8)$$

or equivalently

$$\frac{1}{\log(\text{exposure})} * \log(E(\mu|\lambda) = \log(\text{exposure}) + \alpha + x'\beta * \frac{1}{\log(\text{exposure})}$$

$$\log \left(\frac{E(\mu|\lambda)}{\text{exposure}} \right) = \alpha + x'\beta$$

We take the logarithm of the exposure variable and constrain the parameter to equal 1 so that expected counts from observations are treated as a fixed scale. For example, suppose one wants to know the expected count of street crimes among a sample of released offenders. In this context, someone who committed four crimes and was out of prison for 4 days would have a rate of 1.0 crime per day. Someone who committed four crimes but was out of prison for 40 days would have a rate of 0.1 crimes per day. The ability to express counts as rates provides an important extension to those interested in crime counts by different units like offenders, populations, or time. Statistical software makes this all easy to do now. STATA, for example, will calculate the expected rate as an exposure variable directly in the estimation so that one doesn't have to convert the variable into is logarithmic form (see Stata version 10.0, 2005). Most statistical packages will allow one to declare an offset variable in estimations. In this case, one needs to log the exposure variable first and then declare it as the offset variable.

COUNT MODELS OF ARRESTS AMONG CALIFORNIA YOUTH AUTHORITY PAROLEES

In the following examples, we estimate Poisson and the related negative binomial and zero inflated Poisson GLM models for counts and rates of arrests for a two cohort sample of California Youth Authority (CYA) parolees for their first 3 years following their release from institutions (see Lattimore et al. 1997, 2004 on samples and measures). We first estimate a standard Poisson regression on total crime counts. We then examine how the linear predictors change when one adjusts for offending rates per street time (number of crimes/number of days an offender was on the street).

For these examples, we predict crime counts using a set of variables that attempt to capture individual offender propensity. Specifically, we measure each individual's problem history according to their number of arrests in the previous 3 years, their age at first officially recorded arrest, whether there was any indication in their probation file of alcohol, drug abuse, gang membership while incarcerated in CYA, previous gang membership prior to incarceration, and recorded acts of violence with incarcerated in CYA. We also include measures of their age upon release, their race or ethnicity, and whether they were from Los Angeles County (given that this is the largest county of referral). The basic descriptive statistics for each measure are shown in Table 32.1.

The distribution of arrests in the first 3 years after release from CYA is displayed in Fig. 32.2. This distribution of arrests is highly skewed to the right, ranging from 0 to 20 but

TABLE 32.1. Descriptive statistics of sample of CYA parolees

Description (variable name)	n	Mean	Std. Dev.	Min	Max
Post-release					
Total Arrests 3 years (Arrests3pos)	3,612	2.7267	2.5115	0	20
Days on the street (Daysstreet)	3,612	916.0285	253.0843	0	1095
Cohort (1 = 86/87) (Cohort)	3,612	0.4640	0.4989	0	1
Problem history					
Number of arrests in prior 3 years (Arrests3pre)	3,612	8.0584	5.1910	0	102
Age at first arrest (Agefirst)	3,612	13.5385	2.7095	3	21
Alcohol abuse (0 no, 1 yes) (Alcohol)	3,612	0.6373	0.4808	0	1
Drug abuse (0 no, 1 yes) (Drugabuse)	3,612	0.7674	0.4225	0	1
CYA gang member (0 no, 1 yes) (CYAgang)	3,612	0.2193	0.4138	0	1
Prior gang member (0 no, 1 yes) (Pregang)	3,612	0.3768	0.4846	0	1
CYA violence (0 no, 1 yes) (CYAviolence)	3,612	0.4261	0.4946	0	1
Age at release (years) (Agerel)	3,612	19.3729	2.0160	12	25
White (reference category)	3,612	0.3319	0.4710	0	1
Black (=1)	3,612	0.3735	0.4838	0	1
Hispanic (=1)	3,612	0.2946	0.4559	0	1
Los Angeles County (0 no, 1 yes) (LAcounty)	3,612	0.4236	0.4942	0	1

NOTE: Variables with a range of 0 to 1 are indicator variables

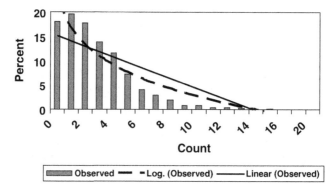

FIGURE 32.2. Distribution of observed crime counts.

TABLE 32.2. Poisson regression of postrelease arrest counts (n = 3,612)

	Coefficient	Std. Err	Z	P > |z|	95% lower CI	95% upper CI	Exp (B)
Cohort	−0.109	0.022	−4.81	0.000	−0.154	−0.064	0.896
Arrests3pre	0.016	0.001	11.43	0.000	0.013	0.0197	1.01
Agefirst	−0.042	0.004	−10.38	0.000	−0.051	−0.034	0.957
Alcohol	−0.085	0.023	−3.62	0.000	−0.131	−0.039	0.918
Drugabuse	0.182	0.027	6.59	0.000	0.128	0.237	1.20
CYAgang	0.127	0.028	4.49	0.000	0.071	0.183	1.13
Pregang	0.023	0.026	0.86	0.390	−0.029	0.075	1.02
CYAviolence	0.128	0.022	5.85	0.000	0.085	0.172	1.13
Agerel	0.030	0.005	5.40	0.000	0.019	0.041	1.03
Black	0.301	0.027	10.89	0.000	0.247	0.356	1.35
Hispanic	0.209	0.029	7.14	0.000	0.152	0.267	1.23
LAcounty	−0.110	0.023	−4.76	0.000	−0.155	−0.0649	0.895
Constant	0.565	0.105	5.35	0.000	0.358	0.772	

Note: Chi-square model fit = 651.56 (df = 12), $p < 0.001$. Pseudo-$R^2 = 0.04$

with a mean value of 2.72, suggesting that a Poisson distribution may provide an appropriate fit to the data. This distribution, as well as observing the log of the trend line, suggests that this may be an appropriate count to estimate using a Poisson distribution. One can also appreciate the log of the trend line for the distribution is closer to the data than the linear trend – again suggesting the Poisson distribution as a useful approximation.

Table 32.2 shows the results from the Poisson regression model of total arrests during the three years after release. One can see that there are a number of statistically significant predictors. This shouldn't be surprising given the relatively large sample size of over 3,000 observations. In fact, if we examine the expected counts from the exponential value of the coefficients (expB), we see that most of the predictors produce relatively small changes in the expected count of arrests. There are some notable exceptions. For example, having a history of drug abuse (Drugabuse) multiplies the expected count by 1.20 or increases it by 20%. Similarly, membership in a gang (CYAgang) and violent behaviors (CYAvio) while detained in CYA facilities, both multiply the expected counts by 1.13 or 13%. There are also differences between Blacks and Hispanics and Whites, but we don't interpret these coefficients because we suspect that these variables may be serving as proxies for variables that are not included in the equation such as household income.

If we are interested in examining how these predictors are related to offending rates and not counts, we can accomplish this by adjusting our estimates for Daysstreet, the time individuals in our sample spent on the street and were, thus, "at risk" of committing crimes and being arrested. For example, parolee A with 10 offenses but who is on the street for 1 month would be a higher rate offender than parolee B who commits 10 offenses while on the street for an entire year. In this example, parolee A would have an offense rate of 0.33 crimes per day (10 crimes/30.4 days), whereas parolee B would have an offense rate of 0.03 crime per day (10/365 days). Parolee B's offense rate is only 1/12th that of parolee A!

Table 32.3 compares the multipliers or incidence ratios (Exp(B)) that were presented in Table 32.2 with the multipliers generated when the same set of predictors are included and we adjust for the days that each parolee was free on the street. This is accomplished by entering the log of the number of days free on the street into the Poisson regression equation as

TABLE 32.3. Comparisons of incidence ratios with
and without adjustments for street time

Variable	Rates (street time adjustment) Exp(B)	Counts (no street time adjustment) Exp(B)
Cohort	0.875***	0.896***
Arrests3pre	1.018***	1.017***
Agefirst	0.951***	0.958***
Alcohol	0.922***	0.918***
Drugabuse	1.236***	1.201***
CYAgang	1.179***	1.136***
Pregang	1.054*	1.023
CYAviolence	1.141***	1.138***
Agerel	1.010*	1.031***
Black	1.408***	1.353***
Hispanic	1.225***	1.233***
LAcounty	0.884***	0.895***
Observations	3,609	3,612

Note: Chi-square model fit $= 880.17$ (df $= 12$), $p <$
0.001. Pseudo-$R^2 = 0.05$
*** $p < 0.01$, ** $p < 0.05$, * $p < 0.1$

an offset variable whose coefficient is fixed to equal one or, where allowed by the statistical package such as STATA declaring an exposure variable that is entered directly into the log-link function. In both estimations, it is important to remember that street time is NOT a predictor variable and should not be absorbed into the direct equation estimation, rather it is an adjustment term (see (32.8) to convince yourself of this). As can be seen in Table 32.3, the results from the model adjusting for street time are materially the same as those presented in Table 32.2, where we did not adjust for street time. In fact, the coefficients change very little. The calculation of rate, however, is useful because it puts every observation's count of arrests on the same scale. In terms of interpretation, we can interpret the multipliers here as increasing the expected count of crime per day. A past history of drug abuse (Drugabuse), for example, multiplies the expected count of crimes per day by 1.236 or increases it by 23.6%, whereas it increases the expected total count over the 3 years post release by 20.1% (IR = 1.201).

Now that we have seen how to interpret the coefficients of predictors of counts and rates of counts from a Poisson model, we need to address the next question of how well the Poisson model approximates the data. Remember that the expected mean and variance from the Poisson distribution should be equal. If we compare the predicted mean and its variance from these models, we find that the expected mean is 2.72, which is the same as the observed mean; but, the estimated variance is less than the mean for both models (0.55 for the count model and 1.24 for the rate model that adjusts for street time).[1] This finding suggests that the conditional variance is underdispersed in our Poisson regression estimations.

The results suggesting that the observed data are underdispersed compared to the dispersion one would expect with a Poisson regression model also suggest that we may want to

---

[1] Most statistical packages have a default routine to save predicted values. Remember this is simply the value of the expected count derived from the model. In STATA there is a default command after model estimations that will allow you to obtain the predicted counts.

estimate a zero-inflated Poisson model in an effort to account for the fact that 18% ($n = 654$) of the parolees in our sample are not observed committing offenses. This group of observations may be driving the variance of the conditional distribution downward. An alternative possibility is that we don't have the right set of predictors to estimate the Poisson model, and if we did have the right set of predictors, the conditional variance would inflate to equal the conditional mean. In any case, we will assume that we have the correct predictors and that the conditional distribution of choice should account for the zero crime counts in our data.

Table 32.4 presents the results from the zero inflated Poisson (ZIP) model and the negative binomial (NB) regressions of crime counts. Column 1 presents the coefficients from the ZIP of the expected counts and column 2 list the inflation estimates which are estimates of the expected zeros of the distribution. Notice that the inflation estimates are in the opposite direction from the expected counts – which is what you would expect, i.e., predictors of positive arrest counts are negatively predictive of zero arrests. As one can see, a past history of drug abuse (Drugabuse) multiples the expected count by 1.13 (increases counts by 13%), but multiplies the expected probability of zero arrests by 0.68 or reduces the expected probability of zero arrests by 32%. There is some noticeable change in the estimated effect of a few predictors when one accounts for the zeros in the empirical distribution. For example, the effect on the expected count of arrests of gang membership in the CYA results in a multiplier of 0.059 in the ZIP model but a multiplier of 1.136 in the standard Poisson model. Similarly, Drugabuse multiplies the expected count of arrests by 1.133 in the ZIP model but 1.201 in the standard Poisson regression model. While these aren't substantial differences, they do provide one with evidence that on the margin the various models could lead to different conclusions.

TABLE 32.4. Zero inflated Poisson (ZIP) and negative binomial (NB) regression of arrests

Variables	ZIP		NB
	(1)	(2)	(3)
	Arrests3pos	Inflate	Arrests3pos
	Exp(B)	Exp(B)	Exp (B)
Cohort	0.924***	1.409***	0.872***
Arrests3pre	1.012***	0.911***	1.026***
Agefirst	0.973***	1.123***	0.956***
Alcohol	0.926***	1.051	0.922**
Drugabuse	1.133***	0.680**	1.203***
CYAgang	1.059*	0.536***	1.126***
Pregang	1.025	1.064	1.021
CYAviolence	1.112***	0.818	1.144***
Agerel	1.050***	1.121***	1.036***
Black	1.247***	0.476***	1.379***
Hispanic	1.243***	1.091	1.229***
LAcounty	0.897***	0.989	0.906***
Constant	1.310**	0.0104***	1.523**
Alpha			0.400***
Observations	3,612	3,612	3,612

Note: Alpha = dispersion parameter likelihood ratio test that Alpha = 0 was 1179.07 ($p < 0.001$).
*** $p < 0.01$, ** $p < 0.05$, * $p < 0.1$

It is often the case in criminology that the counts are so skewed to the right that the conditional variance will exceed the conditional mean (see Osgood 2000 for examples with youth robbery arrests). Under such circumstances, the conventional approach is to estimate a negative binomial regression model. We follow such an approach here for an illustration, not because the data are overdispersed. The results from the NB regression of the counts of arrests are shown in Table 32.4, column 3. The results indicate that the coefficients are similar to the ZIP specification. Column 4 also shows the dispersion parameter, alpha, and indicates that is significantly smaller than 1, indicating that the data are indeed underdispersed. If the dispersion parameter was significantly >1, one would argue that there is evidence of overdispersion.

MODEL DIFFERENCES

Now that we have seen how the Poisson, ZIP, and NB regression models differ, the question arises of which model to use? Unfortunately, there is no correct answer. Specifically, the best model depends on the data and the set of predictors available. One method for choosing between the alternatives is to compare dispersions for each conditional model and examine their relative fit to the data. How dispersed are the data from the conditional mean in each model and how well does each model fit the data? The main problem with this approach is that it assumes that the predictors are correct and complete, providing a basis for comparison and the selection of the right model. In criminology, this is rarely the case; however, we will demonstrate such an approach as a method of model comparison.

Table 32.5 displays the conditional means and variances for the Poisson, ZIP, and NB models, with and without adjustments for street time. Adjusting for street time will inflate the variance by equivalent metrics, such that the dispersion is still less than the mean for the Poisson. One can see that adjusting for street time increases the expected variance for the Poisson model so that it is close to the unadjusted NB model. With the exception of the NB model that adjusts for street time, all models have conditional variances that are substantially lower than their conditional means. This would appear to present prima facie evidence in favor of the NB models. Again, if one assumes that we have all of the correct predictor variables, which is not a reasonable assumption. In fact, given that the coefficients do not change materially it is probably wiser to use the Poisson model than any of the other variants for the simple reason that it provides the most parsimonious approximation and make no assumptions about the error distribution (see Berk and MacDonald 2008 for full exposition).

An alternative approach is described in full in Long (1997) and Long and Freese (2001). This approach involves comparing the fit of each model against their respective probability distribution. In this case, we compare the fit of the estimated Poisson regression model against the theoretical Poisson distribution, the estimated ZIP regression model against the theoretical ZIP distribution, and the NB regression model against the NB distribution. Figure 32.3 displays the fit of each model compared to its respective distribution. These graphs suggest

TABLE 32.5. Conditional means and variances from estimated models

	Poisson	P_Street	NB	NB_Street	ZIP	ZIP_Street
Mean	2.72	2.72	2.74	3.01	2.72	2.80
Variance	0.558	1.23	1.25	3.32	0.534	1.20

that the predicted values from the Poisson regression model underpredicts the lower counts compared to its theoretical Poisson distribution. Given that there were 18% of cases with zero counts of crime, this shouldn't be a big surprise.

Long and Freese (2001) also provide some useful graph commands that allows us to plot the average count from each predicted model against a theoretical distribution. For example, if we select the Poisson distribution as our distribution of choice, we see in Fig. 32.4 how much the expected average count from each of our models deviate from the theoretical Poisson distribution. One can see that the Poisson regression model's deviation (devpois) appears to be underperforming relative to the ZIP (devzip) and NB (devnbreg) models with respect to the lower counts.

DIAGNOSTICS AND RELATED ISSUES

Both the NB and ZIP variants of the Poisson regression model place stringent assumptions with respect to the process generating the excess or dearth of variation relative to the Poisson. Berk and MacDonald (2008) provide clear examples of excess variation and the assumptions imposed by the negative binomial model. In simple terms, both the NB and ZIP assume there is no omitted variable bias driving the over- or under-dispersion. Rarely is it the case in observational studies that one has measured all the relevant predictors. It is useful, therefore, to compare outcomes under both the Poisson and other variants to see how sensitive the findings are to these corrections. In practice, it may be advisable to use the Poisson and work on getting the systematic structure of the model correct before proceeding to other corrections. If the average counts of outcomes are high enough (e.g., 20 or greater) it may be advisable to just use OLS.

Regression diagnostics rarely appear in criminology publications that use Poisson models or the other variants. But the basic assumptions of GLM models regarding collinear predictors and influential observations or outliers on parameter estimates hold for count models as well. Since Poisson regression and its variants are GLM models, the same basic assumptions have to be made that one relies on with other classes like OLS. For example, the negative binomial distribution has an extreme right skew which allows the negative binomial regression model to incorporate particularly high counts, but high counts can also be important outliers in negative binomial models with an observational dataset. In other words, outliers can drive the parameter estimates in count models, as well as traditional OLS. The usual diagnostics for linear regression models can be used to see how well count models hold up. Unfortunately, most statistical software packages don't provide standard regression diagnostics like Cooks D, Dfbetas, and residual plots as default post estimation routines. Residuals can, however, be easily calculated by subtracting the observed counts from those predicted by the model, i.e. $E(Y_i) - Y_i$. One can then inspect residuals for outliers and influential observations. For example, what happens to the model when one drops observations greater than 2.0 or 3.0 standard deviations from the expected mean? One also can easily calculate variance inflation factors (VIF) by regressing each predictor variable on each other and examining the square of the correlation coefficient (R-square) by the following equation: VIF = $1/1$-R-square. VIF values >4.0 may indicate a problem with multicollinearity among the predictors.

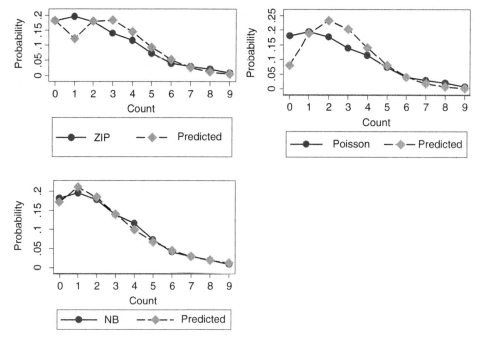

FIGURE 32.3. Predicted vs. theoretical distributions.

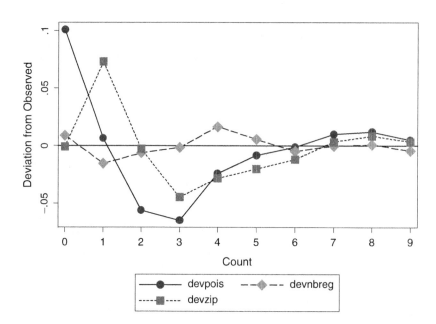

FIGURE 32.4. Predicted values versus Poisson distribution.

CONCLUSIONS

Count models are important to criminology, as so many of the outcomes of interest, such as arrests, take the form of counts in which small counts (and averages) often dominate. Now, most statistical computer software packages offer estimation routines for Poisson, NB and ZIP models, greatly facilitating their use. As is true with all statistical models, the analyst should consider the assumptions underlying the selected model and assess whether these assumptions are reasonable given the data and theory under consideration. Users should follow basic guidelines of regression diagnostics and apply these procedures when they have count outcomes, just as they would with continuous data. The popularity of Poisson regression models has resulted in their use with less focus on their functional utility. For readers with more interest in the limitations of the Poisson regression model and the negative binomial variant, see Berk and MacDonald (2008).

There are several extensions of the class of GLM models for the Poisson that have been developed and applied to good end in criminology. Among these extensions are mixture models that allow one to specify or partition the variance in the Poisson process at different levels of analysis, such as between individuals and the neighborhoods, schools, or prisons under which they are located, or the trajectories or clusters of offenders according to the homogeneity of semi-homogenous groups (Nagin and Land 1993; Nagin 2005; Gellman and Hill 2008; Kreuter and Muthen 2008). The extensions to the GLM of Poisson are discussed in detail elsewhere in this text and offer more flexibility in specification, because they allow the user to test explicit theories that argue the propensity for crime is conditional on different units of analysis. To make appropriate inference with these extensions of the Poisson regression model, it is important that one have a reasonable theory or experiment by which one can attribute independent assignment across different units. For example, within a sample of active offenders, there may exist a subgroup that lived in a set of neighborhoods subjected to a particular police intervention. Under such an example, one could distinguish the covariates for the individual propensity for offending from that generated by the neighborhood-level police intervention. Here, one could use a multilevel Poisson model (commonly referred to among criminologists as a hierarchical linear model). Similarly, there may exist a subgroup of offenders that prefer specific offenses (e.g., burglary vs. violence) and one could estimate Poisson regressions conditional on different offending trajectories. If one has a strong theoretical reason to believe that the process generating the data differs by different units (neighborhood, crime type, or type of offender) one can extend the Poisson regression model to a variety of mixture models. There is also the potential for imbedding a counterfactual model of causal inference using the expected counts as propensities and matching on distance between expected counts or rates between groups of interest. Under such an extension, one could compare the expected count of crimes after each group has been exposed to some treatment. Haviland et al. (2008) provide an example of this by matching on expected crime count propensities for youth prior to joining gangs to compare the difference in subsequent criminal acts between those who join gangs with a group with similar criminal propensities.

Finally, in the absence of compelling evidence, simpler models may be better. As noted earlier, if the average count in the data is large (e.g., >20), OLS may provide an adequate and, likely, best fit to the data. Similarly, Poisson regression may also provide an adequate and, perhaps, best fit even when there is apparent evidence of under- or over-dispersion if the user is not convinced that all (important) parameters have been included in the model. As demonstrated here, there are a number of approaches for examining the fit of alternative models and a thorough analysis should incorporate these.

REFERENCES

Agresti A (2007) An introduction to categorical data analysis, 2nd edn. Wiley, New York

Angrist J (2006) Instrumental variables methods in experimental criminological research: what, why and how. J Exp Criminol 2:23–44

Berk R, MacDonald J (2008) Overdispersion and poisson regression. J Quant Criminol 24:269–284

Blumstein A, Cohen J, Roth JA, Visher CA (eds) (1986) Criminal careers and "career v criminals," vol 2. National Academy Press, Washington DC

Braga A (2003) Serious youth gun offenders and the epidemic of youth violence in Boston. J Quant Criminol 19: 33–54

Cameron AC, Trivedi PK (1998) Regression analysis of count data. Cambridge University Press, Cambridge

Gellman A, Hill J (2008) Data analysis using regression and multilevel/hierarchical models, 5th edn. Cambridge University Press, Cambridge

Good IJ (1986) Some statistical applications of poisson's work. Stat Sci 1:157–170

Greene WH (1997) Econometric analysis, 3rd edn. Prentice Hall, Upper Saddle River, NJ

Greenberg DF (1991) Modeling Criminal Careers. Criminology 29:17–46

Haviland AM, Nagin D, Rosenbaum P, Tremblay R (2008) Combining group-based trajectory modeling and propensity score matching for causal inferences in nonexperimental longitudinal data. Developmental Psychology 44(2):422–436

Kreuter F, Muthen B (2008) Analyzing criminal trajectory profiles: bridging multilevel and group-based approaches using growth mixture modeling. J Quant Criminol 24:1–31

Lattimore PK, Krebs C, Koetse W, Lindquist C, Cowell A (2005) Predicting the effect of substance abuse treatment on probationer recidivism J Exp Criminol 1:159–189

Lattimore PK, Linster RL, MacDonald JM (1997) Risk of death among serious young offenders. J Res Crime Delinq 34:187–209

Lattimore PK, MacDonald JM, Piquero AR, Linster RL, Visher CA (2004) Studying frequency of arrest among paroled youthful offenders. J Res Crime Delinq 41:37–57

Long JS (1997) Regression models for categorical and limited dependent variables. Sage Publications, Thousand Oaks, CA

Long JS, Freese J (2001) Regression models for categorical dependent variables using stata. Stata Press, College Station, TX

Maddala GS (1983) Limited-dependent and qualitative variables in econometrics. Cambridge University Press, New York

Gardner W, Mulvey EP, Shaw ES (1995) Regression analyses of counts and rates: poisson, overdispersed poisson, and negative binomial models. Psychol Bull 118:392–404

Nagin DS (2005) Group-based modeling of development. Harvard University Press, Cambridge, MA

Nagin DS, Land KC (1993) Age, criminal careers, and population heterogeneity: specification and estimation of a nonparametric, mixed poisson model. Criminology 31:327–362

Osgood W (2000) Poisson-based regression analysis of aggregate crime rates. J Quant Criminol 16:21–43

Osgood DW, Chambers JM (2000) Social disorganization outside the metropolis: an analysis of rural youth violence. Criminology 38:81–115

Piquero AR, Farrington DP, Blumstein A (2003) The criminal career paradigm: background and recent developments. In: Tonry M (ed) Crime and justice: a review of research, vol 30. University of Chicago Press, Chicago, pp 359–506

Parker K (2004) Industrial shift, polarized labor markets and urban violence: modeling the dynamics between the economic transformation and disaggregated homicide. Criminology 42:619–645

Paternoster R, Brame R, Bachman R, Sherman L (1997) Do fair procedures matter? The effect of procedural justice on spouse assault. Law Soc Rev 31:163–204

Sampson RJ, Laub JH (1996) Socioeconomic achievement in the life course of disadvantaged men: military service as a turning point, circa 1940–1965. Am Sociol Rev 61:347–367

Stigler S (1986) The history of statistics: the measurement of uncertainty before 1900. The Belknap Press of the Harvard University Press, Cambridge, Massachusetts

CHAPTER 33

Statistical Analysis of Spatial Crime Data

WIM BERNASCO AND HENK ELFFERS

INTRODUCTION

Social scientists become increasingly aware of the relevance of space and place (Goodchild et al. 2000), and criminology is no exception. As a matter of fact, the geography of crime has been a focal concern of criminologists from the very start of the discipline. In nineteenth century Europe, the "moral statistics" of pioneers, Guerry and Quetelet, empirically demonstrated that crime varied across geographical regions. They not only produced maps that visualized these differences, but also studied statistical relations between crime, poverty, and education.

During the early twentieth century, researchers associated with the University of Chicago studied how crime and other social problems varied across urban communities, again mapping the geographical patterns and using community characteristics to explain these distributions. The work on juvenile delinquency has become a classic example (Shaw and McKay 1942).

Interest in the geography of crime decreased somewhat between 1950 and 1980, to some extend possibly because the ecological fallacy (Robinson 1950) hampered the interpretation of aggregated data. Later, the link between communities and crime was revitalized (Bursik and Grasmick 1993; Sampson et al. 1997). In recent years, a new concern has emerged with micro units of place such as addresses or street segments (Eck and Weisburd 1995; St. Jean 2007).

From the very start, geographical criminology has been an area of research where methodological and statistical innovations were either developed or adopted early. In their times, Guerry and Quetelet were pioneers and innovators, and their work is said to have been the launching pad for much of modern social science (Beirne 1987; Friendly 2007). When hierarchical linear (multilevel) models were developed in the 1980s, criminologists and sociologists who studied the links between community and crime quickly embraced and applied them to model community context effects, and even took a lead by developing a new "ecometrics" of crime measurement (Raudenbush and Sampson 1999). When trajectory models were developed to model the criminal development of individuals (Nagin 1999), geographical criminologists soon saw their value for modeling the crime trajectories of geographical entities (Griffiths and Chavez 2004; Weisburd et al. 2004). As another example, spatial econometrics (Anselin 1988) has quickly diffused into the criminology field. In the research on crime

A.R. Piquero and D. Weisburd (eds.), *Handbook of Quantitative Criminology*,
DOI 10.1007/978-0-387-77650-7_33, © Springer Science + Business Media, LLC 2010,
First softcover printing 2011

location choice, developments in discrete choice modeling have been adopted (Bernasco and Nieuwbeerta 2005). The recent focus on small units of analysis creates new methodological challenges for geographic criminology (Weisburd et al. 2009). In sum, geographic criminology has always been at the cutting edge of major methodological and empirical progress.

The purpose of the present chapter is to provide an up-to-date overview of methods for the statistical modeling of spatial crime data, to review some instructive and innovative applications in the field, and to direct the reader to the relevant literature.

The chapter consists of three sections. The first section introduces and delineates the subject matter. It discusses the relevance of spatial analysis, describes what spatial data are, which spatial units of analysis can be distinguished, and how they are sampled. The section further addresses criminological categories that can be geographically referenced, and delineates spatial modeling from descriptive spatial statistics and from visualization techniques ("crime mapping") that are treated elsewhere in this volume.

We distinguish two types of spatial outcomes that can be modeled: spatial distribution, and movement. The second section deals with the analysis of spatial distributions. We discuss how spatial structure is specified in spatial statistics, address the basic concept of spatial autocorrelation, and review a variety of spatially informed regression models and their uses in criminology. The third section addresses the analysis of movement. We address the length of the journey-to-crime, and discuss spatial interaction models, spatial choice models, and the analysis of mobility triads, again highlighting applications in the field of crime and criminal justice.

This chapter resembles and builds upon a review that appeared nearly a decade ago (Anselin et al. 2000). Compared to that review, the present chapter dedicates less space to theory, to geographic information systems (GIS) and to descriptive spatial analysis methods, and more to the analysis of spatial choice and movement.

What are Spatial Crime Data?

All methods discussed in this chapter apply to spatial crime data. Crime data are simply data that bear a direct relation to crime. Often the data apply to people in their roles of offenders, accomplices, fences, victims, bystanders, police officers or judges. They can also be crime targets, such as houses (for burglary), empty walls (for graffiti), cars (for theft), or airplanes (for hijacking). Most often, however, the data are the criminal events themselves: the burglaries, rapes, arsons, robberies, assaults, and murders.

What makes crime data *spatial* crime data is that the units of analysis are geographically referenced. This means that they have attributes (e.g., a pair of geographical coordinates) that can be used to establish where they are situated relative to the other units in the sample. In modeling spatial distributions, a *weight matrix* (see section "Specification of Spatial Structure: The Spatial Weight Matrix and Chap. 6 by Tita and Radil") specifies the spatial relations between all pairs of observations.

Thus, like in network data and in hierarchically structured data, in spatial data the observational units are interrelated. In spatial data, this relation is geographic in nature. For example, two units are adjacent or non-adjacent, they are nearby or distant, they are nearest neighbors or not.

Many textbooks distinguish spatial data by the spatial characteristics of the units of analysis, e.g., whether the data refer to points, to cells of a grid or to areas (depending on the contexts also referred to as zones, lattices, or polygons). For the purpose of the present review, however, it is more useful to make another distinction, namely between stationary (time invariant) spatial distributions on the one hand, and movement between origins and destinations on the other hand. The first type of data may be referred to as spatial distribution data, the second as movement data. Here are some examples of spatial distribution data on crime and criminal justice issues:

- Geographical coordinates of the home addresses of convicted juvenile offenders in Chicago (Shaw and McKay 1942)
- Numbers of homicides per county in the USA (Baller et al. 2001)
- Percentage of residents reporting to be victims of violent assault in their own neighborhood, for each neighborhood cluster in Chicago (Sampson et al. 1997)
- Geographical coordinates and dates of police reported burglary incidents in Liverpool, England (Bowers and Johnson 2005)
- Numbers of police recorded crimes per street segment in Seattle over a period of 14 years (Weisburd et al. 2004)

Spatial mobility data involve movement between two or more locations. Here are some examples of movement data on crime and criminal justice issues:

- The distance between the home and the place of the offence of serial rapists (Warren et al. 1998).
- Robbery incidents in Chicago, georeferenced according to the census tract of residence and the census tract of the robbery incident (Bernasco and Block 2009).
- Homicides in Washington, DC, georeferenced according to the geographical coordinates of the offender's home, the victim's home and the location of the homicide (Groff and McEwen 2007).
- Numbers of crime trips (linking offender's home to crime site) between neighborhoods in The Hague, the Netherlands (Elffers et al. 2008).

What is Spatial Modeling?

Although spatial models require spatial data, spatial data need not necessarily be analyzed with spatial models. As a matter of fact, most spatial crime data have been analyzed without spatial models. For example, with a few exceptions (e.g., Heitgerd and Bursik 1987; Morenoff et al. 2001) spatial models have not been used in the century-old ecological tradition that studies how neighborhood crime rates are influenced by neighborhood conditions, while neighborhoods are clearly spatial entities. Neither have they been used in cross-national comparisons of crime phenomena, although like neighborhoods, countries are spatial entities. The present chapter will obviously focus on the methods of analysis that actually utilize the spatial nature of the data.

We distinguish between two types of spatial analysis methods. The first is often referred to as exploratory spatial data analysis (acronym ESDA) and is concerned with the description and exploration of spatial data. Typically, the results of these analytical methods are visualized with the use of geographic information systems (GIS). Geographical information systems are software tools for digital cartography that help to process, organize, analyze, and visualize geographically referenced information. Applied to crime and justice topics, this is commonly referred to as "crime mapping." Textbooks that discuss ESDA methods are Bailey and Gatrell (1995) and Haining (2003). Visualization and crime mapping issues are comprehensively dealt with in Chainey and Ratcliffe (2005), and more concisely in the chapter by Ratcliffe (Chap. 2) in this volume. Two studies that followed a similar setup analyzed longitudinal data on census tracts in Chicago (Griffiths and Chavez 2004) and on street segments in Seattle (Weisburd et al. 2004). Both first used group-based trajectory analysis (see Chap. 4 by Nagin in this volume) to classify the spatial units according to their temporal crime patterns. Subsequently, the resulting classification was visualized using maps of Chicago and Seattle respectively.

The present chapter addresses only the second type of spatial data analysis: spatial modeling. This term refers to a set of regression analysis techniques that are adapted to spatial data.

When we model *spatial distribution data*, we attempt to predict the outcome variable at each location as a function of variables of the focal location and possibly of variables at other locations as well (typically assuming that a variable measured at nearby locations has a larger influence than the same variable measured at more distant locations). In the following section, we extensively discuss *spatial regression models* and briefly touch upon *spatial filtering models*, *geographically weighted regression models*, and *multilevel models*.

When we model *movement data*, we use either aggregated or disaggregated movement data. In the case of aggregated data, we attempt to predict the number of movements from an origin to a destination as a function of attributes of the origin, the destination, and some measure of impedance (usually distance, or travel time) between the origin and the destination. These models are referred to as *spatial interaction models*. In the case of disaggregated data, we attempt to predict which one of a set of potential destinations an actor will choose as a destination, given that he or she starts from a specific origin. The variables used in the prediction include attributes of all potential destinations and their distance to the origin, possibly in interaction with attributes of the origin or the actor. The models are referred to as *spatial choice models*.

Why is the Spatial Dimension Important?

There are two different reasons why we should care about our crime data being geographically referenced. The first reason is that the spatial arrangement of the data might *bias* the findings of regular statistical analysis, and we need spatial statistics to diagnose the situation or correct for it. The second reason is that the spatial dimension is a necessary element of our findings and conclusions, because we are intrinsically interested in spatial patterns and spatial effects, and need spatial statistics to explore them.

Let us first discuss the spatial arrangement of data as a potential cause of bias. As mentioned earlier, in geographically referenced data, all units of analysis are interrelated. For example, each unit is located at a certain distance from each and every other unit in the data. This implies that they are not independent observations, but that one observation may influence one or all of the others. According to Tobler's First Law of Geography, to the effect that "*everything is related to everything else, but near things are more related than distant things*" (Tobler 1970: 236), we might expect that nearby units influence each other more intensely than distant units. Thus, not only can we expect our observations to be interdependent, but they may also be interdependent to a varying degree.

Because most statistical techniques are based on the assumption of independence between observations, our results may be biased if this assumption is unjustified. Thus, even if we do not have a substantive interest in spatial aspects of the research problem, we may need spatial statistics either to verify that the assumptions hold (diagnostic tests for spatial autocorrelation), or else to correct in a statistically appropriate way for the interdependence between observations. Much recent work in criminology illustrates the increasing awareness of spatial interdependence as a potential source of bias, and of statistical methods and techniques to deal with it (Kubrin and Stewart 2006; McCord and Ratcliffe 2007). Issues of spatial interdependence require special attention as the spatial scale becomes smaller, as is demonstrated in an analysis of spatial autocorrelation of trajectory group membership among nearly 30,000 street blocks in the city of Seattle (Groff et al. 2009).

Instead of being a source of bias and nuisance factor, the spatial arrangement of data is also a potential source of information. It may also provide an opportunity to explore substantive hypotheses. For example, it has been hypothesized that local measures against crime give rise to displacement of crime to nearby locations, i.e., that when offenders find out that their crime opportunities are blocked in one place, they will move to nearby places to commit crime. Alternatively, the beneficial crime-reducing effects may diffuse or spill over to nearby places. In order to test this hypothesis, we need to assert whether after the implementation of the measures, crime increases or decreases more in nearby locations than elsewhere, in more distant locations (Bowers and Johnson 2003; Weisburd et al. 2006). Thus, we can only address the issue empirically if we have geographically referenced crime data.

Another example in which the research question dictates that spatially referenced data are to be analyzed is a study on lynching in the Southern USA in the 1890–1919 era (Tolnay et al. 1996). The authors assessed the effect lynching in one place had on lynching elsewhere, contrasting a "contagion" model – lynching in one place increases the likelihood of lynching in nearby places – with a "deterrence" model, which states that lynching in one place reduces the likelihood of lynching in nearby places. In this research, the authors formulated specific hypotheses on spatial processes assumed to influence the occurrence of crime events, as is the case in many recent analyses of spatial crime data (Andresen 2006; Baller et al. 2001; Hipp 2007; Kubrin and Stewart 2006; Mears and Bhati 2006; Messner et al. 1999; Morenoff et al. 2001; Nielsen et al. 2005; Wilcox et al. 2007).

When we analyze movement, the spatial arrangement of origins relative to destinations is crucial. For example, in a typical application to crime data, movement applies to the journey to crime. Geography is an essential element of travel, and in order to analyze offenders' journeys to crime, we need to know where they live and where they commit crime.

Spatial Units of Analysis

Spatial crime data are crime data that are geographically referenced: we know where the observations are located relative to each other. Spatial crime data can be either point data or areal data. Point data are data for which the geographic reference is a single point, usually a pair of coordinates in a two-dimensional coordinate system that indicates the exact location of the event of interest. As an example, if we have a data set of burglaries and if the geographical coordinates of all burglaries are included, we have point data.

Areal data apply to a continuous subset of the study area. Depending on the discipline where they are used, areas are also denoted as "zones," "spatial lattices" or "polygons." An example of areal data is the numbers of calls for service for all police beats in a city. Although the calls for service originate from a specific point in space, the data are aggregated to the police beat level and, therefore, areal in nature. Areas are typically demarcated by physical or administrative boundaries.

A classic methodological problem in geography is the *modifiable areal unit problem* (MAUP) (Openshaw 1984): there are numerous ways to aggregate individual point data into areas, and the results of the analysis of the aggregated data depend on how the aggregation was done. One aspect of the MAUP is the issue of scale: how large should aggregated units be. In the USA context, for example, the spatial unit of analysis could be as large as a state, a county, or a city. In practice, most studies in criminology use smaller units: they have neighborhood clusters, neighborhoods or census tracts as the spatial unit of analysis. Because even areas as small as census tracts tend to be far from homogeneous, many scholars in geographic criminology have advocated the measurement at still smaller levels of spatial aggregation, such as (again we use terms from the USA context) census block groups, census blocks, street segments, or even addresses (Weisburd et al. 2004, 2009).

When the spatial crime data are georeferenced as points, their spatial relationship to each other can be easily established by calculating the distance between them. When the geographic reference is an area, there are various possibilities. One possibility is to use the centroid of the areas as an approximation and to calculate the distance with the other areas. In most applications, the spatial relation between areas is indicated by some measure of contiguity or adjacency (see section "Specification of Spatial Structure: The Spatial Weight Matrix").

Sampling and Statistical Inference

Spatial data in general and spatial crime data in particular, seldom represent a random sample from a population. In virtually every analysis of spatial crime data, the data are an exhaustive sample of the population, e.g., all cities in a country, all census tracts in a region, or all street segments in a city, so that running a significance test to infer something about a larger population is useless, as there is no larger population, and the "estimates" are truly descriptions (Gould 1970). In practice, researchers often routinely revert significance testing in these cases, because they tend to think of their data as being a sample that could be generalized to other places or to other times. One argument for statistical significance testing in this situation refers to the modifiable areal unit problem (MAUP, see section "Spatial Units of Analysis"): the particular areal subdivision that is used in the analysis is one particular sample from a large number of hypothetical subdivisions (Cliff 1973). This line of argument gives rise to so-called permutation tests (Edgington 1980). For a critique of the application of procedures of classical statistical inference to population data in geography, see Summerfield (1983).

Of course, it is conceivable that true sampling occurs in a spatial context, e.g., when we analyze the numbers of criminal events in randomly chosen street segments in a city, and relate them to characteristics of neighboring segments. In such cases, statistical inference is only logical, because the observed street segments are a random sample from all segments in the city. However, true samples are extremely rare in the statistical analysis of spatial crime data, and we have not been able to find a single instance. In virtually all studies, there is no sample of spatial units, and the complete population is analyzed. Sometimes stratified samples are taken from spatial strata, for example, a population survey stratified by neighborhood (Sampson et al. 1997). In those cases, all neighborhoods are selected, and a random sample of residents is sampled in each neighborhood. In such cases, inferential statistics can logically be applied to the sample units (residents), but the use of inferential statistics for the strata is void, as discussed earlier.

ANALYSIS OF SPATIAL DISTRIBUTIONS

This section deals with the analysis of spatial variation, i.e., with the observation that offenders, victims, crimes, and related events, like many other human phenomena, are not randomly distributed across space, but usually display patterns. Before reviewing a variety of spatially informed regression models and their uses in criminology, we discuss the issue of how spatial structure is incorporated into statistical analysis, how it is used in the calculation of spatial autocorrelation, and how we can test for residual spatial autocorrelation in nonspatial regression models.

Specification of Spatial Structure: The Spatial Weight Matrix

In spatial regression models, an outcome at a focal location is assumed to be influenced not only by its own characteristics, but also by characteristics of other locations. Typically, the strength of these influences is assumed to decay over distance, i.e., the influence of nearby locations is stronger than that of locations further away (this principle is illustrated by the first Law of Geography, see section "Why Is the Spatial Dimension Important?").

To specify the relative strength of these spatial influences and incorporate them in a statistical model, spatial statistics methods use a *spatial weight matrix*, which is sometimes referred to as a *connectivity matrix* (Brunsdon 2001), or *adjacency matrix*. A spatial weight matrix W is a square matrix of dimension n, where n is the number of locations in the dataset. Each element w_{ij} of W is a measure of the strength of the influence of location i on location j. The elements w_{ii} on the diagonal equal zero by definition. Because the strength of the influence is supposed to decay over distance, normally the larger w_{ij}, the closer is i to j.

In spatial models, the weight matrix W is fixed (it is not estimated but defined). Because different weight matrices imply different spatial dependency structures, the outcomes of any model are conditional on the weight matrix used. The specification of the spatial structure is too often chosen as a matter of convenience or dictated by constraints imposed by software. Deane et al. (2008) report an interesting analysis of a single model that is estimated with various differently specified weight matrices.

Figure 33.1 is an example of a simple weight matrix. It depicts a map of an area comprising nine neighborhoods on the left side, and a weight matrix $W^{(1)}$ on the right side.

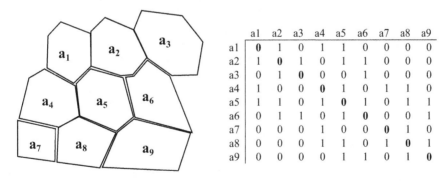

	a1	a2	a3	a4	a5	a6	a7	a8	a9
a1	**0**	1	0	1	1	0	0	0	0
a2	1	**0**	1	0	1	1	0	0	0
a3	0	1	**0**	0	0	1	0	0	0
a4	1	0	0	**0**	1	0	1	1	0
a5	1	1	0	1	**0**	1	0	1	1
a6	0	1	1	0	1	**0**	0	0	1
a7	0	0	0	1	0	0	**0**	1	0
a8	0	0	0	1	1	0	1	**0**	1
a9	0	0	0	0	1	1	0	1	**0**

FIGURE 33.1. Map of area containing 9 neighborhoods (left) and an associated weight matrix $W^{(1)}$ based on first-order adjacency (right)

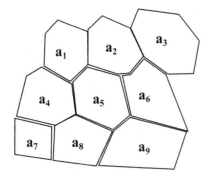

	a1	a2	a3	a4	a5	a6	a7	a8	a9
a1	**0**	1	½	1	1	½	½	½	½
a2	1	**0**	1	½	1	1	⅓	½	½
a3	½	1	**0**	⅓	½	1	¼	⅓	½
a4	1	½	⅓	**0**	1	½	1	1	½
a5	1	1	½	1	**0**	1	½	1	1
a6	½	1	1	½	1	**0**	⅓	½	1
a7	½	⅓	¼	1	½	⅓	**0**	1	½
a8	½	½	⅓	1	1	½	1	**0**	1
a9	½	½	½	½	1	1	½	1	**0**

FIGURE 33.2. Map of area containing 9 neighborhoods (left) and an associated weight matrix $W^{(3)}$ based on inverse of minimal number of borders to be crossed between i and j (right)

The $W^{(1)}$ weight matrix specifies how the nine neighborhoods in the area are expected to influence each other. In this case, $W^{(1)}$ is defined according to *first order adjacency*, i.e., $w^{(1)}_{ij} = 1$ if and only if neighborhoods a_i and a_j have a border in common, otherwise $w^{(1)}_{ij} = 0$. Used in a regression model, this weight matrix claims that an outcome variable in a focal neighborhood is influenced by the characteristics of adjacent neighborhoods, and that each of these influences is equally strong (as the relevant w_{ij} are all equal to 1).

$W^{(1)}$ is by no means the only possible dependency structure. We could, for example, use a second order adjacency matrix $W^{(2)}$, in which case $w^{(2)}_{ij} = 1$ if and only if the number of borders to be crossed between locations i and j equals 1 or 2, and else $w^{(2)}_{ij} = 0$ otherwise.

Still another weight matrix, depicted in Fig. 33.2, uses multiple order adjacencies to define a continuous measure of influence. In $W^{(3)}$, the relationship $w^{(3)}_{ij}$ between two neighborhoods w_i and w_j is quantified as

$$w^{(3)}_{ij} = 1/(\text{minimal number of borders to be crossed between } w_i \text{ and } w_j) \qquad (33.1)$$

Many other spatial weight matrices are possible, and any measure of *proximity* or the *strength of the spatial relation* between w_i and w_i may be considered as an element of W. For example, it could be inverse distance, or the inverse of the traffic intensity from i to j, or a nearest neighbor relation: neighborhood i is the x-order nearest neighbor of neighborhood j if there are no more than x other neighborhoods in the dataset that are closer to i than j is, or the length of the common border between i and j (also see Getis 2007).

The weight matrix plays a pivotal role in the analysis of spatial model, because the results are conditional on the choice of the spatial weight matrix (for a detailed argumentation of this point, see Chap. 6 by Tita and Radil). Therefore, the weight matrix must be carefully chosen by the researcher, legitimated by theoretical arguments, and reported in detail (Anselin 1988).

Spatial Autocorrelation

There is spatial autocorrelation when the spatial distribution of some measure across space is nonrandom, so that there is a spatial pattern (Cliff and Ord 1973; Dubin 1998). Spatial autocorrelation is positive when nearby entities are more similar than entities that are far apart, and thus it embodies Tobler's first Law of Geography. On a map where events are indicated by dots, spatial autocorrelation shows up as the dots form groups. On areal maps, autocorrelation is indicated by the grouping of similarly colored or patterned areas.

Negative spatial autocorrelation is the opposite phenomenon, where nearby entities tend to be different from each other (Griffith 2006). This shows up on maps as evenly spaced patterns of dots or colors (e.g., like on a checkerboard). In the absence of spatial auto-correlation, there is no pattern, neither a clustered pattern nor a uniform (checkerboard) pattern.

There are numerous measures of spatial autocorrelation (for a list, not a discussion, see Getis 2007), the most well-known including Moran's I, Geary's C, and Ripley's K. In order to be informed about the spatial structure of the data, all of these measures require a weight matrix (see section "Specification of Spatial Structure: The Spatial Weight Matrix"). Thus, the level of autocorrelation in a dataset depends on both the specific statistic that is chosen and the weight matrix that is selected. The statistics can be tested against a theoretical distribution, but most contemporary software test the observed values using permutation tests, in which a Monte Carlo simulation is run to construct a sampling distribution using the observed data (Besag and Diggle 1977).

Moran's I is the most commonly used statistic because it is easily computed and adaptable to special situations. For example, it can be used to calculate "local" spatial autocor-relation (Anselin 1995) and can be adapted to take into account variations in the underlying population densities and to situations where the data are points (for an application to fine-grained crime data, see Groff et al. 2009). Its variance–covariance structure is also similar to other well-known statistics.

Regression Analysis in the Presence of Spatial Autocorrelation

As was discussed in section "Why Is the Spatial Dimension Important?," the spatial relations between our observations may be a nuisance rather than an asset. If we are interested in processes within the examined units of analysis, and not between them, then the fact that they may be spatially interdependent is actually a disadvantage from a statistical point of view. Consider the ordinary least squares (OLS) regression model:

$$y = X\beta + \varepsilon \tag{33.2}$$

In this equation, y is a dependent variable (for example, the crime rate) observed in N spatial units (for example, census tracts), $X\beta$ is the matrix representing the independent variables (e.g., population density, affluence, residential stability) and their associated parameters, and ε is a residual (error term).

One of the assumptions of OLS (and many other) regression models is that the residuals ε are uncorrelated with each other. When spatial data are used, residuals are assumed not to be spatially autocorrelated, i.e., the residuals of pairs of nearby observations should not be more similar than the residuals of pairs of observations that are located at greater distance from each other.

The presence of residual spatial autocorrelation can be tested with Moran's I or one of the other test statistics developed for this purpose. If no residual spatial autocorrelation is detected, it means that any existing spatial autocorrelation in the dependent variable is due to spatial autocorrelation in the independent variables, so that the conditional distribution of the dependent variable, i.e., conditional on the values of the independent variables, is not spatially autocorrelated.

If the errors are spatially autocorrelated, and if the substantive interest is in processes within rather than between the observations, the conclusion must be that unobserved variables – the effect of which is captured in the error term – are responsible for the residual spatial autocorrelation. Although an OLS estimate may yield unbiased estimates of the β parameters, the standard errors of the β parameters are unknown and significance is therefore not appropriate.

For this situation, two solutions are available: either filter away autocorrelated error, which is done in the spatial filtering approach (see section "Spatial Filtering below"), or explicitly incorporate spatially autocorrelated error in the model, which is what spatial error regression models do (see section "Spatial Error Regression").

Spatial Filtering

If the researcher is not directly interested in the spatial aspects of the problem under study (i.e., if the spatial arrangement of the data is mainly a potential cause of bias), it may be useful to resort to the spatial filtering approach. Spatial filtering is a method to remove or "filter out" the spatially autocorrelated part of variables in a regression equation. The advantage of this method is that it generates estimates that are not biased by spatial autocorrelation, but allows the analysis to reap all the advantages of the well-known ordinary least squares regression model.

Spatial filtering converts variables that are spatially autocorrelated into spatially independent variables in an OLS regression framework. The conversion requires spatial filtering procedures. Two alternative filtering procedures are available, one devised by Getis (1990, 1995) and one devised by Griffith (2000). Both seem to perform equally well (Getis and Griffith 2002).

Spatial Error Regression

In the spatial error model (Anselin 2003), spatially autocorrelated error is an explicit part of the regression model:

$$y = X\beta + \lambda W\varepsilon + u \tag{33.3}$$

In this equation, y is the dependent variable, $X\beta$ is the matrix representing the independent variables and their associated parameters, ε is a vector of error terms that are subject to the spatial interdependence that is specified in the weight matrix W, λ is a single parameter that measures the amount of spatial interaction, and u is a regular (non-autocorrelated) error term. Thus, in the spatial error model, the error term is split into an autocorrelated part and a non-autocorrelated part. This is an appropriate model if it can be assumed that there are unobserved independent variables that are spatially autocorrelated and affect the value of y. In this sense, the model captures the spatial influence of unobserved (unmeasured) independent variables.

Andresen (2006) analyzed calls for service made to the Vancouver police, utilizing census tracts as the spatial unit of analysis. The purpose was to explain differences in crime rates across census tracts, with a particular focus on using ambient populations as well as resident populations in the denominator of the crime rate equation, in order to measure the population at risk of criminal victimization. After finding that the residuals of OLS regression models displayed spatial autocorrelation, but in the absence of a specific hypothesis of why the crime rate in a focal tract would be affected by the characteristics of adjacent tracts, Andresen used the spatial error model to control for the residual autocorrelation.

In a study of city-level robbery rates (Deane et al. 2008) in 1,056 cities in the United States with 25,000 or more residents, OLS regression was first used to assess the factors that explained variation in robbery rates between cities. When the residuals displayed spatial auto-correlation, a spatial error model was estimated. An interesting feature of this study was that the authors estimated the model with various alternative spatial dependence structures (i.e., weight matrices): one based on distance between the cities, one based on distance between cities in the same state (i.e., the weight of a pair of cities in different states was zero), and one in which all cities are nested in states (i.e., all pairs of cities within a state have a value of 1, and all other pairs 0). The last model, with the nested weight matrix structure, was preferred on the basis of model fit, suggesting that similarity in robbery rates may be a function of processes at the state level (legislation or state level policies) rather than by spatial proximity alone.

Spatial Lag Regression

Spatial filtering procedures and spatial error models are appropriate in situations where spatial interdependence is a nuisance rather than the main topic of inquiry. In many substantive applications, the issue of spatial dependence is at the heart of the research question. In such cases, spatial relations between the units of analysis are actually a necessity because they allow us to assess, for example, whether gang incident rates are affected by gang violence in nearby areas, whether the number of robberies in a block depends on the number of commercial businesses in adjacent blocks, or whether the burglary rate in a community depends on the level of economic deprivation in nearby communities. The observation of adjacent or nearby spatial entities is needed to answer such questions.

Spatial lag models are regression models that incorporate a specification of spatial interdependence not in the error term but in the fixed or predicted part of the regression equation (Anselin 2003). It is useful to distinguish between two separate cases, one in which the hypothesized spatial interdependence runs from the independent variables in nearby areas to the dependent variable in the focal area, and one in which the hypothesized spatial interdependence runs from the dependent variables in nearby areas to the dependent variable in the focal area (so that y is an endogenous variable that appears on both sides of the regression equation). The former model can be written as follows:

$$y = X\beta + \mu WX + \varepsilon \tag{33.4}$$

This model with lagged independent variables is sometimes not specifically referred to as a spatial regression model because it can be estimated with the OLS technique. However, from a substantive point of view it is, because it allows the researcher to assess whether independent variables measured in nearby areas have an effect on a dependent variable in the focal area. In this equation, μWX is a spatially weighted matrix of independent variables in areas "nearby" the focal area where y is measured (where "nearby" is thus defined in the weight matrix W).

In an early application of the idea that extra-community processes affect internal outcomes, Heitgerd and Bursik (1987) demonstrated that local delinquency rates in a community were influenced by racial changes in adjoining communities. More recent examples of this approach are Bernasco and Luykx (2003), who explored whether burglary rates in a reference neighborhood were affected by concentrations of burglars' residences in adjacent neighborhoods, and Mears and Bhati (2006), who explored whether the number of homicides in a neighborhood was affected by resource deprivation in adjacent neighborhoods.

In the other spatial lag model, not the independent variables but the dependent variable is lagged:

$$y = X\beta + \rho W y + \varepsilon \tag{33.5}$$

Here, $\rho W y$ is a spatially weighted matrix of the dependent variable. This is the traditional spatial lag regression model (Anselin 2003) where the dependent variable is endogenous, as it appears on both sides of the equation. This model is often applied when spatial effects are being considered in research on crime and criminal justice. An essential aspect is that it assumes that spatial dependence operates through effects of nearby y variables upon each other, and any spatial effects of the exogenous x variables run indirectly as "spatial multipliers" (Anselin 2003) through their influence on the local y variable. For example, the model could assume that the crime rate in a focal area is affected by the crime rate in surrounding areas. Often, the model is justified by referring to concepts like diffusion, contagion, or displacement, although these concepts assert a sequential process, while the spatial lag model is not sequential.

Some examples of this spatial lag model in research on crime and criminal justice are Baller et al. (2001) who studied the spatial clustering of county-level homicide rates and found evidence for the existence of a diffusion process, and Morenoff et al. (2001) and Kubrin (2003), who studied neighborhood level homicide, and also found spatial proximity to homicide to be related to homicide rates.

The (maximum likelihood) estimation of (33.5) becomes unfeasible in large samples (i.e., in cases where the number of spatial entities N is large, and where the weight matrix W thus contains N^2 cells). A solution for this problem was devised by Land and Deane (1992). They used a Two-Stage-Least-Squares (2SLS) procedure in which they first estimated y using instrumental variables, and subsequently used the predicted y in the right-hand side of the above equation. This procedure is still regularly used in situations where direct estimation of (33.5) is difficult (Hipp 2007; Rosenfeld et al. 2007).

For a discussion on non-linear spatial lag (and error) models (Logit, Poisson, Negative-Binomial), see Anselin (2001). These methods have also been used in panel designs (Anselin 2001; Baltagi et al. 2007).

Geographically Weighted Regression

Geographically weighted regression (GWR) analysis (Brunsdon et al. 1996; Fotheringham et al. 2002; LeSage 2004) is a modeling technique for exploratory spatial data analysis. It estimates (ordinary least squares, logistic or Poisson) regression equations in which the parameters are allowed to vary across space (and it tests whether they do). For example, in estimating a regression model of crime on income in a city, GWR allows the effect of income to be different, even change sign, between different parts of the city. In fact, the effect is allowed to be different at every data point. The (ordinary least squares) equation used in geographically weighted regression analysis, is:

$$y_i = \alpha_i + \beta_i X_i + \varepsilon_i \tag{33.6}$$

The subscript i refers to an individual data point. Because the β has an i subscript, it can have a different value for every observation in the data. To estimate the coefficients of the equation at point i, the other observations in the data set are used as well, but they are spatially weighted to the effect that observations near i weight more heavily in the estimation of β_i than distant observations. The spatial weights can be calculated using a variety of methods.

The estimated coefficients are the output of GWR analysis and can be mapped, because they are all linked to a specific location. The resulting map displays spatial variation in the relationship between two variables (for an example, see Chap. 5 in Chainey and Ratcliffe 2005).

GWR models can also be mixed models, in which the coefficients of some variables are assumed to be global, while others are allowed to vary locally. For example, in the following mixed model, β varies locally, but γ has a single value for all observations:

$$y_i = \alpha_i + \beta_i X_i + \gamma Z_i + \varepsilon_i \tag{33.7}$$

An application of GWR to crime in Portland, Oregon (Cahill and Mulligan 2007) explored spatial variation in the factors that affect the amount of violent crime in block groups. The authors concluded that the GWR method was successful in exploring spatial variation in the relation between structural variables and crime. They found that the effects of some variables were quite stable across the city of Portland, while those of other variables fluctuated substantially across the city. The authors also performed a cluster analysis, using the similarity of coefficients and spatial contiguity as a criterion for placing observations together in a cluster (for a formal method of identifying a mixed model in GWR, see Mei et al. 2004). Malczewski and Poetz (2005) used GWR analysis to study spatial variation of the relation between socioeconomic neighborhood characteristics and the burglary risk in London, Ontario.

Multilevel Regression and Spatial Dependence

Multilevel regression models (also known as *hierarchical linear* models) have been developed for the analysis of hierarchically structured data, i.e., data in which the units of analysis are grouped or *nested*. Examples of such data include gang members grouped by the gang they are part of, offences grouped by the offenders who committed them, and crime victims grouped by their neighborhood of residence. Like spatial data structures, hierarchical data structures violate the standard assumption of OLS regression models that observations are independent. One of the various functions of multilevel models is that they alleviate this assumption, so that the observations within a group are allowed to be interdependent.

Multilevel models are now used routinely in situations where individual crime data that are nested spatially are available (Kubrin and Stewart 2006; Sampson et al. 1997; Velez 2001; Van Wilsem et al. 2006). Typically, such research involves individuals (usually offenders or victims) as the micro level of analysis and census tracts or neighborhoods as the spatially aggregated second level of analysis. The hierarchical structure is thus spatial in nature – the neighborhood encapsulates the individuals – and the multilevel model is used to take into account that all residents of the same neighborhood are subject to the same neighborhood conditions.

Multilevel models were not developed to model spatial processes, and they provide a very crude way of correcting for spatial autocorrelation because neither the influence of neighborhoods on nearby neighborhoods nor the influence of individuals on nearby individuals are modeled. Thus, in a standard multilevel model where spatial data are forced into a hierarchical data structure, both the spatial distribution of subjects within a neighborhood and the spatial arrangement of the neighborhoods themselves become irrelevant. The outcome of the analysis will not change if we were to change the locations of the individuals within the neighborhood, or the locations of the neighborhoods within the study area (Chaix et al. 2005; Elffers 2003).

The spatial aspect of a hierarchy does not always need to dominate its theoretical relevance. For example, if we are to study gun ownership and gun use across the states of the USA, the differences in regulations between states might be considered more salient than their relative spatial positions.

The complete integration of multilevel and spatial modeling is a complex issue. Morenoff (2003) has constructed a partial integration of spatial and multilevel modeling, in which the individuals are nested in neighborhoods but are not directly influenced by a spatial process, while the neighborhoods are subject to influence from adjacent or nearby neighborhoods. Various authors use this approach to test multilevel models for residual autocorrelation (e.g., Kubrin and Stewart 2006; Wyant 2008). If the spatial effects between the neighborhoods are not of substantive interest but a nuisance factor (i.e., potential source of bias) an alternative way to address the issue is by introducing a higher aggregated spatial level. Thus, districts or neighborhood clusters are collections of adjacent neighborhoods that are introduced as a third level in the multilevel model (Van Wilsem 2003; Wilcox et al. 2007). However, this solution solves the problem only partially and reintroduces it at a higher spatial level of aggregation.

ANALYSIS OF MOVEMENT

All methods discussed in the previous section apply to situations in which the units of analysis are stationary objects. As far as the analysis is concerned, they are fixed in space. Various theoretical perspectives require an analysis of movement. For example, routine activity theory (Cohen and Felson 1979) asserts that the convergence in time and space of motivated offenders and attractive and unguarded targets is a necessary and sufficient condition for the occurrence of predatory crime. From this perspective, understanding spatial crime patterns requires the analysis of the movements of potential offenders, potential targets, and potential guardians. Some targets, such as houses and businesses, or guardians like CCTV cameras may of course be immobile.

In the present section, the statistical analysis of criminal movement data is addressed. The distance between the offender's home and the crime location is one of the most studied variables in this field of research. We address the analysis of the length of the journey to crime as a dependent variable in section "Length of the Journey to Crime," and briefly discuss geographic offender profiling, a method that inverts distance decay curves to prioritize the search for an offender. In section "Spatial Interaction Models," we describe how criminologists have taken up the study of the journey to crime using gravity and spatial interaction models that are used in other sciences to study flow between places. In these models, distance is one of the main independent variables. Subsequently, in section "Disaggregate Discrete Location Choice Models," we discuss how explicit models of choice can be used and have been used to study location choice at the individual level. Finally, section "Crime Triads: Convergence of Offenders, Victims and Crimes" deals with methods that can be used to analyze spatial triads, in particular, the offender-victim-crime triad. In each subsection, we address basic methodological literature and discuss applications in research on crime and criminal justice.

Length of the Journey to Crime

One of the applications of Tobler's First Law of Geography, referred earlier, is that, everything else being equal, the amount of interaction between two places declines as the distance between them increases (Fotheringham and Pitts 1995; Haynes and Fotheringham 1984). This phenomenon, *distance decay*, has been found to apply to daily routine journeys for various purposes, such as travel between home, workplace, and shopping and leisure centers, and also to migration. The distribution of the length of these trips is skewed to the left, with the large majority of the trips being relatively short. The general explanation for the distance decay phenomenon is that human movement is governed by the principle of least effort (Zipf 1949). If people travel purposefully towards destinations that provide rewards, they will generally prefer a nearby to a distant destination, unless the distant location provides significantly more rewards than the one nearby.

Criminologists have had a longstanding interest in the offender's journey to crime, in particular in its length: the distance between the offender's home and the location where he or she committed the offence. Starting with Bullock (1955), some studies have also explored the victim's journey to crime, and in the following section, we will discuss the joint analysis of the victim's and the offender's journey to crime in terms of mobility triangles. The length of the journey to crime also displays distance decay. Some studies find a "buffer zone" of decreased criminal activity just around the offender's home (Rossmo 2000), but many other studies do not.

Quite a number of studies relate the length of the journey to crime to features of the crime itself or to characteristics of the offender (Wiles and Costello 2000). For example, various studies demonstrate that juvenile offenders travel shorter distances, that there are systematic differences in the average length of the journey to crime between types of offences and that generally, the criminal rewards of crime increase with its the length of the journey to it. *Geographic offender profiling* (Rossmo 2000) is an investigative method that utilizes the distance decay phenomenon to prioritize the search area for an unknown offender, and it has become the subject of a comprehensive literature (Harries and LeBeau 2007; Wilson and Maxwell 2007). Geographic offender profiling is predicated on the assumption that distance decay, which is a feature of aggregated journeys to crime by different offenders, also holds for multiple crimes committed by the same offender. Recent work that uses multilevel analysis to empirically disentangle the total variation in the length of the journey to crime into within-offender and between-offender components, shows that this is barely the case, and that a large part of the variation is between offenders who have different ranges of operation (Smith et al. 2009).

Spatial Interaction Models

When goods, money, information, or people move between two locations, geographers call it spatial interaction. Spatial interaction models[1] are utilized to explain the quantities of these movements between locations. They can be used to analyze all types of movement flows that have an origin (starting point) and a destination (end). For example, spatial interaction models have been used to study travel between cities in terms of numbers of tickets sold (Zipf 1946), migration in terms of numbers of people moving between cities (Stouffer 1960; Wadycki 1975), trade between countries in terms of monetary value (Bergstrand 1985), inter-city telecommunication in terms of numbers of phone calls (Guldmann 1999), and also the journey to crime, in terms of numbers of offenders' traveling from their homes to the locations where they commit crimes (Elffers et al. 2008; Peeters 2007; Rengert 1981; Reynald et al. 2008; Smith 1976).

There are various textbooks that discuss spatial interaction models in detail (Golledge and Stimson 1997; Haynes and Fotheringham 1984; Wilson and Bennett 1985). Here, we address the main features of these models and their use for understanding crime related movement patterns.

Spatial interaction models are regression models in which the unit of analysis is a *pair of locations*. What is modeled is the size of the interaction between these two locations. The independent variables in the regression equation include characteristics of the origins and the destinations, and one or more measures of the impedance or friction between the origin and the destination. Typically, this is the distance between the two locations, but it could also be formulated in travel time or cost. In one of the first uses of this model (Zipf 1946), it was shown, for travel by bus, by train, and by airplane, that the number of passengers traveling between 29 randomly chosen US cities was roughly proportional to the product of the populations of origin and destination divided by the distance between origin and destination. A simple spatial interaction model is given in (33.8).

$$M_{ij} = k \cdot P_i^\alpha \cdot Q_j^\beta \cdot D_{ij}^\gamma \tag{33.8}$$

In (33.8), P_i is a characteristic of the origin that we assume to represent the propulsiveness of the origin (it is a push factor that generates movement), P_j represents the attractiveness of the destination (a pull factor), D_{ij} is the distance between origin and destination, M_{ij} is the amount of movement from origin to destination, and α, β, and γ, the parameters to be estimated. A more general formulation could include multiple variables that characterize the propulsiveness of the origin (variables with subscript i), the attractiveness of the destination (variables with subscript j), and the impedance or friction between origin and destination (variables with subscripts i and j).

Depending on the substantive questions and data at hand, Wilson (1971) distinguished four variants of the basic spatial interaction model (Pooler 1994, addresses an extended family of spatial interaction models). In the *total flow constrained model*, only the total flow is fixed in advance, and in the *production-constrained model*, the total outflow from all origins is fixed,

---

[1] Some spatial interaction models are also known as *gravity models*, because their mathematical form resembles Newton's Law of Gravitation. This law asserts that the gravitational attraction between two bodies is proportional to the product of their masses divided by the squared distance between them, or $F = g \cdot M_1 \cdot M_2 \cdot D^{-2}$, where g is the gravitational constant. As the physics analogy tends to isolate the model from fruitful application and development in social science (Haynes and Fotheringham, 1984), the term spatial interaction model is preferred here.

so the model is used to estimate "where they go to". In the *attraction-constrained model*, this is reversed. The total inflow into destinations is fixed and the model is used to estimate "where they came from". Finally, in the *doubly constrained model*, the total outflow from all origins and the total inflow is fixed, and the model can be used to estimate the effects of distance, or more generally, the impedance factors.

Although spatial interaction models do include distances between pairs of locations, they do not take into account the role of spatial structure. For example, the potential destinations from a given origin may be spatially clustered, and this clustering may either facilitate travel to the clustered destinations (an agglomeration effect), reduce it (a competition effect) or have no effect at all (the assumption of the standard spatial interaction model). Two conceptually similar adaptations to the spatial interaction model have been proposed (Cascetta et al. 2007). One approach to incorporate these possible effects is to introduce into the model a *competing destination* factor, which measures the accessibility of a destination to other destinations (Fotheringham 1983a, b), i.e., the sum of the distance weighted attractions of other potential destinations.

Alternatively, an *intervening opportunities* factor can be used to incorporate spatial pattern (Stouffer 1940, 1960). According to this approach, the distance effect itself is seen as theoretically redundant, as it represents the absorbing effects of destinations located between the origin and the potential destination (in Stouffer's 1960 formulation), or of destinations located at shorter distances from the origin than the potential origin (in Stouffer's 1940 formulation).

Although various applications of the spatial interaction model exclude the interaction of a spatial unit with itself (e.g., local migration, intra-city phone calls), there is little in the model that prevents it from being applied to such trips. The only issue is that for local trips, the distance in the denominator of the equation may be coded as zero. The solution is to replace the zero value with a small distance, e.g., the average distance between two random points within the origin area.

Spatial interaction methods have been and are often estimated using ordinary least squared regression analysis on the linear equation that results from taking the natural logarithm of both sides of an equation like (33.8):

$$\ln(M_{ij}) = \ln(k) + \alpha \ln(P_i) + \beta \ln(P_j) - \gamma \ln(D) \tag{33.9}$$

When modeling spatial interaction, however, there is often no specific reason to follow the functional specification of (33.9), where the logarithm of the size of the movement stream is a linear function of the logarithms of the other variables. In many cases and for various reasons, including the presence of pairs of locations where the quantity of interaction is zero and logarithms cannot be taken, a Poisson or negative binominal model is to be preferred (Flowerdew and Aitkin 1982; Flowerdew and Lovett 1988). For expositions of the Poisson model family tailored to criminology, see Osgood (2000) and Berk and MacDonald (2008).

In theory, there are quite a number of possible applications for spatial interaction models in criminology and criminal justice. We can model the residential migration of offenders or victims, the journey to crime of victims, offenders or police officers who respond to a call; we can also use spatial interaction models to study co-offending patterns, where the amount of interaction is the number of co-offending relations between these two neighborhoods. In practice, we find only a handful of applications of the spatial interaction model in criminology, and all of them analyze offenders' journey to crime, i.e., the spatial the interaction between the zones where offenders live and the zones where they commit offences (Elffers et al. 2008; Kleemans 1996; Peeters 2007; Rengert 1981; Reynald et al. 2008; Smith 1976).

In the first application of spatial interaction models to crime travel data (Smith 1976), various specifications of spatial interaction models, including Stouffer's intervening opportunities model, were used to analyze the crimes that resulted in arrest in 1972 by the Rochester (New York) Police Department. Offenders' residence and crime site were coded by census tract. Distances were calculated as distances between the centroids of census tracts. Using less elaborate sets of specifications, similar spatial interaction models were applied to burglary in Philadelphia (Rengert 1981) and Enschede, the Netherlands (Kleemans 1996).

More recently, spatial interaction models have been used to study the flow of crime in The Hague, in particular to analyze whether physical barriers (Peeters 2007) and social barriers (Reynald et al. 2008) reduce the criminal movement between neighborhoods, and to test various variants of Stouffer's intervening opportunities theory (Elffers et al. 2008).

Disaggregate Discrete Location Choice Models

Spatial interaction models apply to aggregated crime data. They have been used to explain or predict the total numbers of crimes that originate in one area and take place in another. They do not apply to individual offenders and their specific characteristics, or to individual crimes. While it is possible to estimate spatial interaction models for specific classes of offenders or offences separately (Smith 1976, for example, also performed the analysis separately for property crime only), the model remains an essentially aggregated model.

The models discussed in the following section are similar to production-constrained spatial interaction models, because they assume that the number of journeys to crime that originate from a given location, is fixed. It is not part of what must be explained. The models discussed in the following section are different because they are applied to "disaggregated" data, i.e., to journeys to crime, and they model the behavior of individual actors. They are called *discrete choice models* because they predict which available alternative a decision maker will choose from a set of discrete alternatives. When the choice is between spatial entities (such as the country to visit on holiday, the neighborhood to move to, or the street corner to commit a robbery), it is called spatial (discrete) choice.

Discrete choice models (McFadden 1973) are explicitly based on a theory of random utility maximization (RUM). The first applications of discrete choice models were in the study of travel mode choice (i.e., the choice between train, bus, car, or airplane). Later, the model was also applied to spatial choice (Ben-Akiva and Lerman 1985).

The point of departure of the spatial discrete choice model is an actor who is faced with a choice among J discrete spatial alternatives, of which (s)he must choose only one. The actor could be a motivated offender who is about to choose an area to commit a crime. The actor is supposed to evaluate the utility (net gain, profits, satisfaction) that could be derived from each alternative, and the utility derived by actor i from alternative j is given by the following equation:[2]

$$U_{ij} = \beta P_j + \gamma D_{ij} + \varepsilon_{ij} \qquad (33.10)$$

---

[2] Note that in the aggregate spatial interaction models, we used index i to refer to the origin location. Here, in the disaggregated discrete choice model, i denotes an individual actor.

In this equation, P_j is an attribute that varies across the spatial alternatives (e.g., economic deprivation of a city, or number of bars in a neighborhood), D_{ij} is the distance that varies across spatial alternatives and across individuals, and β and γ are the parameters to be empirically estimated on the basis of the actually observed location choices. They indicate the relative importance of the attributes in the outcome of the utility evaluation. Finally, ε_{ij} is a random error term that contains unmeasured relevant attributes of actors and alternatives, as well as measurement error.

The statistical model used to estimate the theoretical random utility model is the *conditional logit model* (Greene 1997; McFadden 1973), which is also known as the *multinomial logit model*.

The most useful feature of the disaggregated spatial choice model when compared to the aggregated origin-constrained spatial interaction model, is that it can be utilized to study the role of individual characteristics. By including interaction terms of individual characteristics (e.g., age) and destination characteristics (e.g., affluence), we can study whether some destination characteristics have different effects on the spatial choices of different types of offenders.

A feature in the conditional logit model is the assumption of independence from irrelevant alternatives (IIA), which implies that the ratio of two probabilities does not depend on the remaining probabilities. As this assumption is generally considered the main weak spot of the conditional logit model in general and of its application to spatial choice in particular (Pellegrini and Fotheringham 2002; Thill 1992), alternatives have been suggested, such as the *nested logit* model (Greene 1997: 921–926; Heiss 2002), that relaxes the assumption. Used in a spatial choice context (Hunt et al. 2004; Kanaroglou and Ferguson 1996; Pellegrini and Fotheringham 2002), the nested logit model is based on the assumption that the human process of spatial information processing and decision making is hierarchical. This means that spatial alternatives are perceived in more or less homogeneous clusters, and that spatial choice takes place in steps: first decide on a cluster, and once the cluster is chosen, choose a destination from within that cluster. For example, when we decide on where to go on vacation, we would first decide on a country, in the next phase decide on a region, and finally on a specific town or city. In the nested logit model, the IIA assumption is maintained within clusters but not between clusters.

There are various problems with the application of the nested logit model to spatial choice. The most important being that there is usually no way to determine the spatial choice structure, so that the researcher is forced to specify in advance, and often arbitrarily, the hierarchical structure of the spatial choices that individuals are confronted with. This is difficult, sometimes impossible, especially in those cases where the perspective on spatial alternatives may depend on where the origin is. For example, because we are generally most familiar with nearby places, we distinguish between small spatial "pockets" in the nearby environment, while we use larger categories for distant areas. Thus, the actors in our model who live in different locations will have choice sets that are differently structured (Pellegrini and Fotheringham 2002).

The problem of defining the relevant choice set – what is actually the set of alternatives that actors choose from – is a general problem of the discrete spatial choice model (Thill 1992), and another manifestation of the modifiable areal unit problem (MAUP).

In criminology, there have been until now only a few applications of the model (Bernasco 2006; Bernasco and Block 2009; Bernasco and Nieuwbeerta 2005; Clare et al. forthcoming), all of which use the regular multinomial model (conditional logit model). In an analysis of neighborhood destination choice of burglars in the city of the Hague, the Netherlands

(Bernasco and Nieuwbeerta 2005), the authors tested hypotheses on the effects of distance, affluence and social disorganization of neighborhoods on the likelihood of being a target area for burglary, and whether these effects depended on the age and ethnic background of the offenders. Recognizing that quite a number of offences are committed by co-offenders, a subsequent study, using the same data on The Hague but including burglaries committed by co-offenders, established that criteria used in spatial choice of target areas did not differ between solitary offences and group offences (Bernasco 2006). Using the census tract as a spatial unit of analysis, another study addressed location choice of robbers in Chicago (Bernasco and Block 2009). In addition to distance, the authors also used measures of census tract dissimilarity between origin and destination tract as impeding factors to the journey to crime. They showed not only that crime trips are more likely between racially and ethnically similar census tracts, but also that individual robbers prefer to rob in census tracts where the majority of the population is of their own racial or ethnic group.

A study in Perth, Australia (Clare et al. forthcoming) used the model to study the effect of physical barriers and connectors on offenders' choice of a destination for burglary trips.

A complication of the use of multinomial logit models for spatial choice is, that the number of possible choice alternatives becomes unmanageably large when the spatial unit of analysis is small. McFadden (1978) describes a solution in which per individual choice, a random sample of the non-chosen alternatives is deleted from the choice set, and he shows that this procedure will asymptotically yield unbiased estimates.

Crime Triads: Convergence of Offenders, Victims and Crimes

Most studies of the journey to crime have focused on the offender's journey to crime. A handful (Bullock 1955; Caywood 1998; Messner and Tardiff 1985) have, in addition, explored the victim's journey to crime.

Routine activity theory, an influential perspective in criminology, asserts that the necessary and sufficient conditions for a crime are fulfilled when a willing offender and a desirable and unprotected target converge in space and time (Cohen and Felson 1979). This perspective views the journey to crime not as the dyad, but as a triad: it links the offender's home, the victim's home, and the location of the criminal event.

Spatial analyses of crime triads have used either a distance approach or a *mobility triangle* approach. Studies that have used the distance approach typically extend the types of analysis that have been used to study the length of the offender's journey to crime. For example, they explore the distance between the offense and the offender's and the victim's home, and relate these distances to characteristics of the offender, the victim, and the offense (Block et al. 2007; Pizarro et al. 2007).

Another approach focuses on the *mobility triangle*: a typology of the spatial relations between offender, victim and criminal event (Groff and McEwen 2007; Tita and Griffiths 2005). Most studies have used the following five-category typology:

1. Offender and victim both live at the location where the crime takes place (*neighborhood or internal triangle*)
2. Offender and victim live in different locations, and the crime takes place at the victim's address (*offender mobility triangle*)
3. Offender and victim live in different locations, and the crime takes place at the offender's address (*victim mobility triangle*)

4. Offender and victim live at the same location, but the crime takes place elsewhere (*offense mobility triangle*)
5. Offender and victim live in different locations, and the crime takes place at neither's address but elsewhere (*total mobility triangle*)

In this typology, the term "location" is used generically, although most mobility triangle studies have used the census tract or the neighborhood as a spatial unit of analysis. The typology could, however, also be based on a much smaller spatial entity, such as an address. In such a case, for example, the *internal triangle* (type 1) would only apply when committed in the joint home of the offender and the victim (e.g., domestic violence). Groff and McEwen (2006, 2007) propose a distance-based mobility triangle that distinguishes between near (less than a quarter mile apart) and distant (more than a quarter mile apart) location pairs. In another study, they discuss cartographic techniques to visualize mobility patterns in crime triads (Groff and McEwen 2006).

The five-category typology can be related to characteristics of the victim, the offender and the offense. Multivariate approaches have used multinomial regression analysis to explore the relation between these characteristics as the independent variables, and the mobility triangle category as the dependent variable (Groff and McEwen 2007; Tita and Griffiths 2005).

CONCLUSION

There is an increasing spatial awareness in criminology. Testing for residual autocorrelation and utilization of methods that account for spatial autocorrelation have become a routine issue in the analysis of spatial data. Moreover, spatial crime data are more and more the object of theoretically inspired research that focuses explicitly on spatial effects in terms of spillover, diffusion, contagion, and displacement processes. In addition, the analysis of movement and mobility has moved beyond the description of the distance between offenders' home and crime site, and is now used to test theories of travel behavior and target choice. Although the field of crime and criminal justice is certainly not the place where most new analytical methods are discovered and developed, the field is quick to absorb new analytical strategies and apply them to spatial crime data.

At present, there are a few issues that could be addressed to advance the field of spatial analysis of crime data. They include

- The integration of the spatial and the temporal dimensions of crime,
- The empirical measurement of travel of (mobile) targets and offenders,
- The measurement and analysis at lower levels of spatial aggregation, and the utilization of methods that are robust to the skewed distributions resulting from it,
- A greater focus on experimental work, both empirically (field experiments) and theoretically (simulation).

We discuss these four issues below.

There are not only places but also times that are suited for crime. However, the temporal dimension has received far less scholarly attention than the spatial dimension (Grubesic and Mack 2008; Ratcliffe 2006). Still, it is a common observation that crime varies spatio-temporally. For example, because offenders prefer to burgle unoccupied premises, residential burglaries are mostly daytime events while commercial burglaries are nighttime events (Ratcliffe 2001). To capture this variation, research on spatial crime distribution and on spatial movement should take into account spatio-temporal patterns.

All quantitative research on movement and crime location choice has been performed on origin–destination data (whereby the origin is typically the registered home address of an offender as the assumed starting point of the journey to crime). No research has yet studied the concrete spatial behavior of offenders, including routes and travel modes. In other research areas, such as time use and transportation research, instruments have been developed that measure subjects' activities over time (Pentland et al. 1999; Schlich and Axhausen 2003). These time-budgets ask subjects about their activities in terms of what they were doing, when they were doing it, and at what place were, and with whom they were doing it. In a space-time budget instrument, subjects are also asked to indicate at what geographic location the activities took place (Wikström and Sampson 2003: 137–138). Such data would not only specifically document from where and along which roads offenders travel towards and away from their targets (rather than assume a straight line from home to crime site), but also allow us to compare, within the same individual, which time-space patterns are associated with offending and which ones are not.

Ethnographic fieldwork (St. Jean 2007) and quantitative research (Oberwittler and Wikström 2009) show that even at low levels of spatial aggregation, such as block groups or street segments, considerable variation exists. As discussed in this chapter and elsewhere (Weisburd et al. 2009), to capture small-scale variations and interactions, research in geographic criminology should use small spatial units of analysis. As this will generally involve more skewed distributions, they must be analyzed with analytical tools specifically adapted to modeling such skewed data.

Finally, although this is more an issue of methodological than of analytical concern, spatial crime data have very seldom been experimental in nature. Empirically, there is some interesting experimental work on the spatial effects of certain forms of policing, in particular, on spatial displacement effects (for a review, see Braga 2001). On the theoretical front, a start has been made with spatially informed simulation studies (Elffers and van Baal 2008; Groff 2007; Johnson 2008).

REFERENCES

Andresen MA (2006) Crime measures and the spatial analysis of criminal activity. Br J Criminol 46:258–285

Anselin L (1988) Spatial econometrics: methods and models. Kluwer, Dordrecht

Anselin L (1995) Local indicators of spatial association – Lisa. Geogr Anal 27:93–115

Anselin L (2001) Spatial econometrics. In: Baltagi BH (ed) A companion to theoretical econometrics. Blackwell, Oxford, pp 310–330

Anselin L (2003) Spatial externalities, spatial multipliers, and spatial econometrics. Int Reg Sci Rev 26:153–166

Anselin L, Cohen J, Cook D, Gorr W, Tita G (2000) Spatial analysis of crime. In: Duffee D (ed) Measurement and analysis of crime and justice. National Institute of Justice/NCJRS, Rockville, MD, pp 213–262

Bailey T, Gatrell T (1995) Interactive spatial data analysis. Longman, London

Baller RD, Anselin L, Messner SF, Deane G, Hawkins DF (2001) Structural covariates of U.S. county homicide rates: incorporating spatial effects. Criminology 39:561–590

Baltagi BH, Heun Song S, Cheol Jung B, Koh W (2007) Testing for serial correlation, spatial autocorrelation and random effects using panel data. J Econom 140:5–51

Beirne P (1987) Adolphe Quetelet and the origins of positivist criminology. Am J Sociol 92:1140–1169

Ben-Akiva ME, Lerman SR (1985) Discrete choice analysis: theory and applications to travel demand. MIT Press, Cambridge, MA

Bergstrand JH (1985) The gravity equation in international trade: some microeconomic foundations and empirical evidence. Rev Econ Stat 67:474–481

Berk R, MacDonald JM (2008) Overdispersion and Poisson regression. J Quant Criminol 24:269–284

Bernasco W (2006) Co-offending and the choice of target areas in burglary. J Invest Psychol Offender Profiling 3:139–155

Bernasco W, Block R (2009) Where offenders choose to attack: a discrete choice model of robberies in Chicago. Criminology 47:93–130

Bernasco W, Luykx F (2003) Effects of attractiveness, opportunity and accessibility to burglars on residential burglary rates of urban neighborhoods. Criminology 41:981–1001

Bernasco W, Nieuwbeerta P (2005) How do residential burglars select target areas? A new approach to the analysis of criminal location choice. Br J Criminol 45:296–315

Besag J, Diggle PJ (1977) Simple Monte Carlo test for spatial pattern. Appl Stat 26:327–333

Block R, Galary A, Brice D (2007) The journey to crime: victims and offenders converge in violent index offences in Chicago. Secur J 20:123–137

Bowers KJ, Johnson SD (2003) Measuring the geographical displacement and diffusion of benefit effects of crime prevention activity. J Quant Criminol 19:275–301

Bowers KJ, Johnson SD (2005) Domestic burglary repeats and space-time clusters: the dimensions of risk. Eur J Criminol 2:67–92

Braga AA (2001) The effects of hot spots policing on crime. Ann Am Acad Pol Soc Sci 578:104–125

Brunsdon C (2001) Is 'statistix inferens' still the geographical name for a wild goose? Trans GIS 5:1–3

Brunsdon C, Fotheringham AS, Charlton ME (1996) Geographically weighted regression: a method for exploring spatial nonstationarity. Geogr Anal 28:281–298

Bullock HA (1955) Urban homicide in theory and fact. J Crim Law Criminol Police Sci 45:565–575

Bursik RJ Jr, Grasmick HG (1993) Neighborhoods and crime: the dimensions of effective community control. Lexington Books, New York

Cahill M, Mulligan G (2007) Using geographically weighted regression to explore local crime patterns. Soc Sci Comput Rev 25:174–193

Cascetta E, Pagliara F, Papola A (2007) Alternative approaches to trip distribution modelling: a retrospective review and suggestions for combining different approaches. Pap Reg Sci 86:597–620

Caywood TOM (1998) Routine activities and urban homicides: a tale of two cities. Homicide Stud 2:64–82

Chainey S, Ratcliffe J (2005) GIS and crime mapping. Wiley, London

Chaix B, Merlo J, Chauvin P (2005) Comparison of a spatial approach with the multilevel approach for investigating place effects on health: the example of healthcare utilisation in France. J Epidemiol Community Health 59: 517–526

Clare J, Fernandez J, Morgan F (2009) Formal evaluation of the impact of barriers and connectors on residential burglars' macro-level offending location choices. Aust N Z J Criminol 42:139–158

Cliff AD (1973) A note on statistical hypothesis testing. Area 5:240

Cliff AD Ord JK (1973) Spatial autocorrelation. Pion Limited, London

Cohen LE, Felson M (1979) Social change and crime rate trends: a routine activity approach. Am Sociol Rev 44: 588–608

Deane G, Messner S, Stucky T, McGeever K, Kubrin C (2008) Not 'islands, entire of themselves': exploring the spatial context of city-level robbery rates. J Quant Criminol 24:337–421

Dubin RA (1998) Spatial autocorrelation: a primer. J Hous Econ 7:304–327

Eck JE, Weisburd D (1995) Crime places in crime theory. In: Eck JE, Weisburd D (eds) Crime and place. Crime prevention studies, vol 4. Criminal Jutice Press and The Police Executive Forum, Monsey, NY and Washington, DC, pp 1–33

Edgington ES (1980) Randomization tests, vol 31. Marcel Dekker Inc, New York

Elffers H (2003) Analysing neighbourhood influence in criminology. Stat Neerl 57:347–367

Elffers H, Reynald D, Averdijk M, Bernasco W, Block R (2008) Modelling crime flow between neighbourhoods in terms of distance and of intervening opportunities. Crime Prev Community Saf 10:85–96

Elffers H, van Baal P (2008) Realistic spatial backcloth is not that important in agent based simulation research. An illustration from simulating perceptual deterrence. In: Eck JE, Liu L (eds) Artificial crime analysis systems: using computer simulations and geographic information systems. IGI Global, Hershey, PA, pp 19–34

Flowerdew R, Aitkin M (1982) A method of fitting the gravity model based on the Poisson distribution. J Reg Sci 22:191–202

Flowerdew R, Lovett A (1988) Fitting constrained Poisson regression models to interurban migration flows. Geogr Anal 20:297–307

Fotheringham AS (1983a) A new set of spatial interaction models: the theory of competing destinations. Environ Plan A 15:15–36

Fotheringham AS (1983b) Some theoretical aspects of destination choice and their relevance to production-constrained gravity models. Environ Plan A 15:1121–1132

Fotheringham AS, Pitts TC (1995) Directional variation in distance decay. Environ Plan 27:715–729

Fotheringham AS, Brunsdon C, Charlton M (2002) Geographically weighted regression: the analysis of spatially varying relationships. Wiley, West Sussex, UK

Friendly M (2007) A.-M. Guerry's moral statistics of France: challenges for multivariable spatial analysis. Stat Sci 22:368–399

Getis A (1990) Screening for spatial dependence in regression analysis. Pap Reg Sci 69:69–81

Getis A (1995) Spatial filtering in a regression framework: experiments on regional inequality, government expenditures, and urban crime. In: Anselin L, Florax RJGM (eds) New directions in spatial econometrics. Springer, Berlin, pp 172–188

Getis A (2007) Reflections on spatial autocorrelation. Reg Sci Urban Econ 37:491–496

Getis A, Griffith D (2002) Comparative spatial filtering in regression analysis. Geogr Anal 34:130–140

Golledge RG, Stimson RJ (1997) Spatial behavior. The Guilford Press, New York

Goodchild MF, Anselin L, Appelbaum RP, Harthorn BH (2000) Toward spatially integrated social science. Int Reg Sci Rev 23:139–159

Gould P (1970) Is statistix inferens the geographical name for a wild goose? Econ Geogr 46:439–448

Greene WH (1997) Econometric analysis, 3rd edn. Prentice-Hall, Upper Saddle River, NJ

Griffith DA (2000) A linear regression solution to the spatial autocorrelation problem. J Geogr Syst 2:141

Griffith D (2006) Hidden negative spatial autocorrelation. J Geogr Syst 8:335–355

Griffiths E, Chavez JM (2004) Communities, street guns and homicide trajectories in Chicago, 1980–1995: merging methods for examining homicide trends across space and time. Criminology 42:941–978

Groff E (2007) Simulation for theory testing and experimentation: an example using routine activity theory and street robbery. J Quant Criminol 23:75–103

Groff ER, McEwen T (2006) Exploring the spatial configuration of places related to homicide events. Institute for Law and Justice, Alexandra, VA

Groff ER, McEwen T (2007) Integrating distance into mobility triangle typologies. Soc Sci Comput Rev 25:210–238

Groff E, Weisburd D, Morris NA (2009) Where the action is at places: examining spatio-temporal patterns of juvenile crime at places using trajectory analysis and GIS. In: Weisburd D, Bernasco W, Bruinsma GJN (eds) Putting crime in its place: units of analysis in geographic criminology. Springer, New York, pp 61–86

Grubesic T, Mack E (2008) Spatio-temporal interaction of urban crime. J Quant Criminol 24:285–306

Guldmann J-M (1999) Competing destinations and intervening opportunities interaction models of inter-city telecommunication. Pap Reg Sci 78:179–194

Haining RP (2003) Spatial data analysis: theory and practice. Cambridge University Press, Cambridge

Harries K, LeBeau J (2007) Issues in the geographic profiling of crime: review and commentary. Police Pract Res 8:321–333

Haynes KA, Fotheringham AS (1984) Gravity and spatial interaction models. Sage, Beverly Hills, CA

Heiss F (2002) Structural choice analysis with nested logit models. Stata J 2:227–252

Heitgerd JL, Bursik RJ Jr (1987) Extracommunity dynamics and the ecology of delinquency. Am J Sociol 92:775–787

Hipp JR (2007) Income inequality, race, and place: does the distribution of race and class within neighborhoods affect crime rates? Criminology 45:665–697

Hunt LM, Boots B, Kanaroglou PS (2004) Spatial choice modelling: new opportunities to incorporate space into substitution patterns. Prog Hum Geogr 28:746–766

Johnson S (2008) Repeat burglary victimisation: a tale of two theories. J Exp Criminol 4:215–240

Kanaroglou PS, Ferguson MR (1996) Discrete spatial choice models for aggregate destinations. J Reg Sci 36:271–290

Kleemans ER (1996) Strategische misdaadanalyse en stedelijke criminaliteit. Een toepassing van de rationele keuzebenadering op stedelijke criminaliteitspatronen en het gedrag van daders, toegespitst op het delict woninginbraak.. Universiteit Twente, Enschede, the Netherlands

Kubrin CE (2003) Structural covariates of homicide rates: does type of homicide matter? J Res Crime Delinq 40:139–170

Kubrin CE, Stewart EA (2006) Predicting who reoffends: the neglected role of neighborhood context in recidivism studies. Criminology 44:165–197

Land KC, Deane G (1992) On the large-sample estimation of regression models with spatial- or network-effects terms: a two-stage least squares approach. Sociol Methodol 22:221–248

LeSage JP (2004) A family of geographically weighted regression models. In: Anselin L, Florax RJGM, Rey SJ (eds) Advances in spatial econometrics: methodology, tools and applications. Springer, Berlin, pp 241–264

Malczewski J, Poetz A (2005) Residential burglaries and neighborhood socioeconomic context in London, Ontario: global and local regression analysis. Prof Geogr 57:516–529

McCord ES, Ratcliffe JH (2007) A micro-spatial analysis of the demographic and criminogenic environment of drug markets in Philadelphia. Aust N Z J Criminol 40:43–63

McFadden D (1973) Conditional logit analysis of qualitative choice behavior. In: Zarembka P (ed) Frontiers in econometrics. Academic, New York, pp 105–142

McFadden D (1978) Modeling the choice of residential location. In: Karlkvist A, Lundkvist L, Snikars F, Weibull J (eds) Spatial interaction theory and planning models. North-Holland, Amsterdam, pp 75–96

Mears DP, Bhati AS (2006) No community is an island: the effects of resource deprivation on urban violence in spatially and socially proximate communities. Criminology 44:509–548

Mei C-L, He S-Y, Fang K-T (2004) A note on the mixed geographically weighted regression model. J Reg Sci 44:143–157

Messner SF, Anselin L, Baller RD, Hawkins DF, Deane G, Tolnay SE (1999) The spatial patterning of county homicide rates: an application of exploratory spatial data analysis. J Quant Criminol 15:423–450

Messner SF, Tardiff K (1985) The social ecology of urban homicide: an application of the "routine activities" approach. Criminology 23:241–267

Morenoff JD (2003) Neighborhood mechanisms and the spatial dynamics of birth weight. Am J Sociol 108:976–1017

Morenoff JD, Sampson RJ, Raudenbush SW (2001) Neighbourhood inequality, collective efficacy, and the spatial dynamics of urban violence. Criminology 29:517–559

Nagin DS (1999) Analyzing developmental trajectories: semi-parametric, group-based approach. Psychol Methods 4:139–177

Nielsen AL, Lee MT, Martinez R (2005) Integrating race, place and motive in social disorganization theory: lessons from a comparison of Black and Latino homicide types in two immigrant destination cities. Criminology 43:837–872

Oberwittler D, Wikström P-OH (2009) Why small is better: advancing the study of the role of behavioral contexts in crime causation. In: Weisburd D, Bernasco W, Bruinsma GJN (eds) Putting crime in its place: units of analysis in geographic criminology. Springer, New York, pp 35–59

Openshaw S (1984) The modifiable areal unit problem. Geo Books, Norwich

Osgood W (2000) Poisson-based regression analysis of aggregate crime rates. J Quant Criminol 16:21–43

Peeters M (2007) The influence of physical barriers on the journey-to-crime of offenders. Leiden University, Leiden

Pellegrini PA, Fotheringham AS (2002) Modelling spatial choice: a review and synthesis in a migration context. Prog Hum Geogr 26:487–510

Pentland WE, Lawton MP, Harvey AS, McColl MA (eds) (1999) Time use research in the social sciences. Springer, New York

Pizarro JM, Corsaro N, Yu S-sV (2007) Journey to crime and victimization: an application of routine activities theory and environmental criminology to homicide. Vict Offenders 2:375–394

Pooler J (1994) An extended family of spatial interaction models. Prog Hum Geogr 18:17–39

Ratcliffe JH (2001) Residential burglars and urban barriers: a quantitative spatial study of the impact of canberra's unique geography on residential burglary offenders. Criminology Research Council, Canberra

Ratcliffe JH (2006) A temporal constraint theory to explain opportunity-based spatial offending patterns. J Res Crime Delinq 43:261–291

Raudenbush SW, Sampson RJ (1999) Ecometrics: towards a science of assessing ecological settings, with application to the systematic social observation of neighbourhoods. Sociol Methodol 29:1–41

Rengert GF (1981) Burglary in Philadelphia: a critique of an opportunity structure model. In: Brantingham PJ, Brantingham PL (eds) Environmental criminology. Sage, Beverly Hills, CA, pp 189–202

Reynald D, Averdijk M, Elffers H, Bernasco W (2008) Do social barriers affect urban crime trips? The effects of ethnic and economic neighbourhood compositions on the flow of crime in The Hague, The Netherlands. Built Environ 34:21–31

Robinson WS (1950) Ecological correlations and the behavior of individuals. Am Sociol Rev 15:351–357

Rosenfeld R, Fornango R, Renfigo AF (2007) The impact of order-maintenance policing on New York City homicide and robbery rates: 1988–2001. Criminology 45:355–384

Rossmo DK (2000) Geographic profiling. CRC, Boca Raton, FL

Sampson RJ, Raudenbush SW, Earls F (1997) Neighborhoods and violent crime: a multilevel study of collective efficacy. Science 277:918–924

Schlich R, Axhausen K (2003) Habitual travel behaviour: evidence from a six-week travel diary. Transportation 30:13–36

Shaw CR, McKay HD (1942) Juvenile delinquency and urban areas. University of Chicago Press, Chicago

Smith TS (1976) Inverse distance variations for the flow of crime in urban areas. Soc Forces 54:802–815

Smith W, Bond JW, Townsley M (2009) Determining how journeys-to-crime vary: measuring inter- and intra-offender crime trip distributions. In: Weisburd D, Bernasco W, Bruinsma G (eds) Putting crime in its place: units of analysis in geographic criminology. Springer, New York, pp 217–236

St. Jean PKB (2007) Pockets of crime. broken windows, collective efficacy, and the criminal point of view. University of Chicago Press, Chicago

Stouffer SA (1940) Intervening opportunities: a theory relating mobility and distance. Am Sociol Rev 5:845–867

Stouffer SA (1960) Intervening opportunities and competing migrants. J Reg Sci 2:1–26

Summerfield MA (1983) Populations, samples and statistical inference in geography. Prof Geogr 35:143–149

Thill J-C (1992) Choice set formation for destination choice modelling. Prog Hum Geogr 16:361–382

Tita G, Griffiths E (2005) Traveling to violence: the case for a mobility-based spatial typology of homicide. J Res Crime Delinq 42:275–308

Tobler WR (1970) A computer movie simulating urban growth in the Detroit region. Economic Geography 46: 234–240

Tolnay SE, Deane G, Beck EM (1996) Vicarious violence: spatial effects on southern lynchings, 1890–1919. Am J Sociol 102:788–815

Van Wilsem J (2003) Crime and context: the impact of individual, neighborhood, city and country characteristics on victimization. Thela Thesis, Amsterdam

Van Wilsem J, Wittebrood K, De Graaf ND (2006) Socioeconomic dynamics of neighborhoods and the risk of crime victimization: a multilevel study of improving, declining, and stable areas in the Netherlands. Soc Probl 53: 226–247

Velez MB (2001) The role of public social control in urban neighborhoods: a multilevel study of victimization risk. Criminology 39:837–864

Wadycki W (1975) Stouffer's model of migration: a comparison of interstate and metropolitan flows. Demography 12:121–128

Warren J, Reboussin R, Hazelwood RR, Cummings A, Gibbs N, Trumbetta S (1998) Crime scene and distance correlates of serial rape. J Quant Criminol 14:35–59

Weisburd D, Bushway S, Lum C, Yang S-M (2004) Trajectories of crime at places: a longitudinal study of street segments in the city of Seattle. Criminology 42:283–322

Weisburd D, Wyckoff LA, Ready J, Eck J, Hinkle JC, Gajewski F (2006) Does crime just move around the corner? A controlled study of spatial displacement and diffusion of crime control benefits. Criminology 44:549–592

Weisburd D, Bernasco W, Bruinsma GJN (eds) (2009) Putting crime in its place: units of analysis in geographic criminology. Springer, New York

Wikström P-OH, Sampson RJ (2003) Social mechanisms of community influences on crime and pathways in criminality. In: Lahey BB, Moffitt TE, Caspi A (eds) Causes of Conduct Disorder and Juvenile Delinquency. The Guildord Press, New York/London, pp. 118–148

Wilcox P, Madensen TD, Tillyer MS (2007) Guardianship in context: implications for burglary victimization risk and prevention. Criminology 45:771–803

Wiles P, Costello A (2000) The 'road to nowhere': the evidence for traveling criminals (No. Home Office Research Study (HORS) 207). Home Office, Research, Development and Statistics Directorate, London

Wilson AG (1971) A family of spatial interaction models, and associated developments. Environ Plan 3:1–32

Wilson AG, Bennett RJ (1985) Mathematical models in human geography. Wiley, New York

Wilson R, Maxwell C (2007) Research in geographic profiling: remarks from the guest editors. Police Pract Res 8:313–319

Wyant BR (2008) Multilevel impacts of perceived incivilities and perceptions of crime risk on fear of crime: isolating endogenous impacts. J Res Crime Delinq 45:39–64

Zipf GK (1946) The P1P2/D hypothesis: on the intercity movement of persons. Am Sociol Rev 11:677–686

Zipf GK (1949) Human behavior and the principle of least effort. an introduction to human ecology. Addison-Wesley, Cambridge, MA

CHAPTER 34

An Introduction to Statistical Learning from a Regression Perspective

RICHARD BERK

INTRODUCTION

Statistical learning is a loose collection of procedures in which key features of the final results are determined inductively. There are clear historical links to exploratory data analysis. There are also clear links to techniques in statistics such as principle components analysis, clustering, and smoothing, and to long-standing concerns in computer science, such as pattern recognition and edge detection. But statistical learning would not exist were it not for recent developments in raw computing power, computer algorithms, and theory from statistics, computer science, and applied mathematics. It can be very computer intensive. Extensive discussions of statistical learning can be found in Hastie et al. (2009) and Bishop (2006). Statistical learning is also sometimes called machine learning or reinforcement learning, especially when discussed in the context of computer science.

In this chapter, we consider statistical learning as a form of nonparametric regression analysis.[1] The advantage is that novel concepts can be introduced in a setting that many readers will find familiar. The risk is that the advances that statistical learning represents may not be fully appreciated and that important statistical learning procedures not included within a regression perspective will be overlooked. Yet, in a short overview, this is a useful tradeoff and will provide plenty of material. The approach taken relies heavily on a recent book-length treatment by Berk (2008).

Some background concepts will be considered first. Three important statistical learning procedures are then be discussed in turn: random forests, boosting, and support vector

---

[1] Statisticians commonly define regression analysis so that the aim is to understand "as far as possible with the available data how the conditional distribution of some response variable varies across subpopulations determined by the possible values of the predictor or predictors" (Cook and Weisberg 1999: 27). Interest centers on the distribution of the response variable conditioning on one or more predictors. Often the conditional mean is the key parameter.

A.R. Piquero and D. Weisburd (eds.), *Handbook of Quantitative Criminology*,
DOI 10.1007/978-0-387-77650-7_34, © Springer Science + Business Media, LLC 2010,
First softcover printing 2011

machines. Although the exposition makes little use of formal mathematical expressions, some important ideas from mathematical statistics are necessarily assumed. The chapter also necessarily assumes some prior exposure to smoothers and classification and regression trees (CART), and a solid background in the generalized linear model. An attempt is made in several footnotes to provide additional didactic material.

THE BASIC FRAMEWORK

An important, although somewhat fuzzy, distinction is sometimes made between a confirmatory data analysis and an exploratory data analysis. For a confirmatory data analysis, the form of the statistical model is determined before looking at the data. All that remains is to estimate the values of some key parameters. For an exploratory data analysis, there is no model. Statistical tools are used to extract patterns in the data. The distinction is fuzzy because in practice, few statistical analyses are truly confirmatory. More typically, some important parts of the model are unknown before the data are examined. For example, from a large set of potential explanatory variables, a subset may be selected for the "final model" through a procedure such as stepwise regression.

It is sensible, therefore, to think about a continuum from confirmatory to exploratory analyses. This is especially important for an introduction to statistical learning. Let's begin at the confirmatory side of the continuum.

Confirmatory Data Analysis

The poster child for confirmatory data analysis is the ubiquitous linear regression model, which takes the following form.

$$Y_i = \beta_0 + \beta_1 X_{1i} + \beta_2 X_{2i} + \cdots + \beta_{pi} + \varepsilon_i, \tag{34.1}$$

where i is the index for each of N cases, Y_i is the quantitative response variable, X_1 through X_p are the p well-measured predictors, β_0 through β_p are the $p+1$ the regression parameters, and ε_i is a random disturbance. Each ε_i is assumed to behave as if drawn independently of the predictors and of one another from a distribution with a mean of 0 and a variance of σ^2. As a model, (34.1) is a very explicit theory about how the response variable is generated. If a researcher believes that theory, data can be used to estimate the values of the regression coefficients in an unbiased manner. The value of σ^2 can also be properly estimated. Statistical inference can naturally follow.

If one assumes in addition that the disturbances in (34.1) behave as if drawn at random from a normal distribution (34.1) becomes the normal regression special case of the generalized linear model (McCullagh and Nelder 1989). Logistic regression, probit regression, and Poisson regression are other special cases that depend on the nature of the response variable, how the response variable can be transformed, and the distribution assumed for the disturbances. Then as before, the model is known up to the values of the regression coefficients. Estimates of those parameters are obtained from data. Statistical inference can follow as a matter of course.

Equation (34.1) and its generalizations may be interpreted as causal models. One needs to assert that each of the predictors can be independently manipulated. Then, each regression coefficient coveys how much on the average the response variable changes when its associated predictor is changed by one unit. Equation (34.1) is absolutely silent on whether such casual interpretations are appropriate (Freedman 2004). Such claims must be justified with information outside of the model, usually through social science theory, and occasionally because a real experiment was undertaken.

Confirmatory Data Analysis with Some Important Exploratory Components

In a wide variety of applications in criminology and other social sciences, there is a substantial disconnect between (34.1) and how the data were actually generated (Berk 2003; Freedman 2005; Morgan and Winship 2007). The model is substantially wrong. The same problem can arise for the entire generalized linear model. Although this is old news (e.g., Holland 1986), practice has changed slowly.

There have been many suggestions about the way one might tinker with models like (34.1). Transforming the response and/or the predictors, winnowing down the set of predictors, and removing outlier observations are examples (Cook and Weisberg 1999). However, these methods are commonly neglected and are often too little and too late in any case (Berk 2003). For instance, procedures that are meant to provide the proper transformation for Y_i require that all other features of the model are effectively correct. This is a very demanding and often unrealistic requirement.

A bolder step is to make the systematic part of (34.1) far more flexible. One can rewrite (34.1) as

$$Y_i = f(\mathbf{X}_i) + \varepsilon_i, \tag{34.2}$$

where $\mathbf{X}$ is an $N \times p$ matrix of predictors, and $f(\mathbf{X}_i)$ represents how $\mathbf{X}_i$ is related to Y_i. Typically, ε_i is assumed to have the same properties as in (34.1).

The key point is that the $f(\mathbf{X}_i)$ is determined empirically from the data. In other words, the researcher supplies the correct set of well measured predictors, and a computer does the rest. No particular functional forms need to be assumed. The approach is sometimes called function estimation. Just like (34.1), (34.2) can be altered to include the full generalized linear model, but with the $f(\mathbf{X}_i)$ determined by the data.

Equation (34.2), may also be interpreted as a causal model. However, it differs from (34.1) and its generalizations in that there are no longer regression coefficients representing causal effects. Casual effects have to be represented in other ways. We consider this matter later. But, the same basic requirements and concerns apply.

Exploratory Data Analysis

For many applications, the step taken from (34.1) to (34.2) is not bold enough. For example, several important predictors may not be in the data set or may be in the data set but poorly measured. Then, assumptions made about ε_i can be unreasonable, or at least not easily justified. And, because ε_i is unobservable, it is difficult to bring data to bear.

It often makes sense, therefore, to treat (34.1) or (34.2) as descriptions of how in the data on hand, the conditional mean of the response differs depending on the values of each predictor. There is no model stating how the data were generated. Treating regression analysis solely as a descriptive analysis is always formally correct.

The enterprise is now exploratory data analysis. The enterprise is also fully consistent with the definition of a regression analysis. There is nothing in the definition of a regression analysis that requires a model of how the data were generated, let alone a causal model. Further discussion of using regression analysis for description can be found in Berk (2003).

A Few More Definitions

Equation (34.2) represents the kind of statistical learning we will consider. It can be used for function estimation or description, and is called "supervised learning" because there is a response variable. When there is no response variable – one only has predictors – the name is "unsupervised learning.[2]" Unsupervised learning will not be considered in the chapter. Because the most visible and early statistical learning methods built on many passes through the data, "learning" became a metaphor for how the fitted values can improve as the data are revisited.[3]

There are a number of statistical procedures consistent with (34.2) that are not usually considered statistical learning. Smoothers are perhaps the most common example. Classification and regression trees is another instance. As statisticians and computer scientists have examined the properties of statistical learning procedures, however, many earlier approaches have been recast as special cases of statistical learning. Consequently, features of statistical learning once thought to be distinctive are now seen as matters of degree. This chapter will emphasize the more recent and more novel developments that a look to be the most promising for practice. But, there will not be a clear boundary between statistical learning and a number of earlier techniques. A comprehensive examination can be found in the fine book by Hastie et al. (2009).

Statistical Inference

Because there is no model before the data are analyzed, there cannot be any formal statistical inference applied to the $f(\mathbf{X}_i)$ that results. If statistical inference is forced on some feature of the output nevertheless, it is unlikely that the sampling distribution will be known, even asymptotically. This is the same problem that is associated with all model selection procedure (Leeb and Pötscher 2006).

As key problem is that because the definition of a regression parameter depends on the particular model in which it is embedded, and because that model is unknown, conventional statistical criteria such as unbiasedness and consistency are not defined. Moreover, the process of model selection is a form of data snooping, which is well known to compromise statistical tests and confidence intervals. There are solutions to these problems, but they are only practical in certain situations (Berk et al. 2009b) and are beyond the score of this chapter in any case. At this point, statistical inference is usually a suspect and secondary aspect of statistical learning.

---

[2] Under these circumstances, statistical learning is in the tradition of principal components analysis and clustering.

[3] This may seem a lot like standard numerical methods, such as when the Newton–Raphson algorithm is applied to logistic regression. We will see that it is not. For example, in logistic regression, the form of the relationships between the predictors and the response are determined before the algorithm is launched. In statistical learning, one important job of the algorithm is to determine these relationships.

RANDOM FORESTS

Random forests provides a very instructive introduction to statistical learning from a regression perspective. It represents an explicit challenge to modeling by adopting an "algorithmic" approach (Breiman 2001b). There is no model linking inputs to outputs. There are, therefore, no model parameters whose values need to be estimated. Rather, a computer program attempts to directly associate predictors with the response in a manner that is highly sensitive to features of the data. The forecasting accuracy of this approach is impressive (Breiman 2001a; Berk 2008: Chapter 5; Hastie et al. 2009: Chapter 15; Berk et al. 2009a).

Because there is no equivalent of regression parameters to estimate, links between predictors and the response are shown through two other algorithms. These algorithms are considered below. They build directly on a forecasting framework and have intuitively clear meaning.

The random forests algorithm is an integration of several earlier statistical procedures. It uses classification and regression trees (Breiman et al. 1984) as a building block and then takes ideas from the bootstrap (Efron and Tibshirani 1993) and from bagging (Breiman 1996). But, the manner in which the algorithm preforms is not easily anticipated from its component parts.

The seminal paper on random forests is by Leo Breiman (2001a). An interesting interpretation is provided by Lin and Jeon (2006). A very accessible textbook treatment can be found in Berk (2008: Chapter 5). A more formal exposition can be found in Hastie et al. (2009: Chapter 15). Random forest is available in a Fortran program written by Leo Breiman and Ann Cutler, in the programming language R, and in a very user friendly form from Salford Systems (http://www.salford-systems.com/). The random forests procedure in R is the Breiman and Cutler program with some new features. The Salford Systems version of random forests also builds on the Brieman and Cutler program.

The Random Forests Algorithm

Consider now the steps in the random forests algorithm. It is well worth studying carefully. There is a training sample with N observations. There is a response variable and a set of p predictors. Then, the algorithm proceeds in the following sequence.[4]

1. *Draw a random sample of size N with replacement from the training data.*
   Comment: The observations not selected are saved as the "out-of-bag" (OOB) data. These are the test data for the given tree. On the average, about a third of the training data set becomes OOB data. This is the bootstrap step. Some very recent work suggests that the sample size should be a bit smaller than N (Traskin 2008).
2. *Draw a small random sample of predictors without replacement (e.g., three predictors).*
   Comment: Usually the random sample of predictors is much smaller than the number of predictors overall.

---

[4] To provide exact instructions would require formal mathematical notation or the actual computer code. That level of precision is probably not necessary for this chapter and can be found elsewhere (e.g., in the source code for the procedure *randomForest* in R). There are necessarily a few ambiguities, therefore, in the summary of this algorithm and the two to follow. Also, only the basics are discussed. There are extensions and variants to address special problems.

3. *Using the observations sampled, subset the data using CART as usual into two subsets. If the response variable is categorical, the split is chosen to minimize the Gini index. If the response is quantitative, the split is chosen to minimize the residual sum of squares.*

   Comment: This is the first step in growing a classification or regression tree. If the response is categorical, a classification tree is grown. If the response is quantitative, a regression tree is grown.

4. *Repeat Steps 2 and 3 for all later subsets until additional partitions do not improve the model's fit.*

   Comment: The result is a regression or classification tree. There is some debate about how large to grow the tree. Current opinion favors growing the tree as large as possible.

5. *For a classification tree, compute as usual the class to be assigned to each terminal node. For a regression tree, compute as usual the conditional mean of each terminal node.*

   Comment: Both can be thought of as the fitted values from the tree.

6. *"Drop" the OOB data down the tree. For a categorical response variable, assign the class associated with the terminal node in which an observation falls. For a quantitative response variable, assign the conditional mean of the terminal node in which an observation falls.*

   Comment: The key point is that the OOB data were not used to grow the tree. True forecasts are the result.

7. *Repeat Steps 1–6 many times (e.g., 500) to produce many classification or regression trees.*

8. *For a categorical response variable, classify each observation by majority vote over all trees when that observation was OOB. For a quantitative response variable, assign the average conditional mean over all trees when that observation was OOB.*

   Comment: These are the forecasts for each observation averaged over trees.

The output of random forests is a set of forecasts, one for each observation in the training data. From this and the observed value of the response for each observation, one is able to compute various measure of forecasting accuracy. In the categorical case, the measure might be the proportion of cases forecasted incorrectly. For a quantitative response, the measure might be the mean squared error. In practice, however, it is important to unpack these overall measures. With a categorical response variable, for example, it is common to examine separately the proportion in each class (i.e., category) correctly forecasted. Often, some classes are forecasted better than others.

Random forests have some very important assets when compared with the conventional regression models. The CART building blocks are very flexible so that unanticipated nonlinear relationships between the predictors and the response can be inductively discovered. However, individual trees are known to be very unstable. Averaging over trees tends to cancel out the instabilities. The averaging is a form of shrinkage associated with estimators such as the "lasso" (Tibshirani 1996) and a way to smooth the step functions that CART naturally constructs.[5]

---

[5] Shrinkage estimators have a long history starting with empirical Bayes methods and ridge regression. The basic idea is to force a collection estimated values (e.g., a set of conditional means) toward a common value. For regression applications, the estimated regression coefficients are "shrunk" toward zero. A small amount of bias is introduced

Another asset is that by sampling predictors, the fitted values are made more independent across trees. This enhances the impact of the averaging and is another form of shrinkage. It also gives predictors that would otherwise be neglected a chance to contribute to the fitting process. Competition between predictors is greatly reduced with the result that the fitted values can be especially sensitive to highly nonlinear relationships. That is, predictors that are important for only a few observations are not necessarily shouldered aside by predictors that are more important overall. All predictors can help out.[6]

Yet, another asset is that as the number of trees in the random forest increases without limit, the estimate of population generalization error is consistent (Breiman 2001a: 7). That is, one obtains for the binary case a consistent estimate of the probability of a correct classification over trees minus the probability of an incorrect classification over trees. Thus, random forests does not overfit when a large number of trees is grown. This is in important contrast to other highly exploratory methods.[7]

Finally, for categorical response variables, random forests can introduce the relative costs of forecasted false negatives and false positives directly into the algorithm. Most other regression procedures assume that the costs are the same. For example, the costs of failing to identify an individual who will likely commit a serious felony while on parole are assumed to be the same as the costs of falsely identifying an individual as someone who will likely commit a serious felony while on parole. Equal costs are unrealistic in a wide variety of settings and introducing unequal costs can dramatically alter the forecasts that result.

To help fix these ideas, consider the following illustration for a binary response variable. Table 34.1 is a reconstruction from an article in which for individuals in Philadelphia on probation or parole, a forecast was made for whether or not they would be charged with a homicide or attempted homicide within 2 years of intake (Berk et al. 2009a). Predictors included the usual information available at intake. Table 34.1 is essentially a cross-tabulation of the actual outcome against the forecasted outcome. The cell entries are counts with the exception of those on the far right, which are proportions. For ease of labeling, charges of a homicide or an attempted homicide will be denoted by "homicide" in Table 34.1.

---

into the estimates to gain a substantial reduction in the variance of the estimates. The result can be an overall reduction in mean squared error. Shrinkage can also be used for model selection when some regression coefficients are shrunk to zero and some are not. Shrinkage is discussed at some length in the book by Hastie et al. (2009: 61–69) and Berk (2008: 61–69, 167–174). Shrinkage is closely related to "regularization" methods.

[6] Recall that when predictors in a regression analysis are correlated, the covariate adjustments ("partialling") can cause predictors that are most strongly related to the response to dominate the fitting process. Predictors that are least strongly related to the response can play almost no role. This can be a particular problem for nonlinear response functions because the predictors that are more weakly related to the response overall may be critical for characterizing a small but very essential part of the nonlinear function. By sampling predictors, random forests allows the set of relevant predictors to vary across splits and across trees so that some of the time, weak predictors only have to "compete" with other weak predictors.

[7] Overfitting occurs when a statistical procedure responds to idiosyncratic features of the data. As a result, the patterns found do not generalize well. With a new data set, the story changes. In regression, overfitting becomes more serious as the number of parameters being estimated increases for a fixed sample size. The most widely appreciated example is stepwise regression in which a new set of regression coefficients is estimated at each step. Overfitting can also be a problem in conventional linear regression as the number of regression coefficient estimates approaches the sample size. And, overfitting can also occur because of data snooping. The researcher, rather than some algorithm, is the guilty party. The best way to take overfitting into account is to do the analysis on training data and evaluate the results using test data. Ideally, the training data and test data are random samples from the same population. One might well imagine that overfitting would be a problem for random forests. Breiman proves that this is not so.

TABLE 34.1. Random forests confusion table for forecasts of homicide or attempted homicide using the training sample and out-of-bag observations ($N = 30,000$)

	Forecast of no homicide	Forecast of homicide	Forecasting error
No homicide observed	27,914	1,764	0.06
Homicide observed	185	137	0.57

Charges of homicide or attempted homicide are rare events. About 1 in 100 individuals were charged with a homicide or attempted homicide within 2 years of intake. It was very difficult, therefore, to improve on the marginal distribution. If one predicted that all individuals under supervision would not commit such crimes, that forecast would be correct about 99% of time. With so unbalanced a marginal distribution, it is not surprising that when logistic regression was applied to the data, only two cases were forecasted to be charged with a homicide or attempted homicide, and one was a false positive. In fact, 322 individuals were so charged.

Random forests does better. To begin, stakeholders thought that false negatives were about ten times more costly than false positives. The costs of 10 individuals falsely labeled as prospective murderers were about the same as the costs of one prospective murderer who was not labeled as such. This cost ratio was built into the random forests forecasts. Thus, the ratio in Table 34.1 of false negatives to false positives is around 10 to 1 (1,764/185). That ratio, in turn, helps shape the actual forecasts.

When an individual was actually not charged with a homicide or an attempted homicide, 6% of the cases were forecasted incorrectly. When an individual was actually charged with a homicide or an attempted homicide, 57% of the cases were forecasted incorrectly; about 43% of the time when the random forest algorithm forecasted a homicide or attempted homicide, it was correct.[8] Stakeholder found this level of accuracy useful.

Predictor Importance

Although random forests earns it keep through its fitted values, there is naturally an interest in which predictors are most important for forecasting accuracy. This information is obtained through a second algorithm using the following instructions.

1. *For categorical response variables, compute the predicted class over all trees for each case when it is OOB. For quantitative response variables, compute the conditional mean over all trees for each case when it is OOB.*
2. *For categorical response variables, compute the proportion of cases misclassified for each response class. For quantitative response variables, compute the mean squared error.*
   Comment: These serve as a baselines for forecasting accuracy.
3. *Randomly permute all values of a given predictor.*
   Comment: Shuffling makes the predictor unrelated to the response (and all other predictors) on the average.
4. *Repeat Step1.*

---

[8] Table 34.1 raises several other important issues, but they are beyond the scope of this review (see Berk et al. 2009a).

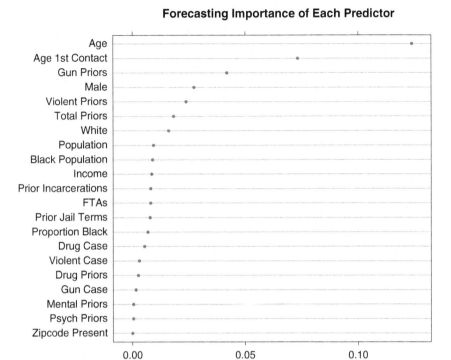

FIGURE 34.1. Predictor importance for forecasting accuracy.

5. *Repeat Step 2.*
   Comment: Steps 4 and 5 provide a performance measure after shuffling.
6. *Compute the increase in forecasting error by comparing the results of Step 5 to the results of step 2.*
   Comment: The increase is a measure of forecasting importance.
7. *Repeat Step 3 through Step 6 for each predictor.*

Figure 34.1 provides importance measures for the predictors used to forecast a charge of murder or attempted murder. Age is the most important predictor. When age was shuffled, the proportion of homicide or attempted homicide cases incorrectly forecasted increased about 12% points (i.e., from 0.57 to 0.69). The increase for the age of first contact with the adult courts was the second most important predictor with an increase of about 8% points. None of the predictors below race ("White") in the table were individually important for forecasting accuracy.

Response Functions

Knowing a predictor's contribution to forecasting accuracy is useful but insufficient. It can also be important to learn how each predictor is related to the response with all other predictors held constant. A third algorithm is required.

1. *For a given predictor with V values, construct V special data sets, setting that predictor's values to each value v in turn and fixing the other predictors at their existing values.*

   Comment: For example, if the predictor is years of age, V might be 40, and there would be 40 data sets, one for each year of 40 years of age. In each dataset, age would be set to one of the 40 age values for all observations (e.g., 21 years old), whether that age was true or not. The rest of the predictors would be fixed at their existing values. The values of the other predictors do not change over data sets and in that fundamental sense are held constant. There are no covariance adjustments as in conventional regression.

2. *Using a constructed data set with a given v (e.g., 26 years of age) and the random forest output, compute the fitted value for each case.*

3. *Average the fitted values over all cases.*

   Comment: This provides the average fitted response for a given v, all other predictors fixed at their actual values. For categorical response variables, the average fitted value is a conditional proportion or a transformation of it. For quantitative response variables, the average fitted value is a conditional mean. The fitted values are analogous to the $\hat{y}_i$ in conventional linear regression.

4. *Repeat Steps 2 and 3 for each of the V values.*

5. *Plot the average fitted values from Step 4 for each v against the V values of the predictor.*

   Comment: This step produces a partial response plot (alternatively called a "partial dependence plot") showing how the average response for a given predictor varies with values of that predictor, all other predictors held constant.

6. *Repeat Steps 1–5 for each predictor.*

To illustrate, Fig. 34.2 shows the partial dependence plot of the age at first contact with the adult court system. The outcome is a charge of homicide or attempted homicide in centered logits. The reasoning for these units is beyond the scope of this chapter but is discussed in Berk's book on statistical learning (2008: 222–226). The circles are the average fitted values, and a smoother is overlaid.

The message is largely in the shape of the response curve. The odds of a charge of homicide or attempted homicide drop precipitously from age 12 to age 30. There is then a gradual and modest increase from age 30 to age 50. Probationers or parolees who get into serious trouble at a young age are at much higher risk to be "shooters." This means that an armed robbery at age 15 is a strong indicator of later violence. That same armed robbery at age 30 is not. The increase between 30 and 50 years of age may represent a different violence etiology, perhaps associated with domestic violence.

The negative slope overall is certainly no surprise. The shape of the response curve, however, was not anticipated by current theory in criminology. Moreover, the strongly nonlinear form was thoroughly misspecified by the logistic regression. Most of the other important quantitative predictors also had dramatically nonlinear response functions, which helps explain why the logistic regression fared so poorly.[9]

---

[9] Although one can construct partial dependence plots for categorical predictors, all one can see is a bar chart. For each category, the height of the bar is the average response value. The order of the bars along the horizontal axis and their distance from one another are necessarily arbitrary.

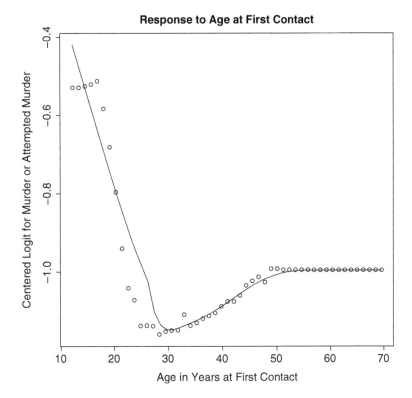

FIGURE 34.2. Partial dependence plot for age at first adult court contact.

BOOSTING

Boosting is often seen as a good alternative to random forests and in practice, it also performs very well. The mathematics behind boosting, however, is somewhat more demanding, and the details of the algorithms require more exposition than can be accommodated here. Fortunately, the broad fundamentals of boosting can be summarized quite easily.

There are many kinds of boosting. But the earliest and most well-known boosting procedure was developed in computer science and in particular, through the work of Freund and Schapire (1996), Schapire (1999, 2002). It is called Adaboost and was originally intended for categorical response variables. We begin with Adaboost. Later, we consider briefly extensions and recent reconceptualizations of boosting by statisticians.

Consider a binary response coded as 1 or -1.[10] The Adaboost algorithm then has the following structure (Hastie et al. 2009: 339). As before, there are N observations in the training data.

1. *Initialize a set of observation weights* $w_i = 1/N, i = 1, 2, \ldots, N$.
   Comment: So, if $N = 1,000$, the initial weight for each observation is 1/1,000.
2. *For $m = 1$ to M:*

---

[10] A coding of 1 and 0 can work too. But the 1 or -1 coding leads to the convenient result that the sign of the fitted value determines class membership.

Comment: There will be M passes through the data.

a. *Fit a classifier $G_m(x)$ to the training data using the weights w_i.*
   Comment: In this context, a "classifier" is essentially any regression statistical procedure for categorical response variables. The subscript m denotes the iteration, and x represents a set of predictors.

b. *Compute:* $\text{err}_m = \frac{\sum_{i=1}^{N} w_i I(y_i \neq G_m(x_i))}{\sum_{i=1}^{n} w_i}$.
   Comment: This is just the weighted proportion of cases misclassified for the mth iteration.

c. *Compute* $\alpha_m = \log[(1 - \text{err}_m)/\text{err}_m]$.
   Comment: This is a logit transformation of the weighted proportion of cases misclassified for the mth iteration.

d. *Set $w_i \leftarrow w_i \cdot \exp[\alpha_m \cdot I(y_i \neq G_m(x_i))], i = 1, 2, \ldots, N$.*
   Comment: I is an indicator ("dummy") variable constructed from the operation within the parenthesis. Thus, new weights are constructed so that cases misclassified in the prior pass through the data are given a larger weight in the next pass through the data.

3. *Output $G(x) = \text{sign}\left[\sum_{m=1}^{M} \alpha_m G_m(x)\right]$.*
   Comment: After M passes through the data, the class assigned to each case is determined by the sign of its averaged fitted values.

Like random forests, Adaboost makes many passes through the data (e.g. 1,000), and each pass through the data produces a set of fitted values. Adaboost also averages its sets of fitted values. But, there is no sampling of the data and no sampling of predictors. And, the averaging is a weighted average, with weights a function of overall fitting accuracy. That is, the better the fit of the output from a given pass through the data, the more weight given to that set of fitted values in the averaging. Adaboost can classify and forecast very accurately, although the forecasting must be undertaken in a subsequent step; it is not built into the algorithm as it is in random forests.

There are now a large number of boosting variants. Perhaps, the most influential of these have been produced by statisticians who have shown that some important features of Adaboost, and boosting in general, can be formulated as a more conventional statistical regression procedure. That is, boosting is "just" another means to minimize a regression loss function and many different loss functions are possible.[11] Thus, Hastie et al. (2009: 343–350) show that Adaboost is doing something very much like logistic regression, but with a somewhat different loss function.

Building on this insight, many different kinds of boosting can be formulated (Friedman 2001, 2002; Friedman et al. 2000, 2004; Bühlmann and Yu 2006), and some properties of boosting can be proved (Mannor et al. 2002; Zhang and Yu 2005). One of the most flexible boosting methods is stochastic gradient boosting (Friedman 2002), which builds on the generalized linear model.[12] There are analogs to logistic regression, Poisson regression, normal regression, Cox proportional hazard regression, quantile regression and others. Software for stochastic gradient boosting can be found in R.

---

[11] Recall that the loss function of least squares regression, for example, is the sum of the squared residuals.

[12] Stochastic gradient boosting samples the training data in the same spirit as random forests.

The statistical view of boosting is not the final word. There are some important features of boosting that at least so far are not "statistical" and are not yet well understood (Wyner 2003; Mease et al. 2007; Mease and Wyner 2008). For example, Adaboost does a fine job capturing the class to which a case belongs (e.g., a reoffender or not), but can easily lead to extremely inaccurate values for the *probability* of belonging to a given class (Buja et al., 2005).

Just like random forests, there is no direct way within the basic algorithm to understand how predictors are related to the response. Just like for random forests, additional algorithms are needed. To date, these algorithms are much like that those used with random forests. There are boosting versions of importance measures and partial dependence plots. Boosting output has much the same look and feel as random forests output.

Perhaps, the major drawback of boosting is that the costs of forecasting errors are not a routine part of the algorithm. But, some potential remedies have been proposed. For example, Kriegler and Berk (2009) develop a form of boosting based on quantile regression in which the quantile specified for the response variable determines the differential costs of forecasting errors.[13]

SUPPORT VECTOR MACHINES

Support vector machines is another very popular statistical learning procedure with roots in computer science. Its rationale is clever and relatively simple. The mathematics is cleverer, but not simple at all. Support vector machines is associated most strongly with the work of Vladimir Vapnick (1996). A discussion of support vector machines from a statistical perspective can be found in Hastie et al. (2009: 423–437). A very accessible exposition is provided by Berk (2008: Chapter 7).

The basic idea is this. Suppose there is a binary outcome: failure on parole or not. Suppose, also there is a risk score serving as a single predictor (although in practice there is usually more than one predictor). For very large risk score values, all of the offenders in fact fail on parole. For very low risk score values, none of the offenders in fact fails on parole. It is for the middle range values of the risk score that the outcomes are mixed. Some offenders fail and some do not. Indeed, some of the offenders in the middle range who fail have lower risk scores than some other offenders in the middle range who do not fail. For the very high and very low risk scores, classification is trivial because for the very low or very high risk scores, the offenders are homogeneous on the outcome. It makes good sense, therefore, to focus on the middle ranges where accurate classification is nontrivial.

Support vector machines builds on this basic logic in two ways. First, its loss function ignores the cases that are easily classified correctly. What matters is how the procedure performs for the cases that are difficult to accurately classify. This is broadly similar to the rationale for boosting. And like boosting, forecasting must be undertaken in a subsequent step. Unlike random forests, it is not part of the basic algorithm. Second, like boosting and random forests, support vector machines can inductively construct highly nonlinear functions for accurate classification. However, the building blocks for these functions are very different for support vector machines. How they are different need not trouble us here. A formal

---

[13] In quantile regression, the fitted values are conditional quantiles, not the conditional mean. For example, the 50th quantile is the conditional median (Keonker 2005). Then, if, say, the 75th quantile is used, overestimates are three times more important (75/25) than underestimates.

discussion of these issues can be found in Hastie et al. (2009: 423–426) and Bishop (2006: 294–299). A more intuitive treatment can be found in Berk (2008: 312–314).

There has been less interest among developers of support vector machines for representing the way predictors are related to the response. Accurate classification and forecasting are the primary goals. Consequently, there is to date little that is comparable to measures of variable important and partial dependence plots. However, there seems to be no principled reason why such procedures would not be helpful. It is likely that importance measures and partial dependence plots will be available in the near future.

Support vector machine can have several operational problems. Most of the developmental work has focused on categorical response variables. For quantitative response variables, support vector machines are less well developed and somewhat harder to justify. In addition, still under development are effective ways to build in the costs of forecasting errors. Finally, support vector machines have several important tuning parameters that can dramatically affect the results. It is not yet clear how best to select the values for these tuning parameters.

Software for support vector machines can be found in a number of stand-alone procedures available over the internet. At last count, there were also three different support vector machines procedures in R. If it does not already exist, there will soon be support vector machines software commercially available. It can be a very powerful procedure.

SUMMARY AND CONCLUSIONS

Statistical learning used as a form of regression analysis has several distinctive features. There is no need for a model in the sense that criminologist use the concept. In addition, how the predictors are related to the response is determined inductively from the data. And, the need to respond to the data in a sensitive fashion leads to computer-intensive algorithms that can respond to highly local, but nonetheless important, features of the data. Finally, statistical learning output differs from conventional regression output. In particular, there are no regression coefficients. Taken together, these features can make statistical inference and casual inference highly problematic. Of course, they are often highly problematic for conventional regression as well although practitioners too often proceed nevertheless. More discussion of statistical inference and causal inference for statistical learning can be found in Berk (2008).

Statistical learning is most model-like when the goal is function estimation. But, the process by which the function is determined falls in the middle ground between confirmatory and exploratory data analysis. In practice, moreover, it will be difficult to make the case that the disturbances have the requisite properties. The enterprise, therefore, is usually very close to exploratory data analysis.

Some might find the inability to proceed in a confirmatory manner a very serious constraint. However, if the form of the model is known with confidence, much of the rationale for statistical learning evaporates. Some form of parametric regression will suffice. And, if the form of the model is unknown, or known only with great uncertainty, exploratory tools can be very liberating.

At a deeper level, statistical learning takes researchers back to first principles. The algorithms stay very close to the data and to the immediate goals of the analysis. There is no model and its attending complications standing between the researcher and the data. There is no model-based recipe either. Rather, the goal is knowledge discovery, and in practice the process is fundamentally inductive.

Acknowledgments Work on this paper was supported in part by a grant from the National Science Foundation: SES-0437169, "Ensemble Methods for Data Analysis in the Behavioral, Social and Economic Sciences." That support is gratefully acknowledged.

REFERENCES

Berk RA (2003) Regression analysis: a constructive critique. Sage Publications, Newbury Park, CA

Berk RA (2008) Statistical learning from a regression perspective. Springer, New York

Berk RA, Sherman L, Barnes G, Kurtz E, Lindsay A (2009a) Forecasting murder within a population of probationers and parolees: a high stakes application of statistical forecasting. J R Stat Soc Ser A 172(part 1):191–211

Berk RA, Brown L, Zhao L (2009b) Statistical inference after model selection. Working Paper, Department of Statistics, University of Pennsylvania

Bishop CM (2006) Pattern recognition and machine learning. Springer, New York

Breiman L (1996) Bagging predictors. Mach Learn J 26:123–140

Breiman L (2001a) Random forests. Mach Learn 45:5–32

Breiman L (2001b) Statistical modeling: two cultures (with discussion). Stat Sci 16:199–231

Breiman L, Friedman JH, Olshen RA, Stone CJ (1984) Classification and regression trees. Wadsworth Press, Monterey, CA

Buja A, Stuetzle W, Shen Y (2005) Loss functions for binary class probability estimation and classification: structure and applications. Unpublished Manuscript, Department of Statistics, The Wharton School, University of Pennsylvania

Bühlmann P, Yu B (2006) Sparse boosting. J Mach Learn Res 7:1001–1024

Cook DR, Weisberg S (1999) Applied regression including computing and graphics. Wiley, New York

Efron B, Tibshirani R (1993) Introduction to the bootstrap. Chapman & Hall, New York

Freedman DA (2004) Graphical models for causation and the identification problem. Eval Rev 28:267–293

Freedman DA (2005) Statistical models: theory and practice. Cambridge University Press, Cambridge

Freund Y, Schapire R (1996) Experiments with a new boosting algorithm. In: Machine learning: proceedings for the 13th international conference. Morgan Kaufmann, San Francisco, pp 148–156

Friedman JH (2001) Greedy function approximation: a gradient boosting machine. Ann Stat 29:189–1232

Friedman JH (2002) Stochastic gradient boosting. Comput Stat Data Anal 38:367–378

Friedman JH, Hastie T, Tibsharini R (2000) Additive logistic regression: a statistical view of boosting (with discussion). Ann Stat 28:337–407

Friedman JH, Hastie T, Rosset S, Tibsharini R, Zhu J (2004) Discussion of boosting papers. Ann Stat 32:102–107

Hastie T, Tibshirani R, Friedman J (2009) The elements of statistical learning, 2nd edn. Springer, New York

Holland P (1986) Statistics and causal inference. J Am Stat Assoc 8:945–960

Keonker R (2005) Quantile regression. Cambridge University Press, Cambridge

Kriegler B, Berk RA (2009) Estimating the homeless population in Los Angeles: an application of cost-sensitive stochastic gradient boosting. Working paper, Department of Statistics, UCLA

Leeb H, Pötscher BM (2006) Can one estimate the conditional distribution of post-model-selection estimators? Ann Stat 34(5):2554–2591

Lin Y, Jeon Y (2006) Random forests and adaptive nearest neighbors. J Am Stat Assoc 101:578–590

Mannor S, Meir R, Zhang T (2002) The consistency of greedy algorithms for classification. In: Kivensen J, Sloan RH (eds) COLT 2002. LNAI, vol 2375. pp 319–333

McCullagh P, Nelder JA (1989) Generalized linear models, 2nd edn. Chapman & Hall, New York

Mease D, Wyner AJ (2008) Evidence contrary to the statistical view of boosting. J Mach Learn 9:1–26

Mease D, Wyner AJ, Buja A (2007) Boosted classification trees and class probability/quantile estimation. J Mach Learn 8:409–439

Morgan SL, Winship C (2007) Counterfactuals and causal inference: methods and principle for social research. Cambridge University Press, Cambridge

Schapire RE (1999) A brief introduction to boosting. In: Proceedings of the 16th international joint conference on artificial intelligence

Schapire RE (2002) The boosting approach to machine learning: an overview. In: MSRI workshop on non-linear estimation and classification

Tibshirani RJ (1996) Regression shrinkage and selection via the LASSO. J R Stat Soc Ser B 25:267–288

Traskin M (2008) The role of bootstrap sample size in the consistency of the random forest algorithm. Technical Report, Department of Statistics, University of Pennsylvania

Vapnick V (1996) The nature of statistical learning theory. Springer, New York

Wyner AJ (2003) Boosting and exponential loss. In: Bishop CM, Frey BJ (eds) Proceedings of the 9th annual conference on AI and statistics, Jan 3–6, Key West, FL

Zhang T, Yu B (2005) Boosting with early stopping: convergence and consistency. Ann Stat 33(4):1538–1579

CHAPTER 35

Estimating Effects over Time for Single and Multiple Units

LAURA DUGAN

INTRODUCTION

As criminologists, we seek to more thoroughly understand the nature of change. That is, we want to know what leads to change and how we can facilitate improved change, such as less crime and more social welfare. Therefore, most of our research questions inherently ask about the changes over time. We may want to know whether crime subsides after implementing a new policy. Or, we might anticipate that delinquents will behave better once they get a college degree. Yet, much of the published research in our field relies on data measured at only one point of time. For instance, when estimating policy effects, we often compare crime rates in jurisdictions with that policy to those without it. Or, we compare the criminal behavior of college graduates to that of nongraduates. By ignoring the temporal dimension in these research questions, we often confound the cause with the effect. Furthermore, we are especially vulnerable to distorted findings when the model excludes important measures that are also related to our predictors. In fact, LaFree (1999) argues that the downturn in violent crime that began in the early 1990s caught criminologists by surprise because we had relied on cross-sectional information for our predictions.

Perhaps, this issue can be best illustrated by turning to the study of criminal hot spots. Hot spots are spatially concentrated areas of crime that are responsible for a large proportion of the crime activity in an area (Sherman et al. 1989). After observing this dynamic, policing strategies were developed to specifically combat hot spots by concentrating patrols in hot spot areas (Sherman and Weisburd 1995). While studies have consistently identified crime clusters, relatively little research examines how stable hot spots are over an extended period of time (Weisburd et al. 2004). Weisburd et al. (2004) examine the distribution of crime at street segments in Seattle annually for 14 years using trajectory analysis (see Chap. 4, in this volume). They show that hot spots are generally stable over time and that the overall crime trend is driven by changes in a relatively small proportion of places. This research is important because it explicitly models the possible changes in hot spots, more fully informing the police about their dynamics. More recently, others have more directly examined patterns of space–time clustering, demonstrating the importance of integrating the space and time

A.R. Piquero and D. Weisburd (eds.), *Handbook of Quantitative Criminology*,
DOI 10.1007/978-0-387-77650-7_35, © Springer Science + Business Media, LLC 2010,
First softcover printing 2011

dimensions to better understand the different spatio-temporal footprints of distinct crimes (Grubesic and Mack 2008), as well as how risk might change once a nearby household is burglarized (Johnson et al. 2007).

While the integration of spatial and temporal analysis is beyond the scope of this chapter, the aforementioned examples raise the importance of connecting our research questions with the appropriate research method. As most of our research questions are inherently dynamic, criminologists have more recently adopted the methods to analyze changes over time. This chapter is designed to introduce the reader to a set of methodological choices to estimate the effects of changes in an independent variable on a dependent variable. I will begin by outlining several methodological options when the scholar has repeated measures of a single unit. I will then discuss several options when many units are repeatedly measured. Finally, this chapter will conclude with a discussion meant to guide the readers' methodological decisions while analyzing dynamic data.

STRATEGIES TO ESTIMATING EFFECTS OF CHANGES IN X ON CHANGES IN Y

This chapter is not intended to imply that by modeling changes over time we can establish causality. It is, however, intended to demonstrate that if experimental data are unavailable, by modeling temporal data, we can improve our efforts to reduce the model's vulnerability to misleading biases and take us closer to establishing causality. By imposing the temporal restriction that changes in X must have occurred prior to changes in Y, we are better able to rule out the possibility that the reverse relationship is driving any correlation (i.e., Y caused X). For example, if we find in a cross-sectional study that youth who work tend to participate in antisocial behavior, it would be naïve to conclude that working causes delinquency. Instead, those youths who are drawn toward antisocial behavior might choose to work in order to finance their activities. By modeling activity before and after work, the causal relationship can be better disentangled (see Paternoster et al. 2003 for a discussion of employment and delinquency).

Many strategies exist to model temporal data. In order to decide upon the best approach, the criminologist must turn to two sources for guidance, the theory and the data. Ideally, theory can direct the type of data collection that is best suited for each research question. Yet, collecting temporal data takes resources and time, which are often not readily available. Thus, it is often more efficient to rely on existing data sources to address research questions. The remainder of this chapter is organized according to the types of data. I begin by discussing several methodological options available when using data on repeated measures of a single unit. I then turn to the options available when using data on repeated measures of multiple units.

Repeated Measures of One Unit

Oftentimes, our research question is directed exclusively toward better understanding changes in a macro condition for an important locality, such as a state or country. Perhaps, the most common criminological example is the study of the changes in the U.S. homicide rate (Pridemore et al. 2008; LaFree 2005; LaFree and Drass 2002; McDowall 2002; Kaminski and Marvell 2002) because it has been consistently measured over a long period. Scholars have also used time series to study changes in other patterns, such as burglaries (Chamlin and Cochran 1998), arrest rates (LaFree and Drass 1996) number of fugitives (Goldkamp and Vilcica 2008), and disparities in sentencing outcomes (Stolzenberg and D'Alessio 1994). By tracking these events over time, we can develop a deeper understanding of the conditions that are related to their rise and fall, or boom and bust. In fact, a large portion of research conducted using time series focuses exclusively on changes in the dependent variable (LaFree 2005; Messner et al. 2005; LaFree and Drass 2002; McDowall 2002; O'Brien 1999). Other research models time trends by estimating their changes after a single intervention using interrupted time series (Pridemore et al. 2008; Goldkamp and Vilcica 2008; D'Alessio and Stolzenberg 1995; Cochran et al. 1994). Others incorporate multiple independent variables, while correcting the error structures due to dependence in the measures over time (Cohn and Rotton 1997; LaFree and Drass 1996; Jacobs and Helms 1996). Finally, criminologists have just begun to examine the mutual relationships between multiple time series (Witt and Witte 2000).

While the focus of this chapter is to present methods to estimate the effects of independent variables on a dependent variable over time, I turn first to a brief discussion on important considerations when modeling changes in a dependent variable. Generally, an ideal dependent variable is *stationary*, which means that the error term has a fixed distribution that remains constant over time. Furthermore, in a stationary series, the covariance between any two values is a function of the amount of time between them, not the specific value of time (i.e., $Cov[y_t, y_s] = f(t - s)$ not $f(t)$ or $f(s)$) (Greene 2008; Banerjee et al. 1993). In essence, we want a dependent variable to appear flat, with a constant variance, without a trend or any evidence of seasonality. To demonstrate the importance of analyzing only stationary series,

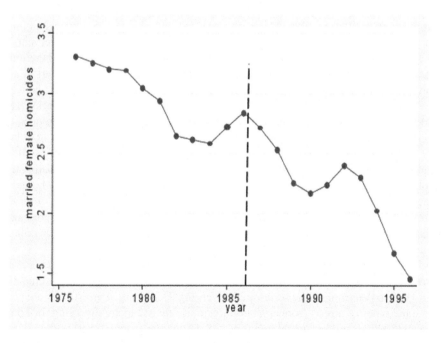

FIGURE 35.1. Nonstationary trend in the married female homicide victimization rate before and after a 1986 intervention. Source: Supplementary Homicide Reports, Uniform Crime Reports.

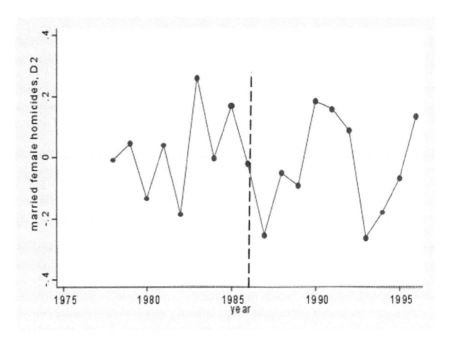

FIGURE 35.2. Stationary trend in the married female homicide victimization rate before and after a 1986 intervention. Source: Supplementary Homicide Reports, Uniform Crime Reports.

consider the following example. Figure 35.1 shows the changing rate of homicides perpetrated against wives from 1976 to 1996. The vertical dashed line around 1986 depicts an intervention. If we were to compare the average homicide rates before and after the intervention, we would conclude that homicide was lower after the intervention, suggesting that the intervention successfully reduced homicides. Yet, the drop in homicide after 1986 is part of a larger nonstationary trend that began well before 1986. Fig. 35.2 shows little difference between the average pre- and post-1986 rates, after transforming the data to a stationary series. Had we not addressed the nonstationarity of the series, the findings would have been erroneous.

Tests for stationarity can be preformed, and if the series fails these tests, the data can usually be transformed into a stationary series, depending on the nature of its nonstationarity. For example, if a nonstationary series is found to have a unit root, then by subtracting the previous observation from the current observation (first-differencing) the series will be stationary (Greene 2008). Once the series is stationary, we are better able to predict future observations. More relevant to this chapter, we are able to estimate changes in the series that are due to the changes in other relevant conditions, which could be discrete such as events or policies, or continuous, such as rates or other values.

As noted earlier, value can be gained by exclusively studying patterns of change in dependent variables. O'Brien (1999) examines the arrest rates for both males and females from 1960 to 1995 to determine if the series are converging. He finds that arrest rates are converging for some types of arrests (robbery, burglary, motor theft) but are diverging for homicide. McDowall (2002) examines annual trends of U.S. homicides from 1925 to 1998 to determine if the series is nonlinear. A nonlinear homicide trend suggests that the mechanisms that lead to more homicides are at least partially self-generating (McDowall 2002). He is unable to detect a nonlinear pattern in homicide. LaFree and Drass (2002) test for booms, or rapid increases, in homicide victimization for 34 nations from 1956 to 1998 to determine the validity of the claim by globalizationalists that crime booms are universal since the Second World War. They found little support for that claim.

Since the purpose of this chapter is to discuss the various methods to estimate the effects of independent variables on dependent variables over time, the remainder of the chapter focuses on this type of modeling. First, I will introduce the basic time series model that allows for multiple independent variables, as it corrects for dependence of the error terms. Then, the chapter introduces interrupted time series, which estimates the effects of a single intervention on the time trend. This section of the chapter ends by introducing vector autoregression (VAR) to examine the relationship between two or more dependent variables.

AUTOREGRESSIVE TIME SERIES.   The simplest of time series models is constructed by simply adding independent variables as predictors of the dependent variable. While simple, since time series data are not generated from a random process, this strategy must consider the inherent dependence across observations that is absent from cross-sectional analysis. The time series process is characterized by its time ordering and the systematic correlation between observations (Greene 2008). Consider the model,

$$y_t = \beta_1 + \beta_2 x_t + \varepsilon_t, \tag{35.1}$$

where $\text{cov}(\varepsilon_t, \varepsilon_s)$ is a function only of $|t - s|$, the distance between the two observations. This stationary assumption allows us to explicitly model the nature of the correlation between error terms. The covariance is often expressed as the matrix, $\sigma^2 \Omega$, where the diagonals of the Ω are all one and the covariance across observations is depicted by the values of the off-diagonals.

Different types of time series processes will produce different Ω matrices. Perhaps, the most commonly used is the first-order autoregressive process, AR(1), which has the following error structure,

$$\varepsilon_t = \rho \varepsilon_{t-1} + u_t, \tag{35.2}$$

where ρ is the correlation between all contiguous error terms, and u_t is stationary and independently distributed (i.i.d.). More generally, according to the AR(1) process, ε_t is a function of $\rho^i \varepsilon_{t-i}$. Thus, for this process, ρ is the only parameter to be estimated, and the effect of prior errors on current errors will fade over time. For example, a relatively large portion of the violent crime rate in January (ρ) might directly affect violence in February. Consequently, that smaller portion of February's violence that was affected by January (ρ^2) might bleed into March's violent crime rate. This indirect effect is much weaker having gone through February to get to March. By June or July, the consequences of the original violence that has passed from month to month is nearly gone (ρ^5 and ρ^6).

Furthermore, the autoregressive model becomes more complicated if we think that the actual process includes separate correlations from errors in earlier periods that directly affect the error in the current period. For example, if a delayed shock from two periods ago directly affects the current period (e.g., violence in January directly affects violence in March), we may model the data using an AR(2) model. This would occur if the data had a cyclical or some other more involved pattern.

There are a number of ways to test for first-order autocorrelation. All methods, however, follow the same general idea of estimating the least squares coefficient of e_t on e_{t-1}, where e is the residual from the sample data (Greene 2008). Common tests include the Lagrange Multiplier test, Box and Pierce's test (Q-test), and the Durbin–Watson test and are found in most statistical packages.[1] Once the tests are completed and autocorrelation is detected, corrected estimates can be generated from transformations (if Ω is know) or by using the Prais–Winsten or Corchrane–Orcutt estimators if Ω is unknown (see Greene 2008 for details).[2]

Perhaps, the most cited criminological piece that uses this autoregressive time series approach is work by Cantor and Land (1985), which estimates the effect of levels and changes in unemployment on several types of crimes in the U.S from 1946 to 1982 by hypothesizing that the relationship is a function of both motivation and opportunity. In this article, the authors explore several strategies to stabilize the data by log transforming it and taking first and second differences. They select the model with the fewest number of transformations that produces a Durbin–Watson statistic that indicates no autocorrelation. Findings demonstrate both the positive and negative effects of economic activity on crime. Others have since explored variations to the Cantor and Land study by including inflation rates as an additional measure of economic distress (Devine et al. 1988), by focusing exclusively on youth (Britt 1994), by disaggregating by age and time period (Britt 1997), and by disaggregating by age and race (Smith et al. 1992). In general, the relationship between unemployment and crime is more equivocal among disaggregated groups.[3]

In another analysis, Jacobs and Helms (1996) use time series to estimate the effects of lagged social, political and economic determinants on yearly shifts in U.S. prison admissions from 1950 to 1990. They begin their investigation by testing the series for unit roots and intercorrelations using the augmented Dickey–Fuller test; and find that they need to first-difference the dependent variable and several independent variables in order to stabilize the series. After the series was stationary, they corrected for autocorrelation by using the Marquardt AR1 procedure available in Micro TSP (Jacobs and Helms 1996). Findings suggest that incarceration rates are driven by social inequality, the strength of the Republican Party and whether it was a presidential election year. Surprisingly, unemployment is unrelated to prison admissions. In another analysis, Cohn and Rotton (1997) used 3 hour intervals as their unit of analysis and test whether the relationship between hot temperatures and assaults is stronger during the evening using data on 911 calls and weather conditions in Minneapolis for 2 years. They include in their analysis controls for important temporal indicators, such as the 7 days, of the week, the 12 months of the year, welfare dispersion days and holidays. They calculated Prais–Winsten estimates to correct the standard errors due to the autoregressive error structure of the data. Results confirmed their hypothesis.

Despite the relative simplicity of testing and correcting for the autoregressive process shown in equation (35.1), criminologists have published relatively few articles using this approach. Instead, the literature suggests that we are more drawn toward modeling

---

[1] If the model includes a lagged dependent variable, the Durbin–Watson statistic will be biased toward no autocorrelation. Turn to Greene (2008: 646) for an adjustment to the Durbin–Watson statistic for the lagged dependent variable. The other two tests produce unbiased estimates regardless of whether the lagged dependent variable is included in the model.

[2] Autocorrelation can also be problematic in panel data. See Greene (2008) for more detail.

[3] This approached used by Cantor and Land (1985) and the others has been criticized by Greenberg (2001). Greenberg explains that nonstationary crime rates are more likely explained by variables that also follow nonstationary processes (unemployment is stationary). Greenberg (2001) shows that while crime and divorce are each nonstationary, when combined they follow a stationary process, suggesting that they are cointegrated (Banerjee et al. 1993). By using error correction models that account for cointegration instead of relying on first- or second-differencing, long term effects can be estimated. See Britt (2001) for continued discussion in this debate.

Autoregressive Integrated Moving Average (ARIMA) models, which more comprehensively address all potential processes of the time series error term. The following section introduces interrupted time series, which is one application of the ARIMA model.

INTERRUPTED TIME SERIES. Oftentimes, we are interested in estimating the impact on a series due to a change in a condition or an intervention. For example, D'Alessio and Stolzenberg (1995) test whether the adoption of sentencing guidelines in Minnesota systematically changed the level of incarceration in that state. For this type of problem, the dependent variable is measured repeatedly both before and after the intervention. If the pattern of incarceration after the intervention differs from the preintervention pattern, then results suggest that the intervention had an impact. However, as noted earlier, the inherent dependence of the error terms of time series data will cause estimation problems. Thus, before estimating any intervention effect, we must first adequately model the structure of the error. After accommodating for the error structure using an ARIMA model, differences between the pre- and postintervention series can be tested (McDowall et al. 1980). The three components of this model, autoregressive, integrative, and moving average can be thought of as three specific forms of dependence that can be found in time series data, often referred to as ARIMA(p,d,q).[4] Furthermore, as with the AR(p) process discussed earlier, this dependence can be between the current and previous measures of any order or length of lag. However, in social science, most orders are rather low, most commonly one and sometimes two (Cook and Campbell 1979; McDowall et al. 1980; Greene 2008).

In practice, we begin by determining whether the series is *integrated*, or summed. If the series is summed, it follows a "random walk" pattern, where the next value of y_t is a summation of the starting value of $Y(y_0)$, all the previous random shocks $(\varepsilon_1 + \varepsilon_2 + \ldots + \varepsilon_{t-1})$, and the current random shock, ε_t. Integrated processes are nonstationary and tend to drift or trend upward or downward depending on the mean of the random shock (McDowall et al. 1980). To formally investigate whether the series is integrated, we can examine the Autocorrelation Function (ACF) which produces the correlations between the current and the lagged values in the series (see McDowall et al. 1980 or Greene 2008 for a derivation of the ACF).[5] If the series is integrated, the correlations will all be large and significant. Integrated series can be made stationary by first-differencing the data, (i.e., $\Delta y_t = y_t - y_{t-1}$). If taking the first differences fails to make the series stationary, the series can be differenced again. In fact, the series should be differenced until the correlations in the ACF are not all large and significant (Greene 2008).[6] In essence, first-differencing removes linear trend, second-differencing removes any quadratic trend, third- removes a cubic trend, and so on (Cantor and Land 1985). The d-value in the ARIMA(p,d,q) model reports the number of times the series is differenced.

---

[4] Most standard statistical packages run ARIMA models.

[5] $ACF(k) = \dfrac{\sum\limits_{i=1}^{N} (Y_i - \bar{Y})(Y_{i+k} - \bar{Y})}{\sum\limits_{i=1}^{N} (Y_i - \bar{Y})^2} \left(\dfrac{N}{N-k}\right)$ (Cook and Campbell 1979; McDowall et al. 1980).

[6] Some of correlations in the ACF can still be large in a stationary series; however, they will follow a pattern consistent with an autoregressive or moving average process.

Once the series is stationary, it can be examined to determine whether it follows an autoregressive process, a moving average process, or both. The first order autoregressive process, ARIMA(1,0,0),[7] takes the following form:

$$y_t = \Phi_1 y_{t-1} + \varepsilon_t, \tag{35.3}$$

where Φ_1 is the correlation between the current and previous value of y. Mathematically, the correlations between the current and earlier lags are $\Phi_1{}^k$, where k is the number of lags (McDowall et al. 1980). Thus, the correlations in the ACF for an ARIMA(1,0,0) process follow the following pattern, Φ_1, $\Phi_1{}^2$, $\Phi_1{}^3$, ... $\Phi_1{}^{t-1}$; such that previous measures have an exponentially decreasing effect on the current value of y. Again, the effects of January's violence decreases as they pass through each additional month. When higher orders of the autoregressive process are present, then previous lags have a direct relationship with the current value of y (e.g., January directly affects March or April). More generally, an ARIMA(p,0,0) process takes the following form:

$$y_t = \Phi_1 y_{t-1} + \Phi_2 y_{t-2} + \ldots + \Phi_p y_{t-p} + \varepsilon_t. \tag{35.4}$$

As noted earlier, most social science series follow rather low orders of autoregressive processes, remaining usually at an ARIMA(1,0,0) and sometimes an ARIMA(2,0,0) process (McDowall et al. 1980). In fact, Greene (2008) states generally that higher order ARIMA(p,0,0) processes usually indicate that the series is nonstationary.

The first order moving average process, ARIMA(0,0,1), takes the following form:

$$y_t = \varepsilon_t - \theta_1 \varepsilon_{t-1}, \tag{35.5}$$

where the value of the current y_t is comprised of the current shock, ε_t and a portion of the preceding shock ε_{t-1}. An important feature of the ARIMA(0,0,1) process is that correlations beyond the first lag drop to zero (McDowall et al. 1980), making it relatively easier to discern between an ARIMA(1,0,0) and an ARIMA(0,0,1) process. The ACF is also a useful tool to identify the order of an ARIMA(0,0,q) process, which is generally written as:

$$y_t = \varepsilon_t - \theta_1 \varepsilon_{t-1} - \theta_2 \varepsilon_{t-2} - \ldots - \theta_q \varepsilon_{t-q}. \tag{35.6}$$

The ACF for the ARIMA(0,0,q) process will only produce significant correlations for q lags, making it relatively easy to identify the order of the moving average process.

It is more challenging to identify the order of an ARIMA(p,0,0) model. Because the subsequent correlations in the lags of the ACF gradually decrease, an ARIMA(1,0,0) looks quite similar to an ARIMA(2,0,0). Here, the Partial Autocorrelation Function (PACF) can be used. The PACF reports only the direct correlation between the current y_t and y_{t-k}. The effects of intervening lags have been "partialed out" of the function (McDowall et al. 1980: 41; Greene 2008). Thus, the PACF for an ARIMA(1,0,0) process only produces a significant correlation for the first lag. That for an ARIMA(2,0,0) process produces significant correlations for the first two lags. In contrast, the correlations in the PACF for an ARIMA(0,0,q)

---

[7] For simplicity, the ARIMA(1,0,0) is written as if the series needed no differencing. The text could also refer a differenced ARIMA(1,d,0) process.

process gradually reduce to zero with later lags. Thus, the combination of the ACF and PACF allows the scholar to discern between ARIMA(p,0,0) and ARIMA(0,0,q) processes (McDowall et al. 1980).[8] Mixed ARIMA(p,0,q) processes are less common, and are often difficult to discern. In fact, the ACFs and PACFs of ARIMA(2,0,1) and (1,0,2) models look similar (Cook and Campbell 1979).[9] Having said that, there may be one or two spikes in first correlations of the ACF (representing the order of the MA process) followed by more gradual declines in the magnitude of the correlations in the later lags (Greene 2008). McDowall et al. (1980) point out that because of parameter redundancy, mixed ARIMA(p,0,q) processes usually simplify to an ARIMA(p,0,0) or an ARIMA(0,0,q) process.[10]

Time series data can also have seasonal correlations that correspond to systematic and cyclical changes over time. For example, crime generally rises on weekends compared to weekdays (Cohn and Rotton 1997). Thus, in a daily time series of criminal activity, positive correlations are found between observations measured 7 days apart. ARIMA models easily account for seasonal correlations by explicitly estimating autoregressive or moving average parameters for the specified lags. In the daily time series mentioned earlier, the ARIMA model can account for correlations between the current y_t and y_{t-7}. See Cook and Campbell (1979), McDowall et al. (1980) or Greene (2008) for a discussion of seasonality.

Once the process has been identified and accounted for, the series is now considered "white noise" or purely random. This allows us to test for a systematic difference between the pre- and postinterruption or intervention period. However, the nature of the intervention effect might differ across contexts. These differences can mostly be characterized in a function that depicts how they begin and how long they lasted (Cook and Campbell 1979; McDowall et al. 1980). Its beginning will be abrupt if the change is immediate once the intervention is implemented. Or the effects of the intervention might be more gradual, slowly or quickly building to its full potential. Furthermore, the intervention might produce permanent or temporary effects. Table 35.1 shows the transfer function, or operationalization, of the intervention used to appropriately estimate the beginning and duration of the effects. Note that I_{t+} is a dummy variable that equal 0 prior to the intervention and 1 after the intervention. Also, I_t is a dummy variable that is 0 for all periods except for that containing the intervention. The parameters ω and δ represent the magnitude of the effect and gradient of its rise or fall, respectively. See Cook and Campbell (1979) for the derivation of these functions.

Notice that no function provides for a gradual, temporary change, which cannot be modeled easily (McDowall et al. 1980). Also notice that the first function is imbedded in the second. Similarly, the second and third are nearly identical. This suggests that the nature of

TABLE 35.1. Operationalization of estimated effects of an intervention

Expected effect	Transfer function
Abrupt, constant change	$Y_t = \omega I_{t+} + noise$
Gradual, constant change	$Y_t = \delta Y_{t-1} + \omega I_{t+} + noise$
Abrupt, temporary change	$Y_t = \delta Y_{t-1} + \omega I_t + noise$

---

[8] Most standard statistical packages will produce ACF and PACF tables. For example, the Stata command corrgram will produce a table the autocorrelations, partial autocorrelations, and the Portmantequ (Q) statistics for time series data. The commands AC and PAC produce a graphical version of the ACF and PACF values.

[9] See Cook and Campbell (1979: 247–250) for a more thorough discussion of mixed models.

[10] By repeated substitution, autoregressive processes can take a moving average form (Greene 2008).

the effect can be empirically determined, absent any guiding theory. McDowall et al. (1980) suggest that the scholar start by modeling the abrupt, temporary intervention component. If the estimate of δ is near one, then the effects of the intervention is likely constant. Next, the scholar should model the gradual, constant change intervention component. If the estimate of δ is too small and insignificant, then the intervention is best modeled using the function for an abrupt, constant change.

This method has been applied by criminologists to a wide variety of situations. Some have modeled changes in policy, such as work by Loftin et al. (1983) who tested the claim that a 1977 gun law in Michigan that imposed an additional 2 years to a felon's sentence would deter criminal behavior. The only crime that seemed to be affected by the intervention was gun homicide. However, since the number of gun assaults was unaffected by the interventions, the authors conclude that the law was ineffective. Goldkamp and Vilcica (2008) use interrupted time series to find a significant rise in the number of fugitives in Philadelphia after a targeted drug enforcement policy was implemented. Work by Stolzenberg and D'Alessio (1994) and D'Alessio and Stolzenberg (1995) estimates the impact of the adoption of Minnesota's sentencing guidelines on changes in unwarranted disparity and the judicial use of the jail sanction. They find less disparity and more incarceration since implementation. Finally, Simpson et al. (2006) use interrupted time series to detect an increase in arrests after the adoption of a pro-arrest policy for domestic violence.

Criminologists have also used this method to test for changes in outcomes after events that were not imposed by policy. For example, recent work by Pridemore et al. (2008) estimates the effects of the Oklahoma City bombing and the September 11th attacks on homicides at the local and state levels. Their findings show that the attacks neither increased nor decreased lethal violence. Cochran et al. (1994) did find evidence that after Oklahoma executed Charles Troy Coleman in 1990, the number of stranger homicides increased, supporting their brutalization hypothesis. Other nonpolicy relationships that have been tested using interrupted time series include changes in oil prices on burglary (Chamlin and Cochran 1998) and the fall of the Soviet Union on homicide and other social ills (Pridemore et al. 2007).

While interrupted time series implies only one interruption, D'Alessio and Stolzenberg (1995) used an ARIMA model to estimate the impact of the initial adoption of sentencing guidelines and two modifications (42 and 111 months after the initial adoption). Furthermore, other covariates can easily be added to the model as controls. In fact, Autoregressive Moving Average with eXogeneous inputs (ARMAX) refers to ARMA models that allow the error structure to also be estimated by a linear combination of independent variables (Stata Press 2005).

MULTIPLE TIME SERIES.   Oftentimes, we are interested in how two or more series relate to each other. For example, Witt and Witte (2000) examined the mutual or endogenous relationships between crime, prison, and economic factors, and found among other things, a long-run negative impact of prison on crime. Also, we may want to estimate the impact of one or more exogenous events on multiple series. When events are exogenous, then their causes are independent of all series outcomes, thus making the causal direction exclusively from the event to the outcomes. Enders and Sandler (1993) estimated the impact of six counter-terrorist interventions on several series of specific terrorist tactical attacks including skyjacking, hostage taking, and others. Their analytical strategy was possible due to research in the early 1970s by Sims (1972) who developed a new approach to examine the causal direction between two dependent variables (money stock and income).[11] With this approach, the inter-dynamics between multiple series of variables avoid relying on the identification assumptions necessary to correctly specify contemporaneous relationships when using structural equation modeling (see Brandt and Williams 2007 for a thorough discussion).

Vector autoregression (VAR) is an interdependent reduced form series of equations where each series is a function of its past values and the past values of the other endogeneous variables.[12] With VAR, the contemporaneous relationships are directly included in the parameterization of the residual covariance (Brandt and Williams 2007). Mathematically, this series of equations is shown as

$$
\begin{aligned}
y_{1t} &= \beta_{10} + \beta_{11} y_{1,t-1} + \ldots + \beta_{1,p} y_{1,t-p} + \ldots + \beta_{1,m} y_{m,t-1} + \ldots + \beta_{1,mp} y_{m,t-p} + \varepsilon_{1t} \\
y_{2t} &= \beta_{20} + \beta_{21} y_{1,t-1} + \ldots + \beta_{2,p} y_{1,t-p} + \ldots + \beta_{2,m} y_{m,t-1} + \ldots + \beta_{2,mp} y_{m,t-p} + \varepsilon_{2t} \\
&\vdots \\
y_{mt} &= \beta_{m0} + \beta_{m1} y_{1,t-1} + \ldots + \beta_{m,p} y_{1,t-p} + \ldots \beta_{m,m} y_{m,t-1} + \ldots + \beta_{m,mp} y_{m,t-p} + \varepsilon_{mt}
\end{aligned}
\tag{35.7}
$$

where m is the number of endogenous variables and p is the number of lags.[13] Brandt and Williams (2007) show that these equations can be simplified by repeating them in their vector form. By allowing y_t to be a vector of all the current measures of all the endogenous variables, $\boldsymbol{\beta}_\ell$ to be a matrix of all the coefficients, and c to be a vector of intercepts, (35.7) can be simplified to the following form,

$$
y_t = c + \sum_{\ell=1}^{p} y_{t-\ell} \boldsymbol{\beta}_\ell + \varepsilon_t.
\tag{35.8}
$$

Since $\varepsilon_t \sim N(0, \Sigma \otimes I)$, meaning that there is no autocorrelation between the residuals and their past values or other variables past residuals, the equations can be estimated as a series of separate Ordinary Least Squares models (Brandt and Williams 2007). However, statistical packages like Stata have built to commands to estimate these models and perform related diagnostics (Stata Press 2005).

The above equations naturally lead to the question of how many lags are appropriate for the model. The general consensus is that the lags should be long enough to capture a full cycle of data as well as any residual seasonality. In fact, by modeling the appropriate number of lags, all autocorrelation is absorbed into the model, leaving the residuals as white noise. Following this logic, quarterly data should include about six quarters, and monthly data should include 13 to 15 lags (Brandt and Williams 2007). If the series is short, it may be necessary to limit the number of lags, as Witt and Witte (2000) did, including only two lags for 38 annual observations. Enders and Sandler (1993) used quarterly data and tested their results for lags of 2, 4, and 8. Likelihood ratio tests and information criteria statistics can more formally determine the optimal number of lags appropriate for the model (Brandt and Williams 2007). Since by

---

[11] He finds that Granger causality is unidirectional from money stock to income, dismissing arguments that changes in income lead to changes in money stock.

[12] This system works better if the variables are stationary. This can be easily determined using the augmented Dickey–Fuller test, which is found in most statistical packages. If the data are nonstationary, it is usually recommended that the analyst estimate Vector Error Correction Models (Stata Press 2005; Greenberg 2001). However, others suggest that there is still value in estimating VAR if the short-term dynamics are the main focus of the analysis (Brandt and Williams 2007).

[13] This notation is borrowed from Brandt and Williams (2007).

using more lags in the model, the residuals are less likely to be autocorrelated (with its own past values) or cross-correlated (with past residuals of other variables), multivariate tests of autocorrelation, such as the Portmanteau test or Legrange multiplier test, can also be used to select the appropriate number of lags. For example, although Witt and Witte (2000) incorporated only two lags, diagnostics show that two lags are sufficient to remove autocorrelation. General practice is to overfit the VAR model with a large number of lags and then to scale back to the most parsimonious model that is absent of autocorrelation (Brandt and Williams 2007). In essence, the lag length should be long enough to produce residuals that are white noise and long enough to produce unbiased and efficient estimates.

Once the lag length is established, it can be determined whether the variables Granger cause one another. Granger causality is described by Brandt and Williams (2007: 32; see also Granger 1969) as "... Y_t Granger causes Z_t if the behavior of past Y_t can better predict the behavior of Z_t than Z_t's past alone." To test for Granger causality, scholars can either conduct a likelihood ratio test or an F-test where the unrestricted model is the full model with all lags from the other exogenous variables, and the restricted model includes only the lagged dependent variable (Sims 1972; Brandt and Williams 2007).[14] We can also think of this as a test for exogeneity, where exogeneity is the null condition. If, indeed, the results of this test favored the unrestricted model, we would conclude that one or more of the variables are mutually related, or endogenous. Witt and Witte (2000) were able to show that durable good consumption and female labor force participation were exogenous to crime.

While it is important to determine whether there are mutual relationships among the variables, exogeneity tests tell us very little about the nature of the relationship between the variables. There are a number of strategies designed to better inform us about the magnitude and dynamics of the estimates generated by the VAR. First, we can decompose the error variance to determine how much of the variance in the predicted path of each variable is due to the past values of the other variables in each equation (Brandt and Williams 2007). In Enders and Sandler's (1993) examination of terrorist tactics, they were able to show that changes in skyjackings explain about 17% of the forecast error variance in attacks against protected persons, such as diplomats and military officials.[15] A second method to estimate the dynamic impact of the variables on one another is to calculate the impulse response function that graphically displays the effect of a shock (usually one standard deviation in magnitude) on itself and other variables. By using confidence bands that incorporate the error generated from the dependent variable as well as that drawn from the covariance between the two variables, we are able to determine the change in the magnitude and significance of all effects over a time horizon (Brandt and Williams 2007).[16] Witt and Witte (2000) present the impulse response functions for their prison-crime model and show, among other things, that the growth in the prison population has a negative impact on crime that disappears by the sixth year.

---

[14] Stata has a post estimation command vargranger that performs pairwise Granger causality tests after running VAR (Stata Press 2005).

[15] This decomposition is done by first inverting the VAR to its Vector Moving Average representation (VMA) and then decomposing the error covariance matrix. This method is sensitive to the ordering of the variables and all orderings should be considered (Brandt and Williams 2007). The Stata post estimation command fevd (forecast-error variance decompositions) calculates these values.

[16] This method also relies on inverting the VAR to its VMA representation and then decomposing the error variance matrix. Once again, all orderings should be considered (Brandt and Williams 2007). The Stata post estimation command irf (impulse-response functions) produce these graphs.

While this section has outlined the value of using VAR to estimate the mutual effects of multiple variables over time, there are limitations to this method. First, all series must be covariance stationary (Brandt and Williams 2007). Nonstationary series, or series with long-memoried processes (unit root or cointegrated) compromise the validity of the Granger causality tests. While solutions to this problem are not as simple as differencing the data, alternate strategies such as fully modified VAR (Freemen et al. 1998) and vector error correction models (VECM) (Brandt and Williams 2007; Greenberg 2001; Banerjee et al. 1993) can be used to estimate the parameters. In fact, Witt and Witte (2000) estimate their model using VECM after an augmented Dickey–Fuller test uncovers cointegration in their series. A second limitation in VAR analysis is that it estimates such a large number of parameters that the estimates could be inefficient and vulnerable to type II error.

OTHER METHODS TO MODEL SINGLE UNITS OVER TIME.   Other methods can be used to estimate the effects of an independent variable on a dependent variable for repeated measures of a single unit over time. For example, spline regression can be used to model structural breaks in any stationary time series (see Marsh and Cormier 2002). A breakdate occurs in the period when one of the parameters in the series changes (Hansen 2001). If there is a known intervention or event, interrupted time series can easily be used to model the structural break. However, if the breakdate or dates are unknown, they can be estimated empirically (Marsh and Cormier 2002; Hansen 2001). Messner et al. (2005) use spline regression to locate structural breaks in city-level homicide trends to identify cities that exhibit a meaningful boom and bust cycle.

Another method that has recently been developed to model the effect of events over time is series hazard modeling (Dugan 2009). Standard hazard models estimate the effect of independent variables on the time until *one* event occurs for *many* units. In this extension of the Cox proportional hazard model, the scholar can model the time between *repeated* events for *one* unit. This strategy was first used in research by Dugan et al. (2005) to estimate the impact of several policies on the hazard of an aerial hijacking by modeling the time until the next hijacking as a function of the current policy profile, and a set of characteristics of the current hijacking event. LaFree et al. (2009) later use this strategy to estimate the impact of several operations implemented by the British government on terrorism by Republicans in Northern Ireland. Most recently, Dugan et al. (2009) use series hazard modeling to examine the effects of a devastating terrorist attack on the continued activity of two Armenian terrorist organizations.

LIMITATIONS.   While time series methods improve our efforts to understand dynamic relationships between variables, they do have their limits. First, because time series models the activity of only one unit, findings are rarely generalizeable beyond that unit. This is especially problematic with smaller units, such as neighborhoods, cities, and states. Generalizeabily is less of an issue when the unit includes the entire country or world. However, modeling large units has its own problems. Macro dynamics tell us very little about the variation across subunits. For example, models that estimate the impact of economic stressors on crime in the U.S. will likely fail to adequately describe how crime responds to economic depression in Atlanta, despite Atlanta's contribution to the data. The overall U.S. trend likely fails to uniformly describe the trends in all U.S. cities, counties, and states. Recall the finding in Weisburd et al. (2004) reporting that macro trends in Seattle were driven by activity in only a few neighborhoods. Finally, a third limitation of time series analysis is that it requires long periods of time in order to efficiently estimate models. Yet, it is often difficult to collect standardized measures over an adequately long period. One strategy to increase the degrees of freedom is to shorten the time of measurement (e.g., from years to quarters or months). However, some measures might be unavailable for the shorter periods. Furthermore, even if the data were available, the pattern in a more refined series might be too sporadic to adequately model.

Repeated Measures of Multiple Units

One strategy to improve upon all of the limitations mentioned above is to model an outcome using repeated measures of multiple units. For example, instead of modeling data in a series for a single state, we can model data from all 50 states, or a subset of states. More locations can be included in the model to improve generalizabilty and efficiency. Once the scholar has decided to use repeated measures of multiple units, the data need to be properly structured for longitudinal analysis. In contrast to cross-sectional data where each row represents one unit (N), for longitudinal data analysis, each row represents one unit (N) for one period of time (T) (e.g., a city-month or a person-year). Thus, instead of having N rows of data, we now have N × T rows.

The next decision is how to analyze the data. One simple method would be to run the analysis on the pooled N × T observations as if the data were cross-sectional as shown in the following equation,

$$y_{it} = \mathbf{X}'_{it}\boldsymbol{\beta} + \mathbf{Z}'_i\boldsymbol{\alpha} + \varepsilon_{it}, \qquad (35.9)$$

where y_{it} is the value of the dependent variable for unit i during period t.[17] $\mathbf{X}'_{it}$ is a vector of the time varying independent variables for that same unit and time period and $\mathbf{Z}'_i$ is a vector of time invariant independent variables for unit i (note that $\mathbf{Z}$ has no subscript t). Here, some variables in $\mathbf{Z}$ might be observed and others may be unobserved. The parameters $\boldsymbol{\beta}$ and $\boldsymbol{\alpha}$ are the corresponding vectors of parameter coefficients for $\mathbf{X}$ and $\mathbf{Z}$; and ε_{it} is the error term for unit i during period t.[18] While this model is rather simple, it will produce misleading results because it ignores the inherent dependence across the rows of data. The value of the error term, ε_{it}, for the same unit will be correlated across time, and error terms for the same time period will be correlated across units. Mathematically, $\mathrm{Cov}(\varepsilon_{it}, \varepsilon_{it}) \neq 0$ for $i = i$ and $t \neq t$ or for $i \neq i$ and $t = t$. By ignoring this dependence, standard errors will be artificially deflated, possibly producing erroneous significance (Greene 2008). Furthermore, if any of the unobserved independent variables in $\mathbf{Z}'_i$ is correlated with any of the observed variables in $\mathbf{X}'_{it}$ or $\mathbf{Z}'_i$, then the estimates for $\boldsymbol{\beta}$ and $\boldsymbol{\alpha}$ will be biased (Hausman and Taylor 1981).

This section formally presents two strategies to addressing the dependence of the error terms in panel data: fixed effects and random effects models. Before choosing the method that is most suitable to the research question, scholar must carefully consider the context of analyses. For example, since the fixed effects model absorbs the variation across units (population heterogeneity), theoretical approaches that make predictions that rely on this variation might be better modeled with random effects. Conversely, if important time-invariant variables are

---

[17] The notation for all equations is borrowed from Greene (2008).

[18] We could easily add another term, $\mathbf{T}'_t\boldsymbol{\gamma}$, to represent those variables that change over time, but are stable across units.

missing from the model and we suspect that these omitted variables are correlated with those in the model, the fixed effects model might be the better choice. These considerations are elaborated upon below.

FIXED EFFECTS LONGITUDINAL ANALYSIS.   Consider the following variation on equation (35.9),

$$y_{it} = \mathbf{X}'_{it}\boldsymbol{\beta} + \alpha_i + \varepsilon_{it}. \tag{35.10}$$

In this model, $\mathbf{Z}'_i\boldsymbol{\alpha}$ is replaced by α_i, which is an individual specific constant term.[19] By including these "fixed effects," we are essentially controlling for all variation across units. Thus, the model is estimated based on the variation in changes within each individual ignoring variation across individuals. In practice, this term is calculated by either producing dummy variables for all but one individual $(N - 1)$ or by subtracting the unit-specific means from all values of $\mathbf{X}'_{it}$ (most statistical packages are now able to automatically run fixed effects models). The fixed effect thus provides a unit-specific intercept vector, α_i, which estimates the deviation of that unit from the overall intercept. Since all of the time-invariant observed and unobserved variables are controlled for, the coefficient estimates are now estimating the effects of changes in $\mathbf{X}$ on changes in $\mathbf{Y}$.

While fixed effects models can be used with any level of analysis, most criminological applications tend to apply it to spatial units rather than to individuals.[20] For example, research by Dugan et al. (1999) combines data from 29 cities over multiple years to produce four time periods between 1976 and 1992 in order to estimate the effects of changes in domestic violence resources on changes in rates of intimate partner homicide (see Dugan et al. 2003 for a more recent analysis). Their model adds a fixed effect for each of the 29 cities (α_i) and a fixed effect for each of the four time periods, effectively removing the common average from every city and wave in the data. It was especially important to add time fixed effects because one could easily imagine many unobserved changes between 1976 and 1992 that are correlated with both domestic violence resources and intimate partner homicide. To reduce any bias due to simultaneity, most of the variables are lagged by one wave. Thus, the estimates are unaffected by the adoption of policies due to salient homicides during the same reporting period. Other criminological research that incorporates fixed effect models examine the effects of state-level unemployment on crime (Levitt 2001; Raphael and Winter-Ebmer 2001), and of individual-level employment on delinquency (Paternoster et al. 2003; Apel and colleagues 2008) and on victimization (Ousey et al. 2008).

Despite the importance of controlling for unobserved variation across units, fixed effects panel models have noteworthy limitations that may preclude scholars from relying exclusively on this analytical strategy. First, by controlling for each unit, the model loses efficiency, possibly dropping statistical power below levels needed to detect significance. This issue is especially problematic for panels with large N, since each fixed effect reduces the model by one degree of freedom. Relatedly, by absorbing the variation across units, little variation is left in the model from which the estimate can be drawn (Levitt 2001). Dugan et al. (2003) addressed this limitation in their more recent city-level analysis of domestic violence resources on intimate partner homicide by estimating the models using no-place effects,

---

[19] Note that we could also add a time specific constant that captures variation that is constant across units, but varies over time.

[20] Exceptions are found in the more recent population heterogeneity versus state dependency literature, which will be discussed below.

city-effects, and state-effects. Since the city-level effects were expected to be suffering least from omitted variable bias, those estimates were used to create upper and lower confidence bounds to test for possible bias in the state and no-place effects models. When the estimates from the no-place model fell within the confidence bounds, that estimate was chosen over that from the state-effects model.

Another limitation is that fixed effects modelers may become overconfident that all omitted variable bias is accounted for by the fixed effects. This model only accounts for time invariant (or unit invariant) omitted variables. It fails to account for unmeasured changes in omitted variables that might be correlated with changes in one or more of the included independent variables. Apel and colleagues (2008) directly address this issue in their study of the effects of youth employment on deviant behavior and academic achievement by using child labor laws as an instrument for within unit changes in the youths' work behavior in the fixed effects model (called fixed effects IV). Results show that the fixed effects IV models are better able to isolate the relationship between work intensity and six different outcomes (Apel and colleagues 2008). IV estimation was also used by Ousey et al. (2008) in their investigation of state dependence in victimizations because the fixed effects transformation produced negative biases in the lagged dependent variable.[21]

The above weaknesses are all methodological and should be carefully considered within the context of all panel research designs. However, at least one important substantive concern should also be carefully considered. Theoretical motivations that rely on variation across individuals cannot be tested using the fixed effects model, since that variation is essentially removed from the model. One prominent example in our literature is the debate on whether the correlation between past and current criminal behavior is more dependent on population heterogeneity, meaning differences across individuals, or on state dependence, which argues that past offending impacts subsequent criminal behavior through its influence on other variables that raise the need or desire to offend (see Nagin and Paternoster 1991, 2000). Fixed effects models essentially remove all population heterogeneity from the data, thus only informing the state dependent side of the debate. Those determined to explicitly estimate the effects of population heterogeneity have turned to random effects models.

RANDOM EFFECTS LONGITUDINAL ANALYSIS. If we can reasonably assume that the unobserved variables, $\mathbf{Z}'_i$, are uncorrelated with those included in the model, then modeling with random effects is a sensible choice. To further understand the random effects model, the following equation expands the $\mathbf{Z}'_i\boldsymbol{\alpha}$ term in (35.9) by adding and subtracting $\mathrm{E}\left[\mathbf{Z}'_i\boldsymbol{\alpha}\right]$ (Greene 2008).

$$y_{it} = \mathbf{X}'_{it}\boldsymbol{\beta} + \mathrm{E}\left[\mathbf{Z}'_i\boldsymbol{\alpha}\right] + \left\{\mathbf{Z}'\boldsymbol{\alpha} - \mathrm{E}\left[\mathbf{Z}'_i\boldsymbol{\alpha}\right]\right\} + \varepsilon_{it} \qquad (35.11)$$

Since $\mathrm{E}\left[\mathbf{Z}'_i\boldsymbol{\alpha}\right]$ is a constant, it can be replaced by α, and interpreted as the mean of the unobserved heterogeneity. The third term shows the deviation of $\mathbf{Z}'_i\boldsymbol{\alpha}$ from its expected value, which is an error term for the cross-sectional observations. By replacing that deviation with u_i, we get the following equation,

$$y_{it} = \mathbf{X}'_{\mathbf{it}}\boldsymbol{\beta} + \alpha + u_i + \varepsilon_{it}. \qquad (35.12)$$

---

[21] Their method differs from that used by Apel and colleagues (2008). Here they incorporated IV estimated with a generalized-method of moments framework.

This equation looks quite similar to the standard regression equation, except that the error term is partitioned into a group specific random element, u_i, and the standard ε_{it}, which is independently and identically distributed normally with a zero mean. We can think of the u_i as the error term that would naturally result from randomly selecting the cross-sectional observations from a larger population (Greene 2008). By modeling with random effects, the number of parameters to be estimated is greatly reduced, compared to the fixed effects model. However, as with standard regression analysis, the disturbance, u_i is assumed to be normal, an assumption that may not always be reasonable (Maddala 1987; Nagin and Paternoster 1991; Bushway et al. 1999).

As noted earlier, when criminologists use individuals as the unit of analysis (rather than geographic units), we tend to apply random effects models more often than fixed effects models. This distinction makes sense because it is more reasonable to assume that individuals are randomly drawn from a larger population than are cities, states, or countries. For example, as an introduction to the debate noted earlier, Nagin and Paternoster (1991) use random effects to discern whether the observed relationship between past and current offending is more driven by unobserved heterogeneity or state dependence. They were the first in our field to model their data using random effects. Their findings strongly suggested that persistent offending is mostly driven by state dependence, which contrasted largely with the common belief at that time that persistence in offending is largely due to population heterogeneity (Nagin and Paternoster 1991). These scholars continued with other colleagues to model individuals using random effects and consistently found evidence that state dependence explains, in part, the continuity in an offending career (Paternoster et al. 1997; Paternoster and Brame 1997; Nagin and Farrington 1992a, b).

As with fixed effects models, the random effects approach has its limitations. Perhaps most important, is that it relies on two very strong assumptions. First, it assumes that the unobserved heterogeneity is unrelated to the covariates in the model (Greene 2008). If u_i is correlated with $\mathbf{X}'_{it}$, then estimates of β will be biased and inconsistent (Hausman and Taylor 1981). This is a strong assumption that modelers face, even with cross-sectional regression analysis, where we are rarely certain that the error term is exogenous to the independent variables. Yet, Hausman and Taylor (1981) argue that by following the cross-section over time, as in panel analysis, we can test for this independence (see also Hausman 1978; Wu 1973; and Durbin 1954). Furthermore, they introduce an instrumental variable strategy that identifies an uncorrelated portion of $\mathbf{X}'_{it}$ to produce a consistent estimate of β (Hausman and Taylor 1981). The key is to use an "instrument" that is correlated with $\mathbf{X}'_{it}$ and $\mathbf{Y}$, but is uncorrelated with omitted variables to isolate the portion of $\mathbf{X}'_{it}$ that is invulnerable to omitted variable bias. Note that this is a similar strategy adopted by Apel and colleagues (2008) to address dependence in the fixed effects model. While finding an adequate instrument will better isolate the "true" effects, such instruments are often very difficult to find, requiring creativity, available data, and much luck. Hence, only a handful of criminological studies have successfully used instrumental variables to reduce omitted variable bias; and the remaining studies cautiously draw conclusions acknowledging their vulnerability to bias.

The second assumption in random effects models is that the u_i term is independently and identically normally distributed (Nagin and Paternoster 1991). Nagin and Paternoster (1991) warn that the results can be very sensitive to this distributional assumption, leading to biased estimates. Bushway et al. (1999) directly address this issue by modeling the same research question (unobserved heterogeneity versus state dependence) using different approaches to see if the results would lead to different conclusions. They compare the estimates generated from a random effects model, a fixed effects model and a semiparametric model (developed in Nagin and Land 1993) of the effect of prior offending on current offending in the 1958 Philadelphia cohort (Tracy et al. 1990). Their findings show that all three methods produce a similar, and therefore robust, estimate of the state dependence parameter (Bushway et al. 1999). Others have similarly compared findings from random and fixed effects models and found that the estimate of within variation for each produces similar results (Paternoster et al. 2003; Phillips and Greenberg 2008).

In summary, when deciding whether to use fixed or random effects, it is necessary to understand how the strengths and weaknesses of each will affect the modeling context. If the covariates in the model are likely to be correlated with the unmeasured heterogeneity, then a fixed effect model may be the best choice. However, this model is problematic if important covariates are constant over time, for they will be washed out by the fixed effects. Also, this model uses a large number of degrees of freedom, making it inefficient, possibly leading to type II errors. Another option is to use the random effects model and address the dependence of covariates on the unobserved heterogeneity by applying IV estimation to the model, as demonstrated by Hausman and Taylor (1981). To be sure that the findings of the random effects model are robust to the distributional assumption, one might follow the lead of other researchers by comparing their estimate of within subject variation to that generated from the fixed effects model. However, caution must be made when estimating the effect of a lagged dependent variable, because estimates from both the random and fixed effects models may produce erroneous results (Ousey et al. 2008).

OTHER LONGITUDINAL METHODS.   Fixed and random effects are by no means the only methods to model panel or longitudinal data. Multilevel, or random coefficient, modeling strategies have also been used to estimate effects using this data. One advantage of multilevel modeling is that it allows linear trends to vary across units (Bryk and Raudenbush 1992).[22] Rosenfeld et al. (2007) use multilevel modeling (hierarchical linear models) to estimate the effect of order-maintenance arresting on robbery and homicide rates for New York City precincts; and find modest effects. Two other methods to model longitudinal data are described in other chapters in this volume. Group-based modeling, or trajectory analysis, was developed by Daniel Nagin as a method to estimate the developmental trajectories of individuals over the life course (Chap. 4 – Nagin 2009). Independent variables can be added to the model as predictors of group membership (Nagin 2005). A similar methodology, latent growth curve trajectories can also be used to model the changes in individuals' developmental trajectories. Petras and Masyn (2009) demonstrates in this book how to analyze longitudinal data using this method in Chap. 5 of this book.

DISCUSSION

Because so much of our theoretical and practical research interests in criminology typically follow the question "If X changed, would Y change too?" this chapter was designed to introduce the basic foundations of estimating the effects of X on Y for time series and longitudinal data. While the universe of modeling options for both of these data types encompasses far

---

[22] Multilevel modeling can be accomplished using a variety of statistical software packages such as Stata, SAS and SPSS. The packages HLM, MLwinN, aML, and WINBUGS were explicitly designed to estimate multilevel models.

more than what could reasonably be included in a single chapter, readers should by now have a reasonable idea of which methods are most appropriate for their research questions, given the available data.

When either the research question or the available data limits the scholar to modeling one unit over time, she or he could choose from several methods of time series. Regardless of methodological choice, all seem to follow the general theme of first assuring that the series is stationary, and then modeling the correlation of the error structure. From the literature, it appears that the decision to use an autoregressive model or an ARIMA model is based on individual preference and discipline. As criminologists, we have used both, while more recently preferring ARIMA. Tests for autocorrelation may not detect moving average processes, making ARIMA modeling the more comprehensive choice. Also, by examining the output from the ACF and PACF functions, we can easily observe the error structure of the uncorrected and corrected models making our modeling decisions more tangible. Further, by including an intervention, interrupted time series allows us to more intuitively estimate the changes in temporal patterns after an event. Finally, since ARIMA models can easily incorporate multiple independent variables, there are fewer advantages to relying only on autoregressive time series.

Finally, we have become increasingly aware of how important it is to account for the intricate relationships between multiple series. Often the causal relationship we hope to model is confounded by mutual dynamics among the predictors. For example, social conditions could be driven by criminal activity which, in turn, might lead to more or less crime, shifting social conditions, and so on. While researchers have found that unemployment is exogenous to crime, it has been shown that divorce rates follow the same patterns as crime rates, suggesting that both series should be modeled together (Greenberg 2001). Also, exogenous variables could affect a series either directly or indirectly through a related series. By modeling multiple series, we can disentangle these relationships and more precisely understand the nature of how X affects Y. Multiple series can easily be modeled using VAR for stationary series and error correction models for nonstationary or cointegrated series.

When the research question is best answered with repeated measures of multiple units, the scholar has several methodological choices. Figure 35.3 maps out a subset of these choices using a decision tree. The bottom of this figure shows only four strategies to modeling longitudinal data (the non-italicized referring to the models discussed in this chapter). As demonstrated by other chapters in this volume, there are more than four ways to model longitudinal data.

The first question raised by this map is *whether the variation across units is theoretically important*. This usually can be answered by whether or not the theory requires the researcher to estimate the effects of time-stable variables. In other words, if the only source of variation for an important theoretical variable is across units, then the answer to this question is likely *yes*. Once it is decided that variation across units is important, then the researcher must decide *how vulnerable the model is to omitted variable bias*. If there is *no* obvious vulnerability, then the researcher could use a *random effects model*. If the model is, *indeed*, vulnerable to such bias (i.e., there are important measures that are likely correlated with both the included variables and the dependent variable), then the researcher should attempt to account for possible bias by incorporating methods such as *IV estimation*.

If the answer to the first question is *no*, meaning that there is *no theoretical reason to account for variation across units*, then the scholar must decide whether it is important to account for *differences in the slopes for each unit*. If *yes*, then *multilevel modeling* might be

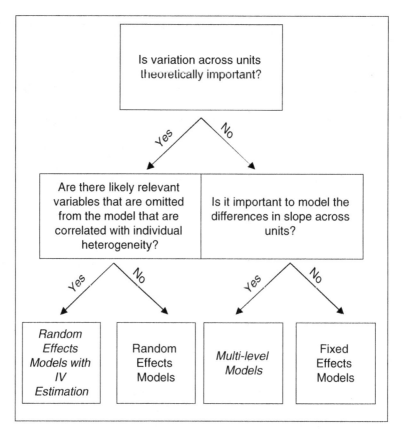

FIGURE 35.3. Decision tree for selecting longitudinal model.

the more efficient choice. While fixed effects models can estimate slopes by including inter-actions, this specification will require many more degrees of freedom, making the results vulnerable to type II errors. If there is *no* theoretical or practical justification for modeling the slopes for the individual units, then the *fixed effects* model may be the best choice. Admit-tedly, this decision tree is unrealistically simplistic, as it fails to account for other important issues that might lead the researcher to another decision, such as low statistical power. It does, however, provide a starting point for exploring methodological options.

REFERENCES

Apel R, Bushway SD, Paternoster R, Brame R, Sweeten G (2008) Using state child labor laws to identify the causal effect of youth employment on deviant behavior and academic achievement. J Quant Criminol 24(4):337–362

Banerjee A, Dolado JJ, Galbraith JW, Hendry DF (1993) Co-integration, error correction, and the econometric analysis of non-stationary data. Oxford University Press, Oxford

Brandt PT, Williams JT (2007) Multiple time series models. Sage Publications, Inc., Thousand Oaks, CA

Britt CL (2001) Testing theory and the analysis of time series data. J Quant Criminol 17(4):343–357

Britt CL (1997) Reconsidering the unemployment and crime relationship: variation by age group and historical period. J Quant Criminol 13(4):405–428

Britt CL (1994) Crime and unemployment among youths in the United States, 1958–1990: a time series analysis. Am J Econ Sociol 53(1):99–109

Bryk AS, Raudenbush SW (1992) Hierarchical linear models. Sage Publications, Inc., Newbury Park, CA

Bushway S, Brame R, Paternoster R (1999) Assessing stability and change in criminal offending: a comparison of random effects, semiparametric, and fixed effects modeling strategies. J Quant Criminol 15(1):23–61

Cantor D, Land KC (1985) Unemployment and crime rates in the post-World War II United States: a theoretical and empirical analysis. Am Sociol Rev 50:317–332

Chamlin MB, Cochran JK (1998) Causality, economic conditions, and burglary. Criminology 36(2):425–440

Cochran JK, Chamlin MB, Seth M (1994) Deterrence or brutalization? An impact assessment of Oklahoma's return to capital punishment. Criminology 32(1):107–134

Cohn EG, Rotton J (1997) Assault as a function of time and temperature: a moderator-variable time-series analysis. J Pers Soc Psychol 72(6):1322–1334

Cook TD, Campbell DT (1979) Quasi-experimentation design & analysis issues for field settings. Houghton Mifflin Company, Boston

D'Alessio SJ, Stolzenberg L (1995) The impact of sentencing guidelines on jail incarceration in Minnesota. Criminology 33(2):283–302

Devine JA, Sheley JF, Smith MD (1988) Macroeconomic and social-control-policy influences on crime rate changes, 1948–1985. Am Sociol Rev 53:407–420

Dugan L (2009) Series hazard modeling: an extension to the cox proportional hazard model to estimate intervention effects on recurrent events for a single unit. Unpublished manuscript. The University of Maryland

Dugan L, Huang J, LaFree G, McCauley C (2009) The Armenian secret army for the liberation of Armenia and the justice commandos of the Armenian genocide. Dynamics of Asymmetric Conflict (forthcoming)

Dugan L, LaFree G, Piquero A (2005) Testing a rational choice model of airline hijackings. Criminology 43(4): 1031–1066

Dugan L, Nagin D, Rosenfeld R (2003) Exposure reduction or retaliation? The effects of domestic violence resources on intimate partner homicide. Law Soc Rev 27(1):169–198

Dugan L, Nagin D, Rosenfeld R (1999) Explaining the decline in intimate partner homicide: the effects of changing domesticity, women's status, and domestic violence resources. Homicide Stud 3(3):187–214

Durbin J (1954) Errors in variables. Rev Int Stat Inst 22:23–32

Enders W, Sandler T (1993) The effectiveness of antiterrorism policies: a vector-autoregression-intervention analysis. Am Polit Sci Rev 87(4):829–844

Freemen J, Houser D, Kellstedt PM, Williams JT (1998) Long-memoried processes, unit roots, and causal inference in political science. Am J Pol Sci 42(4):1289–1327

Goldkamp JS, Vilcica ER (2008) Targeted enforcement and adverse system side effects: the generation of fugitives in Philadelphia. Criminology 46(2):371–409

Granger CWJ (1969) Investigating causal relations by economic models and cross-spectral methods. Econometrica 37(3):424–438

Greenberg DF (2001) Time series analysis of crime rates. J Quant Criminol 17(4):291–327

Greene WH (2008) Econometric analysis, 6th edn. Pearson Prentice Hall, Upper Saddle River, NJ

Grubesic TH, Mack EA (2008) Spatio-temporal interaction of urban crime. J Quant Criminol 24(3):285–306

Hansen BE (2001) The new econometrics of structural change: dating breaks in U.S. labor productivity. J Econ Perspect 15(4):117–128

Hausman J (1978) Specification tests in econometrics. Econometrica 46:1251–1271

Hausman JA, Taylor WE (1981) Panel data and unobservable individual effects. Econometrica 49(6):1377–1398

Jacobs D, Helms RE (1996) Toward a political model of incarceration: a time-series examination of multiple explanations for prison admission rates. Am J Sociol 102(2):323–357

Johnson SD, Bernasco W, Bowers KJ, Elffers H, Ratcliffe J, Rengert G, Townsley M (2007) Space-time patterns of risk: a cross national assessment of residential burglary victimization. J Quant Criminol 23(3):201–219

Kaminski RJ, Marvell TB (2002) A comparison of changes in police and general homicides: 1930–1998. Criminology 40(1):171–190

LaFree G (2005) Evidence for elite convergence in cross-national homicide victimization trends, 1956–2000. Sociol Q 45:191–211

LaFree G (1999) Declining violent crime rates in the 1990s: predicting crime booms and busts. Annu Rev Sociol 25(1):145–68

LaFree G, Drass KA (2002) Counting crime booms among nations: evidence for homicide victimization rates, 1956 to 1998. Criminology 40(4):769–800

LaFree G, Drass KA (1996) The effect of changes in intraracial income inequality and educational attainment on changes in arrest rates for African Americans and whites. Am Sociol Rev 61(3):614–634

LaFree G, Dugan L, Korte R (2009) Is counter terrorism counterproductive? Northern Ireland 1969–1992. Criminology 47(1):501–530

Levitt SD (2001) Alternative strategies for identifying the link between unemployment and crime. J Quant Criminol 17(4):377–390

Loftin C, Heumann M, McDowall D (1983) Mandatory sentencing and firearms violence: evaluating an alternative to gun control. Law Soc Rev 17(2):287–318

Maddala GS (1987) Limited dependent variable models using panel data. J Hum Resour 22(3):307–338

Marsh LC, Cormier DR (2002) Spline regression models. Sage Publications, Inc., Thousand Oaks, CA

McDowall D (2002) Tests of nonlinear dynamics in U.S. homicide time series, and their implications. Criminology 40(3):711–735

McDowall D, McCleary R, Meidinger EE, Hay RA (1980) Interrupted time series analysis. Sage Publications, Inc., Thousand Oaks, CA

Messner SF, Deane GD, Anselin L, Pearson-Nelson B (2005) Locating the vanguard in rising and falling homicide rates across U. S. cities. Criminology 43:661–696

Nagin DS (2009) Group-based modeling: an overview. In: Piquero AR, Weisburd D (eds) Handbook of quantitative criminology. Springer, New York

Nagin DS (2005) Group-based modeling of development. Harvard University Press, Cambridge, MA

Nagin DS, Farrington DP (1992a) The stability of criminal potential from childhood to adulthood. Criminology 30(2):235–260

Nagin DS, Farrington DP (1992b) The onset of persistence of offending. Criminology 30(4) 501–523

Nagin D, Land KC (1993) Age, criminal careers and population heterogeneity: specification and estimation of nonparametric, mixed Poisson, model. Criminology 31(4):581–606

Nagin D, Paternoster R (2000) Population heterogeneity and state dependence: state of the evidence and directions for future research. J Quant Criminol 16(2):117–144

Nagin D, Paternoster R (1991) On the relationship of past and future participation in delinquency. Criminology 29(2):163–190

O'Brien RM (1999) Measuring the convergence/divergence of "serious crime" arrest rates for males and females: 1960–1995. J Quant Criminol 15(1):97–114

Ousey GC, Wilcox P, Brummel S (2008) Déjà vu all over again: investigating temporal continuity of adolescent victimization. J Quant Criminol 24(3):307–335

Paternoster R, Brame R (1997) Multiple routes to delinquence? A test of developmental and general theories of crime. Criminology 35(1):49–84

Paternoster R, Bushway S, Brame R, Apel R (2003) The effect of teenage employment on delinquency and problem behaviors. Soc Forces 82(1):297–335

Paternoster R, Dean CW, Piquero A, Mazerolle P, Brame R (1997) Generality, continuity, and change in offending. J Quant Criminol 13(3):231–265

Petras H, Masyn K (2009) General growth mixture analysis with antecedents and consequences of change. In: Piquero AR, Weisburd D (eds) Handbook of quantitative criminology. Springer, New York

Phillips JA, Greenberg DF (2008) A comparison of methods for analyzing criminological panel data. J Quant Criminol 24(1):51–72

Pridemore WA, Chamlin MB, Cochran JK (2007) An interrupted time-series analysis of Durkheim's social deregulation thesis: the case of the Russian Federation. Justice Q 24(2):271–290

Pridemore WA, Chamlin MB, Trahan A (2008) A test of competing hypotheses about homicide following terrorist attacks: an interrupted time series analysis of September 11 and Oklahoma City. J Quant Criminol 24(4): 381–396

Raphael S, Winter-Ebmer R (2001) Identifying the effect of unemployment on crime. J Law Econ 44:259–283

Rosenfeld R, Fornango R, Rengifo AF (2007) The impact of order-maintenance policing on New York City homicide and robbery rates: 1988–2001. Criminology 45(2):355–383

Sherman LW, Gartin PR, Buerger ME (1989) Hot spots of predatory crime: routine activities and the criminology of place. Criminology 27(1):27–55

Sherman LW, Weisburd D (1995) General deterrent effects of police patrol in crime "hot spots": A randomized, controlled trial. Justice Quarterly 12(4):625–648

Simpson SS, Bouffard LA, Garner J, Hickman L (2006) The influence of legal reform on the probability of arrest in domestic violence cases. Justice Q 23(3):297–316

Sims CA (1972) Money, income, and causality. Am Econ Rev 62(4):540–552

Smith MD, Devine JA, Sheley JF (1992) Crime and unemployment: effects across age and race categories. Sociol Perspect 35(4):551–572

Stata Press (2005) Stata times-series reference manual release 9. Stata Press, College Station, TX

Stolzenberg L, D'Alessio SJ (1994) Sentencing and unwarranted disparity: an empirical assessment of the long-term impact of sentencing guidelines in Minnesota. Criminology 32(2):301–310

Tracy P, Wolfgang ME, Figlio RM (1990) Delinquency careers in two birth cohorts. Plenum, New York

Weisburd D, Bushway S, Lum C, Yang S (2004) Trajectories of crime at places: a longitudinal study of street segments in the city of Seattle. Criminology 42(2):283–321

Witt R, Witte A (2000) Crime, prison, and female labor supply. J Quant Criminol 16(1):69–85

Wu D-M (1973) Alternative tests of independence between stochastic regressors and disturbances. Econometrica 41:733–750

Index

Lightning Source UK Ltd.
Milton Keynes UK
UKOW04f0614090517

300795UK00013B/160/P